Performing with
Microsoft® Office 2007

Iris Blanc
New York City Department of Education

Cathy Vento
Computer Education Consultant

THOMSON

COURSE TECHNOLOGY

COURSE TECHNOLOGY
25 THOMSON PLACE
BOSTON, MA 02210

2-13

#191029002

Australia • Canada • Mexico • Singapore • Spain • United Kingdom • United States

Performing with Microsoft Office 2007

is published by Course Technology.

Authors:
Iris Blanc, Cathy Vento

Contributing Authors:
Jaime Blanc, Katherine T. Pinard

Additional Authors:
Dawna Walls, Laura Story,
Dianne Thompson

Managing Editor:
Donna Gridley

Product Manager:
Jennifer T. Campbell

Developmental Editors:
Karen Porter, Carol Ruhl

Editorial Assistant:
Amanda Lyons

Full-Service Composition:
Newgen, Chennai

Content Project Managers:
Philippa Lehar, Erin Dowler

Copy Editor:
Jeri Freedman

Proofreader:
Kim Kosmatka

Indexer:
Rich Carlson

Marketing Manager:
Tiffany Hodes

Quality Assurance Testers:
John Freitas, Christian Kunciw,
GreenPenQA Tester, Serge
Palladino, Jeff Schwartz, Marianne
Snow, Teresa Storch

Art Director:
Kun-Tee Chang

Cover Designer:
Nancy Goulet

Cover Illustration:
Ferruccio Sardella

The Performing Series Makes a Curtain Call for Microsoft Office 2007!

Give Your Best Performance with Iris Blanc and Cathy Vento!

This book is an innovative instructional tool designed for introductory Office 2007 courses. Students learn more than the software skills—using business documents, they practice writing, problem solving, analysis, critical thinking, and information management. By showing a sample of the finished product at the beginning of a task, students always know what their goal is.

A theatrical structure provides a unique way to teach, and keeps students engaged in what they are learning. Project-based activities go beyond the mechanics of the software, providing students with a higher level of learning through practical application of skills.

An Entertaining, Entrepreneurial Approach:

- **Try out phase:** teaches students the basic steps to perform a task

- **Rehearsal phase:** students apply what is learned for more practice

- **Performance phase:** students use critical thinking skills and problem solving

- **Cues for Reference:** summarizes the skills learned in a task

- **Encore phase:** reinforces the skills learned throughout the lesson

Learning the Craft:

 Students are shown a sample of what they will create at the beginning of a lesson

 A lesson on Microsoft Office Outlook 2007 is added to the book, covering the basics of using e-mail

 An additional Performance exercise after each task, and more Encore projects

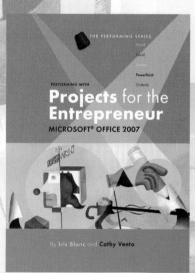

Back by popular demand!

Performing with Projects for the Entrepreneur: Microsoft Office 2007
ISBN 10: 1–4239–0422–2, ISBN 13: 978–1–4239–0422–9

APPROACH

The Performing Series is based on the belief that students successfully learn and retain computer skills when they understand why the skills are useful. Skill sets are presented within the framework of engaging, real-life projects and tasks that teach the software and business competencies needed to succeed in the workplace.

Through this approach, students develop critical thinking, analysis, problem solving, and information and resource management skills. The opportunity to use skills independently and creatively will enable students to survive and thrive in a high-performance workplace.

Performing with Microsoft® Office 2007 teaches Office skills using task-oriented exercises and project-based applications built around a business theme. For additional projects, try *Performing with Projects for the Entrepreneur: Microsoft® Office 2007*.

OBJECTIVES

- To give a complete introductory overview of the Microsoft Office applications for the beginning Office user in a classroom setting or for independent study
- To complete practical, realistic applications and create materials suitable for portfolio evaluation
- To use tasks and projects to develop SCANS competencies

ORGANIZATION

The first three lessons of the book provide an overview of computer concepts, Office, and Internet basics, including coverage of computer software and hardware, and features found in all Office applications, such as opening, saving, and printing files.

Word, Excel, Access, and PowerPoint sections each contain five lessons in the book that build from basic to more advanced skills. An additional sixth lesson for each application is downloadable from the Student Online Companion. There is one new lesson on Microsoft Outlook in the book. The last lesson is a business simulation project that integrates all of the Office applications.

LESSON STRUCTURE

The first phase, **Tryout**, introduces the software features necessary to complete document production in the lesson category, and illustrates them with HOW steps. It also includes software concepts, illustrations, step-by-step directions, and short, easy exercises that provide practice with software features. Students should read all software concepts on a topic before completing the related **Try it Out!** exercise.

In the second phase, **Rehearsal**, students apply the software skills practiced in the Tryout phase to a series of tasks in which they produce model professional documents. **What You Need to Know** information and **Cues for Reference** guide learners in completing the Rehearsal activities on their own, helping them build skills and confidence. The Rehearsal phase produces tangible results that represent actual professional documents.

In the third phase, **Performance**, students complete challenging business-related projects. To complete Performance activities students must apply critical thinking and problem-solving skills and integrate the software skills and business concepts learned to produce the documents required by the company-related scenarios.

The last phase, **Encore**, reinforces the skills learned throughout the lesson using activities that require application of skills as well as independent thought.

ADDITIONAL MATERIALS

The following materials are available on the Student Online Companion and Instructor Resource CD:

- Four additional units on integration pick up where the text leaves off:
  - ✦ Word Lesson 6: Integration: Word and the Web
  - ✦ Excel Lesson 6: Charts, Graphics, and Integration
  - ✦ PowerPoint Lesson 6: Integration: PowerPoint and the Web
  - ✦ Access Lesson 6: Integration
- Appendices: File Management; Using a Pointing Device; the Ribbon; Selection Techniques; Portfolio Basics; Proofreader's Marks; and a Task Reference
- Data files allow learners to complete many of the activities without typing lengthy text

SCANS

The Secretary's Commission on Achieving Necessary Skills (SCANS) from the U.S. Department of Labor is a list of workplace competencies and foundation skills that can be used to ensure that students achieve the level of skills required to enter employment. The workplace competencies are identified as 1) ability to use resources, 2) interpersonal skills, 3) ability to work with information, 4) understanding of systems, and 5) knowledge and understanding of technology. The foundation skills are identified as 1) basic communication skills, 2) thinking skills, and 3) personal qualities.

TEACHING AND LEARNING RESOURCES FOR THIS BOOK

Instructor Resources CD: The Instructor Resources CD contains the following teaching resources:

- Suggested Syllabus with block, two quarter, and 18-week schedule; Annotated Solutions; and Grading Rubrics
- Instructor's Manual with lecture notes for each lesson and task
- PowerPoint presentations for each lesson
- Copies of the figures that appear in the student text
- Grids that show SCANS workplace competencies and skills and activities that apply to cross-curricular topics
- The Data and Solution files for this course

EXAMVIEW®

Also on the Instructor Resource CD: ExamView® tests for each lesson. ExamView is a powerful objective-based test generator that enables you to create paper, LAN, or Web-based tests from test banks designed specifically for your Course Technology text. Utilize the ultra-efficient QuickTest Wizard to create tests in less than five minutes by taking advantage of Course Technology's question banks, or customize your own exams from scratch.

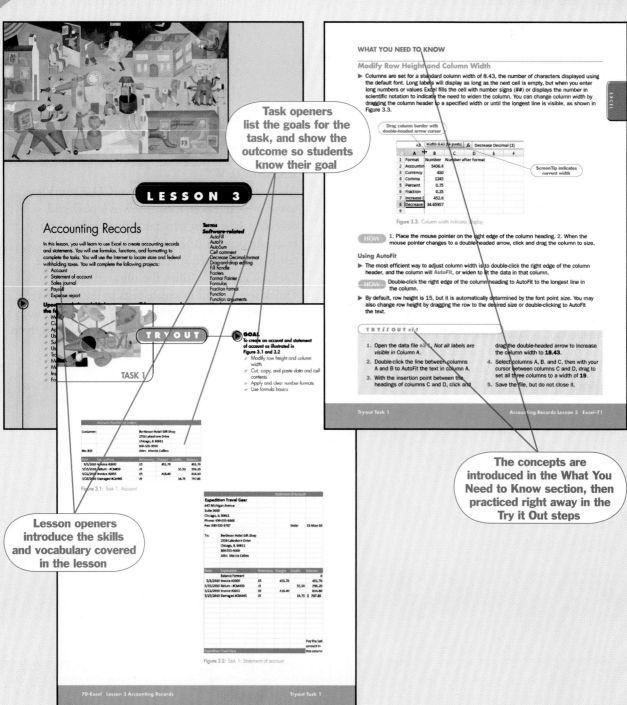

Task openers list the goals for the task, and show the outcome so students know their goal

Lesson openers introduce the skills and vocabulary covered in the lesson

The concepts are introduced in the What You Need to Know section, then practiced right away in the Try it Out steps

LESSON 3

Accounting Records

In this lesson, you will learn to use Excel to create accounting records and statements. You will use formulas, functions, and formatting to complete the tasks. You will use the Internet to locate state and federal withholding taxes. You will complete the following projects:

* Account
* Statement of account
* Sales journal
* Payroll
* Expense report

Terms
Software-related
AutoFill
AutoFit
AutoSum
Cell comment
Decrease Decimal format
Drag-and-drop editing
Fill handle
Footers
Format Painter
Formulas
Fraction format
Function
Function arguments

TRYOUT

TASK 1

GOAL
To create an account and statement of account as illustrated in Figure 3.1 and 3.2
* Modify row height and column width
* Cut, copy, and paste data and cell contents
* Apply and clear number formats
* Use formula basics

Figure 3.1: Task 1: Account

Figure 3.2: Task 1: Statement of account

WHAT YOU NEED TO KNOW

Modify Row Height and Column Width

▶ Columns are set for a standard column width of 8.43, the number of characters displayed using the default font. Long labels will display as long as the next cell is empty, but when you enter long numbers or values Excel fills the cell with number signs (##) or displays the number in scientific notation to indicate the need to widen the column. You can change column width by dragging the column header to a specified width or until the longest line is visible, as shown in Figure 3.3.

Figure 3.3: Column width indicator display

HOW 1. Place the mouse pointer on the right edge of the column heading. 2. When the mouse pointer changes to a double-headed arrow, click and drag the column to size.

Using AutoFit

▶ The most efficient way to adjust column width is to double-click the right edge of the column header, and the column will AutoFit, or widen to fit the data in that column.

HOW Double-click the right edge of the column heading to AutoFit to the longest line in the column.

▶ By default, row height is 15, but it is automatically determined by the font point size. You may also change row height by dragging the row to the desired size or double-clicking to AutoFit the text.

TRYitOUT e3-1

1. Open the data file e3-1. *Not all labels are visible in Column A.*
2. Double-click the line between columns A and B to AutoFit the text in column A.
3. With the insertion point between the headings of columns C and D, click and

   drag the double-headed arrow to increase the column width to **18.43**.
4. Select columns A, B, and C, then with your cursor between columns C and D, drag to set all three columns to a width of **19**.
5. Save the file, but do not close it.

Tryout Task 1   Accounting Records Lesson 3 Excel-71

70-Excel Lesson 3 Accounting Records   Tryout Task 1

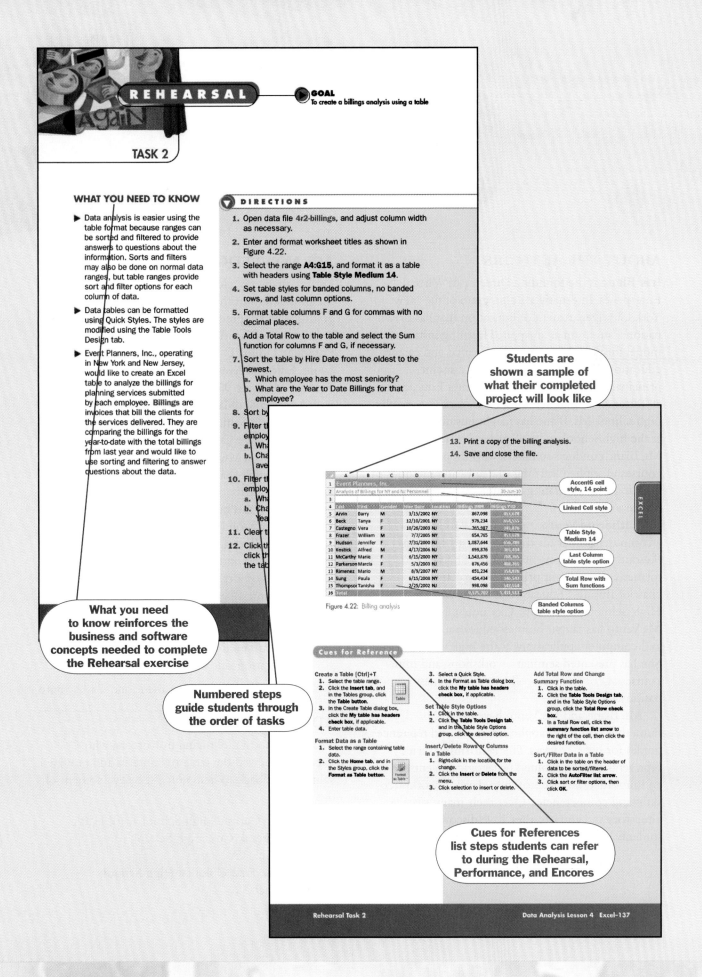

REHEARSAL

GOAL
To create a billings analysis using a table

TASK 2

WHAT YOU NEED TO KNOW

▶ Data analysis is easier using the table format because ranges can be sorted and filtered to provide answers to questions about the information. Sorts and filters may also be done on normal data ranges, but table ranges provide sort and filter options for each column of data.

▶ Data tables can be formatted using Quick Styles. The styles are modified using the Table Tools Design tab.

▶ Event Planners, Inc., operating in New York and New Jersey, would like to create an Excel table to analyze the billings for planning services submitted by each employee. Billings are invoices that bill the clients for the services delivered. They are comparing the billings for the year-to-date with the total billings from last year and would like to use sorting and filtering to answer questions about the data.

What you need to know reinforces the business and software concepts needed to complete the Rehearsal exercise

DIRECTIONS

1. Open data file 4r2-billings, and adjust column width as necessary.

2. Enter and format worksheet titles as shown in Figure 4.22.

3. Select the range **A4:G15**, and format it as a table with headers using **Table Style Medium 14**.

4. Set table styles for banded columns, no banded rows, and last column options.

5. Format table columns F and G for commas with no decimal places.

6. Add a Total Row to the table and select the Sum function for columns F and G, if necessary.

7. Sort the table by Hire Date from the oldest to the newest.
   a. Which employee has the most seniority?
   b. What are the Year to Date Billings for that employee?

8. Sort by

9. Filter the employ
   a. Wha
   b. Cha
      ave

10. Filter the employ
    a. Wha
    b. Cha
       Yea

11. Clear t

12. Click th
    click th
    the tab

Numbered steps guide students through the order of tasks

Students are shown a sample of what their completed project will look like

13. Print a copy of the billing analysis.

14. Save and close the file.

Accent6 cell style, 14 point

Linked Cell style

Table Style Medium 14

Last Column table style option

Total Row with Sum functions

Banded Columns table style option

Figure 4.22: Billing analysis

Cues for Reference

Create a Table [Ctrl]+T
1. Select the table range.
2. Click the **Insert tab**, and in the Tables group, click the **Table button**.
3. In the Create Table dialog box, click the **My table has headers check box**, if applicable.
4. Enter table data.

Format Data as a Table
1. Select the range containing table data.
2. Click the **Home tab**, and in the Styles group, click the **Format as Table button**.

3. Select a Quick Style.
4. In the Format as Table dialog box, click the **My table has headers check box**, if applicable.

Set Table Style Options
1. Click in the table.
2. Click the **Table Tools Design tab**, and in the Table Style Options group, click the desired option.

Insert/Delete Rows or Columns in a Table
1. Right-click in the location for the change.
2. Click the **Insert** or **Delete** from the menu.
3. Click selection to insert or delete.

Add Total Row and Change Summary Function
1. Click in the table.
2. Click the **Table Tools Design tab**, and in the Table Style Options group, click the **Total Row check box**.
3. In a Total Row cell, click the **summary function list arrow** to the right of the cell, then click the desired function.

Sort/Filter Data in a Table
1. Click in the table on the header of data to be sorted/filtered.
2. Click the **AutoFilter list arrow**.
3. Click sort or filter options, then click **OK**.

Cues for References list steps students can refer to during the Rehearsal, Performance, and Encores

ABOUT THE AUTHORS

Iris Blanc is the founding Director of Virtual Enterprises, International, a program of the New York City Department of Education that has drawn national attention as an applied learning instructional model for business, economics, finance, and career education. Formerly, Ms. Blanc was assistant principal/department chair of Business Education at Tottenville High School, a New York City public high school. Ms. Blanc has taught business education at the high school and college levels for over 30 years. Ms. Blanc conducts seminars, workshops, and short courses in applied learning strategies and methods of teaching and integrating technology at conferences nationwide.

Catherine Vento is currently working as a computer trainer for the New Jersey Human Resources Development Division. She was formerly the assistant principal/department chair of Business Education at Susan Wagner High School, a New York City public high school. Ms. Vento has taught business education, accounting, and computer applications at the high school level. She has presented seminars, workshops, and mini-courses at conferences, colleges, and business schools nationwide.

Ms. Blanc and Ms. Vento have co-authored numerous computer application texts and reference guides for over 22 years. The Performing series represents their combined pedagogical talents in an innovative, new approach to develop workplace skills and competencies. Over their many years as educators and authors, they have discovered that students learn best what they need to know!

ACKNOWLEDGMENTS

For the many people who have played a role in the production of this quality book, we owe our gratitude and appreciation. First and foremost among them are the Editorial staff: Nicole Jones Pinard, Vice President; Donna Gridley, Managing Editor; Amanda Lyons, Editorial Assistant; and Jennifer Campbell, Product Manager. We also thank the Production staff: Arunesh Shukla, Full-Service Project Manager, Philippa Lehar, Senior Content Project Manager, and Erin Dowler, Content Project Manager, as well as Jeff Schwartz, MQA Supervisor.

Our heartfelt thanks go to those who have made significant contributions and assisted us with the production of this book:

- To our wonderful editors, Jennifer Campbell, Karen Porter, and Carol Ruhl, who kept everyone on track and on time, and did so with support and guidance all along the way.
- To Jaime Blanc for her review, feedback, and contributions to the PowerPoint section of this text.
- To our families for their love, encouragement, inspiration, and above all, for their patience.

Iris Blanc and Cathy Vento

ADVISORY BOARD

Thank you to the following instructors, who expertly reviewed the table of contents and provided valuable feedback to help guide the development of this book.

Rudell Wert, Carlisle High School, Carlisle, PA
Gail Riffle, Frank Cox High School, Virginia Beach, VA
Janet Kreider, First Colonial High School, Virginia Beach, VA

The exercises in each lesson use various companies to demonstrate the kinds of documents that a real business might produce. A description of each company is outlined below for your reference.

Company Name and Contact Information	Description of Company and Logo	
All Sports Depot *Gaston Store* 543 Gaston Avenue Dallas, TX 75243 Phone: 214-555-1200 Fax: 214-555-1201 *Mesquite Store* 235 Parsons Boulevard Mesquite, TX 75150 Phone: 972-555-1950 Fax: 972-555-1951 E-mail: asd@aom.com Web: www.allsports.com	All Sports Depot is a family-owned-and-operated retailer of sports equipment, and athletic apparel and footwear. All Sports Depot has two large, warehouse-type stores in the Dallas area. The Gaston store is located in downtown Dallas, while the Mesquite store is located in a suburb east of the city.	
BodyWorks Fitness Centers 54 Crabapple Drive Raleigh, NC 27640 Phone: 919-555-1001 Fax: 919-555-1005 E-mail: bodyworks@net.com	BodyWorks Fitness Centers started in Raleigh, North Carolina with one location and quickly grew to four locations in the Raleigh-Durham area. BodyWorks Fitness is a high-quality health and fitness facility, offering a wide range of exercise and fitness programs. The company's success is the result of its innovative fitness programs, well-trained staff, and dedication to quality and service. The president of the company is James Tyler.	
EarthCare Services 32 Braddock Road Cincinnati, OH 45219 Phone: 513-555-0005 Fax: 513-555-0015 E-mail: ecs@network.com Web: www.earthcare.com	EarthCare Services, a full-service landscaping and nursery business, has three locations in and around Cincinnati, Ohio. Kevin Spencer, the president and CEO runs the business with his brother, Lawrence Spencer, the CFO. Lara Morales is their director of Marketing and Sales. They have an office and nursery staff in each store. They also employ workers on a daily basis. The firm handles lawn maintenance programs, tree and shrub planting, pruning, masonry, snow plowing, sanding, and landscape contracting. They carry unique specimen plants and cater to corporate as well as residential markets.	
Expedition Travel Gear Suite 3000 Chicago, IL 60611 Phone: 630-555-8888 Fax: 630-555-8787 E-mail: etg@networld.com Web: www.etg.com	Expedition Travel Gear offers luggage and luggage carts, garment bags, rain gear, money belts, sleep sacks, etc. The company has several retail stores, but most of their business comes from catalog and Internet sales. The retail stores are located in Chicago, Miami, Boston, Dallas, and San Diego. The company's headquarters are located in Chicago Pamela Walters is the president and CEO. The Web site features new products, dozens of reduced-priced items from past catalogs, and lots of valuable information. Their slogan is "Travel in Style."	
Newmark Productions *California* Beverly Hills, CA 90210 Phone: 310-555-8000 Fax: 310-555-8001 E-mail: np@world.com *New York* 350 West 57 Street New York, NY 10106 Phone (212) 555-9999 Fax (212) 555-8900 E-mail: npny@world.com	Newmark Productions is a motion picture and television production company. Alan Newman, the CEO and president, and Mark Cohen, the current CFO formed the company in 1990. Newmark Productions deals with a number of Hollywood's top talent, including writers, directors, and filmmakers. They have released 50 feature films and numerous Emmy-winning television programs. The Motion Picture and Television Divisions are located in the same building in Beverly Hills, California. Newmark also maintains a small office in New York, which primarily handles all marketing and sales distribution. The director of Marketing and Sales is Frank Manning. Mindi Wallace is the manager of the Human Resources Department.	

Company Name and Contact Information	Description of Company and Logo
Palmetto Realtors 450 Flora Boulevard Hollywood, FL 30025 Phone: 954-555-4433 Fax: 954-555-4412 E-mail: palmetto@world.net	Palmetto Realtors is a real estate company located in Hollywood, Florida. It specializes in the sale and rental of residential and commercial properties. Harold Dembar is the president and CEO. The company has a large staff of associates servicing the Hollywood, Florida area and has been selling fine properties for more than 25 years.
Perfect Planning Group *New York* 675 Third Avenue New York, NY 10017 Tel: 212-555-1234 Fax: 212-555-1230 *New Jersey* 1045 Palisades Avenue Fort Lee, NJ 07024 Phone: 201-555-4322 Fax: 201-555-4323 E-mail: ppg@world.com	Perfect Planning Group offers full-service gourmet catering, DJ's, live bands, recreational rentals, entertainment for children's parties, vending machines, appliance rental, and more. Located in New York City, the Perfect Planning Group also plans conferences, seminars, and meetings. Recently, it opened a New Jersey office. Carol McNally is the president of the company.
Transport Travel Services *New York* 505 Park Avenue New York, NY 10010 Phone: 212-555-5555 Fax: 212-555-6767 E-mail: tts@net.com *Boston* One Main Street Boston, MA 11111 Phone: 617-555-6666 Fax: 617-555-7777 E-mail: ttsbos@net.com *California* Los Angeles 46 Beverly Drive Beverly Hills, CA 90210 Phone: 310-555-5555 Fax: 310-555-4444 E-mail: ttsbh@net.com San Francisco 35 Market Street San Francisco, CA 99876 Phone: 415-555-8888 Fax: 415-555-2222 E-mail: ttssf@net.com	Transport Travel Services (TTS) has offices in Boston, New York, and two in California. TTS specializes in both corporate and leisure travel packages. The Corporate Travel department services business clients throughout the country. The company has been in business for over 40 years and is known for its reliable service, great prices, and exclusive offers. The president of the company is Ms. Roslyn Young. The director of the Corporate Travel department in New York is Mr. Robert Ramirez. The director of the Leisure Travel Department is Ms. Jaime Trainor.
Upton Investment Group 34562 Corona Street Reston, VA 20193 Phone: 703-555-6660 Fax: 703-555-6623 E-mail: upton@money.com Web: www.upton.com	Upton Investment Group is a full-service investment company located in Reston, Virginia. They service corporate and individual clients and provide investment, financial planning, and brokerage services. They offer their employees a full benefits package and have been in business 10 years.

GETTING STARTED

Minimum Hardware Configuration
- PC with Pentium processor
- Hard disk with 400 MB free for typical installation
- CD-ROM drive, or access to network drive for downloading and saving Data and Solution Files
- Monitor set at 800x600 or higher-resolution. If your resolution differs, you will see differences in the Ribbon, and may have to scroll up or down to view the information on your screen.
- Printer
- Internet connection. If you are not connected to the Internet, see your instructor.

Software Installation
This book was written and tested using the following settings:
- A typical installation of Microsoft Office 2007
- Microsoft Windows Vista running with Aero off
- Microsoft Internet Explorer 7 browser

FOR WINDOWS XP USERS

The screenshots in this book show Microsoft Office 2007 running on Windows Vista. If you are using Microsoft Windows XP, use these alternate steps.

Starting a Program
1. Click the **Start button** on the taskbar
2. Point to **All Programs**, point to **Microsoft Office**, then click the application you want to use

Saving a File for the First Time
1. Click the **Office Button**, then click Save As
2. Type a name for your file in the File Name text box
3. Click the **Save in list arrow**, then navigate to the drive and folder where you store your Data Files
4. Click **Save**

Opening a File
1. Click the **Office Button**, then click **Open**
2. Click the **Look in list arrow**, then navigate to the drive and folder where you store your Data Files
3. Click the file you want to open
4. Click **Open**

TABLE OF CONTENTS

PREFACE

INTRODUCTION TO COMPUTERS

PERFORMANCE BASICS

PERFORMING WITH WORD

PERFORMING WITH WORD

*Downloadable from the Student Online Companion

PERFORMING WITH EXCEL

PERFORMING WITH EXCEL

*Downloadable from the Student Online Companion

PERFORMING WITH ACCESS

*Downloadable from the Student Online Companion

★Downloadable from the Student Online Companion

FINAL PROJECT

Introduction to Computers

NOTE TO STUDENTS Read this section carefully so that you have an understanding of the computer; its history, hardware, and software applications; the Internet; telecommunications; and related topics.

INTRODUCTION

Forty years ago, computer users were limited to specially trained operators and engineers who interacted with large computers.

Today, approximately 70% of U.S. households have at least one computer. This number is predicted to climb to nearly 85% by the year 2010.

It is important to learn about the parts of a computer, how a computer operates, some of the tasks a computer can perform, and the many responsibilities of being a computer user. It is also important to understand how the computer you are using today evolved and how this incredible tool can give you access to one of the greatest sources of information—the Internet.

BRIEF HISTORY OF COMPUTERS

Computer Hardware History

Although the **microcomputer**, or **PC** (personal computer), was not developed until the early 1980s, non-electronic computing devices, such as the abacus, date back thousands of years. A major step in computer technology came in 1889 with the development of electric machines that could be programmed to read cards with holes punched in them. Other early milestones in computer development are shown in Table 1.1.

Table 1.1 Early computer milestones

DATE	MILESTONE
1890	U.S. Census results were tabulated using an electronic punch-card tabulator.
1944	Howard Aiken of Harvard University worked with engineers from IBM to develop a 50-foot-long, 8-foot-high machine that was able to add, subtract, multiply, divide, and refer to data tables using punched paper tape.
1946	A team from the University of Pennsylvania developed a machine for the U.S. Army's Ballistics Research Lab that weighed approximately 30 tons and covered about 1,000 square feet of floor space. It was the first digital, reprogrammable computing device.
1947	A type of cathode-ray tube was developed to store data electronically. This type of storage was the dominant form for RAM until the 1950s. Before this invention, computers were wired to perform desired tasks and had to be rewired to change the task.
1951	UNIVAC, the first commercial computer, was developed and used to pick presidential winners. Eight of them were sold.
1958	The integrated circuit, the "chip," reduced the cost, size, and processing time of existing computers.
1970	Intel produced the world's first available dynamic RAM chip.

One of the original IBM computers could perform about 2,000 instructions per second. By the late 1980s, computers had begun to be rated in **MIPS** (**millions of instructions per second**). Today, the speed of a supercomputer is measured in **FLOPS** (**FLoating point operations per second**), and IBM is now designing a supercomputer capable of sustained speed of up to 1,000 trillion calculations per second (or one petaflop).

In addition to becoming more versatile, computers became faster, cheaper, and smaller. The development of tiny silicon chips led the way for desktop microcomputers, or PCs. Microcomputers with limited memory and storage ability were first introduced in the mid-1970s. Two major developments occurred in 1975 that led the way for the growth of the computer industry: Steve Jobs and Steve Wozniak started Apple, and Paul Allen and Bill Gates established Microsoft, providing user-friendly software.

Computer Software History

The first software programs were given away free with hardware purchases, as computers could not run without software. Programming languages, such as FORTRAN and COBOL were written in order to adapt software programs written for one machine to be usable on newer machines so that programs and data could be transferred to new hardware. Software engineering became a recognized profession in the 1980s as PCs became more widely used at home and in business. Today, software can run on many different platforms, such as PCs, Macs, and handheld devices, and can be used to provide specific tasks such as accounting or voice recognition, as well as facilitate communication using e-mail and text messaging.

History of the Internet

The Internet was first developed to share information for use by the government and for academic research. In the 1980s, Internet Service Providers started making use of the interconnected networks available for commercial use. The development of e-mail, hypertext, and search engines has made use of the Internet expand.

THE COMPUTER SYSTEM

A **computer** is an electronic device that can perform tasks and calculations based on the instructions it has been given.

How a Computer System Works

Although computers are capable of many complex operations, they can be said to perform three simple tasks:

- Accept input from a person or another outside source
- Interpret and process the input data
- Display the results or perform an action based on the input data or command

Computers can perform these tasks with great speed, accuracy, and reliability. Once data is entered into the computer, the computer processes the data, and the desired information is displayed. How does the computer know what to do with the data? A **software program**, which is a detailed set of instructions, tells the computer what to do.

There are two types of computer software programs: **system software**, which controls the way computer parts work together, and **application software**, which tells the computer how to perform a specific task. (See section "Software" for more information.)

Types of Computers

Computers vary in type, size, speed, and capability. The most common type of computer used in homes, offices, and schools is the **personal computer** (**PC**). A PC is a computer that is small enough to fit on a desk, is relatively inexpensive, and is designed for an individual user. **Laptop computers** (also called **notebooks**) are portable PCs.

Other types of computers include the following:
- The **supercomputer** is the fastest type of computer. It can store data and perform numerous tasks simultaneously at incredible speeds. Supercomputers are used for specialized tasks that require vast amounts of mathematical calculations, such as weather forecasting and medical and weapons research. Usually comprising many computers working in unison, the supercomputer is used only by government agencies, educational institutions, and large corporations.

- **Mainframe** computers are less powerful and cheaper than supercomputers, but they are still capable of storing and processing large amounts of data. Several hundred individuals can access a mainframe simultaneously from their own terminals. Mainframes are used most often by universities, medical institutions, and large companies such as banks and brokerage houses, where they complete millions of daily transactions and save corresponding amounts of data.

- The **minicomputer**, also called a **server**, is smaller than a mainframe and larger than a microcomputer. It can support multiple simultaneous users at their own terminals. Medium-sized companies, such as accounting, advertising, and manufacturing firms, use minicomputers.

Computer Memory

Computer memory is composed of circuits located on tiny computer chips. The number of memory locations is stated in terms of bytes. Table 1.2 describes memory measurements.

Table 1.2 Computer memory measurements

UNIT	DESCRIPTION
byte	Holds a single character, or 8 bits
kilobytes (K or KB)	1,024 bytes
megabytes (M or MB)	1,048,576 bytes. Also called a "meg."
gigabytes (G or GB)	1,073,741,824 bytes. Also called a "gig."

Every computer comes with a certain amount of physical memory, usually referred to as main memory or **random access memory** (**RAM**). Think of RAM as an array of boxes, each of which can hold a single byte of information. A computer that has 1 megabyte of memory, therefore, can hold about 1 million bytes, or characters, of information.

Read-only memory (**ROM**), is computer memory on which data has been recorded on a ROM chip. ROM can be read, but it cannot be deleted. Unlike RAM, ROM preserves its contents even when the computer is shut down. Personal computers contain some ROM memory that stores critical programs, such as those needed for system start-up.

Processing Power

A computer's processing speed (also known as **clock speed**) is measured in **megahertz** (MHz) and **gigahertz** (GHz). In 1993, the average computer processing speed was 25 MHz. By the end of 1994, the average processing speed increased to 66 MHz for the PC. At that time, the 486DX2 chip was new, and there was talk about two new revolutionary chips from Motorola and IBM—the PowerPC and Pentium chips.

The PowerPC chip's speed started at 60 MHz and was capable of running at 120 MHz. The Pentium chip matched these speeds. Within a year, chip speeds increased exponentially. The Pentium 4 line of processors was retired in July 2006, and was replaced by the Intel Core 2 line, a more powerful line of processing chips.

Although processor speed is one major factor in determining a computer's speed, there are others: faster RAM and a data buffer called cache (pronounced "cash"). **Cache** is a region of the hard drive or RAM that temporarily stores frequently accessed data so that it can be retrieved more quickly and efficiently.

As for the future, both Motorola and Intel are working on the next generation of processors, again exceeding current processing speeds. These advancements in technology will be a step toward computers that are 100 billion times as fast as today's most powerful personal computers.

PARTS OF A COMPUTER SYSTEM

A computer system is made up of two principal components: hardware and software.

Hardware

Hardware refers to the physical parts of the computer and includes four main components: input devices, processing unit, output devices, and storage devices.

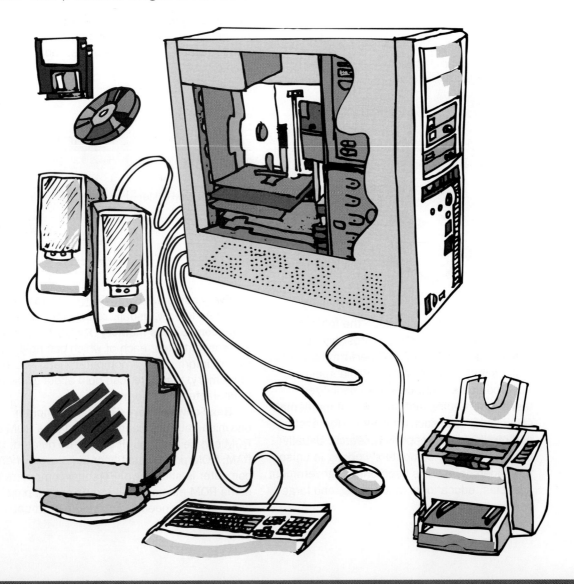

Input Devices **Input devices** feed data into a computer. There are several types of input devices:

- The **keyboard** is the most commonly used input device. It contains typewriter-like keys as well as specialized keys for entering data.

- Mouse, pointing stick, trackball, light pen, puck, and touchpad. (The optical mouse, which uses a laser to detect the motion of the mouse, is quickly replacing the mechanical mouse, which has a rubber or metal ball on its underside.) These small input devices direct the movement of the insertion point on the screen.

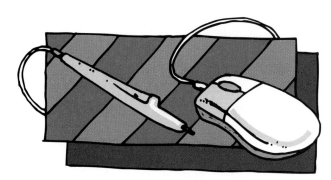

- Optical character recognition (OCR) system: OCRs scan printed pages and translate characters and images into a file that can be edited using a word processor or other application. OCRs accurately translate typewritten or printed data, but are less reliable for handwritten information or musical scores.

- A **scanner** is a device that can read text or illustrations and transmit them in a digital format to the computer screen. Scanners can be small handheld devices or as large as a photocopy machine.

- A **digital camera** captures images in memory storage without using film. The digital images can be transferred to a computer and edited, inserted into a document, or printed. Many cellular phones have digital cameras built in.

- A **digital video camera**, also called a video input camcorder, can record live audio and video, which can then be downloaded into a computer to be edited or viewed using multimedia applications.

- A **microphone** accepts voice input to enter data or execute commands.

Processing Unit The processing unit, also referred to as microprocessor or **CPU** (**central processing unit**), is the brain of the computer. The CPU contains the computer chips and circuits that control and manipulate data to produce information.

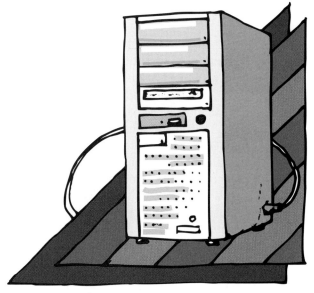

Output Devices **Output devices** allow the user to see or hear the information that the computer compiles.

- **Printers** are devices that print text or graphics onto paper. Printers come in a variety of types and are categorized as either impact or non-impact. An **impact printer** uses a device that strikes a ribbon on paper; **non-impact printers** use laser and ink-jet technology. The quality of the print and the printing speed determine the cost of a printer.

- **Speakers** are internal or external devices that amplify sound.

- A **monitor**, also known as a display, VDT (video display terminal), or computer screen, allows the user to view computer information. There are two main types of monitors: CRT (cathode-ray tube) and LCD (liquid crystal display) monitors. CRT monitors are being phased out as the LCD monitors become the standard. LCD monitors are the screens most commonly used in laptop computers, and often for desktop users because they are typically sharper, brighter, and more economical than CRT monitors. They also take up less room than CRTs, use less energy, and cause less eye fatigue. Plasma and other display technologies are also used for monitors but are more expensive.

Storage Devices **Storage devices** allow instructions and data to be saved and retrieved for future use. Storage devices can be internal or removable, thus allowing data to be transported from one computer to another.

- A **hard drive**, an internal storage device, is also known as a fixed disk. Hard drives can hold huge amounts of information. The size of the drive, which is measured by how much information it can save, affects the price of the computer. A computer that has 1 GB of storage capacity can hold 1 billion bytes of information.

- **Flash drives** are durable, rewritable hard drives that can easily fit in a pocket or on a keychain. They are also called jump drives or thumb drives (because they are the same size as your thumb). Current storage capacity for flash drives exceeds 4 GB. Flash drives use a type of memory called flash memory. Data saved on flash memory has a life span of 10 years.

- **Compact discs (CDs)** can store approximately 650 MB of data. They are commonly used by the software and music industry. CD-R disks (the "R" stands for rewritable) are used by the average computer user to store large amounts of graphics, video, and audio at a relatively inexpensive price, or to store backup data and system files. CD-ROM disks require a CD-ROM drive. Data saved on a CD-ROM has a life expectancy of 5-10 years.

- **DVD (Digital Video Disk)** DVDs can store large amounts of data (approximately 4.7 gigabytes

or 4,700 megabytes). DVDs are most commonly used by the movie industry because they can store and play high-quality video. Data saved on a DVD has a life expectancy of 30-100 years. A Blu-ray disc (also called BD), is a disc used to store digital media and high-definition video. Blu-ray discs can store substantially more data than a DVD.

- A **Digital Audio Tape (DAT)** is a standard magnetic tape that resembles a basic audio-cassette. DATs have the ability to hold tremendous amounts of information on a tape much smaller than an audiocassette and are typically used by businesses to perform daily backups of data. DAT devices can hold up to 10 separate DAT tapes, each of which can hold up to 26 GB of information.

Software

Software is a set of instructions written by programmers in **machine language**, or **programming language**, that tells the computer what to do, how to do it, and when to perform tasks based on input from the user. Examples of programming languages include FORTRAN, COBOL, BASIC, C, C++, Java, JavaScript, Visual Basic, Visual C++, and RPG.

The words software, program, and application are used interchangeably. There are two types of software: operating system software and application software. **Application software** (such as Microsoft Office) interacts with the user to perform tasks and can run only when operating system software (such as Microsoft Windows Vista) is installed and running on a computer. **Operating system software** controls the basic operation of the computer.

Operating System Software Operating system software manages the computer's files and programs using a graphic interface that translates mouse and keyboard actions into appropriate programming code. The most widely used operating systems include Microsoft Windows Vista and Apple Computer's Mac OS. Other operating systems include IBM's Microsoft DOS (Disk Operating System), Linux, and UNIX.

Some operating systems were created specifically for use on a network. These include Novell NetWare, AppleShare IP, and Windows Small Business Server. Handheld devices also use operating systems, such as Palm OS, Symbian OS, and Windows Mobile.

Application Software Application software, sometimes referred to as tool, or end-user software, provides the tools needed to complete a task. Application software types include financial management software, Internet browsers, word processors, and graphic design packages.

Common types of application software include:

- **Word processing** software is used to edit text, and create and print documents such as letters, memos, and reports. Microsoft Word is an example of word-processing software.

charts from statistical information. Microsoft Excel and Lotus 1-2-3 are examples of spreadsheet software.

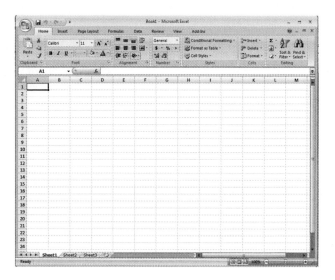

- **Database** software allows the user to collect, store, organize, modify, and extract data. Microsoft Access is an example of database software.

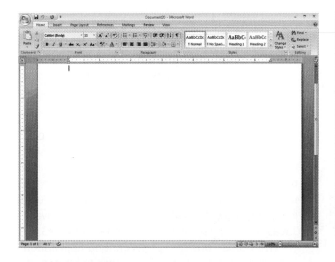

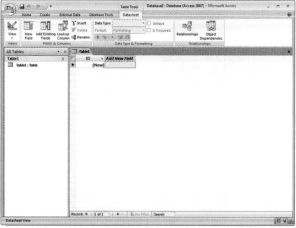

- **Spreadsheet** software is used for analysis and reporting of statistical or numerical data to complete such tasks as preparing budgets, payroll, balance sheets, and profit and loss statements. Spreadsheet software can create

- **Presentation** software is used to create slides that can be shown to accompany a speech or lecture. Slides can be used to summarize data and emphasize highlights. Microsoft PowerPoint is an example of presentation software.

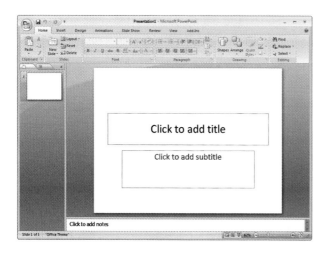

- **Accounting** software is used for organizing and managing money and finances. Quick-Books is an example of accounting software.

- **Collaborative Groupware** is software that helps groups of users communicate and organize activities, meetings, and events using a common interface. Groupware is used within corporations so all employees can share the same common screens on their computers.

- **Communication** software is used to transmit and receive information between computers in real time. For the transfer to take place, both the receiver and the sender must have the software installed. Communication software can be used for online chats and instant messaging, such as AOL Instant Messenger (AIM).

- **Internet browser** software is used to locate, display, and interact with Web pages. Popular Internet browsers include Netscape Navigator, Mozilla Firefox, and Microsoft Internet Explorer.

- **E-mail** software is used to send and retrieve e-mail from a mail server. Microsoft Outlook is an example of an e-mail program. Many e-mail programs are integrated with other software applications. For example, you can send e-mail using Outlook from other Microsoft Office applications.

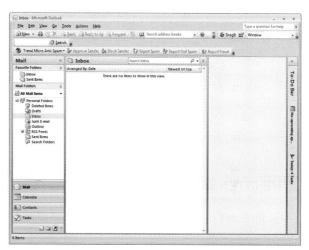

- **Online service** software provides subscribers with the ability to communicate with one another through e-mail, as well as get news, weather, and sports information. America Online and EarthLink are examples of online service software. Access to this information also requires communications equipment. (See the section "Telecommunications.")

- **Voice recognition** software is used to create, edit, and format documents by speaking into a microphone attached to a computer. The dictation is transcribed directly on the computer. Dragon NaturallySpeaking and IBM's ViaVoice are two popular voice recognition software products.

- **Web page** software is used to design and manage Web sites. Microsoft Expression Web and Adobe Dreamweaver are examples of Web page design software.

- **Graphics** software packages can be used to create charts, pictures, illustrations, drawings, and 3-D images. Types of graphic software include: paint, illustration, design, photo editing, and desktop publishing. Adobe Creative Suite contains several types of graphics programs.

THE INTERNET

The **Internet** is a global network of smaller computer networks each with its own unique **IP** (**Internet Protocol**) address. These networks may be located in businesses, schools, research foundations, hospitals, or homes. Businesses use the Internet to share information and to advertise their services and products. Students use the Internet for research and to share information with fellow students and professors. The Internet can be used to book airline flights, buy movie tickets, check your savings account, buy and sell stocks, order a pizza, shop for a gift, apply to a college, find a job, or buy a home. Internet users can also share personal information about themselves through chat groups, blogs, bulletin boards, and e-mail.

To access the Internet, a user must sign up with an **Internet service provider** (**ISP**), which sells access to the Internet. ISP services include e-mail, news on demand, personal Web site hosting, and much more. Connecting via modem to an ISP allows a user access to the **World Wide Web**, a collection of Web pages or **Web sites** that display information over the Internet. Some popular ISPs include The Microsoft Network (MSN), America Online (AOL), EarthLink, net.com, MindSpring, and AT&T Worldnet.

Fee-based online content is available through ISPs by subscription from sources such as Dow Jones News/Retrieval and LexisNexis, which provide legal, financial, and business news that is updated daily.

Web sites reside on a **Web server**, a dedicated computer that stores and delivers Web pages. Every Web server has an IP address, which can correspond to a domain name. **Domain names** are a part of a URL (Uniform Resource Locator), also referred to as a Web address, and are used to locate Web sites. For example, in the URL http://www.microsoft.com, the domain name is microsoft.com. The domain suffix identifies the type of Web site, such as commercial (.com), noncommercial (.org), government (.gov), educational (.edu), U.S. military (.mil), or network (.net) organization.

Information on the Web is created using a programming language called **HTML** (**Hypertext Markup Language**). A Web browser translates HTML into a readable format. Web sites can have a different look when viewed with different Web browsers due to the way the browser reads the HTML code.

You can transmit files between a computer and a file server or a Web server using the **File Transfer Protocol** (**FTP**). Hypertext Transfer Protocol (HTTP) is a protocol used to transfer Web pages from a Web server into a browser. Both FTP and HTTP can be used to transfer data from one computer device to another.

TELECOMMUNICATIONS

To transmit data over a phone line, you need a modem. A **modem** is a device that connects a computer to a phone line or cable, allowing data to be transmitted from one computer to another. For the transmission to work, both computers must have modems and the appropriate communications software. A modem can be internal or external.

Modem speeds vary. Dial-up modems provide online access through telephone lines at speeds up to 57.6 bits per second (bps). A cable modem gives users high-speed Internet access through a cable line at more than 1 million bits per second. DSL and satellite modems provide even faster access to the Internet, but at increased costs, and may not be available in all areas. Downloading files and transmitting data requires fast modem speeds.

A **fax modem** transmits data, graphics, and documents similarly to a facsimile machine. The advantage of a fax modem is that you can receive faxes while the computer is turned off. To transmit faxes via the computer, you need to have the appropriate communications software package installed.

There are various ways to transmit data, sound, and video electronically, including:

- E-mail refers to messages transmitted electronically using a modem or a **network system** called an intranet. Users can send messages to one or more Internet mailboxes simultaneously, and can retrieve messages sent to them. Access to an electronic mailbox is exclusive and limited. Generally, users of the mailbox must know a **password**, or code, to send or retrieve messages. Messages can be transmitted at any time to anyone around the world who has an e-mail address. E-mail addresses are usually formatted in a specific way: user@domain.com. For example, John Doe works for the Pixie Soda Company. His e-mail address might be: john.doe@pixiesoda.com. E-mail can be viewed and sent using e-mail software, via a Web browser, or through a cellular phone or personal digital assistant (PDA).

- A **fax** is a machine connected to a telephone that scans a document and translates the visual image into electronic impulses, which are then transmitted along telephone lines to another fax machine at a different location. The remote machine receives the electronic impulses, reconstructs the visual image of the document, and prints out an exact copy of the original document.

- Information on a variety of topics can be placed on or accessed from an **electronic bulletin board**. Users can exchange information and hold discussions on any topic. Access to some bulletin boards is free; others charge a subscription fee. See the "Future Technologies" section for other ways to share information on the Web.

- **Teleconferencing** allows people in different locations to see and hear one another. A **video-conference** uses television cameras and microphones to transmit voice and video signals through satellite networks.

Using a Computer Responsibly

A great deal of responsibility goes along with personal computing. Working in an office allows you to obtain confidential information that should be used only when you are authorized to do so by your employer or the individual to whom it relates. Private information, such as phone numbers, Social Security numbers, tax records, credit card information, medical histories, and legal records is stored on computers in databases. Access to this information usually requires knowledge of passwords and/or codes, and is limited to those who require this information or are given access to it. Computer databases can be a more secure storage medium than a piece of paper, but in the wrong hands, such information could do great damage.

When irresponsible or unethical individuals, sometimes referred to as **hackers**, discover ways to break codes and gain access to classified files, not only personal but also national security may be threatened. It is a criminal offense to retrieve or view information from a private or limited-access computer or database without permission.

Information, software, and media such as graphics, video, and songs found on the Internet are protected by copyright laws. It is illegal to make copies of software programs or copy, share, or download media without permission of the copyright holder. Information provided on the World Wide Web is usually copyrighted and protected by the creators of the site. When using information from the Internet for independent research, cite the Web site, author, and original source where applicable. Failure to do so is considered plagiarism. Violators of any sort of copyright infringement are subject to prosecution and imprisonment.

TAKING CARE OF YOUR COMPUTER, PERIPHERALS, AND DATA

Part of taking care of your computer is to create plans for maintenance of your systems, devices, and data. Before performing any maintenance task, you should read the specific instructions for that device provided to you by the manufacturer. In addition, never attempt to clean any device without shutting down the computer and unplugging the power source.

Care of Computer and Peripherals

System Care The system case should be cleaned, both inside and out, on a regular basis to prevent buildup of dust.

- Wipe the outside case clean with a damp cloth. Never spray liquids directly on the casing or any part of your computer.
- The inside of the computer can be cleaned by using a compressed-air can to blow out dust, or by using a small handheld vacuum to remove the dust.
- Check the power supply fan periodically to be sure that it has good ventilation and is free of dirt and dust buildup.

Monitors

- Clean monitors using a soft, damp cloth to remove the dust at least once a week.
- Be sure to check that the monitor's cooling vents are never blocked.
- To increase the monitor's life span and protect your system, do not keep monitors turned on overnight or for extended periods of time. Use a screen saver or instruct your computer to hibernate when not in use.

CD Drives Unlike hard disk drives, which are sealed within the central processing unit of the computer, CD drives are exposed to the outside air. The drive's read/write heads should be cleaned every few months using isopropyl alcohol or special cleaning kits.

Keyboards Over time, keyboards will develop keys that stick or repeat if they are not maintained. To avoid these problems, keep food and liquids away from the keyboard.

- Develop a "no eating and drinking" policy while using the computer. If liquids spill into the keyboard, tip it over immediately.
- Clean the key caps at least once every six months, and use compressed air to blow out dust from between the keys.

Mice When the ball inside a mouse becomes dirty, it will not roll properly and the pointer will not react on the screen's surface. Use a damp cloth to clean the mouse and the rollers inside the mouse unit at least once a month. With an optical mouse, there is no way for dirt to get inside the mouse and interfere with the tracking sensors.

Care of Media

- Compact Discs (CDs) Compact discs are durable, and they do not require much special care.
- CDs should not be subjected to temperatures above 100°F.
- Do not handle the surface of a CD. Doing so causes the surface to become scratched, which will interfere with the computer's ability to read the discs.
- Moisture and liquids will not harm a CD. If a CD becomes wet, simply wipe it off with a soft cloth.
- CDs are not affected by magnetic fields.
- CDs can be cleaned using a damp, soft cloth.
- Airport x-ray machines do not affect CDs.

Care of Data

Perform daily backups of your data from your hard drive to a thumb (flash) drive, tape, or CD. To avoid losing data in an unexpected shutdown of your computer, be sure to:

- Save data frequently in all applications.
- Click the Safely Remove Hardware button on the status bar before removing a flash drive from your computer.
- Close all open applications.
- Shut down your operating system according to the instructions given to you by the system.
- Install a virus-scanning program on your computer to protect data from becoming infected.
- Delete unwanted files from your hard drive monthly to increase hard drive performance.

PERFORMANCE BASICS

Exploring Microsoft Office 2007

In this lesson, you will learn to navigate and explore elements of the Microsoft Word 2007 window that are also common in other programs in Microsoft 2007 Office and to use the Help system.

Upon completion of this lesson, you will be introduced to Microsoft Office 2007 and will have mastered the following skill sets

* Learn about Microsoft Office 2007
* Get started with Office programs
* Explore Global Office screen parts and components
* Get help

Terms
Software-related
> Commands
> Desktop
> Dialog box
> Dialog box launcher
> Ellipsis points
> Groups
> Office Button
> Mini toolbar
> Quick Access toolbar
> Ribbon
> ScreenTips
> Shortcut menu
> Start button
> Status bar
> Taskbar
> Title bar
> Window control buttons
> Zoom

T R Y O U T

TASK 1

▶ **GOAL**
To explore common Office screen parts and use Help as shown in Figure 1.1

✴ Introduction to Microsoft Office 2007
✴ Get started
  ✴ Launch an Office program
  ✴ Switch between Office programs
✴ Explore Global Office screen parts and components:
  ✴ Title bar and Window controls
  ✴ Office Button
  ✴ Quick Access toolbar
  ✴ The Ribbon, tabs, and groups
  ✴ Dialog box launcher and dialog boxes
  ✴ Shortcut menu and Mini toolbar
  ✴ Status bar
  ✴ View buttons
  ✴ Zoom
  ✴ ScreenTips
✴ Get help
  ✴ Online help

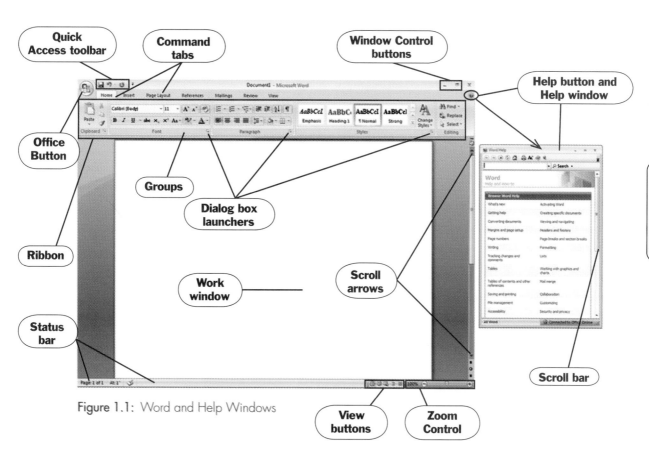

Figure 1.1: Word and Help Windows

BASICS

WHAT YOU NEED TO KNOW

Introduction to Microsoft Office 2007

▶ Microsoft Office Professional 2007 is a system of software programs that provides a full range of powerful computer tools that you can use independently or in an integrated fashion. Table 1.1 lists the tools that are included with the Office Professional 2007 edition.

▶ To use the features in Office, you must be comfortable using the mouse. If you are not familiar with mouse actions and terminology, refer to Appendix E, which is available from your instructor.

▶ Microsoft Office offers you a variety of ways to access most commands. This book will provide the most commonly used methods of using the software tools to complete the job at hand.

Table 1.1: Microsoft Office Programs

PROGRAM	ICON	PROGRAM TYPE
Word		Word processing
Excel		Spreadsheet
Access		Database
PowerPoint		Presentation
Outlook		Desktop information manager
Publisher*		Desktop publishing

*Publisher will not be covered in this book.

Launch an Office program

▶ When you start your computer, the **desktop**, shown in Figure 1.2, is the first window that appears. It displays program and file icons for the programs you use most frequently.

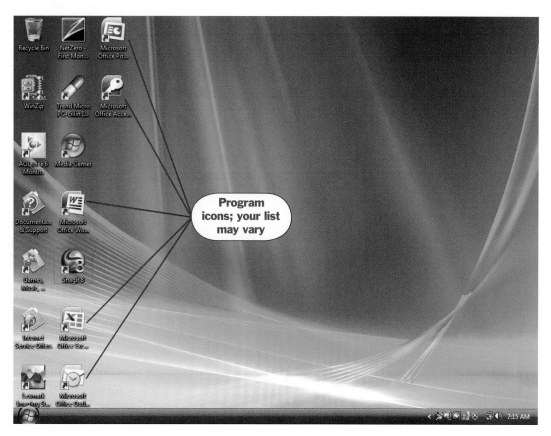

Figure 1.2: Windows desktop

▶ The **taskbar**, located at the bottom of the desktop, displays the **Start button**, as well as open documents and programs. When you click it, the Start button displays menu options to start programs and work with aspects of your computer, as shown in Figure 1.3.

HOW There are two basic ways to start an Office program: from the desktop or from the taskbar.

▶ From the desktop, double-click the program icon on the desktop, if you customized it to include program icons. (See Figure 1.2.)

▶ From the taskbar, **1.** click the **Start button**, **2.** point to **All Programs**, **3.** click **Microsoft Office**, and **4.** select the program you want from the menu. (See Figure 1.3).

Figure 1.3: All Programs menu

T R Y *i t* **O U T** *pb1-1*

1. Click the **Start button**, point to **All Programs**, click **Microsoft Office**, then click **Microsoft Office Excel 2007** to start Excel.

2. Click the **Start button**, point to **All Programs**, click **Microsoft Office**, then click **Microsoft Office Word 2007**.

3. Click the **Start button**, point to **All Programs**, click **Microsoft Office**, then click **Microsoft Office PowerPoint 2007**.

4. Click the **Start button**, point to **All Programs**, click **Microsoft Office**, then click **Microsoft Office Access 2007**.

Switch between Office Programs

▶ After you start a program, a button appears on the taskbar showing the program icon and the document's name, as shown in Figure 1.4 (the program name will be truncated if many buttons are displayed). When you point to a program button, a small window known as a ScreenTip displays the full document and the program's name. *ScreenTips will be discussed later in this lesson.*

Figure 1.4: Taskbar with open programs and ScreenTip

HOW Click the button on the taskbar for the program you want to display.

T R Y *i t* **O U T** *pb1-2*

1. Click the **Word** button on the taskbar to switch to the Word program.
2. Click the **Excel button** on the taskbar to switch to the Excel program.
3. Click the **PowerPoint button**.
4. Click the **Access button**.
5. Click the **Word button**.

Explore Global Office Screen Parts and Components

▶ Many screen parts and commands can be found in all Office programs. The common parts of all Office programs are illustrated and discussed using the Word window (see Figure 1.1). The screen parts that apply to a specific Office program are discussed in the related units of this book.

▶ After launching an Office program, an opening screen appears showing a work window and screen elements needed to work with a specific application.

▶ Each program window contains the following common elements: the title bar, window controls, the Office Button, the Quick Access toolbar, the Ribbon, which includes command tabs, groups, and dialog box launchers, the Help button, and the status bar, which includes View buttons and Zoom options. *A scroll box and scroll arrows allow you to move through a window vertically. Scrolling techniques will be detailed and practiced in each application section.*

Title bar and Window controls

▶ The **title bar**, located at the top of the program window and shown in Figure 1.5, displays the document's name, followed by the program's name. A program-specific generic name will be displayed until you provide a name during the save process.

Figure 1.5: Title bar

▶ The title bar also includes **window control buttons**, which control the way the program window behaves. *When opening a new program, the size of its window will default to the previously used setting.* Table 1.2 describes each window control button.

Table 1.2: Window Control Buttons

CLICKING THIS BUTTON . . .		. . . DOES THIS:
Minimize button	–	Reduces the window to a button on the taskbar
Restore Down button	–	Reduces the size of the window
Maximize button	▭	Replaces the Restore button after you click the Restore Down button and increases the window size to fill the screen
Close button	x	Closes the program

T R Y *i t* **O U T** *pb1-3*

1. The Word window should be displayed. If not, click the **Word button** on the taskbar.

2. Click the **Minimize button**. *The window is reduced to a button on the taskbar.*

3. Click the **Close button** to exit PowerPoint.

4. Click the **Close button** to exit Access.

5. Click the **Word button** on the taskbar to redisplay the Word window.

6. Click the **Restore Down button** to reduce the Word window.

7. Click the **Maximize button** to return the Word window to its original size.

8. Click the **Excel button** on the taskbar.

9. Click the **Close button** to exit Excel.

Office Button

▶ The **Office Button**, located in the upper-left corner of the window, contains commands related to managing documents as a whole. Figure 1.6 shows the commands available after clicking the Office Button.

Figure 1.6: Office Button commands

T R Y *i t* **O U T** *pb1-4*

1. Point to the **Office Button**. *A ScreenTip appears.*

2. Click the **Office Button**. *Note the options that are available.*

3. Click **New**, click **Blank document**, then click **Create**. *You have created a new blank document.*

4. Click the **Office Button**.

5. Click the **Close button**. *The document window closes.*

Quick Access Toolbar

▶ The **Quick Access toolbar**, located to the right of the Office Button, is a customizable toolbar containing a set of frequently used command buttons (see Figure 1.6). *You will use these buttons and learn to customize the toolbar in Performance Basics Lesson 2.*

The Ribbon, Tabs, and Groups

▶ The **Ribbon**, located below the title bar and shown in Figure 1.7, contains the **commands** you need to complete a task. Commands are arranged on command tabs according to the tasks you want to perform. The Home tab is selected by default. Once a tab is selected, command buttons are displayed in **groups**. For example, the Home tab contains buttons related to writing and formatting a document. The buttons are organized on this tab in five groups: Clipboard, Font, Paragraph, Styles, and Editing. Each group contains buttons that provide access to commands related to that group. When your pointer rests on a toolbar button, its name is displayed in a ScreenTip.

▶ Only commands that can be applied to the current document are active. Double-clicking a command tab will hide the command buttons and provide more space for working. To redisplay the tab, double-click it. *Based on your past usage or settings, your tabs and groups may vary.*

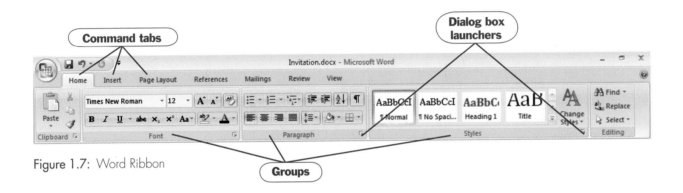

Figure 1.7: Word Ribbon

T R Y *i t* O U T *pb1-5*

1. Point to and rest the pointer on each toolbar button in the Quick Access toolbar to display the ScreenTip.

2. Click the **Insert tab**. *Seven groups are displayed: Pages, Tables, Illustrations, Links, Header & Footer, Text, and Symbols.*

3. In the Illustrations group, click the **Shapes button**. *A gallery of shapes appears. Click away from the gallery to close it.*

4. Click the **Page Layout tab**. *Five groups are displayed: Themes, Page Setup, Page Background, Paragraph, and Arrange.*

5. In the Themes group, click the **Themes button**. *A gallery of themes appears.*

6. In the Page Setup group, click the **Margins button**. *Note the options that appear.*

7. Click the **References tab**. *Six groups are displayed: Table of Contents, Footnotes, Citations & Bibliography, Captions, Index, and Table of Authorities.*

8. In the Table of Contents group, click the **Table of Contents button**. *Note the options that are displayed.*

Continued on next page

9. Click the **Mailings tab**. *Five groups are displayed: Create, Start Mail Merge, Write & Insert Fields, Preview Results, and Finish.*

10. Click the **Review tab**. *Six groups are displayed: Proofing, Comments, Tracking, Changes, Compare, and Protect.*

11. Click the **View tab**. *Four groups are displayed: Document Views, Show/Hide, Zoom, and Window.*

12. In the Show/Hide group, click the **Thumbnails check box** to select it. *A task pane opens on the left side of the window that displays thumbnails of each page, which are miniatures for easy navigation of long documents.*

13. Click the **Thumbnails check box** to deselect it.

14. Double-click the **View tab** to hide all the command buttons. Double-click the **View tab** again to redisplay the command buttons.

15. Click the **Home tab**.

Dialog Box Launcher and Dialog Boxes

▶ Some groups have a **Dialog box Launcher button** in the lower-right corner of the group (see Figure 1.7). Clicking this button will display a **dialog box**, which is a window that presents information about the current settings for a command and allows you to make changes. In the Paragraph dialog box shown in Figure 1.8, note that some command buttons, such as the Tabs button, display **ellipsis points** (. . .). Clicking a button with ellipsis points will display another dialog box.

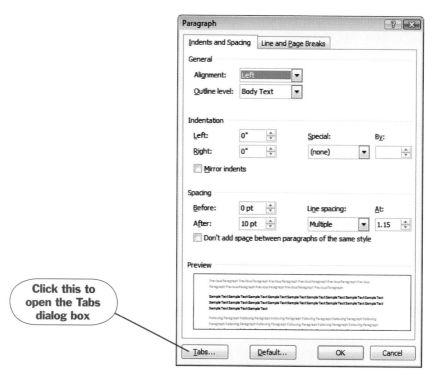

Figure 1.8: Paragraph dialog box

HOW **1.** Click the **dialog box launcher** in the group, or click a command or command button containing ellipsis points. **2.** Make the changes you want, and **3.** click **OK** to save the changes, or click **Cancel** or the **Close button** to close the dialog box without applying changes.

X

T R Y *it* **O U T** *pb1-6*

1. Click the **Home tab** if it is not already selected, and in the Font group, click the **dialog box launcher**.

2. Click the **Character Spacing tab**.

3. Click **Cancel**.

4. In the Paragraph group, click the **dialog box launcher**.

5. Click the **Close button**. **X**

6. Click the **Page Layout tab**, and in the Page Setup group, click the **dialog box launcher**.

7. Click the **Layout tab**.

8. Click **Borders** to display the Borders and Shading dialog box.

9. Click **Cancel** in the Borders and Shading dialog box.

Shortcut Menu and Mini Toolbar

▶ The **Shortcut menu**, shown in Figure 1.9, provides a quick way to display commands you need while working. Shortcut menu options vary, depending on where the mouse is pointing and what task you are performing. The **Mini toolbar**, also shown in Figure 1.9, displays buttons you can use to quickly change the look of text or data. Mini toolbar buttons will vary depending on the Microsoft program you are using.

HOW

▶ Position the insertion point in the work window and right-click.

▶ To hide the menu and toolbar, position the insertion point off the menu and **left-click**. *In Performance Basics Lesson 2, you will learn to work with a semi-transparent Mini toolbar that appears when you select text.*

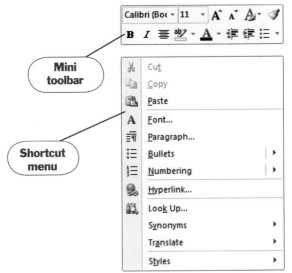

Figure 1.9: Shortcut menu and Mini toolbar

1. Click the **Home tab** if it is not already selected.

2. Position the mouse pointer in the middle of the work window, and **right-click**. *The Shortcut menu and Mini toolbar will display.*

3. Note the commands that contain ellipsis marks (. . .). Click **Font** on the shortcut menu. *The Font dialog box opens.*

4. Click the **Close button** to close the Font dialog box, then right-click the work window again.

5. Move the mouse pointer away from the shortcut menu, then left-click to close it.

Status Bar

▶ The **status bar**, located at the bottom of the program window and shown in Figure 1.10, contains information about the file on which you are working, as well as View shortcut buttons and Zoom control.

Figure 1.10: Status bar

View buttons   Zoom control

▶ You can customize the status bar to display options such as Word Count, line number, page number, the number of spelling and grammar check errors and others.

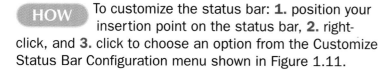 To customize the status bar: **1.** position your insertion point on the status bar, **2.** right-click, and **3.** click to choose an option from the Customize Status Bar Configuration menu shown in Figure 1.11.

View buttons

▶ View shortcut buttons enable you to view your file in different ways. You will learn to use these buttons in application-specific lessons.

Zoom

▶ The **Zoom** feature allows you to get a close-up view of your document or see more of the page at a reduced size. Figure 1.12 shows the Zoom control buttons.

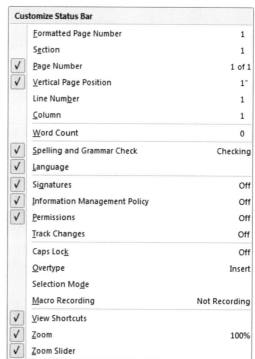

Customize Status Bar	
Formatted Page Number	1
Section	1
✓ Page Number	1 of 1
✓ Vertical Page Position	1"
Line Number	1
Column	1
Word Count	0
✓ Spelling and Grammar Check	Checking
✓ Language	
✓ Signatures	Off
✓ Information Management Policy	Off
✓ Permissions	Off
Track Changes	Off
Caps Lock	Off
Overtype	Insert
Selection Mode	
Macro Recording	Not Recording
✓ View Shortcuts	
✓ Zoom	100%
✓ Zoom Slider	

Figure 1.11: Status bar configuration menu

BASICS

Figure 1.12: Zoom control buttons

HOW

▶ Click and drag the Zoom slider to the right to make the document larger or left to make it smaller, or click the plus and/or minus buttons to increase or decrease the magnification percentage in increments.

▶ To set a particular zoom setting, click the **Zoom level** button. In the Zoom dialog box that appears, as shown in Figure 1.13, choose a zoom setting. You can also access the Zoom dialog box by clicking **View** on the Ribbon, then clicking the **Zoom** button in the Zoom group.

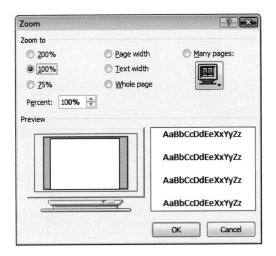

Figure 1.13: Zoom dialog box

TRY it OUT pb1-8

1. Note the information displayed on the Word status bar. Page Number and Word Count should be displayed. If they are not, follow Step 2 in the How section above, display Page Number and Word Count, then complete the remaining steps.

2. Position the insertion point on the status bar, and right-click.

3. Deselect **Page Number** on the menu to remove it from the status bar.

4. Deselect **Word Count**.

5. Click away from the menu to close it.

6. Redisplay the Page Number and Word Count information.

7. Type your first and last name anywhere in the work window.

8. Click the **Zoom level button** on the status bar.

Continued on next page

9. In the Zoom dialog box that displays, select the **75% option button**, then click **OK**.

10. Click the **Zoom In button** on the zoom slider to increase the magnification to 100%.

ScreenTips

▶ **ScreenTips** are small windows that display descriptive information when you rest the mouse pointer on a command or control. Figure 1.14 shows a ScreenTip. An enhanced ScreenTip, shown in Figure 1.15, is a larger window that displays more descriptive text. If the ScreenTip has a Help button, you can click it to link to a Help topic.

Figure 1.14: ScreenTip

Figure 1.15: Enhanced ScreenTip

1. Click the **Home tab**, if it is not already selected.

2. In the Clipboard group, position your insertion point on the top part of the **Paste button**. *A ScreenTip appears.*

3. Position your insertion point on the Paste button arrow (the bottom part of the Paste button). *A ScreenTip appears.*

4. Position your insertion point on the **Format Painter button**. *An enhanced ScreenTip with a Help button appears.*

5. Position your insertion point on the remaining buttons on the Ribbon. *Note each ScreenTip or enhanced ScreenTip.*

BASICS

Get Help

▶ An extensive Help system is provided for each program in the Microsoft Office 2007 system. Each program in Microsoft Office has a separate Help window. If you open Help in Word, then go to Excel and open Help, you will see two separate windows. The Help window, shown for Word in Figure 1.16, stays on top of other windows by default. You can access Help only for the program in which you are working.

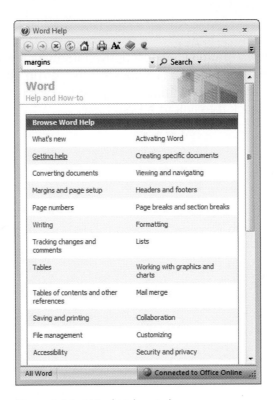

Figure 1.16: Word Help window

HOW F1 **1.** Click the **Help button**. **2.** Enter a Help topic to search in window that displays in the Search text box. To specify which Help resource you want, click the Search arrow, then choose a resource. **3.** Press **[Enter]** or click **Search** to begin the search process. The search results display a list of topics that responds to your search topic. **4.** Click on a topic to view an explanation. **5.** To print a topic, click the **Print button** on the Help window.

Online Help

▶ If you are connected to the Internet, you can get online Help to browse or search for the most up-to-date Help, templates, and training. If you are not connected to the Internet, Office will provide you with those topics installed on your computer.

HOW **1.** Click the **Microsoft Office Word Help button** on the Ribbon. **2.** Click the **Getting help link**. **3.** Click the **Using Microsoft Office Online link**, then **4.** Click to select a topic listed.

T R Y *i t* **O U T** *pb1-10*

1. Press **[F1]**. *The Word Help window appears.*

2. Click the **Close button** on Help window title bar.

   `x`

3. Click the **Microsoft Office Word Help** button on the Ribbon.

   `⊚`

4. Enter **margins** in the Search text box, then press **[Enter]** to start the search.

   Click the **Change or set page margins link**, and read the information that displays.

5. Enter **templates** in the Search text box, then press **[Enter]**. Read the topics that display.

6. Click the **Close button** on the Help window.

REHEARSAL

GOAL
To open several Office programs,
explore global Office screen parts,
and use window controls and the Help
feature with Word

TASK 1

WHAT YOU NEED TO KNOW

▶ When many programs are open at
once the buttons on the taskbar
become smaller.

DIRECTIONS

1. Start **Word**, if necessary.

2. Start **Excel**.

3. Start **PowerPoint**.

4. Start **Access**.

5. Switch to **Excel**. Note the Quick Access toolbar,
Ribbon command tabs, View buttons, and Zoom
control.

6. Minimize the Excel window.

7. Switch to **PowerPoint**.

8. Position your insertion point on the status bar, and
right-click. Note the options in the Customize Status
Bar menu.

9. Minimize the PowerPoint window, then maximize the
Word window.

10. Press **[F1]** to access Help.

11. Enter **ribbon** in the Search text box, as shown in
Figure 1.17, and begin the search.

12. Find information about using the Ribbon.

13. Print the topic.

14. Switch to **Word**, then close the **Word Help** window
if necessary.

15. Enter your first name.

16. Drag the Zoom slider left until the zoom
magnification displays 80%, then click the
Zoom In button to increase the magnification
to 110%.

17. Click the **Page Layout tab**, and in the Page Setup
group, click the **dialog box launcher** to display the
Page Setup dialog box.

18. Click the **Cancel button** in the dialog box to close it.

Continued on next page

19. Remove the Page Number display from the status bar.

20. Redisplay the page numbers on the status bar.

21. Close all programs.

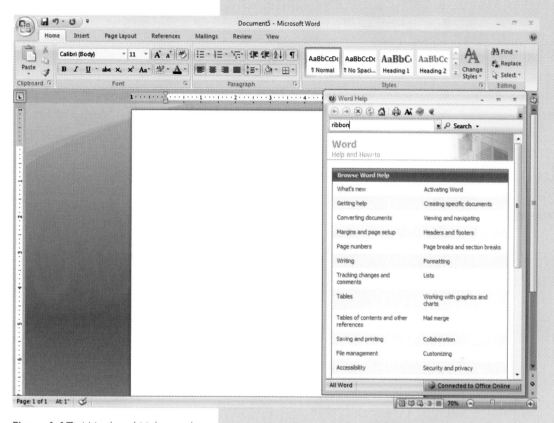

Figure 1.17: Word and Help windows

Start Office
1. Click the **Start button** on the taskbar.
2. Point to **All Programs**.
3. Click **Microsoft Office**.
4. Click the program name.
   Or
- Double-click the **program icon** on the desktop.

Switch Between Office Programs
- Click the desired program or document button on the taskbar.

Zoom
- Click and drag the Zoom slider left to reduce the size of the window or right to increase the size of the window.
  Or
- Click the **Zoom In** and **Zoom Out buttons**.

  Or

1. Click the **Zoom level button**.
2. Choose a Zoom option from the dialog box, then click **OK**.

Close a Program
- Click the **Office Button**, then click Close.
  Or
- Click the **Close** button on the program window.

Use Help
1. Click the **Microsoft Office Program Help button** or press **F1**.
2. Click the desired link.
   Or
- Enter a Help topic in the Search text box, then press **Search**.

BASICS

Working with Files

In this lesson, you will use the basic features common to programs in the Microsoft Office 2007 system to work with files and learn to use keyboard shortcuts.

Upon completion of this lesson, you will have mastered the following skill sets

- About files and folders
- Use keyboard shortcuts
- Start a new file
- Save a file
- Use Save As
- Close a file
- Open a file
- Undo, Redo, and Repeat Tasks
- Quick Print

Terms

Access keys
File
File management
Filename
Folder
Keyboard shortcuts
KeyTips
Read-only
Redo
Repeat
Save As
Undo

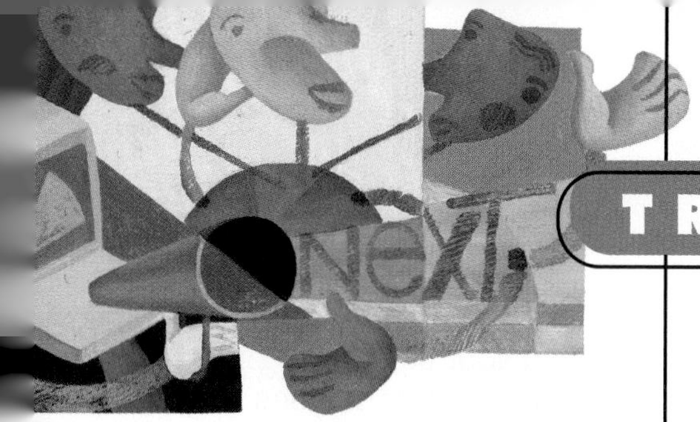

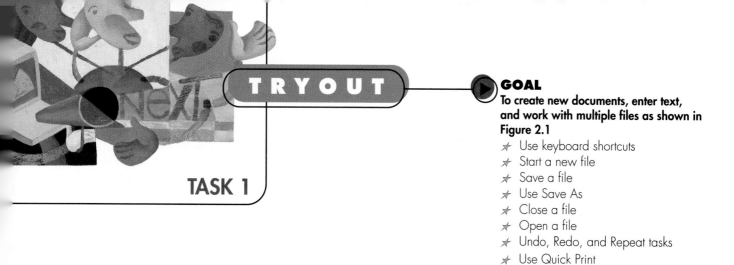

TRYOUT

TASK 1

GOAL

To create new documents, enter text, and work with multiple files as shown in Figure 2.1

- Use keyboard shortcuts
- Start a new file
- Save a file
- Use Save As
- Close a file
- Open a file
- Undo, Redo, and Repeat tasks
- Use Quick Print

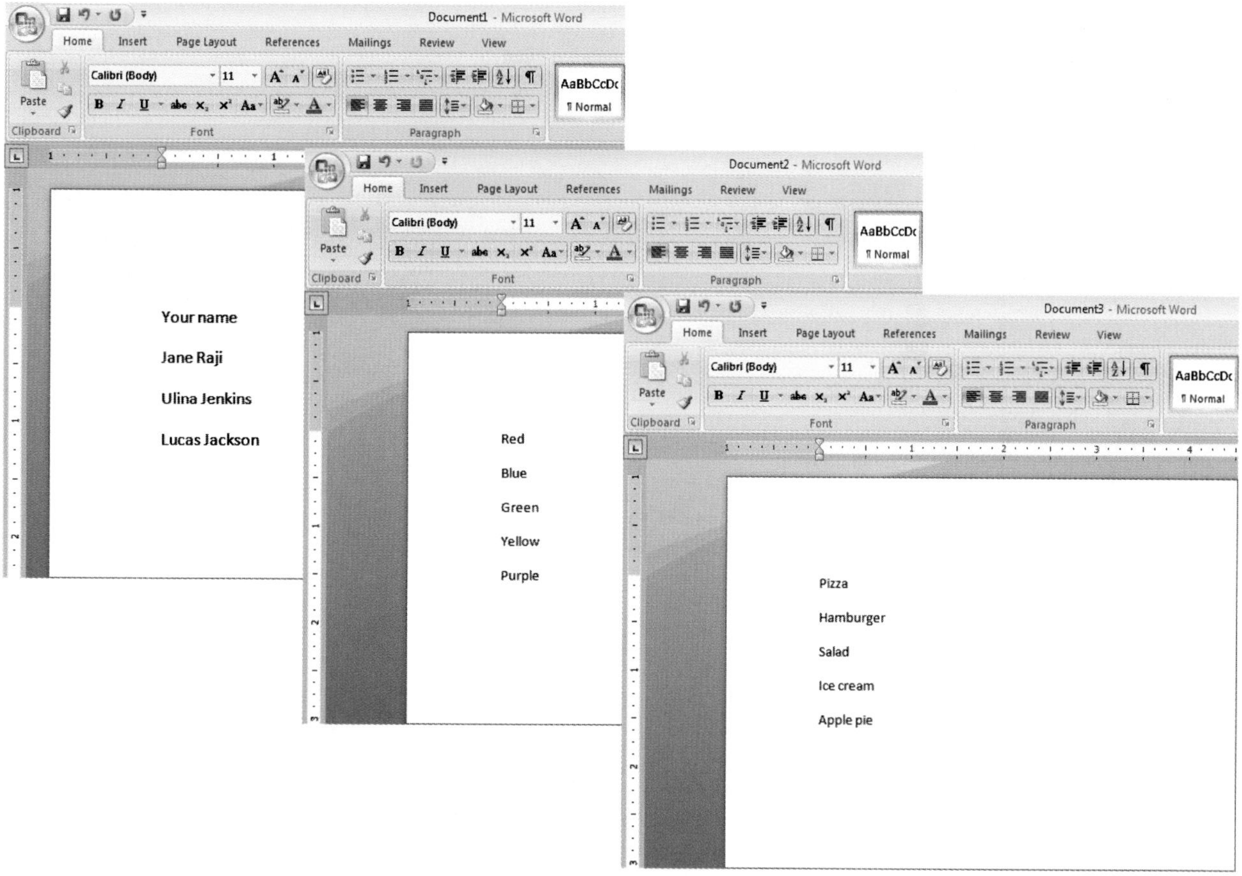

Figure 2.1: Documents created in Word

BASICS

WHAT YOU NEED TO KNOW

About Files and Folders

▶ It is important to understand files and folders and how they are organized on your computer. A **file** is a collection of information, which is named and saved. There are many different types of files, such as data, text, and program. **Folders** are used to organize files. Folders can also contain additional folders. A directory is an organizational unit or container used to organize folders. **File management** is the system of organizing and keeping track of your files and folders.

▶ You can view the overall structure of your files and folders when you open or save a document or you can use Windows Explorer, a Windows Vista tool, to display them. Figure 2.2 shows how files and folders display when you save a document (you will save a file later in this lesson). You can copy, move, rename, and delete files and folders.

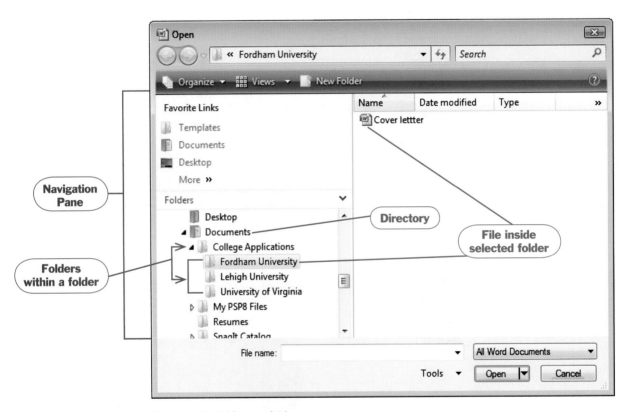

Figure 2.2: Folders and Files

Use Keyboard Shortcuts

▶ The mouse is used to select buttons on the Ribbon and dialog boxes, and help you apply many features. You can also perform many of these functions using the keyboard.

▶ There are two ways to use the keyboard: Access keys and keyboard shortcuts (also known as key combination shortcuts). **Access keys** allow you to use every tab and command on the Ribbon, the Office Button, and the Quick Access Toolbar. To use Access keys, you activate the Ribbon by pressing the Alt key. **KeyTips** appear; these are labels that show the Access key for each tab or command. **Keyboard shortcuts** allow you to perform specific commands and are unrelated to the Ribbon.

Access Keys

HOW **1.** Press **[Alt]** to activate the Ribbon and display KeyTips, as shown in Figure 2.3.
2. Press a key to activate a particular tab. If you press the incorrect key, press **[Esc]** to undo the action.

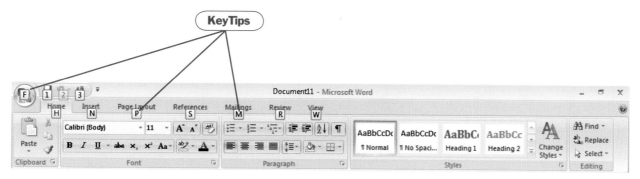

Figure 2.3: KeyTips on the Ribbon

Once you activate the Ribbon using the Alt key, you can move around the Ribbon using the arrow keys or the Tab key.

1. Press **[Alt]** to activate the Ribbon. **2.** Press the left and right arrows to move to the adjacent tabs, the up arrow to move to the Quick Access Toolbar, then press the left arrow as many times as necessary to move to the Office Button. *Once you move around the Ribbon using the arrow keys, the KeyTips disappear. Press [Alt] twice to redisplay the KeyTips.*

You can also:

1. Press **[Alt]** to activate the Ribbon. **2.** Press **[Tab]** to highlight the active tab, then move from group to group.

Keyboard Shortcuts

▶ Keyboard shortcuts require that you press and hold **[Ctrl]** while pressing another key that represents the command. Keyboard shortcuts will be shown in HOW boxes as commands are used in the book.

TRY *it* OUT pb2-1

1. Launch Word if necessary, and open a new blank document.

2. Press **[Alt]**. KeyTips appear on the Ribbon.

3. Press the **W** key to activate the View tab. KeyTips appear on the View tab. Press the **R** key to deactivate the Ruler. If the Ruler is not displayed, click the **View** tab, in the Show/Hide group, select **Ruler**, then repeat Steps 2 and 3.

4. Repeat Steps 2 and 3 to redisplay the Ruler.

5. Press **[Alt]**. Press the left arrow key several times until the Home tab is activated.

6. Press the **down arrow** key to select the **Paste** command in the Clipboard group.

7. Press **[Alt]** twice to redisplay the KeyTips.

8. Press the **F** key to display the Office Button menu.

9. Press **[Esc]** to close the menu.

10. Press **[Esc]** again to hide the KeyTips.

Start a New File

▶ When you launch an Office application, an opening screen appears showing a work window, a new file, and screen elements, which you learned about in Performance Basics Lesson 1.

▶ The new file that opens is assigned a generic name until you save it with a name. As each new file is opened, a corresponding button will appear on the taskbar.

▶ In Word, for example, the opening window contains a blank document, which has been assigned the name **Document1**, as shown in Figure 2.4. Once the application is open, you can create additional blank documents.

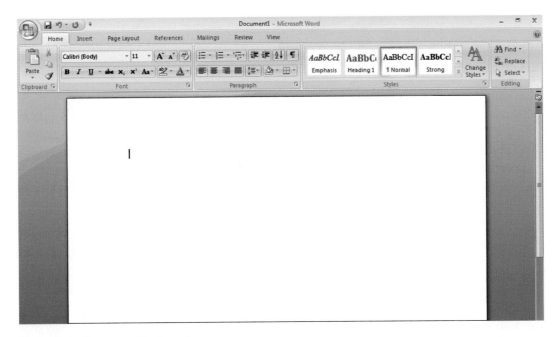

Figure 2.4: Opening Word window

HOW Ctrl+N   **1.** Click the **Office Button**. **2.** Click **New**. **3.** Click **Create**. A new blank document will appear with **Document2** as its name. To switch between open documents, click the desired button on the taskbar.

TRY it OUT *pb2-2*

1. Start **Word**.

2. Enter your first and last name on **Document1**.

3. Click the **Office Button**, click **New**, then click **Create**. *You have created Document2.*

4. Enter your home address, city, and state on **Document2**.

5. Press **[Alt]**, press the **F** key, press the **N** key, then press **[Enter]**. *You have created Document3 using the shortcut keys.*

Continued on next page

6. Enter your telephone number on **Document3**.

7. Click the **Document1 button** on the taskbar.

8. Press **[Ctrl]+N** to create another blank document. *You have created Document4*

using the key combination shortcuts. There is a button on the taskbar for each of the four open documents.

9. Do not close any files.

Save a File

▶ You must name a new file to be able to identify it and easily retrieve it at a later time. A **filename** may contain a maximum of 250 characters and can include spaces. Filenames cannot contain the characters shown in Table 2.1.

Table 2.1: Characters restricted from filenames

CHARACTER(S)	NAME	CHARACTER(S)	NAME
\	Backslash	/	Forward slash
:	Colon	;	Semicolon
*	Asterisk	?	Question mark
[]	Brackets	|	Vertical bar
=	Equals	" "	Quotation marks
.	Period	,	Comma
<	Less than	>	Greater than

▶ To save a file for the first time, you must provide it a unique filename and determine where on your computer you wish to save it. In the Save As dialog box, a filename proposed by Word appears in the File name text box by default. You can choose to accept, edit, or reenter this filename. Since you can save to a folder on your hard drive, a network location, a floppy disk, a flash drive, a CD, the desktop, or another storage location, you must identify the target location in the Navigation Pane of the Save As dialog box. Ask your instructor or lab manager for the preferred saving location.

HOW Ctrl+S 1. Click the **Office Button**. 2. Click **Save**. Or, Click the **Save button** on the Quick Access Toolbar, as shown in Figure 2.5. 3. In the Save As dialog box, shown in Figure 2.6, enter or edit the name of the file in the File name text box. To save a file to a location other than the default, locate the folder you want in the Favorite Links section or click the **Folders** button to find a folder in which you wish to save. *If you always want to save the file to your default location, click **Hide Folders**.* 4. Click **Save** in the Save As dialog box to complete the saving process.

Figure 2.5: Save button (**Save button**) on the Quick Access Toolbar

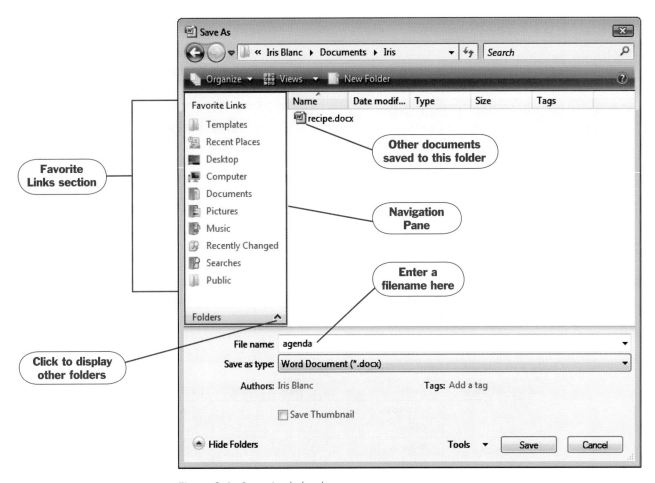

Favorite Links section

Other documents saved to this folder

Navigation Pane

Enter a filename here

Click to display other folders

Figure 2.6: Save As dialog box

▶ Once the file is saved, the filename appears on the title bar.

▶ Save your work frequently to prevent data loss and to save any edits you make. To save a previously saved file, click the **Save button** on the Quick Access Toolbar or press **[Ctrl]+S**.

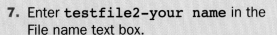

TRY *it* OUT *pb2-3*

1. Display **Document1** if it is not already displayed. *This document contains your first and last name.*

2. Click the **Office Button**, then click **Save**. *Click the **Save in list arrow**, and choose a location in which to save the file, if necessary.*

3. Enter **testfile-your name** in the File name text box.

4. Click **Save**. *Note that the new filename appears in the title bar.*

5. Switch to **Document2**. *This document contains your address.*

6. Click the **Save button** on the Quick Access toolbar.

7. Enter **testfile2-your name** in the File name text box.

8. Click **Save**.

9. Do not close the files.

Use Save As

▶ The **Save As** feature allows you to save a previously saved document under a different filename, in a different file format, or to a different location. The original file will remain intact. Each application in Office contains numerous file formats. You will see a list of available formats when you click the Office Button, choose Save As, then click the Save as type list arrow.

 1. Click the **Office Button**. **2.** Click **Save As**. **3.** In the Save As dialog box, enter a new filename and specify the location. **4.** Click **Save**.

T R Y *i t* **O U T** *pb2-4*

1. Display the file **testfile-your name**.

2. Click the **Office Button**, then click **Save As**.

3. Enter **testfile3-your name** in the File name text box.

4. Click **Save**.

5. Do not close Word.

Close a File

▶ If you attempt to close a file you have not yet saved or that has changed since your last save, you will be prompted to save it.

 1. Click the **Office Button**. **2.** Click **Close** or click the **Close button** on the window, as shown in Figure 2.7.

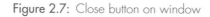

Figure 2.7: Close button on window

T R Y *i t* **O U T** *pb2-5*

1. Display **testfile3-your name**, if it is not already displayed. *This file contains your first and last names.*

2. Click the **Office Button**, then click **Close**.

3. Display **Document3**, if it is not already displayed. *This file contains your phone number.*

4. Click the **Office Button**, then click **Close**. Click **Yes** when prompted to save Document3.

5. Enter the filename **testfile4-your name** in the File name text box, then click **Save**. *The file is saved and closed.*

6. Click the **Close button** on the **testfile2-your name** document window.

7. Display **Document4**, then close it using any method you prefer without saving changes.

8. Press **[Ctrl]+N** to create a new blank document. Enter the name of your school.

Continued on next page

9. Press **[Ctrl]+N** to create another new blank document. Enter a sentence describing today's weather.

10. Click the **Office Button**, then click **Close** to close the document containing today's weather. Click **No** when you are prompted to save your changes.

11. Click the document **Close button** to close the document containing the name of your school. Click **No** when you are prompted to save your changes.

Open a File

▶ When you open a file in Microsoft Office, you have several options for how the file opens. Table 2.2 explains three frequently used ways to open a file.

Table 2.2: File opening options

OPTION	EXPLANATION
Open	Opens the original file for editing.
Open as Read-Only	Opens the original file but does not allow you to save changes to it. If you make changes to a read-only file, you must save it under a new filename, thus allowing the original file to remain intact.
Open as Copy	Creates a duplicate of the file that is opened. Any changes that you make are saved to the copy.

HOW Ctrl+O To open a recently opened file, click the **Office Button**, and click a file on the Recent Documents list shown in Figure 2.8. To open a file not shown on the list, **1.** Click the **Office Button**, then **2.** click **Open**. **3.** In the Open dialog box, shown in Figure 2.9, locate the document you want. **4.** Double-click the filename to open it. To open a file as read-only or as a copy, click the **Open list arrow**, choose an option as shown in Figure 2.9, then click **Open**.

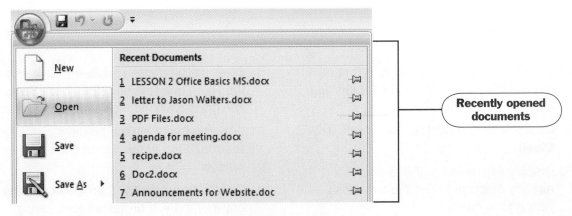

Figure 2.8: Recently opened files

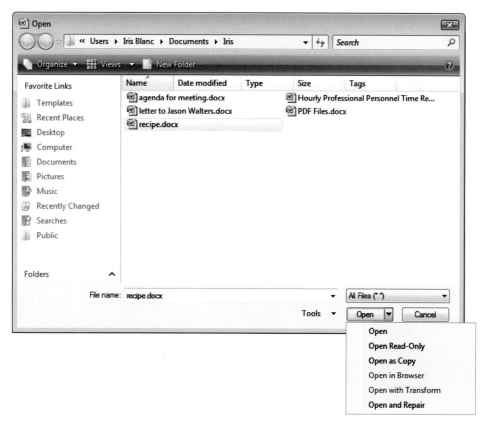

Figure 2.9: Open dialog box

T R Y *i t* O U T *pb2-6*

1. Click the **Office Button**.

2. Click **testfile-your name** on the Recent Documents list.

3. Click the **Office Button**.

4. Click **testfile2-your name** on the Recent Documents list. *You have two open documents.*

5. Press **[Ctrl]+O**.

6. Click **testfile4-your name**. *This file contains your phone number.*

7. Click the list arrow on the **Open button**, then click **Open as Copy**. *You have three open documents.*

8. Enter your first and last name, then press **[Enter]**.

9. Save the file as **testfile5-your name**, then close all files.

Undo, Redo, and Repeat Tasks

Undo

▶ The **Undo** feature lets you reverse an action. If you delete a word by mistake, using the Undo feature will bring back the deleted word. If you click the Undo button repeatedly, you will reverse a series of actions. You can also undo an earlier action or several actions at once.

HOW Ctrl+Z Click the **Undo button** on the Quick Access Toolbar. To undo an earlier action, or group of actions, click the **Undo arrow** as shown in Figure 2.10, then select the action or group of actions to be reversed. The most recent action appears at the top of the list.

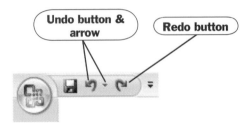

Figure 2.10: Undo and Redo buttons

Redo

▶ Once you undo an action, the Redo button appears, as shown in Figure 2.10. The **Redo** feature lets you reverse the previous undone action. As with Undo, you can redo one or a series of actions.

HOW Ctrl+Y Click the **Redo button** on the Quick Access Toolbar.

Repeat

▶ The **Repeat** action feature allows the user to repeat the last action made.

HOW Ctrl+Y Click the **Repeat button** on the Quick Action Toolbar shown in Figure 2.11.

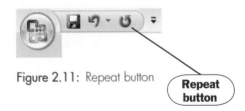

Figure 2.11: Repeat button

Quick Print

▶ The Quick Print option sends your file directly to the printer with the current print settings applied. You will learn to set print options in each program application unit.

 1. Click the **Office Button**, **2.** point to **Print**, and **3.** click **Quick Print** on the menu, as shown in Figure 2.12.

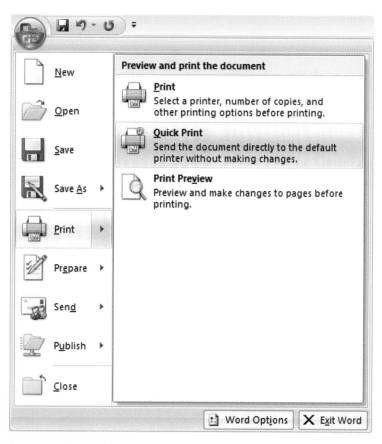

Figure 2.12: Quick Print

T R Y *i t* O U T *pb2-7*

1. Press **[Ctrl]+N** to open a new blank document.

2. Type **Summer**, then press **[Enter]**.

3. Click the **Undo button** once. *Summer should no longer be on your screen.*

4. Click the **Redo button** once. *Summer should be back on your screen.*

5. Type your first and last name, then press **[Enter]**.

6. Click the **Repeat button** twice.

7. Click the **Office Button**, point to **Print**, then click **Quick Print**.

8. Close the file without saving your changes.

REHEARSAL

TASK 1

GOAL
To create new documents, enter text, and work with multiple files

WHAT YOU NEED TO KNOW

▶ To create a list, press [Enter] after each item on the list. Word will automatically insert the spacing amount each time you press [Enter]. You will learn about line spacing in a later lesson.

▶ When working through this activity, use the mouse procedure or a shortcut method to launch a command. The lists shown in Figure 2.13 will differ from those you create.

DIRECTIONS

1. Start **Word** if necessary, and open a new blank document.

2. Enter a list of names starting with your name and adding the names of three other people. Press **[Enter]** after each name.

3. Save the file as **2r1-names**.

4. Open a new blank document.

5. Create a list of your five favorite colors.

6. Save the file as **2r1-colors**.

7. Switch to **2r1-names** and close the file.

8. Create a new blank document.

9. Make a list of your three favorite foods and two favorite desserts.

10. Close the file. When prompted, save the file as **2r1-foods**.

11. Open the file **2r1-names**, and add one additional name to the list.

12. Click the **Undo button**.

13. Click the **Redo button**.

14. Save the file.

15. Switch to **2r1-colors**.

16. Add five more colors to the list.

17. Save the file as **2r1-more colors**.

18. Enter your name at the bottom of the list, then save and print the document.

19. Close all files.

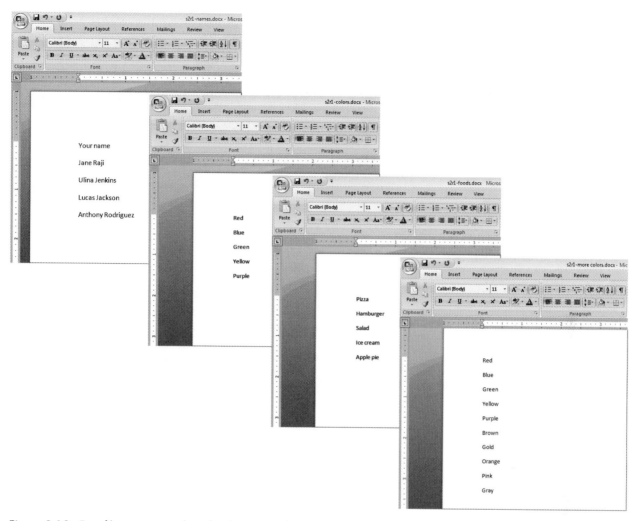

Figure 2.13: Four files: names, colors, foods, more colors

Start a New File

1. Press **[Ctrl]+N**.
   Or
   • Click the **Office Button**.
   • Click **New**.
2. Click **Blank Document** (if it is not already selected).
3. Click **Create**.

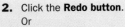

Save a File

To Save a File for the First Time

1. Press **[Ctrl]+S**.
   Or
1. Click the **Save button** on the Quick Access Toolbar.
2. Enter the filename in the File name text box.
3. Click the **Save button**.

To Overwrite or Update a Previously Saved File

1. Click the **Save button** on the Quick Access Toolbar.

Save As

1. Click the **Office Button**.
2. Click **Save As**.

3. Enter the filename in the File name text box.
4. If desired, click the Save as type list arrow and choose a file format.
5. Click the **Save button**.

Open a File

1. Press **[Ctrl]+O**.
   Or
   • Click the **Office Button**.
   • Click **Open**.
2. Double-click the filename.

Close a File

1. Click the **Close button** on the document window.
   Or
1. Click the **Office Button**.
2. Click **Close**.

Undo and Redo

1. Click the **Undo button**.
   Or
1. Press **[Ctrl]+Z**.

2. Click the **Redo button**.
   Or
2. Press **[Ctrl]+Y**.

Quick Print

1. Click the **Office Button**.
2. Point to **Print**.
3. Click **Quick Print**.

Use Ribbon Keyboard Shortcuts

1. Press **[Alt]** once to display the KeyTips.
2. Press a letter to activate a tab.
3. Press a letter to activate a command on a tab.
4. Press **[Esc]** to hide the KeyTips.
   Or
1. Press **[Alt]** once to activate the KeyTips.
2. Use the arrow keys to activate a tab.
3. Use the down arrow keys to activate a command on a tab.
4. Press **[Alt]** twice to reactivate the KeyTips.

LESSON 3

Working with the Web

In this lesson, you will learn the basic concepts of the Internet. You will also learn to use a Web browser to access the World Wide Web, copy text and graphics from Web site pages, print Web site pages, and use search techniques to find information on the Internet.

Upon completion of this lesson, you will be able to use the following skill sets
- Launch Internet Explorer
- Navigate the browser window
- Access a Web site using a Web address (URL)
- Print Web pages
- Save Web pages
- Copy from a Web site
- Exit the browser
- Search the Web
  - Use search engines and directories
  - Advanced search

Terms
Software-related
Bookmark
Directory
Domain name
Downloading
Favorites
Home page
Hyperlink
Internet Explorer
Internet service provider (ISP)
Keyword
Query
Search engine
Text string
URL (Uniform Resource Locator)
Web address
Web browser
Web crawler
Web site
World Wide Web

T R Y O U T

TASK 1

GOALS

To access Web sites using a Web address, as shown in Figure 3.1

To print, save, and bookmark Web pages

To exit the browser

- ✸ Launch Internet Explorer
- ✸ Navigate the browser window
- ✸ Access a Web site using a Web address (URL)
- ✸ Print, save, and bookmark Web pages
- ✸ Copy from a Web site
- ✸ Exit the browser

WHAT YOU NEED TO KNOW

Launch Internet Explorer

▶ The **World Wide Web** is a system of linked documents and files located on computers connected through the Internet. The documents and files are created by companies, individuals, schools, and government agencies around the world.

▶ An **Internet service provider (ISP)** is a service that provides access to the Internet. Using a modem and an ISP service, you can log on to the Internet, browse the World Wide Web, and send and receive e-mail.

Figure 3.1: Internet Explorer window with MSN home page displayed

▶ A **Web browser** is a software program that locates and displays the information you retrieve from the Internet in a readable format. **Internet Explorer** is the Web browser that is included with Microsoft Office. Internet Explorer can display graphics, text, and multimedia such as audio and video. The Internet Explorer icon is located on the desktop or the taskbar, as shown in Figure 3.2.

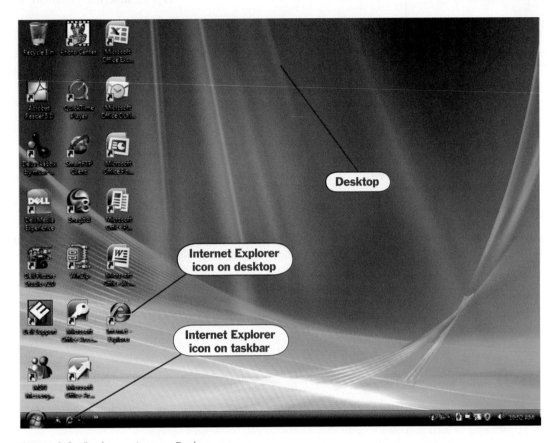

Figure 3.2: Desktop – Internet Explorer icons

Navigate the Browser Window

▶ When you start Internet Explorer, a home page is displayed. The **home page** is the start page of any Web site. A **Web site** is a collection of Web pages.

▶ The top of the Internet Explorer 7 window, shown in Figure 3.3, displays the title bar, address bar, menu bar, links bar, and the toolbar. The page area where the Web page is displayed below the toolbar. The status bar at the bottom of the window displays the status of the information being processed: download percentage, security settings, and zoom setting. **Downloading** is the process of copying files from the Internet to your computer.

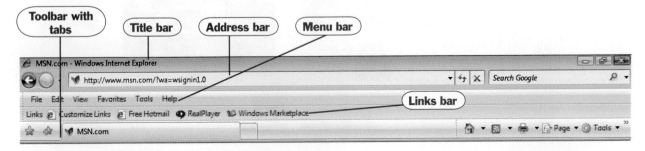

Figure 3.3: Internet Explorer toolbars and buttons

► The address bar contains the Address box and navigation and command buttons, which are described in Table 3.1.

Table 3.1: Address bar buttons

BUTTON		FUNCTION
Back		Returns you to the previous page
Forward		Advances you to the next page
Refresh		Reloads the current Web page to display new or changed content
Stop		Interrupts the search or page download
Search		Returns results based on text you enter in the Search box

► The menu bar is used to access additional commands and features such as a **bookmark** that you can apply to a favorite Web site so that you can revisit it later.

► The links bar contains links to other Web pages, and it can be customized to link to your favorite Web pages. Yours will be different from the one shown in the figures in this lesson.

► The toolbar contains tabs and the commands and features described in Table 3.2. The tabs are used to display and navigate between multiple Web pages in an Internet Explorer window.

Table 3.2: Toolbar buttons

BUTTON		USED TO
Favorites		Access list of your favorite Web sites
Add to Favorites		Add a Web page to your favorites list
Home		Return to the home page, add or change the home page
RSS Feeds		Access sites that provide updated content for news, music, etc.
Print		Print, preview, and change the page setup of a Web site
Page	Page	Access a menu of commands used to manage the Web page
Tools	Tools	Customize toolbars and access other features

► Web pages contain hyperlinks, as shown in Figure 3.1. A **hyperlink** (also referred to as link) appears as underlined or colored text or as a graphic. When clicked, a hyperlink takes you to a new page with related information. The mouse pointer changes to a hand when it finds a link.

1. Double-click the **Internet Explorer icon** on the desktop or click the icon on the taskbar. *Your home page will vary depending on your Internet service provider.*

2. Click a hyperlink on the home page. Click another link.

3. Click the **Back button** to return to the previous page.

4. Click the **Forward** button to advance to the next page.

5. Click the **Home button** to return to the start page.

6. Click the **Tools button** to view the menu. *Note the commands and shortcut keys.*

7. Click the **Page button** to view the menu. *Note the commands and keyboard shortcuts.*

Access a Web Site Using a Web Address (URL)

▶ Every Web site has a unique **Web address**, also called a **URL (Uniform Resource Locator)**. URLs have suffixes called **domain names**, which identify the type of Web site: commercial (.com), noncommercial (.org), government (.gov), educational (.edu), U.S. military (.mil), or network (.net) organization. A typical Web address might look like the ones shown in the history list in Figure 3.4.

▶ Internet Explorer records a history list of the sites you have visited and allows you to jump back to a recently visited site. To view a history list, click the list arrow at the right of the Address box, as shown in Figure 3.4.

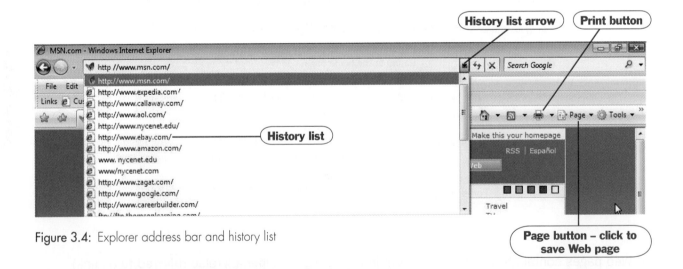

Figure 3.4: Explorer address bar and history list

▶ Each time a Web page downloads, the address appears in the Address box of the Internet Explorer window and on the title bar. To go to another Web page, click a link or enter the correct address in the Address box, and press [Enter]. To use tabbed browsing to have several Web pages open at once, press [Alt]+[Enter] to go to the new address. A rotating circular icon displays on a tab while the page is being located and loaded into your browser. Each Web site will have its title on a tab, as shown in Figure 3.5.

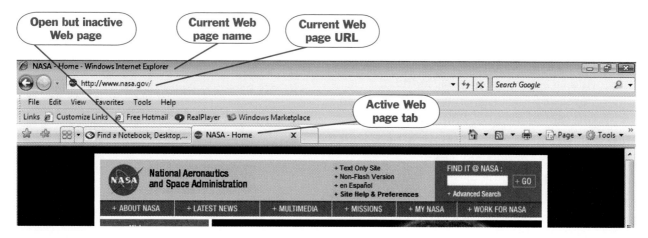

Figure 3.5: Several pages open using tabbed browsing feature

Print Web Pages

▶ Printing Web pages enables you to keep information you research for future reference.

HOW Ctrl+P 1. Click the **Print button** on the toolbar, or 1. click **File** on the menu bar, 2. point to **Print**, 3. then click **Print**.

Save Web Pages

▶ Because Web sites change constantly, it is a good idea to save a page that you find valuable. You can either save the content of a site in a file to your hard drive or other storage medium or create a **Favorites** link to the site so that you can revisit it and view any content changes.

▶ The process of saving a Web page is the same as that for saving a file.

HOW 1. Click **File** on the menu bar, or 1. Click the **Page button**. 2. Click **Save As**, choose a filename and location, and click **Save**.

▶ To create a bookmark or a Favorites link, access the page on the Web site that you wish to revisit, and add the link to your Favorites list.

HOW 1. On the Web page you wish to revisit, click **Favorites** on the menu bar. 2. Click **Add to Favorites**. 3. Edit the name or change the location of the link, if necessary. 4. Click **Add**. *A link to that site will be available when you click Favorites.*

T R Y *i t* **O U T** *pb3-2*

1. Click another link on the Web page, and note the address that is displayed in the Address box.

2. Enter **www.dell.com** in the Address box.

3. Press **Enter**.

4. Enter **www.nasa.gov** in the Address box, then press **[Alt]+[Enter]**.

Continued on next page

BASICS

5. Click **Favorites** on the menu bar, click **Add to Favorites**, then click **Add**. *If necessary, right-click in the blank space to the right of the tabs, then click Menu bar to display the menu bar.*

6. Click the **Address box list arrow**, and view the list of the sites visited. *Click away from the menu to close the list.*

7. Click the **Dell tab**, click **File** on the menu bar, then click **Print**.

8. View the print options, then click **Cancel**.

9. Right-click the **Dell tab**, then click **Close**.

10. Click the **NASA tab** if necessary, press **[Ctrl]+P**, then click **Print** to print the Web page.

11. Save the NASA Web page as **NASA home**.

Copy from a Web Site

▶ You can copy text or a picture from a Web site and paste it into an Office application.

HOW **1.** Select and right-click the graphic or text to be copied. **2.** Click **Copy** on the shortcut menu. *See Figure 3.6.* **3.** Position cursor in the Office document and right-click. **4.** Click **Paste** on the shortcut menu.

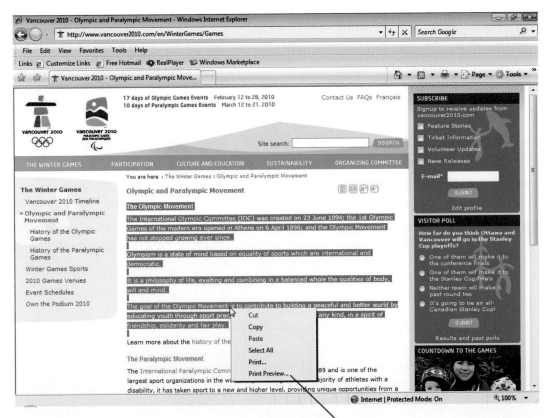

Figure 3.6: Copying text from a Web page

Make selection and right-click to view shortcut menu

► To save a picture, right-click the picture, and click **Save Picture As** on the shortcut menu, as shown in Figure 3.7. You can also e-mail and print the picture from this menu.

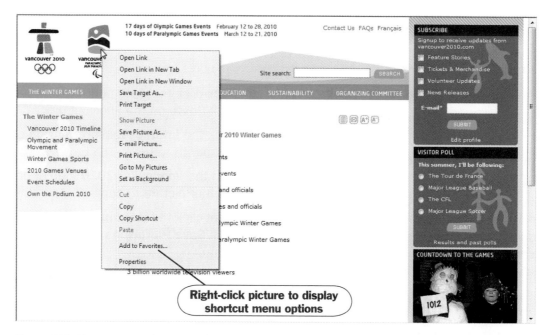

Figure 3.7: Using pictures from a Web page

► In the Save Picture dialog box, shown in Figure 3.8, choose the folder in which to save the file, enter a name for the picture, and click Save. Saved picture files may be inserted into a document.

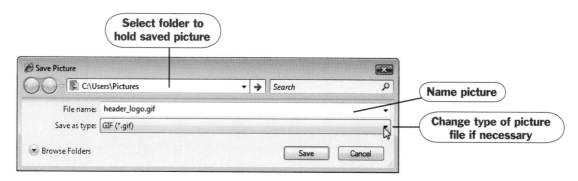

Figure 3.8: Save Picture dialog box

Exit the Browser

▶ To exit Internet Explorer, click the **Close button** or click **File** on the menu bar, and click **Exit**.

T R Y *i t* **O U T** *pb3-3*

1. Open a new blank document in Word.

2. Click the **Internet Explorer button** on the taskbar or launch it, if necessary.

3. Enter **www.vancouver2010.com** in the Address box, then press **[Enter]**.

4. Click the **The Winter Games tab** or a link to an article. *Web sites are updated constantly, so the page you see when you access this Web site may not resemble Figures 3.6 and 3.7.*

5. Select the text in the first paragraph shown in Figure 3.6 or any text.

6. Right-click the selection, then click **Copy** on the shortcut menu.

7. Click the **Microsoft Word button** on the taskbar to switch to the blank document.

8. Right-click the document window, then click **Paste** on the shortcut menu.

9. Click the **Internet Explorer button** on the taskbar to return to the browser window.

10. Find the **Vancouver 2010 logo** or choose another picture to copy.

11. Right-click the **Vancouver 2010 logo**, then click **Save Picture As** on the shortcut menu.

12. Select a folder in which to save the file, enter **2010logo** as the filename, then click **Save**.

13. Click the **Close button** to exit Internet Explorer.

14. Close Word without saving the file.

REHEARSAL

TASK 1

 GOALS
To access Web sites using a Web address

To print and save Web pages, and exit the browser

WHAT YOU NEED TO KNOW

▶ Because Web sites are updated, a Web site may display a different home/start page each time you access it.

▶ Be sure to cite the source of any Internet material you use in a document. Failing to do so is called plagiarism.

▶ If you cannot copy a picture, it may be that the picture has been copyrighted. A copyrighted picture has legal protection and cannot be used unless you obtain written permission from the publisher. Be sure to read Web pages carefully for this information.

DIRECTIONS

1. Launch Internet Explorer, if necessary.

2. Enter **www.baseballhalloffame.org** in the Address box, then press **[Enter]**.
   a. As shown in Figure 3.9, click **Baseball History**. *Web sites are updated constantly, so the page you see when you access this Web site may not resemble Figure 3.9.*
   b. Click and follow another link that interests you from the baseball history page.
   c. Click the **Back button**. Click the **Forward button**.

3. Enter **www.ed.gov/finaid** in the Address box, then press **[Alt]+[Enter]**. *The ed.gov site and the Baseball site are on different tabs, as shown in Figure 3.10.*
   a. Click the **Students** link or another link that interests you.
   b. Click a link to a feature that you are interested in learning more about.
   c. Print a copy of the article.
   d. Return to the home page.

4. Click the **Address box list arrow** to view your history, then click anywhere in the window to close the history list.

5. Return to the Baseball Web page.

6. Access the Web site www.nasa.gov using **[Alt]+[Enter]** to open another tab.
   a. Click the **WORK FOR NASA** link or another link that interests you.
   b. Right-click a picture from the page, then copy and paste it into a new blank Word document.
   c. Return to Internet Explorer.
   d. Copy a paragraph or an article from the page, then paste it into your Word document.
   e. Save the NASA Web page in a folder named **nasa**.

Continued on next page

7. Return to the Baseball Web page, and right-click the tab. Click **Close Other Tabs**.

8. Select a picture from the site and save it as a picture.

9. Close the browser and the Word file without saving it.

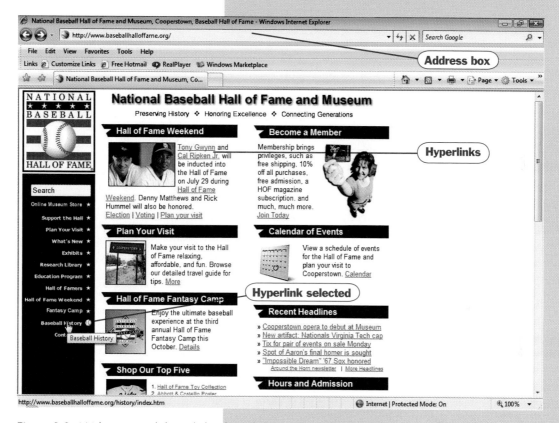

Figure 3.9: Web page with hyperlink selected

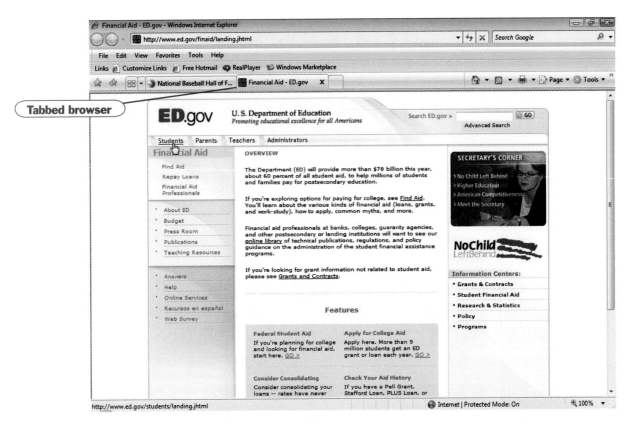

Tabbed browser

Figure 3.10: Web site, tabbed browser, link selected

Cues for Reference

Start Internet Explorer
1. Click the **Internet Explorer button** on the taskbar or double-click the **Internet Explorer icon** on your desktop.

Access a Web Site
1. Enter the URL in the Address box, then press **Enter**.
   Or
1. Click a link on the displayed Web page.

Print Web Pages
1. Click the **Print button** on the toolbar.

Copy from a Web Site
1. Select the text or point to the picture on the Web page to copy.
2. Right-click, then click **Copy** on the shortcut menu.
3. Position the insertion point in the document to paste the copied text or picture.
4. Right-click, then click **Paste** on the shortcut menu.

Save a Picture
1. Right-click the picture to save.
2. Click **Save Picture As** from the shortcut menu.

3. Select a folder to save, enter a filename, then click **Save**.

Save a Web Page
1. Click **File** on the menu bar.
2. Click **Save As**.
3. Select a folder to save, enter a filename, then click **Save**.

Exit the Browser
1. Click **File** on the menu bar, then click **Exit**.

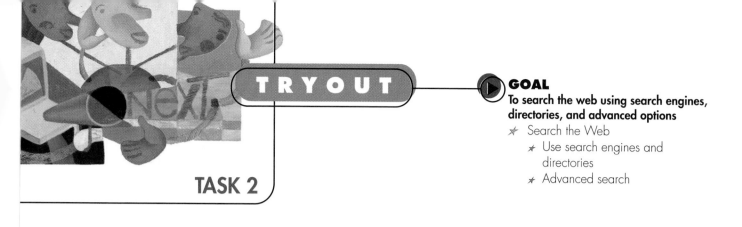

TRYOUT

TASK 2

GOAL
To search the web using search engines, directories, and advanced options
* Search the Web
  * Use search engines and directories
  * Advanced search

WHAT YOU NEED TO KNOW

Search the Web

▶ When you are researching a topic and do not know the URL that contains the information you need, you can search the Web using **keywords**. Keywords are terms that identify the information you are seeking. When you enter a keyword, a group of keywords, or a phrase, you are creating a **query**. A search will return sites relevant to your query.

▶ It is important to note the following when working with the Web:

- Use reliable sources. Anyone can publish information on the Web, and not all information you find is accurate.

- Many search engines are supported by advertising revenue and rank sites from their advertisers higher in the search results.

- Any program or file downloaded from the Internet can have a virus. Be sure that the computer you are using has updated virus-protection software installed.

Use Search Engines and Directories

▶ One of the tools you can use to search for information is a **search engine**, which is a software program that searches the Web and returns a list of relevant sites based on the search criteria you use. Search engines try to come up with the most relevant and substantial site at the top of each search no matter what the category may be. The people who maintain the search engines constantly review Web sites and index them using keywords with hyperlinks to new pages. Search engines are often called **Web crawlers** or "spiders," because they crawl the Web looking for information. Popular search engines include Google, Lycos, AltaVista, Yahoo! Search, and Ask.com.

▶ A **directory** displays information by major topic headings or categories, which are broken down into smaller topics that are then broken down further. A directory is handled by a service that will list your site, describe it, and possibly rank it. Yahoo!, About.com, and Google Directory are examples of popular directories. Yahoo! and Google offer both types of search capabilities so that if you are looking for a directory, you should add the word "directory" to your search word.

▶ On the address bar in Internet Explorer 7, there is a Search box with a list of search engines. One of them is set as the default, but you may change the default or try other options, as shown in Figure 3.11. Click the Search button to begin the search or press [Alt]+[Enter] to search and place the results on a new tab.

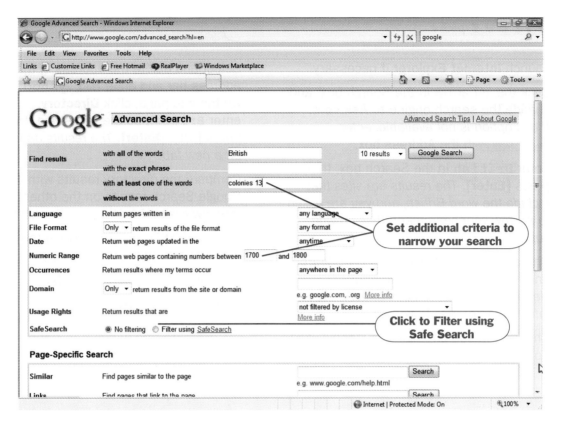

Figure 3.13: Advanced search screen

TRY it OUT pb3-5

1. Return to Internet Explorer.

2. Enter **British** in the Search box, and use **Ask.com** as the search engine to search for results.

3. In the Narrow Your Search section, scroll if necessary, select **British Colonies**, then narrow the search to **13 British Colonies**. Check several sites until you find a list of the colonies.

4. Enter **British History** in the Search box, and use **Google** as the search engine.

5. Click **Advanced Search** on the Google screen. and make the following settings:

a. Under Find results, enter: with **at least one** of the words **colonies 13**.

b. Under Numeric Range, enter: Return web pages containing numbers between **1700** and **1800**.

c. Under SafeSearch, click the **Filter using SafeSearch option button** as shown in Figure 3.13.

d. Click **Google Search**. *You have narrowed the search results to a topic and time period.*

6. Close all open Web pages.

GOAL
To search the Internet using search engines/directories, and advanced options

TASK 2

WHAT YOU NEED TO KNOW

▶ Use multiple sites when you research a topic. Directories and search engines vary in their content and accuracy and will often yield different results. Therefore, use a directory when you have a broad topic to research; use a search engine when you have a narrow topic to research.

▶ In this Rehearsal activity, you will search the Internet and print Web pages to research the 2010 Winter Olympics in Vancouver. Your report will include the history of the Olympic movement, the 2010 Olympic events, and touring information for Vancouver including a list of accommodations.

▼ DIRECTIONS

1. Start Internet Explorer.

2. Enter `Olympics` in the Search box, and use **Google** as the search engine.

3. Visit the official Web site for the Olympic movement, as shown in Figure 3.14.

4. Click the **Back button** to return to the Google screen, then click **Advanced Search**.

5. Add `History` to the with the exact phrase section, and add `Winter Olympics` to the with at least one of the words section. Click **Google Search**.

6. Follow links to find the history of the Winter Olympics. Copy and paste an appropriate article into Word. *Note the name of the Web page for citation purposes.*

7. Enter `2010 Olympics` in the Search box, and use **Live Search** as the search engine.

8. Click on the **Images tab**, select one of the pictures, and copy it into your Word document. Save the picture as a picture file.

9. Enter `Vancouver Olympics travel` in the Search box, and use **Yahoo! Search** as the search engine. *Use another provider or click Find More Providers if Yahoo! Search is not an option.*

10. Locate information about Vancouver as a travel destination, and find information about accommodations. Print the pages.

11. Close the browser.

Figure 3.14: Official Web site of the Olympic Movement

Access a Search Engine
1. Start Internet Explorer.
2. Enter a search string, then click the list arrow in the Search box.
3. Select the search engine, then press **[Enter]**.

Use a Search Engine to Refine the Search
1. Enter a text string in the Search box.
2. Press **[Enter]** or click the **Search button**.

3. Click **Advanced Search** on the Search Engine site.
4. Add additional criteria to refine the search.
5. Click Search on the Web page.

Use a Directory
1. Enter the name of a directory site in the address box. *For example: dir.yahoo.com*

2. Enter the search string on the directory site.
3. Click **Directory Search**, if necessary.
4. Click **Search**.

BASICS

* Downloadable from the
Student Online Companion

Word Basics

In this lesson, you will be introduced to Word and its basic features.
You will complete the following projects:

✻ Guidebook page
✻ Announcement
✻ Newsletter article

Upon completion of this lesson, you will have mastered the following skill sets

✻ Start Word
✻ Explore the Word window
✻ Create a new document
✻ Enter text
✻ Check spelling and grammar
✻ Change document and window views
✻ Display window elements
✻ Navigate through a document
✻ Select text/data
✻ Insert and delete text
✻ Show/hide codes
✻ Move and copy text

✻ Use the Office Clipboard
✻ Use Print Preview
✻ Print
✻ Format text
✻ Set text alignments
✻ Set line and paragraph spacing
✻ Work with fonts
✻ Use symbols
✻ Use Format Painter
✻ Highlight text
✻ Change case
✻ Change character spacing

Terms
Software-related

Active document
Click and type
Clipboard
Cut and paste
Defaults
Drag and drop
Font
Font face
Font size
Font style
Format Painter
Gridlines
Insertion point
Justified text
Landscape orientation
Portrait orientation
Sans serif
Script
Serif
Subscripts
Superscripts
Symbols
Thumbnails
Word-wrap

TRYOUT

TASK 1

GOALS

To explore and navigate the Word window
* About Word
* Start Word
* Explore the Word window

To open a document, then use the AutoCorrect and spelling and grammar features to finalize it, as shown in Figure 1.1
* Create a new document
* Enter text
* Change default settings

To create the document shown in Figure 1.2 and use word-wrap, AutoFormat As You Type, and spelling and grammar features
* Use AutoCorrect
* Use AutoFormat As You Type
* Check spelling and grammar

> **Default font: Calibri, 11 point**
> **Note default line spacing: 1.15**
> **Note default paragraph spacing:**
> **10 point after each paragraph**

Grammar Check Limitations

Grammar check, just like spell check, is not always correct and can be misleading.

Language is complex. It is difficult for a program to identify everything that is incorrect in a document. In fact, grammar check can be totally wrong. You MUST proofread a document and not depend on the computer to flag errors for you.

Use grammar check to correct the following sentences:

1. She wore two hats.

2. The girls are from a city near the ocean.

3. The books were written by an author.

4. A painting was stolen from the museum.

5. There are two of us going to the fair.

Using AutoCorrect

The AutoCorrect feature corrects com
once you press the spacebar. You mu
corrections you want. The AutoForm
typing these fractions and ordinals: ½

> **Use AutoCorrect to change abbreviations to complete words**

Event planning requires much of your time and energy. It requires a dependable network of suppliers. Assigning an inexperienced person to this type of work can be time-consuming.

ppg will help you with your event-planning needs. We coordinate all aspects of the event to ensure that it is ON TIME and ON BUDGET. Let ppg plan your next party!

Time is money. In the time it takes for an inexperienced person to plan an event, you may end up spending more money than it would have cost you to hire ppg.

Hiring an event planner to manage an event means you can relax and enjoy the party. Call us Monday through Friday from 8:00 a.m. to 5:30 p.m.

Figure 1.1: Task 1: Corrected document

Figure 1.2: Task 1: New Word document

WHAT YOU NEED TO KNOW

About Word

Microsoft Word 2007 is the word processing application within the Microsoft Office 2007 Suite that enables you to create letters, memos, reports, and other text-based documents. The features found in Word allow you to perfect and enhance your document and share it among workgroups. In addition, Word 2007 provides you with quick access to the Internet to support and share the documents you create.

Start Word

▶ There are two basic ways to start Word. Use the method that you find easiest.

 Using the first method, double-click the **Microsoft Word icon** on the desktop, as shown in Figure 1.3.

Using the second method, **1.** click the **Start button** on the Windows taskbar, **2.** point to **All Programs**, **3.** click **Microsoft Office**, then **4.** click **Microsoft Office Word 2007**, as shown in Figure 1.4.

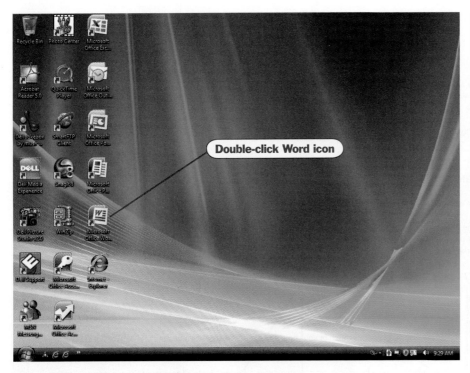

Figure 1.3: Start Word from desktop

Figure 1.4: Start Word from Windows taskbar

1. Click the **Start button**.

2. Point to **All Programs**.

3. Click **Microsoft Office**.

4. Click **Microsoft Office Word 2007**.
   A blank page appears in the Word window.

Explore the Word Window

▶ After launching Word, a new blank page appears in the Word window ready for you to enter text. Figure 1.5 shows the Word window, and Table 1.1 identifies and explains window elements that are basic for using Word. *Your Word window might look different from Figure 1.5 if a previous user changed screen elements or default settings.*

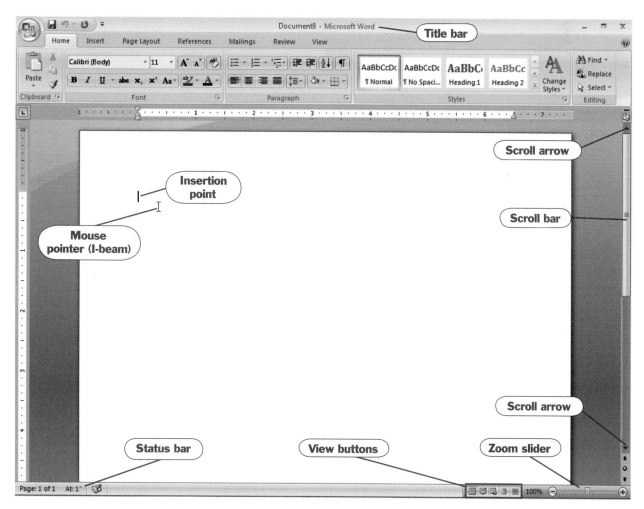

Figure 1.5: Word window

Table 1.1: Word window elements

WINDOW ELEMENT	EXPLANATION
Document window	Displays a blank page where you can insert text, graphics, tables or anything else to create your document.
Insertion point	Blinking line that displays to indicate where text will be inserted as you type.
Mouse pointer	As you move your mouse on the mouse pad, a corresponding movement of the pointer shows on-screen. The mouse pointer changes its shape depending on the task you are performing and the object on the screen to which you are pointing. *See Appendix E for a description of mouse pointer shapes and customizing options.*
Scroll bars, scroll arrows	Allows you to move the page to view different parts of a document. Scroll bars move the page horizontally and vertically. Scroll arrows move the document in incremental amounts.
Status bar	Displays information about the document (Page 1 of 6, for example); contains View buttons and Zoom control buttons. The type of information that is displayed depends on the options you select from the Customize Status Bar menu shown in Figure 1.6. Right-click the status bar to display this menu.
View buttons	Allows you to changes view of your document. *Changing document views will be covered in Task 2.*
Zoom slider	Allows you to get a close-up view of a document, see more of a page at a reduced size, or view multiple pages on the screen.

Customize Status Bar	
Formatted Page Number	1
Section	1
✓ Page Number	1 of 1
✓ Vertical Page Position	1"
Line Number	1
Column	1
Word Count	0
✓ Spelling and Grammar Check	Checking
✓ Language	
✓ Signatures	Off
✓ Information Management Policy	Off
✓ Permissions	Off
Track Changes	Off
Caps Lock	Off
Overtype	Insert
Selection Mode	
Macro Recording	Not Recording
✓ View Shortcuts	
✓ Zoom	100%
✓ Zoom Slider	

Figure 1.6: Customize Status Bar menu

TRY *it* OUT *w1-2*

1. Word should be open. Open the data file **w1-2**.

   a. Move your mouse on any text in the document area, and notice that the mouse pointer is in the shape of an "I-beam."

   b. Move your mouse on the graphic, and notice that the pointer's shape changes to a move handle.

   c. Move your mouse anywhere on the Ribbon, and notice that the pointer's shape changes to an arrow.

Continued on next page

TRY *it* **OUT** *w1-2 Continued*

d. Click and drag the **vertical scroll bar** up, then down. *Note that you can see other parts of your document.*

e. Point to the status bar, and right-click to display the Customize Status Bar menu.

f. Click to select **Page Number**, **Vertical Page Position**, and **Word Count**, if they are not already selected. If these options are selected, deselect them one at a time. *Note each change on the status bar.*

2. Locate the five **View buttons** and the Zoom slider on the right side of the status bar. These will be discussed in Task 2.

3. Close the file, and do not save it.

Create a New Document

▶ A new blank page is displayed when you open Word. Word assigns Document1 as the document name until you name it during the saving process. The document's name is displayed on the title bar (see Figure 1.5).

HOW [Ctrl]+N To create additional new documents without closing or exiting Word, 1. click the **Office Button**, 2. click **New**, then 3. click **Create**. Or, you can use the shortcut keys **[Ctrl]+N**. Word numbers each new document consecutively (Document2, Document3, etc.) until you provide a name during the saving process.

TRY *it* **OUT** *w1-3*

1. Press **[Ctrl]+N** to create a new blank document. *Notice the document number that is assigned by Word and displayed in the title bar.*

2. Enter your first and last name.

3. Press **[Ctrl]+N** to create another new blank document. *Notice the document number in the title bar.*

4. Enter a friend's name.

5. Close both files, and do not save them.

Enter Text

▶ When text is entered beyond the right margin, the insertion point automatically advances to the next line. This is called **word-wrap**. Press **[Enter]** only at the end of a short line or to begin a new paragraph.

Change Default Settings

▶ Characters are displayed in a specific font and font size, and other settings are in effect when you start Word. These preset settings are known as **defaults**.

▶ In Word 2007, the default font is set to Calibri, 11 point. Line spacing is set to 1.15, and paragraph spacing is set to 10 point after each paragraph. *This means that each time you press [Enter], 10-point spacing will be applied. A point is ¹⁄₇₂ of one inch in height.*

▶ When you change a default setting, the new setting will be applied to every subsequent document until you make another change. If you change a setting for a document but do not change the default, the setting will apply to that document only.

HOW To change a default setting, **1.** display the appropriate dialog box, **2.** make the changes you want in the dialog box, **3.** click the **Default button**, and click **4. Yes**. To change the default font, for example, **1.** click the **Home tab** and in the **Font group**, **2.** click the **dialog box launcher** to display the Font dialog box shown in Figure 1.7. **3.** Make the changes you want, **4.** click **Default**, then **5.** click **Yes**.

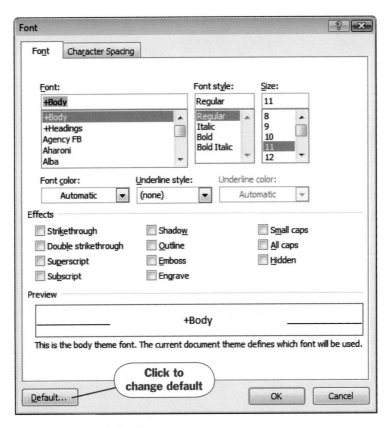

Figure 1.7: Font dialog box

Use AutoCorrect

▶ As you enter text, the AutoCorrect feature automatically replaces common capitalization, spelling, grammatical errors, and mistyped words with the correct text as you type.

▶ You can set this feature to insert specific words by entering an abbreviation in the AutoCorrect dialog box, which is shown in Figure 1.8. For example, you can enter "Mr." and have AutoCorrect replace it with "Mr. Snufulufougus." You can also enter words you commonly misspell into the AutoCorrect dictionary.

▶ When a word is corrected by the AutoCorrect feature, a blue horizontal line appears below the corrected word. Placing your insertion point on the line displays an AutoCorrect options button, as shown in Figure 1.9. Clicking the button displays options related to the corrected word.

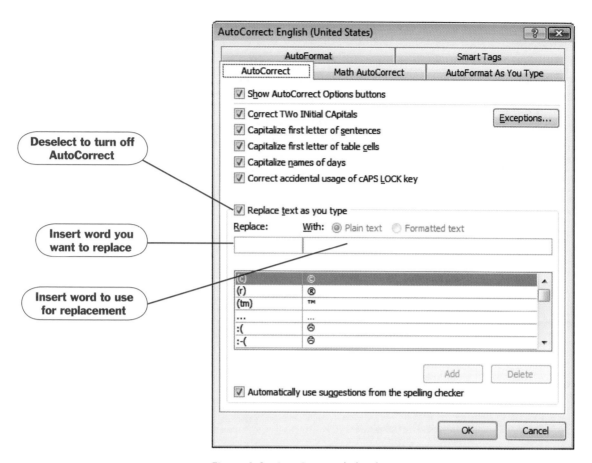

Deselect to turn off AutoCorrect

Insert word you want to replace

Insert word to use for replacement

Figure 1.8: AutoCorrect dialog box

HOW To set AutoCorrect preferences, **1.** click the **Office Button**, **2.** click **Word Options**, **3.** select **Proofing**, then **4.** click **AutoCorrect Options**. **5.** In the AutoCorrect dialog box, click the **AutoCorrect tab**, make the changes you want, **6.** click **OK** to close the AutoCorrect dialog box, then **7.** click **OK** to close Word options.

▶ The AutoCorrect feature is on by default. If you find this feature annoying, deselect the **Replace text as you type check box** within the AutoCorrect dialog box to turn the feature off (see Figure 1.8).

AutoCorrect Options button

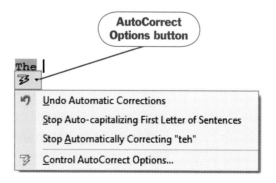

Figure 1.9: AutoCorrect Options button

Use AutoFormat As You Type

▶ The AutoFormat As You Type feature automatically formats text as you type it. You can set the AutoFormat As You Type options as you want. For example, you can choose to automatically change two hyphens (–) to a dash (–), fractions such as 1/2 to ½, and ordinals such as 2nd to a superscript (2nd).

HOW To set formatting options as you type, **1.** click the **Office Button**, **2.** click **Word Options**, **3.** select **Proofing**, then **4.** click **AutoCorrect Options**. **5.** In the AutoCorrect dialog box, click the **AutoFormat As You Type tab**, shown in Figure 1.10, **6.** make the changes you want, **7.** click **OK** to close the AutoCorrect dialog box, then **8.** click **OK** to close Word options.

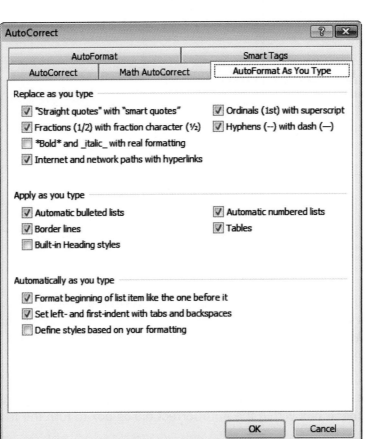

Figure 1.10: AutoFormat As You Type tab in the AutoCorrect dialog box

---

T R Y it O U T w1-4

A blank document should be open on screen. If not, press [Ctrl]+N to display a new blank document.

1. Click the **Home tab** and in the **Font group**, click the **Font dialog box launcher**. *Note the selected font and font size.*

a. Select **Times New Roman** in the Font list box and **12** in the Size box.

b. Click **Default**. When prompted, click **Yes**.

c. Enter your first and last name. Press **[Ctrl]+N** to display a new blank document.

Continued on next page

2. Enter each word exactly as shown. AutoCorrect will automatically correct the incorrectly typed word after you press the space bar.

   `teh  accomodate  adn  acheive`

3. Click the **Office Button**, **Word Options**, **Proofing**, and **Autocorrect Options**, then click the **AutoCorrect tab**.

4. Enter **usa** in the Replace text box.

5. Enter `United States of America` in the With text box. Click **Add**.

6. Click the **AutoFormat As You Type tab**.
   a. Select the following options if they have not already been selected: **Ordinals (1st) with superscript** and **Fractions (1/2) with fraction character (½)**.
   b. Deselect the following option if it is selected: **Set left- and first-indent with tabs and backspaces**. Note the other options. Click **OK**, then click **OK** again to close the Word options dialog box.

7. Enter the following text. Allow the text to word-wrap at the end of the line. Press **[Enter]** once when you see the paragraph symbol (¶). Do not be concerned with spelling errors at this time.

   `On May 1st I will be going to the usa. I will be there for 6 1/2 months. During my stay in the usa, I hope to visit many cities across the country, including New York, Los Angeles, Miami, and Chicago—the home town of my dearest friend, Jane. ¶ I hope we have a chance to see each other while I am in the usa.`

   Notice that because the default paragraph spacing is set to leave 10 points after each paragraph, you only had to press **[Enter]** once to create the paragraph.

8. Change the default font to **Calibri** and the font size to **11 point**.

9. Close the file, and do not save it.

Check Spelling and Grammar

As You Type (Shortcut Method)

▶ As you enter text, Word checks the text for spelling and grammar errors. A word with a possible spelling error is underlined with a wavy red line, a grammatical error is underlined with a wavy green line, and an error in word usage and style is underlined with a wavy blue line.

▶ When a spelling or grammar error is detected, the Proofing button on the status bar at the bottom of the Word window shows an "X" on the book rather than a writing pencil, to alert you that there is a possible error in your text. *If the spelling and grammar button is not displayed, right-click the* **status bar** *and choose* **Spelling and Grammar Check** *from the Customize Status Bar menu.*

HOW To correct a spelling error, **1.** right-click the underlined word, and a shortcut menu, shown in Figure 1.11, appears, displaying a list of suggested corrections. **2.** Click the correctly spelled word on the menu to replace the incorrectly spelled word in the document, or click the option button to ignore the error. You can also choose to add the word to the custom dictionary so that the word will not be flagged as an error if you use it again.

To correct a grammatical error, **1.** right-click the underlined word, and a shortcut menu, shown in Figure 1.12, appears, displaying suggested corrections. **2.** Click a listed suggestion, click the option button to ignore the error, or click **About This Sentence** to find out why Word finds the word or phrase to be an error. You can also click the **Proofing button** on the status bar, and Word will identify an error and open a shortcut menu with suggested corrections.

▶ Figure 1.13 shows the shortcut menu that is displayed when you right-click an error identified by a wavy blue line. Click the correctly spelled word on the menu to replace the incorrectly spelled word.

We was having a great conversasion when the bell rang.
Hats is worn by women.
As a matter of fact we were hopeing
One thing follow another.
I have a sugggestion that hers is as g
She are alone in this world.

| conversation |
| conversations |
| Ignore |
| Ignore All |
| Add to Dictionary |
| AutoCorrect ▶ |
| Language ▶ |
| Spelling... |
| Look Up... |
| Cut |
| Copy |
| Paste |

Figure 1.11: Spelling shortcut menu

We was having a great conversasion when the bell rang.   their.
Hats is worn by women.

| Hats are |
| A hat is |
| Ignore Once |
| Grammar... |
| About This Sentence |
| Look Up... |
| Cut |
| Copy |
| Paste |

re hopeing to see you their.

ers is as good as yours.

| there |
| Ignore |
| Ignore All |
| Add to Dictionary |
| Language ▶ |
| Spelling... |
| Look Up... |
| Cut |
| Copy |
| Paste |

Figure 1.13: Usage shortcut menu

Figure 1.12: Grammar shortcut menu

Entire Document at Once

▶ In addition to checking individual errors as you type, you can check your entire document or parts of the document at one time using the Spelling and Grammar feature.

▶ Because language is complex, it is difficult for a computer to identify everything that is incorrect in a document. Remember that neither the grammar nor the spelling check eliminates the need for you to carefully proofread a document.

How F7 **1.** Click the **Review tab**, and in the **Proofing group**, **2.** click the **Spelling & Grammar button** shown in Figure 1.14. In the Spelling and Grammar dialog box that is displayed, as shown in Figure 1.15, **3.** choose a correction option. Each option is explained in Table 1.2.

Figure 1.14: Spelling & Grammar button

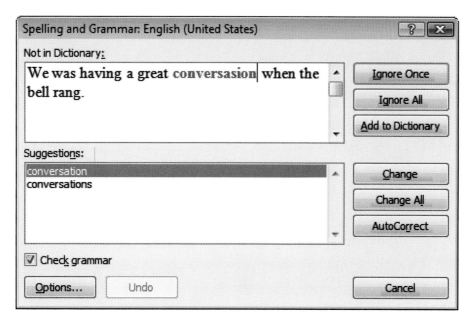

Figure 1.15: Spelling and Grammar dialog box

Table 1.2: Spelling and grammar correction options

OPTION	EXPLANATION
Ignore Once	Ignores the error.
Ignore All	Ignores all instances of the error.
Add to Dictionary	Adds the highlighted word to Word's custom dictionary.
Change	Changes the flagged error to the selected suggestion.
Change All	Changes all instances of the error to the selected suggestion.
AutoCorrect	Adds the word to the AutoCorrect dictionary.

TRY *it* OUT w1-5

1. Open the data file **w1-5**.

2. Right-click the first misspelled word, and choose the correct spelling from the shortcut menu.

3. Right-click the first grammatical error, and choose the correct usage from the shortcut menu.

4. Click the **Proofing button** on the status bar. Choose the correction from the shortcut menu.

5. Click the **Review tab** and in the **Proofing group**, click the **Spelling and Grammar button**. Using the Spelling and Grammar dialog box, correct the remaining errors.

6. Close the file, and do not save it.

REHEARSAL

TASK 1

GOALS

To open the document shown in Figure 1.16 and use the AutoCorrect and Spelling and Grammar features to finalize it

To create the new document shown in Figure 1.17 and use word wrap, AutoFormat As You Type, and spelling and grammar features

WHAT YOU NEED TO KNOW

▶ A document is also called a file.

▶ Space twice after punctuation that ends a sentence.

▶ A **draft document** is one that is not yet finalized.

DIRECTIONS

1. Open the data file **w1r1-draft document**, which is shown in Figure 1.16.

2. Use the shortcut method to check the spelling errors indicated.

3. Use the shortcut method to check the grammatical errors indicated.

4. Open the AutoCorrect dialog box, and select the **AutoFormat As You Type tab**. Make sure that all the options are checked in the Replace as you type section.
   a. Click the **AutoCorrect tab**.
   b. Enter **ac** in the Replace text box. Enter **AutoCorrect** in the With text box, and click **OK** twice.

5. Click below the paragraph that reads "Using AutoCorrect." Enter the following paragraph exactly as shown, including the misspelled words that are highlighted. Allow the text to word-wrap at the end of each line.

   THe ac feature corrects common capitalization, spelling, and grammatical errors as you type once you press teh spacebar. You must be sure the ac menu has been set to make the corrections yuo want. The AutoFormat As You Type option (which is part of the ac feature) allows you to set formatting options. Try typing these fractions and ordinals: 1/2, 1/4, 1ST, 2ND. did the ac feature work for you?

6. Save the file. Name it **1r1-corrected**, then close it.

7. Click **[Ctrl]+N** to create a new blank document.

Continued on next page

8. Open the AutoCorrect Options dialog box. Enter **ppg** in the Replace text box. Enter **Perfect Planning Group** in the With text box.

9. Enter the paragraphs shown in Figure 1.17. Press **[Enter]** once to start a new paragraph.

10. Check the spelling and grammar for the entire document.

11. Save the document. Name it **1r1-wordwrap**, then close the file.

Grammar Check Limitations

Grammar check, just liike spell check, is not alwaays correct correct and can be misleeading.

Language is complex. It is difficult for a programm to identify everything that is incorrect in a document. In fact, Grammar check can be totally wrong. You MUST proofread a document and not depend on the computer to flagg errors for you.

Use grammar check to correct the following sentences:

1. She wore two hat.

2. The girl are from a city near the ocean.

3. The book were written by an author.

4. A painting were stolen from the museum.

5. Their are two of us going to the fair.

Using AutoCorrect

Figure 1.16: Uncorrected document–Draft document

Event planning requires much of your time and energy. It requires a dependable network of suppliers. Assigning an inexperienced person to this type of work can be time-consuming.

ppg will help you with your event-planning needs. We coordinate all aspects of the event to ensure that it is ON TIME and ON BUDGET. Let ppg plan your next party!

Time is money. In the time it takes for an inexperienced person to plan an event, you may end up spending more money than it would have cost you to hire ppg.

Hiring an event planner to manage an event means you can relax and enjoy the party. Call us Monday through Friday, from 8:00 a.m. to 5:30 p.m.

Figure 1.17: New word document–New Word document

Start Word (and Open a New Blank Document)
1. Click **Start**.
2. Point to **All Programs**.
3. Click **Microsoft Office**.
4. Click **Microsoft Office Word 2007**.

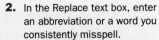

Create a New Document
1. Click the **Office Button**, click **New**, click **Create**.
   Or
1. Click **[Ctrl]+N**.

Use AutoCorrect
1. Click the **Office Button**, click **Word Options**, select **Proofing**, click **AutoCorrect Options**.

2. In the Replace text box, enter an abbreviation or a word you consistently misspell.
3. In the **With text box**, enter the correctly spelled word.
4. Click **OK** twice.

Check Spelling and Grammar
As You Type (Shortcut method)
1. Right-click the misspelled word or usage error, and choose a correctly spelled word or usage correction from the shortcut menu.

Entire document at once
1. Click the **Review tab**, and in the **Proofing group**, click the **Spelling & Grammar button**.

2. Make your desired changes in the Spelling and Grammar dialog box.
3. Click **OK**.

TASK 1

You work for the Perfect Planning Group, a company that offers full-service gourmet catering for parties and other events. This year, the company has decided to publish a magazine filled with articles about cooking, cooking tips, catering menus, food health issues, and other information that would be of interest to someone hosting a party. You have been asked to finalize a draft article and make any spelling and grammatical corrections necessary.

Follow these guidelines:

1. Open the data file **w1p1-article**.

2. Enter the abbreviation `carb` in the AutoCorrect dictionary for the word `carbohydrates`.

3. Enter the following paragraph beneath the last paragraph in the document. Leave the same spacing after the last paragraph as in the previous paragraphs.

   ```
   Carb

   Carb are your body's primary fuel. In the body, carb are broken down
   into simple sugar glucose. The glucose is carried by the blood and
   stored as glycogen in your liver and muscles. Complex carb, found in
   unrefined whole grains, beans, and vegetables, are high in fiber,
   while simple carb are sugars for the most part and generally have
   almost no nutritional value.
   ```

4. Check the spelling and grammar for the entire document.

5. Save the file, then close it.

TRYOUT

TASK 2

GOAL
To finalize and print edited documents, as shown in Figure 1.18

- Change document and window views
- Display window elements
- Navigate through a document
- Select text/data
- Insert and delete text
- Show/hide codes
- Move and copy text
- Use the Office Clipboard
- Use Print Preview
- Print

HOW TO STUDY EFFECTIVELY

How do you study? If your studying consists of reading and rereading the material, you are not studying effectively.

In order to study productively, you must become actively involved in the process. and You should usetilize as many senses as you can: sight, sound, and touch if possible. This means that in addition to reading the material, you should be writing, speaking and thinking about everything what you are studying.

Here are some helpful tips for studying effectively:

When studying from text, prepare an outstanding outline of the material according to the structure of the text. Use the main topics as the different levels of the outline.

Take wonderfulgood class notes. Keep a separate notebook for each class. Write the date and page number for each page you use. Teachers usually write all the key points on the board or on a overhead projector. Wait to write each point until your teacher begins to talk about the lesson it. In this way, you will have room to fill in the details. That's the way to do it.

Reread the material. Look back and carefully read any material you still do not understand. Always look for the main points, further details and questions you can answer as you read.

Read your notes after class,: while Yyour memory is fresh soand you may be able to supply more details. Underline or highlightEmphasize important points and write down questions and the key terms included in the lesson.

Good study skills not only help us achieve good grades in school, but they are invaluable tools that will allow us to be more productive in our professional lives.

HOW TO STUDY EFFECTIVELY

How do you study? If your studying consists of reading and rereading the material, you are not studying effectively.

In order to study productively, you must become actively involved in the process. You should use as many senses as you can: sight, sound, and touch if possible. This means that in addition to reading the material, you should be writing, speaking and thinking about what you are studying.

Good study skills not only help us achieve good grades in school, but they are invaluable tools that will allow us to be more productive in our professional lives.

Here are some helpful tips for studying effectively:

Take good class notes. Keep a separate notebook for each class. Write the date and page number for each page you use. Teachers usually write the key points on the board or on a projector. Wait to write each point until your teacher begins to talk about it. In this way, you will have room to fill in the details.

Reread the material. Look back and carefully read any material you still do not understand. Always look for the main points, further details, and questions you can answer as you read.

Read your notes after class, while your memory is fresh so you may be able to supply more details. Emphasize important points and write down questions and key terms included in the lesson.

When studying from text, prepare an outline of the material according to the structure of the text. Use the main topics as the different levels of the outline.

Figure 1.18: Task 2: Edited and final documents

WHAT YOU NEED TO KNOW

Change Document and Window Views

Document Views

▶ Word provides several ways to view a document on-screen. There are five views in Word, which are useful in different situations. Table 1.3 describes each document view.

Table 1.3: Document views

VIEW		DESCRIPTION
Print Layout	Print Layout	Shows how a document will look when it is printed. This view, which is the default and is shown in Figure 1.19, allows you to see headers and footers, columns, and graphics. Most users prefer this view when working with Word. *Headers and footers will be covered in Lesson 3.*
Full Screen Reading	Full Screen Reading	Maximizes the reading experience by hiding all toolbars and increasing the size of the text without affecting the size of the font in the document. All pages of a multi-page document may not be visible in this view. Figure 1.20 shows two pages of a three-page document. You can edit text in this view.
Web Layout	Web Layout	Shows how a document will look as a Web page, as shown in Figure 1.21.
Outline	Outline	Displays heading levels in an outline, as shown in Figure 1.22. *Outlines will be covered in Lesson 4.*
Draft	Draft	Allows you to view a document as a draft and quickly make corrections. Graphics, headers, and footers are not displayed in this view, which is shown in Figure 1.23.

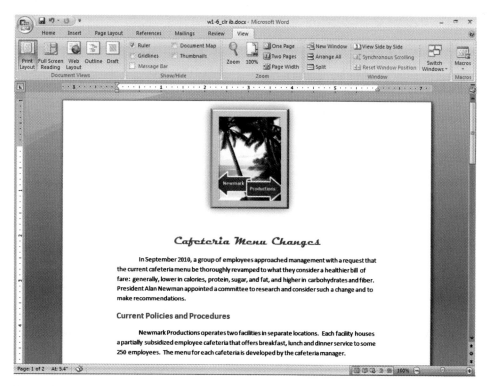

Figure 1.19: Print Layout view

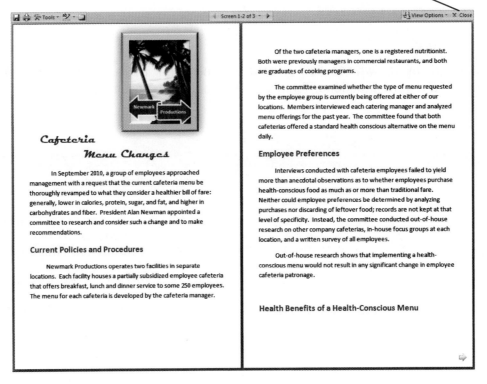

Figure 1.20: Full Screen Reading view

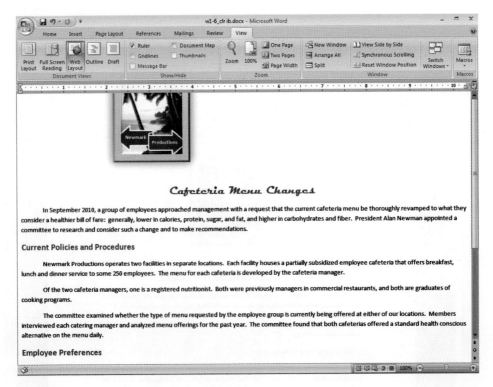

Figure 1.21: Web Layout view

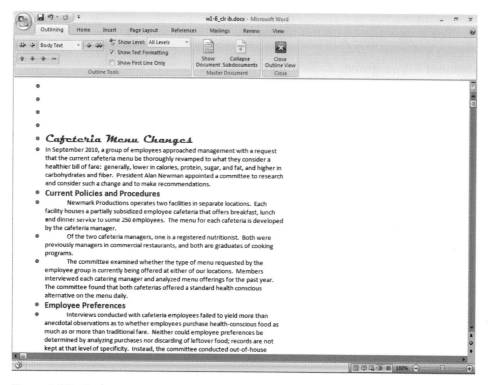

Figure 1.22: Outline view

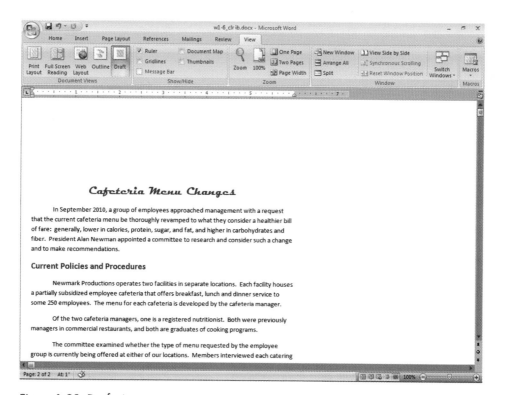

Figure 1.23: Draft view

View buttons

Figure 1.24: View buttons on status bar

HOW **1.** Click a view button on the status bar, as shown in Figure 1.24, or **1.** click the **View tab** and in the **Document Views group**, **2.** click a view button, as shown in Figure 1.25.

Figure 1.25: View buttons on Ribbon

Zoom

▶ As you learned in Performance Basics Lesson 1, you can use the Zoom feature to get a close-up view of your document or see more of a page at a reduced size. You can also use the Zoom feature to view multiple pages on the screen.

HOW **1.** Click and drag the **Zoom slider** on the status bar to the right to make the document larger and to the left to make it smaller. You can also **1.** click the **View tab**, and in the **Zoom group** shown in Figure 1.26, **2.** click the **Zoom button** for the option you want.

Zoom

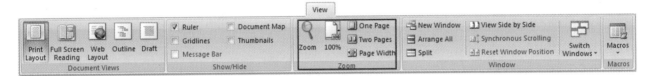

Figure 1.26: Zoom options on View tab

T R Y i t O U T w1-6

1. Open the data file **w1-6.** *You should be in Print Layout view.* Notice that the graphic and footer are displayed in this view (scroll down to see the footer). *Headers and footers will be covered in Lesson 3.*

2. Click the **Draft view button.** Notice that the graphic and footer are not displayed in this view.

   Draft

3. Click the **Outline view button.** Notice that the Outline toolbar appears. *This view does not apply to this document. Outlines will be covered in Lesson 4.*

   Outline

4. Click the **Print Layout view button.** Notice that the vertical ruler appears.

   Print Layout

5. Click the **Full Screen Reading view button.** The entire page is displayed; however, only half of the text that is actually on the page is displayed. The footer is not displayed at all. Click the **Close button** in the upper-right corner of the screen or press **[Esc]** to exit Full Screen Reading view.

   Full Screen Reading

6. Click the **View tab,** and in the **Zoom group,** click the **Two Pages button.** The document is displayed in a reduced size so that two pages can be viewed.

   Two Pages

7. Click the **Page Width button.** The document is displayed as wide as possible in the document window.

   Page Width

Continued on next page

8. Click the **One Page button**. The document is displayed in a reduced size as one page.

 One Page

9. Click the **100% button**. The document returns to the default size.

100%

10. Click the **Zoom button**. The Zoom dialog box is displayed, allowing you to make other zoom choices. Click **Cancel** to close the dialog box.

Zoom

11. Close the file, and do not save it.

Window Views

▶ Word provides a number of ways to split the screen, allowing you to view two different portions of a document at one time or multiple documents at one time. It is particularly helpful to display two parts of a document or multiple documents at once if you want to move or copy text between pages of a long document or between documents.

HOW To split a document, arrange all open documents on-screen or view a document side by side, **1.** click the **View tab**, and in the **Window group**, **2.** click either the **Split button**, **Arrange All button**, or **View Side by Side button**, as shown in Figure 1.27.

Split

Arrange All   View Side by Side

Figure 1.27: Window buttons on View tab

Split Windows

▶ After clicking the **Split button** on the **View tab** (see Steps 1 and 2 above), position your insertion point where you want the split to occur, then left-click. Figure 1.28 shows a split document. Notice that each document window contains its own scroll bar.

HOW You can also split the window by positioning the mouse pointer on the split bar at the top of the vertical scroll bar, as shown in Figure 1.29, until the pointer changes to a resize pointer. Then **1.** drag the pointer down, and then **2.** release the mouse button.

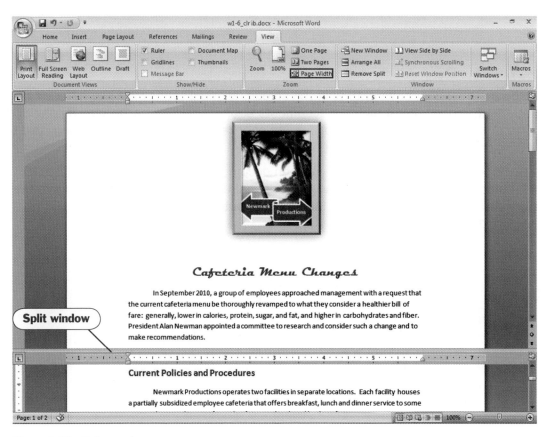

Figure 1.28: Split window

To remove a split window, **1.** click the **Remove Split button** *(the Split button changes to the Remove Split button)*, or double-click the **split bar**.

Arrange All Open Documents

▶ Figure 1.29 shows three documents in multiple windows after Arrange All was selected. Notice that the documents are tiled from top to bottom. The **active document** contains the insertion point and displays a darkened title bar. In Figure 1.29, the top document is the active document.

▶ To make one of the arranged documents fill the entire screen, click the **Maximize button** in that window. To switch to another document and maximize it, click the **Switch Windows button** on the **View tab**, select a document to display, then click its **Maximize button**.

Figure 1.29: Multiple windows after Arrange All selection

Side-by-Side Documents

▶ The documents you want displayed side by side should be open when you make this selection. If you have multiple documents on-screen, Word will assume that you want the active document compared with another one. After you click the View Side by Side button, a dialog box will appear prompting you to select the open document you wish to display next to the active one.

▶ Figure 1.30 shows documents displayed side by side. Note that the Ribbon is displayed in each window. To return to one window, click the **Window button**, and select **Side by Side** from the menu, as shown in Figure 1.31.

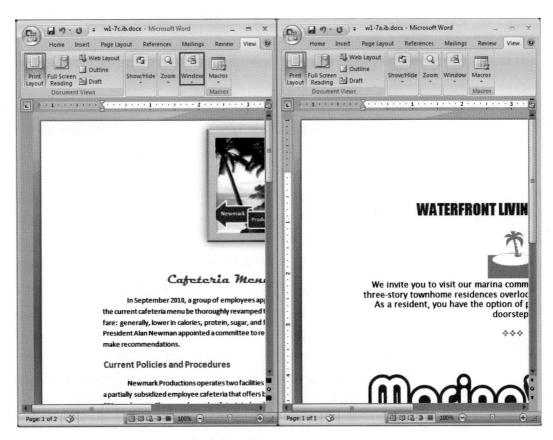

Figure 1.30: Documents displayed side by side

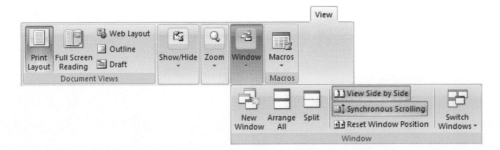

Figure 1.31: Window menu

1. Open data documents **w1-7a**, **w1-7b**, and **w1-7c**.

2. Click the **View tab**, and in the **Window group**, click **Arrange All**.

   a. Scroll to view each document.

   b. Click the **Maximize button** on **w1-7a** to return the document to full size.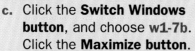

   c. Click the **Switch Windows button**, and choose **w1-7b**. Click the **Maximize button**.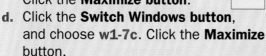

   d. Click the **Switch Windows button**, and choose **w1-7c**. Click the **Maximize button**.

3. Click the **Switch Windows button** and select **w1-7a**.

4. Click the **View Side by Side button**. Select  **w1-7b**, and click **OK**. Scroll up and down the document. *Both documents will move together if the Synchronous Scrolling option is on. To turn this feature off, click the* **Synchronous Scrolling button**. *When the feature is turned off, you can scroll each document independently of each other.*

5. Maximize **w1-7a**. Click the **View tab**, and in the **Window group**, click the **Split button**. Move your insertion point where you want the split, then left-click. Scroll each part of the document up and down, then click the **Remove Split button**.

6. Close all files, and do not save them.

Display Window Elements

▶ Window elements such as the horizontal and vertical rulers, gridlines, document map, and thumbnails make it easier for you to create and navigate through documents. Word allows you to display or hide these elements.

▶ Horizontal and vertical **rulers**, shown in Figure 1.32, are used to gauge the position of text on a page. Use the horizontal ruler to set tab stops, adjust page margins, indent paragraphs, and adjust column widths.

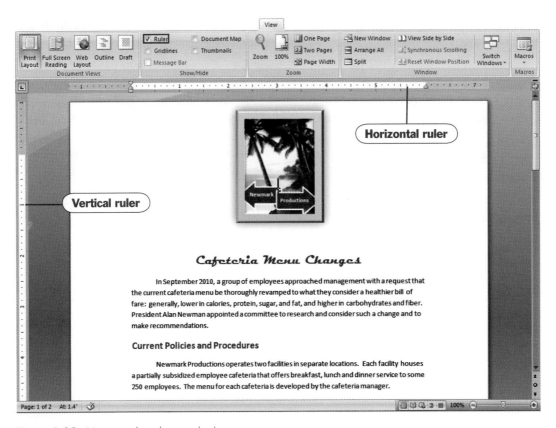

Figure 1.32: Horizontal and vertical rulers

▶ **Gridlines**, shown in Figure 1.33, are horizontal and vertical lines that form a grid, which can help you with the placement of graphics. Gridlines appear only in Print Layout view and within your margins. *Gridlines will be covered in more detail in Lesson 4.*

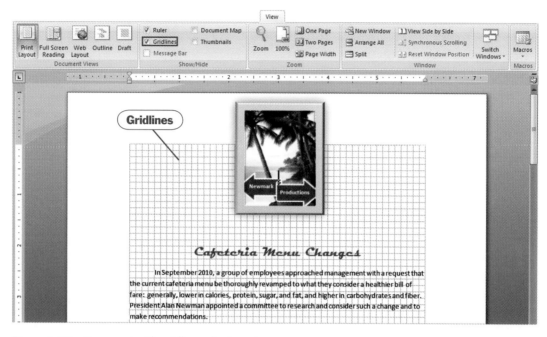

Figure 1.33: Document with gridlines displayed

▶ The **Document Map** allows you to see a structural view of your document, as shown in Figure 1.34. You can click any item in the Document Map pane to quickly get to it into the document.

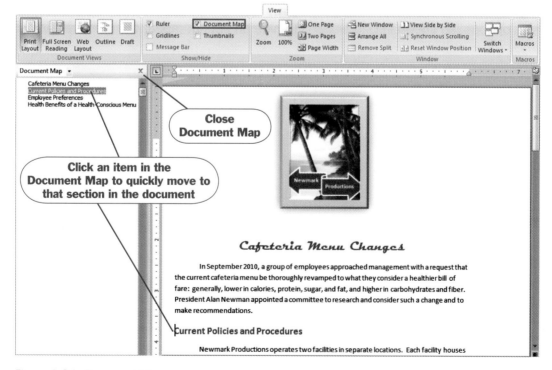

Figure 1.34: Document Map

▶ **Thumbnails** display each document page in miniature in the Thumbnails pane on the left of your screen, as shown in Figure 1.35. A border around the thumbnail indicates the displayed page. You can click on a thumbnail to quickly display a page in a document.

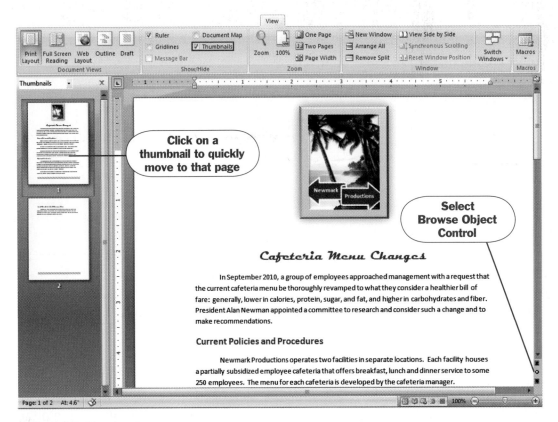

Figure 1.35: Thumbnails

HOW **1.** Click the **View tab**, and in the **Show/Hide group**, **2.** click one of the Show/Hide options, as shown in Figure 1.36. To hide an option, repeat the process and deselect the option.

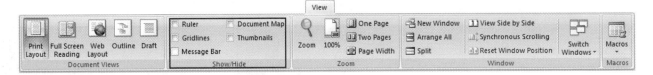

Figure 1.36: Show/Hide options on View tab

TRY*it*OUT *w1-8*

1. Open the data file **w1-8**.

2. Click the **View tab** and in the **Show/Hide group**, click to select **Ruler**, if it is not already displayed. If the rulers are displayed, skip this step. *The horizontal and vertical rulers are displayed at the top and side of the page.*

3. Select **Document Map**. *The Document Map is displayed in the pane on the left side of your screen.*
   a. Click the **Current Policies and Procedures link** on the document map. *This will quickly move your*

Continued on next page

insertion point to that part of the document.

b. Click the **Close button** on the Document Map pane to close the window.

4. Select **Gridlines**. Scroll to the top of the page. *Notice where the graphic is*

positioned on the page in relation to the margins. Deselect **Gridlines**.

5. Select **Thumbnails**. Click the second page on the thumbnail pane, then deselect **Thumbnails**.

6. Close the file, and do not save it.

Navigate through a Document

▶ The easiest way to move the insertion point around a document is to place the insertion point where you want it and click. This is called **click and type**.

▶ If you are working on long documents, however, you must be able to scroll through the pages quickly. As you just learned, to quickly display a page, click on its thumbnail. Once you display a page, you can use the keyboard and/or mouse movements described in Table 1.4 to navigate through it.

Table 1.4: Express navigation options

KEYBOARD MOVEMENTS		MOUSE MOVEMENTS	
PRESS	**TO MOVE**	**DO THIS**	**TO**
[Ctrl]+left or right arrow	One word to the left or right	Click above or below the scroll box.	Scroll up or down one screen
[Ctrl]+up or down arrow	One paragraph up or down	Drag the scroll box.	Scroll to a specific page
[End]	To the end of a line	Hold **[Shift]** and click the left scroll arrow at the bottom of the screen.	Scroll left, beyond the margin
[Home]	To the beginning of a line	Click the **Select Browse Object Control** (the circle at the bottom of the vertical scroll bar), as shown in Figure 1.35. Click the **Go To arrow**. Enter page number and click **Go To**.	Go to a specific page
[Page Up] or [Page Down]	Up or down one screen	Click on a thumbnail.	Quickly display a page
[Ctrl]+[Page Down]	To the top of the next page	Rotate the center wheel forward or backward through a document.	Scroll up or down using the IntelliMouse
[Ctrl]+[Page Up]	To the top of the previous page	Press down on the center wheel. When you see the scroll symbol, move the mouse up or down. Press down on the center wheel to stop AutoScroll.	Quickly scroll up or down using AutoScroll on the IntelliMouse
[Ctrl]+[End]	To the end of the document		
[Ctrl]+[Home]	To the beginning of the document		

1. Open the data file **w1-9**.
2. Click the **View tab**, and in the **Show/Hide group**, click **Thumbnails**.
3. Click on the thumbnail of page two, then click the thumbnail of page one.
4. Drag the vertical scroll box down to view the entire document.
5. Press **[Ctrl]+[Home]** to return to the top of the document.
6. Press **[Ctrl]+[End]** and **[Ctrl]+[Home]** again.
7. Click at the beginning of paragraph 1.
8. Press **[End]**, then press **[Home]**.
9. Press **[Ctrl]+[PageDown]**, then **[Ctrl]+[PageUp]**.
10. Click the arrow below the vertical scroll box.

11. Click at the beginning of paragraph 2.
12. Press **[Ctrl]+[Home]**.
13. Click the **Select Browse Object control** (circle) located on the vertical scroll bar, and roll your mouse pointer over each option to view its purpose.
    a. Click the **Go To button**.
    b. Enter page 2, click **Go To**, then click **Close**.
14. If you have an IntelliMouse, click the center wheel and watch the document scroll down.
    a. Slide the mouse downward to scroll the document faster.
    b. Click the center wheel to stop AutoScroll.
15. Close the file, and do not save it.

Select Text/Data

▶ Before you can edit text or data (format, delete, move, or copy it), you must first select it. Selecting text highlights a character, word, or block of text or data, as shown in Figure 1.37. The most frequently used selection techniques are explained in Table 1.5. Other techniques are detailed in Appendix G.

▶ When you select text, the Mini toolbar appears, quickly giving you access to formatting options. You will learn to use the Mini toolbar to change formatting in Task 3.

HOW Table 1.5: Text selection techniques

TO SELECT	ACTION
A word	Double-click the word.
A sentence	Press and hold **[Ctrl]** as you click in the sentence.
A paragraph	Triple-click anywhere in the paragraph.
Entire document	Triple-click in the left margin. Or Click the **Home tab** and in the **Editing group**, click the **Select button**, then choose **Select All** from the menu. [⬚ Select]

SCROLLING THROUGH TWO-PAGE PRACTICE TEXT

This is practice text that you can use for importing, placing, and "playing" purposes. Practice text is useful when you are planning a layout or trying out the features of Microsoft Word. Using practice text rather than real text is a good way to concentrate on the form and design of your layout without reading the text itself. Consider this **paragraph one** (this might change, of course).

This is paragraph two. Practice text should have paragraphs so you can manipulate them and move them as you desire. Practice text also encourages you to experiment with changing typefaces, type styles, type sizes and leading. You become less intimidated experimenting with your software's design elements if you know that it is merely practice and not the real text.

This is paragraph three. When working with practice text, you should have at least four paragraphs. This will enable you to move them and experiment with at least four different formats. The paragraphs should be long enough so that you can see the effects of a line spacing or paragraph spacing change, for example. You might also want

Figure 1.37: Selected text

T R Y *i t* **O U T** *w1-10*

1. Open the data file **w1-10**.

2. Double-click **SCROLLING** in the title to select the word. *Notice that the Mini toolbar appears.*

3. Double-click **THROUGH** in the title to select the word.

4. Click and drag the mouse over the first paragraph to select it.

5. Position the insertion point in the second paragraph. Triple-click in rapid succession to select the paragraph.

6. Position the insertion point in the first sentence of the first paragraph. Press **[Ctrl]**, and click once to select a sentence.

7. Click the **Home tab** and in the **Editing group**, click the **Select button**, then choose **Select All** to select the entire document.

8. Close the file, and do not save it.

Insert and Delete Text

▶ After creating a document, it is likely that you will make changes to it. The most frequent changes include inserting and/or deleting text. The Delete feature allows you to remove text, graphics, or codes from a document. The user must select text before using the delete feature. See Appendix G for various text selection techniques.

HOW [Ctrl]+X (delete text) To insert text, **1.** position the insertion point to the left of the character that will follow the inserted material, then **2.** enter the new text. *When you enter new text, the existing text moves to the right.*

To delete a character or close up spaces to the left of the insertion point, press **[Backspace]**. To delete blocks of text, you must **1.** select the text you want to delete, **2.** then press **[Delete]**, or **2.** click the **Home tab**, and in the **Clipboard group**, **3.** click the **Cut button**, as shown in Figure 1.38.

Figure 1.38: Cut button on Home tab

T R Y *i t* **O U T** *w1-11*

1. Open a new blank document.

2. Enter the following without pressing **[Enter]**:

   ```
   Admission to all Conference
   events is free. Please
   join us.
   ```

3. Double-click the word "all" to select it, then press **[Delete]**.

4. Double-click the word "events" and enter **sessions**.

5. Position the insertion point anywhere in the sentence "Please join us." Press **[Ctrl]**, and click to select it, then press **[Delete]**.

6. Open the data file **w1-11**. Insert and delete words, as shown in Figure 1.39 (insert underlined words; delete words that are crossed out).

7. Close the files, and do not save them.

We <u>now</u> have <u>growth</u> opportunities ~~available~~ in our ~~new~~ company for managers ~~and associate managers~~ who are ~~very~~ interested in a ~~fast-track~~ career with a<u>n</u> industry leader<u>.</u> ~~in the industry.~~ Please ~~send a~~ fax your resume to me <u>as soon as possible.</u>

Figure 1.39: Text with insertions and deletions

Show/Hide Codes

▶ As you create a new document, Word inserts nonprinting codes. You can choose to display these codes at any time. Figure 1.40 shows several paragraphs with Show/Hide codes displayed. The codes represent paragraph marks (¶), tabs (→), and spaces (·). It is recommended that you display codes when editing.

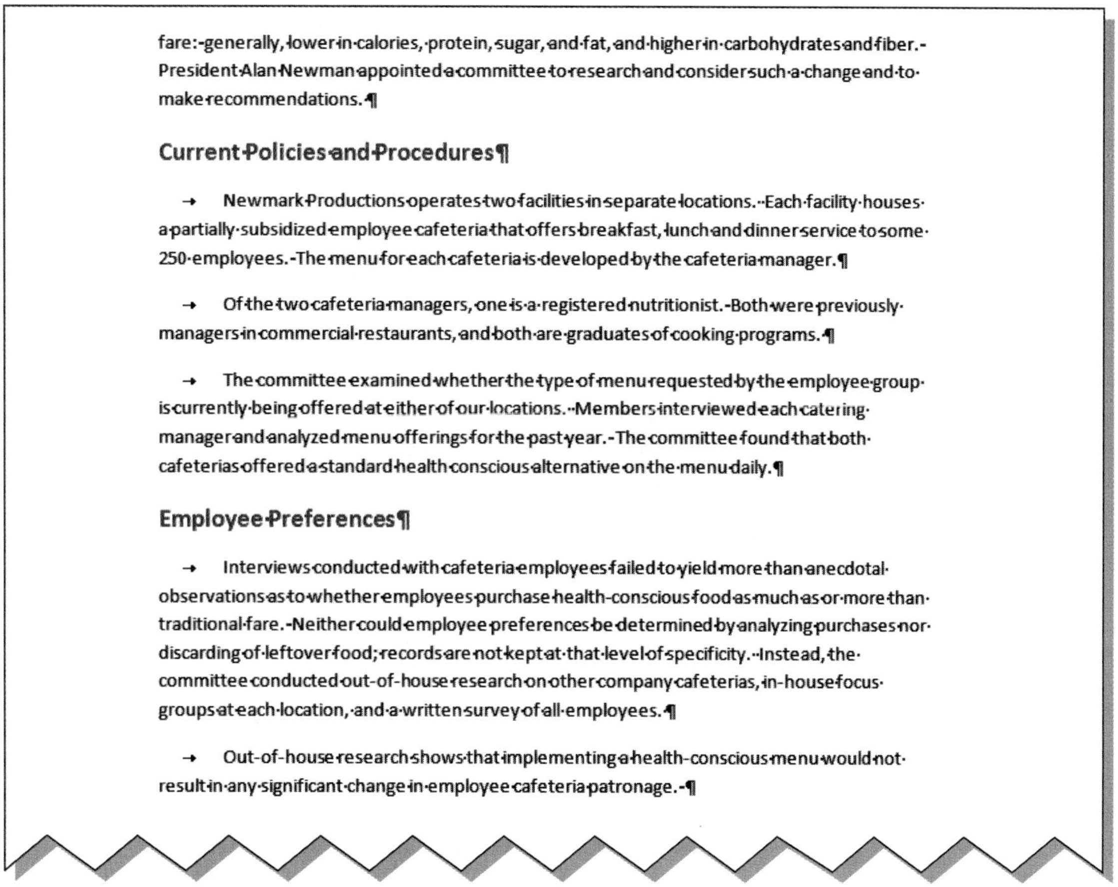
fare: generally, lower in calories, protein, sugar, and fat, and higher in carbohydrates and fiber. President Alan Newman appointed a committee to research and consider such a change and to make recommendations.¶

Current Policies and Procedures¶

→ Newmark Productions operates two facilities in separate locations. Each facility houses a partially subsidized employee cafeteria that offers breakfast, lunch and dinner service to some 250 employees. The menu for each cafeteria is developed by the cafeteria manager.¶

→ Of the two cafeteria managers, one is a registered nutritionist. Both were previously managers in commercial restaurants, and both are graduates of cooking programs.¶

→ The committee examined whether the type of menu requested by the employee group is currently being offered at either of our locations. Members interviewed each catering manager and analyzed menu offerings for the past year. The committee found that both cafeterias offered a standard health conscious alternative on the menu daily.¶

Employee Preferences¶

→ Interviews conducted with cafeteria employees failed to yield more than anecdotal observations as to whether employees purchase health-conscious food as much as or more than traditional fare. Neither could employee preferences be determined by analyzing purchases nor discarding of leftover food; records are not kept at that level of specificity. Instead, the committee conducted out-of-house research on other company cafeterias, in-house focus groups at each location, and a written survey of all employees.¶

→ Out-of-house research shows that implementing a health-conscious menu would not result in any significant change in employee cafeteria patronage.¶

Figure 1.40: Document with Show/Hide codes displayed

HOW **1.** Click the **Home tab**, and in the **Paragraph group**, **2.** click the **Show/Hide button**.

TRY *it* OUT *w1-12*

1. Open the data file **w1-12**.
2. Click the **Home tab**, and in the **Paragraph group**, click the **Show/Hide button**. *Note the paragraph, tab, and spacing codes that are displayed.* ¶
3. Repeat Step 2 to hide the codes.
4. Close the file, and do not save it.

Move and Copy Text

▶ Moving text allows you to remove text from one location and reinsert it in another.

▶ Copying text leaves text or data in its original location, while placing a duplicate in another location. Text cut or copied from the screen is placed temporarily on the Office Clipboard, a temporary storage area in the computer's memory. *You will learn more about the Office Clipboard later in this lesson.*

▶ When moving or copying text, it is recommended that you display screen codes. This will help you select the space following a word or sentence, and/or the paragraph mark following a paragraph or line that you plan to move or copy, as shown in Figure 1.41.

▶ The paragraph mark stores the formatting you apply to a paragraph. Therefore, it is particularly important to include the paragraph marks in your selected text to ensure that the paragraph formatting is moved or copied along with the text.

Figure 1.41: Selected paragraph

Move Text

▶ The easiest way to move text is to use the **cut-and-paste** method.

HOW [Ctrl]+X (cut) **[Ctrl]+V (paste)** **1.** Select the text to move, then **2.** click the **Home tab**, and in the **Clipboard group**, click the **Cut button**. **3.** Click in the location where you want to insert the text, then **4.** click the **Paste button**, as shown in Figure 1.42.

You can also use the *drag-and-drop* method to move text. To do so, **1.** place the insertion point on the selected text, **2.** drag the selected text to its new location, then **3.** release the mouse button. This method does not place text on the Office Clipboard.

Figure 1.42 Cut and Paste buttons on Home tab

Copy Text

HOW [Ctrl]+C **1.** Select the text to copy, **2.** click the **Home tab**, and in the **Clipboard group**, **3.** click the **Copy button**. **4.** Click in the location where you want to insert the text, then **5.** click the **Paste button**, as shown in Figure 1.43.

▶ To copy text using the drag-and-drop method, hold down **[Ctrl]** as you drag a selection.

Figure 1.43: Copy and Paste buttons on Home tab

1. Open the data file **w1-13**.

2. Click the **Home tab**, then click the **Show/Hide button**.

3. Move the paragraphs into numerical order as follows:
   a. Select the paragraph numbered ONE, including the two paragraph marks following the paragraph, as shown in Figure 1.44.
   b. Click the **Home tab**, then click the **Cut button**.
   c. Position the insertion point to the left of the paragraph numbered FOUR.

   d. On the Home tab, click the **Paste button**.
   e. Select the paragraph numbered THREE, including the two paragraph marks following the paragraph.
   f. Drag and drop it in front of the paragraph numbered FIVE.
   g. Move the remaining paragraphs into order using any method you prefer.

4. Do not close the file. You will use this file for _Try it Out w1-14_.

Five·Great·Websites·for·Start-up·Entrepreneurs¶

¶
¶

FOUR.·**Business·Start-Ups·Magazine:**·www.bizstartups.com.¶
An online magazine for new entrepreneurs, with information on start-up strategies, hot· opportunities, financing and more.¶
¶

TWO.·**HomeOfficeMag.com:**·www.homeofficemag.com.¶
An "e-zine" that features articles on running a home-based business or working for· someone else from your home office.¶
¶

ONE.·**SBA:**·www.sbaonline.sba.gov¶
Find out all the ways the Small Business Administration can help you, plus click on links· to other valuable resources.¶
¶

FIVE.·**Entrepreneur·Magazine:**·www.entrepreneur.com¶
Interesting articles and links to resources for those starting their own business.¶
¶

THREE.·**Small·Business·Exchange:**·www.americanexpress.com/smallbusiness.¶
Browse an array of American Express products and services, including merchant status,· corporate cards and equipment financing, plus a wide range of articles on various aspects· of starting and running a business.¶
¶

To·Summarize,·the·Five·Great·Websites·for·Entrepreneurs·are:¶
¶

Figure 1.44: Paragraph to be moved

Use the Office Clipboard

▶ When you cut or copy text, it is temporarily placed on the Clipboard. The Office **Clipboard** is a temporary storage area that can hold up to 24 items.

▶ The contents of the Clipboard can be viewed, which is particularly useful if you cut and/or copy multiple items and want to paste one item or the entire collection into a new location. After pasting an item from the Clipboard, it still remains on the Clipboard should you want to paste it into another location.

HOW To view the Clipboard contents, **1.** click the **Home tab**, and in the **Clipboard group**, **2.** click the **dialog box launcher**, as shown in Figure 1.45. The Clipboard task pane, shown in Figure 1.46, lists each copied or cut item. **3.** Position the insertion point where you wish to reinsert the cut or copied item, and **4.** click the item in the Clipboard task pane. A list box next to each item gives you a delete option.

▶ To Paste All or Clear All of the selections, click the appropriate button in the Clipboard task pane (see Figure 1.46).

▶ To display the task pane automatically after you have cut or copied more than one selection, click **Options**, and choose **Show Office Clipboard Automatically**.

Figure 1.45: Clipboard dialog box launcher on Home tab

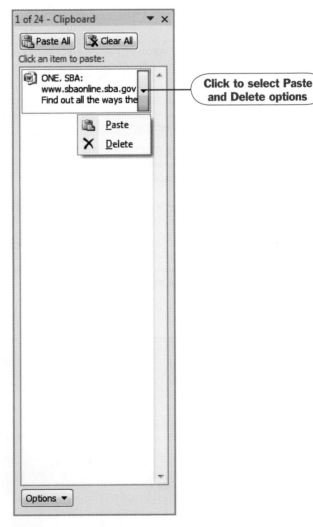

Figure 1.46: Clipboard task pane

w1-13 *should still be displayed on your screen. If it is not, repeat Try it Out w1-13 before completing this Try it Out activity.*

1. Click the **Home tab**, and in the **Clipboard group**, click the **dialog box launcher** to display the Clipboard.

2. Copy the first line of each paragraph. *You are copying multiple items, which you will then paste in Step 3.*

3. Paste each line individually below the words "To Summarize, . . ." as shown in Figure 1.47. Press **[Enter]** after each pasted item.

4. Click **Close** on the Clipboard task pane.

5. Close the file, and do not save it.

¶

To·Summarize,·the·Five·Great·Websites·for·Entrepreneurs·are:¶

¶

ONE.··SBA:··www.sbaonline.sba.gov¶

¶

TWO.··HomeOfficeMag.com:··www.homeofficemag.com¶

¶

THREE.··Small·Business·Exchange:··www.americanexpress.com/smallbusiness¶

¶

FOUR.··Business·Start-Ups·Magazine:··www.bizstartups.com¶

¶

FIVE.··Entrepreneur·Magazine:··www.entrepreneur.com¶

¶

Figure 1.47: Copy and Paste solution

Use Print Preview

▶ **Print Preview** allows you to see how a document will look on the page before you print it. In this view, your document will be displayed in a reduced size.

▶ In Print Preview, you can edit text, change margins, view multiple pages, change the page orientation, change the document size, and reduce the document to fit on a single page and print it.

▶ The Print Preview window displays its own tab, groups, and buttons, as shown in Figure 1.48. The buttons used most frequently and their functions are described in Table 1.6.

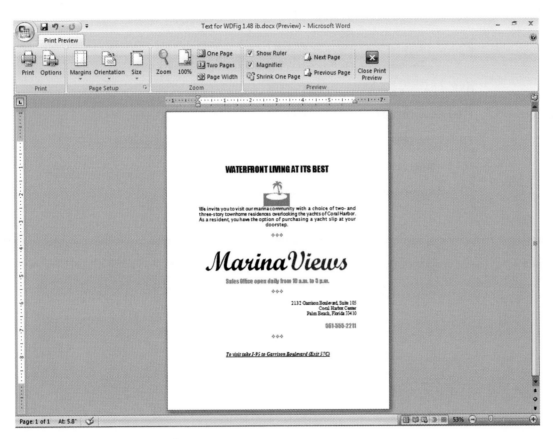

Figure 1.48: Print Preview window

Table 1.6: Print Preview options

CLICKING THIS BUTTON	WILL CAUSE THIS ACTION
Print	Prints the document on screen.
Margins	Allows you to set margins from this view. Setting margins will be detailed in Lesson 2.
Orientation	Allows you to switch between Portrait and Landscape orientation. **Portrait orientation** positions a page so that it is taller than it is wide. **Landscape orientation** positions a page so that it is wider than it is tall. Page orientation options are shown in Figure 1.49.
Size	Allows you to select a paper size for the document.
Zoom	Opens the Zoom dialog box and allows you to specify a magnification amount.
100%	Zooms the document to 100% of its normal size.
One page	Shows one page of the document.
Two pages	Shows two pages of the document.
Page width	Zooms the document so the width of the page matches the width of the window.
Show Ruler check box	Shows/hides the ruler on the Print Preview window.
Magnifier check box	Turns the mouse pointer into a magnifying glass, which can be used to quickly change magnification. Deselecting this option will allow you to edit the document.
Shrink One Page	Fits text/data onto one page.
Close Print Preview	Closes the Print Preview window.

HOW **1.** Click the **Office Button**, **2.** highlight **Print**, then **3.** click **Print Preview**.

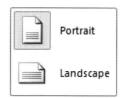

Figure 1.49: Portrait and Landscape orientation options

1. Open the data file **w1-15**.

2. Click the **Office Button**, highlight **Print**, then click **Print Preview**.

3. Select the **Magnifier check box** if it is not already selected. Position the mouse pointer, which appears as a magnifying glass, on the smallest text, and click to enlarge it.

4. Click again to reduce the page.

5. Click the **Zoom button**. *This will open the zoom dialog box.*

6. Change the Zoom to option to **100%**, and click **OK**.

7. Deselect the **Show Ruler check box** to hide the ruler.

8. Select the **Show Ruler check box** to show the ruler.

9. Change the page orientation to **landscape**. *Notice that the document does not fit on one page in this view.*

10. Change the page orientation back to **portrait**.

11. Click the **Close Print Preview button** on the **Print Preview tab**.

12. Close the file, and do not save it.

Print

▶ You learned earlier that you can quickly print a document by clicking the Office Button, highlighting Print, and clicking Quick Print. This method sends your document directly to the printer without giving you any printing options. You can, however, display a print dialog box and choose from several printing options, as shown in Figure 1.50.

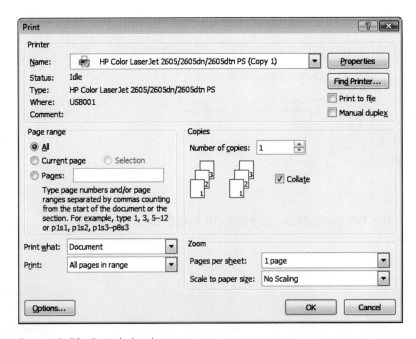

Figure 1.50: Print dialog box

HOW [Ctrl]+P To print a document, **1.** click the **Office Button**, **2.** highlight **Print**, then **3.** click **Print**. In the Print dialog box that appears, shown in Figure 1.50, **4.** choose one of the options described in Table 1.7. **5.** Click **OK** to send the document to the printer.

To print a portion of a document, **1.** select the text you want to print, **2.** repeat Steps 1–3 above, **3.** click **Selection**, then click **OK**.

Table 1.7: Print options

PRINT OPTION	EXPLANATION
Print range	Click **All** to print the entire document. Click **Current page** to print the page containing the insertion point. Click **Pages**, then enter the page numbers you wish to print. To print consecutive pages, click the **Pages** option and enter the pages you want printed, separated by a hyphen. (To print pages 1 through 3, for example, you would enter 1-3 in the text box.) To print individual pages, enter the page numbers, separated by a comma (1,5). Click **Selection** to print a portion of a document.
Copies	To print a single copy or multiple copies of a document, enter the number you want in the Number of copies text box.
Print	To print all pages or just odd- or even-numbered pages, click the **Print list arrow** and choose an option.
Collate	To specify how you want the document collated, select or deselect the **Collate check box**.

T R Y *i t* O U T *w1-16*

1. Open the data file **w1-16**.

2. Select the summary information, including the sentence "To Summarize . . . ."

3. Click the **Office Button**, highlight **Print**, then click **Print**.

4. Click the **Selection** option.

5. Click **Cancel**.

6. Click the **Office Button**, highlight **Print**, then click **Print**.

7. Click to deselect the **Collate check box** to view the other collating options.

8. Click the **Print list arrow** to view the options.

9. Click **Cancel**.

10. Close the file, and do not save it.

REHEARSAL

 GOAL
To edit and print a document, as shown in Figure 1.51

TASK 2

WHAT YOU NEED TO KNOW

▶ An edited document contains proofreader's marks, which indicate corrections that need to be made to the text.

▶ The proofreader's mark to indicate a new paragraph is ¶.

▶ The proofreader's mark to indicate an insertion is ∧ or <u>underlined text</u>.

▶ The proofreader's mark to indicate a deletion is crossed out text ~~crossed out text~~ ℓ.

▶ The proofreader's mark to indicate a move is ◯→.

▶ Click the Undo button immediately after an edit to reverse the action and restore the text to its unedited form.

▼ DIRECTIONS

1. Open the data file **w1r2-study points**.

2. Click the **Home tab**, and in the **Paragraph group**, click the **Show/Hide button**.

3. Make the revisions shown in Figure 1.51. Use any move method to move the paragraphs.

4. Correct grammar and spelling, if necessary.

5. Display the document in **Full Screen Reading view**.

6. Display the document in **Print Layout view**.

7. Preview the document, then print one copy.

8. Close the file, and save the changes.

HOW TO STUDY EFFECTIVELY

How do you study? If your studying consists of reading ~~and rereading~~ the material, you are not studying effectively.

In order to study productively, you must become actively involved ~~in the process.~~ ~~and~~ ~~Y~~you should u~~se~~tilize as many senses as you can: sight, sound, ~~and touch~~ if possible. This means that in addition to reading ~~the material~~, you should be writing, speaking and thinking about ~~everything~~ ~~what~~ you are studying.

Here are some helpful tips for studying ~~effectively~~:

When studying from text, prepare an ~~outstanding~~ outline of the material according to the structure of the text. Use the main topics as the different levels of the outline.

Take ~~wonderful~~good class notes. Keep a ~~separate~~ notebook for each class. Write the date and page number ~~for each page you use~~. Teachers usually write ~~all~~ the key points on the board or ~~on~~ a ~~overhead~~ projector. Wait to write each point until your teacher begins to talk about ~~the~~ ~~lesson~~ ~~it~~. In this way, you will have room to fill in the details. ~~That's the way to do it.~~

~~Reread the material. Look back and carefully read any material you still do not understand. Always look for the main points, further details and questions you can answer as you read.~~

Read your notes after class~~,~~ ~~while~~ ~~Y~~your memory is fresh ~~so~~~~and~~ you may be able to supply more details. ~~Underline or highlight~~Emphasize important points and write down questions and ~~the~~ key terms included in the lesson.

Good study skills not only help us achieve good grades in school, but they are invaluable tools that will allow us to be more productive in our professional lives.

Figure 1.51: Rehearsal Task 2–Edited document

Change Document Views

1. Click a view button on the status bar:
   - **Print Layout**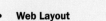
   - **Full Screen Reading**
   - **Web Layout**
   - **Outline**
   - **Draft**

Change Window Views

Split Windows

1. Click **View tab, Split window button**.
2. Move insertion point where split should occur.
3. Click the **left mouse button**.
4. Click the **View tab, Remove Split button** to redisplay entire document.

Arrange All or View Side by Side

1. Click the **View tab, Arrange All button** or **View Side by Side button**.
   If you chose View Side by Side, select the document to which you want the active document compared.
2. Click in a window to make it the active document.
3. To redisplay the entire document, click the **maximize button** in a window.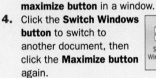
4. Click the **Switch Windows button** to switch to another document, then click the **Maximize button** again.

Display Window Elements

1. Click the **View tab**, and in the **Show/Hide group**, click to select an element (Ruler, Gridlines, Document Map, Thumbnails, and Message Bar) to display.

Zoom

1. Click and drag the **Zoom slider** on the status bar right to enlarge the document and left to make the document smaller.

Insert Text

1. Position the insertion point to the left of the character where you want to insert text.
2. Click and enter the new text.

Delete Text

1. Select the text to delete.
2. Press **[Delete]** or click the **Cut button** or press **[Ctrl]+X**.

Show/Hide Codes

1. Click the **Home tab**, and in the **Paragraph group**, click the **Show/Hide button**.

Move and Copy Text

Cut/Copy-and-Paste Method

1. Select the text to move.
2. Click the **Home tab**, and in the **Clipboard group**, click the **Cut button** or **Copy button**.
   Or
2. Press **[Ctrl]+X** (cut) or **[Ctrl]+C** (copy).
3. Position the insertion point where you want the text inserted.

4. Click the **Home tab**, and in the **Clipboard group**, click the **Paste button**.
   Or
2. Press **[Ctrl]+V**.

Drag-and-Drop Method

1. Select the text to move or copy.
2. Point to the selected text.
3. To move, hold down the **left mouse button** and drag the text to the new location. To copy, hold down **[Ctrl]** and the **left mouse button** as you drag the text to the new location.
4. Release the mouse button.

Print Preview

1. Click the **Office Button**, highlight **Print**, then click **Print Preview**.

Print

1. Click the **Office Button**, highlight **Print**, then click **Print**.
   Or
1. Press **[Ctrl]+P**.

PERFORMANCE

TASK 2

BodyWorksFitnessCenters plans to publish a monthly newsletter. You have been asked to edit some of the articles to be included in the first issue. They also will use some of the text in the article to create posters as a way to encourage members to read the newsletter.

Follow these guidelines:

1. Open the data file **w1p2-tips**.

2. Click the **Show/Hide button**.

3. Make the revisions shown in Figure 1.52.

4. Move the paragraphs in alphabetical order.

5. Correct spelling and grammar, if necessary.

6. Save the file, and do not close it.

7. Create a new blank document.

8. View the documents side by side.

9. Display the codes.

10. Copy the title and paste it into a new blank document, as shown in Figure 1.52.

11. Copy each tip (CARE FOR YOURSELF, for example) and paste it below the title in the blank document as shown. Figure 1.52 shows the first two tips copied for your reference. You should copy all six tips.

12. Save the second document. Name it **w1p2-tips summary**.

13. Close both files.

Six Tips for the Workaholic

SLOW DOWN. Make a~~n all out~~ conscious effort to eat, talk<u>,</u> <u>walk</u> and drive more slowly. Give yourself ~~extra~~ extra time to get to appointments ~~and dates~~ so you are not always rushing<u>.</u> ~~around.~~

DRAW THE LINE. When you are already overloaded<u> and need more personal time</u>, do not take on any other projects. You will just be causing yourself more stress.

LEARN TO DELEGATE. Let others share the load—you don't have to do everything yourself. You will have <u>more </u>energy, and the <u>end</u> result will be better <u>for everyone</u>.

TAKE BREAKS. Take frequent <u>work </u>breaks. Short walks or meditating for a few minutes ~~a day~~ can help you unwind and clear your head.

CARE FOR YOURSELF. Eat properly, get enough sleep and exercise regularly. Do what you can so that you are healthy, both mentally and physically.

CUT YOUR HOURS. Be <u>well </u>organized, but do not let your schedule run your life. Also, try to limit yourself to working eight hours a day<u>--and not a minute more</u>.

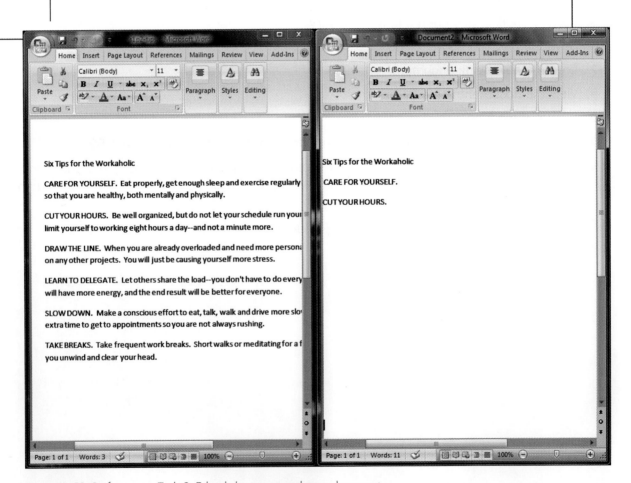

Figure 1.52 Performance Task 2—Edited document and new document

TRYOUT

TASK 3

GOAL
To format paragraphs and characters, as shown in Figure 1.53

✴ Format Text
✴ Set text alignments
✴ Set line and paragraph spacing
✴ Work with fonts
✴ Use symbols
✴ Use Format Painter
✴ Highlight text
✴ Change case
✴ Change character spacing

WATERFRONT LIVING AT ITS BEST

We invite you to visit our marina community with a choice of two-and three-story town home residences overlooking the yachts of Coral Harbor. As a resident, you have the option of purchasing a yacht slip at your doorstep.

Marina Views

sales Office open daily from 10 a.m. to 5 p.m.
2132 garrison boulevard, Suite 105
coral Harbor Center
palm beach, florida 33410

561-555-2211

To visit take I-95 to Garrison Boulevard (Exit 57C)

WATERFRONT LIVING AT ITS BEST

Character spacing
Apply font and color

Insert symbols

We invite you to visit our marina community with a choice of two-and three-story town home residences over looking the yachts of Coral Harbor. As a resident, you have the option of purchasing a yacht slip at your doorstep.

❖❖❖

Line spacing

MarinaViews

Sales Office open daily from 10 a.m. to 5 p.m.

❖❖❖

Align text

Copy formatting

2132 Garrison Boulevard, Suite 105
Coral Harbor Center
Palm Beach, Florida 33410

561-555-2211

To visit take I-95 to Garrison Boulevard (Exit 57C)

Figure 1.53: Task 3: Unformatted document and formatted document

WHAT YOU NEED TO KNOW

Format Text

▶ Formatting allows you to change the appearance of a paragraph or characters including letters, numbers, and symbols. By formatting characters, you can emphasize individual letters, words, or a block of text and/or improve the readability of text in a document.

▶ Formatting includes text alignments, line and paragraph spacing, fonts, font styles, font colors, case, highlighting, and character spacing.

▶ You can apply formatting before or after entering text. To apply formatting to existing text, you must first select it or position your insertion point anywhere on the word or in the paragraph.

▶ Formatting buttons can be found on the Ribbon or on the Mini toolbar. The Mini toolbar is displayed when you select text. It is also displayed with the shortcut menu when you right-click (which you can do when applying formatting to new text).

▶ Word 2007 shows you a live preview of how most formatting changes will look when you point to a selection. You do not have to actually apply the formatting to see its effect. The live preview works only when you select the option from the Ribbon.

▶ You should return to your original settings after applying formatting. Otherwise, the new format will remain in effect as you continue to work on your document until you make another change.

Set Text Alignments

▶ You can align text left (the default), right, and center. Text is aligned between existing margins. You can also justify text. **Justified text** displays lines that are even at the left and right margins (except for the last line). Figure 1.54 shows the effect of different text alignments.

Left-Aligned Paragraph One. **This is practice text that you can use for importing, placing and "playing" purposes. Practice text is useful when you are planning a layout. Using practice text rather than real text is a good way to concentrate on the form and design of your layout without reading the text itself.**

Center-Aligned Paragraph Two. **From now on, this file will be referred to as the "pf" (practice file) file. Have fun!**

Right-Aligned Paragraph Three. **Practice text should have paragraphs so you can manipulate them and move them as you desire. Practice text encourages you to experiment with alignments, typefaces, type styles, type sizes and leading.**

Justified Paragraph Four. **When working with practice text, you should have at least four paragraphs. This will enable you to move them and experiment with at least four different formats. The paragraphs should be long enough so that you can see the effects of a line spacing or paragraph spacing change, for example.**

Figure 1.54: Text alignments

HOW 1. Click the **Home tab**, and in the **Paragraph group**, 2. click an **alignment button**, as shown in Figure 1.55. To center text quickly, 1. Select the text to center and 2. choose the **Center button** from the Mini toolbar, as shown in Figure 1.56. You can also use shortcut keys: [Ctrl]+L (left), [Ctrl]+E (center), [Ctrl]+R (right), and [Ctrl]+J (justify).

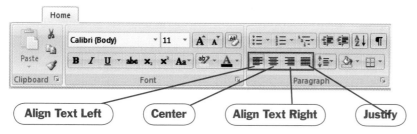

Figure 1.55: Alignment buttons on Home tab

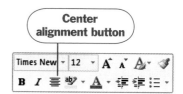

Figure 1.56: Center alignment button on Mini toolbar

T R Y *i t* **O U T** *w1-17*

1. Open the data file **w1-17**.

2. Position your insertion point anywhere paragraph two. Click the **Home tab**, and in the **Paragraph group**, click the **Center button**.

3. Position your insertion point anywhere paragraph three. In the **Paragraph group**, click the **Align Text Right button**.

4. Position your insertion point anywhere in paragraph four. In the **Paragraph group**, click the **Justify button**.

5. Position your insertion point anywhere in paragraph one. In the **Paragraph group**, click the **Center button**, then click the **Align Text Left button**.

6. Position your insertion point after the last word in paragraph four. Press **[Enter]** twice.

7. Enter your first and last name.

8. Right-click and select the **Center button** from the Mini toolbar.

9. Press **[Enter]** twice.

10. Enter today's date.

11. In the **Paragraph group**, click the **Align Text Right button**.

12. Print one copy.

13. Close the file, and do not save it.

Set Line and Paragraph Spacing

Line Spacing

▶ **Line spacing** is the amount of vertical space between lines of text. The default line spacing in Word 2007 is set to 1.15 lines. *Line spacing is measured in "lines" or "points." Line spacing measured in points (a more precise measurement) is referred to as* leading (*pronounced "ledding"*).

HOW **1.** Click the **Home tab**, and in the **Paragraph group**, **2.** click the **Line spacing button**, then, **3.** choose a line spacing, as shown in Figure 1.57. You can also use shortcut keys: [Ctrl]+1 (single), [Ctrl]+5 (1.5), and [Ctrl]+2 (double).

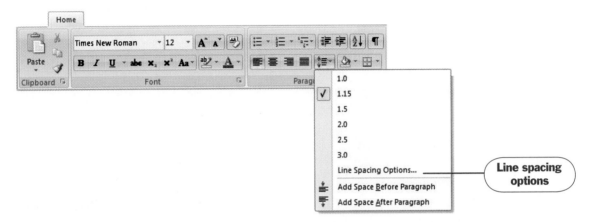

Figure 1.57: Line spacing list on the Home tab

For additional line spacing options,
1. display the Paragraph dialog box
shown in Figure 1.58. To do so,
click the **Line Spacing button**, then
choose **Line Spacing Options** from
the menu that appears (see Figure
1.57), or click the **Paragraph dialog
box launcher**, or right-click and select
Paragraph from the shortcut menu.
2. Choose **Exactly** from the Line
spacing list box, and **3.** enter an
amount in the **At text box**.

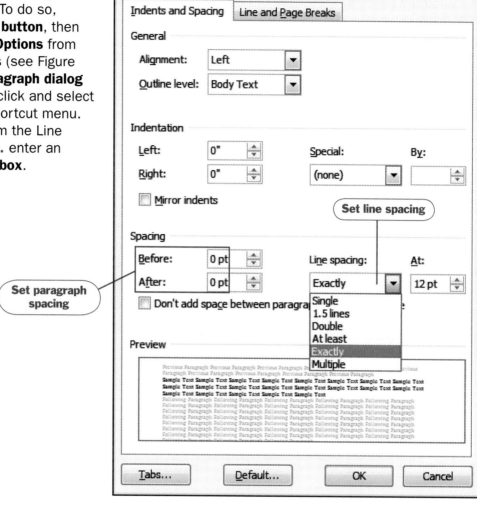

Figure 1.58: Paragraph dialog box

T R Y *it* O U T *w1-18*

1. Open the data file **w1-18**.

2. Position the insertion point in the first
   paragraph.

3. Click the **Home tab**, and in the
   Paragraph group, click the **Line
   spacing button**, then select **2.5 lines**.

4. Position the insertion point in the second
   paragraph.

5. Click the **Home tab**, and in the **Paragraph
   group**, click the **dialog box launcher** to
   display the Paragraph dialog box.

6. In the **Paragraph dialog box**, click the
   Line spacing list arrow and click **Exactly**.

7. Enter 15 in the **At text box**, and click **OK**.

8. Select the last two paragraphs.

9. Press **[Ctrl]+2**.

10. Close the file, and do not save it.

Paragraph Spacing

▶ **Paragraph spacing** determines the amount of space above or below a paragraph. Paragraph spacing is measured in points (there are 72 points to an inch).

▶ The default paragraph spacing is 0 points before a paragraph and 10 points after a paragraph. If you use the default paragraph spacing, you just need to press **[Enter]** once to create a new paragraph.

HOW Paragraph spacing is set in the Paragraph dialog box (see Figure 1.58). Enter a spacing amount in the Before and/or After text box.

T R Y *i t* **O U T** *w1-19*

1. Open the data file **w1-19**.

2. Select all the paragraphs.

3. Click the **Home tab**, and in the **Paragraph group**, click the **dialog box launcher**.

4. In the **Spacing section**, click the **Up increment arrow** three times in the

After box, which will change the spacing amount to **24 pt**, and click **OK**. *Notice the change in the spacing between paragraphs.*

5. Close the file, and do not save it.

Work with Fonts

▶ A **font** is a complete set of characters designed in a specific face, style, and size.

Change the Font Face

▶ Each font design has a name and is intended to convey a specific feeling. The design is called a **font face**.

▶ There are basically three types of font faces—serif, sans serif, and script. A **serif** face has lines, curves, or edges extending from the ends of the letters (serif font), whereas a **sans serif** face is straight-edged (sans serif font), and **script** looks like handwriting (script font).

▶ The default font in Word 2007 is Calibri (sans serif font), 11 point. Figure 1.59 illustrates a document that contains all three types of font faces.

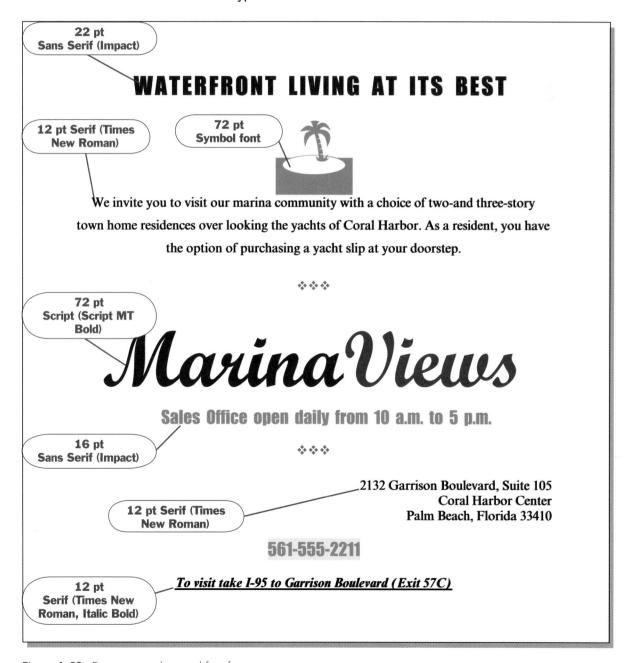

Figure 1.59: Document with varied font faces

HOW **1.** Click the **Home tab**, and in the **Font group**, **2.** click the **Font list arrow**, and **3.** choose a font face from the list shown in Figure 1.60. You can also select the font list from the Mini toolbar shown in Figure 1.61.

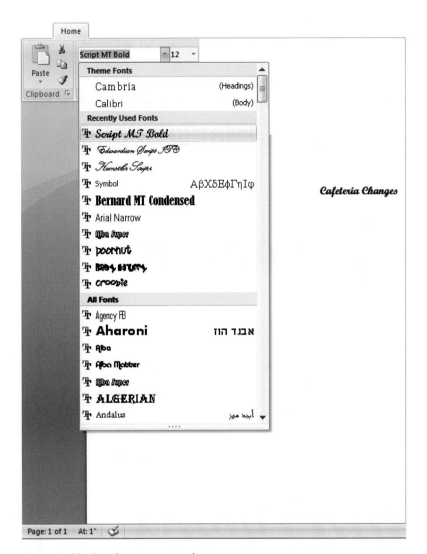

Figure 1.60: Font list on Home tab

Grow font   Shrink font

Times New ▾ 12 ▾ A A A ▾ 🖌
B *I* ≣ ᵃᵇⁿ ▾ **A** ▾ 雷 雷 ≣ ▾

Font list arrow   Font size list arrow

Figure 1.61: Font list on Mini toolbar

T R Y *i t* **O U T** *w1-20*

1. Open the data file **w1-20**.

2. For each line of text:
   a. Select the line, then select the **Font list arrow** from the Mini toolbar.
   b. Select the font face indicated by the font name.

3. For the last three lines of text:
   a. Select the word, then click the **Home tab** and in the **Font group**, click the **Font list arrow**.

   b. Point to several font options to display the live preview, then click the font face indicated by the font name.

4. Close the file, and do not save it.

Font Size

▶ **Font size** refers to the height of the font, usually measured in points. There are 72 points to an inch.

HOW **1.** Click the **Home tab**, and in the **Font group**, **2.** click the **Font Size list arrow**, and **3.** choose a font size, as shown in Figure 1.62. You can also select the font size from the Mini toolbar.

To increase or decrease the font incrementally, click the **Grow Font button** or the **Shrink Font button** on the Home tab or the Mini toolbar (see Figure 1.61).

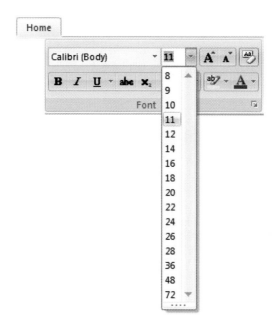

Figure 1.62: Font size list on Home tab

T R Y *i t* O U T *w1-21*

1. Open the data file **w1-21**.

2. For each line of text listed:
   a. Select the word.
   b. Click the **Home tab**, and in the **Font group**, click the **Font Size list arrow**, point to several font size options to display the live preview, then click the font size indicated by the text.

3. Select the text **14 point**. Click the **Grow Font button** in the **Font group** until the font grows to **72 points**. *Notice that the font size increased incrementally each time you clicked the mouse button.*

4. Close the file, and do not save it.

Font Style

▶ **Font style** refers to the appearance of text. Bold, italic, and underline are the most common examples of styles. Styles are generally used to emphasize text.

HOW **1.** Click the **Home tab**, and in the **Font group**, **2.** click the **Bold button**, **Italic button**, or **Underline button**, as shown in Figure 1.63. To select an underline style other than a single solid line, click the list arrow on the button (see Figure 1.63). You can also use the bold and italic buttons on the Mini toolbar, or use shortcut keys: Ctrl+B (bold), Ctrl+I (italic), and Ctrl+U (underline).

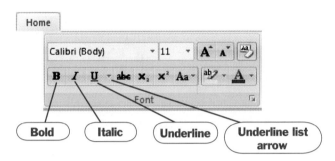

Figure 1.63: Style buttons on the Home tab

T R Y *it* O U T *w1-22*

1. Open the data file **w1-22**.

2. Select the first paragraph. Click the **Bold button** on the Mini toolbar. **B**

3. Select the second paragraph. Click the **Italic button** on the Mini toolbar. **I**

4. Select the third paragraph. Click the **Home tab**, and in the **Font group**, click the **Underline button**. **U**

5. Select the last paragraph. Click the **Underline list arrow**, and choose the **double-underline** option.

6. Close the file, and do not save it.

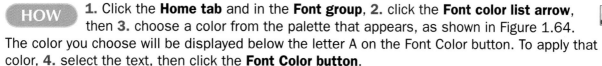

Font Color

▶ Font colors are also used to emphasize text and give it a professional look.

HOW **1.** Click the **Home tab** and in the **Font group**, **2.** click the **Font color list arrow**, then **3.** choose a color from the palette that appears, as shown in Figure 1.64. The color you choose will be displayed below the letter A on the Font Color button. To apply that color, **4.** select the text, then click the **Font Color button**.

You can also click the **font color list arrow** on the Mini toolbar and choose a color.

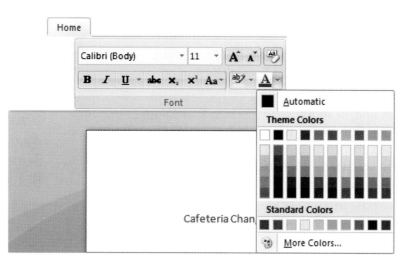

Figure 1.64: Font Color button on Home tab

T R Y *it* O U T *w1-23*

1. Open the data file **w1-23**.

2. Select the word **Blue**. Click the **Font color list arrow** on the Mini toolbar, and click any shade of blue.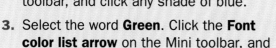

3. Select the word **Green**. Click the **Font color list arrow** on the Mini toolbar, and click any shade of green.

4. Select the word **Red**. Click the **Font color list arrow** on the Mini toolbar, then click **More Colors**. On the **Standard tab**, click any shade of **red**, and click **OK**.

5. Select the word **Yellow**. Click the **Home tab**, and in the **Font group**, click the **dialog box launcher** to display the Font dialog box.

6. Click **Arial** as the font, **Bold** as the style, **24** as the font size, and **Yellow** as the color, then click **OK**.

7. Close the file, and do not save it.

Font Effects

▶ In addition to the capability to emphasize text using bold, italics, underlining, and color, Word provides other effects that you can apply to characters. These include small caps, all caps, strikethrough, double strikethrough, shadow, outline emboss, engrave, subscript, and superscript.

▶ **Superscripts** are characters that print slightly above the normal typing line. **Subscripts** are characters that print slightly below the typing line.

▶ Figure 1.65 shows examples of other font effects available. The **Hidden** option allows you to hide text in your document.

HOW To apply strikethrough, subscript, or superscript, **1.** click the **Home tab**, and in the **Font group**, **2.** select the **Strikethrough button**, **Subscript button** or **Superscript button**.

To apply font effects and/or fonts, styles, sizes, and colors simultaneously, **1.** click the **dialog box launcher** in the **Font group**. In the **Font dialog box** that is displayed, as shown in Figure 1.66, **2.** choose the option you want. You can also display the Font dialog box by right-clicking and choosing **Font** from the **Shortcut menu**.

To remove character formatting from paragraphs in one step, **1.** select all the paragraphs that contain formatting, **2.** click the **Home tab**, and in the **Font group**, **3.** click the **Clear Formatting button** or press **[Ctrl]+[Spacebar]**.

~~Strikethrough~~
~~Double strikethrough~~
SMALL CAPS
ALL CAPS
Shadow
Outline
Emboss
Engrave
Superscript: x^2
Subscript: H_2O

Figure 1.65: Sample font effects

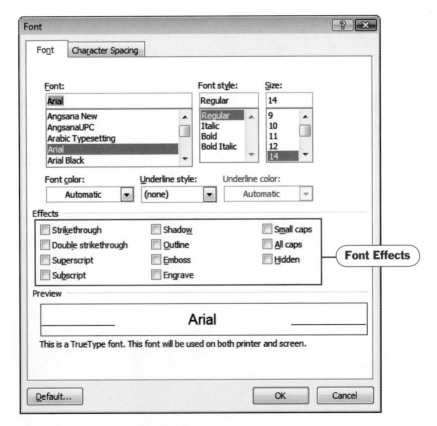

Figure 1.66: Font dialog box

1. Open the data file **w1-24**.

2. Select the word **Strikethrough**. Click the **Home tab**, and in the **Font group**, click the **Strikethrough button**.

3. Select the **2** in H20. Click the **Home tab**, and in the **Font group**, click the **Subscript button**.

4. Select the words **in this sentence**.
   a. Display the **Font dialog box**.
   b. Select **Hidden**, then click **OK**.

5. Select all the text. Press **[Ctrl]+[spacebar]** to remove the applied formatting.

6. Close the file, and do not save it.

Use Symbols

▶ **Symbols** are ornamental font collections or special characters that you can use to separate items on a page, emphasize items on a list, or enhance a document.

▶ Symbols behave like fonts; therefore, you can change the point size, color, or emphasis style of a symbol just as you did with other fonts. Figure 1.67 illustrates some ways to use symbols.

Figure 1.67: Ornamental font uses

1. Click the **Insert tab** and in the **Symbols group**, **2.** click the **Symbol button**, and **3.** choose a symbol that is displayed, or click **More Symbols** to display the Symbol dialog box shown in Figure 1.68. **4.** Click a symbol you want to insert, then **5.** click **Insert**. *Notice that the selected Font is* Wingdings. *Clicking the list arrow will display other font collections such as* Wingdings2, Wingdings3, *and* Webdings. *You can also access symbol collections by clicking the Font list arrow on the Home tab, the Mini toolbar, or the Font dialog box.*

Ω Symbol ▾

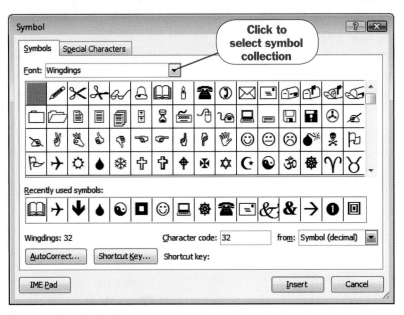

Figure 1.68: Symbol dialog box

T R Y *it* O U T *w1-25*

1. Open a new blank document.

2. Create the heading shown below by completing the following steps.
   📖📖📖The Reading Club📖📖📖
   a. Key the words **The Reading Club**.
   b. Position the insertion point before "The."
   c. Click the **Insert tab**, and in the **Symbols group**, click the **Symbol button**, then click **More Symbols** to open the Symbol dialog box. *Be sure the Wingdings font collection is selected. If it is not, click the **Font list arrow** and select it.*

   Ω Symbol ▾

   d. Click the **Book** symbol (found in the first row), click **Insert** three times, then click **Close**.
   e. Copy the three book symbols, and paste them after the word "Club."
   f. Select the symbols, and apply a **red** font color from the Mini toolbar.
   g. Select the text and symbols, center them, then change the font size to **18 point**.

3. Close the file, and do not save it.

Use Format Painter

▶ The **Format Painter** feature allows you to copy formatting such as the font face, style, and size from one block of text to another.

HOW **1.** Select the text or data that contains the formatting you wish to copy, **2.** click the **Format Painter button** on the Mini toolbar (*After clicking the Format Painter button, the insertion point becomes a paintbrush.*), then **3.** select the text to receive the formatting. *In essence, you are "painting" the new text with formatting you copied from the old text.* Or **1.** click the **Home tab**, and in the **Clipboard group**, **2.** click the **Format Painter button**, then **3.** select the text to receive formatting.

To copy formatting from one location to several locations, **1.** select the text with the formatting you wish to copy, **2.** then double-click the **Format Painter button**. You can now "paint" the formatting on several blocks of text or data. To turn off this feature, click the **Format Painter button** again.

T R Y *i t* **O U T** *w1-26*

1. Open the data file **w1-26**.

2. Select the word **Blue**.

3. Click the **Format Painter button** on the Mini toolbar. *Note that the insertion point changes to a paintbrush.*

4. Click **blueberries**. *Note that the formatting font face, color, and size have been copied to the word "blueberries."*

5. Copy the formatting from the word "Red" to "apples."

6. Select the word **Green**.

7. Click the **Home tab**, and in the **Clipboard group**, double-click the **Format Painter button**.

8. Click **lettuce**, then click **grapes**, then click **cabbage**.

9. Click the **Format Painter button** again to turn off the feature.

10. Close the file, and do not save it.

Highlight Text

▶ The Text Highlight Color feature allows you to mark text or graphics for emphasis as though they were marked with a highlighter pen.

HOW **1.** Click the **Home tab**, and in the **Font group**, **2.** click the **Text Highlight Color list arrow** to display a palette of colors, as shown in Figure 1.69. **3.** Click to select a highlight color, then **4.** select the text you wish to highlight. *After clicking the Text Highlight Color button, the insertion point changes to a highlighter pen.* Word applies the color displayed on the highlight button.

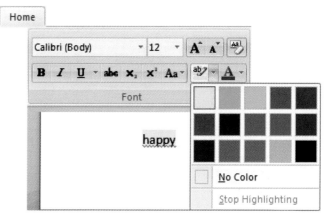

Figure 1.69: Highlight color palette

1. Open the data file **w1-27**.

2. Click the **Home tab**, and in the **Font group**, click the **Highlight Color list arrow**. Click **Bright Green** on the palette.

3. Select the first paragraph to highlight it.

4. Click the **Highlight list arrow**, and change the highlight color to **Turquoise**.

5. Select the second paragraph to highlight it.

6. Click the **Highlight list arrow**, and change the highlight color to **Yellow**.

7. Select the third paragraph to highlight it.

8. Close the file, and do not save it.

▶ To see a live preview of the highlight color before you apply it, select the text, and then move the pointer over each color to see a preview. You can also apply highlight on the Mini toolbar.

Change Case

▶ The Change Case feature allows you to easily convert one case (uppercase, lowercase, sentence case, title case) to another.

HOW 1. Select the text you wish to convert, 2. click the **Home tab**, and in the **Font group**, 3. click the **Change Case button**, then 4. choose the case you want from the menu that displays, as shown in Figure 1.70. You can also use shortcut keys to change case: [Shift]+[F3] once to capitalize each word, [Shift]+[F3] twice for uppercase, and [Shift]+[F3] three times for lowercase.

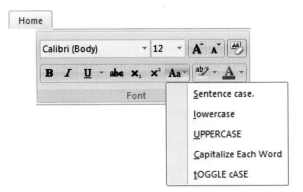

Figure 1.70: Change Case menu

1. Open a new document.

2. Enter the following on separate lines as shown.
   ```
   technology forum
   third annual summer conference
   embassy hotel, detroit,
   michigan
   ```

3. Select **technology forum**. Press **[Shift]+[F3]** as many times as necessary to change it to uppercase.

4. Select **third annual summer conference**. Click the **Home tab**, and in the **Font group**, click the **Change Case button**, and select **Capitalize Each Word**.

5. Select the last line. Press **[Shift]+[F3]** as necessary to capitalize the first letter of each word.

6. Close the file, and do not save it.

Change Character Spacing

▶ Word sets a default for the amount of space it leaves between letters and words. You can adjust the spacing between characters for selected text or for particular characters by using the character spacing feature. Setting character spacing can affect the readability of text, particularly headlines. The effects of character spacing are shown in Figure 1.71.

▶ Word provides three character spacing options:

1. Expanded or condensed spacing evenly alters the spacing between all selected letters by the same amount. Expanded or condensed spacing is measured in points.

2. Scale text changes the shapes of characters by percentages and allows you to set their width. Percentages above 100% stretch the text; percentages below 100% compress the text.

3. Kern characters fit letters closer together and is used to refine letter spacing, particularly when working with large or decorative letters. Kerning alters the spacing between particular pairs of letters.

Look	Normal
L o o k	Expanded by 10 points
Look	Condensed by 2 points
Look	Scaled by 200%
Look	Scaled by 33%
Look	Kerned "o"

Figure 1.71: Character spacing options

HOW 1. Select the text to affect. 2. Click the **Home tab**, and in the **Font group**, click the **Font dialog box launcher**. In the Font dialog box, 3. click the **Character Spacing tab** and 4. make the selections you want.

1. Open the data file **w1-29**.

2. Select **Joan**.

3. Click the **Home tab**, and in the **Font group**, click the **Font dialog box launcher**. In the Font dialog box, click the **Character Spacing tab**.

4. Click the **Spacing list arrow**, and click **Expanded**.

5. Enter 2 in the **By text box**, and click **OK**.

6. Select **Mary**, right-click, and select **Font** from the shortcut menu. Click the **Character Spacing tab**, if necessary.

7. Click the **Spacing list arrow**, and click **Condensed**.

8. Enter **.5** in the **By text box**, and click **OK**.

9. Select **Paul**.

10. Display the Font dialog box and click the **Character Spacing tab**, if necessary.

11. Click the **Spacing list arrow**, and click **Expanded**.

12. Enter 2 in the **By text box**.

13. Click the **Scale list arrow**, and click **200%**.

14. Click **OK**.

15. Select **Fran**.

16. Apply any letter spacing option.

17. Close the file, and do not save it.

REHEARSAL **GOAL**
To apply basic formatting to paragraphs and characters

TASK 3

WHAT YOU NEED TO KNOW

▶ It is important to remember to select existing text before you apply formatting.

▶ A serif font is typically used for document text because it is more readable. A sans serif font is often used for headlines or technical material. A script font is usually reserved for formal invitations and announcements.

▶ You should choose typefaces that will make your document attractive and communicate its particular message most effectively. As a rule, use no more than two or three font faces in any one document.

▶ You will apply formatting to unformatted text so that it matches the advertisement in Figure 1.72. You will use the Format Painter to copy formatting from one block of text to another.

▼ DIRECTIONS

1. Open the data file **w1r3-ad**.

2. Change the page orientation to **landscape**.

3. Use the Change Case feature to change the capitalization to match the text shown in Figure 1.72.

4. Format each paragraph with the font face, size, style, color, character spacing, and line spacing indicated in Figure 1.72. *If you do not have the exact font faces indicated in the Figure, you may substitute others.*

5. Use the Format Painter to copy the formatting from the descriptive paragraph ("We invite you to visit . . . .") to the three lines of the address.

6. Change the line spacing to **single** for the three lines of the address.

7. Use the Format Painter to copy the formatting from the Sales Office opening hours information to the phone number.

8. Delete "community" in the paragraph text.

9. Undo the deletion.

10. Change the page orientation to **portrait**.

11. Center a graphic symbol below the main heading, and set it to **72** point.

12. Insert any desired symbols between text as shown.

13. Highlight the phone number in **yellow**.

14. Set the magnification to **200%**.

15. Underline the last line of text.

16. Use Print Preview.

17. Print one copy.

18. Set the magnification to **100%**.

19. Save and close the file.

**Impact, 22 pt
Character Spacing:
Expanded 2 pts**

WATERFRONT LIVING AT ITS BEST

**72 pt
Symbol font**

We invite you to visit our marina community with a choice of two-and three-story town home residences over looking the yachts of Coral Harbor. As a resident, you have the option of purchasing a yacht slip at your doorstep.

**Times New Roman,
12 pt
Line Spacing: 2.0**

❖ ❖ ❖

**Script MT
Bold, 72 pt**

Marina Views

Sales Office open daily from 10 a.m. to 5 p.m.

❖ ❖ ❖

Impact, 16 pt

2132 Garrison Boulevard, Suite 105
Coral Harbor Center
Palm Beach, Florida 33410

561-555-2211

**Times New
Roman, 12 pt
Italic, Bold**

To visit take I-95 to Garrison Boulevard (Exit 57C)

**Times New
Roman, 12 pt
Right-aligned**

Figure 1.72: Rehearsal Task 3—Formatted advertivsement

PERFORMANCE

TASK 3

Your supervisor at Transport Travel Services has asked you to format a flyer to send to customers who have expressed an interest in traveling to Arizona. You want the document to be attractive and communicate its message effectively.

Follow these guidelines:

1. Open the data file, **w1p3-resort**.

2. Apply the fonts, sizes, colors, styles, and alignments shown in Figure 1.73. If you do not have the fonts indicated, you can substitute others.

3. Insert the **clock** symbol shown from the Wingdings collection, and size it to **48 point**. Apply a **yellow** highlight.

4. Insert the symbols shown from the Webdings collections before each sentence, and size it to **36 point**.

5. Copy the formatting for "Essex Hotel and Resort" from the first occurrence in the first sentence to the last occurrence in the last sentence.

6. Insert one space immediately after the graphic in paragraphs 1, 3, 6, and 7.

7. Save the file.

8. Preview the file, then print one copy.

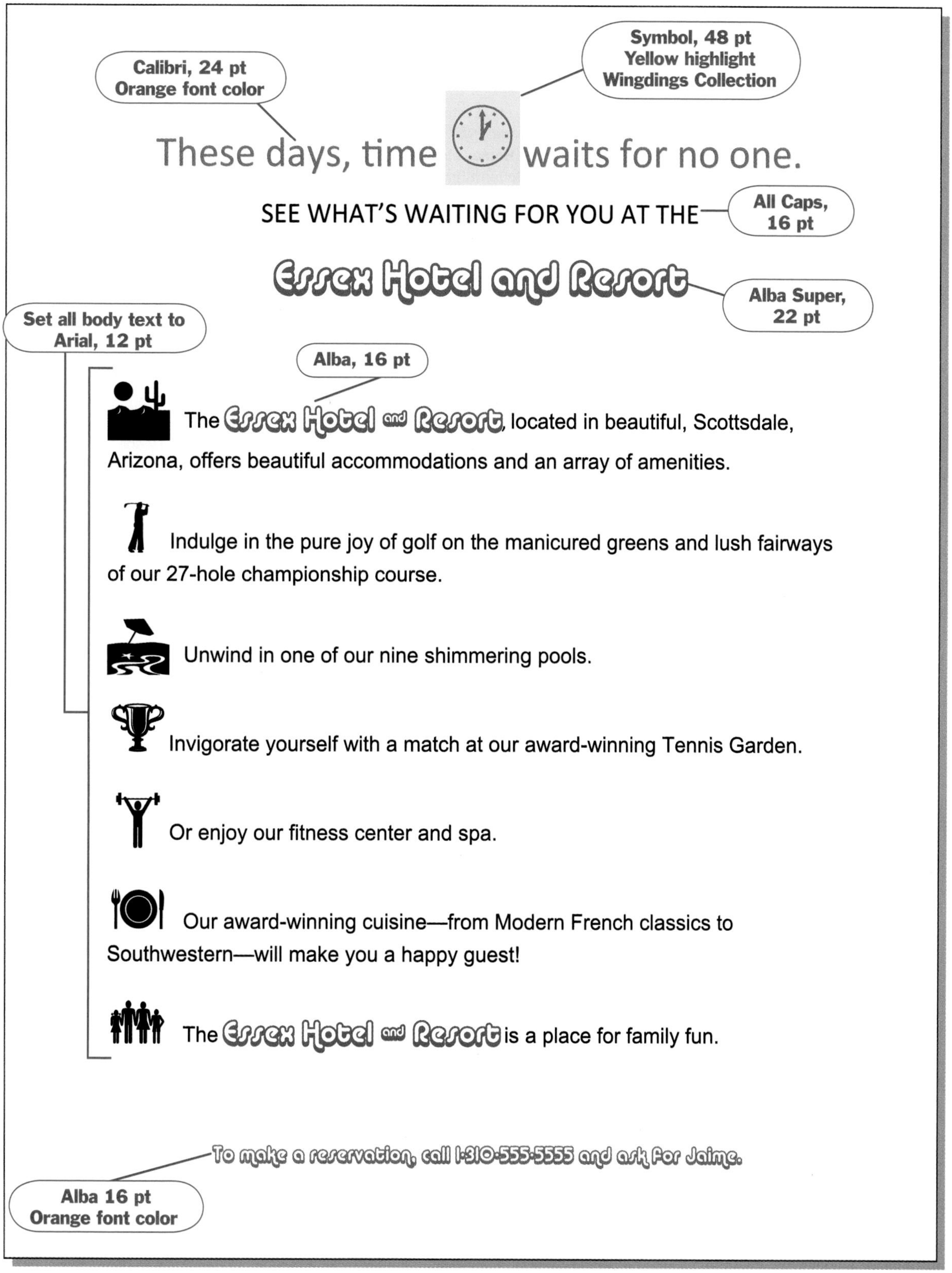

> **Calibri, 24 pt**
> **Orange font color**

> **Symbol, 48 pt**
> **Yellow highlight**
> **Wingdings Collection**

These days, time ⏰ waits for no one.

SEE WHAT'S WAITING FOR YOU AT THE —

> **All Caps,**
> **16 pt**

Essex Hotel and Resort —

> **Alba Super,**
> **22 pt**

> **Set all body text to**
> **Arial, 12 pt**

> **Alba, 16 pt**

The **Essex Hotel and Resort**, located in beautiful, Scottsdale, Arizona, offers beautiful accommodations and an array of amenities.

Indulge in the pure joy of golf on the manicured greens and lush fairways of our 27-hole championship course.

Unwind in one of our nine shimmering pools.

Invigorate yourself with a match at our award-winning Tennis Garden.

Or enjoy our fitness center and spa.

Our award-winning cuisine—from Modern French classics to Southwestern—will make you a happy guest!

The **Essex Hotel and Resort** is a place for family fun.

To make a reservation, call 1-310-555-5555 and ask for Jaime.

> **Alba 16 pt**
> **Orange font color**

Figure 1.73: Performance Task 3

Change Font, Size, Style, and Color

1. Select the text to be formatted or position the insertion point where the new formatting is to begin.
2. Click the **Home tab**, and in the **Font group**, click the appropriate list arrow or button.
3. Make the desired changes.
   Or
1. Click the **Home tab**, and in the **Font group**, click the **dialog box launcher**.
2. Make the selections you want.
3. Click **OK**.

Apply Bold, Italics, Underlining

1. Click the **Bold button** or press **[Ctrl]+B**.
   Or
1. Click the **Italic button** or press **[Ctrl]+I**.
   Or
1. Click the **Underline button** or press **[Ctrl]+U**.

Format Painter

1. Select the text with the formatting you wish to copy.
2. Click the **Home tab**, and in the **Clipboard group**, click the **Format Painter button** once to copy formatting from one location to another.
3. Select the text to receive the copied formatting.

Copy Formatting to Multiple Locations

1. Select the text with the formatting you wish to copy.
2. Click the **Home tab**, and in the **Clipboard group**, double-click the **Format Painter button**.
3. Select text to receive the copied formatting.
4. Click the **Format Painter button** to turn the option off.

Highlight Text

1. Select the text you want to affect.
2. Click the **Home tab**, and in the **Font group**, click the **Text Highlight Color button**.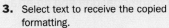

Change the Highlight Color

1. Click the **Text Highlight Color list arrow**.
2. Select a color from the palette.

Insert Symbols

1. Click the **Insert tab**, and in the **Symbols group**, click the **Symbol button**, then click **More Symbols**.
2. Click the **Font list arrow** and choose a symbol font collection.
3. Click the desired symbol, and click **Insert**.

Act I

Newmark Productions will hold its annual three-day convention in Las Vegas, Nevada. The publications director is preparing a guide for conference attendees that includes the conference program, restaurant listings, scheduled sessions, a diagram of the exhibit area, and contact phone numbers. You have been asked to format the list of "other things to do," which will be included in the guide.

Follow these guidelines:

1. Open the data file **w1e1-guide page**.

2. Follow the guidelines below to format the guide page as shown in Figure 1.74. Use your own judgment with regard to font face, but be sure that the document does not exceed one page.
   a. Select all the text, then set the line spacing to 1.15 and the paragraph spacing to 10 point after each paragraph.
   b. Center the heading, then apply a 12-point script bold font and set the character spacing to Expanded By 3 point. Apply a yellow highlight to the text.
   c. Apply a 12-point sans serif bold font to the word "Museums." Set the font color to red. Copy the formatting to "Movies" and "Shopping."
   d. Apply an 11-point serif font to "Elvis-a-Rama Museum." Set the font color to green. Copy the formatting to the other subheadings.
   e. Apply a 10-point sans serif font to the first paragraph below each subheading. Set the font color to blue. Copy the formatting to the other paragraphs.
   f. Set each address and phone number to bold and italic.

3. Save the file, then print one copy.

Other Things to Do While in Las Vegas

MUSEUMS

Elvis-a-Rama Museum

3401 Industrial Road, 702-309-7200. This museum features more than $3 million of authentic inventory of Elvis' personal items. Open 10 a.m. – 6 p.m. daily. Admission is $9.95 general admission and $7.95 for senior citizens, Nevada residents, and students.

Liberace Museum

1775 East Tropicana Avenue, 702-7908-5595. This museum houses exhibits of the late pianist's belongings, including his car collection. Hours are 10 a.m. – 5 p.m. Mondays-Saturdays and 1-5 p.m. Sundays. General admission is $6.95; $4.95 for senior citizens and students.

Guinness World of Records Museum

2780 Las Vegas Boulevard South, 702-792-3766. This museum features hands-on displays and the "World of Las Vegas" exhibit of superlatives and records set in Las Vegas. Hours are 9 a.m. – 6 p.m. daily. General admission is $4.95; $3.95 for senior citizens, military personnel, and students.

Elephants are Forever Museum

650 West Sunset Road, Henderson, 702-566-7600. This museum features more than 2,500 items, from elephants made of shells and crystal to handmade rugs from Burma. The museum is open 10 a.m. – 5 p.m. Mondays-Saturdays and 11 a.m. – 4 p.m. Sundays.

MOVIES

Fiesta Silent Film Series

2400 North Rancho Drive, 702-631-7000. This movie theatre features Silent Film Night 4-8 p.m. Tuesdays and Thursdays. Silent films featuring Charlie Chaplin, Buster Keaton, Harold Lloyd, and Clara Bow will be accompanied by a vintage Kimball pipe organ. Admission is free.

Figure 1.74: Encore Act 1–Formatted guide page

Act II

You are employed by the Johnson & Renaldo legal firm. Because you have become so skilled working with the formatting features found in Word, you have been asked to design an announcement informing clients that the office has been relocated. Mr. Johnson has asked that you create two versions (both in landscape orientation) so he can decide which one best meets his needs.

Johnson & Reynoldo
ATTORNEYS – AT - LAW

Follow these guidelines:

1. Create a new document.
2. Enter the text shown in Figure 1.75. The formatting shown is merely a guide. You may use any formatting features, alignments, and symbols to create two versions of the announcement.
3. Check grammar and spelling.
4. Save version one as **w1e2-announcement one**.
5. Print a copy and close the file.
6. Create version two, using formatting different from version one.
7. Check grammar and spelling.
8. Save version two as **w1e2-announcement two**, then print one copy.

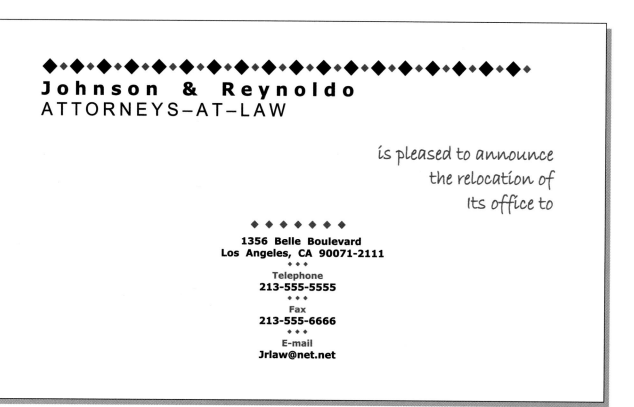

Figure 1.75: Encore Act II—Formatted announcement

Act III

Previously, you edited an article to appear in the first newsletter published by BodyworksFitnessCenters. Now, you have been asked to put your skills in formatting text to work by enhancing that article with appropriate font faces, colors, alignments, and the like.

Follow these guidelines:

1. Open the data file **w1e3-tips**.

2. Center-align the title, and change the case to all caps. Use a font color and size of your choice.

3. Insert and center four symbols of your choice below the heading. Select an appropriate font size and color.

4. Set the first side heading to 14 point using any font you want, then apply a color of your choice.

5. Copy the formatting from the first side heading to the remaining five.

6. Format the paragraph text as needed.

7. Print preview the file, and make any changes necessary.

8. Save the file, then print one copy.

Insert the Date and Time

▶ The Date and Time feature allows you to insert the current date and/or time into a document.

HOW **1.** Type the current month followed by a space. A ScreenTip showing today's date will display, as shown in Figure 2.5. **2.** Press **[Enter]** to insert it. The default format is month, date, year.

> March 1, 2010 (Press ENTER to Insert)
> March|

Figure 2.5: Date ScreenTip

▶ To change the date format, or to insert or change the time format, **1.** click the **Insert tab** and in the **Text group**, **2.** click the **Date & Time button**, as shown in Figure 2.6. **3.** In the Date and Time dialog box that displays, as shown in Figure 2.7, select the format you want, and then click **OK**.

Date & Time

Insert

> Text Box ▼ A▤
> 🗐 Quick Parts ▼ 📝 Signature Line ▼
> 🖋 WordArt ▼ 🔂 Date & Time
> A≡ Drop Cap ▼ 📇 Object ▼
>
> Text

Figure 2.6: Date & Time button

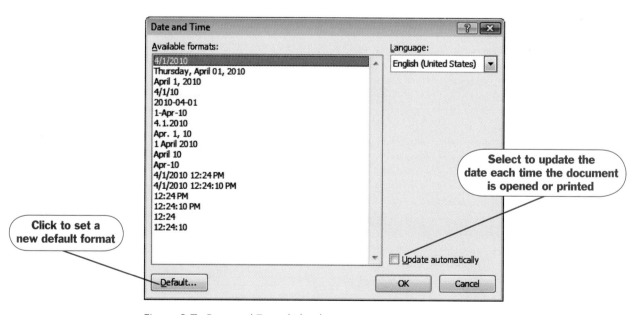

Figure 2.7: Date and Time dialog box

1. Click the **Office Button**, then click the **New button**.

2. Click **Blank document**, and then click **Create**.

3. Enter the letters of the current month, press **[space bar]**, and then press **[Enter]**. *Notice that the date and year were inserted automatically.*

4. Close the file, and do not save changes.

5. Open a new blank document.

6. Click the **Insert tab**, and in the **Text group**, click the **Date & Time button**.

7. Enter today's date again using this format: 1/28/10.

8. Close the file, and do not save changes.

Use Quick Parts

▶ The **Quick Parts** feature allows you to save and quickly insert frequently used text and graphics, which are considered building blocks since they help you build your document.

HOW To create a new Quick Part, **1.** select the text or graphic you want to save as a building block entry. *Include the paragraph mark in your selection if you wish to save paragraph formatting with the entry.* **2.** Click the **Insert tab**, and in the **Text group**, click the **Quick Parts button**, as shown in Figure 2.8. **3.** Select **Save Selection to Quick Part Gallery** on the menu that appears, as shown in Figure 2.9. **4.** Enter a name for the new Quick Part in the Create New Building Block dialog box, as shown in Figure 2.10, then **5.** click **OK** to save it.

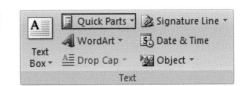

Figure 2.8: Quick Parts button

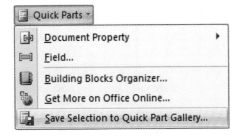

Figure 2.9: Quick Parts menu

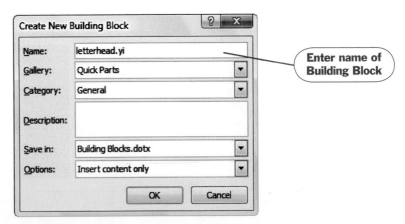

Figure 2.10: Create New Building Block dialog box

HOW To insert a Quick Part into a document, **1.** click to position the insertion point where you want to insert the entry, then **2.** click the **Quick Parts button**. Select the desired entry which was added to the Quick Parts menu, as shown in Figure 2.11.

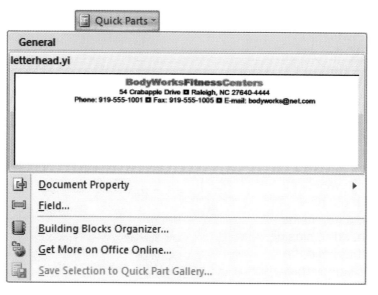

Figure 2.11: Quick Parts menu with listed Building Block

T R Y *i t* O U T *w2-3*

1. Open a new blank document.

2. Create the BodyWorksFitnessCenters letterhead, and center it at the top of the page. Use the text and settings shown in Figure 2.12.

3. Select all the text.

4. Click the **Insert tab**, and in the **Text group**, click the **Quick Parts button**.

5. Select **Save Selection to Quick Part Gallery**.

6. Enter `letterhead` in the Name text box. *When saving a document, include your initials or name as part of the filename, so*

you can easily identify it in the future as your file.

7. Click **OK** to save.

8. Close the file, and do not save changes.

9. Open a new blank document.

10. Click to position the insertion point at the top of the page, if necessary.

11. Click the **Insert tab**, then click the **Quick Parts button**.

12. Click to insert the letterhead Quick Part you want.

13. Close the file, and do not save changes.

Figure 2.12: BodyWorks FitnessCenters logo text

REHEARSAL

GOAL
To create a block business letter, as shown in Figure 2.13

TASK 1

WHAT YOU NEED TO KNOW

▶ The layout of a letter is called a **format**. There are a variety of letter formats, but most have the following parts: date, inside address, salutation, body, closing, writer's name and title, and the writer's initials followed by the preparer's initials.

▶ In the **block business letter**, all parts begin at the left margin. The margins depend on the length of the letter.

▶ A **letterhead** is a heading that includes the contact information (name, address, phone number, e-mail address, and/or Web address) of an individual or company that is printed at the top, side, or bottom of stationery. Some company letterheads also contain a **logo**, which is a symbol, picture, or saying that creates an image of that company. Most companies use stationery with preprinted letterheads.

▶ The date generally begins about 2.5" down from the top of the page. (The At indicator on the status bar displays the exact position.)

▶ "Sincerely" is generally used to close a letter. "Cordially," "Yours truly," and "Very truly yours," can also be used.

▶ An **enclosure notation** is indicated on a letter when something in addition to the letter

▼ DIRECTIONS

1. Open a new blank document.
2. Use the following settings:

Margins	Any desired
Line Spacing	1.0
Paragraph Spacing	
Before	0
After	0
Font	Times New Roman, 12 point

3. Create a Quick Parts entry for the word **Enclosure** and name it `enclos`.

4. Create a Quick Parts entry for the following closing and name it `closing`.

```
Yours truly,

↓4x


Benjamin Chasin
President

bc/yo (yo="your own" initials)
```

5. Close the file, and do not save changes.
6. Open another new blank document.
7. Use the following settings:

Margins	Normal
Line Spacing	1.0
Paragraph Spacing	
Before	0
After	0
Font	Times New Roman, 12 point

8. Insert the Quick Parts entry **letterhead** at the top of the page.

Continued on next page

is included in the envelope. The notation is generally placed at the left margin, two lines below the reference initials.

▶ A ZIP Code can be five or nine digits. The four-digit add-on number identifies a geographic segment within the five-digit delivery area, such as a city block, office building, or any other unit that would aid efficient mail sorting and delivery. Use of the four-digit add-on is helpful but not mandatory, according to the U.S. Postal Service. To find a ZIP Code, use ZIP Code Lookup at www.usps.com.

9. Press **[Enter]** to advance the insertion point to about 2.5". *If necessary, customize the status bar to display the vertical position from the top of the page.*

10. Use the Date feature to insert the current date with the format September 3, 2010.

11. Enter the letter shown in Figure 2.13. Insert spacing between letter parts as shown.

12. Insert the Quick Parts entry for the closing.

13. Insert the Quick Parts entry for the enclosure notation.

14. Correct any spelling errors, and then preview the document.

15. Save the file, and name it **2r1-employment**.

16. Close the file.

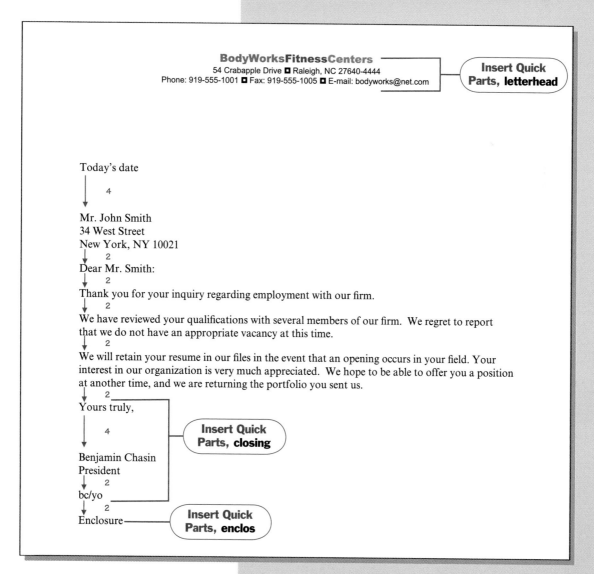

BodyWorksFitnessCenters
54 Crabapple Drive ◻ Raleigh, NC 27640-4444
Phone: 919-555-1001 ◻ Fax: 919-555-1005 ◻ E-mail: bodyworks@net.com

> **Insert Quick Parts, letterhead**

Today's date

↓ 4

Mr. John Smith
34 West Street
New York, NY 10021
↓ 2
Dear Mr. Smith:
↓ 2
Thank you for your inquiry regarding employment with our firm.
↓ 2
We have reviewed your qualifications with several members of our firm. We regret to report that we do not have an appropriate vacancy at this time.
↓ 2
We will retain your resume in our files in the event that an opening occurs in your field. Your interest in our organization is very much appreciated. We hope to be able to offer you a position at another time, and we are returning the portfolio you sent us.
↓ 2
Yours truly,

↓ 4

> **Insert Quick Parts, closing**

Benjamin Chasin
President
↓ 2
bc/yo
↓ 2
Enclosure

> **Insert Quick Parts, enclos**

Figure 2.13: Business letter

Set Margins

1. Click the **Page Layout tab**, and in the **Page Setup group**, click the **Margins button**.

2. Select margin format from the gallery.

   Or

2. Click **Custom Margins**, and in the Page Setup dialog box, enter the desired margins in appropriate text boxes.

3. Click **OK**.

Insert Date and Time

1. Type the month, press [**space bar**], and then press [**Enter**].

   Or

1. Click the **Insert tab**, and in the **Text group**, click the **Date & Time button**.

2. Select the Date and Time format you want, and then click **OK**.

Create a New Quick Part

1. Select the text you want to save as a Quick Part.

2. Click the **Insert tab**, and in the **Text group**, click the **Quick Parts button**.

3. Click **Save Selection to Quick Part Gallery**.

4. Enter a name in the **Name text box**, and then click **OK**.

Insert a Quick Part into a Document

1. Position the insertion point where you want to insert the Quick Part.

2. Click the **Insert tab**, and in the **Text group**, click the **Quick Parts button**.

3. Click to select the Quick Part you want to insert.

TASK 1

BodyWorksFitnessCenters is selling the RideTheTrack exercising machine for home use and wants to market this product to current members of its clubs. You have been asked to prepare a letter telling a member about this product.

Follow these guidelines:

1. Create an AutoCorrect entry as follows:
   a. Click the **Office Button**, then click **Word Options**.
   b. Click **Proofing**, then click **AutoCorrect Options**.
   c. In the AutoCorrect dialog box, select the **AutoCorrect tab**, if necessary.
   d. Enter **ri** in the Replace box, and then enter **RideTheTrack Exerciser** in the With box.
   e. Click **OK** to close the dialog box, and then click **OK** to close Word Options.

2. Create a new blank document. Use the following settings:

Margins	Any desired
Line Spacing	1.0
Paragraph Spacing	
Before	0
After	0
Font	Times New Roman, 12 point

3. Insert the Quick Parts entry, **letterhead** at the top of the page. *You created this entry in Try it Out w2-3.*

4. Format a block business letter using the text shown in Figure 2.14. *When you type "ri" as shown in the letter, it will be replaced with your AutoCorrect entry.*

5. Insert the Quick Parts entry **closing** where appropriate. *You created this entry in Try it Out w2-3.*

6. Save the file, and name it **2p1-exerciser letter**.

7. Print one copy.

8. Close the file.

Insert Quick Parts, letterhead

Today's date Ms. Joanna Newman, 12 Amsterdam Avenue, New York, NY 10023

Dear Ms. Newman: According to medical fitness experts, regular aerobic exercise is essential for achieving all-around wellness. Aerobic exercise helps you prevent illness, feel better physically and mentally, boost your energy level, and increase the years of your life. That's why you need the ri for your home. The ri will provide you with the following benefits:

You can burn more fat than on other exercisers.

You can improve your cardiovascular fitness and lower your cholesterol level.

With regular work outs at home using the ri, you will feel wonderful because you are doing something positive for yourself. Speak to one of the trainers the next time you come in. They will provide you with all the purchasing details

Insert Quick Parts, closing

Figure 2.14: Unarranged business letter

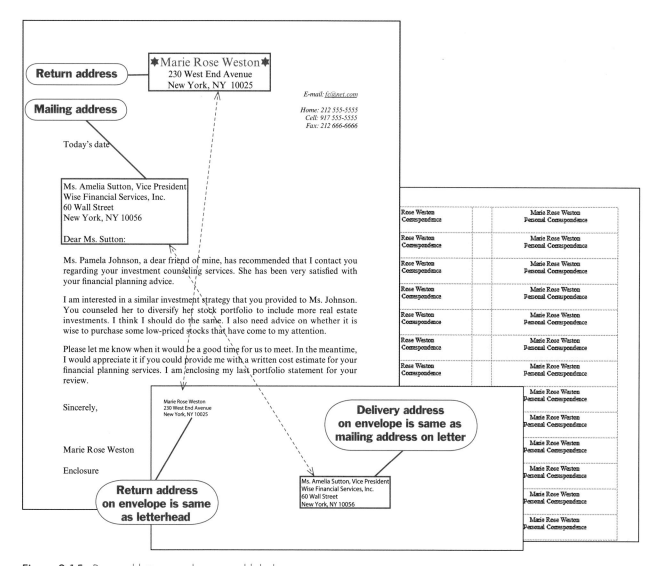

Figure 2.15: Personal letter, envelopes, and labels

WHAT YOU NEED TO KNOW

Create Envelopes and Labels

Envelopes

▶ The Envelopes feature allows you to print a delivery address as well as your return address directly on the envelope. The **delivery address** indicates to whom the letter is going and is the same as the inside address on a letter. The **return address** is the address of the sender. Once you have set up your envelope the way you want, you can print it as well as save it so that you can reuse it at a future time.

HOW 1. Click the **Mailings tab**, and in the **Create group**, 2. click the **Envelopes button**, as shown in Figure 2.16. The Envelopes and Labels dialog box displays with the Envelopes tab selected, as shown in Figure 2.17. 3. Enter the address of the person to whom the letter is going in the Delivery address window. If a letter is on screen, Word automatically places the inside address into the Delivery address window. 4. Insert the envelope into your printer as shown in the Feed window, and then 5. click **Print** in the Envelopes and Labels dialog box.

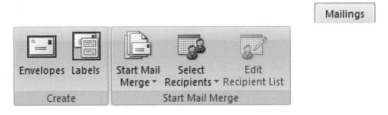

Figure 2.16: Envelopes and Labels buttons on the Mailings tab

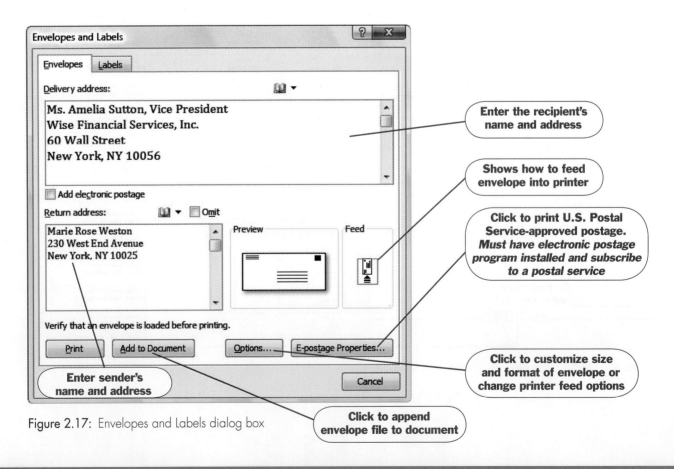

Figure 2.17: Envelopes and Labels dialog box

▶ Do not enter a return address if you are using envelopes that have a preprinted address.

▶ Other envelope printing options are explained in Table 2.1.

Table 2.1: Envelope printing options

CLICK THIS	IF YOU WANT TO
Add to Document button	Append the envelope file to the beginning of the document so that the envelope prints along with the document, making it unnecessary to re-create the envelope the next time you print the document.
Options/Envelope Options tab	Customize the size and format of an envelope. The default envelope size is letter (No. 10), measuring 4⅛ x 9½ inches.
Options/Printing Options tab	Change printing feed options.
E-postage Properties button	Print U.S. Postal Service–approved postage on the envelope. Users must install an electronic postage program and subscribe to www.stamps.com to use this service.

T R Y *i t* O U T *w2-4*

1. Open the data file **w2-4**.

2. Click the **Mailings tab**, and in the **Create group**, click the **Envelopes button**. *The Envelopes tab should be automatically selected, and the inside address on the letter should appear in the Delivery address window.*

3. On the **Envelopes tab**, click **Options**.

4. Click the **Envelope Options tab**. *Size 10 envelope should be selected.*

5. Click the **Printing Options tab**.

6. Select the feed method that is compatible with your printer, and then click **OK**.

7. Click **Add to Document**.

8. Insert an envelope into your printer. *It is not necessary to use an actual envelope for this tryout. You can print the envelope using plain paper.*

9. Click the **Office Button**, and then click the **Print button**.

10. Close the file, and do not save changes.

Labels

▶ The Labels feature allows you to create labels for mailings, file folders, business cards, or name badges. Once address labels are printed, they can be affixed to an envelope for mailing.

HOW **1.** Click the **Mailings tab**, and in the **Create group**, **2.** click the **Labels button**. The Envelopes and Labels dialog box is displayed with the Labels tab selected, as shown in Figure 2.18. **3.** Click **Options** to specify the type of label you wish to use. **4.** Select the label vendor and product number in the Label Options dialog box that appears, as shown in Figure 2.19, and then **5.** click **OK**. **6.** Click **New Document** in the Envelope and Labels dialog box (blank labels appear, ready for you to begin entering text). *Product numbers and vendors are typically indicated on the box of labels you purchase.*

> To print labels with the same information, enter text in Address window and select Full page of the same label

> Click Options to specify label type, then click New Document to display labels

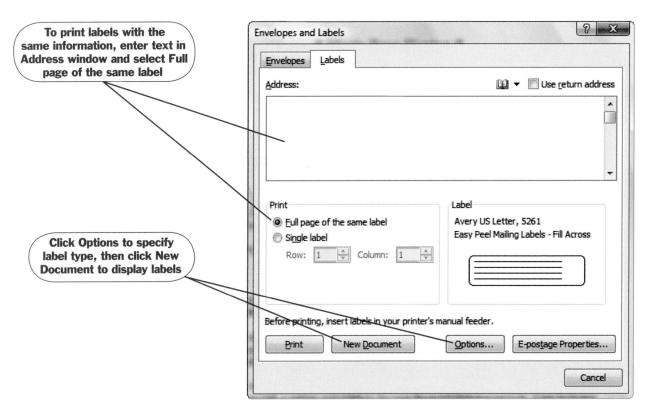

Figure 2.18: Labels tab in Envelopes and Labels dialog box

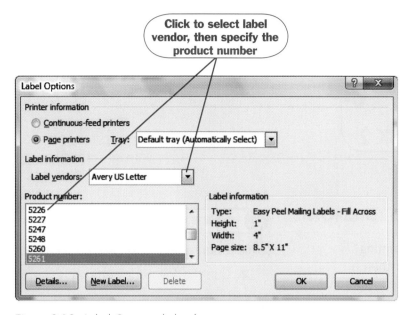

Figure 2.19: Label Options dialog box

▶ To print the labels, load the printer with the size and type of label paper you specified. When you print a single page, the entire physical page is printed.

▶ To print a sheet of labels with the same information, enter the information in the Address window of the Envelopes and Labels dialog box, and click the **Full page of the same label option** (see Figure 2.18).

▶ Once you create and save a page of labels, you can use it in the future.

T R Y _it_ O U T _w2-5_

1. Open a new blank document.

2. Click the **Mailings tab**, and in the **Create group**, click the **Labels button**. _The Labels tab should be automatically selected._

3. On the Labels tab, click **Options**.

4. Click the **Label vendors list box**, and choose **Avery US Letter**.

5. Scroll the **Product number list**, and select **5261**.

6. Click **OK**. _You will now return to the Envelope and Labels dialog box._

7. Click **New Document**.

8. Enter the following address:

   ```
   Ms. Wendy Ng
   78 Jason Lane
   East Meadow, NY 11545-4456
   ```

9. Press **[Tab]** twice to advance to the next label.

10. Enter the following address:

    ```
    Mr. Harmon Jones
    33 Pine Street
    Middletown, NJ 01154-3711
    ```

11. If you have the specified label type, insert a sheet of labels (or a sheet of letter-size paper) into the printer. Click the **Office Button**, click the **Print button**, select the desired print options, then click **OK**.

12. Close the file, and do not save changes.

REHEARSAL

TASK 2

 GOAL
To create a personal letter with an envelope and labels, as shown in Figure 2.20

WHAT YOU NEED TO KNOW

▶ Individuals representing themselves rather than a business firm write a **personal letter**.

▶ In the block personal letter, all parts begin at the left margin. The margins of the letter depend on the length of the letter.

▶ In this rehearsal activity, you will format a block personal letter.

▼ DIRECTIONS

1. Open a new blank document.

2. Use the following settings:

Margins	1.5" left and right (custom)
Line Spacing	1.0
Paragraph Spacing	
Before	0
After	0
Font	Times New Roman, 12 point

3. Format the letterhead shown in Figure 2.20 as follows:
   a. Center and set the individual's name to **16-point bold** using any font color.
   b. Center and set the address information to **12-point** using any font color.
   c. Insert any symbol before and after the individual's name.
   d. Right-align and set the communication information to **9-point italic** using any font color.

4. Press **[Enter]** to advance the insertion point to approximately 2.5".

5. Left-align and insert the current date.

6. Enter the remainder of the letter. Insert the Quick Parts entry **enclos** for the enclosure notation.

7. Justify the paragraph text.

8. Proofread the document, and correct all errors.

9. Preview the document.

10. Prepare an envelope (size 10) with a return address (the name and address on the letterhead), and append the envelope to the letter.

11. Save the file, and name it `2r2-financial planning`.

12. Print the letter and envelope.

Continued on page 98

✷Marie Rose Weston✷
230 West End Avenue
New York, NY 10025

E-mail: fc@net.com

Home: 212 555-5555
Cell: 917 555-5555
Fax: 212 666-6666

Today's date

Ms. Amelia Sutton, Vice President
Wise Financial Services, Inc.
60 Wall Street
New York, NY 10056

Dear Ms. Sutton:

Ms. Pamela Johnson, a dear friend of mine, has recommended that I contact you regarding your investment counseling services. She has been very satisfied with your financial planning advice.

I am interested in a similar investment strategy that you provided to Ms. Johnson. You counseled her to diversify her stock portfolio to include more real estate investments. I think I should do the same. I also need advice on whether it is wise to purchase some low-priced stocks that have come to my attention.

Please let me know when it would be a good time for us to meet. In the meantime, I would appreciate it if you could provide me with a written cost estimate for your financial planning services. I am enclosing my last portfolio statement for your review.

Sincerely,

Marie Rose Weston

Enclosure

Figure 2.20a: Personal letter

13. Prepare a full page of **Avery US Letter**, **5866 filing labels** with the following information:

```
Marie Rose Weston
Personal Correspondence
```

a. Center the text on the label.

b. Print the label file (use plain paper for this Rehearsal).

14. Do not save, but close all files.

Figure 2.20b: Envelope and labels

PERFORMANCE

TASK 2

You and a friend are interested in traveling to Dallas, Texas, in May. Write a personal letter to Ms. Robin Betts of the Transport Travel Services, 505 Park Avenue, New York, NY 10010. Transport Travel Services specializes in leisure travel packages. You would like a copy of *Travel Guide 2010* to help with your planning. You are particularly interested in visiting the Arts District, Civic Center, and the well-known Farmer's Market and would like any information available about those areas. Ask that the materials be sent to your home address.

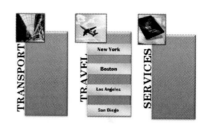

Follow these guidelines:

1. Create a letterhead using your own name, address, and phone information. Include a symbol of your choice as part of the design.

2. Write a letter to Ms. Betts using appropriate margins, any desired font, and an appropriate closing.

3. Save the file, and name it `2p2-dallas`.

4. Prepare an envelope, and append the envelope to the letter.

5. Print one copy of the letter and envelope.

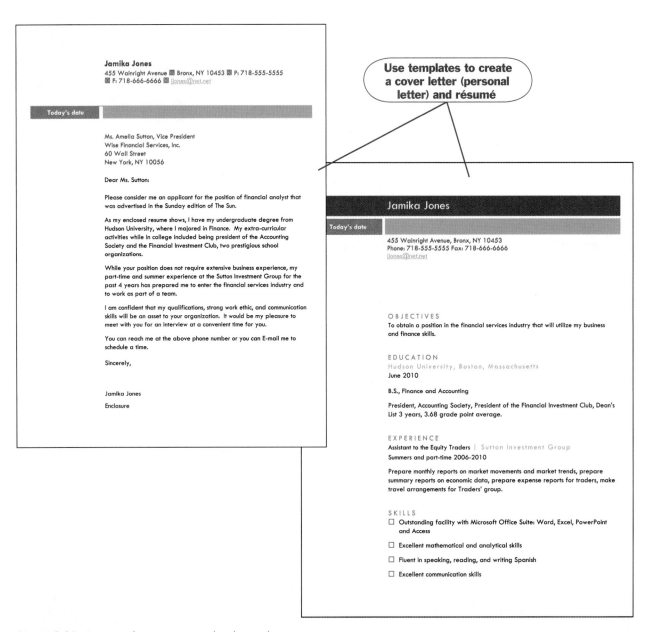

Use templates to create a cover letter (personal letter) and résumé

Figure 2.21: Letter and résumé created with templates

WHAT YOU NEED TO KNOW

Use Templates

Open Existing Templates

▶ A **template** is a document that contains a predefined page layout, fonts, formatting, pictures, or text, which may be used as the structure for a new document. Word installs with numerous templates that you can use to create a variety of different documents. Other Word templates can be found on Microsoft Office Online (www.microsoft.com).

▶ After opening a Word template, you fill in the information that is specific to your document, then save it.

HOW **1.** Click the **Office Button**, then **2.** click the **New button**. **3.** Click **Installed Templates** in the New Document dialog box, as shown in Figure 2.22. *Thumbnails of each template installed on your computer are listed in the middle pane.* **4.** Click a template to select it. *The selected template will be displayed in the preview window in the right pane.* **5.** Click **Create** to open the template.

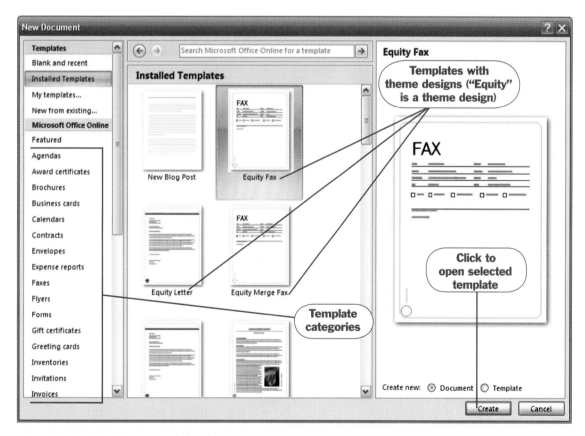

Figure 2.22: New Document dialog box

► If you are connected to the Internet and wish to find templates in a specific category, click the template category that you want in the left pane (Award certificates, for example) to display thumbnails of templates available on Microsoft Office Online.

► For each template type, there are usually several formats from which to choose, as shown in Figure 2.23.

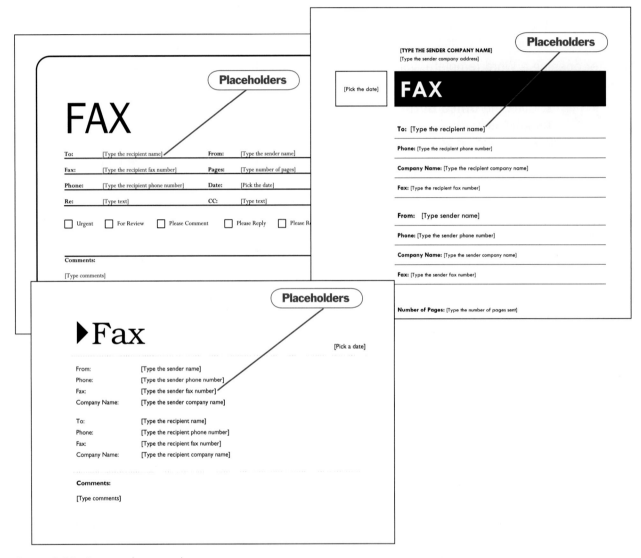

Figure 2.23: Fax template samples

► Templates are typically designed with a theme and a style. A theme is a collection of overall colors, fonts, and effects. A style combines different colors, formats, fonts, and effects and determines which effect is dominant. Figure 2.24 illustrates a letter, fax, and résumé template that use the Oriel theme. *You will learn more about themes and styles in a later lesson.*

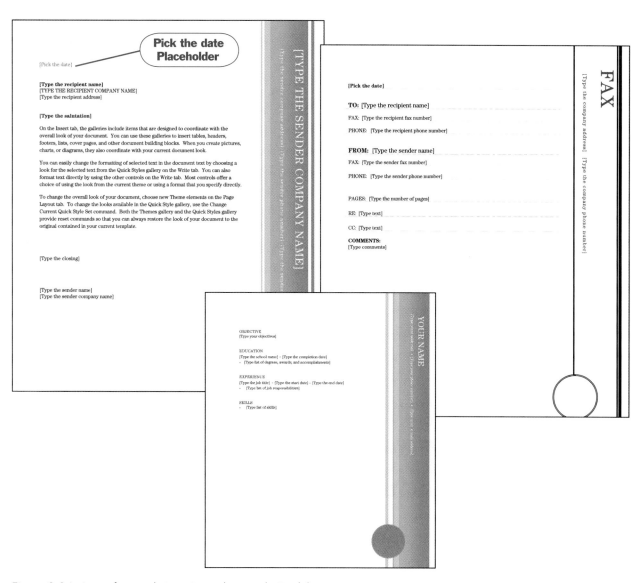

Figure 2.24: Letter, fax, and résumé templates with Oriel theme

▶ Templates contain **placeholders**, which are boxes that identify the placement and location of text and contain preset text formats. (See the fax template samples in Figure 2.23.) Click in the placeholder to select it, then follow the directions in the placeholder to insert the appropriate information. To replace sample text, highlight the existing text, then enter the new text.

▶ Some placeholders once selected, will provide a drop-down list of options. For example, to enter a date, click the [Pick a date] placeholder, which will display a drop-down calendar for you to choose the date to be inserted, as shown in Figure 2.25. Other placeholders automatically insert information from the computer's memory, such as your name, your school or company name.

▶ To delete a placeholder, click to select it, then press **[Delete]**.

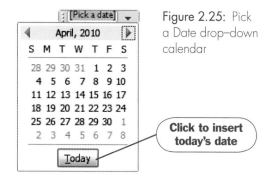

Figure 2.25: Pick a Date drop-down calendar

Click to insert today's date

1. Click the **Office Button**, then click the **New button**.

2. Click **Installed Templates**.

3. Click **Equity Fax**, and view the document in the preview window. *Fax cover sheets accompany other documents being faxed and indicate for whom the fax is intended, the sender, and the number of pages being faxed.*

4. Click **Equity Letter**, and view the document in the preview window.

5. Click **Equity Resume**, and view the document in the preview window.

6. Click the **Memos** category. Review the memo templates available. *If you do not have an Internet connection, skip this step.*

7. Click **Installed Templates**, click **Median Fax**, and then click **Create** to open the fax template, as shown in Figure 2.26.

8. Click in each placeholder, and replace placeholder text with the information shown in Table 2.2.

9. Close the file, and do not save the changes.

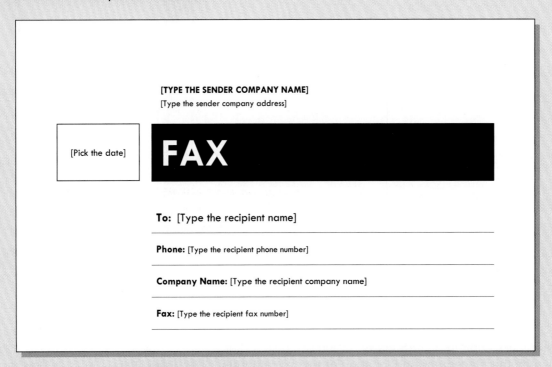

[TYPE THE SENDER COMPANY NAME]
[Type the sender company address]

[Pick the date]

FAX

To: [Type the recipient name]

Phone: [Type the recipient phone number]

Company Name: [Type the recipient company name]

Fax: [Type the recipient fax number]

Figure 2.26: Fax template with Median theme

Table 2.2: Placeholder replacement text

PLACEHOLDER TEXT	REPLACE WITH
[TYPE THE SENDER COMPANY NAME]	Travels Unlimited
[Type the sender company address]	505 Park Avenue, New York, NY 10010
TO: [Type the recipient name]	Ira Morre
[Pick the date] Select the option	Today's date
Phone: [Type the recipient phone number]	212-555-5555
Company Name: [Type the recipient Company name]	Vista Planning Group
Fax: [Type the recipient fax number]	212-555-5556
From: Your Name	Your name
Phone: [Type the sender phone number]	212-555-7777
Company Name: [Type the sender company name]	Same as above
Fax: [Type the sender fax number]	212-555-7776
Number of Pages: [Type the number of pages sent]	2
Urgent: [Select the option]	No
Action Requested: [Type the action required]	Please respond by next Friday

Create Your Own Template

▶ You can create your own template by customizing an existing one or by creating a new one from scratch. For example, you can create your own letterhead and save it as a template. Each time you want to send a letter, you can easily access your saved letterhead template.

▶ You can customize an existing template by changing the fonts, font colors, font sizes, themes, and line and paragraph spacing.

HOW To make adjustments to an existing template, select the placeholder first. To adjust spacing between paragraphs text, **1.** select the placeholder. **2.** Click the **Page Layout tab**, and in the **Paragraph group**, **3.** select the Before and After spacing you want.

To save a document as a template, **1.** click the **Office Button**, and **2.** point to (but do not click) **Save As**. **3.** Select **Word Template** from the *Save a copy of the document list*, as shown in Figure 2.27. **4.** The Templates folder is automatically selected as the save location, as shown in Figure 2.28. **5.** Enter a filename, and click **Save**. Since you are saving the file in the Templates folder, Word automatically enters "Word Template" as the *Save as type*. The file extension for a Word template is .dotx.

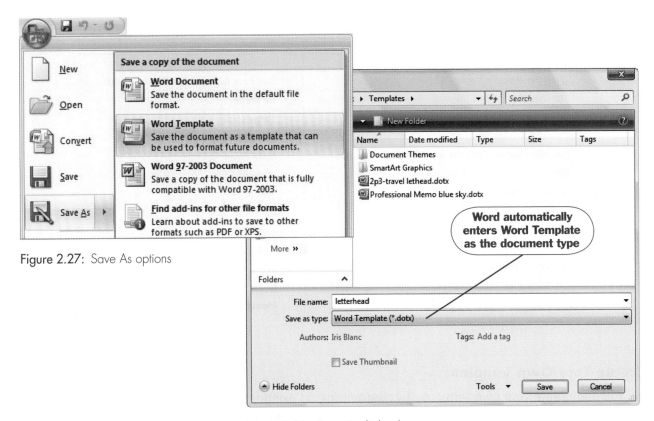

Figure 2.27: Save As options

Figure 2.28: Save As dialog box

Word automatically enters Word Template as the document type

T R Y *i t* **O U T** *w2-7*

1. Open a new blank document.

2. Create your own letterhead. Include your name, address, city, state, ZIP Code, phone and fax numbers, and e-mail address. Use any desired font, font style, font colors, and alignments.

3. Click the **Office Button**, point to **Save As**, and then click **Word Template**.

4. In the **Save As dialog box**, click **Templates**.

5. In the **File name text box**, enter My letterhead, then click **Save**.

6. Click the **Office Button**, then click **Close**.

7. To access your newly created template, click the **Office Button**, then click **Open**.

8. Click the **Templates folder**, if necessary.

9. Select **My letterhead**, and then click **Open**. *If you were to type a letter at this*

point, you could use your letterhead. When you save the letter, you will be prompted to save it under a new filename, thus leaving your letterhead template intact for future use.

10. Close the file, and do not save changes.

11. Click the **Office Button**, then click the **New button**.

12. Click **Installed Templates**.

13. Click **Oriel Letter**, then click **Create**.

14. Select the **[Pick the date] placeholder**. Click the **Page Layout tab**, and in the **Paragraph group**, increase the After spacing to **24 pt**. *Note the effect of the spacing after the dateline.*

15. Select the **[Type the recipient address] placeholder**. Repeat Step 14, but change the After spacing to **12 pt**.

16. Close the file, and do not save changes.

REHEARSAL

GOAL
To modify templates, then create a letter and résumé as, shown in Figures 2.29 and 2.30

TASK 3

WHAT YOU NEED TO KNOW

▶ A **résumé** is a summary of your background and qualifications and is used to gain employment. Most résumés include some or all of the following: identifying information (name, address, and contact numbers), career objective, education, experience, skills, and abilities. The purpose of a résumé is to identify what you can do for a prospective employer with the experience you have acquired and the skills you have developed.

▶ A résumé is typically enclosed with a **cover letter** (also called an application letter). The purpose of a cover letter is to provide a summary of what you have to offer a prospective employer and to gain an interview.

▶ The line and paragraph spacing on letter templates will vary, and there may not be traditional spacing between the parts of the letter. You can adjust this, however. Check the line spacing setting in the Paragraph dialog box when you use a template. Pressing **[Enter]** once may leave more than one blank line.

▶ Some résumé templates contain a picture placeholder.

▼ DIRECTIONS

1. Click the **Office Button**, then click the **New button**.
2. Click **Installed Templates**, and use the **Median Letter template** to create the cover letter, as shown in Figure 2.29.
3. Make the following modifications to the template:

   Select the **[Type the Closing] placeholder**. Change the paragraph spacing Before to **12 pt** and After to **36 pt**.
4. Enter the information shown in Figure 2.29. Use a symbol of your choice in the letterhead. Insert the Quick Parts **enclos** for the enclosure notation. Apply the formatting used in the body of the letter to the Enclosure notation.
5. Check the spelling and grammar in the document.
6. Save the file and name it `2r3-cover letter`.
7. Print one copy, then close the file.
8. Click the **Office Button**, then click the **New button**.
9. Click **Installed Templates**. Use the **Median Resume template** to create the résumé, as shown in Figure 2.30.
10. Make the following modifications to the template:
    a. Delete the picture placeholder. Select the picture, then press **[Delete]**.
    b. Delete the **[Type your website address] placeholder**.
11. Type the information shown in Figure 2.30.
12. Save the file, and name it `2r3-resume`.
13. Print one copy, and close the file.

Jamika Jones
455 Wainright Avenue 🔲 Bronx, NY 10453 🔲 P: 718-555-5555
🔲 F: 718-666-6666 🔲 jjones@net.net

Today's date	

Ms. Amelia Sutton, Vice President
Wise Financial Services, Inc.
60 Wall Street
New York, NY 10056

Dear Ms. Sutton:

Please consider me an applicant for the position of financial analyst that was advertised in the Sunday edition of The Sun.

As my enclosed resume shows, I have my undergraduate degree from Hudson University, where I majored in Finance. My extra-curricular activities while in college included being president of the Accounting Society and the Financial Investment Club, two prestigious school organizations.

While your position does not require extensive business experience, my part-time and summer experience at the Sutton Investment Group for the past 4 years has prepared me to enter the financial services industry and to work as part of a team.

I am confident that my qualifications, strong work ethic, and communication skills will be an asset to your organization. It would be my pleasure to meet with you for an interview at a convenient time for you.

You can reach me at the above phone number or you can E-mail me to schedule a time.

Sincerely,

Jamika Jones

Enclosure

Figure 2.29: Cover letter

Jamika Jones

Today's date

455 Wainright Avenue, Bronx, NY 10453
Phone: 718-555-5555 Fax: 718-666-6666
jjones@net.net

OBJECTIVES

To obtain a position in the financial services industry that will utilize my business and finance skills.

EDUCATION

Hudson University, Boston, Massachusetts
June 2010

B.S., Finance and Accounting

President, Accounting Society, President of the Financial Investment Club, Dean's List 3 years, 3.68 grade point average.

EXPERIENCE

Assistant to the Equity Traders | Sutton Investment Group
Summers and part-time 2006-2010

Prepare monthly reports on market movements and market trends, prepare summary reports on economic data, prepare expense reports for traders, make travel arrangements for Traders' group.

SKILLS

☐ Outstanding facility with Microsoft Office Suite: Word, Excel, PowerPoint and Access

☐ Excellent mathematical and analytical skills

☐ Fluent in speaking, reading, and writing Spanish

☐ Excellent communication skills

Figure 2.30: Résumé

PERFORMANCE

TASK 3

You work for Wilson Jones, director of corporate travel at Transport Travel Services in the Los Angeles office. He has asked you to prepare a letter to Mr. Alan Newman, CEO of Newmark Productions, 101 Sunset Boulevard, Beverly Hills, CA 90210. He has also asked you to customize the Oriel Letter template to be used as the new template for the company.

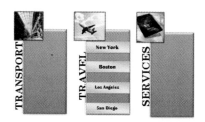

Follow these guidelines:

1. Use the **Oriel Letter template** to create a new letter template for Transport Travel Services, as shown in Figure 2.31. The California office is located at 46 Beverly Drive, Beverly Hills, CA 90210, Phone: 310-555-5555, e-mail: ttsbh@net.com.

2. Modify the template as follows:
   - Replace the **[TYPE THE SENDER COMPANY NAME] placeholder** text. Set the font color to dark blue.
   - Replace the placeholders for sender company address, phone number, and e-mail address. Set the contact information to Arial Narrow, **10 pt**. Set the font color to dark blue.
   - Center the company name and contact information.
   - Select the **[Pick the date] placeholder**. Change the paragraph spacing After to **36 pt**.
   - Select the **[Type the recipient address] placeholder**, and set the paragraph spacing After to **12 pt**.
   - Select the **[Type the closing] placeholder**, and set the paragraph spacing Before to **0 pt** and After to **36 pt**.
   - Delete "Transport Travel Services" below your name in the template.

3. Save the document as a template, and name it `2p3-TTS letter template`.

Continued on next page

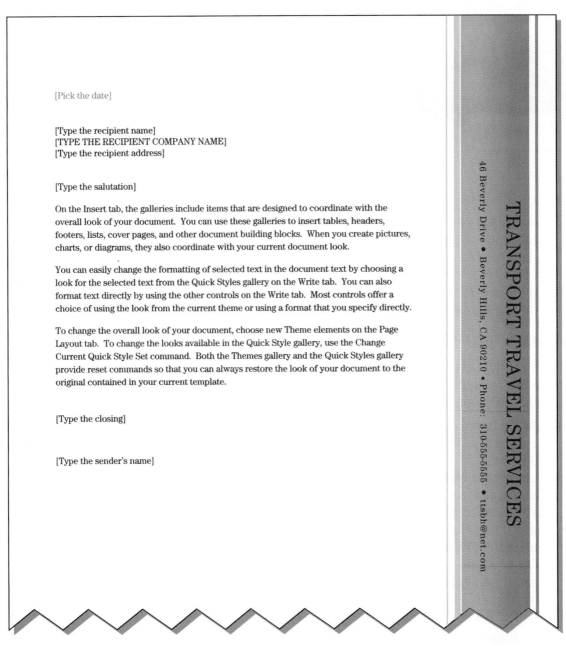

[Pick the date]

[Type the recipient name]
[TYPE THE RECIPIENT COMPANY NAME]
[Type the recipient address]

[Type the salutation]

On the Insert tab, the galleries include items that are designed to coordinate with the overall look of your document. You can use these galleries to insert tables, headers, footers, lists, cover pages, and other document building blocks. When you create pictures, charts, or diagrams, they also coordinate with your current document look.

You can easily change the formatting of selected text in the document text by choosing a look for the selected text from the Quick Styles gallery on the Write tab. You can also format text directly by using the other controls on the Write tab. Most controls offer a choice of using the look from the current theme or using a format that you specify directly.

To change the overall look of your document, choose new Theme elements on the Page Layout tab. To change the looks available in the Quick Style gallery, use the Change Current Quick Style Set command. Both the Themes gallery and the Quick Styles gallery provide reset commands so that you can always restore the look of your document to the original contained in your current template.

[Type the closing]

[Type the sender's name]

46 Beverly Drive • Beverly Hills, CA 90210 • Phone: 310-555-5555 • ttsbh@net.com

TRANSPORT TRAVEL SERVICES

Figure 2.31: TTS Letter template

4. Using the customized letter template you just created, complete the letter. Enter today's date (do not use the Pick a Date feature), the inside address, and an appropriate salutation. Then enter the body of the letter (shown on the next page) and an appropriate closing. Include your reference initials (yo).

Latifa Capra has referred your letter to me. You had asked her to provide you with a list of hotels in the San Francisco area that have a business center, laptop rentals, fax services, and teleconferencing capabilities.

I have compiled a list of hotels that offer the services you requested. They appear below:

Regency Central

Surry Hotel

Fairmont Hotel

Renaissance Center

Marriott Mark

Grand Hyatt

The Fairmont Hotel and Grand Hyatt are located nearest to where your meetings will take place. Please call our office when you have decided where to stay so we can finalize your bookings to San Francisco.

5. Check spelling.

6. Make the following modifications to the letter:
- Unbold the date and change the font color to match the document font color.
- Unbold the recipient name and salutation.

7. Save the file as a Word document, and name it `2p3-sanfran`.

8. Prepare an envelope and append it to the file. Do not include a return address. *The recipient's name appears in a larger bold font, which is part of the theme of this template.*

9. Print the letter and the envelope.

Cues for Reference

Use Templates
1. Click the **Office Button**, then click the **New button**.
2. Click **Installed Templates** or a Microsoft Office Online template category.

3. Click the desired template, then click **Create**.

Save a Document as a Template
1. Click the **Office Button**.
2. Point to **Save As**, then click **Word Template**.

3. In the Save as dialog box, click the **Templates** folder, if necessary.
4. Enter a filename, and click **Save**.

TRYOUT

GOAL
To create a memo and labels for mass mailing, as shown in Figure 2.32
* Use basic mail merge
* Merge labels with a data source

TASK 4

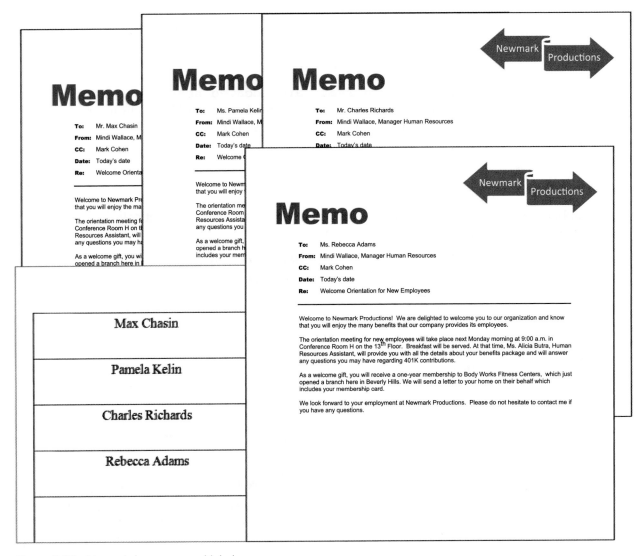

Figure 2.32: Merged documents and labels

WHAT YOU NEED TO KNOW

Use Basic Mail Merge

▶ The Mail Merge feature allows you to mass-produce letters, envelopes, mailing labels, and other documents so they appear personalized. The **merge** process combines two documents: a main document and a data source document.

▶ The **main document** contains information that does not change as well as merge codes where variable information will be inserted. A **merge field code** acts as a placeholder for the variable information. All formatting, graphics, and paper size information should be included in the main document. Figure 2.33 illustrates a portion of a main document with merge field codes inserted.

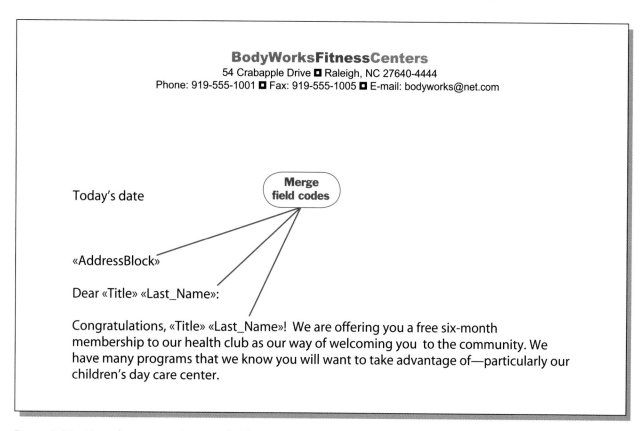

Figure 2.33: Main document with merge fields

▶ When you insert a mail merge field into the main document, the field name is always surrounded by *chevrons* (<< >>). The **AddressBlock** is a combination of several fields that includes Title, First Name, Last Name, Company, Address, City, State and Postal code (ZIP Code).

▶ The **data source** document contains variable information (information that does change) which is inserted into the main document during the merge process. Figure 2.34 illustrates a data source document.

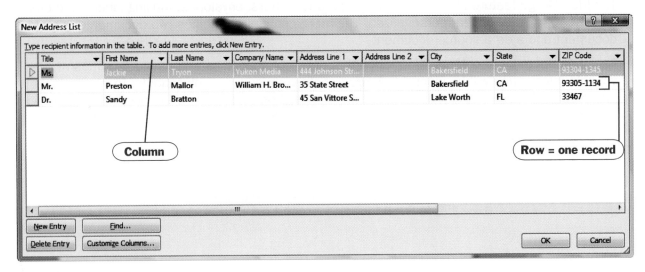

Figure 2.34: Data source document

▶ Think of a data source as a table of columns and rows. Each column in the data source corresponds to a category of information or a data field—for example, first name, last name, title, etc. Each row in the table contains one data **record**, which is a complete set of related information about one person or thing—for example, the name and address of a single person. The data source document many contain many records.

HOW There are four steps to the mail merge process:

Step **1:** Create the main document.

Step **2:** Create or identify a data source document.

Step **3:** Insert merge field placeholders into the main document.

Step **4:** Merge the main document and data source to create new documents.

Word provides you with a Help feature called a wizard to guide you step by step through the mail merge process. To activate the wizard, **1.** click the **Mailings tab**, and in the **Start Mail Merge group**, **2.** click the **Start Mail Merge button**, then **3.** select **Step-by-Step Mail Merge Wizard**, as shown in Figure 2.35. The Mail Merge task pane, as shown in Figure 2.36, takes you step by step through the mail merge process.

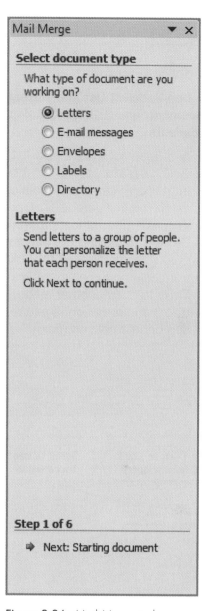

Figure 2.36: Mail Merge task pane

Figure 2.35: Start Mail Merge button and menu

TRY it OUT w2-8

Main Document

1. Open a new blank document.

2. Use the following settings:

Margins	Any desired
Line Spacing	1.0
Paragraph Spacing	
Before	0
After	0
Font	Any desired

3. Click the **Mailings tab**, and in the **Start Mail Merge group**, click the **Start Mail Merge button**, then select **Step-by-Step Mail Merge Wizard**. *The Mail Merge task pane appears. You will complete the steps necessary to complete the merge process from this task pane.*

4. In Step 1 on the Mail Merge task pane, select **Letters** as the document type, and click **Next: Starting document**.

Continued on next page

Data Source Document

5. In Step 2, select **Use the current document**, and click **Next: Select recipients**.

6. In Step 3, select **Type a new list**, and then click **Create**.

   a. In the New Address List dialog box, as shown in Figure 2.37, type the recipient information shown here. Be sure to include the punctuation marks shown. Press **[Tab]** to advance from column to column. Click **New Entry** to start another record. Be sure that the information is entered in the appropriate column (field).

Figure 2.37: New Address List dialog box

```
Ms. Jackie Tryon
Yukon Media
444 Johnson Street
Bakersfield, CA 93304-1345

Mr. Preston Mallor
William H. Brown & Company
35 State Street
Bakersfield, CA 93305-5545

Dr. Sandy Bratton
45 San Vittore Street
Lake Worth, FL 33467
```

   b. Click **OK**.
   c. Enter the file name w2-8, and then click **Save**.
   d. Click **OK** to accept the listed recipients. *If you do not wish to send*

a document to one of the recipients, deselect the check mark next to his/her name.

   e. Click **Next: Write your letter**.

Insert Merge Field Placeholders

7. At approximately 2.5" from the top of the page, enter today's date at the left margin. Then press **[Enter]** four times.

8. In Step 4, insert your merge codes as follows:

   a. Click **Address block**, which will display the Insert Address Block dialog box, as shown in Figure 2.38. Specify address elements by selecting the check boxes you want, which will display in the Preview window.

   b. Click the **Next button** on the top of the preview window to see that your inside addresses display correctly.

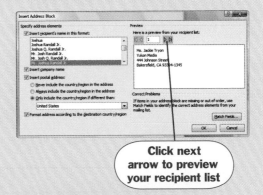

Figure 2.38: Insert Address Block dialog box

   c. Click **OK**, then press **[Enter]** twice.
   d. Click **Greeting line**. In the Insert Greeting Line dialog box, as shown in Figure 2.39, click the **Punctuation list arrow**, and then choose a colon. *In a business letter, the proper punctuation after the salutation (greeting line) is a colon; a comma may be used for less formal correspondence.*

Continued on next page

e. Click **OK**, and then press **[Enter]** twice.

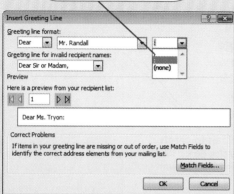

Colon selected from the punctuation list options

Figure 2.39: Insert Greeting Line dialog box

9. Enter the remaining letter text shown below. To insert the merge code for the first name, in the Mail Merge task pane, click **More items**. . . . Select **First Name**, click **Insert**, then click **Close**. Type a comma **[,]**, press **[space bar]**, and then type the remainder of the letter.

As you know, <<First Name>>, we are holding a private sale for our most valued customers, which will take place on

June 10. We look forward to welcoming you then.

Sincerely,

Trent Preston
Sales Manager

tp/yo

Merge to Create New Documents

1. Click **Next: Preview your letters**.

2. In Step 5, click the forward arrow to preview the rest of your letters. If the merge is correct, click **Next: Complete the merge**.

3. In Step 6, click **Print** to print all the letters at once or click **Edit individual letters**. *If you select **Edit individual letters**, the Merge to New Document dialog box appears. Choose **All**, then click **OK**. Each letter appears on a separate page. Scroll down to edit individual letters and/or you can print one or all of the letters and/or you can save the file.*

4. Close the file, and do not save changes.

Merge Labels with a Data Source

▶ You can use the mail merge feature to create labels or envelopes for mailing your new documents. The label (or envelope) is the main document, which will be merged with a data source.

HOW Use the Step-by-Step Mail Merge Wizard to create labels and envelopes in the same way you created your merged letters. **1.** Click the **Mailings tab**, and in the **Start Mail Merge group**, **2.** click the **Start Mail Merge button**, and then **3.** select **Step-by-Step Mail Merge Wizard**. **4.** In the Mail Merge task pane, select **Labels (or Envelopes)** as the document type, as shown in Figure 2.40. **5.** Select the label product or envelope size when you are prompted, then **6.** select your recipients, which will be the same list of recipients that you used for your letter.

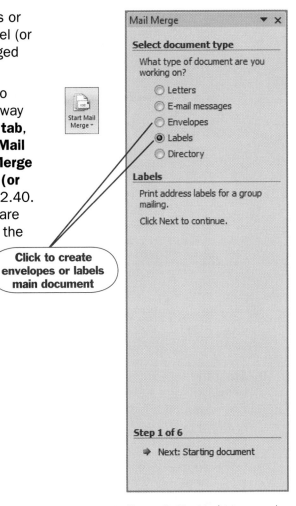

Click to create envelopes or labels main document

Figure 2.40: Mail Merge task pane

TRY *it* OUT *w2-9*

Main Document

1. Open a new blank document.

2. Use the following settings:

Margins	Any desired
Line Spacing	1.0
Paragraph Spacing	
Before	0
After	0
Font	Any desired

3. Click the **Mailings tab**, on the **Start Mail Merge group**, click the **Start Mail Merge button**, and then select **Step-by-Step Mail Merge Wizard**.

4. Select **Labels** as the document type, and then click **Next: Starting document**.

5. Click **Label options**.

6. In the Label Options dialog box, click the **Label vendors list box**, and then click **Avery US Letter**. Scroll down in the product numbers window, choose **5161**, and then click **OK**. If label borders do not display, select the entire page, and click the **Home tab**. In the **Paragraph Group**, click the **Borders button list arrow**, and choose **All Borders**.

Continued on next page

Data Source Document

1. Click **Next: Select recipients**.

2. Click **Use an existing list**.

3. Click **Browse**, select **w2-8** as the file, and then click **Open**.

4. Click **OK**.

Insert Merge Field Placeholders

1. Click **Next: Arrange your labels**.

2. Position the insertion point in the first label.

3. Click **Address block**, select the format for the name, and then click **OK**.

4. Click **Update all labels**.

Merge to Create New Documents (Labels)

1. Click **Next: Preview your labels**.

2. Click **Next: Complete the merge**. *You need not print these labels for this activity. However, if you wish to do so, click **Print**.*

3. Close the file, and do not save changes.

GOAL
To merge a memo and label main documents with a data source document, as shown in Figure 2.41

WHAT YOU NEED TO KNOW

▶ Once you create and save a data source document, it can be used for merging with other main documents.

▶ In this Rehearsal activity, you will create two main documents—a memo and labels. In each main document, you will insert the appropriate merge field codes. You will merge each with the same data source document you create from scratch.

▶ You will use a memo template provided to you in the data files to prepare a **memorandum**, or memo, which is a written communication within a company. "Re" in the memo heading means "in reference to" or "subject." The initials "CC" in the memo heading refer to "courtesy copy" or "copies."

▶ *The memo template used in this activity was downloaded from* www.microsoft.com, *saved as a Word 2007 template, then modified for this activity.*

▶ You will use the same data source to prepare file folder labels.

▼ DIRECTIONS

Memo

1. Open the data file **w2r4-memo**.

2. Replace the From, CC, Date, and Re placeholder text in the memo header, as shown in Figure 2.41. You will replace the To placeholder with a merge code during the merge process.

3. Start the Mail Merge Wizard. When prompted in Step 2, select **Use the current document**.

4. When prompted in Step 3, select **Type a new list**, and create the data source document, as shown in Figure 2.42. Save the file as `2r4-new employees`.

5. When prompted in Step 4, position your insertion point in the [To] placeholder, then click **More items**. . . . Insert the Title, First Name, and Last Name field codes. Be sure to insert a space between the codes.

6. Preview your memos and complete the merge.

7. Print one copy (optional).

8. Save the file as a Word document, and name it `2r4-merged memos`.

Labels

1. Create a new blank document.

2. Start the **Mail Merge Wizard**. When prompted in Step 1, select **Labels** as the document type.

3. When prompted in Step 2, select **Avery US Letter**, product number **5205** as the labels options. *If necessary, apply border lines to the labels*.

4. When prompted in Step 3, select `2r4-new employees` as your data source document.

Continued on next page

5. Position your insertion point in the first label. When prompted in Step 4, click **More items**. . . . Insert the **First Name** and **Last Name** field codes, and click **Update all labels**.

6. Preview your labels, and then complete the merge.

7. Center the names on the labels, and change the font size to **14 point**.

8. Print one copy (use regular paper).

9. Save the labels, and name the file `2r4-merged labels`.

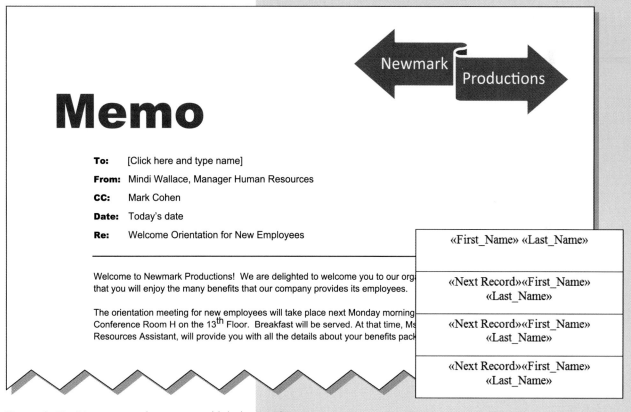

Figure 2.41: Memo main document and label main document

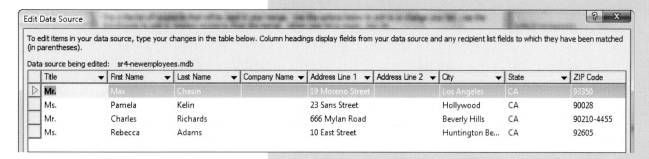

Figure 2.42: Data source of new employees

Basic Mail Merge

1. Click **Mailings**, and in the **Start Mail Merge group**, click the **Start Mail Merge button**.
2. Select **Step-by-Step Mail Merge Wizard**.
3. Follow the prompts on the Mail Merge task pane to complete the merge.
   a. In Step 1, select the document type, and click **Next: Starting document**.

b. In Step 2, Select the starting document type, and click **Next: Select recipients**.
c. In Step 3, select **Use an existing list**, and click **Browse** to locate it, or select **Type a new list** and click **Create**.
d. Enter the names and addresses for the recipients.
e. Click **New Entry** to start a new record, and then click **OK** when finished.

f. Enter a filename and click **Save**.
g. Click **Next: Write your letter**.
h. In Step 4, insert merge codes into your document, and click **Next: Preview your letters**.
i. In Step 5, click the **forward button** to preview each document, and click **Next: Complete the merge**.
j. In Step 6, click **Print** or **Edit individual letters**.

PERFORMANCE

TASK 4

You work for Ms. Mindi Wallace, human resources manager at Newmark Productions. She has asked you to merge a letter she has prepared with a previously developed data source document of new employees. You will also prepare mailing labels for the letters.

Follow these guidelines:

1. Open the data file **w2p4-gym membership**. This will be your main document.

2. Start the Mail Merge Wizard:
   a. Use the **2r4-new employees** file that you created earlier as your data source document.
   b. Insert the field code placeholders into the letter, as shown in Figure 2.43 on the next page.
   c. Print one letter for each person in the data source document.
   d. Save the merged file as **2p4-gym membership final**.

3. Use the Mail Merge Wizard to create labels. Select **Avery US Letter**, product number **5161**, as the label options. Preview your labels and then complete the merge.
   a. Print one copy (use regular paper).
   b. Save the merged label file as **2p4-gym membership labels**.

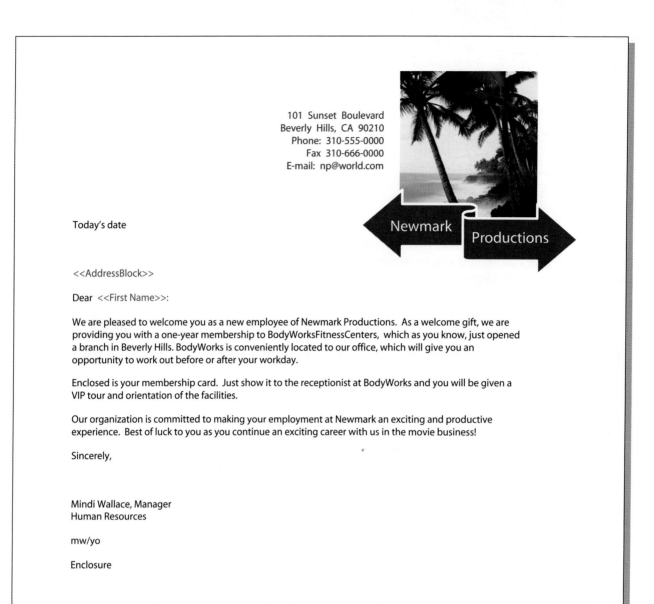

101 Sunset Boulevard
Beverly Hills, CA 90210
Phone: 310-555-0000
Fax 310-666-0000
E-mail: np@world.com

Today's date

<<AddressBlock>>

Dear <<First Name>>:

We are pleased to welcome you as a new employee of Newmark Productions. As a welcome gift, we are providing you with a one-year membership to BodyWorksFitnessCenters, which as you know, just opened a branch in Beverly Hills. BodyWorks is conveniently located to our office, which will give you an opportunity to work out before or after your workday.

Enclosed is your membership card. Just show it to the receptionist at BodyWorks and you will be given a VIP tour and orientation of the facilities.

Our organization is committed to making your employment at Newmark an exciting and productive experience. Best of luck to you as you continue an exciting career with us in the movie business!

Sincerely,

Mindi Wallace, Manager
Human Resources

mw/yo

Enclosure

Figure 2.43: Letter main document

ENCORE

Act I

Ms. Mindi Wallace, human resources manager at Newmark Productions, has given you another assignment—to prepare a memo to members of your department who are working on Welcome Kits for new employees. In the memo, she wants you to remind them to include the summary of the most important employer responsibilities from the Occupational Safety and Health Act of 1970 in all printed material. You will search the Internet and copy and paste some of this information into your memo. You can find the information at: www.osha.gov/as/opa/worker/employer-responsibility.html. *While the OSHA legislation was passed in 1970, this important law still applies in the workplace today.*

Follow these guidelines:

1. Open the data file **w2e4-memo form**.

2. Send the memo to Human Resources Department Members.
   a. The memo is from Mindi Wallace, Human Resources Manager.
   b. Send a copy to Alice Butra.
   c. Use today's date.
   d. Include an appropriate subject (Re:).

3. Use the following settings for the body of the memo:

Margins	.5" left and right
Line Spacing	1.0
Paragraph Spacing	
Before	0
After	4
Font	As per template

4. The body of the memo should read as follows:

   Please be sure that all Welcome Kits indicate that employers have certain responsibilities under the Occupational Safety and Health Act of 1970. Employees must be aware of these. The information below summarizes the most important employer responsibilities.

   The Welcome Kits should inform employees that they can find more information about workers rights and responsibilities by visiting OSHA's Web site at www.osha.gov.

Continued on next page

5. Go online to the Osha Website. Copy the bulleted information listed below "Employer Responsibilities," and paste it two lines below the last paragraph of the memo text. Set the bulleted text to 10 point and format it so that the font matches the other paragraph text. *If you do not have an Internet connection, you can copy this information from the data file,* **w2e4-osha**.

6. Save the file as a Word document (not as a template), and name it `2e4-osha`.

7. Print one copy.

Act II

You work in the marketing department of Transport Travel Services. Your company has organized a special travel package for people interested in attending the 2010 World Figure Skating Championships in Minneapolis. You have been asked to send letters to members of the local figure skating association telling them about this special travel package and the informational brochure that you will be enclosing. Transport Travel Services has decided on a new letterhead design for the company, which will now be used by all of their offices.

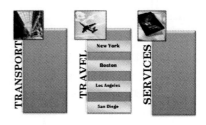

Follow these guidelines:

1. Open the data file **w2e4-figure skating**. Save the file as **2e4-figure skating final**. This file contains the company letterhead and the text of the letter.

2. Use any margin settings you want.

3. Start the Mail Merge Wizard. Using the **w2e4-figure skating** file as your main document, finalize the letter to include today's date appropriate merge codes, a letter closing, and an enclosure notation. The letter is from Roslyn Young, President.

4. Create a data source document with the following skating association members; name the file `2e4-skating assn. members` and use it for the merge.

```
Ms. Joan Marker      Ms. Beverly Adams      Mr. Bruce Spitz      Mr. Fritz Spiegel
123 East End Road    345 Tyler Way          321 Barker Road      45 Broadway
Harvard, MA 01451    Swampscott, MA 01432   Nashua, NH 89348     Manchester, NH 89847
```

5. Print one letter for each person in the data source document. Make any formatting modifications necessary to finalize the document.

6. Save the merged letters.

7. Use the Mail Merge Wizard and the data source document to create mailing labels. Select **Avery US Letter**, product number **5161**, as the label options. Preview your labels, and complete the merge.

8. Print one copy (use regular paper).

9. Save the merged label file as `2e4-skating labels`.

LESSON 3

Lists, Meeting Documents, Schedules, and Forms

In this lesson, you will learn to use the list and table features found in Word to create bulleted and numbered lists, meeting documents, schedules, and forms. Meeting documents include those that are used to prepare for a meeting, such as an agenda, a program, and minutes. Schedules include documents that list dates, times, and events. Forms are documents that contain fill-in blanks in which you enter information. You will complete the following projects:

✴ Agenda and planning list
✴ Minutes of a meeting
✴ Schedule
✴ Itinerary
✴ Expense report form
✴ Letter with an inserted table

Upon completion of this lesson, you will have mastered the following skill sets

✴ Create lists
✴ Modify lists
✴ Sort lists
✴ Create tables
✴ Modify tables
✴ Format tables
✴ Apply table borders and shading

✴ Apply table styles
✴ Use Quick Tables
✴ Create tabular columns
✴ Set tabs within table cells
✴ Convert text to and from a table
✴ Sort table data
✴ Perform calculations in a table

Terms
Software-related
Cells
Columns
Custom tabs
Leader
Quick Tables
Rows
Table
Tabs
Document-related
Agenda
Expense report form
Itinerary
Minutes

TRYOUT

TASK 1

GOAL
To create an agenda and planning list, as shown in Figure 3.1

✦ Create bulleted, numbered, and multilevel lists
✦ Modify lists
✦ Sort lists

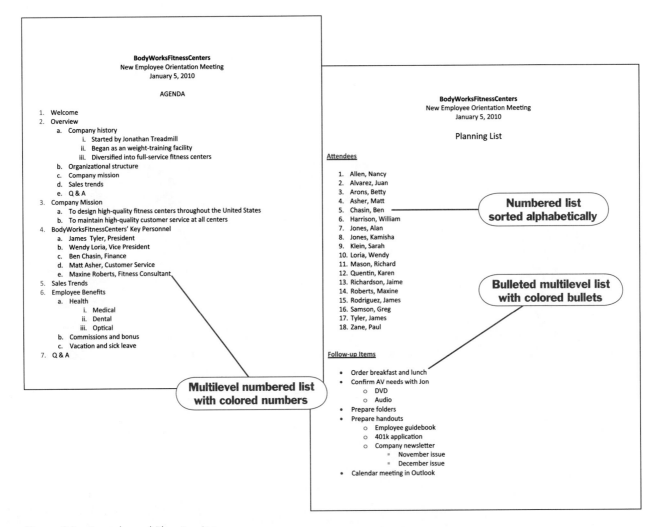

BodyWorksFitnessCenters
New Employee Orientation Meeting
January 5, 2010

AGENDA

1. Welcome
2. Overview
   a. Company history
      i. Started by Jonathan Treadmill
      ii. Began as an weight-training facility
      iii. Diversified into full-service fitness centers
   b. Organizational structure
   c. Company mission
   d. Sales trends
   e. Q & A
3. Company Mission
   a. To design high-quality fitness centers throughout the United States
   b. To maintain high-quality customer service at all centers
4. BodyWorksFitnessCenters' Key Personnel
   a. James Tyler, President
   b. Wendy Loria, Vice President
   c. Ben Chasin, Finance
   d. Matt Asher, Customer Service
   e. Maxine Roberts, Fitness Consultant
5. Sales Trends
6. Employee Benefits
   a. Health
      i. Medical
      ii. Dental
      iii. Optical
   b. Commissions and bonus
   c. Vacation and sick leave
7. Q & A

Multilevel numbered list with colored numbers

BodyWorksFitnessCenters
New Employee Orientation Meeting
January 5, 2010

Planning List

Attendees

1. Allen, Nancy
2. Alvarez, Juan
3. Arons, Betty
4. Asher, Matt
5. Chasin, Ben
6. Harrison, William
7. Jones, Alan
8. Jones, Kamisha
9. Klein, Sarah
10. Loria, Wendy
11. Mason, Richard
12. Quentin, Karen
13. Richardson, Jaime
14. Roberts, Maxine
15. Rodriguez, James
16. Samson, Greg
17. Tyler, James
18. Zane, Paul

Numbered list sorted alphabetically

Bulleted multilevel list with colored bullets

Follow-up Items

- Order breakfast and lunch
- Confirm AV needs with Jon
  - DVD
  - Audio
- Prepare folders
- Prepare handouts
  - Employee guidebook
  - 401k application
  - Company newsletter
    - November issue
    - December issue
- Calendar meeting in Outlook

Figure 3.1: Agenda and Planning List

WHAT YOU NEED TO KNOW

Create Lists

▶ Lists allow you to summarize information in an organized way and have many different uses. You can create a numbered list to sequence information, a bulleted list to emphasize points of information that do not need a sequence, or a multilevel list to organize information in a hierarchical structure. Multilevel lists can be bulleted, numbered, or an outline.

▶ Figure 3.2 illustrates the different types of lists you can create in Word.

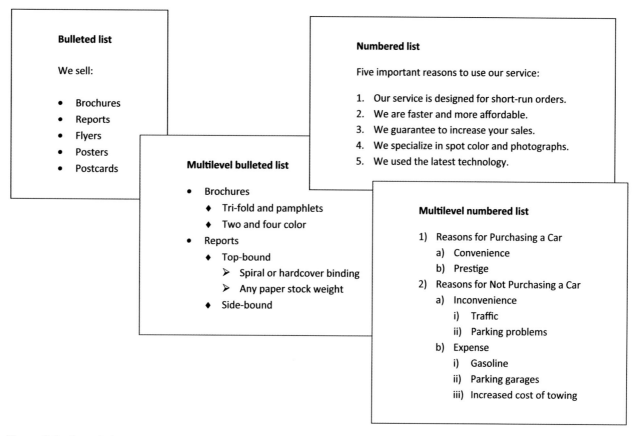

Figure 3.2: Sample lists

Bulleted Lists

HOW **1.** To create a bulleted list, enter an asterisk (*) at the beginning of a paragraph, then **2.** press **[Spacebar]** or **[Tab]**. You can also **1.** click the **Home tab**, and in the **Paragraph group**, **2.** click the **Bullets button**.

Numbered Lists

HOW **1.** Enter the number 1 followed by a period (**1.**) at the beginning of a paragraph, then **2.** Press **[Spacebar]** or **[Tab]**. Or, you can click the **Home tab**, and in the **Paragraph group**, click the **Numbering button**.

▶ For both bullets and numbers, each time you press **[Enter]**, a new bullet or number appears automatically; numbers increase sequentially.

▶ To end a list, press **[Enter]** twice, or press **[Enter]** then **[Backspace]**, or click the **Bullets button** or **Numbering button** on the Ribbon to deactivate the feature.

Multilevel Lists

HOW **1.** Click the **Home tab**, and in the **Paragraph group**, **2.** click the **Multilevel List button**, and **3.** choose a multilevel list style from the library shown in Figure 3.3. **4.** Enter the first line of text, **5.** press **[Enter]** once to stay on the same level or press **[Enter]** and then **[Tab]** to indent text to the next level. To move back a level, press **[Enter]**, then click the **Decrease Indent button** in the **Paragraph group**. You can also press **[Enter]** more than once to move back levels.

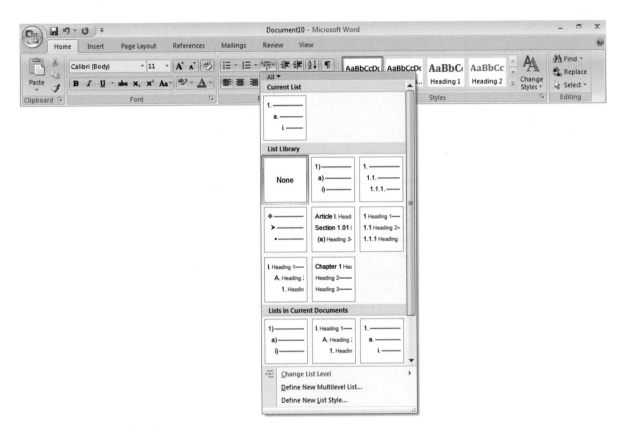

Figure 3.3: Multilevel List library

T R Y *it* **O U T** *w3-1*

1. Open a new blank document.

2. Type an asterisk (*), then press **[Spacebar]** to start the bulleted list. Type the word **Red**.

3. Press **[Enter]**, and type **Blue**.

4. Press **[Enter]**, type **Green**.

5. Press **[Enter]** twice to end the bulleted list.

6. Type the number 1 followed by a period (**1.**), then press **[Spacebar]**. Type **First day**.

7. Press **[Enter]**, and type **Second day**.

8. Press **[Enter]**, and type **Third day**.

9. Press **[Enter]** twice to end the numbered list.

Continued on next page

10. Close the file, and do not save the changes.

11. Open a new blank document.

12. Create the multilevel numbered list shown in Figure 3.2 by following these steps:

   a. Click the **Home tab**, and in the **Paragraph group**, click the **Multilevel List button**. Then, select the thumbnail that shows the number 1 followed by a parenthesis: **1)**.

   b. Type **Reasons for Purchasing a Car**. Press **[Enter]** and then **[Tab]**. Notice that the new item is indented to the next level and is automatically assigned the next number style.

   c. Type **Convenience**, then press **[Enter]**.

   d. Type **Prestige**, then press **[Enter]**.

   e. Press **[Shift]+[Tab]** to return to the previous level.

   f. Type **Reasons for Not Purchasing a Car**. Press **[Enter]**, then press **[Tab]**.

   g. Type **Inconvenience**. Press **[Enter]**, then **press [Tab]**.

   h. Type **Traffic**, then press **[Enter]**.

   i. Type **Parking problems**, then press **[Enter]**.

   j. Click the **Decrease Indent button**. Type **Expense**, press **[Enter]**, and then press **[Tab]**.

   k. Type **Gasoline**, then press **[Enter]**.

   l. Type **Parking garages**, then press **[Enter]**.

   m. Type **Increased cost of towing**, then press **[Enter]** as many times as necessary to end the multilevel list.

13. Close the file, and do not save the changes.

Modify Lists

▶ After creating a list, you can modify it by moving, inserting, or deleting text. When you insert and/or delete text from a numbered list, Word automatically adjusts the numbers.

▶ You can change the default round bullet or number style to one of the styles that Word provides in the bullets and numbering libraries. A bulleted list can be changed to a numbered list and vice versa. In addition, you can format bullets or numbers separately from text in the list so that you could, for example, create green bullets and black text.

▶ It is easy to change an ordinary list of text to a bulleted or numbered one. Bullet and numbering styles can be changed before or after creating a list. The style you choose will remain in effect for subsequent documents until you make another change.

HOW To change the bullet symbol, **1.** click the **Home tab**, and in the **Paragraph group**, **2.** click the **Bullets button list arrow**, then **3.** click to choose a bullet style from the Bullet Library shown in Figure 3.4. *You can see a live preview of the bullet style before making your selection by placing your insertion point over each bullet style.* **4.** Type your text, then **5.** press **[Enter]** to start each new bullet.

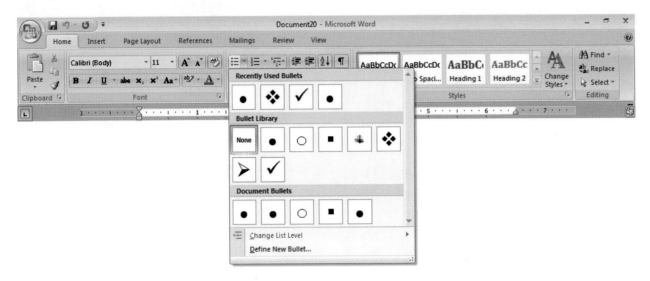

Figure 3.4: Bullet Library

To change the numbering style, **1.** click the **Home tab**, and in the **Paragraph group**, **2.** click the **Numbering button list arrow**, then **3.** click to choose a style from the Numbering Library shown in Figure 3.5.

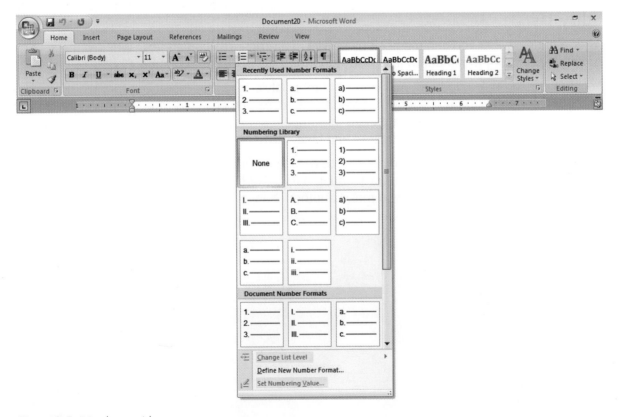

Figure 3.5: Numbering Library

To format bullets or numbers differently from text, **1.** select the bullets or numbers (not the text), then **2.** format them the way you would any other text.

TRY *it* OUT *w3-2*

1. Open the data file **w3-2**.

2. Make the following edits to the text in the section titled "Steps to Maintaining a Healthy Weight."
   a. Add an item to the list.
      - Position your insertion point after the period in Step 4, press **[Enter]**, and type **Choose a variety of grains daily**. *Notice that Word automatically renumbered the list.*
   b. Delete Step 8 (Exercise every day). *Notice that Word automatically renumbered the list.*
   c. Change the color of the numbers to red.
      - Position your insertion point on the number 1, left-click to select the numbers (not the text), then change the number color.

3. Make the following edits to the text below the section titled "Vegetable Choices."
   a. Apply bullets to the list.
      - Select the nine items in the list. On the **Home tab**, and in the **Paragraph group**, click the **Bullets button**.

   b. Add items to the list.
      - Position your insertion point after the word "Okra." Press **[Enter]**, and type **Cucumber**. Repeat the process to enter **Eggplant** and **Lettuce**. *You should now have three additional bulleted items.*
   c. Change the bullet style for the list.
      - Select the list, click the **Bullets button list arrow**, then click to select the check mark (✓) from the Bullets Library.

4. Make the following edits to the text below the section titled "Making Vegetable Soup."
   a. Select the 11 items listed below "Ingredients," apply any bullet style, and change the color of the bullets to green.
   b. In the list below "Preparation," select the sentence in Item 3, and move it so that it becomes Item 2.

5. Close the file, and do not save the changes.

Sort Lists

▶ The Sort feature allows you to rearrange a bulleted list or text in a numbered list in alphabetic (ascending) or reverse alphabetic (descending) order.

HOW **1.** Select the text to be sorted. Then **2.** click the **Home tab**, and in the **Paragraph group**, **3.** click the **Sort button**. In the **Sort Text dialog box** that appears, as shown in Figure 3.6, **4.** click to select the **Ascending** or **Descending** option, then **5.** click **OK**. *By default, Paragraphs should be selected as the Sort by option and Text should be selected as the Type option.*

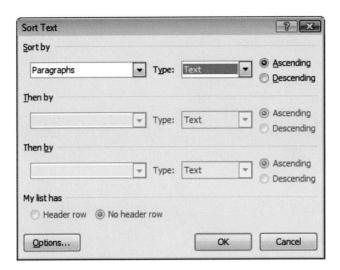

Figure 3.6: Sort Text dialog box

TRY *it* OUT *w3-3*

1. Open the data file **w3-3**.
   a. Select the list below "Steps to Maintaining a Healthy Weight."
   b. On the **Home tab** in the **Paragraph group**, click the **Sort button** with the **Ascending** option selected. Then click **OK**.

2. Select the eight items listed below "Vegetable Choices," and sort the list in alphabetic (ascending) order.

3. Close the file, and do not save the changes.

REHEARSAL

TASK 1

WHAT YOU NEED TO KNOW

▶ An **agenda** is a plan or a list of things to be done, events to occur, or matters to bring before a committee, council, or board.

▶ The format of an agenda can vary. It is often created as a multilevel outline list. Regardless of the format used, an agenda always includes the date and time and sometimes the location of the planned activities.

▶ A planning list contains items that relate to the planning of a meeting or event.

▼ DIRECTIONS

1. Open a new blank document.

2. Use the following settings:

Margins	Default
Line Spacing	1.0
Paragraph Spacing	
Before	0
After	0
Font	Default

3. Use a multilevel list with a traditional outline format to create the agenda shown in Figure 3.7.

4. Select the Numbers (not the letters or the Roman numerals), and change the font color to red.

5. Move the Company Mission heading and its subtext after the subtext below "Overview."

6. Print one copy.

7. Save the file, and name it **3r1-agenda**.

8. Close the file.

9. Open the data file **w3r1-planning list**.

10. Number the list of attendees, then sort the list in alphabetical order.

11. Set the headings "Attendees" and "Follow-up Items" to a red font, then bold and underline them.

12. Enter the text below "Follow-up Items" in Figure 3.8 shown on page 140. Use multilevel bullets, and color the bullets as shown.

13. Print one copy.

14. Save the file, and name it **3r1-completed list**.

15. Close the file.

BodyWorksFitnessCenters
New Employee Orientation Meeting
January 5, 2010

AGENDA

1. Welcome
2. Overview
   a. Company history
      i. Started by Jonathan Treadmill
      ii. Began as an weight-training facility
      iii. Diversified into full-service fitness centers
   b. Organizational structure
   c. Company mission
   d. Sales trends
   e. Q & A
3. BodyworksFitnessCenters' Key Personnel
   a. James Tyler, President
   b. Wendy Loria, Vice President
   c. Ben Chasin, Finance
   d. Matt Asher, Customer Service
   e. Maxine Roberts, Fitness Consultant
4. Company Mission
   a. To design high-quality fitness centers throughout the United States
   b. To maintain high-quality customer service at all centers
5. Sales Trends
6. Employee benefits
   a. Health
      i. Medical, dental, optical
      ii. Major medical
   b. Commissions and bonus
   c. Vacation and sick leave
7. Q & A

Figure 3.7: Agenda

BodyWorksFitnessCenters
New Employee Orientation Meeting
January 5, 2010

Planning List

Attendees

1. Allen, Nancy
2. Alvarez, Juan
3. Arons, Betty
4. Asher, Matt
5. Chasin, Ben
6. Harrison, William
7. Jones, Alan
8. Jones, Kamisha
9. Klein, Sarah
10. Loria, Wendy
11. Mason, Richard
12. Quentin, Karen
13. Richardson, Jaime
14. Roberts, Maxine
15. Rodriguez, James
16. Samson, Greg
17. Tyler, James
18. Zane, Paul

Follow-up Items

- Order breakfast and lunch
- Confirm AV needs with Jon
  - DVD
  - Audio
- Prepare folders
- Prepare handouts
  - Employee guidebook
  - 401k application
  - Company newsletter
    - November issue
    - December issue
- Calendar meeting in Outlook

Figure 3.8: Planning List

PERFORMANCE

TASK 1

Expedition

Travel Gear

Ms. Jane McBride of Expedition Travel Gear plans to meet with the staff of her marketing department to discuss a new market strategy proposal. Their plan is to increase product sales by partnering with travel agencies. Jane has asked you to create an agenda for the meeting, which will take place on June 15, 2010.

Follow these guidelines:

1. Use any line and paragraph spacing you want, but be sure the document fits on one page.

2. Create an appropriate heading for the agenda.

3. Use a multilevel bulleted list with the following topics and subtopics:

   Welcome

   History of Expedition Travel Gear

          Success speaks for itself

          Catalog and internet sales

          Retail stores

                 West coast

                 East coast

   New market strategy proposal

          Linkage to travel agencies

          Benefits of the partnership

   Strategies for making it happen

   The partnership

          What we'll offer

          Product discounts

          Travel specials insert

          Client referrals

   Questions and answers

4. Change the bullets to a multilevel numbered list using any style that uses numbers (not Roman numerals).

Continued on next page

5. Set the color of the numbers (not the letters or the Roman numerals) to any color you want.

6. Print one copy.

7. Save the file, and name it **3p1-etg agenda**.

8. Close the file.

Cues for Reference

Create Bullets, Numbering, and Multilevel lists

1. Click the **Home tab**, and in the **Paragraph group**, click the **Bullets button** or **Numbering button** or **Multilevel List button**.

2. Choose a bullets, numbering, or multilevel list style from the library.

3. Press **[Enter]** to create a new bullet or number; press **[Tab]** to indent text to the next level; click the **Decrease indent button**, or press **[Enter]** more than once to move back levels.

4. Press **[Enter]** as many times as necessary to end the list.

Sort Lists

1. Select the list to sort.

2. Click the **Home tab** and in the **Paragraph group**, click the **Sort button**.

3. Click the **Ascending** or **Descending** option.

4. Click **OK**.

TRYOUT

GOAL
To create minutes of a meeting shown in Figure 3.9

* Create a table
* Modify a table
    * Change column width
    * Change row height
    * Insert and delete columns and rows
    * Position a table on a page
    * Merge and split table cells

TASK 2

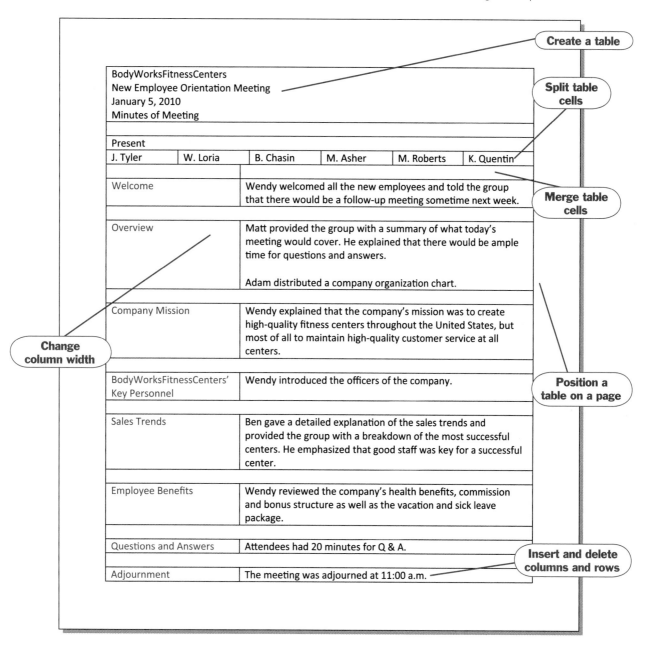

Create a table

Split table cells

Merge table cells

Change column width

Position a table on a page

Insert and delete columns and rows

BodyWorksFitnessCenters
New Employee Orientation Meeting
January 5, 2010
Minutes of Meeting

Present					
J. Tyler	W. Loria	B. Chasin	M. Asher	M. Roberts	K. Quentin

Welcome	Wendy welcomed all the new employees and told the group that there would be a follow-up meeting sometime next week.
Overview	Matt provided the group with a summary of what today's meeting would cover. He explained that there would be ample time for questions and answers. Adam distributed a company organization chart.
Company Mission	Wendy explained that the company's mission was to create high-quality fitness centers throughout the United States, but most of all to maintain high-quality customer service at all centers.
BodyWorksFitnessCenters' Key Personnel	Wendy introduced the officers of the company.
Sales Trends	Ben gave a detailed explanation of the sales trends and provided the group with a breakdown of the most successful centers. He emphasized that good staff was key for a successful center.
Employee Benefits	Wendy reviewed the company's health benefits, commission and bonus structure as well as the vacation and sick leave package.
Questions and Answers	Attendees had 20 minutes for Q & A.
Adjournment	The meeting was adjourned at 11:00 a.m.

Figure 3.9: Minutes of a meeting

WHAT YOU NEED TO KNOW

Create Tables

▶ The **Table** feature lets you organize information into columns and rows. **Rows** run horizontally; **columns** run vertically. The rows and columns intersect to form a grid, made up of **cells**. Table cells display with gridlines. *Gridlines* are light gray lines that define the structure of a table.

▶ All the cells are created of equal size, and columns adjust themselves to fit between the left and right margins. You can, however, modify the table structure at any time.

▶ Once you create a table, the Ribbon displays the Table Tools Design and Layout contextual tabs, giving you access to table-related features as shown in Figure 3.10. You will learn to use these tabs later in this lesson.

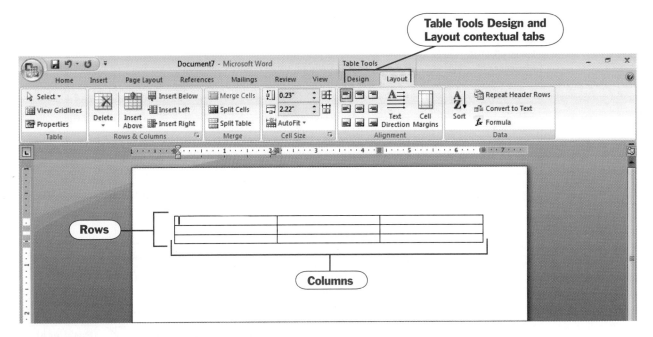

Figure 3.10: Table Tools, Layout Tab

▶ The insertion point moves within a table in the same way it moves within a document. You can use the mouse to click in the appropriate cell, or use **[Tab]** to move to the next cell. Pressing **[Tab]** when the insertion point is in the last cell in the last row adds a new row to the bottom of the table. The new row will take on the same formatting as the previous one.

▶ As you enter text in a table cell, the cell expands downward to accommodate the text. Pressing **[Enter]** in a cell also expands the cell downward; it does not move the insertion point to the next cell.

HOW **1.** Click the **Insert tab**, and in the **Tables group**, **2.** click the **Table button**. **3.** Point to the upper-left box, and move the pointer across the number of columns and down the number of rows you want in your table, as shown in Figure 3.11. *Notice that Word highlights the cells and at the same time creates a table in the document to show you what your selection will look like.* **4.** Click the lower-right cell in your selection to enter the table into your document.

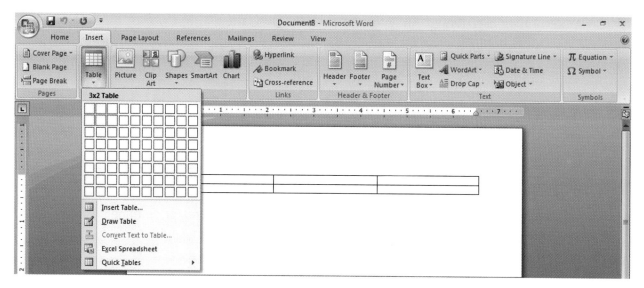

Figure 3.11: Insert table

You can also **1.** click the **Table button**, then **2.** choose **Insert Table** from the menu to display the Insert Table dialog box shown in Figure 3.12. **3.** Enter the number of columns and rows in the appropriate text boxes, and **4.** click **OK**.

Figure 3.12: Insert Table dialog box

1. Open a new blank document.

2. Click the **Insert tab**, and in the **Table group**, click the **Table button**.

3. Point to the upper-left cell, move the pointer across four columns and down two rows, then click the lower-right cell in the selection to enter the table in the

document. _Notice that the insertion point appears in the first cell of the first column._

4. Enter the text shown below into your table. Press **[Tab]** to advance from column to column.

5. Close the file, and do not save the changes.

First Term	Second Term	Third Term	Final Grade
Pass with honors	Pass	Pass	A

Modify Tables

▶ You can modify a table by changing its column width, by inserting and/or deleting columns and/or rows, or by changing the position of the table on the page.

Change Column Width

▶ There are several ways to change the width of a column. You can also adjust column width to fit the contents of a cell.

HOW To change column width on the ruler, **1.** click inside a table cell. **2.** Display the ruler, if necessary, which will display column markers. **3.** Position the insertion point on the column marker until you see a two-headed arrow. **4.** Click and drag the marker on the ruler left or right to the position you want, as shown in Figure 3.13.

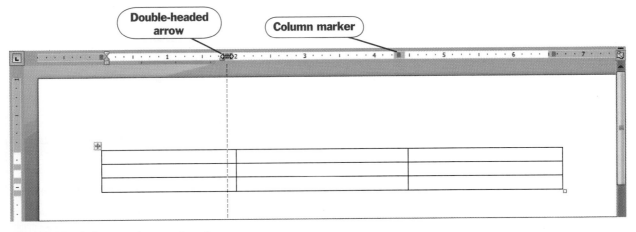

Figure 3.13: Column markers on the ruler

To change column width by a specific measurement, **1.** click in the column or select the columns to affect. This will display the Table Tools Design and Layout tabs. **2.** Click the **Layout tab**, and in the **Cell Size group**, **3.** enter a column width in the **Table Column Width box**, as shown in Figure 3.14, or use the increment arrows in the Table Column Width box to see a live preview of the change on the table cell. *You can also use the Table Properties dialog box and enter a specific measurement on the Column Tab. To open the Table Properties dialog box quickly, double-click a column marker on the ruler.*

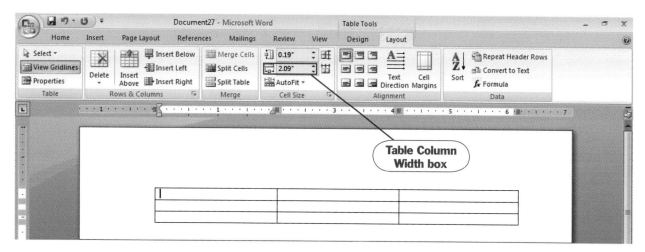

Figure 3.14: Table Column Width box on the Layout tab

To change the column width by dragging vertical lines between columns, **1.** position the mouse pointer on a vertical line bordering a column. When the pointer changes to the table-sizing arrow, **2.** press and hold the mouse button as you drag the line left or right, as shown in Figure 3.15.

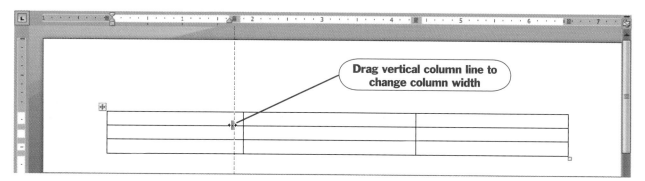

Figure 3.15: Table with vertical column lines

To adjust column width to fit cell contents, **1.** click anywhere in the table. **2.** Click the **Layout tab**, and in the **Cell Size group**, **3.** click the **AutoFit button**, then choose **AutoFit Contents** from the menu, as shown in Figure 3.16.

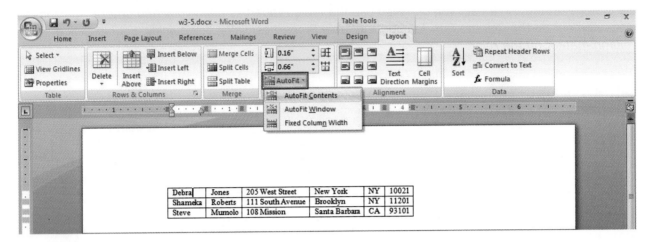

Figure 3.16: AutoFit to cell contents

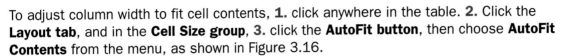

TRY*it* OUT w3-5

1. Open the data file **w3-5**.

2. Position the insertion point on the vertical line between columns 2 and 3 until the pointer becomes a two-headed arrow.

3. Drag the second vertical line left to widen column 3 so that the addresses fit on one line.

4. Position the insertion point anywhere in the second column.

5. Click the **Layout tab**, and in the **Cell Size group**, enter **.75** in the **Table Column Width text box**.

6. Position the insertion point anywhere in the table.

7. Click the **Layout Tab**, and in the **Cell Size group**, click **AutoFit**, **AutoFit Contents**. *Note that the columns adjust to fit the longest entries in a cell.*

8. Close the file, and do not save the changes.

Change Row Height

▶ The height of each row adjusts to the font size of the text. Adjusting the row height can make text more readable or can add special effects. You can change the row height by a specific amount or you can drag the horizontal table lines up or down.

HOW 1. Click in the row or select the rows to affect. This will display the Table Tools Design and Layout tabs. 2. Click the **Layout tab**, and in the **Cell Size group**, 3. enter a row height in the **Table Row Height box**, as shown in Figure 3.17, or use the increment arrows in the Table Row Height box to see a live preview of the change on the table cell. *You can also use the Table Properties dialog box and enter a specific measurement on the Row Tab. To open the Table Properties dialog box, quickly double-click a column marker on the ruler.*

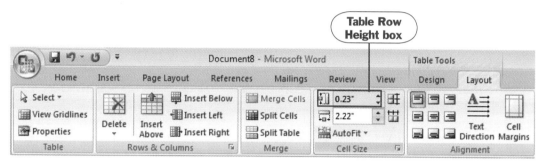

Figure 3.17: Table Row Height box on the Ribbon

T R Y *it* O U T *w3-6*

1. Open the data file **w3-6**.

2. Position the insertion point on the second horizontal line until the pointer becomes a two-headed arrow.

3. Drag the line down to increase the height of the cell so that the text is more readable. Do the same to the third horizontal line.

4. Close the file, and do not save the changes.

5. Reopen the data file **w3-6**.

6. Position your insertion point anywhere in the table.

7. Click the **Layout tab**, and in the **Cell Size group**, enter **.25** in the **Table Row Height box**.

8. Close the file, and do not save the changes.

Insert and Delete Columns and Rows

▶ Word sets columns in a table to spread out evenly between margins, whether the table contains two or ten columns. When you insert columns, all existing columns will become smaller to allow the newly inserted column to fit in. When you delete a column or row, its contents are also deleted.

HOW To insert a column or row, **1.** click in a column or row next to the location where you want to make the insertion. **2.** Click the **Layout tab**, and in the **Rows & Columns group**, click the **Insert Above, Insert Below, Insert Left,** or **Insert Right button,** as shown in Figure 3.18.

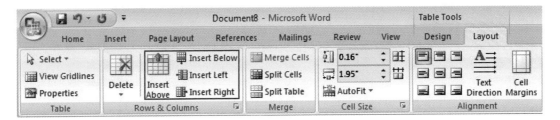

Figure 3.18: Table insert buttons

To delete a column or row, **1.** click in a column or row you want to delete. **2.** Click the **Layout tab**, and in the **Rows and Columns group**, click the **Delete button**, then **3.** choose a deletion option from the menu that appears, as shown in Figure 3.19.

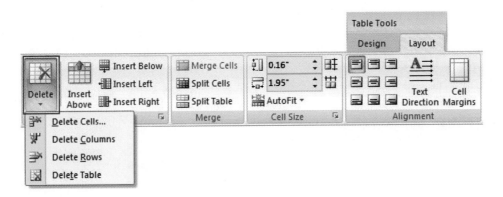

Figure 3.19: Deletion options

Position a Table on a Page

▶ When you change column width or delete a column, Word keeps the same left margin. This means that the table is no longer centered across the page. You can, however, align the table left, right, or center on the page. You can also move a table to any position on the page.

HOW To position a table, **1.** click in a table cell. **2.** Click the **Layout tab**, and in the **Table group**, click the **Properties button**. In the Table Properties dialog box, shown in Figure 3.20, **3.** click the **Table tab**, choose an alignment option, then **4.** click **OK**.

Properties

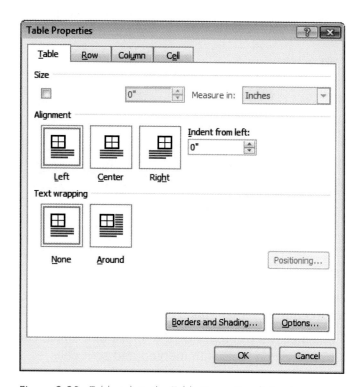

Figure 3.20: Table tab in the Table Properties dialog box

To move a table, **1.** switch to Print Layout view, if necessary. **2.** Position the mouse pointer over the table until the Move handle appears at the top-left corner of the table, as shown in Figure 3.21. **3.** Position your insertion point over the move handle. When a four-headed arrow appears, **4.** click and drag the table to its new location.

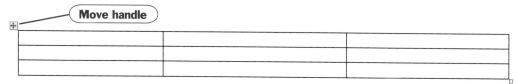

Figure 3.21: Table with Move handle

1. Open the data file **w3-7**.

2. Click anywhere in the last column.

3. On the **Layout tab**, and in the **Rows & Columns group**, click the **Delete button**, and choose **Delete Columns**.

4. Click anywhere in the second row ("Annual Appeal").

5. On the **Layout tab**, and in the **Rows & Columns group**, click the **Insert Above button**.

6. Click in the last cell of the last row ("107.0").

7. Press **[Tab]** to create a new row.

8. Click in the row containing the word "Benefit."

9. On the **Layout tab**, and in the **Rows & Columns group**, click the **Delete button**, and choose **Delete Rows**.

10. Click the **Layout tab**, if necessary, and in the **Tables group**, click the **Properties button**.

11. Click the **Table tab**, if necessary. Click **Center**, then click **OK**. _The table should be horizontally centered between the left and right margins._

12. Position your insertion point over the move handle. When a four-headed arrow displays, click and drag the table to the bottom of the page.

13. Close the file, and do not save the changes.

Merge and Split Table Cells

▶ Removing vertical lines between table cells creates a single larger "merged" cell. Merged cells are useful when you want to enter text that spans more than one column.

▶ You can also split cells, which allows you to divide the space of a single cell into a specified number of cells. Figure 3.22 shows a table with merged and split cells.

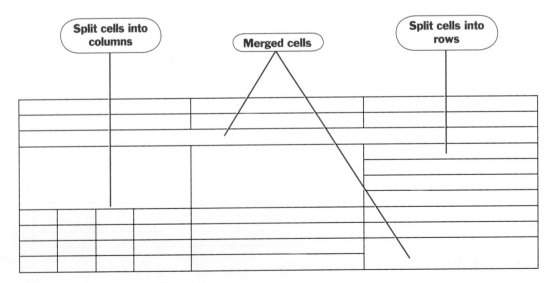

Figure 3.22: Table with merged and split cells

HOW 1. Select the cells to merge or split. 2. Click the **Layout tab**, if necessary, and in the **Merge group**, 3. click the **Merge Cells button** or the **Split Cells button**. 4. After clicking the **Split Cells button**, enter the number of columns and/or the number of rows to split in the **Split Cells dialog box**, and 5. Click **OK**.

You can also select most editing options from the shortcut menu shown in Figure 3.23. 1. Click in a row or column you want to affect, 2. right-click, then 3. choose an option from the shortcut menu that appears.

Figure 3.23: Editing options on the shortcut menu

TRY it OUT w3-8

1. Open the data file **w3-8**.

2. Position your insertion point in the first row, and click the **Layout tab**. Insert a row above.

3. Select the first five cells in the top row.

4. In the **Merge group**, click the **Merge Cells button**.

5. Click in the last column of the last row. Press **[Tab]** to create a new row.

6. In the **Merge group**, click the **Split Cells button**. Enter 3 in the **Number of columns box**, and click **OK**.

7. Close the file, and do not save the changes.

GOAL
To create and finalize the minutes shown in Figure 3.24

WHAT YOU NEED TO KNOW

▶ **Minutes** are a summary of points discussed and decided upon at a meeting. The summary points closely follow the agenda.

▶ The document in this activity uses a two-column table format to create parallel columns. Parallel columns are used to create a list, script, itinerary, minutes of a meeting, a schedule, or any other document in which text in the left column relates to the text in the right column.

 DIRECTIONS

1. Open a new blank document.

2. Use the following settings:

Margins	Default
Line Spacing	1.0
Paragraph Spacing	
Before	0
After	0
Font	Default

3. Create the table shown in Figure 3.24 using **2** columns and **25** rows.

4. Set the column width for column 1 to **1.89"**. Set the column width for column 2 to **4.16"**.

5. Merge the cells in the first row, and enter the text for the heading as shown.

6. Split the cells in the 4th row into **6** columns. Enter the names as shown.

7. Merge the cells in the second and third rows.

8. Enter the text for the remainder of the table as shown in Figure 3.24.

9. Merge the cells between each topic, as shown.

10. Delete any blank rows at the bottom of the table.

11. Position your insertion point in the row you split, and insert two rows below. Enter each of the following names in a cell:

    G. Samson, J. Richardson, J. Rodriguez, J. Alvarez, S. Klein, A. Jones, R. Mason, B. Arons, K. Jones, N. Allen, W. Harrison, P. Zane.

12. Change the font color to red for the topics in the first column.

Continued on next page

13. Center the table horizontally.

14. Print one copy.

15. Save the file, and name it **3r2-minutes**.

16. Close the file.

BodyWorksFitnessCenters New Employee Orientation Meeting January 5, 2010 Minutes of Meeting					
Present					
J. Tyler	W. Loria	B. Chasin	M. Asher	M. Roberts	K. Quentin
Welcome	Wendy welcomed all the new employees and told the group that there would be a follow-up meeting sometime next week.				
Overview	Matt provided the group with a summary of what today's meeting would cover. He explained that there would be ample time for questions and answers. Adam distributed a company organization chart.				
Company Mission	Wendy explained that the company's mission was to create high-quality fitness centers throughout the United States, but most of all to maintain high-quality customer service at all centers.				
BodyWorksFitnessCenters' Key Personnel	Wendy introduced the officers of the company.				
Sales Trends	Ben gave a detailed explanation of the sales trends and provided the group with a breakdown of the most successful centers. He emphasized that good staff was key for a successful center.				
Employee Benefits	Wendy reviewed the company's health benefits, commission and bonus structure as well as the vacation and sick leave package.				
Questions and Answers	Attendees had 20 minutes for Q & A.				
Adjournment	The meeting was adjourned at 11:00 a.m.				

Figure 3.24: Minutes

PERFORMANCE

TASK 2

Several meetings have been scheduled for members of the Newmark Productions sales staff attending the three-day annual sales convention in Las Vegas. You have been asked to create the meeting schedule, which will be included in a conference guide to be distributed to participants.

Follow these guidelines:

1. Enter the appropriate number of columns and rows to create the meeting schedule shown in Figure 3.25.

2. Merge and split columns and rows as shown.

3. Enter the text using the default font. Bold the heading and column headings.

4. Size the columns to fit the contents of the cells.

5. Adjust the row height for the text in the last column to **.3**.

6. Center the table horizontally on the page.

7. Print one copy.

8. Save the file, and name it **3p2-schedule**.

9. Close the file.

Newmark Productions
Meeting Schedule
Annual Sales Convention
January 22-24, 2010

Date	Time	Location	Who Will Be Attending
January 22	9:30 a.m.	Bella Hotel Conference Room H	Janis Huff
			Max Ryan
			Lorraine Jackson
			Rayon Vikos
	12:30 p.m.	Bella Hotel Conference Room J	Phyllis Ashton
			Max Ryan
			Vince Lori
January 23	12:30 p.m.	Palace Hotel Balm Restaurant	Janis Huff
			Lorraine Jackson
			Thomas Bergman
			Pamela Tricia
			Rayon Vikos
January 24	9:30 a.m.	Bella Hotel Conference Room C	Larry Robbins
			Janis Huff
			Vince Lori
	1:00 p.m.	Man Bay Hotel Axis Restaurant	Phyllis Ashton
			Max Ryan
	3:30 p.m.	Bella Hotel Conference Room B	Thomas Bergman
			Phyllis Ashton
			Max Ryan
			Vince Lori
			Rayon Vikos

Figure 3.25: Meeting Schedule

Create a Table

1. Click the **Insert tab**, and in the **Tables group**, click the **Table button**.
2. Point to the upper-left box, and move the pointer across and down to indicate the number of columns and rows you want. Click the lower-right cell in the selection to enter the table into the document.
   Or
2. Click **Insert Table**.
3. Enter the number of columns and rows in the appropriate text boxes.
4. Click **OK**.

Change the Column Width

1. Place the mouse pointer on a vertical line separating the column until it changes to the table-sizing arrow.
2. Drag the arrow left or right to adjust the column width.
   Or
1. Place the insertion point in the table.
2. Drag the column markers on the ruler left or right to the desired column size.

Change the Column Width by a Specific Measurement

1. Position the insertion point in a column or select the columns to change.
2. Click the **Layout tab** and in the **Cell Size group**, enter a column width in the **Table Column Width**

box or use the increment arrows to see a live preview of the change.
   Or
1. Double-click a column marker on the ruler to open the **Table Properties dialog box**.
2. Click the **Column tab**.
3. Click the **Preferred width text box** and enter an amount.
4. Click **Next Column**.
5. Repeat Steps 3 and 4 for remaining columns.

Adjust the Width to Fit the Cell Contents

1. Click in a table cell.
2. Click the **Layout tab**, and in the **Cell Size group**, click the **AutoFit button**.
3. Choose **AutoFit Contents** from the menu.

Position a Table on a Page

1. Click in a table cell.
2. Click the **Layout tab**, and in the **Tables group**, click the **Properties button**.
3. Click the **Table tab**.
4. Choose an alignment option.
5. Click **OK**.

Insert and Delete Columns and Rows

1. Place the insertion point in a row or column next to where you want

to insert a row or column or in the column or row you want to delete.
2. Click the **Layout tab**, and in the **Rows & Columns group**, click the desired Insert button or click the **Delete button**.
   Or
1. Select a column or row.
2. Click **Delete Cells** or **Delete Columns**. (The choices will display differently depending on your selection.)
   Or
2. Click Delete Cells.
3. Choose a delete option.
4. Click **OK**.

Merge and Split Table Cells

1. Select the cells to merge or split.
2. Click the **Layout Tab**, and in the **Merge group**, click the **Merge Cells button**.
   Or
2. Click the **Split Cells button**.
3. Enter the number of columns and/or the number of rows to split.
4. Click **OK**.

T R Y O U T

TASK 3

GOAL
To use formatting features to enhance the appearance of tables created previously, as shown in Figure 3.26

✱ Format tables
✱ Align data within table cells
✱ Apply borders and shading
✱ Apply table styles
✱ Use Quick Tables

WORD

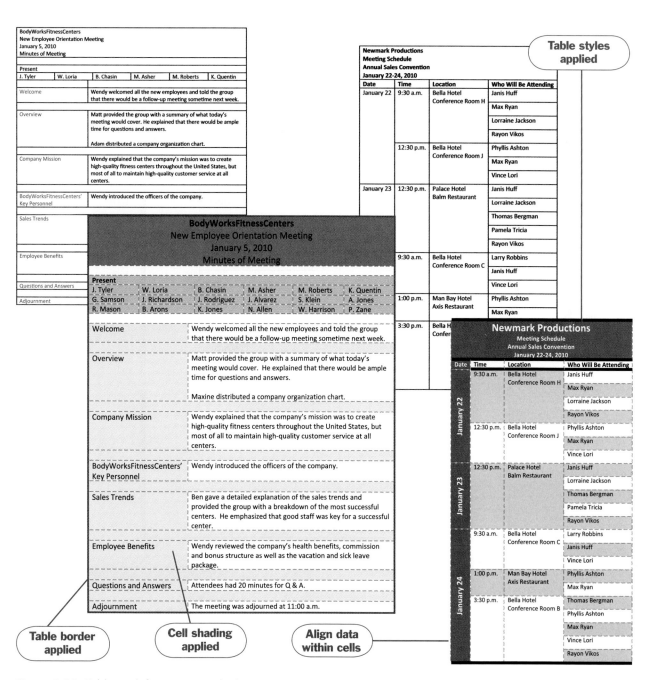

Figure 3.26: Tables with formatting applied

WHAT YOU NEED TO KNOW

Format Tables

▶ After you create a table, Word provides many formatting tools to enhance the appearance of that table. You can align data within cells, apply borders and shading, or use one of Word's predesigned formats to make your table more attractive. Word provides a live preview of what your table will look like before actually applying a format.

Align Data within Table Cells

▶ You can align cell data in various ways during the table creation process or afterward. Figure 3.27 illustrates data alignments within table cells.

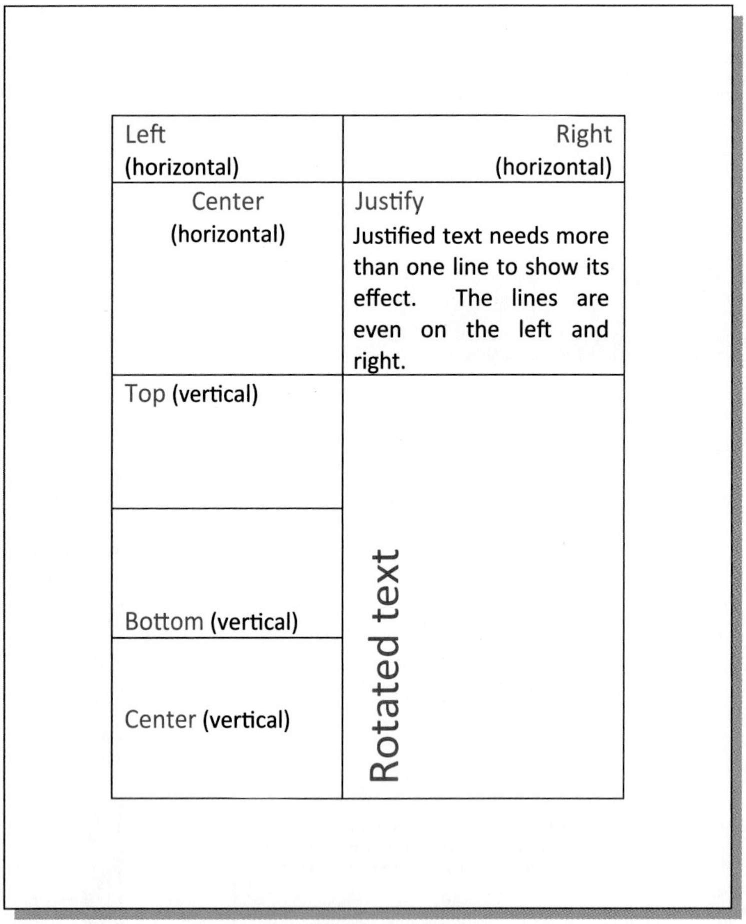

Left (horizontal)	Right (horizontal)
Center (horizontal)	Justify Justified text needs more than one line to show its effect. The lines are even on the left and right.
Top (vertical) Bottom (vertical) Center (vertical)	Rotated text

Figure 3.27: Alignment options in table cells

HOW To align text horizontally, **1.** click in any cell or select several cells or columns in which you wish to align data. **2.** Click the **Home tab**, and in the **Paragraph group**, click the **Center alignment button**.

You can also select an alignment option from the Mini toolbar that is displayed when you select text, as shown in Figure 3.28.

Center alignment button

Figure 3.28: Center alignment button on the Mini toolbar

To align text vertically, **1.** click in any cell, or select the cells to affect. **2.** Click the **Layout tab**, and in the **Alignment group**, **3.** click an alignment button, as shown in Figure 3.29.

You can also **1.** right-click, **2.** choose **Cell Alignment**, and **3.** click a vertical alignment option from the shortcut menu that appears.

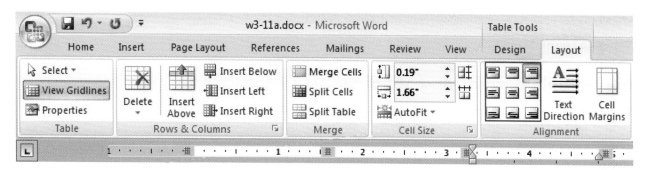

Figure 3.29: Vertical alignment buttons

To change the direction of text, **1.** click in the cell containing the text you want to affect. **2.** Click the **Layout tab**, and in the **Alignment group**, **3.** click the **Text Direction button** until the text is displayed in the direction you want. Each time you click the button, the text will rotate in a different direction.

You can also **1.** right-click, and **2.** choose **Text Direction**. In the Text Direction dialog box that appears, as shown in Figure 3.30, **3.** click the box containing the text orientation you want. The Preview window displays the text in the new direction.

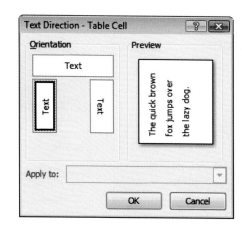

Figure 3.30: Text Direction dialog box

1. Open the data file **w3-9**.

2. Select the first row.

3. Click the **Home tab**, and in the **Paragraph group**, click the **Center button**, then click the **Bold button**.

4. Click in the cell that contains the word "Campaign."

5. Click the **Layout tab**, and in the **Alignment group**, click the **Text Direction button** twice. Click the **Text Direction button** again to return the text to its original position.

6. Select the cells in the first row.

7. Click the **Layout tab**, and in the **Alignment group**, click the **Align Center button**.

8. Select the cells containing numbers.

9. Click the **Home tab**, and in the **Paragraph group**, click the **Align Text Right button**.

10. Close the file, and do not save the changes.

Apply Table Borders and Shading

▶ By default, tables appear with ½-point border lines. Changing line characteristics of cell borders and adding shading to cells are effective ways to emphasize data.

▶ You can modify the line style, color, and width of borders around a table or around individual cells, and you can add shading to cells, as shown in Figure 3.31. You can also remove some or all borders. If you remove borders, you can still view the boundaries of the cells or gridlines. Gridlines do not print.

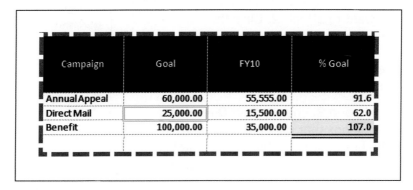

Figure 3.31: Table with borders and shading applied

Table Borders

HOW **1.** Select the table by positioning the mouse over the table, then click the **Move box** at the top-left corner of the table. **2.** Click the **Design tab**, and in the **Table Styles group**, **3.** click the **Borders button list arrow**, then **4.** click **Borders and Shading**. In the Borders and Shading dialog box that appears, as shown in Figure 3.32, **5.** click a line Style, and/or click the line **Color list arrow** and choose a color from the gallery that appears, and/or click the line **Width list arrow** and choose a line width from the options that are displayed. *Your new line style will be added to the Style list for easy access in the future.* **6.** Click one of the following options below Setting to apply modifications:

a. **None** to remove all table and cell borders
b. **Box** to apply modifications to the table border and remove the inside cell borders
c. **All** to apply modifications to the table and cell borders
d. **Grid** to apply style, color, and width modification to the table borders but only color to the cell borders

If you like the result of your selections as shown in the Preview window, **7.** click **OK**.

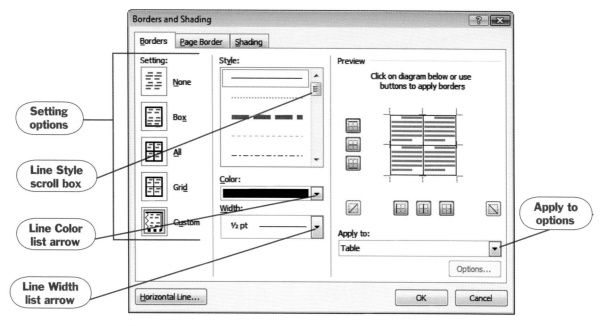

Figure 3.32: Borders and Shading dialog box

Cell Borders

HOW **1.** Select the cells to affect. **2.** Click the **Design tab**, and in the **Table Styles group**, **3.** click the **Borders button list arrow**, then **4.** click **Borders and Shading**. In the Borders and Shading dialog box, **5.** click a line style in the **Style list box**, and/or click the **Color list arrow** and choose a line color from the gallery that displays, and/or click the **Width list arrow** and choose a line width from the options that display. **6.** Click one of the following options below Settings. The modifications will apply to selected cells only.

a. **None** to remove cell borders
b. **Box** to apply modifications to the outside cell border(s)
c. **All** to apply modifications to all cell borders
d. **Grid** to apply style, color, and width modification to the outside cell borders, but only color to the inside cell borders

If you like the result of your selections as shown in the Preview window, **7.** click **OK**.

HOW To modify lines surrounding an individual cell, **1.** click in the cell you want to affect. **2.** Display the **Borders and Shading dialog box**. **3.** Select the line style, and/or line color and/or line width. **4.** Click the **Apply to list arrow**, and choose **Cell**. **5.** Click a cell border button in the Preview window twice to apply the modifications. *The first time you click a border button, you will remove the existing line; the second time you click, you will apply the new settings. You can observe these changes in the Preview window.* You can also click **Box** from the Setting options to apply the border to the cell. If you like the result of your selections as shown in the Preview window, **6.** click **OK**.

Shading

▶ Colors are displayed in a gallery as *Theme Colors*, which are a set of tints and shades of unique colors or as Standard Colors, as shown in Figure 3.33. By selecting a theme color, you can make formatting choices for pieces of document content that follow a theme. You will learn to use themes later in this text.

HOW **1.** Select the cell or cells you want to shade. **2.** Click the **Design tab**, and in the **Table Styles group**, **3.** click the **Shading button list arrow**, and **4.** choose a color from the gallery that appears, as shown in Figure 3.33.

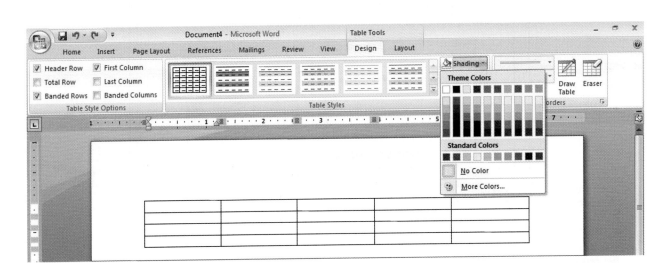

Figure 3.33: Shading gallery

1. Open the data file **w3-10**.

2. Insert a new row to become the last row.

3. Select the table.

4. Click the **Design tab** and in the **Table Styles group**, click the **Borders button list arrow**, then choose **Borders and Shading** from the menu.

5. In the Borders and Shading dialog box, select a **dotted line** style, a **red** line color, and a **4½ pt** line width.

6. Click the **Box** setting to apply the modifications to the table border, and click **OK**.

7. Position the insertion point in the cell containing the number "107.0."

8. Click the **Shading button list arrow**, then under Standard Colors, click **Yellow**.

9. Click the **Borders button**. *This will display the Borders and Shading dialog box, the*

last menu choice you made. Remember that selections remain in effect until you make another selection.

10. In the **Style list**, click the **double-line** option.

11. Click the **Color list arrow**, and select any shade of **Blue**.

12. Click the **Width list arrow**, and select **1½ pt**.

13. Click the **Apply to list arrow**, and choose **Cell**.

14. Click the **Top**, **Left**, and **Right buttons** once to remove the lines, then click **OK**.

15. Select the first row.

16. Click the **Shading button**, and select **Black**. *Notice that the text turns white.*

17. Close the file, and do not save the changes.

Apply Table Styles

▶ Using Word's predesigned formats called table styles, you can quickly change the look of a table to include a variety of borders, colors, shading, and text alignments. You can see a live preview of what your table will look like before actually applying a style. Once you apply a style, you can tweak it by selecting other table style options.

HOW 1. Click anywhere in the table, 2. click the **Design tab**, and in the **Table Styles group**, 3. point to each style shown to see a live preview (click the down list button to see more styles), or click the **More arrow** to display the Table Styles gallery shown in Figure 3.34. 4. Click to select a style. Optional: 5. In the **Table Style Options group**, click one of the options to display or hide a style element.

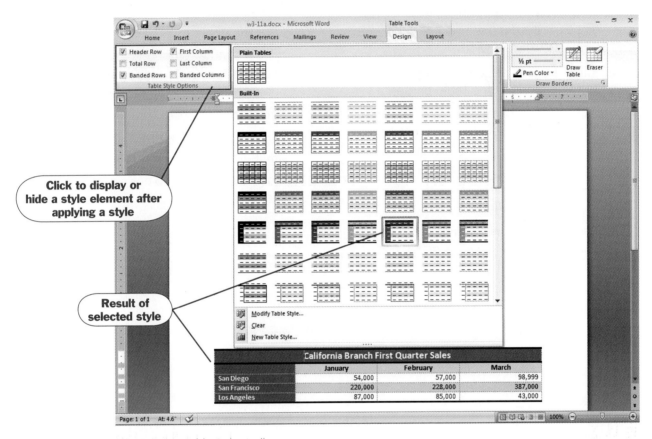

Figure 3.34: Table Styles gallery

TRY it OUT w3-11

1. Open the data file **w3-11**.

2. Click anywhere in the table.

3. Click the **Design tab**, and in the **Table Styles group**, click the **More button**, and point to each style shown to see a live preview.

4. Scroll down to and click the **Medium Shading 2-Accent 4** thumbnail.

5. In the **Table Style Options group**, click to select or deselect each option and note the effect on the table style.

6. Close the file, and do not save the changes.

Use Quick Tables

▶ **Quick Tables** are predesigned tables with sample data that you can customize. You can apply one of the table styles to a quick table or just replace the sample data with your own.

HOW **1.** Open a new blank document. **2.** Click the **Insert tab**, and in the **Tables group**, click the **Table button**, then **3.** point to (but do not click) **Quick Tables**, which will open the Quick Tables gallery shown in Figure 3.35. **4.** Scroll through the gallery and choose a table that best suits your needs. **5.** Replace the sample data with your own.

Table

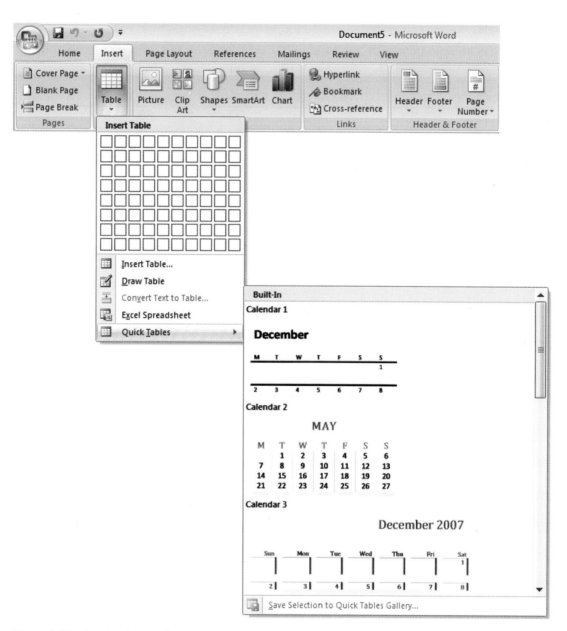

Figure 3.35: Quick Tables gallery

1. Open a new blank document.

2. Click the **Insert tab** and in the **Tables group**, click the **Table button**, then click **Quick Tables** on the menu.

3. Scroll down the gallery and select the **Matrix** style.

4. Replace the sample data with the data shown below:

5. Delete the blank rows, then click anywhere in the table.

6. In the **Table Style Options group**, select and deselect each option to see its effect on the table.

7. Apply another style from the Table Styles gallery.

8. Close the file, and do not save the changes.

STUDENT	EXAM 1	EXAM 2	EXAM 3	EXAM 4	AVERAGE
Burns, J.	83	72	77	88	
Alfred, W.	88	77	81	90	
West, R.	90	92	97	95	

REHEARSAL

 GOAL
To enhance the minutes of a meeting and schedule created previously, as shown in Figures 3.36 and 3.37

TASK 3

WHAT YOU NEED TO KNOW

▶ In this Rehearsal activity, you will add borders and shading and other enhancements to the documents you created in Task 2.

 DIRECTIONS

Minutes

1. Open **3r2-minutes**, if you completed it in Task 2. If this file is unavailable, open the data file **w3r3-minutes**.

2. Enhance the document as follows. Use Figure 3.36 as a guide.
   a. Apply shading to the cell containing the heading lines using any color you want.
   b. Apply a table border using any style, color, and line width.
   c. Set the font for the first column to sans serif **12 point**, and set the font color to **black**.
   d. Shade the row containing the word "Present" and the cells containing attendee names to a color that complements the heading row. Bold the word "Present."

3. Save the file as **3r3-minutes updated**.

4. Print one copy.

5. Apply any table style you think best presents the data. Make any modification necessary to the results if you feel that it better presents the data.

6. Print one copy.

7. Save the file as **3r3-minutes1**.

8. Close the file.

Schedule

1. Open **w3r3-schedule**, if you completed it in Task 2. If this file is unavailable, open the data file **3r3-schedule**.

2. Enhance the document as shown in Figure 3.37.
   a. Center the heading text in the first row, and set the company name to **18 point**.
   b. Change the text direction of the dates as shown on page 166, and set the text to **14 point**.
   c. Apply the **Medium Shading 2 - Accent 2** table style.

Continued on next page

3. Make the following changes to the borders and shading to better emphasize the data:
    a. Apply shading to the cells containing time and location information for Bella Hotel (9:30 a.m.) using **White**, **Background 1**, **Darker 15%**.
    b. Remove the shading from the last cells containing time and location information for Bella Hotel (3:30 p.m.).
    c. Add a black line border using a **2¼"** line width below cells containing the headings Time, Location, and Who Will Be Attending headings and remove the gray shading.

4. Center the table horizontally on the page.

5. Print one copy.

6. Save the file as **3r3-schedule updated**.

BodyWorksFitnessCenters
New Employee Orientation Meeting
January 5, 2010
Minutes of Meeting

Present

J. Tyler	W. Loria	B. Chasin	M. Asher	M. Roberts	K. Quentin
G. Samson	J. Richardson	J. Rodriguez	J. Alvarez	S. Klein	A. Jones
R. Mason	B. Arons	K. Jones	N. Allen	W. Harrison	P. Zane

Welcome	Wendy welcomed all the new employees and told the group that there would be a follow-up meeting sometime next week.
Overview	Matt provided the group with a summary of what today's meeting would cover. He explained that there would be ample time for questions and answers. Maxine distributed a company organization chart.
Company Mission	Wendy explained that the company's mission was to create high-quality fitness centers throughout the United States, but most of all to maintain high-quality customer service at all centers.
BodyWorksFitnessCenters' Key Personnel	Wendy introduced the officers of the company.
Sales Trends	Ben gave a detailed explanation of the sales trends and provided the group with a breakdown of the most successful centers. He emphasized that good staff was key for a successful center.
Employee Benefits	Wendy reviewed the company's health benefits, commission and bonus structure as well as the vacation and sick leave package.
Questions and Answers	Attendees had 20 minutes for Q & A.
Adjournment	The meeting was adjourned at 11:00 a.m.

Figure 3.36: Enhanced minutes

Newmark Productions
Meeting Schedule
Annual Sales Convention
January 22-24, 2010

Date	Time	Location	Who Will Be Attending
January 22	9:30 a.m.	Bella Hotel Conference Room H	Janis Huff
			Max Ryan
			Lorraine Jackson
			Rayon Vikos
	12:30 p.m.	Bella Hotel Conference Room J	Phyllis Ashton
			Max Ryan
			Vince Lori
January 23	12:30 p.m.	Palace Hotel Balm Restaurant	Janis Huff
			Lorraine Jackson
			Thomas Bergman
			Pamela Tricia
			Rayon Vikos
January 24	9:30 a.m.	Bella Hotel Conference Room C	Larry Robbins
			Janis Huff
			Vince Lori
	1:00 p.m.	Man Bay Hotel Axis Restaurant	Phyllis Ashton
			Max Ryan
	3:30 p.m.	Bella Hotel Conference Room B	Thomas Bergman
			Phyllis Ashton
			Max Ryan
			Vince Lori
			Rayon Vikos

Figure 3.37: Enhanced schedule

Palmetto Realtors wants to inform customers who have purchased homes through their agency that the Hollywood Planning Commission will hold hearings in May to discuss zoning and land uses. You have been asked to create a letter that includes a table of dates, times, and locations for these hearings.

Follow these guidelines:

1. Open the data file **w3p3-palmetto letterhead**.

2. Begin the dateline at **2"**.

3. Use the following settings:

Margins	Default
Line Spacing	1.0
Paragraph Spacing	
Before	0
After	0
Font	Default

4. Create the letter and table shown in Figure 3.38.

   To create the table shown:
   a. Use the **Double Table style** in Quick Tables to create the table.
   b. Delete the last three columns and last four rows.
   c. Delete the sample data.
   d. Set the row height to **.3"**.
   e. Merge rows 2 and 3, 5 and 6, 8, and 9 in the first column.
   f. Enter the text shown. Leave a blank row between dates.
   g. Rotate the dates.
   h. AutoFit the cell to contents.
   i. Center the table.
   j. Shade the cells containing the dates in any color you want.

5. Print one copy.

6. Save the file as **3p3-hearings**.

7. Close the file.

Palmetto Realtors

450 Flora Boulevard ◆Hollywood, FL 30035
Phone: 954-555-4412 ◆ Fax: 954-555-4412◆ E-mail: palmetto@world.net

Today's date

Ms. Sara Mosler
768 Harbor Way
Hollywood, FL 33035

Dear Homeowner:

We wanted to inform all those who have purchased homes through our agency that the Hollywood Planning Commission will hold a series of public hearings on zoning and land uses throughout our county.

The hearings will be held on the dates and locations indicated below:

Date	Location	Time
May 1	Hollywood High School	7:30 – 9:00 p.m.
	Hollywood Community Center	6:00 – 7:30 p.m.
May 2	Hollywood College	7:30 – 9:00 p.m.
	Hollywood Community Center	6:00 – 7:30 p.m.
May 3	Hollywood High School	6:00 – 7:30 p.m.
	Hollywood College	7:30 – 9:00 p.m.

We encourage you to attend these important hearings. While we feel that the proposals will have a major positive effect on homeowners, it is the homeowners who must decide on the outcomes.

Cordially,

Harold Dembar
President and CEO

hd/yi

Figure 3.38: Letter with inserted table

Horizontal Alignment within Table Cells

1. Select the cells to affect.
2. Click the **Home tab**, and in the **Paragraph group**, click an alignment button.

Vertical Alignment within Table Cells

1. Click in any cell or select the cells to affect.
2. Click the **Layout tab**, and in the **Alignment group**, click an alignment button.
   Or
2. Right-click, choose **Cell Alignment**, then click a vertical alignment button from those that display.

Table Borders and Shading

Borders

1. Select the table or individual cells to receive borders.

2. Click the **Design tab**, and in the **Table Styles group**, click the **Borders button list arrow**. Then click **Borders and Shading**.
3. In the **Borders and Shading dialog box**, click a line **Style** and/or a **Color**, and/or a line **Width**. Your selection in Step 1 will automatically select Table or Cell in the **Apply to** box. Be sure to check that the selection is correct.
4. Click an option below Setting, or click a line button in the Preview window twice to apply modifications to a selected cell or group of cells.
5. Click **OK**.

Shading

1. Select the cell or cells to receive shading.

2. Click the **Design tab**, and in the **Table Styles group**, click the **Shading button list arrow**.
3. Click a color.

Table Styles

1. Click anywhere in the table.
2. Click the **Design tab**, and in the **Table Styles group**, scroll down to see styles line by line, or click the **More arrow** to display the Table Styles gallery.
3. Click to select a style.

GOAL
To create an itinerary and expense report form, as shown in Figure 3.39
- ✳ Create tabular columns
- ✳ Set and modify tabs
- ✳ Set tabs with leaders
- ✳ Set tabs within table cells
- ✳ Convert text to and from a table
- ✳ Sort table data
- ✳ Perform calculations in a table

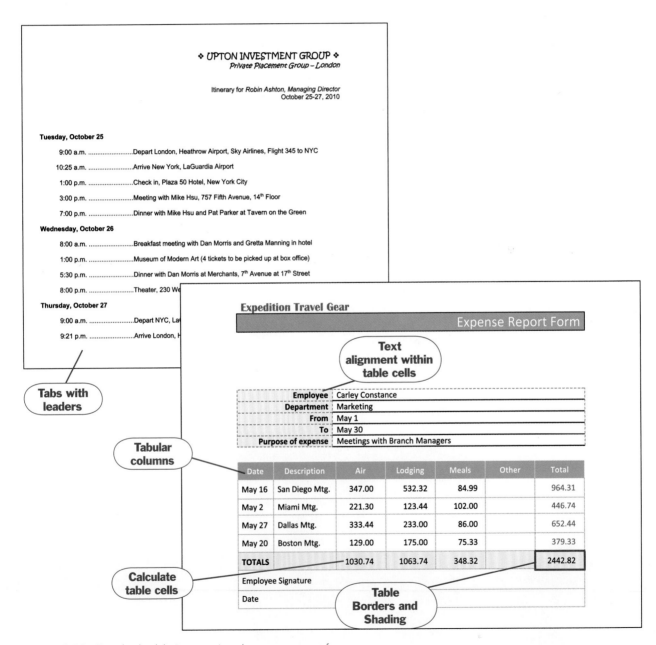

Figure 3.39: Travel schedule (itinerary) and expense report form

WHAT YOU NEED TO KNOW

Create Tabular Columns

▶ In previous tasks, you learned to use tables to organize information into columns. You can also use tabular columns, which arrange text in columns that are separated by tabs. **Tabs** are stopping points for the insertion point when [Tab] is pressed.

Set and Modify Tabs

▶ By default, tab stops are left-aligned and set every half inch. Default tab markers are indicated on the ruler by gray vertical tick marks, and the tab type is represented on the tab type selector at the left end of the ruler, as shown in Figure 3.40.

Figure 3.40: Tab markers on the ruler

▶ You can, however, change the distance between settings or you can create custom tabs. **Custom tabs** are settings that affect the way text behaves once you begin typing.

▶ Each custom tab type is represented on the tab type selector by a different indicator and has a different effect on text. Figure 3.41 shows text organized into tabular columns using custom tabs. Table 3.1 illustrates the tab buttons and explains the different tab types.

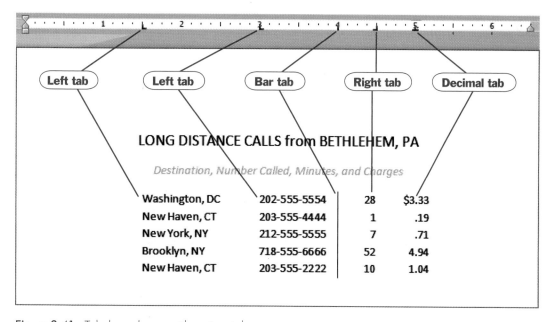

Figure 3.41: Tabular columns with custom tabs

Table 3.1: Custom tab types

TAB TYPE	INDICATOR	EXPLANATION
Left tab	L	Aligns text left at the tab stop (moves text right of tab as you enter text)
Center tab	⊥	Centers text at the tab stop
Right tab	⅃	Aligns text right at the tab stop (moves text left of the tab as you enter text)
Decimal tab	⊥	Aligns text at the decimal point (moves text left before the decimal point, then right after the decimal point)
Bar tab			Does not align text, but adds a vertical line to selected paragraphs to further define tabular columns

HOW 1. Click the **Tab type selector** at the left side of the ruler (see Figure 3.40) until it displays the button for the type of tab stop you wish to create. 2. Click the ruler at the position where you want a custom tab stop. You will notice that once you set a custom tab, default tabs to the left of it are deleted. 3. Press **[Tab]** to move the insertion point to a tab stop.

▶ To delete a tab, drag the tab marker off the ruler.

▶ To move a tab, drag the tab marker left or right on the ruler.

▶ Tab settings become part of paragraph formatting, and all paragraph formatting is stored in the paragraph mark (¶) at the end of the paragraph. If you delete the paragraph mark, or if you move the insertion point to another paragraph, you might not have the tab settings you expect.

TRY it OUT w3-13

1. Open a new blank document.

2. Display the ruler, if necessary.

3. Click the **Tab Type selector** to the left of the ruler to display the **Left Tab indicator**, if necessary.

4. Click the ruler at **1"** to insert a left tab stop.

5. Drag the Left Tab stop marker to **2"**.

6. Drag the Left Tab stop marker off the ruler to remove it.

7. Click the ruler at **1.5"** to insert a left tab stop.

8. Click the ruler at **3"** to insert another left tab stop.

9. Click the **Tab Type selector** until a **Right Tab indicator** appears.

10. Click the ruler at **4.5"** to insert a right tab.

11. Click the **Tab Type selector** until a **Bar Tab indicator** appears.

12. Click the ruler at **4"** to insert a bar tab.

13. Click the **Tab Type selector** until the **Decimal Tab indiator** appears.

14. Click the ruler at **5"** to insert a decimal tab.

15. Press **[Tab]** and enter: Washington, DC.

16. Press **[Tab]** and enter: 202-555-5554.

17. Press **[Tab]** and enter 28.

18. Press **[Tab]**, enter $3.33, then press **[Enter]**.

Continued on next page

19. Enter the text shown below at each tab stop as appropriate to complete the table. Refer to Figure 3.41, if necessary.

20. Close the file, and do not save the changes.

New Haven, CT	203-555-4444	1	.19
New York, NY	212-555-5555	7	.71
Brooklyn, NY	718-555-6666	52	4.94
New Haven, CT	203-555-2222	10	1.04

Set Tabs with Leaders

▶ You can set tabs that contain leaders. A **leader** is a series of dotted, dashed, or solid lines that connects one column to another to keep the reader's eyes focused.

▶ The settings are made in the Tabs dialog box, which can also be used to set custom tab stops. Figure 3.42 shows tabular columns with dot leaders and the corresponding settings in the Tabs dialog box.

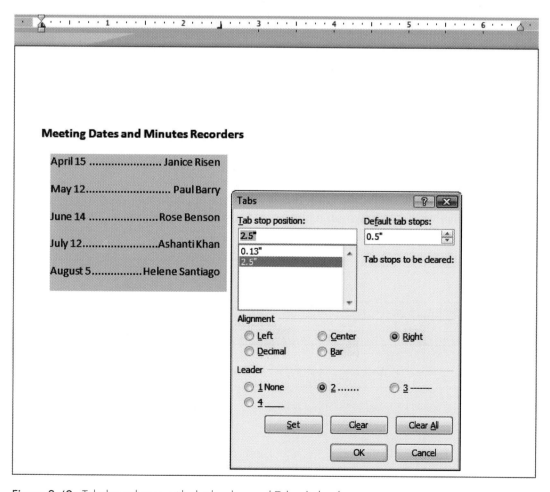

Figure 3.42: Tabular columns with dot leaders and Tabs dialog box

HOW 1. Click the **Home tab** or the **Page Layout tab**, and in the **Paragraph group**, 2. click the **Paragraph dialog box launcher**. In the Paragraph dialog box that appears, 3. click the **Tabs button** to display the Tabs dialog box, (see Figure 3.42). 4. For each tab to set, enter the tab position (1", 2", 2.5", for example) in the **Tab stop position text box**, 5. click a **tab type** below Alignment, and if you want to set a leader, 6. click a **leader style** in the Leader section, 7. click **Set**, and 8. click **OK**. Then, 9. press **[Tab]** to move the insertion point to each column. The leaders automatically appear preceding those columns that contain a tab setting with a leader. *The default tab stops remain in place to the right of the custom tab.*

T R Y i t O U T *w3-14*

1. Open a new blank document.

2. Center the title **Meeting Dates and Minutes Recorders** using a sans serif **12-point** bold font. Press **[Enter]**.

3. Click the **Home tab** and in the **Paragraph group**, click the **Paragraph dialog box launcher**. In the Paragraph dialog box, click the **Tabs button**.

4. Enter **.13"** in the Tab stop position text box, click **Left** as the Alignment option, then click **Set**.

5. Enter **2.5"** in the Tab stop position text box, click **Right** as the Alignment option, and click **2** as the Leader style.

6. Click **Set**, then click **OK**.

7. Press **[Tab]**, then enter **April 15** at the first tab stop.

8. Press **[Tab]**, enter **Janice Risen**, and press **[Enter]**.

9. Enter the text shown below to complete the table:

   May 12 . . . . Paul Barry

   June 14 . . . . Rose Benson

   July 12 . . . . Ashanti Kahn

   August 5 . . . . . Helene Santiago

10. Print one copy.

11. Close the file, and do not save the changes.

Set Tabs within Table Cells

▶ You can create tab stops within table cells using the same techniques used to create them in tabular columns. Figure 3.43 shows an example of tabs within table cells.

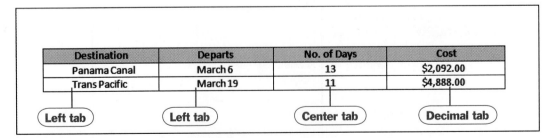

Figure 3.43: Tabs within table cells

HOW 1. Position the insertion point in the cell or select the cells to affect. 2. Use the same procedures you learned earlier to set a tab type. 3. Press [Ctrl]+[Tab] to advance the insertion point to a tab stop for all tab types except the decimal tab. Press [Tab] to advance to a decimal tab setting.

T R Y i t O U T *w3-15*

1. Open the data file **w3-15**.
2. Display the ruler, if necessary.
3. Click the **Tab Type selector** to the left of the ruler until it displays the **Left Tab indicator**, if necessary.
4. Select the blank cells below "Destination," and then click at **.3"** on the ruler to set a left tab.
5. Select the blank cells below "Departs," and then click at **2"** on the ruler to set a left tab.
6. Click the **Tab Type selector** to the left of the ruler until it displays the **Center Tab indicator**.
7. Select the cells below "No. of Days," and click at **4"** on the ruler to set a center tab.
8. Click the **Tab Type selector** to the left of the ruler until it displays the **Right Tab indicator**.
9. Select the cells below "Cost," and click at **5.5"** on the ruler to set a right tab.

10. Click in the first row below "Destination."
11. Press [Ctrl]+[Tab] and enter `Panama Canal`.
12. Press [Tab], [Ctrl]+[Tab], and enter `March 6`.
13. Press [Tab], [Ctrl]+[Tab], and enter `13`.
14. Press [Tab], [Ctrl]+[Tab], and enter `$2,092.99`.
15. Click in the first column of the third row.
16. Enter the following in the proper columns, using [Tab] and [Ctrl]+[Tab] as appropriate:

`Trans Pacific`
`March 19`
`11`
`$4,888.00`

17. Print one copy.
18. Close the file, and do not save the changes.

Convert Text To and From a Table

▶ You can convert text to a table so that the text is inserted into columns and rows. This is useful when you have typed text that you feel would be better presented in a more organized way. Figure 3.44 illustrates text that would be better organized in a table format. You can also convert data in a table to text organized by separators.

Debra, Jones, 205 West Street, New York, NY, 10021-9876
Shameka, Roberts, 111 South Avenue, Lake Worth, FL, 33467
Steve, Mumolo, 108 Mission Street, Santa Barbara, CA, 93101

Figure 3.44: Text to be converted to a table

HOW **1.** Separate the text with a comma, a tab, or other separator character you designate to indicate where to begin a new column. Use a paragraph mark to indicate where to begin a new row (see Figure 3.44). **2.** Select the text to be converted, **3.** click the **Insert tab** and in the **Tables group**, **4.** click the **Table button**, then **5.** click to **Text button**. In the Convert Table to Text to Table dialog box that appears (shown in Figure 3.45), **6.** verify the number of columns you want. Also indicate the separator character, and **7.** click **OK**.

To change data in a table to text with separators, **1.** select the table. **2.** Click the **Layout tab** and in the **Data group**, **3.** click the **Convert to Text button**. In the Convert Table to Text dialog box that appears, shown in Figure 3.46, **4.** click to indicate the separator you want, then **5.** click **OK**.

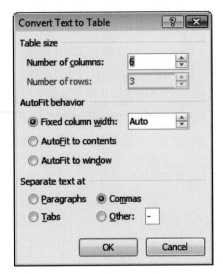

Figure 3.45: Convert Text to Table dialog box

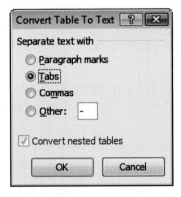

Figure 3.46: Convert Table to Text dialog box

T R Y *it* **O U T** *w3-16*

1. Open a new blank document.

2. Enter the text shown below, including the commas (separator characters). Press **[Enter]** at the end of each line.
   ```
   Debra, Jones, 205 West Street,
   New York, NY, 10021-9876
   Shameka, Roberts, 111 South Avenue,
   Lake Worth, FL, 33467
   Steve, Mumolo, 108 Mission Street,
   Santa Barbara, CA, 93101
   ```

3. Select the text.

4. Click the **Insert Tab**, and in the **Tables group**, click the **Table button**, then click **Convert Text to Table**.

5. In the Convert Text to Table dialog box, verify that the number of columns is six, and click the **Commas option** below "Separate text at." *The number of columns is automatically inserted based on the number of commas Word detects in your selected text.*

6. Click **OK**.

7. Close the file, and do not save the changes.

8. Open the data file, **w3-16**.

9. Select the table.

Continued on next page

10. Click the **Layout tab**, and in the **Data group**, click the **Convert to Text button**. In the Convert Table to Text dialog box, click **Commas**.

日≣ Convert to Text

11. Click **OK**.

12. Close the file, and do not save the changes.

Sort Table Data

▶ Using Word's sort feature, you can rearrange data in a table so that it is presented in alphabetic or numeric order.

HOW **1.** Select the data to sort, **2.** click the **Layout tab**, and in the **Data group**, **3.** click the **Sort button**. In the Sort dialog box that appears, shown in Figure 3.47, **4.** click **Header row** or **No header row**. *This will depend on whether or not your selected text contains such a row.* **5.** Click the **Sort by list box**, and choose a column title to sort, and **6.** click the **Type list box**, and choose the content type. Then, **7.** click **Ascending** or **Descending**. To conduct a second- or third-level sort, enter your selections in the second- and third-tier sort options boxes, choose a sort direction (Ascending or Descending), then **8.** click **OK**. *If you do not like the results of your sort, click the Undo button.*

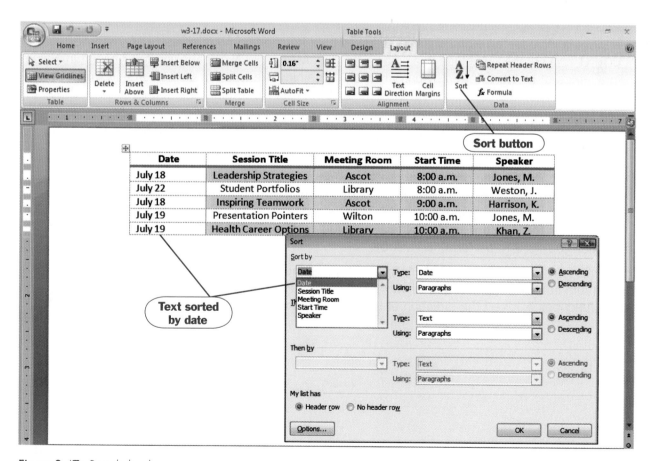

Figure 3.47: Sort dialog box

1. Open the data file **w3-17**.

2. Select the table.

3. Click the **Layout tab**, and in the **Data group**, click the **Sort button**.

4. In the Sort dialog box, do the following:
   a. Click **Header row** below "My list has," if necessary.
   b. Click the **Sort by list arrow**, and choose **Date**, if necessary. Click **Ascending**, if necessary.
   c. Click the **Then by list arrow**, and choose **Speaker**. Click **Ascending**, if necessary.
   d. Click **OK**. Note the result of your sort.

5. Click the **Undo button** on the Quick Access toolbar.

6. Click the **Sort button** again.

7. Click **Header row**, if necessary.

8. Sort by **Start Time**, then by **Date** in **Ascending** order.

9. Click **OK**. Note the result of your sort.

10. Close the file, and do not save the changes.

Perform Calculations in a Table

▶ You can perform basic calculations (addition, subtraction, multiplication, and division) when numbers are in table cells by using and of Word's built-in formulas, or you can construct the formula from scratch.

▶ A formula includes an equal sign (=), followed by a function name such as SUM, AVERAGE, COUNT (the number of values in a column or row), MAX, or MIN (the maximum or minimum value in a series of cells), followed by parentheses containing the location of the cells on which you want to perform the calculation. The formula =SUM(ABOVE) totals the amounts in cells above the cell containing the formula.

▶ This lesson will cover simple calculations using Word's built-in formulas. For complex calculations, use the features found in Excel, which you will learn to use later in this text.

HOW **1.** Click in the cell where the answer should appear. **2.** Click the **Layout tab** and in the **Data group**, click the **Formula button**. *ƒx* Formula In the Formula dialog box that displays, as shown in Figure 3.48, Word automatically inserts the SUM formula and intuitively adds the direction of the calculation (LEFT or ABOVE), in the Formula box. If this is the calculation you want to perform, **3.** click **OK**.

To enter a function other than SUM, **1.** follow steps 1 and 2 above. Then, **2.** delete the formula in the Formula box, **3.** enter an equal sign (=), **4.** click the **Paste function list arrow**, **5.** choose a built-in function, **6.** insert the direction of the calculation within the parentheses, then **7.** click **OK**.

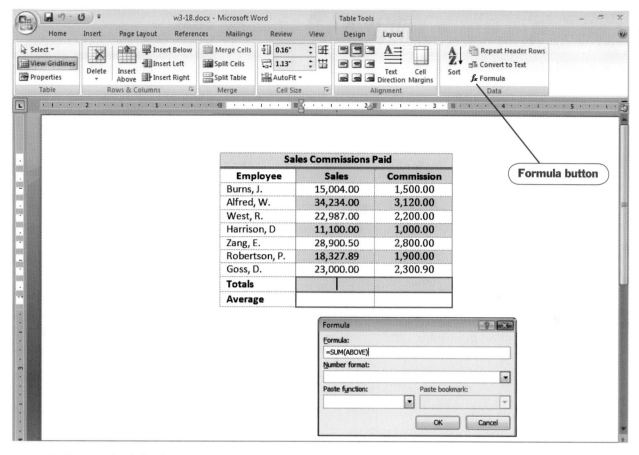

Figure 3.48: Formula dialog box

1. Open the data file **w3-18**.

2. Position your insertion point in the Average row of the Sales column.

3. Click the **Layout tab** and in the **Data group**, click the **Formula button**.

4. Delete the formula in the Formula box.

5. Enter an equal sign (=) in the formula box, then click the **Paste function list arrow**, and select **AVERAGE**. Enter the word **ABOVE** between the parentheses so that the formula reads **=AVERAGE(ABOVE)**.

6. Click **OK**.

7. Position your insertion point in the Average row of the Commission column. Repeat Steps 3–6.

8. Position your insertion point in the Totals row of the Sales column.

9. Click the **Layout tab**, and in the **Data group**, click the **Formula button**.

10. Enter the formula **=SUM(ABOVE)** in the formula box, if necessary.

11. Click **OK**.

12. Position your insertion point in the Totals row of the Commission column. Repeat Steps 9, 10 and 11.

13. Close the file, and do not save the changes.

REHEARSAL

 GOAL
To create an itinerary (travel schedule) and an expense report form, as shown in Figures 3.49 and 3.50

TASK 4

WHAT YOU NEED TO KNOW

▶ An **itinerary** details the travel arrangements, meeting schedule, and contact information for the person making a trip.

▶ Companies often develop forms to collect information from their employees. Forms are often printed, filled out on paper, and collected.

▶ An **expense report form** summarizes expenses incurred by an employee, which is submitted to a company for reimbursement.

▼ DIRECTIONS

Itinerary

1. Open a new blank document.
2. Display the ruler, if necessary.
3. Use the following settings:

Margins	1" left and right
Line Spacing	1.0
Paragraph Spacing	
Before	0
After	0
Font	Arial

4. Create the itinerary shown in Figure 3.49.
5. Right-align the headings; use any font, font size, and symbol.
6. Set a **10-point** font for the body of the itinerary.
7. Set a right tab at **1"** from the left margin; set a left tab with a dot leader at **2"** from the left margin.
8. Enter the itinerary text as shown.
9. Print one copy.
10. Save the file, and name it **3r4-itinerary**.
11. Close the file.

Expense Report Form

1. Open a new blank document.
2. Use the following settings:

Margins	1.25" left and right
Line Spacing	1.0
Paragraph Spacing	
Before	0
After	0
Font	Default

Continued on next page

❖ UPTON INVESTMENT GROUP ❖
Private Placement Group – London

Itinerary for Robin Ashton, Managing Director
October 25-27, 2010

Tuesday, October 25

9:00 a.m. ....Depart London, Heathrow Airport, Sky Airlines, Flight 345 to NYC

10:25 a.m. ....Arrive New York, LaGuardia Airport

1:00 p.m. ....Check in, Plaza 50 Hotel, New York City

3:00 p.m. ....Meeting with Mike Hsu, 757 Fifth Avenue, 14th Floor

7:00 p.m. ....Dinner with Mike Hsu and Pat Parker at Tavern on the Green

Wednesday, October 26

8:00 a.m. ....Breakfast meeting with Dan Morris and Gretta Manning in hotel

1:00 p.m. ....Museum of Modern Art (4 tickets to be picked up at box office)

5:30 p.m. ....Dinner with Dan Morris at Merchants, 7th Avenue at 17th Street

8:00 p.m. ....Theater, 230 West 44th Street (4 tickets at box office)

Thursday, October 27

9:00 a.m. ....Depart NYC, LaGuardia Airport, Sky Airlines, Flight 33 to London

9:21 p.m. ....Arrive London, Heathrow Airport

Figure 3.49: Itinerary

3. Create the expense report form shown in Figure 3.50 on page 189. This form consists of three tables—a single column table that contains the name of the form, a two-column, five-row table that contains the employee information, and a seven-column, eight-row table containing expense information.

4. Enter the company name using any font in **14 point**.

5. For the single column table:
   a. Enter the title (**Expense Report Form**) using any desired font, font size, font color, and shading.
   b. Align the data as shown.

Continued on next page

6. For the table containing employee information:
   a. Set the width of the left column to **1.7"**. Set the width of the right column to **4.45"**.
   b. Enter the text as shown. Set the font size to **11 point**. Use any desired font and font color for the text.
   c. Apply text alignments to cells as shown. Use any color shading you want.
   d. Remove table lines as shown.

7. For the table containing expense information:
   a. Set the column widths to **.88"**. Set the row height to **.3"**.
   b. Enter the text as shown. Use any desired font and font color for the text. Set the font size to **11 point**.
   c. Decimal-align the cells containing currency amounts. Apply other alignments and shading to the cells as shown.
   d. Center-align all cell text vertically.
   e. Sort the data in numeric order by Date.
   f. Adjust the width of the Description column so that the text fits on one line (create a narrower Date column).
   g. Enter the signature and date text as shown.
   h. Find the sum of each of the currency columns. Decimal align the totals.
   i. Apply a red border around the last TOTALS cell, as shown. Use any border width.
   j. Apply a **1/2"** dotted green border to the table, as shown.

8. Print one copy of the form.

9. Save the file, and name it **3r4-expense form**.

10. Close the file.

Expedition Travel Gear

Expense Report Form

Employee	Carley Constance
Department	Marketing
From	May 1
To	May 30
Purpose of expense	Meetings with Branch Managers

Date	Description	Air	Lodging	Meals	Other	Total
May 16	San Diego Mtg.	347.00	532.32	84.99		964.31
May 2	Miami Mtg.	221.30	123.44	102.00		446.74
May 27	Dallas Mtg.	333.44	233.00	86.00		652.44
May 20	Boston Mtg.	129.00	175.00	75.33		379.33
TOTALS						
Employee Signature						
Date						

Enter formula

Figure 3.50: Expense Report Form

PERFORMANCE

TASK 4

BodyWorksFitnessCenters is offering new weekend classes that should be quite popular with members of all ages. Wendy Carroll, director of the Weekend Fitness Program, has asked you to create a schedule of classes to send to all members.

Follow these guidelines:

1. Open a new blank document.
2. Use landscape orientation and the default margins.
3. Create a table using six columns and eight rows.
4. Enter the fitness schedule heading text as shown in Figure 3.51.
   a. Merge columns 1–4 and 5–6.
   b. Set the heading text to any font and size, and shade the cells using any colors you want.
   c. Vertically and horizontally center the text in row 1.
   d. Set row height to 2" for row 1.
5. Merge the cells in row 2.
6. Enter the text in the columns.
   a. Set the row heights to **.5"**.
   b. Set the text for "Instructor," "Saturday," and "Sunday" to a serif, **22-point** font.
   c. Set the font size for the body text to a serif **11 point**.
   d. In Columns 4 and 6, set a custom center tab in the middle of the column and a right tab with a dot leader at the end of the column.
   e. Make the class titles ("Body Sculpt," "Yoga," etc.) bold.
   f. Shade the cells in any color.
   g. Set the column widths for all the columns containing schedule information to AutoFit the Contents.
7. Print one copy.
8. Save the file, and name it **3p4-fitness schedule**.
9. Close the file.

Instructor		Saturday		Sunday	
		BodyWorksFitnessCenters Weekend Schedule		**Weekend Fitness Director Wendy Carroll** Note: Classes will be held in either Studio 1, 2 or Studio Right (SR)	
	Ronnie	8:15-9:00	**Body Sculpt** 2	8:30-9:30	**Yoga** 2
	John	9:00-10:00	**Yoga** 2	9:00-10:00	**Step** 2
	Ronnie	10:00-11:00	**Spin** 1	9:30-10:30	**Body Sculpt** 1
	Felicia	11:00-12:00	**Cardio** .... SR	11:00-12:00	**Step** .... SR
	Forrest	12:00-1:00	**Stretch** 1	12:30-1:30	**Spin** 1
	Jessica	3:30-5:30	**Ballet** .... SR	4:30-5:30	**Yoga** 2

Figure 3.51: Fitness Schedule

ENCORE

Act I

Ms. Roslyn Young, president of the Transport Travel Services, is traveling from New York to Belgium on business from June 14 to June 17, 2010. You have been asked to prepare an itinerary for her. Ms. Young wants the heading of the itinerary to include the company name, the words "Itinerary for" followed by her name, and the dates of travel.

Follow these guidelines:

1. Organize the following information as an itinerary for Ms. Young.

   Ms. Young is leaving on Tuesday, June 14, at 9:00 p.m. from New York's LaGuardia Airport on American Airlines Flight 225, arriving in Brussels, Belgium, on Wednesday, June 15, at 8:00 a.m. She is staying at the Hotel Amigo, located at rue de l'Amigo, where she is scheduled to check in at 9:00 a.m. At 10:30 a.m., she is meeting with Ramone Valdez of the European Travel Society, 213 Place de la Rosa. At 6:30 p.m., she is having dinner with the Private Travel Group at Les Brigittines, 5 Place de la Chapelle. On Thursday, June 16, Ms. Pierce is scheduled to meet with Phillippe Haas of ARB SA Corporation at 8:30 a.m. The ARB SA offices are located at Chaussee de La Hulpe 185. At 12:15 p.m., she is meeting Laurence Volpe for lunch at the ARB offices. She is returning to her hotel at 6:30 p.m. On Friday, June 17, she will be leaving Brussels at 8:00 a.m. on American Airlines Flight 225 and is scheduled to land at New York's LaGuardia Airport at 1:00 p.m.

2. Use a two-column table to create parallel columns for the itinerary.

3. Insert the heading in a merged cell.

4. Format the table using any desired table border, cell border, and shading.

5. Adjust column widths as desired.

6. Print one copy.

7. Save the file, and name it **3e1-brussels**.

8. Apply a style from the Table Styles gallery that best presents the data. Remember, once you apply a style, you can tweak it by selecting other table style options.

9. Print one copy.

10. Save the file, and name it **3e1-brussels1**.

11. Close the file.

Act II

Each year, Newmark Productions sponsors a technology conference to which clients in the surrounding area are invited. This year's conference is scheduled for Monday, February 4 through Wednesday, February 6. As coordinator of special events at Newmark, it is your responsibility to coordinate the conference, which includes notifying guest speakers of their topics and speaking times. You have been asked to prepare a letter to one of the speakers, Ms. Irene Quincy, director of sales, NVC Arts, 9145 Sunset Boulevard, Los Angeles, CA 90069.

Follow these guidelines:

1. Use the following settings:

Margins	1.25" left and right.
Line Spacing	1.0
Paragraph Spacing	
Before	0
After	0
Font	Default

2. Start the document at approximately 2". Include today's date, an appropriate salutation, and a closing.

3. The body of the letter should read as follows:

   We are delighted that you are able to be a featured presenter at our upcoming conference on February 4, 5, and 6. ¶You are scheduled to present "The History and Future of TV and the Internet" on Monday, February 4 at 2:00 p.m. We will be contacting you by phone very shortly to discuss the details of your presentation and to coordinate any audiovisual requests you may have.¶ A schedule of Monday's events is provided here for your reference.¶

   1 p.m.......Webstation Lounge Box Lunch

   2 p.m.......The History and Future of TV and the Internet

   3:30 p.m.......How to Create Award-Winning Websites

   Once again, thank you for your participation at this year's conference. I look forward to meeting you in February.

4. Insert the schedule as tabular columns with leaders, as shown in Figure 3.52. Set a right tab for time of the session approximately 1" from the left margin (after p.m.). Set a right tab for the session titles 1" from the right margin.

Continued on next page

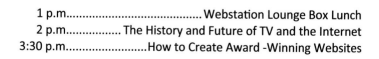

Figure 3.52: Tabular table for letter

5. Use your name as the sender of the letter, and include your title.

6. Print one copy.

7. Save the file, and name it **3e2-conference**.

8. Close the file.

Act III

Upton Investment Group holds an annual fund-raising event to help needy children. After all pledges have been received, the company publishes the results as a means of thanking the contributors. You have been asked to use your formatting skills to prepare the table of contributors for publication in next month's newsletter.

Follow these guidelines:

1. Open the data file **w3e3-table**.

2. Insert and delete the columns and rows indicated in Figure 3.53.
   a. In the newly inserted column, enter the column heading and state abbreviations shown in Figure 3.54.
   b. Merge the cells for the heading row and enter the heading shown using any font and font size.
   c. Sort the data alphabetically by name.
   d. Enter data for the additional contributors in the last two rows:
      Giles, Robert, 45 Icon Place, Richmond, VA 23220, 2,000
      Berber, Sarah, 98-98 Nancy Lane, Richmond, VA 23223, 1,200
   e. Re-sort the data alphabetically by name.
   f. Insert a row at the end of the table, and enter the word **TOTAL**.
   g. Center the table horizontally.
   h. Use a formula to calculate the total in the Contribution column.
   i. Align the data horizontally and vertically in the cells as shown.
   j. Use a red font for the total.

3. Format the table. Apply any table lines and shading or a table style to enhance the table. Figure 3.54 is merely a guide; you can enhance the table using any table tools you have learned thus far.

4. Save the file, and name it **3e3-fundraising event**.

5. Print one copy.

6. Sort the rows in descending order by Contribution.

7. Print one copy.

8. Undo the sort.

9. Save the changes, and close the file.

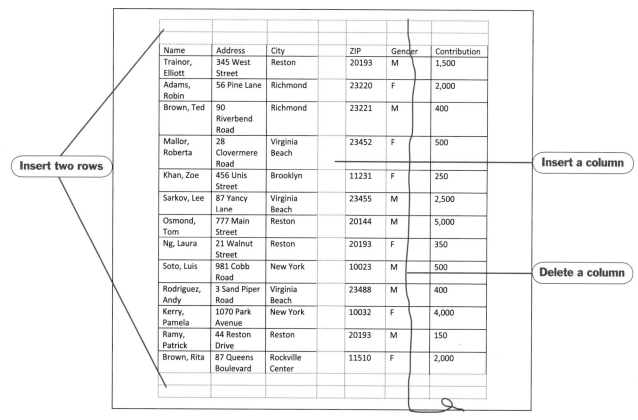

Insert two rows

Insert a column

Delete a column

Name	Address	City		ZIP	Gender	Contribution
Trainor, Elliott	345 West Street	Reston		20193	M	1,500
Adams, Robin	56 Pine Lane	Richmond		23220	F	2,000
Brown, Ted	90 Riverbend Road	Richmond		23221	M	400
Mallor, Roberta	28 Clovermere Road	Virginia Beach		23452	F	500
Khan, Zoe	456 Unis Street	Brooklyn		11231	F	250
Sarkov, Lee	87 Yancy Lane	Virginia Beach		23455	M	2,500
Osmond, Tom	777 Main Street	Reston		20144	M	5,000
Ng, Laura	21 Walnut Street	Reston		20193	F	350
Soto, Luis	981 Cobb Road	New York		10023	M	500
Rodriguez, Andy	3 Sand Piper Road	Virginia Beach		23488	M	400
Kerry, Pamela	1070 Park Avenue	New York		10032	F	4,000
Ramy, Patrick	44 Reston Drive	Reston		20193	M	150
Brown, Rita	87 Queens Boulevard	Rockville Center		11510	F	2,000

Figure 3.53: Unformatted table

Upton Investment Group
Fundraising Event
November 12, 2010

Name	Address	City	State	ZIP	Contribution
Adams, Robin	56 Pine Lane	Richmond	VA	23220	2,000
Berber, Sarah	98-98 Nancy Lane	Richmond	VA	23223	1,200
Brown, Rita	87 Queens Boulevard	Rockville Center	NY	11510	2,000
Brown, Ted	90 Riverbend Road	Richmond	VA	23221	400
Giles, Robert	45 Icon Place	Richmond	VA	23220	2,000
Kerry, Pamela	1070 Park Avenue	New York	NY	10032	4,000
Khan, Zoe	456 Unis Street	Brooklyn	NY	11231	250
Mallor, Roberta	28 Clovermere Road	Virginia Beach	VA	23452	500
Ng, Laura	21 Walnut Street	Reston	VA	20193	350
Osmond, Tom	777 Main Street	Reston	VA	20144	5,000
Ramy, Patrick	44 Reston Drive	Reston	VA	20193	150
Rodriguez, Andy	3 Sand Piper Road	Virginia Beach	VA	23488	400
Sarkov, Lee	87 Yancy Lane	Virginia Beach	VA	23455	2,500
Soto, Luis	981 Cobb Road	New York	NY	10023	500
Trainor, Elliott	345 West Street	Reston	VA	20193	1,500
TOTAL					22,750

Figure 3.54: Formatted table

Set a Custom Tab on the Ruler

1. Position the insertion point in the paragraph or select the paragraphs in which to set the tab.
2. Click the **Tab Type selector** to the left of the ruler to select the tab:

Left

Center

Right

Decimal

Bar

3. Click the ruler where the tab is to be set.
4. Press **[Tab]** to advance to the next tab stop.

Set a Custom Tab with Leaders

1. Click the **Home tab** or the **Page Layout tab**, and in the **Paragraph group**, click the **Paragraph dialog box launcher**.
2. In the **Paragraph dialog box**, click **Tabs**.
3. Enter a tab position in the Tab stop position text box.

4. Click an **Alignment option** (Left, Center, Right, Decimal, or Bar).
5. Click a Leader option.
6. Click **Set**.
7. Repeat Steps 3–6 for each tab to set.
8. Click **OK**.
9. Press **[Tab]** to advance to the next tab stop.

Remove a Custom Tab

1. Drag the tab indicator off the ruler.

Move a Tab

1. Drag the tab indicator left or right on the ruler to the appropriate location.

Set Tabs within Table Cells

1. Position the insertion point in the cell or select the columns.
2. Set tabs as outlined above ("Set a Custom Tab on the Ruler," "Set a Custom Tab with Leaders").
3. Press **[Ctrl]+[Tab]** to advance to the next tab stop. Press **[Tab]** to advance to a decimal tab stop.

Sort Table Data

1. Select the data to sort.
2. Click the **Layout tab**, and in the **Data group**, click the **Sort button**.
3. In the Sort dialog box, click **Header row** or **No header row**.
4. Select the column title to sort in the **Sort by box** and the **content Type** in the **Type box**.
5. Click **Ascending** or **Descending**.
6. Repeat Steps 4 and 5 for second and/or third-tier sorts.
7. Click **OK**.

Perform Calculations in a Table

1. Click in the cell where the answer should appear.
2. Click the **Layout tab**, and in the **Data group**, click the **Formula button**.
3. Enter a formula in the Formula box.
4. Click **OK**.

LESSON 4

Sales and Marketing Documents

In this lesson, you will learn to use features found in Word to format sales and marketing documents. Sales and marketing documents include anything that helps sell or promote a product or service. Examples include flyers, advertisements, newsletters, brochures, and catalogs. You will complete the following projects:

✴ Flyer
✴ Advertisement
✴ Newsletter
✴ Catalog page

Upon completion of this lesson, you will have mastered the following skill sets

✴ Work with text boxes
✴ Wrap text around a text box
✴ Work with Clip Art
✴ Wrap text around a graphic
✴ Work with shapes, lines, WordArt, and SmartArt
✴ Layer and group graphics
✴ Create a section break
✴ Create columns
✴ Create a drop cap
✴ Use page borders and page colors

Terms
Software-related
AutoShapes
Clip art
Crop
Group
Layer
Organization chart
SmartArt
Text box
WordArt
Style
Document-related
Flyer
Advertisement
Catalog
Newsletter

TRYOUT

GOAL
To create a flyer and advertisement, as shown in Figure 4.1

* Work with text boxes
* Create a text box and enter text
* Size and reposition a text box
* Format a text box
* Wrap text around a text box

TASK 1

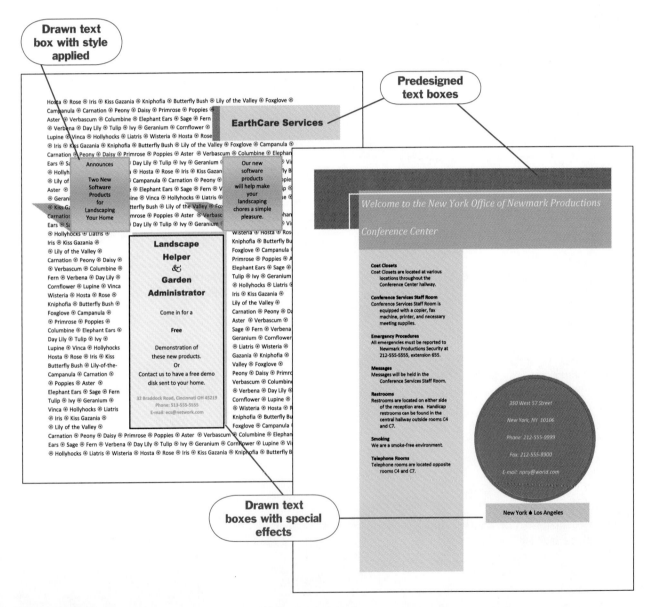

Figure 4.1: Flyers

WHAT YOU NEED TO KNOW

Work with Text Boxes

▶ A **text box** allows you to set off text in a box, which you can then position anywhere on a page. A text box is considered an object. You will learn to work with other objects later in this lesson.

▶ Text entered inside a text box becomes part of the box and moves as you move the box. You can position and format texts boxes, as well as align the text within the box, to create interesting effects. Before actually applying formatting options to a text box, you can see a live preview.

Create a Text Box and Enter Text

▶ Text boxes can be created from scratch, or you can use one of Word's built-in predesigned text boxes. Predesigned text boxes are particularly useful for pull quotes or sidebars—interesting text used to add interest to a design or attract a reader's attention to the story. Figure 4.2 shows several predesigned text boxes, while Figure 4.3 shows drawn text boxes with different outlines, fills, and text alignments.

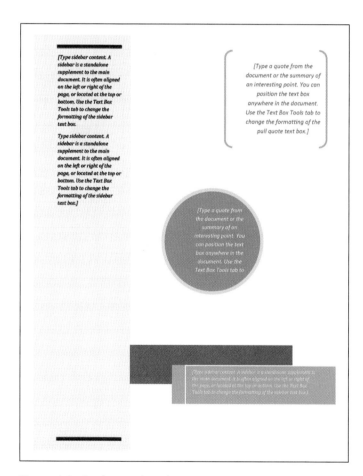

Figure 4.2: Predesigned text boxes

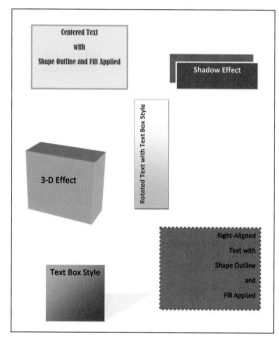

Figure 4.3: Drawn text boxes with applied effects

HOW 1. Click the **Insert tab**, and in the **Text group**, 2. click the **Text Box button**. In the menu that displays, 3. click **Draw Text Box**, as shown in Figure 4.4. 4. Drag the mouse pointer to the required box size, as shown in Figure 4.5. *You will notice that the text box initially appears with sizing handles, small circles and squares that appear at the corners and sides of a selected box, and a contextual tab on the Ribbon that provides tools to help you work with text boxes.* 5. Enter the text. 6. Click outside the text box to deactivate it and inside the box to activate it.

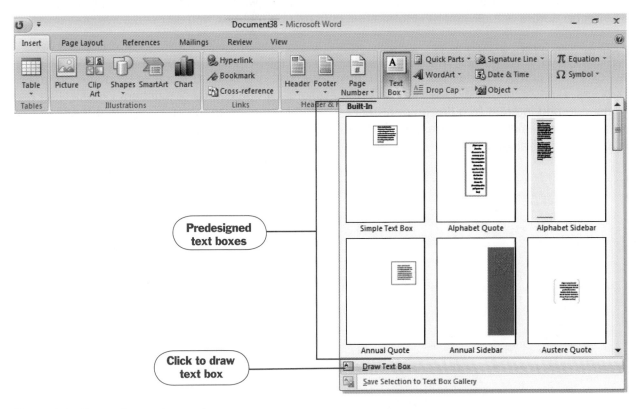

Figure 4.4: Options for creating text boxes

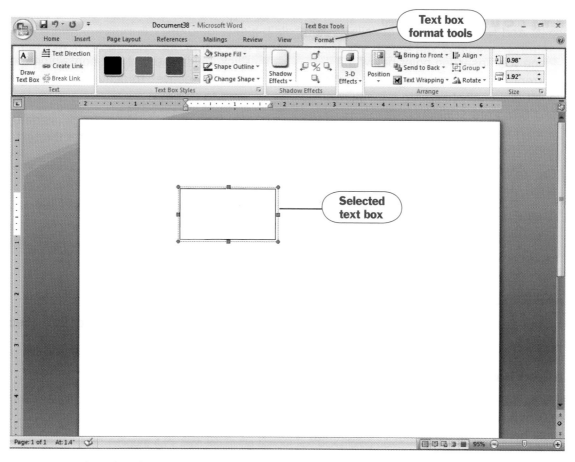

Figure 4.5: Selected text box with text box tools displayed

HOW To use a predesigned text box, **1.** click the **Insert tab**, and in the **Text group**, **2.** click the **Text Box button**. In the Built-In gallery that appears, **3.** scroll down to view the predesigned text boxes (see Figure 4.4), and click to select one. **4.** Select the sample text in the box, and enter your replacement text. **5.** Click outside the box to deactivate it and inside the box to activate it. *You will learn to position the box and change the colors and box effects later in this lesson.*

T R Y _it_ O U T *w4-1*

1. Open a new blank document.

2. To create a text box using a built-in style, click the **Insert tab** and in the **Text group**, click the **Text Box button**.

3. Scroll down to view the built-in styles. Select the **Contrast Sidebar text box**. *Notice that the Format tab appears with text box tools.*

4. Select the text inside the box, and enter **Upton Investment Group**. Notice that the sample text is replaced with the new text. Press **[Enter]**, then enter **Marketing Department**.

5. To draw a text box, click the **Insert tab** and in the **Text group**, click the **Text Box button**, and click **Draw Text Box**.

Continued on next page

Reposition a Text Box

1. Select the box, then **2.** position your mouse pointer over the box until it turns into a four-headed arrow. **3.** Click and drag the box to any location on the page.

You can also apply the Copy, Cut, and Paste commands to copy, delete, and reposition a text box.

TRY *it* OUT w4-2

1. Open the data file **w4-2**.

2. Click inside the box containing the word "Communications." *The text box tools appear*.
   a. Click the **Format tab**, if necessary, and in the **Size group**, enter **2"** in the Shape Width box.
   b. In the **Text group**, click the **Text Direction button** twice to rotate text.
   c. Click the **Format tab**, if necessary, and in the **Size group**, enter **1.65"** in the **Shape Height box** and **.47"** in the **Shape Width box**.

3. Click inside the box containing the word "Clear."
   a. Click the **Format tab** (if necessary), and in the **Size group**, click the **dialog box launcher**.

   b. In the Format Text Box dialog box that appears, click the **Size tab**, if necessary, and enter **.38"** in the Absolute Height box and **.65"** in the Absolute Width box, then click **OK**.

4. Click inside the box containing the words "is Essential."

   Repeat Steps 3a and 3b, and enter **.38"** in the Absolute Height box and **1.10"** in the Absolute Width box, and click **OK**.

5. Drag each box to position it in the order shown in Figure 4.9.

6. Print one copy.

7. Close the file, and do not save the changes.

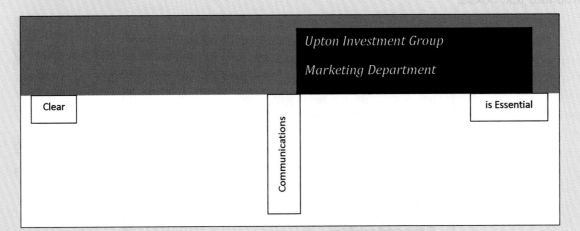

Figure 4.9: Results of Try it Out w4-2

7. Print one copy.
8. Save the file, and name it **4r1-plant flyer**.
9. Close the file.

Hosta ❀ Rose ❀ Iris ❀ Kiss Gazania ❀ Kniphofia ❀ Butterfly Bush ❀ Lily of the Valley ❀ Foxglove ❀ Campanula ❀ Carnation ❀ Peony ❀ Daisy ❀ Primrose ❀ Poppies ❀ Aster ❀ Verbascum ❀ Columbine ❀ Elephant Ears ❀ Sage ❀ Fern ❀ Verbena ❀ Day Lily ❀ Tulip ❀ Ivy ❀ Geranium ❀ Cornflower ❀ Lupine ❀ Vinca ❀ Hollyhocks ❀ Liatris ❀ Wisteria ❀ Hosta ❀ Rose

EarthCare Services

❀ Iris ❀ Kiss Gazania ❀ Kniphofia ❀ Butterfly Bush ❀ Lily of the Valley ❀ Foxglove ❀ Campanula ❀ Carnation ❀ Peony ❀ Daisy ❀ Primrose ❀ Poppies ❀ Aster ❀ Verbascum ❀ Columbine ❀ Elephant Ears ❀ Sa...

Announces

Two New Software Products for Landscaping Your Home

...Day Lily ❀ Tulip ❀ Ivy ❀ Geranium ❀ ...Vinca
❀ Hollyh... ...a ❀ Hosta ❀ Rose ❀ Iris ❀ Kiss Gazan... ...fly Bush
❀ Lily of... ...❀ Campanula ❀ Carnation ❀ Peony ❀ ...ppies ❀
Aster ❀ ...❀ Elephant Ears ❀ Sage ❀ Fern ❀ V... ...ip ❀ Ivy
❀ Gerani... ...ine ❀ Vinca ❀ Hollyhocks ❀ Liatris ... ...se ❀ Iris
❀ Kiss Ga... ...tterfly Bush ❀ Lily of the Valley ❀ Fo...
Carnation ...mrose ❀ Poppies ❀ Aster ❀ Verbasc... ...hant
Ears ❀ Sa... ...Day Lily ❀ Tulip ❀ Ivy ❀ Geranium ❀ ... ❀ Vinca

Our new software products will help make your landscaping chores a simple pleasure.

❀ Hollyhocks ❀ Liatris ❀
Iris ❀ Kiss Gazania ❀
❀ Lily of the Valley ❀
Carnation ❀ Peony ❀ Daisy ❀
❀ Verbascum ❀ Columbine ❀
Fern ❀ Verbena ❀ Day Lily ❀
Cornflower ❀ Lupine ❀ Vinca ❀
Wisteria ❀ Hosta ❀ Rose ❀
Kniphofia ❀ Butterfly Bush ❀
Foxglove ❀ Campanula ❀
❀ Primrose ❀ Poppies ❀
Columbine ❀ Elephant Ears ❀
Day Lily ❀ Tulip ❀ Ivy ❀
Lupine ❀ Vinca ❀ Hollyhocks ❀
Hosta ❀ Rose ❀ Iris ❀ Kiss
Butterfly Bush ❀ Lily-of-the-
Campanula ❀ Carnation ❀
❀ Poppies ❀ Aster ❀
Elephant Ears ❀ Sage ❀ Fern
Tulip ❀ Ivy ❀ Geranium ❀
Vinca ❀ Hollyhocks ❀ Liatris
❀ Iris ❀ Kiss Gazania ❀
❀ Lily of the Valley ❀

Landscape Helper & Garden Administrator

Come in for a

Free

Demonstration of these new products.
Or
Contact us to have a free demo disk sent to your home.

32 Braddock Road, Cincinnati OH 45219
Phone: 513-555-5555
E-mail: ecs@network.com

Wisteria ❀ Hosta ❀ Rose ❀
Kniphofia ❀ Butterfly Bush
Foxglove ❀ Campanula ❀
Primrose ❀ Poppies ❀ Aster ❀
Elephant Ears ❀ Sage ❀
Tulip ❀ Ivy ❀ Geranium ❀
❀ Hollyhocks ❀ Liatris ❀
Iris ❀ Kiss Gazania ❀
Lily of the Valley ❀
Carnation ❀ Peony ❀ Daisy ❀
Aster ❀ Verbascum ❀
Sage ❀ Fern ❀ Verbena ❀
Geranium ❀ Cornflower ❀
❀ Liatris ❀ Wisteria ❀
Gazania ❀ Kniphofia ❀
Valley ❀ Foxglove ❀
Peony ❀ Daisy ❀ Primrose ❀
Verbascum ❀ Columbine ❀
❀ Verbena ❀ Day Lily ❀
Cornflower ❀ Lupine ❀
❀ Wisteria ❀ Hosta ❀ Rose ❀
Kniphofia ❀ Butterfly Bush
Foxglove ❀ Campanula ❀

Carnation ❀ Peony ❀ Daisy ❀ Primrose ❀ Poppies ❀ Aster ❀ Verbascum ❀ Columbine ❀ Elephant Ears ❀ Sage ❀ Fern ❀ Verbena ❀ Day Lily ❀ Tulip ❀ Ivy ❀ Geranium ❀ Cornflower ❀ Lupine ❀ Vinca ❀ Hollyhocks ❀ Liatris ❀ Wisteria ❀ Hosta ❀ Rose ❀ Iris ❀ Kiss Gazania ❀ Kniphofia ❀ Butterfly Bush

Figure 4.16: Flyer 1

Flyer 2

1. Open a new blank document.

2. Use the default margins.

3. Create the flyer shown in Figure 4.17, using three predesigned text boxes and one drawn text box (for company locations).

   a. Use the **Tiles Sidebar** style predesigned text box for the Welcome information.

   b. Use the **Annual Sidebar** style predesigned text box for the information about the conference center. Set line spacing to **single** and paragraph spacing to **0** before and after. Use the default font. Bold the text where shown. *Note that the second and subsequent sentences of each paragraph are automatically formatted as indented from the left margin. This is called a "hanging indent," which you will learn to create in a later lesson.*

   c. Use the **Mod Quote** text box for the contact information.

   d. Draw a text box below the **Mod Quote** (circle), and add the locations.

4. Align the text as shown. Make any adjustments necessary to better present the information.

5. Size the circle to **2.94"** high by **2.94"** wide and position it where shown.

6. Change the fill and outline colors, if you want.

7. Use any desired symbol between "New York" and "Los Angeles" in the bottom-right text box.

8. Print one copy.

9. Save the file, and name it **4r1-conference flyer**.

10. Close the file.

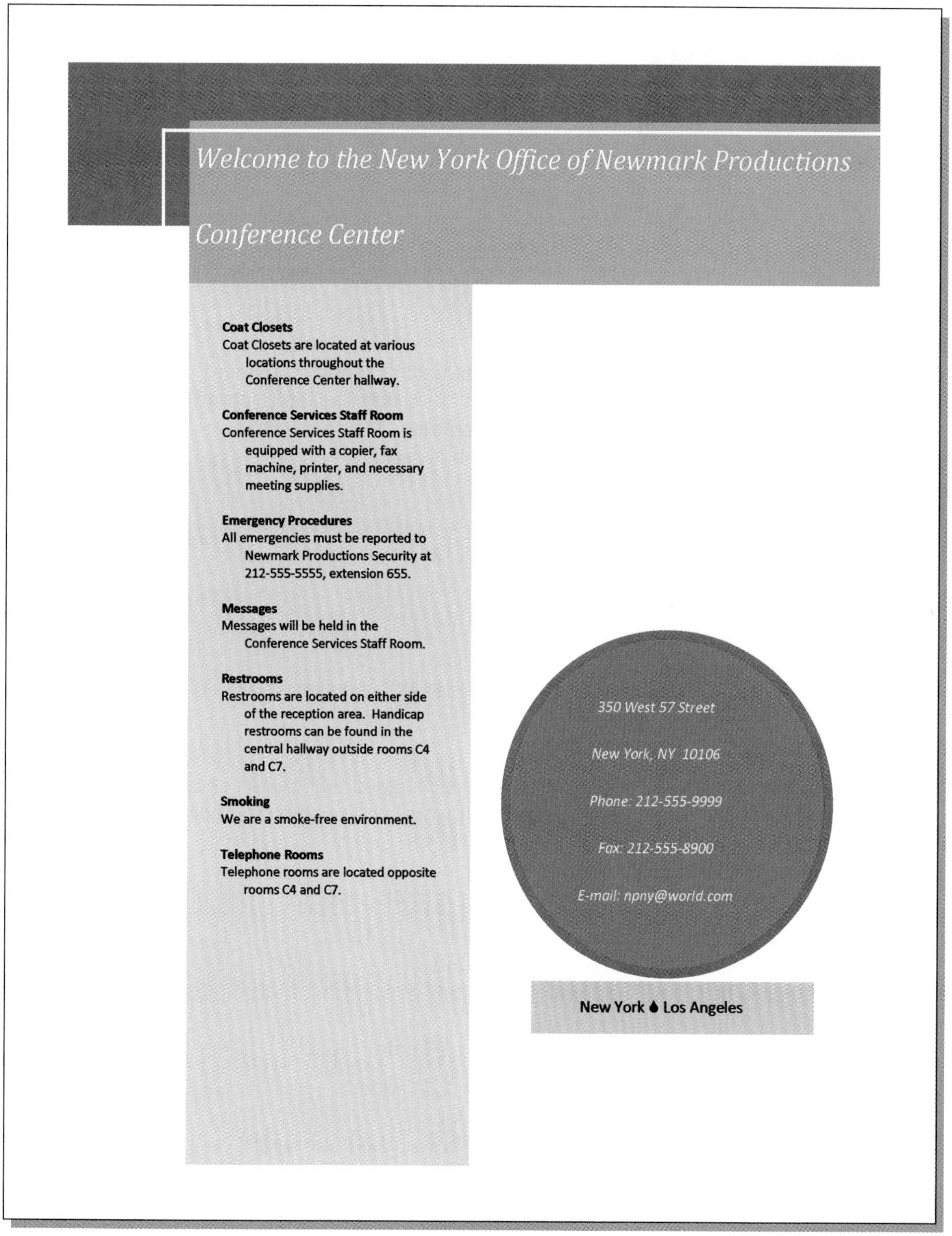

Welcome to the New York Office of Newmark Productions

Conference Center

Coat Closets
Coat Closets are located at various locations throughout the Conference Center hallway.

Conference Services Staff Room
Conference Services Staff Room is equipped with a copier, fax machine, printer, and necessary meeting supplies.

Emergency Procedures
All emergencies must be reported to Newmark Productions Security at 212-555-5555, extension 655.

Messages
Messages will be held in the Conference Services Staff Room.

Restrooms
Restrooms are located on either side of the reception area. Handicap restrooms can be found in the central hallway outside rooms C4 and C7.

Smoking
We are a smoke-free environment.

Telephone Rooms
Telephone rooms are located opposite rooms C4 and C7.

350 West 57 Street

New York, NY 10106

Phone: 212-555-9999

Fax: 212-555-8900

E-mail: npny@world.com

New York ♦ Los Angeles

Figure 4.17: Flyer 2

PERFORMANCE

TASK 1

BodyWorksFitnessCenters is committed to preserving the health and well being of the employees of local area businesses. As part of that commitment, BodyWorks is instituting a new fitness program. You have been asked to create a flyer to announce a special offer for corporate members. The flyer will be posted in all area fitness centers and sent to local businesses.

Follow these guidelines:

1. Open the data file **w4p1-fitness**.

2. Create the flyer shown in Figure 4.18.

3. Set a **4"** left margin.

4. Set line spacing to **double**.

5. Set the title to **14 point**.

6. Use the default font. Justify the text.

7. For the Corporate Fitness Sale seal, insert a predesigned text box as shown, and size it to **4.31"** high by **4.31"** wide. Apply a **Tight** text wrap, and position the box so that it overlays the text.
   a. Apply any color fill (or style) and any outline color and style you want.
   b. Replace the sample text as shown, and set it to **48-point** italic. Use any font face you want.

8. Draw a text box and size it to **1"** high by **1"** wide.
   a. Apply any text box fill, style, or color you want.
   b. Apply a **Square** text wrap, and position the box at the top left of the first paragraph as shown.
   c. Enter the text shown using any font color in **16 point**.

9. Draw another text box and size it to **1"** high by **1.1"** wide.
   a. Apply any text box fill, style, or color you want.
   b. Apply a **Square** text wrap, and position the box at the bottom right of the last paragraph as shown.
   c. Enter the text shown using any font color. Set "Call," "Today," and the phone number to **10 point**.

10. Print one copy.

11. Save the file, and name it **4p1-fitness flyer**.

12. Close the file.

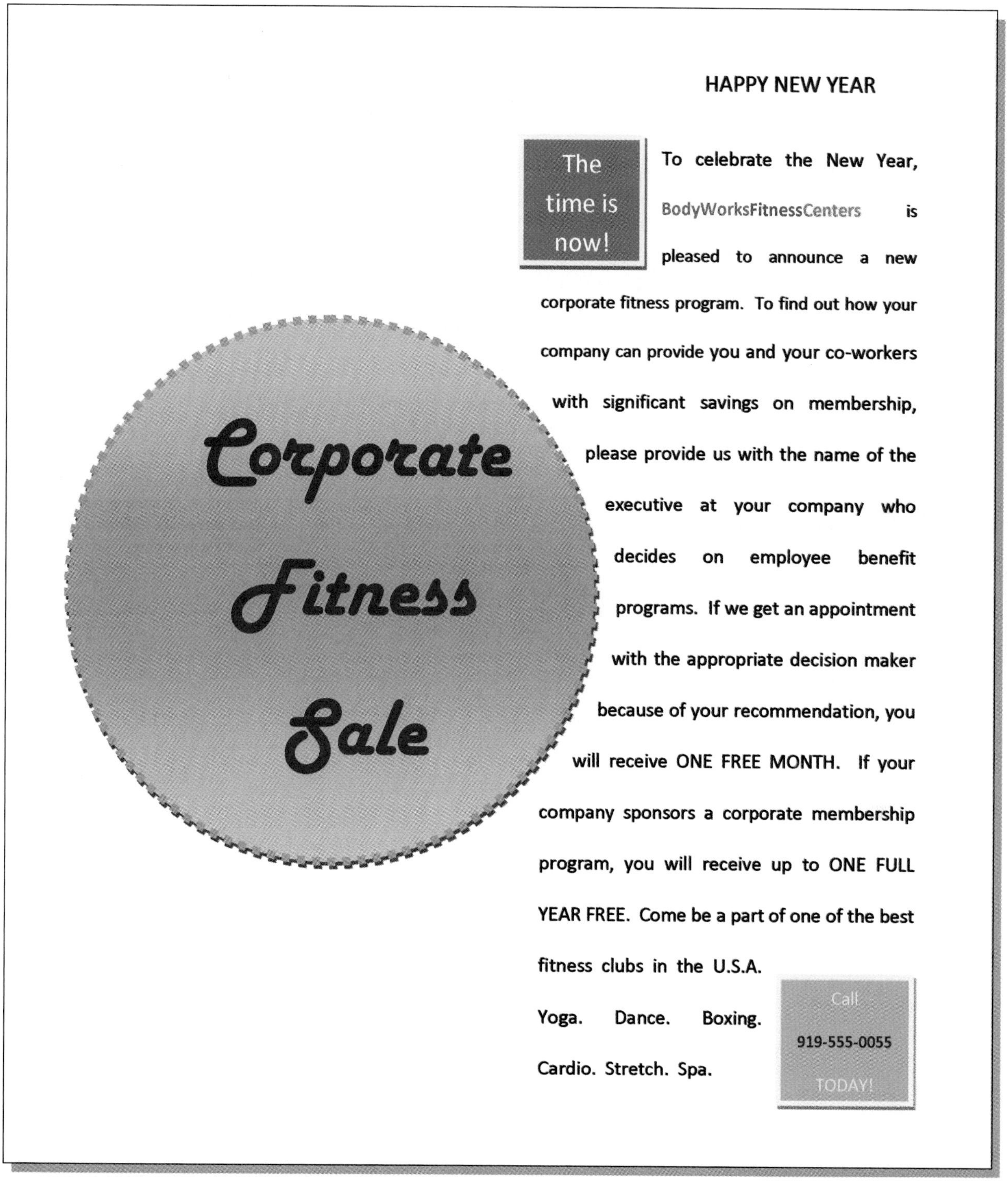

HAPPY NEW YEAR

The time is now!

To celebrate the New Year, BodyWorksFitnessCenters is pleased to announce a new corporate fitness program. To find out how your company can provide you and your co-workers with significant savings on membership, please provide us with the name of the executive at your company who decides on employee benefit programs. If we get an appointment with the appropriate decision maker because of your recommendation, you will receive ONE FREE MONTH. If your company sponsors a corporate membership program, you will receive up to ONE FULL YEAR FREE. Come be a part of one of the best fitness clubs in the U.S.A.

Yoga. Dance. Boxing. Cardio. Stretch. Spa.

Corporate Fitness Sale

Call
919-555-0055
TODAY!

Figure 4.18: Fitness flyer

Draw a Text Box

1. Click the **Insert tab**, and in the **Text group**, click the **Text Box button**.
2. Click **Draw Text** box, then drag the mouse to the required box size. Enter text in the box.
   Or
1. Click a built-in, predesigned text box from the gallery that appears.
2. Select the sample text, and enter new text to replace it.
3. Click outside the text box to deactivate it (and inside the box to activate it).

Size a Text Box

1. Click to select the box.
2. Click the **Format tab**, and in the **Size group**, enter an amount in the Shape Height and Shape Width boxes.
   Or
1. Drag a corner handle to size the object proportionally, or drag a middle handle to size the height or width, or drag the object to the appropriate position on the page.

Format a Text Box

1. Click to select the box, then proceed with steps in each of the categories below.

Outline Color, Weight, and Style

1. Click the **Format tab**, and in the **Text Box Styles group**, click the **Shape Outline button**.
2. Select a line color, point to **Weight**, and select a line weight, and/or point to **Dashes**, and select a line style.

Text Box Style

1. Click the **Format tab**, and in the **Text Box Styles group**, click the **More arrow** to display the Text Box Styles gallery.
2. Select a style.

Fill

1. Click the **Format tab**, and in the **Text Box Styles group**, click the **Shape Fill button**.
2. Select a color or color effect.

Shadow/3-D Effect

1. Click the **Format tab**, and in the **Shadow Effects group**, click the **Shadow Effects button** to display the Shadow Effects gallery.
   Or
1. Click the **Format tab**, and in the **3-D Effects group**, click the **3-D Effects button** to display the 3-D Effects gallery.
2. Click the shadow effect or the 3-D effect desired.

Wrap Text

1. Click to select the box.
2. Click the **Format tab**, and in the **Arrange group**, click the **Text Wrapping button**.
3. Select a wrapping style.

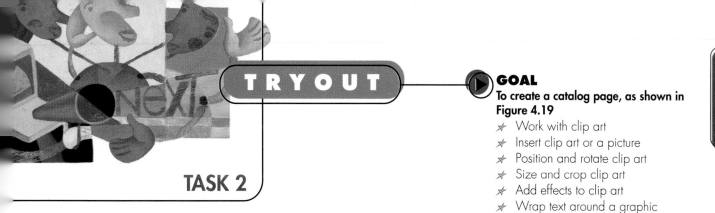

GOAL
To create a catalog page, as shown in Figure 4.19

✴ Work with clip art
✴ Insert clip art or a picture
✴ Position and rotate clip art
✴ Size and crop clip art
✴ Add effects to clip art
✴ Wrap text around a graphic

TASK 2

WORD

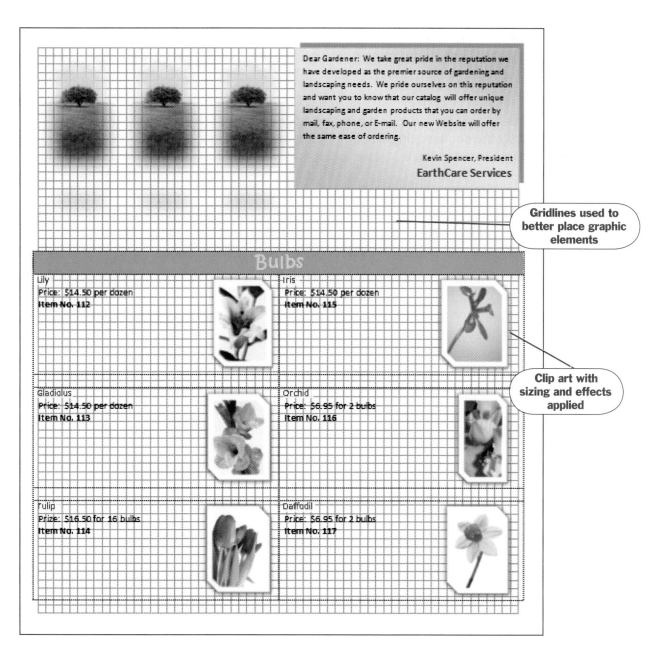

Gridlines used to better place graphic elements

Clip art with sizing and effects applied

Figure 4.19: Catalog page

WHAT YOU NEED TO KNOW

Work with Clip Art

▶ To enhance the visual aspects of your document, you can insert graphic elements that include clip art, pictures, charts, diagrams, shapes, and drawn lines.

▶ **Clip art** includes various media types such as drawn images, photographs, movies, and sounds that are available in Word. Pictures are images that you download from a digital camera or the Internet and save on your computer.

▶ Graphic images come in different file formats and carry a filename extension that identifies the image type. For example, you might see .bmp as a filename extension, which indicates that the image is a Windows bitmap, a format that almost all Windows applications recognize and use for photographs and illustrations. Other common image formats include .gif, .jpg, .wmp, and .tif.

▶ Most Web browsers support .gif and .jpg file formats, so these image types are popular for use on Web pages.

▶ This task will focus on working with clip art and photographs that can be accessed through Word. You can apply the same editing features that relate to clip art to pictures that you have downloaded to your computer.

Insert Clip Art or a Picture

▶ When you insert clip art or a picture, it appears in your document at the insertion point location. The image initially displays with sizing handles and a rotation handle, and the Ribbon displays Picture Tools to help you work with your image, as shown in Figure 4.20.

▶ When you are inserting clip art, the Clip Art task pane also appears to allow you to search for the type of clip art that you want.

▶ You can edit an image (size, trim, add an effect, position, copy, or delete), which you will learn to do later in this lesson.

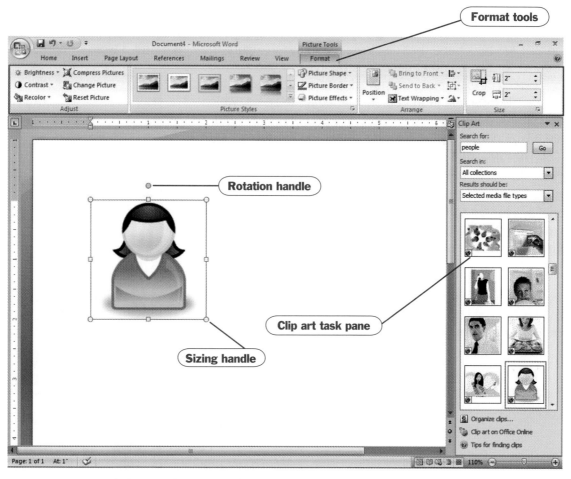

Figure 4.20: Inserted clip art with Picture Tools displayed

HOW To insert a picture, **1.** click in the document where you want to insert the image. **2.** Click the **Insert tab**, and in the **Illustrations group**, **3.** click the **Picture button**, as shown in Figure 4.21. Then, **4.** navigate to the folder that contains the picture you want, and **5.** click **Insert** to insert it.

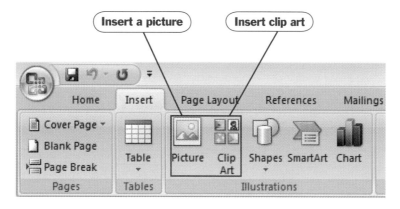

Figure 4.21: Illustrations group on the Insert tab

To insert clip art, **1.** click in the document where you want to insert the image, **2.** click the **Insert tab**, and in the **Illustrations group**, **3.** click the **Clip Art button** (see Figure 4.21). **4.** In the Clip Art task pane that displays, as shown in Figure 4.22, **5.** enter a word or phrase in the Search for text box that describes the type of clip art you want to insert. (For example, you may wish to search using the word *people*.) The default is to search All media file types, which includes clip art, photographs, movies, and sounds. To search for one media type only, click the **Results should be list arrow**, and select the type you want or deselect the type you do not want. Then, **6.** click **Go**. **7.** Click the image on the task pane to insert it.

If Word does not have the images you want, you can find additional images on the Web. Click the **Clip art on Office Online link** in the Clip Art task pane to display the Microsoft Office Online home page in your Web browser.

Figure 4.22: Clip Art task pane

1. Open a new blank document.

2. Click the **Insert tab**, and in the **Illustrations group**, click the **Clip Art button**.

3. In the Clip Art task pane that appears, click the **Results should be list arrow**, and select **Clip Art** and **Photographs** (deselect other choices, if necessary). Click the **Search in list arrow**, and select **Everywhere**.

4. Enter **people** in the Search for text box, and click **Go**.

5. Click an image to insert it into your document. Notice that square sizing handles and the Picture Tools Format tab appear. *If you get a message that the image is only available on the CD-ROM, select another image.*

6. Do not close the file. You will continue to work with this file as you complete the next Try it Out activity.

Position and Rotate Clip Art

▶ Word inserts an image at the insertion point location and automatically applies an *Inline with text* wrapping style, which positions the image so that it becomes part of the paragraph. You can horizontally align an inline graphic by using alignment buttons found on the Home tab or on the Mini toolbar.

▶ To position an image at a specific location in a document, you must change its wrapping style. By default, the image is aligned relative to the margin. You can, however, align the graphic relative to the edge of the paper.

▶ To fine-tune the placement of images on the page, it is recommended that you work with the gridlines displayed.

HOW 1. Select the image, if it is not already selected. 2. Click the **Picture Tools Format tab**, if necessary, and in the **Arrange group**, 3. click the **Text Wrapping button**, and select either **Square** or **Tight** as the wrapping style. 4. Drag the image to the desired location on the page, or click the **Align button**, and choose an alignment option, as shown in Figure 4.23. *You can also display gridlines from this menu and choose whether you want the graphic to align relative to the edge of the paper or to the margin.*

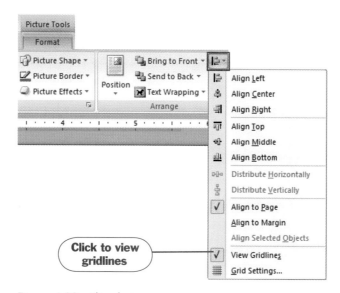

Figure 4.23: Align button menu

To rotate an image, click and drag the green rotation handle left or right to the appropriate angle. To set the rotation by a specific amount, **1.** click the **Format tab**, if necessary, and **2.** click the **dialog box launcher** in the **Size group. 3.** In the Size dialog box, enter a rotation measurement, as shown in Figure 4.24.

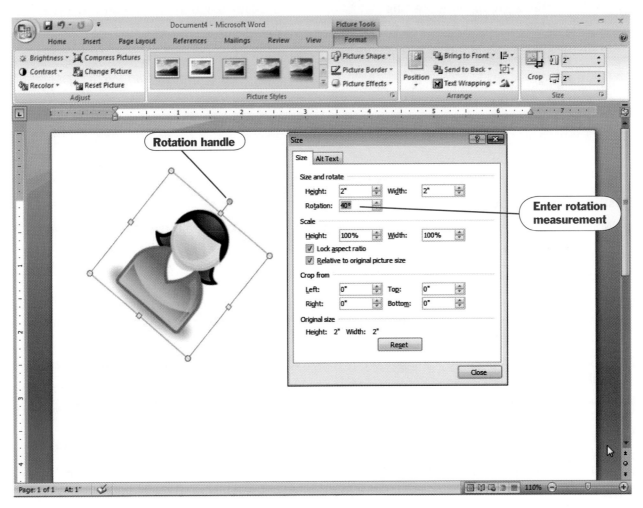

Figure 4.24: Size dialog box

TRY *it* OUT *w4-6*

Note: The image from Try it Out 4-5 should be displayed on your screen. If it is not, complete Try it Out w4-5 before completing this one.

1. Select the image, if necessary.

2. Click the **Format tab**, if necessary, and in the **Arrange group**, click the **Text Wrapping button**, and select **Square**. *You have created a floating image and now can easily move it.*

3. Drag the image to the middle of the page.

4. Click to select the image again, if necessary.

5. Click the **Format tab**, if necessary, and in the **Arrange group**, click the **Align button**. *Notice that the graphic is aligned relative to the margin.*

6. Click **View Gridlines**.

7. Click the **Align button** again, and click **Align Right**. Notice that the graphic is aligned to the right margin.

8. Click the **Align button** again, and click **Align to Page**. When you next select an alignment option, the graphic will be aligned to the page.

9. Click the **Align button** again, and click **Align Left**. Notice that the graphic is aligned to the edge of the page.

10. Select the image, if necessary. Drag the rotation handle, and turn the image upside down.

11. Deselect **View Gridlines**.

12. Close the file, and do not save the changes.

Size and Crop Clip Art

▶ You can change the size of a clip art image or crop it, which allows you to trim parts of the image to eliminate those you do not want.

HOW To change the size of an image, **1.** select the image, and **2.** drag a corner handle to size the image proportionally, or drag a middle handle to size its height or width.

To size an image by a specific measurement, **1.** select the image. **2.** Click the **Picture Tools Format tab**, and in the **Size group**, enter a measurement in the Shape Width and Shape Height boxes, as shown in Figure 4.25.

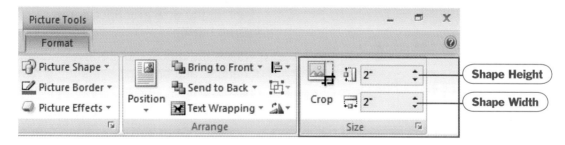

Figure 4.25: Size group tools on the Format tab

To crop an image, **1.** select the image. Click the **Picture Tools Format tab**, and in the **Size group**, **2.** click the **Crop button** (see Figure 4.25), which changes the mouse pointer to a cropping tool. **3.** Place the cropping mouse pointer over a cropping handle, as shown in Figure 4.26, and drag the sides, top, or bottom of the picture to crop off the parts you do not want. **4.** Click the **Crop button** again to turn off cropping.

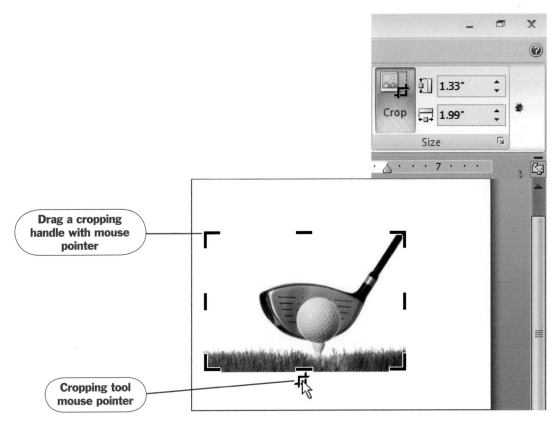

Drag a cropping handle with mouse pointer

Cropping tool mouse pointer

Figure 4.26: Cropping an image

TRY*it***OUT** *w4-7*

1. Open a new blank document.

2. Click the **Insert tab**, and in the **Illustrations group**, click the **Clip Art button**.

3. Click the **Results should be list arrow**, and select Photographs.

4. Click the **Search in list arrow**, and select **Everywhere**.

5. Enter golf ball in the Search for text box, and click **Go**.

6. Click to insert an image containing a golf ball.

7. Position the mouse pointer on a corner handle of the selected image until it changes to a two-headed arrow.
   a. Drag the handle diagonally to create a medium-sized image.
   b. Select the picture, if necessary.

8. Click the **Format tab**, and in the **Size group**, enter 2" in the **Shape Height** box and 2" in the **Shape Width** box.

9. Select the image, if necessary. Click the **Format tab**, if necessary, and in the **Size group**, click the **Crop button**.

10. Place the mouse pointer over a cropping handle, and drag the sides top or bottom of the picture to crop out most of the image except the golf ball.

11. Click the **Crop button** again to turn off cropping.

12. Close the file, and do not save the changes.

Add Effects to Clip Art

▶ After you insert an image, you can modify it by adding special effects. You can adjust the image's brightness and contrast, change its border, and/or apply an effect or style.

▶ Picture styles offer you a combination of different picture borders, orientations, and effects. You can see a live preview of many of Word's effects before you actually apply them.

HOW To adjust the brightness or contrast, **1.** select the image. **2.** Click the **Format tab**, if necessary, and in the **Adjust group**, **3.** click the **Brightness button** or the **Contrast button**, as shown in Figure 4.27. In the Brightness gallery or the Contrast gallery that appears when you click the related button, **4.** point to each option to preview its effect, then **5.** click to select an effect.

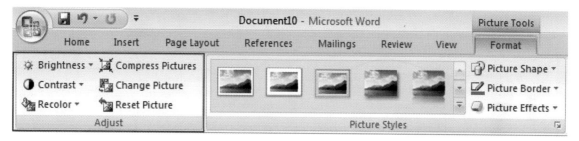

Figure 4.27: Adjust group on the Format tab

To apply a border effect, **1.** select the image. **2.** Click the **Format tab**, if necessary, and in the **Picture Styles group**, **3.** click the **Picture Border button**. **4.** Move your mouse through the gallery, as shown in Figure 4.28, to see the effects of different borders, weights, or border styles (dashes). **5.** Select an effect or effects.

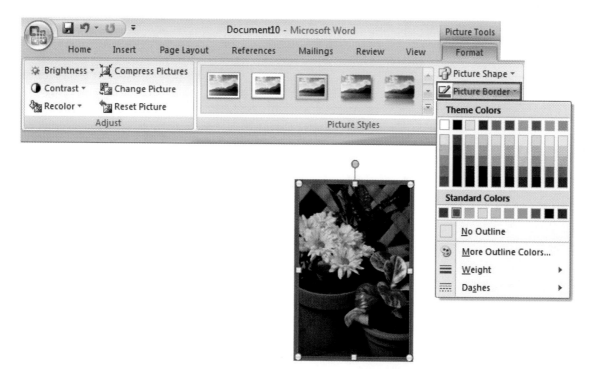

Figure 4.28: Picture Border gallery

To apply a special effect, **1.** select the image. **2.** Click the **Format tab**, if necessary, and in the **Picture Styles group**, **3.** click the **Picture Effects button**. **4.** Highlight an effect option, and **5.** move your mouse through the effect gallery, as shown in Figure 4.29, to see the different effects for that option. Then, **6.** select an effect or effects.

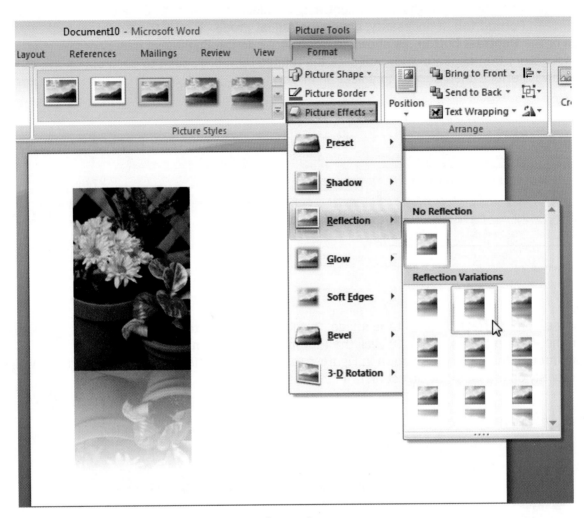

Figure 4.29: Picture Effects options and Picture Effects gallery

To apply a style, **1.** select the image. **2.** Click the **Format tab**, if necessary, and in the **Picture Styles group**, **3.** click the **More arrow** to display the styles gallery, as shown in Figure 4.30. **4.** Move your mouse through the gallery to see the effects. Then, **5.** select an effect.

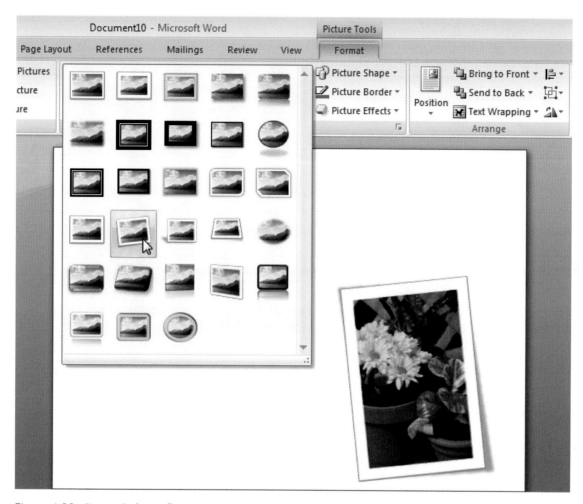

Figure 4.30: Picture Styles gallery

T R Y *i t* **O U T** *w4-8*

1. Open a new blank document.

2. Click the **Insert tab**, and in the **Illustrations group**, click the **Clip Art button**.

3. Click the **Results should be list arrow** and, if necessary, select **Photographs**.

4. Click the **Search in list arrow** and, if necessary, select **Everywhere**.

5. Enter `people` in the **Search for text box**, and click **Go**.

6. Select any picture you want.

7. Click the **Format tab**, if necessary, and in the **Picture Styles group**, click the **Picture Border button**.

   a. Select a **red** color; highlight **Weight**, and select **4½ point**; highlight **Dashes**, and select **Round Dot**.

   b. Click the **Picture Border button** again, and click **No Outline** to remove all border effects.

8. Click the **Picture Effects button**.

Continued on next page

a. Highlight **Shadow**, and move your mouse through the different shadow effects. Select a shadow effect.

b. For each effect, highlight the option, and move your mouse through the different effects, then select one.

9. Click the **More arrow** to display the Picture Styles gallery. Move your mouse through the different styles, then select one.

10. Close the file, and do not save the changes.

Wrap Text around Graphics

▶ Earlier in Task 2, you learned to apply a Square or Tight text wrap option to a graphic in order to create a floating image that you could position anywhere on the page. You can wrap text around images using the same techniques you used for creating a floating image and for wrapping text around text boxes.

▶ After applying a text wrap option, you may need to adjust the position of the graphic to avoid awkward line breaks in the text.

 1. Select the graphic. **2.** Click the **Format tab**, and in the **Arrange group**, click the **Text Wrapping button**. **3.** Click to select a text-wrapping option from the menu that appears.

You can also **1.** select the graphic, **2.** right-click the mouse, **3.** highlight **Text Wrapping**, and **4.** click a text-wrapping option.

1. Open the data file **w4-9**.

2. Click the **Insert tab**, and in the **Illustrations group**, click the **Clip Art button**.

3. In the Clip art task pane that appears, enter **flower** in the Search for text box, and click **Go**. Select a flower to insert into the document.

4. In the **Size group**, enter **1.25"** in the Shape Width box and **1.25"** in the Shape Height box.

5. Select the graphic. Then, click the **Format tab**, if

necessary, and in the **Arrange group**, click the **Text Wrapping button**. Select the **Tight** wrapping style.

6. Drag the image to the middle of the text.

7. Select the graphic again, if necessary. Click the **Text Wrapping button** again, and select another wrapping option.

8. Close the file, and do not save the changes.

REHEARSAL

GOAL
To create a catalog page, as shown in Figure 4.31

TASK 2

WHAT YOU NEED TO KNOW

▶ A **catalog** is a booklet that includes product photos, product sheet captions, prices, and an order form. A catalog is often sent to homes and businesses and is considered a direct-mail sales tool.

▶ Catalogs use a lot of color, which tends to increase their selling power. The inside page of a catalog usually describes the company. Sometimes there is a letter from the president explaining the company's philosophy of doing business.

▼ DIRECTIONS

1. Create a new blank document.

2. Use the following settings:

Margins	.5" left, right, top and bottom
Line Spacing	default
Paragraph Spacing	
Before	0
After	0
Font	default

3. Click the **View tab**, and in the **Show/Hide group**, select **Gridlines** to display them.

4. Draw a text box that measures **2.1" high** by **3.5" wide**, as shown in the catalog page in Figure 4.31 on page 232.
   a. Enter the "Dear Gardener" text shown using the default font and size. For "EarthCare Services," apply a purple font color and set the text to **14 point**.
   b. Apply any text box style that uses a green fill.
   c. Add a shadow effect.
   d. Move the text box to the top right of the grid.

5. Insert a relevant clip art photograph.
   a. Size it to approximately **2" high** by **1.3" wide**.
   b. Click the **Picture Effects button**, and apply **Soft Edges, 25% Point effect**.
   c. Copy the picture, and paste it two times, as shown in Figure 4.31.

6. Begin the table at approximately **3.5"**, as noted by the At indicator on the Status bar.

7. Create the table using two columns and seven rows.
   a. Merge Row 1, and center the word **Bulbs** in a sans serif **18-point** font. Fill the row with a **green** color.
   b. Set the row height for rows 2, 4, and 6 to **1.5"**.

Continued on next page

   c. Enter the text as shown. Apply a **red** color to the bulb names.

   d. Apply a **dotted** border to the table, as shown.

8. Insert the flower photograph in each column and row as follows:

   a. Position the insertion point in the row and column where you will insert the photograph.

   b. Click the **Insert tab**, and in the **Illustrations group**, click the **Clip Art button**. Search for each flower type (Lily, Tulip, and so forth), and select **Photographs** as the media type. If the flower types are unavailable to you, open the data file **w4r2**, copy each picture from the Word document, then paste each into the document.

   c. Click to insert the photo. Size each photograph to approximately **1.2"** high by **1"** wide. (Some photos may require a different width to keep the photo in proportion and some may need cropping. Crop where you feel it is necessary, and adjust the width appropriately.)

   d. Apply a **Square** text wrap, and move the photograph to the right edge of the row. Use the gridlines to help you guide the placement of the photographs so that they are aligned.

   e. Apply the **Snip Diagonal Corner, White picture style** to each flower photograph.

9. Preview the document.

10. Print one copy.

11. Save the file, and name it **4r2-bulbs page**.

12. Close the file.

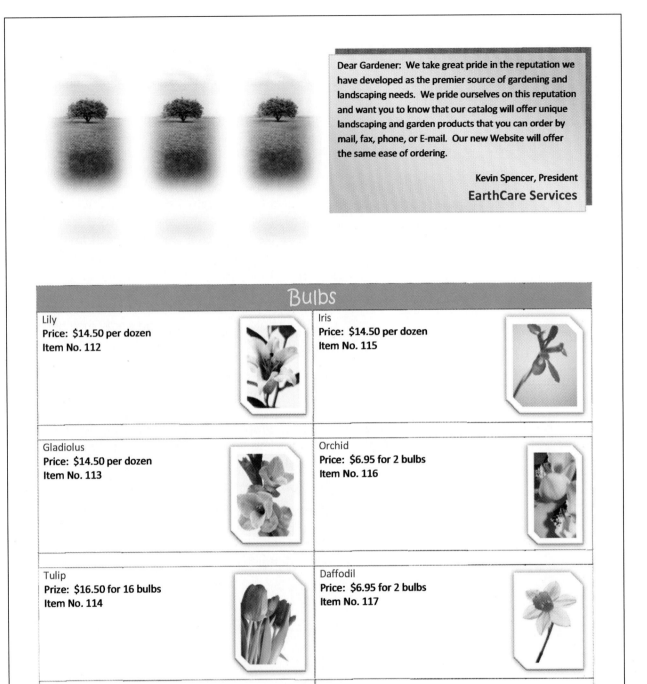

Dear Gardener: We take great pride in the reputation we have developed as the premier source of gardening and landscaping needs. We pride ourselves on this reputation and want you to know that our catalog will offer unique landscaping and garden products that you can order by mail, fax, phone, or E-mail. Our new Website will offer the same ease of ordering.

Kevin Spencer, President
EarthCare Services

Bulbs

Lily
Price: $14.50 per dozen
Item No. 112

Iris
Price: $14.50 per dozen
Item No. 115

Gladiolus
Price: $14.50 per dozen
Item No. 113

Orchid
Price: $6.95 for 2 bulbs
Item No. 116

Tulip
Prize: $16.50 for 16 bulbs
Item No. 114

Daffodil
Price: $6.95 for 2 bulbs
Item No. 117

Figure 4.31: Bulbs catalog page

PERFORMANCE

TASK 2

EarthCare Services has expanded its product line to include decorative garden pots and containers. You have been asked to create a special catalog page that features these items. Lara Morales, director of marketing and sales, will provide you with three photographs of products that will be featured in this catalog page. The remaining photographs that you need can be found in Word's clip art collection. Ms. Morales will also provide you with introductory text for this new line of products. The catalog page that you are to create, including the introductory text and photographs, is shown in Figure 4.32. The layout shown in the figure is merely a guide.

Follow these guidelines:

1. Open a new document. Use any page layout that you feel will feature the products most effectively. *The layout shown was created using a one column table; all table borders were removed.*

2. Copy the introductory text provided in the data file **w4p2-introductory text** into your document. You might wish to include the text in a text box or wrap the text around a graphic, as shown. Size and color the text as you wish.

3. Enter the product description, prices, order numbers, and types, as shown in Figure 4.32.

4. Locate the photograph you used in the Rehearsal task, and use it to represent EarthCare Services. Insert the photo into the document, and include it in your page design. Size the graphic, and rotate it if you wish.

5. Insert the four photographs, and position them attractively on the page.
   a. Insert three of the photographs from data file **w4p2-garden photos**.
   b. Insert the photograph of the two terra-cotta pots from Word's clip art collection. Enter **flower pot** in the Search for text box, and you will find the picture in the task pane. *If this photo does not appear in the clip art collection installed on your computer, or if you cannot access it, you can copy the picture from the data file **w4p2-garden photos**.*
   c. Size the photographs as you wish as long as the document is no more than one page.
   d. The photograph of the Spanish beige pot requires that you crop the bottom of it.
   e. Apply any border or special effects to the photographs.

6. Save the file, and name it **4p2-garden pots page**.

7. Print one copy.

8. Close all files.

EarthCare Services is introducing garden pots from around the world, made of ceramics, glass, china, and terra-cotta—for all your indoor or outdoor planting needs.

With no weeding or strenuous digging to do, it is no wonder that container gardening is riding the crest of a wave.

There is also an ever-increasing range of tempting plants to fill your pots, so why not be a bit adventurous and devise your own unique recipe? In the summer, it is breathtaking to look at pots that include tender annuals that are in a blended-color scheme. Focus your palette on pink, blue, and purple, for example, to create a splendid effect. Choose a really big pot (about 16" in diameter) and pack in the plants for an excellent show.

Keep these planting tips in mind: 1. Buy young annuals.

2. Add a water-retaining gel to the potting medium to reduce the pot's watering requirements. 3. Choose a warm sunny spot for your planter.

Container gardening is great for use on balconies, patios, or anywhere in the garden.

Spanish Beige	
	Thick-walled planter, decorated with vines below the top rim. Sophisticated design. *21" diameter x 21" H.* *Price: $225.00* *Order #CE 28* *Type: Ceramic*

Spanish Beige

Thick-walled planter, decorated with vines below the top rim. Sophisticated design.
21" diameter x 21" H.
Price: $225.00
Order #CE 28
Type: Ceramic

Sleek Ceramic

Blue ceramic planter with glossy finish.
11" diameter.
Price: $133.00
Order # CE93
Type: Ceramic

Terra-Cotta Clay

Classic terra-cotta. Porous material allows roots to breathe and moss to grow.
9" – 11" diameters
Price: $15.00-- $60.00
Order # TA63
Type: Terra-cotta

Figure 4.32: Garden pots catalog page

Insert a Picture or Clip Art

1. Click the **Insert tab**, and in the **Illustrations group**, click the **Picture button**.

   a. Navigate to the folder containing the picture file.

   b. Select the file, and click **Insert**.

   Or

1. Click the **Insert tab**, and in the **Illustrations group**, click the **Clip Art button**.

2. Enter a word or phrase in the Search for text box to describe the clip art you want to insert.

3. Click **Go**.

Position a Graphic

1. Select the graphic.

2. On the **Format tab** and in the **Arrange group**, click the **Text Wrapping button**.

3. Select a **Square** or **Tight** wrap option.

4. Drag the graphic where you want it on the page.

Crop a Graphic

1. Select the graphic.

2. On the **Format tab**, and in the **Size group**, click the **Crop button**.

3. Place the cropping mouse pointer over a cropping handle, then drag the sides, top, or bottom of the picture to crop off the parts you do not want.

4. Click the **Crop button** again to turn off cropping.

Wrap Text around a Graphic

1. Select the graphic.

2. Click the **Format tab** and in the **Arrange group**, click the **Text Wrapping button**.

3. Select a text-wrapping option.

4. Position the graphic as desired.

Add Effects

1. Select the graphic.

2. Click the **Format tab**, and in the **Picture Styles group**, click the **Picture Border button** or the **Picture Effects button** or the **Picture Styles More arrow**, and select an effect or effects.

TRYOUT

GOAL
To create an advertisement, as shown in Figure 4.33
* Work with shapes, lines, WordArt, and SmartArt
* Group and layer objects

TASK 3

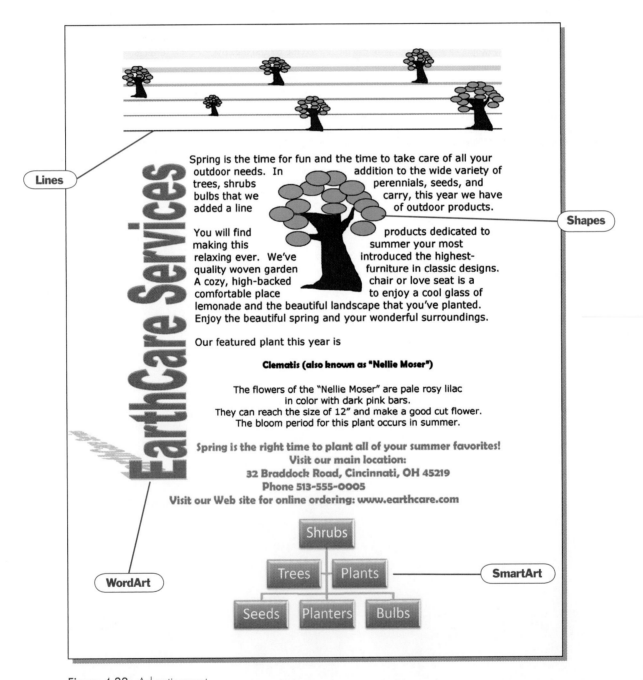

Figure 4.33: Advertisement

WHAT YOU NEED TO KNOW

Work with Shapes, Lines, WordArt, and SmartArt

▶ In addition to clip art, pictures, and text boxes, graphic elements also include shapes, lines, WordArt, and diagrams. Word classifies diagrams as SmartArt. You can use these graphic elements to create a document that is both professional and eye-catching.

▶ Shapes, lines, WordArt, and SmartArt behave the same way as other graphic elements. That is, you can size, position, and edit them (change fill and border lines, add special effects, and wrap text around, copy, delete, and move them) using the same techniques you used previously.

Shapes

▶ Shapes can be used to create interesting effects in your document. You can also insert text into a shape for flyers or advertisements or any other communication that requires attention-grabbing results.

▶ A drawn shape displays with sizing, adjustment, and rotation handles. Figure 4.34 shows a newly drawn shape (a circular arrow) and others that have been enhanced with borders, fills, and special effects. After you draw or select the shape, the Drawing Tools Format tab displays tools to help you customize the appearance of the shape.

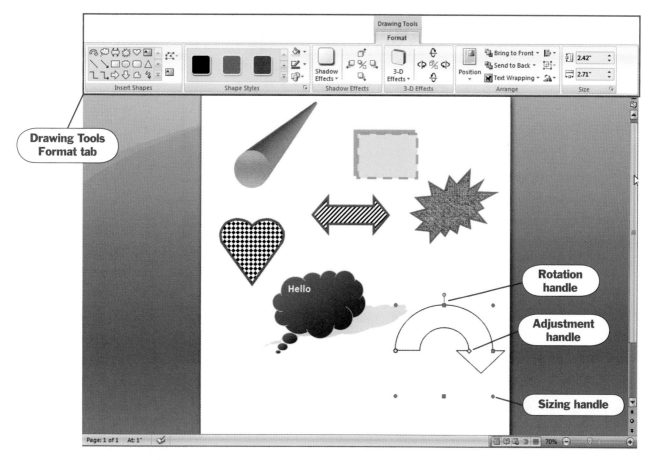

Figure 4.34: Shape samples and Drawing Tools Format tab

HOW To draw a shape, **1.** click in the document where you want to insert the shape. **2.** Click the **Insert tab**, and in the **Illustrations group**, click the **Shapes button** shown in Figure 4.35. **3.** Select a shape from the gallery that appears. **4.** Hold down the left mouse button, and drag diagonally to create the shape.

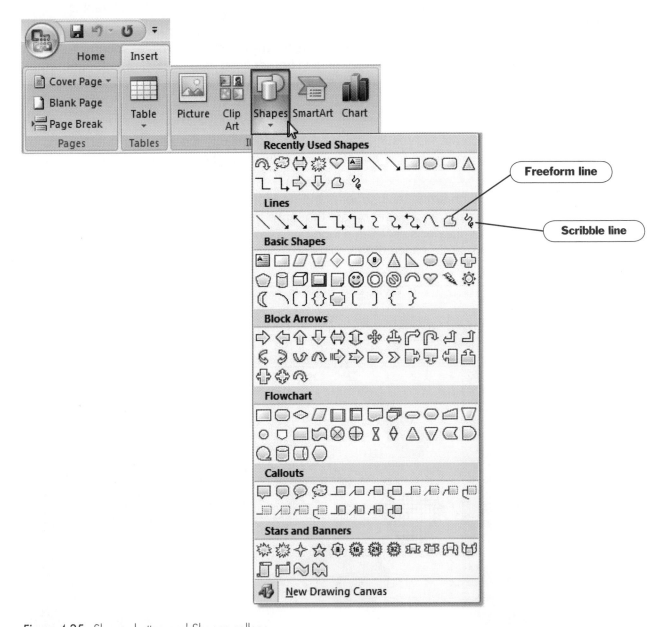

Figure 4.35: Shapes button and Shapes gallery

To adjust the shape, drag a **sizing handle** to change the size of the shape, the **adjustment handle** to reshape the drawing, or the **rotation handle** to rotate the shape (see Figure 4.34).

To change the size of a shape by a specific amount, enter an amount in the Shape Height and Shape Width boxes in the **Size group** on the **Drawing Tools Format tab**.

To draw a perfect circle or square, hold down **[Shift]** as you drag the mouse.

1. Open a new blank document.

2. Click the **Insert tab**, and in the **Illustrations group**, click the **Shapes button**.

3. Click the **Oval** shape in the **Basic Shapes group**.

4. Position the mouse pointer in a blank area of the page.

5. Hold down **[Shift]**, then click and hold down the mouse button as you drag the mouse (which becomes a crosshairs symbol) diagonally until you create a medium-sized circle. Release the mouse button.

6. Select the circle, and drag to move the circle to the upper-right corner of the page.
   a. On the **Drawing Tools Format tab**, click the **Shape Fill list arrow**, and select **yellow** from the palette.
   b. Click the **Shape Outline list, arrow** highlight **Weight**, then select **4½ point**.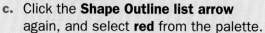
   c. Click the **Shape Outline list arrow** again, and select **red** from the palette.

7. Select the circle to display the **Drawing Tools Format tab**, if necessary. In the **Insert Shapes group**, click the **More arrow** to display the **Shapes group**.

8. Click the **Right Arrow** shape in the **Block Arrows group**.
   a. Position the mouse pointer in a blank area of the document, and click and

drag the mouse diagonally until you create an arrow.
   b. Click the **Shape Fill list arrow**, and select **red.**
   c. Click the **Shape Fill list arrow**, and click **Pattern**.
   d. Click any desired pattern, and click **OK**.

9. Select the **Right Arrow** shape. Position the mouse pointer on a sizing handle. When the pointer turns to a two-headed arrow, drag it to make the arrow longer. Select the shape again. Enter 1 in the Shape Height box and 1 in the Shape Width box.

10. Select the **Right Arrow** shape. Position the mouse pointer on the adjustment handle (the yellow diamond). When the mouse pointer turns to an arrowhead, drag it left and right to see the effect.

11. Drag the arrow so that it overlaps the circle.

12. Select one of the shapes. In the **Insert Shapes group**, click the **More arrow**.

13. Click the **Rectangle** shape, and draw a small rectangle in a blank area of the document.
   a. In the **3-D Effects group**, click the **3-D Effects button**, and select a 3-D effect.
   b. In the **Shadow Effects group**, click the **Shadow Effects button**, and select a shadow effect.

14. Close the file, and do not save the changes.

Lines

▶ You can create a variety of horizontal, vertical, and curved lines in a document using the line tools available on the Shapes gallery (see Figure 4.35). Figure 4.36 illustrates lines created with the line tools in Word.

▶ You can use the same techniques to change a line style, color, or line size as you did when you worked with shapes.

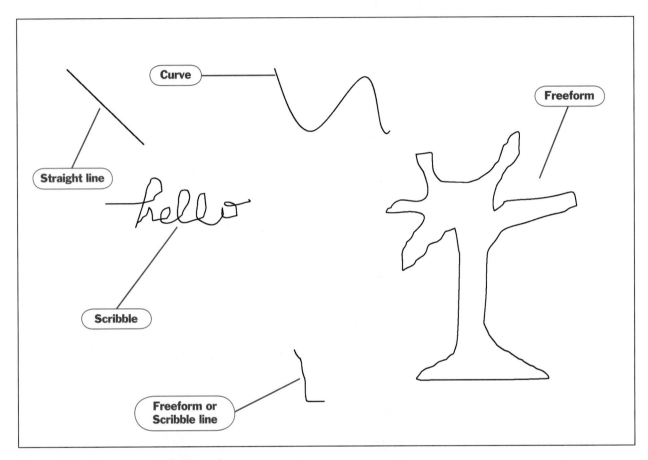

Figure 4.36: Lines created with line tools

HOW To draw a straight line (or line with arrowhead), **1.** click the **Insert tab**, and in the **Illustrations group**, **2.** click the **Shapes button**, then **3.** click a line shape in the Lines group. **4.** Drag the insertion point (which becomes a cross symbol) to the length you want. You can angle the line in any direction or adjust the size of the line when Word displays the handles.

To draw a Freeform or Scribble line, **1.** click the **Freeform** or **Scribble** line style in the **Lines group**. When you click to create the line, the crosshairs symbol becomes a pen. **2.** Use the mouse as a pen to draw the line, and **3.** double-click to end the line. *When drawing a curve, you must click each time you create an angle, then click again to close the shape.*

To apply line style and color options in one step, **1.** select the line, and **2.** click the **Shape Styles dialog box launcher**. In the Format AutoShape dialog box that appears, as shown in Figure 4.37, **3.** select the options that you want.

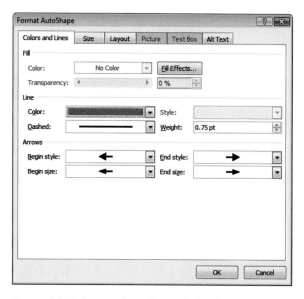

Figure 4.37: Format AutoShape dialog box

TRY *it* OUT *w4-11*

1. Open a new blank document.

2. Click the **Insert tab**, and in the **Illustrations group**, click the **Shapes button**.

3. Click a line shape, and drag to create a small, straight horizontal line. Before you release the mouse, be sure that the line is straight.

4. Select the line, if necessary. Click the **Format tab**, if necessary.

5. Enter **4** in the Shape Width box.

6. Copy the line, then paste it below the other.

7. Select the first line. Click the **Format tab**, if necessary.

8. Click the **Shape Outline list arrow**, highlight **Weight**, and select **2¼-point**.

9. Click the **Shape Outline list arrow** again, and select **green**.

10. Click to select the second line. Click the **Format tab**, if necessary.

11. Click the **Shape Styles dialog box launcher**.

12. Click the **Color list arrow** in the Line section, and select a color; click the **Dashed list arrow**, and select a dashed style; enter **2 pt** in the Weight text box, and click **OK**.

13. Click the **Insert tab**, and in the **Illustrations group**, click the **Shapes button**, then select the **Freeform** line shape.

14. Create a **diamond** shape. Click to begin the line and click at each angle.

15. Close the file, and do not save the changes.

WordArt

▶ The **WordArt** feature lets you create text as art. Using Word's predesigned WordArt styles, you can create eye-catching effects. As with clip art, WordArt is inserted into your document as an inline graphic. Apply a text wrap to it to create a floating graphic so that you can easily position it on the page.

▶ You can change WordArt's shape, character spacing, size, or position, as well as copy, delete, or apply effects just as you did with other graphic elements.

HOW **1.** Click the **Insert tab**, and in the **Text group**, **2.** click the **WordArt button**. In the WordArt gallery that appears, shown in Figure 4.38, **3.** click a WordArt style. **4.** Enter the text that you want to appear as WordArt in the Edit WordArt Text dialog box, then **5.** choose a font, font size, and emphasis style, as shown in Figure 4.39. *The new text will replace the words "Your Text Here."* **6.** Click **OK** to insert the WordArt into your document.

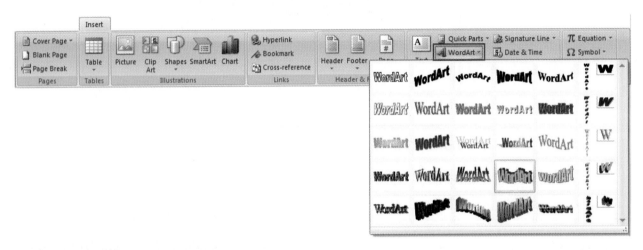

Figure 4.38: WordArt button and gallery

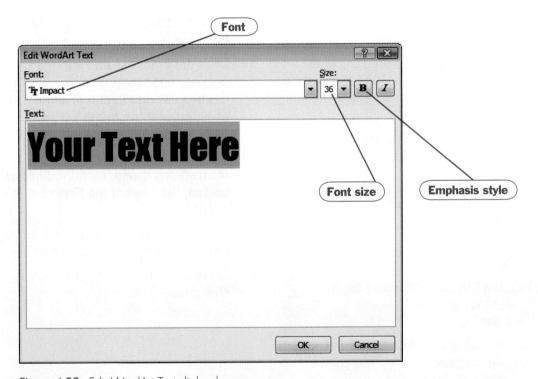

Figure 4.39: Edit WordArt Text dialog box

After WordArt is inserted into the document or selected, the WordArt Tools Format tab appears, as shown in Figure 4.40, to help you customize the WordArt shape.

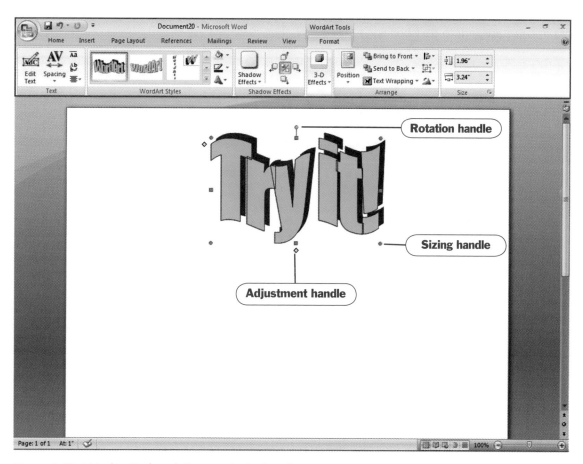

Figure 4.40: WordArt Tools with Format tab displayed

To apply line style and fill color options in one step, **1.** select the WordArt. **2.** Click the **Format tab**, if necessary, then **3.** click the **Size dialog box launcher**. In the Format WordArt dialog box that appears, as shown in Figure 4.41, **4.** click the **Colors and Lines tab**, and **5.** select the options you want. *You can also set the size in this dialog box by clicking the **Size tab** and entering the size amounts in the appropriate text boxes.*

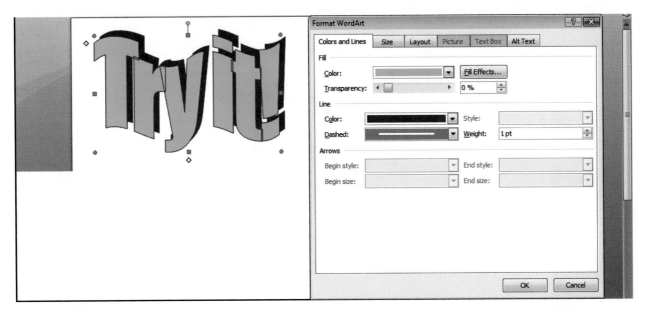

Figure 4.41: Format WordArt dialog box

TRY *it* OUT w4-12

1. Open a new blank document.

2. Click the **Insert tab**, and in the **Text group**, click the **WordArt button**.

3. Click any WordArt style. The Edit WordArt Text dialog box appears.

4. Enter **Congratulations!** in the Text window, and click **OK.**

5. Select the WordArt if necessary.

6. Click the **Format tab**, if necessary, and in the **Arrange group**, click the **Text Wrapping button**, and select **Square**. Move the WordArt to another location on the page.

7. Select the WordArt, if necessary. Click the **Format tab**, if necessary, and in the **WordArt Styles group**, click the **Change WordArt Shape button**.

8. Click the **Triangle Up** shape.

9. Select the WordArt, if necessary.

10. Click the **Format tab**, if necessary, then click the **Size dialog box launcher**.

11. Click the **Colors and Lines tab**, click the **Fill Color list arrow**, and select **red**; click the **Line Color list arrow**, and select **yellow**, then click **OK**.

12. Select the WordArt, if necessary.

13. Click the **Format tab**, if necessary, and in the **Text group**, click the **Edit Text button**. Replace the current word with **Try it!** and click **OK**.

14. Select the WordArt, if necessary.

15. Click the **Format tab**, if necessary. Experiment with different WordArt styles and shadow effects.

16. Close the file, and do not save the changes.

SmartArt

▶ A **SmartArt** graphic is a conceptual diagram that helps you visualize information. Before selecting from the many graphic layouts available, think about what type and layout are best for displaying your data.

▶ Word provides various SmartArt graphic types (Process, Hierarchy, Cycle Relationship, Matrix, or Pyramid), and each type contains several different layouts, as shown in Figure 4.42. For example, you would select "Hierarchy" and choose an **organization chart** layout to illustrate hierarchical structures, such as department reporting relationships within a company. You can also use an organization chart to show the flow of a project or family tree.

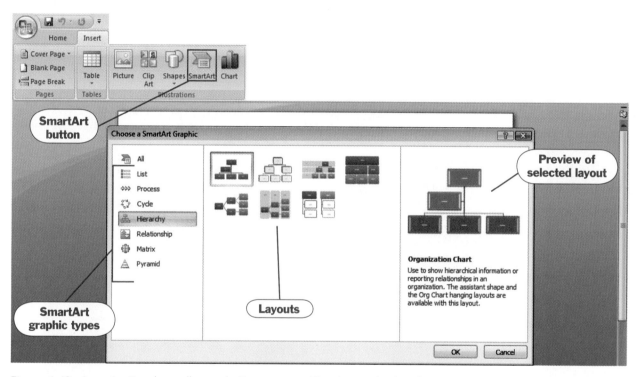

Figure 4.42: SmartArt Graphic gallery with Organization Chart layout displayed

▶ After SmartArt is inserted into the document (or after the SmartArt graphic is selected), a frame appears around the graphic, and the SmartArt Tools Design and Format tabs also display (the Design tab is selected) to help you customize the SmartArt graphic, as shown in Figure 4.43. Figure 4.44 shows the tools that appear on the Format tab.

▶ You can format a SmartArt graphic with preset styles, or you can format portions of it as you would format shapes. That is, you can add fill color and text, and change the line weight and style.

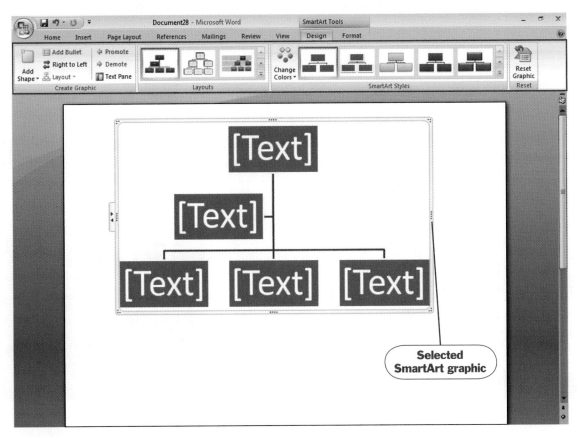

Figure 4.43: SmartArt Tools with Design tab displayed

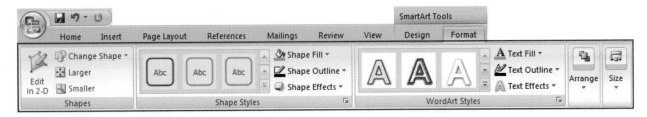

Figure 4.44: SmartArt Tools Format tab

▶ You can also wrap text around, position, modify the size, add special effects, copy, or delete it as you did with the other graphics you learned previously. Figure 4.45 shows a formatted organization chart with wrapped text that has been sized and positioned.

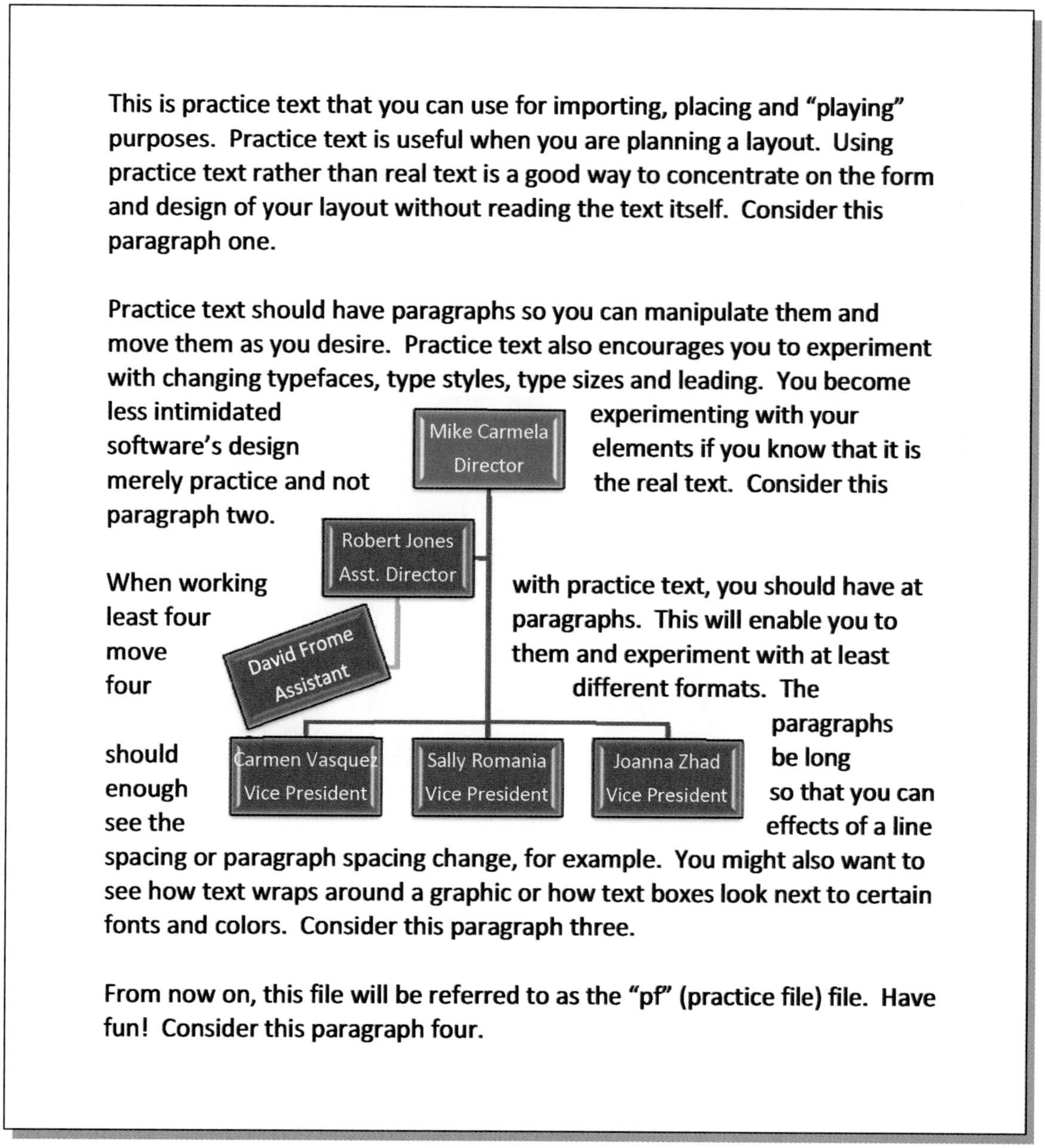

This is practice text that you can use for importing, placing and "playing" purposes. Practice text is useful when you are planning a layout. Using practice text rather than real text is a good way to concentrate on the form and design of your layout without reading the text itself. Consider this paragraph one.

Practice text should have paragraphs so you can manipulate them and move them as you desire. Practice text also encourages you to experiment with changing typefaces, type styles, type sizes and leading. You become less intimidated experimenting with your software's design elements if you know that it is merely practice and not the real text. Consider this paragraph two.

Mike Carmela
Director

Robert Jones
Asst. Director

David Frome
Assistant

When working with practice text, you should have at least four paragraphs. This will enable you to move them and experiment with at least four different formats. The paragraphs should be long enough so that you can see the effects of a line spacing or paragraph spacing change, for example. You might also want to see how text wraps around a graphic or how text boxes look next to certain fonts and colors. Consider this paragraph three.

Carmen Vasquez
Vice President

Sally Romania
Vice President

Joanna Zhad
Vice President

From now on, this file will be referred to as the "pf" (practice file) file. Have fun! Consider this paragraph four.

Figure 4.45: Formatted organization chart in a document

HOW To create a SmartArt graphic, **1.** click the **Insert tab**, and in the **Illustrations group**, **2.** click the **SmartArt button**. **3.** In the Choose a SmartArt graphic gallery that appears (see Figure 4.42 on page 245), **4.** select a SmartArt graphic type (List, Process, Hierarchy, Cycle Relationship, Matrix, or Pyramid). **5.** Select a layout. **6.** Click in a shape to enter text directly into it, or click the first item in the text pane shown in Figure 4.46, and enter the text for that item. *If the text pane is not displayed, click the Text Pane button on the SmartArt Tools Design tab.* **7.** Format the layout using the SmartArt Tools found on the Design and Format tabs.

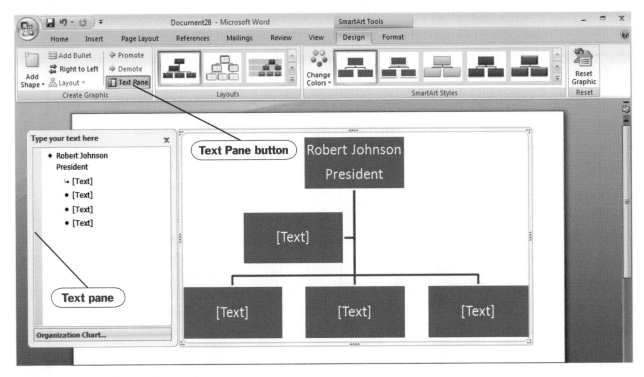

Figure 4.46: SmartArt graphic and text pane

T R Y *i t* O U T *w4-13*

1. Open the data file **w4-13**.

2. Position your insertion point anywhere in the text.

3. Click the **Insert tab**, and in the **Illustrations group**, click the **SmartArt button**.

4. In the Choose a SmartArt Graphic gallery, click **Hierarchy**, click the **Organization Chart** layout, then click **OK**. *Notice that the Design tab is selected.*

5. **Right-click** on the chart, highlight **Text Wrapping**, and select **Tight**. *Remember*

that you must select a Square or Tight text wrap in order to position the graphic.

6. Click in the top shape, and enter **Mike Carmela**. Press **[Enter]**, and type **Director**.

7. Click in the box to the left and below the top shape, and enter **Robert Jones**. Press **[Enter]**, and type **Asst. Director**.

8. Click in the bottom-left box, and enter **Carmen Vasquez**. Press **[Enter]**, and type **Vice President**.

Continued on next page

9. Click in the bottom-middle box, and enter `Sally Romania`. Press **[Enter]**, and type `Vice President`.

10. Click in the bottom-right box, and enter `Joanna Zhad`. Press **[Enter]**, and type `Vice President`.

11. Click in the box containing "Robert Jones."

12. To add a shape to the chart, click the **Design tab**, if necessary, and in the **Create Graphic group**, click the **Add Shape button list arrow**. Click **Add Assistant**.

13. Click in the newly inserted box. Enter `David Frome`. Press **[Enter]**, and type `Assistant`.

14. Click in the box containing "Mike Camela."

15. Select the box.
    a. Click the **Format tab**, and in the **Shape Styles group**, click the **Shape Fill list arrow**, and click **green**.
    b. Click the **Shape Outline button list arrow**, highlight **Weight**, and select **4½ point**. Click the **Shape Outline list arrow** again, then click **dark blue**.

16. Click in the box containing the name "David Frome." Rotate the box slightly to the left, as shown in Figure 4.45.

17. Click the **Design tab**, and in the **SmartArt Styles group**, click the **More button** and choose any 3-D effect. In the **SmartArt Styles group**, click the **Change Colors button list arrow**, and select any colorful option.

18. Click on the edge of the box containing the name "David Frome." Press **[Delete]** to delete the box.

19. Print one copy.

20. Close the file, and do not save the changes.

Layer and Group Graphics

▶ When you **layer** or stack graphics on top of each other, you create shadowing and other effects, as shown in Figure 4.47.

▶ You can arrange the order of layered graphics by moving an item to the bottom or to the top of all the other items in the stack. You can also move an item back or forward one level in the stack.

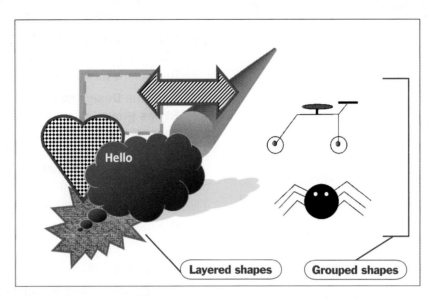

Figure 4.47: Layered and grouped graphics

▶ When you **group** shapes, you create one object out of individual parts. Grouped shapes behave like a single object. Grouping is particularly useful when you want to move or copy a graphic as a single item.

▶ If you want to edit part of a grouped graphic, you must first *ungroup* it. Figure 4.48 shows ungrouped and grouped shapes.

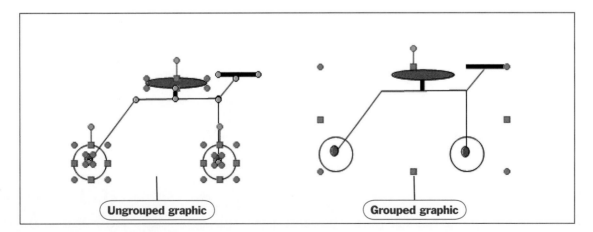

Figure 4.48: Ungrouped and grouped graphics

HOW To layer graphics, **1.** arrange the graphics where you want to position them. *Remember, to position a graphic, you must first apply a Square or Tight text-wrapping option.* **2.** Select the graphic you want to move to another level in the stack. **3.** Click the **Format tab**, if necessary, and in the **Arrange group**, **4.** click the **Send to Back list arrow** or the **Bring to Front list arrow**. **5.** Select **Send to Back** to move the graphic behind all other objects in the stack, **Send Backward** to move the graphic back one level, **Bring to Front** to move the graphic on top of all other objects in the stack, or **Bring Forward** to move the graphic up one level.

To group shapes, **1.** hold down **[Ctrl]** as you select the individual parts of the shape. *You can select individual parts at once by clicking the **Home tab**, and in the **Editing group**, clicking the **Select list arrow**, selecting the **Select Objects button**, then dragging the pointer around all the objects (as shown in Figure 4.48).* **2.** Click the **Format tab**, if necessary, and in the **Arrange group**, click the **Group button**.

To ungroup, **1.** select the grouped object, **2.** click the **Format tab**, if necessary, and in the **Arrange group**, click **Ungroup**.

T R Y *i t* **O U T** *w4-14*

1. Open the data file **w4-14**.

2. Select the **text box**.

3. Click the **Format tab**, if necessary, and in the **Arrange group**, click the **Bring to Front button**.

4. Select the **Star** shape.

5. Right-click, highlight **Order**, and click **Send to Back**.

6. Select the **Heart** shape.

7. Click the **Format tab**, if necessary, and in the **Arrange group**, click the **Send to Back button list arrow**, and click **Send to Back**.

8. Click the **Home tab** in the **Editing group**, click the **Select button list arrow**, then click **Select Objects**.

9. Position the pointer at the top left of the bike. Drag to draw a box around the bike to select all the bike's parts.

10. Click the **Format tab**, and in the **Arrange group**, click the **Group button list arrow**, and click **Group**.

11. Select the **Bike** graphic. Drag a corner handle to increase its size.

12. Drag the bike to the lower-right corner of the page.

13. Select the **Bike**, if necessary.

14. Click the **Format tab**, if necessary, and in the **Arrange group**, click the **Group list arrow**, and click **Ungroup**.

15. Select the **red circle** on top of the bike seat. Press **[Delete]**.

16. Using the Select Objects pointer, select all the bike's parts, then click the **Format tab**, and in the **Arrange group**, click the **Group list arrow**, and select **Regroup**.

17. Close the file, and do not save the changes.

REHEARSAL

TASK 3

GOAL
To create an advertisement, as shown in Figure 4.49

WHAT YOU NEED TO KNOW

▶ An **advertisement** is a sales tool that conveys a message about a product or service and thus helps to market it.

▶ Advertisements may appear in magazines and newspapers and on billboards. The goal for a good advertisement is to have a clear, uncluttered presentation. Images should be relevant and relate to the subject or product advertised.

DIRECTIONS

1. Open the data file **w4r3-ad text**. Enhance the text with images as follows to create the advertisement shown in Figure 4.49 on page 254.

2. Display **gridlines**.

3. Create a WordArt graphic using the words **EarthCare Services**.
   a. Rotate the text direction as shown in the figure.
   b. Apply a **Tight** text wrap, and position the box at the left margin.
   c. Apply an **orange** fill and **green** outline color.
   d. Size the figure to **1"** high by **5.2"** wide.

4. Create the tree in a blank area at the bottom of the page as follows:
   a. Use the **Freeform shape line tool** to draw the tree trunk. Apply a **brown** fill to the trunk.
   b. Create an **Oval** shape to represent one leaf. Apply a **green** fill to the leaf.
   c. Copy the leaf several times, and position the copies around the tree trunk as shown in the figure.
   d. Use the **Select Objects tool** to select the tree parts, then group the parts.
   e. Size the image to **2"** high by **2"** wide.
   f. Apply a **Tight** text wrap, then position the image in the middle of the text, as shown.

5. Center the name of the featured plant. Center the contact information text. Color the contact information text **green** as shown.

6. Create the design at the top of the page as follows:
   a. Draw a straight horizontal line from the left to the right margin, and position it at the top of the grid.
   b. Copy the line five times, and position each line slightly below the other as shown.

Continued on next page

c. Color each line a darker shade of **gray**. *Hint: Select the first line, click the **Format tab**, and in the **Shape Styles group**, click the **Shape Outline button** and apply the first shade of gray below Theme Colors. Apply a darker shade to each subsequent line.*

d. Set the line width to **10 point** for the first line; set the second line to **6 point**, the third line to **3 point**, the fourth line to **2.25 point**, and the fifth and sixth line to **1 point**.

e. Copy and paste the tree image once. Position it on the sixth line on the right as shown, then size it to approximately **.8"** high by **.9"** wide.

f. Apply an **In Front of Text** wrap option so the image sits on top of the line.

g. Copy the small tree five more times.

h. Size and position each to resemble the figure.

7. Create a SmartArt graphic using the **Organization Chart** layout.

a. Click in the top box, and add an **Assistant** shape.

b. Enter the text as shown.

c. Size the graphic to approximately **1.8"** high by **3.8"** wide.

d. Apply an **In Front of Text** text wrap, and position the graphic at the bottom middle of the grid.

e. Apply any SmartArt graphic style.

8. Preview the document.

9. Print one copy.

10. Save the file, and name it **4r3-advertisement**.

11. Close the file.

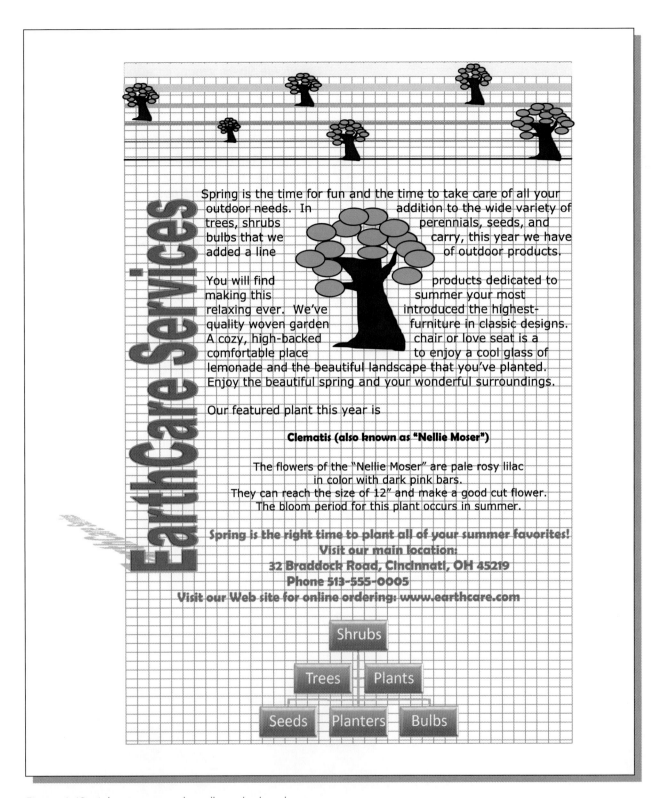

Figure 4.49: Advertisement with gridlines displayed

Transport Travel Services is pleased to publish a popular travel magazine. You have been asked to create an advertisement that will be featured in several upcoming issues. The travel information provided will help clients have a more pleasant journey. This popular magazine is sent to all TTS clients who book travel packages. Figure 4.50 on page 256 is shown as a guide. You may create any design you want.

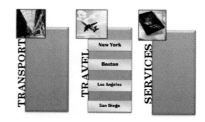

Follow these guidelines:

1. Open the data file **w4p3-airlines**, which contains the body text for the advertisement.

2. Display gridlines to help you place the graphics and text.

3. Use the default margins.

4. Draw the airplane using the drawing tools. Size and position it as desired.

5. Use WordArt to create the words "Bon Voyage."
   a. Apply an appropriate text wrap depending on where you position the graphic.
   b. Apply any WordArt style and color.
   c. Size and position it as desired.

6. Create a SmartArt graphic using a **list** layout.
   a. Enter the text shown.
   b. Apply a **Square** text wrap.
   c. Apply any SmartArt style and color to the shapes and text.
   d. Size and position it as desired.

7. Use any font, font color, font size, and style for the text. However, be sure to keep to one page.

8. Save the file, and name it **4p3-airlines**.

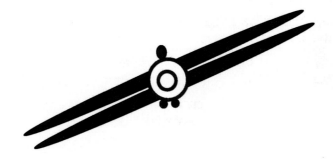

All of us at Transport Travel Services wish you a pleasant journey. Here are some topics and related travel tips that we hope will make your journey more enjoyable:

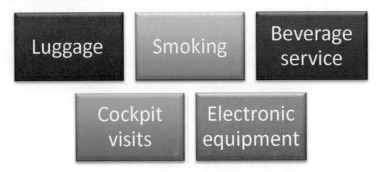

Luggage. Attach your name to each piece of baggage—particularly checked baggage. We provide all our clients with bag identification tags. Pack identification inside your bags, too, and carry all valuables, medicines, and keys with you onto the plane. You may not, however, take any liquids with you on the plane.

Smoking. Not permitted on any domestic or international flights. It is a Federal crime to smoke in lavatories.

Beverage service. Available on all flights. Only liquor served by your flight attendant may be consumed on board, however. Only passengers twenty-one or older will be served alcoholic beverages.

Cockpit visits. Available while the aircraft is parked at the airport gate. Ask one of your flight attendants if you're interested in seeing it. While the aircraft is in motion, however, the cockpit door must remain closed.

Bon Voyage!

Electronic equipment. Electronic devices are not allowed to be used during taxi, takeoff, and landing. Following takeoff and the flight crew's approval announcement, all portable electronic devices may be used, except the following: cellular telephones, radios, TV cameras, TV sets, electronic games and/or toys with remote control.

We welcome your comments! We at TTS would like you to write us about your trip, your flight, and your overall time. You can email us tts@net.com. Or fax your comments to 212-555-6767. Remember, we at Transport Travel Services want you to go away—again, and again and again!

Figure 4.50: Advertisement

Create a Shape

Shape

1. Click the **Insert tab**, and in the Illustrations group, click the **Shapes button**.
2. Select a shape from the gallery.
3. Drag diagonally to create a shape. (Hold down **[Shift]** as you drag to create a perfect circle or square.)

Create WordArt

1. Click the **Insert tab**, and in the Text group, click the **WordArt button**.

2. Click to select a WordArt style in the WordArt gallery.
3. Enter the text to appear as WordArt, and click **OK**.

Create SmartArt

1. Click the **Insert tab**, and in the **Illustrations group**, click the **SmartArt button**.
2. Select a SmartArt graphic type, then select a layout.
3. Click in the shape to enter the text directly in it, or click the first item in the Text pane and enter the text for that item.

4. Format the layout using the SmartArt tools found on the Design and Format tabs.

Group/Ungroup Shapes

1. Hold down **[Ctrl]** as you click each shape to group, or click the **Select button** (found on the Home tab, Editing group), click **Select Objects**, and then drag a box around all parts.
2. Click the **Format tab**, and in the **Arrange group**, click the **Group** or **Ungroup button**.

T R Y O U T

TASK 4

▶ **GOAL**
To create a newsletter, as shown in Figure 4.51

✦ Create a section break
✦ Create columns
✦ Create a drop cap
✦ Use Page Borders and Page Colors

Healthwatch

A Newsletter from BodyWorksFitnessCenters

Fall 2010

Drop cap

Columns

Page border

In This Issue

Vitamin C Shown to Reduce Heart Disease

Beta-carotene Alert: It May Clear Your Arteries

Vitamin C Shown to Reduce Heart Disease

New studies have shown that high blood levels of vitamin C are associated with higher levels of "good" cholesterol in the blood and lower the risk of coronary heart disease. Research shows that vitamin C appears to prevent cholesterol from being oxidized in the blood; this may decrease the chance that the cholesterol circulating in the blood will end up in the arteries, increasing one's risk of acquiring heart disease.

Vitamin C can be found in one whole papaya, mango, orange, half of a cantaloupe, one cup strawberries, broccoli, orange or grapefruit juice, brussel sprouts, or

cauliflower. Be sure to maintain your vitamin C intake—your life depends on it!

Beta-carotene Alert: It May Clear Your Arteries!

Beta-carotene, processed by the body to form vitamin A, has been noted as useful in treating fatty-cholesterol deposits in arteries that lead to heart attacks and strokes. Beta-carotene is found in yellow-orange or red foods, such as oranges, peaches, sweet potatoes, and carrots. It is also found in leafy, dark-green vegetables; the green color of chlorophyll masks the color of the beta-carotene.

For these reasons, it is important to consume fruits and vegetables as part of your regular diet. In fact, six servings of fruits and vegetables are recommended daily. If you choose one fruit

and one vegetable high in vitamin C every day, your remaining portions should include some dark green vegetables, yellow vegetables, and fruit. Fresh fruit and vegetables provide more nutrients to the body than canned ones.

To maintain a healthy diet, one should eat moderately from the five basic food groups (fruits and vegetables, dairy, grains, meats, and fats) with low fats, simple sugars, low cholesterol, high carbohydrates, moderate protein, high fiber, and an adequate supply of vitamins, minerals and water. It's too bad we never followed our mothers' advice about eating vegetables. As more and more research is done, we are finding that Mom was smart to force us to eat that one last bite of broccoli at the dinner table. She was adding years to our lives.

Tips for Your Overall Diet

1. Always eat breakfast, even if you have only a piece of fruit and a glass of milk. Your blood sugar level is very low in the morning.
2. Eat five or six small meals during the day. This will help keep your energy levels high.
3. Avoid overeating. Large amounts of food require a lot of time to digest, thus draining the body of energy. Eat until you are satisfied and then stop.
4. Drink plenty of water throughout the day, especially after exercising.
5. Above all, listen to your body.

Figure 4.51: Newsletter

WHAT YOU NEED TO KNOW

Create a Section Break

▶ By default, a document contains one section. You can use section breaks to split your document into multiple sections, which will allow you change the layout or format of each section differently. Figure 4.52 shows a document that uses section breaks to format sections differently.

Figure 4.52: Sample document with inserted section breaks

HOW **1.** Position the insertion point where you want to create a new section.
2. Click the **Page Layout tab**, and in the **Page Setup group**, click the **Breaks button**. In the Breaks menu that appears, shown in Figure 4.53, **3.** click the section break type that you want in the section breaks group. The section break types are explained in Table 4.1.

Section break marks store section formatting in the same way paragraph marks store paragraph formatting. Therefore, removing a section break may also delete all section formatting preceding the break.

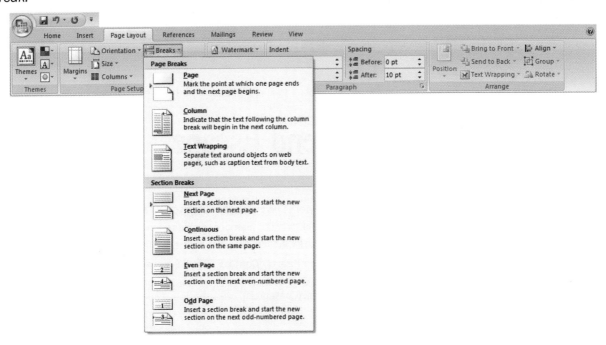

Figure **4.53**: Section Break options

Table **4.1**: Section break types

TYPE	DESCRIPTION
NEXT PAGE	Creates a new section on the next page
CONTINUOUS	Creates a new section at the insertion point
EVEN PAGE	Creates a new section on the next even-numbered page (usually a left-hand page)
ODD PAGE	Creates a new section on the next odd-numbered page (usually a right-hand page)

T R Y *i t* **O U T** *w4-15*

1. Open a new blank document.

2. Enter the following text:

   `The Highland Grand Hotel is located on 17 acres in the historic Woodland Hills. Guests are offered a range of accommodations.`

3. Press **[Enter]** twice.

4. On the **Home tab**, click the **Show/Hide button** to display codes.

5. Click the **Page Layout tab**, and in the Page Setup group, click the **Breaks button**, then click **Continuous**.

6. Change the left and right margins to **2"**.

7. Enter these bulleted paragraphs:
   * `Rooms combine into family units to allow a small group or family to vacation in comfort within the privacy of their own spacious unit.`

Continued on next page

T R Y _it_ O U T _w4-15 Continued_

- Five-minute drive to beach.
- Great value, well priced.

8. Press **[Enter]** twice.

9. Click the **Page Layout tab**, and in the **Page Setup group**, click the **Breaks button**, then click **Continuous**.

10. Reset the left and right margins to **1"**.

11. Enter the text:

    The Highland Grand Hotel also offers a newly created exercise gym and one of the most famous restaurants in the area.

12. Print preview.

13. Close the file, and do not save the changes.

Create Columns

▶ The Columns feature allows text to flow down one column and into the next column. Word formats columns with even widths and gutter space (space between columns). You can, however, create custom column widths and insert a vertical line between adjacent columns.

▶ Columns are particularly useful when creating manuals, newsletters, pamphlets, brochures, and lists.

▶ You can force text to start a new column by entering a Column break. You can also change the number of columns in the same document as long as you insert a section break before and/or after each section. Figure 4.54 shows a document with columns that have been formatted with column and section breaks.

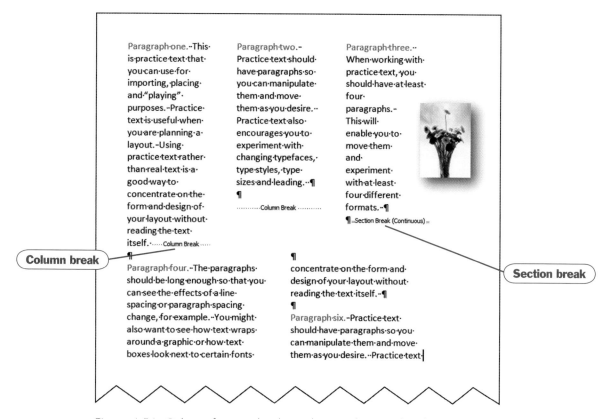

Figure 4.54: Columns formatted with a column and section breaks

HOW 1. Click the **Page Layout tab**, and in the **Page Setup group**, 2. click the **Columns button**. 3. Click the layout you want from the list that appears, as shown in Figure 4.55.

To create custom columns, 1. click **More Columns** (see Figure 4.55). In the Columns dialog box that appears, as shown in Figure 4.56, 2. enter the column widths and spacing you want below the Width and spacing section. If you want to include a line between columns, check the **Line between check box**.

To turn the Columns feature off, 1. click the **Page Layout tab**, and in the **Page Setup group**, 2. click the **Columns button**, then 3. click **One**.

To force text to wrap to the next column before it reaches the bottom of the current column, 1. click the **Page Layout tab**, and in the **Page Setup group**, 2. click the **Breaks button list arrow**, and 3. click **Column**.

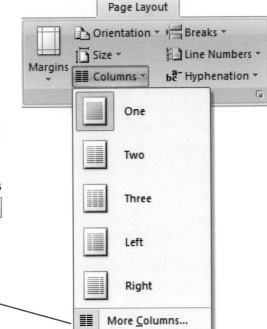

Figure 4.55: Columns button and layout options list

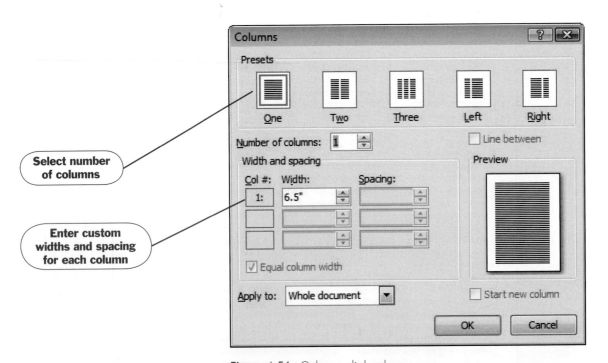

Figure 4.56: Columns dialog box

1. Open the data file **w4-16**.

2. Position the insertion point in the first paragraph.

3. Click the **Page Layout tab**, and in the **Page Setup group**, click the **Columns button list arrow**, then select **Two**.

4. Position your insertion point before the first letter in Paragraph three.

5. Click the **Page Layout tab**, and in the **Page Setup group**, click the **Breaks button list arrow**, then select **Column**. Notice that this break forced the text to the next column.

6. Click the **Home tab**, and in the **Paragraph group**, click the **Show/Hide button**

if necessary, to show formatting marks. Notice the Column break indicator in your document.

7. Delete the **Column break indicator**, which will fill the entire first column (and a small portion of the second column) with text.

8. Position your insertion point in the first paragraph.

9. Click the **Page Layout tab**, and in the **Page Setup group**, click the **Columns button list arrow**, and select **One**. Notice that your document is now one column.

10. Close the file, and do not save the changes.

Create a Drop Cap

▶ A "drop cap" (or "drop capital") is an enlarged capital letter that drops below the first line of body text. It is usually the first letter of a paragraph (see Figure 4.57).

▶ You can choose a drop capital style from those Word provides, or you can customize your drop capital to drop below text by a specific amount.

HOW **1.** Select the character on which to apply the drop cap. **2.** Click the **Insert tab**, and in the **Text group**, **3.** click the **Drop Cap button list arrow**, and **4.** select the drop cap style from the list that displays, as shown in Figure 4.57.

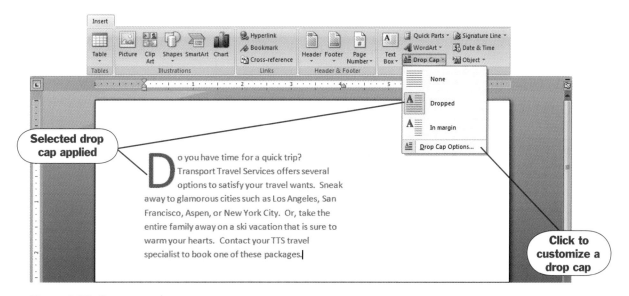

Figure 4.57: Drop capital options

To customize your drop cap, **1.** click **Drop Cap Options** (see Figure 4.57). In the Drop Cap dialog box that appears, shown in Figure 4.58, select **Dropped** or **In Margin**, and enter the desired options.

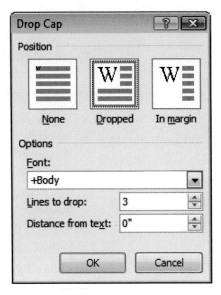

Figure 4.58: Drop Cap dialog box

TRY*it*OUT *w4-17*

1. Open the data file **w4-17**.

2. Select the "D" in the first paragraph.

3. Click the **Insert tab**, and in the **Text group**, click the **Drop Cap button list arrow**, and select the **Dropped** option.

4. Select the "O" in the second paragraph.

5. Repeat Step 3, but select the **In margin** option.

6. Close the file, and do not save the changes.

Use Page Borders and Page Colors

▶ To add a final touch to your document, you can place a border around a page or apply a background color.

▶ Word provides numerous page border styles including interesting art borders. Figure 4.59 shows a document with an art border and a background page color.

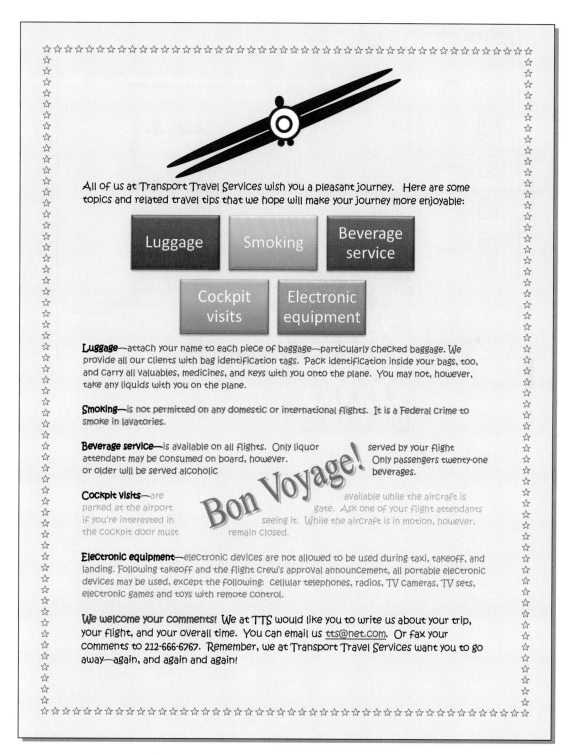

Figure 4.59: Document with page border and background color

To apply a page border, **1.** click the **Page Layout tab**, and in the **Page Background group**, **2.** click the **Page Borders button**. In the Borders and 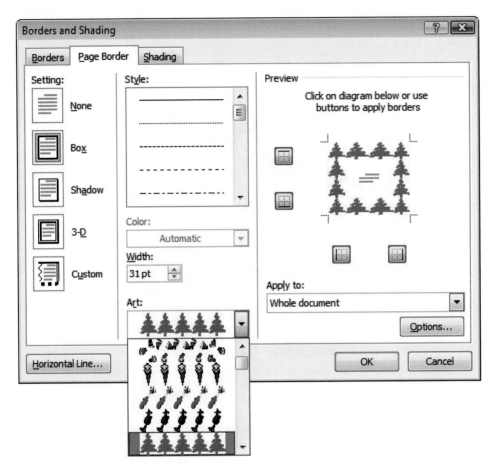 Shading dialog box that appears, as shown in Figure 4.60, **3.** click the **Page Border tab**. **4.** Click **Box** in the Setting section. **5.** Select a line style, color, and width. To apply an Art border, click the **Art box list arrow**, and choose an art style. Then, **6.** click **OK**.

Figure 4.60: Borders and Shading dialog box

To apply a page color, **1.** click the **Page Layout tab**, and in the **Page Background group**, **2.** click the **Page Color button list arrow**, and **3.** select a color from the gallery that appears, as shown in Figure 4.61.

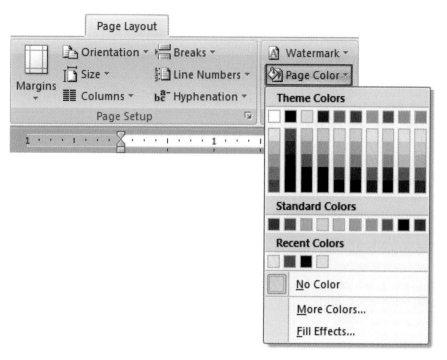

Figure 4.61: Page Color gallery

TRY*it*OUT *w4-18*

1. Open the data file **w4-18**.

2. Click the **Page Layout tab**, and in the **Page Background group**, click the **Page Color list arrow**, then highlight each light background color to see a live preview. Select a color you want.

3. Click the **Page Layout tab**, and in the **Page Background** **group**, click the **Page Borders button**. In the Borders and Shading dialog box that appears, do the following:
   a. Click the **Box** setting.
   b. Click the **Art list arrow**, select any Art border, and click **OK**.

4. Close the file, and do not save the changes.

REHEARSAL

 GOAL
To create a newsletter, as shown in
Figure 4.62

TASK 4

WHAT YOU NEED TO KNOW

▶ A **newsletter** is a communication that allows people who share a common interest to exchange ideas, developments, and information on a regular basis. Business organizations use newsletters to deliver a message about new products, promotions, achievements, and announcements.

▶ Although the format of newsletters varies, the following basic parts can be found on the first page of most newsletters:

- **Masthead**: Includes the newsletter title, the division or organization publishing the document, the volume or issue number, and the current date of the issue

- **Contents**: Includes a listing of the articles or topics featured in the issue

- **Headline**: Summarizes the contents of the articles that follow

- **Body copy**: Includes the text of the articles

▶ After applying a text wrap option, adjust the position of graphics to avoid awkward line breaks.

▼ DIRECTIONS

1. Open the data file **w4r4-newsletter text**, which contains the newsletter text. Format it to create the newsletter shown in Figure 4.62 on page 270.

2. Position the insertion point before the first word, "In," and press **[Enter]** enough times so the At indicator on the status bar reads **3"**.

3. Insert a continuous section break at this point in the document. (*Hint*: Display codes. Then, click the **Page Layout tab** and in the **Page Setup group**, click the **Breaks button list arrow** and select **Continuous**).

4. Create three columns (*Hint*: Click **Page Layout tab**, click the **Columns button list arrow**, and select **Three**).

5. Format "In This Issue" in **sans serif 10 point**. Apply an **orange** color to the text, as shown (apply a lighter shade of orange to "In This Issue").

6. Set the two headlines to sans serif **12-point** bold. Apply a **blue** color to the headline text.

7. Set the body text to **11 point**. Create a drop cap on the letter "N" in the first paragraph.

8. Draw a **3-point**, horizontal, dashed line before and after "In This Issue," as shown.

9. To create the masthead, do the following:
   a. Draw a text box, and enter the text as shown. Right-align "Fall 2010."
   b. Set the text within the box to sans serif.
   c. Set "Health" to **48 point**, then set character spacing to **condensed by 2 points**. Apply a **dark orange** font color. Set "watch" to **36-point bold**, and set the character spacing to **condensed by 0.7** and scaled to **150%**. Apply a **light orange** font color.

Continued on next page

    d. Position the masthead, as shown.

    e. Create a **12-point** solid horizontal line below "Healthwatch."

    f. Set "A Newsletter from BodyWorksFitnessCenters" to **12 point**.

    g. Remove the text box border.

10. Insert relevant images, where shown. Size them to keep the text on one page. Apply a **Square** text wrap to each image.

11. Apply any picture style or effect to the images.

12. Draw the text box shown at the bottom of the newsletter as follows:

    a. Enter the text, as shown. Center and underline the heading, using a sans serif **11-point** font. Set the remaining text as **9 point**.

    b. Apply a **4½ point** dotted border, and apply a **light yellow** fill color.

    c. Apply a **Tight** text wrap.

    d. Stretch the text box to span two columns.

13. Apply a **2¼-point orange** page border.

14. Preview the document.

15. Save the file, and name it **4r4-newsletter**.

16. Print one copy.

17. Close the file.

Healthwatch

A Newsletter from BodyWorksFitnessCenters

Fall 2010

Vitamin C Shown to Reduce Heart Disease

New studies have shown that high blood levels of vitamin C are associated with higher levels of "good" cholesterol in the blood and lower the risk of coronary heart disease. Research shows that vitamin C appears to prevent cholesterol from being oxidized in the blood; this may decrease the chance that the cholesterol circulating in the blood will end up in the arteries, increasing one's risk of acquiring heart disease.

Vitamin C can be found in one whole papaya, mango, orange, half of a cantaloupe, one cup strawberries, broccoli, orange or grapefruit juice, brussel sprouts, or

cauliflower. Be sure to maintain your vitamin C intake—your life depends on it!

Beta-carotene Alert: It May Clear Your Arteries!

Beta-carotene, processed by the body to form vitamin A, has been noted as useful in treating fatty-cholesterol deposits in arteries that lead to heart attacks and strokes. Beta-carotene is found in yellow-orange or red foods, such as oranges, peaches, sweet potatoes, and carrots. It is also found in leafy, dark-green vegetables; the green color of chlorophyll masks the color of the beta-carotene.

For these reasons, it is important to consume fruits and vegetables as part of your regular diet. In fact, six servings of fruits and vegetables are recommended daily. If you choose one fruit and one vegetable high in vitamin C every day, your remaining portions should include some dark green vegetables, yellow vegetables, and fruit. Fresh fruit and vegetables provide more nutrients to the body than canned ones.

To maintain a healthy diet, one should eat moderately from the five basic food groups (fruits and vegetables, dairy, grains, meats, and fats) with low fats, simple sugars, low cholesterol, high carbohydrates, moderate protein, high fiber, and an adequate supply of vitamins, minerals and water. It's too bad we never followed our mothers' advice about eating vegetables. As more and more research is done, we are finding that Mom was smart to force us to eat that one last bite of broccoli at the dinner table. She was adding years to our lives.

Tips for Your Overall Diet

1. Always eat breakfast, even if you have only a piece of fruit and a glass of milk. Your blood sugar level is very low in the morning.
2. Eat five or six small meals during the day. This will help keep your energy levels high.
3. Avoid overeating. Large amounts of food require a lot of time to digest, thus draining the body of energy. Eat until you are satisfied and then stop.
4. Drink plenty of water throughout the day, especially after exercising.
5. Above all, listen to your body.

Figure 4.62: Newsletter

PERFORMANCE

TASK 4

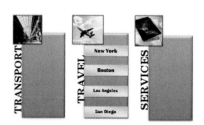

Transport Travel Services has just opened a new office in San Diego. Now that the company has expanded, management would like to create a monthly newsletter to be distributed to employees in all the branch offices, as well as to many TTS travel clients. As the newly hired public relations director, you have been asked to create the first company newsletter. This assignment will require you to design a masthead, find appropriate graphics, and format the newsletter. The masthead should read: Club News A Newsletter of Transport Travel Services. Include the month (December) and year (2010). Figure 4.63 on page 272 is provided as a guide. You may use your own judgment as you design the newsletter.

Follow these guidelines:

1. Open the data file **w4p4-tts news text**, which contains the newsletter text.

2. Format the newsletter using three or four columns. Set the column widths as you prefer.

3. Include a Contents section.
   a. Use at least three images and place them wherever you choose. Ideally, one of the images should be of Paris; another should be of Rome. (If you cannot find images of these cities, substitute other relevant images).
   b. Apply any picture style or effect to the images.

4. Use at least one text box. Apply any font, font size, font colors, or fills to the text box. You can decide what text you would like to insert into the box.

5. Emphasize headline text.

6. Apply an appropriate page border.

7. Apply a light background page color.

8. Print one copy.

9. Save the file, and name it **4p4-tts news**.

10. Close all files.

A Newsletter of Transport Travel Services ◆ December 2010

In This Issue

- ❖ Unpredictable International Travel
- ❖ See More of the World, Weekend by Weekend
- ❖ Travel Values for the Whole Family
- ❖ Best Buys of the Month

UNPREDICTABLE INTERNATIONAL TRAVEL

One of the unfortunate aspects of international travel is the possibility of natural disasters or political turmoil that can disrupt the best-made plans. That is certainly true with any travel organization. Since TTS travels to nearly every destination in the world, some trips will undoubtedly be affected at one time or another. However, since TTS offers such a wide array of destinations, if such a need arises to cancel a trip due to natural or political problems, clients can switch to another comparable available destination so they do not miss out on a long-anticipated vacation or trip deposit. We do try to accommodate our members' wishes and will offer members a full refund if booking another trip isn't possible.

SEE MORE OF THE WORLD, WEEKEND BY WEEKEND

For less than the cost of a cross-country trip, members can explore the Arctic, view the Old Masters in Brussels, dine at a historic Irish Castle, or see a new production in London's West End.

Over the course of five to six days, members can experience a true getaway, with most prices starting at less than $100 a day per person, double occupancy, including roundtrip international airfare, first-class accommodations, breakfasts, and airport transfers. Most programs offer optional tours and plenty of recommendations for activities to enjoy on your own. In 2020, clients can travel to Iceland, Ireland,

Brussels, Amsterdam, Paris, Rome, London,

Madrid, Lisbon, or Switzerland's lovely lake region for a long weekend. See more of the world, weekend by weekend.

TRAVEL VALUES FOR THE WHOLE FAMILY

Family travel programs are increasingly popular as hectic schedules for both parents and children can limit quality time together.

Our Caribbean and Mexico tours offer some of the best values for family travel. Families should also consider cruise travel as an excellent family vacation, especially for parents with children over 12.

☆ **BEST DEALS** ☆

While all our tours are designed to offer excellent value, the following are the Best Deals, which you shouldn't miss:

Rome Weekend
5 days from $399

☆

Sorrento, Rome and Florence
10 days from $999

☆ **Alaska Cruises**
7 Nights from $1229

☆ **Barcelona and Paris**
8 days from $999

Figure 4.63: Newsletter

Create a Section Break

1. Position the insertion point you want at the beginning of the paragraph that starts a new section.
2. Click the **Page Layout tab**, and in **the Page Setup group**, click the **Breaks button list arrow**.
3. Click the section break type you want in the Section Breaks group from the list that appears.

Create Columns

1. Click the **Page Layout tab**, and in the **Page Setup group**, click the **Columns button list arrow**.
2. Click the layout you want. To create custom columns, click **More Columns**, and enter the column widths and spacing you want in the Columns dialog box that appears.

To force text to wrap to the next column:

1. Click the **Page Layout tab**, and in the **Page Setup group**, click the **Breaks button list arrow**.
2. Click **Column** under Page Breaks.

Create a Drop Cap

1. Select the character on which to apply the drop cap.
2. Click the **Insert tab**, and in the **Text group**, click the **Drop Cap button list arrow**.
3. Select the drop cap style from the list that appears, or click **Drop Cap Options** to customize the drop cap.

Use Page Borders and Page Colors

Page Border

1. Click the **Page Layout tab**, and in the Page Background group, click the **Page Borders button**.
2. Click the **Page Border tab** in the Borders and Shading dialog box that appears.
3. Click **Box** in the Setting section.
4. Select the line style, color, and width. To apply an Art border, click the **Art list box arrow**, and choose an art style.
5. Click **OK**.

Page Color

1. Click the **Page Layout tab**, and in the **Page Background group**, click the **Page Color button list arrow**.
2. Select a color from the gallery that displays.

ENCORE

Act I

To foster a sense of camaraderie and enhance employee morale, Alan Newman, the CEO of Newmark Productions, has invited the staff from the California offices to a company barbeque that he is hosting at his home. The barbeque is scheduled for Saturday, June 17, at 1:00 p.m. Alan lives at 400 Beverly Glen in Beverly Hills, California. You have been asked to create a flyer providing this information and encouraging all employees to "come and join in the fun." Alan would like everyone to R.S.V.P. to his assistant, Jim Bronson, at Extension 444, by Thursday, June 15.

Follow these guidelines:

1. Use any font style(s), font color(s), and font size(s).

2. Use at least one text box.

3. Include relevant clip art or pictures, two shapes, and WordArt.
   a. Use any fill and outline color for the shapes and WordArt.
   b. Apply an appropriate text wrap to each graphic.

4. Apply any style or effect to the clip art or pictures.

5. Use an appropriate page border and page background color.

6. Print one copy.

7. Save the file, and name it **4e1-barbeque**.

Act II

BodyWorksFitnessCenters wants to increase public awareness of its personal training options, spa facilities, fitness classes, and special programs. You have been asked to use your creativity to create an advertisement to be included in the next mailing to new members. Figure 4.64 on page 276 is provided as a guide. However, you are encouraged to use your own judgment as you design the flyer. Use any of the Word features that you learned in this lesson.

Follow these guidelines:

1. Open the data file **w4e2-fitness offerings text**, which contains the flyer text.

2. Use margins that you feel will work best for your page design.

3. Include the BodyWorksFitness logo, which can be found in the **Logos** folder in the data files. Apply any effect to the logo.

4. Enter The **Complete Fitness Facility** in a text box. You can format the text box using any colors or design you want. Position it where it best supports your design.

5. Format the text in columns. You can use two or three columns. You must insert a continuous section break before you start the columns.

6. Use WordArt to create the four headings, or, if you prefer, use a SmartArt graphic that includes each offering. Then position the SmartArt graphic within the text with an InLine with Text text wrapping. Apply any fill or outline color to the WordArt or SmartArt graphic.

7. Include at least three relevant images, and apply a picture effect to each one.

8. Include a drop capital before each paragraph, as shown in Figure 4.64.

9. Include shapes as part of your design.

10. Print one copy.

11. Save the file, and name it **4e2-fitness offerings**.

The Complete Fitness Facility

Personal Training

Personal training is the best way to get the most out of your time. Find out why BodyWorksFitnessCenters is rated number one in personal training programs.

At BWFC, all of our personal trainers have either national certificatins or college degrees in exercise physiology; many have both. At BWFC, we believe personal training is one of

the best ways we have to help members reach their fitness goals. Whether you want to lose weight, gain lean muscle mass, or just increase your strength, stamina and energy, personal training is a great

way to get the most out of your workout time.

Spa Facilities

Our spa services include massage therapy, body treatments, facials, tanning booths, and hair and nail salons.

Come in and relax with one of our treatments.

Fitness Classes

We offer the most innovative classes taught by the best fitness instructors. Whether you choose kickboxing, fencing, yoga, or spinning, you will get results and have fun at the same time!

Visit us online at www.bwfc.com to check out our fitness schedule.

Special Programs

The new sports-specific training programs offer you six weeks of hard-core training for maximum performance.

The equestrian training program will hone your riding skills and techniques for maximum performance on the trails or in the ring, whether you're a novice or competitive rider.

The ski and snowboard program is a six-week, specialized training program designed to develop all aspects of conditioning for skiing and snowboarding performance.

Figure 4.64: Fitness flyer

LESSON 5

Reports and Long Documents

In this lesson, you will learn to use features found in Word to format and edit reports and long documents. You will complete the following projects:

- ✴ Multiple-page reports
- ✴ Cover page
- ✴ Bibliography
- ✴ Handbook pages

Upon completion of this lesson, you will have mastered the following skill sets

- ✴ Insert a page break
- ✴ Indent text
- ✴ Insert headers, footers, and page numbers
- ✴ Insert a cover page
- ✴ Use Research services
- ✴ Apply and modify a Quick Style
- ✴ Apply a theme
- ✴ Apply paragraph borders and shading
- ✴ Set vertical centering
- ✴ Insert a watermark
- ✴ Find and replace text
- ✴ Insert a file
- ✴ Insert a citation and create a bibliography
- ✴ Insert, view, and edit comments
- ✴ Track changes in a document
- ✴ Compare and combine changes
- ✴ Use Word Count

Terms
Software-related
Citation
Comments
First-line indent
Footer
Hanging indent
Header
Page break
Style
Theme
Watermark

Document-related
Bibliography
Manuscript
Report

TRYOUT

TASK 1

GOAL
To create a multiple-page report with a cover page, as shown in Figure 5.1

- ✴ Insert a page break
- ✴ Indent text
- ✴ Insert headers, footers, and page numbers
- ✴ Insert a cover page
- ✴ Use Research services

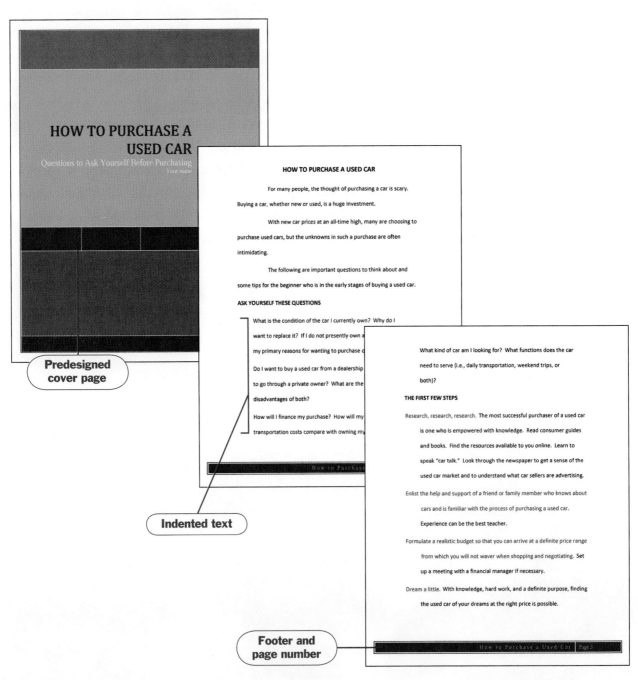

Predesigned cover page

Indented text

Footer and page number

Figure 5.1: Report with cover page

WHAT YOU NEED TO KNOW

Insert a Page Break

▶ A **page break** is the location on a page where that page ends and the next page begins. Word automatically inserts a page break when text goes beyond the bottom margin of a page. You can also insert a page break manually at any point in a document.

▶ A page break entered manually appears as a dotted horizontal line with the words "Page Break," as shown in Figure 5.2, when codes are displayed.

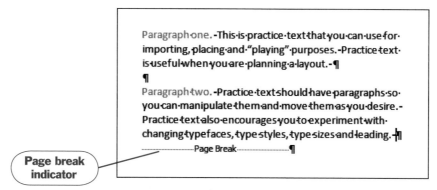

Figure 5.2: Page break in Print Layout view

HOW [Ctrl]+[Enter] To insert a page break, **1.** click **Page Layout**, and in the **Page Setup group**, **2.** click the **Breaks button**, and **3.** select **Page** from the gallery that appears, as shown in Figure 5.3.

To delete a page break, **1.** click on the page break line, and **2.** press **[Delete]**.

Figure 5.3: Breaks button and Page Breaks gallery

1. Open the data file **w5-1.**

2. Position the insertion point after paragraph two.

3. Press **[Ctrl]+[Enter]** to insert a page break.

4. Click the **Show/Hide button** to display the document codes.

5. Scroll up and note the dotted horizontal line that indicates the page break.

6. Click on the page break line, and press **[Delete]** to remove the break.

7. Hide codes.

8. Position the insertion point after paragraph three.

9. Click the **Page Layout tab**, and in the **Page Setup group**, click the **Breaks button**, and click **Page** in the gallery.

10. Close the file, and do not save the changes.

Indent Text

▶ The *Indent feature* allows you to set a temporary left, right, or left and right margin for paragraph text. In addition, you can set a **first-line indent**, which indents each new paragraph at the indented setting. You can also set a **hanging indent**, which indents all lines in a paragraph except the first line. Figure 5.4 shows examples of indented text.

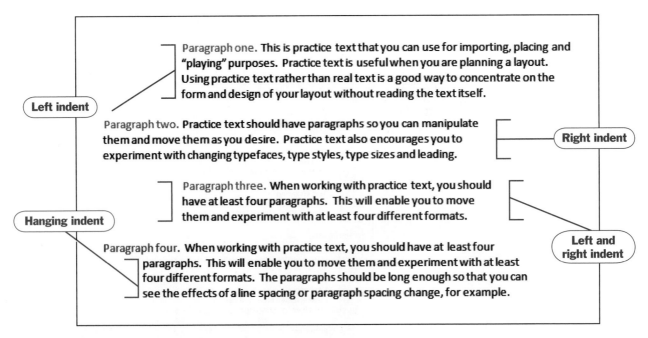

Figure 5.4: Examples of indented text

HOW To set a left indent, **1.** click the **Home tab**, and in the **Paragraph group**, **2.** click the **Increase Indent button** shown in Figure 5.5. *Each click advances the insertion point .5".* (Click the **Decrease indent button** to decrease the indent level of the paragraph.)

To set a left and right indent, a hanging indent, or a first-line indent, **1.** click the **Home tab**, and in the **Paragraph group**, **2.** click the **Paragraph dialog box launcher**. In the Paragraph dialog box that appears, shown in Figure 5.6, **3.** click the **Indents and Spacing tab**, **4.** enter the indent amount in the Left and/or Right text boxes of the Indentation section (or click the **Special list arrow**, and select **First line** or **Hanging**, enter the amount in the **By text box**), then **5.** click **OK**.

Figure 5.5: Decrease and Increase Indent buttons on the Home tab

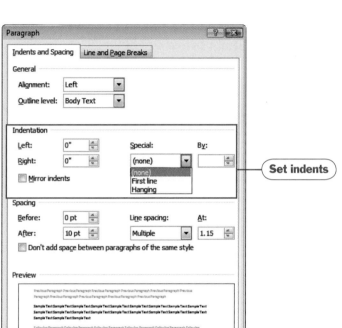

Figure 5.6: Paragraph dialog box

You can also set left and right indents by dragging Indent markers on the ruler, as shown in Figure 5.7.

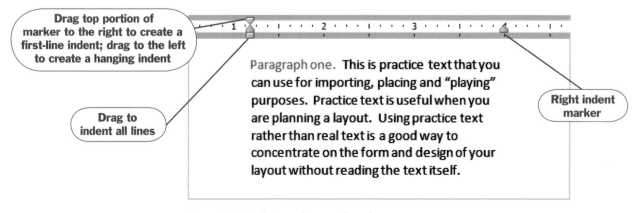

Figure 5.7: Indent markers on the ruler

1. Open a new blank document.

2. If necessary, click the **Home tab**, and in the **Paragraph group**, click the **Paragraph dialog box launcher** to display the paragraph dialog box.

3. Click the **Special list arrow**, and click **First line**.

4. Click the **increment arrow** in the By text box, and select **1.5"**.

5. Click **OK**.

6. Enter these paragraphs:

   We are happy to announce that we are expanding our services by building a second sports center, allowing us to offer several more fitness classes.¶ When we open the second center this summer, we will finally be able to provide the advanced classes that our most loyal clients have requested, such as:

7. Press **[Enter]** twice.

8. Click the **Paragraph dialog box launcher** again.

9. On the **Indents and Spacing tab**, enter 1.5 in the Left and Right text boxes.

10. Click **OK**.

11. Enter this paragraph:

    Yoga Long and Lean combines the benefits of yoga and stretching and blends them together to create a total body/mind workout.

12. Close the file, and do not save the changes.

13. Open the data file **w5-2**.

14. Position the insertion point in the first paragraph.

15. If necessary, click the **Home tab**, and in the **Paragraph group**, click the **Increase Indent button** twice. *You have just indented the paragraph 1" from the left margin.*

16. Position the insertion point in the second paragraph.

17. Click the **Paragraph dialog box launcher** to display the paragraph dialog box.
    - On the **Indents and Spacing tab**, click the **Special list arrow**, select **Hanging**, and click **OK**.

18. Position the insertion point in the third paragraph.

19. Display the paragraph dialog box.
    - On the **Indents and Spacing tab**, enter 1" in the Left and Right text boxes below **Indentation**, and click **OK**.

20. Close the file, and do not save the changes.

Insert Headers, Footers, and Page Numbers

▶ A **header** is identical text that appears at the top of every page or specified pages. A **footer** is identical text that appears at the bottom of every page or specified pages. A header or footer might include the document title or filename, the page number, the current date or time, or any other text, graphic, or symbol. You can format header and footer text in the same way as any other text.

▶ Headers, footers, and page numbers usually appear on the second and subsequent pages of a document; they generally do not appear on the first page. You can make the first page header or footer different from the rest of the pages or use no header or footer on the first page.

▶ When you insert a header or footer, Word provides Header and Footer contextual design tools to help you work with headers and footers.

▶ To view headers and footers (and page numbers) on screen, you must be in Print Layout view.

HOW **1.** Click the **Insert tab**, and in the **Header & Footer group**, **2.** click the **Header button** or **Footer button**, as shown in Figure 5.8. In the gallery that appears, as shown in Figure 5.9, **3.** select the layout and content you want in the header or footer. If there are placeholders in the header design, click the placeholder, and enter your information. **4.** Click the **Close Header and Footer button** to return to the document.

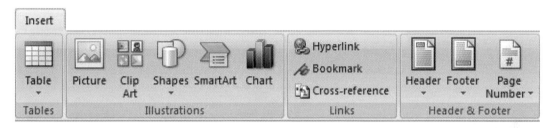

Figure 5.8: Header and Footer button on the Insert tab

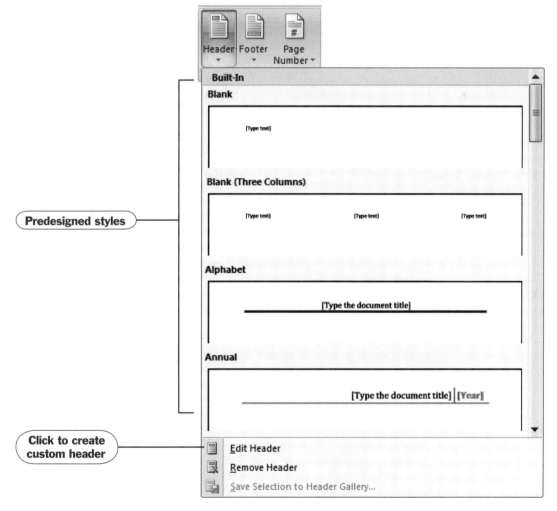

Figure 5.9: Header gallery

To create a custom header (or footer), **1.** click the **Insert tab**, and in the **Header & Footer group**, **2.** click the **Header button** (or the **Footer button**), if necessary, and **3.** click **Edit Header** (or **Edit Footer**) in the gallery (see Figure 5.9). On **Header & Footer Tools**, **4.** click the **Design tab**, if necessary, and in the **Insert group**, **5.** click an appropriate button to insert the Date and Time, Quick Parts, Picture, or Clip Art into the Header or Footer area, as shown in Figure 5.10. **6.** Click the **Close Header and Footer button** to return to the document area.

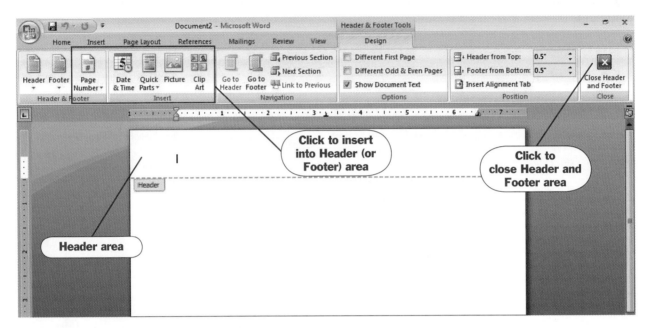

Figure 5.10: Header & Footer tools, Design tab

To insert a page number within a header or footer, **1.** click the **Page Number button** in the **Header & Footer group** (see Figure 5.10). In the menu that appears, **2.** point to a page number position option, then **3.** select a page number design from the gallery that appears, as shown in Figure 5.11.

To insert header or footer content in front of the page number, **1.** press **[HOME]**, **2.** enter the content, and then **3.** press **[TAB]** to position the page number.

To insert page numbers without header/footer text and footers, **1.** click the **Insert tab**, and in the **Header & Footer group**, **2.** click the **Page Number button list arrow**, then **3.** follow Steps 2 and 3 above under *To insert a page number within a header or footer.*

To make the first page header or footer different from the rest, or to use no header (or footer) on the first page, **1.** double-click the Header (or Footer) area. **2.** On the **Design tab**, and in the **Options Group**, select the **Different First Page check box**, as shown in Figure 5.11, then in the **First Page Header** (or **First Page Footer**) area, **3.** delete the contents of the header (or footer) or make changes to the existing header or footer.

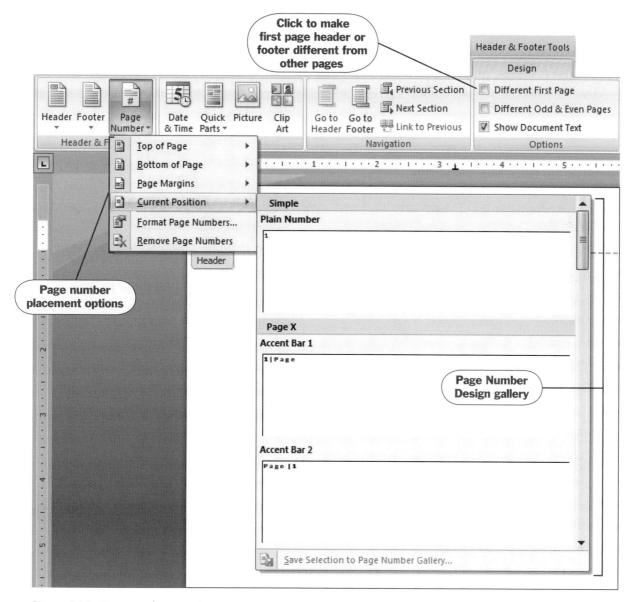

Figure 5.11: Page number insertion options

1. Be sure you are in Print Layout view; open the data file **w5-3**.

2. Click **[Ctrl]+A** to select all the paragraphs; set the line spacing to **double**.

3. Click the **Insert tab**, and in the **Header & Footer group**, click the **Header button**, then click **Edit Header**.

4. Enter **Practice Text** in the header box, and press **[Tab]** twice.

5. Click the **Page Number button**, highlight **Current Position**, and click **Accent Bar 1** in the gallery of predesigned headers/footers. *Page 2 will appear.* Scroll up to see that the header and page number are also inserted on Page 1.

6. Click the **Close Header and Footer button**.

7. Double-click the **Header area** to open the Header box.

8. In the **Navigation group**, click the **Go to Footer button**, which will open the Footer box.

9. To insert the filename into the footer, click the **Quick Parts list button** in the **Insert group**.
   a. Click **Field**.
   b. Select **FileName** from the Field names list.
   c. Click **OK**.

10. Click the **Close Header and Footer button**.

11. Scroll down to see the header and footer on both pages.

12. Double-click the **Header area** to open the header box.

13. In the **Options group**, select **Different First Page**.

14. Click the **Close Header and Footer button**. Notice that the header and footer appear only on Page 2.

15. Close the file, and do not save the changes.

Insert a Cover Page

▶ Word provides a gallery of predesigned cover pages. Regardless of where you insert the page, Word places it at the beginning of the document.

 1. Click the **Insert tab**, and in the **Pages group**, **2.** click the **Cover Page button list arrow**, as shown in Figure 5.12. In the gallery that appears, shown in Figure 5.13, **3.** select a design and **4.** replace the sample text with your own.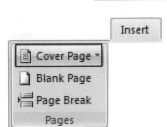

Figure 5.12: Cover Page button

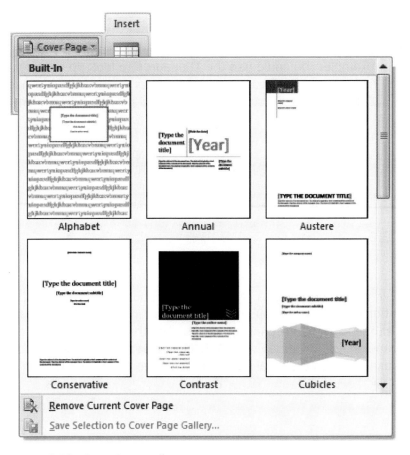

Figure 5.13: Cover Page gallery

TRY *it* **OUT** *w5-4*

1. Be sure you are in Print Layout view, then open the data file **w5-4**.

2. Click the **Insert tab**, and in the **Pages group**, click the **Cover Page button list arrow**.

3. Select the **Exposure** design. Scroll through the design to view the various placeholders.

4. Select each placeholder and enter the text shown below. The Author and Year placeholders will automatically display information that has been pulled from your computer's memory.

5. Print preview the document.

6. Close the file, and do not save the changes.

PLACEHOLDER	ENTER THIS TEXT
Title (at the left margin)	Garden Advice
Abstract (below the picture)	Tricks and Tips for Planting
Company (bottom of the page)	EarthCare Services
Address (bottom of the page)	32 Braddock Road
Phone (bottom of the page)	513-555-0005
Fax (bottom of the page)	513-555-0015

Use Research Services

▶ Word's Research feature provides useful services for you to use while you are working on your document. For example, you could use the Thesaurus to look up a synonym for the word "thorny." Once you have found the word you are looking for, you can easily insert it into your document. Table 5.1 identifies the Research features and provides an explanation of each.

Table 5.1: Research features

Dictionary	Provides definitions of words and phrases
Thesaurus	Lists synonyms, sometimes antonyms, and parts of speech for a selected word
Encyclopedia	Allows you to research a subject and click links to related articles
Translation	Translates single words or short phrases into 12 different languages
Stock quotes and company information	Accesses stock quotes and company information while you work

HOW **1.** Click in a word (or select a group of words about which you want information or enter what you are searching for in the **Search for text box**).
2. Click the **Review tab**, and in the **Proofing group**, **3.** click the **Research button**, which will display the Research task pane shown in Figure 5.14. **4.** Click the **Search for list arrow**, and choose a service you want to use, Encarta Dictionary, for example (see Figure 5.14), and **5.** click the **Start searching arrow**.

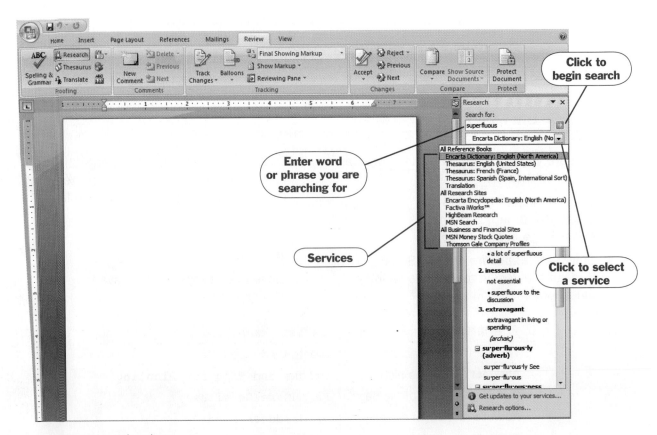

Figure 5.14: Research task pane

► You can also use a shortcut method to select the Search for word or phrase, as indicated in Table 5.2.

Table 5.2: Shortcuts to Access Research Services

SERVICE	SHORTCUT TO SEARCH FOR WORD OR PHRASE
Dictionary	Press **[ALT]**, and click the word you want to look up.
Thesaurus	Select the word you want to look up, and press **[Shift]+[F7]**. To replace the word you looked up with the one listed in the Thesaurus, position your insertion point on the word in the list, click the list arrow, and select **Insert**, or right-click the word, point to **Synonyms**, and select a word from the list.
Encyclopedia	Press **[ALT]**, and click the word or select the phrase you want to look up.
Translation	Press **[ALT]**, and click the word or select the phrase you want to translate.

T R Y *i t* **O U T** *w5-5*

1. Open the data file **w5-5**.

2. Position the insertion point on the first highlighted word.

3. Press **[Shift]+[F7]**. *This will launch the Thesaurus in the Research task pane.*

4. Position your insertion point on an appropriate replacement word in the Research task pane, and click its list arrow. Then click **Insert**.

5. Use the Thesaurus to substitute the remaining yellow highlighted words.

6. Print one copy. *The Research task pane should still be open.*

7. Click the **Search for list arrow** to select the **Translation** service. *Note: If you do not have this feature installed or if you do not have online access, skip Steps 8–11.*

8. Select to translate from **English** to **Italian**.

9. Press and hold **[Alt]**, while you click the first green highlighted word. Note the results in the Research task pane.

10. Use the Translation feature to translate the remaining green highlighted words.

11. Close the Research task pane.

12. Close the file, and do not save the changes.

REHEARSAL

TASK 1

GOAL
To create a report with a page cover, as shown in Figure 5.15

WHAT YOU NEED TO KNOW

▶ A **report** or **manuscript** communicates information about a topic. The topic may be formal or informal. Although most reports require research, others include the writer's opinion or position on the topic.

▶ The margins for a report depend on how the report is bound. The recommended margin requirements for different bindings are as follows:

- **Unbound**: 1" or 1.25" left and right, 2" or 2.5" top, 1" bottom
- **Left-bound**: 1.5" left, 1" right, 2" or 2.5" top, 1" bottom
- **Top-bound**: 1" left and right, 2" or 2.5" top, 1" bottom

▶ The start line for the first page is generally 2" or 2.5".

▶ A report is generally double-spaced. Each paragraph starts 0.5" or 1" from the left margin.

▶ A report should include a cover or title page and a bibliography. It may also include a table of contents. (You will learn to create a bibliography in Task 2.) Informational reports do not necessarily include a bibliography.

DIRECTIONS

Note: Figure 5.15 shows two pages; however, your final document, including the page cover, will span three pages.

1. Be sure you are in Print Layout view, then open the data file **w5r1-car**.

2. Use the following settings:

Margins	1.25" left and right
Line Spacing	2.0
Paragraph Spacing	
Before	6 pt
After	6 pt
Font	Default, 14 point

3. Begin the document approximately **2.0"** from the top edge of the page.

4. Format the title and the first two paragraphs as follows:
   a. Center the title, and set it to a **16-point bold** font.
   b. Set a **1"** first-line indent for the first three paragraphs.

5. Format the side headings and paragraphs below the side headings as follows:
   a. Set the two side headings to bold. (Use **Format Painter** to copy the formatting from the first side heading to the second side heading.)
   b. Set a **0.5"** left and right indent on the paragraphs shown in Figure 5.15.
   c. Create a **.05"** hanging indent, and set the font color to **red** for the first sentence of each paragraph as shown in the figure.

6. Click the **Insert tab**, and in the **Header & Footer group**, click the **Footer button**.

Continued on next page

▶ A **title page** typically contains the report's title, the writer's name, and the date the report was submitted. It may also contain the school's name, class, company's name, or division.

a. Select the **Tiles** design. If this design is not available, choose another.
b. Enter `How to Purchase a Used Car` in the **Address** placeholder. Note that the page number is entered automatically.
c. Close the Footer box.

7. Click the **Insert tab**, and in the **Pages group**, click the **Cover Page list arrow**, and select the **Tiles** page design.
   a. Delete the placeholders for **Company**, **Year**, and **Company Address**.
   b. Insert the subtitle text `Questions to Ask Yourself`.
   c. Replace the name, if necessary, in the **Author** placeholder with your own.

8. Spell check.

9. Use the Thesaurus feature to substitute the words that are highlighted in yellow.

10. On Page 3, position your insertion point before the last paragraph ("Formulate a realistic budget . . .") Press **[Ctrl]+[Enter]** to force the last paragraph to the last page.

11. Display codes. Delete the page break.

12. Press **[Ctrl]+[Home]** to move your insertion point to the top of the document. Scroll down to Page 2. Delete lines from the top of the document so that the title starts at 1", allowing the document to fit on three pages.

13. Preview all pages.

14. Save the file, and name it **5r1-buycar**.

15. Print one copy.

16. Close the file.

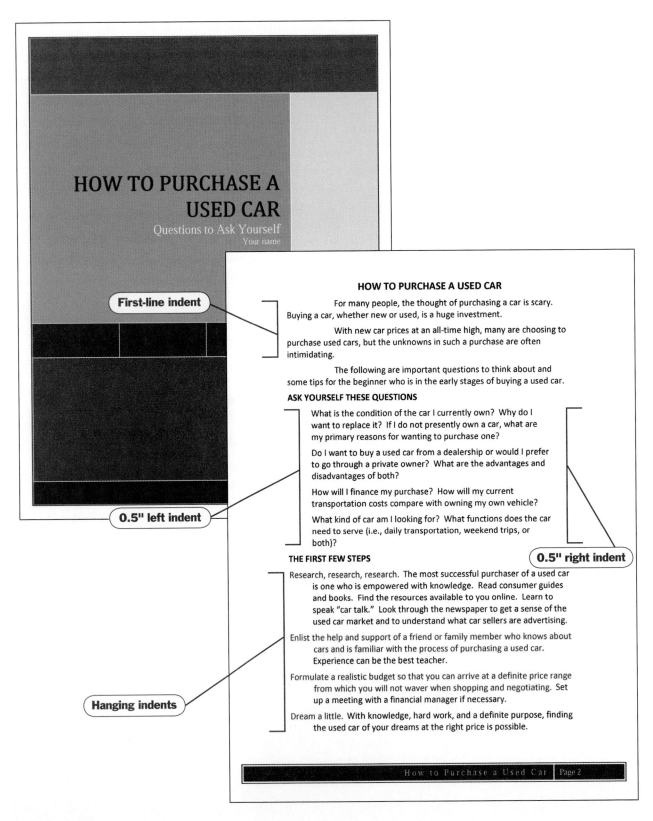

Figure 5.15: Report with a cover page

PERFORMANCE

TASK 1

As part of their promotion to encourage travelers to visit the islands of the Caribbean, Transport Travel Services is preparing an informational report titled "Cruising the Islands of the Caribbean." You have been asked to prepare the report so that that it will attract readers and inform them about the wonderful cruises available through TTS. A sample layout is shown in Figure 5.16. Use the skills you have learned thus far to replicate the sample.

Follow these guidelines:

1. Open the data file **w5p1-cruise**.

2. Select all the text in the document, then apply the following settings:

Margins	1.5" left and 1" right
Line Spacing	2.0
Paragraph Spacing	
Before	12 pt
After	12 pt
Font	Default

3. Enter a page break before the text "Any cruise you select will . . ." to position it on Page 3.

4. Format Page 3 as follows:
   a. Click the **Page Layout tab**, and in the **Page Setup group**, click the **Columns button**, then click **More Columns**. Select **Left** as the column format. Click the **Apply to list arrow**, choose **This point forward**, and click **OK**.
   b. Insert a column break after the word "reservation."
   c. Click the **Home tab**, and in the **Paragraph group**, click the **Show/Hide button** to display the document codes. Delete the paragraph symbol (¶) at the top of the second column to align the second paragraph with the first.
   d. Set the first column to a script font. Set the second column to single space.
   e. Insert a relevant clip art graphic, as shown in Figure 5.16. Apply a **Behind Text** wrap. Then, size the graphic so that it is as large as possible.
   f. Select the graphic. Click the **Format tab**, and in the **Adjust group**, click the **Brightness button**, then select **+40%**.
   g. Set the cruise type headings to a **blue** font.

5. Insert a custom header that reads, "Cruising to the Islands of the Caribbean." Center the text, and set the font to **14-point blue script**. Press **[Enter]** once.
   * Insert a page number in the **Current Position** (centered below the centered header text), using the **Accent Bar 1** page number design.

Continued on next page

6. Insert a cover page using the **Transend** design.
   a. Replace the car graphic with a graphic depicting sailing. Size and position it as you want.
   b. Delete the **Author** and **Date** placeholders.
   c. Insert the text (shown in the figure) in the **Document Title** and **Document Subtitle** placeholders.

7. Insert two drop capitals as shown in the figure. Use any drop capital style you want.

8. Print preview the file. Save the file, and name it **5p1-cruise**.

9. Print one copy, and close the file.

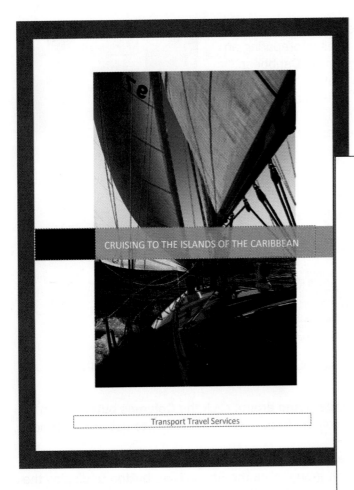

Figure 5.16a: Cover page and Page 1 of an informational report

Page 3 content:

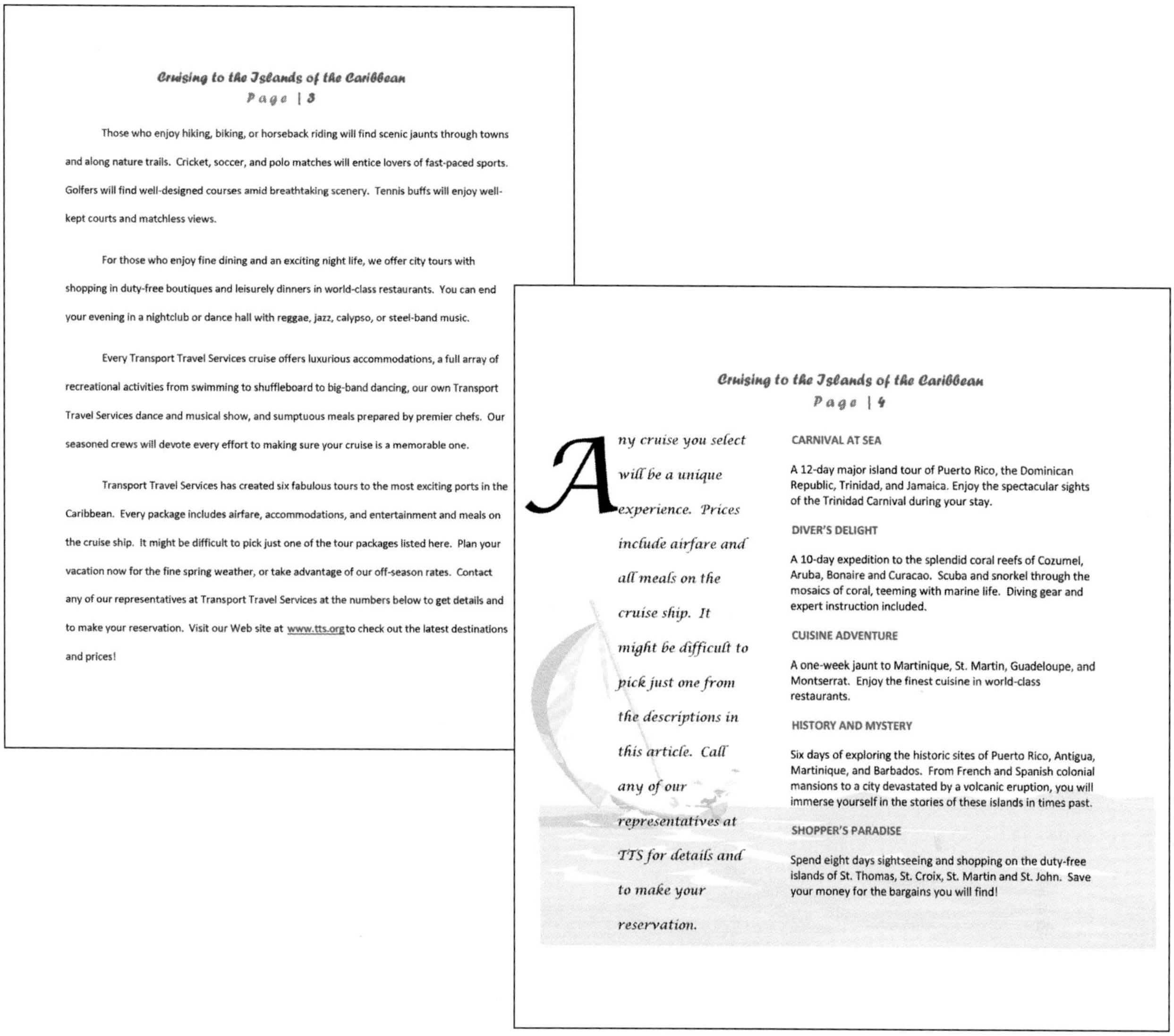

Cruising to the Islands of the Caribbean
Page | 3

Those who enjoy hiking, biking, or horseback riding will find scenic jaunts through towns and along nature trails. Cricket, soccer, and polo matches will entice lovers of fast-paced sports. Golfers will find well-designed courses amid breathtaking scenery. Tennis buffs will enjoy well-kept courts and matchless views.

For those who enjoy fine dining and an exciting night life, we offer city tours with shopping in duty-free boutiques and leisurely dinners in world-class restaurants. You can end your evening in a nightclub or dance hall with reggae, jazz, calypso, or steel-band music.

Every Transport Travel Services cruise offers luxurious accommodations, a full array of recreational activities from swimming to shuffleboard to big-band dancing, our own Transport Travel Services dance and musical show, and sumptuous meals prepared by premier chefs. Our seasoned crews will devote every effort to making sure your cruise is a memorable one.

Transport Travel Services has created six fabulous tours to the most exciting ports in the Caribbean. Every package includes airfare, accommodations, and entertainment and meals on the cruise ship. It might be difficult to pick just one of the tour packages listed here. Plan your vacation now for the fine spring weather, or take advantage of our off-season rates. Contact any of our representatives at Transport Travel Services at the numbers below to get details and to make your reservation. Visit our Web site at www.tts.org to check out the latest destinations and prices!

Page 4 content:

Cruising to the Islands of the Caribbean
Page | 4

*A*ny cruise you select will be a unique experience. Prices include airfare and all meals on the cruise ship. It might be difficult to pick just one from the descriptions in this article. Call any of our representatives at TTS for details and to make your reservation.

CARNIVAL AT SEA

A 12-day major island tour of Puerto Rico, the Dominican Republic, Trinidad, and Jamaica. Enjoy the spectacular sights of the Trinidad Carnival during your stay.

DIVER'S DELIGHT

A 10-day expedition to the splendid coral reefs of Cozumel, Aruba, Bonaire and Curacao. Scuba and snorkel through the mosaics of coral, teeming with marine life. Diving gear and expert instruction included.

CUISINE ADVENTURE

A one-week jaunt to Martinique, St. Martin, Guadeloupe, and Montserrat. Enjoy the finest cuisine in world-class restaurants.

HISTORY AND MYSTERY

Six days of exploring the historic sites of Puerto Rico, Antigua, Martinique, and Barbados. From French and Spanish colonial mansions to a city devastated by a volcanic eruption, you will immerse yourself in the stories of these islands in times past.

SHOPPER'S PARADISE

Spend eight days sightseeing and shopping on the duty-free islands of St. Thomas, St. Croix, St. Martin and St. John. Save your money for the bargains you will find!

Figure 5.16b: Pages 3 and 4 of an informational report

Indent Text

1. Click the **Home tab**, then click the **Paragraph dialog box launcher**.
2. Click **Indents and Spacing tab**, if necessary.
3. Make your selections and/or enter amount of the indent.
4. Click **OK**.

Hanging Indent

1. Place the insertion point in affected paragraph or select desired paragraphs.
2. Drag the hanging indent marker on the ruler to the appropriate position.
   Or
1. Click the **Home tab**, and in the **Paragraph group**, click the **dialog box launcher**.
2. Click the **Indents and Spacing tab**.
3. Click the **Special list arrow**, and select **Hanging** or **First line**.
4. Click the increment arrow in the By text box to enter a hanging indent amount or enter an amount in the Left and/or Right text box below Indentation to set a left/right indent.
5. Click **OK**.

Headers and Footers

1. Click the **Insert tab**, and in the **Header & Footer group**, click the **Header button** or **Footer button**.
2. Select a header or footer design from the gallery, and replace or delete the placeholder text, or click **Edit Header** or **Edit Footer** to create a custom header/footer, and enter and format header or footer text as you prefer.
3. Click an appropriate button to insert the Date and Time, Quick Parts, Picture, or Clip Art in the header or Footer area.
4. Click the **Page Number button** to add a page number.
   - Point to a placement position.
   - Select a page number style from the gallery.
5. Click the **Close Header and Footer button**.

Suppress the Header/Footer on First Page

1. Double-click the **Header or Footer area**.
2. On the **Design tab**, and in the **Options group**, select the **Different First Page check box**.
3. Click the **Close Header and Footer button**.

Insert Page Numbers (Independently of Headers and Footers)

1. Click the **Insert tab**, and in the **Header & Footer group**, click the **Page Number button list arrow**.
2. Point to a placement position.
3. Select a page number style from the gallery.

Insert a Cover Page

1. Click the **Insert tab**, and in the **Pages group**, click the **Cover Page button**.
2. Select a design from the gallery.
3. Replace placeholder text with your own or delete the placeholder.

TRYOUT

TASK 2

GOAL

To create a research report with cover page and bibliography, as shown in Figure 5.17

* Apply and modify a Quick Style
* Apply a theme
* Insert a watermark
* Set vertical centering
* Apply paragraph borders and shading
* Find and replace text
* Insert a file
* Insert a citation and create a bibliography

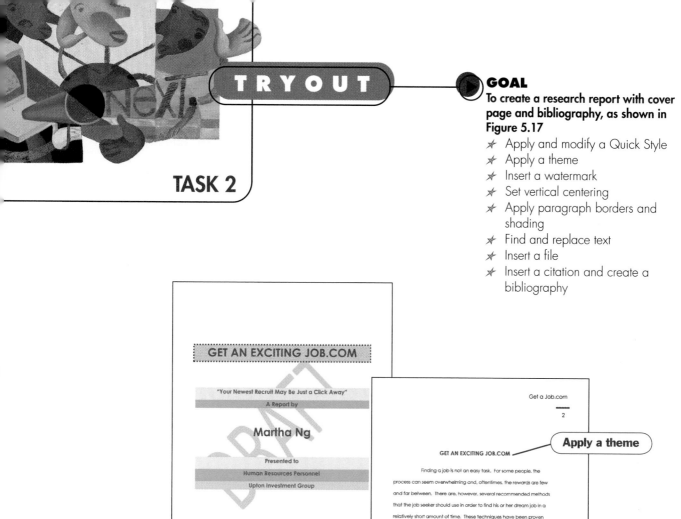

Apply a theme

Cover page vertically centered with paragraph borders and shading

Bibliography

Citation

Watermark

Figure 5.17: Cover page, Page 2, Page 3, and Bibliography of a research report

WHAT YOU NEED TO KNOW

Apply and Modify a Quick Style

▶ A **style** is a collection of formats you can apply to selected text. For example, one style might specify 16-point Arial bold and single spacing. By using a style, you can apply several formats (font size, font style, and line spacing) in one step and ensure consistency in formatting.

▶ You can use or modify one of Word's Quick Styles, or you can create your own. Styles are displayed on the Home tab, as shown in Figure 5.18. Additional styles can be displayed by clicking the More arrow (see Figure 5.18).

▶ Once you make a change to a style, any text based on that style is updated automatically with the modified characteristics.

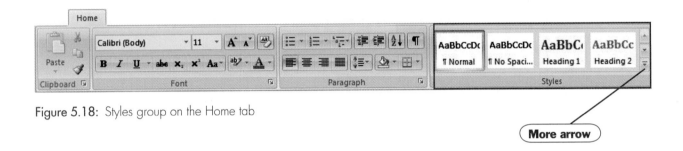

Figure 5.18: Styles group on the Home tab

More arrow

HOW To apply an existing style, **1.** select the text to which you want to apply a style. **2.** Click the **Home tab**, and in the **Styles group**, **3.** click the style you want. To see additional styles, click the **More arrow** (see Figure 5.18), which will display the **Quick Styles gallery** shown in Figure 5.19.

Figure 5.19: Quick Styles gallery

To create a new style, **1.** format some text on which you want to base the style, **2.** right-click the selection, **3.** point to **Styles**, then **4.** click **Save Selection as a New Quick Style** on the menu, as shown in Figure 5.20. The word "HELLO" is the formatted text on which the style is based. **5.** In the Create New Style from Formatting dialog box, enter a name for your new style, then **6.** click **OK**. The style you just created will appear in the Quick Styles gallery, ready for you to use.

Figure 5.20: Create a new Quick Style

To modify or delete a style, **1.** right-click the style you want to modify, and **2.** click **Modify** on the menu. **3.** In the Modify Style dialog box that displays shown in Figure 5.21, **4.** make the modifications you want, then **5.** click **OK**.

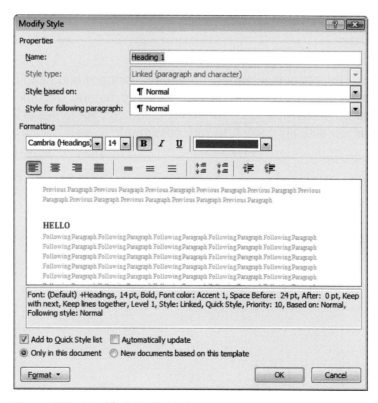

Figure 5.21: Modify Style dialog box

To view the attributes of a particular style (Heading 1, perhaps), click the **Styles dialog box launcher** and point to a style in the list, which will display a pop-up box with the style information.

TRY*it*OUT *w5-6*

Apply an Existing Style

1. Open the data file **w5-6**.

2. Select the words "TOUR IN EGYPT."

3. Click the **Home tab**, if necessary, and in the **Styles group**, click the **Heading 1** style.

4. Select the words "TOUR IN PERU."

5. Repeat Step 3.

Create a New Style

1. Select the words "July 14-July 22."

2. Change the font to **10-point Comic Sans MS**, the style to **italic**, and the font color to **Red**.

3. Select the words "July 14–July 22," then right-click the selection, point to **Styles**, and click **Save Selection as a New Quick Style**.

4. In the Create New Style from Formatting dialog box, click in the **Name** text box, and enter: `Date Head`.

5. Click **OK**.

6. Select the words "June 14-June 22."

7. Click **Date Head** in the **Style group**.

Modify an Existing Style

1. On the **Home tab**, in the **Styles group**, right-click the **Heading 1 style**, and select **Modify**.

2. Change the font color to **green**.

3. Click **OK**. *The two headings that were based on the Heading 1 style automatically change to green.*

4. Close the file, and do not save the changes.

Apply a Theme

▶ A **theme** is a combination of color schemes, fonts used for body and heading text, and shading effects on graphics that creates the look for your entire document. Document themes that you apply immediately affect the styles you have applied. You can see a live preview of the theme to see its effect before you actually apply it to your document.

HOW **1.** Click the **Page Layout tab**, and in the **Themes group**, **2.** click the **Themes button list arrow** to display the Themes gallery shown in Figure 5.22. **3.** Point to each theme to see a live preview, then **4.** select one to apply it.

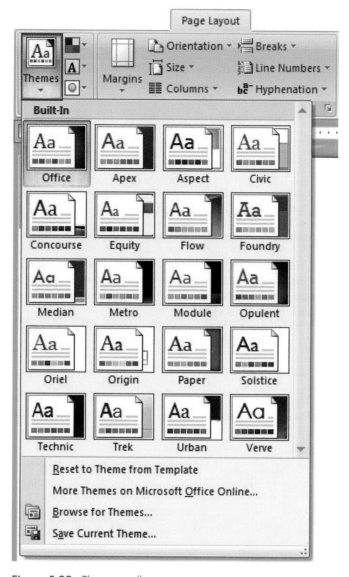

Figure 5.22: Themes gallery

T R Y *i t* **O U T** *w5-7*

1. Open the data file **w5-7**.

2. Click the **Page Layout tab**, and in the **Themes group**, click the **Themes button list arrow**.

3. Point to each theme to see a live preview.

4. Select the **Equity** theme.

5. Close the file, and do not save the changes.

Apply Paragraph Borders and Shading

▶ You learned previously to apply borders and shading to a shape, graphic, or a page to add emphasis or create an interesting effect. Using the same techniques, you can also apply borders and shading to a paragraph or selected text, as shown in Figure 5.23.

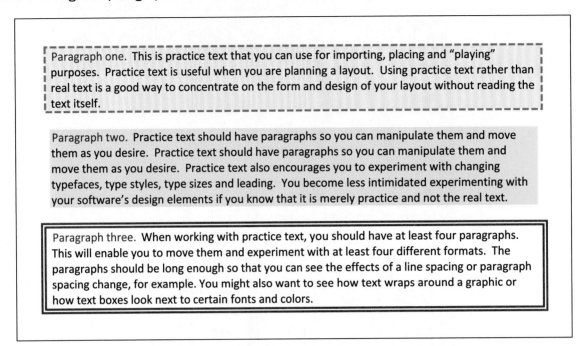

Figure 5.23: Paragraph border and shading examples

HOW To apply a border and/or shading, **1.** select the paragraph or text. **2.** Click the **Home tab**, and in the **Paragraph group**, **3.** click the **Borders button list arrow** (The button displays the most recently used border, but other borders can be accessed by using the list arrow.), and **4.** select **Borders and Shading**, as shown in Figure 5.24. In the Borders and Shading dialog box that appears, as shown in Figure 5.25, **5.** click the **Borders and/or Shading tab**, and select the options you want (be sure **Paragraph** is selected in the Apply to box), then **6.** click **OK**.

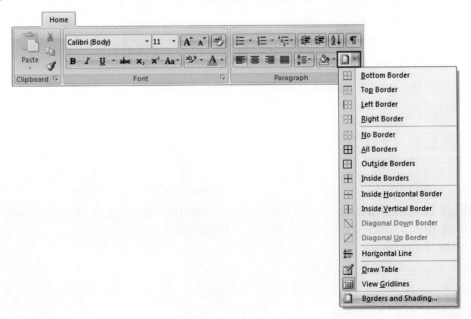

Figure 5.24: Borders button on Home tab

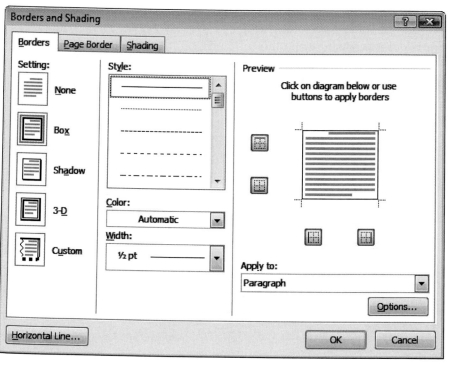

Figure 5.25: Borders and Shading dialog box

TRY *it* OUT w5-8

1. Open the data file **w5-8**.

2. Select the first paragraph.

3. Click the **Home tab**, and in the **Paragraph group**, click the **Borders button list arrow**, and select **Borders and Shading**.

4. In the Borders and Shading dialog box that appears, click the **Borders tab**, if necessary.

5. Select **Box** below **Setting**.

6. Select a dotted line from the Style list.

7. Click the **Apply to list arrow**, and select **Paragraph**.

8. Click the **Color list arrow**, and click **red**.

9. Click the **Width list arrow**, and click **2 1/4 pt**.

10. Click the **Shading tab**, and select a **light yellow** fill.

11. Click **OK**.

12. Close the file, and do not save the changes.

Tryout Task 2

Set Vertical Centering

▶ You can center text vertically between the top and bottom margins or between the top and bottom edges of the page. This is particularly useful if you are centering text on a cover page that you created from scratch. Figure 5.26 shows a cover page that has been vertically centered on the page.

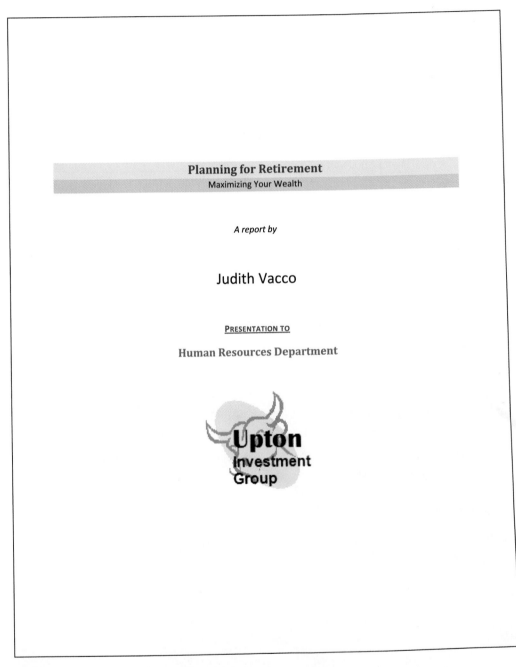

Figure 5.26: Text centered vertically on the page

HOW 1. Click the **Page Layout tab**, and in the **Page Setup group**, click the **Page Setup dialog box launcher**. In the Page Setup dialog box that appears, 2. click the **Layout tab**, as shown in Figure 5.27, 3. click the **Vertical alignment list arrow**, 4. click **Center**, then 5. click **OK**.

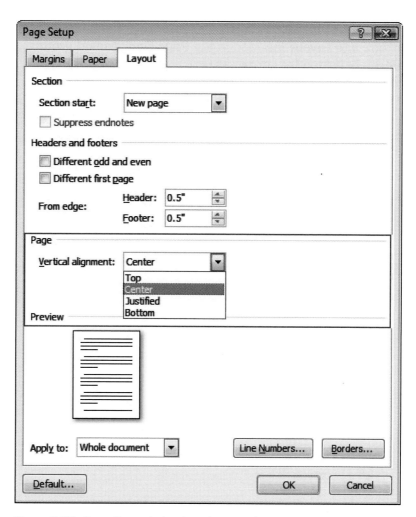

Figure 5.27: Page Setup dialog box, Layout tab

T R Y *it* O U T *w5-9*

1. Open the data file **w5-9**.

2. Click the **Page Layout tab**.

3. Click the **Page Setup dialog box launcher**.

4. Click the **Layout tab**.

5. Click the **Vertical alignment list arrow**.

6. Click **Center**.

7. Click **OK**.

8. Print preview the file.

9. Close the file, and do not save the changes.

Insert a Watermark

▶ A **watermark** is text or pictures that appear behind document text. It appears on every printed page. You can create a picture watermark or a text watermark, but you cannot include both on the same page.

▶ Word provides a gallery of predesigned watermarks from which you can choose.

HOW 1. Click the **Page Layout tab**, and in the **Page Background group**, 2. click the **Watermark button list arrow**, as shown in Figure 5.28. 3. Select a watermark from the gallery shown in Figure 5.29 (or click **Custom Watermark**), and in the Printed Watermark dialog box that appears, as shown in Figure 5.30, 4. make your selections, and 5. click **OK**.

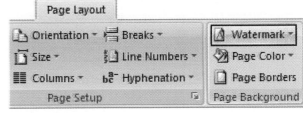

Figure 5.28: Watermark button

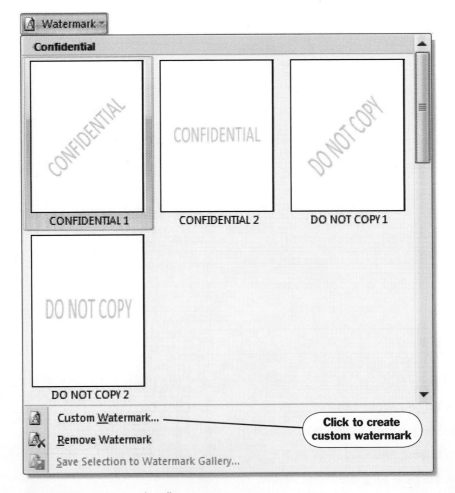

Figure 5.29: Watermark gallery

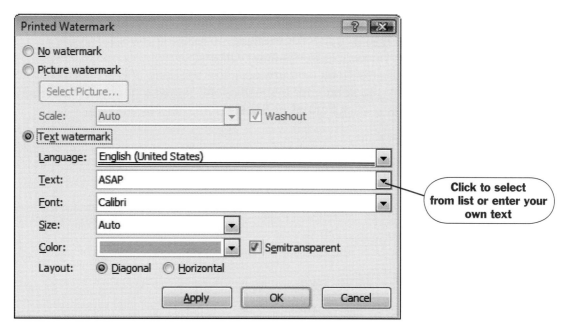

Figure 5.30: Printed Watermark dialog box

TRY it OUT *w5-10*

1. Open the data file **w5-10**.

2. Click the **Page Layout tab**, and in the **Page Background group**, click the **Watermark button list arrow**.

3. Scroll down, and select the **URGENT 1** predesigned watermark.

4. Close the file, and do not save the changes.

5. Open the data file again.

6. Repeat Step 2.

7. Click **Custom Watermark**.

8. Click the **Text watermark** option.

9. Click the **Text** box, and enter **FOR REVIEW**. Click the **Color list arrow**, select **Red**, then click **OK**.

10. Close the file, and do not save the changes.

Find and Replace Text

▶ The *Find feature* scans a document and searches for occurrences of specified text, symbols, or formatting.

▶ The *Replace feature* allows you to locate all occurrences of certain text and replace it with different text, special characters, or symbols.

HOW [Ctrl]+H **1.** Click the **Home tab**, and in the **Editing group, 2.** click the **Replace button**, as shown in Figure 5.31. In the Find and Replace dialog box that appears, shown in Figure 5.32, **3.** click the **Replace tab**, and **4.** enter text to find and/or replace in the appropriate text boxes. **5.** Click **More** for advanced searches, as shown in Figure 5.32. **6.** Click **Find Next**, then **Replace**, to replace one word at a time, or click **Replace All** to replace all occurrences at once.

To conduct an advanced search, select the appropriate check boxes in the advanced search dialog box (see Figure 5.33). For example, to locate the word "The," select "Match case" and "Find whole words only." Otherwise, your search will not only find "The" but also "the," "otherwise," "thesis," and any other word of which "the" is a part. To search for a specific font, paragraph, tab, style, or other specialized mark, click **Format** or **Special** for other options.

Figure 5.31: Replace button on the Home tab

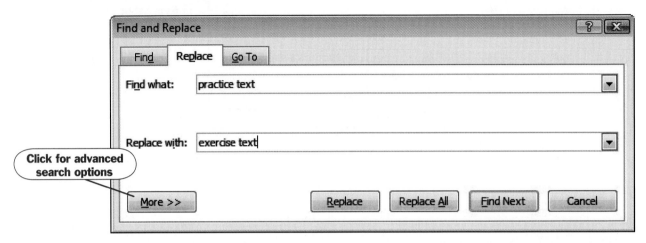

Figure 5.32: Find and Replace dialog box

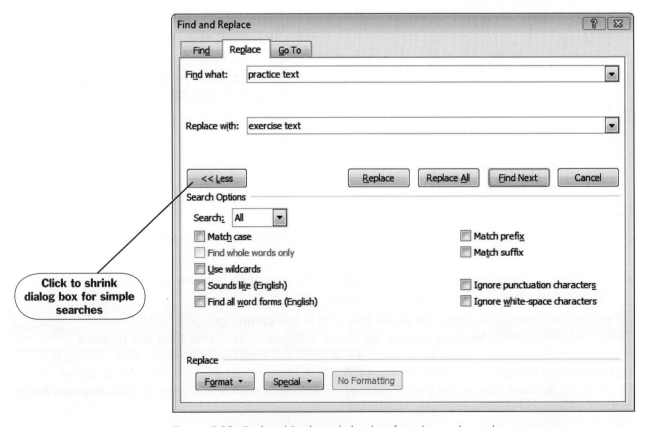

Figure 5.33: Find and Replace dialog box for advanced searches

TRY *it* OUT *w5-11*

1. Open the data file **w5-11**.

2. Click the **Home tab**, and in the **Editing group**, click the **Replace button**.

3. Enter **intimidated** in the Find what box, and click **Find Next**.
   a. Close the dialog box.
   b. Use the Thesaurus to substitute another word.

4. Click the **Replace button** again.

5. Enter **practice text** in the Find what box and **exercise text** in the Replace with box.

6. Click **More**.
   a. Click **Format**, then click **Font**.
   b. Enter **14** in the Size box, then click **OK**.
   c. Click **Replace All**, then click **OK**.

7. Find the abbreviation "pf" and replace it with **ef**.

8. Close the file, and do not save the changes.

Insert a File

▶ The *Insert File feature* allows you to insert a file into the current document, which then becomes part of that document. The file you insert remains intact, enabling you to use it again as needed.

HOW 1. Position the insertion point at the location in the document where you want the insert to appear. 2. Click the **Insert tab**, and in the **Text group**, 3. click the **Object button list arrow** and 4. select **Text from File**, as shown in Figure 5.34. 5. Select the file you wish to insert, and 6. click **Insert**.

Figure 5.34: Object button on Insert tab

TRY *it* OUT *w5-12*

1. Open the data file **w5-12**.

2. Position the insertion point in front of the word "As" at the start of the second paragraph.

3. Click the **Insert tab**, and in the **Text group**, click the **Object button list arrow**, and select **Text from File**.

4. Select the data file **w5-12a**.

5. Click **Insert** to insert the file into the current document.

6. Close the file, and do not save the changes.

Insert a Citation and Create a Bibliography

▶ Research reports usually contain quoted material from another source (a book, newspaper, magazine, encyclopedia, or the Web, for example). A **citation** references the source of quoted material. *It is necessary to cite someone else's ideas, words, statistics, artwork, or lab results. Failing to do so constitutes plagiarism.*

▶ Citations generally appear at the bottom of a page as footnotes or at the end of the report as endnotes. They may also appear as *internal citations,* that is, references that immediately follow the quoted or paraphrased material.

▶ In the internal citation, just the author's name and year of publication is listed. When using the internal citation for Web references, however, list the author's last name, the Web site, and the date of Web posting.

▶ A **bibliography**, or references page, is a summary list of the sources used, quoted, or paraphrased within a document. A bibliography is generally the last page in a report.

▶ Each bibliographical entry contains the author's last name and first name, the name of the article and the publication, the publisher, and the date of publication. The sources are generally listed in alphabetical order by author's last name. If you used internal citations in the report, the bibliographical reference should include the page number of the quoted material.

▶ Word's Citation feature allows you to enter information about each source, which is then properly formatted (based on a writing style you choose) and inserted as an internal citation at the location in your document that you specify.

▶ The Bibliography tool automatically generates a list of sources you entered as citations and formats them based on your selected writing style. Table 5.3 lists the different writing styles and by whom they are typically used. *Professional organizations provide styles for the mechanics of writing, such as punctuation, quotation, and documentation of sources.*

Table 5.3: Writing styles

STYLE	USED BY
AMA (American Medical Association)	Writers in the fields of medicine, health, and biological sciences
APA (American Psychological Association)	Writers in the fields of psychology, education, and other social sciences
Chicago	Publishing and research communities
MLA (Modern Language Association)	Writers in the fields of literature, arts, and humanities
Turabian	College students with all subjects

HOW To create each internal citation, **1.** click the **References tab**, and in the **Citations & Bibliography group**, **2.** click the **Style button list arrow**, as shown in Figure 5.35, and **3.** select a writing style for your citations. **4.** Click in the document where you want the citation to appear. **5.** Click the **Insert Citation button list arrow** (see Figure 5.35). **6.** Select **Add New Source**. In the Create Source dialog box that appears, shown in Figure 5.36, **7.** click the **Type of Source list arrow**, and select the type of source from which you are citing. **8.** Enter the information for the citation in the **Bibliography Fields** section, and **9.** click **OK**.

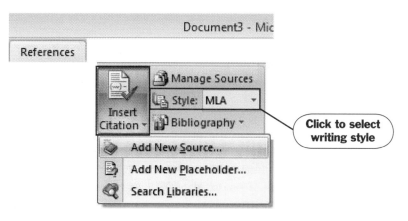

Figure 5.35: Citations & Bibliography group, References tab

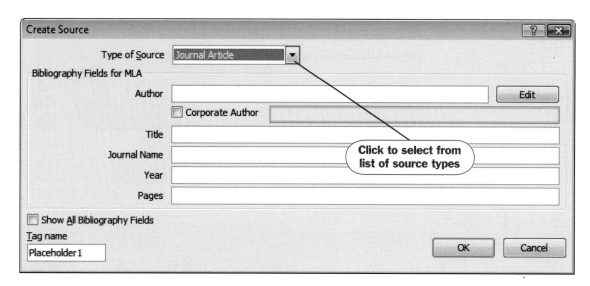

Figure 5.36: Create Source dialog box

To create a bibliography, **1.** click in the document where you want the bibliography to appear (generally the last page). **2.** Click the **References tab**, and in the **Citations & Bibliography group**, **3.** click the **Style button list arrow**, and select the same writing style you used to create the citation. **4.** Click the **Bibliography button list arrow**. **4.** Click **Bibliography**, as shown in Figure 5.37. The format will vary depending on the writing style you select.

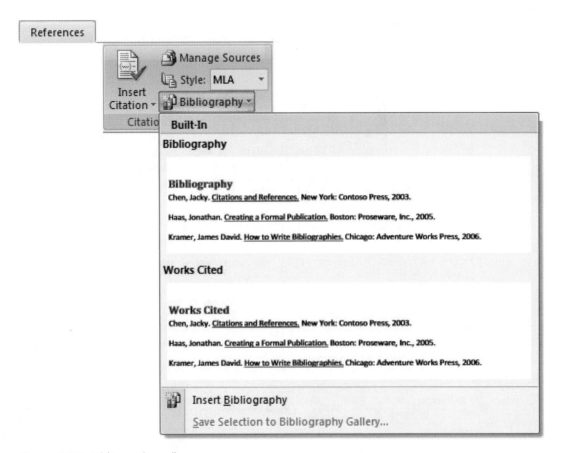

Figure 5.37: Bibliography gallery

T R Y *i t* **O U T** *w5-13*

1. Open the data file **w5-13**.

2. Position your insertion point at the end of the first paragraph.

3. Click the **References tab**, and in the **Citations & Bibliography group**, click the **Style button list arrow**, and select **MLA**.

4. Click the **Insert Citation button list arrow**, then click **Add New Source**.

5. Click the **Type of Source** list box, and select **Web site**.

6. Select the **Corporate Author** check box to indicate that the author works for the company.

7. Enter the information into the text boxes, as shown in Figure 5.38, then click **OK**.

8. Position your insertion point at the end of the second paragraph.

9. Repeat Steps 3 and 4.

10. Click the **Type of Source list arrow**, and select **Article in Periodical**.

Continued on next page

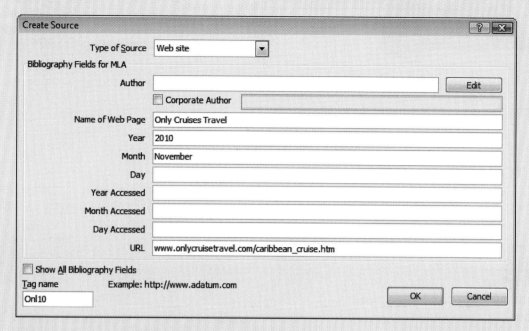

Figure 5.38: Create Source dialog box for Web site

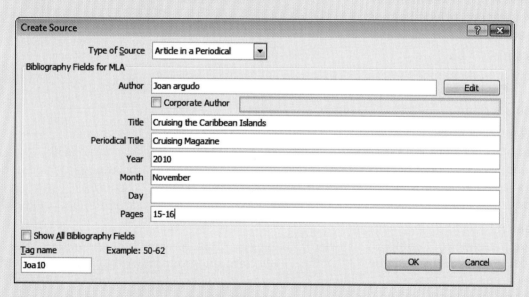

Figure 5.39: Create Source dialog box for an article in a periodical

11. Enter the information into the text boxes as shown in Figure 5.39, then click **OK**.

12. Position your insertion point at the end of the last paragraph.

13. Press **Ctrl+[Enter]** to create a new page.

14. Position your insertion point where you want the bibliography to begin.

15. Click the **Bibliography button list arrow**, and select **Bibliography** from the gallery that displays. *Note: Page numbers will be displayed as part of the bibliography only if you choose certain writing styles.*

16. Close the file, and do not save the changes.

REHEARSAL

GOAL
To create a multiple-page report with cover page, headers and footers, internal citations, and a bibliography, as shown in Figure 5.40

TASK 2

WHAT YOU NEED TO KNOW

► A *style* is a collection of formats you can apply to selected text.

► A *theme* is a combination of color schemes, fonts used for body and heading text, and shading effects on graphics that creates the look for your entire document.

► You can create a picture watermark or a text watermark, but you cannot include both on the same page.

► The *Find feature* scans a document and searches for occurrences of specified text, symbols, or formatting.

► The *Replace feature* allows you to locate all occurrences of certain text and replace it with different text, special characters, or symbols.

► Research reports usually contains quoted material from another source. It is necessary to cite someone else's ideas, word, statistics, or artwork. Failing to do so constitutes plagiarism.

► When quoted material is more than two lines, it is indented 0.5" or 1" from the left and right margins and single spaced; the quotation marks are omitted.

► A bibliography is generally the last page in a report.

DIRECTIONS

1. Open the data file **w5r2-job**. This text is single-spaced and unformatted. Your final copy will look like Figure 5.40.

2. Create the report shown in Figure 5.40. Select all the text in the document and apply the following settings:

Margins	1.25" left and 1.25" right
Line Spacing	2.0
Paragraph Spacing	
Before	0
After	0
Font	Default, 12 point

3. Start the document approximately **2.5"** from the top of the page.

4. Apply the **Heading 1** style to the title.

5. Set a **1"** first-line indent for the paragraphs.

6. Insert a header using the **Stacks** design and enter `Searching for a Job`.
   a. Suppress the header on the first page.
   b. Close the header box.

7. Click the **Page Layout tab**, and in the **Page Background group**, click the **Watermark button list arrow**, scroll down, and select the **DRAFT 1** design from the gallery.

8. Position your insertion point in front of the paragraph that reads, "There's another huge advantage . . ."
   a. Click the **Insert tab**, and in the **Text group**, click the **Object button list arrow**, and select **Text from File**. Insert the data file **w5r2-quote**. Insert a blank line after the insert, if necessary.
   b. Indent the quoted material **0.5"** from the left and right margins.

9. Single-space the numbered list at the end of the report.

Continued on next page

10. Insert a bullet for the paragraphs shown.

11. Click the **Home tab**, and in the **Editing group**, click the **Replace button**.
    a. Enter `concentration` in the Find what box; enter `focus` in the Replace with box.
    b. Click **Replace** once to find the word; click **Replace** again the replace the word; then click **OK**.

12. Find the word "customary" and replace it with `traditional`.

13. Spell check.

14. Double-click the Header area to open the header box. Edit the header to read `Get a Job.com`.

15. Click the **Page Layout tab**, and in the **Themes group**, click the **Themes button**, and apply a **Verve** theme. Center the heading.

Continued on next page

Get a Job.com

—

2

GET AN EXCITING JOB.COM

Finding a job is not an easy task. For some people, the process can seem overwhelming and, oftentimes, the rewards are few and far between. There are, however, several recommended methods that the job seeker should use in order to find his or her dream job in a relatively short amount of time. These techniques have been proven successful and can help the person seeking a job to focus on the task at hand.

It is important to begin a job search with a self-assessment. There are several books and tests available at the library, in career placement offices, at bookstores, and online that can help an individual begin to form a list of the kinds of jobs that she or he is seeking based on personal and professional goals. The job seeker should also begin by talking to a wide variety of individuals in several different fields to learn more about what types of jobs are available and at what level and salary range. This will help the seeker narrow her or his focus so that the search is more effective.

Figure 5.40a: Page 2 of job search report

16. Insert a citation at the end of paragraph three.
    a. Click the **References tab**, and in the **Citations & Bibliography group**, click the **Style button list arrow**, and select **MLA**.
    b. Click the **Insert Citation button**, and select **Add New Source**.
    c. Fill in the Create Source dialog box using the information shown below. Click the **Show All Bibliography Fields check box** to expand the dialog box.

FIELDS	SELECT OPTION/ENTER THIS TEXT
Type of Source	**Book Section**
Author	**John Nobel**
Title	**The Elements of Job Hunting**
Year	**2009**
City	**Boston**
Publisher	**Hinton-Hall**
Pages	**45**

17. Insert a citation at the end of paragraph four.
    a. Repeat Steps 16a and 16b.
    b. Fill in the Create Source dialog box as shown below.

FIELDS	SELECT OPTION/ENTER THIS TEXT
Type of Source	**Web site**
Author	**David Colson**
Name of Web Page	**Jobs Jobs Jobs**
Year	**2010**
Month	**January**
URL	**www.zdmag.com**

18. Insert a citation at the end of the single-spaced quotation.
    a. Repeat Steps 16a and 16b.
    b. Fill in the **Create Source dialog box** using the information shown below.

FIELDS	SELECT OPTION/ENTER THIS TEXT
Type of Source	**Article in Periodical**
Author	**Vicky G. Lamorte**
Title	**Classifieds on the Web**
Periodical Title	**PC Journal**
Year	**2010**
Month	**November**
Pages	**127**

Continued on next page

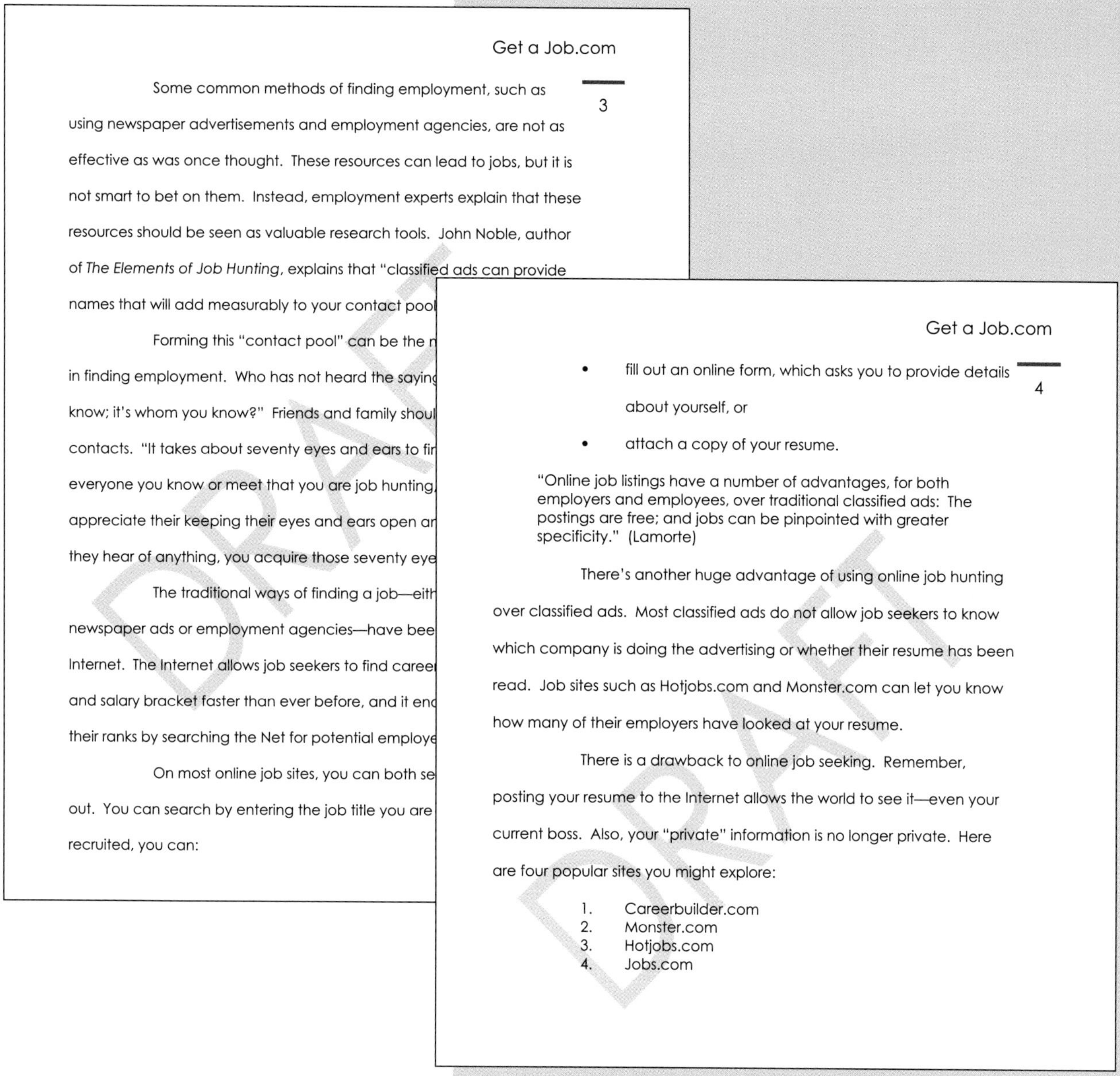

Get a Job.com
___
3

Some common methods of finding employment, such as using newspaper advertisements and employment agencies, are not as effective as was once thought. These resources can lead to jobs, but it is not smart to bet on them. Instead, employment experts explain that these resources should be seen as valuable research tools. John Noble, author of *The Elements of Job Hunting*, explains that "classified ads can provide names that will add measurably to your contact pool

Forming this "contact pool" can be the m in finding employment. Who has not heard the saying know; it's whom you know?" Friends and family shoul contacts. "It takes about seventy eyes and ears to fir everyone you know or meet that you are job hunting, appreciate their keeping their eyes and ears open ar they hear of anything, you acquire those seventy eye

The traditional ways of finding a job—eith newspaper ads or employment agencies—have bee Internet. The Internet allows job seekers to find caree and salary bracket faster than ever before, and it en their ranks by searching the Net for potential employe

On most online job sites, you can both se out. You can search by entering the job title you are recruited, you can:

Get a Job.com
___
4

- fill out an online form, which asks you to provide details about yourself, or
- attach a copy of your resume.

"Online job listings have a number of advantages, for both employers and employees, over traditional classified ads: The postings are free; and jobs can be pinpointed with greater specificity." (Lamorte)

There's another huge advantage of using online job hunting over classified ads. Most classified ads do not allow job seekers to know which company is doing the advertising or whether their resume has been read. Job sites such as Hotjobs.com and Monster.com can let you know how many of their employers have looked at your resume.

There is a drawback to online job seeking. Remember, posting your resume to the Internet allows the world to see it—even your current boss. Also, your "private" information is no longer private. Here are four popular sites you might explore:

1. Careerbuilder.com
2. Monster.com
3. Hotjobs.com
4. Jobs.com

Figure 5.40b: Pages 3 and 4 of job search report

19. Create the bibliography as follows:
   a. Insert a page break at the end of the last page.
   b. Set the first line indent to **0**.
   c. Begin the bibliography at approximately **2.5"** from the top of the page.
   d. Click the **References tab**, and in the **Citations & Bibliography group**, click the **Style button list arrow**, and select **MLA**.
   e. Click the **Bibliography button list arrow**. Click **Bibliography** from the gallery that appears.

Continued on next page

Get a Job.com

5

Bibliography

Colson, David. Jobs Jobs Jobs. January 2010. <www.zdmag.com>.

Lamorte, Vicky G. "Classifieds on the Web." PC Journal November 2010: 127.

Nobel, John. The Elements of Job Hunting. Boston: Hinton-Hall, 2009.

Figure 5.40c: pages 5 (Bibliography) of job search report

20. Create the Cover Page as follows:
   a. Position your insertion point in front of the title. Press **[Ctrl]+[Enter]** to create a new page.
   b. Insert a **continuous section break**. (*Hint:* Click the **Page Layout tab**.) This is necessary since you will format the newly created first page differently from the remaining pages.
   c. Press **[Ctrl]+[Home]** to move your insertion point to the top of the first page.

Continued on next page

d. Enter the text shown in Figure 5.40. Use any line spacing between parts that you want.
e. Center and set the title and author's name to **28-point bold**. Center and set the remaining text to **14 point**. Use a font color that complements the applied theme.
f. Apply paragraph shading around the title and subtitles using any color(s) you want.
g. Apply a dotted paragraph border around the title using any appropriate color.

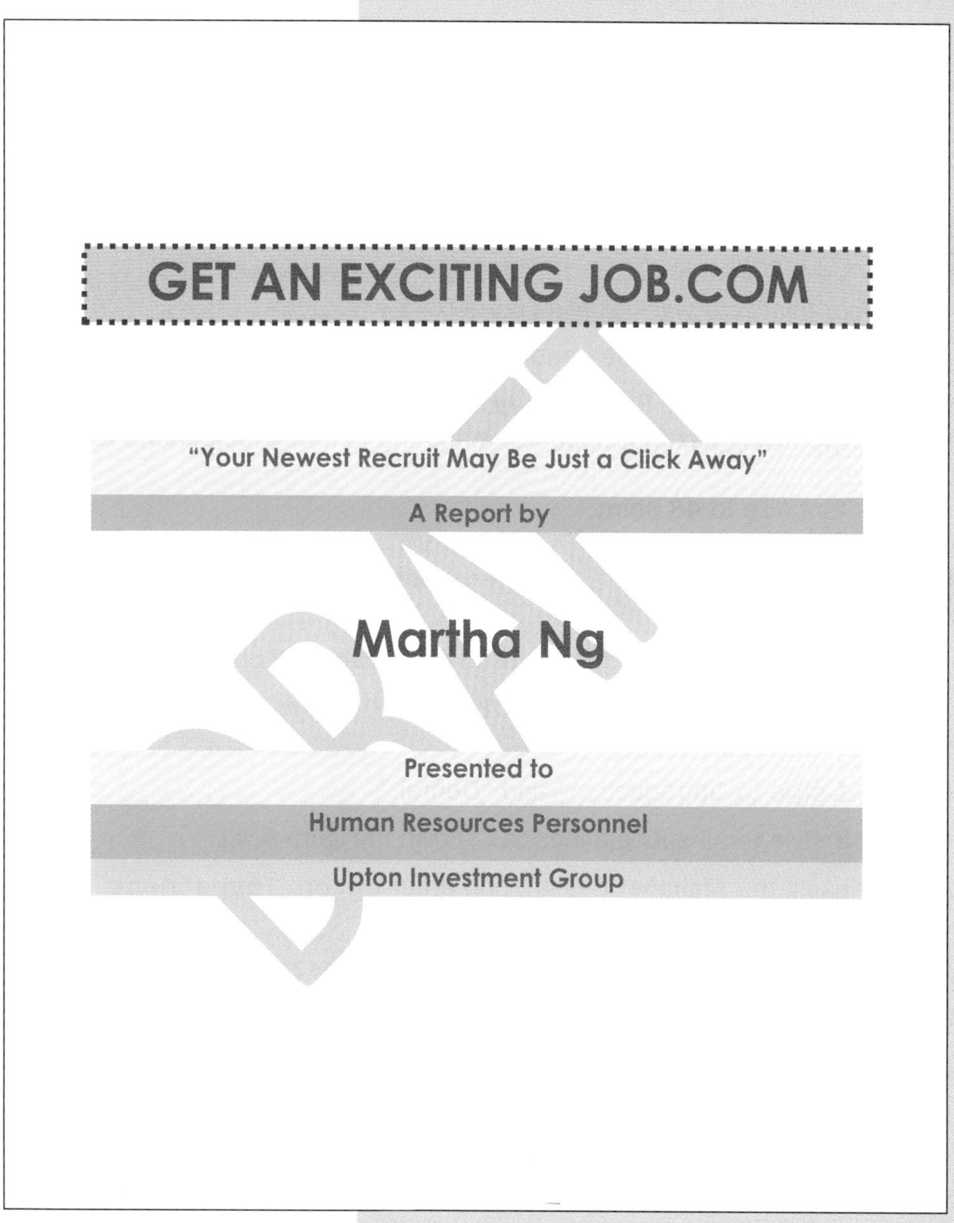

GET AN EXCITING JOB.COM

"Your Newest Recruit May Be Just a Click Away"

A Report by

Martha Ng

Presented to

Human Resources Personnel

Upton Investment Group

Figure 5.40d: Cover page of job search report

21. Center the text vertically on the page.

22. Save the file, and name it **5r2-jobsearch**.

23. Preview, print, and then close the file.

PERFORMANCE

TASK 2

As the human resources manager at Upton Investment Group, you have been asked to create an employee manual, a handbook which contains information about company procedures, policies, and benefits. Using Styles will help you maintain a consistent format for the handbook pages.

Follow these guidelines:

1. Open the data file **5p2-benefits text**. *This text is single-spaced and unformatted. Your final copy will look like Figure 5.41.*

2. Insert a page break before the side heading "Dental."

3. Click the **Home tab**, and in the **Styles group**, right-click the **Heading 1** style, and select **Modify**. In the Modify Style dialog box that appears, make the following selections to modify the Heading 1 style:
   a. Change the font size to **48 point**.
   b. Click **Format**, and click **Border**.
   c. Create a custom bottom border using a **4½-point blue dotted line**, and click **OK**.
   d. Click **OK**.

4. Modify **Heading 2** by changing the font color to **dark blue**, and click **OK**.

5. Modify **Normal style** by changing the font size to **Arial 11 point**. Set the paragraph spacing to **6 point** before and after.

6. Apply **Heading 1** style to "Introduction" and "Dental."

7. Apply **Heading 2** style to all subheadings, as shown in Figure 5.41.

8. Insert a footer using the **Alphabet** design, and enter Upton Investment Group—Benefits Handbook.

9. Position the insertion point below the last paragraph of the last page.

10. Insert the data file **w5p2-education**.

11. Insert a page break before "Education."

12. Apply the styles necessary to format the newly inserted file so that it is consistent with the rest of the document. *After the styles are applied, you will have three pages.*

13. Replace all occurrences of "Upton Group" with "Upton Investment Group."

14. Find the word "accumulate." Use the Thesaurus to substitute another word.

15. Position your insertion point at the top of the document.
    a. Click the **Insert tab**, and in the **Pages group**, click **Blank Page**.
    b. Press **[Ctrl]+[Home]** to move the insertion point to the top of the first page. The dotted underline, which is part of the Heading 1 style, will be automatically applied.

   c. Enter the heading for the title page, as shown in the figure.

   d. Enter the subheading, and apply a **Heading 2** style. Center the text and set it to **28 point**.

   e. Apply a **green** paragraph shading to the text.

16. Insert the **Upton logo**, which can be found in Logos folder in the data files. Position and size it appropriately. Apply any desired picture effects.

17. Insert a watermark using the **Confidential** design.

18. Save the file as **5p2-benefits1**.

19. Click the **Page Layout tab**, and in the **Page Background group**, click the **Watermark list arrow**. Select **Remove Watermark**. Resave the file.

20. Preview, print, and then close the file.

Upton Investment Group

Benefits Handbook

Education

EDUCATION INCENTIVE PLAN

The Upton Investment Group Benefits Program will help you pay for your children's education. The Education Incentive Plan helps you plan ahead for the day tuition bills begin to arrive.

WHO IS ELIGIBLE FOR EDUCATION BENEFITS?

The Education Incentive Plan is designed to help you save from $5,000 to $40,000 (over a 5- to 15-year period) toward the education costs you anticipate for each of your children. You may choose to set aside an amount needed to reach your savings goal for one or more children in the selected time period as follows:

   ✓ The maximum goal is $40,000 per child; the minimum is $5,000.

   ✓ You may have a maximum of four plan accounts per child.

   ✓ The company contributes 15% of the amount of your payroll toward Education Benefits.

The funds will accrue over a period of 5 to 15 years, but not beyond your child's twenty-fifth birthday. When a plan reaches the level of money you want, the funds are paid to you. You can request that the account be canceled and paid out earlier.

HOW TO GET THE MOST OUT OF THE EDUCATION PLAN

The matching contributions from Upton Investment Group are reported as ordinary income on your W-2 tax form. That means that any money you earn through our investment is subject to taxes until all the proceeds are paid out to you.

Your savings and the company matching contributions are invested in stocks and bonds. The full amount of your account will automatically be paid to you upon cancellation of this plan.

Upton Investment Group-Benefits Handbook   Page 4

Figure 5.41a: Cover page and page 4 of Benefits Handbook

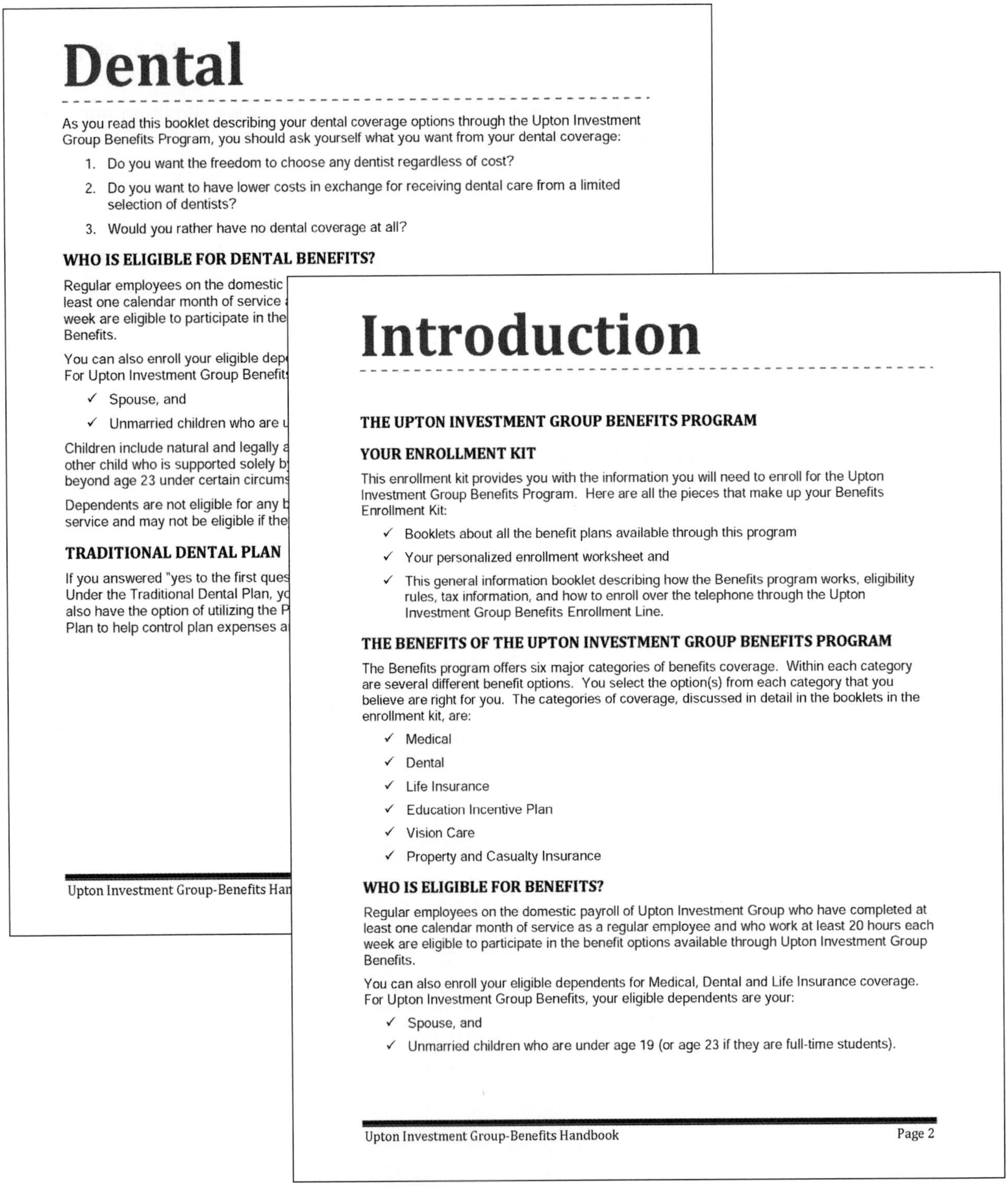

Dental

As you read this booklet describing your dental coverage options through the Upton Investment Group Benefits Program, you should ask yourself what you want from your dental coverage:

1. Do you want the freedom to choose any dentist regardless of cost?
2. Do you want to have lower costs in exchange for receiving dental care from a limited selection of dentists?
3. Would you rather have no dental coverage at all?

WHO IS ELIGIBLE FOR DENTAL BENEFITS?

Regular employees on the domestic [payroll] least one calendar month of service [as] week are eligible to participate in the [benefit options] Benefits.

You can also enroll your eligible dep[endents] For Upton Investment Group Benefit[s]

- ✓ Spouse, and
- ✓ Unmarried children who are u[nder]

Children include natural and legally a[dopted] other child who is supported solely by beyond age 23 under certain circums[tances]

Dependents are not eligible for any b[enefit] service and may not be eligible if the[y]

TRADITIONAL DENTAL PLAN

If you answered "yes to the first ques[tion] Under the Traditional Dental Plan, yo[u] also have the option of utilizing the P[referred] Plan to help control plan expenses a[nd]

Upton Investment Group-Benefits Han[dbook]

Introduction

THE UPTON INVESTMENT GROUP BENEFITS PROGRAM

YOUR ENROLLMENT KIT

This enrollment kit provides you with the information you will need to enroll for the Upton Investment Group Benefits Program. Here are all the pieces that make up your Benefits Enrollment Kit:

- ✓ Booklets about all the benefit plans available through this program
- ✓ Your personalized enrollment worksheet and
- ✓ This general information booklet describing how the Benefits program works, eligibility rules, tax information, and how to enroll over the telephone through the Upton Investment Group Benefits Enrollment Line.

THE BENEFITS OF THE UPTON INVESTMENT GROUP BENEFITS PROGRAM

The Benefits program offers six major categories of benefits coverage. Within each category are several different benefit options. You select the option(s) from each category that you believe are right for you. The categories of coverage, discussed in detail in the booklets in the enrollment kit, are:

- ✓ Medical
- ✓ Dental
- ✓ Life Insurance
- ✓ Education Incentive Plan
- ✓ Vision Care
- ✓ Property and Casualty Insurance

WHO IS ELIGIBLE FOR BENEFITS?

Regular employees on the domestic payroll of Upton Investment Group who have completed at least one calendar month of service as a regular employee and who work at least 20 hours each week are eligible to participate in the benefit options available through Upton Investment Group Benefits.

You can also enroll your eligible dependents for Medical, Dental and Life Insurance coverage. For Upton Investment Group Benefits, your eligible dependents are your:

- ✓ Spouse, and
- ✓ Unmarried children who are under age 19 (or age 23 if they are full-time students).

Upton Investment Group-Benefits Handbook   Page 2

Figure 5.41b: Pages 2 and 3 of Benefits Handbook

Apply and Modify a Quick Style

Apply

1. Select the text to which you want to apply a style.
2. Click the **Home tab**, and in the **Styles group**, click the style you want. Click **More** to view additional styles.
3. Click on a style to apply it.

Modify

1. Right-click the style you want to modify.
2. Click **Modify**.
3. Make the modifications you want.
4. Click **OK**.

Apply a Theme

1. Click the **Page Layout tab**, and in the **Themes group**, click the **Themes button list arrow**.
2. Point to each theme to see a live preview; click to select one.

Set Vertical Centering

1. Click the **Page Layout tab**, then click the **Page Setup dialog box launcher**.
2. Click the **Layout tab**.
3. Click the **Vertical alignment list arrow**, then click **Center**.
4. Click **OK**.

Insert a Watermark

1. Click the **Page Layout tab**, and

in the **Page Background group**, click the **Watermark button**.
2. Select a watermark from the gallery, or click **Custom Watermark**.
   a. Select **Picture watermark** or **Text watermark**.
   b. Make your selections.
   c. Click **OK**.

Find and Replace Text

1. Position the insertion point at the top of the document.
2. Click the **Home tab**, and in the **Editing group**, click the **Replace button**.
3. Click the appropriate tab.
4. Enter text to find and/or replace.
5. To find text, click **Find Next**. To replace text, click **Replace** (to replace one occurrence at a time) or **Replace All** (to replace all occurrences at once).
6. Click **Close**.

Insert a File

1. Position the insertion point at the insert location.
2. Click the **Insert tab**, and in the **Text group**, click the **Object button list arrow**.
3. Select **Text from File**.
4. Click the file to insert.
5. Click **Insert**.

Insert a Citation and Create a Bibliography

Insert a Citation

1. Click the **References tab**, and in the **Citations & Bibliography group**, click the **Style button list arrow**.
2. Select a writing style.
3. Click in the document where you want the citation.
4. Click the **Insert Citation button list arrow**.
5. Select **Add New Source**.
6. Click the **Type of Source list arrow**, and select the type of source from which you are citing.
7. Enter the information for the citation in the Bibliography Fields section.
8. Click **OK**.

Create a Bibliography

1. Click in the document where you want the bibliography to appear.
2. Click the **References tab**, and in the **Citations & Bibliography group**, click the **Style button list arrow**, and select the same writing style you used to create the citation.
3. Click the **Bibliography button list arrow**.
4. Click **Bibliography**.

TRYOUT

GOAL
To edit a report, as shown in Figure 5.42
✻ Insert, view, and edit comments
✻ Track changes in a document
✻ Compare and combine changes
✻ Use Word Count

TASK 3

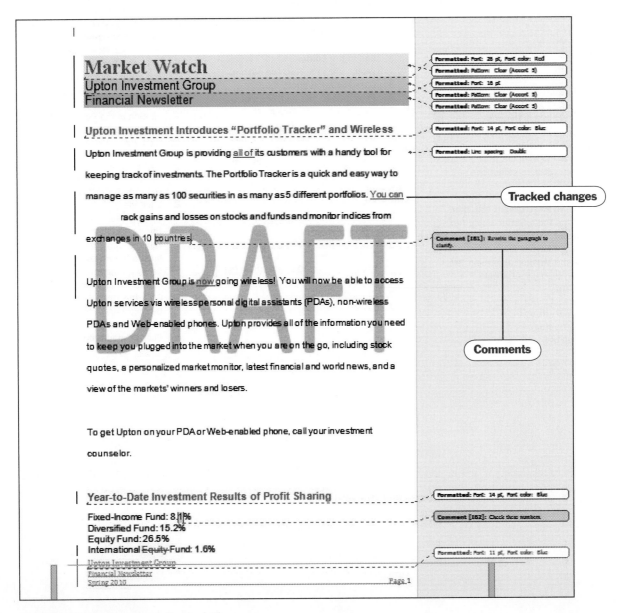

Figure 5.42: Document with Tracked Changes

WHAT YOU NEED TO KNOW

Insert, View, and Edit Comments

▶ **Comments** are hidden notes or annotations that you or a reviewer can add to a document. The Comments feature is useful for facilitating the online review of documents. You can read comments on-screen, hide them when the document is printed, or print them with the document. You can also delete the comment.

▶ When comments are inserted, a balloon appears in which you can enter your comment. The balloon is numbered and includes the author's initials. Positioning your mouse on the balloon will display a pop-up with additional information, including the author's full name, and the date and time the comment was entered. You can display a Reviewing pane, which contains a summary of the comments entered. Figure 5.43 shows a document with Track Changes turned on, comments inserted, and the Reviewing pane displayed.

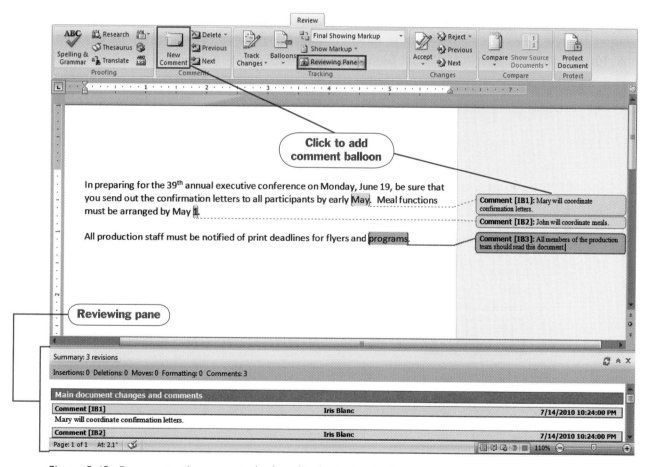

Figure 5.43: Document with comments displayed in the Reviewing Pane

1. Position the insertion point where you want to insert the comment, **2.** click the **Review tab**, and in the **Comments group**, click the **New Comment button**. **3.** Enter the comment in the comment balloon that opens (see Figure 5.43).

To see the author of the comment, as well as the date and time the comment was made, **1.** position the insertion point over the balloon, and a pop-up window displays this information.

To edit a comment, **1.** click in the comment balloon, and **2.** make your change.

To view a summary of all the comments in a document, **1.** click the **Review tab**, and in the **Tracking group**, **2.** click the **Reviewing Pane button list arrow** (see Figure 5.43), and **3.** select the direction (horizontal or vertical) that you want the Reviewing pane to display. You can also edit a comment directly in the Reviewing pane. A change made to a comment in the Reviewing pane automatically changes the comment in the corresponding comment balloon. **4.** Click the **Reviewing Pane button** again to hide the pane.

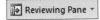

To delete a comment, **1.** right-click the comment balloon, and **2.** click **Delete Comment** from the menu.

To print a document with comments, **1.** click the **Microsoft Office button**, and **2.** click **Print**. In the Print dialog box, shown in Figure 5.44, **3.** select **Document showing markup** from the Print what list box. To print without comments, select **Document** from the Print what list box, then **4.** click **OK**.

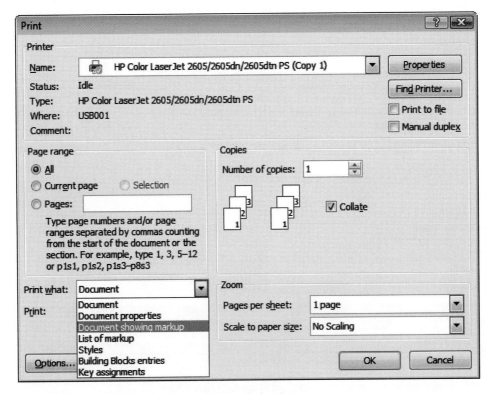

Figure 5.44: Print with comments in the Print dialog box

T R Y *it* O U T *w5-14*

1. Open the data file **w5-14**.

2. Position the insertion point after the first sentence that ends with the word "May."

3. Click the **Review tab**, and in the **Comments group**, click the **New Comment button**.

4. Enter the following in the comment balloon: `Mary will coordinate confirmation letters.`

5. Position the insertion point after the second sentence that ends with "May 1."

6. Click the **New Comment button**.

7. Enter the following in the comment balloon: `John will coordinate meals.`

8. Position the insertion point after the last sentence, which ends with the word "programs."

9. Click the **New Comment button**.

10. Enter the following in the comment balloon: `All members of the production team should read this document.`

11. On the **Review tab** in the **Tracking group**, click the **Reviewing Pane button list arrow**, and select **Reviewing Panel Horizontal**.

12. Click in the second comment balloon, and change the comment to: `John and Amy will coordinate meals.`

13. Right-click the third comment balloon, and click **Delete Comment**.

14. Click the **Microsoft Office button**, then click **Print**.
    a. Select **Document showing markup** from the Print what list.
    b. Click **Cancel**.

15. Close the file, and do not save the changes.

Track Changes in a Document

▶ The Track Changes feature allows you to see where a deletion, insertion, or other formatting change has been made in a document. This feature is a useful tool when editing an online document.

► When you turn on Track Changes, insertions are indicated in red as underlined text; deletions are shown with a strikethrough. By default, a balloon (like the one used for comments) displays formatting changes. You can set the balloon to show revisions. Figure 5.45 shows an edited document in which Track Changes has been turned on. By positioning your insertion point on the balloon, you can see the person and the date the change was made.

► As with comments, you can print the document showing the marked up changes or print a list of changes.

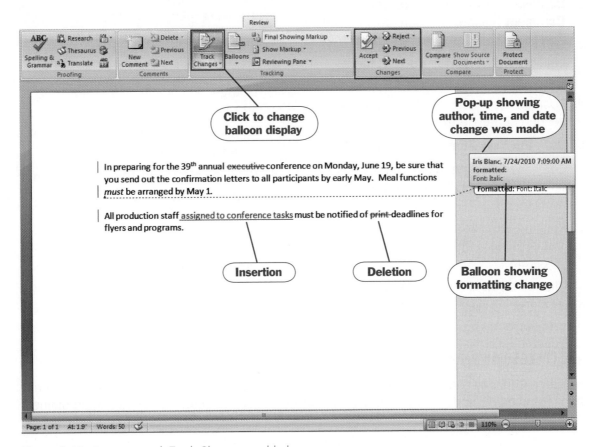

Figure 5.45: Document with Track Changes enabled

HOW [Ctrl]+[Shift]+E To turn on track changes, **1.** click the **Review tab**, and in the **Tracking group**, click the **Track Changes button** (see Figure 5.45). When the Track Changes feature is enabled, the Track Changes button remains highlighted. **2.** Repeat Steps 1 and 2 to turn off the feature. *Turning off the Track Changes feature does not remove any changes that have already been tracked.*

To accept or reject changes and remove tracking, **1.** click the **Review tab**, and in the **Changes group**, **2.** click the **Accept button** or **Reject button**, which will accept or reject your change and move to the next change. You can also right-click the change, and select **Accept Change** or **Reject Change** from the menu.

To accept or reject all changes in a document, **1.** click the **Accept** or **Reject button list arrow**, and **2.** select **Accept** (or **Reject**) **All Changes in Document**.

To set what changes are displayed in the balloon, **1.** click the **Balloons button**, and **2.** make the changes you want.

To print showing the document with tracking or a list of changes, click **Document showing markup** or **List of markup** in the Print what section of the Print dialog box (see Figure 5.44).

TRY it OUT *w5-15*

1. Open the data file **w5-15**.

2. Click the **Review tab**, and in the **Tracking group**, click the **Track Changes button**.

3. Delete the word "executive" in the first sentence.

4. Italicize the words "must be" in the second sentence.

5. Enter the words **assigned to conference tasks** after the word "staff" in the third sentence.

6. Delete the word "print" in the last sentence.

7. Position your insertion point on the first change. (Deleted: executive). Click the **Accept button** to accept the revision.

8. Right-click the insertion (assigned to conference tasks), and select **Reject Change**.

9. Click the **Next button** to move to the last change (Deleted: print). Click the **Reject button** to reject the revision.

10. Close the file, and do not save the changes.

Compare and Combine Changes

▶ The Compare feature allows you to compare any two versions of the same document, the differences of which are shown as tracked changes (comment balloons will also be displayed). The source documents that are being compared are not changed.

▶ The Merge Comments feature allows you to combine revisions from multiple reviewers into a single document. You can then review each change from the single document.

HOW To compare two versions of the same document, **1.** click the **Review tab**, and in the **Compare group**, **2.** click the **Compare button list arrow**, then **3.** click **Compare**, as shown in Figure 5.46. **4.** In the Compare Documents dialog box, **5.** select (or browse for) the **Original document**, **6.** select (or browse for) the **Revised document** you want to compare, then **7.** click **More** to expand the dialog box, as shown in Figure 5.47. **8.** Under **Show changes in**, select **New document**, then **9.** Click **OK**. **10.** Click **Yes** when prompted. Word displays a new third document in which tracked changes in the original document are accepted, and previously made changes in the revised document are shown as tracked changes (see Figure 5.49).

Figure 5.46: Compare button, Review tab

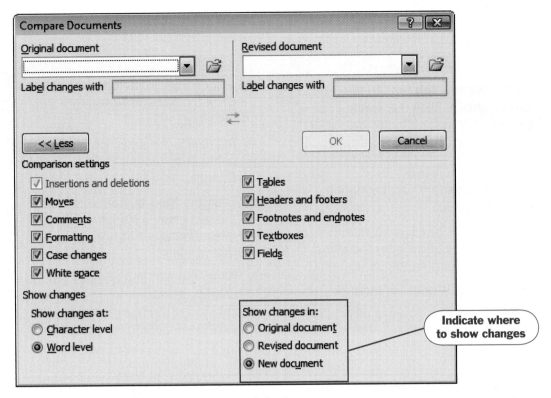

Figure 5.47: Expanded Compare Documents dialog box

To combine changes and comments from several reviewers, **1.** click the **Review tab**, and in the **Compare group**, **2.** click the **Compare button list arrow**, then **3.** click **Combine**. **4.** In the Combine Documents dialog box that displays, shown in Figure 5.48 (which has been expanded), under **Original document**, select a document in which you want to combine the changes from multiple sources. **5.** Under **Revised document**, select the document that contains the changes

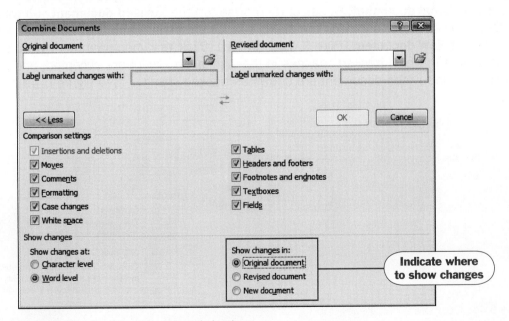

Figure 5.48: Combine Documents dialog box

by one of the reviewers. **6.** Click **More**, if necessary. **7.** In the **Show changes** section, select the options you want to compare. **8.** In the **Show changes in** section, click **Original document**, then **9.** click **OK**. Word displays the combined document and compares it to the original, as shown in Figure 5.48. Repeat Steps 1–9 to merge other reviews into the combined final document. Then, use the previously discussed methods to accept or reject changes in the document.

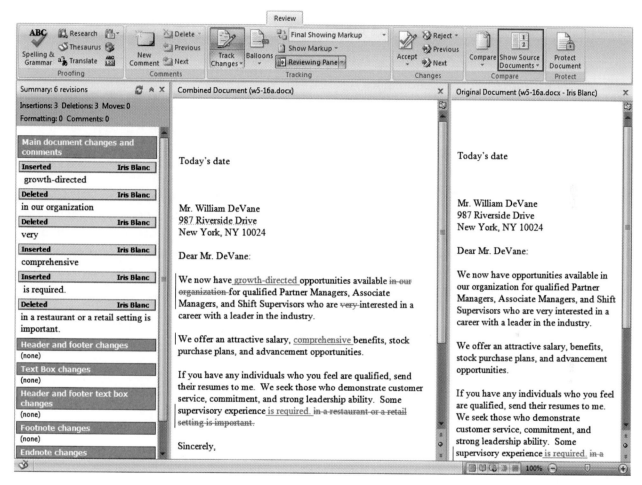

Figure 5.49: Compared documents

To compare changes

1. Open the data file **w5-16**. Note that comments are included in the document.

2. Save the file as **5-16-compare documents**.

3. Make the following changes to the document:
   a. Insert `growth-directed` before "opportunities" in the first sentence.
   b. Delete "in our organization" in the first sentence.
   c. Delete "very" in the first sentence.
   d. Insert `comprehensive` before "benefits" in the second sentence.

4. Save the file, but do not close it.

5. Click the **Review tab**, and in the **Compare group**, click the **Compare button list arrow**, and select **Compare**.
   a. Select the data file **w5-16** as the Original document, and select **5-16-compare documents** as the Revised document.
   b. In the Compare documents dialog box, click **More**, if necessary, and select

New document in the **Show changes in** section.
   c. Click **OK**, then **Yes** when prompted, to continue with comparison.

6. Close the files, and do not save the changes.

To combine changes

7. Click the **Compare button list arrow** again, and select **Combine**.
   a. Select the data file **w5-16-reviewer 1** as the **Original** document, and select the data file **w5-16-reviewer 2** as the **Revised** document.
   b. In the Combine Documents dialog box, click **More**, if necessary, and select **Original document** in the **Show changes in** section.
   c. Click **OK**, then **Yes**, if prompted.
   d. In the **Compare group**, click the **Show Source Documents button list arrow**, and select **Show Both**.

8. Close all files, and do not save the changes.

Use Word Count

▶ When working on a long document, you might want to know how many words, characters, paragraphs, and/or lines it contains—particularly if you have a page or word limit for the document.

▶ The *Word Count feature* calculates the pages, characters, paragraphs, and lines in a document or in the selected text. The insertion point can be anywhere in the document when you use this feature.

HOW **1.** Right-click the **status bar**, and **2.** select **Word Count**, which will display the Word count indicator on the status bar. **3.** Click the **Word Count area** on the status bar to display the Word Count dialog box, which will show the statistics for the document, as shown in Figure 5.50. **4.** Click **Close**.

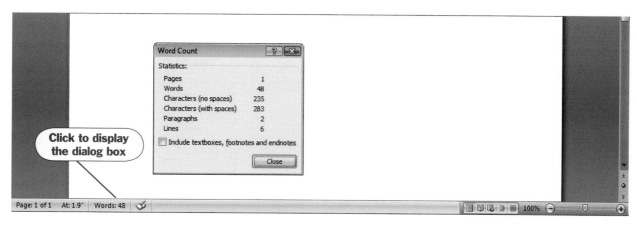

Figure 5.50: Word Count dialog box

T R Y *it* **O U T** *w5-17*

1. Open the data file **w5-17**.

2. Right-click the **status bar**, and select **Word Count**, if Word Count is not currently displayed on the status bar.

3. Click the **Word Count area** on the status bar to open the Word Count dialog box. Note the statistics for the document.

4. Close the file, and do not save the changes.

REHEARSAL

GOAL
To edit a document using comments and tracking, as shown in Figure 5.51

TASK 3

WHAT YOU NEED TO KNOW

▶ Documents go through many editing cycles.

▶ You can use the Track Changes feature to edit a document by marking changes and reviewing them before actually making the changes.

▶ You will edit a document, insert comments, and compare the original and revised documents.

DIRECTIONS

1. Open the data file **w5r3-draft document original**. Note that comments are included in the document.

2. Click the **Review tab**, and in the **Tracking group**, click the **Track Changes button**.

3. Edit the document as shown in Figure 5.51 by doing the following:
   a. Insert a watermark with the word "Draft" using any design you want.
   b. Insert text shown as underlined; delete text shown with a strikethrough.
   c. Change the font size of "Market Watch" to **26 point**; change the font color to **red**.
   d. Change the font size of "Upton Investment Group" and "Financial Newsletter" to **16 point**.
   e. Apply paragraph shading to each line of the title as shown using any shade of **blue**.
   f. Change the first side heading to **14 point**; change the font color to **medium blue**.
   g. Copy the formatting to the other side headings.
   h. Set the line spacing for each paragraph to **double** except for the Year-to-Date paragraph text.

4. Add a footer with the following information:
   Upton Investment Group
   Financial Newsletter
   Spring 2010

   Use the **Pinstripes** design for the footer, as shown.

5. Position your insertion point at the end of the first paragraph.
   a. Click the **Review tab**, and in the **Comments group**, click the **New Comment button**, and enter the following text in the balloon: **Rewrite the paragraph to clarify**.

6. Save the file as **5r3-revised draft**.

Continued on next page

334–Word Lesson 5 Reports and Long Documents   **Rehearsal Task 3**

7. Combine changes and comments.
   a. Click the **Review tab**, and in the **Compare group**, click the **Compare button list arrow**, then click **Combine**.
   b. Enter **w5r3-draft document original** as the Original document and **5r3-revised draft** as the Revised document.
   c. Show the changes in the **Original document**, and click **OK**.

8. Edit the footer by removing the company name.

9. Print one copy of the combined document showing markups.

10. Accept all the changes, and delete the comments.

11. Save the file as **5r3-revised draft1**.

12. Determine the word count for the document. Close all files.

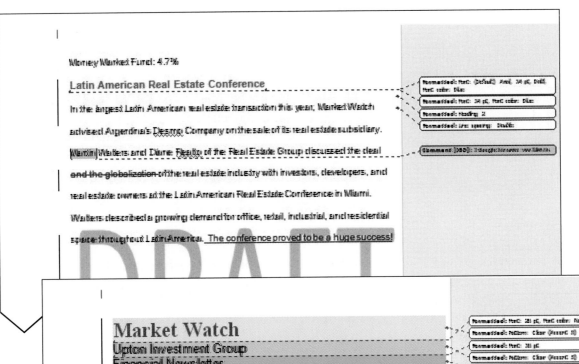
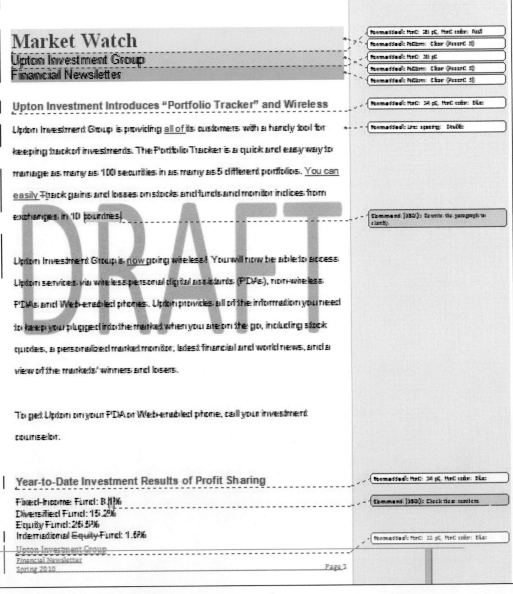

Figure 5.51: Revised draft of newsletter

PERFORMANCE

TASK 3

To honor the many contributions of Walt Disney, Newmark Productions is planning a Walt Disney festival. To promote the festival, Newmark is planning to publish several special editions of its newsletter—each edition will feature an article devoted to the lifetime achievement of this great man. You have been asked to format and edit one of the articles. Several people will be reviewing it before it is submitted for publication.

Follow these guidelines:

1. Open the data file **w5p3-living graphics**.

2. Turn Track Changes on.

3. Find each occurrence of "Walte," and replace it with **Walt**.

4. Find the words "for example" in the last paragraph. Then delete them.

5. Find both occurrences of "depicts," and replace them with "shows."

6. In the "STAGING PRINCIPLE" paragraph, insert "clearly" before "understood," and delete the last sentence.

7. Modify the **Heading 1 style** as follows:
   a. Set the font to **Arial 14 point**.
   b. Set paragraph spacing to **6 pt** before and after.

8. Modify the **No spacing** style as follows:
   a. Set the line spacing to **1.5"**.
   b. Set the font to **Calibri, 11 point**.

9. Apply the **Title style** to the title.

10. Apply the **Heading 1 style** to the side headings.

11. Apply the **No spacing** style to the paragraph text.

12. Insert a comment on the last word in the document, which reads **Check references.**

13. Apply a new theme to the document.

14. Insert a page number as a footer using a predesigned style. Suppress the header on the first page.

15. Save the file as **5p3-living graphics final**.

16. Combine **w5p3-living graphics** with **5p3-living graphics final**. Show changes in the original document.

Continued on next page

17. Save the combined document as **5p3-animation**. Accept all the changes in the document. Delete the comment to apply paragraph shading. Save the file.

18. Print one copy of **5p3-animation**, and close all files.

ANIMATION

One of the many reasons Walt Disney became successful was that he was able to give life to his cartoon characters. Once the character has a personality, the audience can identify with it and believe it. Walt believed the "true interpretation of caricature is the exaggeration of an illusion of the actual, possible, or probable." This belief developed into several fundamental principles for Disney animators, which include squash and stretch, staging, secondary action, exaggeration, anticipation, and follow-through and overlapping action.

CONCEPT OF SQUASH AND STRETCH

One of the most important innovations in animation is the concept of "squash and stretch." This technique involves creating several drawings for one action to show flexibility and pliability. The squashed position shows the form either squeezed up and bunched together or flattened out by great pressure. The stretched position then shows the same form lengthened to a very extended condition. Arms and legs, for example, swell and they bend and extend into long and flexible limbs. A character chewing food has ballooned cheeks, a jaw with extended stretching motions, and a mouth that moves from well below the nose to up beyond the nose.

STAGING PRINCIPLE

Staging is a general but essential principle in animation. It is the presentation of an idea, a mood, or an expression so that it is clearly recognizable and clearly understood. Staging a spooky scene means including appropriate imagery: a full moon, a threatening sky, looming shadows, and an old house.

ANTICIPATION

Perhaps one of the oldest theater devices, anticipation, is what keeps the audience interested and prepared for upcoming scenes. If an action or a scene is not set up properly, the audience can miss the humor. Anticipatory moves, such as crouching before running or winding up before pitching, show the audience what the character will be doing next.

SECONDARY ACTION

Secondary actions emphasize the primary actions and provide greater richness and dimension to the character or the action in the scene. If the primary action is a flustered character jumping up and down, his arm movements and hand gestures, following a different pattern from his moving body, can

Figure 5.52a: Page 1 of final newsletter

accentuate the character's confusion. If the primary focus is a mood or expression, such as a character crying, the secondary action might be a hand wiping a tear away.

EXAGGERATION

The purpose of exaggeration is not to distort, but to present a scene or character in an unreal way to make it seem more real. Lightning would not be convincing if it were drawn as it appears in a photograph. By exaggerating the bolts and adding flashes of light, animated lightning can seem more dramatic than the real thing.

FOLLOW THROUGH AND OVERLAPPING ACTION

Once many of these elements are combined, the best way to bring life and magic to the scene is to make the action look natural by using "follow through" or "overlapping action." If a moving figure stops, appendages continue to move, such as hair, ears, fleshy cheeks, hats, or clothes. The final result is animation with more vitality, realism, and life.

Figure 5.52b: Page 2 of final newsletter

Cues for Reference

Insert, Delete, and Edit Comments
Insert
1. Position the insertion point where you want to insert the comment.
2. Click the **Review tab**, and in the **Comments group**, click the **New Comment button**.
3. Enter your comment in the comment balloon.

Delete
1. Right-click the comment balloon, and click **Delete Comment**.

Edit
1. Click in the comment balloon, and edit the text as appropriate.

Tracking Changes
1. Open the document you want to revise.
2. Click the **Review tab**, and in the **Tracking group**, click the **Track Changes button**.
3. Repeat Step 2 to turn off the feature.

Review Tracked Changes
1. Click the **Review tab**, and in the **Changes group**, click the **Accept button** or **Reject button**.

Accept/Reject All Changes at Once
1. Click the **Accept button list arrow** or **Reject button list arrow**.
2. Click **Accept All Changes in Document** or **Reject All Changes in Document**.

Compare and Combine Changes
To compare two versions of the same document
1. Click the **Review tab**, and in the **Compare group**, click the **Compare button list arrow**, and select **Compare**.
2. Select (or browse for) the **Original document**, and select (or browse for) the **Revised document** you want to compare.
3. Click **More** to expand the dialog box.
4. Click **New document** under **Show changes in**.
5. Click **OK**.
6. Click **Yes** when prompted.

To combine changes and comments from several reviewers
1. Click the **Review tab**, and in the **Compare group**, click the **Compare button list arrow**, and click **Combine**.
2. Select a document in which you want to combine the changes, to enter in the Original document text box.
3. Select the document that contains the changes by one of the reviewers to enter in the Revised document text box.
4. In the **Show changes section**, select the options you want to compare.
5. In the **Show changes in section**, click **Original document**.
6. Click **OK**.

Word Count
1. Right-click the **status bar**.
2. Select **Word Count** to display the counter on the **status bar**.
3. Click the **status bar** counter area.
4. View the statistics for the document in the dialog box.

Act I

You work in the marketing department at Transport Travel Services in New York. Your department is responsible for updating *Travel Guide 2010*, a handbook of practical information for the traveler. As a courtesy to its loyal customers, Transport Travel Services plans to provide them with a free copy of this popular handbook. You have been asked to format four pages of text using Figure 5.53 as a guide. *Note: The text is provided to you unformatted. After applying formatting, the text may span five or six pages, depending on the font sizes and styles you choose.*

Follow these guidelines:

1. Open the data file **w5e1-travel guide text**. Section, column, and page breaks have been inserted. Review the entire file.

2. Create a header and/or footer that includes the name of the publication and the company name. Format the header and/or footer using any font, color, and alignment, or use a predesigned header and/or footer.

3. Include page numbers and position them as you prefer. The page numbers may be part of the header/footer text. You may use a predesigned page number, if you want.

4. Create or modify styles to format the headings, short quotes, author's name, and body text, as shown in Figure 5.53. You can design the styles for the headings, short quotes, and body text using any desired formatting, line spacing, and paragraph spacing.

5. Create citations where shown in the figure using the information shown on page 5 (the Works Cited page). Insert a bibliography on the last page of the document as "Works Cited."

6. Save the file as **5e1-travel guide**.

7. Preview all pages.

8. Print one copy.

9. Optional: Create a page that contains a list of 10 words or phrases you think are important when traveling. Then, translate the words/phrases into French, Spanish, and a third language of your choice. Use any desired format to best display this list. Insert this page so that it becomes the fifth page of the travel guide.

PACKING: THE CHECKLIST OF ESSENTIALS

"We were very tired, we were very merry—
We had gone back and forth all night on the ferry." (Gilford)
Edna St. Vincent Millay

- adapter
- alarm
- binoculars
- camera with batteries and film
- credit cards
- driver's license
- earplugs
- flashlight
- guidebooks
- hanger
- itineraries
- laundry bag
- lock
- maps

- money belt
- passport
- pen
- plastic bags
- safety pins
- sewing kit
- sleeping bag
- sunglasses
- swimsuit
- traveler's checks
- travel iron
- umbrella
- walking shoes

Insert citation

You might consider taking other things with you such as a small photo album, chewing gum, picture postcards from home (to show other people you meet where you come from), a calling card, and small packaged snacks (in case you get hungry and are nowhere near food).

PACKING TIPS

"She who travels lightest travels without shoulder pain. " (Fairechild)
Robin Mason

- Keep your color scheme simple.
- Select everything you think you should bring – then eliminate half.
- Fold delicate clothing in plastic bags to avoid wrinkles.
- Keep accessories to a bare minimum.
- Do not bring jewelry or other valuables.

Figure 5.53a: Page 1 of Travel Guide 2010

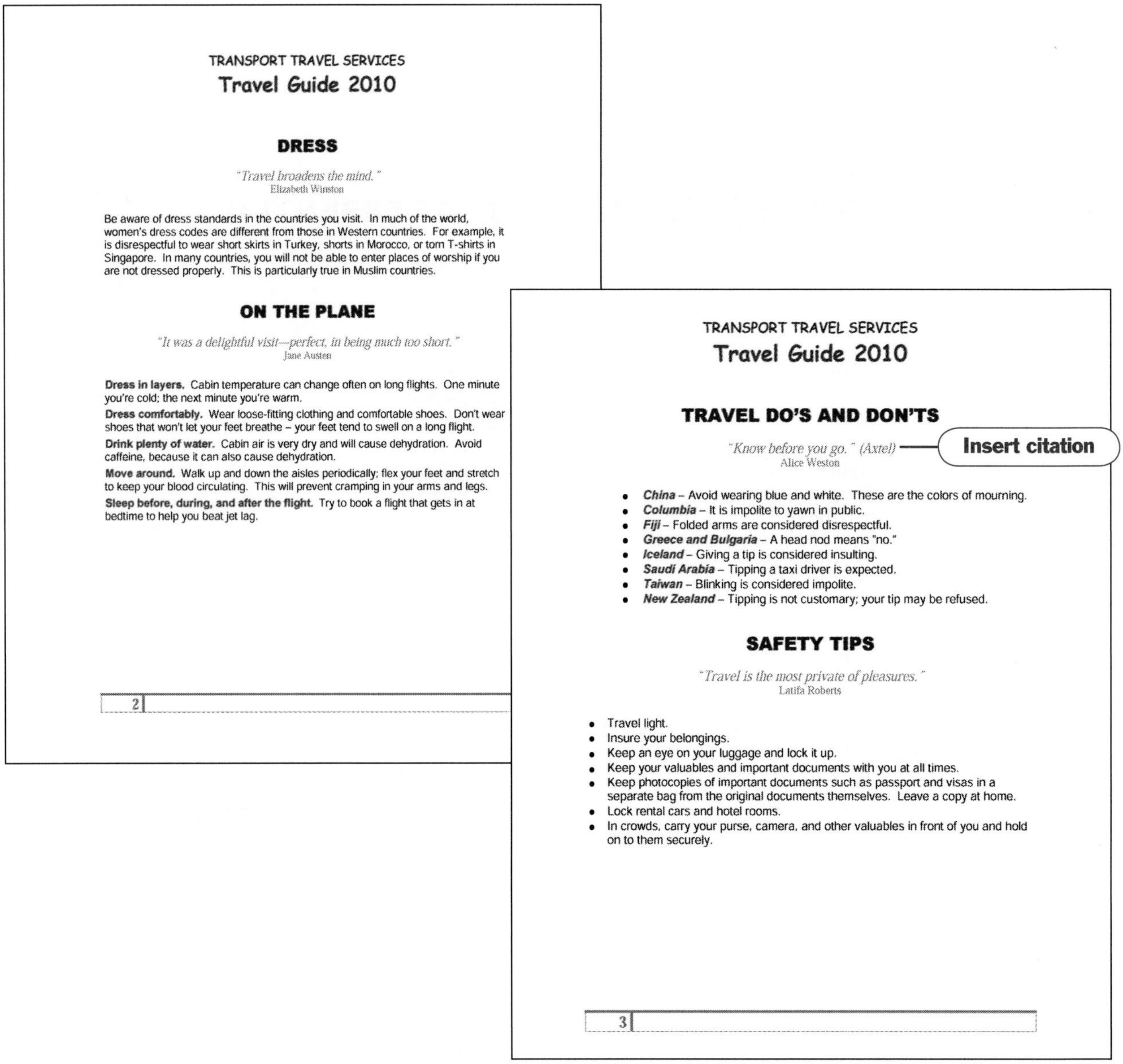

TRANSPORT TRAVEL SERVICES
Travel Guide 2010

DRESS

"Travel broadens the mind."
Elizabeth Winston

Be aware of dress standards in the countries you visit. In much of the world, women's dress codes are different from those in Western countries. For example, it is disrespectful to wear short skirts in Turkey, shorts in Morocco, or torn T-shirts in Singapore. In many countries, you will not be able to enter places of worship if you are not dressed properly. This is particularly true in Muslim countries.

ON THE PLANE

"It was a delightful visit—perfect, in being much too short."
Jane Austen

Dress in layers. Cabin temperature can change often on long flights. One minute you're cold; the next minute you're warm.

Dress comfortably. Wear loose-fitting clothing and comfortable shoes. Don't wear shoes that won't let your feet breathe – your feet tend to swell on a long flight.

Drink plenty of water. Cabin air is very dry and will cause dehydration. Avoid caffeine, because it can also cause dehydration.

Move around. Walk up and down the aisles periodically; flex your feet and stretch to keep your blood circulating. This will prevent cramping in your arms and legs.

Sleep before, during, and after the flight. Try to book a flight that gets in at bedtime to help you beat jet lag.

2

TRANSPORT TRAVEL SERVICES
Travel Guide 2010

TRAVEL DO'S AND DON'TS

"Know before you go." (Axtel) —— **Insert citation**
Alice Weston

- *China* – Avoid wearing blue and white. These are the colors of mourning.
- *Columbia* – It is impolite to yawn in public.
- *Fiji* – Folded arms are considered disrespectful.
- *Greece and Bulgaria* – A head nod means "no."
- *Iceland* – Giving a tip is considered insulting.
- *Saudi Arabia* – Tipping a taxi driver is expected.
- *Taiwan* – Blinking is considered impolite.
- *New Zealand* – Tipping is not customary; your tip may be refused.

SAFETY TIPS

"Travel is the most private of pleasures."
Latifa Roberts

- Travel light.
- Insure your belongings.
- Keep an eye on your luggage and lock it up.
- Keep your valuables and important documents with you at all times.
- Keep photocopies of important documents such as passport and visas in a separate bag from the original documents themselves. Leave a copy at home.
- Lock rental cars and hotel rooms.
- In crowds, carry your purse, camera, and other valuables in front of you and hold on to them securely.

3

Figure 5.53b: Pages 2 and 3 of Travel Guide 2010

TRANSPORT TRAVEL SERVICES
Travel Guide 2010

CURRENCIES AND LANGUAGES OF POPULAR DESTINATIONS

"We all ended up with our pockets full of foreign coins." (Brandenburger) — **Insert citation**
Kate Emily

Country
Currency
Language

Australia
Dollar
English

Austria
Euro
German

Belgium
Euro
Dutch, French, German

Brazil
Real
Portuguese

Bulgaria
Lev
Bulgarian

Canada
Dollar
English, French

Chile
Peso
Spanish

China
Yuan
Chinese dialects

Colombia
Peso
Spanish

Cuba
Peso
Spanish

Czech Republic
Koruna
Czech

Denmark
Krone
Danish

Egypt
Pound
Arabic

Finland
Euro
Finnish, Swedish

France
Euro
French

Germany
Euro
German

Greece

Israel
Shekel
Hebrew, Arabic, Yiddish

Italy
Euro
Italian

Japan
Yen
Japanese

Luxembourg
Euro
French, German, Luxembourgish

Mexico
Peso
Spanish

Netherlands
Euro
Dutch, Frisian

Russia
Ruble
Russian

4

TRANSPORT TRAVEL SERVICES
Travel Guide 2010

Works Cited
Axtel, Roger E. <u>Do's and Taboos Around the World.</u> Boston: John Williams & Sons, 2005.
Brandenburger, Caroline. "The Traveler's Handbook." <u>The Essential Guide for International Travelers</u> (2002): 101-107.
Fairechild, Diana. <u>Jet Smart.</u> Celestial Arts, 2002.
Gilford, Judith. <u>The Packing Book.</u> Ten Speed Press, 2004.

Figure 5.53c: Pages 4 and 5 of Travel Guide 2010

Act II

The manager of the marketing department is pleased with the development of the *Travel Guide 2010* handbook so far. She has given you a file that contains maps of Europe, South America, and Asia and has asked you to insert them as the last three pages of the guide. She has also asked you to create a cover page for the guidebook using a predesigned page.

Follow these guidelines:

1. Open the **5e1-travel guide** that you completed in Act I.

2. Insert the data file **w5e2-maps** so that it becomes the last three pages.

3. Create a heading for each of the newly inserted pages that identifies the continent that the map depicts.

4. Format the headings on these pages to be consistent with the subheadings on the other pages.

5. Insert a cover page using a predesigned format. Include the name of the guidebook, the company information (given below), and the year of this guidebook. Delete any other placeholders from the cover page.

   ```
   Transport Travel Services
   505 Park Avenue
   New York, NY 10020
   Phone: 212-555-5555
   Fax: 212-555-6767
   E-mail: tts@net.com
   ```

6. Preview all pages.

7. Save the file as **5e2-travel guide final**.

8. Print one copy.

PERFORMING WITH EXCEL

* Downloadable from the
Student Online Companion

Excel Basics

In this lesson, you will learn about the Excel screen, including the Office Button, Ribbon, and band of tabs that take you to the commands you need. You will open new and existing files, use navigation techniques, and enter text, dates, and values. Then you will learn how to select cells and change the views of a worksheet according to your needs. You will complete the following projects:

✴ Explore and navigate the Excel screen
✴ Create a grade sheet

Upon completion of this lesson, you will have mastered the following skill sets

✴ Learn about Excel
✴ Start Excel
✴ Explore the Excel screen
✴ Explore the Excel workbook
✴ Explore worksheet elements
✴ Navigate the worksheet
✴ Enter text, dates, and numbers
✴ Use Save and Save As
✴ Open a file
✴ Open a new workbook
✴ Select worksheet cells
✴ Proof data and check spelling
✴ Change workbook views

Terms
Software-related

Active cell
Active cell reference
Cell
Cell address
Column
Formula bar
Full Screen
Label
Left-aligned
Name Box
New Window
Office Button
Pane
Quick Access Toolbar
Range
Ribbon
Right-aligned
Row
Scroll bar
Sheet tab
Split screen
Status bar
Title bar
Value
Workbook
Worksheet

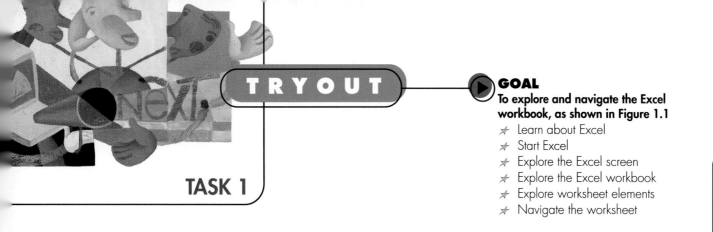

TRYOUT

GOAL
To explore and navigate the Excel workbook, as shown in Figure 1.1
- Learn about Excel
- Start Excel
- Explore the Excel screen
- Explore the Excel workbook
- Explore worksheet elements
- Navigate the worksheet

TASK 1

WHAT YOU NEED TO KNOW

Learn About Excel

▶ Excel is a powerful spreadsheet tool you can use to analyze, chart, share, and manage data for personal, business, and financial use.

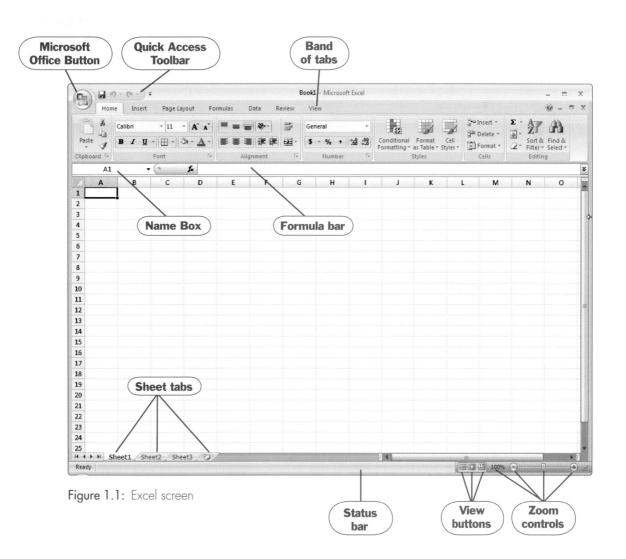

Figure 1.1: Excel screen

Start Excel

▶ If you have customized your desktop or Start menu, double-click the Excel icon, or follow the steps below:

TRY *it* OUT e1-1

1. Click the **Start button** on the Windows taskbar.

2. Click **All Programs**.

3. Click **Microsoft Office**.

4. Click **Microsoft Office Excel 2007**.

Explore the Excel Screen

▶ As shown in Figure 1.2, the top portion of the screen contains the **Office Button**, the Quick Access Toolbar, and the title bar. The **Office Button** provides access to basic open, save, and print commands. The customizable **Quick Access Toolbar** provides a set of commands independent of the **tab** you have open. The **title bar** displays the name of the active workbook. The **Ribbon** is made up of **tabs** that group commands by function. Each of the **tabs** represents a core task you perform in Excel.

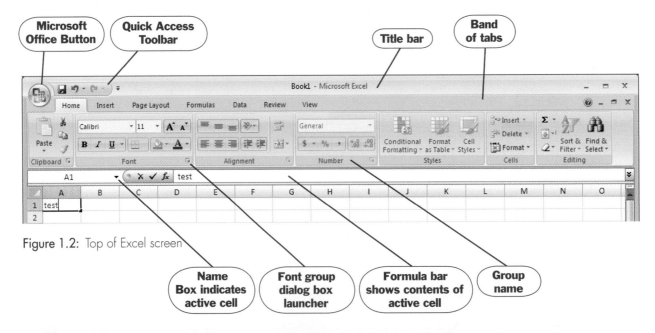

Figure 1.2: Top of Excel screen

▶ Below the Ribbon is the **Name Box** on the left, the **Function Wizard button**, and the **formula bar**, which displays the contents of the active cell. The **active cell** is the location of the worksheet insertion point where you are currently working. The name of the active cell appears in the **Name Box**.

1. In cell **A1**, enter `test`. Press **[Enter]**.

2. Click in cell **A1**. *Reference to A1, the active cell, appears in the Name Box, and* `test` *appears in the formula bar.*

3. Click the **Office Button** and view the commands.

4. Click away from the menu once to close it.

5. Click each **tab** on the Ribbon to view the groups of commands.

6. Click the **Insert tab**, and position the mouse pointer over the Clip Art button. *A ScreenTip appears.*

7. Click the **Home tab**, and at the bottom of the Font group, click the **dialog box launcher**.

8. Close the dialog box.

Explore the Excel Workbook

▶ An Excel file is called a **workbook**. Each workbook contains one or more **worksheets**, which are separate documents within your workbook. When you start Excel, a new workbook called Book1 appears, containing three worksheets. The worksheets are identified by the **sheet tabs** at the bottom of the workbook. The active sheet is Sheet1, but you can click another **sheet tab** to make it the active sheet. You can increase the number of sheets in a workbook by clicking the **Insert Worksheet tab** at the bottom of the Excel window.

▶ The bottom of the screen, as shown in Figure 1.3, also contains the **status bar**, which provides **workbook view buttons** and the Zoom controls, and indicates if certain options are turned on or off.

▶ The **worksheet view buttons** are Normal view, Page Layout view, and Page Break Preview view. Page Layout view shows the worksheet as it will print with margins, headers and footers, and rulers. Use this view to make or change settings before printing a worksheet.

▶ The Zoom controls consist of the Zoom slider, Zoom In, Zoom Out, and **Zoom level buttons**. Use the slider and **buttons** to change magnification levels as desired. Use the **Zoom level button** to open the **Zoom dialog box** to set a specific level of magnification.

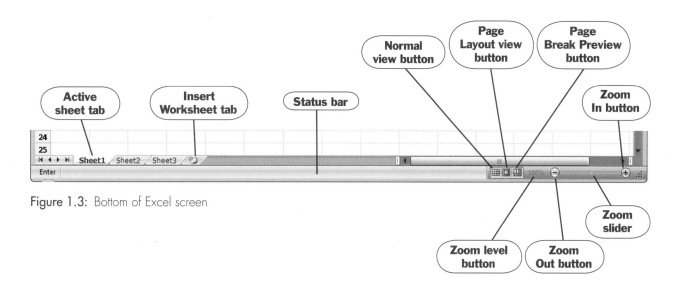

Figure 1.3: Bottom of Excel screen

1. Click the **Sheet2 sheet tab**.

2. Click the **Sheet3 sheet tab**.

3. Click the **Sheet1 sheet tab**.

4. Click the **Insert Worksheet tab**. *A new worksheet, Sheet4, appears*.

5. Click the **Page Layout view button** on the status bar.

6. Click the **Normal view button** on the status bar.

7. Click the **Sheet1 sheet tab** on the status bar.

8. Use the **Zoom slider** to increase and decrease magnification levels. *The Zoom level reflects the change as a percentage as you move the slider*.

9. Move the **Zoom slider** to **100%** magnification.

Explore Worksheet Elements

▶ A worksheet has vertical alphabetical **columns** and horizontal numbered **rows**. The intersection of a column and row is called a **cell**. A worksheet contains 16,384 columns and 1,048,576 rows. Over 17 billion cells are available for data. As you will see after the Try it Out, only a small part of the worksheet is visible on the screen at one time.

▶ A cell is referenced by its unique **cell address**, which is made up of the column letter and row number. The cell address for the active cell is called an **active cell reference**. Cell B2, as shown in Figure 1.4, has a heavy border indicating that it is the active cell. The active cell is also identified in the Name Box on the formula bar, which always displays the active cell reference, and by the highlighted column and row of the active cell. The mouse pointer is a plus sign when on the worksheet, as shown in Figure 1.4.

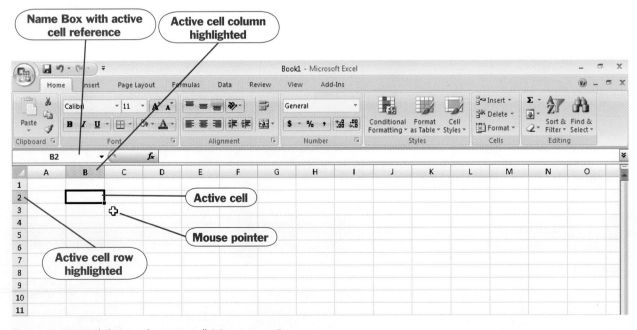

Figure 1.4: Worksheet with active cell B2 in Name Box

1. Click cell **D5** to make it active. *The column and row are highlighted.*

2. Press the left arrow key until cell **B5** is selected.

3. Press the arrow keys to select cell **H20**.

Navigate the Worksheet

▶ There are many ways to move efficiently around the worksheet. You can press the arrow keys or press both an arrow key and [Ctrl] for express movements. As you move through the worksheet, the active cell changes, as does the active cell reference in the Name Box. Table 1.1 provides keystroke shortcuts to navigate the worksheet.

Table 1.1: Navigating the worksheet

NAVIGATE TO:	KEYSTROKE SHORTCUTS:
One cell in any direction	The left arrow [←], right arrow [→], up arrow [↑], or down arrow [↓] keys
One screen up or down	[Page Up] or [Page Down]
First cell in worksheet	[Ctrl]+[Home]
First cell in current row	[Home]
First cell in current column	[Ctrl]+[↑]
Last cell in current row	[Ctrl]+[→]
Last cell in current column	[Ctrl]+[↓]

H20 should be the active cell.

1. Press **[Ctrl]+[Home]**.

2. Use navigation shortcuts to go to:
   a. Last cell in current row: **[Ctrl]+[→]**
   The last column is XFD or 16,384 columns.

   b. First cell in current row: **[Home]**
   c. Last cell in current column: **[Ctrl]+[↓]**
   The last row is 1048576.

3. Press **[Ctrl]+[↑]** to return to the first cell in the worksheet.

4. Click any cell to deselect it.

Use Scroll Bars

▶ To scroll to different areas in a worksheet, use the mouse pointer and the **scroll bars** at the right and bottom of the worksheet window as summarized in Table 1.2, and illustrated in Figure 1.5. Scrolling does not change the active cell.

Table 1.2: Using scroll bars

TO SCROLL:	DO THIS:
One column left or right	Click the left or right scroll arrows
One row up or down	Click the up or down scroll arrows
Scroll quickly	Press and hold [Shift] while dragging the scroll bar

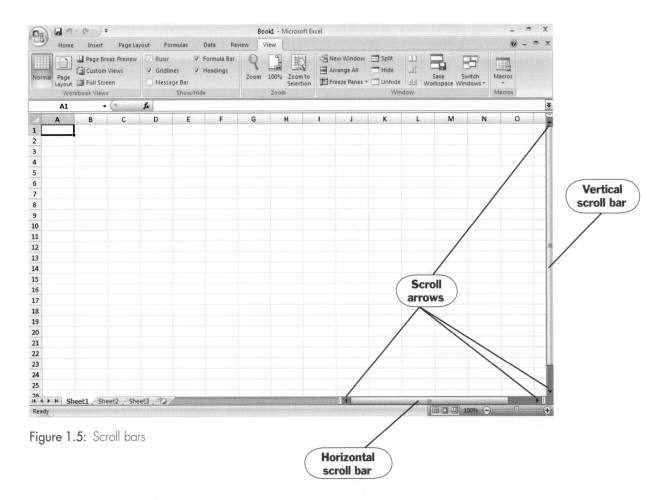

Figure 1.5: Scroll bars

T R Y *it* O U T *e1-6*

1. Click the **down scroll arrow** on the vertical scroll bar.

2. Click the **right scroll arrow** on the horizontal scroll bar.

3. Click and hold the **horizontal scroll bar**, press **[Shift]**, and drag to the right.

4. Click and drag the **horizontal scroll bar** to the left to view column A.

5. Click the **up scroll arrow** on the vertical scroll bar.

Go to a Specific Cell

▶ You can move directly to a specific cell by entering the cell address in the Name Box or by using the Go To dialog box as shown in Figure 1.6.

HOW **1.** Enter the cell address in the Name Box. **2.** Press **[Enter]**.

HOW **1.** Press **[F5]**. **2.** Enter the cell address. *You may also select a location from your list of previously selected locations.* **3.** Click **OK**. *The dollar signs displayed with the cell addresses indicate that the address is an absolute reference to that specific location. Absolute references will be covered in depth in Lesson 4.*

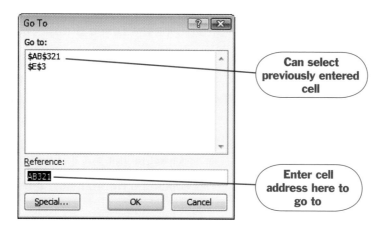

Figure 1.6: Go To dialog box

T R Y *it* O U T *e1-7*

1. Press **[F5]**, enter **AB321**, then click **OK**.

2. Click the **Name Box** on the left side of the formula bar.

3. Enter **E15**, then press **[Enter]**.

4. Press **[F5]**, then double-click **$AB$321** to select cell **AB321** from the Go To list.

5. Press **[Ctrl]+[Home]** to return to cell **A1**.

REHEARSAL

GOAL
To explore and navigate the Excel workbook and screen

TASK 1

WHAT YOU NEED TO KNOW

▶ In this Rehearsal activity, you will explore and navigate the Excel workbook, as shown in Figure 1.7, using shortcut keys and express movements.

▶ The active cell reference, in the Name Box, changes as you move through the worksheet.

DIRECTIONS

1. Click the **Office Button**. *View Menu selections*.
2. Click the worksheet to close the menu.
3. Click the **Page Layout View button**.
4. Click the **Page Layout tab**, and position the mouse over the **Margins button** to view the ScreenTip.
5. Click the **Margins button** to open the Margins gallery.
6. Click the **Normal view button**.
7. Click **Sheet3**.
8. Click **Sheet1**.
9. On the **Home tab**, locate the **Bold button**.
10. On the Quick Access Toolbar, locate the **Save button**.
11. Click cell **E5** to make it active.
12. Use navigation shortcuts to go to the following locations:
    a. Last cell in the current row
    b. Last cell in the current column
    c. First cell in the current row
    d. First cell in the worksheet
13. Click and hold the **horizontal scroll bar**, press **[Shift]**, and drag slowly to the right until you can see column CT.
14. Drag the **horizontal scroll bar** to the left, until you can see column A.
15. Use **[F5]** to go to cell **J33**.
16. Repeat Step 15 to go to cells **BB159** and **J33** again.
17. Enter G5 in the **Name box**, and press **[Enter]**.
18. Move one screen down. *Use [Page Down]*.
19. Return to cell **A1**.

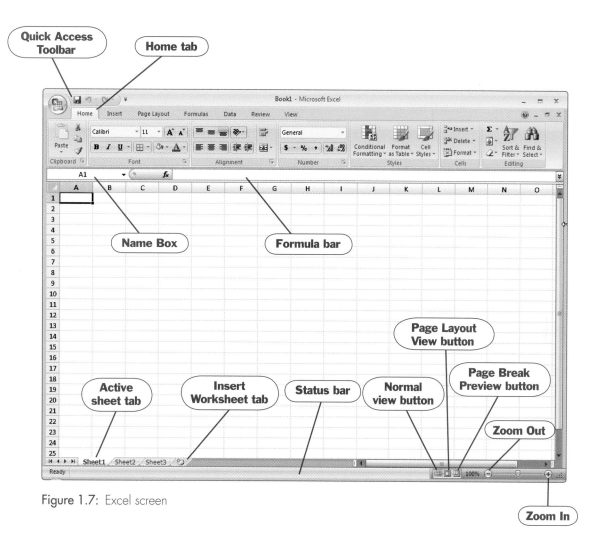

Figure 1.7: Excel screen

Cues for Reference

Start Excel

- Double-click the **Microsoft Excel 2007** icon on the desktop or Windows taskbar.

  or

1. Click the **Start button**.
2. Click **All Programs**.
3. Click **Microsoft Office**, then **Microsoft Office Excel 2007**.

Set Zoom

1. Click the **Zoom In button** to increase magnification.
2. Click the **Zoom Out button** to decrease magnification.

  or

- Click the **Zoom level button** to set magnification. `100%`

  or

- Move the **Zoom slider** as desired.

Use Navigation Shortcuts

  Refer to Table 1.1 Navigating the worksheet.

Scroll Through a Worksheet

- Click the **scroll arrow** to move worksheet view.

  or

- Press **[Shift]** and drag **scroll bar** to scroll quickly through worksheet.

  Refer to Table 1.2 Using scroll bars.

Use Go To

1. Press **[F5]**.
2. Enter the **cell address**, and click **OK**.

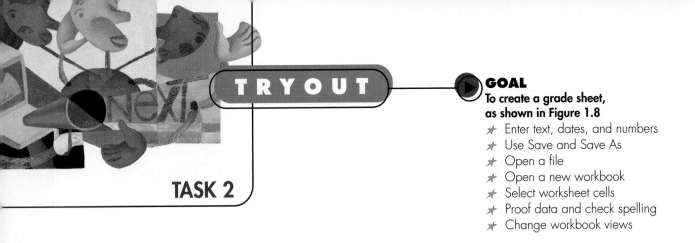

TRYOUT

TASK 2

GOAL
To create a grade sheet,
as shown in Figure 1.8

- ✷ Enter text, dates, and numbers
- ✷ Use Save and Save As
- ✷ Open a file
- ✷ Open a new workbook
- ✷ Select worksheet cells
- ✷ Proof data and check spelling
- ✷ Change workbook views

WHAT YOU NEED TO KNOW

Enter Text, Dates, and Numbers

▶ **Labels** are cells that contain text, such as an alphabetic character or non-mathematical symbols, as the first character. Labels are **left-aligned** in the cell by default.

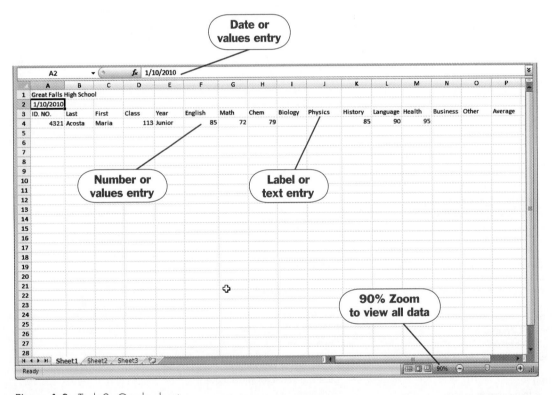

Figure 1.8: Task 2: Grade sheet

▶ When you enter a number or date as the first character in a cell, the cell contains a **value**. Values are **right-aligned** in the cell by default. Note the alignment of label and value entries in Figure 1.9.

▶ After you enter a label or value in a cell, you enter the data by pressing the Enter key or the arrow key that points to the location of the next entry.

▶ The default cell width displays approximately nine characters, depending on the font, but you can enter over 32,000 characters in each cell. If you enter text beyond the default cell width, it appears in the next cell's space as long as no other data is there. In Figure 1.9, the label **Half Marathon Training Record** in cell A1 would be truncated if there were data in B1. The formula bar for A1 would show the full label stored there.

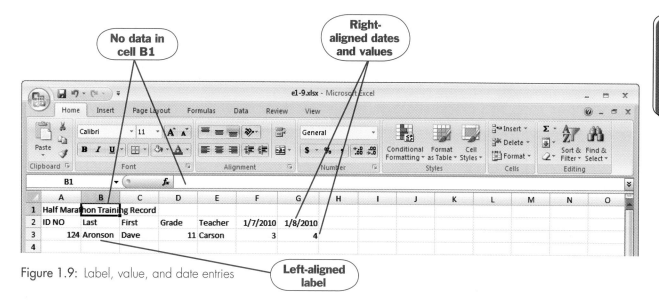

Figure 1.9: Label, value, and date entries

TRY it OUT e1-8

1. Enter the label Half Marathon Training Record in cell **A1**, as shown in Figure 1.9.

2. Press [↓] to enter the label and move to cell **A2**.

3. Enter the label data in cells **A2, B2, C2, D2,** and **E2** as shown in Figure 1.9. *Use the right arrow key to enter data and move to the next cell.*

4. Enter the dates in cells **F2** and **G2**. *Dates are right-aligned.*

5. Enter the data in row 3, as shown in Figure 1.9. *Numbers are right-aligned.*

6. Click cell **A1**, then click cell **B1**. *The label is stored only in cell A1.*

7. Do not close or save the file.

Use Save and Save As

▶ Excel workbooks are named Book1, Book2, and so forth, until you save them with a descriptive filename. When you use the Save command you can save a new file or overwrite an existing file.

HOW Ctrl+S Click the **Save button** on the Quick Access Toolbar.

▶ When you click the **Save button** to save a new file, the Save As dialog box opens. Naming a file in the Save As dialog box creates an Excel 2007 Worksheet file with an .xlsx extension.

▶ You can save Excel files with different names, in different locations, and in different file formats using the settings in the Save As dialog box. If it is necessary to save a worksheet for use in a previous version of Excel, use the Save as type list, as shown in Figure 1.10.

HOW F12 1. Click the **Office Button**. 2. Click **Save As**. 3. Enter the filename. 4. Choose the appropriate settings, then click **OK**.

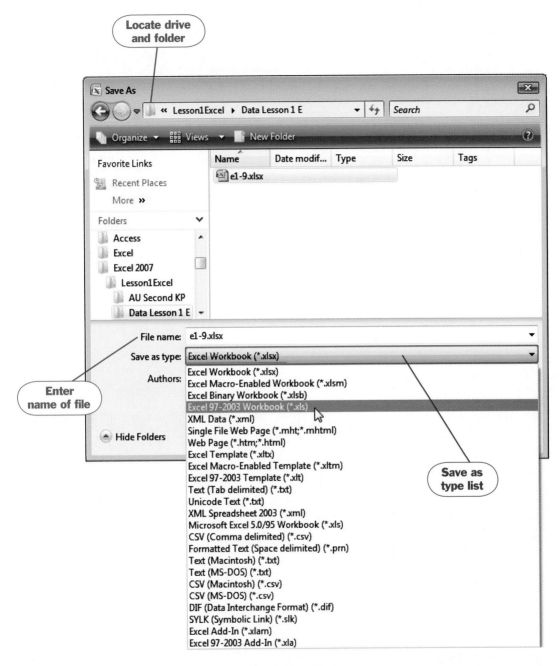

Figure 1.10: Save As dialog box with list of file formats

TRY *it* OUT *e1-9*

1. Continue to work in the open file.

2. Click the **Save button** on the Quick Access Toolbar. *The Save As dialog box appears.*

3. Open the folder where you save your Data Files.

4. Enter **e1-9** as the filename.

Continued on next page

5. Click **Save**. *The filename is displayed on the title bar.*

6. Enter `Total` in cell **P2**.

7. Click the **Save button**. *The new data overwrites the original file.*

8. Press **[F12]**. *This displays the Save As dialog box. You may also click Office Button and Save As.*

9. Enter **e1-9A** as the filename to save the file with a new name.

10. Click the **Save as type list arrow**, then select **Excel 97-2003 Workbook (*.xls)**. *This file can be used with the earlier version of the software.*

11. Click **Save**. Click the **Office Button**, then click **Close**.

Open a File

▶ You can open recently saved documents from the list on the **Office Button** menu or you can display the Open dialog box, as shown in Figure 1.11, to locate other files. To open a file as a copy to use as the basis for a new worksheet, click the Open list arrow, and click Open as Copy.

Figure 1.11: Open dialog box

1. Click the **Office Button**. **2.** Click **Open**. **3.** Click the folder, drive, or location on the Favorite Links pane. **4.** Click and open the folder that contains the file. **5.** Click the file, then click **Open**.

TRY *it* **OUT** *e1-10*

1. Press **[Ctrl]+[O]** to open the Open dialog box, then click **Cancel**.

2. Click the **Office Button** and view the list of Recent Documents.

3. Click **e1-9** on the Recent Documents list.

4. Click the **Office Button**, then click **Open**.

5. Select **e1-9** from the correct folder.

6. Click the **Open list arrow**. Click **Open as Copy**. *Filename displays as Copy (1)e1-9 on the title bar.*

7. Close both files, and do not save.

Open a New Workbook

▶ When you want to open a blank workbook, you can use the **Office Button**, but it is faster to use the keyboard shortcut.

1. Click the **Office Button**. **2.** Click **New**. **3.** Click **Blank Workbook** in the New Workbook dialog box, and click **Create**.

Select Worksheet Cells

▶ You can print, format, or apply styles to cell data. First, you must select the cell or cell range that contains the data.

▶ A **range** is a group of cells in a row, column, or block. The beginning and ending cell addresses identify a range. For example, the range A2:C5 is selected in Figure 1.12.

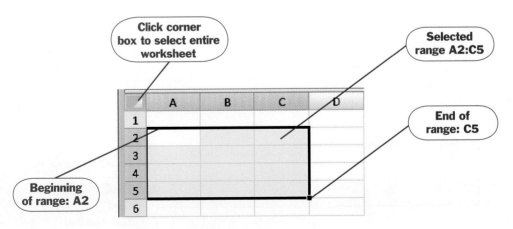

Figure 1.12: Selected range

HOW **1.** Click the first cell in the range. **2.** Click and hold the left **mouse button**. **3.** Drag to select all the cells in the range. A dark border outlines the range. Table 1.3 outlines the ways to select cells.

Table 1.3: Selecting worksheet cells

TO SELECT:	DO THIS
Cell	Click the **cell**.
Row	Press **[Shift]+[Space]** anywhere in row to be selected.
Column	Press **[Ctrl]+[Space]** anywhere in column to be selected.
Worksheet	Press **[Ctrl]+[A]**, or click the **corner box** as shown in Figure 1.12.
Range	Click the first cell in the range, press and hold the left mouse button, and drag until all the cells in the range are selected.

TRY *it* OUT e1-11

1. Open a new Excel workbook. *[Ctrl]+[N]*.

2. Select cell **B7**.

3. Select row 2.

4. Select column C.

5. Select the worksheet. *All the rows and columns are shaded to show that worksheet is selected.*

6. Select the cell range **A2:C5**.

7. Click on any cell to deselect the range.

8. Close the file, and do not save. Do not close the Excel program.

Proof Data and Check Spelling

▶ You can use the Proofing group in the **Review tab**, as shown in Figure 1.13, to check spelling, research reference materials, refer to a thesaurus, or translate data. In Excel, there is no indication of a spelling error until you use the Spelling feature. The Spelling feature compares the words in your file to the words in the Excel dictionary.

HOW F7 **1.** Click the **Review tab**. **2.** Click the **Spelling button**.

ABC
✓
Spelling

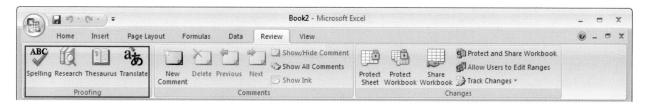

Figure 1.13: Review tab and Proofing group

1. Open the data file **e1-12**.

2. Return to cell **A1**. *Press [Ctrl]+[Home] to start checking from the beginning of the worksheet.*

3. Click the **Review tab** and in the Proofing group, click the **Spelling button**.

4. Click **OK** when the spell check is complete. *There were no errors.*

5. In cell **A5**, enter `marothon`, then press **[Enter]**.

6. Press **[F7]**.

7. Click **Yes** to continue checking from the beginning of the sheet.

8. Select **marathon** in the Suggestions box, if necessary, then click **Change**.

9. Click **OK**.

10. Close the file, and do not save.

Change Workbook Views

▶ Use the **View tab** to set display options for your Excel workbook. In the Workbook Views group, there are five views, as shown in Figure 1.14. Three of the views are also available on the status bar.

▶ **Full Screen** view hides all the commands and provides a full view of just the worksheet. To return to Normal view, click the **Restore Down button** on the top right of the screen.

▶ In the Show/Hide group, the Gridlines, Formula Bar, and Headings check boxes are selected, which means that they are displayed. Deselect the check marks to remove the features from the display.

▶ In the Zoom group, you can set the Zoom magnification or use Zoom to Selection to magnify the cells selected.

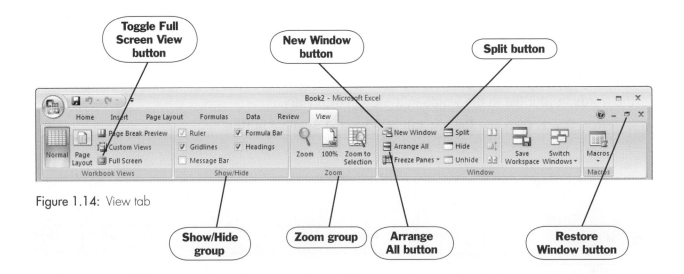

Figure 1.14: View tab

1. Open the data file **e1-13**.

2. Click the **View tab** and place the mouse over each of the Show/Hide options to read the ScreenTips.

3. Deselect the **Gridlines**, **Formula Bar**, and **Headings check boxes**.

4. Click the **Gridlines**, **Formula Bar**, and **Headings check boxes** to select them.

5. In the Workbook Views group, click the **Toggle Full Screen View button**.

6. Click the **Restore Down button** to return to Normal view.

7. In the Zoom group, click **Zoom** to display the dialog box.

8. Select **50%** magnification, and then click **OK**.

9. Click **Zoom to Selection** to magnify cell **G8**, the active cell.

10. Click the **100% button** to return to normal size.

11. Close the file, and do not save.

Add Windows to Change View

▶ In the **View tab**, in the Window group, you can create a **New Window**, which is a copy of the worksheet. The copy will use the current filename with the suffix :2, and the original file will have a :1 suffix. Use the Arrange All button to arrange the two files on the screen to see different parts of the same worksheet, as shown in Figure 1.15.

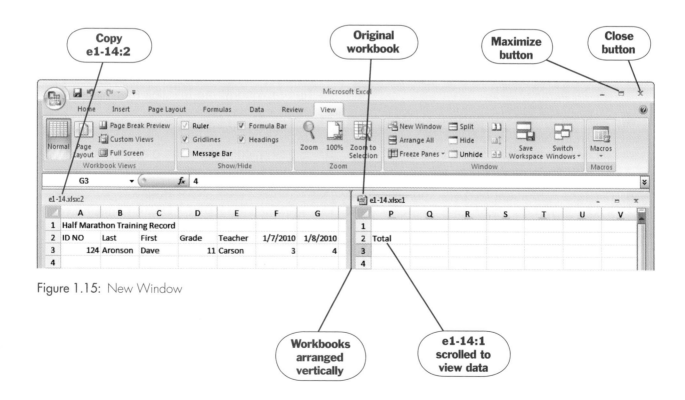

Figure 1.15: New Window

▶ You can also use the Split tool to create a **split screen** with multiple resizable panes to view all parts of a worksheet, as shown in Figure 1.16. Resize the **panes**, or sections of the window, by dragging the frame with the mouse. To remove the split, click the Split tool again.

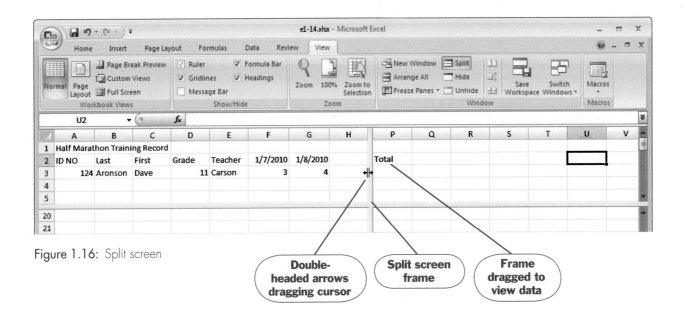

Figure 1.16: Split screen

Double-headed arrows dragging cursor

Split screen frame

Frame dragged to view data

T R Y *it* **O U T** *e1-14*

1. Open the data file **e1-14**.

2. Press **[Ctrl]+[Home]** to return to **A1**.

3. Click the **View tab** and in the Window group, click the **New Window button**. *e1-14:2 will appear in the title bar.*

4. Click the **Arrange All button** and in the dialog box, click **Vertical**, then click **OK**. *e1-14:1 and e1-14:2 are arranged vertically.*

5. Click the worksheet **e1-14:2**, then click **e1-14:1**. *The scroll bars appear in the active copy.*

6. Use the scroll bar at the bottom of the screen of the copy at the right to display column P.

7. Click in **e1-14:2**, then click the **Close button**.

8. Click the **Maximize button** to restore the worksheet and **[Ctrl]+[Home]** to return to cell **A1**.

9. In the Window group, click the **Split button**. *The worksheet splits into four panes.*

10. Scroll to column P, and drag the vertical frame so that columns C and P are side by side.

11. To remove the split, click the **Split button** again.

12. Save and close the file.

REHEARSAL

TASK 2

GOALS

To create a grade sheet

To open a file, enter and proof data, change workbook views, and save the file

WHAT YOU NEED TO KNOW

▶ By default, labels are left-aligned in a cell, and dates and values are right-aligned.

▶ You can change worksheet views to help you view a large worksheet.

▶ In this Rehearsal activity, you will enter labels, values, and dates into a grade sheet for Great Falls High School. You will change worksheet views on the **View tab** and status bar and save the file.

▼ DIRECTIONS

1. Open the data file **1r2-grades**. *The label is left-aligned.*

2. Enter the date 1/10/2010 in cell **A2**. *The date value is right-aligned.*

3. Enter the data from Figure 1.17 in rows 3 and 4. *The values in Row 4 are right-aligned.*

4. Move to cell **A1**, and check the spelling in the worksheet.

5. Use the **Zoom buttons** on the status bar to zoom out to 90%.

6. On the **View tab**, use Zoom to return to 100% magnification.

7. Use the Split command to view all parts of the worksheet.

8. Drag the frame and use the scroll bar so that columns E and P are side by side.

9. Remove the split.

10. Use the New Window command to make a copy of the worksheet.

11. Arrange the worksheets vertically and scroll to view all data.

12. Close the worksheet **1r2-grades:2** and maximize the **1r2-grades:1** window. Return to **A1**.

13. Click the **Full Screen button**. Restore the screen to Normal view.

14. Click the **Page Layout View button** on the status bar. *The worksheet will print on two pages unless you change print specifications.*

15. Return to Normal view.

16. Save the file as **1r2-gradesA**.

17. Save the file as **1r2-gradesA** in Excel 97-2003 format.

18. Close the file.

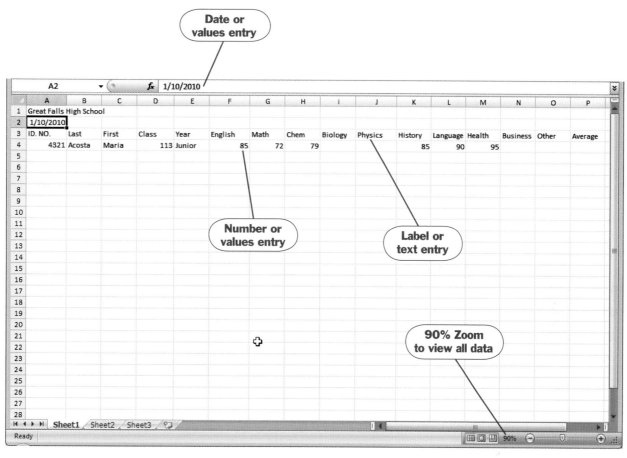

Figure 1.17: Grade sheet

Cues for Reference

Open a New Workbook [CTRL]+[N]
1. Click the **Office Button**.
2. Click **New**.
3. Double-click **Blank Workbook**.

Open a File [CTRL]+[O]
1. Click the **Office Button**.
2. Click **Open**.
3. Click the folder, drive, or location in the Favorite Links pane.
4. Click and open the folder that contains the file.
5. Click the file, then click **Open**.

Enter a Label or Value
1. Click cell to make it active.
2. Enter the label or value.
3. Press **[Enter]** or press an **arrow key** to move to the next cell.

Save [CTRL]+[S]
- Click the **Save button** on the Quick Access Toolbar.

Save As [F12 To Step 3]
1. Click the **Office Button**.
2. Click **Save As**.
3. In the **Save As box**, click a location in the Favorite Links pane to open, if available.
4. Double-click a folder to open it.
5. Enter filename in **File name box**.
6. Click **Save as type** down arrow, and choose file type, if necessary.
7. Click **Save**.

Change Workbook Views
- Views: Use the **buttons** on the status bar to change to Page Layout, Page Break Preview, or Normal view.
  Or
- Full Screen: Click on the **View tab**, and in the Workbook Views group, click on the **Full Screen button**. Click the **Restore Down button** to return to Normal view.

- Zoom Levels: Click on the **View tab**, and in the Zoom group, click the **Zoom button**, select a level of magnification, then click **OK**.
- Zoom to Selection: Select the cells to be magnified. Click on the **View tab**, and in the Zoom group, click the **Zoom to Selection button**.
- New Window: Click on the **View tab**, and in the Windows group, click the **New Window button**.
- Arrange Windows: Click on the **View tab**, and in the Windows group, click the **Arrange All button**, click the desired layout, then click **OK**.
- Split Window: Click on the **View tab**, and in the Windows group, click the **Split button**. Drag frame to size sections. Click the **Split button** again to deselect.

The Computer Specialist at Great Falls High School has added a formula to find the grade average on the grade sheet you have previously prepared, as shown in Figure 1.18. You have been asked to enter data for two more students and to view the worksheet to answer questions about the grades.

Follow these guidelines:

1. Open the data file **1p2-grades**. *The average is in cell **P4,** and there are formulas in **P5** and **P6**.*

2. Enter the grades and data for the following students in the appropriate columns:

ID. NO.	Name	Class	Year	English	Math	Physics	History	Language	Health	Business	Other
5435	Adams, Mark	115	Senior	70	75		75		85	80	85
5874	Ahearn, Patrick	113	Junior	85	85	80	80	85	90	90	

3. Use the Split Screen command to view all parts of the worksheet.

4. Drag the frame and use the scroll bar so that columns E and P are side by side. *Which student has the highest average? Which has the lowest?* Remove the split.

5. Click the **Toggle Full Screen View button**. *Who had the highest Health grade? Who had the lowest History grade?* Restore the screen to Normal view.

6. Save the file as **1p2-grades**. Close the file.

	A	B	C	D	E	P	Q
1	Great Falls High School						
2	1/10/2010						
3	ID. NO.	Last	First	Class	Year	Average	
4	4321	Acosta	Maria	113	Junior	84	
5	5435	Adams	Mark	115	Senior	78	
6	5874	Ahearn	Patrick	113	Junior	85	
7							
8							
9							
10							
11							
12							
13							
14							

Figure 1.18: Split screen view of grade sheet

LESSON 2

Business Forms

In this lesson, you will learn to use Excel to design business forms and to customize both software and online templates. You will format and edit data, insert data using AutoFill, print worksheets, and work with templates. You will complete the following projects:

- Invoice for services
- Time sheet
- Purchase order
- Sales invoice
- Price quotation

Upon completion of this lesson, you will have mastered the following skill sets

- Format cell data
- Apply and modify cell styles
- Edit cell data
- Insert cell data
- Print
- Work with templates

Terms
Software-related
Accounting format
AutoComplete
AutoFill
Cell style
Comma format
Currency format
Default printer settings
Edit mode
Fill handle
Format
Number format
Portable Document Format (PDF)
Template
Theme
Wrap Text

Document-related
Business form
Invoice for services
Purchase order
Sales invoice
Time sheet
Transaction
Vendor

TRYOUT

GOAL
To create an invoice for services,
as shown in Figure 2.1
* Format cell data
* Apply and modify cell styles

TASK 1

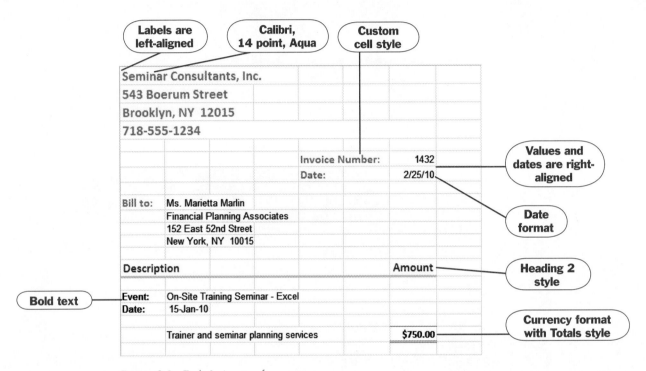

Figure 2.1: Task 1: Invoice for services

WHAT YOU NEED TO KNOW

Format Cell Data

Apply Number Format

▶ **Formats** change the appearance of numbers without changing the value used in calculations. For example, if you enter a number such as 1234.567 and format it for two decimal places, it will appear as 1234.57, but the full number remains in the cell's memory and is used in calculations.

► By default, numbers will be displayed with no specific format (General). In this Lesson, you will be applying the following number formats:

- **Accounting format**: $ aligned in the column
- **Currency format**: $ to the immediate left of the number
- **Comma format**: 2 decimal places and commas
- **Number format**: 2 decimal places

► Look at Figure 2.2 for examples of how these formats change the number display.

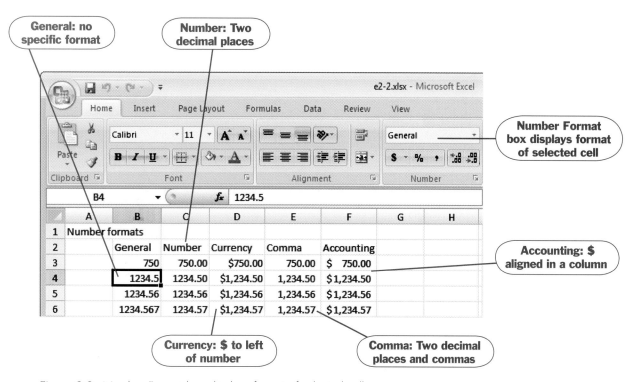

Figure 2.2: Number Format box displays format of selected cell

► Number format tools can be found in numerous places:
- In the Home tab, in the Number group, shown in Figure 2.3a

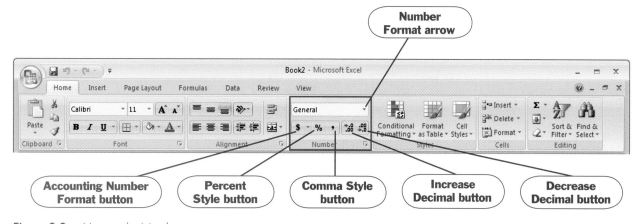

Figure 2.3a: Home tab, Number group

- In the Number Format gallery, shown in Figure 2.3b, displayed when you click on the Number Format arrow
- In the shortcut menu and Mini toolbar, shown in Figure 2.4, displayed when you right-click on a cell
- In the Format Cells dialog box, shown in Figure 2.5, accessed through the Shortcut menu, by clicking the dialog box launcher arrow in the Number group, or by pressing [Ctrl]+[1]

Once data is formatted using any method, the format style will be displayed in the Number format box, as shown in Figure 2.2.

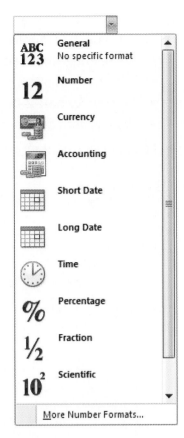

Figure 2.3b: Number Format gallery

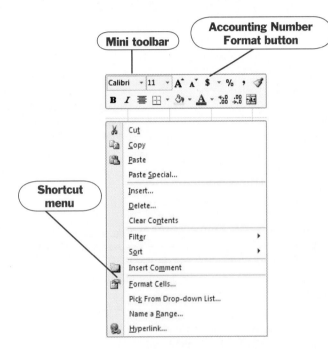

Figure 2.4: Shortcut menu and Mini toolbar

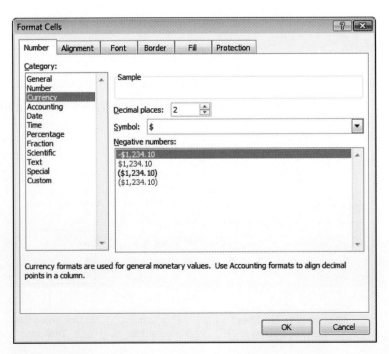

Figure 2.5: Format Cells dialog box

HOW Ctrl+1 1. Select cell(s) to be formatted. 2. Right-click and select desired **number format button** on Mini toolbar, or 2. Press **[Ctrl]+[1]**, and in the Number tab, click the appropriate category and number format, or 2. Click the **Number Format arrow** and click the format in the Number Format gallery.

T R Y *i t* **O U T** *e2-1*

1. Launch Excel.

2. Open the data file **e2-1**. *Press [Ctrl]+[O], then locate folder and select file to open.*

3. Select the range **C3:C6**.

4. Click the **Home tab**, and in the Number group, click the **Number Format arrow** and click the **Number category** in the Number Format gallery.

5. Select the range **D3:D6**. Press **[Ctrl]+[1]**, and in the Number tab, click the Currency category. Click **OK**.

6. Select the range **E3:E6**. Click the **Comma Style button** in the Number group.

7. Select the range **F3:F6**. Right-click and click the **Accounting Number Format button** in the Mini toolbar.

8. Save the file, but do not close it.

Format Dates

▶ You can enter a date in any format and reformat it in one of 17 date formats, as shown in Figure 2.6, or use the Short Date or Long Date formats from the Number Format gallery, shown in Figure 2.3b.

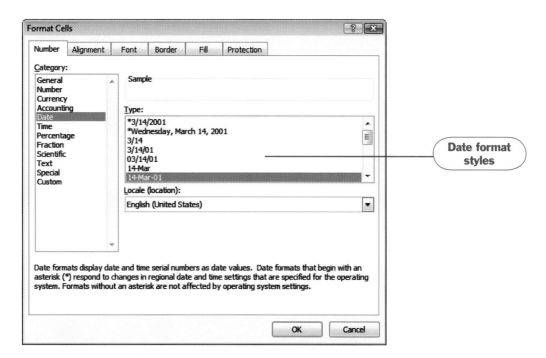

Figure 2.6: Format Cells: Date

HOW Ctrl+1 1. Click the **date**. 2. Press **[Ctrl]+[1]**. 3. In the Number tab in the Format Cells dialog box, click **Date**. 4. Click a date format from the Type list.

TRY*it* OUT e2-2

1. Continue to work in the open file, or open the data file **e2-2**.

2. Click cell **B9**.

3. Enter today's date. *Press [Ctrl]+[;] to enter the current date.*

4. Repeat Step 3 for **B10** and **B11**.

5. Format the date in **B9** with the Short Date format. *Click the **Number Format arrow**, and in the Number Format gallery, click the **Short Date format**.*

6. Format the date in **B10** with the Long Date format, using the Number Format gallery.

7. Format the date in **B11** with the 14-Mar-01 format. *Select **B11**, and press [Ctrl]+[1]. In the Number tab, click the **Date category**, click the **14-Mar-01 format**, then click **OK**.*

8. Save the file, but do not close it.

Format Text

▶ The default font is Calibri, 11 point. To change the font and font size, select the cell(s), and use the Font group on the Home tab, as shown in Figure 2.7, or right-click to display the Mini toolbar, as shown in Figure 2.4. As with numbers and dates, the Format Cells dialog box can be used to customize the settings for text. To make changes this way, press [Ctrl]+[1], and go to the Font tab.

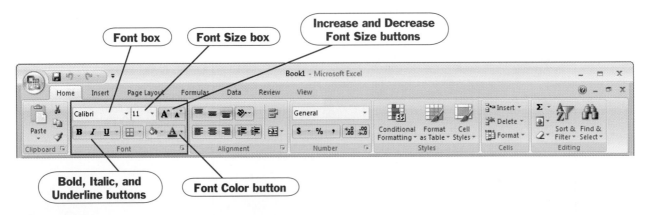

Figure 2.7: Home tab, Font group

► You can also use the **buttons** in the Home tab, in the Font group, shown in Table 2.1 to format text. Except for the **Underline button**, all the text **formatting buttons** also appear on the Mini toolbar.

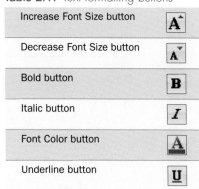

Table 2.1: Text formatting buttons

Increase Font Size button	A‸
Decrease Font Size button	A▾
Bold button	**B**
Italic button	*I*
Font Color button	A
Underline button	U

HOW Ctrl+1

1. Select text. **2.** Click the **Home tab**, and in the Font group, click the **Font list arrow**. **3.** Select font. **4.** Click the **Font Size list arrow** to select font size.

T R Y *it* O U T *e2-3*

1. Continue to work in the open file or open the data file **e2-3**.

2. Right-click cell **A1**.

3. Use the Mini toolbar to change the font to **Arial Black, 22 point**.

4. Click the **Home tab**, and in the Font group, click the **Decrease Font Size button** to scale down to **Arial Black, 18 point**.

5. Select row 2.

6. Change the font to **Arial**, **12 point**, using the Mini toolbar.

7. In the Home tab, in the Font group, click the **Bold button** and the **Underline button**.

8. Change the font color of row 2 to **Orange** using the **Font Color button**.

9. Save the file as **e2-3**, and close the file.

Apply and Modify Cell Styles

▶ **Cell styles** define a set of formats, such as font, font size, or font color, that can be applied to cells. The **Cell Styles button** on the Home tab in the Styles group displays the Cell Styles gallery, shown in Figure 2.8. In the Cell Styles gallery, you will find predefined formats that you can apply or modify.

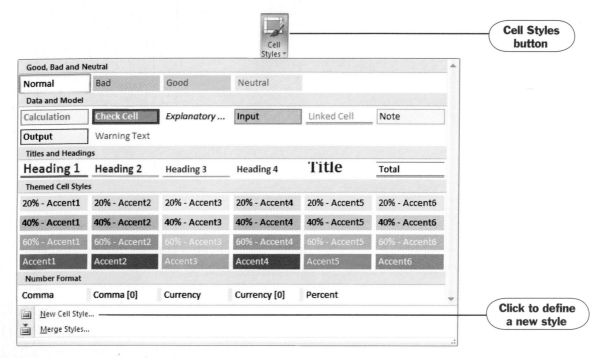

Figure 2.8: Home tab, Styles group, Cell Styles: Cell Styles gallery

Apply a Cell Style

 1. Select the cell(s) to be formatted. **2.** Click the **Home tab**, and in the Styles group, click the **Cell Styles button**. **3.** Select a style.

T R Y *i t* **O U T** *e2-4*

1. Open the data file **e2-4**. This is a sample of an invoice for professional services.

2. Select the range **A1:G4**.

3. Click the **Home tab**, and in the Styles group, click the **Cell Styles button**. *At monitor settings above 1024 X 768, the gallery displays in the Ribbon area.*

4. Move your mouse over the styles and note the effect on your text.

5. Click the **Heading 3 cell style button**.

6. Apply Heading 3 to the range **A14:G14**.

7. Save the file, but do not close it.

Create a Custom Cell Style

▶ You can create your own cell style by modifying an existing cell style or by selecting all the settings in a cell and then naming the style. Once the new style has been named in the Style dialog box, shown in Figure 2.9, it will appear in the Cell Styles gallery.

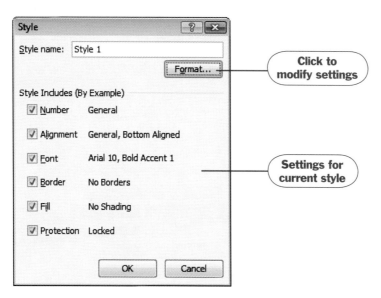

Figure 2.9: Style dialog box

HOW 1. Format the cell as desired using the font, style, or number settings. 2. Click the **Home tab**, and in the Styles group, click the **Cell Styles button**. 3. Click **New Cell Style**. 4. Enter a cell style name, confirm the settings, then click **OK**. *If necessary, click Format to change any settings that appear.*

T R Y *i t* O U T *e2-5*

1. Continue to work in the open file, or open the data file **e2-5**.

2. Right-click on cell **E6** and format the text for **Arial**, **10 point**, **Bold**, **Blue**.

3. Click the **Home tab**, and in the Styles group, click the **Cell Styles button**.

4. Click **New Cell Style**.

5. Type **Blue** as the Style name in the Style dialog box.

6. Click **OK**.

7. Click the **Cell Styles button**. *There is a new Blue setting under the Custom category.*

8. Use the new Blue cell style to format cells **E7** and **A9**.

9. Save the file as **e2-5** and close it.

Modify a Cell Style

▶ An existing cell style may be duplicated and then modified to create a new style. The shortcut menu that displays when you right-click a style, shown in Figure 2.10, also allows you to delete a style.

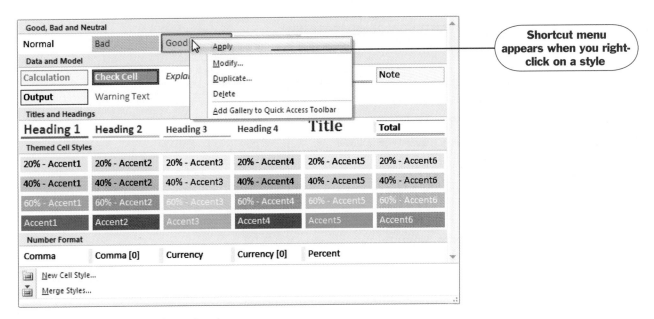

Figure 2.10: Shortcut menu for Cell Style

HOW 1. Right-click a cell style to modify. 2. Select **Duplicate**. 3. Click **Format**. 4. Change settings as desired. 5. Click **OK**, then **OK** again.

TRY it OUT e2-6

1. Open the data file **e2-6**.

2. Click the **Home tab**, and in the Styles group, click the **Cell Styles button**. *The Blue cell style is located under Custom styles.*

3. Right-click the **Blue cell style button**. Click **Duplicate**. *Blue 2 is the duplicate style name.*

4. Click the **Format button**, and in the **Alignment tab**, change the horizontal text alignment to **Center**.

5. Click **OK**, then **OK** again.

6. Apply the Blue 2 cell style to **E6**, **E7**, and **A9**.

7. In the Cell Styles gallery, right-click the **Blue 2 cell style button**, then click **Delete**. *The formatted text changes back to the default settings.*

8. Apply the Blue cell style to **E6**, **E7**, and **A9**.

9. Save the file, but do not close it.

Apply a Theme

▶ A **theme** is a set of font, color, and style formatting choices for an entire worksheet. Companies generally use one theme in all documents for a uniform look.

HOW
1. Click the **Page Layout tab**, and in the Themes group, click the **Themes button**.
2. Click the predefined theme you prefer.

T R Y _it_ O U T _e2-7_

1. Continue to work in the open file, or open the data file **e2-7**.

2. Click the **Page Layout tab**, and in the Themes group, click the **Themes button**.

3. Click the **Aspect theme**. _See the change in the font, font size, and colors._

4. Save the file as **e2-7**, and close it.

REHEARSAL

TASK 1

GOAL
To create an invoice for services

WHAT YOU NEED TO KNOW

▶ A **business form** is a document format that you develop to standardize the appearance of business data. Most business forms are numbered consecutively for reference in records or communications.

▶ Consultants and professionals in fee-based businesses use an **invoice for services** to bill their clients for a service or for their time.

▶ You can use preprinted forms or predesigned Excel worksheets for business forms or you can create your own forms with Excel.

▶ In this Rehearsal activity, you will create an invoice for planning services for Seminar Consultants, Inc. Data will be entered first and then formatted.

DIRECTIONS

1. Open the data file **2r1-proinv**.

2. Use Figure 2.11 as a guide and enter the missing data without formatting in cells **A1**, **G6**, **G7**, **B11**, **B12**, **G14**, **B17**, and **B19**. *Press the arrow keys to enter data and move to the next cell.*

3. Select the range **A1:G4** and right-click. Change the font settings to **Calibri**, **16 point**, **Bold**, **Blue**, **Accent 1 font color**.

4. With the same range selected, decrease the font size to **14 point**.

5. Select the range **A14:G14**, and apply the Heading 2 cell style.

6. Select cell **E6**. In the Home tab, use the Font group to format the cell for **Calibri**, **12 point**, **Bold**, **Blue**, **Accent 1 font color**.

7. With **E6** selected, click the **Cell Styles button**. Use **New Cell Style** to name the style `Title2`.

8. Apply the Title2 cell style to cells **E7** and **A9**.

9. Bold the text in cells **A16** and **A17**.

10. Format the dates in cells **G7** and **B17** using the 14-Mar-01 format.

11. Format cell **G19** for currency, and apply the Total cell style.

12. Save the file in your solutions folder as **2r1-proinv**.

13. On the Page Layout tab, change the theme from Office to Module and save the file as **2r1-proinv2**. *After the file is saved, the new cell style can be removed from the gallery if the computer will be used by others. Right-click the style, and click **Delete** to remove a style.*

14. Close the file.

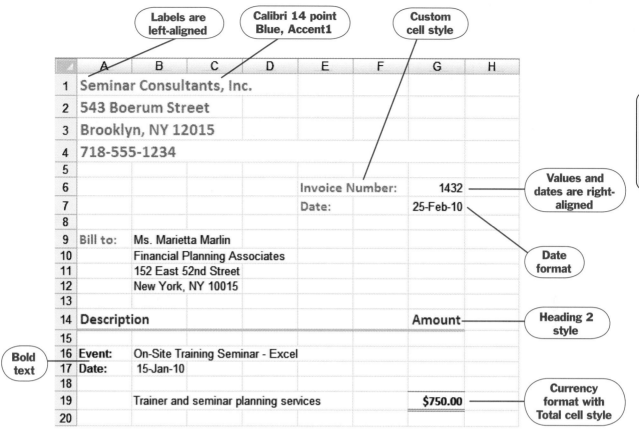

Figure 2.11: Invoice for services

Cues for Reference

Format Currency
1. Select the value to format.
2. Click the **Accounting Number Format button**. $
   Or
2. Press **[Ctrl]+[1]**.
3. In the Number tab, click the **Currency category**.
4. Click **OK**.

Format Dates
1. Select the date.
2. Press **[Ctrl]+[1]**.
3. In the Number tab, click the **Date category**.
4. Select a date format.
5. Click **OK**.

Format Text
1. Select the text to format.
2. Right-click to display the Mini toolbar.
   Or

2. In the Home tab, use the Font group buttons.
3. Select the font, font size, and font color.
4. Use the **Increase Font Size button** or the **Decrease Font Size button** to adjust text, if necessary.

Apply a Cell Style
1. Select the cell(s) to be formatted.
2. Click the **Home tab**, and in the Styles group, click the **Cell Styles button**.
3. Select a Cell Style.

Create a Custom Cell Style
1. Format the cell as desired using font, style, or number settings.

2. Click the **Home tab**, and in the Styles group, click the **Cell Styles button**.
3. Click **New Cell Style**.
4. Enter a name for the style in the Style dialog box.
5. Check the settings. If necessary, click **Format** to modify any settings that appear, then click **OK**.
6. Click **OK** to close the Style dialog box.

Apply a Theme
1. In the Page Layout tab, in the Themes group, click the **Themes button**.
2. Click the desired theme.

PERFORMANCE

TASK 1

The Corporate Travel department of Transport Travel Services wants you to create an invoice for arrangements and travel bookings for a company conference in Scottsdale, Arizona.

Follow these guidelines:

1. Open a new blank worksheet.

2. Use Figure 2.12 as a guide, and enter the data without formatting into the worksheet in the locations shown.

3. Apply the Heading 1 cell style to the heading information in the range **A1:G3**.

4. In Cell Styles, right-click the **Heading 2 cell style button**, and make a duplicate of the style.

5. Remove the bottom border from the style by deselecting the Border format checkbox. Click **OK**.

6. Apply the new Heading 2 2 cell style to **E6**, **E7**, and **A9**.

7. Apply the Heading 2 cell style to the range **A14:G14**.

8. Bold text in the range **A16:A19**.

9. Format the date in cell **G7** in the 14-Mar-01 format.

10. Format data in cell **G21** in Accounting Number format and apply the Total cell style.

11. Change the theme from Office to **Equity**, and save the file as **2p1-inv**.

12. Close the file.

Invoice data
before formatting

	A	B	C	D	E	F	G	H
1	Transport Travel Services							
2	46 Beverly Drive							
3	Beverly Hills, CA 90210							
4								
5								
6					Invoice Number:		65342	
7					Date:		2/5/2010	
8								
9	Bill to:	Mr. Martin Halliday						
10		Proxaar Pharmaceuticals						
11		543 Longacre Drive						
12		Los Angeles, CA 90013						
13								
14	Description						Amount	
15								
16	Event:	Corporate Conference - Scottsdale, AZ						
17	Location:	Resorts Conference Center of Scottsdale						
18	Dates:	February 10-13, 2010						
19	Group:	4 participants - Marketing Department						
20								
21		Flight and hotel arrangements for the group						3575	
22								

Figure 2.12: Invoice for services

EXCEL

TRYOUT

GOAL
To create a time sheet, as shown in Figure 2.13
- Edit cell data
- Insert cell data
- Print

TASK 2

Edited data

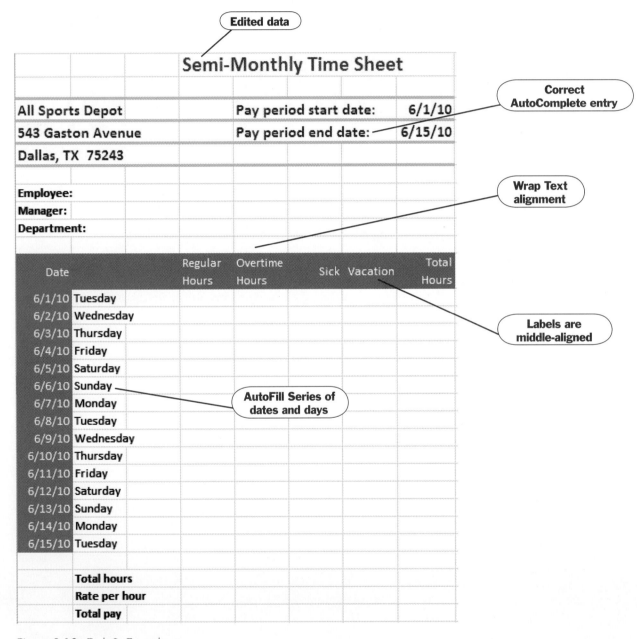

Semi-Monthly Time Sheet

All Sports Depot		**Pay period start date:**		6/1/10		
543 Gaston Avenue		**Pay period end date:**		6/15/10		
Dallas, TX 75243						
Employee:						
Manager:						
Department:						

Date	Regular Hours	Overtime Hours	Sick	Vacation		Total Hours
6/1/10 Tuesday						
6/2/10 Wednesday						
6/3/10 Thursday						
6/4/10 Friday						
6/5/10 Saturday						
6/6/10 Sunday						
6/7/10 Monday						
6/8/10 Tuesday						
6/9/10 Wednesday						
6/10/10 Thursday						
6/11/10 Friday						
6/12/10 Saturday						
6/13/10 Sunday						
6/14/10 Monday						
6/15/10 Tuesday						
Total hours						
Rate per hour						
Total pay						

Correct AutoComplete entry

Wrap Text alignment

Labels are middle-aligned

AutoFill Series of dates and days

Figure 2.13: Task 2: Time sheet

WHAT YOU NEED TO KNOW

Edit Cell Data

Edit Cell Contents

▶ To edit data before you complete an incorrect entry, press the Backspace key. To edit after incorrect data is entered, use one of these methods:

- Redo the entry to overwrite the original data.
- Press the F2 key. This will activate **Edit mode**, which places the insertion point at the end of the incorrect label.
- Double-click in the cell at the editing location.

T R Y *it* O U T *e2-8*

1. Open the data file **e2-8** and make edits as shown in Figure 2.14.

2. Change **75423** to **75243**:
   a. Click cell **A5**.
   b. Press **[F2]**. *The insertion point is at the end of the label.*
   c. Press **[Backspace]** to delete **423** and enter **243**.

3. Change **Time Sheet** to **Bi-Weekly Time Sheet**:
   a. Place the mouse pointer at the beginning of cell **D1** and double-click. *You should be in Edit mode with the insertion point at the beginning of the cell.*
   b. Enter **Bi-Weekly**, press the **spacebar**, then press [**Enter**].

4. Edit before entering data:
   a. Click in cell **L1** and enter **130**. *Do not press [Enter]*.
   b. Press **[Backspace]** once and enter **5** to make it **135**.
   c. Press **[Enter]**.

5. Edit after entering data:
   a. In cell **L2**, enter **182**, and press **[Enter]**.
   b. In cell **L2**, enter **185** to overwrite existing entry, and press **[Enter]**.

6. Save the file, but do not close it.

	A	B	C	D	E	F	G	H
1				Time Sheet				
2								
3	CarWorld					Pay period start date:		
4	67 Viscount Street					Pay period end date:		
5	Dallas, TX 75423							
6								
7	Employee:							
8	Manager:							
9	Department:							
10								

To change to Bi-Weekly Time Sheet, place insertion point at the beginning of the cell

Change to 75243

Figure 2.14: Items to edit

Align Cell Data

▶ As previously discussed, the default alignment for label text is left-aligned, while values and dates are right-aligned in the cell. However, you can change the alignment of data to improve the appearance of the worksheet by using the tools in the Alignment group on the Home tab, shown in Figure 2.15.

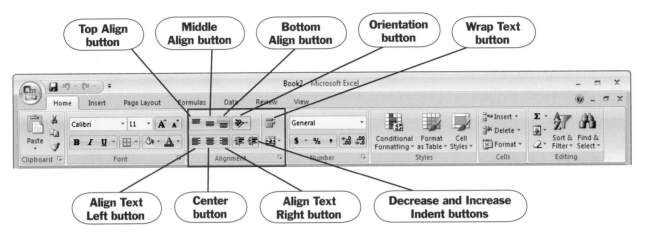

Figure 2.15 Home tab, Alignment group

HOW 1. Select the cell(s) to be aligned. 2. Click the **appropriate alignment button**, shown in Table 2.2.

▶ The **Orientation button** allows you to rotate cell text to diagonal or vertical orientation. If you have text that is too long for the column size and wish to display it all, use the **Wrap Text button**, which displays the text on more than one line. The **Increase Indent and Decrease Indent buttons** move text in or back approximately two spaces.

Table 2.2: Alignment buttons

Align Text Left button	
Center button	
Align Text Right button	
Top Align button	
Middle Align button	
Bottom Align button	

TRY it OUT e2-9

1. Continue working in the open file or open the data file **e2-9**.

2. Click cell **A11**, and click the **Center button**.

3. Right-align the label in **H11**.

4. Select the range **A7:A9**, and click the **Increase Indent button** once.

5. Select the range **D11:E11**, and click the **Wrap Text button**.

6. Select the range **F11:H11** and click the **Top Align button**.

7. Select **L1**, and click the **Orientation button**, then click through the list to test the different orientations provided. *Click the **Undo button** on the Quick Access Toolbar, until data is returned to its original position.*

8. Save the file, but do not close it.

Clear Cell Contents

▶ If you want to remove entered data, select the cell and press the Delete key, or right-click the data and click Clear Contents from the Shortcut menu.

TRY it OUT e2-10

1. Continue working in the open file or open the data file **e2-10**.

2. Click cell **L1**.

3. Press **[Delete]**.

4. Right-click cell **L2**, and select **Clear Contents** from the Shortcut menu.

5. Save the file as **e2-10**, and close it.

Insert Cell Data

Use AutoComplete

▶ The **AutoComplete** feature enters labels automatically if you have previously entered them in the same column. When you enter the first letter or letters of repeated data, Excel completes the label from your previously entered data, as shown in Figure 2.16. If the label is correct, press the Enter key to confirm the entry. If it is not correct, continue entering the new label or edit the AutoComplete text.

| Pay period start date: | 4/5/10 |
| Pay period start date: | 4/16/10 |

AutoComplete entry appears highlighted or selected so that the text can be entered or edited

Figure 2.16: AutoComplete

EXCEL

1. Open the data file **e2-11**.

2. In cell **F4** begin to enter **Pay period end date:** . *The AutoComplete feature will complete the label with the information from F3.*

3. In the suggested label select the word **start** and replace it with **end**.

4. Press **[Enter]**.

5. Save the file, but do not close it.

Use AutoFill

▶ The **AutoFill** feature, using the fill handle, will automatically continue a series based on a pattern you establish. The **fill handle** is the small black square in the lower-right corner of a selection, as shown in Figure 2.17. When you point to the fill handle, the pointer changes to a black cross. In the examples of AutoFill series in Table 2.3, you will note that when there is a number series or a variation of a normal sequence, you need to select the first two items to define the series.

Table 2.3: AutoFill series

INITIAL SELECTION:	EXTENDED SERIES:
8:00	9:00, 10:00, 11:00 . . .
Monday	Tuesday, Wednesday . . .
Jan	Feb, Mar, Apr . . .
Qtr 1	Qtr 2, Qtr 3 . . .
10, 20 *	30, 40, 50 . . .
March, June *	September, December . . .

*You need to select the first two cells in the range to create this series.

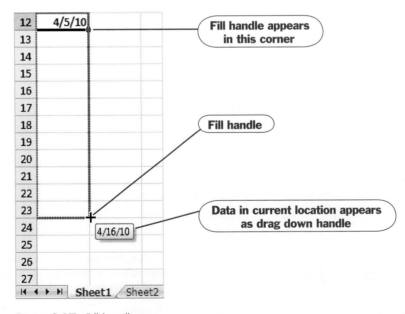

Figure 2.17: Fill handle

HOW 	**1.** Select the cell or cells that contain the starting values. **2.** Drag the fill handle through the range that you want to fill. *To fill in increasing order, drag down or to the right. To fill in decreasing order, drag up or to the left.*

T R Y *i t* **O U T** *e2-12*

1. Continue working in the open file or open the data file **e2-12**.

2. In cell **A12**, enter the date **4/5/10**. *After the date is entered, right-click the **date**, and select **Format Cells**. Format the date in 3/14/01 format. Click **OK**.*

3. In cell **A12**, drag the fill handle down and release it when the ScreenTip displays

4/16/10, the end of the pay period, as shown in Figure 2.17.

4. In cell **B12**, enter **Monday**.

5. Use the fill handle to fill down to **B23**.

6. Save the file, but do not close it.

Print

▶ From the Print gallery on the **Office Button** menu, you can select Print, Quick Print, or Print Preview, as shown in Figure 2.18. If you select Quick Print, the worksheet prints immediately with the default settings.

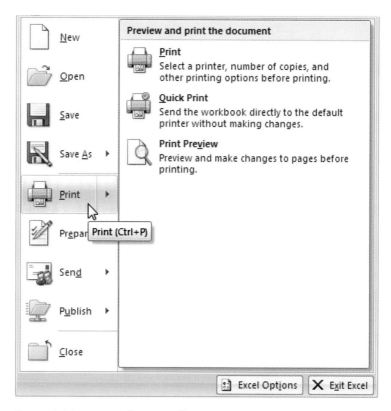

Figure 2.18: Print Gallery on Office Button menu

Use Print Preview

▶ Before printing, it is advisable to preview the worksheet to check the settings.

HOW Ctrl+F2 **1.** Click the **Office Button**. **2.** Click **Print**. **3.** Click **Preview**.

▶ If the layout is satisfactory, you can print the worksheet using the **Print button** on the Print Preview tab, as shown in Figure 2.19.

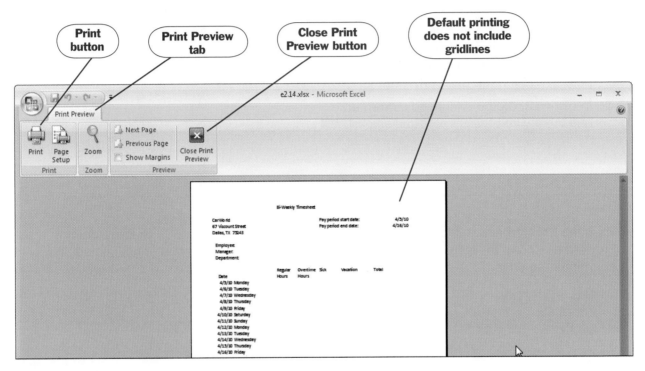

Figure 2.19: Print Preview screen

T R Y i t O U T e2-13

1. Continue working in the open file or open the data file **e2-13**.

2. Press **[Ctrl]+[F2]**. *The Print Preview screen appears.*

3. Close the Print Preview screen.

4. Click the **Office Button**, and point to, but do not click, **Print**, then click **Print Preview**.

5. Click on the **worksheet** to zoom in. Click again to zoom out.

6. Click the **Print button**.

7. Click **OK** in the Print dialog box. *The worksheet prints as previewed.*

Change Print Settings

▶ When you use Quick Print or do not customize print settings, the worksheet prints with default settings. The **default printer settings** are portrait orientation without gridlines or row and column headings. If this is satisfactory, Quick Print is the most efficient way to print.

▶ To customize print settings, click Page Setup on the Print Preview screen and use the dialog box, shown in Figure 2.20. If you wish to view settings as you make changes, work in Page Layout view, and use the Page Layout tab, shown in Figure 2.21.

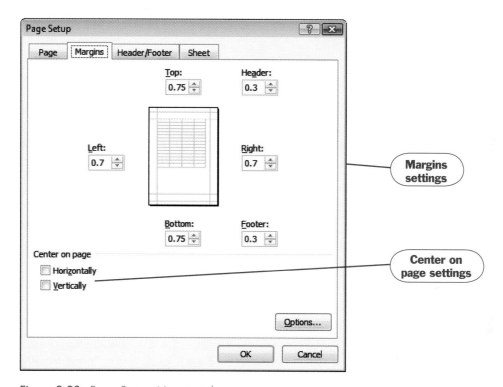

Figure 2.20: Page Setup, Margins tab

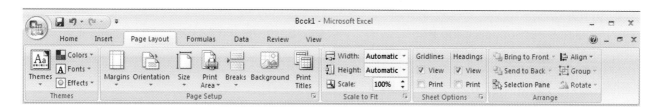

Figure 2.21: Page Layout tab

 HOW 1. Click the **Page Layout view button** on the status bar.
2. Click the **Page Layout tab**. 3. Make and preview customized settings.

Set Print Area

▶ To print only part of a worksheet, you must define the print area, as shown in Figure 2.22. If you wish to print any other selection, you must clear the print area.

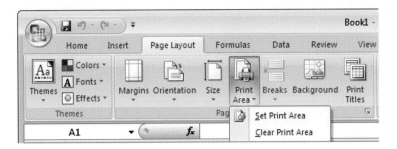

Figure 2.22 Set Print Area

HOW 1. Select range to be printed. 2. Click **Page Layout tab**, and in the Page Setup group, click **Print Area**, then **Set Print Area**. *You can clear the print area by clicking **Print Area** and **Clear Print Area**.*

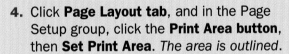

1. Continue working in the open file or open the data file **e2-14**.

2. Select the range **A1:J23**.

3. Click the **Page Layout button** on the status bar.

4. Click **Page Layout tab**, and in the Page Setup group, click the **Print Area button**, then **Set Print Area**. *The area is outlined.*

5. In the Sheet Options group, in the Gridlines section, click the **Print check box**.

6. In the Page Setup Group, click the **Orientation button**, then click **Landscape**. *The worksheet is not centered.*

7. In the Page Setup group, click the **Margins button**, then **Custom Margins**. *The Page Setup dialog box opens.*

8. Click the **Center on Page Horizontally check box**, then click **Print Preview**.

9. Click the **Print button** on the Print Preview toolbar.

10. Click **OK**. *The worksheet prints as previewed with area and gridline settings.*

11. Save the file as **e2-14**, and close it.

WHAT YOU NEED TO KNOW

▶ A **time sheet** is a record of employee hours for use with payroll systems. Employee hours may also be tracked using time clocks that record the hours on cards or into payroll software.

▶ In this Rehearsal activity, you will create a time sheet for All Sports Depot. Employees are paid on a semi-monthly basis and may work weekends in this retail store.

All Sports Depot

▼ DIRECTIONS

1. Open the data file **2r2-time**.

2. With the cursor at the beginning or left side of cell **D1**, double-click to switch to Edit mode. Change the label to `Semi-Monthly Time Sheet`.

3. Format the label in **Calibri**, **18 point**, **Bold**, **Blue**, **Accent 1 Daskar 25%**.

4. In cell **E4**, enter the label, as shown in Figure 2.23, and notice the AutoComplete effect. Correct the label, and enter the corrected text.

5. Enter the dates in **H3** and **H4**, and format them in the 3/14/01 date format.

6. Select the range **A3:H5**, and apply the Heading 2 cell style.

7. **Right-align** the labels in **A11**, **F11**, **G11**, and **H11**.

8. Select cells **D11:E11**, and click the **Wrap Text button** on the Home tab.

9. Overwrite data in cell **H11**, changing `Total` to `Total Hours`. Wrap the text in cell **H11**.

10. Middle-align the labels in cells **A11**, **F11**, and **G11**.

11. Select the range **A11:H11**, and apply the Accent1 cell style.

12. Enter the start date, 6/1/10, in **A12** and format it in the 3/14/01 date format.

13. Enter `Tuesday` in cell **B12**.

14. Select the range **A12:B12** and use the fill handle in **B12** to fill the series to **B26**.

15. Apply the Accent1 cell style to the range **A12:A26**.

16. Click the **Page Layout tab**, and set gridlines to print.

Continued on next page

17. Click the **Margins button**, use Custom Margins to center the page horizontally, and click **Print Preview**.

18. Print the time sheet with gridlines and centered horizontally.

19. Save the file as **2r2-time**, and close it.

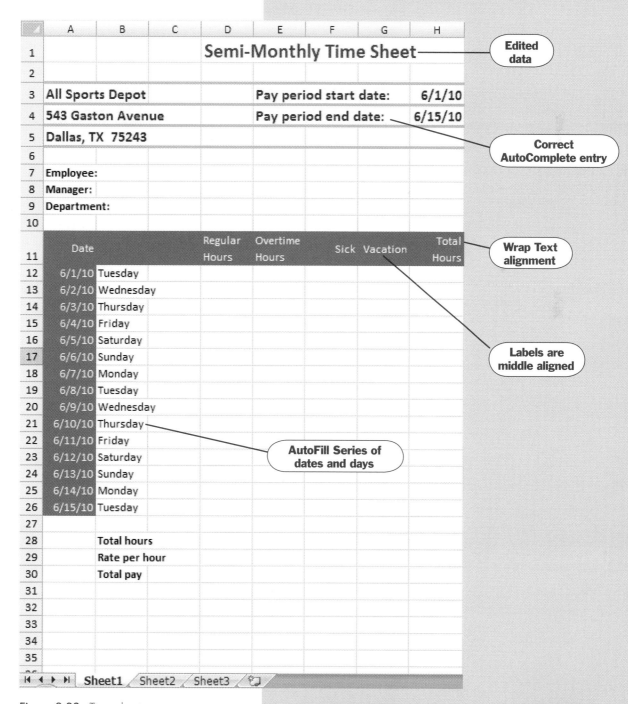

Figure 2.23: Time sheet

Align Labels

1. Select the cell to align.
2. Click the appropriate alignment button:
   - Align Text Left
   - Center
   - Align Text Right
   - Top Align
   - Middle Align
   - Bottom Align
   - Wrap Text

Format Text Font

1. Right-click the cell(s) to format.
2. Click the **Font List arrow** on the Mini toolbar.

3. Select the font.
4. Click the **Font Size arrow**.
5. Select the size.
6. Click the **Font Color arrow** and Select the color.

Edit Data

1. Double-click the cell in the location you wish to edit.
   Or
1. Press **[F2]**.
2. Edit the data using backspace, arrows, or other edit keys.

Clear Cell Contents

1. Right-click on the cell and select Clear Contents from the shortcut menu.
   Or
1. Click the cell.
2. Press **[Delete]**.

AutoFill Data

1. Select the cell or cells that contain the starting values.
2. Drag the fill handle through the range that you

want to fill. *To fill in increasing order, drag down or to the right. To fill in decreasing order, drag up or to the left.*

Set Print Area

1. Select the range to be printed.
2. Click the **Page Layout tab**, and in the Page Setup group, click the **Print Area button**, then **Set Print Area**.

Clear Print Area

1. Click the **Page Layout tab**, and in the Page Setup group, click the **Print Area button**, then **Clear Print Area**.

Print with Gridlines

1. Click the **Page Layout tab**.
2. In the Sheet Options group, in the Gridlines section, click the **Print check box**.

PERFORMANCE

TASK 2

BodyWorks Fitness Centers would like you to create a time sheet for the pay period 7/5/10 through 7/18/10. Employees are paid on a bi-weekly basis and may work weekends.

Follow these guidelines:

1. Open the data file **2p2-hours**.

2. Use Figure 2.24 and your knowledge of entering and formatting data to complete the time sheet.

3. On the Page Layout tab, set the print area for the range A1:I9 to print the heading. *In Page Layout view, note the outlined print area*. Then, clear the print area.

4. Use Custom Margins to center the page horizontally, and click **Print Preview**.

5. Print the time sheet without gridlines and centered horizontally.

6. Save and close the file.

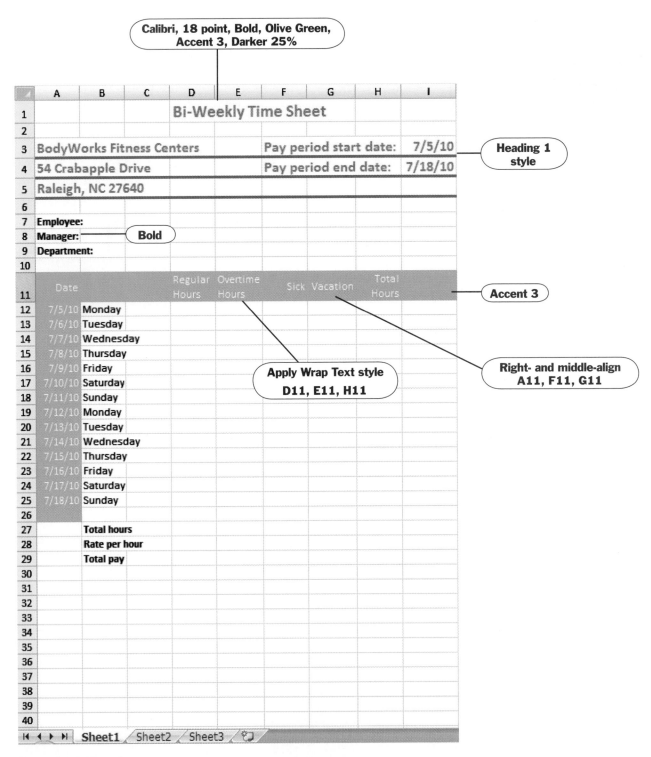

Calibri, 18 point, Bold, Olive Green, Accent 3, Darker 25%

	A	B	C	D	E	F	G	H	I
1				Bi-Weekly Time Sheet					
2									
3	BodyWorks Fitness Centers					Pay period start date:			7/5/10
4	54 Crabapple Drive					Pay period end date:			7/18/10
5	Raleigh, NC 27640								
6									
7	Employee:								
8	Manager:								
9	Department:								
10									
11	Date			Regular Hours	Overtime Hours		Sick Vacation	Total Hours	
12	7/5/10	Monday							
13	7/6/10	Tuesday							
14	7/7/10	Wednesday							
15	7/8/10	Thursday							
16	7/9/10	Friday							
17	7/10/10	Saturday							
18	7/11/10	Sunday							
19	7/12/10	Monday							
20	7/13/10	Tuesday							
21	7/14/10	Wednesday							
22	7/15/10	Thursday							
23	7/16/10	Friday							
24	7/17/10	Saturday							
25	7/18/10	Sunday							
26									
27		Total hours							
28		Rate per hour							
29		Total pay							
30									
31									
32									
33									
34									
35									
36									
37									
38									
39									
40									

Sheet1 / Sheet2 / Sheet3

Heading 1 style

Bold

Accent 3

Apply Wrap Text style D11, E11, H11

Right- and middle-align A11, F11, G11

Figure 2.24: Time sheet

TRYOUT

GOALS
To create a sales invoice from a customized template, as shown in Figure 2.25

To create a purchase order and a price quotation from templates

✳ Work with templates

TASK 3

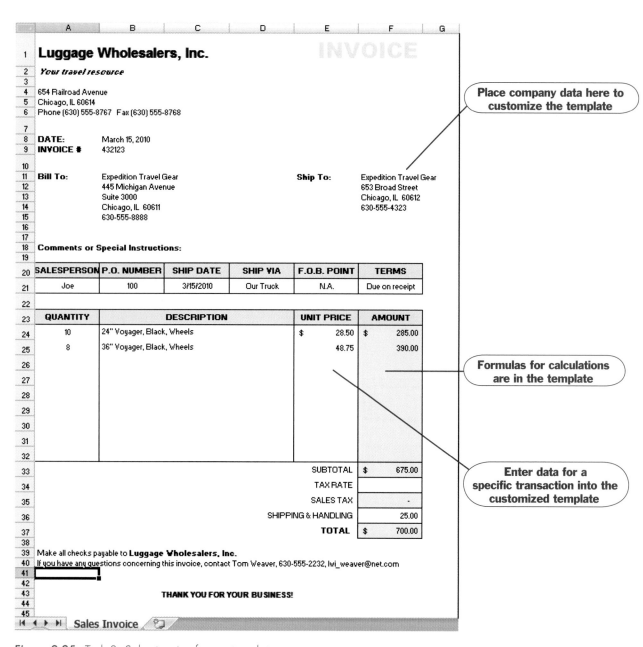

	A	B	C	D	E	F	G
1	**Luggage Wholesalers, Inc.**				INVOICE		
2	*Your travel resource*						
3							
4	654 Railroad Avenue						
5	Chicago, IL 60614						
6	Phone (630) 555-8767 Fax (630) 555-8768						
7							
8	**DATE:**	March 15, 2010					
9	**INVOICE #**	432123					
10							
11	**Bill To:**	Expedition Travel Gear			**Ship To:**	Expedition Travel Gear	
12		445 Michigan Avenue				653 Broad Street	
13		Suite 3000				Chicago, IL 60612	
14		Chicago, IL 60611				630-555-4323	
15		630-555-8888					
16							
17							
18	**Comments or Special Instructions:**						
19							
20	**SALESPERSON**	**P.O. NUMBER**	**SHIP DATE**	**SHIP VIA**	**F.O.B. POINT**	**TERMS**	
21	Joe	100	3/15/2010	Our Truck	N.A.	Due on receipt	
22							
23	**QUANTITY**	**DESCRIPTION**			**UNIT PRICE**	**AMOUNT**	
24	10	24" Voyager, Black, Wheels			$ 28.50	$ 285.00	
25	8	36" Voyager, Black, Wheels			48.75	390.00	
26							
27							
28							
29							
30							
31							
32							
33					SUBTOTAL	$ 675.00	
34					TAX RATE		
35					SALES TAX	-	
36					SHIPPING & HANDLING	25.00	
37					TOTAL	$ 700.00	
38							
39	Make all checks payable to **Luggage Wholesalers, Inc.**						
40	If you have any questions concerning this invoice, contact Tom Weaver, 630-555-2232, lwi_weaver@net.com						
41							
42							
43		**THANK YOU FOR YOUR BUSINESS!**					
44							
45							

Sales Invoice

Place company data here to customize the template

Formulas for calculations are in the template

Enter data for a specific transaction into the customized template

Figure 2.25: Task 3: Sales invoice from a template

WHAT YOU NEED TO KNOW

Work with Templates

View Online Templates

▶ Excel provides templates for common business forms. A **template** is a model worksheet design, containing permanent worksheet settings for fonts, formatting, styles, and formulas.

▶ To use Excel templates, open the New Workbook dialog box, shown in Figure 2.26. You can view installed templates, create a new template from an existing file, or search Microsoft Office Online for additional templates.

▶ The search feature for Microsoft Office Online allows you to enter the type of template you need. Click the Start searching **arrow button** or press the Enter key to connect you to the site and display the results of the search. You can then view, download, customize, and save the template to your computer.

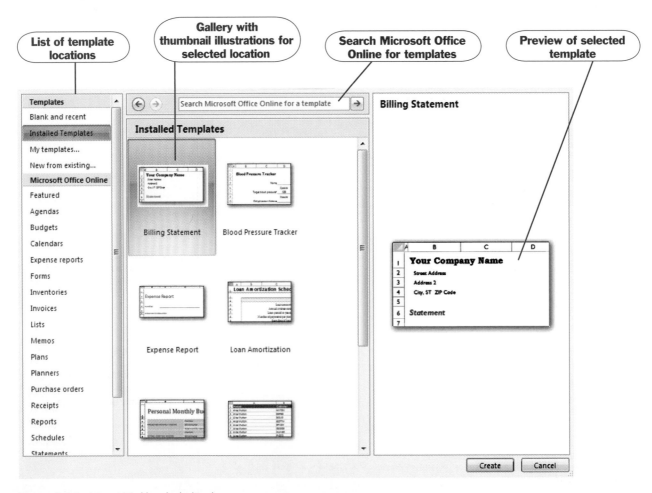

Figure 2.26: New Workbook dialog box

HOW 1. Click the **Office Button**. 2. Click **New**. 3. Click the desired template from the Templates pane on the left.

TRY*it* **OUT** *e2-15*

1. Click the **Office Button**, and click **New**. *A blank workbook and recently used templates appear in the middle pane of the dialog box.*

2. Click **Installed Templates** in the left pane to view the templates installed in Excel.

3. Click each one of the seven templates, and view a sample in the Preview pane on the right.

4. In the **Search Microsoft Office Online box**, enter Car Loan. Press **[Enter]**. *Various loan calculator templates*

appear including a vehicle loan payment calculator.

5. In the left pane, click **Invoices** to view the templates from Microsoft Office Online.

6. Click **Purchase orders** and double-click the **Purchase order with sales tax** template.

7. Click **Continue** on the Microsoft dialog box. *The template is downloaded.*

EXCEL

Customize a Template

▶ Once a template has been opened or downloaded, you can customize it with your permanent data to create a business form for your company, as shown in Figure 2.27. The **purchase order** is a form used to order merchandise or supplies from a **vendor** or supplier/wholesaler. The data that is specific to the **transaction**, or recordable business event, will be entered when the form is used.

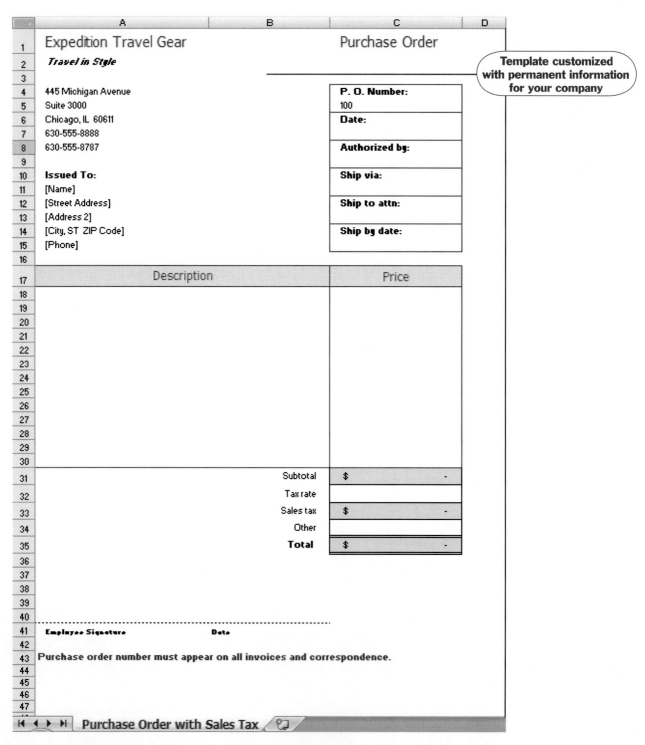

Figure 2.27: Customized purchase order template

1. You should be in the Purchase order template from **e2-15**.

2. Click in each cell to be customized **(A1, A2, A4:A8)**, and enter the data shown in Figure 2.27.

3. Format the slogan in **A2** in Bold, Italic style.

4. Do not save or close the file.

Save a File as a Template

▶ Once you customize a template with your permanent data, you should save it as a template file so that it will remain intact after each use. Select Excel Template from the Save as type list, as shown in Figure 2.28. The new template can then be found under My templates in the New Workbook dialog box. When you open and make entries into your customized template, you will save it under a new name so that the template will remain as a form.

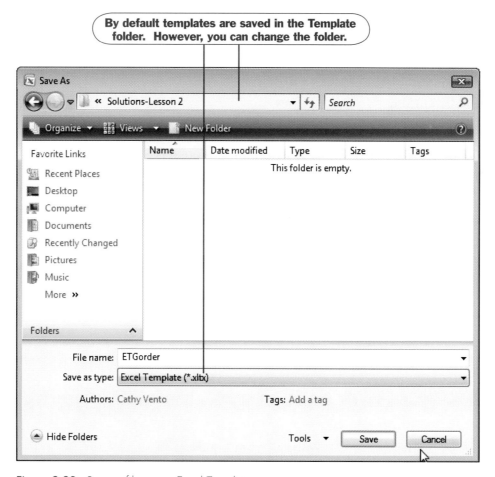

Figure 2.28: Save a file as an Excel Template

HOW F12 **1.** Press **[F12]**. **2.** Enter the name of the template file. **3.** Select **Excel Template** in the Save as type box. *You can locate your folder and save the template there, but it will not appear in My templates.* **4.** Click **Save**.

TRY *it* **OUT** *e2-17*

1. Continue working in the purchase order template from **e2-16**, or open the data file **e2-17**.

2. Press **[F12]**. In the Save As dialog box, enter the file name **ETGorder**.

3. Click the **Save as type arrow**, and click **Excel Template (*.xltx)**.

4. Click **Save**, and close the file. *The file is saved in the Templates folder.*

5. Click the **Office Button**, click **New**, and click **My templates**. *View your template location.*

6. Double-click the **ETGorder** template and enter **Luggage Wholesalers** into cell **A11**.

7. Press **[F12]**. *You should select your solution folder. The file name is ETGorder1 and the file type is Excel Workbook.*

8. Click the **Save button**, and close the file.

Save a File as a PDF

▶ **Portable Document Format (PDF)** is a file format that preserves document formatting. If you wish to share a worksheet and ensure that it keeps all its formatting, you can save it as a PDF file, shown in Figure 2.29. Once the worksheet is in PDF format, data cannot be easily changed and it can only be viewed if Acrobat Reader is installed on the computer. This is a good file type to use to send a form to a printer for publication. *If your network administrator approves, you may have to click **Find add-ins for other file formats** in the Save As gallery to add PDF or XPS to the Save As list.*

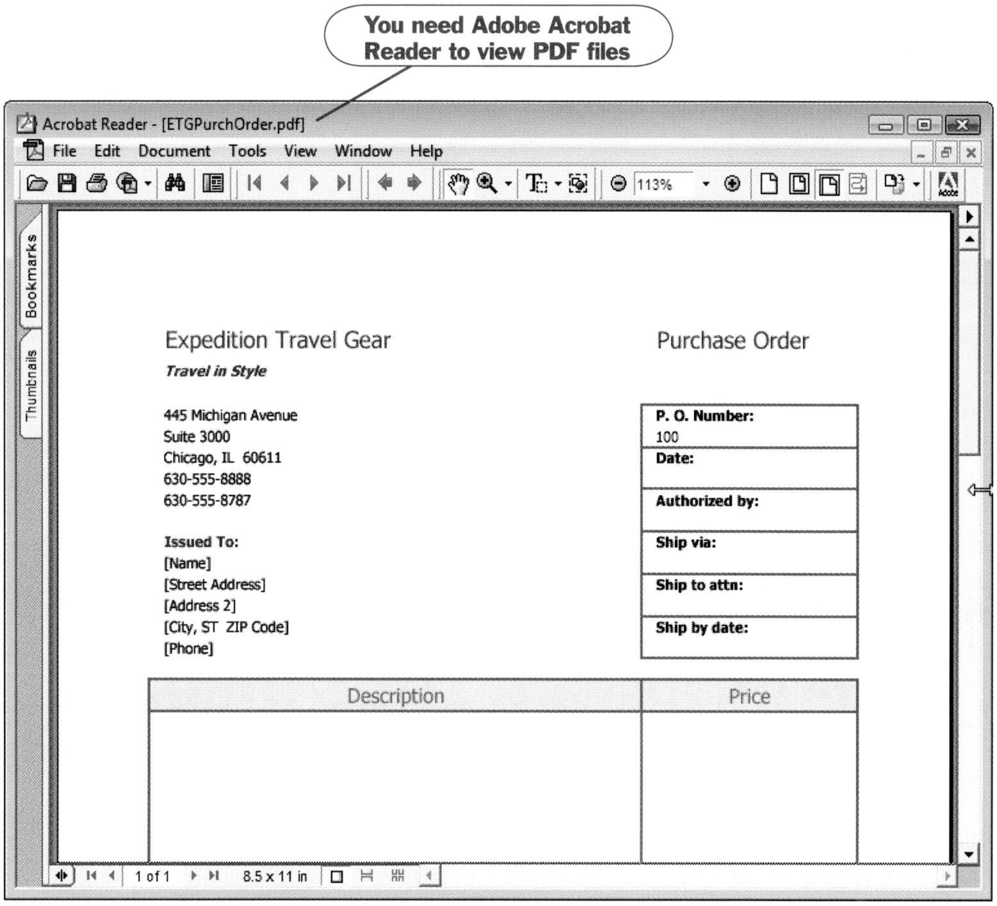

Figure 2.29: PDF file format

HOW **1.** Click the **Office Button**. **2.** Point to **Save As**. **3.** Click **PDF or XPS**. **4.** Enter a name for the file. **5.** In the Save as type box, click **PDF**. **6.** Click **Publish**.

T R Y i t O U T *e2-18*

1. Click the **Office Button**, click **New**, then click **My templates**.

2. Open the **ETGorder** template.

3. Click the **Office Button**, and point to, but do not click, **Save As** to display the Save As gallery, then click **PDF or XPS**.

4. Name the file **ETGPurchorder**, and click **PDF** in the Save as type box. Click **Publish**. *If you have Acrobat Reader loaded, the publication will appear.*

5. Close the PDF file and the template.

6. Repeat step 1, and right-click the **ETGorder** template icon.

7. Click **Delete**, then click **Yes**.

8. Click **Cancel** to close the New dialog box.

9. Click **Cancel** to close the New Workbook dialog box.

REHEARSAL

TASK 3

WHAT YOU NEED TO KNOW

▶ A **sales invoice** is a bill that a seller prepares and sends to a customer for goods supplied by the seller. It usually contains an itemized list of goods sold, as well as shipping and payment information, and may contain the customer's purchase order number.

▶ After you customize a sales invoice template for your company and save it as a template, you can use it to prepare all future company invoices. Because the template contains formulas, it automatically calculates the total bill.

▶ In this Rehearsal activity, you will customize the invoice template for Luggage Wholesalers, Inc. They do not include the sales tax rate unless they are selling retail. The company will be shipping luggage ordered by Expedition Travel Gear and needs to prepare the invoice for the sale.

DIRECTIONS

1. Open the **Sales Invoice with tax and shipping and handling calculations** template in the Invoices section of Microsoft Office Online templates.

2. Enter the company information for Luggage Wholesalers in cells **A1:A6**, as shown in Figure 2.30.

3. Scroll to the bottom of the invoice, and edit the data in **A39** and **A40**, as illustrated, to complete the permanent data for the invoice.

4. Save the file as a template, and name it **LWIinvoice**. *Save the file in your solutions folder*.

5. Save the file as a PDF file and name it **2r3-LWIinv**. You want to send a sample to the sales personnel. *Save the file in your solutions folder*.

6. Close both of the files.

7. Open the **LWIinvoice** template file in your solutions folder. *Be sure to change the file type to Templates*.

8. Complete the invoice, as illustrated, deleting the sales tax rate and adding the shipping charge of $25. *The total price for each item and final totals are automatically calculated. The sales tax rate is deleted because this is not a retail sale.*

9. Print the invoice.

10. Save the file as an Excel Workbook file in your solutions folder, and name it **2r3-invoice**. Close the file.

11. Delete the LWIinvoice template from My Templates. *This step is necessary in an environment where several classes are using the same computers.*

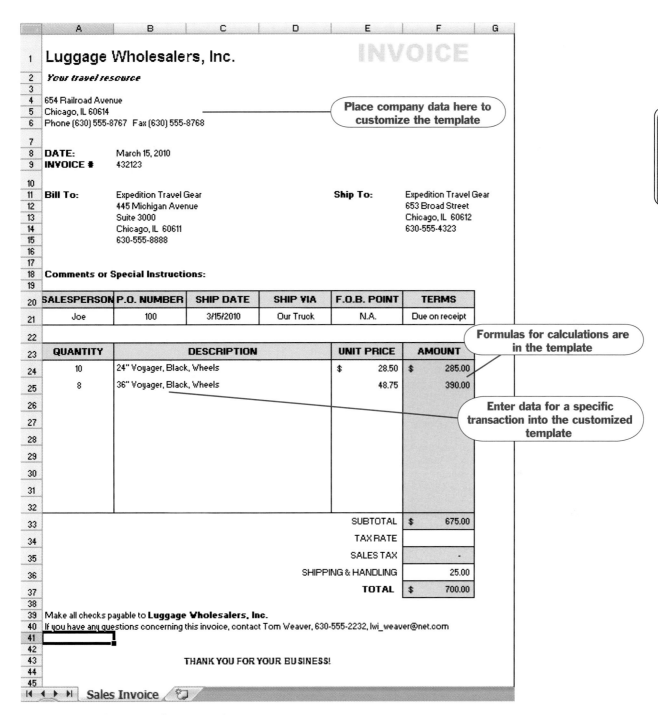

Figure 2.30: Sales invoice from a template

Open Templates Dialog Box
1. Click the **Office Button**.
2. Click **New**.
3. Select desired templates from templates pane on the left.

Customize Template
1. Select the cell to customize.
2. Enter the custom information.

Save File as Template
1. Press **[F12]**.
2. Enter the name of the template file.

3. Select **Excel Template** in Save as Type box. *If you do not wish to have the template appear in My Templates, you can change the folder here to another folder. When you try to open the template from another folder, you will have to change the Files of type setting to Templates.*
4. Click the **Save button**.

Save File as a PDF File
1. Click the **Office Button**.
2. Point to **Save As**.
3. Click **PDF or XPS**.
4. Enter a name for the file.
5. In the Save as type box, click **PDF**.
6. Click **Publish**.

PERFORMANCE

TASK 3

You work for Marilyn Proctor in the Marketing Department at Expedition Travel Gear. ETG has started to use a catalog to market its merchandise wholesale to hotel gift shops, and retail to their mailing list. You are asked to prepare a customized invoice template for catalog sales and an invoice for a sale made today.

Expedition

Travel Gear

Follow these guidelines:

1. Use the **Sales invoice with stock number** template to create a new invoice template for Expedition Travel Gear. *Earlier, you created a purchase order for ETG.*

2. Enter the permanent information as shown in Figure 2.31. *Since sales are generally retail, you should include the tax rate in the template.*

3. Save the file as a template in your folder, and name it **2p3-ETGinvoice**.

4. Create an invoice for the sale made today, using the template. Use today's date and the following information:

The sale was made to:　　**Marcie Collins**

　　　　　　　　　　　　Bertleson Hotel

　　　　　　　　　　　　Gift Shop

　　　　　　　　　　　　2356 Lakeshore Drive

　　　　　　　　　　　　Chicago, IL 60611

　　　　　　　　　　　　800-555-9000

Invoice No.:　　　　　　**2000**

Shipping Address:　　　　**Same**

Qty	Stock #	Description	Unit Price
12	432	**Leather waist packs**	12.35
6	1654	**Collapsible luggage carts**	18.50
12	211	**Travel alarm clocks**	14.50

Shipping is $18.50. Delete the sales tax rate because this is a wholesale transaction.

5. Save the document and name it **2p3-bertle**. Close the file.

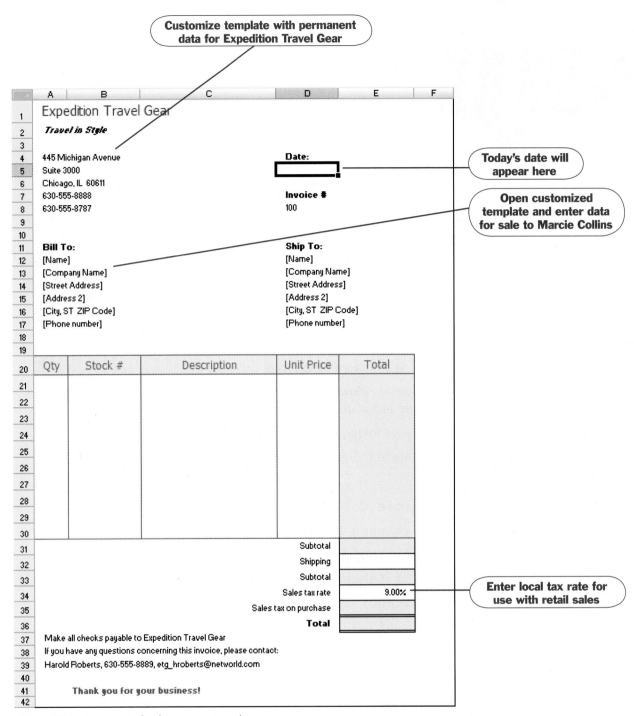

Customize template with permanent data for Expedition Travel Gear

Today's date will appear here

Open customized template and enter data for sale to Marcie Collins

Enter local tax rate for use with retail sales

Figure 2.31: Customized sales invoice template

ENCORE

Act I

Grace Lin is a Certified Fitness Trainer who has just started training and billing her clients. She needs to complete her training log sheet, to format an invoice to bill for her services, and to create invoices for this week.

Follow these guidelines:

1. Open the data file **2ep1-log**, and apply the Module theme to the worksheet. Use Figure 2.32 as a guide to format the worksheet. Save the file.

2. Open the data file **2ep1-inv** where all permanent information has been entered. Use the Module theme and cell styles to enhance the appearance of the invoice. Format cell **G18** in the Total cell style. Save the invoice as a template in your folder, and name it **2ep1-invtmp**.

3. Prepare an invoice for services for BodyWorks for the week ending July 24, 2010. Use Invoice #100 to start. Save the file as **2ep1-bw724**. Print a copy without gridlines and centered horizontally.

4. Use the template to create invoice numbers 101 and 102 for the other clients to complete the week's billings. Name the files so that the client and date are included, as in Step 3.

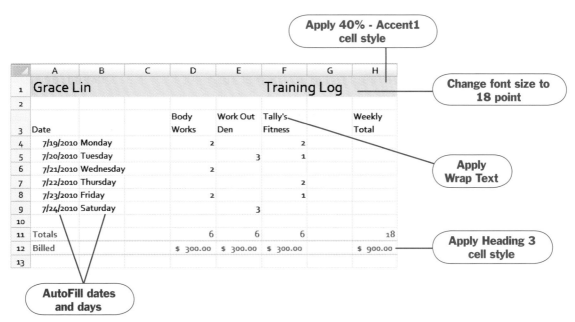

Figure 2.32: Training log

Act II

You work for the sales manager, Kelly Thompson, in the New York office of Newmark Productions. A small independent film company has requested a price quotation for the use of the studios and editing facilities.

Follow these guidelines:

1. Search for a Quotation template on Microsoft Online.
   Use the Price quotation without tax template.

2. Enter Newmark Production information for the New York office found in the *To the Student section*. Delete the company slogan line. The contact information for the bottom of the form is Kelly King, 212-555-9991, kknewmark@world.com.

3. Save the file as a template in your folder, and name it **2ep2-quote**. Save the file as a PDF file for publication purposes, and name it **2ep2-quotation**.

4. Use the template to create a quotation using the following information:

Date:	8/10/2010
Quotation #:	100
Customer ID:	346
Quotation valid until:	9/10/2010
Prepared by:	[Your name]
Bill to:	Jamal Carson
	Carson Films, Inc.
	432 Christopher Street
	New York, NY 10012
	212-555-4388
Comments:	Customer will provide personnel.

Description		Amount
2 days	Use of studio for filming short subject	$4200.00
1 day	Use of editing facilities	$1000.00

5. Preview the worksheet, and make any adjustments that are necessary before printing a copy.

6. Save the worksheet as **2ep2-quotecarson**.

LESSON 3

Accounting Records

In this lesson, you will learn to use Excel to create accounting records and statements. You will use formulas, functions, and formatting to complete the tasks. You will use the Internet to locate state and federal withholding taxes. You will complete the following projects:

✴ Account
✴ Statement of account
✴ Sales journal
✴ Payroll
✴ Expense report

Upon completion of this lesson, you will have mastered the following skill sets

✴ Modify row height and column width
✴ Cut, copy, and paste data and cell contents
✴ Apply and clear number formats
✴ Use formula basics
✴ Summarize data using formulas
✴ Use Format Painter
✴ Troubleshoot a formula
✴ Modify page setup options
✴ Move selected cells
✴ Insert, view, edit, and delete cell comments
✴ Format or modify text using formulas

Terms
Software-related

AutoFill
AutoFit
AutoSum
Cell comment
Decrease Decimal format
Drag-and-drop editing
Fill handle
Footers
Format Painter
Formulas
Fraction format
Function
Function arguments
Headers
Increase Decimal format
Insert Function button
Mathematical priority
Office Clipboard
Order of mathematical operations
Percent Style format

Document-related

Account
Accounts payable
Accounts receivable
Expense report
General ledger
Journal
Payroll register
Reimburse
Sales journal
Statement of account
Tax status

TRYOUT

TASK 1

GOAL
To create an account and statement of account as illustrated in Figure 3.1 and 3.2

* Modify row height and column width
* Cut, copy, and paste data and cell contents
* Apply and clear number formats
* Use formula basics

Accounts Receivable Ledger						
Customer:		Bertleson Hotel Gift Shop				
		2356 Lakeshore Drive				
		Chicago, IL 60611				
		800-555-9000				
No: B15		Attn: Marcie Collins				
Date	Explanation		Reference	Charges	Credits	Balance
5/3/2010	Invoice #2000		S5	451.70		451.70
5/15/2010	Return - #CM450		J9		55.50	396.20
5/22/2010	Invoice #2055		S5	418.40		814.60
5/25/2010	Damaged #CM465		J9		16.75	797.85

Figure 3.1: Task 1: Account

				Statement of Account		
Expedition Travel Gear						
445 Michigan Avenue						
Suite 3000						
Chicago, IL 60611						
Phone: 630-555-8888						
Fax: 630-555-8787				Date:	31-May-10	
To:	Bertleson Hotel Gift Shop					
	2356 Lakeshore Drive					
	Chicago, IL 60611					
	800-555-9000					
	Attn: Marcie Collins					
Date	Explanation		Reference	Charges	Credits	Balance
	Balance Forward					0
5/3/2010	Invoice #2000		S5	451.70		451.70
5/15/2010	Return - #CM450		J9		55.50	396.20
5/22/2010	Invoice #2055		S5	418.40		814.60
5/25/2010	Damaged #CM465		J9		16.75	$ 797.85
						Pay the last
						amount in
Expedition Travel Gear						this column

Figure 3.2: Task 1: Statement of account

WHAT YOU NEED TO KNOW

Modify Row Height and Column Width

▶ Columns are set for a standard column width of 8.43, the number of characters displayed using the default font. Long labels will display as long as the next cell is empty, but when you enter long numbers or values Excel fills the cell with number signs (##) or displays the number in scientific notation to indicate the need to widen the column. You can change column width by dragging the column header to a specified width or until the longest line is visible, as shown in Figure 3.3.

Drag column border with double-headed arrow cursor

	A	B	C	D	E	F
	Width: 8.43 (64 pixels)	f_x	Decrease Decimal (2)			
1	Format	Number	Number after format			
2	Accountin	5436.4				
3	Currency	450				
4	Comma	1245				
5	Percent	0.75				
6	Fraction	0.25				
7	Increase [	452.6				
8	Decrease	34.65957				
9						

ScreenTip indicates current width

Figure 3.3: Column width indicator display

 HOW **1.** Place the mouse pointer on the right edge of the column heading. **2.** When the mouse pointer changes to a double-headed arrow, click and drag the column to size.

Using AutoFit

▶ The most efficient way to adjust column width is to double-click the right edge of the column header, and the column will **AutoFit**, or widen to fit the data in that column.

HOW Double-click the right edge of the column heading to AutoFit to the longest line in the column.

▶ By default, row height is 15, but it is automatically determined by the font point size. You may also change row height by dragging the row to the desired size or double-clicking to AutoFit the text.

TRY it OUT e3-1

1. Open the data file **e3-1**. *Not all labels are visible in Column A.*

2. Double-click the line between columns A and B to AutoFit the text in column A.

3. With the insertion point between the headings of columns C and D, click and drag the double-headed arrow to increase the column width to **18.43**.

4. Select columns A, B, and C, then with your cursor between columns C and D, drag to set all three columns to a width of **19**.

5. Save the file, but do not close it.

Align Data Vertically

▶ Once row height is larger, data can be aligned vertically to the top, middle, or bottom of a row. We have already used the Alignment group on the Home tab to align data horizontally to the left, right, or center of a column.

 1. Select the cell or row. **2.** Click the **Middle Align button**, **Top Align button**, or **Bottom Align button**.

T R Y *i t* **O U T** *e3-2*

1. Use the open file or open the data file **e3-2**.

2. Select row **1** by clicking the row number, and change the font size to **14**. *Notice the change in the row height.*

3. Place cursor between rows 1 and 2 and drag until row height is **30**.

4. With row 1 still selected, click the **Middle Align button**, then click the **Top Align button**.

5. Change the font size back to **11**.

6. Double-click the bottom edge of row **1** to adjust the row height back to **15**.

7. Save the file, but do not close it.

Cut, Copy, and Paste Data and Cell Contents

▶ Cut, Copy, and Paste are tools to move or copy data from one location and place it in another. You can use the shortcut menu, keystrokes, or the buttons on the Home tab in the Clipboard group, as shown in Figure 3.4.

▶ The Cut tool removes the data from the location.

HOW Ctrl+X **1.** Select and right-click data to be cut. **2.** Select **Cut** on the shortcut menu. The data is placed temporarily on the Office Clipboard, a temporary storage area.

▶ The Copy tool copies the data in the location.

HOW Ctrl+C **1.** Select and right-click data to be copied. **2.** Select **Copy** on the shortcut menu. *The data is placed temporarily on the Office Clipboard, a temporary storage area.*

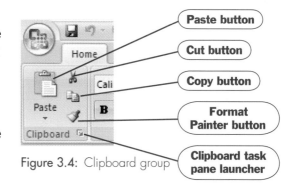

Figure 3.4: Clipboard group

▶ In both cases, the Paste tool places the data in a new location.

HOW Ctrl+V **1.** Select the first cell of the new location. **2.** Select **Paste** on the shortcut menu. *The data is placed in the new location.*

T R Y *i t* **O U T** *e3-3*

1. Use the open file or open the data file **e3-3**.

2. Select the range **A3:A7** and click the **Cut button** on the Home tab.

3. Select cell **A10** and click the **Paste button** on the Home tab to move the data.

Continued on next page

---

4. Click the **Undo button** on the Quick Access Toolbar to restore the data.

5. Select the range **B2:B8**. Right-click and click **Copy** on the shortcut menu.

6. Click cell **C2** and press **[Ctrl]+[V]** to paste the copied data.

7. Save the file, but do not close it.

Use the Office Clipboard to Cut, Copy, and Paste

▶ When you copy data in Excel, it is stored in a memory location called the **Office Clipboard**. If you plan to copy more than one group of data, you should display the Clipboard task pane by clicking the task pane launcher in the Clipboard group on the Home tab, shown in Figure 3.4. Use the Clipboard if you are reordering or reassigning locations for several items of data or if you want to paste items several times. As shown in Figure 3.5, after each row is copied the sample appears on the Clipboard, with the last selection shown on top.

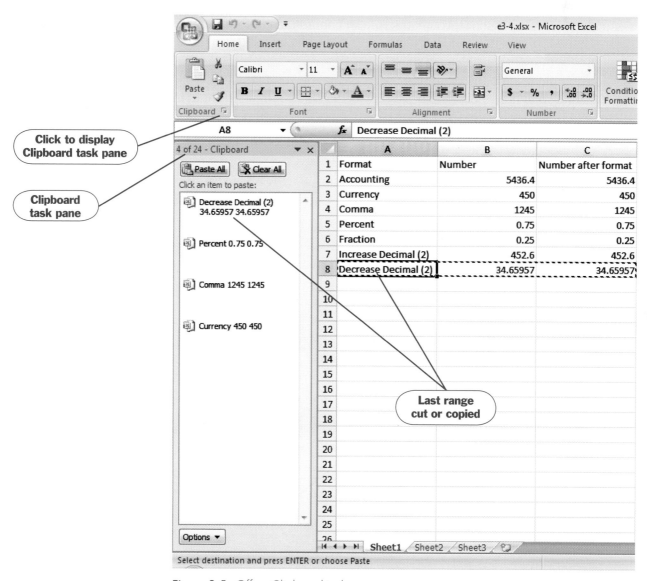

Figure 3.5: Office Clipboard task pane

1. Use the open file or open the data file **e3-4**.

2. Click the **Home tab**, and in the Clipboard group click the **Clipboard task pane launcher**. *The Clipboard task pane appears. Click **Clear All** if it is not empty.*

3. Cut the data in the following ranges one at a time: **A3:C3**, **A4:C4**, **A5:C5**, **A8:C8**. *Each range appears on the Clipboard task pane after it is cut, as shown in Figure 3.5.*

4. Select cell **A3** and click the Comma data on the Clipboard. *The data is pasted*.

5. Select cell **A4** and click the Currency data on the Clipboard.

6. Paste the Decrease Decimal data in **A5** and Percent data in **A8**. Clear the Clipboard and close it.

7. Save the file, and name it **e3-4**. Close the file.

Apply and Clear Number Formats

▶ As discussed in Lesson 2, you can format numbers using the formats in the Number group on the Home tab, as shown in Figure 3.6, or by right-clicking and using the Mini toolbar. Additional number formats are explained below:

- Accounting Number Format adds two decimal places and aligns dollar signs in a column. As shown in Figure 3.7, the list arrow displays Accounting formats in other monetary systems.

- **Percent Style format** changes the value to a percentage.

- **Increase Decimal format** adds one decimal place.

- **Decrease Decimal format** decreases one decimal place. *Values are rounded when decimals are decreased.*

- **Fraction format**, found on the Format Cells dialog box or the Number format gallery, changes a decimal to its fractional equivalent.

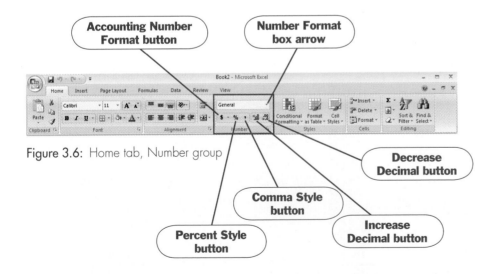

Figure 3.6: Home tab, Number group

Figure 3.7: Accounting Number Format list arrow displays other monetary formats

HOW **1.** Select the data to format. **2.** Click the appropriate format button.

▶ General format means there is no specific formatting. Therefore, you can clear number formats without deleting the values in a selected cell by clicking General format.

T R Y *i t* **O U T** *e3-5*

1. Open the data file **e3-5**.

2. Click cell **C2**, then click the **Home tab**, and in the Number group click the **Accounting Number Format button**. [$] *Notice the location of the dollar sign. Click the list arrow to view other monetary accounting formats.*

3. Click cell **C3**, then in the Number group click the **Number Format box arrow**. In the Number Format gallery, click **Currency**. *Notice the location of the dollar sign.*

4. Format cell **C4** in Comma style and **C5** in Percent style. [,] [%]

5. Format cell **C6** as a Fraction using the Number Format gallery. *The name of the format appears in the Number Format box.*

6. The numbers in **C7** and **C8** should have two decimals. Use the Increase or Decrease decimal buttons appropriately. *The value in C8 is rounded.*

7. Select the range **C2:C8** and clear all formats by clicking **General** in the Number Format gallery.

8. Click the **Undo button** to reverse the clearing of formats.

9. Deselect the range by clicking another cell.

10. Save the file, and close the file.

Use Formula Basics

▶ **Formulas** are equations or instructions to calculate values on the worksheet. All formulas start with an equal sign (=), contain no spaces, and include the cell addresses or values, and mathematical operators necessary to complete the formula. For example, =B5+B6 adds the values in B5 and B6.

▶ The standard mathematical operators used in formulas are shown in Table 3.1.

Table 3.1: Standard mathematical operators

+	Addition
–	Subtraction
*	Multiplication
/	Division
^	Exponentiation

▶ To enter formulas correctly, you need to understand the way the computer processes an equation. The computer executes all operations from left to right, in order of mathematical priority. The **order of mathematical operations**, or **mathematical priority**, is listed in Table 3.2.

Table 3.2: Order of mathematical operations

1st	Parentheses ( )
2nd	Exponents ^
3rd	Multiplication * and/or Division /
4th	Addition + and/or Subtraction –

▶ For example, in the formula =A1*(B1+C1), the formula in parentheses, B1+C1, is calculated first, before the multiplication is performed. If the parentheses were omitted, A1*B1 would be calculated first and C1 would be added to that answer. This would result in a different outcome.

▶ You can input a formula by entering the symbols and cell addresses. Or, you can enter the symbols and select the cell addresses as they appear in the formula. Selecting the cell addresses minimizes the possibility of entry errors. When you enter a formula into a cell, it displays in the formula bar while the answer appears in the cell, as shown in Figure 3.8.

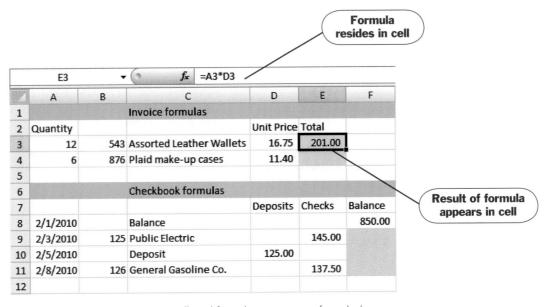

Figure 3.8: Answer appears in cell and formula appears on formula bar

Use AutoFill

▶ Once a formula is entered, you can copy it down a column or across a row using **AutoFill** as a copy tool. Select the cell to be copied, and place your insertion point on the **fill handle**, the small square at the bottom right of the cell. When the mouse pointer changes to a thin black plus sign, click and drag the cell border to fill the appropriate range.

T R Y *it* **O U T** e3-6

1. Open the data file **e3-6**.

2. In cell **E3**, enter a formula to multiply the quantity by the price:
   a. Enter = (equal sign).
   b. Click cell **A3**.
   c. Enter * (asterisk for multiply).
   d. Click cell **D3**.
   e. Press [Enter].

3. Click cell **E3**, and notice the formula in the formula bar.

4. Copy the formula in **E3**, and paste it into **E4**. *The formula in cell E4 copies relative to the new location.*

5. In cell **F9**, enter a formula to subtract the check in **E9** from the balance in **F8**. *Hint: =F8-E9*

6. In cell **F10**, enter a formula that can be copied and will work for either deposits or checks. *New Balance = Old Balance + Deposits – Checks (hint: =F9+D10–E10).*

7. Use the fill handle in **F10** to fill the formula down to **F11**.

8. Click in cell **F11**. *The formula in cell F11 is copied relative to the new location.*

9. Save the file, and name it **e3-6**. Close the file.

REHEARSAL

GOAL
To create an account and statement of account

TASK 1

WHAT YOU NEED TO KNOW

▶ An **account** is an accounting record that keeps track of the increases and decreases in the value of an item in a business. It is set up in a bankbook-style arrangement that contains columns for increases, decreases, and balances. Account data comes from journals or business forms such as invoices.

▶ The **general ledger** contains all the accounts of a business. In addition, there are supplemental ledgers: the **accounts receivable** (AR) ledger containing records of customers, the people who owe the business money, and the **accounts payable** (AP) ledger containing records of creditors, the people to whom the business owes money.

▶ Customers' accounts are used to create the **statement of account** or bills that are sent out each month. This is similar to a monthly credit card bill.

DIRECTIONS

1. Open the data file **3r1-account**.

2. Adjust column width as necessary, and apply the Accent2 cell style as shown in Figure 3.9.

3. Format numbers in the range **D10:F13** in Comma style.

4. In cell **F10**, calculate the balance on 5/3. *Because the first invoice is also the balance on 5/3, enter =D10 in cell* **F10**.

5. Enter a formula in cell **F11** that can be used for any balance calculation in this account. *Hint: Previous balance + charges – credits: =F10+D11–E11.*

6. Use the fill handle in **F11**, and fill the formula down to **F13**.

7. Clear all formats in cell **E11** by changing to General format. Click **Undo** to keep the format.

8. Save the file as **3r1-account**.

9. In the Home tab, click the **Clipboard task pane launcher** to display the Office Clipboard.

10. Copy the following ranges to the clipboard to create the account statement, as shown in Figure 3.10:
    a. **C3:C7** Name and address of customer
    b. **A9:F9** Column headings
    c. **A10:F13** Account data

11. Open the data file **3r1-statement**.

12. Paste the following data to the locations listed below:
    a. Name and address to cell **B9**
    b. Column headings to cell **A16**
    c. Account data to cell **A18**

13. Adjust column width as necessary, and clear and close the Clipboard task pane.

14. Apply the Accent2 cell style to the ranges **A1:F1** and **A32:E32**.

Continued on next page

► In this Rehearsal activity, you will create an account and a statement of account for an Expedition Travel Gear customer. On accounts receivable accounts, invoices (which increase the account) and credits and returns (which decrease the account) are used to tabulate the account balance. The account statement or bill is sent out at the end of the month to every customer, based on the activity in the account.

15. Format the final balance in cell **F21** as accounting number and bold.

16. Print the account statement centered vertically and horizontally without gridlines.

17. Save the file as **3r1-statement**. Close both files.

EXCEL

Expedition

Travel Gear

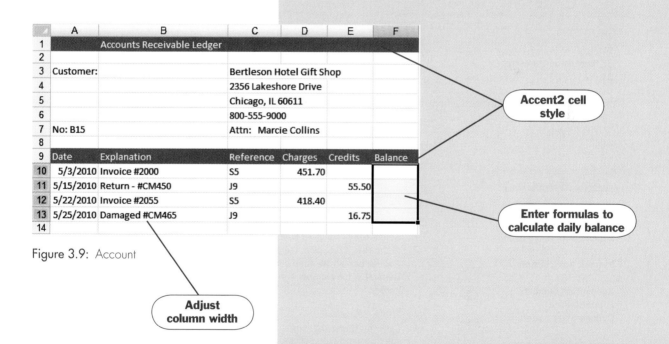

Figure 3.9: Account

Accent2 cell style

Enter formulas to calculate daily balance

Adjust column width

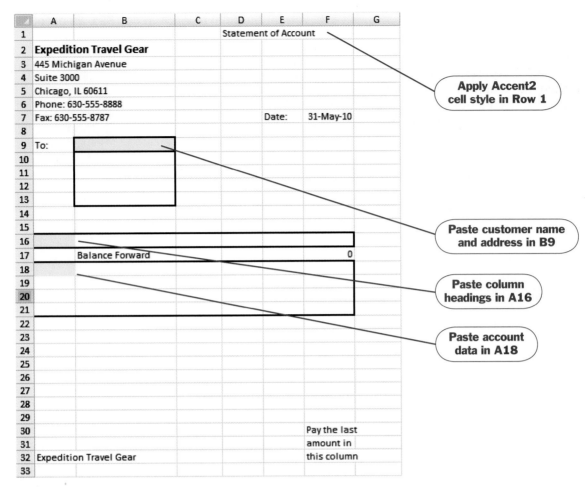

Figure 3.10: Statement of account

Cues for Reference

Apply Number Formats
1. Select cell or range of cells.
2. Click format button:

Percent Style button

Accounting Number Format button

Comma Style button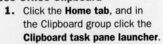

Increase Decimal button

Decrease Decimal button

Clear Number Formats
1. Select cell or range of cells.
2. In the Home tab, click the **Number Format box arrow**, then click **General** in the Number Format gallery.

Use Office Clipboard
1. Click the **Home tab**, and in the Clipboard group click the **Clipboard task pane launcher**.
2. Cut or copy data.
3. Select location for pasted data.

4. Click the data sample on the Clipboard task pane.

Enter Formulas
1. Enter the equal sign, =.
2. Select formula data.
3. Enter a mathematical operator.
4. Select formula data.
5. Repeat Steps 3 and 4 until the formula is complete.
6. Press [Enter].

TASK 1

Hardy's Department store has started its own charge account system for its customers. They want you to complete a customer account and prepare a statement of account to bill for the monthly activity.

Follow these guidelines:

1. Open the data files **3p1-account** and **3p1-statement**.

2. In the account: Apply the Technic theme, apply Accent1 cell style to rows 1 and 9, columns A:F. Format **B9** for wrapped text, and adjust the row height and column width as necessary. Format values in Comma style.

3. Enter a formula in cell **F11** that can be used for any balance calculation in this account, and fill it to **F15**. *Hint: Previous balance + charges – credits*.

4. Save the file and display the Office Clipboard.

5. Copy three ranges to the clipboard to create the account statement. (The name, address block, and account number; the column headings; and the account data.)

6. In the statement file, **3p1-statement**, paste the address block to **B9**, the column headings to **A15**, and the account data to **A16**. Clear and close the Clipboard task pane.

7. Apply the theme and cell styles used on the account to the statement. Adjust column width and format the final balance.

8. Print the account statement centered vertically and horizontally without gridlines.

9. Save and close both files.

TRYOUT

TASK 2

GOAL
To create a sales journal, as shown in Figure 3.11
* Summarize data using formulas
* Use Format Painter

	A	B	C	D	E	F	G
2				SALES JOURNAL			Page 5
3	Date	Taxable	Invoice #	Customer	Sales Income	Sales Taxes	Accounts Receivable
4	5/3/2010	N	6545	Valley H.S. - Health Department	557.65		557.65
5	5/4/2010	N	6546	Royal Fitness Center	550.00		550.00
6	5/7/2010	N	6547	Eastern H.S. - Gym	515.00		515.00
7	5/9/2010	N	6548	Barbell Gym	1,255.00		1,255.00
8	5/11/2010	Y	6549	George Driver	175.00	10.94	185.94
9	5/14/2010	N	6550	Eastern H.S. - Gym	356.50		356.50
10	5/14/2010	N	6551	Royal Fitness Center	385.00		385.00
11	5/16/2010	N	6552	Barbell Gym	155.00		155.00
12	5/17/2010	Y	6553	George Driver	295.00	18.44	313.44
13	5/18/2010	N	6554	Eastern H.S. - Gym	660.70		660.70
14	5/21/2010	Y	6555	Polly Wilson	135.00	8.44	143.44
15	5/22/2010	N	6555	Valley H.S. - Health Department	1,015.45		1,015.45
16	5/24/2010	N	6555	Royal Fitness Center	451.43		451.43
17	5/31/2010	Y	6555	Polly Wilson	95.89	5.99	101.88
18							
19				Totals	6,602.62	43.81	6,646.43
20							
21				Averages	471.62	10.95	474.74
22				Highest	1,255.00	18.44	1,255.00
23				Lowest	95.89	5.99	101.88
24				Count	14	4	14
25							

Sheet1 Sheet2 Sheet3

Formulas to create data

Formulas to summarize data

Format painted from G2

Figure 3.11: Task 2: Sales journal

WHAT YOU NEED TO KNOW

Summarize Data Using Formulas

Enter Functions

▶ A **function** is a built-in formula that performs a specific calculation automatically. Function formulas contain an equal sign, a function name, an opening parenthesis, a range of arguments, and then a closing parenthesis. For example, =SUM(B4:B7) adds all the values, or arguments, in the range specified.

AutoSum

▶ The **AutoSum** feature automatically enters a function to find the total of a group of cells. Excel selects the cells it thinks you want to add and surrounds them with a moving dotted line, as shown in Figure 3.12.

▶ In the cell where the total is to appear, you see the automatic sum formula used to add the cells, =SUM(B4:B7).

Enter the Range in a Formula

▶ You can enter a range in a formula by selecting it. If the range suggested by AutoSum is not correct, enter the correct range by selecting the range with the mouse pointer.

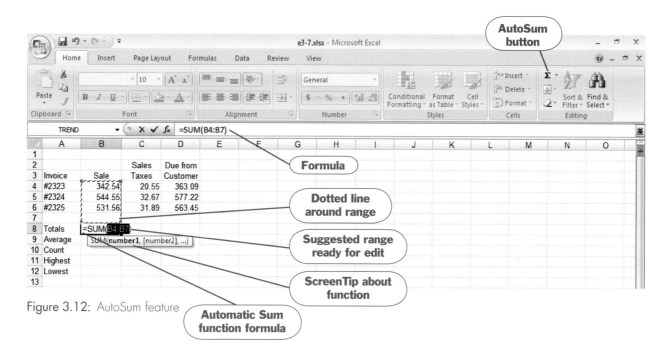

Figure 3.12: AutoSum feature

HOW Alt+= 1. Click the cell to receive the total. 2. Click the **Home tab**, and in the Editing group, click the **AutoSum button**. 3. Press **[Enter]** if the formula is correct or select the correct range.

TRY it OUT e3-7

1. Open the data file **e3-7**.

2. In cell **B8**, click the **Home tab**, and in the Editing group, click the **AutoSum button**. *The formula is in the cell and appears on the formula bar.*

3. Press **[Enter]**.

4. In cell **C8**, press **[Alt]+[=]**. If the range is correct press **[Enter]**.

5. Use the fill handle in **C8**, and fill the formula to **D8**.

6. In cell **F8**, add the Sales Taxes and Sales totals horizontally to see if they equal the "Due from Customer" total:
   a. Click the **AutoSum button**. *Notice that the range is incorrect.*
   b. Drag to select the range **B8:C8**, the correct range.
   c. Press **[Enter]**.

7. Select the range **B8:F8** and format it in Comma style.

8. Save the file, but do not close it.

AutoSum Functions List

▶ To the right of the AutoSum button is a list arrow, as shown in Figure 3.13, that provides other commonly used functions you can select for a range of data. The functions available are listed in Table 3.3.

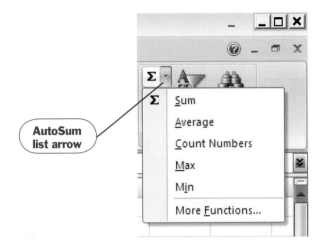

Figure 3.13: AutoSum functions list

Table 3.3: AutoSum functions list

COMMON FUNCTIONS	PURPOSE
Sum	Calculates the total of numbers in a range
Average	Calculates the average, or mean, of numbers in a range
Count Numbers	Counts the number of values in a range
Max	Calculates the highest value in a range
Min	Calculates the lowest value in a range

HOW 1. Click the cell to receive the formula. 2. Click the **Home tab**, and in the Editing group, click the **AutoSum list arrow**. 3. Select the appropriate function. 4. Press [Enter] if the formula is correct or correct the range, then press [Enter].

TRY it OUT e3-8

1. Use the open file or open the data file e3-8.

2. Click cell **B9**, then click the **AutoSum list arrow**.

3. Click **Average**.

4. Select **B4:B6** and press [Enter] to correct the range.

5. For the following, be sure to correct the range to **B4:B6** before pressing [Enter].

a. In cell **B10**, find the **Count Numbers**, or number of values.

b. In cell **B11**, find the **Max**, or highest value.

c. In cell **B12**, find the **Min**, or lowest value.

6. Format the range **B9:D12** in Comma style.

7. Save the file, but do not close it.

Formula Bar

▶ Formulas may also be entered using the formula bar. When you press the equal sign, the formula bar provides Cancel and Enter buttons, and the Insert Function button. You can click the **Insert Function button** to search for uncommon functions and to view an explanation and argument screen for the function selected. Or, a list of commonly-used functions is accessible by clicking on the Functions list arrow, as shown in Figure 3.14.

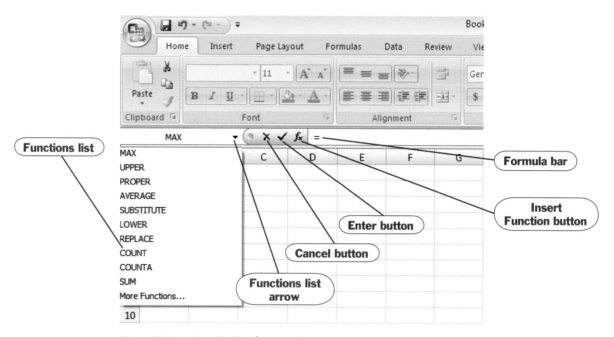

Figure 3.14: Formula bar functions list

▶ When you select a function from the list, Excel enters the function name automatically in the formula and prompts you for the **function arguments**, the cell ranges that supply the data for the formula. The Function Arguments dialog box, shown in Figure 3.15, displays the arguments or range, the result of the formula, explains the function, and provides Help features.

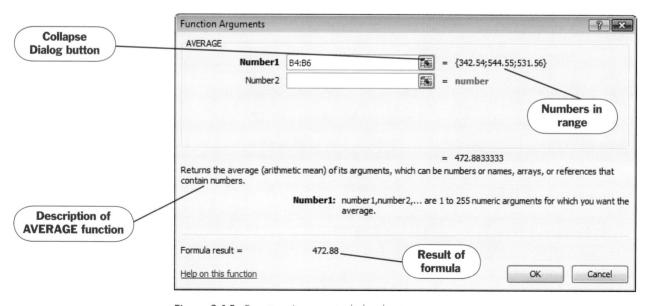

Figure 3.15: Function Arguments dialog box

▶ The Collapse Dialog button, at the right of the range, collapses the dialog box to help you select the correct range. When the dialog box is collapsed, if it still obstructs the range, move it away by dragging its title bar with the mouse pointer. After you make your selection, you can click the Expand Dialog button to redisplay the dialog box.

HOW 1. Enter the equal sign, **=**. 2. Click the **Functions list arrow** on the formula bar. 3. Click desired function. 4. In the Function Arguments box, select the range for arguments. *You may have to collapse and expand the dialog box to select the range.* 5. Click **OK**.

T R Y *i t* **O U T** e3-9

1. Use the open file or open the data file **e3-9**.

2. Enter a formula to calculate the average of numbers in **C4:C6**:
   a. In cell **C9**, enter the equal sign, **=**.
   b. Click the **Functions list arrow**, then click **AVERAGE** from the list of functions.
   c. In the Function Arguments dialog box, click the **Collapse Dialog button**.
   d. Drag the dialog box title bar out of the way, if necessary.

   e. Select the range **C4:C6**.
   f. Click the **Expand Dialog button**.
   g. Click **OK**.

3. Use the same method to complete the formulas for cells **C10**, **C11**, and **C12**.

4. Select the range **C9:C12**, and use the fill handle to fill formulas in **D9:D12**.

5. Format the range **B10:D10** to General number format.

6. Save the file, but do not close it.

Use Format Painter

▶ After entering formulas, you may have to format numbers and/or text. Rather than making repeated settings for formats, you can copy formats from one cell to another by using **Format Painter** on the Home tab in the Clipboard group, or on the Mini toolbar, as shown in Figure 3.16. When you are in Format Painter mode, the mouse pointer includes a paintbrush icon.

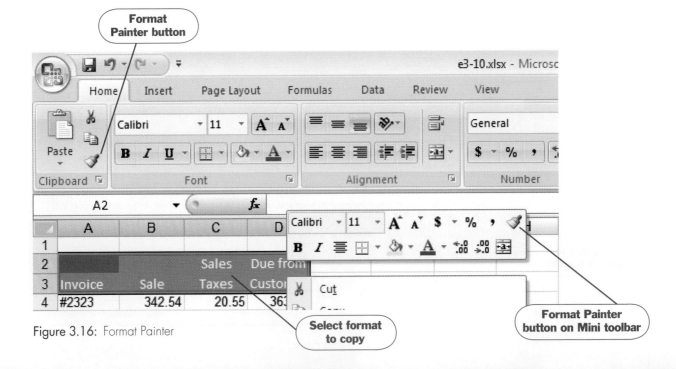

Figure 3.16: Format Painter

HOW 1. Click cell with format to be copied. 2. Click the **Home tab**, and in the Clipboard group, click the **Format Painter button**. 3. Click cell to receive format.

▶ To format more than one area of the worksheet with the Format Painter option, double-click the button. After formatting is complete, click the Format Painter button again, or press the Escape key, to exit Format Painter mode.

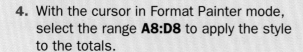

T R Y *i t* **O U T** *e3-10*

1. Use the open file or open the data file **e3-10**.

2. Select **A2:D3** and apply the Accent4 cell style.

3. Right-click the range, and click the **Format Painter button** on the Mini toolbar.

4. With the cursor in Format Painter mode, select the range **A8:D8** to apply the style to the totals.

5. Click **B8** and format it in Accounting style.

6. Click the **Home tab**, and on the Clipboard group, click the **Format Painter button**.

7. Select **C8:D8** to apply the format to the totals.

8. Adjust the column width.

9. Right-click **D8** and double-click the **Format Painter button**. With the cursor in paintbrush mode, select the range **B9:D9**, then **B11:D12** to apply the style from **D8** to the totals.

10. Press **[Esc]** to turn off Format Painter mode.

11. Save the file as **e3-10**, and close the file.

REHEARSAL

GOAL
To create a sales journal

TASK 2

WHAT YOU NEED TO KNOW

▶ Accounting records, such as **journals**, keep track of financial events or transactions for money management and decision-making purposes. One type of journal, a **sales journal**, is a record of the sales made to customers on credit.

▶ The sales invoice, created when a sale is made on credit, is the basis for the entry in the journal. Entries from the journal are then transferred to each customer's account, as discussed in Task 1. In some businesses, the journal and ledger accounts are generated from the preparation of the invoice, using accounting system software.

▶ The final (retail) consumer of merchandise pays sales tax, whereas wholesale customers who are resellers and/or nonprofit organizations are tax exempt.

▶ In this Rehearsal activity, you will prepare a sales journal for All Sports Depot to record sales for its credit business, which is a small part of its total sales.

▼ DIRECTIONS

1. Open the data file **3r2-journal**.

2. Select the range **A3:G3**, and set the Wrap Text alignment.

3. Adjust column widths for columns A, D, and G, and center the data in column B.

4. Format rows 1, 2, and 3 as shown in Figure 3.17.

5. Enter the additional invoices as follows:

    a. Select **C13:C14**, and use AutoFill to fill in the three new invoice numbers.
    b. Enter data in rows 15, 16, and 17 as shown. *AutoComplete will help you enter the customers' names.*

6. In cell **F8**, enter a formula to calculate sales tax of 8.25%. *Hint: Sales Income*8.25%, or =E8*8.25%.*

7. Copy the sales tax formula and paste it to those customer sales that are taxable as noted in column B. *Sales to George Driver and Polly Wilson are taxable.*

8. In cell **G4**, enter a formula to add Sales Income and Sales Taxes to get the total Accounts Receivable amount.

9. Use the Fill handle in **G4** to fill the formula down to **G17**.

10. Use the AutoSum feature to find the total in cell **E19**. Use AutoFill to fill the formula to **F19** and **G19**.

11. Use the AutoSum functions list to find the average of the range **E4:E17** in cell **E21**. Use the mouse to correct the range in the function.

12. Enter the equal sign in cell **E22**, and use the function list on the formula bar to find the highest value (MAX). Click the **Collapse Dialog button** to select the range **E4:E17**.

13. Use the method you prefer to find the remaining data.

14. Select the range **E4:G23**, and format it for two decimal places, using the **Comma Style button**.

Continued on next page

15. Select the range **E21:E24**, and use the Fill handle to fill the formulas to column G.

16. Right-click on cell **G2**, and click Format Painter. Paint the format to the range **D21:G24**. *Reformat E21:G23 in Comma style if necessary.*

17. Use Format Painter to copy the format from **C3** to the total line **D19:G19**. *Reformat the totals in Comma style if necessary.*

18. Print the journal with gridlines.

19. Save the file **3r2-journal**. Close the file.

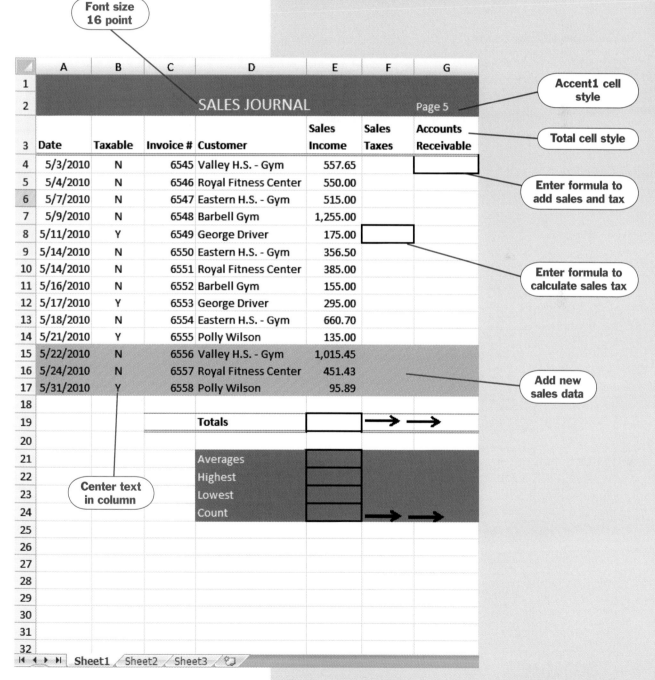

Figure 3.17: Sales journal

Use AutoSum
1. Select cell to display answer.
2. Click the **AutoSum button**.
3. If range is correct, press **[Enter]**. Otherwise, use the mouse pointer to reselect the correct range, then press **[Enter]**.

Enter Range in a Formula
1. Place mouse pointer on first cell in range.
2. Click, hold, and drag to last cell in range.

Use Functions on AutoSum List
1. Select cell to display answer.
2. Click **AutoSum list arrow**.
3. Select function.

4. Correct the range.
5. Press **[Enter]**.

Use Functions from the Formula Bar
1. Select cell to display answer.
2. Enter the equal sign, **=**.
3. Click on **Functions list arrow**, then select function from list.
4. Click the **Collapse Dialog button**.
5. Drag the dialog box title bar out of the way, if necessary.
6. Select the range.
7. Click the **Expand Dialog button**.
8. Click **OK**.

Use Format Painter
1. Select cell with format to copy.
2. Click the **Format Painter button**.
3. Select cell to receive format.

Use Format Painter Multiple Times
1. Select cell with format to copy.
2. Double-click **Format Painter button**.
3. Apply formats to cells.
4. Click the **Format Painter button** or press **[Esc]** to exit Format Painter mode.

PERFORMANCE

TASK 2

Lawrence Spencer, the CFO of EarthCare Services, has asked you to work on a Sales Journal to record credit sales. This journal, for their smallest nursery, divides sales into the services provided at that location; that is, nursery, maintenance contracts, and landscaping. Use 6.5 percent for the sales tax which is only applied to nursery sales. Mr. Spencer would like summary data on June 15 to help make business decisions.

EarthCare Services

Follow these guidelines:

1. Open the data file **3p2-salejour**. Format the column headings with Wrap Text, and adjust column width as needed.

2. Invoice number column: Use AutoFill to fill in the series.

3. Sales Income column: Enter the formula in **G4** to add all services.

4. Sales Tax column: Enter the formula in **H4** to calculate taxes on nursery sales only. *If there is no nursery sale, a zero or dash will appear.*

5. Accounts Receivable column: Enter the formula in **I4** to add tax to sales.

6. Fill the formulas down the columns.

7. Find totals and statistics for all columns.

8. Format numbers in Comma style, except for the Count row (General format), and use cell styles, alignments, column widths, and text formats to improve the appearance of the worksheet.

9. Print the journal using the landscape orientation and with gridlines.

10. Save the file, and close it.

TRYOUT

GOAL
To create a payroll, as shown in Figure 3.18
★ Troubleshoot a formula
★ Modify page setup options

TASK 3

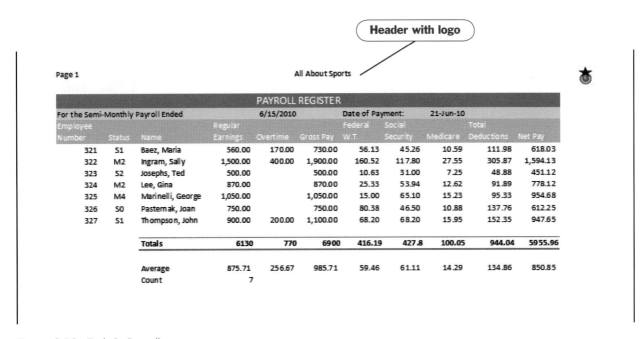

Header with logo

All About Sports

PAYROLL REGISTER									
For the Semi-Monthly Payroll Ended			6/15/2010		Date of Payment:		21-Jun-10		
Employee Number	Status	Name	Regular Earnings	Overtime	Gross Pay	Federal W.T.	Social Security	Medicare	Total Deductions	Net Pay
321	S1	Baez, Maria	560.00	170.00	730.00	56.13	45.26	10.59	111.98	618.03
322	M2	Ingram, Sally	1,500.00	400.00	1,900.00	160.52	117.80	27.55	305.87	1,594.13
323	S2	Josephs, Ted	500.00		500.00	10.63	31.00	7.25	48.88	451.12
324	M2	Lee, Gina	870.00		870.00	25.33	53.94	12.62	91.89	778.12
325	M4	Marinelli, George	1,050.00		1,050.00	15.00	65.10	15.23	95.33	954.68
326	S0	Pasternak, Joan	750.00		750.00	80.38	46.50	10.88	137.76	612.25
327	S1	Thompson, John	900.00	200.00	1,100.00	68.20	68.20	15.95	152.35	947.65
		Totals	6130	770	6900	416.19	427.8	100.05	944.04	5955.96
		Average	875.71	256.67	985.71	59.46	61.11	14.29	134.86	850.85
		Count		7						

Figure 3.18: Task 3: Payroll

WHAT YOU NEED TO KNOW

Troubleshoot a Formula

▶ Excel will display a triangle in the top-left corner of the cell, as shown in Figure 3.19, to indicate an error in a formula or one that does not follow formula rules. The description of the error is highlighted on the Error Checking list along with solutions.

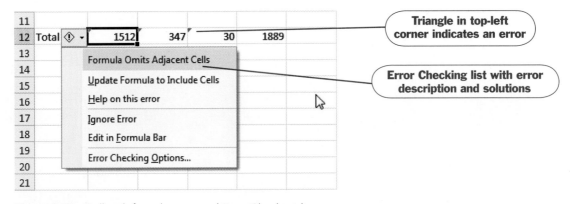

Triangle in top-left corner indicates an error

Error Checking list with error description and solutions

Figure 3.19: Cell with formula error and Error Checking list

Display and Print Formulas

▶ Common formula errors are flagged by Excel, like spelling errors in Word, but errors in logic may not be picked up by the system. You can check formulas by displaying and printing them and then edit them in the formula bar.

> **HOW Ctrl+`** **1.** Click the **Formulas tab**, and in the Formula Auditing group, click the **Show Formulas button**. **2.** Click **[Ctrl]+[P]** to print.

TRY it OUT e3-11

1. Open the data file **e3-11**.

2. Double-click cell **B12**, and notice the range. Press **[Esc]** to exit the formula display.

3. Point to the Error Checking triangle, then click the **Error Checking list arrow**. Click **Update Formula to Include Cells**. *The error marker vanishes and the range is correct: B5:B11.*

4. Click the **Formulas tab**, and in the Formula Auditing group, click the **Show Formulas button**. *There are other formulas that are wrong, but the errors are in the logic, not in the syntax. This can be printed.*

5. Click **Show Formulas button** again to return to Normal view.

6. Save the file, but do not close it.

Edit Formulas Using the Formula Bar

▶ To edit or revise a formula in Edit mode, press the F2 key or double-click the formula. Excel uses color for the arguments in the cell formula and on the formula bar to match a border around the actual arguments, as shown in Figure 3.20. This clearly identifies each part of the formula and may highlight errors that need correction.

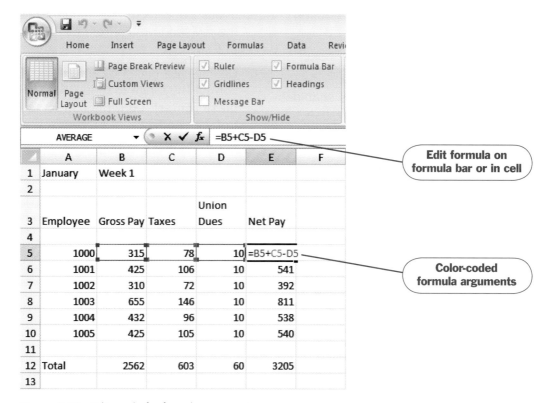

Figure 3.20: Edit mode for formula arguments

► Once you are in Edit mode, you can drag the border of the range or cell, or backspace to correct errors. Figure 3.21 shows how a range of formula arguments appears in Edit mode.

	A	B	C	D	E	
1	January	Week 1				
2						
3	Employee	Gross Pay	Taxes	Union Dues	Net Pay	
4						
5	1000	315	78	10	383	
6	1001	425	106	10	541	
7	1002	310	72	10	392	
8	1003	655	146	10	811	
9	1004	432	96	10	538	
10	1005	425	105	10	540	Reselect the correct range
11						
12	Total	2562	=SUM(C8:C10)		1889	
13			SUM(**number1**, [number2], ...)			ScreenTip for SUM function
14						

Figure 3.21: Edit mode for arguments in a range

T R Y *it* **O U T** *e3-12*

1. Continue to work in the open file or open the data file **e3-12**.

2. Double-click cell **E5** to edit the formula.

3. Revise the formula to read **=B5–C5–D5** because both the taxes and dues should be subtracted from the Gross Pay. *Use the left arrow and the backspace keys to make the change from plus to minus.*

4. Press **[Enter]**.

5. In cell **E5**, click the **fill handle** to AutoFill the revised formula from cell **E5** down to **E10**.

6. Double-click in cell **C12**. Reselect to correct the range to read **C5:C10**, and press **[Enter]**. Copy the correct formula to **D12** and **E12**.

7. Save and close the file.

Modify Page Setup Options

Orientation and Scale

▶ If you print preview your worksheet and note that it is wider than the page width, use landscape orientation to print the worksheet horizontally on the page. Or, on the Page Layout tab, as shown in Figure 3.22, you can scale the data to fit on one page, which reduces the font size.

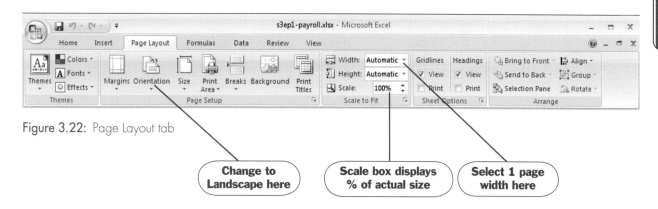

Figure 3.22: Page Layout tab

Change to Landscape here

Scale box displays % of actual size

Select 1 page width here

T R Y *it* O U T *e3-13*

1. Open the data file **e3-13**.

2. Click the **Page Layout view button** on the status bar. *The worksheet is too large to fit on one page.*

3. Click the **Page Layout tab**. In the Page Setup group, click the **Orientation button**, then click **Landscape**. *If you scroll right, you will see that the worksheet is still too large to fit on one page.*

4. In the Scale to Fit group, click the **Width list arrow** and set Width to **1 page**. *The scale changes to 77% of the original size.*

5. Click the **Page Setup dialog box launcher** and notice the Page settings.

6. Click **Print Preview**. *Note that the full worksheet is displayed on one page with a smaller font.*

7. Close the Print Preview screen.

8. Save the file, but do not close it.

Set Page Margins and Centering

▶ In the Margins tab of the Page Setup dialog box, shown in Figure 3.23, you can center the worksheet on the page and set the margins. Or, you can manually adjust the margins on the Print Preview screen, as shown in Figure 3.24, after you select the Show Margins check box on the toolbar.

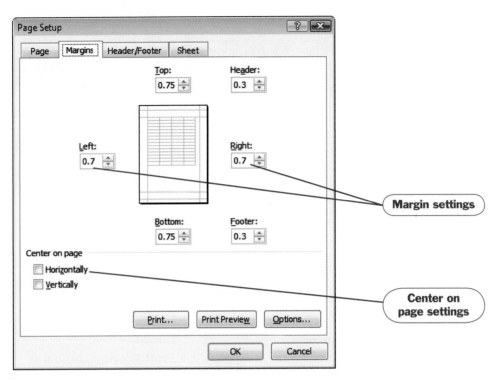

Figure 3.23: Page Setup dialog box, Margins tab

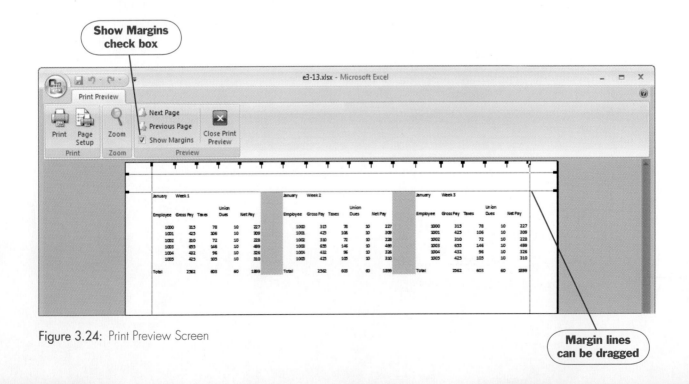

Figure 3.24: Print Preview Screen

1. Continue working in the open file or open the data file **e3-14**.

2. Click the **Page Layout tab**, and in the Page Setup group, click the **Margins button**, then click **Custom Margins**.

3. In the Page setup dialog box, in the Center on page section, click the **Horizontally check box**.

4. Click the **Print Preview button**.

5. In the Preview group, click the **Show Margins check box**.

6. Drag the margin grids toward the edge of the page to make them wider.

7. Click the **Close Print Preview button**.

8. Save the file, but do not close it.

Add and Modify Headers and Footers

▶ **Headers** and **footers** allow you to repeat the same information at the top (header) or bottom (footer) of every page. You use this feature to enter a company name, date, filename, sheet name, or any other identifying information. There are three text boxes that make up both headers and footers. You can select from built-in headers or footers on the Header & Footer Tools Design tab, as shown in Figure 3.25.

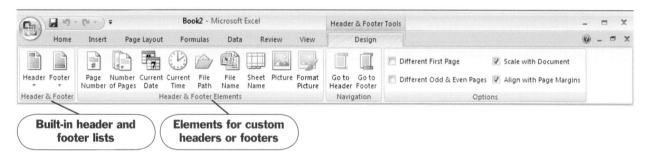

Figure 3.25: Header & Footer Tools Design tab

HOW 1. Click the **Page Layout view button**. 2. Click in the **Click to add header box** at the top of the worksheet. *The Header & Footer Tools Design tab appears*. 3. Click the **Header button** to display built-in headers. 4. Click selection.

1. Continue working in the open file or open the data file **e3-15**.

2. Click **Page Layout view button** on the status bar.

3. On the worksheet, click in the **Click to add header box**.

4. In the Header & Footer Tools Design tab, click the **Header button** and select

the **e3-15.xlsx** or filename header. *The filename appears in the center box.*

5. Scroll down to the bottom of the worksheet, and click in the **Click to add footer box**. *You may need to use the arrow key to get to the bottom of the page to enter the footer.*

6. Click the **Footer button**, and select the **Sheet1, Page1 footer**.

Continued on next page

7. Click the **Office Button**, point to **Print**, then click **Print Preview**. *Notice the headers and footers.*

8. Close the preview screen.

9. Save and close the file.

Add Customized Headers and Footers

▶ To enter a customized header or footer, click in the section and then click the header or footer element you wish to include. The elements enter a code that displays the desired result when you deselect the section. As shown in Figure 3.26, text entered into the left, center, and right sections is aligned in that section. You can use the picture option to insert a logo or graphic and the Format Picture button to customize settings once the picture is in place.

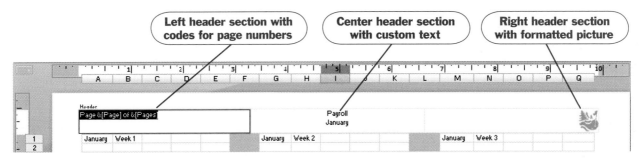

Left header section with codes for page numbers

Center header section with custom text

Right header section with formatted picture

Figure 3.26: Customized Header

HOW **1.** In Page Layout view, click in the header or footer section to customize. *The Header & Footer Tools Design tab appears.* **2.** In the Header & Footer Elements group, click the desired element. **3.** Repeat 1 and 2 until complete.

1. Open the data file **e3-16**.

2. Click the **Page Layout view button** on the status bar.

3. In the center header section, enter **Payroll**, press **[Enter]** and enter **January**.

4. In the left header section, enter **Page**, press **[Spacebar]**, then click the **Page Number button**, press **[Spacebar]**, enter **of** followed by a space, and click the **Number of Pages button**. *The entry will look like: Page &[Page] of &[Pages].*

Page Number

Number of Pages

5. In the right header section, click the **Picture button** and select data file **e3-16logo.tif**. Click **Insert**.

Picture

6. Click the **Format Picture button**.

7. Set picture height to **.54"**, and click **OK**.

Format Picture

8. Click away from the header line to view the custom header.

9. Save the file and close it.

REHEARSAL

TASK 3

GOAL
To create a payroll

WHAT YOU NEED TO KNOW

▶ Company payrolls may be completed by outside services or by the Accounting Department in a large firm. A **payroll register** is a form used to calculate the salaries, taxes, and net pay due each employee for the pay period.

▶ To complete payroll calculations, you need to know the employee's **tax status**; that is, marital status and the number of dependents claimed. Using the tax status and the salary you can look up the federal and state withholding taxes on tax tables. State tax rates vary with each state having different tables and rules. Social Security and Medicare taxes are deducted from all payrolls at the rates of 6.2% and 1.45%, respectively.

▶ You will calculate gross pay (the salary before taxes), the taxes on gross pay, and the net pay (the salary less all the deductions). Once you complete a payroll register, you can save the worksheet as a template to use for each week's payroll. Internet sites also provide paycheck calculators for small businesses.

DIRECTIONS

1. Open data file **3r3-payroll**. Wrap text in **A3:K3** and adjust column width as necessary.

2. Employee Number: Select the range **A4:A5**, and use the fill handle to drag the series of numbers to every employee.

3. Gross Pay: In cell **F4**, enter a formula to find gross pay. *Hint: =Regular Earnings+Overtime. Use cell addresses in the formula.* Use the fill handle in cell **F4** to copy the formula down to each employee's payroll.

4. Social Security: In cell **H4**, enter a formula to find the Social Security tax, which is 6.2% of the gross pay. *Hint: =Gross Pay*6.2%.*

5. Medicare: In cell **I4**, enter a formula to find the Medicare tax, which is 1.45% of the gross pay.

6. Total Deductions: In cell **J4**, use AutoSum to enter a formula to find the total of all the payroll deductions in the range G4:I4.

7. Net Pay: In cell **K4**, enter a formula to find net pay, which is the gross pay less the total deductions.

8. As shown in Figure 3.27, select the range **H4:K4**, and use the fill handle to fill all the formulas for the payroll.

9. In cell **D12**, use AutoSum to find the total of the column.

10. In cell **D14**, enter the equal sign, **=**, and use the formula bar function list to enter the formula for the column average. *Be sure to select the correct range.*

11. In cell **D15**, use the AutoSum drop-down list to find the count. *Be sure to correct the range.*

12. Display the formulas, check them, and turn off Show Formulas.

Continued on next page

► In this Rehearsal activity, you will prepare a semi-monthly payroll for All Sports Depot, located in Texas. There is no state or local income tax in this state.

13. Select the range **D12:D14**, and use the fill handle to copy the formulas across to all columns.

14. Format payroll data in the range **D4:K14** in Comma style.

15. Format the worksheet as shown in Figure 3.27.

16. Custom header and footer:
   a. Header:
      • Left section: Page number
      • Center section: **All Sports Depot**
      • Right section: Company logo, using **3r3-logo.tif** formatted to a height of **.32"**
   b. Footer:
      • Center section: Filename
      • Right section: Date

17. Print the payroll in landscape orientation, centered horizontally.

18. Save the file **3r3-payroll**. Close the file.

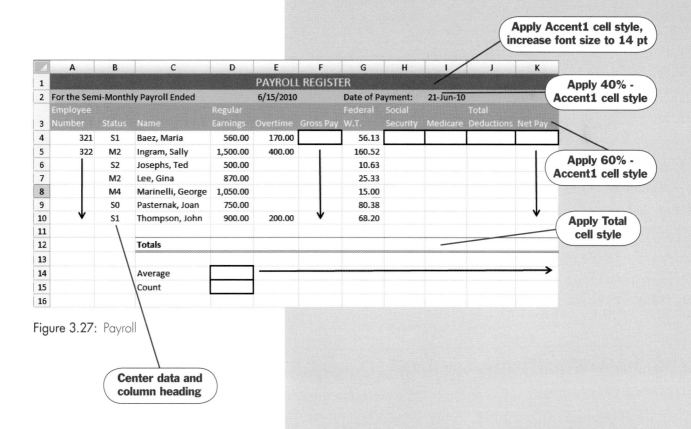

Figure 3.27: Payroll

Apply Accent1 cell style, increase font size to 14 pt

Apply 40% - Accent1 cell style

Apply 60% - Accent1 cell style

Apply Total cell style

Center data and column heading

Edit Formulas
1. Select formula.
2. Press **[F2]**.
3. Edit range by dragging border, or edit operators in formula.

Display Formulas
1. Click the **Formulas tab**, and in the Formula Auditing group, click the **Show Formulas button**.

Modify Page Orientation
1. Click the **Page Layout tab**, and in Page Setup group, click the **Orientation button**.
2. Click **Landscape**.

Modify Scale
1. Click the **Page Layout tab**, and in the Scale to Fit group, click the **Width list arrow**.
2. Set the desired page width.

Set Page Margins and Centering
1. Click the **Page Layout tab**, and in the Page Setup group, click the **Margins button**, then click **Custom Margins**.
2. Set margins or centering. Click **OK**.
   Or
2. Click **Print Preview**.

3. Click the **Show Margins check box**, and drag margins to appropriate location.

Add Headers or Footers
1. Click the **Page Layout view button**.
2. Click in the **Click to add header box** or **Click to add footer box**.
3. Click the **Header** or **Footer button**, and click selection.
   Or
3. Select each section of header or footer, and click the desired element in the Header & Footer Elements group.

P E R F O R M A N C E

TASK 3

You have completed an employee timesheet for BodyWorks Fitness Center, and now you need to complete a bi-weekly payroll register for their four locations. The state withholding tax in North Carolina and the federal taxes are provided, since they had to be obtained from tax tables.

Follow these guidelines:

1. Open the data file **3p3-payroll**. Adjust column width and wrap text in the column headings.

2. Formulas: Enter appropriate formulas in **F4**, I4, **J4**, **K4**, and **L4**. Enter formulas to summarize data in **D20**, **D22**, **D23**, and **D24**. Use AutoFill. *Social Security Tax is 6.2% and Medicare Tax is 1.45% of the Gross Pay. Use the MAX function for Highest and the MIN function for Lowest. Be careful with ranges in formulas.*

3. Formats: Format values in Comma style. To match the timesheet prepared in Lesson 2, use the Accent3 cell style, and its variations, and the Totals cell style for the Total line. Make the font size larger for the title.

4. Footer: (Left section) Date, (Center Section) **BodyWorks Fitness Center**, (Right section) filename.

5. Print two copies of the payroll set to one page wide, landscape orientation, with gridlines. Copy 1: Print it with the formulas displayed. Copy 2: Print the completed payroll.

6. Save the file **3p3-payroll** and close it.

TRYOUT

▶ **GOAL**
To create an expense report, as shown in Figure 3.28
✴ Move selected cells
✴ Insert, view, edit, and delete cell comments
✴ Format or modify text using formulas

TASK 4

		Perfect Planning Group 675 Third Avenue New York, NY 10017					
EXPENSE REPORT							
Employee:		Jennifer Hodges					
Purpose:		Meetings with sponsor, vendors, and hotel for computer conference					
Date (s):		September 7 and 8, 2010					
Date	Description	Meals	Travel	Lodging	Telephone	Other	Total
9/7/2010	Taxi to terminal		5.00				5.00
9/7/2010	NJ Transit		29.50				29.50
9/7/2010	Employee	35.00		185.00	23.00	15.00	258.00
9/7/2010	Entertainment*	158.75					158.75
9/8/2010	Taxi to vendor/hotel meeting		7.50				7.50
9/8/2010	Employee	87.50			21.00	22.00	130.50
9/8/2010	NJ Transit		29.50				29.50
9/8/2010	Taxi- home		5.00				5.00
	Totals						623.75
					Less: Advance		250.00
					Net due		373.75
Entertainment Expenses Detail*							
Date	Client/Company Entertained	Purpose		Restaurant		Amount	
9/7/2010	Tech-Solutions, Inc.	Planning meeting		Bock's Oyster House		158.75	
	Martin Greenwich						
Expense Report							
Approval:							
	Carol McNally, President						

Figure 3.28: Task 4: Expense report

WHAT YOU NEED TO KNOW

Move Selected Cells

▶ Moving data removes it from the first location and pastes it to the new location. You can use the cut-and-paste tools or you can use **drag-and-drop editing**, where you select the range and drag it to the paste location. As shown in Figure 3.29, as you drag the data, the new range or location appears in a ScreenTip. Data formats move with the data, but you must check that formulas are correct after a move operation.

HOW **1.** Select the data to move. **2.** Place the mouse pointer on the edge of the range until it changes to a four-headed arrow. **3.** Drag the outline of the range to the first cell in the new location's range.

	A	B	C	D	E	F
1	Expense Report for March business trips					
2		Baltimore	Washingt¢	Richmond		
3					3/18/2010	3/16/2010	3/15/2010
4	Hotel				315	189	165
5	Meals				94	141	75
6	Air Fare				155	210	195
7	Car Renta					56	
8	Telephon¢				28	22	18
9	Entertain				185		135
10	Misc.				27	43	17
11				B3:B12			
12	Totals				804	661	605
13							

Select range to drag to new location

New range address

Outline of range in new location

Figure 3.29: Selected range moved to new location

TRY it OUT e3-17

1. Open data file **e3-17**.

2. Select the range **E3:E12**, and right-click and click the **Cut button** on the shortcut menu.

3. Select cell **C3**, and right-click and click the **Paste button** on the shortcut menu.

4. Select the range **F3:F12**.

5. Place the mouse pointer at the edge of the range until the pointer becomes a four-headed arrow.

6. Click, hold, and drag the range to **B3:B12**. Adjust column widths.

7. Click on **B12**. *The Error Checking button appears.* Point to the Error Checking triangle, click the **Error Checking list arrow**, then click **Ignore Error**. Repeat for **C12**.

8. Save the file, but do not close it.

Insert, View, Edit, and Delete Cell Comments

▶ You can attach a text **cell comment** to document formulas or assumptions built into the worksheet, or to comment on data sent to you by someone else. Because this feature is used when sharing workbooks, the user's name will also be included on the comment.

▶ A red triangle appears in the top corner of the cell to indicate the presence of a cell comment, as shown in Figure 3.30. Comments are displayed when the mouse moves over a cell with a comment indicator. To edit or delete a comment, right-click the comment cell and select the desired action.

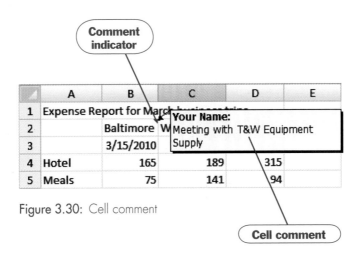

Figure 3.30: Cell comment

HOW   **1.** Right-click in cell. **2.** Click **Insert Comment** on the shortcut menu. **3.** Enter a comment. **4.** Click away from the comment cell.

T R Y _it_ O U T *e3-18*

1. Continue working in the open file or open data file **e3-18**.

2. Right-click in cell **B2**, and click **Insert Comment**.

3. Enter the text **T&W Equipment Supply**.

4. Click on any cell to exit Comment mode.

5. Right-click cell **C2**, click **Insert Comment**, and enter **Sailboat Show and Conference**.

6. Right-click cell **B2**, click **Edit Comment**.

7. Edit the comment to read **Meeting with T&W Equipment Supply**.

8. Enter the comment in cell **D2 Meeting with Michael Collins**.

9. Right-click cell **D2**, and click **Delete Comment**.

10. Save the file as **e3-18**, and close it.

Format or Modify Text Using Formulas

▶ You have used functions to calculate values but there are also text functions that allow you to format or modify text entries. If want to copy text, but in a different way, you can apply a text function to modify the text rather than retyping data. There are many text functions, as shown in Figure 3.31, but the text functions in Table 3.4 will be practiced.

Table 3.4: Text functions

TEXT FUNCTION	PURPOSE
UPPER(text reference)	Converts text in cell to uppercase
LOWER(text reference)	Converts text in cell to lowercase
PROPER(text reference)	Converts first letter in a text string to uppercase and all other letters in string to lowercase
SUBSTITUTE(text,new_text,old_text)	Substitutes new text for specific text in a text string

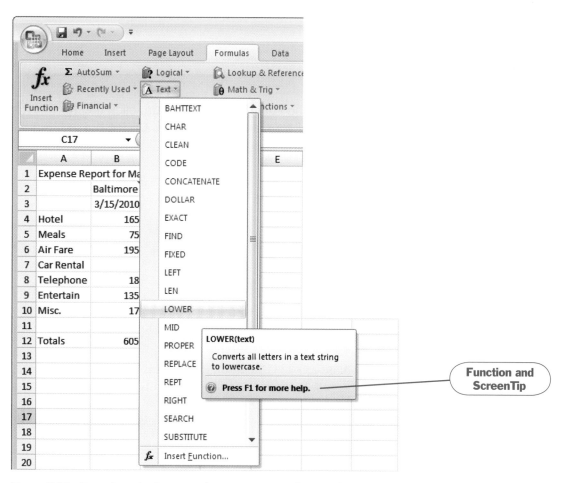

Figure 3.31: Formulas tab, Function Library group, Text function list

▶ Once you select a function from the function list, you enter the formula arguments on the Function Arguments dialog box that appears, as shown in Figure 3.32.

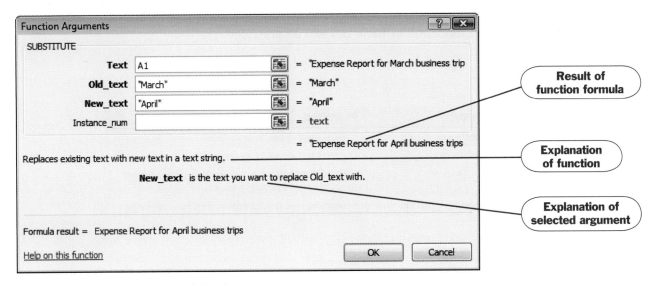

Figure 3.32: Function Arguments dialog box

 1. Click the **Formulas tab**, and in the Function Library group, click the **Text button**.
2. Select the text function. **3.** Enter formula arguments. **4.** Click **OK**.

T R Y i t O U T *e3-19*

1. Open data file **e3-19**, and place your cursor in cell **G12**.

2. Click the **Formulas** tab, and in the Function Library group, click the **Text button**.

3. Select **LOWER**, enter or select **A12**, and click **OK**. *The totals entry copies to the cell in lowercase.* Delete the result in **G12**.

4. In cell **G12**, apply the **UPPER** function to the text in **A12**. *TOTALS appears.*

5. In cell **G1**, click **SUBSTITUTE** on the Text function list.

6. To copy the text in **A1** to **G1**, substituting April for March, make the entries shown in Figure 3.32 in the Function Arguments dialog box. Click **OK**.

7. In cell **G15**, select the **PROPER** function and the text in **G1** to change the heading to Proper format. *The title displays with uppercase letters for each text string.*

8. Save and close the file.

GOAL
To create an expense report

TASK 4

WHAT YOU NEED TO KNOW

▶ When employees travel on company business, the company usually **reimburses**, or refunds, their expenses. Employees may get a cash advance before the trip, which reduces the reimbursement amount.

▶ When employees return from the trip, they submit an **expense report**, listing all expenses and their receipts for reimbursement. Tax laws require detailed records for business entertainment and travel because they are deductible business expenses that reduce profit.

▶ In this Rehearsal activity, you will prepare an expense report for Jennifer Hodges, an employee of Perfect Planning Group. She is applying for reimbursement of expenses for her business trip to Atlantic City, New Jersey, to meet with the hotel, vendors, and sponsor of the computer software conference she is planning.

Perfect Planning Group

▼ DIRECTIONS

1. Open data file **3r4-expense**. Adjust column width as necessary and enter data in **C6** and **C7**, as shown in Figure 3.33.

2. Change the theme of the worksheet to **Metro**. *Use the Page Layout tab.*

3. Select the range **A1:A3**, and move it using drag and drop to **C1**. Apply the Accent3 cell style to **C1:H3**. Increase the font size to **18 pt**.

4. Apply Accent3 cell style to **A4:B4**, and increase the font size to **14 pt**.

5. Click the logo in **J1**, and when the cursor appears as a four-headed arrow, move the graphic to the right side of column B, as illustrated.

6. Formats: Apply the 40% - Accent3 cell style to the range **A10:H10**, right-click, and, on the Mini toolbar, double-click the **Format Painter button**. Apply the format from the range to the ranges **A32:B32** and **A33:H33**. Press **[Esc]** to turn off format painting mode. Bold text in **A6:A8**.

7. Select the range **A26:H35**, and move the range to cell **A20**.

8. In cell **H11**, use AutoSum to find the total of all the expenses in the row. *Be sure to use C11:G11 as the range in the formula.*

9. Use the fill handle to extend the formula to cell **H18**.

10. In cell **C20**, enter a formula to find the total of the column. *Use the range C11:C18.* AutoFill the formula across to **H20**.

11. In cell **H23**, enter a formula to find the amount due Jennifer Hodges. *Hint: =Total–Advance.*

12. Format all numeric data in Comma style, and apply Total cell style to **C20:H20** and **H23**.

Continued on next page

13. Right-click cell **H22**, click **Insert Comment**, and enter the comment **Receipt #86 9/6**.

14. In cell **A32**, enter the **PROPER** text function, using the text in **A4** to enter **Expense Report** as shown.

15. Enter the text in **A33** and **B34** from Figure 3.33 for approval of the report.

16. Edit the comment in **H22** to add the year to the date.

17. Print the expense report on one page with gridlines and centered horizontally on the page.

18. Save the file **3r4-expense**. Close the file.

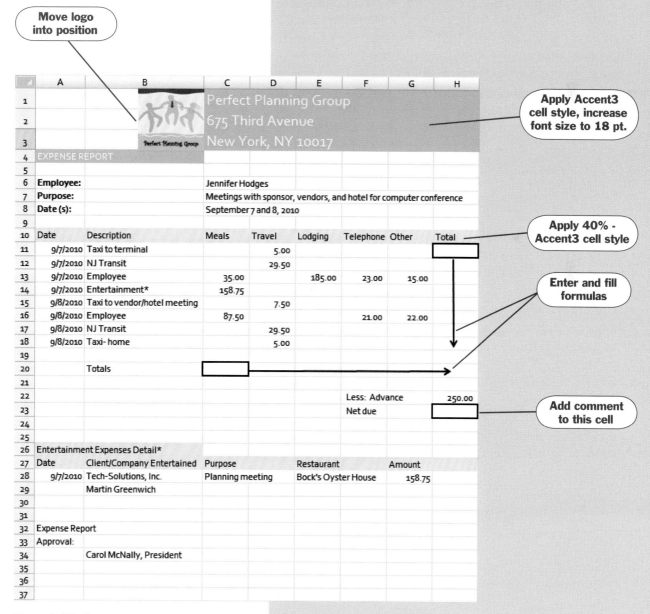

Figure 3.33: Expense report

Move Data

1. Select data to move.
2. Place mouse pointer at edge of selection until the four-arrow cursor appears. Click, hold, and drag to new location.

Insert Cell Comment

1. Right-click in the cell.
2. Click **Insert Comment** on the shortcut menu.
3. Enter comment.
4. Click on any cell to exit Comment mode.

Edit Cell Comment

1. Right-click the cell with the comment to edit.
2. Click **Edit Comment** on the shortcut menu.
3. Edit comment.
4. Click on any cell to exit Comment mode.

Delete Cell Comment

1. Right-click cell with comment to edit.
2. Click **Delete Comment** on the shortcut menu.

Use Text Functions

1. Click the **Formulas tab**, and in Function Library, click the **Text button**.
2. Click the text function.
3. In Function Arguments dialog box, enter arguments.
4. Click **OK**.

PERFORMANCE

TASK 4

Frank Manning, director of marketing and sales for NewMark Productions, has just returned from a business trip to San Diego, California, where he met with local stations and sponsors. He needs an expense report for the trip made October 13 to October 15, 2010. When a meeting is held over a meal, it is an Entertainment expense and should be detailed as per IRS guidelines. The company reimburses him for his mileage at $.485 per mile.

Follow these guidelines:

1. Open data file **3p4-expense**. Format the worksheet using Wrap text for the column headings, cell styles, bold style, and adjustments to column width and row height as needed. A sample format is shown in Figure 3.34.

2. Mr. Manning provides you with the receipts and list of expenses, shown in Table 3.5. Enter and place the expense amounts in the appropriate columns and enter the Entertainment details in the section below the report.

Table 3.5: Expense report information

10/13	Employee expenses: Meals: $37.50, Fuel:$35.76, Hotel: $165, Miscellaneous: $18
10/13	Dinner Meeting: Meals/Tips: $325.64 - SDTV Marketing Team, Meeting at Ocean View Restaurant
10/14	Employee expenses: Meals: $15.65, Hotel: $165, Miscellaneous: $72.89
10/14	Luncheon meeting: Meals/Tips: $114.95 - Carson Willers, screenwriter, XY Project, at LaTavola
10/15	Breakfast meeting: Meals/Tips: $79.55 - AutoMart and Bright Jewelry, sponsor meeting at Hotel Coffee Shop
10/15	Employee expenses: Meals/Tips: $18, Fuel $33.54, Miscellaneous: $24.92
10/15	Mileage for trip: Estimate - 300 miles. Or, calculate: Check the distance of this trip on the Internet by going to www.mappoint.msn.com. Mr. Manning drove from Sunset Boulevard in Beverly Hills, CA 90210 to Federal Boulevard in San Diego, CA 92102. Determine the one-way mileage for this trip. Then, on an unused area of the worksheet, calculate the mileage by doubling the one-way mileage and adding 50 miles for in-town driving.

3. Enter a comment in the cell where you entered the mileage to note either "Estimate" or "Mileage calculated at ___ each way plus 50 miles of in-town driving."

4. In **D15**, enter a formula to calculate Mileage Reimbursement by multiplying the miles by the reimbursement rate of $.485.

5. In **K9**, enter a formula to find the total for each row, including columns D:J. In **D18**, enter a formula to total expense items and AutoFill the formulas. Mr. Manning had an advance of $300. Enter formulas to find the total expenses and the amount of reimbursement due. Format all values.

6. Print the expense report, changing the print settings if necessary. Save the file as an Excel workbook file and name it **3p4-expense**. Close the file.

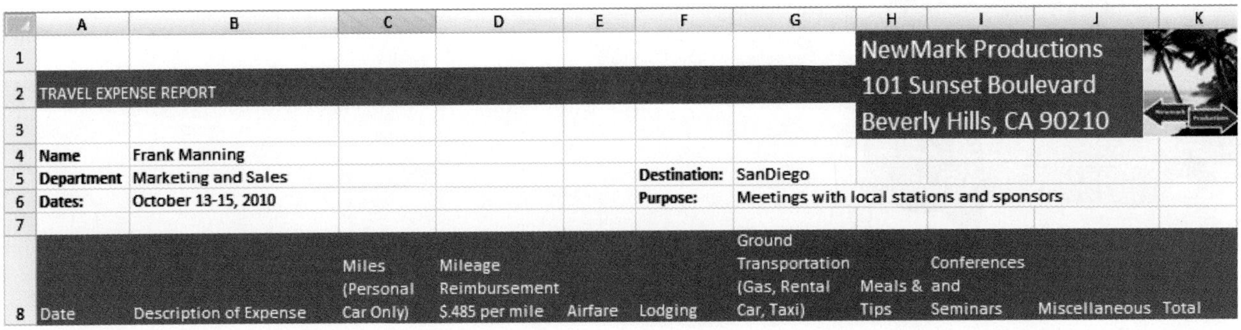

	A	B	C	D	E	F	G	H	I	J	K
1								NewMark Productions			
2	TRAVEL EXPENSE REPORT							101 Sunset Boulevard			
3								Beverly Hills, CA 90210			
4	Name	Frank Manning									
5	Department	Marketing and Sales				Destination:	SanDiego				
6	Dates:	October 13-15, 2010				Purpose:	Meetings with local stations and sponsors				
7											
8	Date	Description of Expense	Miles (Personal Car Only)	Mileage Reimbursement $.485 per mile	Airfare	Lodging	Ground Transportation (Gas, Rental Car, Taxi)	Meals & Tips	Conferences and Seminars	Miscellaneous	Total

Figure 3.34: Example of formatting for expense report

ENCORE

Act I

Expedition Travel Gear has asked you to complete the weekly payroll for the Chicago store for the week ending July 20. Store employees are paid based on an hourly rate.

Expedition

Travel Gear

Deductions for federal and state income taxes are based on the salary and tax status of the employee and are obtained from tax tables or from online services. The tax status M2, for example, is made up of the marital status (M = married, S = single) and the number of federal exemptions. Social Security (6.2%) and Medicare (1.45%) taxes are calculated using the current tax rate.

Follow these guidelines:

1. Open data file **3ep1-payroll**, adjust column widths as necessary, and apply the Accent2 cell style and other styles in that color to enhance the worksheet.

2. The employees' hours for the week are: Montez, Carlo, 40; Vaughn, Tamika, 40; Soto, Linda, 35; Wong, Sam, 38; Kingsley, Mary, 40. Insert formulas to calculate Gross Pay. *Hint: Hours*Rate.*

3. Federal and state taxes are included for the first three employees. Use the Paycheck Calculator on the Personal Calculator link on www.paycheckcity.com to look up the federal and state taxes for the last two employees. *On the Web site, you must enter the State (Illinois), Gross Pay for the pay period, Pay Frequency (weekly), Married or Single for federal filing status, and enter the number of federal exemptions. When you click Calculate, the detailed paycheck will appear. Copy the state and federal taxes and enter them on your worksheet.*

4. Enter formulas for Social Security Tax, Medicare Tax, Total Deductions, and Net Pay. Fill in the formulas for all employees, and format the values.

5. Find summary values for the payroll, including Totals, Averages, Highest, and Lowest. Format all values except Hours in Comma style.

6. Add a footer that includes the Date, Filename, and Page number. In Print Preview, change the orientation to print the worksheet on one page, then print, save, and close the file **3ep1-payroll**.

Act II

Palmetto Realtors manages some commercial and residential properties and acts as an agent for leasing these units. The management fee is 5% of the monthly rent, which reduces the amount the owner receives. Also, when a new lease is signed, the agency gets one month's rent as their fee and they hold the security deposit until the end of the lease.

Palmetto Realtors

They have started to prepare a journal to record their receipts for rental income that needs formatting and formulas. They also want to prepare an entry to summarize the journal on the 15th of the month.

Follow these guidelines:

1. Open data file **3ep2-journal**. Set the Median theme, and use Accent4 cell style and its variations to format headings and titles. Set Wrap Text alignment for the column headings, and adjust column and row sizes as necessary.

2. Cash Received: In cell **I5**, enter a formula to calculate total Cash Received. *Hint: Add columns F:H.*

3. Management Fee: In cell **J5**, enter a formula to calculate the management fee of 5 percent of the monthly rent.

4. Owner's Rent Payable: In cell **K5**, enter a formula to calculate the amount to send to the owner. *Hint: Monthly Rent-Management Fee.*

5. Total Rental Income: In cell **L5**, enter a formula to calculate the total income from rentals. *Hint: Management Fee+Rental Fee.*

6. Enter all summary formulas in cells **F15:F18**. AutoFill all formulas to fill in the worksheet. Format the values in Comma style.

7. Move the summary titles in **A15:A18** to **E15**. Apply the Total cell style to the Totals line.

8. In each cell in the range **A21:A25**, use the UPPER text function to place the headings for columns G:K, in the order shown in Figure 3.35, in uppercase into the Journal entry list. Move the totals into the appropriate spaces. The four totals on the right (credits) should equal the Cash Received total on the left (debit). *You can check this with a formula in **E26**.*

9. Save the file **3ep2-journal**. Close the file.

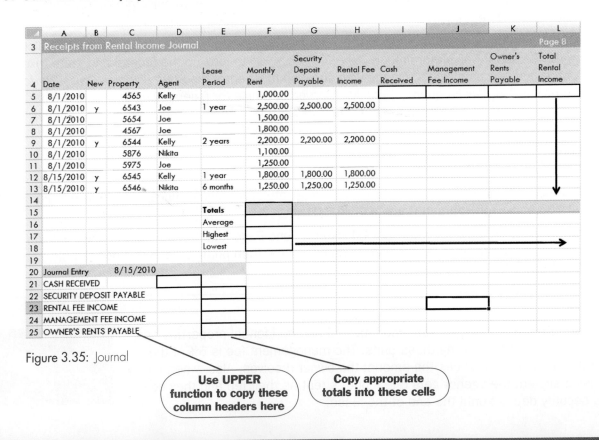

Figure 3.35: Journal

Use UPPER function to copy these column headers here

Copy appropriate totals into these cells

LESSON 4

Data Analysis

In this lesson, you will learn to use Excel features, functions, and multiple
worksheet workbooks to create and complete analyses of business data.
Completed worksheets and workbooks will be saved as a Web page.
You will complete the following projects:
* Budget analysis
* Billings analysis
* Income statement analysis
* Revenue analysis on multiple sheets

Upon completion of this lesson, you will have mastered the following skill sets
* Apply and modify cell formats
* Insert and delete cells, columns, and rows
* Format data as a table
* Sort and filter data
* Use formulas with absolute and relative references
* Add a background pattern
* Save a workbook as a Web page
* Manage workbooks
* Use Paste Special

Terms
Software-related
Absolute reference
AutoFilter
Background
Banded rows or columns
Border
Group sheets
Label prefix
Negative numbers
Numeric label
Paste Special
Paste Values
Quick Styles
Relative reference
Sort
Table
Tab scrolling buttons
Transpose
Web page

Document-related
Billings
Budget
Income statement
Listing
Quarterly
Revenue

GOAL
To create a budget analysis, as shown in Figure 4.1
* Apply and modify cell formats
* Insert and delete cells, columns, and rows

Fancy Flowers, Inc.

Comparison of Budgeted Income Statement
with Actual Income Statement
For the year ended December 31, 2010

	Budget 2010	Actual 2010	Increase/ Decrease	% Increase/ Decrease
Operating Revenue:				
Sales	1,188,000	1,212,321	24,321	2.0%
Cost of Goods Sold	522,720	532,220	9,500	1.8%
Gross Profit on Operations	$ 1,710,720	$ 1,744,541	$ 33,821	2.0%
Operating Expenses:				
Selling Expenses:				
Advertising Expense	9,900	10,124	224	2.3%
Delivery Expense	18,700	19,425	725	3.9%
Depr. Expense - Delivery Equip.	23,650	24,290	640	2.7%
Miscellaneous Expense - Sales	6,600	6,600	-	0.0%
Salary Expense - Sales	315,040	320,700	5,660	1.8%
Supplies Expense - Sales	21,340	21,980	640	3.0%
Total Selling Expenses	395,230	403,119	7,889	2.0%
Administrative Expenses:				
Bad Debts Expense	5,940	5,930	(10)	-0.2%
Depr. Expense - Off. Equip.	4,720	4,720	-	0.0%
Insurance Expense	1,200	1,320	120	10.0%
Miscellaneous Expense - Admin.	2,810	2,725	(85)	-3.0%
Payroll Taxes Expense	31,450	31,865	415	1.3%
Rent Expense	19,800	19,800	-	0.0%
Salary Expense - Admin.	78,100	77,610	(490)	-0.6%
Supplie Expense - Office	2,430	2,489	59	2.4%
Utilities Expense	5,060	5,170	110	2.2%
Total Administrative Expenses	151,510	151,629	119	0.1%
Total Operating Expenses	$ 546,740	$ 554,748	$ 8,008	1.5%
Net Income Before Federal Income Tax	1,163,980	1,189,793	25,813	2.2%
Federal Income Tax	34,232	34,876	644	1.9%
Net Income After Federal Income Tax	$ 1,129,748	$ 1,154,917	$ 25,169	2.2%

Figure 4.1: Task 1: Budget analysis

WHAT YOU NEED TO KNOW

Apply and Modify Cell Formats

▶ In addition to cell styles and text formats previously discussed, Excel provides additional features to format the cells in a worksheet to create professional-looking documents. You can add cell borders, font and fill colors, and number formats for decimals and negative numbers.

Cell Borders

▶ There are a variety of line styles that **border** the edge of a cell or range of cells to outline or separate data. The Borders button can be found on the Home tab, in the Font group, or on the Mini toolbar, as shown in Figures 4.2 and 4.3. The button displays the most recently used border, but other borders can be accessed by using the list arrow.

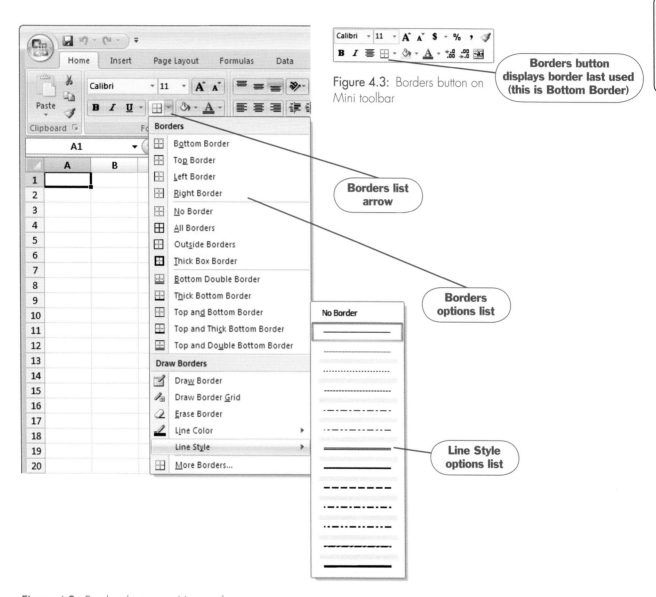

Figure 4.3: Borders button on Mini toolbar

Figure 4.2: Borders button on Home tab

HOW **1.** Select and right-click the range. **2.** Click the **Borders list arrow** on the Mini toolbar. *See below if you need to use Line Styles.* **3.** Click a border style.

▶ Border formats remain when you clear cell contents. Therefore, you must clear border settings separately by using the Erase Border tool or by formatting the range for No Border in the Borders options list, shown in Figure 4.2.

HOW **1.** Right-click range to be cleared. **2.** Click the **Borders list arrow**, and in the Borders options list, click **No Border** or **Erase Border**.

▶ Borders can also be set, previewed, and edited using the Border tab in the Format Cells dialog box, as shown in Figure 4.4. The dialog box contains three preset border formats and other styles illustrated around a preview box that displays your settings. Line Style and Color settings allow you to customize the preset border styles.

HOW 1. Select the range to receive borders. 2. Press **[Ctrl]+1**. 3. Click the **Border tab**. 4. Make settings. 5. Click **OK**.

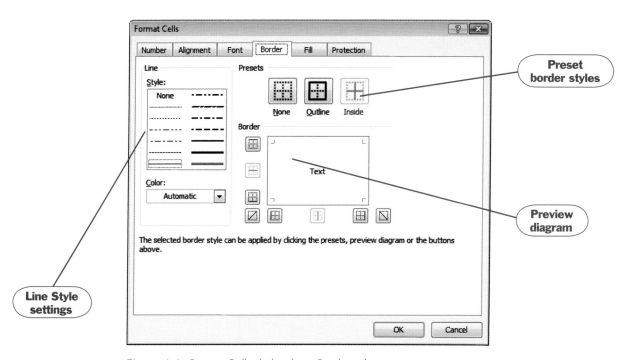

Figure 4.4: Format Cells dialog box, Border tab

TRY *it* **OUT** *e4-1*

1. Open data file **e4-1**. Select columns B:F and double-click between columns F and G to AutoFit the data.

2. Select and right-click the range **A4:F4**, click the **Borders list arrow** on the Mini toolbar, and click **Thick Bottom Border**.

3. Select the range **C34:F34** and press **[Ctrl]+1**.

4. Click the **Border tab** in the Format Cells dialog box.

5. In Line Style, click the double line, and in Preset, click **Outline**. *Note the preview*. Click **OK** and click outside the range to view the setting.

6. Select **C34:F34**, and clear the borders. *Click **No Border** on the Borders options list.*

7. Click the **Undo button** to reverse the No Border style.

8. Select and right-click the range **F5:F32**, and apply the **Left Border style**.

9. On the Home tab, click the **Borders list arrow**, then click **Erase Border**.

10. Erase the border by selecting the range **F5:F32**. *The Borders button will display the last tool used so that it can berepeated. Press **[Esc]** to exit Erase Border mode.*

11. Save the file, but do not close it.

Indent Text

▶ The indent text feature allows you to align text away from the left edge of the cell. Use indentations to set text off from lists or headers, as shown in Figure 4.7.

7	INCOME:		
8		Salary	$ 3,854.34
9		Other	$ 215.00
10		Total Income	$ 4,069.34
11			

Indented text

Figure 4.7: Indent text feature

HOW **1.** Select text to indent. **2.** Click the **Home tab**, and in the Alignment group, click the **Increase Indent button**. *Adjust or undo indentation by clicking the **Decrease Indent button**.*

T R Y *i t* O U T e4-4

1. Continue to work in the open file, or open data file **e4-4**.

2. Select the range **B8:B10**.

3. Click the **Home tab**, and in the Alignment group, click the **Increase Indent button**.

4. Select the range **B8:B9** and click the **Decrease Indent button**.

5. Select B10 and indent the text a second time by clicking the Increase Indent button. Use the Format Painter to apply the same indent format to **B18**, **B30**, and **B34**. Adjust the column width as necessary.

6. Save the file, and close it.

Insert and Delete Cells, Columns, and Rows

▶ You can insert or delete cells, columns, or rows to change the layout of data on a worksheet, using the Insert or Delete buttons on the Home tab, as shown in Figure 4.8.

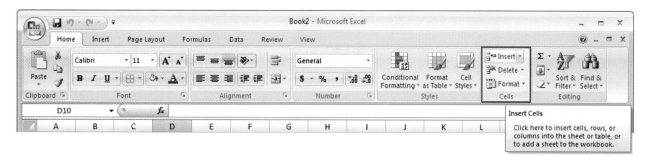

Figure 4.8: Home tab, Cells group, Insert button

Insert

▶ When you make insertions, existing data shifts to allow for the new space. If you want to insert more than one cell, column, or row, select that number of locations, starting with the location where the new spaces begin. An Insert Options button will appear with format options when columns or rows are inserted, as shown in Figure 4.9.

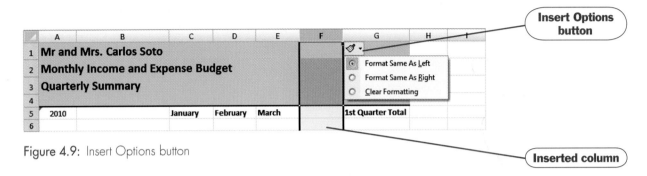

Figure 4.9: Insert Options button

HOW **1.** Select the column(s) or row(s) where you want the new space. **2.** Click the **Home tab**, and in the Cells group, click the **Insert list arrow**. **3.** Click the item to insert. *You can also right-click the location, click **Insert**, and make a selection to shift cells up or down, or insert columns or rows.*

Delete

▶ When you delete a cell, column, or row, all data in that space is eliminated and existing data shifts to fill in the space. Always save a workbook before doing this to avoid deleting data in error. If you attempt to delete data by selecting cells, and not the entire row or column, the Delete dialog box opens, as shown in Figure 4.10, to provide options to clarify the request.

Figure 4.10: Delete dialog box

1. Open data file **e4-5**.

2. Select column F.

3. Click the **Home tab**, and in the Cells group, click the **Insert list arrow**, then click **Insert Sheet Columns**. *Note the Insert Options button.*

4. Click the **Insert Options button**, then click **Clear Formatting**.

5. Select row 6, right-click, and click **Delete** on the shortcut menu. *The row and data, if present, are deleted.*

6. Select **C11:E11**. Click the **Home tab**, and in the Cells group, click the **Delete button**. *Note that the cells are deleted and that the data shifts upward, causing an error. Click the **Undo button**.*

7. Right-click the range **F8:F34**, and click **Delete**. Click **Cancel** on the Delete dialog box.

8. Select and delete column F using the **Delete list arrow**.

9. Select columns C and D, right-click, and click **Insert**. *Two columns were selected and two are inserted in the location of the first selected column. Click the **Undo button**.*

10. Save and close the file.

WHAT YOU NEED TO KNOW

▶ A **budget** is an analysis of the projected income and expenses for a future period. Companies create budgets based on past history and projections of future trends. Budgets are the basis for management decisions and plans for expenditures.

▶ Businesses analyze data **quarterly**, which is every three months, or four times a year, using percentages for ease of comparison. To calculate the percent of increase or decrease over or under the budget, you divide the increase or decrease by the budgeted amount and express the answer as a percent.

▶ Fancy Flowers, Inc. created a budgeted income statement in January of 2010. They now wish to compare the actual numbers in December 2010 with the estimates they made at the beginning of the year.

DIRECTIONS

1. Open data file **4r1-budget**. Drag and drop data in **C13:C19** and **C21:C30** from column C to column B.

2. Delete column C and adjust the width of column B.

3. Set the following formats, as shown in Figure 4.11:
   a. Indent lists of expenses and total labels.
   b. Change the theme to **Origin** and make cell style settings in rows **1:5**.
   c. Add a thick bottom border to rows 4 and 5 and set Wrap Text alignment for column headings.

4. Enter formulas on the worksheet as listed below:
   a. In cell **E7**, find the Increase/Decrease from Budget. *Hint: Actual-Budget.*
   b. Format result for Commas with no decimal places. *Use the Comma Style button and Decrease Decimal button.*
   c. In cell **F7**, find the % Increase/Decrease and format for Percent style with one decimal place. *Hint: E7/Budget. Use the Percent button and Increase Decimal button.*
   d. Fill formulas from the range **E7:F7** down to **E35:F35**.
   e. In cell **C9**, find the Gross Profit on Operations. *Hint: Sales-Cost of Goods Sold.*
   f. In cell **C19** and **C30**, enter formulas to add expenses.
   g. In cell **C31**, enter the formula to add Total Selling Expenses and Total Administrative expenses.
   h. In cell **C33**, enter formula to find Net Income. *Hint: Gross Profit on Operations-Total Operating Expenses.*
   i. In cell **C35**, enter formula to find Net Income after Federal Income Tax. *Hint: Net Income before Federal Income Tax-Federal Income Tax.*
   j. AutoFill formulas across from column C to column D.

Continued on next page

5. Complete and correct formats for worksheet, as necessary:
   a. Delete dashes or zeros in columns E and F where there are no entries in Column C.
   b. Format any negative numbers in column E for red with parentheses and column F for red with no parentheses.
   c. Use Border tools to extend borders for rows 9, 19, 30, 31, and 35.
   d. Format numbers in columns C and D for commas, no decimals.
   e. Correct formats for borders and apply cell styles for totals rows as illustrated.
   f. Adjust the widths of columns C, D, and F to match Figure 4.11.

6. On the Page Layout tab, set to print the worksheet without gridlines and set Margins to center the worksheet horizontally and vertically.

7. Save the file **4r1-budget**, and close it.

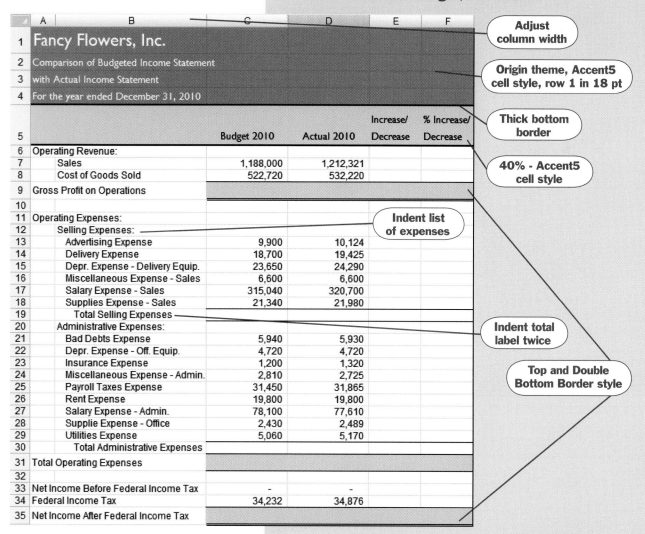

Figure 4.11: Budget analysis

Apply Borders
1. Select and right-click the range.
2. Click the **Borders list arrow** on the Mini toolbar.
3. Click a border style.

Apply Custom Borders
1. Select the range to receive borders.
2. Press **[Ctrl]+1**.
3. Click the **Border tab**.
4. Select the settings and click **OK**.

Remove Borders
1. Right-click range to clear.
2. Click the **Borders list arrow** on Mini toolbar.
3. Click **No Border**.

Format Decimals and Negative Numbers
1. Select data to format.
2. Press **[Ctrl]+1**, and click the **Number tab**.

3. Click the **Number category**.
4. Use arrows to set Decimal places.
5. Click desired negative numbers setting.
6. Click **comma indicator check box**, if appropriate, and click **OK**.

Indent Text
1. Select cells with data to indent.
2. Click **Home tab**, and in the Alignment group, click the **Increase Indent button**.

Add Font Color and Fill Color
1. Right-click cells to format.
2. Click **Font Color list arrow** or **Fill Color list arrow** on the Mini toolbar.
3. Click the color.

Insert Cells, Columns, or Rows
1. Select cell(s), column(s), or row(s) at the insertion point.
2. Click the **Home tab**, and in the Cells group, click the **Insert list arrow**.
3. Click to select item to insert.

Delete Columns or Rows
1. Select column(s) or row(s) to delete.
2. Click the **Home tab**, and in the Cells group, click the **Delete list arrow**.
3. Select item to delete.

Enter Numeric Label
1. Enter apostrophe (').
2. Enter a value and press **[Enter]**.

At the beginning of the year, All Sports Depot prepared a budgeted income statement for the first quarter. At the end of the quarter, March 31, they wish to compare their budget with actual data to find the areas where unexpected changes took place. You are to complete the budget analysis and format the report.

Follow these guidelines:

1. Open data file **4p1-budget**. Adjust column A to a width of 24, format row 5 for Wrap Text alignment, and adjust widths of columns D and E as necessary.

2. Use variations of the Accent1 cell style for headings in rows 1:5, as shown in Figure 4.12. Apply the All Borders setting to row 5 and increase font size of the company name in row 1.

3. Enter formulas listed below and AutoFill to column C:
   a. **B12**: Find Gross Profit. *Sales-Cost of Goods Sold.*
   b. **B27**: Find Total Expenses.
   c. **B29**: Find Net Income before Taxes. *Gross Profit-Expenses.*
   d. **B31**: Find Net Income after Taxes. *Net Income before Taxes-Taxes.*

4. Enter analysis formulas listed below and AutoFill down to calculate all data. Delete zeros or error messages where no data is present.
   a. **D7:** Find Increase/Decrease over budget. *Actual 1st Qtr-Budget 1st Qtr.*
   b. **E7:** Find % Increase/Decrease over budget. *D7/Budget 1st Qtr.* Format for Percent style with two decimal places.

5. Format worksheet as follows:
   a. Indent text in **A7**, **A10**, **A15:A27**.
   b. Format columns B, C, and D for commas with no decimal places.
   c. Extend the borders in rows 12, 27, and 31 to columns D and E.
   d. Format the negative numbers in column D in red with parentheses.
   e. Format totals in rows 12, 27, and 31 using an appropriate cell style.

6. Print a copy of the analysis without gridlines centered horizontally on the page.

	A	B	C	D	E
1	All Sports Depot				
2	Comparison of Budgeted Income Statement with Actual Income Statement				
3	For Quarter Ended March 31, 2010				
4					
5		Budget 1st Qtr	Actual 1st Qtr	Increase/ Decrease from Budget	% of Increase/ Decrease from Budget

Figure 4.12: Formatted headings

TRYOUT

GOAL

To create a billings analysis using a table, as shown in Figure 4.13

✵ Format data as a table
✵ Sort and filter data

TASK 2

Event Planners, Inc.

Analysis of Billings for NY and NJ Personnel   30-Jun-10

Last	First	Gender	Hire Date	Location	Billings 2009	Billings YTD
Arvin	Barry	M	3/15/2002	NY	867,098	453,678
Beck	Tanya	F	12/10/2001	NY	976,234	654,555
Castegno	Vera	F	10/26/2003	NJ	765,987	345,876
Frazer	William	M	7/7/2005	NY	654,765	453,678
Hudson	Jennifer	F	7/31/2000	NJ	1,087,644	656,789
Kostick	Alfred	M	4/17/2006	NJ	699,876	365,434
McCarthy	Marie	F	6/15/2000	NY	1,543,876	768,765
Parkerson	Marcia	F	5/3/2003	NJ	876,456	488,765
Rimenez	Mario	M	8/9/2007	NY	651,234	354,876
Sung	Paula	F	6/15/2008	NY	454,434	346,543
Thompson	Tanisha	F	2/25/2002	NJ	998,098	542,554
Total					9,575,702	5,431,513

Sort/Filter Arrow

Excel table

Total line

Figure 4.13: Task 2: Billings analysis

WHAT YOU NEED TO KNOW

Format Data as a Table

▶ Data arranged in columns with headers or in a list is called a **table**. You can summarize, format, sort, or filter tables to arrange or find data. You can create a table using the Table button, as shown in Figures 4.14 and 4.15, and then enter the data.

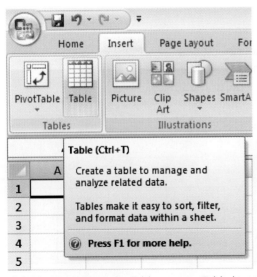

Figure 4.14: Insert tab, Tables group, Table button

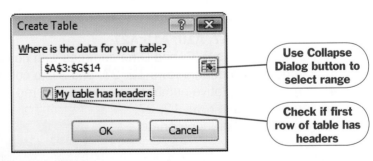

Use Collapse Dialog button to select range

Check if first row of table has headers

Figure 4.15: Create Table dialog box

 **HOW Ctrl+t** **1.** Select the table range. **2.** Click the **Insert tab**, and in the Tables group, click the **Table button**. **3.** In the Create Table dialog box, click the **My table has headers check box**, if applicable. **4.** Enter table data.

T R Y *i t* **O U T** *e4-6*

1. On a new Excel worksheet, select the range **A1:E10**.

2. Click the **Insert tab**, and in the Tables group, click the **Table button**.

3. Click the **My table has headers check box**, and click **OK**. *A table ready for data appears.*

4. Close and do not save the file.

Apply and Change Quick Styles

▶ You can also create the data first and then format it as a table. Use predefined table styles, or **Quick Styles**, to format a table, as shown in Figure 4.16. Once a table style is set it can be changed by selecting another style while in the table.

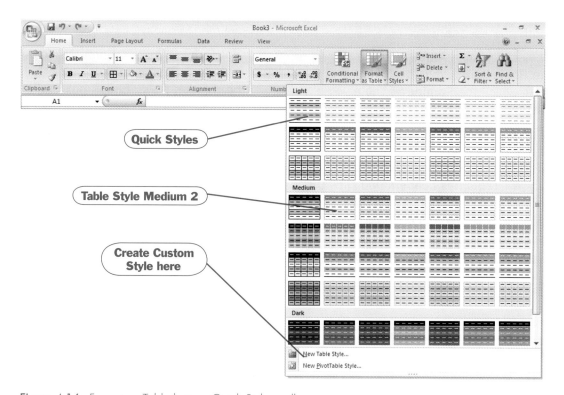

Figure 4.16: Format as Table button, Quick Styles gallery

HOW **1.** Select the range containing table data. **2.** Click the **Home tab**, and in the Styles group, click the **Format as Table button**. **3.** Click a Quick Style. **4.** In the Format As Table dialog box, click the **My table has headers check box**, if applicable.

Table Style Options

▶ Once you create the table or are in a table, the Table Tools Design tab appears, as shown in Figure 4.17. In the Table Style Options group, you can display or delete the header row, total row, banded rows, first column, last column, and/or banded columns. **Banded rows or columns** are displayed with alternating colors to make the data easier to read.

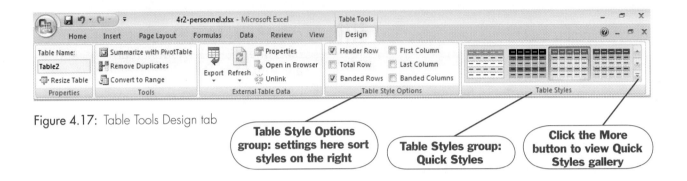

Figure 4.17: Table Tools Design tab

Table Style Options group: settings here sort styles on the right

Table Styles group: Quick Styles

Click the More button to view Quick Styles gallery

T R Y *it* O U T e4-7

1. Open data file **e4-7** and adjust column width as necessary.

2. Select the range **A2:E9** and click the **Home tab**, and in the Styles group, click the **Format as Table button**. *The Quick Styles gallery appears.*

3. Click **Table Style Medium 2** in the Quick Styles gallery, as shown in Figure 4.16. *If the Format as Table dialog box appears, click **My table has headers** and click **OK**. The data displays in table format, and the Table Tools Design tab appears.*

4. With the cursor in any table cell, change the Quick Style to **Table Style Medium 3**.

Click the arrow in the Table Styles group to see the Quick Styles gallery.

5. On the Table Tools Design tab, in the Table Style Options group, click to select the **Banded Rows check box** and the **Banded columns check box**. *Note the change and the change in the Quick Styles displayed.*

6. Click to deselect the **Header Row check box**, note the change, and then reselect **Header Row**.

7. Select and deselect **Last Column** and **First Column** and note the bolding.

8. Close and do not save the file.

Insert and Delete Rows and Columns

▶ You may insert or delete columns or rows in a table by selecting the location for the change and using the shortcut menu, as shown in Figure 4.18. Columns will insert to the left or right and rows will be inserted above or below the cell depending on the location.

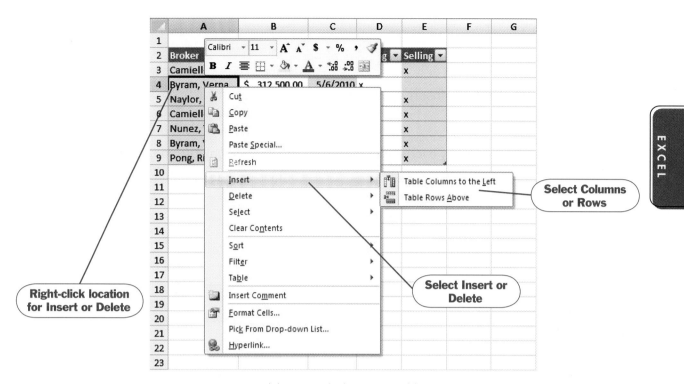

Figure 4.18: Insert or delete rows/columns in a table

Add Total Row and Change Summary Function

▶ When you add a total row to a table, each cell in the total line will have a summary functions list that you may select for the data, as shown in Figure 4.19.

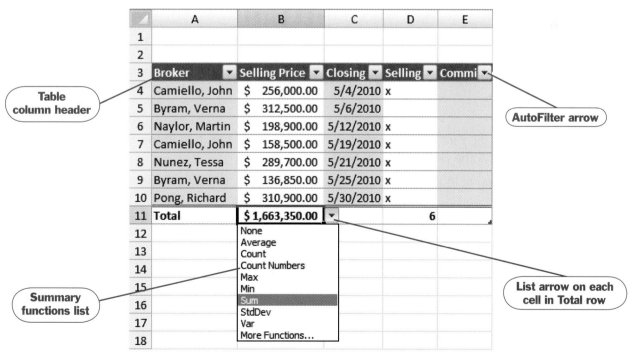

Figure 4.19: Total row and summary functions list

HOW **1.** Click any cell in the table. **2.** Click the **Table Tools Design tab**, and in the Table Style Options group, click **Total Row**. **3.** In any cell in Total row, click the **summary functions list arrow** and select a summary function.

1. Open data file **e4-8**.

2. Right-click in cell **E3** and insert a column to the right of the cell.

3. In the new column, enter **Commission** as the column heading by overwriting the default heading.

4. Click the **Table Tools Design tab**, and in the Table Style Options group, click **Total Row**.

5. In cell **B10**, click the **summary functions list arrow** and click **Sum**.

6. In cells **D10** and **E10**, summarize using the Count function, if necessary.

7. Right-click cell **D2** and delete the column.

8. Close and do not save the file.

Sort and Filter Data

Sort Data

▶ Sorting and filtering data is an important part of data analysis. When you apply a **sort**, you order data alphabetically, from highest to lowest, or the reverse. You can sort data in a non-table range using the Sort and Filter group on the Data tab, as shown in Figure 4.20.

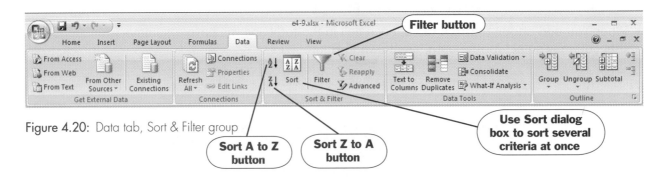

Figure 4.20: Data tab, Sort & Filter group

HOW 1. Select the range to be sorted. 2. Click the **Data tab**, and in the Sort & Filter group, click the **Sort A to Z** or **Sort Z to A button**.

▶ You will use the filtering tools discussed in the next segment to sort data in tables.

1. Open data file **e4-9**. *The workbook contains two sheets: Normal Range: data in a normal Excel range, and Table Range: data in an Excel table.*

2. On the Normal Range sheet, select **A3:E9**.

3. Click the **Data tab**, and in the Sort & Filter group, click the **Sort A to Z** **button**. *The records are sorted by the brokers' last names.*

4. With the range still selected, click the **Sort Z to A button**.

5. Click the **Undo button**.

6. Save the file, but do not close it.

Filter Data

▶ **AutoFilter** is the system for sorting provided in Excel tables. It hides all items that do not meet the criteria you set. For example, if you select Byram, Verna, the broker, as the criterion, only those records are displayed, and all others are filtered out. To remove the filter, click Clear Filter. Filters are included on the sort/filter list for each column in a table, as shown in Figure 4.21.

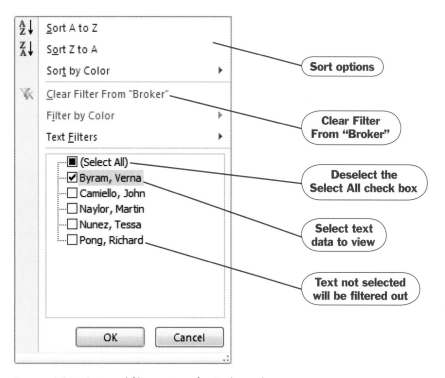

Figure 4.21: Sort and filter options for Broker column

HOW **1.** Click the **AutoFilter arrow** in a table column heading. **2.** Click to deselect **Select All check box**. **3.** Make criteria settings, and click **OK**.

TRY it OUT *e4-10*

1. Continue to work in the open file or open data file **e4-10**.

2. Click the **Table Range sheet tab**, and click the **AutoFilter arrow** in table header cell **A3**. Click **Sort A to Z**.

3. Click cell **B3** and sort largest to smallest.

4. Click cell **C3** and sort oldest to newest. Click the **Undo button**.

5. Click the **AutoFilter list arrow** in **A3**, deselect the **Select All check box**, and click **Byram, Verna**. Click **OK**. *Only the records for Verna Byram appear and are totaled.*

6. Click the same **AutoFilter list arrow**, then click **Clear Filter From "Broker"**.

7. Click the **AutoFilter list arrow** in D3, and set criteria to show only X data.

8. Clear the filter.

9. Click the **Data tab**, and in the Sort & Filter group, click **Filter**. *Note that the filter arrows are disabled.* Click **Filter** again to enable AutoFilter.

10. Close the file, but do not save it.

WHAT YOU NEED TO KNOW

▶ Data analysis is easier using the table format because ranges can be sorted and filtered to provide answers to questions about the information. Sorts and filters may also be done on normal data ranges, but table ranges provide sort and filter options for each column of data.

▶ Data tables can be formatted using Quick Styles. The styles are modified using the Table Tools Design tab.

▶ Event Planners, Inc., operating in New York and New Jersey, would like to create an Excel table to analyze the billings for planning services submitted by each employee. **Billings** are invoices that bill the clients for the services delivered. They are comparing the billings for the year-to-date with the total billings from last year and would like to use sorting and filtering to answer questions about the data.

DIRECTIONS

1. Open data file **4r2-billings**, and adjust column width as necessary.

2. Enter and format worksheet titles as shown in Figure 4.22.

3. Select the range **A4:G15**, and format it as a table with headers using **Table Style Medium 14**.

4. Set table styles for banded columns, no banded rows, and last column options.

5. Format table columns F and G for commas with no decimal places.

6. Add a Total Row to the table and select the Sum function for columns F and G, if necessary.

7. Sort the table by Hire Date from the oldest to the newest.
   a. Which employee has the most seniority?
   b. What are the Year to Date Billings for that employee?

8. Sort by Last name in A to Z order.

9. Filter the Location column so that only NJ employees display.
   a. What is the Total Year to Date billings for NJ?
   b. Change the function to Average. What is the average billing for NJ employees?

10. Filter the Location column so that only NY employees display.
    a. What is the average billing for NY employees?
    b. Change the function to Sum. What is the Total Year to Date billings for NY?

11. Clear the filter from the Location column.

12. Click the **Data tab**, and in the Sort & Filter group, click the **Filter button** to turn off AutoFilter arrows in the table.

Continued on next page

13. Print a copy of the billing analysis.

14. Save and close the file.

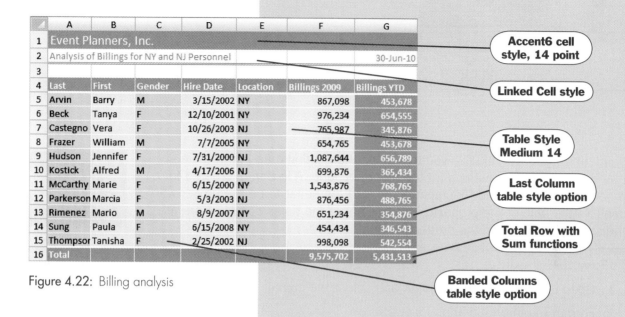

Figure 4.22: Billing analysis

Cues for Reference

Create a Table [Ctrl]+T
1. Select the table range.
2. Click the **Insert tab**, and in the Tables group, click the **Table button**.
3. In the Create Table dialog box, click the **My table has headers check box**, if applicable.
4. Enter table data.

Format Data as a Table
1. Select the range containing table data.
2. Click the **Home tab**, and in the Styles group, click the **Format as Table button**.

3. Select a Quick Style.
4. In the Format as Table dialog box, click the **My table has headers check box**, if applicable.

Set Table Style Options
1. Click in the table.
2. Click the **Table Tools Design tab**, and in the Table Style Options group, click the desired option.

Insert/Delete Rows or Columns in a Table
1. Right-click in the location for the change.
2. Click the **Insert** or **Delete** from the menu.
3. Click selection to insert or delete.

Add Total Row and Change Summary Function
1. Click in the table.
2. Click the **Table Tools Design tab**, and in the Table Style Options group, click the **Total Row check box**.
3. In a Total Row cell, click the **summary function list arrow** to the right of the cell, then click the desired function.

Sort/Filter Data in a Table
1. Click in the table on the header of data to be sorted/filtered.
2. Click the **AutoFilter list arrow**.
3. Click sort or filter options, then click **OK**.

PERFORMANCE

TASK 2

Palmetto Realtors would like you to change their listing data into a table so that they can analyze listings for the month of June. A **listing** is created for a property when an agency has contracted with the seller to be the broker who controls the sale of the property. They will share the sales commission with the selling broker when the property is sold.

Follow these guidelines:

1. Open the data file **4p2-listings**, and adjust the column width as necessary.

2. Format the information as follows:
   a. **Title line**: Use the Accent3 cell style and increase the font size as desired.
   b. **Data range**: Format as a table in Table Style Light 11.
   c. **Price column**: Accounting style with no decimal places.

3. In A9, insert a row into the table and add the following data:

Dembar	6/30/2010	876 No. Ocean Drive	Hallandale	Condo	3	2	$ 475,000

4. Format the table using the Last Column and Total Row options.

5. Add the **Palmetto Realtors.tif** picture file to the right header of the report, and format the picture so that it is scaled to 50%. Add the filename to the center footer area. Set the report to print in landscape centered horizontally.

6. Answer the following questions by using total functions, and/or by sorting and filtering the data:
   a. Average, maximum, and minimum value of all listings.
   b. Total listings for each broker: Barona, Dembar, Garcia, Lincoln.
   c. Total and average the listings for Hallandale and Hollywood.
   d. Which properties are available with three or more bedrooms? Print a copy of that filtered list.

7. Print a copy of the table with all filters cleared.

8. Close and save the file.

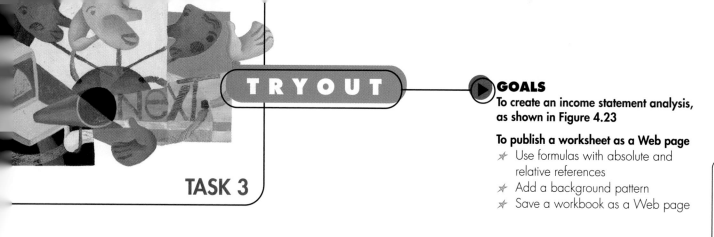

TRYOUT

GOALS
To create an income statement analysis, as shown in Figure 4.23

To publish a worksheet as a Web page
* Use formulas with absolute and relative references
* Add a background pattern
* Save a workbook as a Web page

TASK 3

EXCEL

File saved and published as a Web page

Management Update

	2009 Summary	2010 Summary	Increase/ Decrease	% Increase/ Decrease		2009 Summary	% of Sales	2010 Summary	% of Sales
Income:									
Net Sales	1,647,778	1,548,911	(98,867)	-6.00%		1,647,778	100%	1,548,911	100%
Less: Cost of Goods Sold	1,045,212	990,543	(54,669)	-5.23%		1,045,212	63%	990,543	64%
Gross Profit	602,566	558,368	(44,198)	-7.33%		602,566	37%	558,368	36%
Expenses:	446,049	415,789	(30,260)	-6.78%		446,049	27%	415,789	27%
Net Income before Taxes	156,517	142,579	(13,938)	-8.91%		156,517	9%	142,579	9%
Less: Taxes	46,955	42,774	(4,181)	-8.91%		46,955	3%	42,774	3%
Net Income after Taxes	109,562	99,805	(9,757)	-8.91%		109,562	7%	99,805	6%

Miami Swimwear, Inc.
Income Statement Summary Comparison
For Years Ended December 31, 2009 and 2010

Figure 4.23: Task 3: Income statement analysis

Formulas using relative reference

Formulas using absolute reference

WHAT YOU NEED TO KNOW

Use Formulas with Absolute and Relative References

▶ When you copy formulas from one cell to another, the cell references change, relative to their new location, as shown in Figure 4.24. This is called a **relative reference**, the most commonly used technique of entering and copying formulas.

▶ However, in some cases a value in a formula must remain constant when copied to other locations. This is called an **absolute reference**. To identify a cell value as an absolute reference, or a constant, a dollar sign ($) must precede the column and row references for that cell.

▶ For example, you need an absolute reference to find the percentage that each value in a list represents of the total, because the total must be the constant in each formula. Therefore, in the formula =E5/$E$17, $E$17 represents the total and is an absolute reference to that row and column number. When this formula is copied, E17 remains constant in the formula, but E5, with no absolute reference code, changes relative to the formula location for each value in the list.

1. Press [=]. **2.** Enter cell addresses in formula. **3.** Press **[F4]** after any cell entry that should be an absolute reference. Or, if you wish to have a mixed reference, press the $ as required. **4.** Press **[Enter]**.

	A	B	C	D	E	F	G	H	I
1	EXPENSE ANALYSIS								
2									
3		2009	2010	Increase/Decrease	2009	% of Total	2010	% of Total	
4	Expenses:								
5	Advertising/promotions	12701	14689	=C5-B5	12701	=E5/$E$17	14689	=G5/$G$17	
6	Depreciation	21544	21544	=C6-B6	21544	=E6/$E$17	21544	=G6/$G$17	
7	Insurance	18000	18000	=C7-B7	18000	=E7/$E$17	18000	=G7/$G$17	
8	Legal/accounting	13165	15965	=C8-B8	13165	=E8/$E$17	15965	=G8/$G$17	
9	Loan interest payments	25500	25500	=C9-B9	25500	=E9/$E$17	25500	=G9/$G$17	
10	Miscellaneous expenses	8576	10644	=C10-B10	8576	=E10/$E$17	10644	=G10/$G$17	
11	Payroll expenses	10322	11434	=C11-B11	10322	=E11/$E$17	11434	=G11/$G$17	
12	Rent	204000	225000	=C12-B12	204000	=E12/$E$17	225000	=G12/$G$17	
13	Repairs/maintenance	5439	6547	=C13-B13	5439	=E13/$E$17	6547	=G13/$G$17	
14	Salaries/wages	81342	82434	=C14-B14	81342	=E14/$E$17	82434	=G14/$G$17	
15	Supplies	5765	6805	=C15-B15	5765	=E15/$E$17	6805	=G15/$G$17	
16	Utilities	6987	7487	=C16-B16	6987	=E16/$E$17	7487	=G16/$G$17	
17	Total Expenses	=SUM(B5:B16)	=SUM(C5:C16)	=C17-B17	=SUM(E5:E16)	=E17/$E$17	=SUM(G5:G16)	=G17/$G$17	
18									

Figure 4.24: Data file e4-11 with formulas displayed

Relative reference formulas that change depending on location

Absolute reference formula with Total (E17) as a constant

TRY it OUT e4-11

1. Open data file **e4-11**.

2. Click cell **D5**, and note the formula on the formula bar.

3. Copy the formula down to cell **D17**, and view the formulas. *The formulas are copied relative to their locations, as shown in Figure 4.24.*

4. Enter a formula in cell **F5** to find the percentage each expense is of the total. *Hint: = E5/$E$17: press [=], click E5, press [/], click cell E17, press the F4 key to enter the dollar signs, and press [Enter].*

5. Format the value for Percent style with no decimal places.

6. Use the fill handle to copy the formula down to cell **F17**.

7. View the formulas for each expense. *The formulas are copied with an absolute reference for cell E17 since all numbers should be divided by the same number.*

8. Complete the formulas for column **H** and format for Percent style with no decimal places. *You can click the Formulas tab, and click Show Formulas to compare your worksheet to Figure 4.24.*

9. Save and close the file.

Add a Background Pattern

▶ A **background** is a pattern that is added to a worksheet to enhance its display for a visual presentation, using a picture file. The background pattern does not print, will fill the sheet, and will be retained in the saved file. To further enhance the display you may want to remove the gridlines and headings and use the full screen setting. Remove the background by clicking the Page Layout tab, and in the Page Setup group, click Delete Background.

HOW **1.** Click the **Page Layout tab**, and in the Page Setup group, click the **Background button**. **2.** Move to the correct folder. *The system will default to a Picture folder.* **3.** Double-click the picture file. *The picture will either fill the screen or repeat until the screen is filled.*

Background

TRY*it*OUT *e4-12*

1. Open data file **e4-12**.

2. Click the **Page Layout tab**, and in the Page Setup group, click **Background**.

3. In the Sheet Background dialog box, locate your data file folder and double-click **golf.jpg**. *The picture fills the screen background.*

4. On the Page Layout tab, in the Sheet Options group, deselect the **Gridlines** and **Headings View check boxes**.

5. Click the **View tab**, and, in the Workbook Views group, click the **Full**

Screen button. *You can use this screen for a presentation.* Click the **Restore Down button**.

6. Press **[Ctrl]+[F2]** to print preview the worksheet. *Note that the background will not print.* Close the preview screen.

7. Click the **Page Layout tab**, and in the Page setup group, click the **Delete Background button**.

8. Close and do not save the file.

Save a Workbook as a Web Page

▶ A **Web page** is a location on an Internet server, part of the World Wide Web, which can be reached and identified by a Web address. You can make workbooks available to employees or stockholders by saving all or part of a workbook as a Web page, so that users can view the worksheet without Excel. Before you save an Excel workbook as a Web page, however, carefully edit and check the content.

▶ Web pages have an .htm or .html file extension. When you save a worksheet as a Web page, Excel creates a folder where it saves all the page's supporting files. This may create a problem if you move files because the supporting folder has to be moved as well. To avoid the problem, you can save the page as a Single File Web page with the .mht or .mhtml extension. In this case, all the supporting files are part of the Web page file.

► You can create a title for your Web page by clicking the Change Title button in the Save As dialog box. The Set Page Title dialog box opens, as shown in Figure 4.25, and the title you enter will display centered over your worksheet on the Web page.

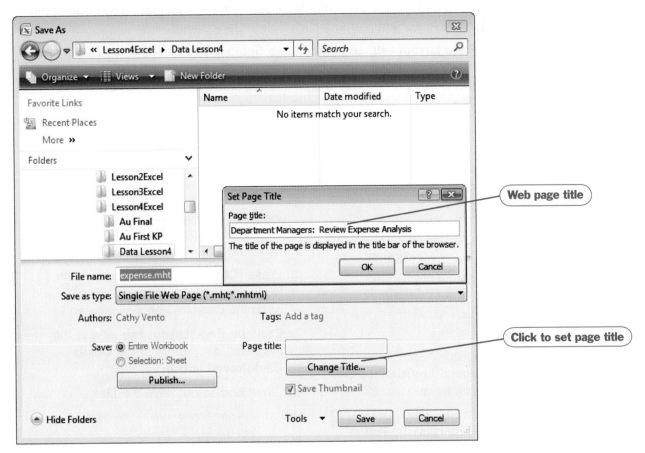

Figure 4.25: Save as a Single File Web Page with Set Page Title dialog box

► When you click **Publish** in the Save As dialog box, the Publish as Web Page dialog box displays, as shown in Figure 4.26. You can elect to AutoRepublish every time the workbook is updated and saved. The published page is saved to your local drive, and the Web page opens in Internet Explorer or your Web browser for you to preview. To publish it directly to the Internet, your company or school would need to have an account with a Web site hosting company.

HOW 1. Press **[F12]**. 2. In the Save as type box, click **Single File Web Page (*.mht;*.mhtml)**. 3. Name the page. 4. Click **Change Title** and enter Web page title. 5. Click **OK**, and click **Publish** twice.

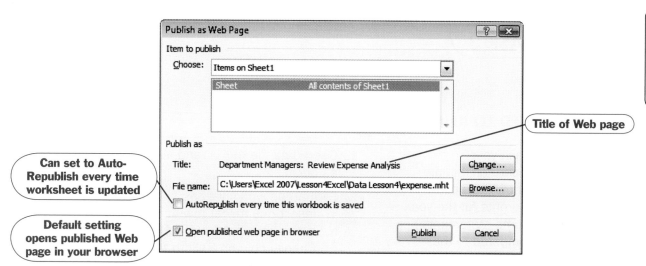

Title of Web page

Can set to Auto-Republish every time worksheet is updated

Default setting opens published Web page in your browser

Figure 4.26: Publish as Web Page dialog box

TRY it OUT e4-13

1. Open data file **e4-13**.

2. Press **[F12]**, and in the Save as type box, click **Single File Web Page (*.mht;*.mhtml)**.

3. Name the Web page **Expense**.

4. Click **Change Title**, enter **Department Managers: Review Expense Analysis**, and click **OK**.

5. Click **Publish**.

6. On the Publish as Web Page dialog box, click **Open published web page in browser check box**, and click **Publish**. *The file will open in Internet Explorer or your default browser.*

7. Close the browser and the file. Do not save the file.

▶ GOALS

To create an income statement analysis with absolute reference formulas

To save the file as a Web page

TASK 3

WHAT YOU NEED TO KNOW

▶ At the end of each year businesses prepare an **income statement** to show the income, expenses, and profits for the year. The current income statement data may be compared to the statement for the previous year to determine trends.

▶ To make a comparison, we can compare the percentage each item is of net sales for each year. Because net sales are used as a constant in every formula for this analysis, it is necessary to use an absolute reference.

▶ In this Rehearsal activity, you will prepare a comparison of summary income statements for Miami Swimsuits, Inc. for two years, add a background for a presentation for an office meeting, and save it as a Web page for distribution to off-site staff members.

▽ DIRECTIONS

1. Open data file **4r3-is**, and adjust the column width as necessary.

2. Format the worksheet as shown in Figure 4.27:
   a. Insert one row at row 4.
   b. Indent text in **A8** and **A16**.
   c. Change column F width to **3.00**.
   d. Copy data in the range **B7:C17** to **G7**.
   e. Insert a column at column H.
   f. Add column headings as shown and use Wrap text alignment.
   g. Use the Paper theme and cell styles shown to format the worksheet.
   h. Format numbers for commas with no decimal places.

3. Enter a formula in cell **D7**, to find the increase/decrease between the two years' data. *Hint: =2010 Summary–2009 Summary.*

4. Press **[Ctrl]+1** and use the Format Cells dialog box to format negative numbers in black font with parentheses.

5. Enter a formula in cell **E7** to find the % Increase/Decrease and format for Percent style with two decimal places. *Hint: =(Increase/Decrease)/2009 Summary.*

6. Copy the formula down for each item, and delete unnecessary formula results.

7. In cell **H7**, enter a formula using an absolute reference, to find the percentage each line is of net sales. *Hint: =G7/$G$7.*

8. Format the result for Percent style with no decimal places. *The answer in cell **H7** should be 100%, because the sales are 100% of the sales.*

Continued on next page

9. Copy the formula down for each item, and delete unnecessary formula results. *The values are percentages that each value is of sales, creating a basis for comparison.*

10. Repeat Steps 7–9 for column J data.

11. Delete row 12.

12. Check your formats and results.

13. Save the worksheet as a Single File Web page, using **4r3-isweb** as the filename. Add the title **Management Update** and publish the analysis. Close the browser.

14. Add a background pattern to the worksheet using the data file **beachbackground.jpg**. Remove the gridlines and headings and change your worksheet to Full Screen view. *This background will not print but can be saved with the file.*

15. Restore the screen, gridlines, and headings. Delete the background.

16. Save the file as **4r3-is**, and close it.

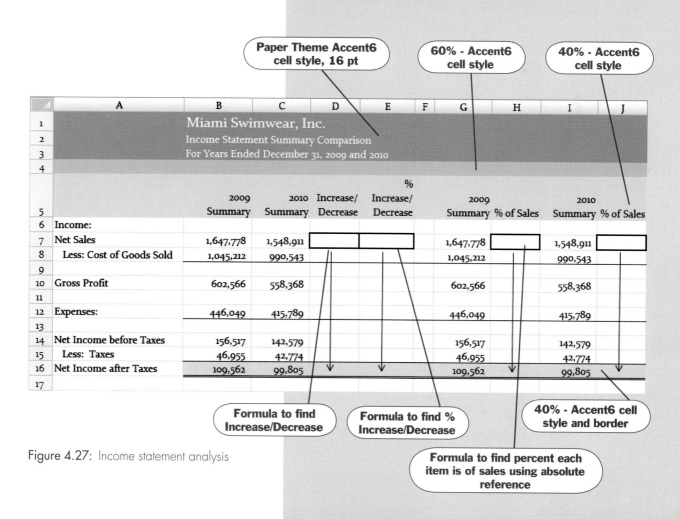

Figure 4.27: Income statement analysis

Use Absolute Reference Formulas

1. Enter a formula, including an absolute reference cell.
2. Press **[F4]** to insert dollar signs to make the reference absolute.

Add Background Pattern

1. Click the **Page Layout tab**, and in the Page Setup group, click the **Background button**.

2. Double-click the graphic.

Save as Web Page and View in Browser

1. Press **[F12]**, and in the Save as type box, click **Single File Web Page (*.mht, *mhtml)**.
2. Click **Change Title**, and enter a Web page title, then click **OK**.

3. Name the file.
4 Click **Publish**.
5. In the Publish as Web Page dialog box, click **Open published web page in browser**, then click **Publish**.

Barlow Foods, Inc., a large food producer and distributor, has prepared an analysis of their income sources comparing this year's data to last year. You are to complete the analysis using Figure 4.28 as a guide and publish the worksheet as a Web page.

Follow these guidelines:

1. Open data file **4p3-income**.

2. Format the worksheet as shown, adding column headings, fill color, borders, alignments, and totals for columns **B** and **C**.

3. Enter appropriate formulas in columns **D** and **E**. Format column **E** for Percent style with one decimal place, and copy formulas down for all data rows.

4. Change column **F** to a width of 3.00 and use fill color as shown. Copy data from column **C** to column **G**.

5. Enter an absolute reference formula in **H6** to find the percentage that each revenue item is of the total. Format the information for Percent style with one decimal place, and copy the formula down for all items. Check formatting and correct if necessary.

6. Save the file, and then save it again as **4p3-incomeweb.mht** in Single File Web Page format. Enter **Annual Income Analysis** as the Web page title, and publish the page.

7. Close the browser and the file.

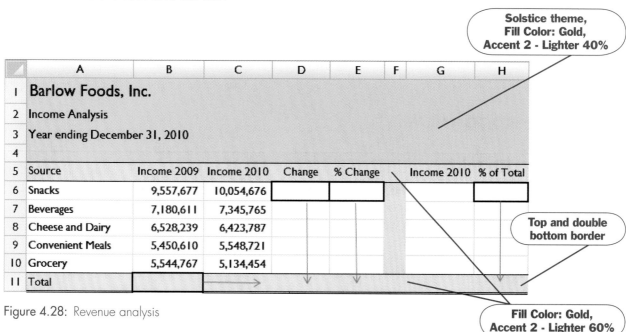

Figure 4.28: Revenue analysis

GOAL
To create a revenue analysis on multiple worksheets, as shown in Figure 4.29
* Manage workbooks
* Use Paste Special

TASK 4

	A	B	C	D	E
1	PERFECT PLANNING GROUP				
2	Revenue and Billings Analysis				
3		January	February	March	Total
4	Billings for Contract Vendors:				
5	Food/Catering	53,445	43,766	33,232	130,443
6	Hotels/Venues	87,543	65,888	73,455	226,886
7	Printing/Advertising	13,232	10,533	8,564	32,329
8	Music/Entertainment	45,865	45,865	45,865	137,595
9	Personnel/Speakers/Security	56,454	43,566	44,345	144,365
10	Audio/Visual	17,654	15,433	13,245	46,332
11	Computers/Special Equipment	54,333	54,678	32,122	141,133
12	Miscellaneous	11,342	9,453	6,590	27,385
13	Total	339,868	289,182	257,418	886,468
14					
15	Revenue:				
16	Fees on Contracts	61,176	52,053	46,335	159,564
17	Consultation Revenues	10,540	11,450	11,340	33,330
18	Total	71,716	63,503	57,675	192,894
19					
20					
21					

1st Qtr. / 2nd Qtr. / 3rd Qtr. / 4th Qtr. / Summary

Multiple worksheets in workbook

Figure 4.29: Task 4: Revenue analysis

WHAT YOU NEED TO KNOW

Manage Workbooks

▶ You can create the same worksheet for several months or for several divisions of the same company by using multiple worksheets in the same workbook. You can delete, insert, rename, move, copy, and hide sheets in a workbook.

Insert and Delete Worksheets

▶ A new workbook opens with three sheet tabs, labeled Sheet1 through Sheet3, and the Insert Worksheet button. The active sheet tab is white, and the inactive sheet tabs are shaded. The **tab scrolling buttons** allow you to scroll hidden sheets into view, as shown in Figure 4.30.

▶ You can insert and delete sheets by right-clicking a sheet tab and clicking Insert or Delete on the shortcut menu, as shown in Figure 4.31.

Figure 4.30: Sheet tabs and tab scrolling buttons

HOW Shift+F11   Insert Sheet: Click Insert Worksheet button.

HOW   Delete Sheet: **1.** Right-click the sheet tab. **2.** Click **Delete**.

Figure 4.31: Shortcut menu: Right-click any sheet tab

Reposition Worksheets

▶ You can move sheets by using the drag-and-drop method. When you drag the sheet tab, the mouse pointer displays a black arrowhead and a sheet icon that you can drop in any location.

Copy Data Between Worksheets

▶ You can copy ranges of data from one worksheet to another in the same workbook by using the sheet tab to locate the paste location.

HOW   **1.** Select and right-click range of data to be copied from source sheet. **2.** Click **Copy**. **3.** Click the sheet tab of the paste location. **4.** Right-click in cell, and then click **Paste**.

T R Y *i t* **O U T** *e4-14*

1. Open data file **e4-14**.

2. Click the **Insert Worksheet tab**. *The active sheet is a new sheet labeled Sheet4.*

3. Right-click the **Sheet3 tab**, click **Insert**, and click **OK** in the Insert dialog box. *The active sheet is a new sheet labeled Sheet5, and they are out of order.*

4. Right-click **Sheet4 tab**, then click **Delete**.

5. Click and drag the **Sheet5 tab** to the position after the **Sheet3 tab**.

6. Click on the **Sheet1 tab**, select and right-click the range **C14:F17**, then click **Copy**.

7. Click the **Sheet2 tab**, and then right-click in cell **C14**. Click **Paste**. The summary formulas are copied to Sheet 2.

8. Click the **Sheet1 tab**. Do not close the file.

Rename and Format Worksheet Tabs

▶ Select Rename on the shortcut menu to rename a worksheet tab, as shown in Figure 4.31, or double-click the sheet tab and enter the new name.

▶ You can format the color of the sheet tab by clicking Tab Color on the shortcut menu. Then, select the color from the palette that appears, as shown in Figure 4.32. The color displays at the bottom of the tab if it is active, or, the color will fill the tab of inactive sheets.

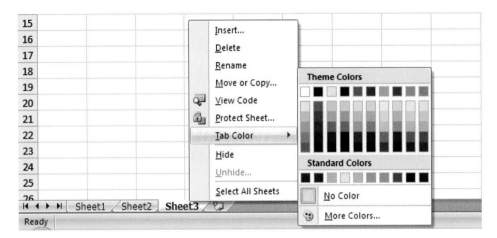

Figure 4.32: Format tab color

Hide and Unhide Worksheets

▶ You may wish to hide worksheets from view to simplify the workbook or to remove sheets from the view of other users.

HOW Hide: **1.** Right-click the sheet to be hidden. **2.** Click **Hide**.

HOW Unhide: **1.** Right-click on any tab. **2.** Click **Unhide**. **3.** Select the sheet to unhide, and click **OK**.

TRY it OUT e4-15

1. Continue to work in the open file, or open data file **e4-15**.

2. Rename Sheet1 to January: double-click the tab and enter **January**.

3. Rename Sheet2 to **February** and Sheet3 to **March**.

4. Format tab colors for January, February, and March to Red, Green, and Blue, using the Standard colors section of the palette.

5. Right-click **Sheet5**, and click **Hide**.

6. Right-click on any tab and click **Unhide**. Click **OK**.

7. Do not close the file.

Use Paste Special

▶ When you used the Copy and Paste functions in previous tasks, you copied the entire contents of a cell. If you want to copy and paste specific cell contents, use the Paste options list on the Home tab, as shown in Figure 4.35 and as listed in Table 4.1.

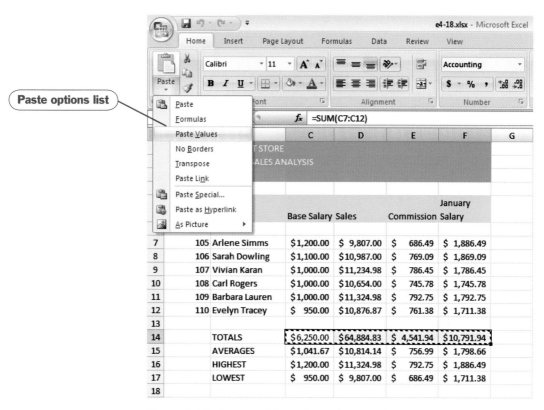

Figure 4.35: Copy and Paste Special options list

Table 4.1: Paste options list

PASTE OPTION	RESULT
Formulas	Formulas are pasted relative to the new location
Paste Values	Numeric values are pasted without formulas in cases where location will not support formulas
No Borders	Formulas, values, and formats are pasted without borders
Transpose	Vertical data is pasted as horizontal data or vice versa
Paste Link	Values are pasted and linked so that if one is changed the other will change

▶ If you have custom pasting requirements, click Paste Special, or right-click and click **Paste Special**, which displays the Paste Special dialog box, shown in Figure 4.36.

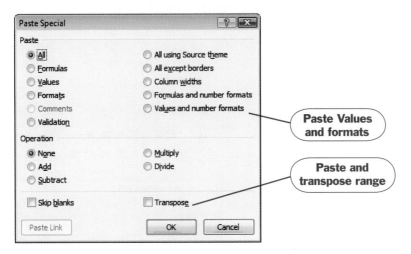

Figure 4.36: Paste Special dialog box

1. Continue to work in the open file or open data file **e4-18**.

2. On the January sheet, select and right-click the range **C14:F14**, the formulas for totals on the January sheet, and click **Copy**.

3. Click the **Summary sheet tab**, right-click in cell **C6**, then click **Paste**. *Zeros or a #REF error appears because the formulas do not work in this location.*

4. Click the **Home tab**, and in the Clipboard group, click the **Paste button list arrow**, then click **Paste Values**. Adjust the column width as necessary. *Only the resulting values of the formulas appear.*

5. Repeat Steps 2, 3, and 4 for the February and March data. Format the data for Accounting style with two decimal places.

6. To transpose employee names: On the January sheet, copy the range **B7:B12**, and then right-click in cell **G5** on the Summary sheet. Click **Paste Special**, and in the Paste Special dialog box, click **Transpose**, then click **OK**. *The employee names are transposed to row 5.* Format the column headings for Wrap text.

7. To paste employee salary totals from each month's sheet to the Summary sheet: On the January sheet, copy the range **F7:F12**, and then right-click in cell **G6** on the Summary sheet. Click **Paste Special**, and in the Paste Special dialog box, click **Transpose** and **Values and number formats**, then click **OK**. *The salary total values and their formats are transposed.* Adjust the column width as necessary.

8. Repeat Step 7 for February and March, pasting the values to **G7** and **G8** on the Summary sheet.

9. On the Summary sheet, in cell **C10**, enter a formula to find the total. AutoFill the formula across to cell **L10**.

10. Save the file **e4-18**. Close the file.

REHEARSAL

TASK 4

GOAL
To create a revenue analysis on multiple worksheets

WHAT YOU NEED TO KNOW

▶ **Revenue**, or income, for a business will vary depending on seasonal or economic factors. Business owners analyze revenue figures to note trends and warning signs, and to make management decisions.

▶ Perfect Planning Group plans conferences, parties, seminars, meetings, and the like. The company makes arrangements with vendors such as hotels, food caterers, printers, and so on, to plan clients' events. Its revenues come from charges for consultation hours and a charge of 18% of all contract vendor bills.

▶ In this Rehearsal activity, you will create a revenue analysis workbook using a quarterly analysis on multiple worksheets.

DIRECTIONS

1. Open data file **4r4-revenue**, adjust column width as necessary, and set workbook to Origin theme.

2. Insert an additional worksheet at the end of the workbook.

3. Copy column A from Sheet1 to remaining sheets:
   a. Copy column A on Sheet1.
   b. Group Sheets2–4 by clicking the **Sheet2 tab**, pressing and holding **[Shift]**, and clicking the **Sheet4 tab**.
   c. Paste data to cell **A1** on Sheet2. Column A data will be shown on all sheets, and the column will be AutoFitted.

4. Rename Sheets 1–4: **1st Qtr.**, **2nd Qtr.**, **3rd Qtr.**, and **4th Qtr.** and color the sheet tabs in shades of yellow and orange.

5. Cut and paste April, May, and June data, in the range **E3:G17**, as shown in Figure 4.37, from the 1st Qtr. sheet to the 2nd Qtr. sheet in cell **B3**.

6. Group all sheets. *Select* **1st Qtr.**, *press and hold* **[Shift]**, *and click* **4th Qtr**.

7. Enter the following labels, formats, and formulas on all grouped sheets:
   a. In cell **E3**, enter a column heading: **Totals**.
   b. In cell **E5**, enter a formula to add the values for the three months.
   c. AutoFill the formula down to cell **E12**.
   d. In cell **B13**, enter a formula to add the values for the month.
   e. AutoFill the formula for all months and for the Totals column.
   f. In cell **B16**, enter a formula to find Fees on Contracts. *Hint: 18% of total billings for the month: =Total*18%.* AutoFill across for all months.
   g. In cell **B18**, enter a formula to find Total Revenue by adding Fees and Consultation Revenues. AutoFill across for all months.

Continued on next page

h. In cell **E16:E18**, enter formulas to total monthly values.

i. Format all values for commas with no decimal places.

j. Format the sheets as shown in Figure 4.37.

8. Format totals in rows 13 and 18, in columns B:E, with Total cell style and the same color as the heading.

9. Ungroup sheets by clicking the **3rd Qtr. sheet tab**. *Note that the formulas and headings are on that sheet and will be calculated when data is added.*

10. Add a new sheet to the workbook and name it **Summary**.

11. Use Figure 4.38 as a guide to create the summary data. *Be sure to use the appropriate Paste Special options.* Copy and paste special the totals from **E16:E18** for the 1st and 2nd quarters to the summary sheet.

12. Total the summary columns, and format the sheet as shown.

13. Group all sheets and print workbook by clicking **Entire workbook** in the Print dialog box in the Print what section.

14. Save the file **4r4-revenue**.

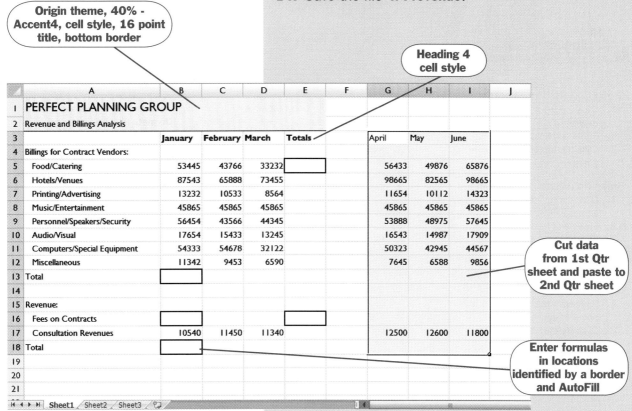

Figure 4.37: Revenue analysis on multiple sheets

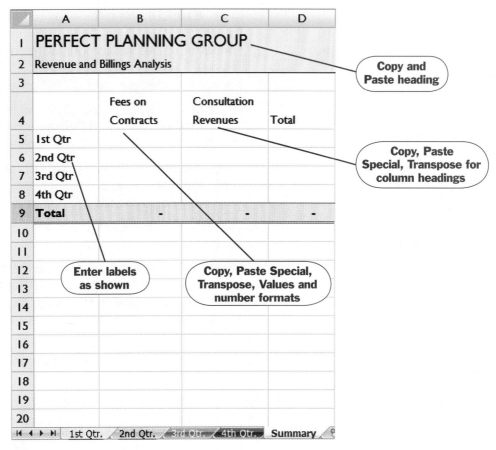

Figure 4.38: Summary sheet: Create with Paste Special

Group Consecutive Sheets
1. Click the tab of the first sheet to group.
2. Press and hold **[Shift]**.
3. Click the tab of the last sheet to group.

Group Nonconsecutive Sheets
1. Click the tab of the first sheet to group.
2. Press and hold **[Ctrl]**.
3. Click the tab of the second sheet to group.
4. Repeat as necessary.

Delete Sheet
1. Right-click the sheet tab of the sheet to delete.
2. Click **Delete**, then click **OK**.

Insert Sheet
1. Click **Insert Worksheet tab**.

Rename Sheet
1. Double-click the sheet tab and type new name.
   Or
1. Right-click the sheet tab of sheet to rename.
2. Click **Rename**.
3. Enter new name.

Format Tab Color
1. Right-click the sheet tab to format.
2. Click **Tab Color**.
3. Click color, then click **OK**.

Paste Special
1. Select and right-click item to copy, then click **Copy**.
2. Right-click the paste location, then click **Paste Special**.

3. Click the desired paste options, for example: **Values and number formats** and/or **Transpose**.
4. Click **OK**.

Paste Options on Home Tab
1. Select and right-click item to copy, then click **Copy**.
2. Click Paste location.
3. Click the **Home tab**, and in the Clipboard group, click the **Paste list arrow**.
4. Select the Paste option.
   Or
4. Click **Paste Special**, click the desired options, then click **OK**.

ENCORE

Act I

You analyze accounting data for the Boston office of Transport Travel Services. The office manager has asked you to develop an expense analysis comparing expense data for the last two years with an estimate of expenses for this year. This report will be e-mailed to the other offices in California and New York, so that they can complete similar analyses to consolidate later into one report.

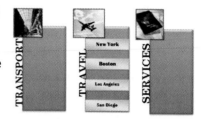

Follow these guidelines:

1. Open data file **4ep1-budget**, and adjust column width as necessary.

2. Create title lines for the report that include the company name, report name "Expense Budget Analysis," and "Boston Office." Insert rows if necessary, and format the worksheet in the Equity theme using Accent1 cell styles. Use Wrap Text alignment for the column headings.

3. Enter and fill formulas to complete the Projected Change and % Change columns, and Totals row:
   a. The Projected Change column shows the change the 2010 budget is from the 2009 actual numbers.
   b. The % Change is the percentage the Projected Change is of the 2009 Actual data. *Include the Total line when you copy down the formula in cell* **F5**, *to get the % Change for the Total line.*

4. Enter formulas in the total row to total columns B:E. Format numbers and percentages, and the total line, as appropriate.

5. Check your work and save the file. Attach the worksheet to an e-mail to the other offices (using an address provided by your instructor). Write a note to accounting personnel requesting that they complete a similar analysis for their office so that all the reports can be consolidated.

6. Save the file, and close the file.

Act II

Earlier, you created a table to analyze property listings for Palmetto Realtors. Now, your supervisor is asking you to analyze sales data, using the table format, to obtain summary data. When a property is sold, it means that the agency has brokered a contract with the seller and a qualified buyer for a listed property.

Follow these guidelines:

1. Open data file **4ep2-sales**, and adjust column width as necessary.

2. Format the information as shown in Figure 4.40, and add the last row of new data. Format the table using the Last Column and Total Row options. Format the last column for Accounting style with no decimals.

3. Enter a formula to calculate days on the market and format the answers in General format. *Hint: =date sold-date listed.*

4. Answer the summary questions on the worksheet by using total functions, and/or by sorting and filtering the data.

5. Add the **Palmetto Realtors.tif** picture file to the right header for the report and format the picture so that it is scaled to 50%. Add the filename to the center footer area. Print the report on one page, in landscape, centered horizontally, with all filters cleared.

6. Save the file, and close it.

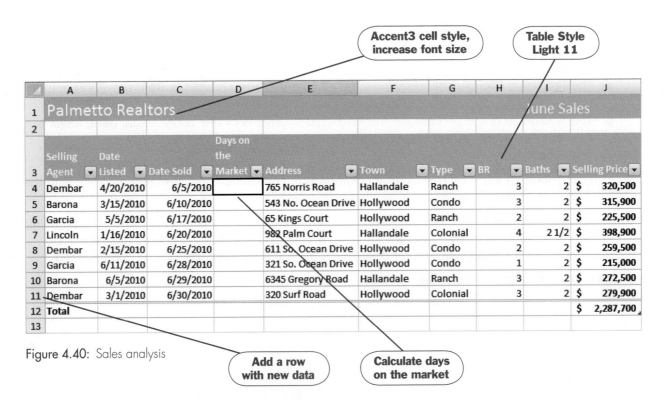

Figure 4.40: Sales analysis

Act III

EarthCare Services has received income statement results from their three locations, Barlow, Central, and Lincoln, for the six months ended June 30, 2010. They want you to format these results, prepare a summary sheet, and prepare sheets for the data for the next six month period.

Follow these guidelines:

1. Open data file **4ep3-netincome** and group all sheets. Adjust the column width and format headings using Accent3 cell styles and bold labels in **A4**, **A15**, and **A22**; increase font size for headings appropriately.

2. Copy each sheet so that it appears at the end, and then group the new sheets. *You will have three new sheets with the same name and a (2) indicating a copy.* Delete the data in the cells in column B, and edit the title of the report to read: **For six months ended December 31, 2010.**

3. Add a new worksheet and name it **Summary**. Prepare the sheet as shown in Figure 4.41. *Note that headings are copied and the title modified, and the labels in column A are placed in* **A5.** *Do not delete any rows until the data has been pasted.* Use Values and number formats in Paste Special, to copy the data from column C on each June data sheet to the summary sheet. As shown in Figure 4.41, delete the rows that do not contain values or headings for values to create the report as illustrated. Find the semi-annual June 30 total. Extend borders and formats for the width of the worksheet.

4. Set footers for all sheets as follows: filename, sheet name, page number.

5. Make print settings for the summary sheet to print in landscape mode, and print a copy of that sheet.

6. Close and save the file.

> After data is pasted, delete rows shown as missing here to create this report

	A	B	C	D	E (Semi-Annual June 30)	F	G	H	I (Semi-Annual December 31)	J (Annual total)
1	EarthCare Services									
2	Income Statement									
3	Summary for the year ended December 31, 2010									
4		Barlow	Central	Lincoln		Barlow	Central	Lincoln		
5	Income									
6	Services Income:									
9	Total Services Income	189,141	400,446	284,200						
10	Sales Income:									
13	Net Sales Income	45,777	146,514	68,666						
14	Total Income from all sources	234,918	546,960	352,866						
15										
16	Expenses									
21	Total Expenses	157,942	349,549	236,913						
22										
23	Net Income Before Taxes	76,976	197,411	115,953						
24										
25										
26										
27										
28										
29										

Barlow / Central / Lincoln / Barlow (2) / Central (2) / Lincoln (2) / **Summary**

Figure 4.41: Summary sheet

LESSON 5

Financial Reports

In this lesson, you will learn to use logical functions, 3-D formulas, print settings, and the linking and formatting features in Excel to prepare financial reports.

▶ **Upon completion of this lesson, you will have mastered the following skill sets**
- ✳ Merge, center, and split cells
- ✳ Work with multiple workbooks and links
- ✳ Work with hyperlinks
- ✳ Modify row and column layout
- ✳ Modify page setup options
- ✳ Use conditional logic functions in formulas
- ✳ Create formulas that reference data from other worksheets or workbooks
- ✳ Find, select, and replace cell data and formats

Terms
Software-related
3-D reference
Bookmark
Find and Replace
External reference
Freeze Panes
Hyperlink
Logical functions
Merge & Center button
Paste Link
Print titles
Splitting a merged cell
Document-related
Balance sheet
Consolidated income statement
Credit balances
Debit balances
Gross profit
Net profit
Sales and commission schedule
Schedule of accounts payable
Schedule of accounts receivable
Trial balance
Worksheet

TRYOUT

TASK 1

GOAL

To create a trial balance with linked accounts receivable and payable schedules, as shown in Figure 5.1

* Merge, center, and split cells
* Work with multiple workbooks and links
* Work with hyperlinks

EXCEL

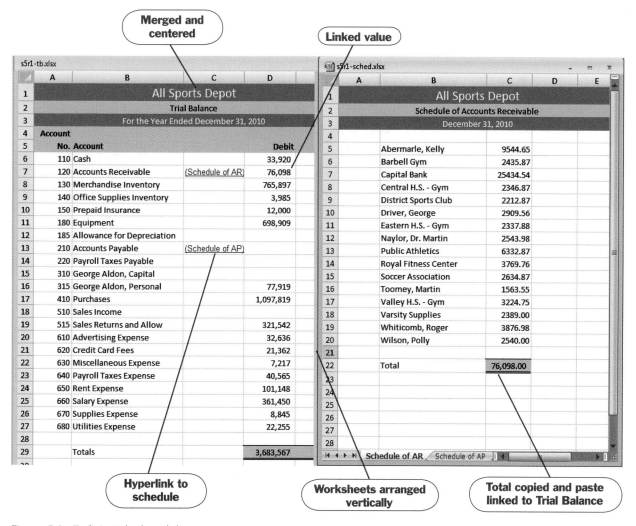

Figure 5.1: Task 1: Linked worksheets

WHAT YOU NEED TO KNOW

Merge, Center, and Split Cells

▶ In the Alignment group on the Home tab, the **Merge & Center button**, shown in Figure 5.2, centers text over a selected range by merging the cells, as shown in Figure 5.1. The title remains in the first column of the range, but it is centered in one large cell you create by merging the cells across the range. You can merge only one line at a time.

 1. Enter title in leftmost cell in heading row. **2.** Select title and the range over which to center it. **3.** Click the **Home tab**, and in the Alignment group, click the **Merge & Center button**.

▶ Returning a cell to its normal width is called **splitting a merged cell**.

 1. Select merged cell. **2.** Click the **Merge & Center button**. Or, Click the **Merge & Center list arrow**. **3.** Click **Unmerge Cells**.

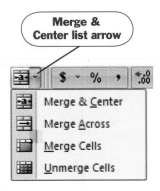

Merge &
Center list arrow

Figure 5.2: Merge &
Center button

T R Y *it* O U T e5-1

1. Open data file **e5-1**.

2. Group the AR and AP worksheets.

3. Select the range **A1:B1**, change the font size to 14 point, and bold the text.

4. Click the **Home tab**, and in the Alignment group, click the **Merge & Center button** to merge the cells and center the text.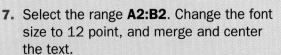

5. Click the **Merge & Center button** again, or click the **Merge & Center list arrow** and click **Unmerge Cells** to split the cells.

6. Click the **Undo button** to keep the merge and center setting.

7. Select the range **A2:B2**. Change the font size to 12 point, and merge and center the text.

8. Ungroup the sheets by clicking on the **Sheet3 tab**, and check the headings on the AR and AP sheets.

9. Save but do not close the file.

Work with Multiple Workbooks and Links

Switch and Arrange Multiple Workbooks

▶ When working with more than one workbook, you can switch between workbooks by using the Switch Windows button, shown in Figure 5.3.

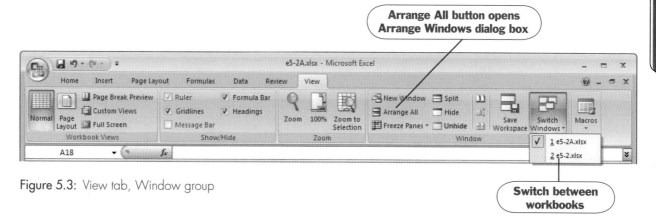

Figure 5.3: View tab, Window group

▶ To view multiple workbooks, click the Arrange All button and use the options in the Arrange Windows dialog box, shown in Figure 5.4, to arrange multiple files or to view windows of the active workbook. When multiple files or sheets are on the screen, you can determine the active sheet by finding the title bar with all control buttons at the right and by the highlighted column and row of the active cell. In an inactive window these are grayed out. Click any cell in a window to make it active or use the Switch Windows button.

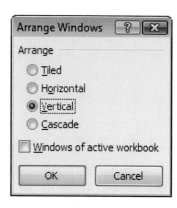

Figure 5.4: Arrange Windows dialog box

TRY it OUT e5-2

1. Continue to work in the open file or open data file **e5-2**. *Note the total on the AR sheet*.

2. Open data file **e5-2A** and notice the total on the AR sheet. *You are looking for the reason that the two files do not agree*.

3. Click the **View tab**, and in the Window group, click the **Switch Windows button** and click **e5-2**, or **e5-1**.

4. To arrange both files on the screen vertically, in the [Arrange All]

Window group, click the **Arrange All button**, click **Vertical**, then click **OK**. *Find the value that causes the difference*.

5. To change the arrangement option, click the **Arrange All button**, click **Horizontal**, then click **OK**.

6. Click in each worksheet and notice the different appearance of the active and inactive sheet.

7. Close the files without saving them.

Paste Link between Workbooks

▶ In the last lesson, you used Paste Special and the Values feature to copy and paste the values or answer in a formula cell. Another Paste Special feature is the Paste Link option. You use **Paste Link** to link a cell to another worksheet or workbook. The linked cell will change if the source cell changes. This feature is invaluable when combining schedules or data from various workbooks into a summary workbook, because any corrections you make to the source data will be reflected in the summary worksheet.

▶ Paste Link is from the options list, shown in Figure 5.5, which appears when the Paste list arrow is clicked.

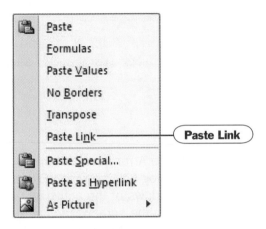

Figure 5.5: Paste Options list

HOW **1.** Right-click the cell to be linked, and click **Copy**. **2.** Go to the paste link location. *This could be on another workbook, another sheet, or on the same sheet.* **3.** Click the **Home tab**, and in the Clipboard group, click the **Paste list arrow**, then click **Paste Link**.

▶ In the formula bar of a linked cell, you will see a reference to the original file. For example, **='[e5-3.xlsx]AR'!$B$10** means that the cell is linked to cell B10 on the AR sheet of the e5-3 file.

► Links between files are saved when you save and close the files. When you open a linked file, a security warning may appear in the message bar above the formula bar, as shown in Figure 5.6. When you click Options, a Security Alert - Links message appears, requesting permission to update the file by activating the link. You can set links to be updated automatically, without a prompt, by using Excel Options, Advanced options on the Office Button menu.

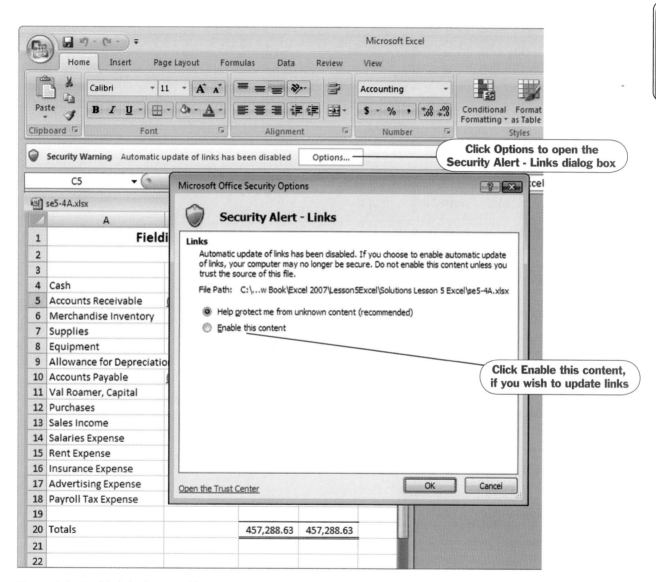

Figure 5.6: Enable links Security Alert

1. Open data files **e5-3** and **e5-3A**, and arrange them vertically on the screen.

2. In **e5-3** on the AR sheet, copy the total in cell **B10** and click in **e5-3A** in cell **C5**.

3. Click the **Home tab**, and in the Clipboard group, click the **Paste list arrow**, then click **Paste Link** to link the data. *Notice the paste link reference on the formula bar.*

4. In **e5-3**, click the **AP sheet tab** and copy cell **B7**.

5. In **e5-3A**, click in cell **D10**, click the **Paste list arrow** and click **Paste Link** to link the

data. *Notice that the Totals row. Debits and Credits do not match.*

6. In **e5-3**, click the **AR sheet tab** and correct Mary Cainter's balance (cell **B5**) to: 1311.55.

7. Notice the updated Accounts Receivable total on both worksheets and the Totals in **e5-3A**.

8. Save both files **e5-3** and **e5-3A**, and close them.

Work with Hyperlinks

Insert a Hyperlink

▶ A **hyperlink** is a shortcut that allows you to jump to another location that provides additional or related information. When you click a hyperlink, it can open another workbook, a file on your hard drive or network, or an Internet address.

▶ The Insert Hyperlink dialog box, shown in Figure 5.7, provides a choice of link locations and a pane to identify the specific link.

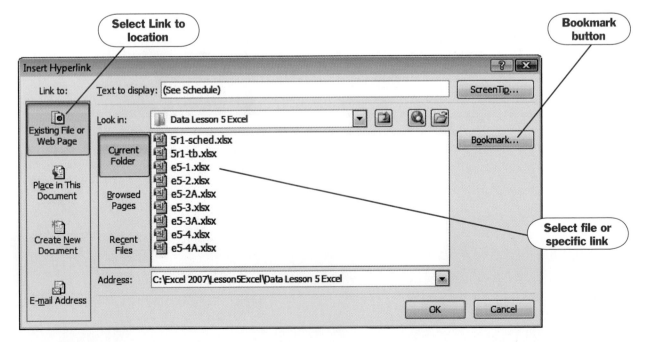

Figure 5.7: Insert Hyperlink dialog box

HOW **1.** Enter the text that will lead to the link. **2.** Right-click the text, and click **Hyperlink** on the shortcut menu. **3.** On the Insert Hyperlink dialog box, in the Link to pane, select the hyperlink location, and then select the file or reference. **4.** Click **OK**.

▶ You can link to a specific location in a workbook with multiple sheets by using a **bookmark** to the sheet or to a specific cell. The Select Place in Document dialog box, shown in Figure 5.8, appears when you click Bookmark on the Insert Hyperlink dialog box.

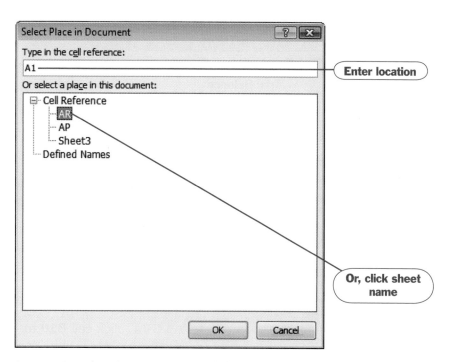

Figure 5.8: Select Place in Document dialog box

HOW **1.** In the Insert Hyperlink dialog box, after you select the workbook, click **Bookmark**. **2.** Enter a cell reference or click the sheet name. **3.** Click **OK**.

T R Y *i t* O U T *e5-4*

1. Open data files **e5-4** and **e5-4A**, and enable the link if you get the Security Alert message. Arrange the files on the screen vertically.

2. In cells **B5** and **B10** of **e5-4A**, enter (See Schedule) and adjust column width if necessary.

3. Right-click cell **B5**, and click **Hyperlink** on the shortcut menu.

4. In the Insert Hyperlink dialog box, click **e5-4** in the current folder.

5. Click **Bookmark** and click **AR**. *A specific cell is not necessary in this case.*

6. Click **OK** twice. *The hyperlinked text is underlined and in a blue font.*

7. Repeat Steps 3-6 for cell **B10**, except change step 5 to select **AP**.

8. Do not close the files.

Use a Hyperlink

▶ When you point to text or a graphic that contains a hyperlink, the mouse pointer becomes a hand to indicate the link. A ScreenTip appears, containing the link reference and instructions for using a hyperlink, as shown in Figure 5.9. You can click once to follow the link or click and hold to select and edit the cell. After you view and close the file referenced by the hyperlink, you are taken back to the original location.

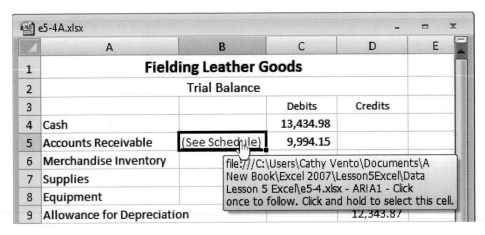

Figure 5.9: Hyperlink path and instructions

TRY*it* OUT *e5-5*

1. Continue to work in the open files.

2. In **e5-4A**, point to, but do not click, cell **B5** to view the ScreenTip.

3. Click cell **B5** to jump to the AR sheet in **e5-4**, then close the file.

4. In **e5-4A**, click cell **B10** to jump to the AP sheet in **e5-4**, then close the file **e5-4**.

5. Do not close **e5-4A**.

Edit a Hyperlink

▶ To edit the hyperlink text without activating the link, click the hyperlink, hold the mouse button down until the pointer changes to a plus sign, as shown in Figure 5.10, then release the mouse button and edit the text on the formula bar.

Figure 5.10: Edit mode for hyperlink

▶ To open the Edit Hyperlink dialog box, shown in Figure 5.11, to edit any part of the hyperlink, right-click the hyperlink and click Edit Hyperlink from the shortcut menu. The Remove Link button differentiates this dialog box from the Insert Hyperlink dialog box.

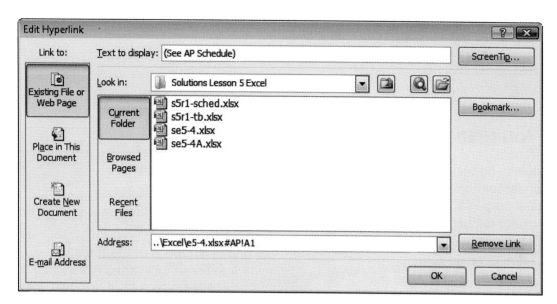

Figure 5.11: Edit Hyperlink dialog box

TRY it OUT e5-6

1. Continue to work in the open file.

2. Click and hold the mouse pointer on the hyperlink text in cell **B5** until it changes to a plus sign.

3. In the formula bar, edit the hyperlink text to read **(See AR Schedule)**, and press **[Enter]**. Adjust column width.

4. Right-click the hyperlink text in cell **B10**, and click **Edit Hyperlink**.

5. In the Text to display box, edit the text to read **(See AP Schedule)**. Click **OK**.

6. Save the file as **e5-6A**, and close it.

REHEARSAL

TASK 1

 GOAL
To create a trial balance with linked accounts receivable and payable schedules

WHAT YOU NEED TO KNOW

▶ Schedules and trial balances are lists of account balances that a business prepares at the end of each month to check the accuracy of its accounts.

▶ The **schedule of accounts receivable** (AR) is a list of all the customers that owe the business money. The **schedule of accounts payable** (AP) is a list of all the business's creditors, or suppliers, that it must pay.

▶ The **trial balance** is a list of all the accounts in the ledger, with a record of the balances for the end of the month. Accounts either have **debit** (left side) or **credit** (right side) **balances**, depending on the type of account. For example, Accounts Receivable and Cash have debit balances and Accounts Payable and Sales have credit balances. In a trial balance, the debit and credit balances must be equal to prove the accuracy of the ledger, or book of accounts.

DIRECTIONS

1. Open data file **5r1-sched**.

2. Adjust column width as necessary, and group the Schedule of AR and the Schedule of AP sheets, shown in Figure 5.12 and 5.13.

3. Merge and center each of the three title rows over columns A to E and format the rows as shown. Format values in Comma style with two decimal places.

4. Click the **Sheet3 tab** to ungroup the sheets and check the titles on both sheets.

5. Use AutoSum to find the totals on each schedule and format totals as shown.

6. Open data file **5r1-tb**, shown in Figure 5.14.

7. Merge and center each of the three title rows over columns A to E and apply consistent cell styles rows 1 through 5.

8. Practice splitting the cells for row 1 to return to the original settings.

9. Merge and center row 1 again.

10. Use AutoSum to find the total of all the debits in column D and all the credits in column E. Format the Totals line as illustrated.

11. Arrange both worksheets on the screen vertically.

12. Copy the total of the Schedule of AR (**5r1-sched**, cell **C22**) and paste link it to cell **D7** on the trial balance, as shown in Figure 5.14.

13. Switch to the Schedule of AP sheet and copy the total of the Schedule of AP (**5r1-sched**, cell **C14**) and paste link it to cell **E13** on the trial balance. *Check to see if the trial balance debits equal the credits.*

14. To find the error, the bookkeeper first checked the schedules and found an error in the Martin Toomey AR account. The amount should be $1563.55, not

Continued on next page

▶ In this rehearsal activity, All Sports Depot wants to check its schedules and trial balance for the year ended December 31, 2010. You will merge and center the headings, paste link the schedule totals, correct the schedules, and create and edit hyperlinks on the trial balance.

$1063.55. Make the correction on the Schedule of AR sheet as shown and notice the automatic update to the trial balance in **5r1-tb**.

15. Save the **5r1-sched** and **5r1-tb** files.

16. Enter hyperlink text in column C of the trial balance to refer users to the schedules. Adjust column width as necessary.
    a. In cell **C7**, enter: **(see Schedule of AR)**.
    b. In cell **C13**, enter: **(see Schedule of AP)**.

17. Create hyperlinks for each text string, using bookmarks to send the user to the correct sheet. Check the hyperlinks.

18. Edit the hyperlink text to delete the word "see" on both hyperlinks.

19. Print a copy of the trial balance.

20. Save the **5r1-tb** and **5r1-sched** files. Close both files.

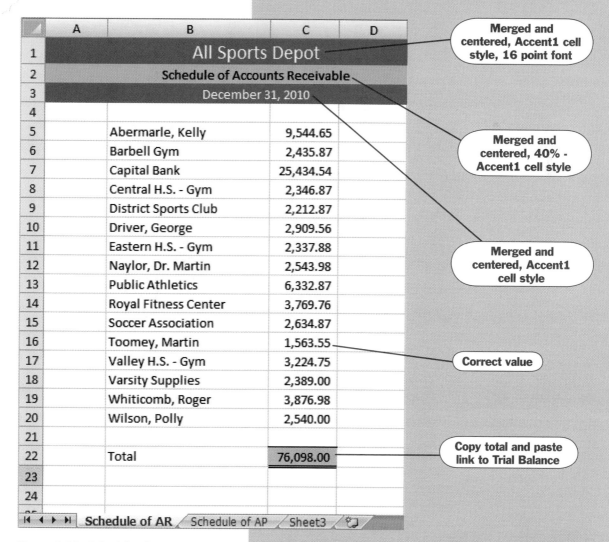

Figure 5.12: Schedule of AR

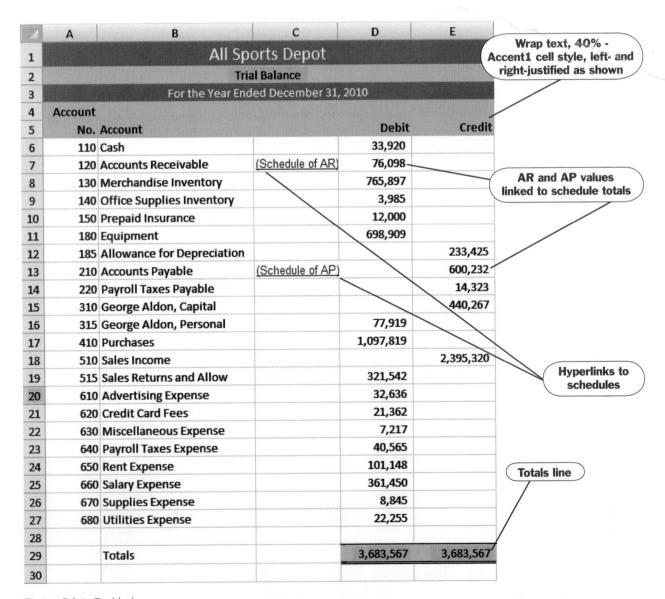

	A	B	C	D	E
1		All Sports Depot			
2		Schedule of Accounts Payable			
3		December 31, 2010			
4					
5		Ace Sporting Goods, Inc.	43,234.00		
6		B and G Wholesalers, Inc.	118,654.00		
7		Brazil Shoe Imports, Inc.	34,212.00		
8		Equipment Suppliers Unlimited	124,675.00		
9		GBS Wholesalers	98,768.00		
10		JCV Athletic Equipment	109,654.00		
11		Modern Sports Wholesalers	45,322.00		
12		Sports Apparel Warehouse	25,713.00		
13					
14		Total	600,232.00		
15					

Copy total and paste link to Trial Balance

Figure 5.13: Schedule of AP

	A	B	C	D	E
1		All Sports Depot			
2		Trial Balance			
3		For the Year Ended December 31, 2010			
4	Account				
5	No.	Account		Debit	Credit
6	110	Cash		33,920	
7	120	Accounts Receivable	(Schedule of AR)	76,098	
8	130	Merchandise Inventory		765,897	
9	140	Office Supplies Inventory		3,985	
10	150	Prepaid Insurance		12,000	
11	180	Equipment		698,909	
12	185	Allowance for Depreciation			233,425
13	210	Accounts Payable	(Schedule of AP)		600,232
14	220	Payroll Taxes Payable			14,323
15	310	George Aldon, Capital			440,267
16	315	George Aldon, Personal		77,919	
17	410	Purchases		1,097,819	
18	510	Sales Income			2,395,320
19	515	Sales Returns and Allow		321,542	
20	610	Advertising Expense		32,636	
21	620	Credit Card Fees		21,362	
22	630	Miscellaneous Expense		7,217	
23	640	Payroll Taxes Expense		40,565	
24	650	Rent Expense		101,148	
25	660	Salary Expense		361,450	
26	670	Supplies Expense		8,845	
27	680	Utilities Expense		22,255	
28					
29		Totals		3,683,567	3,683,567
30					

Wrap text, 40% - Accent1 cell style, left- and right-justified as shown

AR and AP values linked to schedule totals

Hyperlinks to schedules

Totals line

Figure 5.14: Trial balance

Merge and Center Cells

1. Select cells to merge.
2. Click the **Home tab**, and in the Alignment group, click the **Merge & Center button**.

Split Cells

1. Select merged cells to split.
2. Click the **Home tab**, and in the Alignment group, click the **Merge & Center button**.

   Or

2. Click the **Home tab**, and in the Alignment group, click the **Merge & Center list arrow**, then click **Unmerge Cells**.

Arrange Workbooks

1. Open workbooks.
2. Click the **View tab**, and in the Window group, click the **Arrange All button**.

3. In the Arrange Windows dialog box, click the arrange option, then click **OK**.

Paste Link Cells

1. Right-click cell to paste, and click **Copy**.
2. Select link location.
3. Click the **Home tab**, and in the Clipboard group, click the **Paste list arrow**.
4. Click **Paste Link**.

Insert a Hyperlink

1. Enter the text to be hyperlinked.
2. Right-click the cell and click **Hyperlink**.
3. Select location in the Look in box.
4. Click **Bookmark**, if a specific location is necessary.
5. Select a bookmark, then click **OK**.
6. Click **OK** again.

Edit a Hyperlink

1. Right-click hyperlink text and click **Edit Hyperlink**.

   Or

1. Click and hold the mouse over the hyperlink.
2. Make corrections in the formula bar as necessary.
3. Press **[Enter]**.

PERFORMANCE

TASK 1

You work in the accounting department of Expedition Travel Gear in Chicago, and at the end of the year your department combines accounts from all stores and outlets into one trial balance. You have been asked to prepare the schedules of accounts receivable and accounts payable and use the Paste Link and Hyperlink features to link the data to the trial balance.

Expedition

Travel Gear

Expedition Travel Gear has thousands of customers, or accounts receivable that are billed on a 20-day cycle. The accounts are organized alphabetically into billing groups; for example, customers with names from Aa to Be are billed on the first day of the cycle. The total due from each billing group is summarized on the schedule of accounts receivable, as shown in Figure 5.15, which represents the total due from all customers.

Follow these guidelines:

1. Open data files **5p1-schedules** and **5p1-trialbal**. In both files, group sheets where possible, and format the titles and column headings using Merge and Center, cell styles, and font formats. *This company uses variations of the Accent2 cell style.* Format workbook values for commas with no decimal places.

2. In the schedules file, rename and color the tabs. Find the total for each schedule, and add a top and double bottom border.

3. Arrange the files vertically, and copy the Accounts Receivable and Accounts Payable totals from the schedules and paste link them to the proper location on the trial balance. *Link the totals in the correct row,* in the Debit column for Accounts Receivable and in the Credit column for Accounts Payable.

4. Total the trial balance and add a top and double bottom border. *The debits and credits should balance.* Insert a column to the right of the Account column. Insert hyperlinks to the correct schedule sheet in the file **5p1-schedules**, using appropriate hyperlink text.

5. Enter appropriate footers, save both files, print a copy of the trial balance and both schedules, and close the files.

	A	B	C
1		**Expedition Travel Gear**	
2		Schedule of Accounts Receivable	
3		December 31, 2010	
4			
5	Cycle	Customer Billing Groups	Amount
6	1	Aa-Be	45,346
7	2	Bf-Cr	46,543
8	3	Cr-D	50,764
9	4	E-F	29,765
10	5	G	32,456
11	6	H	43,566
12	7	I-J	43,235
13	8	K	38,796
14	9	L	42,687
15	10	M	48,769
16	11	Mo-N	40,443
17	12	O	34,561
18	13	P-Q	29,432
19	14	R	50,840
20	15	R	26,544
21	16	S	49,076
22	17	S	23,343
23	18	T	31,854
24	19	U-V	24,345
25	20	W-Z	36,543
26			768,908
27			
28			
29			
30			
31			
32			
33			

Total amount due from customers in each alphabetical billing group

Accounts Receivable / Accounts Payable

Figure 5.15: Accounts Receivable schedule with billing groups

GOALS

To create a sales and commissions schedule using conditional logic formulas, as shown in Figure 5.16

To print nonadjacent sections of a worksheet

✴ Modify row and column layout
✴ Modify page setup options
✴ Use conditional logic functions in formulas

Upton Investment Group
Sales and Commission Schedule
For the quarter ended March 31, 2010

Salesperson	Client Sales	New Business	Total Sales	Commission	Bonus	Total	President's Club	Business Development Program
Abrams, Sally	2,000,738	465,012	2,465,750	24,657.50	4,828.75	29,486	*	
Baer, Buddy	1,501,045	42,855	1,543,900	15,439.00	219.50	15,659		6/15
Gomez, John	1,940,075	55,915	1,995,990	19,959.90	2,479.95	22,440		6/15
Jackson, Robert	1,345,876	40,224	1,386,100	13,861.00	-	13,861		6/15
Keyes, Tracy	1,024,045	25,015	1,049,060	10,490.60	-	10,491		6/15
Lee, Randy	1,900,785	356,000	2,256,785	22,567.85	3,783.93	26,352	*	
Martino, Jack	1,707,606	380,054	2,087,660	20,876.60	2,938.30	23,815	*	
Nunez, Debra	1,470,350	74,500	1,544,850	15,448.50	224.25	15,673		6/15
Okowski, Bill	930,555	68,000	998,555	9,985.55	-	9,986		6/15
Ringold, Diane	1,765,876	376,984	2,142,860	21,428.60	3,214.30	24,643	*	
Souten, Tyler	1,959,076	500,804	2,459,880	24,598.80	4,799.40	29,398	*	
Sullivan, Tara	2,065,343	677,017	2,742,360	27,423.60	6,211.80	33,635	*	
Watson, George	1,676,985	43,255	1,720,240	17,202.40	1,101.20	18,304		6/15
Totals	21,288,355	3,105,635	24,393,990	243,940	29,801	273,741		

Figure 5.16: Task 2: Sales and commission schedule

Formulas using conditional logic

WHAT YOU NEED TO KNOW

Modify Row and Column Layout

Hide and Unhide Rows and Columns

▶ You can hide detail columns and rows on the screen display to simplify a complicated worksheet or for security purposes. When you hide a column or row, the worksheet border does not display the column letter or row number, and hidden data does not print.

 1. Select and right-click columns or rows to hide. **2.** Click **Hide** on the shortcut menu.

▶ You can display hidden columns by selecting the columns or rows before and after the hidden area, and using the shortcut menu.

HOW **1.** Select and right-click columns or rows before and after hidden data. **2.** Click **Unhide** on the shortcut menu.

T R Y *i t* **O U T** *e5-7*

1. Open data file **e5-7**, and close the security warning message bar above the formula bar.

2. Select and right-click columns B:F. Click **Hide**.

3. Select and hide rows 23:28.

4. Select and right-click rows 22 and 29, and click **Unhide**.

5. Press **[Ctrl]+[F2]** to Print Preview the worksheet. *Note that the hidden columns will not print.* Close the preview screen.

6. Select and right-click columns A:G, and click **Unhide**.

7. Do not close the file.

Freeze and Unfreeze Rows and Columns

▶ When you work with a large worksheet, you may find that the column headings or row labels that identify the data scroll out of view. You can keep them in view by freezing them.

▶ The **Freeze Panes** command locks the pane, which is a group of rows or columns above or to the left of the cell you select, so that area does not move during scrolling. There are three options on the Freeze Panes button, and once the panes are frozen the first option changes to Unfreeze, as shown in Figure 5.17.

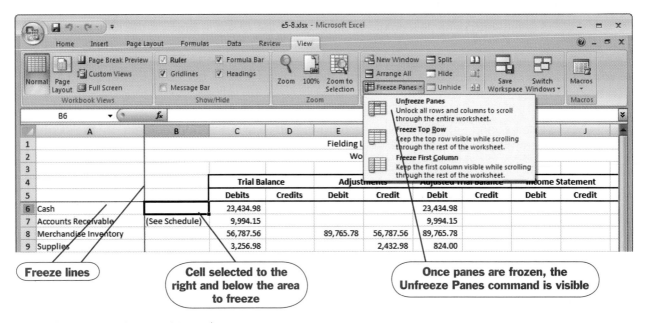

Figure 5.17: Freeze Panes on View tab

HOW **1.** Place cursor in location below and/or to the right of freeze area. **2.** Click the **View tab**, and in the Window group, click the **Freeze Panes button**, then select the desired option.

T R Y *it* O U T *e5-8*

1. Continue to work in the open file or open data file **e5-8**. *Close the security warning message bar.*

2. Click anywhere in column A and click the **View tab**, and in the Window group, click the **Freeze Panes button**, then click **Freeze First Column**. *A line appears at the right edge of column A.*

3. Use the horizontal scroll bar to scroll across the page, and notice the frozen column on the left side of the screen.

4. Click the **View tab**, and in the Window group, click the **Freeze Panes button**, then click **Unfreeze Panes**. *The line is cleared.*

5. Click in cell **B6**, which is below the column headings and to the right of the first column. Click the **Freeze Panes button**, then click **Freeze Panes**. *Freeze lines appear above row 6 and to the left of column B.*

6. Use the horizontal and vertical scroll bar to scroll to the right and down to view the frozen column and row headings.

7. Clear the freeze.

8. Close the file, without saving it.

Modify Page Setup Options

Print Nonadjacent Sections of a Worksheet

▶ If you want to print sections of a worksheet that are not adjacent, hide the columns or rows that are not needed and print the data as displayed. As discussed previously, if a worksheet is wider or longer than the width of the page, use tools in the Page Layout tab to scale the worksheet to fit on one page.

T R Y *i t* O U T *e5-9*

1. Open data file **e5-9**. *Close the security warning message bar*.

2. Hide Columns **C:F** and click the **Page Layout view button**. *Note that the worksheet is wider than the page.*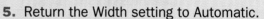

3. Click the **Page Layout tab**, and in the Scale to Fit group, set Width to **1 page**. Print the worksheet as displayed. Only Columns A, B, G, H, I, J, K, and L will print.

4. Click the **Normal view button**, select and right-click columns B and G, and unhide the columns.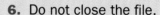

5. Return the Width setting to Automatic.

6. Do not close the file.

Print Titles

▶ The **Print Titles** feature allows you to print column or row titles on subsequent pages of a multiple page worksheet. For example, if the worksheet in **e5-9** were not modified to fit on one page, it would require two pages to print. To print a multipage worksheet, you can set column titles to repeat at the left of all pages or rows to repeat at the top, so that you can identify the values on each page. Settings are made in the Page Setup dialog box, shown in Figure 5.18.

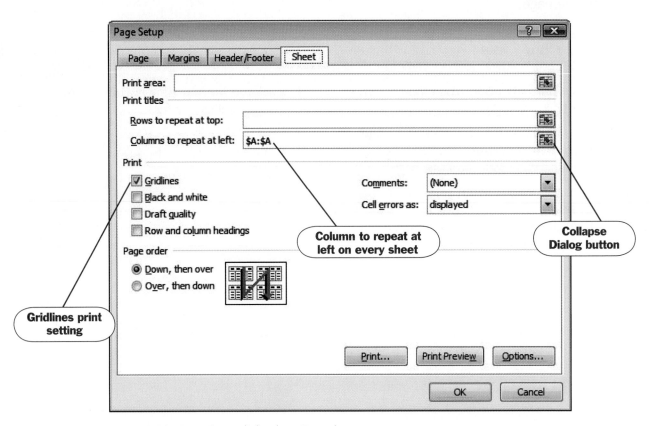

Figure 5.18: Page Setup dialog box: Print titles

HOW **1.** Click the **Page Layout tab**, and in the Page Setup group, click the **Print Titles button**. **2.** Click the **Collapse Dialog button** in the Rows to repeat at top box or the Columns to repeat at left box. **3.** Select the columns or rows, and click the **Expand Dialog button**. **4.** Click **Print**, then click **OK**.

1. Continue to work in the open file or open data file **e5-10**. *Close the security warning message bar in* **e5-10**.

2. Click each merged title row and click the **Merge & Center button** to unmerge the cells.

3. Click the **Page Layout tab**, and in the Page Setup group, click the **Print Titles button**.

4. Click the **Collapse Dialog button** in the Columns to repeat at left box.

5. Click column A and click the **Expand Dialog Button**. Click **Gridlines** to print.

6. Click the **Print Preview button**. Click the **Next Page button** on the Print Preview tab to see Page 2. *Note that there are two pages in the preview and both have column titles at the left*.

7. Close the preview screen.

8. Save the file, and close it.

Use Conditional Logic Functions in Formulas

▶ The Insert Function dialog box contains a category of functions called Logical functions, as shown in Figure 5.19. **Logical functions** test data and determine actions based on the outcome of the test. We will discuss AND, IF, OR, and IFERROR functions. A description of the function and help in entering it are provided when you select the function on the Insert Function dialog box.

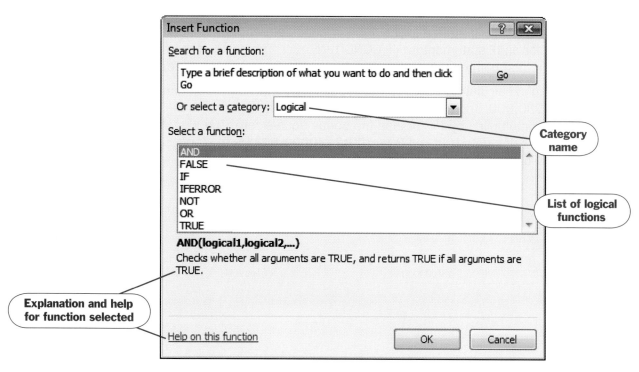

Figure 5.19: Insert Function: Logical functions category

▶ Logical functions use the conditional operators shown in Table 5.1 to state the conditional question.

Table 5.1: Conditional operators

CONDITIONAL OPERATOR	QUESTION
=	Equal to
>	Greater than
<	Less than
<>	Not equal to
<=	Less than or equal to
>=	Greater than or equal to

▶ A summary of the logical functions we will use is shown in Table 5.2.

Table 5.2: Logical functions

FUNCTION	DESCRIPTION
AND	Used to check several conditions to see if all are TRUE conditions
IF	Used to check if condition is TRUE or FALSE and to provide an action for each condition
IFERROR	Returns a value or error message you specify if there is an error, otherwise it returns the result of the formula
OR	Used to check several conditions to see if any one of them is TRUE

IF Statements

▶ Use an IF statement to state a logical test, or condition, and return values based on the results. The format for an IF statement is =IF(CONDITION,X,Y). The parts of the function are separated by commas: the first comma represents "then," and the second comma represents "else."

▶ As an example, calculate a bonus for salespeople who get a 1% bonus on sales if they make sales over $30,000. The formula would state: if sales are greater than $30,000, then the bonus equals sales multiplied by 1%, or else the bonus equals zero. The IF statement would read as follows if the sales data is in cell B2: **=IF(B2>30000,B2*1%,0)**. Table 5.3 details the translation of each part of this statement.

Table 5.3: Explanation of IF function formula

FORMULA	FUNCTION	CONDITION OR LOGICAL TEST	X	Y
Excel	=IF	(B2>30000,	B2*1%,	0)
Translation	If	sales are greater than $30,000, then	multiply sales by 1% to get bonus, else	the bonus equals 0.

▶ To enter an IF statement, click the Insert Function button on the formula bar, select IF from the Logical category, and click OK. There are Collapse Dialog buttons to select cells from the worksheet, or you can enter the function directly into the cell. Notice the entries in the dialog box in Figure 5.20.

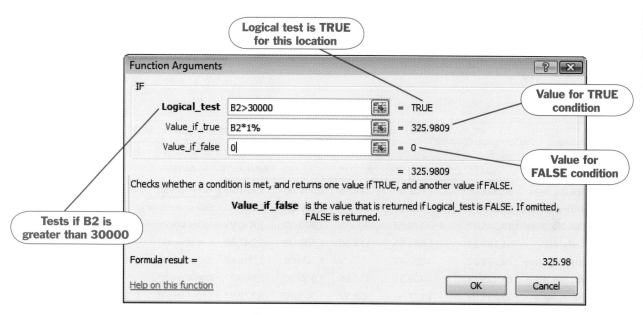

Figure 5.20: IF statement function arguments

T R Y *i t* O U T *e5-11*

1. Open data file **e5-11**.

2. In cell **D2**, enter an IF statement to calculate the bonus.
   a. Click the **Insert Function button** on the formula bar.
   b. Select the **Logical category** and the **IF function**. Click **OK**.
   c. In Logical_test, enter: **B2>30000**.
   d. In the Value_if_true, enter: **B2*1%**.

   e. In the Value_if_false, enter: **0**.
   f. Click **OK**.

3. In cell **D2**, view the resulting formula on the formula bar.

4. AutoFill the formula for all salespeople. *Notice how the bonuses were applied.*

5. Save but do not close the file.

▶ You can use an IF statement to insert text according to a condition or the result of a logical test. For example, if the sales are greater than a certain amount, you can insert "Great work"; if not, you can insert "Sales seminar on 5/15." When you use an IF statement to enter text, the text appears within quotation marks in the formula. Excel automatically inserts quotation marks if you use the Insert Function dialog box, but if you enter the formula directly into the cell you must include the punctuation. If you wish to enter no text as a result, place a space between quotation marks, that is " ". Notice the formula bar and the Earnings and Note columns in Figure 5.21.

IF statement:
(test, value if true, value if false)

	G2	▼	*fx*	=IF(B2>30000,"Great work!","Sales seminar on 5/15")				
	A	B	C	D	E	F	G	H	I
1	SALES STAFF	SALES	COMMISSION	BONUS	SALARY	EARNINGS	NOTE		
2	Acosta, Sam	32,598.09	651.96	325.98	1,500.00	2,477.94	Great work!		
3	Billings, Mary	28,321.32	566.43	-	1,500.00	2,066.43	Sales seminar on 5/15		
4	Camino, Juan	18,545.77	370.92	-	1,500.00	1,870.92	Sales seminar on 5/15		
5	Kelly, Joe	51,567.54	1,031.35	515.68	1,500.00	3,047.03	Great work!		
6	Lincoln, Terry	29,921.22	598.42	-	1,500.00	2,098.42	Sales seminar on 5/15		
7	Parson, Alice	35,325.78	706.52	353.26	1,500.00	2,559.77	Great work!		
8	Sulfa, Sally	55,896.95	1,117.94	558.97	1,500.00	3,176.91	Great work!		

Figure 5.21: IF statement with text output

TRY *it* OUT e5-12

1. Continue to work in the open file or open data file **e5-12**.

2. In cell **F2**, enter a formula to add the Commission, Bonus, and Salary values to find the Earnings. AutoFill the formula.

3. In cell **G2**, enter an **IF** statement to generate the notes.
   a. Click the **Insert Function button**.
   b. Select the **Logical category** and the **IF function**. Click **OK**.
   c. In the Logical_test box, enter: B2>30000.

   d. In the Value_if_true box, enter: Great work!
   e. In the Value_if_false box, enter: Sales seminar on 5/15. *Quotation marks will be inserted by Excel for d and e.*
   f. Click **OK**.

4. In cell **G2**, view the resulting formula on the formula bar. *Note the quotation marks.*

5. AutoFill the formula for all salespeople.

6. Save and close the file.

AND and OR Statements

▶ You may wish to test two or more conditions to determine the results. When you use AND in a function, all conditions must be TRUE before the action will take place. When you use OR in a function, one or the other must be TRUE before the action takes place.

▶ Examples of Excel formulas using OR and AND with IF statements are shown in Table 5.4 with their translations. In this example, B2 is the number of new clients, and C2 is the sales figure.

Table 5.4: Explanation of OR and AND functions

FORMULA	FUNCTION	CONDITION OR LOGICAL TEST	X	Y
Excel	=IF	AND(B2>2,C2>30000,	C2*1%,	0)
Translation	If	new clients are greater than 2 AND sales are greater than $30,000, then	multiply sales by 1% to get bonus, else	the bonus equals 0.
Excel	=IF	OR(B2>3,C2>30000,	C2*1%,	0)
Translation	If	new clients are greater than 3 OR sales are greater than $30,000, then	multiply sales by 1% to get bonus, else	the bonus equals 0.

T R Y i t O U T e5-13

1. Open data file **e5-13**.

2. In cell **E2**, enter an **IF** statement to calculate the bonus if the new clients are over 2 AND the sales are over $30,000.
   a. Click the **Insert Function button**.
   b. Select the **Logical category** and the **IF function**. Click **OK**.
   c. In the Logical_test box, enter: `AND(B2>2,C2>30000)`.
   d. In the Value_if_true box, enter: `C2*1%`.
   e. In the Value_if_false box, enter: `0`.
   f. Click **OK**.

3. In cell **E2**, view the resulting formula on the formula bar and use the fill handle to copy the formula for all salespeople.

4. Copy the range **A1:H8** and paste it to **A12**.

5. Double-click on **E2**, and edit the formula to calculate the bonus if the new clients are greater than **3 OR** the sales are over $30,000. The formula should be: `=IF(OR(B2>3,C2>30000),C2*1%,0)`.

6. AutoFill the formula and compare results with the copied worksheet in **A12**. *The OR statement allowed more staff to qualify for the bonus.*

7. Save and close the file.

IFERROR Statement

▶ You can use the IFERROR statement to calculate a result and to display a specific message for any formula where there is an error, as shown in Table 5.5.

Table 5.5: Explanation of IFERROR function

FORMULA	FUNCTION	VALUE	VALUE IF ERROR
Excel	=IFERROR	C3/B3,	"no quota"
Translation	If there is an error when	the value is present or formula is calculated, then	print the error message.

1. Open data file **e5-14**.

2. In cell **D3**, enter a formula to calculate what percent quotas are of sales. *Hint =sales/quota and format as a percent.*

3. AutoFill the formula down to cell D10 and note the error messages.

4. Delete formula in **D3** and enter a formula to calculate the percent quotas are of sales, but if there is an error, the words "no quota" should be displayed. *fx*
   a. Click the **Insert Function button**.
   b. Select the **Logical category** and the **IFERROR function**. Click **OK**.

c. In the Value box, enter: **C3/B3**.

d. In the Value_if_error box, enter: **no quota**. *Quotation marks will be inserted by Excel.*

e. Click **OK**.

5. In cell **D3**, view the resulting formula on the formula bar and AutoFill the formula for all salespeople. *Note the error message for those rows where dividing by zero creates an error.*

6. Save and close the file.

REHEARSAL

GOALS

To create a sales and commission schedule and link the data into a worksheet

To print nonadjacent sections of a worksheet

TASK 2

WHAT YOU NEED TO KNOW

▶ In Excel, spreadsheets are called worksheets. In accounting terminology, however, a **worksheet** is a form used by accountants to gather trial balance and adjustments information at the end of an accounting period to plan the preparation of the income statement and balance sheet.

▶ The worksheet adjustments, usually prepared by the accountant, are corrections that are made at the end of the period so that the accounts will reflect their true balances. The net income is calculated and the income statement and balance sheet are planned on the worksheet, using the adjusted trial balance data.

▶ The **sales and commission schedule** calculates the sales, commissions, and bonuses for the period. Conditional logic statements are used to calculate the commissions and bonuses for each salesperson. The commission expense for the period is linked to the appropriate location on the worksheet.

▽ DIRECTIONS

1. Open data file **5r2-bonus**.

2. Use cell styles and formats as shown in Figure 5.22.

3. Enter the formulas as follows, AutoFill appropriately, and format numbers to Comma style with no decimals:
   a. **D6**: Total Sales
   b. **E6**: Commission: Calculate a 1% commission on sales. *Hint: Total Sales*1%.*
   c. **F6**: Bonus: Staff receives a .5% bonus on all sales over $1,500,000. *Hint: Logical test: Total sales greater than 1500000. If true: (Total Sales -1500000)*.5%, If false: 0.*
   d. **G6**: Total: Total of commission and bonus
   e. **H6**: President's Club: Staff is honored if their total sales are over $2,000,000 AND their new business is over $50,000. An asterisk is entered if they are in the President's Club. *Hint: Logical test: AND(Total sales>2000000,New business >50000) If true: "*" If false:" " Right-align data in column.*
   f. **I6**: Business Development Program: Staff must take a seminar on the date specified (6/15) if their total sales are less than $1,200,000 OR their new business is less than $75,000. *Hint: Logical test: OR(Total sales <1200000,New business<75000) If true: "6/15" If false:" " Right-align data in column.*
   g. **B20**: Total

4. Save the file **5r2-bonus**, but do not close it.

5. Open data file **5r2-worksheet** and format as shown in Figure 5.23. *The column headings over each set of Debit and Credit columns should be Merged and Centered over the two columns.*

6. Switch to **5r2-bonus**, and copy the total in cell **G20**.

7. Switch back to **5r2-worksheet**, and paste link the total to the Commissions Expense location in cell **B22**.

Continued on next page

▶ In this Rehearsal activity, Upton Investment Group wants you to prepare and format the quarterly sales and commission schedule, as shown in Figure 5.22, and link the data to the worksheet, as shown in Figure 5.23.

8. Click the column B header, click the **Insert list arrow**, then click **Insert Sheet Columns** to add a new column B.

9. In cell **B22**, enter a hyperlink to **5r2-bonus** using "(See Schedule)" as the hyperlink text.

10. Freeze panes in cell **B7** and find totals for columns C:L. *Note: Columns C and D, E and F, and G and H should match or balance with each other.*

11. In a blank area below the worksheet, subtract the Income Statement totals, column I from column J (J-I). This value, the net income, should be placed in cells **I31** and **L31**.

12. In cell **I32**, add cells **I30** and **I31**. AutoFill this formula across to columns J:L. *Note: Columns I and J, and K and L should be in balance.*

13. Include borders and lines, as shown, and format totals lines.

14. Unfreeze panes, hide columns B:F, and print the worksheet to fit on one page.

15. Unhide the columns and print the worksheet on two pages with column A titles.

16. Save the file **5r2-worksheet**. Close both files.

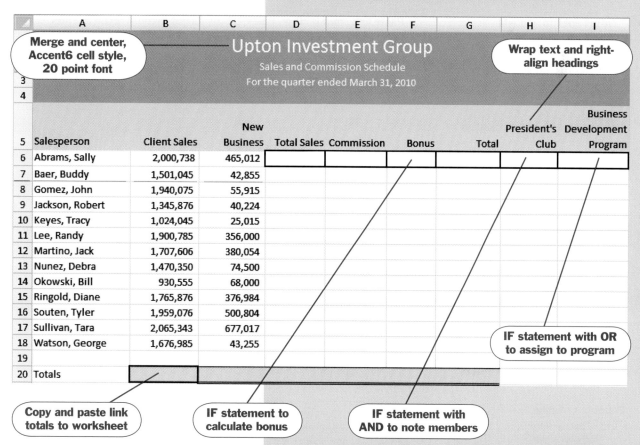

Figure 5.22: Sales and commission schedule

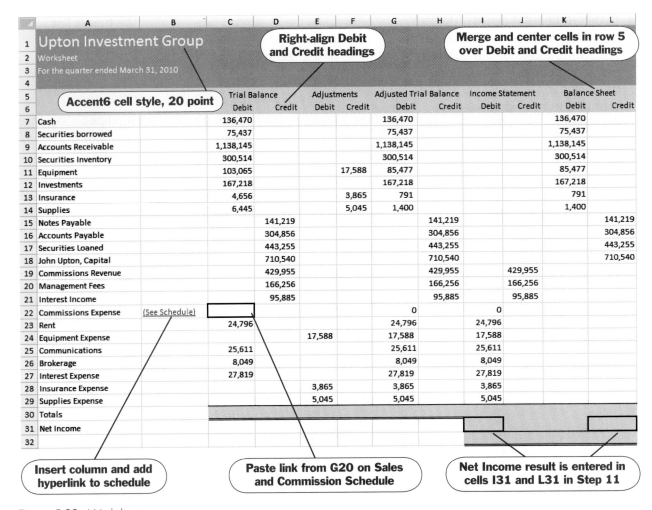

Figure 5.23: Worksheet

The worksheet shows:

Upton Investment Group
Worksheet
For the quarter ended March 31, 2010

Callouts on the worksheet:
- Right-align Debit and Credit headings
- Merge and center cells in row 5 over Debit and Credit headings
- Accent6 cell style, 20 point
- Insert column and add hyperlink to schedule
- Paste link from G20 on Sales and Commission Schedule
- Net Income result is entered in cells I31 and L31 in Step 11

		Trial Balance		Adjustments		Adjusted Trial Balance		Income Statement		Balance Sheet	
		Debit	Credit	Debit	Credit	Debit	Credit	Debit	Credit	Debit	Credit
7	Cash	136,470				136,470				136,470	
8	Securities borrowed	75,437				75,437				75,437	
9	Accounts Receivable	1,138,145				1,138,145				1,138,145	
10	Securities Inventory	300,514				300,514				300,514	
11	Equipment	103,065			17,588	85,477				85,477	
12	Investments	167,218				167,218				167,218	
13	Insurance	4,656			3,865	791				791	
14	Supplies	6,445			5,045	1,400				1,400	
15	Notes Payable		141,219				141,219				141,219
16	Accounts Payable		304,856				304,856				304,856
17	Securities Loaned		443,255				443,255				443,255
18	John Upton, Capital		710,540				710,540				710,540
19	Commissions Revenue		429,955				429,955		429,955		
20	Management Fees		166,256				166,256		166,256		
21	Interest Income		95,885				95,885		95,885		
22	Commissions Expense	(See Schedule)				0		0			
23	Rent	24,796				24,796		24,796			
24	Equipment Expense			17,588		17,588		17,588			
25	Communications	25,611				25,611		25,611			
26	Brokerage	8,049				8,049		8,049			
27	Interest Expense	27,819				27,819		27,819			
28	Insurance Expense			3,865		3,865		3,865			
29	Supplies Expense			5,045		5,045		5,045			
30	Totals										
31	Net Income										
32											

Cues for Reference

Hide Columns or Rows
1. Select and right-click row(s) or column(s) to hide.
2. Click **Hide**.

Unhide Columns or Rows
1. Select and right-click rows or columns on either side of hidden area.
2. Click **Unhide**.

Freeze Columns or Rows
1. Select the cell below and/or to the right of the column(s) or row(s) to freeze.
2. Click the **View tab**, and in the Window group, click the **Freeze Panes button**.

Unfreeze Columns or Rows
1. Click the **View tab**, and in the Window group, click the **Freeze**

Panes button, then click **Unfreeze Panes**.

Enter IF Statement
1. Click the **Insert Function button** on the formula bar.
2. Click the **Logical category** and the **IF function**, then click **OK**.
3. In Logical_test, enter or select condition.
4. In Value_if_true, enter or select data or a formula.
5. In Value_if_false, enter or select data or a formula.
6. Click **OK**.

Print Nonadjacent Sections of a Worksheet
1. Hide columns or rows that are not needed.
2. Press **[Ctrl]+P** and click **OK**.

Print Titles
1. Clear merged cells, if necessary.
2. Click the **Page Layout tab**, and in the Page Setup group, click **Print Titles**.
3. Click the **Collapse Dialog button** in the Rows to repeat at top box or the Columns to repeat at left box.
4. Select the columns or rows and click the **Expand Dialog button**.
5. Click **Print**.

PERFORMANCE

TASK 2

Perfect Planning Group

▶ The accountant for Perfect Planning Group has prepared a worksheet for the quarter ending March 31, 2010, in preparation for preparing financial reports. The Salary Expense number will be calculated on a salary and bonus schedule and linked to the worksheet.

▶ To encourage consulting activity, the firm is giving a 15% bonus on consulting revenues earned over $4,000 for the quarter, if billings are over $130,000. In addition, the staff members that have billings over $150,000 or consulting revenues over $6,500 will be recognized at the quarterly dinner.

Follow these guidelines:

1. Open data files **5p2-salarysched** and **5p2-qtrworksheet**, and adjust column widths as necessary.

2. Use borders, cell styles, and formats as shown in Figure 5.24 to format **5p2-salarysched**. Both worksheets should be in the Origin theme using variations of Accent4 cell style and numbers should set to Comma style with no decimals. On **5p2-qtrworksheet**, use Merge & Center, and align column headings as shown in Figure 5.23.

3. Enter formulas on the salary and bonus schedule, and AutoFill as necessary:
   a. **E6**: Bonus: Staff receives a 15% bonus on all consulting revenues over $4,000, if their billings are greater than $130,000 AND their consulting revenues are greater than $4,000. *Hint: Logical test: AND (Billings greater than 130000, Consulting Revenues greater than 4000). If true: (Consulting Revenues-4000)*15%, If false: 0.*
   b. **F6**: Total Salary includes salary and bonus.
   c. **H6**: Sales Leader's Club: Staff is honored if their billings are greater than $150,000 OR their consulting revenues are greater than $6,500. "Dinner 4/18" is entered if they meet requirements or else no text is entered. *Hint: Logical test: OR (Billings>150000, Consulting revenues>6500). If true: "Dinner 4/18." If false:" "*
   d. **B13**: Total row 13.

4. Save the file and copy the total salary in cell **F13**, and paste link it to cell **B28** in the worksheet. *Use the Paste list arrow on the Home tab and click **Paste Link.***

5. Click the column B header, click the **Insert list arrow**, then click **Insert Sheet Columns** to insert a new column. Create a hyperlink to the schedule. Use Freeze Panes to complete the totals for the worksheet and apply an appropriate cell style and borders.

6. Unfreeze panes, hide columns B:F, and print the worksheet on one page. Unhide the columns, and print the worksheet on two pages with column A titles. Save and close both files.

	A	B	C	D	E	F	G	H
1	PERFECT PLANNING GROUP							
2	Salary and Bonus Schedule							
3	For the quarter ended March 31, 2010							
4								
5		Billings for Contract Vendors	Consulting Revenues	Salary	Bonus	Total Salary		Sales Leader's Club
6	Hodges, Jennifer	155,556	4,985	13,500				
7	Martinez, Sam	143,456	6,520	12,700				
8	McNally, Carol	174,678	5,000	15,500				
9	Rogers, Monica	158,765	7,205	11,625				
10	Williamson, Trey	121,878	3,495	11,900				
11	Wu, Patricia	132,135	6,125	11,750				
12								
13	Total							
14								

Callout: Origin theme, 40% - Accent4 cell style, 16 point font

Callout: Copy and paste link total to worksheet cell B28

Callout: Alphabetize names

Figure 5.24: Salary and Bonus Schedule

TRYOUT

TASK 3

GOALS

To create a consolidated income statement using 3-D references, as shown in Figure 5.25

To create a balance sheet using Find and Replace features, as shown in Figure 5.26

✳ Create formulas that reference data from other worksheets or workbooks

✳ Find, select, and replace cell data and formats

All Sports Depot
Consolidated Income Statement
For Year Ended December 31, 2010

Income:		
Sales Income	2,395,320	
Less: Sales Returns	321,542	
Net Sales		2,073,778
Less: Cost of Goods Sold	1,162,482	1,162,482
Gross Profit		911,296
Expenses:		
Advertising Expense	32,636	
Credit Card Fees	21,362	
Depreciation Expense	17,000	
Insurance Expense	10,000	
Miscellaneous Expense	7,217	
Payroll Taxes Expense	40,565	
Rent Expense	101,148	
Salary Expense	361,450	
Supplies Expense	9,295	
Utilities Expense	22,255	
Total Expenses		622,928
Net Income before Taxes		288,368
Less: Taxes	65,250	65,250
Net Income after Taxes		$ 223,118

▶ ▶│ Gaston / Mesquite / **Consolidated Income Statement** / Sh

Sheets summarized using 3-D references

Figure 5.25: Task 3: Consolidated income statement

All Sports Depot

Balance Sheet

December 31, 2010

Assets			
Current Assets:			
	Cash	33,920	
	Accounts Receivable	76,098	
	Merchandise Inventory	701,234	
	Office Supplies Inventory	3,535	
	Prepaid Insurance	2,000	
	Total Current Assets		816,787
Fixed Assets:			
	Equipment	698,909	
	Allowance for Depreciation	250,425	
	Total Fixed Assets		448,484
Total Assets			$ 1,265,271
Liabilities			
Current Liabilities:			
	Accounts Payable	600,232	
	Payroll Taxes Payable	14,323	
	Income Taxes Payable	65,250	
	Total Liabilities		679,805
Owner's Equity			
	John Aldon, Equity 1/1/2010	440,267	
	Add: Net Income	223,118	
	Less: John Aldon, Personal	77,919	
	John Aldon, Equity 12/31/2010		585,466
Total Liabilities and Owner's Equity			$ 1,265,271

External reference

Figure 5.26: Task 3: Balance sheet

WHAT YOU NEED TO KNOW

Create Formulas that Reference Data from other Worksheets or Workbooks

3-D References to Worksheets

▶ If you want to summarize data from several sheets onto a totals sheet within a workbook, you can use a formula in the **3-D reference** style. The style is called 3-D, or three-dimensional, because it is used to calculate values through the sheets of a workbook to a summary worksheet at the end of the workbook.

▶ A 3-D reference includes the sheet names followed by an exclamation point, and the cell or range reference, as shown in the examples in Table 5.6.

Table 5.6: Examples of 3-D reference formulas

EXAMPLES OF 3-D REFERENCE FORMULAS	EXPLANATIONS
=January!C7+February!C7+March!C7	Adds the values in C7 from the January, February, and March sheets
=SUM(Sheet1:Sheet3!D7)	Adds the values in D7 from sheets 1 to 3
=AVERAGE(Sheet3:Sheet5!D7:D12)	Averages values in D7:D12 from sheets 3 to 5

▶ You can enter a 3-D reference directly in the formula, or select the sheets and cells involved, and enter the mathematical operators, as necessary. Notice the formula in Figure 5.27, which was entered by selection. When 3-D references are copied down using AutoFill on a summary sheet, the cell references change, relative to the new location, but the sheet names remain constant. For example, in cell C8 the copied formula would change to January!C8+February!C8.

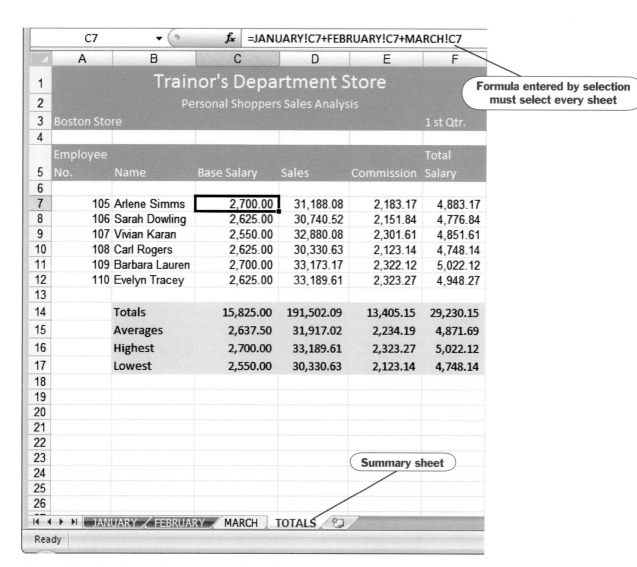

Figure 5.27: 3-D reference formula entered by selection

1. Open data file **e5-15**.

2. Rename Sheet3: **TOTALS**.

3. Use the selection method to enter a 3-D reference to add the values from the JANUARY, FEBRUARY, and MARCH sheets onto the TOTALS sheet:
   a. In cell **C7** on the TOTALS sheet, enter: =
   b. Click cell **C7** on the JANUARY sheet.
   c. Enter: +
   d. Click cell **C7** on the FEBRUARY sheet.
   e. Enter: +
   f. Click cell **C7** on the MARCH sheet.
   g. Press **[Enter]** and go to cell **C7** in the TOTALS sheet to view the formula.

4. In cell **D7**, enter a 3-D reference to add the values in cell **D7** from the JANUARY thru MARCH sheets. *Hint: =Sum(JANUARY: MARCH!D7). When you enter the formula you can use the SUM function.*

5. Use AutoFill to copy cell **D7** to cells through to **F7**, and copy all four formulas down to row 12. *The summary data will be computed because the formulas were copied from the monthly sheets.*

6. Format the copied cells to two decimal places. Adjust column width as necessary.

7. Save the file **e5-15** and close it.

References between Workbooks

▶ Using similar steps you can create an **external reference**, which is a reference to a cell in another workbook. This is like a link, but the references can be used in formulas. External references are useful when you want to combine data from several workbooks into one streamlined report, or if you keep data in one workbook and then use it in formulas in other workbooks.

▶ It is best to use the selection method to create an external reference formula so that the references to the workbook, sheet, and cell location are properly entered with the required punctuation. An external reference formula entered by selection is shown in Figure 5.28.

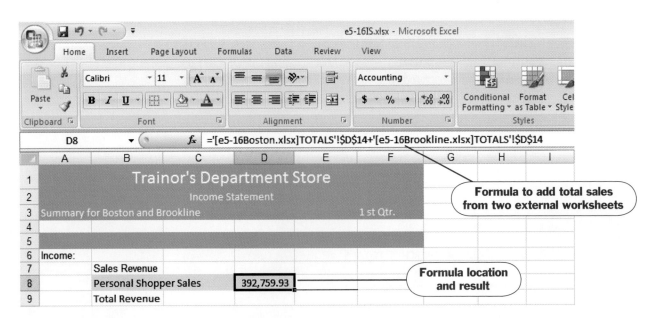

Figure 5.28: External reference formula entered by selection

▶ In an external reference, the filename is always in brackets and the sheet name always is followed by an exclamation point. External reference formulas are displayed in two different ways, depending on whether the workbook that contains the source data is open. Samples of external references are shown in Table 5.7.

Table 5.7: Examples of External Reference formulas

EXAMPLES OF EXTERNAL REFERENCE FORMULAS	EXPLANATIONS
=SUM([Sales.xlsx]Annual!C10:C25) *Source file open*	Finds total of C10:C25 on the Annual sheet in the Sales.xlsx file. The filename is in brackets with no further information if the file is open.
=SUM('C:\Reports\[Sales.xlsx]Annual'!C10:C25) *Source file closed*	Finds the same result as above, but since the source file is not open, the path to the Sales file appears before the filename in brackets.
='[e5-16.xlsx]TOTALS'!$D$14+[e5.16B.xlsx]TOTALS!$D$14 *Source files open*	Entered by selection. Finds the total of cell D14 on the TOTALS sheets from e5-16 and e5-16B.

T R Y *i t* O U T *e5-16*

1. Open data files **e5-16Boston**, **e5-16Brookline**, and **e5-16IS**. *On e5-16IS, you will gather information to create the quarterly income statement.*

2. Enter a formula to add the total personal shopper sales from the TOTALS sheet in the Boston and Brookline store files.
   a. In cell **D8** in **e5-16IS**, enter: =
   b. Click cell **D14** in the **e5-16Boston** file on the TOTALS sheet.
   c. Enter: +
   d. Click cell **D14** in the **e5-16Brookline** file on the TOTALS sheet.
   e. Press **[Enter]** and go to cell **D8** in **e5-16IS** to view the formula.

3. In cell **D21** in **e5-16IS**, find the total Personal Shopper Salaries. Use the selection method to enter a formula with external references to add the values from the TOTALS sheets in cell **F14** from the Boston and Brookline files. *You can instead copy the formula from **D8** and edit it to include the data from **F14** instead of **D14**.* The answer should be $59,143.20.

4. Save and close all the files.

Find, Select, and Replace Cell Data and Formats

▶ The Find & Select button, on the Home tab, displays a list of types of data and tools to find data and edit your worksheets. You can also find cells that match the format of a specific cell, formulas, or comments, as shown in Figure 5.29.

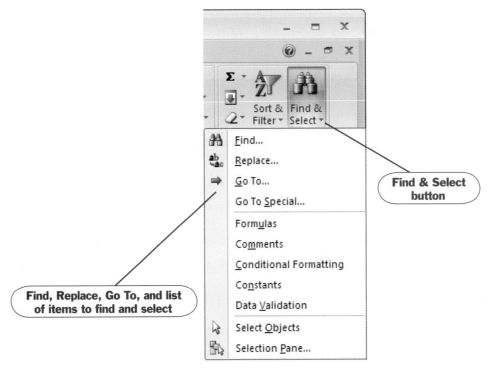

Figure 5.29: Find & Select button and list

Find Cell Data

▶ To find data, press [Ctrl]+[F] to display the Find and Replace dialog box. When you click the Options button, you can narrow your search to a sheet, the workbook, by columns or rows, or to look for formulas, values, or comments, as shown in Figure 5.30. In addition, you can select options to match the case or the contents of the entire cell, and/or you can search for specific formats.

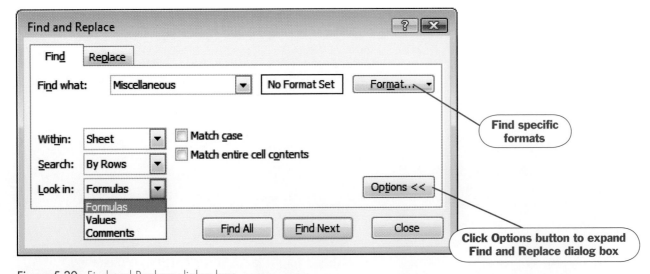

Figure 5.30: Find and Replace dialog box

▶ Once you set your options, you can click Find All or Find Next. When you click Find All, you get a list of all the cell addresses that contain a match. When you click Find Next, you go to each location as it appears in the worksheet.

T R Y *i t* O U T *e5-17*

1. Open data file **e5-17**.

2. Press **[Ctrl]+[F]**, and click the **Options button**.

3. Enter **Miscellaneous** in the Find what box.

4. Set the search to Within: Workbook, and click the **Match case check box**.

5. Click **Find Next**, and keep clicking it until you find all occurrences. *There are four occurrences. It occurs once in each sheet.*

6. Click **Find All** to see a list of all the locations at the bottom of the dialog box.

7. Click the **Close button** in the dialog box.

8. Do not close the file.

Find and Replace Data and Formats

▶ **Find and Replace** is a feature used to search for specific data for review or edit, and to replace it, if necessary. After entering the Find and Replace information, as shown in Figure 5.31, you can click Replace All or Replace. Clicking Replace All replaces all occurrences without giving you a chance to view each change. Clicking Replace lets you view each instance before it is replaced, so you can be sure that you want to replace it. You can undo a Find and Replace operation.

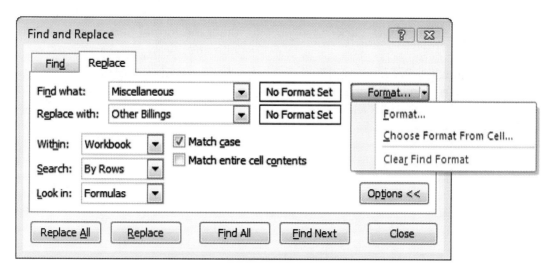

Figure 5.31: Replace tab and Format button

HOW 1. Click the **Home tab**, and in the Editing group, click the **Find & Select button**. 2. Click **Replace**. 3. Enter text to find and text with which to replace it. 4. Click **Replace**. You can view each replace location before the change is made.

1. Continue to work in the open file or open data file **e5-18**.

2. Click the **Home tab**, and in the Editing group, click the **Find & Select button**, then click **Replace**.

3. Enter the information shown in Figure 5.31, but do not press the Format button. *If the Format & Replace dialog box does not look like the one shown in Figure 5.31, click the **Options button.***

4. Click **Replace All**, and notice the changes. Click **OK**.

5. Click the **Undo button**, then click the **Redo button**.

6. Select and delete the text in the Find what and Replace with boxes.

7. Save, but do not close, the file.

▶ To search for a certain format, you can select a cell with the format you want, click the Format list arrow, and click Choose Format From Cell, and that format becomes the search criteria. You can then change the format of the Replace terms with line by clicking Format to set the new format.

1. Continue to work in the open file or open data file **e5-19**, and perform Step 2 from **e5-18**.

2. Click the **Format list arrow** on the Find what line, and click **Choose Format From Cell**.

3. With the Choose cell pointer, click cell **B3**.

4. Click the **Format list arrow** on the Replace with line, and click **Format**.

5. In the Font tab, set the Color to Dark Red, and click **OK**. *Notice the preview.*

6. Click **Replace** each time to view the corrections.

7. Click the **Format list arrow** on the Find what line, and click **Clear Find Format**. Clear the format setting on the Replace with line.

8. Click the **Close button**.

9. Save and close the file.

REHEARSAL

GOALS

To create a consolidated income statement using 3-D references

To create a balance sheet with external references using Find and Replace features

TASK 3

WHAT YOU NEED TO KNOW

▶ Corporations must report their financial data to their stockholders quarterly and annually. If a company has branches or divisions in various parts of the country, they need to combine income statement data into one financial report called a **consolidated income statement**.

▶ An income statement is prepared at the end of a financial period using income, cost, and expense accounts from the worksheet. It calculates **gross profit**, the profit margin over the cost of the merchandise, and **net profit**, which is the final profit for the period after deducting expenses from the gross profit.

▶ A business also prepares a **balance sheet**, which is a financial report that shows the value of the firm's assets and liabilities, owner's worth, or stockholder's equity on a certain date. The balance sheet is based on the basic accounting equation: assets = liabilities + capital (owner's worth or equity).

▼ DIRECTIONS

1. Open data file **5r3-income**, and group the Gaston and Mesquite sheets and format as shown in Figure 5.32.

2. With the sheets still grouped, enter formulas in the cells listed below to calculate the following income statement items.
   a. **C9**: Net Sales. *Hint: Sales - Sales Returns.*
   b. **C13**: Gross Profit. *Hint: Net Sales - Cost of Goods Sold.*
   c. **C26**: Total Expenses.
   d. **C28**: Net Income before Taxes. *Hint: Gross Profit - Total Expenses.*
   e. **C30**: Net Income after Taxes.

3. Ungroup the sheets by using the worksheet tab shortcut menu.

4. Create a copy of the Gaston sheet, and place it after the Mesquite sheet.

5. Rename it: `Consolidated Income Statement`. Format the worksheet tabs with colors.

6. Adjust column widths as necessary, and change the second title in the new sheet to read: `Consolidated Income Statement`.

7. Delete the values in Column B on the Consolidated Income Statement sheet.

8. In cell **B7**, on the Consolidated Income Statement sheet, enter a 3-D formula to add the values from the Gaston sheet and Mesquite sheet in cell **B7**. *Hint: =Gaston!B7+Mesquite!B7.*

9. Use AutoFill to copy the formula down to cell **B29**. Delete all zeros or dashes where the formula did not find values. Fix borders, as necessary.

10. Check your work by looking at a value on the consolidated sheet to see if it totaled the two sheets correctly.

Continued on page 208

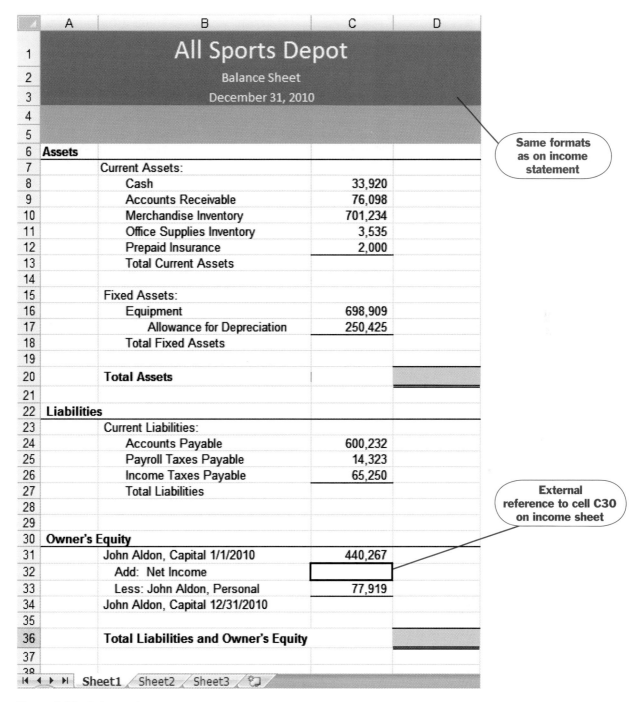

	A	B	C	D
1		All Sports Depot		
2		Balance Sheet		
3		December 31, 2010		
4				
5				
6	Assets			
7		Current Assets:		
8		Cash	33,920	
9		Accounts Receivable	76,098	
10		Merchandise Inventory	701,234	
11		Office Supplies Inventory	3,535	
12		Prepaid Insurance	2,000	
13		Total Current Assets		
14				
15		Fixed Assets:		
16		Equipment	698,909	
17		Allowance for Depreciation	250,425	
18		Total Fixed Assets		
19				
20		Total Assets		
21				
22	Liabilities			
23		Current Liabilities:		
24		Accounts Payable	600,232	
25		Payroll Taxes Payable	14,323	
26		Income Taxes Payable	65,250	
27		Total Liabilities		
28				
29				
30	Owner's Equity			
31		John Aldon, Capital 1/1/2010	440,267	
32		Add: Net Income		
33		Less: John Aldon, Personal	77,919	
34		John Aldon, Capital 12/31/2010		
35				
36		Total Liabilities and Owner's Equity		
37				
38				

Same formats as on income statement

External reference to cell C30 on income sheet

Sheet1 / Sheet2 / Sheet3

Figure 5.33: Balance sheet

Enter 3-D References

1. Enter the reference.
   Or
   Use the mouse:
1. Enter the equal sign, function, and parentheses, if necessary.
2. Select the sheet and cell to reference.
3. Enter the mathematical operator.
4. Repeat Steps 2 and 3 and close the parentheses, if necessary.
5. Press **[Enter]**.

Enter External References

1. Enter the reference.
   Or
   Use the mouse:
1. Enter the equal sign, function, and parentheses, if necessary.
2. Select the workbook, sheet, and cell to reference.

3. Enter the mathematical operator, if necessary.
4. Repeat Steps 2 and 3 and close the parentheses, if necessary.
5. Press **[Enter]**.

Find and Replace Data

1. Click **Home tab**, and in the Editing group, click the **Find & Select button**.
   Or

1. Press **[Ctrl]+F**.
2. Enter data in the Find what box.
3. Enter data in the Replace with box.
4. Click **Options** and set, if appropriate.
5. Click **Replace** to make changes one item at a time.
   Or
5. Click **Replace All** to replace all occurrences.

Find and Replace Formats

1. Click the **Home tab**, and in the Editing group, click the **Find & Select button**.
   Or

1. Press **[Ctrl]+[F]**.
2. Clear text in the Find what and Replace with boxes.
3. On the Find what line, click the **Format list arrow**, then click **Choose Format From Cell**.
4. Select cell with format to find.
5. On Replace with line, click the **Format button**, then click **Format** or **Choose Format From Cell**.
6. Set the new format.
7. Click **Replace** or **Replace All**.

PERFORMANCE

TASK 3

Transport Travel Services has agencies in Boston, New York, Los Angeles, and San Diego. Each agency has sent its quarterly income statement data, which has been copied into one worksheet. Ms. Roslyn Young, the president of the company, would like you to prepare a consolidated income statement along with the supporting agency reports and a consolidated balance sheet. The net income from the consolidated income statement will be referenced to the appropriate location on the balance sheet for June 30, 2010.

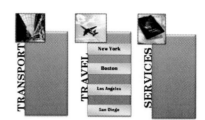

Follow these guidelines:

1. Open data files **5p3-balancesheet** and **5p3-cis**.

2. In **5p3-cis**, copy any sheet and place it after Sheet4, and name it **Consolidated Income Statement**. Name and color the tabs for Sheets 1 through 4 using the city name.

3. Group the city sheets and the Consolidated Income Statement sheet and format columns C and D in Comma style with no decimals. Enter formulas for calculating Total Income (**D11**), Total Expenses (**D26**), Net Income before taxes (**D28**), and Net Income (**D31**). Include borders where necessary, and use the **Accent1** cell style for Net Income. Apply formats as shown in Figure 5.34, including changing the theme to **Equity**, and indenting the Income section.

4. Ungroup the sheets, and on the Consolidated Income Statement sheet, clear the data from column C, leaving the formulas in column D. Correct the title to read: **Consolidated Income Statement**. Use 3-D references in column C to combine all the data from the four agencies onto the Consolidated Income Statement sheet. Clear any unnecessary formulas, and check to make sure that the existing formulas in column D are working correctly. Correct formats as necessary.

5. Group the sheets and add footers with the sheet name, date, and filename. Set the sheets to print centered horizontally and vertically on the page. Format **5p3-balancesheet** in the same styles as the income statements, using indents for lists of assets and for total labels, as shown in the Rehearsal Figure 5.33, the **Heading 1** cell style for the Assets, Liabilities, and Owner's Capital section heading rows, and the **Total** cell style for **C20** and **C34**.

6. Use the Find and Replace feature to find the word Capital and replace it with the word Equity in all occurrences. In cell **B30**, enter an external reference to the Net Income on the Consolidated Income sheet of **5p3-cis**.

7. Complete formulas for Total Current Assets (**C13**), Total Fixed Assets (**C18**) *(The depreciation is subtracted from the asset value)*, Total Assets (**C20**), Total Liabilities (**C26**), Roslyn Young, Equity (**C32**) *(Current equity is calculated by adding the profit and subtracting the withdrawals from the beginning equity)*, and Total Liabilities and Owner's Equity (**C34**).

Continued on next page

    c. **H6**: 2010 % Raise. Use an IF AND statement. The percent raise is "7.25%" if years of seniority are greater than 4 AND productivity rating is greater than 3; otherwise, the raise percentage is "5.25%".

    d. **I6**: 2010 Raise *Multiply 2009 salary by percentage in* **H6.**

    e. **J6**: 2010 Salary *Add raise in* **I6** *to 2009 salary.*

    f. **L6**: In-service course *Print an asterisk* "*" if the Productivity rating is less than 4; otherwise, print " ".

3. Find the totals for all money columns, adjust columns as necessary, and add cell styles to the total line.

4. Hide columns B:C and F:H. Merge and center the headings, and print a copy of the report. Save and close the file.

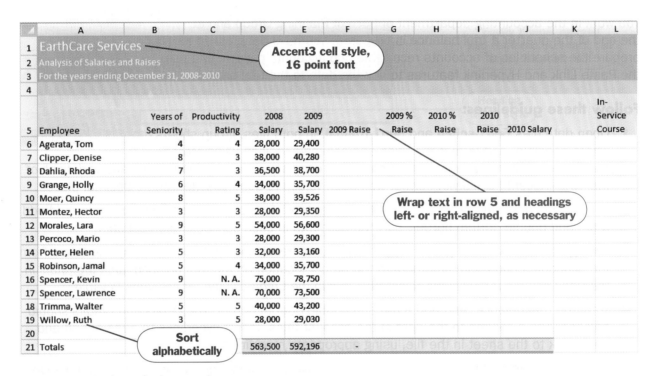

Figure 5.35: Analysis of salaries and raises

Act III

EarthCare Services' chief financial officer, Lawrence Spencer, has started to prepare the worksheet, income statement, and balance sheet for the year. He has asked you to complete and format the reports. Lawrence Spencer needs the reports for meetings with bankers and the president, Kevin Spencer, because EarthCare Services is contemplating an expansion and requires additional funding.

Follow these guidelines:

1. Open data files **5ep3-worksheet**, **5ep3-is**, and **5ep3-balsheet**. Also, open your solution to **5ep2-salinc**.

2. Format the three new files in the styles shown in Figure 5.36, and format values in the Comma style with no decimal places.

3. In cell **B31** of the worksheet (**5ep3-worksheet**), enter an external reference to the 2010 Salaries, in cell **J21** in your solution file **5ep2-salinc**.

4. Freeze panes in cell **B7** to be able to work in the worksheet. Find totals in cells **B33:C33** and in cells **D35:K35**. *The values in each set of debit and credit columns, beginning with Columns B and C, should be equal.*

5. On the Income Statement (**5ep3-is**), merge and center the titles. Create a duplicate for Heading 3 and change the bottom border to green. Apply Heading 3 2 to the section headings in rows 5, 15, and 28. Enter all formulas necessary to complete the income statement, and remove the yellow highlights from the formula cells.

Continued on next page

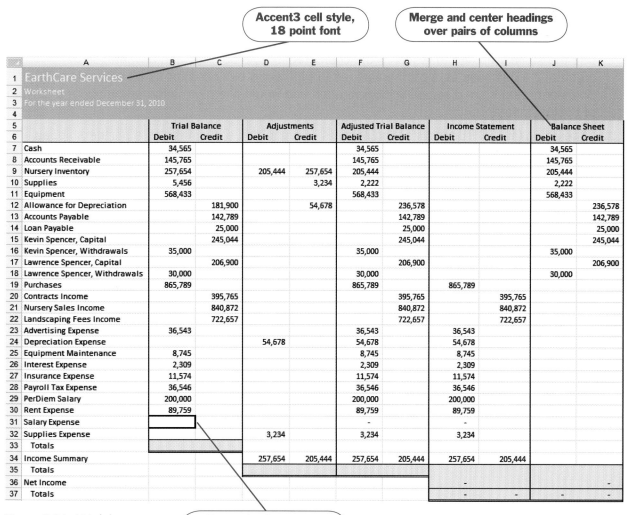

Accent3 cell style, 18 point font

Merge and center headings over pairs of columns

	Trial Balance		Adjustments		Adjusted Trial Balance		Income Statement		Balance Sheet	
	Debit	Credit	Debit	Credit	Debit	Credit	Debit	Credit	Debit	Credit
7 Cash	34,565				34,565				34,565	
8 Accounts Receivable	145,765				145,765				145,765	
9 Nursery Inventory	257,654		205,444	257,654	205,444				205,444	
10 Supplies	5,456			3,234	2,222				2,222	
11 Equipment	568,433				568,433				568,433	
12 Allowance for Depreciation		181,900		54,678		236,578				236,578
13 Accounts Payable		142,789				142,789				142,789
14 Loan Payable		25,000				25,000				25,000
15 Kevin Spencer, Capital		245,044				245,044				245,044
16 Kevin Spencer, Withdrawals	35,000				35,000				35,000	
17 Lawrence Spencer, Capital		206,900				206,900					206,900
18 Lawrence Spencer, Withdrawals	30,000				30,000				30,000	
19 Purchases	865,789				865,789		865,789			
20 Contracts Income		395,765				395,765		395,765		
21 Nursery Sales Income		840,872				840,872		840,872		
22 Landscaping Fees Income		722,657				722,657		722,657		
23 Advertising Expense	36,543				36,543		36,543			
24 Depreciation Expense			54,678		54,678		54,678			
25 Equipment Maintenance	8,745				8,745		8,745			
26 Interest Expense	2,309				2,309		2,309			
27 Insurance Expense	11,574				11,574		11,574			
28 Payroll Tax Expense	36,546				36,546		36,546			
29 PerDiem Salary	200,000				200,000		200,000			
30 Rent Expense	89,759				89,759		89,759			
31 Salary Expense					-		-			
32 Supplies Expense			3,234		3,234		3,234			
33 Totals										
34 Income Summary			257,654	205,444	257,654	205,444	257,654	205,444		
35 Totals										
36 Net Income							-			-
37 Totals							-	-	-	-

EarthCare Services
Worksheet
For the year ended December 31, 2010

Figure 5.36: Worksheet

External reference to 5ep2-salinc total for 2010

EXCEL

6. On the Balance Sheet (**5ep3-balsheet**), merge and center the titles. Use the Format Painter button to apply the Heading 3 2 style from the Income Statement to the Balance sheet section headers in rows 6, 21, and 29. Divide the Net Income (**D28**) from the income statement in half, and place half the net income under each partner's equity to calculate their new equity. Enter all formulas necessary to complete the balance sheet, and remove the yellow highlights from the formula cells. Add lines and borders, as necessary. Find and replace all occurrences of the word "Equity" with "Capital."

7. Lawrence Spencer needs the following printouts: *Add appropriate footers and center worksheets horizontally.*
   a. Income Statement.
   b. Balance Sheet.
   c. Partial worksheet with the Trial Balance and Adjustments columns hidden.
   d. Full worksheet on two pages using the Print Titles feature.
   e. Full worksheet in landscape orientation adjusted to fit on one page.

8. Save and close all files.

Group Projects

1. Search the www.entrepreneurmag.com site, under the Money category, to develop a list of the "best banks for small businesses" for the state of Ohio.

2. Use the same Web site to research the characteristics, problems, and advantages of organizing a business as a partnership (as in this family business) or as a corporation. The Spencer brothers are discussing incorporation and would like more information about this type of business organization.

3. Write an essay that summarizes the aspects of organizing a business as a partnership, as compared to a corporate form of organization. *You can use "advantages of incorporation" as keywords.*

PERFORMING WITH ACCESS

Access Basics

In this lesson, you will be introduced to databases, and to Access and its basic features.

Upon completion of this lesson, you will have mastered the following skill sets

* Learn about Access and database concepts
* Learn about database management systems
* Start Access and explore the Access opening screen
* Learn about database objects
* Open a database and explore the Access database screen
* Explore the Navigation Pane and close a database
* Understand database design
* Understand database views

Terms
Software-related

Access opening screen
Categories
Datasheet view
Design view
Groups
Navigation Pane
PivotChart view
PivotTable view
Shutter Bar Open/Close button
Templates
Views
Work pane

Database-related

Database
Database management system
Database objects
Datasheets
Field content
Field name
Fields
Forms
Primary key
Queries
Record
Relational database management system
Reports
Table

TRYOUT

TASK 1

GOAL

To start Access and to explore the Access screens and database objects, as shown in Figure 1.1

✻ Learn about Access and database concepts
✻ Learn about database management systems
✻ Start Access and explore the Access opening screen
✻ Learn about database objects
✻ Open a database and explore the Access database screen
✻ Explore the Navigation Pane and close a database
✻ Understand database design
✻ Understand database views

Tabs for working in Access

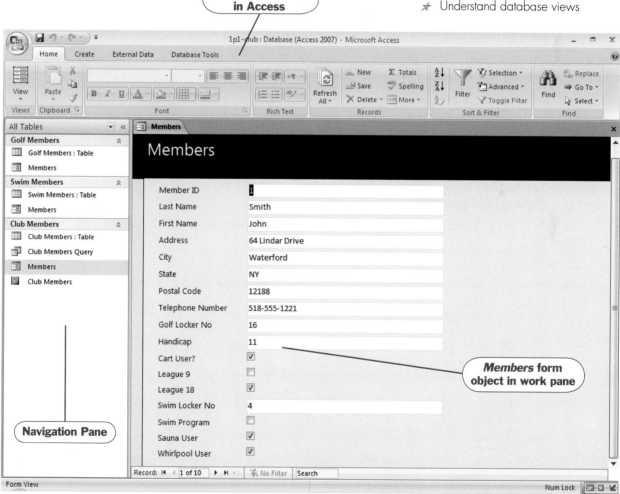

Navigation Pane

Members form object in work pane

Figure 1.1: Task1: Access screen with open database

WHAT YOU NEED TO KNOW

Learn about Access and Database Concepts

▶ Access 2007 is a database management system that you can use independently or as part of the Office suite. Data management can be done manually, with index cards, files, folders, and/or file cabinets. With Access, however, you can organize facts and maintain and look up the data electronically. An Access database is the equivalent of an electronic file cabinet.

▶ A **database** is an organized collection of facts about a particular subject. For example, databases provide the information about your account when you call your telephone company, your bank, or your credit card company for information. A database is a way to organize vast amounts of data so that you can access, analyze, or update it easily.

Learn about Database Management Systems

▶ A **database management system** provides functions to store, search, filter, query, and report on the data in a database. For example, to locate all the books in the library that were published in the year 2000, you would have to review each card in the card catalog and write down the name and call number of every book that meets the search criterion. With an automated database management system, once the information is in the database, you can identify the books with a few keystrokes.

▶ Access provides many additional functions besides data maintenance and storage. Access is a **relational database management system** where your data is divided into separate, subject-based tables that you can bring together in reports as you need it. For example, one table might contain customer names and addresses, and another might contain sales information. By using the customer number to link the data between the two databases, you can generate invoices or reports, as shown in Figure 1.2.

Customer Table	Sales Detail Table						
ID	Cust ID	Company Name	Contact	Address	City	State	Zip Code
1	4321	Willens Co.	Will Collins	51 Front Street	San Diego	CA	90900
2	3421	F and J Limited	Frank Miller	21 Billings Road	Tustin	CA	90883
3	1234	McConnell Associates	Roger McConnell	752 Patricia Street	Sonoma	CA	98789

Customer Table	Sales Detail Table			
Purchase Or	Cust ID	Item Description	Quantity	Amount
101	1234	Ink Jet Printer Model #CW543	1	$243.55
102	3421	Leather Border desk blotter	1	$125.00
103	4321	Laser Printer Model #2544	1	$954.33
104	1234	Printer stand	1	$150.00
105	1234	Printer Cartridges #CW5-B	2	$35.68

INVOICE

Roger Mc Connell
McConnell Associates
752 Patricia Street
Sonoma, CA 98789

Customer Number: 1234

Purchase Order #	Description	Quantity	Price	Total
101	Ink Jet Printer Model #CW543	1	243.55	243.55
104	Printer Stand	1	150.00	150.00
105	Printer Cartridges #CW5-B	2	35.68	71.36

Total $ 464.91

Figure 1.2: Database tables related by Customer ID to produce an invoice

Start Access and Explore the Access Opening Screen

▶ If you have customized your desktop or Start menu, double-click the Access 2007 icon, or follow the steps in Try it Out a1-1.

TRY it OUT a1-1

1. Click the **Start button** on the Windows taskbar.

2. Click **All Programs**.

3. Click **Microsoft Office**.

4. Click **Microsoft Office Access 2007**.

5. Do not close the program.

▶ The Getting Started with Microsoft Office Access screen appears, as shown in Figure 1.3. The **Access opening screen** contains links to help and training; to templates and a blank database, so you can create databases; and a list of recently saved databases. **Templates** are model databases in categories that you may be able to adapt to your needs. There are Local Templates, which are available in your installed software, and Online templates.

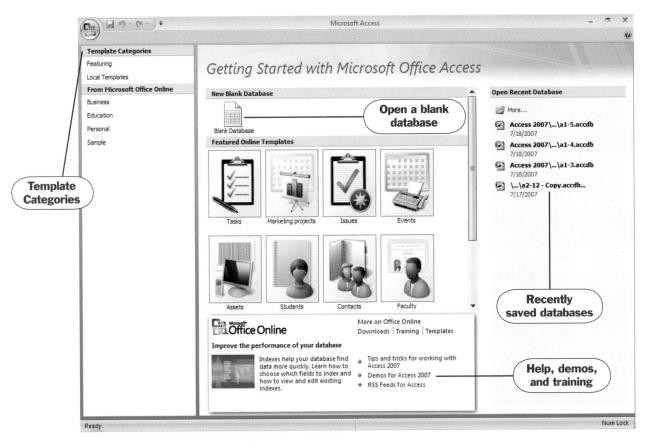

Figure 1.3: Access opening screen

TRY *it* **OUT** *a1-2*

Access should be open.

1. If time permits and if you are online, in the bottom section of the middle panel, click **Training** under More on Office Online and view the online training.

2. In the Template Categories list, click **Local Templates**. *Note the database templates that are available on your computer.*

3. Point to, but do not click, each database to view an explanation of its purpose.

4. If you are online, click each of the Microsoft Office Online categories and view the choices.

5. Do not close Access.

Learn about Database Objects

▶ **Database objects** are tools that you create to store, maintain, search, analyze, and report on data in a database program such as Access. All the objects are created and saved within one database file. In this lesson you will learn about four database objects: tables, forms, queries, and reports. The icon displayed with the explanatory text for each database object will identify the object type on lists of objects.

▶ A **table** appears in a spreadsheet format, and each row in a table represents one **record** in a database. The table shown in Figure 1.4 contains a list of friends, and each friend's data is a record. The items of data that make up each record, such as the ID, First, Last, Address, and so on, are called **fields**. Each field is identified by a **field name**. A table can have up to 255 fields. Specific data in a field is called the **field content**. Tables are sometimes referred to as **datasheets**.

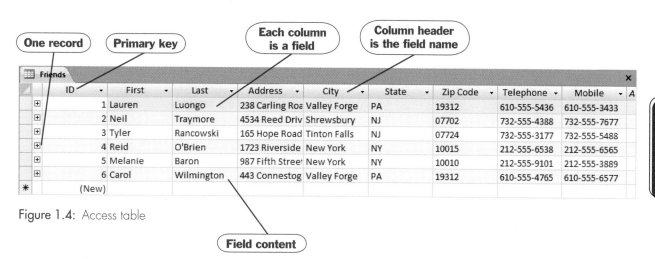

Figure 1.4: Access table

▶ When designing a database, you should provide at least one field in each table that provides a unique code or number to identify each record. This field, called a **primary key**, may be used in other related tables. In Figure 1.4, the primary key is the ID. This field also exists in another table containing birthdays, shown in Figure 1.5. The ID primary key in the *Birthdays* table provides the key to relate the information to the *Friends* table.

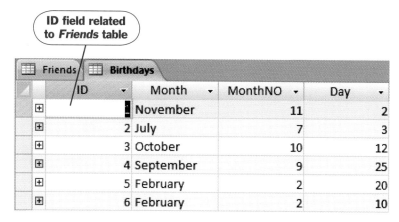

Figure 1.5: Linked table

▶ **Forms** are used to display one record at a time and can contain fields from several different tables. It is easier to enter or update data with a form than on the row of a table, where records may be changed in error. The form illustrated in Figure 1.6 shows data from the first record in the *Friends* table and the related data from the *Birthdays* table. *See Figures 1.4 and 1.5.*

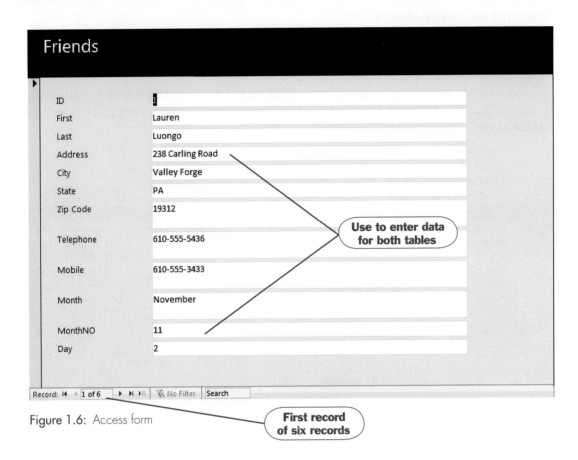

Figure 1.6: Access form

► **Queries** are a structured way to tell Access to search the records and retrieve data that meets certain criteria from one or more database tables. For example, a query may request that Access retrieve data from the *Friends* table to display names and mobile telephone numbers along with birthdays from the *Birthdays* table. The data is displayed in a table format, as shown in Figure 1.7.

Last	First	Mobile	Month	Day
Wilmington	Carol	610-555-6577	February	10
Baron	Melanie	212-555-3889	February	20
Traymore	Neil	732-555-7677	July	3
O'Brien	Reid	212-555-6565	September	25
Rancowski	Tyler	732-555-5488	October	12
Luongo	Lauren	610-555-3433	November	2

Figure 1.7: Access query

Query to display friends and their mobile telephone numbers, listed in birthday order

► **Reports** display information retrieved from the database. A report analyzes the data you specify. Notice that in the report shown in Figure 1.8, the data from the query is displayed, formatted, and arranged in month and day order.

Birthdays

Month	Day	Last	First	Mobile
February	10	Wilmington	Carol	610-555-6577
February	20	Baron	Melanie	212-555-3889
July	3	Traymore	Neil	732-555-7677
September	25	O'Brien	Reid	212-555-6565
October	12	Rancowski	Tyler	732-555-5488
November	2	Luongo	Lauren	610-555-3433

Report on query results

Figure 1.8: Access report

Open a Database and Explore the Access Database Screen

▶ When you create or open a database, the Access database screen appears, as shown in Figure 1.9. The Quick Access toolbar, the Microsoft Office Button, and the Ribbon of tabs that you used in other Office 2007 applications are available here with application-specific commands. The **Navigation Pane**, on the left side of the screen, lists the database objects present in the file, and the **work pane** on the right side of the screen is the display area for the active object. Objects can be opened by dragging them from the Navigation Pane to the work pane, or by double-clicking the object.

▶ Tabs appropriate to the task will be displayed. In Figure 1.9, the Table Tools Datasheet tab appears because a datasheet/table is in the work pane.

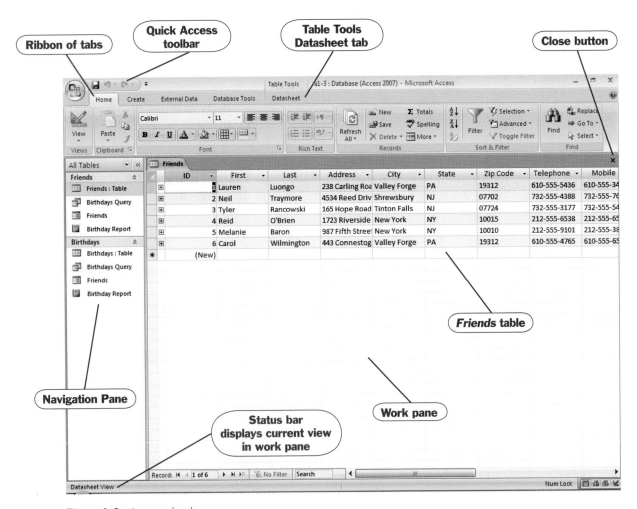

Figure 1.9: Access database screen

▶ You can use the Office Button to open an existing database file, or if the file is on the list of recently saved databases, double-click the database to open it. Access 2007 databases have an **.accdb** extension.

HOW [Ctrl]+O **1**. Click the **Office Button**. **2**. Click **Open**. **3**. Locate the folder that contains the database, and double-click the file.

T R Y *it* O U T *a1-3*

1. Press **[Ctrl]+O** and locate your data folder. Double-click data file **a1-3.accdb**. *Note the Navigation Pane and the list of objects with their icons in both groups.*

2. Click **Friends : Table**, and drag and drop it into the work pane. *The Table Tools Datasheet tab appears.*

3. Double-click **Birthdays : Table** to place it in the work pane. *Note the Friends table and Birthdays table are arranged as tabbed datasheets.* Close both tables using the Close button at the top right of the table.

4. View the *Friends* form by double-clicking or dragging it into the work

pane. *Note that some objects appear in more than one group on the Navigation Pane.*

5. View and close the *Birthdays* query.

6. Click the **Home tab**, if necessary, to view the set of commands. Click the **Create**, **External Data**, and **Database Tools tabs** to view each set of commands.

7. Double-click **Birthdays Report** to view the report version of the *Birthdays* query.

8. Close each of the objects in the work pane using the Close button in the upper-right corner of the work pane.

9. Do not close the database.

Explore the Navigation Pane and Close a Database

▶ The Navigation Pane is used to view and manage the objects in your database. Database objects are organized into a category and then further divided into groups. The default category is Tables and Related Views, and the default group in that category is All Tables, which appears in the menu at the top of the Navigation Pane.

► The Tables and Related Views category groups the objects in a database by the tables to which they are related. For example, if the table named *Friends* is bound to a form, a query, and a report, the Navigation Pane places those objects in a group called *Friends*. Objects may appear in more than one group if they are related to other tables. As shown in Figure 1.10, the Navigation Pane contains the elements listed in Table 1.1.

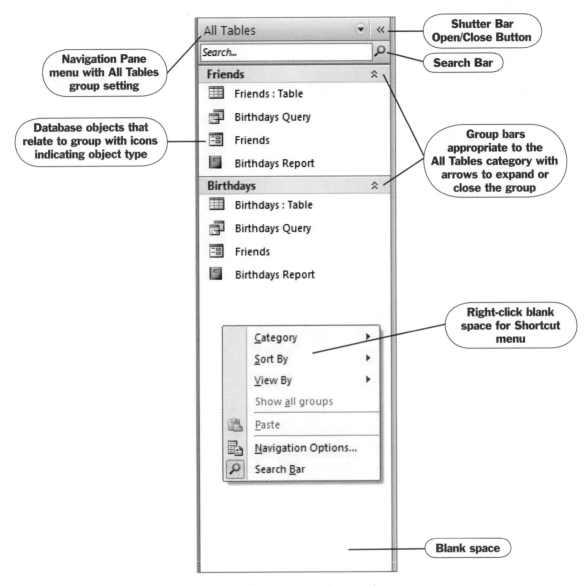

Figure 1.10: Navigation Pane and shortcut menu

Table 1.1: Navigation Pane elements

Menu	The menu displays the group setting. Click it to change categories and to view the new group setting. Right-click the menu to perform other tasks, such as opening the Navigation Options dialog box.
Shutter Bar Open/ Close Button	Expands or collapses the Navigation Pane. The collapsed Navigation Pane will still be visible at the left of the screen and can be expanded again using the same button.
Search Bar	Find objects quickly by entering part or all of an object name. Objects that do not match the search string are hidden. The Search Bar may have to be added to the Navigation Pane by right-clicking the blank space and selecting Search Bar.
Group bars	The Navigation Pane displays each group under a bar containing the name of the group. For example, in Figure 1.10, the groups are *Friends* and *Birthdays*, which are tables and reflect the All Tables category setting. To expand or close a group, click the up or down arrows on the group bar. The groups will change when you change categories.
Database objects	The tables, forms, reports, queries, and other objects in a database are represented by their name and the object icon. The objects that appear in a group are determined by the category. Each group includes the objects that belong there or are related in some way, which may result in some objects being listed in more than one group.
Blank space	Right-click the blank space at the bottom of the Navigation Pane to use the shortcut menu to change categories, sort the items in the pane, and show or hide the details (such as creation date) for the objects in each group.

▶ The Navigation Pane menu appears when you click the list arrow, as shown in Figure 1.11. As detailed in Table 1.2, there are two sections to the menu: Navigate to Category, which lists the categories, and Filter by Group, which lists groups. **Categories** are ways you can organize your objects into sets that make managing the database easier. **Groups** are subsets of the category selected. For example, if you are in the Object Type category, the groups would be Tables, Forms, Queries, and Reports.

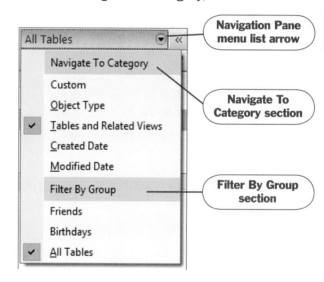

Figure 1.11: Navigation Pane menu

Table 1.2: Navigation Pane menu

Navigate To Category section	Displays the categories for the open database with the current category checked. In Figure 1.11, the database is set to the default category of Tables and Related Views. You can change the category here.
Filter By Group section	Lists the groups that are contained in the selected category. In Figure 1.11, the groups are set to All Tables for this database, which becomes the title of the menu.

► When you close a database file, you are returned to the Access opening screen. If you use the Close button at the top right of the Access screen, you will close the database and Access.

HOW **1**. Click the **Office Button**. **2**. Click **Close Database**. *You are returned to the Access opening screen.*

TRY *it* **OUT** *a1-4*

1. Use the open database or open data file **a1-4**.

2. Double-click **Birthdays Report**. Click the **Shutter Bar Open/Close Button** to collapse the Navigation Pane and get a full view of the *Birthdays* report. Click it again to redisplay the Navigation Pane.

3. In the Search Bar box, enter **query**. *If the Search Bar is not visible, right-click on the menu bar and click **Search Bar**. Note that all other objects are cleared, and you can see only the query object.* Click the **Clear Search String button** to the right of the Search Bar box.

4. Click the **up arrow** at the end of the Friends group bar to close the group. Click the **down arrow** to expand the group.

5. Click the **Navigation Pane menu list arrow**, and click the category **Object Type**. *Note the new groupings on the Navigation Pane and the new menu title. Click the menu to view the change in the group setting.*

6. Right-click the blank space of the Navigation Pane, and point to **Category**, then click **Tables and Related Views**. *This is the default setting for databases.*

7. Close the *Birthdays* report.

8. Click the **Office Button**, then click **Close Database**. *You are returned to the Access opening screen.*

Understand Database Design

▶ Before creating a database, you must determine what type of information the database will contain and how you will organize it. Plan your database on paper first by determining the purpose of the database and listing the fields that best identify the information you plan to enter. For example, if you want to create a mailing list, you should include first name, last name, address, and so on.

▶ Follow these guidelines when designing a database:

1. Divide data into subject-based tables to reduce duplication. With the exception of primary key fields, a table should not contain information duplicated in another table.

2. Determine field names and content. Each field should relate to the subject of the table.

3. Determine the primary keys that will link tables. The primary key is a unique field with unique values that identify the record.

4. Determine the links between tables. Tables must share a field so that they can be related.

5. Store information in its smallest segment. For example, names should be stored in First and Last fields.

6. Do not include calculated data. You can calculate data in Access reports and queries.

▶ When you are satisfied that the table structures meet your goals, you can create a form for data entry, add your data, and create any queries and/or reports required.

▶ In the database planning phase for the database in Try it Out a1-4, it was decided that there was a need for two tables and that the data would be stored in the tables as follows:

FRIENDS	BIRTHDAYS
ID	ID
First	Month
Last	MonthNO (the number of the month)
Address	Day
City	
State	
Zip	
Telephone	

T R Y i t O U T a1-5

1. On the Access opening screen, under Open Recent Database, double-click to open **a1-4**, or use **[Ctrl]+O** to open data file **a1-5**.

2. Notice that there are two tables: *Friends* and *Birthdays*.

3. Click and drag **Friends : Table** to the work pane, and notice that there are two fields for the name: First and Last. Notice that there are four fields for the address: Address, City, State, and Zip Code. *This allows for sorting and creating reports using each field independently.*

4. Close the *Friends* table.

5. Open the *Birthdays* table, and notice that the only field duplicated from the *Friends* table is ID.

6. Close the *Birthdays* table.

7. Close the database.

Understand Database Views

▶ Database **views** are ways to look at the data or the structure of a table, form, query, or report. Some views are common to all database objects, and some are unique. Click the list arrow on the View button on the Home tab to determine the views available for each object, as shown in Figure 1.12. Or, if you right-click the object, such as a report, in the Navigation Pane, or right-click on the object's tab in the work pane, you can change the view, as shown in Figure 1.13.

▶ The views available for a table are Datasheet, PivotTable, PivotChart, and Design. The View button will display an icon for a view other than the one you are in. This allows you to switch to that view without using the list arrow. The views for tables are listed in Table 1.3.

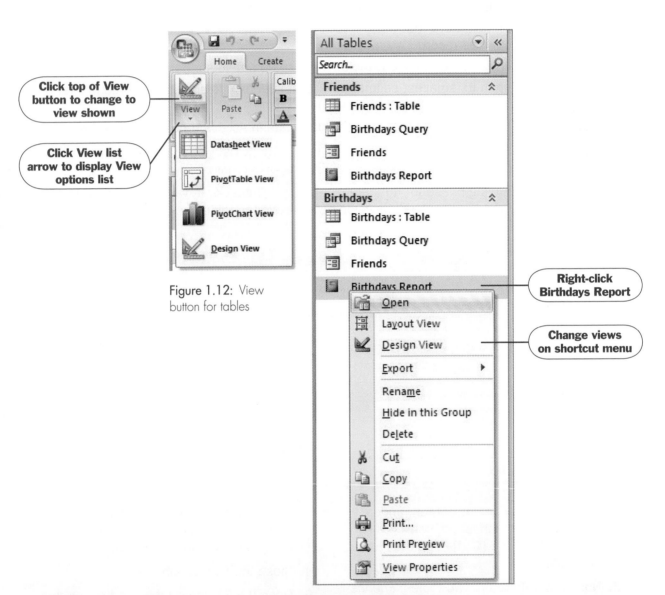

Figure 1.12: View button for tables

Figure 1.13: Right-click object in Navigation Pane to change view

Table 1.3: Table views and uses

Datasheet View		Add, edit, delete, and view data
PivotTable View		Interactively summarize and analyze data from tables
PivotChart View		Graphically represent the information in a PivotChart
Design View		Create and modify table structures

T R Y _it_ O U T _a1-6_

1. On the Access opening screen, under Open Recent Database, double-click to open **a1-4**.

2. Double-click **Friends : Table** in the Navigation Pane to open the _Friends_ table.

3. Click the **Home tab**, and in the Views group, click the **View list arrow**. _Note the icons for each view and the icon currently on the button._

4. Click **Design View** to change to Design view. _Note the view name on the status bar at the bottom left._

5. Click the **Datasheet View button**, which should be displayed on the View button. _Click each of the other two views._

6. Close the _Friends_ table.

7. Double-click **Birthdays Query**, click the **view list arrow** and note the View options list. _A SQL view is available for queries._ Close the query.

8. Open the _Friends_ form. Click the **View list arrow**, and open the Layout and Design views. Close the form.

9. Double-click **Birthdays Report**. Right-click the **Birthdays Report tab**, and click **Design View** on the shortcut menu. Close the report by clicking the **Close button** for the Birthdays Report bar.

10. Close the database file.

11. Close Access.

REHEARSAL

AGAIN

TASK 1

WHAT YOU NEED TO KNOW

▶ Access files have an **.accdb** extension.

▶ A table is also called a datasheet. You can set a primary key, of unique data, to identify records and link tables.

▶ In this Rehearsal activity, you will familiarize yourself with navigating the database screen and with Access database objects, in a database for a swim and golf club.

▼ DIRECTIONS

1. Start Access.

2. Open the data file **1r1-club.accdb**.

3. In the *Club Members* group, double-click **Club Members : Table**, as shown in Figure 1.14. *Note that there are eight fields. The field named "Member ID" is the primary key.*

4. Close the table.

5. In the *Golf Members* group, click and drag **Golf Members : Table** to the work pane, as shown in Figure 1.15. *Note the field named "Member ID" and the golf-specific data.*

6. Close the table.

7. In the *Swim Members* group, double-click **Swim Members : Table**, as shown in Figure 1.16. *Note the field named "Member ID" and the swim-specific data.* The three tables are linked by the Member ID field.

8. Close the table.

Primary key field

Club Members									✕
Member ID ▾	Last Name ▾	First Name ▾	Address ▾	City ▾	State ▾	Postal Code ▾	Telephone ℕ ▾	Add New Field	
⊞	1	Smith	John	64 Lindar Drive	Waterford	NY	12188	518-555-1221	
⊞	2	Johansen	James	100 Circle Drive	Melrose	NY	12121	518-555-2657	
⊞	3	Keith	Kenny	1715 Milton Av	Scotia	NY	12302	518-555-6328	
⊞	4	Smith	Brian	23 Renwick Roa	Melrose	NY	12121	518-555-6599	
⊞	5	Dennis	Patricia	45 Corner Ave	Ravena	NY	12143	518-555-9876	
⊞	6	Hurley	Michael	45 Candle Stree	Ravena	NY	12143	518-555-7054	
⊞	7	Martens	Tracy	32 West Ave	Ravena	NY	12143	518-555-4655	
⊞	8	Palardi	Martha	65 Acorn Street	Soctia	NY	12302	518-555-0654	
⊞	9	Hansen	Kelly	765 Lake Drive	Scotia	NY	12302	518-555-8232	
⊞	10	Vasquez	Robert	32 Sapling Ave	Melrose	NY	12121	518-555-3265	
✳	(New)								

Figure 1.14: *Club Members* table

Continued on page 20

Relates to *Club Members* table

Golf Members

Golf Locker No ▾	Member ID ▾	Handicap ▾	Cart User? ▾	League 9 ▾	League 18 ▾	Add New Field
5	8	19	☑	☑	☐	
10	9	15	☑	☐	☑	
15	7	24	☑	☑	☐	
16	1	11	☑	☐	☑	
20	10	19	☑	☐	☐	
24	3	23	☑	☐	☐	
32	2	14	☑	☐	☑	
*			☐	☐	☐	

Figure 1.15: *Golf Members* table

Relates to *Club Members* and *Golf Members* tables

Swim Members

Swim Locker ▾	Member ID ▾	Swim Progra ▾	Sauna User ▾	Whirlpool U ▾	Add New Field
5	1	☐	☑	☑	
8	5	☑	☐	☑	
10	8	☐	☑	☑	
12	2	☑	☑	☐	
15	6	☐	☐	☑	
21	4	☑	☑	☑	
*		☐	☐	☐	

Figure 1.16: *Swim Members* table

Club Members Query

City ▾	Last Name ▾	First Name ▾	Telephone N ▾
Melrose	Johansen	James	518-555-2657
Melrose	Smith	Brian	518-555-6599
Melrose	Vasquez	Robert	518-555-3265
Ravena	Dennis	Patricia	518-555-9876
Ravena	Hurley	Michael	518-555-7054
Ravena	Martens	Tracy	518-555-4655
Scotia	Hansen	Kelly	518-555-8232
Scotia	Keith	Kenny	518-555-6328
Soctia	Palardi	Martha	518-555-0654
Waterford	Smith	John	518-555-1221

Figure 1.17: *Club Members* query

9. In the *Club Members* group, open the *Club Members* query, as shown in Figure 1.17. This query answers the question, "What are the names and telephone numbers of the members arranged by city?"

10. Close the query.

11. Open the *Members* form from any group, as shown in Figure 1.18. *Note that this form appears in all three groups and contains data from all three tables. This form displays one record of the Club Members table.*

12. Close the form.

13. Open the *Club Members* report, as shown in Figure 1.19. This report lists the names of the members by City.

14. Close the report and the database file.

15. Close Access.

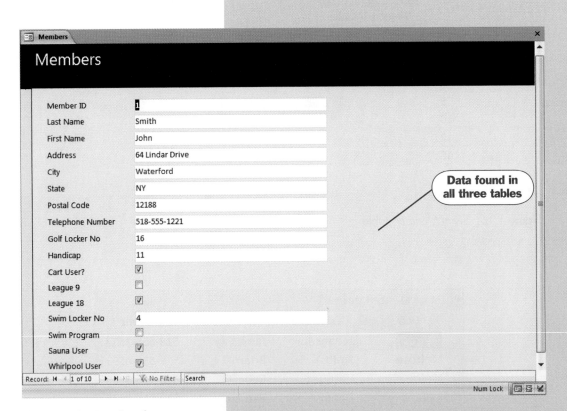

Figure 1.18: *Members form*

Club Members

City	Last Name	First Name	Telephone Number
Melrose			
	Johansen	James	518-555-2657
	Smith	Brian	518-555-6599
	Vasquez	Robert	518-555-3265
Ravena			
	Dennis	Patricia	518-555-9876
	Hurley	Michael	518-555-7054
	Martens	Tracy	518-555-4655
Scotia			
	Hansen	Kelly	518-555-8232
	Keith	Kenny	518-555-6328
	Palardi	Martha	518-555-0654
Waterford			
	Smith	John	518-555-1221

Figure 1.19: *Club Members* report

Cues for Reference

Start Access
1. Double-click the **Microsoft Access 2007 icon** on the desktop or Windows taskbar.
   Or
1. Click the **Start button**.
2. Click **All Programs**.
3. Click **Microsoft Office**, then **Microsoft Office Access 2007**.

Design a Database
1. Plan the database before you begin.
2. Identify the tables by dividing the data into subject-based groups.
3. Define fields in each table, breaking information into its smallest segments.
4. Determine the primary keys (unique fields with unique values to identify records).
5. Define the relationships between the tables.
6. Create a form.
7. Enter data into tables or the form.
8. Create queries and reports as needed.

Open a Database File
1. Click [Ctrl]+O.
   Or
1. Click the **Office Button**, then click **Open**.
2. Locate the folder that contains the database, and double-click the file.

Change the Navigation Pane Category
1. Click the **Navigation Pane menu list arrow**.
2. Click a new category.
   Or
1. Right-click the blank space on the Navigation Pane.
2. Point to **Category** on the shortcut menu.
3. Click a new category.

Open Table/Form/Query/Report
1. Double-click an object in the Navigation Pane, or click and drag it into the work pane.

Open Table/Form/Query/Report in Design View
1. Right-click an object in the Navigation Pane, then click **Design View**.
   Or
1. Right-click an object tab in the work pane, then click **Design View**.
   Or
1. Click the **Home tab**, and in the Views group, click the **View list arrow**, then click **Design View**, if necessary.

Change View
1. Right-click an object in the Navigation Pane, and select a view.
   Or
1. Right-click an object tab in the work pane, and select a view.
   Or
1. Click the **Home tab**, and in the Views group, click the **View list arrow**, then click the desired view.

PERFORMANCE TASK 1

The Club database has been explored but each database object has multiple views. You will open the objects, switch views, note the available views, and look closely at the Design view for each object.

Follow these guidelines:

1. Start Access and open the data file **1p1-club.accdb**.

2. Change the Navigation Pane category to Object Type. *Use the Navigation Pane menu list arrow.*

3. Open the *Club Members* table.

4. Right-click on the table tab and click **Design View**, as shown in Figure 1.20. *Note the Table Tools Design tab.*

5. Read the explanation of the Field Name column in the bottom-right corner of the Field Properties section. Tab to each of the remaining two columns, and read the explanations.

6. Click the **Home tab**, and in the Views group, click the **View button** to change back to Datasheet view. Close the table.

7. Use the search feature on the Navigation Pane to search for: `query`. *Use the Navigation Pane menu list arrow to open the Search Bar if necessary.*

8. Open the *Club Members* query and change to Design view, as shown in Figure 1.21. *Note the Query Tools Design tab and that the City and Last Name fields are set to sort in ascending order.* Close the query, and clear the search string.

9. Open the *Members* form and change to Design view, as shown in Figure 1.22. *Note the Form Design Tools Design tab. You need to use the scroll bar to view the entire form design.* Close the form.

10. Open the *Club Members* report, right-click on the **report tab**, and change to Design view, as shown in Figure 1.23. *Note the Report Design Tools Design tab.*

11. Use the Shutter Bar Open/Close Button on the Navigation Pane to collapse the Navigation Pane. Expand the pane.

12. Close the database and Access.

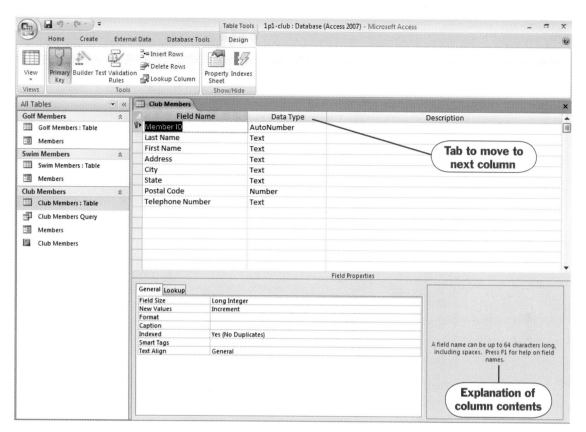

Figure 1.20: *Club Members* table in Design View

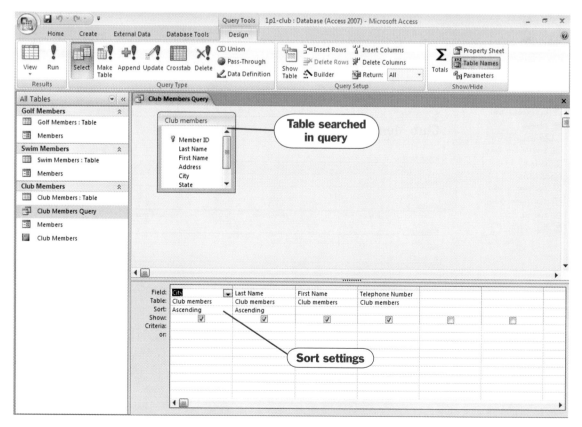

Figure 1.21: *Club Members* query in Design view

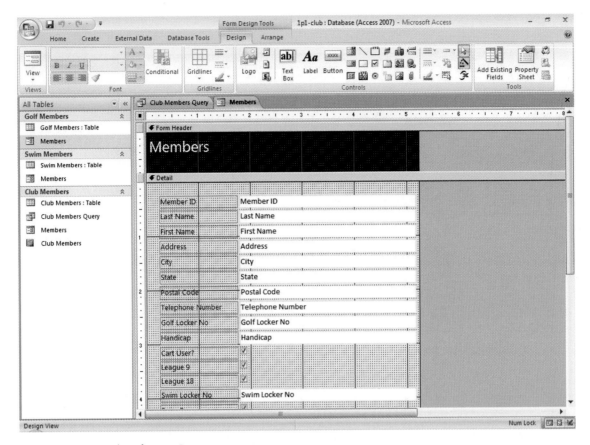

Figure 1.22: *Members* form in Design view

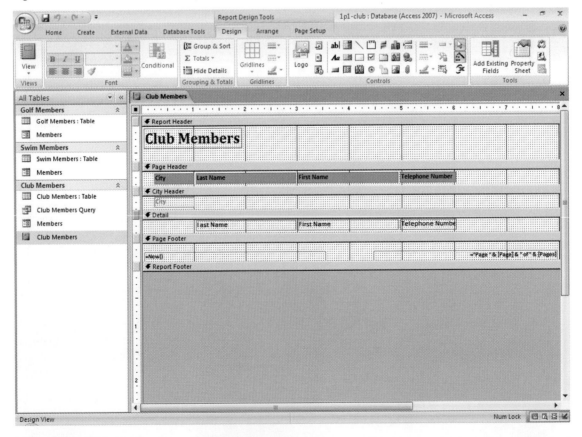

Figure 1.23: *Club Members* report in Design view

Access Tables and Datasheets

In this lesson, you will learn to use features in Access to create and modify tables and table relationships. You will learn about field data types and properties, and how to enter and edit data.

Upon completion of this lesson, you will have mastered the following skill sets

- ✶ Create a new file with a blank database
- ✶ Create tables from templates
- ✶ Create tables in Datasheet view
- ✶ Add, set, change, and remove the primary key
- ✶ Set data types
- ✶ Enter data using a datasheet
- ✶ Create tables in Design view
- ✶ Modify table and field properties
- ✶ Use the Lookup Wizard
- ✶ Use the Input Mask Wizard
- ✶ Create, modify, and print relationships

Terms
- Attachment
- AutoNumber
- Caption
- Currency
- Data type
- Date/Time
- Field properties
- Field templates
- Foreign key
- Hyperlink
- Indexed
- Inner join
- Input mask
- Input Mask Wizard
- Left outer join
- Lookup field
- Lookup Wizard
- Many-to-many
- Memo
- Number
- OLE Object
- One-to-one
- One-to-many
- Record selector
- Relationship
- Right outer join
- Row Source Type
- Table properties
- Table templates
- Text
- Yes/No

T R Y O U T

TASK 1

GOAL

To create an Employee database with two tables, several data types, and a primary key, as shown in Figure 2.1

✴ Create a new file with a blank database
✴ Create tables from templates
✴ Create tables in Datasheet view
✴ Add, set, change, and remove the primary key
✴ Set data types
✴ Enter data using a datasheet

Table created by entering data into datasheet

Table created using table templates

Emp ID	Last Name	First Name	E-mail	Home Phone	Address	City	State	ZIP	N
1	Williams	Charles	wmsch@world.net	480-555-6534	43 Voight Street	Phoenix	AZ	85006	
2	Popper	Karen	poppk@globe.net	480-555-1654	92 Carson Drive	Tempe	AZ	85281	
3	Carlyle	Terry	carter@world.net	480-555-3522	490 Bard Avenue	Phoenix	AZ	85003	
5	Thompson	Michael	thomic@globe.net	480-555-3009	543 Ray Road	Chandler	AZ	85224	
*(New)									

Payroll

Payroll ID	SSNO	Emp ID	Title	Status	Exemptions	Rate	Add New Field
1	143-00-7643	1	Manager	M	3	$20.00	
2	196-00-2345	2	Bookkeeper	M	4	$15.00	
3	156-00-4568	3	Sales Associate	S	1	$12.00	
*(New)						$0.00	

Currency field template

Figure 2.1: Task 1: Database with two tables

WHAT YOU NEED TO KNOW

Create a New File with a Blank Database

▶ A database file can be created by using a blank database and building your own database objects, as an alternative to using one of the database templates provided by Access. Tables are the first objects to create in a new database because all the other objects rely on their data. Access provides several ways to develop tables, which we will practice in this lesson.

▶ When you use a blank database to create a new file, you must name it first, as shown in Figure 2.2. After you enter the name, you will locate the folder where the file should be saved.

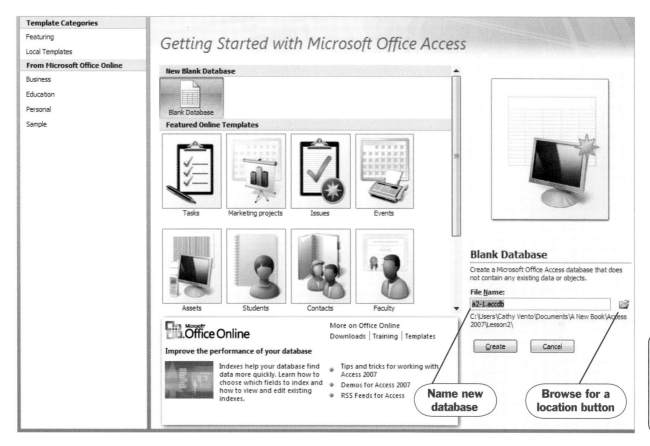

Figure 2.2: Name and save a new blank database

HOW 1. On the Getting Started with Microsoft Office Access page, click the **Blank Database button**. 2. In the Blank Database pane, enter a filename. 3. Click the **Browse for a location button**, and locate the appropriate folder. Click **OK**. 4. Click **Create**.

TRY _it_ OUT _a2-1_

1. Open Access and on the Getting Started with Microsoft Office Access page, click the **Blank Database button**.

2. In the Blank Database pane, enter **a2-1**. *Access will add the .accdb extension.*

3. Click the **Browse for a location button**, and locate your solutions folder. Click **OK**.

The path to your location appears under the filename.

4. Click **Create**. *The database opens with a blank table in the work pane.*

5. Do not close the database.

Create Tables from Templates

▶ Access provides table templates for Contacts, Tasks, Issues, Events, and Assets, as shown in Figure 2.3. Each **table template** provides a table with field names and data types organized to provide all necessary information on that subject. A template may be customized to meet your specific requirements, or it can be named, saved, and used as it appears.

▶ To base a new table on a template you can delete the blank new table (Table1). If a table is closed without using or saving it, it will be deleted and you can begin with the template-based table.

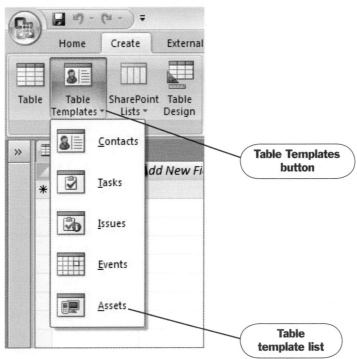

Figure 2.3: Create tables from templates

HOW **1.** In an open database, click the **Create tab**, and in the Tables group, click the **Table Templates button**. **2.** Select an available template from the list. A new table based on the template is added to your database and appears on the work pane.

TRY*it*OUT a2-2

1. You should have the **a2-1** database on the Access screen.

2. Click the **Close button** on **Table1**. *The table is deleted because no changes were made or saved.*

3. Click the **Create tab**, and in the Tables group, click the **Table Templates button**.

4. Click **Contacts** in the list of table templates. *A new table appears on the work pane with fields related to contact information.*

5. Click and move the scroll bar at the bottom of the work pane to the right to view all the fields in the new Table1.

Continued on next page

6. Click the **Save button** on the Quick Access Toolbar. *A Save As dialog box appears where you can enter the table name.*

7. Enter `Contacts` as the table name, and click **OK**. *The table tab displays the new name.*

8. Do not close the file.

Modify Tables

▶ A table may be modified by inserting, deleting, or renaming a column. You can right-click and use the shortcut menu on any column, shown in Figure 2.4, or use the buttons in the Fields & Columns group of the Table Tools Datasheet tab, shown in Figure 2.5.

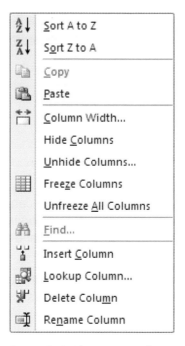

Figure 2.4: Shortcut menu from any column header

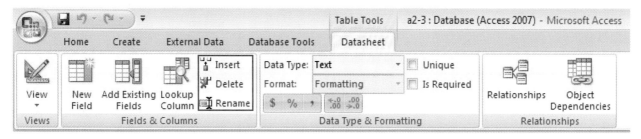

Figure 2.5: Modify tables using Table Tools Datasheet tab

1. Use the open database or open data file **a2-3** and double-click on **Contacts : Table**.

2. Right-click the **Contacts tab** and click **Design View**. *Note that the ID field is identified as the Primary Key field with the Primary Key icon. View the list of field names.*

3. Right-click the **Country/Region field row** and on the **Table Tools Datasheet tab**, click **Delete Rows**. Click the **Save button** to save the change.

4. Click the **View button** on the Home tab to return to Datasheet view.

5. Delete the **Home Phone, Fax Number, and Web Page columns**:
   a. Click on the **Home Phone column header** to delete.
   b. Click the **Table Tools Datasheet tab**, and in the Fields & Columns group, click the **Delete button**.
   c. Repeat for the Fax Number and Web Page field columns.

6. Right-click the **Notes column header** and click **Rename Column**. Name the field column header **Other**.

7. Click on the **Last Name column header**, and click the **Insert Column button** in the Fields & Columns group on the Table Tools Datasheet tab. *A new column called Field1 is added*. Click the **Delete button**.

8. Save, click the **Office Button**, and click **Close Database**, but do not close Access.

Create Tables in Datasheet View

▶ When you need to create a table without a template, you can add a table and Access will create the table structure while you enter data. It is similar to working in an Excel worksheet. Each field's data type will be set based on the data you enter and fields will be named Field1, Field2, and so on.

 1. In an open database, click the **Create tab**, and in the Tables group, click the **Table button**. *A table is created with the cursor in the Add New Field column.*

▶ When you add a new field you can enter actual data or use the **New Field button** to view the Field Templates pane, as shown in Figure 2.6. **Field templates** are field definitions for commonly used field types and specific types organized by table template categories. Double-click a field template to create a field with the desired characteristics for your table.

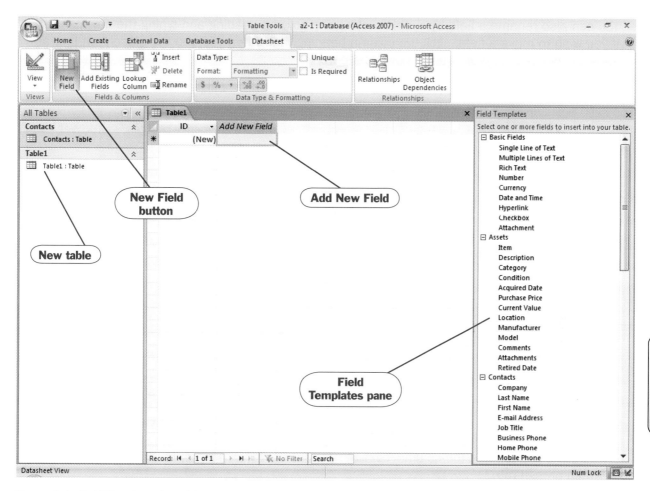

Figure 2.6: Field Templates for table

HOW   **1.** In a new table, click the **New Field button**. **2.** Double-click each field to add to the table.

New Field

TRY it OUT a2-4

1. Open data file **a2-4**. *Note the Contacts table created earlier. We need another table to record billings.*

2. Click the **Create tab**, and in the Tables group, click the **Table button**. *A new table appears named Table1, and the Table Tools Datasheet tab becomes active.*

3. In the Fields & Columns group, click the **New Field button**, and scroll to view all the field templates.

4. Double-click on the **Currency field template** under Basic Fields to add the field. *A field titled Currency is added.* Add another Currency field.

5. Do not close the table or the database.

► You can also rename a field by double-clicking the column heading and typing the new name. If you wish to move a field, click the column heading, and when you see the placement bar, as shown in Figure 2.7, drag it to its new location.

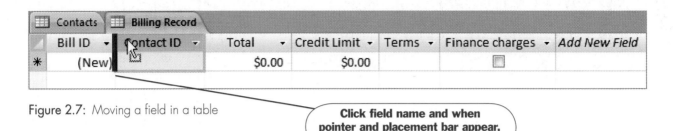

Figure 2.7: Moving a field in a table

Click field name and when pointer and placement bar appear, drag the column to new location

TRY it OUT a2-5

1. Use the open database file from **a2-4**.

2. Double-click the **ID column header**, and rename it `Bill ID`.

3. Double-click each of the Currency column headers to rename the columns `Total` and `Credit Limit`.

4. Double-click the **Add New Field column header**, and rename the column `Terms`, then press **[Tab]**.

5. In the Field Templates list, double-click to add the Checkbox field template under Basic Fields. *The checkbox field template provides a check box for Yes/No data.*

6. Rename the Checkbox column header `Finance charges`.

7. Double-click the **Add New Field column header**, rename the column `Contact ID`, then press **[Tab]**.

8. Click the **Contact ID column header**, and drag the column so that it appears to the right of the Bill ID column, as shown in Figure 2.7. *You cannot drag the column until the vertical bar appears. Click back into the middle of the column to get the bar.*

9. Close the Field Templates pane.

10. Click the **Save button** on the Quick Access toolbar. Name the table `Billing Record`. Click **OK**.

11. Do not close the table or the database.

Add, Set, Change, and Remove the Primary Key

► The primary key is a field that is a unique identifier for each record. It always contains a value, and that value never changes for that record. The primary key is used to bring information in different tables together by using the key to refer back to that table. For example, in the Contacts database, we used the ID number from the *Contacts* table in the *Billing Record* table. When a primary key from one table appears in another table, it is called a **foreign key**, as shown in Figure 2.8.

Figure 2.8: Primary and Foreign keys

▶ When you create a table with a template or in Datasheet view, Access assigns the first field as the primary key. In Design view, the primary key field is identified by the Primary Key icon, as shown in Figure 2.9. You will note, in the Field Properties pane, that primary key fields are **indexed**, or placed in order for easy access, with no duplicates so that the values are unique for each record.

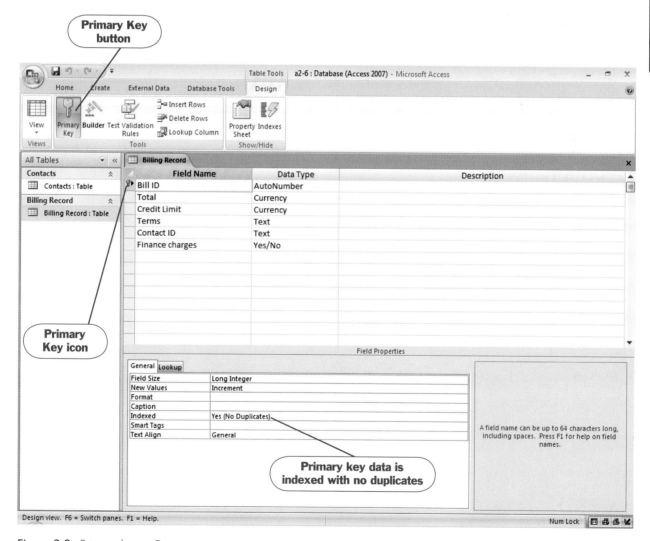

Figure 2.9: Primary key in Design view

► If you click the Primary Key button on the Table Tools Design tab, you can add, remove, set, or change the primary key designation. The determination of primary key designations should be done during the database design phase, but you may change the design later in the process, if necessary.

Primary
Key

TRY *it* OUT *a2-6*

1. Use the open database or open data file **a2-6**.

2. With the *Billing Record* table in the work pane, right-click the **Billing Record tab** and click **Design View**. *You will see the screen in Figure 2.9.*

3. Click the **Bill ID field name**, and notice that in the Field Properties pane, the primary key data is indexed with no duplicates.

4. Click the **Primary Key button** to remove the designation and icon. *Note that the Indexed field property is set to No.*

5. Click the **Contact ID field name**, and click the **Primary Key button**. Note the

Indexed field property. Since this is a table of billing records and contacts will have more than one billing, there will be duplicates.

6. Click the **Bill ID field name**, and click the **Primary Key button**. *The primary key designation and the icon is removed from the Contact ID field row and moved to the Bill ID field row.*

7. Switch to the *Contacts* table, and click the **View button** for Design view. *Note the primary key and the field properties.*

8. Do not close the tables or database.

Set Data Types

► All fields, including those you choose when using Table or Field templates, have a specific data type. A **data type** is an attribute that determines what type of information a field can contain. Table 2.1 lists the 11 data type settings, the type of data defined, and the size of the field. The data types are presented in the order in which they appear in Design view.

Table 2.1: Data type settings

Text	The default setting; text or a mix of text and numbers (e.g., street addresses), or numbers that are not calculated (e.g., ZIP codes)	255 characters or less; unused space is not reserved
Memo	Long text, such as notes or descriptions; may include numbers	63,999 characters or less
Number	Numeric data used for calculations, except involving money	Size may be set
Date/Time	Date and time values	8 characters
Currency	Currency format for numbers used in calculating money values	15 digits to left of decimal and 4 to the right
AutoNumber	Identification number Access automatically enters, in sequential (incrementing by one) or random order, when you add a record	
Yes/No	Data that is one of two values, such as Yes/No, True/False, On/Off	Can use a check box for this data
OLE Object	Data linked to an object in another file, such as an Excel worksheet, created using the object linking and embedding procedure	Limited by space available
Hyperlink	A path to a file on a hard drive, a LAN Server, or an Internet address	A hyperlink can contain the text to display, the address, a sub-address, and a ScreenTip
Attachment	Any file that is supported by Access, such as images, spreadsheets, charts, and the like	More efficient than using OLE
Lookup Wizard	A feature that defines a field that looks up values from another table or list of values	After the field is created by Lookup Wizard, the data type is set automatically

▶ Field data types are displayed in Table Design view. Each data type has different field properties. A drop-down list appears when you click the arrow in the Data Type column, as shown in Figure 2.10.

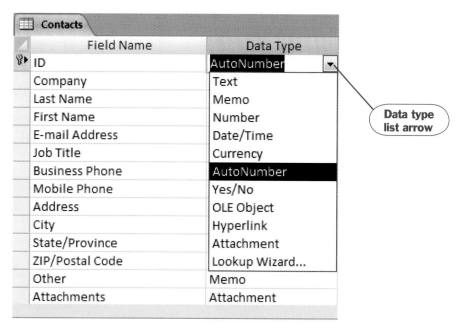

Figure 2.10: Data type list in Table Design view

1. The open database should have the *Contacts* table in Design view in the work pane, or open data file **a2-7** and move to that location. *Note the Primary Key icon next to the ID field.*

2. Click the **ID field name** in the Field Name column. *Note that this field is an AutoNumber field and look at the field properties.*

3. Click the **Last Name field** in the Data Type column. *Note that this field is a Text field and the field properties show a Field Size of 255.*

4. Click the **data type list arrow**. *Note the 11 data type options.*

5. Switch to the *Billing Record* table in Design view, and click the **Total field name**. *Note that this field is a Currency field and the field properties show Decimal Places set to automatic.*

6. Click the **Finance charges field name**, and note the settings for a Yes/No data type.

7. Do not close the table.

Enter Data Using a Datasheet

▶ You can use a datasheet, in Datasheet view, to enter data, or records, into your database. Enter the data below each field name as you would in a spreadsheet. You can adjust column width as in Excel by dragging the column header to size, or by double-clicking the field column header to AutoFit the data. Use the Tab key to advance from column to column. To advance to the next row, press the Enter key, press the Tab key, or use the arrow keys. Once you go to the next record, Access automatically saves the previously completed record.

▶ It is not necessary to enter data in an AutoNumber field, because Access automatically assigns a consecutive number. Therefore, as shown in Figure 2.11, you begin entry with the second field. It is important to check the accuracy of your entries because table data is used by all other objects. If you make a mistake, select the entry and press the Delete key to empty the contents of the field.

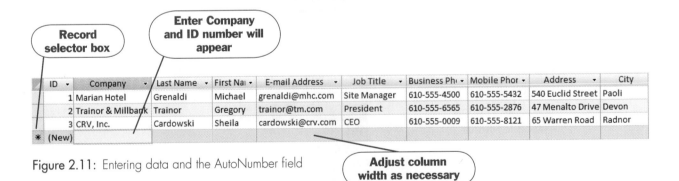

ID	Company	Last Name	First Nai	E-mail Address	Job Title	Business Pho	Mobile Phor	Address	City
1	Marian Hotel	Grenaldi	Michael	grenaldi@mhc.com	Site Manager	610-555-4500	610-555-5432	540 Euclid Street	Paoli
2	Trainor & Millbank	Trainor	Gregory	trainor@tm.com	President	610-555-6565	610-555-2876	47 Menalto Drive	Devon
3	CRV, Inc.	Cardowski	Sheila	cardowski@crv.com	CEO	610-555-0009	610-555-8121	65 Warren Road	Radnor
(New)									

Figure 2.11: Entering data and the AutoNumber field

1. Use the open database or open data file **a2-8**. Open the *Contacts* table in Datasheet view.

2. Enter the information below. Do not enter anything in the ID field; the records will be automatically numbered. *Note that the records are arranged vertically in the table below, and you will be entering one record at a time horizontally. Check the field names carefully.*

3. Check your entries for accuracy.

4. Save the table, but do not close the table or database.

	RECORD 1	**RECORD 2**	**RECORD 3**
Company	Marian Hotel	Trainor & Millbank	CRV, Inc.
Last Name	Grenaldi	Trainor	Cardowski
First Name	Michael	Gregory	Sheila
E-mail Address	grenaldi@mhc.com	trainor@tm.com	cardowski@crv.com
Job Title	Site Manager	President	CEO
Business Phone	610-555-4500	610-555-6565	610-555-0009
Mobile Phone	610-555-5432	610-555-2876	610-555-8121
Address	540 Euclid Street	47 Menalto Drive	65 Warren Road
City	Paoli	Devon	Radnor
State/Province	PA	PA	PA
Zip/Postal Code	19301	19333	19087
Other			

Edit or Delete Records in a Table

▶ If you enter invalid data in a field, such as text in a number field, Access displays an error message indicating that the value is not valid for the field. You can respond to the message and enter the data correctly.

▶ To edit an entry in a table, click in the edit location and make the edit or press the F2 key to select the data and retype the entry. When you move to the next record, the edits are saved.

▶ To delete a record, select the row by clicking the **record selector**, the small box to the left of the first field in a record, as shown in Figure 2.11. You can delete the record by pressing the Delete key or by right-clicking the row and selecting Delete record. Since there is no Undo option within Access, you will be asked to confirm the deletion.

Use Navigation Controls to Move through Records in Datasheets

▶ Access provides buttons on the bottom of the datasheet window that allow you to move efficiently through a datasheet or table. The Navigation bar, shown in Figure 2.12, also indicates which record is active and how many records are in the table.

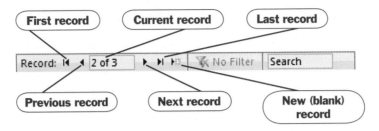

Figure 2.12: Datasheet navigation bar

T R Y *it* **O U T** *a2-9*

1. Use the open database, or open data file **a2-9** and open the *Contacts* table in Datasheet view.

2. Click the Navigation buttons to view each record and the ScreenTip for each button.

3. Edit Grenaldi's mobile phone number to read **610–555–5438**. Place the cursor at the end of the number, backspace, and replace the last number.

4. In record ID 3, click the **Mobile Phone field** and press **[F2]**. Enter **610–555–8181** *Note that the previous entry is cleared*.

5. Click the **record selector box** to the left of record ID 3, and press **[Delete]**.

6. Click **Yes** when Access asks "Are you sure you want to delete these records?" *Note that there is no Undo for this operation*.

7. Close the table and the database. Saving the data changes is unnecessary as Access automatically saves data as it is edited.

REHEARSAL AGAIN

 GOAL
To create an employee database with two tables, several data types, and a primary key

TASK 1

WHAT YOU NEED TO KNOW

▶ Businesses keep detailed records about their employees to provide information for various reasons, including government reports. In this Rehearsal activity, you will begin to create a database with two tables, one to provide contact information for employees and another that contains payroll information. The information technology person in this company has planned the fields for each of the two tables.

▼ DIRECTIONS

1. Open a blank database. Name it **2r1-EMP**, locate your data folder, and click **Create**. *A blank Table1 appears*.

2. Click the **Create tab**, and using Table Templates, create a *Contacts* table.

3. **PLAN:** *Contacts* **table:** Emp ID, Last Name, First Name, E-mail, Home Phone, Address, City, State, ZIP, Notes.
   a. Rename the ID field **Emp ID**. Save and name the table **Contacts**.
   b. Continue to customize the *Contact* table to match the plan by deleting or renaming fields on the Contact table template. *Delete the column that appears as a paper clip, as this is an attachment field*.
   c. Save the table.

4. Switch to Design view, and check that the Emp ID field is the primary key. Return to Datasheet view.

5. **PLAN:** *Payroll* **table:** Payroll ID, SSNO, Emp ID, Title, Status, Exemptions, Rate. Click the **Table1 tab**, and tab to each field column header to enter the field names from the plan for the Payroll table. For the Rate field, use the **New Field button** and the Field Templates pane to add a Currency field from Basic Fields. Rename the field **Rate**. Close the Field Templates pane.

6. Save the table and name it **Payroll**.

7. Right-click the **Payroll tab**, and click **Design View**. Save the Design and return to Datasheet view.

8. Enter the following information in the *Contacts* table. *Note that the data is arranged by record vertically*.

Continued on next page

Emp ID	1	2	3	4
Last Name	Williams	Popper	Carlyle	Thompson
First Name	Charles	Karen	Terry	Michael
E-mail	wmsch@world.net	poppk@globe.net	carter@world.net	thomic@globe.net
Home Phone	480-555-6534	480-555-1654	480-555-3522	480-555-3009
Address	43 Voight Street	92 Carson Drive	451 Bard Avenue	543 Ray Road
City	Phoenix	Tempe	Phoenix	Chandler
State	AZ	AZ	AZ	AZ
ZIP	85006	85281	85003	85224
Notes				

9. Edit the record for Terry Carlyle, as shown in Figure 2.13. His address should be **490 Bard Avenue**, with the same ZIP code.

10. Delete the record for Michael Thompson. He left the company.

11. Close the table.

12. Enter the following information in the *Payroll* table.

SSNO	143-00-7643	196-00-2345	156-00-4568
Emp ID	1	2	3
Title	Manager	Bookkeeper	Sales Associate
Status	M	M	S
Exemptions	3	4	1
Rate	20.00	15.00	12.00
Other			

13. Close the table and the database.

Figure 2.13: *Contacts* and *Payroll* tables

Create a Blank Database

1. On the Getting Started with Microsoft Office Access page, click the **Blank Database button**.
2. In the Blank Database pane, enter a filename.
3. Click the **Browse for a location button**, and locate the appropriate folder. Click **OK**.
4. Click **Create**.

Create a Table with Table Templates

1. In an existing database file, click the **Create tab**, and in the Tables group, click the **Table Templates button**.
2. Click a table template.
3. Rename or delete fields as necessary.
4. Click the **Save button** and name the table. Click **OK**.

Rename a Field

In Design view:

1. Double-click the **field name**.
2. Enter the new name.
3. Press **[Enter]**.

In Datasheet view:

1. Double-click the **field column header**.
2. Enter the new name.
3. Press **[Enter]**.

Delete a Field

In Design view:

1. Right-click the **field row**.
2. Click **Delete Rows**.
3. Click **Yes** to permanently delete the selected field and all data in the field.

In Datasheet view:

1. Right-click the **field column header**.
2. Click **Delete Column**.
3. Click **Yes** to permanently delete the selected field and all the data in the field.

Enter Data Using a Datasheet

1. Open the table in Datasheet view.
2. Press **[Tab]** or **[Enter]** or use the arrow keys to proceed from field to field.

Delete a Record

1. In Datasheet view, right-click the **record selector box** at the left of the row.
2. Click **Delete Record**.
3. Click **Yes** to confirm the deletion.

Name a Table

1. In Datasheet view, right-click the **table tab**.
2. Click **Save**, and enter the table name.
3. Click **OK**.

Edit a Record

1. Overtype or correct data, or, with the insertion point in the field, press **[F2]** to select data and then overtype it.

PERFORMANCE

TASK 1

Expedition Travel Gear has stores in five locations and some records are located in each store. They would like to create a database so that they can access the information for reports on all the employees. They will begin by planning the database, creating tables, and entering data for the Chicago employees.

Expedition

Travel Gear

Follow these guidelines:

1. The database plan for the tables is as follows:
   Contacts table: Employee ID, Last, First, Home Phone, Address, City, State, Postal Code, Notes
   Payroll table: Payroll ID, SSNO, Emp ID, Store, Status, Exemptions, Birth Date, Rate, Other

2. Create a blank database, and name it **2p1-ETG-EMPS**.

3. Create the tables according to the plan. Use templates for the tables or fields if possible. Rename, delete, or move fields so that the names are exactly as written in the plan and in the order specified.

4. In Design view, check that the primary keys are set to the underlined fields in the plan and that both are AutoNumber data types. In the *Payroll* table make the following data type settings: SSNO field set to Text data type, Birth Date field to Date/Time, and Rate field to Currency. Save the tables.

5. Switch to Datasheet view, and enter the data in each table, as shown in Figure 2.14.

6. Edit Linda Soto's telephone number to read **312–555–0685** and Sam Wong's address to **548 Hartland Court**.

7. Close the tables and the database.

Employee ID	Last	First	Home Phone	Address	City	State	Postal Code	No
1	Montez	Carlo	312-555-3241	65 East 5th Street	Chicago	IL	60604	
2	Vaughn	Tamika	773-555-8723	321 Lakeview Road	Chicago	IL	60618	
3	Soto	Linda	312-555-8218	2398 Barton Drive	Chicago	IL	60604	
4	Wong	Sam	773-555-1990	543 Hartland Court	Chicago	IL	60624	
5	Kingsley	Mary	773-555-6621	543 South Michigan Avenue	Chicago	IL	60616	
(New)								

SSNO	Emp ID	Store	Status	Exemptions	Birth Date	Rate	Other	Add New F
143-00-6598	1	C	M	2	11/12/1965	$14.50		
132-00-4321	2	C	M	1	3/6/1978	$10.95		
210-00-3234	3	C	S	0	6/10/1989	$9.00		
154-00-8712	4	C	S	2	12/14/1985	$9.00		
127-00-7165	5	C	M	0	8/14/1982	$8.25		

Figure 2.14: ETG-EMPS tables

ACCESS

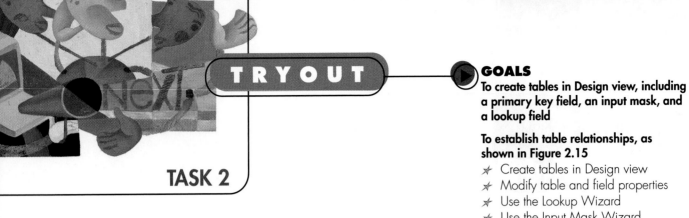

TRYOUT

TASK 2

GOALS

To create tables in Design view, including a primary key field, an input mask, and a lookup field

To establish table relationships, as shown in Figure 2.15

✴ Create tables in Design view
✴ Modify table and field properties
✴ Use the Lookup Wizard
✴ Use the Input Mask Wizard
✴ Create, modify, and print relationships

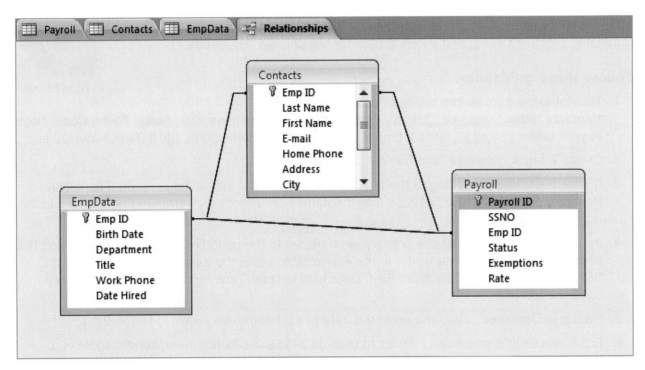

Figure 2.15: Task 2: Table Relationships window

WHAT YOU NEED TO KNOW

Create Tables in Design View

▶ You have created tables using Table templates, and directly in Datasheet view. It is beneficial, however, to create a table directly in Design view so that data types can be set and field names entered according to your design. You can switch to the Design view of a new table and begin or click the New Object: Table button on the Create tab, as shown in Figure 2.16.

Figure 2.16: New Object: Table button

▶ The steps to create a table in Design view are:

1. **Enter the field name first**. It can contain up to 64 characters. Valid characters include letters, numbers, non-leading spaces, and special characters, except the period (.), exclamation point (!), accent grave (`), and brackets ([ ]). Each field name must be unique.

2. **Set the data type next**. The default data type is Text. To change it, click the data type list arrow and select the data type you want. You learned about the 11 data types earlier in this lesson.

3. **The Description field is optional**. You can identify a field with a description of up to 255 characters.

4. **Define field properties**. These will be discussed in the next section.

5. **Determine and set the primary key**. If you do not set a primary key, Access will prompt you to do so when you save the table, and will enter one if you wish. This is not required but is recommended if you want to link the table to another table.

6. **Save and name the table**. If you do not save the table, Access prompts you to do so.

7. **Enter data**. Change to Datasheet view to enter data.

► If you need to insert or delete a row in Design view, right-click the selector box at the left of the row, and click Insert Rows or Delete Rows, as shown in Figure 2.17. In Design view, each row represents a field.

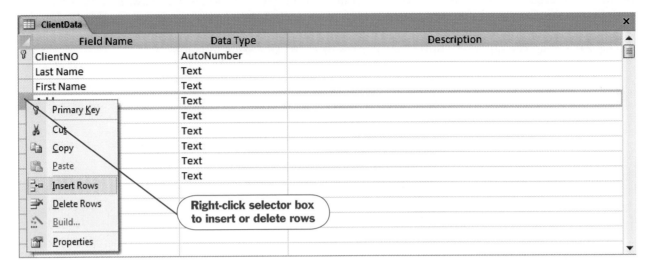

Figure 2.17: Insert or delete rows in Design view

TRY it OUT a2-10

1. Open a blank database and name it **a2-10**.

2. Click the **Create tab**, and in the Tables group, click the **New Object: Table button** labeled Table Design. *Note that you are in Design view, and the insertion point is at the top of the screen under Field Name.*

3. Enter the following fields and set the indicated data types.

FIELD NAME	DATA TYPE
ClientNO	Number
Last Name	Text
First Name	Text
Address	Text
City	Text
State	Text
ZIP Code	Text
Business Number	Text
Mobile Number	Text

4. Change the ClientNO field to an AutoNumber data type and make it the primary key. *Click the **record selector box** and click the **Primary Key button**.*

5. Right-click the **record selector box** at the Address field, and click **Insert Rows**. Add a field named **Birth Date** with a Date/Time data type.

6. Save the table, and name it **ClientData**.

7. Leave the table open in Design view.

Modify Table and Field Properties

Table Properties

▶ **Table properties** provide descriptive information, such as date created, date modified, and a description of the table. You can modify table properties or any object's properties by right-clicking the object and selecting Properties. The Table Properties dialog box, shown in Figure 2.18, is used to document table information.

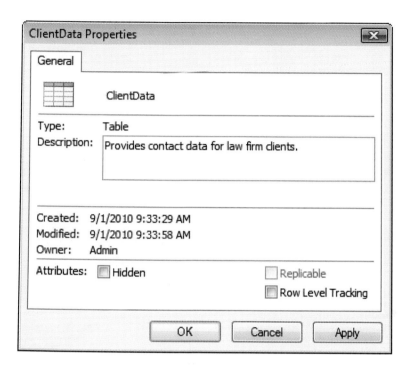

Figure 2.18: Table Properties dialog box

Field Properties

▶ **Field properties** define how Access stores, manipulates, and displays data. In Design view, you can set or modify field properties by selecting the field in the table, and then selecting the property you want in the Field Properties pane. To switch between panes, press [F6] or move the insertion point.

▶ The field property settings depend on the data type you select for the field. For example, Text data type fields have a field size property, and AutoNumber data type fields do not. All field data types have a **caption** property, which allows you to assign a name to a field other than its field name, for use in reports.

► The Date/Time, Currency, and Yes/No data types provide a format property instead of field size properties. You use field properties to select a format for each of these data types by clicking the list arrow on the right side of the Format box. Note the Date/Time and Currency data type formatting options, as shown in Figures 2.19 and 2.20. You must save a table each time you make a property change to fields.

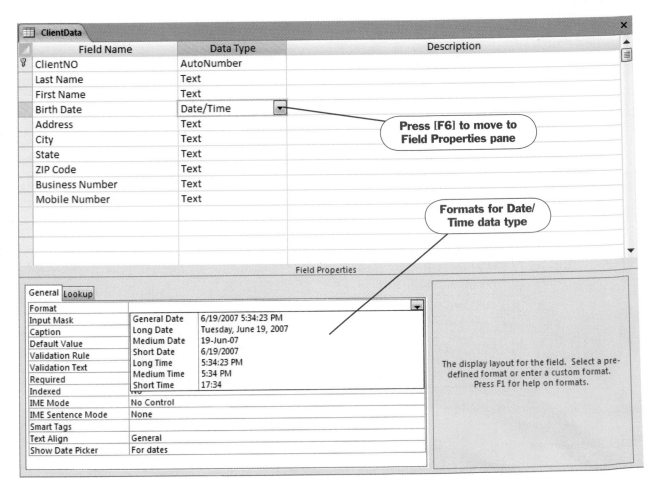

Figure 2.19: Set Date/Time Format field properties in Design view

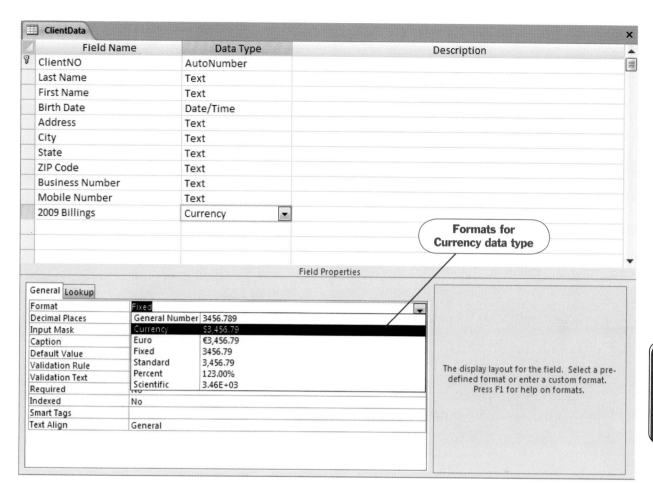

Figure 2.20: Set Currency Format field properties in Design view

HOW [F6] 1. Click the **field name** in the work pane of Design view, and press **[F6]**.
2. Replace the setting, or 2. click the **list arrow** at the right side of the property
row and select a setting from the list. 3. Click the **Save button**.

1. The *ClientData* table in **a2-10** should be in the work pane in Design view; if not, open data file **a2-11** and move it to that location.

2. Right-click **ClientData : Table** in the Navigation Pane, and click **Table Properties**.

3. Enter the Description: `Provides contact data for law firm clients`. Click **OK**.

4. Click the **ClientNO field name**, if necessary, in the Field Name column. *Note that the data type is AutoNumber and that there are seven properties under the General tab in the Field Properties pane.*

5. Click the **Last Name field name**. *Note that this field is a Text field and that there are 14 properties in the General tab in Field Properties pane.* Press **[F6]**.

6. Change the field size from the default of 255 to **30**. *Since Access saves only data in each field and does not save excess blank spaces, it is not really necessary to change the field size.*

7. Click the **Birth Date field name**. Press **[F6]**, and click the list arrow on the Format property. Click **Short Date** in the Format property options list. *Note the different settings that are available with the Date/Time data type.*

8. Add a new field to the table titled: `2009 Billings`.

9. Set the data type to Currency. Press **[F6]**, click the Format property list arrow, and set the format to **Fixed**. *Note the different settings that are available with the Currency data type.*

10. Leave the table open in Design view.

Use the Lookup Wizard

▶ One of the data types is the Lookup Wizard, which automates the process of creating a lookup field. A **lookup field** allows you to enter the value for the field from a list of values you enter or from another table and is used when there are a limited number of values for the field. For example, if you have employees who work in one of five states, you can create a list or table of those states. When you use the Tab key to move to the State field, Access displays a list or column, as shown in Figure 2.21, from which you can choose one entry. This eliminates both the need to enter it each time and the possibility of keyboarding errors. Or, if you enter the first letter or letters of the entry, a lookup field will complete the entry.

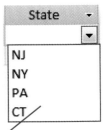

Figure 2.21: Lookup field in Datasheet view

Select value from lookup value list

▶ The Lookup Wizard guides you through the process of identifying where to obtain the values to create a lookup column. It can reference a column in an existing table, or you can enter the values you need, as shown in Figure 2.22. To enter the values, select I will type in the values that I want, and click Next.

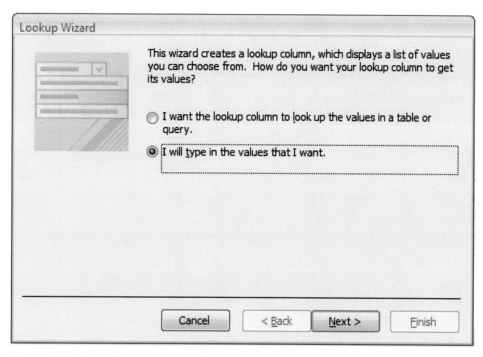

Figure 2.22: Set values source in Lookup Wizard dialog box

▶ The Lookup Wizard dialog box lets you set up one or more columns, as shown in Figure 2.23. The Wizard will then ask you for the field name; the name you provided in the design is the default setting. The field data type will then be changed to the appropriate setting. In this example, it is Text.

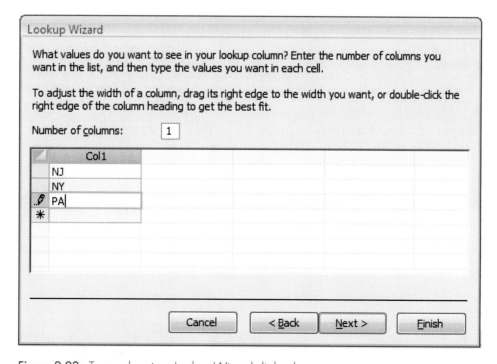

Figure 2.23: Type values in a Lookup Wizard dialog box

▶ To view or edit the lookup value list that you created, click the field and then click the Lookup tab in the Field Properties pane of Design view. The list is stored in, and can be edited in, the Row Source property, as shown in Figure 2.24. The **Row Source Type**, located above Row Source, is the property that specifies the source Access will use for a lookup field, which is the value list you entered.

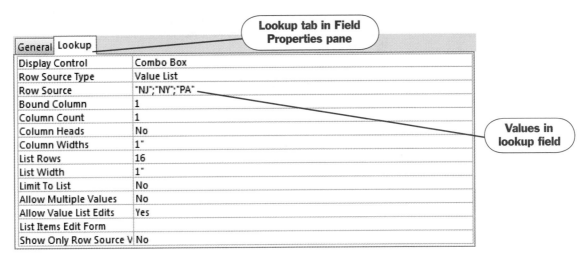

Figure 2.24: Field Properties pane, Lookup tab, Row Source property

TRY it OUT a2-12

1. The *ClientData* table should be in the work pane in Design view; if not, open data file **a2-12** and move to that location.

2. Click the data type column for the State field, click the **Data Type list arrow**, then click **Lookup Wizard**. *The Wizard screens are shown in Figures 2.22 and 2.23.*

3. Click **I will type in the values that I want.** Click **Next**.

4. Leave the number of columns at 1, and click the cell under Col1.

5. Enter the states, pressing **[Tab]** after each:

   NJ, NY, PA

6. Click **Next**, and note that State is the field label, and click **Finish**. *Note that the State data type is still Text.*

7. Click the **Lookup tab** in the Field Properties pane. Note that the states you entered are listed in the Row Source property setting. Add **"CT"** to the list.

8. Save the file, and switch to Datasheet view. Click the **State field** to view the lookup list, as shown in Figure 2.21.

9. Do not close the database.

Use the Input Mask Wizard

▶ Another data type setting is the **input mask**, which controls how data is entered in a field to ensure that it is entered in a consistent format. An input mask provides a pattern, or template, to which data must conform.

▶ For example for telephone numbers, you can set a Text format that automatically requires the spaces for the numbers and enters the separators automatically, (315) 555-1212. This reduces data entry keystrokes and errors.

▶ To assist you in defining input masks, Access provides an **Input Mask Wizard**, to work with the Text or Date/Time data types. You must be in Design view and have the field selected to use the Wizard. In the Field Properties pane, click the Build button in the Input Mask property field, as shown in Figure 2.25. You may be prompted to save your design before beginning.

Figure 2.25: Field Properties pane, Input Mask property with Build button

▶ The Input Mask Wizard opens a dialog box with available formats. If you are working with a Date/Time field, the dialog box appears as shown in Figure 2.26. If you are working with a Text field, the dialog box appears as shown in Figure 2.27.

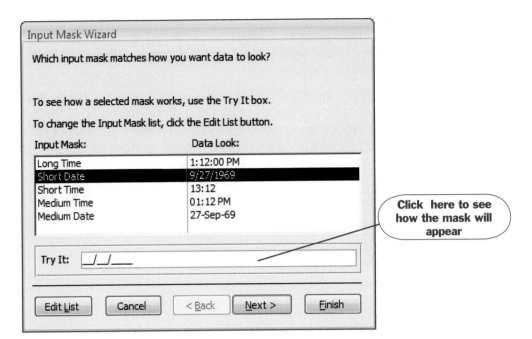

Figure 2.26: Input Mask Wizard for Date/Time data type

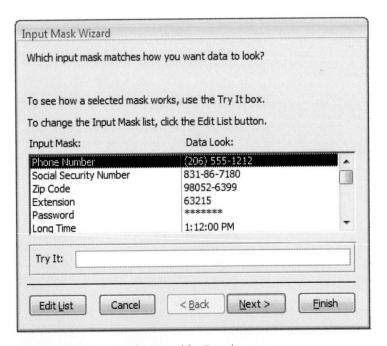

Figure 2.27: Input Mask Wizard for Text data type

▶ The Input Mask Wizard allows you to customize the mask and choose the placeholder characters, which disappear as you enter data in the field. In Text fields, you also have the option of deciding if you want to store the symbols with the data.

T R Y *i t* **O U T** *a2-13*

1. The *ClientData* table should be in the work pane; if not, open data file **a2-13** and move it to that location. Switch to Design view.

2. Click the **Birth Date field**. *Note that the Birth Date field is a Date/Time field.*

3. Press **[F6]** and in the Field Properties pane, click the **Input Mask property field**.

4. Click the **Build button** in the Input Mask property field.

5. Click **Short Date**. *Click the blank box next to Try It to see the format.*

6. Click **Next**. *Note that you can change the input mask, and you can choose the placeholder character. The placeholder character is an underscore.*

7. Click **Next**, and then click **Finish**.

8. Repeat the procedures from Step 2 for the **Business Number** and **Mobile Number fields** to set a Phone Number input mask. Elect not to store the symbols with the data. Save the table when prompted.

9. Switch to Datasheet view.

10. Enter the data from the table below into the datasheet. In the State field, click the lookup list arrow to view the values, and click the correct one. Enter the dates and telephone numbers without the symbols, since they are provided by the input mask.

11. Close the table and the database.

FIELD NAMES	RECORD 1	RECORD 2	RECORD 3
ClientNO	1	2	3
Last Name	LiBecci	Peterson	Perry
First Name	Barbara	Charles	Michael
Birth date	07/09/1987	09/08/1986	03/11/1990
Address	12 Carling Lane	654 East 67 Street	60 Main Street
City	Fort Lee	New York	New Haven
State	NJ	NY	CT
ZIP	07024	10021	06513
Business Number	(201) 555-2540	(212) 555-7800	(203) 555-9230
Mobile Number	(201) 555-2398	(917) 555-9112	(203) 555-2987
2009 Billings	$2600	$8600	$5400

Create, Modify, and Print Relationships

Create Relationships

▶ Once all the data has been placed in several subject-related tables, you must provide a means to bring that information together for queries, forms, and reports that use data from several tables. To establish how the tables relate, you use relationships.

▶ A **relationship** is a correlation established between shared fields or columns in two tables. Relationship commands are found on the Database Tools tab, as shown in Figure 2.28. You create a table relationship by using the Relationships window, as shown in Figure 2.29. The common field does not have to have the same name in both tables but must have the same data type or field size setting.

Figure 2.28: Relationships button

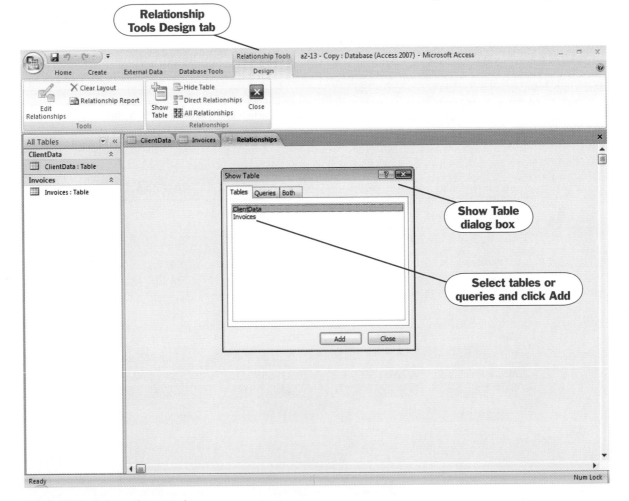

Figure 2.29: Relationships window

▶ The Edit Relationships dialog box appears when you identify the field that will be in both tables, allowing you to make settings for the relationship. The Edit Relationships dialog box shown in Figure 2.30 identifies the type of relationship as one-to-many.

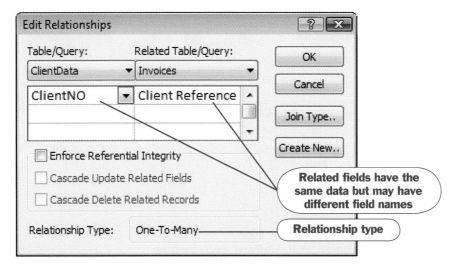

Figure 2.30: Edit Relationships dialog box

▶ There are three kinds of relationships you can build in the Relationships window, as detailed in Table 2.2.

Table 2.2: Types of relationships

One-to-one	Each record in the first table can have only one matching record in the second table, and each record in the second table can have only one matching record in the first table. Both tables must share a common field because this relationship is generally used to divide a table with many fields. For example, use a one-to-one relationship to segment a table for security reasons, or to store information that applies only to some of the main table's data.
One-to-many	A record in one table can match many records in a second table. However, each record in the second table can only have one match in the first table. For example, although there is one record for each client, there may be many invoices for each of them throughout the year.
Many-to-many	For each record in the one table, there can be many records in the other table, and vice versa. For example, if you have an *Inventory* table and an *Orders* table, there can be many orders for each inventory item and many items in each order.

▶ After you create the relationship, the tables will be joined as shown in Figure 2.31. Although the joined fields have different names in this example, the field data is the same.

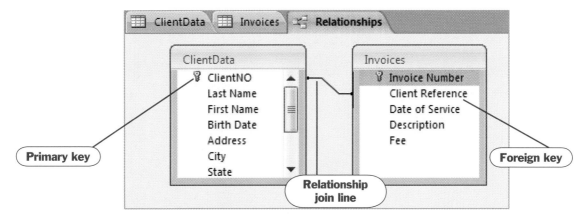

Figure 2.31: Related tables joined by a common field

HOW **1.** In an open database, click the **Database Tools tab**, and in the Show/Hide group, click the **Relationships button**. **2.** Click the **Show Table button**, and in the Show Table dialog box select one or more tables or queries, click **Add**, and then click **Close**. **3.** Drag a field (normally the primary key) from one table to become the foreign key in the other table. **4.** In the Edit Relationships dialog box, make any additional settings, and then click **Create**. *A line is drawn between the two tables.*

Relationships

Show Table

T R Y i t O U T *a2-14*

1. Open data file **a2-14**, where a table and more data have been added. *Note the new Invoices table and its data.*

2. Click the **Database Tools tab**, and in the Show/Hide group, click the **Relationships button**.

3. In the Relationships group, click the **Show Table button**, and in the Show Table dialog box, click **ClientData**, then click **Add**.

4. Add the *Invoices* table in the same manner, and click **Close**.

5. Click **ClientNO** in the *ClientData* table field list, and drag it to **Client Reference** in the *Invoice* table field list. *Note that the Edit Relationships dialog box opens with both fields listed.*

6. Click **Create**. *Note that the tables are joined.*

7. Do not close the Relationships document tab or the database.

Modify Relationships

▶ One method of modifying a relationship is to delete it and reselect the join fields. To delete a relationship, right-click the relationship join line, click Delete, and confirm the deletion.

▶ You can also modify the relationship by creating join type settings in the Edit Relationships dialog box. Clicking Join Type in the Edit Relationships dialog box opens the Join Properties dialog box, shown in Figure 2.32.

Figure 2.32: Join Properties dialog box

▶ The choices create an inner join, left outer join, or a right outer join. The differences are subtle but may be important for the report or query you are trying to produce. If you select join type 2 or 3, an arrow appears on the relationship join line and points to the table with matching rows. Table 2.3 defines the terms using the database in data file **a2-15** as an example.

Table 2.3: Join types

Join type 1	Inner join	Includes only records in left table (*ClientData*) that match records in right table (*Invoices*)
Join type 2	Left outer join	Includes all records from *ClientData* (the table on the left) and only those from *Invoices* where the joined fields are equal
Join type 3	Right outer join	Includes all records from *Invoices* (table on the right) and only those records from *ClientData* where the joined fields are equal

T R Y *i t* O U T *a2-15*

1. Use the open database, in the Relationships window, or open data file **a2-15**, click the **Database Tools tab**, and click the **Relationships button**.

2. Right-click the **relationship join line** between the tables, and click **Delete**. Confirm the deletion. *The line is deleted, but the tables remain in the window.*

3. Click and drag the **ClientNO field** from the *ClientData* table field list to the **Client Reference field** on the *Invoices* table field list.

4. In the Edit Relationships dialog box, click **Join Type**.

5. In the Join Properties dialog box, read and click option **2**, and then click **OK**.

Click **Create**. *Note the arrow showing a left outer join, which will join all the records from the **ClientData** table with the information from the **Invoices** table.*

6. Right-click the **relationship join line**, and click **Edit Relationship**.

7. In the Edit Relationships dialog box, click **Join Type**.

8. In the Join Properties dialog box, read and click option **1**, and then click **OK**. Click **OK**. *Note the inner join line, which will only join records when the joined fields are equal.*

9. Save the Relationships window.

10. Do not close the database.

Print Table Relationships

▶ To document the current database table relationships, you may wish to print a report to keep with your database plan. On the Relationship Tools Design tab, click the Relationship Report button to view the report and the Print Preview tab, as shown in Figure 2.33.

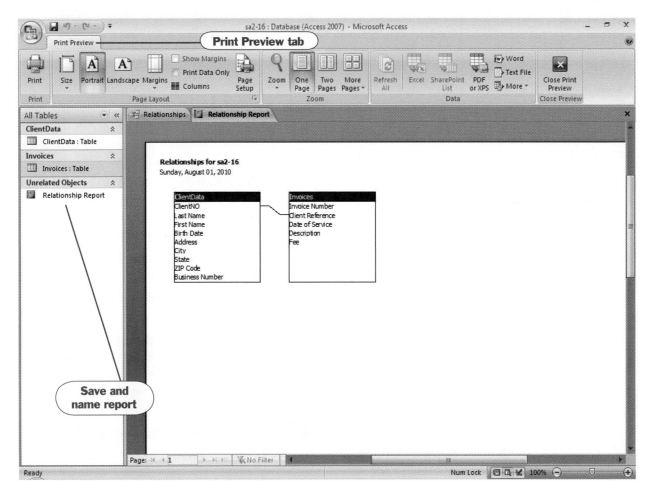

Figure 2.33: Relationship Report and Print Preview tab

TRY it OUT *a2-16*

1. Use the open database, in the Relationships window, or open data file **a2-16**, click the **Database Tools tab**, and click the **Relationships button**.

2. On the Relationship Tools Design tab, in the Tools group, click the **Relationship Report button**.

3. Click the **Save button**, and name the report: **Relationship Report**. Click **OK**.

4. On the Print Preview tab, click the **Print button**, then click **OK**.

5. Close the database.

REHEARSAL

TASK 2

GOALS

To create tables in Design view, including a primary key field, an input mask, and a lookup field

To establish table relationships

WHAT YOU NEED TO KNOW

▶ A business depends on the accuracy of its data. Data in databases must be reliable so that the business can make decisions with confidence. For this reason, Access provides tools to restrict data formats and limit data entry mistakes.

▶ Database tables are organized by subject, but reports or queries may require data from all of the tables. Relationships between tables provide the means by which data from several tables can be combined.

▶ In this Rehearsal activity, you will use Design view to create a table, with a primary key, to add to an existing database. You will use the Input Mask Wizard to restrict the format of a field, and you will use the Lookup Wizard to create a lookup field that will improve the accuracy of data entry. You will also create table relationships to join the tables.

▼ DIRECTIONS

1. Open data file **2r2-EMP** or use your solution to Task 1, **2r1-EMP**.

2. Create a new table in Design view to store the information shown in the table plan below:

FIELD NAME	DATA TYPE	FIELD PROPERTY SETTINGS
Emp ID	Number (Primary Key)	
Birth Date	Date/Time	Input mask for date __/__/____
Department	Lookup Wizard	Row Source Values: "Administration", "Maintenance", "Sales Staff"
Title	Text	
Work Phone	Text	Input mask for telephone number
Date Hired	Date/Time	Input mask for date __/__/____

Note that there is a Title field that we have used in another table already.

a. Set the Emp ID field as the primary key, and save the table as **EmpData**.

b. Use an Input Mask to format the Birth Date and Date Hired data types for dates with the format shown.

c. Set the Department data type to Lookup Wizard, and use the values shown in the plan.

d. Use an Input Mask for the Work Phone field, using the Phone Number input mask. Store the symbols with the data.

e. Save the table and switch to Datasheet view.

3. Right-click each of the tables in the Navigation Pane, and enter the following text as Table Properties:

a. *Payroll* **table**: Contains data to complete weekly payroll.

b. *Contacts* **table**: Contains employee home contact information.

c. *EmpData* **table**: Contains employee office contact and personnel information.

Continued on next page

4. Enter the data shown in Figure 2.34 into the table.

5. Open the *Payroll* table, right-click the **Title column header**, and click **Delete Column**. Confirm the deletion. *Note that we included this data in the EmpData table.*

6. Click the **Database Tools tab**, and in the Show/Hide group, click the **Relationships button**.

7. In the Relationships window, do the following:
   a. Add all three tables to the window using the Show Table dialog box.
   b. Create a one-to-one relationship between the **Emp ID fields** in the *Contacts* table and the *EmpData* table. *Drag the Emp ID field from one table to the other.*
   c. Create a one-to-many relationship between the **Emp ID fields** in the *Contacts* table and the *Payroll* table.
   d. Create a one-to-many relationship between the **Emp ID fields** in the *Payroll* table and the *EmpData* table.
   e. Move the tables so that you can see the join lines as shown in Figure 2.35.
   f. Save the Relationships window.

Continued on next page

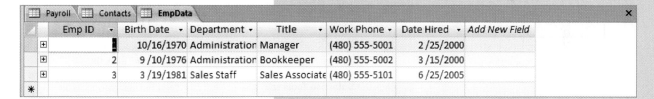

Emp ID	Birth Date	Department	Title	Work Phone	Date Hired	Add New Field
1	10/16/1970	Administration	Manager	(480) 555-5001	2/25/2000	
2	9/10/1976	Administration	Bookkeeper	(480) 555-5002	3/15/2000	
3	3/19/1981	Sales Staff	Sales Associate	(480) 555-5101	6/25/2005	

Figure 2.34: *EmpData* table

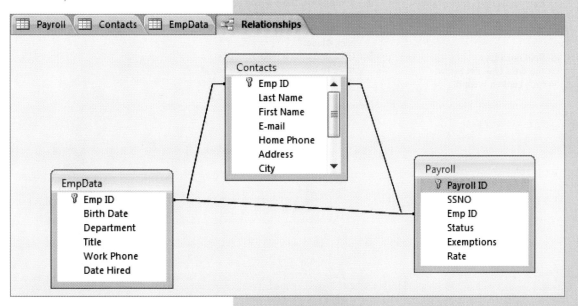

Figure 2.35: Relationships window

8. Click the **Relationship Tools Design tab**, and in the Tools group, click the **Relationship Report button**.

9. Save the report, naming it `Relationship Report`.

10. Close the database.

Create a Table in Design View
1. Create a blank database, or open an existing database file.
2. Click the **Create tab**, and in the Tables group, click the **New Object: Table button**.

Table Design

3. Enter the field names and data types.
4. Set the field properties, if necessary.
5. Save and name the table.

Set the Primary Key in Design View
1. Click field to designate as primary key.
2. Click the **Table Tools Design tab**, and click the **Primary Key button**.

Set Field Properties
1. In Design view, press **[F6]** to move to Field Properties pane.
   Or
1. Click in the Field Properties pane.
2. Set desired properties.

Create a Lookup Field Using Value List
1. Click **field name** and press **[Tab]** or use arrow keys to move to the Data Type column.
   Or
1. Click **field data type**.
2. Click the **data type list arrow**, then click **Lookup Wizard**.

3. Click **I will type in the values that I want**, then click **Next**.
4. Enter values and click **Next**.
5. Assign labels to values, and click **Finish**.

Use the Input Mask Wizard
1. In Design view, click the field you want to mask.
2. Click the **Input Mask property field**, then click the **Build button**.
3. Select the desired mask style, then click **Next**.
4. Make appropriate settings, clicking **Next** each time. Click **Finish**.

Set Table Properties
1. Right-click the table name in the Navigation Pane.
2. Click **Table Properties** on the shortcut menu.
3. Make desired settings, and click **OK**.

Create Table Relationships
1. Click the **Database Tools tab**, and in the Show/Hide group, click the **Relationships button**.
2. In the Show Table dialog box, select one or more tables or queries, click **Add** after each, then click **Close**.
3. Click and drag a field from one table to become the foreign key in the other table.

4. In the Edit Relationships dialog box, make any additional settings, then click **Create**.

Delete Table Relationships
1. Right-click the **relationship join line**, then click **Delete**.

Modify Relationship Join Line Properties
1. Right-click the **relationship join line**, then click **Edit Relationship**.
2. Click **Join Type**.
3. In the Join Properties dialog box, click join property option, and then click **OK**.
4. Click **OK**.

Print Table Relationships
1. Click the **Relationship Tools Design tab**, and click the **Relationship Report button**.
2. Click the **Save button**, name the report, and click **OK**.
3. On the Print Preview tab, click the **Print button**, then click **OK**.

TASK 2

Expedition Travel Gear has continued to build its database by adding the Miami employees to its *Contact* table. You are asked to edit the existing tables to improve data entry by adding input and lookup fields. You will add data to the *Payroll* table, add a new table in Design view, and set table relationships.

1. Open data file **2p2-ETG-EMPS**. *Note the new names on the Contact table.*

2. In the *Contact* table in Design view, add an input mask to the Home Phone field, and store the symbols with the data. Save the table design.

3. In the *Payroll* table in Design view, make the following changes:
   a. Remove the Primary key from the SSNO field. Add a Social Security Number input mask to the field and store the symbols with the data.
   b. Make Emp ID the primary key field and drag the field up to the first row position.
   c. Change the Store field to a Lookup Wizard data type, and enter store locations in the value list: **Boston, Chicago, Dallas, Miami, San Diego**.
   d. Add a Short Date input mask to the Birth Date field.

4. In the *Payroll* table in Datasheet view, correct the data in the Store field for the first five records and add the additional data, as shown in Figure 2.36.

Continued on next page

Emp ID	SSNO	Store	Status	Exemptions	Birth Date	Rate	Other
1	143-00-6598	Chicago	M	2	11/12/1965	$14.50	
2	132-00-4321	Chicago	M	1	3/6/1978	$10.95	
3	210-00-3234	Chicago	S	0	6/10/1989	$9.00	
4	154-00-8712	Chicago	S	2	12/14/1985	$9.00	
5	127-00-7165	Chicago	M	0	8/14/1982	$8.25	
6	237-00-8711	Miami	M	3	6/9/1975	$13.50	
7	185-00-5167	Miami	S	2	1/7/1985	$12.50	
8	214-00-6548	Miami	S	0	9/21/1989	$9.00	
9	165-00-4387	Miami	M	4	7/5/1982	$10.00	
10	132-00-2198	Miami	S	1	11/5/1988	$9.00	

Figure 2.36: *Payroll table*

5. Add a new table named **Weekly** in Design view, using the fields and data types listed below, saving the table when prompted.

FIELD NAME	DATA TYPE	FIELD PROPERTIES
Payroll ID	AutoNumber	
Emp ID	Number	
Week ending	Date/Time	Short Date input mask
Hours	Number	
Dues	Currency	
Other-1	Currency	
Other-2	Currency	

6. Save the *Weekly* table.

7. Create and save table relationships as follows:
   a. **Contact table and Payroll table**: Join the Employee ID and Emp ID fields in a one-to-one relationship.
   b. **Contact table and Weekly table**: Join the Employee ID and Emp ID fields in a one-to-many relationship.
   c. **Weekly table and Payroll table**: Join the Emp ID fields in a one-to-many relationship.
   d. Arrange the tables so that you can view the relationships.

8. Create a relationship report and print a copy.

9. Save and close the database.

ENCORE

Act I

EarthCare Services is beginning to create a database for its clients. They have retail and wholesale clients in each of their three locations in and around Cincinnati, Ohio, and many of them have landscaping maintenance contracts. They have made a list of some of the data they require and have asked you to create the database. They would like to open a table for customers and one for maintenance contracts, and have given you some sample data for testing purposes.

EarthCare Services

Follow these guidelines:

1. The database plan includes the following fields and tables.

CUSTOMERS TABLE	
CustID	AutoNumber
Company	
Last	
First	
Address	
City	
State	
ZIP	
Telephone	Input mask
Wholesale?	Yes/No

CONTRACTS TABLE	
ContractNO	AutoNumber
CustID	Number
Type of Service	Lookup Wizard*
Other Description	Memo
Renewal Date	Date/Time Input mask
Monthly Rate	Currency

*Full, Lawn, Lawn/Fertilize, Snow, Trim, Trim/Fertilize

2. Create a new database, and name it **2ep1-EarthCare**.

3. Create the tables as listed in the plan, and set data types using input masks or the Lookup Wizard as indicated. Use a table template if you wish or create the tables in Design view. Set the primary key for each table using the AutoNumber fields.

4. Create a table relationship between the two tables, using the CustID field. Create a relationship report and print a copy.

Continued on next page

5. Enter the sample data as listed below, and adjust column width as necessary. *Note that all the data is in the table and arranged vertically. Blank spaces indicate no data because not all customers are corporate clients or have contracts.*

FIELD NAME	RECORD	RECORD	RECORD
CustID	1	2	3
Company	Township WaterWorks		Barstow and Valmont
Last	Reilly	Granger	Valmont
First	Benjamin	Carl	Patricia
Address	432 Beachmont Avenue	65 Circle Drive	761 Crescent Circle
City	Milford	Cincinnati	Amelia
State	OH	OH	OH
ZIP	45150	45255	45102
Telephone	(513) 555-7878	(513) 555-6126	(513) 555-8117
Wholesale?	Y	N	N
ContractNO	1		2
Type of Service	Full		Lawn/Fertilize
Other Description	Includes snow removal		Trim as per customer request only
Renewal date	5/15/2011		7/15/2011
Monthly rate	$350		$125

6. Save and close the database.

Act II

You work for NewMark Productions in New York City, where they maintain a small office that primarily handles all marketing and sales distribution. Your supervisor is Ms. Mindi Wallace, the manager of the human resources department. The company is preparing to expand and is planning to hire 20 people over the next two months.

Ms. Wallace has asked you to develop a database to store all the employee contact and payroll information for NewMark employees in New York and California. You have been given a sample of employee index cards, shown in Figure 2.37, showing some of the data to be included in the database.

Follow these guidelines:

1. Review the existing data, and make a list of all the fields you think you should include in this database. Add a Birth Date field and a Salary field to the list. Any missing data will have to be obtained. Decide on at least two tables, and divide the data by subject. *Use Employees and Payroll as the tables. Office telephone and location data should be kept with employee contact information.* Determine the primary key for each table.

2. Review each field in terms of data type, and input mask or lookup field requirements. *Note that the Emp NO data is not incremental and should be a Number data type.* You should use an input mask setting for dates, telephone fields, and Social Security numbers. Use lookup fields for the State and Office fields. The states of residence are: CA, NY, or NJ, and the offices are California or New York.

```
Name:      Alan Newman          Emp NO: 1      Title: CEO and President
Status:    M          Exemptions: 2    Social Security No: 434-00-4323   Office: CA
Address:   54 Culver Drive    City: Beverly Hills   State: CA   ZIP: 90211
Office Phone: 310-555-8005    E-mail: alne@world.com   Home Phone: 310-555-5434
Emergency contact: Jamie Newman    Emergency phone: 310-555-7622
```

```
Name:      Mark Cohen          Emp NO: 10    Title: CFO
Status:    S          Exemptions: 2    Social Security No: 543-00-7698   Office: CA
Address:   654 Mountain Road    City: Beverly Hills   State: CA   ZIP: 90211
Office Phone: 310-555-8006    E-mail: maco@world.com   Home Phone: 310-555-5765
Emergency contact: Jane Young        Emergency phone: 310-555-0987
```

```
Name:      Frank Manning        Emp NO: 12    Title: Director Marketing and Sales
Status:    M          Exemptions: 4    Social Security No: 657-00-0980   Office: NY
Address:   456 East 67 Street    City: New York   State: NY   ZIP: 10021
Office Phone: 212-555-9996    E-mail: frma@world.com   Home Phone: 212-555-9871
Emergency contact: Michele Manning   Emergency phone: 917-555-7612
```

```
Name:      Mindi Wallace        Emp NO: 14    Title: Manager Human Resources
Status:    S          Exemptions: 1    Social Security No: 231-00-7658   Office: NY
Address:   345 Christopher Street    City: New York   State: NY   ZIP: 10009
Office Phone: 212-555-9995    E-mail: miwa@world.com   Home Phone: 212-555-9112
Emergency contact: Jenna Jamison        Emergency phone: 917-555-9187
```

Figure 2.37: Employee card file

3. Create a database named **2ep2-NEWMARK** and create the two tables. Use any table templates that suit your needs or use Design view, if you prefer. Add primary key designations, and save the tables as *Employees* and *Payroll*. Add input masks and lookup fields according to your plan, saving as you change the design. Create a table relationship to link the tables.

4. Enter the data in both tables. *Leave the missing Birth Date and Salary data fields blank until you can obtain that data.*

5. Save and close the database.

LESSON 3

Access Forms

In this lesson, you will learn how to create, use, and modify forms using Access form tools and all form views. You will learn about field controls, including calculated controls, and how to enter records using a form.

Upon completion of this lesson, you will have mastered the following skill sets

- ✦ Create a form using form tools
- ✦ AutoFormat a form
- ✦ Create forms using the Form Wizard
- ✦ Enter and edit records using a form
- ✦ Print database objects
- ✦ Modify a form in Layout view
- ✦ Create a form using the Blank Form tool
- ✦ Use Form Design view
- ✦ Add, size, and move controls
- ✦ Modify the properties of specific controls on a form
- ✦ Modify the properties of a form
- ✦ Add a calculated control to a form

Terms
Software-related
Bound control
Calculated control
Controls
Expression
Form footer
Form header
Form selector
Form tool
Form Wizard
Label control
Multiple items form
Split form
Text box
Unbound control

TASK 1

GOAL

To create a form for a real estate office to enter new home listings, update current listings, and delete listings that have sold, as shown in Figure 3.1

* Learn about forms
* Create a form using form tools
* AutoFormat a form
* Create forms using the Form Wizard
* Enter and edit records using a form
* Print database objects

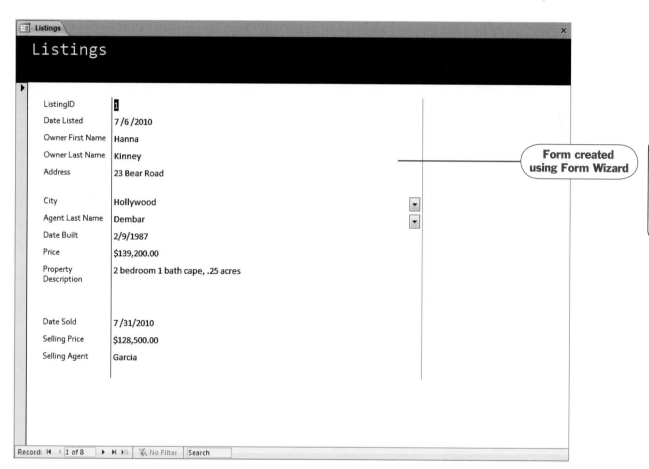

Figure 3.1: Task 1: *Listings* form

WHAT YOU NEED TO KNOW

Learn about forms

▶ Form objects are used to enter, edit, or display data in a database. A form can be created to update or enter records, or it can be customized specifically for certain users to limit access to sensitive data such as Social Security numbers or credit card information. Form objects have three views: Form view, Layout view, and Design view. You will work in Form view and Layout view in this task.

▶ The Create tab, shown in Figure 3.2, contains a Forms group that provides different form tools and features to create a form.

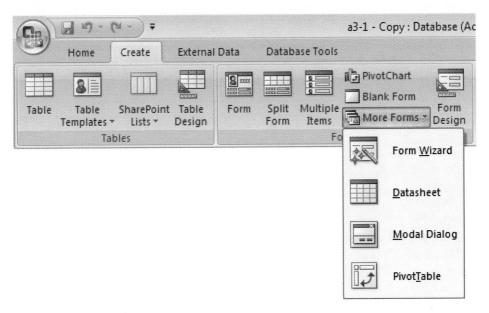

Figure 3.2: Create tab, Forms group

Create a Form Using Form Tools

▶ A **form tool** automatically creates a form to display all the fields in a table. If you press the Form button, a form is created that displays one record at a time, as shown in Figure 3.3. The form appears in Layout view, where you can add formats, change the design, or change the size or location of fields. You will learn to modify forms in Design view in Task 2.

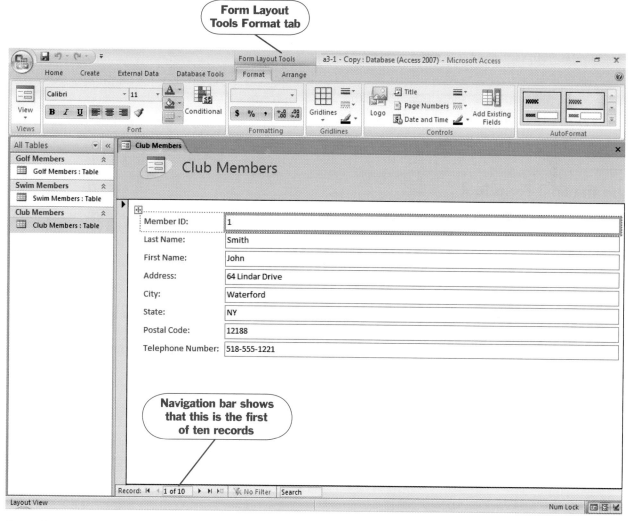

Figure 3.3: Form in Layout view

HOW **1.** In the Navigation Pane, click the table to be used to create a form, or move the table into the work pane. **2.** Click the **Create tab**, and in the Forms group, click the **Form button**. The form is created and displayed in Layout view.

▶ If the selected table has a relationship, a datasheet is added to the bottom of the form showing the data from the related table that applies to that record. You can delete the datasheet if you want. If more than one table is related to the form, no datasheets are added.

1. Start Access.

2. Open data file **a3-1**, the club members' database, and open the *Club Members* table. Note the fields in the table.

3. Click the **Create tab**, and in the Forms group, click the **Form button**. *The form appears, showing the first record and all the fields from the Club Members table.*

4. Click the **Database Tools tab**, and in the Show/Hide group, click the **Relationships**

button. *Note that several tables are related to the Club Members table. Therefore, no datasheets were added to the form.*

5. Close the Relationships window.

6. Click the **Format Layout Tools Format tab**, and note the format tools for Layout view.

7. Close the form. Do not name or save the form.

8. Do not close the table or database.

Use the Split Form Tool

▶ A **split form**, shown in Figure 3.4, gives you the form view and datasheet view of the data at the same time, and is created automatically using the Split Form tool. The two views are synchronized at all times so that if you select a field in one view, the same field is selected in the other. This allows you to quickly locate a record and then use the form to edit it.

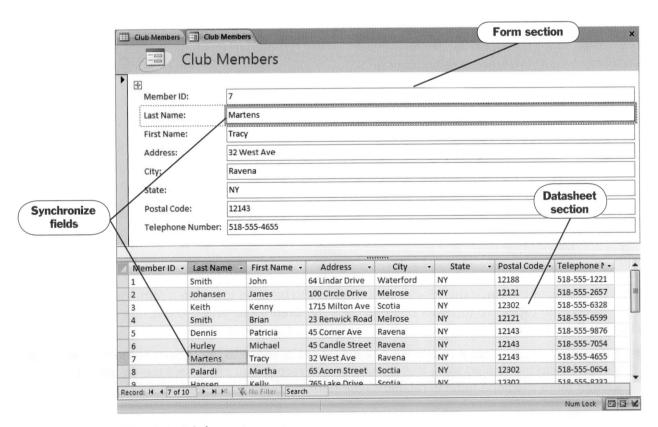

Figure 3.4: Split form in Layout view

HOW 1. Select or open the table to be used. 2. Click the **Create tab**, and in the Forms group, click the **Split Form button**. *The form is created and displayed in Layout view.*

T R Y *i t* O U T *a3-2*

1. Use the open database or open **a3-2**, and open the *Club Members* table.

2. Click the **Create tab**, and in the Forms group, click the **Split Form button**. *The form appears, showing the first record and a datasheet of the Club Members table.*

3. In the datasheet section, click the **record selector box** for Tracy Martens. *The*

record for Tracy Martens appears in the Forms section.

4. Click the **record selector box** for Member ID 4.

5. Close the form but do not save or name it.

6. Do not close the table or the database.

Use the Multiple Items Tool

▶ A **multiple items form** resembles a datasheet, showing all items in the table, but has more customization and format options than a datasheet provides. A multiple items form is created using the same techniques as other forms, and appears in Layout view, as shown in Figure 3.5.

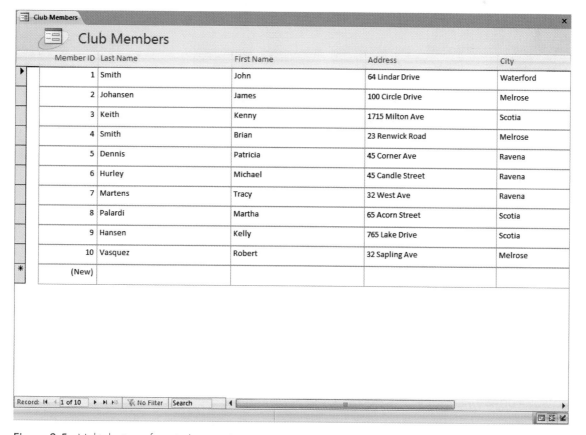

Figure 3.5: Multiple items form in Layout view

1. Use the open database or open **a3-3**, and open the *Club Members* table.

2. Click the **Create tab**, and in the Forms group, click the **Multiple Items button**. *The form displays showing the first record and all the fields* 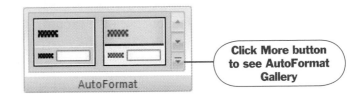 *from the Club Members table in a format that resembles a datasheet.*

3. Close the form, but do not save or name it. Close the table.

4. Do not close the database.

AutoFormat a Form

▶ You can use the AutoFormat feature, shown in Figure 3.6, on the Form Layout Tools Format tab, to select a format for a form with preset colors and font styles. The AutoFormat gallery displays the name of each format as you position your mouse over the style in a ScreenTip, as shown in Figure 3.7.

Click More button to see AutoFormat Gallery

Figure 3.6: Form Layout Tools Format tab, AutoFormat group

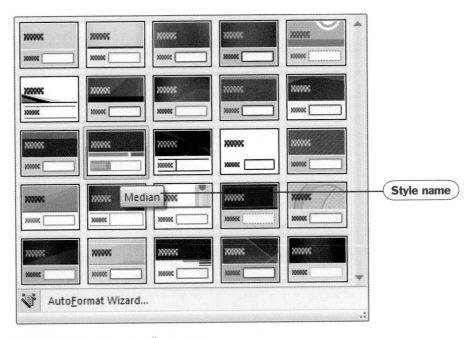

Style name

Figure 3.7: AutoFormat gallery

HOW   **1.** In a form in Layout view, click the **Form Layout Tools Format tab**, and in the AutoFormat group, click the **More button** to view the AutoFormat gallery. **2.** Click the desired AutoFormat.

1. Use the open database or open **a3-4**. Open the *Swim Members* table.

2. Click the **Create tab**, and in the Forms group, click the **Form button**.

3. Click the **Form Layout Tools Format tab** if necessary, and in the AutoFormat group, click the **More button** to display the AutoFormat Gallery.

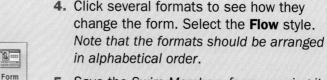

4. Click several formats to see how they change the form. Select the **Flow** style. *Note that the formats should be arranged in alphabetical order.*

5. Save the *Swim Members* form, naming it **Swim Members Form**.

6. Close the form and the table, but do not close the database.

Create Forms Using the Form Wizard

▶ Unlike using the form tools, which include all the fields from a table, the **Form Wizard** provides a series of steps to create a customized form. It is useful when:

- All the fields in a table are not required.
- You want to choose the layout and style.
- Fields from more than one table will be used.

▶ To use the Form Wizard, click the Create tab, and in the Forms group, click the More Forms button, then click Form Wizard. The Form Wizard dialog box, shown in Figure 3.8, asks you to select the data source table(s) and the fields to include. You can select the fields to include or click the double arrow [>>] to include all the fields. If you click Finish, a basic form appears and the Wizard names and saves the form with the same name as the table.

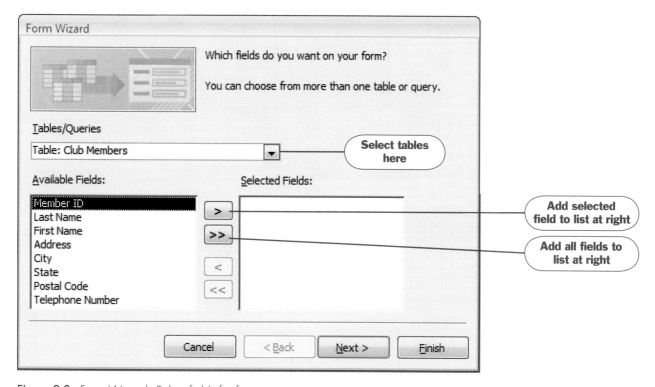

Figure 3.8: Form Wizard: Select fields for form

1. Use the open database or open data file **a3-5**. Open the *Club Members* table.

2. Click the **Create tab**, and in the Forms group, click the **More Forms button** and then click **Form Wizard**. *Note the Club Members table appears selected under Tables/Queries.*

3. Double-click the following fields in the order listed to move them to the Selected Fields box:
   a. **Member ID**
   b. **First Name**
   c. **Last Name**
   d. **Telephone Number**

4. Click **Finish**. *A form appears with the selected fields, and the form is named, saved, and appears on the Navigation Pane.*

5. Close the form. Right-click the *Club Members* form name in the Navigation Pane, click **Delete**, then click **Yes** to confirm the deletion.

6. Do not close the database.

Use the Form Wizard to Apply a Layout and Style

► The Form Wizard also provides preset layouts and styles you can apply to a form. If you continue with the Form Wizard by pressing Next, you are asked to select a layout, as shown in Figure 3.9. The layout options are: Columnar, Tabular, Datasheet, and Justified. When you select an option, an example appears in the left portion of the window.

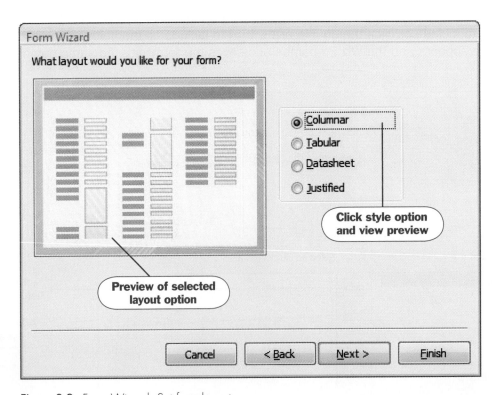

Figure 3.9: Form Wizard: Set form layout

▶ When you click the layout option you want and click Next, the wizard asks, "What style would you like?" as shown in Figure 3.10. Click to preview each style; an example appears in the left portion of the window. You can click Finish to produce a form or continue with wizard settings by clicking Next. On the last screen, you can rename the form and choose to open it in Form or Design view, as shown in Figure 3.11.

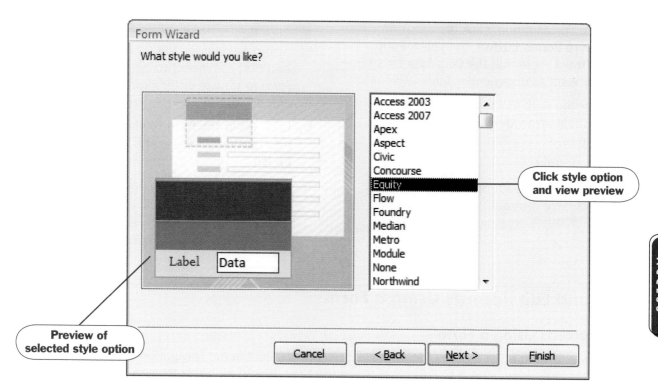

Figure 3.10: Form Wizard: Set form style

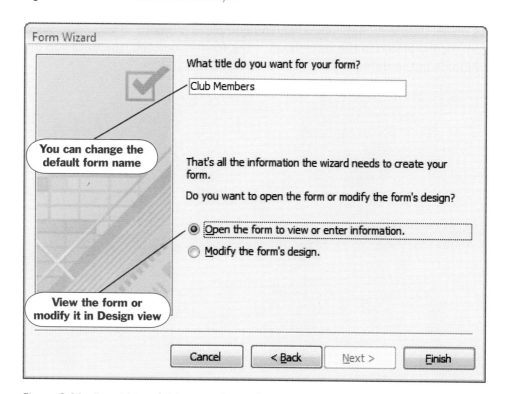

Figure 3.11: Form Wizard: Name and view form

1. Use the open database or open data file **a3-6**.

2. Click the **Create tab**, and in the Forms group, click the **More Forms button**, then click **Form Wizard**. *Note that the Club Members table appears selected under Tables/Queries.*

3. For the *Club Members* table, click the double arrow to include all the fields in the form.

4. Click **Next**.

5. Click each layout option to preview available formats.

6. Click **Columnar**, then click **Next**.

7. Click each style option to preview available styles.

8. Click **Equity**, then click **Next**. *Note that the wizard has named the form Club Members and that you have two options: "Open the form to view or enter information" and "Modify the form's design."*

9. Click **Open the form to view or enter information** if necessary, then click **Finish**.

10. Close the form, but do not close the database.

Enter and Edit Records Using a Form

Enter Records Using a Form

▶ To use a form to enter records, double-click the Forms object in the Navigation Pane, or if the form is in the work pane, switch to Form view. Click the New (Blank) record button on the Navigation bar to add a record. Enter field data, and press the Tab key to move from field to field. Press the Tab key to move to the next record, or click the New (blank) record button on the Navigation bar.

▶ Access saves data automatically when you complete a record. If you add a record using a form, it is automatically stored in the datasheet. If the form is deleted, the data you entered through the form remains in the datasheet.

1. Use the open database or open data file **a3-7**.

2. Double-click the *Club Members* form.

3. Click the **New (blank) record button** on the Navigation bar (see Figure 3.13).

4. Add the two records shown in the table below, pressing **[Tab]** to move from field to field, and to a new record. *AutoNumber data need not be entered, and fields with input masks do not require the entry of data separators.*

5. Close and reopen the *Club Members* table and note the new entries.

6. Switch back to the form using the tab. Do not close the database.

MEMBER ID	PRESS [TAB] TO INSERT AUTONUMBER 11	PRESS [TAB] TO INSERT AUTONUMBER 12
Last Name	Deer	Pappas
First Name	James	Sophia
Address	23 Still River Road	78 Shaker Road
City	Melrose	Scotia
State	NY	NY
Postal Code	12121	12302
Telephone Number	(518) 555-0476	(518) 555-1054

Edit Records Using a Form

▶ Maintaining a database requires that fields be updated with current data. When you click the name of the field to edit, Access selects its contents so that you can overwrite the data. Access saves changes to a field when you move to the next record.

▶ You must be certain that you have located the correct record, because several records may contain similar information. There are several methods to locate the record you want to edit:

- Click the Next Record or Previous Record button to move through the records consecutively.
- Click the Home tab, and in the Find group, click the Find button to use the Find feature, as shown in Figure 3.12.

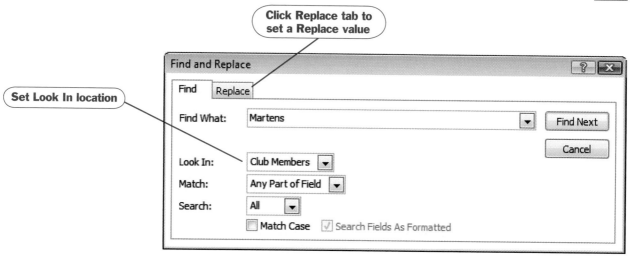

Figure 3.12: Find and Replace dialog box

- Enter the search text in the Search box on the Navigation bar, shown in Figure 3.13, and it will immediately find the text. Press [Enter] to look for additional occurrences of the same text.

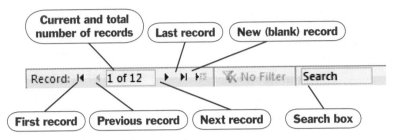

Figure 3.13: Form Navigation bar

TRY it OUT a3-8

1. Use the open database or open data file a3-8.

2. In the *Club Members* form, in the Search box, enter **Keith** and press **[Enter]**.

3. In Kenny Keith's record, click the **Address field label** to select the field data, then enter: **54 Scott Lane**.

4. Click the **Home tab**, and in the Find group, click the **Find button**. *You want to change Tracy Martens to Tracy Collingswood.*

   a. Enter **Martens** in the Find What box. Be sure the Look I: location is set to Club Members, as shown in Figure 3.12.

   b. Click **Find Next**. *Check to see that this is a record containing information about Tracy Martens, moving the dialog box, if necessary. If not, click **Find Next** again.*

   c. Click the **Replace tab**, and enter **Collingswood** in the Replace With box. Click **Replace**, then click the **Close button**.

5. Do not close the database.

Print Database Objects

▶ You can easily print datasheets, forms, or selected records of either object, as shown in Figure 3.14. If you use the Print command to print a form, it will print all the forms unless you click Selected Record(s). You can also select specific records on a datasheet and click Selected Record(s) to print part of a table.

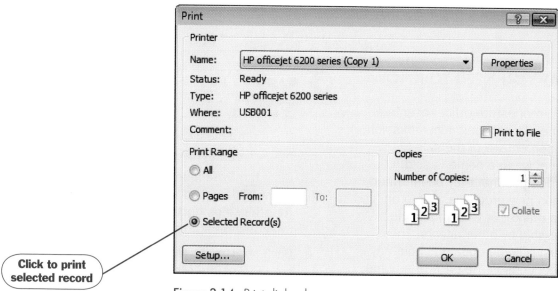

Click to print selected record

Figure 3.14: Print dialog box

HOW **1.** In a table or form, click the **Office Button**, point to **Print**, then click **Print**. **2.** Click **Selected Record(s)** on the Print dialog box, to limit your print result. **3.** Click **OK**.

TRY it OUT a3-9

1. Use the open database, or open data file **a3-9**.

2. With the *Club Members* table open, click the **Office Button**, point to **Print**, then click **Print Preview**. *Note that in Portrait orientation some of the columns are cut off on the right of the page. The Print Preview tab is now active.*

3. Click the **Landscape button** on the Print Preview tab and click **Print**, then **OK**. Close the preview screen.

4. Open the *Club Members* form and select the last record, Sophia Pappas.

5. Click the **Office Button**, point to **Print**, then click **Print**. In the Print dialog box, click **Selected Record(s)**, then click **OK**.

6. Switch to the *Club Members* table, and select the record selector boxes for records 11 and 12. *To select multiple records, drag through the selection boxes or press and hold [Shift] while clicking each record selector box.*

7. Click the **Office Button**, point to **Print**, and click **Print**. In the Print dialog box, click **Selected Record(s)**, then click **OK**.

8. Close the database.

REHEARSAL

TASK 1

WHAT YOU NEED TO KNOW

▶ In a real estate office, agents are generally only paid a commission, or percentage of the sales price, when a home is sold. It is imperative that they be informed when new properties come on the market or when properties are sold by other agents. They must also be updated about any reductions in the price of a home.

▶ In this Rehearsal activity, you will create a form for Palmetto Realtors of Hollywood, Florida. The purpose of the form is to allow agents to enter new property listings, edit existing listings, and update and later delete the listings that have sold.

▼ DIRECTIONS

1. Start Access.

2. Open data file **3r1-Palmetto**, and open the *Agents* and *Listings* tables to view the fields and data.

3. Click the **Database Tools tab**, and Show/Hide Group, click the in the **Relationships button** to review the table relationships. Close the window.

4. Click the **Create tab**, and in the Forms group, click the **More Forms button**, then click **Form Wizard**.
   a. Use the *Listings* table and all its fields for the form. Use the Columnar layout, apply the Metro style, and name the form **Listings**.
   b. Click **Open the form to view or enter information**, if necessary, then click **Finish**.

5. In Form view, click the **New (blank) record button** on the Navigation bar.

6. Add the two new listings, as shown below.

Date Listed	07/28/2010	07/29/2010
Owner First Name	Margie	Lorenzo
Owner Last Name	Kelley	Vargas
Address	750 Ocean Ave	21 Green Street
City	Hollywood	East Hollywood
Agent Last Name	Olsen	Barona
Date Built	12/12/1990	10/10/1998
Price	575,000	270,000
Property Description	3 bedroom, 2 bath condo, ocean view	2 bedroom, 1 bath cottage .25 acres

7. The price of ListingID 3 has been reduced to $395,000. Click the **Previous Record button** until ListingID 3 is displayed, and update the price.

Continued on next page

8. ListingID 1 sold on 07/31/2010 for $128,500 and the selling agent was Garcia. Update the record as shown in Figure 3.15, then print a copy. *The record will be deleted after the contract closing.*

9. Create a split form for the *Agents* table, as shown in Figure 3.16 and name it **Agents**. Use AutoFormat, and apply the Metro style. Save the form.

10. In Form view, update the record for Agent Garcia. He has changed his mobile telephone number to 754-555-3498.

11. Close the form and close the database and exit Access.

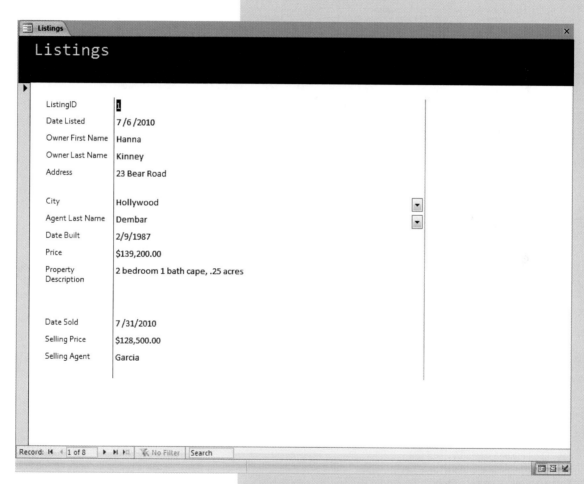

Figure 3.15: *Listings* form

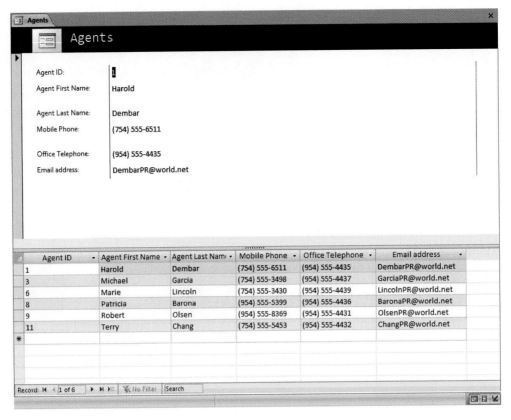

Figure 3.16: *Agents* split form

Create a Form Using Form Tools
1. In the Navigation Pane, click the table to be used to create a form.
2. Click the **Create tab**, and in the Forms group, click the **Form button**, or the **Split Form button**, or the **Multiple Items button**.

Create a Form Using the Form Wizard
1. Click the **Create tab**, and in the Forms group, click the **More Forms button**, then click **Form Wizard**.
2. Double-click the fields you want. Click **Next**.
3. Choose a layout and click **Next**.
4. Choose a style and click **Next**.
5. Enter a title, select how to open the form, and click **Finish**.

Enter Records Using a Form
1. Double-click the form in the Navigation Pane to open it in Form view.

2. Click the **New (blank) record button**.
3. Press [Tab] to move from field to field while entering data.

Edit Records Using a Form
1. Double-click the form in the Navigation Pane to open it in Form view.
2. Locate the record by entering a text string in the Search box on the Navigation bar of the form.
3. Select the field name and overwrite the data.

Locate Form Data Using the Find Feature
1. Double-click the form in the Navigation Pane to open it.
2. Click the **Home tab**, and in the Find group, click the **Find button**.
3. In the Find and Replace dialog box, enter the Find What text.
4. In the Look In box, set the field or form name.
5. Click **Find Next** and check if record is correct; if not, click **Find Next**.

6. Click the **Replace tab**, enter new text, then click **Replace**. Or, close the dialog box and make edits in the form.

Print Database Objects
1. Select the record, form, or datasheet.
2. Click the **Office Button**, point to **Print**, then click **Print**.
3. Click **Selected Record(s)**, if applicable. Click **OK**.
   Or
2. Click the **Office Button**, point to **Print**, then click **Print Preview**.
3. Change settings on the Print Preview tab.
4. Click the **Print button** to print from Print Preview.

TASK 1

Expedition Travel Gear wants to continue to build its database by adding its Boston employees to the *Contact* and *Payroll* tables. They have decided to create forms for each of the tables and use them for data entry and record updates.

Expedition

Travel Gear

Follow these guidelines:

1. Open data file **3p1-ETG-EMPS**, open the *Contact* table, and note the new records.

2. Use the Form Wizard to create a form for the *Contact* table. Use the columnar layout and the Equity style. Name the form **Contact Form**.

3. Open the *Payroll* table and create a form using the Form button. Use AutoFormat to apply the Equity style. *Note that this table has not been updated with the Boston employee data and that the related Weekly datasheet appears at the bottom.* Save the form as **Payroll Form**, and close the *Payroll* table.

4. In Form view, enter the data below into the *Payroll* form. Save the form, and then open the *Payroll* table to check your entries. *Note that when entering* **Boston**, *you can select the city from the list or just enter* **B** *and Access will complete the entry. There are no entries for Boston in the related Weekly table at this time.*

5. Close the database.

EMP ID	11	12	13	14	15
SSNO	112-00-8711	102-00-4511	176-00-8733	213-00-0564	195-00-8926
Store	Boston	Boston	Boston	Boston	Boston
Status	M	M	S	S	M
Exemptions	1	3	1	1	3
Birth Date	10/12/1978	9/25/1985	2/18/1989	07/07/1990	11/22/1988
Rate	14.50	13.75	11.50	11.50	10.00

TRYOUT

TASK 2

GOALS

To modify the format and properties of a form in Design view, as shown in Figure 3.17

To modify the form header and footer and to add a calculated control

* Modify a form in Layout view
* Create a form using the Blank Form tool
* Use Form Design view
* Add, size, and move controls
* Modify the properties of specific controls on a form
* Modify the properties of a form
* Add a calculated control to a form

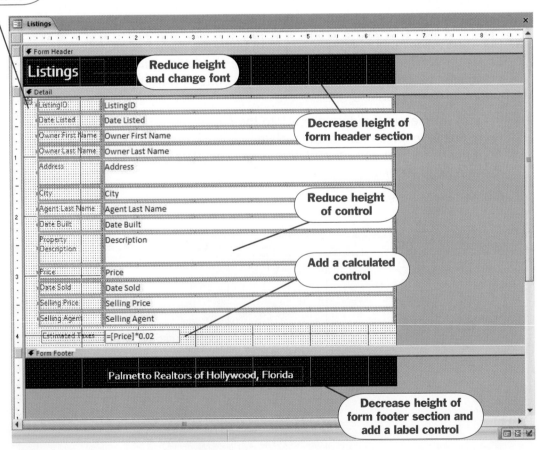

Figure 3.17: Task 2: Modify form in Design view

WHAT YOU NEED TO KNOW

Modify a Form in Layout View

▶ When you worked in Layout view, the Form Layout Tools tabs were available. We used the AutoFormat tool on the Format tab, shown in Figure 3.18, and will now utilize the other features on this tab.

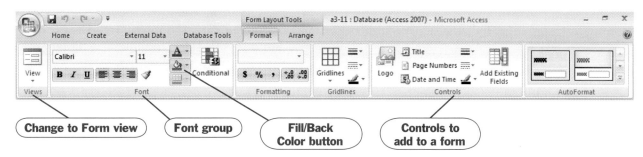

Figure 3.18: Form Layout Tools Format tab

▶ The most basic formatting tools are those in the Font, Formatting, and Gridlines groups. They are used to change the format of data or field names in a form, using the same techniques as in Word and Excel.

▶ In the Controls group on the Form Layout Tools Format tab, we can modify the form by adding or editing a form title or a logo, or by adding existing fields. Each object you see on a form is called a control. **Controls** display data, perform actions, and enhance the view of form data. Field labels and the field values are both types of controls. Other formats have been added to the form shown in Figure 3.19.

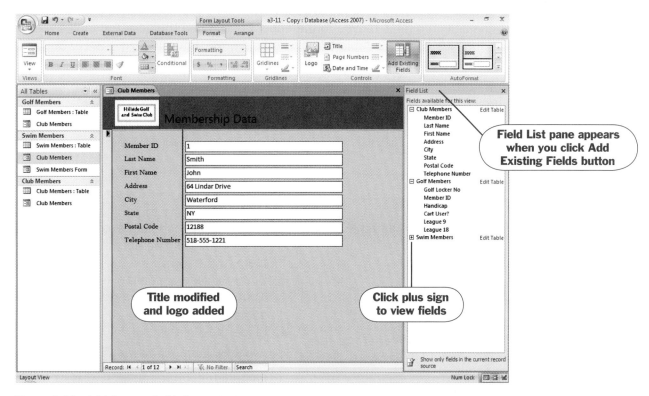

Figure 3.19: Add Existing Fields button

1. Open data file **a3-10**, and open the *Club Members* form in Layout view.

2. Click anywhere on the form background to select it. Click the **Form Layout Tools Format tab**, and in the Font group, click the **Fill/Back Color list arrow**, then click **Brown 3**. *Brown 3, a peach color, is applied to the form background.*

3. Click on the **Member ID field label**. *Note that the Font tools are active.* Click the **Bold button**, then click the **Align Text Right button**. Click the **Undo button** on the Quick Access toolbar twice. *Try this with field data as well.*

4. Double-click the *Club Members* form title, select the text, and enter the new title: **Membership Data**.

5. On the Form Layout Tools Format tab, in the Controls group, click the **Logo button**. Locate your data folder, select **clublogo.tif**, and click **Open**. *You may have to change the file type to All Files to locate the logo. The logo appears on the left side of the form header. Click and drag the sides to make it a bit larger, then drag it to the right side of the header text.*

6. In the Controls group, click the **Date & Time button**. Click the **Include Date check box** if necessary, deselect the **Include Time check box**, then click **OK**. *The date appears on the right side of the form header.* Right-click the date, and click **Delete**.

7. Do not close the database.

Add Existing Fields to a Form

▶ When you click the Add Existing Fields button in the Controls Group, a list of related tables appears from which you can add existing fields to your form. When you select a field from a table in the bottom pane, the selected table moves to the upper pane. Once the selected tables are in the upper pane, click the plus sign on a table to view its fields, as shown in Figure 3.19. Double-click a field to add it to the form. If a field is added in error, right-click the field and click Delete.

HOW 1. In a form in Layout view, click the **Form Layout Tools Format tab**, and in the Controls group, click the **Add Existing Fields button**. 2. In the Field List pane, click the plus sign next to the table that contains the field you want to add. 3. Double-click a field name to add it to the form.

1. Use the open database or open data file **a3-11** and open the *Club Members* form in Layout view.

2. In the Controls group, click the **Add Existing Fields button**. All the related tables will appear.
   a. Click the plus sign next to the *Golf Members* and the *Swim Members* tables to display the fields.
   b. Double-click each field except Member ID from the *Golf Members* table to add them to the form.
   c. Double-click each field except Member ID from the *Swim Members* table to add them to the form.
   d. Close the Field list.

3. Save the *Club Members* form.

4. Do not close the database.

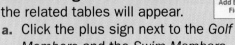

Create a Form Using the Blank Form Tool

▶ You can create a new form from scratch, using the Blank Form tool, as shown in Figure 3.20. You will add fields to the form using the Field List pane and use Layout view and its tools to format and customize the form.

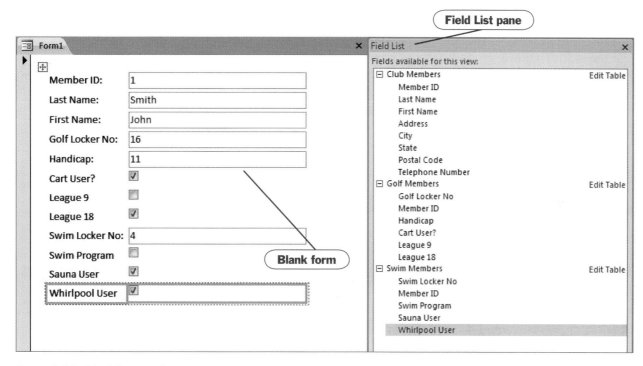

Figure 3.20: Blank Form tool

TRY *it* OUT a3-12

1. Use the open database or open data file **a3-12**. *The club needs a form for the receptionist to look up golf and swim club information.*

2. Click the **Create tab**, and in the Forms group, click the **Blank Form button**. *A blank form appears with the Field List pane at the right.*

3. Click the plus signs on all the tables in the Field List pane to show the fields.

4. Double-click the first three fields from the *Club Members* table, and the fields other than Member ID from the *Golf* and *Swim Members* tables, as shown in Figure 3.20.

5. Save the form as **Swim and Golf Data**.

6. Switch to Layout view if necessary, and format the table to match the *Club*

Members table: Use AutoFormat to set Equity style, use the form name as a title by clicking the **Title button** in the Controls group. Insert the club logo, then change background fill to Brown 3. *Adjust size and placement of logo and title if necessary.*

7. Compare the new form to the *Club Members* form. *Reapply the Equity style to the Club Members form and reset the background, if necessary.*

8. Save and close all forms.

9. Right-click the *Swim Members* form and click **Delete**. *This form is no longer necessary.*

10. Do not close the database.

Use Form Design View

▶ You have used Form view and Layout view. However, you can also create or modify a form in Design view. To work in Design view, right-click the form tab and click Design View. In Design view you can see the controls, the objects that display or organize data on a form, which you used earlier in Layout view.

▶ Controls can be bound, unbound, or calculated. A **bound control** is connected to a field in a table. In general, a **text box** is the control used for viewing and editing data on forms and reports. In Figure 3.21, the text box controls and their attached labels are bound controls because they represent fields in the database. The text labeling the data control may be changed by changing the caption for the label control. However, the data itself is bound to the table data. You will learn about unbound and calculated controls later in this lesson.

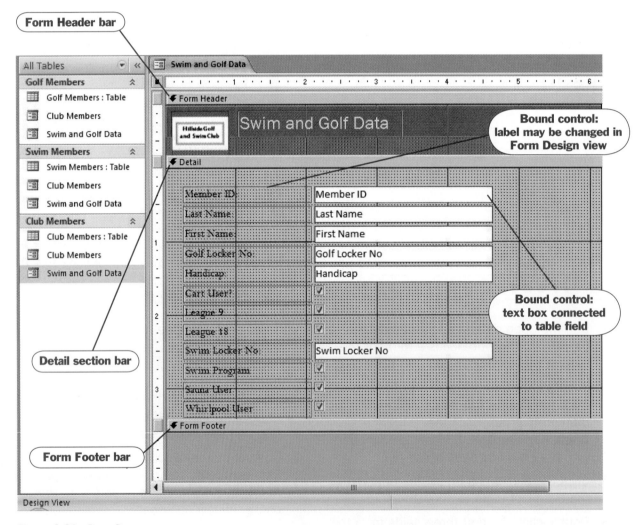

Figure 3.21: Form Design view

► In Design view, the Form Design Tools Design tab appears, as shown in Figure 3.22. On the Form Design Tools Design tab, the Controls group contains 25 objects you can add to a form, such as Text Box, Check Box, Option Button, Combo Box, and List Box. As you position your mouse over each control, a ScreenTip will display the control's name.

Figure 3.22: Form Design Tools Design tab

T R Y *i t* **O U T** *a3-13*

1. Use the open database or open data file **a3-13**.

2. Right-click the *Swim and Golf Data* form in the Navigation Pane, and click **Design View**. *Note how the fields, or bound controls, appear in Design view.*

3. Position the mouse pointer over each control in the Form Design Tools Design tab to display its ScreenTip.

4. Do not close the form.

Add, Size, and Move Controls

▶ You may customize forms by adding a title, dates, or notes for the user to every form. To accomplish this, add a label control to the header, footer, or detail section of a form in Form Design view. A **label control** displays a title or caption and is an **unbound control**, which is not connected to a data source. Unbound controls are used to display information such as text, lines, rectangles, and pictures.

▶ To add a label control, click the Label (Form Control) button on the Form Design Tools Design tab and click the location where you want the upper-left corner of the control to be. A small box appears, shown in Figure 3.23, and as you enter the information you want to display, the box expands as necessary. If you right-click the control, you can position or add formats or styles to the control, such as a shadow. If you switch to Form view, you can see how your design looks in the form.

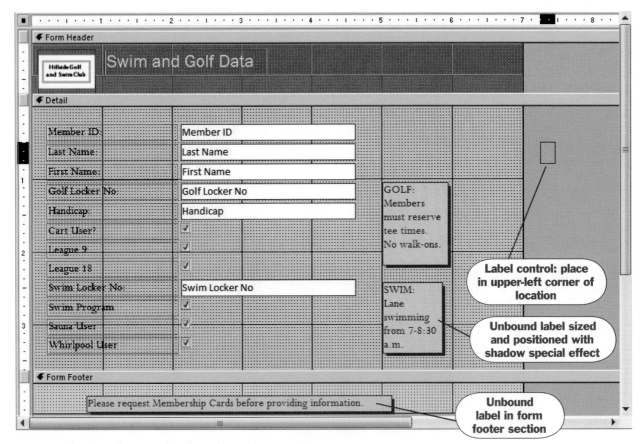

Figure 3.23: Form design with unbound controls

▶ When you select a control in Design view, handles appear, as shown in Figure 3.24. The mouse pointer can be used to stretch, shrink, or size the control by dragging the handles. When the mouse pointer is a four-headed arrow you can move the control.

▶ It may be necessary to expand the area in Design view where you want to place a label. If you need to expand the form header or form footer section, click on the edge of the header or footer bar and drag it to size. **Form headers** and **form footers** are sections that appear at the top and bottom of each form where you can include identification data or data to be repeated on each form. If you want to move the footer section, click the bar and drag it to the new location.

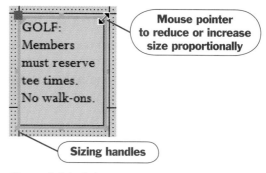

Figure 3.24: Select control to move and size

TRY *it* OUT a3-14

1. Use the open database with the *Swim and Golf Data* form in Design view, or open the data file **a3-14** to that location. *Try expanding the form header section and the form footer section.*

2. Click the **Form Design Tools Design tab** if necessary, and in the Controls group, click the **Label (Form Control) button**.

3. As shown in Figure 3.23, click the location in the form footer section where you want the upper-left corner of the control to be placed. Enter: `Please request Membership Cards before providing information.`

4. Add two unbound labels to the right of the Golf and Swim data in the detail section as shown.

5. Select and size the label boxes so that they fit to the right of the relevant data.

6. Right-click the **Golf label control**, then point to **Special Effect**, and click the **Shadow Effect button**. Repeat this step for the Swim label and the footer label controls. *The Special Effects button will be set for the last effect and can be clicked directly.*

7. Right-click the **Swim and Golf Data tab**, and click **Form View**. Save the form when you are satisfied with your changes.

8. Scroll through the records and note that the form header, form footer, and unbound labels appear on every form.

9. Close the form, but do not close the database.

Modify the Properties of Specific Controls on a Form

▶ Every control on a form has properties. These properties determine a control's format, appearance, and behavior. They also detail the characteristics of the text or data contained in the control.

▶ You modify the properties of a control in Design view by making changes to its property sheet, as shown in Figure 3.25. You can change a label by entering the new caption on the Format tab on the Property Sheet pane. To change the width of a control, double-click Width, delete the existing value, and enter the new value.

HOW 1. Click the control you want to change in Design view. 2. Click the **Form Design Tools Design tab**, and in the Tools group, click the **Property Sheet button**, or right-click the control and click **Properties**. 3. Make the desired changes. 4. Close the Property Sheet pane to view the change.

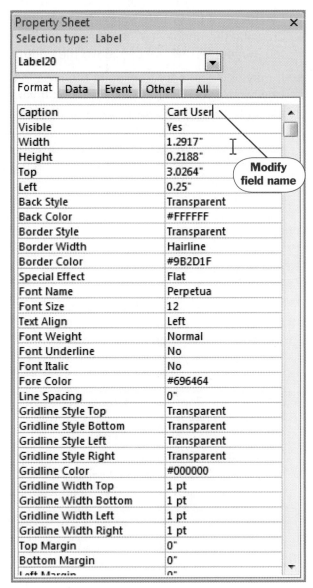

Figure 3.25: Property Sheet pane for field label

1. Use either the open database or data file **a3-15** and open the *Club Members* form in Design view.

2. Right-click the **Cart User? field label**, then click **Properties**. Notice the five tabs of the Label Property Sheet pane. Click each tab and scroll through the property settings.

3. In the Property Sheet pane, click the **Format tab** and click **Caption**.

4. Delete the question mark from the caption, so that it reads **Cart User**.

5. Close the Property Sheet pane, and check the change in the label in the Design, Layout, and Form views.

6. Switch to Design view, and note the size of the controls that contain data.

7. Right-click the bound control for the **Address field data box** (on the right), and click **Properties**.

8. Click the **Format tab**, and double-click the **Width property field**. Change the width to 3".

9. Close the property sheet, and notice the size of all the data controls.

10. Close the form, and save your changes.

Modify the Properties of a Form

▶ We have already set control properties, but the form itself has properties that define the form's characteristics. Use the **form selector**, which is the box where the rulers meet in a form's Design view, to view the properties of a form, as shown in Figure 3.26.

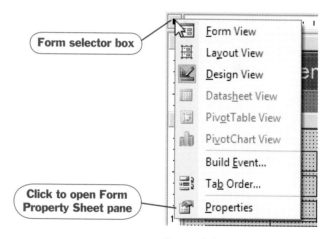

Form selector box

Click to open Form Property Sheet pane

Figure 3.26: Design view shortcut menu

▶ Double-click the form selector and the form's property sheet appears, as shown in Figure 3.27. Use the scroll bar on the right side of the Property Sheet pane and click other tabs to view property sheet settings. Click the name of the property to select and then change the setting. When you make a change to the form, it is only to the display of the data, not to the underlying data source or table.

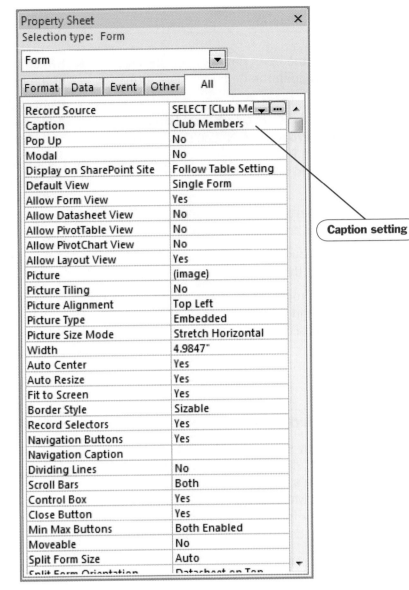

Figure 3.27: Form Property Sheet pane

1. Use the open database or open data file **a3-16** and open the *Club Members* form in Design view.

2. Double-click the **form selector box**. Notice the five tabs of the Form Property Sheet pane. Click each tab and scroll through the property settings.

3. In the Property Sheet pane, click the **Format tab** and double-click the **Caption property field**.

4. Enter: `Club Members : Form`.

5. Close the Property Sheet pane, and save the design. Switch to Form view. *Note that the caption on the tab of the form has changed to: Club Members : Form.*

6. Switch back to Design view, and note that the tab has not been changed in Design view.

7. Save and close the database.

Add a Calculated Control to a Form

▶ There are times when you want to display a calculated value on a form. For example, unit price and quantity ordered data can be used to calculate the total price.

▶ A **calculated control** uses an expression as its source of data rather than a field. An **expression** can be made up of operators (such as = and *), control names, field names, functions, and constant values. For example, =[Total Price]*.08 calculates an eight percent sales tax on the price. Percent values must be changed to their decimal equivalent for the expression.

▶ In a calculated control, preface each expression with the = operator and place control names in brackets. In the expression, **=[UnitsOnOrder]*[UnitPrice]**, [UnitsOnOrder] and [UnitPrice] represent the values in the controls, * is the multiplication operator, and the result is the value of outstanding orders.

▶ A text box is the most common type of control used to display a calculated value. Two boxes appear: the label and the unbound control. To make this field a calculated field, modify the Control Source property of the unbound control, found under the Data tab of the Property Sheet pane, as shown in Figure 3.28. If you need help with the expression, click the Expression Builder button and in the Expression Builder dialog box, use the buttons and list of segments to create the expression. When you click OK, the expression is entered into the Control Source property field.

HOW 1. In Form Design view, click the **Form Design Tools Design tab**, and in the Controls group, click the **Text Box button**. 2. Place the box in the desired location on the form. *Two boxes appear: a text label and an unbound control.* 3. Right-click the label, click **Properties**, and modify the Caption property. 4. Right-click the unbound control, then click **Properties**. 5. In the Property Sheet pane, click the **Data tab** and enter the expression in the Control Source property setting.

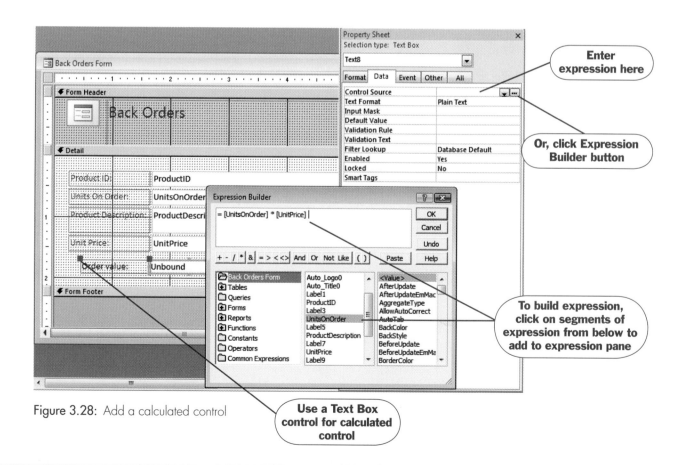

Figure 3.28: Add a calculated control

▶ The formula appears in the calculated control in Design view. Go to Form view to see the contents of calculated controls.

T R Y *i t* **O U T** *a3-17*

1. Open the data file **a3-17**, and view the table and form. *Click the arrowhead at the left to view the form better.*

2. Open the form in Design view. To make room for another field, click and drag the top edge of the Form Footer bar down to the next horizontal gridline.

3. Click the **Form Design Tools Design tab**, and in the Controls group, click the **Text Box button**.

4. Click a location under the last data field (on the right). *The text box appears with a label Access assigns.*

5. Double-click the text box label and enter `Order Value`.

6. If the Property Sheet pane is not visible, right-click the text box unbound control, and click **Properties**.

7. Click the text box unbound control. In the Property Sheet pane, click the **Data tab**, then click the **Control Source property field**. Enter: `=[UnitsOnOrder]*[UnitPrice]`. *Or, you can click the Expression Builder button and click the segments of the expression, as shown in Figure 3.28.*

8. Click the **Format tab**, click the **Format property field list arrow**, and change the number format to **Currency**.

9. Close the Property Sheet pane, and switch to Form view.

10. Use the navigation controls to view each form and the value in the calculated control.

11. Save and close the form and the database.

REHEARSAL

 GOALS

To modify the format and properties of a form in Design view

To modify a form header and footer and to add a calculated control

TASK 2

WHAT YOU NEED TO KNOW

▶ Earlier you created a listings form for Palmetto Realtors of Hollywood, Florida. The form is used to enter new property listings, edit existing listings, and delete listings that have sold, after the contract closing.

▶ In this Rehearsal activity, you will modify that form as follows:

- Add the company name in the form footer.
- Calculate the estimated annual taxes on the form for each house. Taxes in the three towns that Palmetto covers are based on the selling price of the home, which is not determined until the sale takes place. The estimated taxes will be calculated based on the asking price and using the tax rate of two percent of the selling price.

▼ DIRECTIONS

1. Open your solution to **3r1-Palmetto** or open data file **3r2-Palmetto**. Close the security warning message bar if necessary.

2. Open the *Listings* form in Design view. Drag the bottom edge of the Form Footer bar down to open the footer section. *You will see a shaded area to match the header section.*

3. Click **Form Design Tools Design tab** if necessary, and in the Controls group, click the **Label (Form Control) button**.

4. In the form footer section, place the label for the name of the company. Enter: `Palmetto Realtors of Hollywood, Florida`. Press **[Enter]**.
   a. Select the text and set the text color to **White** and font to **Corbel, 14 point**.
   b. Move and size the label box so that it is aligned under the field data boxes in the form.

5. Select the text in the form header, and change the font to **Corbel**. Switch to Form view to check your changes.

6. In Design view, to make room for another control in the detail section, click and drag the top edge of the Form Footer bar down about one inch.

7. Click **Form Design Tools Design tab**, and in the Controls group, click the **Text Box button**. *The steps below will add the calculated control.*
   a. Click under the last field data box where you want to place a calculated control for the taxes.
   b. Right-click the text label box, and click **Properties**. Modify the Caption property to read `Estimated Taxes`.
   c. Click the text box unbound control box.
   d. In the Property Sheet pane, click the **Data tab**, then click the **Control Source property field** and enter: `=[Price]*.02.` *You cannot use a percent sign in Access expressions.*

Continued on next page

e. Click the **Format tab**, and using the Format property field list arrow, set the format to **Currency**.

f. Modify the size and location of the label and unbound control boxes so that they are aligned under the other data.

8. Switch to Form view, and note that you need to scroll to see all the data.

9. Return to Design view, and make the following modifications in the design:

a. Reduce the height of the text box for the form header text and then reduce the size of the form header by dragging the upper edge of the Detail bar upward.

b. Click on any field to display the Select All button in the top-left corner, as shown in Figure 3.29. Click it to select all fields, and drag the fields upward to the bottom of the Detail bar.

c. Clear the Select All button by clicking outside the fields, and click on the **Description field data box**. Change the Height property to read **.5"**.

d. Move the Estimated Taxes control directly below the last field.

Continued on next page

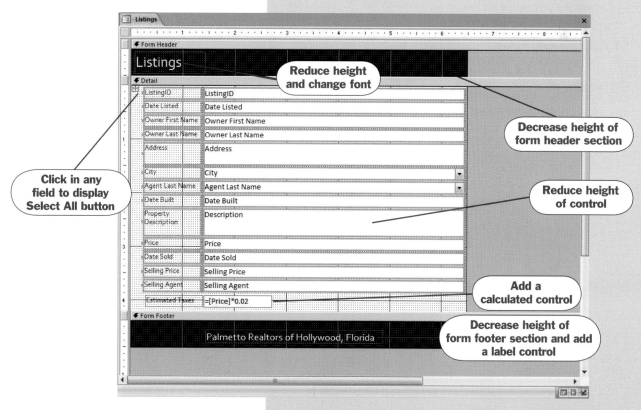

Figure 3.29: Design view of *Listings* form

e. Move the form footer section upward to meet the bottom of the detail section.

f. Switch to Form view, and save the form.

10. In Form view, use the Navigation controls to view each record and the value in the calculated control.

11. Print a copy of the form for ListingID 7, being sure to click **Selected Record(s)**.

12. Close the form, and close the database.

PERFORMANCE

TASK 2

Expedition Travel Gear would like to modify the structure of its database by deleting its *Weekly* table and its relationships, adding fields to another table, modifying its forms, and adding a calculated field. You will also format the forms in Design view to add a logo and footer text.

Expedition

Travel Gear

Follow these guidelines:

1. Open your solution to **3p1-ETG-EMPS**, or open the data file **3p2-ETG-EMPS**.

2. Delete the *Weekly* table: Click the **Database Tools tab**, then click the **Relationships button**. Note the fields in the *Weekly* table. Right-click both relationship join lines between the *Weekly* table and the other tables, and delete the relationships. Right-click the *Weekly* table, and click **Hide Table**. Save and close the window. Right-click **Weekly : Table** in the Navigation Pane, and delete it.

3. Open the *Payroll* form. You will get error messages because the *Weekly* table was part of this form. Click **OK** to all. You will be correcting the problem. Switch to Design view, and right-click the bottom datasheet area titled Table.Weekly, and click **Delete**. Save and close the form.

4. Modify the *Payroll* table by adding a column for **Dues** and changing Other to **Other Deductions** (for weekly deductions in addition to payroll taxes). Both fields should be Currency data types. *You will get a warning about field size that does not matter in this case.* Use Figure 3.30 as a guide, and enter the new data shown.

Continued on next page

Emp ID	SSNO	Store	Status	Exemptions	Birth Date	Rate	Dues	Other Deduc
1	143-00-6598	Chicago	M	2	11/12/1965	$14.50	$8.00	$15.00
2	132-00-4321	Chicago	M	1	3/6/1978	$10.95	$8.00	$0.00
3	210-00-3234	Chicago	S	0	6/10/1989	$9.00	$5.00	$0.00
4	154-00-8712	Chicago	S	2	12/14/1985	$9.00	$5.00	$0.00
5	127-00-7165	Chicago	M	0	8/14/1982	$8.25	$8.00	$0.00
6	237-00-8711	Miami	M	3	6/9/1975	$13.50	$8.00	$15.00
7	185-00-5167	Miami	S	2	1/7/1985	$12.50	$5.00	$0.00
8	214-00-6548	Miami	S	0	9/21/1989	$9.00	$5.00	$0.00
9	165-00-4387	Miami	M	4	7/5/1982	$10.00	$8.00	$0.00
10	132-00-2198	Miami	S	1	11/5/1988	$9.00	$5.00	$0.00
11	112-00-8711	Boston	M	1	10/12/1978	$14.50	$8.00	$15.00
12	102-00-4511	Boston	M	3	9/25/1985	$13.75	$8.00	$0.00
13	176-00-8733	Boston	S	1	2/18/1989	$11.50	$5.00	$0.00
14	213-00-0564	Boston	S	1	7/7/1990	$11.50	$5.00	$0.00
15	195-00-8926	Boston	M	3	11/22/1988	$10.00	$8.00	$0.00

Add new fields and data

Figure 3.30: *Modify Payroll table*

5. Modify the *Payroll* form in Design view, as shown in Figure 3.31. Delete the Other field remaining from the earlier table and add the logo (**ETGlogo.tif**) and footer as shown. Add the two new fields to the form. *Expand the form footer section to accept the footer label.* Add a calculated control for a Total control, which adds the Dues and Other Deductions field values. Format the calculated field for Currency, and add the text box label as shown. Save the form.

6. Modify the *Contact* form in Design view by adding the logo and footer to match the *Payroll* form.

7. Save the form and close the database.

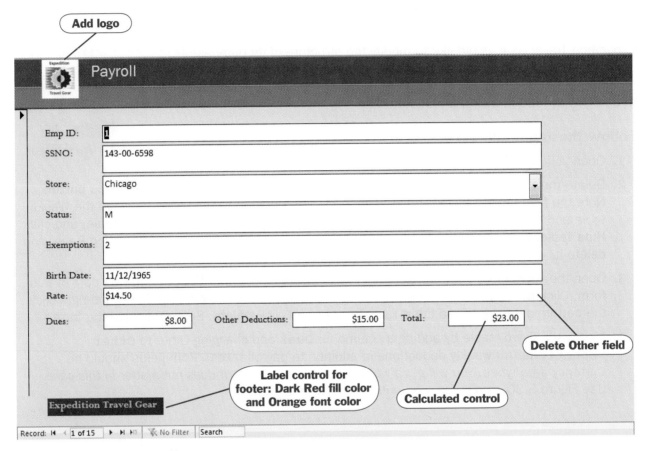

Figure 3.31: Modified *Payroll* form

EarthCare Services

Act I

You work for EarthCare Services, a full-service landscape contractor. The company is interested in keeping accurate information on each of their customers and their contracts. Data has been added to the database, and you will add more today. You have been asked to build a form that they can use to enter data as well as to update the customer database.

Follow these guidelines:

1. Open data file **3ep1-EarthCare**.

2. Create a *Customers* form with the fields and formats shown in Figure 3.32. Save the form, and add the following information to the database in Form view.

Customer ID	10	11
Company		Sullivan Volvo
Last	Ericson	Sullivan
First	Anthony	Michael
Address	23 Stone Hill Drive	73 Kingsley Road
City	Cincinnati	Milford
State	OH	OH
ZIP	45255	45150
Telephone	513-555-4324	513-555-6300
Wholesale		Yes
Contract No		9
Type of Service		Full
Other Description		Full snow removal.
Renewal Date		09/10/2011
Monthly Rate		$500

3. Make the following updates to customers' records in the *Customers* form:
   a. Correct the telephone number for Customer ID 4 to **513–555–7126**.
   b. Alfred Montez has just signed a monthly contract for the Trim/Fertilize service, renewable on 09/20/2011, for a monthly rate of $75.
   c. Change the first name at 250 Sparrow Drive to: **Katherine**.

4. Save the database but do not close it.

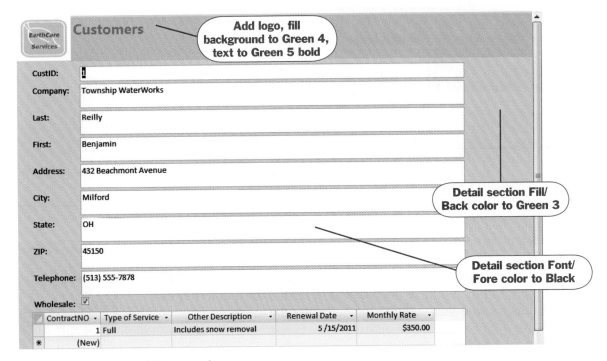

Figure 3.32: Customized *Customers* form

Act II

Kevin Spencer, the CEO of EarthCare Services is happy with the new look of the database form and the ease of updating and viewing customers and their contracts. He would like you to add a *Contracts* form and to calculate the yearly contract fee.

Follow these guidelines:

1. Continue to work in the same database. Create a *Contracts* form including all of the fields. Add a calculated control to the form that multiples the monthly rates by 12 to display a yearly rate. Format the yearly rate for currency. Change the label name to: **Yearly:**. Format the form to match the *Customers* form.

2. The company has received a call from Alfred Montez, who wants a record of his change in service. Print a copy of his form.

3. Save and close the database.

Act III

Ms. Wallace of Newmark Productions wants to continue to improve the employee database started earlier. Additional employees have been added to the database in the *Employees* table. They would like you to add an *Employees* form and a *Payroll* form, format the forms, and add additional data.

Follow these guidelines:

1. Open data file **3ep3-NEWMARK**, and look at the tables to review the database. *Note that employees have been added but that data has not been entered for them on the Payroll table.*

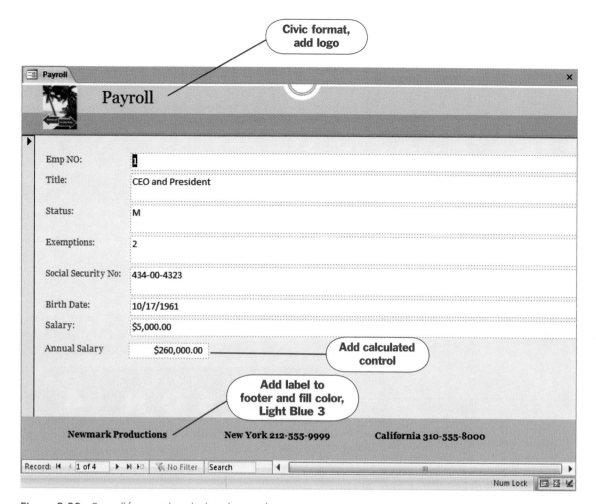

Figure 3.33: *Payroll* form with calculated control

Emp NO	18	22	28	30
Title	Television Production	Director Sales	Movie Production	Manager Sales
Status	S	M	M	S
Exemptions	2	3	4	1
Social Security No.	543-00-0787	234-00-6376	654-00-3434	154-00-0825
Birth Date	5/12/1980	11/24/1982	4/7/1980	3/30/1979
Salary	$2500	$2500	$3000	$1500

2. Create and format a form for the *Payroll* table, as shown in Figure 3.33. The calculated control multiplies the weekly salary by 52 weeks to get the annual salary.

3. Create a matching form for the *Employees* table.

4. Use the *Payroll* form to enter data for the employees already added to the *Employees* table.

5. Save and close the form and all the tables. Close the database.

LESSON 4

Getting Information

In this lesson, you will learn how to obtain the information you need from a database. You will learn more about finding and sorting records, and you will learn to create, use, modify, and format queries.

Upon completion of this lesson, you will have mastered the following skill sets

- Find and replace a record
- Sort records in a datasheet
- Apply and remove filters
- Create a query object
- Create select queries using the Simple Query Wizard
- Create select queries with calculations
- Create crosstab, duplicates, and unmatched queries
- Modify queries in Design view
- Use aggregate functions
- Add a calculated field to queries in Query Design view
- Format and sort query results
- Create a multi-table query

Terms
Software-related

Aggregate functions
Ascending order
Calculated field
Criteria
Crosstab query
Descending order
Duplicates query
Filter by form
Filter by selection
Filter
Match box
Match Case
Multi-table select query
Query
Query design grid
Query Design view
Query Wizards
Select query
Simple Query Wizard
Sort
Summary query
Total row
Unmatched query

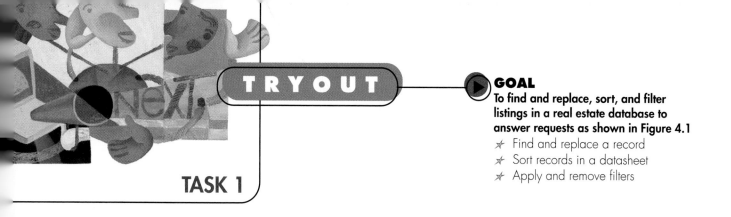

TRYOUT

GOAL
To find and replace, sort, and filter listings in a real estate database to answer requests as shown in Figure 4.1

⁎ Find and replace a record
⁎ Sort records in a datasheet
⁎ Apply and remove filters

TASK 1

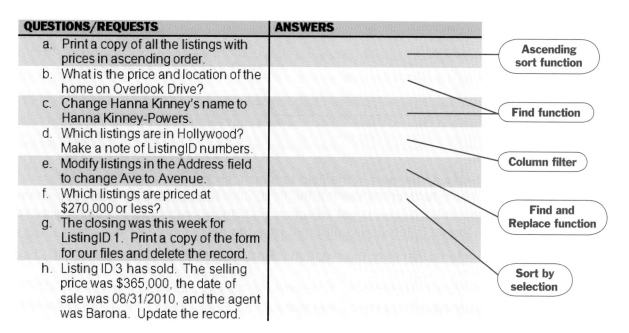

QUESTIONS/REQUESTS	ANSWERS
a. Print a copy of all the listings with prices in ascending order.	
b. What is the price and location of the home on Overlook Drive?	
c. Change Hanna Kinney's name to Hanna Kinney-Powers.	
d. Which listings are in Hollywood? Make a note of ListingID numbers.	
e. Modify listings in the Address field to change Ave to Avenue.	
f. Which listings are priced at $270,000 or less?	
g. The closing was this week for ListingID 1. Print a copy of the form for our files and delete the record.	
h. Listing ID 3 has sold. The selling price was $365,000, the date of sale was 08/31/2010, and the agent was Barona. Update the record.	

Callouts (right side): Ascending sort function • Find function • Column filter • Find and Replace function • Sort by selection

Figure 4.1: Task 1: Use tools to find, sort, and filter data

ACCESS

WHAT YOU NEED TO KNOW

Find and Replace a Record

▶ Sometimes you need to update field contents in many records. For example, the telephone company may decide to change an area code. This means that you need to find each record containing a field with that area code and update it. There are also times when you need to replace some, but not all, of the information. You used the Find and Replace dialog box in the last lesson to search forms to locate data. You can speed up a search in a datasheet by selecting a field and just searching that data.

▶ To search for data in a specific field, with a datasheet displayed, click the column representing the field to search. This will limit the search to that column. Press [Ctrl]+[F] to display the Find and Replace dialog box, shown in Figure 4.2. Enter the data or criteria for the search in the Find What box. The selected column appears in the Look In box.

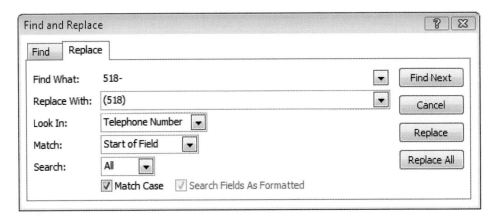

Figure 4.2: Find and Replace dialog box

▶ In the **Match box**, which sets the part of the field to match, click the list arrow to select any part of the field, the whole field, or the start of the field. Click **Match Case** to match uppercase and lowercase entries; if Match Case is not selected, Find ignores case. Click Search Fields As Formatted if the data format in the view is different from the defined format.

▶ After you select your criteria, you have three options: Find Next, Replace, and Replace All. Click Find Next to go to the next occurrence. Click Replace to replace one occurrence at a time. Click Replace All to change all occurrences automatically. Access will ask you to confirm all replacement choices because there is no Undo feature.

TRY *it* OUT *a4-1*

1. Open data file **a4-1**, and open the *Club Members* table.

2. Click the **Telephone Number column header** to select it.

3. Press **[Ctrl]+[F]**. *Notice that Telephone Number appears in the Look In box, or you may select it using the list arrow.*

4. Click the **Replace tab**, and enter **518-** in the Find What box. *We set an input mask in the middle of data entry, and the telephone number formats do not match.*

5. In the Replace With box, enter **(518)**, then press the spacebar to add a space.

6. Click the **Match list arrow**, and click **Start of Field**.

7. Click the **Search list arrow** and click **All**, if necessary.

8. Click the **Match Case check box**, and click **Replace**. *Notice that Access replaces the first instance.*

9. Click **Replace All**. *Access will ask you to confirm replacements.* Click **Yes**.

10. Click **Cancel** to close the dialog box.

11. Do not close the table or the database.

Sort Records in a Datasheet

▶ You often enter records into a datasheet in random or chronological order. There are times when you need to **sort**, or rearrange the sequence in which records are displayed. This might be the case, for example, if you were asked to present a membership list in alphabetical order. It is also useful to sort records when you need to arrange data into groups. For example, you might want to group the records of all the people who live in a specific town.

▶ **Ascending order** displays data in alphabetical order from A to Z, or in numerical order from lowest to highest, and can be applied using the Ascending button on the Home tab, as shown in Figure 4.3. Dates and times are sorted from earliest to latest in ascending order. **Descending order** is the opposite of ascending order, and it is applied by using the Descending button on the Home tab.

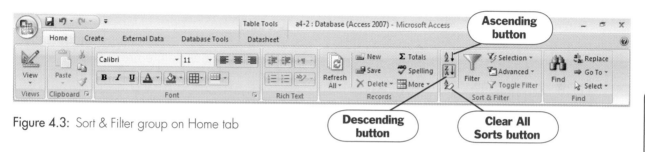

Figure 4.3: Sort & Filter group on Home tab

▶ Alternatively, you can click the list arrow on the column header to display the Sort/Filter shortcut menu, shown in Figure 4.4. You can save the table to make the sorted version of the datasheet permanent or you can print the sorted datasheet. The sorts may be cleared by clicking the Clear All Sorts button on the Home tab.

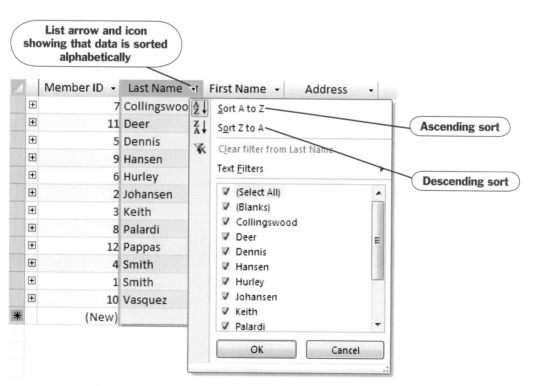

Figure 4.4: Sort features on Sort/Filter shortcut menu

HOW 1. In Datasheet view, click the **column header list arrow** of the column to reorder it.
2. On the Sort/Filter shortcut menu, click the Sort option desired.

TRY *it* **OUT** *a4-2*

1. Use the open database or open data file a4-2 and open the *Club Members* table.

2. Click the **Last Name column header list arrow**, and click **Sort A to Z**. *Note that the Last Name column is now in alphabetical order.*

3. Click the **Office Button,** point to **Print**, then click **Print Preview**. Change to Landscape mode, and print a copy of the datasheet. Close Print Preview.

4. Click the **Home tab**, and in the Sort & Filter group, click the **Clear All Sorts button**.

5. Click the **Member ID column header list arrow**, and click **Sort Smallest to Largest**. *This restores chronological order by Member ID. Note the Up arrow that shows the sort that was done.*

6. Click the **City column header** to select the City fields.

7. Click the **Home tab**, and in the Sort & Filter group, click the **Descending button**. *Note that the cities are grouped in reverse alphabetical order.*

8. Do not close the table or the database.

Apply and Remove Filters

▶ Occasionally, you may want to view only records that satisfy a specific set of conditions. For example, to provide a list of members from two towns, you would use a **filter**, which isolates records meeting a certain set of conditions. You can use the Sort/Filter shortcut menu on each column, as shown in Figure 4.5, or the Sort & Filter group buttons on the Home tab.

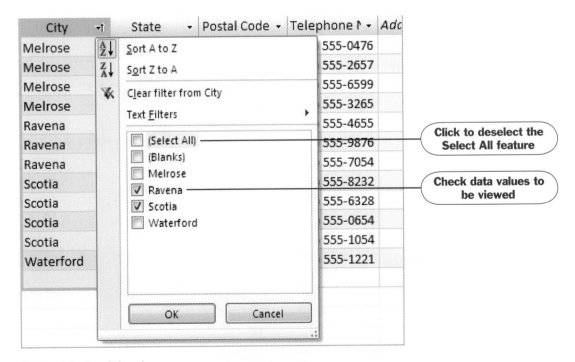

Figure 4.5: Sort/Filter shortcut menu

▶ When you have selected the text you want using the check boxes, all other data will be filtered out. When the filter is complete, you will only see those data items selected. The column header will contain icons to indicate that there is a sort and a filter present, as shown in Figure 4.6. Click the Toggle Filter button, on the Home tab, in the Sort & Filter group, to cancel the filter and restore the excluded data.

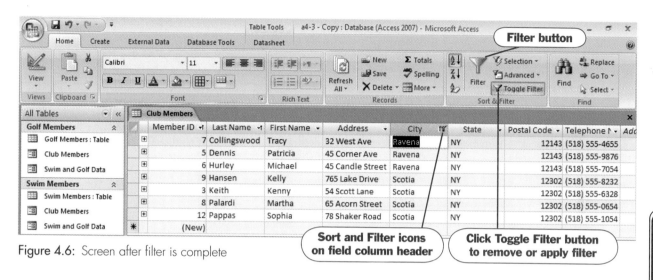

Figure 4.6: Screen after filter is complete

TRY *it* OUT *a4-3*

1. Use the open database or open data file **a4-3** and open the *Club Members* table.

2. Click the **City column header**, and click the **Ascending button** in the Sort & Filter group on the Home tab.

3. Click the **City column header list arrow** to display the Sort/Filter menu.

4. Click the **Select All check box** to deselect it, click the **Ravena** and **Scotia check boxes**, and click **OK**. *All field values other than those selected will be filtered out.*

5. Click the **Toggle Filter button** to remove the filter.

6. Click the **Home tab**, and in the Sort & Filter group, click the **Filter button**. *Note that the Sort/Filter shortcut menu appears for the field.*

7. Make a filter setting to display only members from the city of Melrose.

8. Remove the filter. Do not close the table or database.

Filter Datasheets by Selection

▶ Another method of filtering datasheets and forms is **filter by selection**. This feature allows you to filter all or part of a value to obtain those values that meet the criteria of the selection. When you click the Selection button, as shown in Figure 4.7, you can select the criteria for the selection.

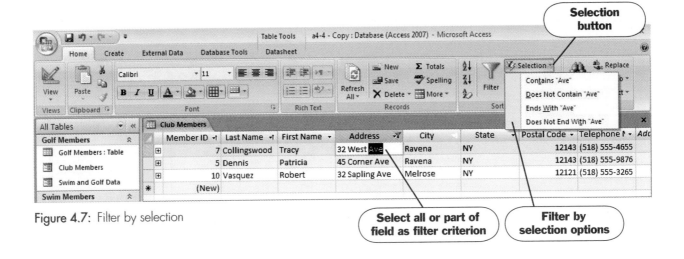

Figure 4.7: Filter by selection

HOW 1. Select all or part of a value in the field you want. 2. Click the **Selection button** and set the criterion. 3. Click the **Toggle Filter button** to remove the filter.

T R Y *it* **O U T** *a4-4*

1. Use the open database or open data file **a4-4** and open the *Club Members* table. *You are looking for someone who has Ave in their address.*

2. Select "Ave" in the Address field of Member ID 7.

3. Click the **Home tab**, and in the Sort & Filter group, click the **Selection button**, then click the **Contains "Ave" criterion**. *The result is a list of those entries with Ave in the address.*

4. Press **[Ctrl]+[F]**, and replace all occurrences of Ave with Avenue. Set the Match setting to **Any Part of Field**. Close the Find and Replace dialog box.

5. Click the **Toggle Filter button** to remove the filter.

6. Do not close the database.

Filter Datasheets by Form

▶ **Filter by form** is a method that allows you to use a sample of the form or datasheet to indicate your selection criteria. Use this method to filter records when you want to filter more than one field. In a datasheet or form, click the Advanced Filter Options button on the Home tab, in the Sort & Filter group, and click Filter By Form, to use this feature. A version of the datasheet or form you are working with appears, as shown in Figure 4.8.

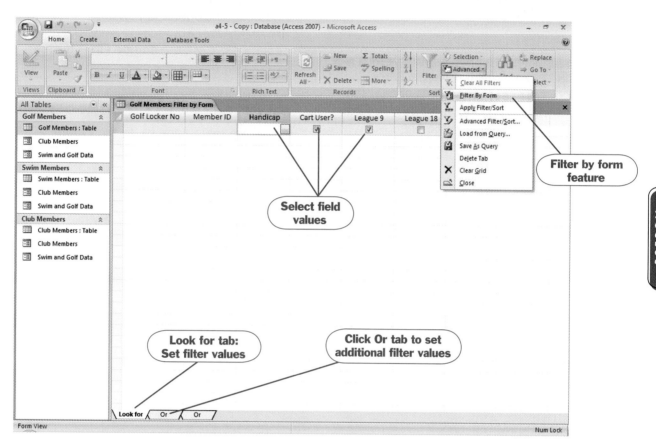

Figure 4.8: Filter by form

▶ Click the down arrow of each field to see the list you can use to filter the datasheet. You can select values in more than one field as the filtering criteria. To specify multiple sets of values involving the same fields, click the Or tab at the bottom of the pane and enter another criteria. For example, if you wanted to see cart users in the 9 league or the 18 league, you would need to set the Or criteria.

▶ To apply the filter, click the Toggle Filter button. The filter displays records only if they meet the criteria you specify for each of the fields in the Look for tab or in the Or tabs. Click the Toggle Filter button again to remove the filter. The table and underlying data are not changed, but the filter settings are saved in the file.

1. Use the open database, or open data file **a4-5**. Open the *Golf Members* table.

2. Click the **Home tab**, and in the Sort & Filter group, click the **Advanced Filter Options button**, then click **Filter By Form**. *A form appears where you can set your filter values.*

3. Click the **Cart User** and **League 9 field check boxes**. Click the **Toggle Filter button**. *Note that two records appear that meet those criteria.* Click the **Toggle Filter button** again to remove the filter.

4. Click the **Home tab**, and in the Sort & Filter group, click the **Advanced Filter Options button**, and then click **Filter By Form**. *Note that the filter you set appears.*

5. Click the **Or tab**, and click the **Cart User** and **League 18 field check boxes**. *You are asking for cart users in League 9 or in League 18.* Click the **Toggle Filter button**. *Check that the results meet the criteria.*

6. Click the **Toggle Filter button** to return to the unfiltered table.

7. Close the tables and close the database.

REHEARSAL

Again

TASK 1

GOAL
To find and replace, sort, and filter listings in a real estate database

WHAT YOU NEED TO KNOW

▶ In real estate sales, it is very important to identify properties that meet the requirements of prospective buyers. Often buyers have a specific town they are interested in, as well as an acceptable price range. Sometimes the most important requirement is the size of the home or the number of bedrooms in the house. Some clients require new homes, while others want older homes.

▶ A real estate agent must be able to search listings quickly to identify the ideal properties to present to his or her clients. An agent must also be able to update the listings when they change.

▶ In this Rehearsal activity, you will search and update the listing database for Palmetto Realtors. Additional listings have been added to the database. Use a copy of the questions list to keep track of the information you will gather and the changes you will make to the database.

▼ DIRECTIONS

1. Open data file **4r1-Palmetto**.

2. Open the *Listings* table and note the new listings.

3. Answer or respond to the requests listed on your copy of the questions, or as found in the data file **4r1-PalmettoQuestions.docx**.

QUESTIONS/REQUESTS	ANSWERS
a. Print a copy of all the listings with prices in ascending order.	
b. What is the price and location of the home on Overlook Drive?	
c. Change Hanna Kinney's name to Hanna Kinney-Powers.	
d. Which listings are in Hollywood? Make a note of ListingID numbers.	
e. Modify listings in the Address field to change Ave to Avenue.	
f. Which listings are priced at $270,000 or less?	
g. The closing was this week for ListingID 1. Print a copy of the form for our files and delete the record.	
h. Listing ID 3 has sold. The selling price was $365,000, the date of sale was 08/31/2010, and the agent was Barona. Update the record.	

Use the guidelines below:

a. Use the Sort feature to create this list and print a copy.

b. Your client saw a Palmetto Realtors sign in the front yard of a property. Use the Find feature to locate the record and make note of the location and price.

Continued on next page

c. Hanna Kinney, a homeowner in the database, has remarried and her last name is now Kinney-Powers. Use Find and Replace, but confirm that the replacement will be made in the record of the Kinney who owns the house at 23 Bear Road.

d. Use the Sort/Filter menu on the City field to find the listings in Hollywood, Florida. Use Toggle Filter to remove the filter.

e. Use the Find and Replace feature and match any part of field and match case.

f. Use the Filter by Selection feature, click on **$270,000**, and use the Filter option of Less Than or Equal To $270,000 to find these listings. Make a note of the ListingID numbers.

g. Be sure to click **Selected Record(s)** to print only the ListingID 1 form. Delete the record in the table.

h. Update the record.

4. Close the table, but do not save the changes to the design. Close the database.

Cues for Reference

Find a Record

1. With a table open in Datasheet view, press **[Ctrl]+[F]**.
   Or
1. Click the **Home tab,** and in the Find group, click the **Find button**.
2. Enter the value in the Find What box.
3. Choose a Look In list option.
4. Choose a Match list option.
5. Choose a Search list option.
6. Click **Match Case** and/or **Search Fields As Formatted** to restrict search, as desired.
7. Click **Find Next**.
8. Click **Cancel** to close the dialog box.

Find and Replace a Record

1. With a table open in Datasheet view, click **[Ctrl]+[F]**.
   Or
1. Click the **Home tab**, and in the Find group, click the **Find button**.
2. Click the **Replace tab** in the Find and Replace dialog box.
3. Enter the find value in the Find What box.
4. Enter the replacement value in the Replace With box.
5. Choose a Look In list option.
6. Choose a Match list option.

7. Choose a Search list option.
8. Click **Match Case** and/or **Search Fields As Formatted** to restrict search, as desired.
9. To replace next field, click **Find Next**, then click **Replace**.
10. To replace all matching fields at once, click **Replace All**.
11. Click **OK** to confirm changes.

Sort Records
With a table open in Datasheet view:
1. Click the **column header list arrow** in the column to sort.
2. Click the appropriate option to sort in ascending or descending order.

Filter Records
With a table open in Datasheet view:
1. Click the **column header list arrow** in the column to filter.
2. Click to deselect the **Select All check box**, and click the values you wish to see.

Filter Records by Selection
With a table open in Datasheet view:
1. Click selected item in a field location.

2. Click the **Home tab**, and in the Sort & Filter group, click the **Selection button**.
3. Click a filter option.

Filter Records by Form
With a table open in Datasheet view:
1. Click the **Home tab**, and in the Sort & Filter group, click the **Advanced Filter Options button**, then click **Filter By Form**.
2. Enter items required in appropriate fields.
   Or
2. Click on the appropriate field list box arrow.
3. Click the data item. Use the Or tab if you are filtering more than one value for a field.
4. Click the **Toggle Filter button** to apply the filter.

Remove a Filter from Records
1. Click the **Toggle Filter button**.

PERFORMANCE

TASK 1

Expedition Travel Gear has added the Dallas store employees to its database but would like you to add the Payroll data. Also, the human resources manager in Chicago wants you to find answers to various questions that have come up about employees. Use the sort, find and replace, and filter features to answer the questions.

Expedition

Travel Gear

Follow these guidelines:

1. Open data file **4p1-ETG-EMPS**, and add the following information using the *Payroll* form. Be sure to enter the zero values in the Other Deductions column. Save the data.

EMPID	16	17	18	19	20
SSNO	321-00-6545	214-00-8564	201-00-9879	189-00-9823	097-00-4545
Store	Dallas	Dallas	Dallas	Dallas	Dallas
Status	M	S	M	M	S
Exemptions	3	1	0	4	1
Birth Date	12/14/1984	01/13/1987	10/09/1991	03/06/1989	07/03/1990
Rate	14.50	14.00	11.50	11.50	11.00
Dues	8.00	5.00	8.00	8.00	5.00
Other Deductions	15.00	20.00	0.00	0.00	0.00

2. Using the *Contact* and *Payroll* tables, respond to or act on the following requests using the appropriate tools and providing the result requested. Be sure to clear a filter before handling another request. Make a copy of this list so that you can enter your responses, or use **4p1-ETG-Questions.docx**.

QUESTIONS/REQUESTS	ANSWERS
a. Print a list of employees arranged alphabetically by last name. Sort the first names then the last names alphabetically.	
b. EmpID numbers of employees earning $10 or less per hour. Use filter by selection.	
c. In the *Contact* table, use the column filter to find those records and print a copy of the filter.	
d. EmpID numbers of employees earning $14.50 per hour. Use filter by selection.	
e. Print a copy of the contact information for those employees.	
f. Dues for married employees have increased for Chicago and Boston employees to $9.00. Use filter by form to find Chicago or Boston employees with $8 dues and make changes to $9.	

3. Clear filters, and return *Contact* table to EmpID order.

4. Save and close the database.

TRYOUT

TASK 2

GOAL

To build queries to search a property listings database to answer questions, as shown in Figure 4.9

* Create a query object
* Create select queries using the Simple Query Wizard
* Create select queries with calculations
* Create crosstab, duplicates, and unmatched queries
* Modify queries in Design view

Agent Last Name ▾	Total Listings ▾	East Hollywood ▾	Hollywood ▾	West Hollywood ▾
Barona ▾	$1,210,000.00	$1,210,000.00		
Chang	$725,000.00	$375,000.00		$350,000.00
Dembar	$980,000.00		$980,000.00	
Lincoln	$1,155,000.00		$830,000.00	$325,000.00
Olsen	$1,365,000.00		$730,000.00	$635,000.00

Figure 4.9: Task 2: Crosstab query

WHAT YOU NEED TO KNOW

Create a Query Object

▶ In addition to the search tools you have used, Access provides a more powerful tool called a **query**. A **query** is a database object that you create to answer questions or to view, modify, delete, manage, or analyze data in a database. A saved query can be run any time and will include any new data added to the database. You can perform calculations in a query, ask it to find data, or use it to sort or total fields.

▶ A query that is used to find data or to make calculations is called a **select query.** Access provides **Query Wizards,** which are step-by-step dialog boxes that request the needed information to develop four different types of select queries that retrieve and analyze data from the fields you specify within one or more tables or queries. Click the Query Wizard button on the Create tab, in the Other group, as shown in Figure 4.10, to display the New Query dialog box.

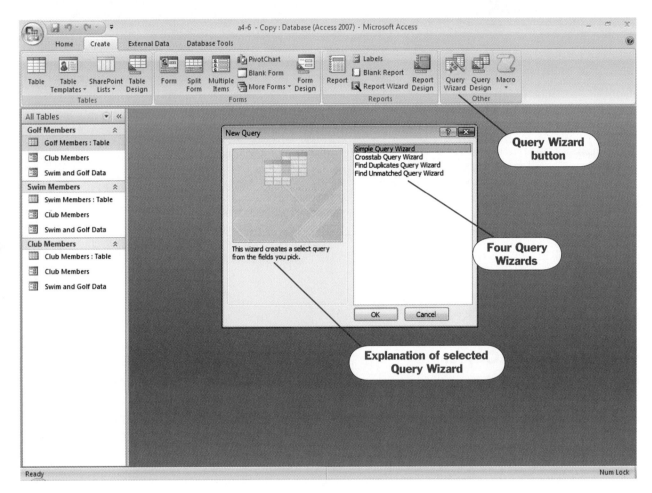

Figure 4.10: New Query dialog box: Query Wizards

TRY it OUT a4-6

1. Open data file **a4-6**. Open the *Club Members* table.

2. Click the **Create tab**, and in the Other group, click the **Query Wizard button**. *The New Query dialog box appears.*

3. Click each of the four query wizards, and review the descriptions displayed in the left pane:
   - Simple Query Wizard
   - Crosstab Query Wizard

   - Find Duplicates Query Wizard
   - Find Unmatched Query Wizard

4. Click **Cancel**.

5. Do not close the database.

Create Select Queries Using the Simple Query Wizard

▶ The **Simple Query Wizard** creates a select query, which asks a question about the data stored in one or more tables. It returns a result set in the form of a datasheet and does not change the original data. Once the results appear, you can view and, in some cases, modify the data in the underlying tables.

▶ To use the Simple Query Wizard, double-click the Simple Query Wizard selection on the New Query dialog box. The Simple Query Wizard dialog box appears, as shown in Figure 4.11.

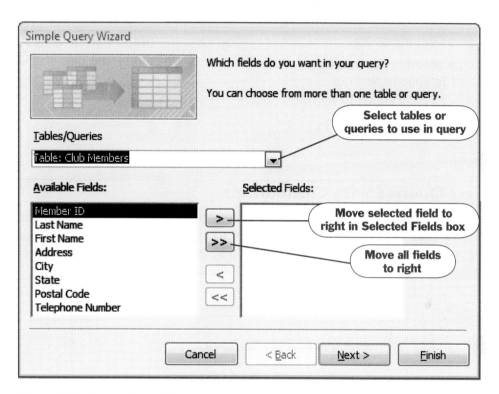

Figure 4.11: Simple Query Wizard

▶ Click to select a table and double-click the fields to be added to the query. To choose fields from more than one table or query, click each table or query and double-click the fields to include. Repeat this step until you have selected all the fields you want. Click Next, then Finish to view the select query.

▶ Queries can be printed just like datasheets, using the Office Button and Print tools.

1. Use the open database or open data file **a4-7**.

2. Click the **Create tab**, and in the Other group, click the **Query Wizard button**.

3. Double-click **Simple Query Wizard**.

4. Click the list arrow under **Tables/Queries**.

5. Click **Table: Club Members**.

6. Double-click **Member ID, Last Name, First Name**, and **Telephone Number** to move them from Available Fields to Selected Fields.

7. Click **Next** and on the next screen, change the title of the query to **Member Telephone Numbers**.

8. Click **Finish**. *A query appears showing the names and telephone numbers of the members. It is listed on the Navigation Pane so that it can be opened again.*

9. Click the **Office Button**, click **Print**, and click **OK** to print the query.

10. Save and close the query but do not close the database.

Create Select Queries with Calculations

▶ The Simple Query Wizard can create summary values of a numeric field. If you choose fields that are Number data types, the wizard asks you if you would like a detail or summary query, as shown in Figure 4.12. You used the Detail query to show every record in the *Member Telephone Numbers* query. The summary query only shows summary values.

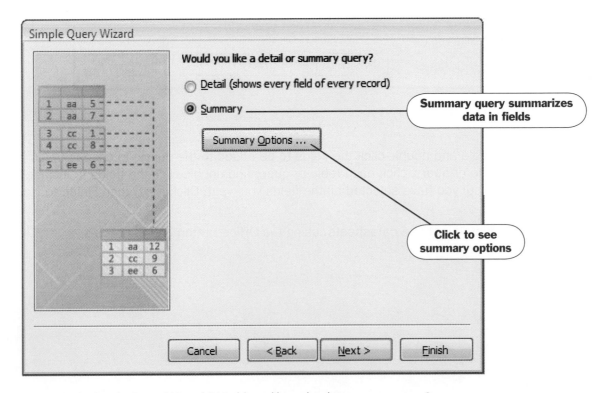

Figure 4.12: Simple Query Wizard: Would you like a detail or summary query?

▶ A **summary query** will sum, count, average, or calculate minimum or maximum values, as shown on the Summary Options screen in Figure 4.13. Click the Summary Options button to see this screen and make settings.

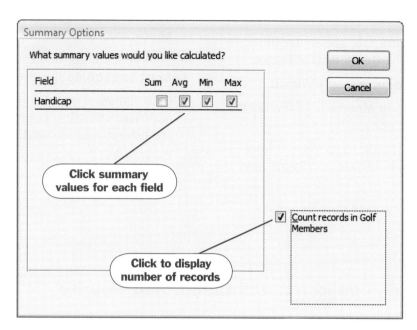

Figure 4.13: Summary Options: What summary values would you like calculated?

▶ On the last screen of the Simple Query Wizard, shown in Figure 4.14, you give your query a title and decide how to open the query. Name your query appropriately so that you know what it produces.

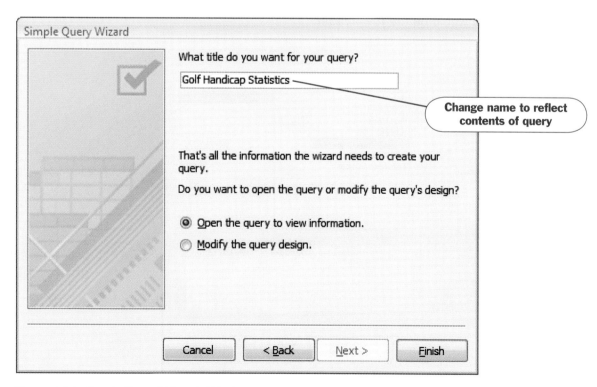

Figure 4.14: Simple Query Wizard: Title the query

1. Use the open database or open data file **a4-8**.

2. Click the **Create tab**, and in the Other group, click the **Query Wizard button**.

3. Double-click **Simple Query Wizard**.

4. Click **Table: Golf Members** on the list of tables and queries.

5. Double-click **Handicap** to move it from Available Fields to Selected Fields, and click **Next**.

6. Click **Summary**, then click **Summary Options**.

7. Click the **Avg**, **Min**, and **Max check boxes** and the **Count records in Golf Members check box**. Click **OK**.

8. Click **Next**. Enter `Golf Handicap Statistics` as the title for this query.

9. Click **Finish**. *A query appears, showing handicap statistics. Double-click between the column headers to AutoFit data.*

10. Save and close the query, but do not close the database.

Create Crosstab, Duplicates, and Unmatched Queries

Crosstab Query

▶ A **crosstab query** arranges fields in a spreadsheet format and provides summary options. When you double-click Crosstab Query Wizard on the New Query dialog box, the Crosstab Query Wizard dialog box appears; here you select the table, query, or report to use for the query.

▶ After making your selection and clicking Next, you are asked to select up to three fields to be row headers, as shown in Figure 4.15. The row headers depend on the question you are asking in the query. For example, if you want to find the number of club members in each city by postal codes, the City field would be the row header.

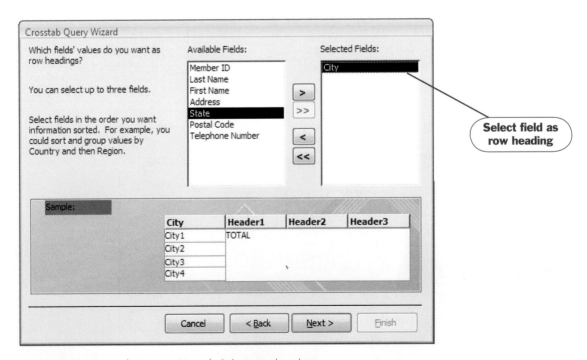

Figure 4.15: Crosstab Query Wizard: Select row headings

▶ The next screen asks you to select column headings, as shown in Figure 4.16. This could be a field related to the City row headers, such as Postal Code, where there are a limited number of different entries.

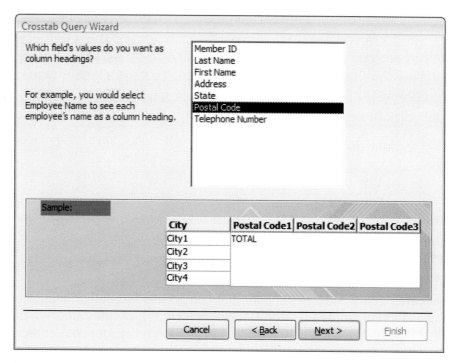

Figure 4.16: Crosstab Query Wizard: Select column headings

▶ Next, you select the field to be calculated and the function to use. In the example, you would select Member ID and apply the Count function. You can select the option to get a sum of the rows as well, as shown in Figure 4.17.

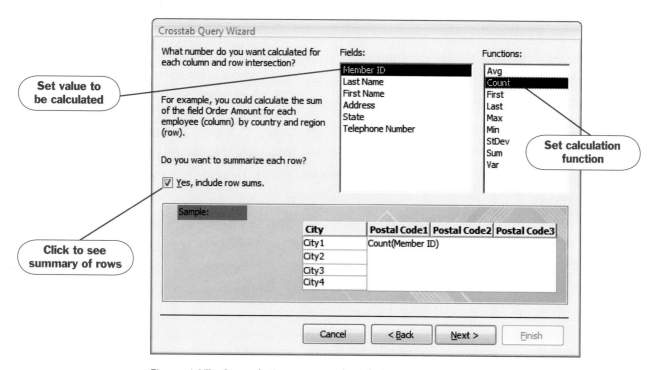

Figure 4.17: Crosstab Query Wizard: Calculation options

A crosstab query will be created to find the number of members in various cities and postal codes.

1. Use the open database or open data file **a4-9**. Click the **Query Wizard button** on the Create tab.

2. Double-click **Crosstab Query Wizard**.

3. Select the *Club Members* table, and click **Next**.

4. Double-click **City** to select it as the row header, and click **Next**.

5. Click to select **Postal Code** as the column header, and click **Next**.

6. Select **Member ID** as the field and **Count** as the function, to summarize the number of members in each category. Click **Next**.

7. Name the query Count by City and Postal Code, and click **Finish**.

8. View, save, and close the query and the database.

Duplicates Query

▶ The **duplicates query** is a select query that can be used to detect duplicate entries in a field, when duplication presents an error. Double-click Find Duplicates Query Wizard in the New Query dialog box, and on the screens that follow, select the table, queries, or reports to use; select the field where duplicates might be found; and then select fields to identify the duplicates data, such as Name or Address. You can then name and view the query.

We want to check for duplicates in our Friends database.

1. Open data file **a4-10**. Click the **Query Wizard button** on the Create tab.

2. Double-click **Find Duplicates Query Wizard**.

3. Click **Table: Friends**, then click **Next**.

4. Double-click to select the **Last** and **Address fields** to search for duplicates. Click **Next**.

5. Click the double arrow to select all remaining fields to identify the data and error. Click **Next**.

6. Accept the name **Find duplicates for Friends**, and click **Finish**.

7. Check the entries and note that they are the same except for the first name. *The record for Member ID 7 is a duplicate.*

8. Save and close the query. Switch to the *Friends* table, and delete the duplicate record for Member ID 7.

9. Close the table and the database.

Unmatched Query

▶ The **unmatched query** is a select query that finds records in one table that do not match records in another. This query can be used to find records from one segment of your database that you may wish to solicit for additional services, or to check why they are not on the other table.

▶ When you select Find Unmatched Query Wizard, you will have to complete the following screens:

- Select the table or query that might have unmatched records.
- Select the table or query that contains the related records.
- Select the field that is the same in both tables, as shown in Figure 4.18.
- Select the fields you need to see in the results table.
- Name the table.

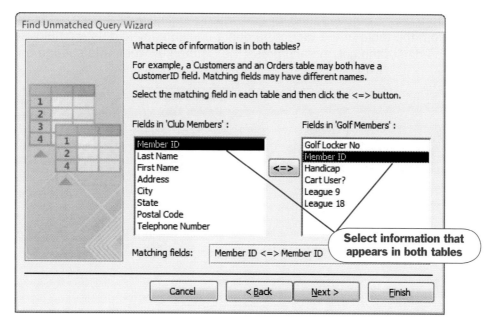

Figure 4.18: Find Unmatched Query Wizard: Matching fields

TRY it OUT a4-11

The club wants a telephone list for non-golf members to be able to call them to promote golf membership.

1. Open data file **a4-11**, and click the **Query Wizard button**.

2. Double-click **Find Unmatched Query Wizard**.

3. Select the *Club Members* table, and click **Next**.

4. Select the *Golf Members* table to match with the first table. Click **Next**.

5. Select the **Member ID field** in each table. Click the **<=> button**. Click **Next**.

6. Select the following fields necessary for the telephone promotion: **Member ID, Last Name, First Name, Telephone Number**. Click **Next**.

7. Name the query: `Non-golf members telephone list`. Click **Finish**.

8. Print a copy of the query, if a printer is available.

9. Save and close the query. Do not close the database.

Modify Queries in Design View

▶ You can create and modify queries in **Query Design view**, which shows the structure of a query. To open a query in Design view, right-click the query name on the Navigation Pane and click Design View. If the query is already open, select the Design view from the View button on the Home tab.

▶ **Criteria** are restrictions you place on a query to specify the records with which you want to work. For example, instead of viewing the handicaps of all golf members, you can view members whose handicaps are less than 15. To specify criteria in a query, use the query design grid, as shown in Figure 4.19. The **query design grid** is the area in Design view where you can set criteria, indicate if a field is to be shown or not, and add the totals, which will be discussed in the next task.

▶ It is convenient to create a query using a wizard and then modify or tailor it in Design view. You may add a field to a query, delete a field, or add criteria to limit your search. To add a field, drag the field name from the table at the top to the query design grid. To delete a field, select it in the middle of the top edge of the column and press the Delete key when it is shaded and selected.

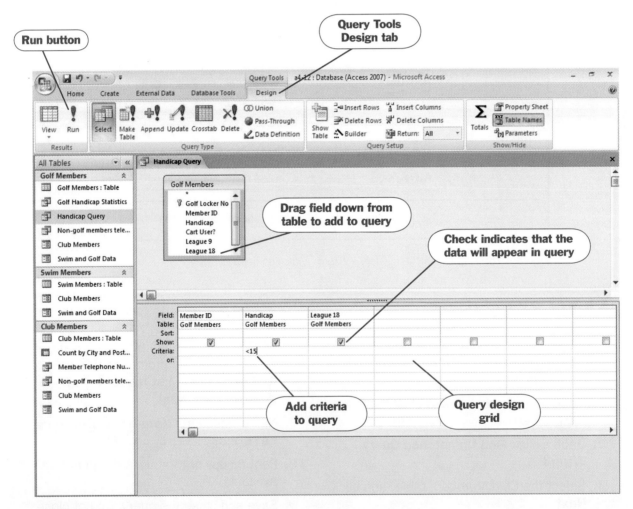

Figure 4.19: Query Design view

▶ In the example shown in Figure 4.19, the table is *Golf Members*, and the fields are Member ID and Handicap. The League 18 field is being added to the query for informational purposes. A criteria is set, in the Criteria row of the Handicap field, to view members whose handicaps are less than 15. You can add additional criteria for the same field or different fields on the query design grid. Click the Run button on the Query Tools Design tab to see the query results.

T R Y *it* O U T *a4-12*

1. Use the open database or open data file **a4-12**.

2. Open the *Handicap* query. *Note that Access displays handicaps ranging from 11 through 24.*

3. Click the **Home tab** if necessary, and click the **View button** to switch to Design view. *The View button was set to Design view.*

4. Click and drag the **League 18 field** from the table list in the work pane to the third column position on the query design grid.

5. Click the **Criteria cell** in the Handicap column.

6. Enter: **<15**. *The < symbol means "less than," and the criterion states "less than 15."*

7. Click the **Query Tools Design tab**, and in the Results group, click the **Run button**. *Only records showing a handicap less than 15 appear.*

8. Click the **View button** to return to Design view.

9. Edit the Criteria for Handicap to read **<=15** to find handicaps equal to or less than 15. Click the **Run button**. *Note that members with handicaps of 15 or less appear.*

10. Save and close the query and the database.

GOAL
To build queries to search the property listings in the Palmetto Realtor database to answer questions

WHAT YOU NEED TO KNOW

▶ Property listings change on a daily basis. New properties are added, properties are sold, and the prices of listings change. What does not change is the type of information that real estate agents and customers want from a property listing database. Building queries allows you to answer the standard questions that agents and customers have quickly. You can run these queries repeatedly, and any new or updated data will be included.

▶ In this Rehearsal activity, you will build queries that agents can use on a daily basis. Use a copy of the table shown as an outline and a place to record answers.

▼ DIRECTIONS

1. Open your solution to **4r1-Palmetto** or open **4r2-Palmetto**. A copy of the outline can be found in **4r2-PalmettoQueries.docx**.

NAME OF QUERY	TYPE OF QUERY	ANSWERS/ ACTIONS
Pricing Statistics	Simple query	Print
Agents Without Listings	Unmatched query with all fields of *Agents* table	Name(s):
Agents Total Listings	Crosstab query (see illustration)	Compare to illustration
Listings Query	Simple query	Save query
Listings Query (Step 5 d.)	Add criteria to query as specified	Address(es):

2. Provide a query to calculate pricing statistics for the homes in the database by city. Use the **Simple Query Wizard** with the *Listings* table.
   a. Move the **City** and **Price fields** to the Selected Fields box.
   b. Select the **Summary query** and the **Sum**, **Avg**, **Max**, and **Min** summary options.
   c. Name the query **Pricing Statistics**.
   d. Print the query.

3. The owner of the agency, Harold Dembar, would like to be able to quickly check to see which agents have no listings. Use the **Find Unmatched Query Wizard** with the *Agents* and *Listings* tables, using the agent's last name field.
   a. The results of the query should show all the information about the agent.
   b. Name the query **Agents Without Listings**.
   c. Write the name(s) of the agent(s) with no listings on a copy of the table shown.

Continued on next page

4. Mr. Dembar needs a list of agents with their total listings broken down by city. Use the **Crosstab Query Wizard** with the *Listings* table.
   a. Use Figure 4.20 as a guide to prepare the query. Find the total of the Price field.
   b. Name the query **Agents Total Listings**.
   c. Switch to Design view, and change the title of the total column to **Total Listings**.
   d. Switch to Datasheet view, and compare your query to the illustration.
   e. Modify your query or delete and prepare a new query if yours is not correct.

5. Create a *Listings* query that agents can use to search for properties with specific criteria. Use the **Simple Query Wizard** and the *Listings* table.
   a. Include the fields in the order listed: Price, City, Description, Address, Date Built, Date Listed.
   b. Name the query **Listings Query**.
   c. Switch to Design view. Modify the query by moving the Description column to the right of the Address column so that it is the fourth column. *Select the column and drag it into position. Move it when a dark vertical bar appears at the left of the selected column.* Save the query.
   d. In the Criteria row, set criteria to find homes for less than or equal to $300,000 in Hollywood. *Hint: Enter* **<=300000** *under Price and* **Hollywood** *under City.*
   e. Run the query and record the address(es) in your copy of the queries table. Do not save the criteria to the query so that agents can enter their own criteria as necessary.

6. Close the database.

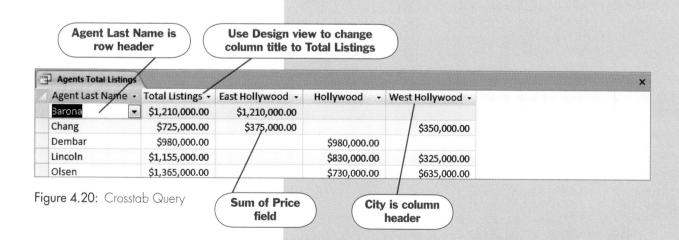

Figure 4.20: Crosstab Query

Agent Last Name is row header

Use Design view to change column title to Total Listings

Agent Last Name	Total Listings	East Hollywood	Hollywood	West Hollywood
Barona	$1,210,000.00	$1,210,000.00		
Chang	$725,000.00	$375,000.00		$350,000.00
Dembar	$980,000.00		$980,000.00	
Lincoln	$1,155,000.00		$830,000.00	$325,000.00
Olsen	$1,365,000.00		$730,000.00	$635,000.00

Agents Total Listings

Sum of Price field

City is column header

Use the Simple Query Wizard

1. Click the **Create tab**, and in the Other group, click the **Query Wizard button**.
2. Click **Simple Query Wizard**. Click **OK**.
3. Choose a table or query.
4. Double-click fields to move from Available Fields to Selected Fields, then click **Next**.
5. Name the query, then click **Finish**.

Use the Simple Query Wizard with Summary Options

1. Click the **Create tab**, and in the Other group, click the **Query Wizard button**.
2. Click **Simple Query Wizard**, then click **OK**.
3. Choose a table or query.
4. Double-click fields to move from the Available Fields to the Selected Fields. *You need a numeric field for summary options.* Click **Next**.
5. Click **Summary**, then click **Summary Options**.
6. Click values to be calculated, then click **OK**.
7. Click **Next**.
8. Name the query, then click **Finish**.

Use the Unmatched Query Wizard

1. Click the **Create tab**, and in the Other group, click the **Query Wizard button**.
2. Click **Find Unmatched Query Wizard**, then click **OK**.
3. Choose a table or query that contains unmatched records, then click **Next**.
4. Choose a table or query that contains the search records, then click **Next**.
5. Click the arrows to select matching fields between tables, then click **Next**.
6. Select fields to appear in the results table, then click **Next**.
7. Name the query, then click **Finish**.

Use the Crosstab Query Wizard

1. Click the **Create tab**, and in the Other group, click the **Query Wizard button**.
2. Click **Crosstab Query Wizard**, then click **OK**.
3. Select the table or query containing the data to search, then click **Next**.
4. Select the field(s) for row headers, then click **Next**.
5. Select the field for column headers, then click **Next**.
6. Select the field to calculate and function for calculation, then click **Next**.
7. Name the query, then click **Finish**.

Modify a Query

1. In Design view, click and drag fields from the table listing to the query design grid to add to the query.
2. Click to select a field column and press **[Delete]** to remove from the query.
3. Click to select a field column, and when a dark vertical bar appears to the left of the column, drag it to change the location of data.

Specify Criteria in a Query

1. Right-click the query in the Navigation Pane or the **Query tab**, and click **Design View**.
2. Set criteria under appropriate field.
3. Click the **Run button**.

TASK 2

The human resources manager of Expedition Travel Gear has asked you to find answers to several questions that require that you use queries on the employees' database. Make a copy of the table with the data requests, create the queries in the database, and indicate your answers.

Expedition

Travel Gear

Follow these guidelines:

1. Open your solution to **4p1-ETG-EMPS** or open data file **4p2-ETG-EMPS**.
2. Create the queries listed in the table, and enter your responses to the questions on a copy of the table or in **4p2-ETG-Queries.docx**.
3. Use Figure 4.21 as a guide to create the last two queries.
4. Close and save the database.

NAME OF QUERY	TYPE OF QUERY	ANSWERS
Rate Statistics	Simple Query with summary options AVG, MIN, MAX to determine the statistics for payroll hourly rates	What are the average, minimum, and maximum rates?
Birth Date 1990 or Later	Simple Query with criteria for >=1/1/1990 to determine which employees are born on or after January 1, 1990	Emp ID numbers?
Rates by Store	Simple Query with summary options SUM, AVG, MIN, MAX to compare hourly rate statistics by store	Compare to illustration
Dues by Store	Simple Query with summary options SUM, AVG, MIN, MAX to determine dues structure by store	Which store(s) collect(s) the most dues?

Rates by Store				
Store	Sum Of Rate	Avg Of Rate	Min Of Rate	Max Of Rate
Boston	$61.25	$12.25	$10.00	$14.50
Chicago	$51.70	$10.34	$8.25	$14.50
Dallas	$62.50	$12.50	$11.00	$14.50
Miami	$54.00	$10.80	$9.00	$13.50

Figure 4.21: Select Query with summary options

GOAL
To add a calculated field to a query, and to build a multi-table based query, as shown in Figure 4.22

✻ Use aggregate functions
✻ Add a calculated field to queries in Query Design view
✻ Format and sort query results
✻ Create a multi-table query

TASK 3

Calculated control

Listings-Estimated Tax

ListingID	Date Listed	Owner Last	Address	City	Agent Last	Date Built	Price	Estimated Tax
2	7/8/2010	Davids	23 Easton Avenue	Hollywood	Olsen	9/9/1999	$155,000.00	$3,100.00
3	7/12/2010	Angeli	2 Woodside Avenue	East Hollywood	Barona	8/18/1987	$395,000.00	$7,900.00
4	7/12/2010	Lee	12 Gale Way	West Hollywoc	Chang	2/7/2000	$350,000.00	$7,000.00
5	7/19/2010	Taylor	1 Somers Road	Hollywood	Dembar	2/12/2001	$320,000.00	$6,400.00
6	7/25/2010	Davis	8 Overlook Drive	Hollywood	Lincoln	1/1/2006	$355,000.00	$7,100.00
7	7/28/2010	Kelley	750 Ocean Avenue	Hollywood	Olsen	12/12/1990	$575,000.00	$11,500.00
9	7/29/2010	Vargas	21 Green Street	East Hollywooc	Barona	10/10/1998	$270,000.00	$5,400.00
10	8/1/2010	Rielly	1200 North Ocean Avenue	Hollywood	Lincoln	5/15/2008	$475,000.00	$9,500.00
11	8/5/2010	Greaves	548 Greenleaf Street	East Hollywooc	Chang	2/10/2007	$375,000.00	$7,500.00
12	8/7/2010	Mulholland	24 Breezy Point Road	West Hollywoc	Olsen	3/31/2005	$310,000.00	$6,200.00
13	8/12/2010	Vargas	432 Blossom Road	Hollywood	Dembar	10/23/2006	$295,000.00	$5,900.00
14	8/16/2010	Kinney	925 Prescott Circle	East Hollywooc	Barona	11/17/2007	$545,000.00	$10,900.00
15	8/19/2010	Umberto	76 Grand Avenue	West Hollywoc	Lincoln	10/12/2005	$325,000.00	$6,500.00
16	8/26/2010	Pilgrim	651 North Ocean Avenue	Hollywood	Dembar	12/10/2007	$365,000.00	$7,300.00
17	8/29/2010	Thompson	39 Hibiscus Lane	West Hollywoc	Olsen	6/5/2006	$325,000.00	$6,500.00
*	(New)							

Figure 4.22: Task 3: Multi-table query with a calculated control

WHAT YOU NEED TO KNOW

Use Aggregate Functions

▶ **Aggregate functions**, are used to calculate a summary value for grouped data in queries and can be set up in Query Design view. When you are using an aggregate function, you usually use two fields, one to group the data and the other, a numeric field, for calculations.

▶ To group data, in Query Design view, click the Totals button on the Query Tools Design tab, shown in Figure 4.23. A Total row will appear in the query design grid. The **Total row** is used to perform calculations on the values in a field. Click the list arrow of the relevant Total row cell to view and set the available calculations.

▶ For example, if you want to count or total the number of units on order for each department in a Products database, you can set up a query displaying the Department field (for grouping) and the UnitsOnOrder field (for calculating). Click the Totals button, and then, in the query design grid, select Group By in the Total row cell for the Department column. Next, select Sum in the Total row cell for the UnitsOnOrder column. Click the Run button or display the results in Datasheet view. Access will rename the calculated field with a title such as Sum of Units Ordered. If necessary, you can bring down another copy of the UnitsOnOrder column to get an average of values in that group.

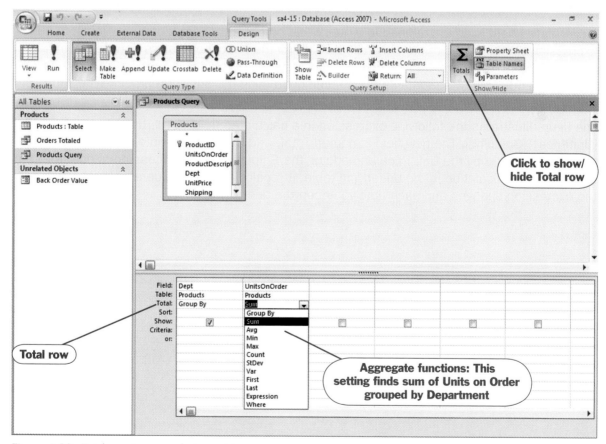

Figure 4.23: Total row in query design grid

1. Open data file **a4-13** and open the *Products* query. *Note that the query presents a list of departments and the number of units ordered. You will use aggregate functions to group data by departments and get the total for each department.*

2. Click the **View button** to switch to Design view.

3. On the Query Tools Design tab, in the Show/Hide group, click the **Totals button** to display the Total row on the query design grid.

Σ
Totals

4. In the Dept column, click the **Total row cell list arrow**. *Note the choices but leave it set to Group By since we will group data by departments.*

5. In the UnitsOnOrder column, click the **Total row cell list arrow**. Click **Sum** on the list of aggregate functions.

6. Click the **Run button**. *Note that the units are totaled by department.*

7. Close and save the *Products* query and the database.

Add a Calculated Field to Queries in Query Design View

▶ You can add calculated fields to a database to perform calculations as part of a query on the entire database, on selected groups of data, or on data that meet specific criteria.

▶ A **calculated field** is a field defined in a query that displays the result of an expression. An expression contains field names in brackets with mathematical operators between items, as shown in Figure 4.24, and that you used earlier in forms. Expressions are entered in the Field row of the grid. If you wish to name the column containing the answers, precede the expression with the column name and a colon.

▶ The figure illustrates the following expression in a calculated field: Total:[UnitsOnOrder]*[UnitPrice]+[Shipping]. The new field is named Total, and the result is obtained by multiplying the Units on Order by the Unit Price and adding the Shipping Costs. Access does not store the results of the calculation in the underlying table. It recalculates the value each time a value in the expression changes and each time you open the query.

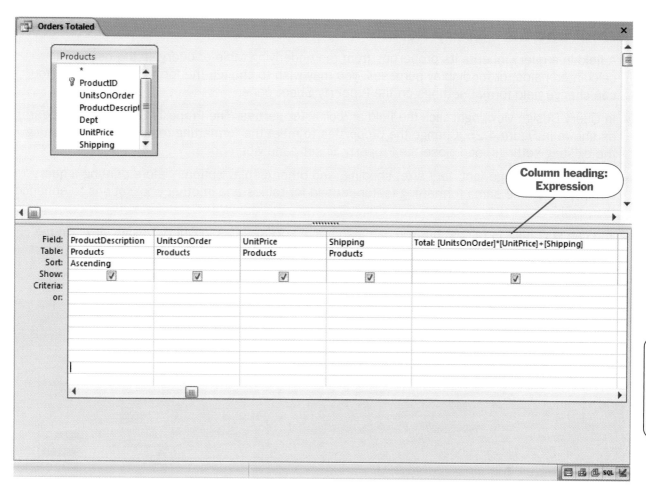

Figure 4.24: Adding a calculated control, Query Design view

TRY*it*OUT a4-14

1. Open data file **a4-14**. *This is a Products database.*

2. Open the *Orders Totaled* query in Design view.

3. Click the first empty cell in the top row of the query design grid.

4. Enter the expression and column title as shown in Figure 4.24:
   ```
   Total: [UnitsOnOrder]*
   [UnitPrice]+[Shipping]
   ```

5. Click the **Run button**.

6. Notice the total order amounts in the last column.

7. Save the query, and do not close the database.

Format and Sort Query Results

▶ A field in a query inherits its properties from the underlying table or query. In the case of calculated fields, or for display purposes, you may wish to change the format of field data. You can change field format settings on the Property Sheet pane.

▶ In Query Design view, right-click the field and click Properties. The Property Sheet pane appears, as shown in Figure 4.25. Change the properties to meet the formatting requirements by editing the existing settings, and close the Property Sheet pane when done.

▶ You can also change font, font size, shading, and other display options before printing a query result. Use all the same formatting features used for tables and in other applications to enhance the result.

▶ You can sort data in tables, but you can also make sort settings in Query Design view. On the query design grid, shown in Figure 4.25, note the sort settings that were made for the Product Description field.

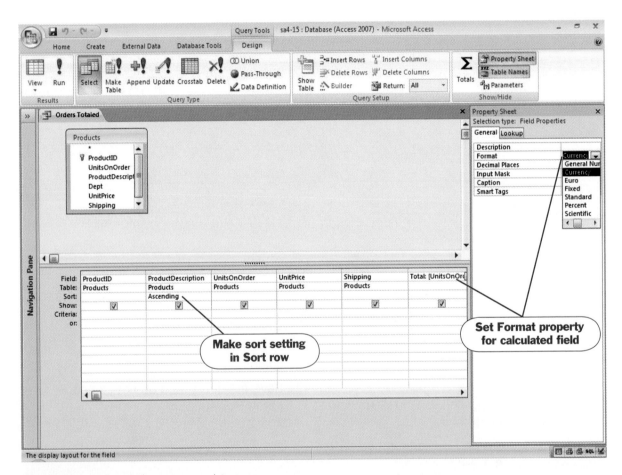

Figure 4.25: Property Sheet pane and Sort settings

1. Use the open database or open data file **a4-15**.

2. Open the _Orders Totaled_ query and note the number formats.

3. Click the **View button** to switch to Design view.

4. Click the **Sort row list arrow** for the ProductDescription field. Click **Ascending**.

5. Right-click the calculated field cell in the Field row. Click **Properties**.

6. In the Property Sheet pane, change the Format to **General Number**. Close the Property Sheet pane.

7. Click the **View button** to switch to Datasheet view. _Note the change in format_.

8. Click the **View button** to switch back to Design view. Right-click the calculated field, click **Properties**, and change the Format back to **Currency**. Close the Property Sheet pane.

9. Click the **View button** to switch to Datasheet view. _Note the change in format_.

10. On the Home tab, click the **Fill/Back Color list arrow** and click **Green 3**.

11. Change the font to **Euphemia**, **11 point**, or another font you prefer.

12. Close and save the query and the database.

Create a Multi-Table Query

▶ The query feature is especially powerful when you build a **multi-table select query**, which is a query based on more than one table. When tables are related in the Relationship window, you can create a multi-table select query by using a wizard in the same way you did to create a single table query.

▶ After you click the Query Wizard button and select a Simple Query, you click the first table to include in the query, and double-click each field to add to the query. When you are done, click the down arrow in the Tables/Queries list box and click the next table to include. Double-click each field to be included in the query. Then complete the process in the normal way.

1. Open data file **a4-16** and, on the Create tab, click the **Query Wizard button**. _This is a supplier's database_.

2. Double-click **Simple Query Wizard**.

3. Click the **Tables/Queries box list arrow**, and click **Table: Products**.

4. Double-click the following fields: **ProductID**, **ProductName**, and **UnitPrice**.

5. Click the **Tables/Queries box list arrow** in Tables/Queries, and click **Table: Suppliers**.

6. Double-click the following fields: **SupplierName**, **ContactName**, and **PhoneNumber**.

7. Click **Next** twice. Name the query `Order Information`. Click **Finish**. _Note the results. The query appears under both the Products and Suppliers tables in the Navigation Pane._

8. Save and close the query and the database.

REHEARSAL

 GOAL
To add a calculated field to a query, and
to build a multi-table query

TASK 3

WHAT YOU NEED TO KNOW

▶ Every real estate agent is
concerned with selling homes and
acquiring new listings, because
commissions are split between
the listing firm and the selling
firm. If the listing firm sells the
property, it earns the entire
commission.

▶ Palmetto Realtors has
established a relationship
between the *Listings* table and
the *Agents* table. This will enable
you to build a multi-table query
that provides agent information
with listing data. You will create
another query with a calculated
field to provide agents with
approximate real estate taxes for
their buyers.

▶ In this Rehearsal activity, you will
use a copy of the questions in
Step 5 to record the information
you will gather using the queries
you build.

▼ DIRECTIONS

1. Open your solution to **4r2-Palmetto**, or open data
file **4r3-Palmetto**.

2. Click the **Database Tools tab**, and in the Show/
Hide group, click the **Relationships button**. Check
the relationship between the *Agents* table and the
Listings table.

3. Create a multi-table query that produces listings by
agent with their contact information:
   a. Click the **Create tab**, and in the Other group,
   click the **Query Wizard button** and open the
   Simple Query Wizard.
   b. Select the *Agents* table and double-click the
   Agent Last Name, **Office Telephone**, and **Mobile
   Phone fields**.
   c. Select the *Listings* table, double-click the
   ListingID, **Owner Last Name**, **Address**, **City**, and
   Price fields.
   d. Name the query **Agents and Listings**. Click
   Finish.
   e. In Design view, set the sort to **Ascending** for the
   Agent Last Name field.
   f. Run, save, and close the query.

4. Create a query that produces a table of listings
information to calculate approximate real estate
taxes, as shown in Figure 4.26.
   a. Click the **Create tab**, and in the Other group,
   click the **Query Wizard button** and open the
   Simple Query Wizard.
   b. From the *Listings* table, move **ListingID**, **Date
   Listed**, **Owner Last Name**, **Address**, **City**,
   Agent Last Name, **Date Built**, and **Price** to the
   Selected Fields list. Click **Next** twice.
   c. Name the query: **Listings-Estimated Tax**.
   Click **Finish**.
   d. In Design view, add a calculated field to calculate
   the estimated tax. Enter an expression that
   includes the column name (**Estimated Tax**)

Continued on next page

ListingID	Date Listed	Owner Last	Address	City	Agent Last	Date Built	Price	Estimated Tax
2	7/8/2010	Davids	23 Easton Avenue	Hollywood	Olsen	9/9/1999	$155,000.00	$3,100.00
3	7/12/2010	Angeli	2 Woodside Avenue	East Hollywood	Barona	8/18/1987	$395,000.00	$7,900.00
4	7/12/2010	Lee	12 Gale Way	West Hollywood	Chang	2/7/2000	$350,000.00	$7,000.00
5	7/19/2010	Taylor	1 Somers Road	Hollywood	Dembar	2/12/2001	$320,000.00	$6,400.00
6	7/25/2010	Davis	8 Overlook Drive	Hollywood	Lincoln	1/1/2006	$355,000.00	$7,100.00
7	7/28/2010	Kelley	750 Ocean Avenue	Hollywood	Olsen	12/12/1990	$575,000.00	$11,500.00
9	7/29/2010	Vargas	21 Green Street	East Hollywood	Barona	10/10/1998	$270,000.00	$5,400.00
10	8/1/2010	Rielly	1200 North Ocean Avenue	Hollywood	Lincoln	5/15/2008	$475,000.00	$9,500.00
11	8/5/2010	Greaves	548 Greenleaf Street	East Hollywood	Chang	2/10/2007	$375,000.00	$7,500.00
12	8/7/2010	Mulholland	24 Breezy Point Road	West Hollywood	Olsen	3/31/2005	$310,000.00	$6,200.00
13	8/12/2010	Vargas	432 Blossom Road	Hollywood	Dembar	10/23/2006	$295,000.00	$5,900.00
14	8/16/2010	Kinney	925 Prescott Circle	East Hollywood	Barona	11/17/2007	$545,000.00	$10,900.00
15	8/19/2010	Umberto	76 Grand Avenue	West Hollywood	Lincoln	10/12/2005	$325,000.00	$6,500.00
16	8/26/2010	Pilgrim	651 North Ocean Avenue	Hollywood	Dembar	12/10/2007	$365,000.00	$7,300.00
17	8/29/2010	Thompson	39 Hibiscus Lane	West Hollywood	Olsen	6/5/2006	$325,000.00	$6,500.00
*	(New)							

Set Fill/Back Color to Light Gray 2

Calculated control

Figure 4.26: Multi-table query with a calculated control

and a formula that multiplies Price by the county tax rate of two percent. *Hint: Estimated Tax: [Price]*.02.*

e. Click the **Run button** to see the change. *Only one property has sold.*

f. Switch back to Design view, and set the Format property of the Estimated Tax data to **Currency**.

g. In Datasheet view, format the query datasheet using the Fill/Back Color **Light Gray 2**.

h. Print a copy of the query in Landscape orientation and Normal margins. Save and close the query.

5. Answer the questions in the table below or in data file **4r3-PalmettoQuestions.docx** using any one of the queries in this database.

6. Close the database.

QUESTIONS	ANSWERS
a. What are the approximate taxes on the house at 12 Gale Way?	
b. Mr. Mulholland, an owner, wants the mobile telephone number of his listing agent.	
c. Any agent(s) without listings are being asked to come in this Saturday for telephone duty. Who will be called to come in to work?	
d. Which agent has the highest value in listings? Provide the agent's name and value of listings.	
e. What is the average price of the homes we have listed in West Hollywood?	
f. Which city has the highest value in listings? What is the average price of a home in that city?	

ACCESS

Use Aggregate Functions in a Query

1. Design a query with two fields: one for grouping and the other to be summarized with aggregate functions.
2. In Design view, click the **Query Tools Design tab**, and in the Show/Hide Group, click the **Totals button**.
3. In the query design grid, click in the Total row cell for the field to be grouped. Click the **list arrow**, and click **Group By**.
4. In the Total row cell for the field to be summarized, click the **list arrow** and select the aggregate function.
5. Click the **Run button** to view the results.

Make Sort Settings in Query Design

1. Open a query, and switch to Design view using the **View button**.
2. In the query design grid, click the **Sort row cell** for the field to be sorted.

3. Click the **list arrow**, and click **Ascending** or **Descending**.

Add a Calculated Field to Queries

1. Open a query, and switch to Design view using the **View button**.
2. Enter the expression in the top cell of the first blank column in the query design grid.
3. Click the **Run button** to view the results.

Format Results Displayed in a Calculated Field

1. Open a query, and switch to Design view using the **View button**.
2. In the query design grid, right-click the calculated field, and click **Properties**.
3. In the Property Sheet pane, click the property to modify.
4. Delete any contents and replace them with the necessary value or format.
5. Close the Property Sheet pane.
6. Click the **Run button** to view the change in format.

Create a Multi-Table Select Query

1. Click the **Create tab**, and in the Other group, click the **Query Wizard button**.
2. Double-click the Query Wizard you want to use.
3. In the Tables/Queries box, click the **list arrow** and select the first table to include.
4. Double-click the fields in the Available Fields list to move them to the Selected Fields list.
5. Click the **list arrow** in the Tables/Queries list box, and click the next table to include.
6. Double-click the fields in the Available Fields list to move them to the Selected Fields list.
7. Click **Next** twice, name the query, and click **Finish**.

TASK 3

The Craftoy Shoppe sells a selection of crafts and toys in a boutique setting in a tourist area in Connecticut. They have started a database for their products, suppliers, and orders. You are being asked to sort, filter, and query the data to answer questions.

Craftoy Shoppe

Follow these guidelines:

1. Open data file **4p3-Craftoy**, and review the tables and their relationships.

2. The owner needs a query that provides a list of orders, with products and quantities so that he can give the list to the Receiving Department. Use all of the tables to include the following fields in the order listed: **ItemID**, **Purchase Order Number**, **Order Date**, **SupplierName**, **ProductID**, **ProductName**, and **Quantity**. Name the query `Orders Receiving List`.

3. Run an unmatched query to find out who the suppliers are that do not have matching orders. Use the *Suppliers* and *Orders* tables, and include all fields in the *Suppliers* table as the result. Name the query `Suppliers Without Matching Orders`.

4. Sort the *Suppliers* table in ascending order by Supplier Name and print a copy of the sorted list. Return the table to SupplierID order.

Continued on next page

5. Create a query to perform order calculations, as shown in Figure 4.27.
   a. Use the following fields in the order specified from all the tables: **Purchase Order Number, SupplierName, Quantity, Unit Price,** and **Discount**.
   b. Name the query **Orders Calculations**.
   c. In Design view, add the following calculated fields:
      Total: Multiply the Unit Price by Quantity
      Less Discount: Multiply the Total by Discount
      Net Price: Subtract Less Discount from Total
   d. Set Format field property to **Currency** for all the calculated fields.
   e. Deselect the **Show check box** for the Discount field.
   f. Run the query. Save and close it.

6. Save and close the database.

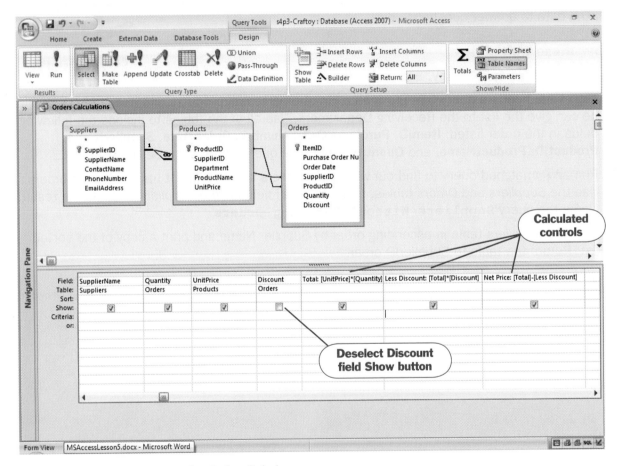

Figure 4.27: Query Design view for *Orders Calculations* query

Act I

Transport Travel Services has offices in Boston, New York, and California. They specialize in both corporate and leisure travel packages. The director of the Corporate Travel Department in New York is Mr. Robert Ramirez, and the director of the Leisure Travel Department is Ms. Jaime Trainor.

You work for Ms. Trainor in the Leisure Travel Department. She would like to begin a direct mail campaign in conjunction with a cruise company, but before investing in the campaign she wants to analyze the customer survey results.

Ms. Trainor has listed some questions about existing customers that she would like you to answer by using information stored in the customer database. She has also recommended a method of obtaining the information from the database.

Use a copy of the Questions table to keep track of the information you gather using the sorts, filters, and queries you build.

Follow these guidelines:

1. Open the data file **4ep1-Transport**. Use the table that contains questions and the suggested method for obtaining the answers to complete this project. A copy of the table is in the data file **4ep1-TransportQuestions.docx**. Additional information is listed below the table.

Continued on next page

QUESTIONS	HOW	ANSWERS
a. Where does Richard McCarthy live?	Search	
b. What are the Customer Numbers of our NY clients?	Filter	
c. What is the satisfaction level of our customers for the last trip they took? How many customers recently took cruises?	Crosstab query: Satisfaction Recent Trip	How many recently took cruises:
d. Would you print out a list of our customers in alphabetical order by last name within each state?	Filter	
e. Can we find out how many customers prefer each type of travel? What is the most popular travel preference?	Group by Travel Preference: Travel Preference Count	Most popular travel preference:
f. Which travel partners have our customers used? How many customers used the services of the most popular travel partner? How many customers have used Davis Tours?	Group by Company Name: Travel Partners Count	Clark's Cruises: Davis Tours:
g. What are the locations and counts for each future travel destination? What are the two most popular destinations?	Group by Next Travel Interest: Next Travel Interest Count	Most popular destinations:

2. Use Find and Filter tools to answer the questions as listed. To answer the questions that have a Query indication, create four queries and name them as listed below:
   - **Satisfaction Recent Trip** (Crosstab Query): Use the *Most Recent Travel* and the Satisfaction fields, and use the Count function on the Customer Number field.
   - **Travel Preference Count** (Query): Use only the Travel Preference field. In Design view, drag another copy of the field down to the design grid and use a Total row to set the Group by and the Count function, as shown in Figure 4.28.
   - **Travel Partners Count** (Query) and **Next Travel Interest Count** (Query): Use the same method as described above.

3. Save but do not close the database.

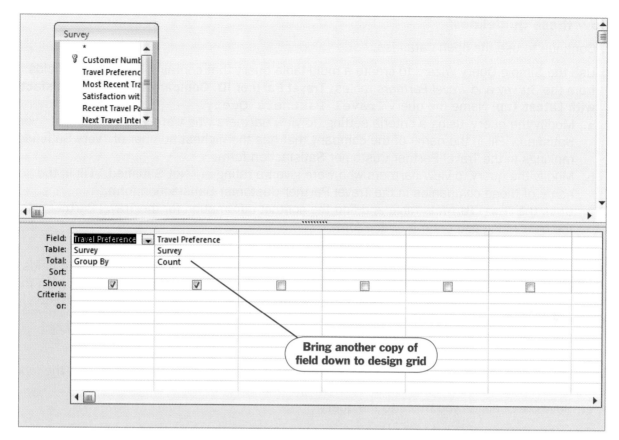

Figure 4.28: Query Design view for Travel Preference Count

Act II

Based on your analysis of the customer database, Ms. Trainor, of Transport Travel Services, is moving forward with a Travel Partners Cruise Promotion, targeted to the customer base. In addition, an important corporate account has asked Robert Ramirez, the director of the Corporate Travel Department, to arrange a cruise for one of its key executives. Mr. Ramirez has asked Ms. Young for some information, and she has asked you to provide the information to her in the form shown below, and found in data file **4ep2-TransportQuestions.docx**.

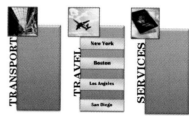

QUESTIONS	ANSWERS
a. Name of the company with the highest number of Very Satisfied customers?	
b. Names of companies with a Not Satisfied rating?	
c. Name of contact for the company with the highest number of Very Satisfied customers?	

Follow these guidelines:

1. Continue to use the open database.

2. Use the Simple Query Wizard to create a multi-table query that contains the following fields from the *Survey* and *Travel Partners* tables: **Travel Partner ID**, **CompanyName**, and **Satisfaction with Latest Trip**. Name the query `Travel Partners Query`.

   a. Modify the query, using a criteria setting, to view partners who were given a rating of "Very Satisfied." Fill in the name of the company that has the highest number of "Very Satisfied" rankings in the Travel Partner Customer Satisfaction form.

   b. Modify the query to view partners who were given a rating of "Not Satisfied." Fill in the name of those companies in the Travel Partner Customer Satisfaction form.

   c. Open the *Travel Partners* table and find the contact information for the Travel Partner with the best rating and enter it on the form.

   d. Close the query and save the modifications you made.

3. Create another query for Jaime Trainor for her cruise promotion. She would like all the fields from the *Customers* table, and the **Travel Preference** and **Next Travel Interest fields** from the *Survey* table. Name the table `Cruise Promotion List`.

   a. Modify the query to set the criteria of "Cruise Ship" in the Travel Preference field.

   b. Deselect the **Show button check box** for the Travel Preference field.

   c. Set the Sort option in the Next Travel Interest column to **Ascending**.

   d. Print a copy of the list. *You may have to narrow the width of some columns to print the table on one page. Use Print Preview and Landscape orientation.*

   e. Save the changes you made to the query.

4. Close the database. Exit Access.

Access Reports

In this lesson, you will learn how to create, modify, preview, and print reports based on a database using the Report Wizard. You will use Report Design view to add and modify controls, report sections, and properties, and to add a calculated field to a report.

Upon completion of this lesson, you will have mastered the following skill sets

- ⚹ Learn about reports
- ⚹ Create a report using the Report button
- ⚹ Create a report using the Label Wizard
- ⚹ Create and format reports using the Report Wizard
- ⚹ View, modify, and print reports
- ⚹ Use report sections
- ⚹ Modify report format properties
- ⚹ Modify reports in Design view
- ⚹ Modify reports in Layout view
- ⚹ Add aggregate functions using calculated controls

Terms
Software-related

Aggregate function
Design view
Detail section
Group footer
Group header
Label Wizard
Layout view
Over All
Over Group
Page footer
Page header
Print Preview
Report footer
Report header
Report sections
Report selector
Report Wizard
Report view
Reports
Section selector

▶ **GOAL**

To create reports based on a database, including a mailing label report, and to print the reports you create, as shown in Figure 5.1

❋ Learn about reports

❋ Create a report using the Report button

❋ Create a report using the Label Wizard

❋ Create and format reports using the Report Wizard

❋ View, modify, and print reports

Weekly Listings Report

City   East Hollywood

	Price	Address	Property Description	Estimated Tax
	$270,000.00	21 Green Street	2 bedroom, 1 bath cottage .25 acre	$5,400.00
	$375,000.00	548 Greenleaf Street	3 bedroom, 2 bath ranch	$7,500.00
	$395,000.00	2 Woodside Avenue	5 bedroom 2.5 bath Tudor .5 acres	$7,900.00
	$545,000.00	925 Prescott Circle	5 bedroom, 2 1/2 bath colonial with lake view	$10,900.00

Summary for 'City' = East Hollywood (4 detail records)

Avg $396,250.00

City   Hollywood

	Price	Address	Property Description	Estimated Tax
	$155,000.00	23 Easton Avenue	2 bedroom 1.5 bath ranch on .25 acre. Recently upgraded kitchen	$3,100.00
	$295,000.00	432 Blossom Road	2 bedroom, 2 bath cottage	$5,900.00
	$320,000.00	1 Somers Road	4 bedroom 2 bath cape .25 acres	$6,400.00
	$355,000.00	8 Overlook Drive	3 bedroom 2 bath condominium	$7,100.00
	$365,000.00	651 North Ocean Avenue	2 bedroom, 1 1/2 bath condo with intercoastal view	$7,300.00
	$475,000.00	1200 North Ocean Avenue	2 bedroom, 2 bath condominium	$9,500.00
	$575,000.00	750 Ocean Avenue	3 bedroom, 2 bath condo, ocean view	$11,500.00

Summary for 'City' = Hollywood (7 detail records)

Avg $362,857.14

City   West Hollywood

	Price	Address	Property Description	Estimated Tax

Figure 5.1: Task 1: Report Wizard report with summary options

WHAT YOU NEED TO KNOW

Learn About Reports

▶ **Reports** are database objects that use data from tables and queries to create a presentation-quality printout. You can build reports from more than one table or query. Additional information, such as headings or logos, can be part of the design of the report.

▶ Report objects are extremely valuable business tools because once they are created and saved, you can open them later to present a report with any new or updated information.

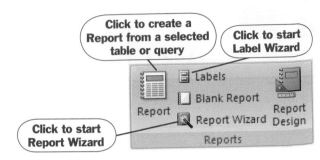

Figure 5.2: Create tab, Reports group

▶ You can create a report or labels using the tools in the Reports section of the Create tab, shown in Figure 5.2.

Create a Report Using the Report Button

▶ The Report button automatically creates a basic report to display all the fields in a selected table or a query. The report data is arranged in columnar fashion with report and page headers and footers, as shown in Figure 5.3.

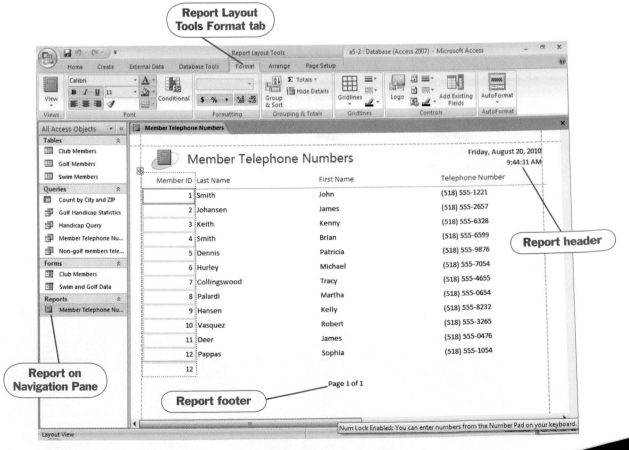

Figure 5.3: Report Layout Tools Format tab and Report

1. Start Access.

2. Open data file **a5-1**.

3. In the Navigation Pane, click the *Member Telephone Numbers* query.

4. Click the **Create tab**, and in the Reports group, click the **Report button**. *Note that this is a single-page report with header and footer information.*

5. Save the report with the name **Member Telephone Numbers** and note its appearance on the Navigation Pane.

6. Close the report but do not close the database.

Create a Report Using the Label Wizard

▶ The **Label Wizard** tool allows you to create mailing and other label types in standard and custom sizes, based on the data in a database.

▶ To create labels, select the data source table, and click the Labels button in the Reports group on the Create tab. On the first Label Wizard screen, shown in Figure 5.4, you select the label size, unit of measure, label type, and manufacturer. The wizard lists the most popular product numbers for the leading label manufacturers. Click the manufacturer and then click the product number of the labels you are using. Also, click the appropriate Unit of Measure and Label Type.

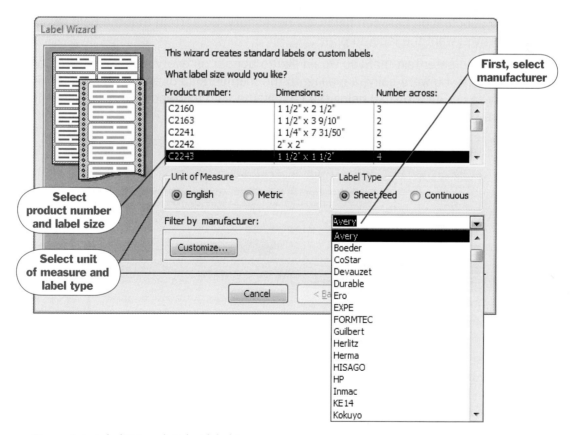

Figure 5.4: Label Wizard: Select label type

▶ Click the Next button to open the dialog box where you can set the font, font size, and font weight. You can also set text color and italic and underline formats. A preview appears at the left, as shown in Figure 5.5.

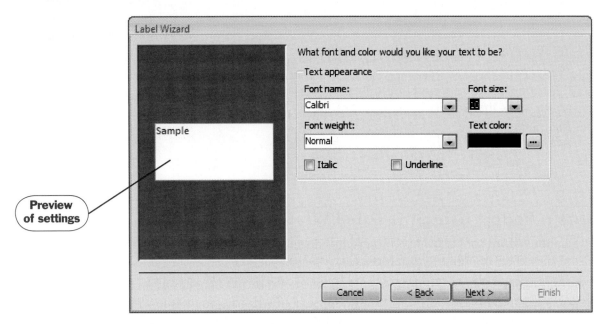

Figure 5.5: Label Wizard: Font and color settings

▶ Click Next, and a dialog box opens to assist you in constructing the label, shown in Figure 5.6. Double-click each field you want to include, in the order you want them to print. As you complete each line in the address, use the Enter or Tab key to move to the next line. Add spaces, returns, other text, and punctuation between fields, as necessary. Be certain that the field layout represents how you want the label to print.

▶ In addition, you can enter text that you would like to appear on every label in the Prototype label box. For example, if you were doing a mailing to the membership of a club about a family event, you might want to create the label using the Last Name field followed by the word Family, as shown in Figure 5.6.

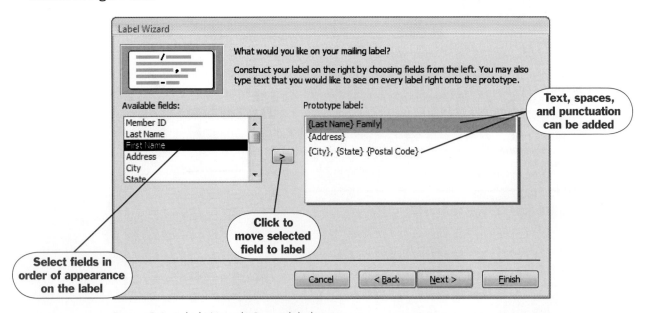

Figure 5.6: Label Wizard: Create label prototype

▶ Click Next, and a dialog box opens, prompting you to choose sort order, as shown in Figure 5.7. You may choose to sort your mailing by postal code to take advantage of the post office's special mailing rates. You can also sort by more than one field. Double-click the Sort by choice or choices, and click Next to display the last step of the wizard. Title the report and click Finish to open the label report.

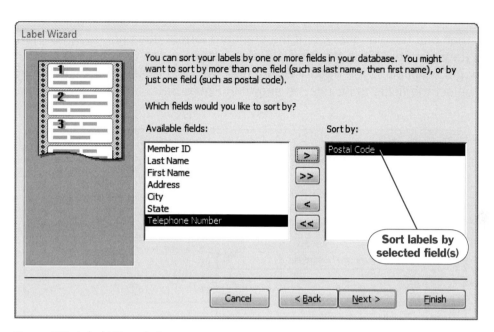

Figure 5.7: Label Wizard: Sort settings

TRY *it* OUT *a5-2*

1. Use the open database or open data file **a5-2**.

2. Click the *Club Members* table in the Navigation Pane.

3. Click the **Create tab**, and in the Reports group, click the **Labels button**.

4. If necessary, click the **Filter by Manufacturer list arrow**, and then click **Avery**, click **English** under Unit of Measure, and **Sheet feed** under Label Type.

5. Click Product number **C2243** in the What label size would you like? box. *Note that this choice prints four labels across a page.*

6. Click **Next**. Set the font to **Calibri, 10, Normal** font weight, and, if necessary, set the color to **black**.

7. Click **Next**. Double-click the **Last Name field** in the Available fields box to place it in the Prototype label box.

8. Press **[Spacebar]**. Enter `Family`, then press **[Enter]**.

9. Double-click **Address**, then press **[Enter]**.

10. Double-click **City**. Enter a comma and press **[Spacebar]**.

11. Double-click **State** and press **[Spacebar]**. Double-click **Postal Code**.

12. Click **Next**. Double-click **Postal Code** to move it to the Sort by box.

13. Click **Next**, name your report **Labels Club Members**, then click **Finish**. *Note that the information appears in label format with four labels across.*

14. Close the report. *Note that it appears on the Navigation Pane as a report object.*

Create and Format Reports Using the Report Wizard

▶ You can build a report using the Report Wizard. Similar to other wizards, the **Report Wizard** asks you questions about what information you want to include in a report and how you want to present and format it. You can modify the resulting report, if changes are necessary.

▶ Use the Report Wizard to create reports if you do not require all the fields in a table, if you require a specific layout and orientation, if the report contains fields from more than one table or query, or if the standard format does not meet your requirements. To use the Report Wizard, click the Report Wizard button on the Create tab, and the first Report Wizard dialog box appears. The Report Wizard first asks you to select the data source table or query and select the fields to include, as shown in Figure 5.8.

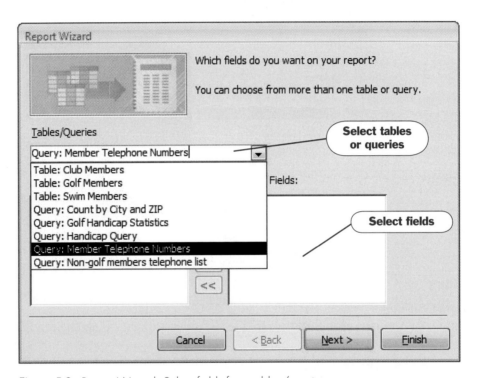

Figure 5.8: Report Wizard: Select fields from tables/queries

▶ Click the data source table or query and double-click the fields to include. If the report is based on more than one table or query, click the additional data source and double-click the fields to add. Tables must have established relationships before you can include them, or a related query, in a report.

▶ Click Next and the grouping level options appear, shown in Figure 5.9. You can group records in a report based on the values of up to four fields. If you use more than one grouping field, select the most significant group first. In our example, we are creating a telephone list grouped by City using fields from the *Members Telephone Numbers* query and the *Club Members* table.

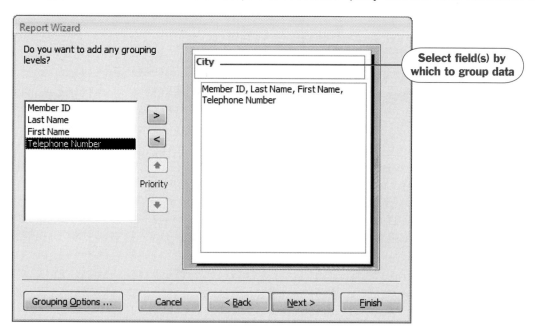

Figure 5.9: Report Wizard: Grouping levels

▶ Click Next to enter any sort requirements, as shown in Figure 5.10. You can sort records by up to four fields in ascending or descending order. Click the list arrow in each box to select the fields by which to sort. Click the button to the right of the appropriate box to set ascending or descending order. If any of the fields selected are numeric, a Summary Options button will appear on this screen. The summary settings are similar to those used in the Query Wizard except that you have the option to show Detail and Summary data together.

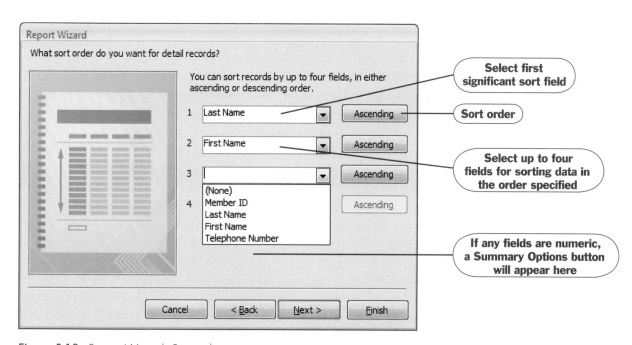

Figure 5.10: Report Wizard: Sort order

► Click Next and layout options appear, shown in Figure 5.11. The wizard provides three layout options, and the choice of a portrait or landscape page orientation. Click each layout to see a preview of the format and then select the layout and orientation you want.

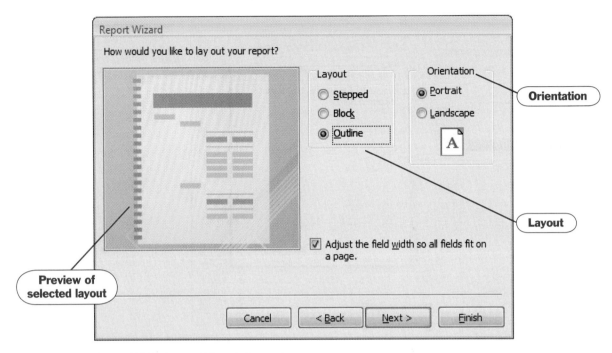

Figure 5.11: Report Wizard: Report layout settings

► Click Next and you can select style options for the report, shown in Figure 5.12. Click a style to preview it. Once you have selected a style, click Next to provide a title for the report, as shown in Figure 5.13. Click Finish, and the new report appears in the Print Preview. The Report Wizard adds a footer to the report which includes the date, the page number, and the number of pages.

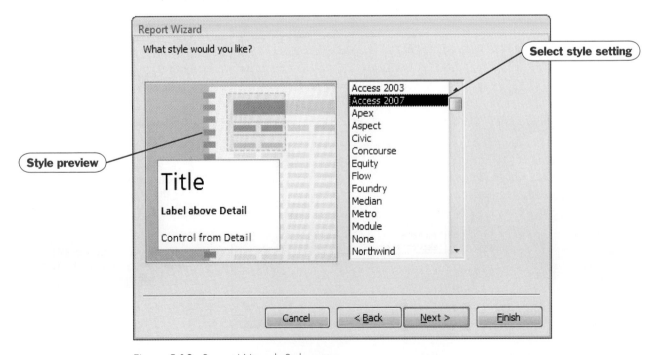

Figure 5.12: Report Wizard: Style setting

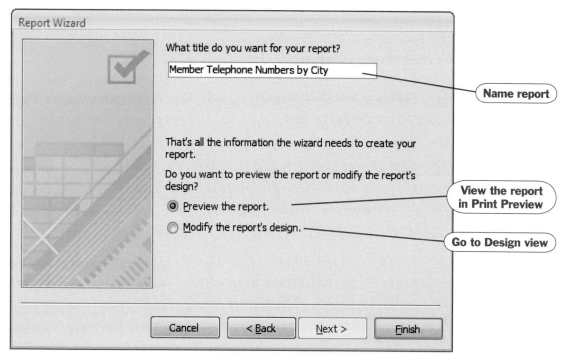

Figure 5.13: Report Wizard: Final screen

TRY*it*OUT a5-3

1. Use the open database or open data file **a5-3**.

2. Click the **Create tab**, and in the Reports group, click the **Report Wizard button**.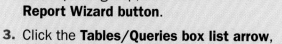

3. Click the **Tables/Queries box list arrow**, and click **Query: Member Telephone Numbers**.

4. Move all fields to the Selected Fields box using the double arrow button.

5. Click the **Tables/Queries box list arrow**, and click **Table: Club Members**.

6. Move the City field to the Selected Fields box, and click **Next**.

7. Double-click the **City field** to group by city. Click **Next**.

8. Click the list arrow in the first sort box. Click **Last Name**. *Note that Ascending*

is the default. You can click and change to Descending, if necessary. Click **First Name** in the second box. Click **Next**.

9. Click each layout option to preview the available layouts. Click the **Outline layout option**, and the **Portrait orientation option**, then click **Next**.

10. Click each style option to preview available styles. Click **Access 2007** and then click **Next**.

11. Name the report **Member Telephone Numbers by City**. Click **Finish** to preview the report.

12. Close the report, but do not close the database. *Note that the report is now listed on the Navigation Pane.*

View, Modify, and Print Reports

Change Report Views and Modify Reports

▶ Reports have four views: Report view, Layout view, Print Preview, and Design view, as outlined in Table 5.1. You can change the report view by right-clicking the report tab and selecting the view or by clicking the View button on the Home tab.

Table 5.1: Report views

Report view	Used to display report. No modifications may be made.
Layout view	May use Report Layout Tools Format and Arrange tabs to change report layout.
Print Preview	View upon completion of Report Wizard. Make print settings and navigate to all pages in the report.
Design view	Use to create report or to modify a report created with report tools.

▶ In Layout view, you can modify reports using the Format and Arrange tabs in the same manner as you did with the other database objects. Additional modifications available in Layout view will be discussed in Task 2.

TRY it OUT a5-4

1. Use the open database or open data file **a5-4**.

2. Open the *Member Telephone Numbers by City* report.

3. Right-click the **report tab**, then click **Print Preview**. *Note the Print button, and the Page Layout, Zoom, and Data groups on the tab.* Click the **Close Print Preview button**.

4. Click the **Home tab**, and in the Views group, click the **View button** to switch to Layout view. *If the Field List pane opens at the right, click the **Close button** on the pane.*

5. Click the **Member ID column header** and on the Report Layout Tools Format tab, in the Font group, click the **Center button**. Repeat this step for the data fields in the Member ID column.

*For some screen settings, you may have to click the **Font group list arrow** to find the Center button.*

6. Click the **First Name column header**, and use the double-arrow cursor to move the left side of the column to the right to create space after the Last Name column.

7. Click the **City name column header** (the second control box), and change the font size to **14 point**. Switch to Report view to view your changes. *The city name is in a larger font.*

8. Switch to Design view to see how the elements of the report are placed in sections in the design.

9. Switch back to Report view and close and save the report. Do not close the database.

Modify Page Settings and Print a Report

▶ You can print a report from the Navigation Pane by right-clicking the report name and selecting Print or Print Preview, shown in Figure 5.14. The Print Preview screen allows you to set margins or orientation, and you can make additional page setup and column settings.

Figure 5.14: Print a report from the Navigation Pane

T R Y *i t* O U T *a5-5*

1. Use the open file or open data file **a5-5**.

2. Right-click the *Members Telephone Numbers by City* report, then click **Print Preview**. *You see a full page view of the report.*

3. Click the **Margins button** and click **Wide**.

4. Click the **Page Setup button**, and change the Left margin to **1.3** and the Right margin to **1.0**. Click **OK**.

5. Click the **Print button**, then click **OK**.

6. Close the report and close the database.

REHEARSAL

TASK 1

GOAL

To create reports based on Palmetto Realtors listings database, to create a mailing label report to use for a company family outing, and to print the reports you create

WHAT YOU NEED TO KNOW

▶ Real estate agents are often out of the office showing properties and may not have the ability to connect to the office database while they are on the road. In that case, they rely on printed reports that they carry with them.

▶ You have been asked to produce a report that presents all of the property listings by town, in order of price. This report will be printed weekly.

▶ Every year Palmetto Realtors has a company picnic to which each agent's family is invited. You have been asked to prepare mailing labels for the family invitations.

▶ In this Rehearsal activity, you will create two reports using the Report Wizard and the Label Wizard. You will preview and print both reports.

DIRECTIONS

1. Open your solution to **4r3-Palmetto** or open data file **5r1-Palmetto**.

2. Create a report with the Report Wizard tool using the *Listings* table and the *Listings-Estimated Tax* query and the following fields in the order indicated: **City**, **Price**, **Address**, **Description**, **Estimated Tax**.
   a. Group by **City**.
   b. Sort by **Price** in ascending order, and click **Summary Options**. Click **Avg** for the Price field and under Show click **Detail and Summary**.
   c. Use the Outline layout, Landscape orientation, and Metro style.
   d. Rename the report **Weekly Listings Report**. Note that Price and Average Price data are not showing.
   e. Right-click the **report tab** and switch to Layout view. Click and reduce the size of the Address field by moving the left edge of the text box to the right so that it aligns under the City name. *Close the Field List pane if it opens. The Price data should now be visible.*
   f. Click on the first Average value and drag the right edge of the text box to align under the right edge of the Price field.
   g. Switch to Design view, and check that no fields or sections extend beyond the 10" mark on the horizontal ruler. If they do, move the edges back to the 10" mark. Save the design.
   h. Switch to Print Preview using the View button, and compare your printout with the report in Figure 5.15.
   i. Print a copy of the report and close it.

Continued on next page

Adjust size of Address text box by moving to the right to make room for Price data

Outline layout, Landscape orientation, Metro style

Weekly Listings Report

City		East Hollywood		
	Price	Address	Property Description	Estimated Tax
	$270,000.00	21 Green Street	2 bedroom, 1 bath cottage .25 acre	$5,400.00
	$375,000.00	548 Greenleaf Street	3 bedroom, 2 bath ranch	$7,500.00
	$395,000.00	2 Woodside Avenue	5 bedroom 2.5 bath Tudor .5 acres	$7,900.00
	$545,000.00	925 Prescott Circle	5 bedroom, 2 1/2 bath colonial with lake view	$10,900.00

Summary for 'City' = East Hollywood (4 detail records)
Avg $396,250.00

Adjust size of Avg value text box in Layout view

City		Hollywood		
	Price	Address	Property Description	Estimated Tax
	$155,000.00	23 Easton Avenue	2 bedroom 1.5 bath ranch on .25 acre. Recently upgraded kitchen	$3,100.00
	$295,000.00	432 Blossom Road	2 bedroom, 2 bath cottage	$5,900.00
	$320,000.00	1 Somers Road	4 bedroom 2 bath cape .25 acres	$6,400.00
	$355,000.00	8 Overlook Drive	3 bedroom 2 bath condominium	$7,100.00
	$365,000.00	651 North Ocean Avenue	2 bedroom, 1 1/2 bath condo with intercoastal view	$7,300.00
	$475,000.00	1200 North Ocean Avenue	2 bedroom, 2 bath condominium	$9,500.00
	$575,000.00	750 Ocean Avenue	3 bedroom, 2 bath condo, ocean view	$11,500.00

Summary for 'City' = Hollywood (7 detail records)
Avg $362,857.14

City		West Hollywood		
	Price	Address	Property Description	Estimated Tax

Figure 5.15: Report Wizard report with summary options

3. Create a label report to use to address the invitations for the annual beach party to the agents and their families. Use the Label Wizard and the *Agents* table.
   a. Set the Unit of Measure to **English** and the **Avery** Product Number to **C2160**.
   b. Use the **Comic Sans MS font** in **10 point**, and **Normal font weight**.
   c. Use the prototype illustration in Figure 5.16 to add the appropriate fields, text, and punctuation to create the labels for the invitation envelopes.
   d. Sort by Agent Last Name.
   e. Rename the report: `Labels Agent Beach Party`.
   f. Print and close the report and the table.

4. Close the database.

ACCESS

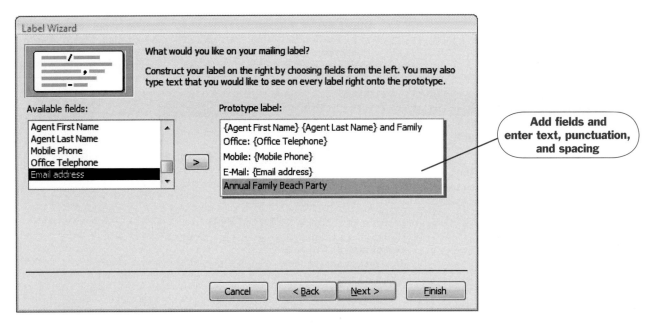

Figure 5.16: Prototype for label

Create a Report Using Report Button

1. With the table open or selected, click the **Create tab**, and in the Reports group, click the **Report button**.

Create a Report Using the Label Wizard

1. With the table open or selected, click the **Create tab**, and in the Reports group, click the **Labels button**.
2. Click the **Filter by manufacturer list arrow**, and select the label company name.
3. Click to select a Product number, a Unit of Measure, and Label Type, then click **Next**.
4. Use the list arrows to select the Font, Font size, and Font weight. Change the Text color, and click to select **Italic** or **Underline** format, if desired. Click **Next**.
5. Click the field names in the Available fields list and use the arrow button to arrange them in the Prototype label box. Add additional text, punctuation, or spaces as needed. Click **Next**.
6. Click to select an Available field to Sort by, then click **Next**.
7. Name the report, then click **Finish**.

Create and Format Reports Using the Report Wizard

1. Click the **Create tab**, and in the Reports group, click the **Report Wizard button**.
2. Click the **Table/Queries box list arrow**, and click a table or query.
3. Double-click the fields to include.
4. Repeat steps two and three if you are using more than one table/query.
5. Click **Next**.
6. Double-click grouping level fields, then click **Next**.
7. Click the **sort box list arrow** to select Sort by fields. Select the sort order, if necessary.
8. If there are numeric fields, click the **Summary Options button** if necessary. Select summary functions and make a selection in the Show section. Click **OK**, then click **Next**.
9. Click to make selections for Layout and Orientation, then click **Next**.
10. Select the style, then click **Next**.
11. Name the report, then click **Finish**.

Change Report Views

1. Right-click the **report tab**, and click the desired view.
   Or
1. Click the **Home tab**, and in the Views group, click the **View list arrow** and select the view.

Modify a Report in Layout View

1. Right-click the **report tab**, and click **Layout View**.
2. Use the Report Layout Tools Format tab to make modifications.
   Or
2. Click to select the field and move or resize the data.

Print a Report

1. Right-click the **report tab** or the report name on the Navigation Pane.
2. Click **Print Preview**.
3. Make any margin or orientation settings.
4. Use the Zoom or page features to view report.
5. Click the **Print button**.

TASK 1

Expedition Travel Gear has added the contact data for its last store in San Diego. You are asked to add the payroll data. They also want to analyze hourly wages to adjust them to maintain employee morale while staying within the prevailing rates for each store location. Employees pay dues that entitle them to union coverage for health and welfare. The company would like a report on hourly rates and a similar report on the dues structure for each store. In addition, the human resources manager needs mailing labels for all employees.

Expedition

Travel Gear

Follow these guidelines:

1. Open data file **5p1-ETG-EMPS** and note the new data in the *Contact* table.

2. Add the following information using the *Payroll* form. *Be sure to enter zeros in the Other Deductions field as indicated. You may wish to drag the edge of the Navigation Pane to the left to reduce the width to allow you to see more of the form as you make data entries.* Save the data.

Continued on next page

EMPID	21	22	23	24	25
SSNO	165-00-7645	216-00-9757	301-00-8645	265-00-0363	217-00-0445
Store	San Diego	San Diego	San Diego	San Diego	San Diego
Status	M	S	S	M	S
Exemptions	2	1	0	3	1
Birth Date	01/06/1986	07/19/1985	04/18/1978	08/22/1990	06/30/1989
Rate	14.50	14.25	12.50	11.50	11.50
Dues	8.00	5.00	5.00	8.00	5.00
Other Deductions	20.00	10.00	0.00	0.00	0.00

3. Create an *Hourly Rates by Store* report and format it in Layout view, as shown in Figure 5.17. Use the *Rates by Store* query and the **Report button**.

4. Create a similar report for the *Dues by Store* query.

5. Prepare mailing labels for the employees using **Avery J8160 labels** and using the appropriate fields in the prototype label. Set the font to **Calibri**, **9 point**, **Medium weight**. Sort them by Postal Code.

6. Save and close the report and the database.

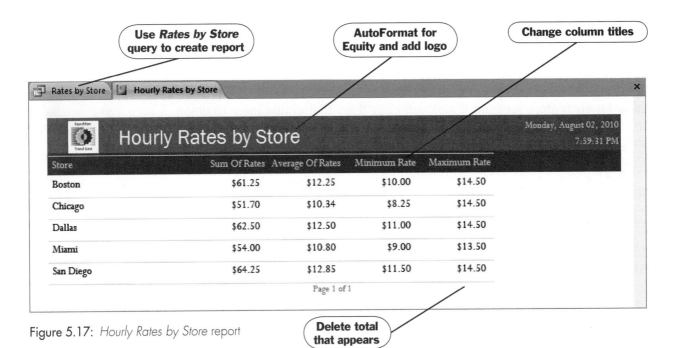

Figure 5.17: *Hourly Rates by Store report*

▶ **GOAL**

To modify existing reports by adding calculated controls and changing the properties of the report controls and sections, as shown in Figure 5.18

★ Use report sections
★ Modify report format properties
★ Modify reports in Design view
★ Modify reports in Layout view
★ Add aggregate functions using calculated controls

TASK 2

ACCESS

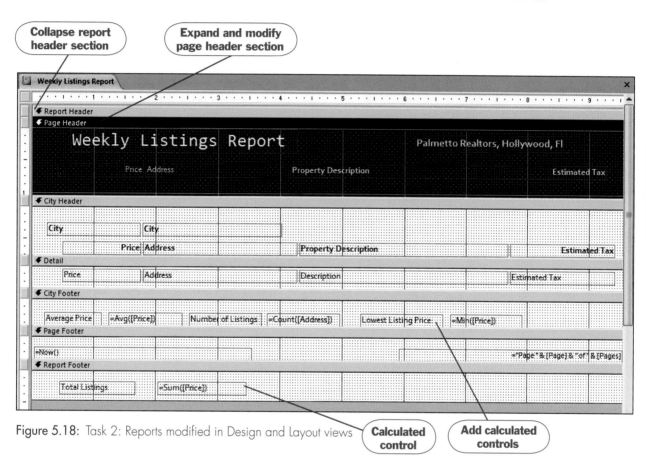

Collapse report header section

Expand and modify page header section

Figure 5.18: Task 2: Reports modified in Design and Layout views

Calculated control

Add calculated controls

WHAT YOU NEED TO KNOW

Use Report Sections

▶ **Report sections** are separate areas of the report that have various purposes to improve the report's design and usefulness. The report **detail section** appears in every report, is the main body of the report, and shows the fields that repeat once for each record. The other sections may be added or used as required. The sections are explained in Table 5.2 and can be viewed in Design view, as shown in Figure 5.19.

Table 5.2: Report sections

REPORT SECTION	LOCATION IN REPORT	PURPOSE
Report header section	Top of first printed page	Report title, logo, current date
Report footer section	Bottom of last printed page, above the page footer	Summary values for the report
Page header section	Top of every report page	Report title, page number
Page footer section	Bottom of every report page	Current date, page number
Group header section	Preceding each group of data; for example, if the data is grouped by city, each city title would be the group header.	A grouped data field value
Group footer section	Following each group of data	Summary values for the grouped data

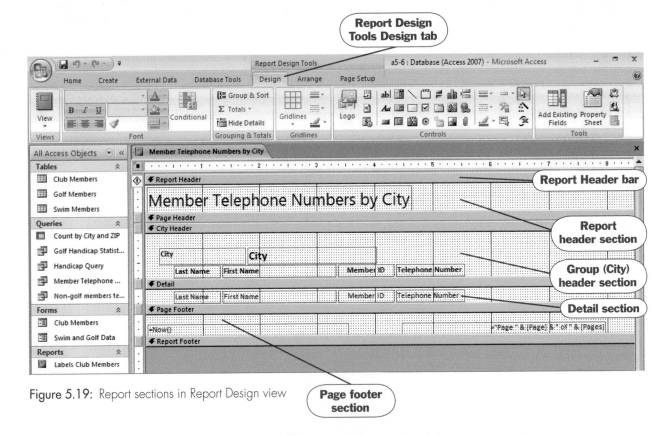

Figure 5.19: Report sections in Report Design view

▶ As you will note in Figure 5.19, the report header section contains the report title. There is no page header section data in this example. If this was a multipage report, page header information should be included. The group header and footer take on the name of the field that you are grouping; in this example it is the City Header. That header will repeat for every city in the database.

► There is no summary data and thus no group footer displayed. You can display the footer by right-clicking the field to summarize, pointing to Total, then clicking a summary option. The detail section is the main body of the report, and each record in the group will appear in that layout. The page footer, printing at the end of the page, contains the date and page number.

T R Y *i t* O U T *a5-6*

1. Open data file **a5-6**.

2. Open the *Member Telephone Numbers by City* report.

3. Right-click the **report tab** and click **Design View**. Close the Property Sheet pane if necessary.
   a. Note the location and contents of the report header and the page footer.
   b. Note that the detail section contains the fields of the report.
   c. Note the location of the group header, named City Header, and that the group footer is not displayed.
   d. Right-click in the **First Name field** in the City header section, point to **Total**, then click **Count Records**. Note that the City footer section and the report

   footer section appear with a control using the Count function.
   e. Note also that the Report Wizard adds two controls to the page footer section:
      • **=Now()** contains the date the report is printed, and
      • **="Page" & [Page] & "of" & [Pages]** contains the page number and how many pages are in the report.

4. Switch to Report view to see the count of records in each group, and then return to Design view.

5. Save the report changes. Do not close the report or the database.

Modify Report Format Properties

▶ A report has properties, which are stored in a property sheet that defines the report's characteristics. Use the report selector to view the properties of a report. The **report selector** is the box where the rulers meet in the upper-left corner of a report in Design view (see Figure 5.21). Double-click the report selector and a Property Sheet pane for the report appears, as shown in Figure 5.20.

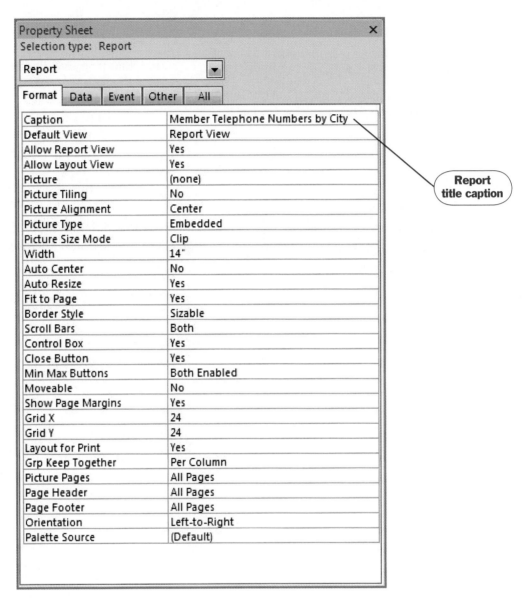

Figure 5.20: Modify the properties of a report

▶ The properties fall into four categories represented by the tabs: Format, Data, Event, and Other. To view all the properties, click the All tab. Use the scroll bar on the right side of the Property Sheet pane to view property sheet options. Click the name of the property to select it, then enter the new setting. When you make a change to the report, you do not make a change to the underlying data source or table.

▶ Each section of a report also has properties. To view the properties of a section, click the **section selector**, which is the box to the left of a section bar. Double-click this box to select the section and to open the section's Property Sheet pane. The property sheet for a group header section is shown in Figure 5.21.

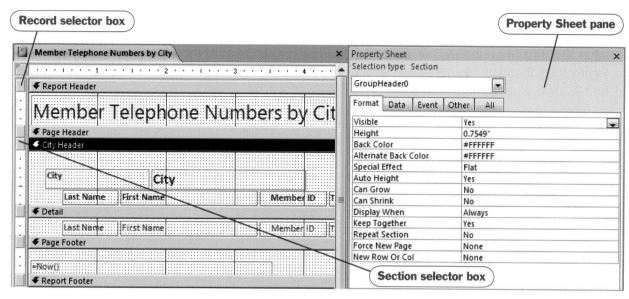

Figure 5.21: Modify the properties of a report section

▶ To change the height of a report section, click Height in the Property Sheet pane Format tab. Delete the existing value and replace it with the height you want. You can also change the size of report header/footer, group header/footer, or page header/footer sections using the mouse. Place the mouse pointer on the bottom edge of the section and drag the pointer up or down to change the height of the section.

▶ You can change the width of a section by placing the mouse pointer on the right edge of the section and dragging the pointer to the left or right. Report sections can have different heights; however, the report has one width. When you change the width of one section, you change the width of the entire report.

T R Y *it* O U T *a5-7*

1. Use the open database or open data file **a5-7** and open the *Members Telephone Numbers by City* report in Design view.

2. Place the mouse pointer on the bottom edge of the **report header section**, which is at the top edge of the Page Header bar. Drag the pointer down to approximately one inch.

3. Double-click the **page header section selector box**, and the Property Sheet pane appears.

4. Click **Height** on the Format tab of the Property Sheet pane, and replace the contents with: **1"**.

5. Close the Property Sheet pane, and switch to Report view. *Note the increased height at the top of the report.*

6. Switch back to Design view, and click **Undo** to reverse the page header property setting.

7. Save the design. Do not close the report or the database.

Modify Reports in Design View

▶ To customize a report, you may want to have an additional title or a date appear on every page. To accomplish this, add a label control to the page header or page footer section of a report to display a title or caption. It is unbound and remains the same for each page.

▶ To add an unbound label control, use the Report Design Tools Design tab, and click the Label (Form Control) button, in the Controls group, as shown in Figure 5.22. You can add a label, text box, date, button, or any of the controls in the group to the report. Note also in Figure 5.22 that you can right-click report sections to change fill/back color using the shortcut menu.

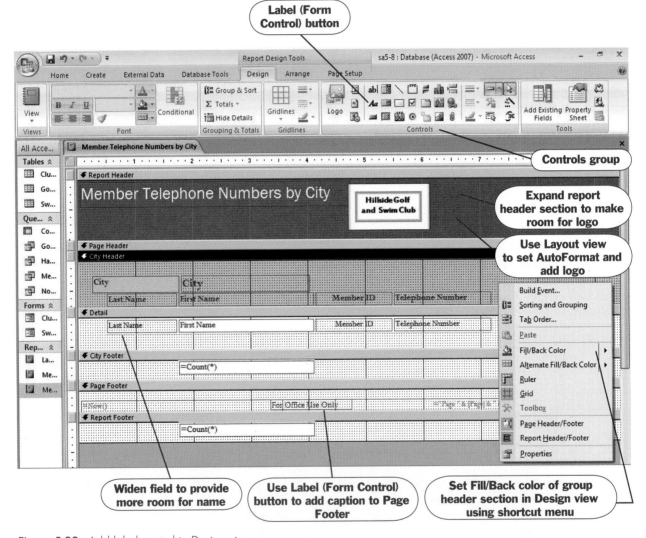

Figure 5.22: Add label control in Design view

T R Y i t O U T *a5-8*

1. Use the open database or open data file **a5-8**. You should be in Design view of the *Member Telephone Numbers by City* report. *The height of the report header should be 1" to accommodate the logo.*

2. Switch to Layout view and set AutoFormat to the **Equity style**. Add the logo data file **clublogo.tif** to the report header section, and place and expand it as shown in Figure 5.22.

Continued on next page

3. Switch back to Design view and note the appearance of the new design.

4. Right-click the **City header section**, point to **Fill/Back Color**, and change the back fill to **Brown 3**, a light peach color.

5. Click the **Report Design Tools Design tab**, and in the Controls group, click the **Label (Form Control) button**.

   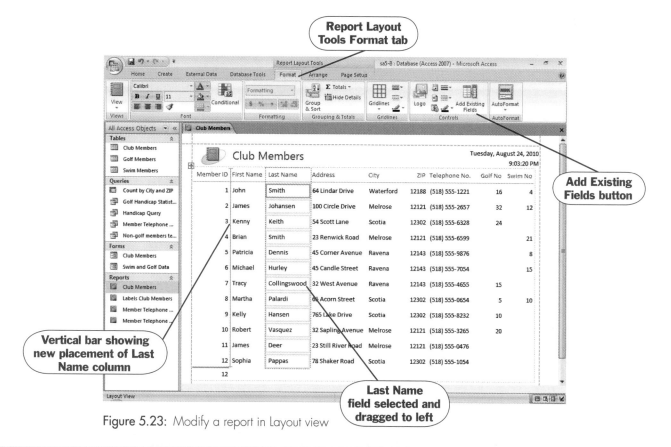

   (Labels)

6. In the page footer section, click a location at 3½" on the horizontal ruler line where you want the upper-left corner of the

control to appear. Enter: `For Office Use Only`.

7. Click the right edge of the Last Name field in the Detail section, and drag the edge to the right to widen the field. Drag the right edge of the First Name field to shorten it. *Note that the City Header fields move with the Detail fields.*

8. Click the **View list arrow** and click **Print Preview**.

9. Close and save the report and the database.

Modify Reports in Layout View

▶ When you create a report using the Report Wizard, it may be necessary to add or delete fields, reposition fields, or resize fields to fit the data on one page. This is easy to do in Layout view. When you click in a column or field the field control will be highlighted and you can then move, delete, resize, or position the control using drag and drop, shortcut menus, or the tools on the Report Layout Tools Format tab. When you begin to drag a control to move or reposition it, a vertical bar appears to show you where it will be placed, as shown in Figure 5.23. The dotted line at the right edge shows the page break so that you know the available space on the page.

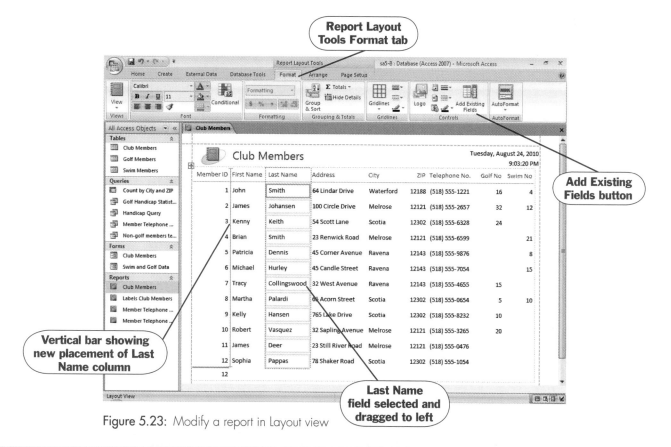

Figure 5.23: Modify a report in Layout view

▶ You can also add a field in Layout view by clicking the Add Existing Fields button in the Controls group of the Report Layout Tools Format tab, shown in Figure 5.24. The new field will be added and all fields adjusted to fit. The Field List pane is used in the same manner that it was used with forms. If a field is deleted the columns will adjust to fit the margins as well.

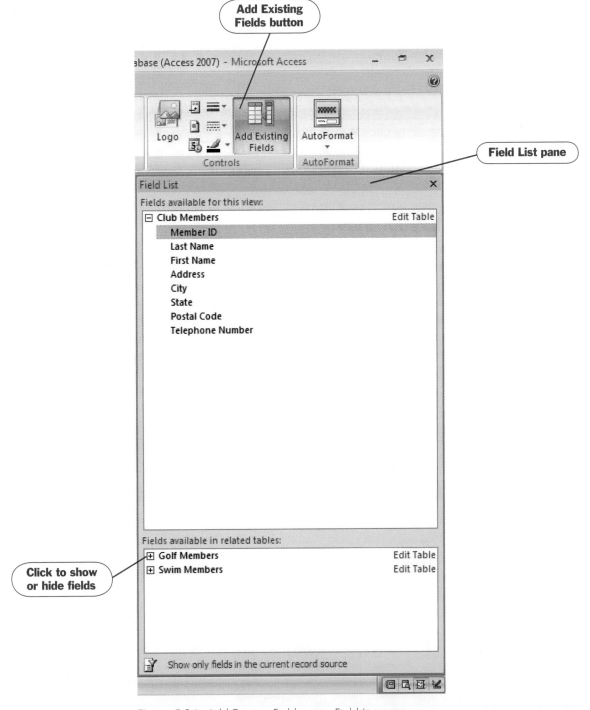

Figure 5.24: Add Existing Fields using Field List pane

1. Open data file **a5-9** and open the *Club Members* report in Layout view. *Scroll to the right, and note by the page break line that the report is wider than one page and that there is a lot of space between fields.*

2. Click anywhere in each column, and when the column is selected use your mouse to narrow each field width at the field name box. *Be sure that all the data and column headings can be read. All the data should now fit.*

3. Right-click the **State field column header**. Click **Delete**.

4. Click the **Last Name field column**, and move it to the right of the First Name field. *Note the vertical bar that appears when you drag the field to the right.*

5. Click the **Member ID field column** and center the values using the Center button on the Report Layout Tools Format tab.

6. Click on the last field in the report and then click the **Add Existing Fields button**, in the Controls group on the Report Layout Tools Format tab.

7. In the Fields available in related tables section of the pane, display the fields in the Golf and Swim Members tables by clicking the plus sign for each table.

8. Double-click the **Golf Locker No**. and the **Swim Locker No. fields** to add them to the report. Close the Field List pane.

9. Adjust column widths further and modify column headers to reduce column width to fit all columns on the page. *Hint: Change column titles to make room: Postal Code to ZIP Code, Telephone Number to Telephone, Golf Locker No. to Golf #, and Swim Locker No. to Swim #.*

10. Center values in the Golf # and Swim # columns.

11. Save and close the report and the database.

Add Aggregate Functions Using Calculated Controls

▶ After a report is designed, you may decide to calculate numeric data. For example, you may want to total the values in a list or calculate the average value. To do so, you can add a calculated control using aggregate functions to the report. An **aggregate function** is used to calculate totals and includes functions such as Sum, Count, Average, or Variance.

▶ As you learned in the Forms lesson, a calculated control uses an expression as its source of data. An expression can use data from a field in an underlying table or from another control on the report. A text box is the most common type of control used to display a calculated value.

▶ To add a calculated control, click the Text Box button in the Controls group of the Report Design Tools Design tab. You can place controls in all sections of a report; however, if you want to total the value of all the records in a report, you must place the control in the report footer section. The text box appears with a label that Access assigns, as shown in Figure 5.25.

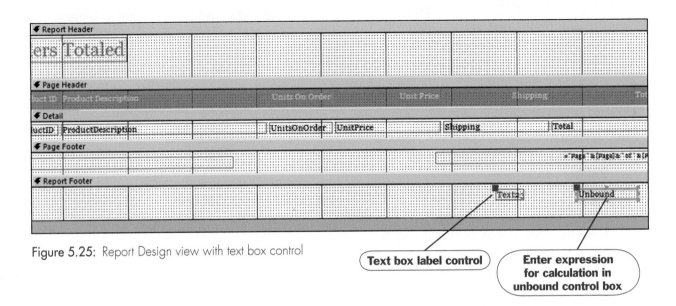

Figure 5.25: Report Design view with text box control

Text box label control

Enter expression for calculation in unbound control box

▶ As you did in Form Design view, to make this field a calculated field, you modify the Control Source, found in the Data tab of the Property Sheet pane, by entering the appropriate expression, as shown in Figure 5.26. Expressions begin with the = operator, as in the expression =Sum([Total]):

• =*Sum( )* is the aggregate function that totals the values in a control.

• *[Total]* represents the field name of the value in the control.

▶ Click Over All in the Running Sum property box to total the entire list. **Over All** displays a running sum of values that accumulate until the end of the report. You use the **Over Group** property to calculate record-by-record or group-by-group totals in a report. A group footer control must be placed in the group footer section.

▶ Close the Property Sheet pane and the expression appears in a calculated control in Design view. Switch to Print Preview to see the results of the calculated control.

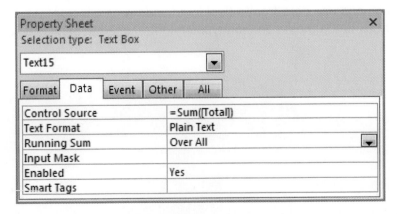

Figure 5.26: Property Sheet pane for text box control

1. Open data file **a5-10** and open the *Orders Totaled* report. *Note the size of the Product Description field and the data in the report.*

2. Switch to Design view and double-click the **report footer section selector**. In the Property Sheet pane, change the height setting to **.5"**. Close the Property Sheet pane.

3. In the Report Design Tools Design tab, in the Controls group, click the **Text Box button**.

4. Click to place the control in the report footer section, at the 8½" position on the horizontal ruler. The text box appears with a label that Access assigns.

5. Right-click the **Unbound text box** and click **Properties**. In the Property Sheet pane, click the **Data tab**, then click **Control Source**.

6. Enter: **=Sum([Total])** in the Control Source property box.

7. Click **Running Sum**, then click the list arrow of the box, and click **Over All**.

8. Close the Property Sheet pane.

9. Right-click the **report tab** and click **Report View**. *Note that the total format does not include a dollar sign and that the text label for the calculated control has been assigned by Access.*

10. Switch to Design view. Do not close the report or the database.

Modify Controls

▶ Every control on a report has properties. These properties determine a control's format, appearance, and behavior. They also detail the attributes of the text or data contained in the control.

▶ You modify the properties of a control in Design view by making changes in the Property Sheet pane. Right-click the control you want to change, and click Properties. The Property Sheet pane appears, as shown in Figure 5.27. To change a caption assigned by Access, in the Caption property, delete the contents of the property box, and enter the new caption. To change the format of a calculated control to Currency, click the Format tab, and in the Format box, select Currency.

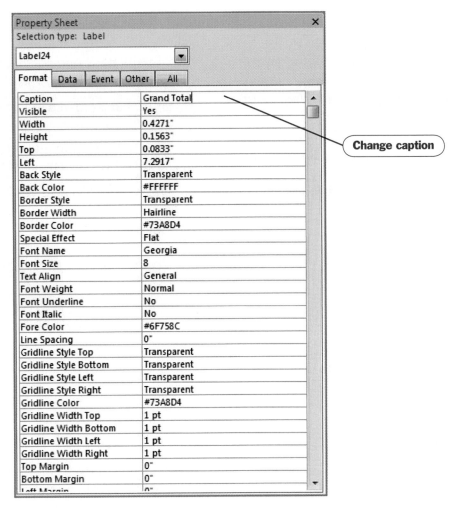

Property Sheet
Selection type: Label

Label24 ▾

| Format | Data | Event | Other | All |

Caption	Grand Total
Visible	Yes
Width	0.4271"
Height	0.1563"
Top	0.0833"
Left	7.2917"
Back Style	Transparent
Back Color	#FFFFFF
Border Style	Transparent
Border Width	Hairline
Border Color	#73A8D4
Special Effect	Flat
Font Name	Georgia
Font Size	8
Text Align	General
Font Weight	Normal
Font Underline	No
Font Italic	No
Fore Color	#6F758C
Line Spacing	0"
Gridline Style Top	Transparent
Gridline Style Bottom	Transparent
Gridline Style Left	Transparent
Gridline Style Right	Transparent
Gridline Color	#73A8D4
Gridline Width Top	1 pt
Gridline Width Bottom	1 pt
Gridline Width Left	1 pt
Gridline Width Right	1 pt
Top Margin	0"
Bottom Margin	0"
Left Margin	0"

Change caption

Figure 5.27: Property Sheet pane for text box control: Label

TRY*it*OUT a5-11

1. Use the open database or open data file **a5-11**. The *Orders Totaled* report should be open in Design view.

2. Right-click the calculated control text box containing the aggregate function, and click **Properties**.

3. In the Property Sheet pane, click the **Format tab**, if necessary and click **Format**. Click the **Format property box list arrow**, and click **Currency**. Close the Property Sheet pane.

4. Right-click the label for the text box, and click **Properties**.

5. In the Property Sheet pane, in the Format tab, click **Caption**. Delete the contents

of the caption box, and enter: **Grand Total**. Close the Property Sheet pane.

6. Switch to Layout view. Expand the size of the Grand Total label box to display the entire caption.

7. Click the right edge of the Product Description field, and make it narrower.

8. Adjust the position of the Unbound control that shows the total so that the right edge of the box aligns with the right edge of the Total field. This may require that the footer control is moved to the left.

9. Save the report and close the database.

REHEARSAL

GOAL
To modify existing reports by adding calculated controls and changing the properties of the report controls and sections

TASK 2

WHAT YOU NEED TO KNOW

▶ There has been significant activity in the office during the past month, and Palmetto Realtors has added new listings to its database and several properties have sold. You have been asked to update the *Listings* table and to delete any sold properties that have closed.

▶ The agents have also requested that "Number of Listings" and "Lowest Listing Price" be added to each City section of the *Weekly Listings Report* in addition to the average price that is already there.

▶ In this Rehearsal activity, you will modify a report and report controls. You will use report sections, and you will add calculated controls to report sections and preview and print the report.

DIRECTIONS

1. Open data file **5r2-Palmetto**.

2. Use the *Listings* form to make the following updates:
   a. ListingID 2 – Sold on 09/01/2010 by Olsen for $140,000.
   b. ListingID 7 – Sold on 09/02/2010 by Dembar for $545,000.
   c. Print a copy of ListingID 3. The sale has closed, and it is no longer available. Switch to the *Listings* table and delete the record.

3. Open the *Weekly Listing Report* in Print Preview and zoom out so that you can view each page of the multiple page report. *Note that there are no page headers for the pages after the first page with a title and the column headers.*

4. Switch to Design view and make the modifications shown in Figure 5.28. Check your modifications in Layout view and move controls so that they align appropriately.
   a. Expand the page header section. Move the title down, and collapse the report header section. Add the company name and increase the font to 12 point. Add column titles using label controls, align as shown, and format for a black background and bold text in white.
   b. In the City footer section, change the label text from Avg to **Average Price**. Add text box controls to calculate Number of Listings (=Count) and Lowest Listing Price (=Min) as shown. Format results appropriately using the Property Sheet pane. Expand and move controls to accommodate the new labels in Layout view. Position controls so that the labels and aggregate function results are visible.

Continued on next page

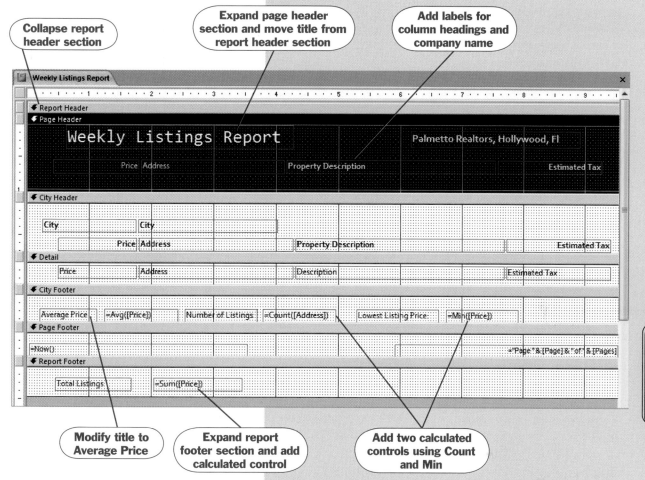

The following callouts appear around the figure:

- **Collapse report header section**
- **Expand page header section and move title from report header section**
- **Add labels for column headings and company name**
- **Modify title to Average Price**
- **Expand report footer section and add calculated control**
- **Add two calculated controls using Count and Min**

Figure 5.28: Design view for *Weekly Listings Report*

c. In Design view, expand the report footer section to include an aggregate function to total all the prices to get a Total Listings value. Format results for currency on the property sheet pane for the control.

5. Switch to Layout view and check that you have the group summary data, the top of page headings, page footers, and the final total at the end of the report.

6. Scroll down to review the average price of homes in each city.

7. Print the report in landscape orientation, close it, and close the database.

Modify Report Format Properties: Height

1. Place mouse pointer on bottom edge of report section.
2. Click and drag the pointer down or up.
   Or
1. Click the **section selector box**.
2. In the Property Sheet pane, click **Height**.
3. Replace contents of Height property box and close the Property Sheet pane.

Add a Control to a Report

1. In Design view, click the **Report Design Tools Design tab**, and in the Controls group, click a control.
2. Click the location for the upper-left corner of the control.
3. Enter label text or modify properties appropriately.

Modify Control Properties

1. If the Property Sheet pane is not open, right-click the control and click **Properties** to open it.
2. Modify the properties as desired:
   - To change label text, modify the Caption property.

- To place a formula in an unbound control, modify the Control Source property.
- To change font size, color, etc., modify Format properties.

Modify a Report in Layout View

1. To move columns: click in the column and drag until vertical bar is in the correct position, then release.
2. To delete columns: right-click in the column, then click **Delete**.
3. To size columns: click the **field column header** and drag right or left edge to resize.

Add an Existing Field to a Report

1. Place cursor in location to the left of the new field location in Layout view.
2. Click the **Report Layout Tools Format tab**, and in the Controls group, click **Add Existing Fields**.
3. In the Field List pane, click **Show all tables** if necessary to show related tables.
4. To view fields of related tables, click the plus sign next to the table name.

5. Double-click the **field name** to add to the report.
6. Close the Field List pane. Resize and move fields and labels as necessary.

Add Calculated Controls to a Report Section

1. In Design view, click the **Report Design Tools Design tab**, and in the Controls group, click the **Text Box button**. `abl`
2. Click the location where you want to place the control.
3. Click the label box and modify the title.
4. Right-click the Unbound control, and, if necessary, click **Properties** to open the Property Sheet pane.
5. In the Property Sheet pane, click the **Data tab**, then click **Control Source** and enter an expression.
6. Close the Property Sheet pane.
7. Switch to Layout view to see the modification.

PERFORMANCE

TASK 2

Expedition Travel Gear has all its employees in the database now and would like a report showing contact data for all employees. They want the list grouped by store and arranged alphabetically by last name within each store grouping.

Expedition

Travel Gear

All reports will continue using the Equity style with the company logo to match the queries and reports prepared earlier.

Follow these guidelines:

1. Open your solution to **5p1-ETG-EMPS** or open data file **5p2-ETG-EMPS**.

2. Use the Report Wizard to create a report using the following fields in the order listed and from the tables as indicated.
   - *Payroll* table: Store
   - *Contact* table: Employee ID, Last, First, Address, City, State, Postal Code, Home Phone
   - Group by Store
   - Sort by Last and then First names in Ascending order
   - Use Outline layout and Landscape orientation
   - Apply the Equity style, and name the report `Contact List by Store`

3. Modify the design of the report in Layout view so that all fields are fully visible by moving and resizing fields as necessary. Be sure that the report does not extend past one page wide, and center the data in the Employee ID column. Add the company logo, **Expedition Travel Gear.tif**. In Design view, expand the page header section to add label controls for column headings for the second page of the report, and format the font color as orange, as shown in Figure 5.29. Make sure that the report and page header sections do not extend beyond the 10" marker on the ruler.

4. Save and print a copy of the report. Close the database.

Contact List by Store

| Last | First | Employee ID | Address | City | State | Postal Code | Home Phone |

Store   Boston

Last	First	Employee ID	Address	City	State	Postal Code	Home Phone
Benson	Tyrone	12	760 Stuart Street	Boston	MA	02116	(617) 555-8154
Nolte	Carol	13	64 Leyden Street	East Boston	MA	02128	(617) 555-7306
Nunez	Maria	15	734 Shawmut Street	Boston	MA	02118	(617) 555-5489
O'Connell	Robert	14	87 Peacevale Road	Dorchester	MA	02124	(617) 555-0376
Wharton	Phyllis	11	912 Greenville Street	Roxbury	MA	02119	(617) 555-1984

Page header section

Store   Chicago

Last	First	Employee ID	Address	City	State	Postal Code	Home Phone
Kingsley	Mary	5	543 South Michigan Avenue	Chicago	IL	60616	(773) 555-6621
Montez	Carlo	1	65 East 5th Street	Chicago	IL	60604	(312) 555-3241
Soto	Linda	3	2398 Barton Drive	Chicago	IL	60604	(312) 555-0685
Vaughn	Tamika	2	321 Lakeview Road	Chicago	IL	60618	(773) 555-8723
Wong	Sam	4	548 Hartland Court	Chicago	IL	60624	(773) 555-1990

Store   Dallas

| Last | First | Employee ID | Address | City | State | Postal Code | Home Phone |

Figure 5.29: *Contact List by Store* report

ENCORE

Act I

The president of Transport Travel Services, Ms. Roslyn Young, has signed a strategic agreement with Clark's Cruise Company. The director of the Leisure Travel Department, Jaime Trainor, has been charged with managing this relationship for the Leisure Travel Department.

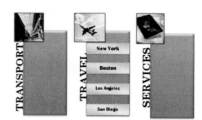

Ms. Trainor anticipates the need for more standard reporting to support pending marketing campaigns and has asked you to create reports that she can provide to Ms. Young on a weekly basis.

Follow these guidelines:

1. Open data file **5ep1-Transport**. The company prefers an Outline layout and the Module style for their reports.

2. Create a report showing all customers grouped by travel preference. The report should contain no more than five fields, but must include last name and state. You need to use data from more than one table. Name the report **Customer Travel Preferences** and print a copy.

3. Make the following modifications in Design view:
   a. Right-click the **Last Name field** in the Detail section, point to **Total**, then click **Count Records**. A Travel Preference Footer is added with a calculated control to count the number in the group. Right-click the **Count control field** in the Travel Preferences footer, and click **Set Caption**. Do the same for the Count control field in the Report footer.
   b. Expand the page header section and move the title of the report into that section. Add a label control to the report header section, and enter **Transport Travel Services**. Format appropriately. Save the design.

4. Prepare a mailing label report, using the Cruise Promotion query for your data. The label product used is an Avery, C2242, English Unit of Measure, and the company font is Calibri, 10 point, Normal weight, color dark navy blue. The label should be addressed to the family, not to a specific person. The labels should be sorted by ZIP code and last name. Name this report **Labels Cruise Promotion**.

5. Close and save the database.

Act II

Craftoy Shoppe created a query earlier, in data file **5ep2-Craftoy**, to calculate the prices of their purchase orders, entitled *Orders Calculations* query. They would now like a report using that query but grouped by supplier and sorted by purchase order number, so that they can get the sum of the total order, the discount, and the net price for the order from that supplier. You need to use the Summary Options function in the Report Wizard for these totals. A sample of the report is shown in Figure 5.30. They use the Technic style and have added their company name to the report header section. Use Layout view to align the totals and data properly.

Craftoy Shoppe

Craftoy Shoppe
Orders Calculations

SupplierName	Beads 'R Us				
Purchase Order Number		Unit Price	Quantity	Total	Less Discount	Net Price
235		$12.00	5	$60.00	$3.00	$57.00

Summary for 'SupplierName' = Beads 'R Us (1 detail record)
Sum

				$60.00	$3.00	$57.00

SupplierName	China Novelties, Inc.				
Purchase Order Number		Unit Price	Quantity	Total	Less Discount	Net Price
240		$5.00	6	$30.00	$6.00	$24.00
240		$5.00	6	$30.00	$6.00	$24.00
240		$2.50	12	$30.00	$6.00	$24.00

Summary for 'SupplierName' = China Novelties, Inc. (3 detail records)
Sum

				$90.00	$18.00	$72.00

SupplierName	Fabric Universe				
Purchase Order Number		Unit Price	Quantity	Total	Less Discount	Net Price
237		$12.00	12	$144.00	$21.60	$122.40
237		$18.00	6	$108.00	$16.20	$91.80

Figure 5.30: Report with group summary options

Act III

Expedition Travel Gear would like you to create a report to assist in payroll preparations.

Expedition

Travel Gear

Follow these guidelines:

1. Open your solution to **5p2- ETG-EMPS** or open data file **5ep3-ETG-EMPS**.

2. Create a *Payroll* report with the following fields: Store, Emp ID, Last(name), First(name), SSNO, Status, Exemptions, Rate, Dues, Other Deductions.
   a. You are to group the data by Store.
   b. Use Summary Options to obtain totals for the Rate, Dues, and Other Deductions fields in the group.
   c. Use Landscape orientation, and the style the company prefers (Equity).
   d. Use Layout view to position data and align totals properly under the columns, including the grand totals.
   e. Add the Birth Date field to the report after SSNO.

3. Save and print the report.

4. Close the database.

PERFORMING WITH POWERPOINT

LESSON 1

PowerPoint Basics

In this lesson, you will be introduced to PowerPoint and its basic features. You will complete the following projects:

✳ Conference presentation
✳ Marketing presentation
✳ Travel tips presentation

Upon completion of this lesson, you will have mastered the following skill sets

✳ Start PowerPoint
✳ Explore the PowerPoint window
✳ Open a presentation
✳ Navigate through a presentation
✳ Close a presentation and exit PowerPoint
✳ Create and save a presentation
✳ Apply slide layouts
✳ Add slides to a presentation
✳ Work with placeholders
✳ Create placeholders
✳ Change presentation views
✳ Run a slide show
✳ Change the orientation and select page setup options
✳ Move, copy, duplicate, and delete slides
✳ Check spelling
✳ Change text alignment and direction

Terms
Software-related
Blank Presentation
Handle
Landscape orientation
Layout
Normal view
Notes Page view
Notes pane
Outline and Slides tab pane
Placeholder
Portrait orientation
Presentation
Rotate
Slide pane
Slide Show view
Slide Sorter view
Text box

GOALS

To explore and navigate the PowerPoint window

To open a presentation and navigate slides as shown in Figure 1.1

* Start PowerPoint
* Explore the PowerPoint window
* Open a presentation
* Navigate through a presentation
* Close a presentation
* Exit PowerPoint

Figure 1.1: Six-slide presentation

WHAT YOU NEED TO KNOW

About PowerPoint

▶ PowerPoint is the **presentation** program within the Microsoft Office 2007 suite that lets you create and save on-screen slide shows, slides for transparencies, and handouts.

▶ The features of PowerPoint allow you to enhance the slides in your presentation with graphics, charts, animation, sound, transitions, and video to create an exciting slide show that supports and complements an oral report. You can even record and time your oral report so that it is delivered automatically when you run the slide show.

▶ PowerPoint also allows you to publish your presentation to the Web so that others can view it.

Start PowerPoint

▶ There are two basic ways to start PowerPoint:

HOW **1.** Click the **Start button** on the taskbar. **2.** Point to **All Programs**. **3.** Click **Microsoft Office**. **4.** Click **Microsoft Office PowerPoint 2007**, as shown in Figure 1.2. Or, **1.** double-click the **PowerPoint program icon** on the desktop, as shown in Figure 1.3.

Figure 1.2: Start PowerPoint from the Start menu

Figure 1.3: Start PowerPoint from desktop

TRY*it*OUT *p1-1*

1. Click the **Start button.**

2. Point to **All Programs**.

3. Click **Microsoft Office**.

4. Click **Microsoft Office PowerPoint 2007**.

Explore the PowerPoint Window

▶ After PowerPoint starts, the PowerPoint window appears, as shown in Figure 1.4. Your window might look different if a previous user changed screen elements or default settings.

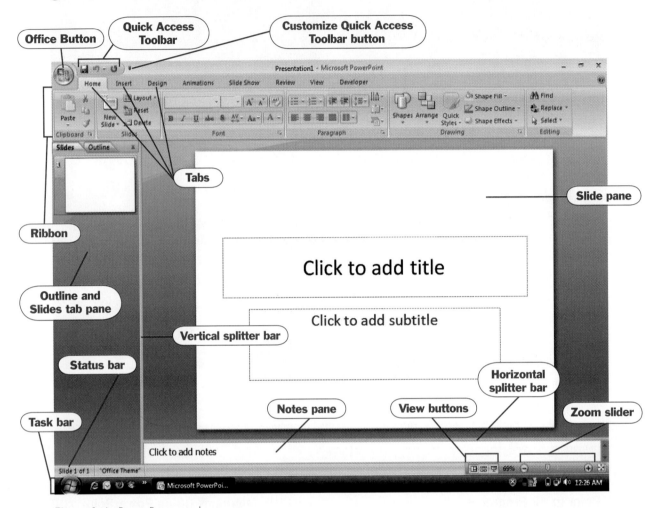

Figure 1.4: PowerPoint window

▶ The main window contains three panes unique to PowerPoint:

1. The **Slide pane** contains the current slide. In a new presentation it contains a new blank slide for you to begin creating a presentation.

2. The **Outline and Slides tab pane** is to the left of the Slide pane and is used to navigate through slides or topics.

3. The **Notes pane** is below the Slide pane and contains additional notes for the speaker that do not show up in the slide presentation.

▶ Parts of the window are described below:

- The **title bar** displays the program and presentation names.

- The **Quick Access toolbar** contains buttons that execute commands commonly used in all Office programs.

- The **Customize Quick Access Toolbar button** allows you to quickly add commands to the Quick Access toolbar, change the position of the toolbar, and hide the Ribbon.

- The **Ribbon** displays buttons to execute commands to accomplish many common Office tasks, such as formatting text, and also contains buttons unique to PowerPoint.

- **Tabs** on the Ribbon organize the commands into categories and divide the commands on each tab into groups.
- The **Rulers** display the horizontal and vertical measurements of a slide and allow you to change margins, text indentations, and tabs. By default, the rulers are not displayed, but you will see them on your screen if someone turned them on.
- The **Slide pane** displays the current slide.
- The **Outline and Slides tab pane** contains the Outline and Slides tabs. When selected, the Slides tab displays miniatures, called thumbnails, of all the slides in a presentation; the Outline tab displays an outline of the text on each slide.
- The **vertical splitter bar** divides the Slide pane from the Outline and Slides tab pane.
- The **horizontal splitter bar** divides the Slide pane from the Notes pane.
- The **Notes pane** allows you to add speaking notes to accompany the current slide.
- The **view buttons** allow you to change presentation views.
- The **Zoom slider** allows you to magnify (zoom in) or reduce (zoom out) the size of the text and items on the screen.
- The **status bar** displays the current slide number and the total number of slides in the presentation (Slide 1 of 1), as well as the name of the current design (Office Theme in this case).
- The **taskbar** displays the Start button, as well as open documents and programs.

▶ You can make the Slide pane larger to display more of the slide by closing or reducing the size of the Outline and Slides tab pane and/or hiding the Ribbon.

HOW To close the Outline and Slides tab pane and the Notes pane, click the **Close button** in the Outline and Slides tab pane.

To reduce the size of the Outline and Slides tab pane and the Notes pane, drag the vertical splitter bar to the left or the horizontal splitter bar down.

To hide the Ribbon, **1.** click the **Customize Quick Access Toolbar button**. **2.** Click **Minimize the Ribbon**. Or, **1.** right-click a tab. **2.** Click **Minimize the Ribbon**. Or, press **[Ctrl]+[F1]**.

T R Y *it* O U T *p1-2*

1. Start PowerPoint, if necessary.

2. Click each tab. *Note that the commands on each tab are divided into groups.*

3. Move the mouse pointer over several of the commands on the Ribbon to display their ScreenTips.

4. To make the slide pane larger:
   a. Move the pointer on top of the vertical splitter pane so that it changes to two vertical lines with double arrows pointing to the left and right. Drag the vertical splitter bar all the way to the left side of the screen.
   b. Move the pointer on top of the horizontal splitter pane so that it changes to two horizontal lines with

   double arrows pointing up and down. Drag the horizontal splitter bar all the way to the bottom of the screen.
   c. Click the **Customize Quick Access Toolbar button**. Click **Minimize the Ribbon** on the menu to hide the Ribbon.

5. Click the **Customize Quick Access Toolbar button**. Click **Minimize the Ribbon** on the menu again to redisplay the Ribbon.

6. Click the **View tab**, and in the **Presentation Views group**, click the **Normal button**. *The Outline and Slides tab pane and the Notes pane reappear.*

Continued on next page

7. On the **View tab**, and in the **Show/Hide group**, click the **Ruler check box**, if necessary, to display the ruler.

8. Click the **Ruler check box** to deselect it. *The check mark is removed and the rulers are no longer visible.*

Open a Presentation

▶ As with other Office applications, presentations can be opened by using the Office menu or clicking a filename in the Recent Documents list.

▶ When you click the **Office Button**, documents you have recently opened appear in the Recent Documents list on the right side of the Office menu, similar to Figure 1.5. You can use the Recent Documents list to open one of the files listed there, or you can use the Open dialog box to find and open any file on your computer.

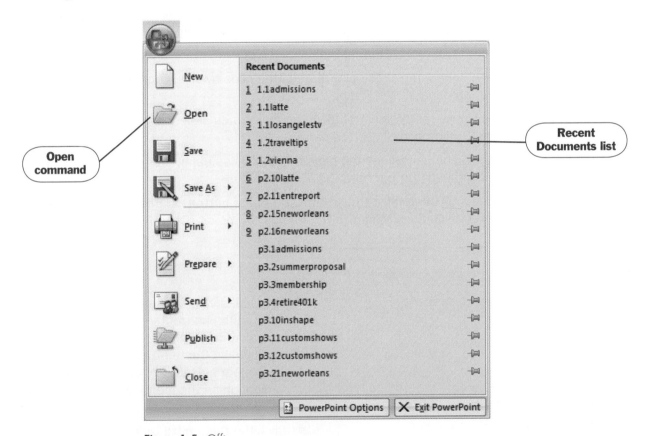

Figure 1.5: Office menu

HOW [Ctrl]+O **1.** Click the **Office Button**. **2.** Click **Open**. **3.** Select the file location in the list in the left pane of the dialog box. **4.** Double-click the folder containing the file. **5.** Click the file. **6.** Click **Open**. Or, **2.** click the filename in the Recent Documents list.

1. Click the **Office Button**.

2. Click **Open**.

3. Select the data file **p1-3**, then click **Open**.

4. Click the **Outline tab** in the Outline and Slides tab pane to view the presentation in Outline view.

5. Click the **Slides tab** in the Outline and Slides tab pane to view the presentation as slides.

6. Do not close the presentation.

Navigate through a Presentation

▶ You can move from slide to slide using several methods.

HOW

- Click the slide thumbnail displayed on the Slides tab, or

- Drag the scroll box in the vertical scroll bar up or down until the desired slide appears. *As you drag the scroll box, a slide label appears, indicating the slide number and slide name, as shown in Figure 1.6, or*

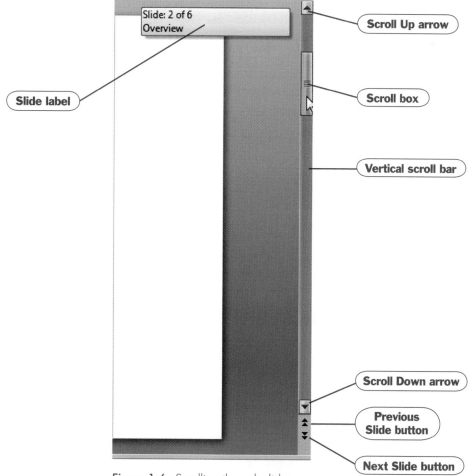

Figure 1.6: Scrolling through slides

- Click above the scroll box in the vertical scroll bar to scroll up one slide or below the scroll box to scroll down one slide, or
- Click the **scroll up arrow** to scroll up one slide or the **scroll down arrow** to scroll down one slide, or
- Click the **Next Slide button** or the **Previous Slide button** at the bottom of the vertical scroll bar. *These buttons appear on the scroll bar when a presentation contains multiple slides.*
- Press **Page Down** to display the next slide or **Page Up** to display the previous slide.

T R Y *it* **O U T** *p1-4*

*Note: The data file **p1-3** presentation should be displayed. If it is not, open the data file **p1-4**.*

1. Click **Slide 3** on the Slides tab to display Slide 3 in the Slide pane.

2. Click below the scroll box in the vertical scroll bar in the Slide pane to display Slide 4 in the Slide pane.

3. Drag the scroll box in the vertical scroll bar up to display Slide 2.

4. Click the **Next Slide button** at the bottom of the vertical scroll bar four

times to display Slides 3 through 6 one at a time.

5. Click the **Previous Slide button** at the bottom of the vertical scroll bar twice to display Slide 5 then Slide 4.

6. Press **Page Down** twice to display Slide 5 then Slide 6.

7. Press **Page Up** once to display Slide 5.

8. Do not close the presentation.

Close a Presentation and Exit PowerPoint

▶ You can close a presentation without exiting PowerPoint.

HOW [Ctrl]+W To close a presentation and leave PowerPoint running, **1.** click the **Office Button**. **2.** Click **Close**. *The presentation closes but the*
PowerPoint program window remains open.

▶ There are two ways to exit PowerPoint.

HOW [Ctrl]+Q or [Alt]+[F4] To exit PowerPoint, click the **Close button** in the upper-right corner of the program window. Or, **1.** click the **Office Button**. **2.** Click **Exit PowerPoint**. *If a presentation is open when you exit PowerPoint, the presentation and PowerPoint close. You will be prompted to save any changes to open presentations before PowerPoint closes them.*

T R Y *it* **O U T** *p1-5*

*Note: The data file **p1-3** should be displayed. If it is not, open the data file **p1-5**.*

1. Click the **Office Button**.

2. Click **Close** to close the presentation but leave PowerPoint open.

3. Click the **Close button** in the upper-right corner of the program window to exit PowerPoint.

REHEARSAL

GOAL
To start PowerPoint, open a presentation as shown in Figure 1.7, navigate through slides, close the presentation, then exit PowerPoint

TASK 1

WHAT YOU NEED TO KNOW

▶ When moving from slide to slide, use the navigation techniques with which you are most comfortable.

▼ DIRECTIONS

1. Start PowerPoint.
2. Open the data file **p1r1-losangelestv**.
3. Click the **Outline tab** in the Outline and Slides tab pane.
4. Widen the **Slide pane**, but do not completely hide the Outline and Slides tab pane.
5. Click the **Slides tab** in the Outline and Slides tab pane.
6. Hide both the **Outline and Slides tab pane** and the **Notes pane**.
7. Redisplay the **Outline and Slides tab pane** and the **Notes pane**.
8. Use any method to display Slide 2 in the Slide pane.
9. Use another method to display Slide 4.
10. Use another method to display Slide 1.
11. Close the file, and leave PowerPoint open.
12. Exit PowerPoint.

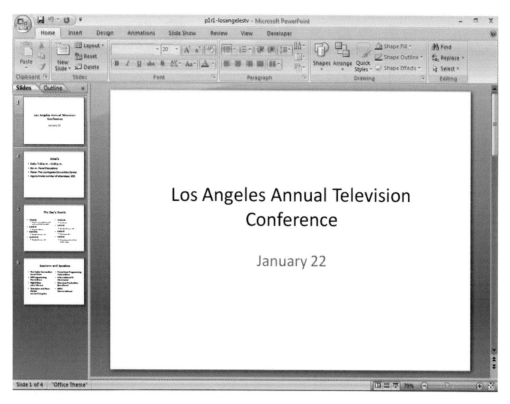

Figure 1.7: Presentation open in PowerPoint

Start PowerPoint
1. Click the **Start button**.
2. Select **All Programs**.
3. Select **Microsoft Office**.
4. Click **Microsoft Office PowerPoint 2007**.
   Or
1. Double-click the **Microsoft PowerPoint icon** on the desktop.

Hide/Show the Outline and Slides Tab Pane
Hide
1. Drag the vertical splitter bar all the way to the left edge of the screen.
   Or
1. Click the **Close button** in the pane.

Show
1. Click the **View tab**, and in the **Presentation Views group**, click the **Normal button**.

Hide/Show the Notes Pane
Hide
1. Drag the horizontal splitter bar all the way to the bottom edge of the screen.

Show
1. Click the **View tab**, and in the Presentation Views group, click the **Normal button**.

Hide/Show the Ribbon
1. Click the **Customize Quick Access Toolbar button**, then click **Minimize the Ribbon**.
   Or
1. Right-click a tab.
2. Click **Minimize the Ribbon**.
   Or
1. Press **[Ctrl]+[F1]**.

Open a Presentation
1. Click the **Office Button**.
2. Click file in Recent Documents list.
   Or
1. Click the **Office Button**.
2. Click **Open**.
3. Click the filename to open.
4. Click **Open**.

Navigate through a Presentation
1. Click the slide thumbnail displayed on the Slides tab.
   Or

1. Drag the vertical scroll box up or down.
   Or
1. Click above the scroll box to move up one slide or below the scroll box to move down one slide.
   Or
1. Click the **scroll up arrow** and the **scroll down arrow** on the scroll bar.
   Or
1. Click the **Next Slide** or the **Previous Slide button** on the scroll bar.
   Or
1. Press **Page Up** or **Page Down**.

Close a Presentation
1. Click the **Office Button**.
2. Click **Close**.

Exit PowerPoint
1. Click the **Close button** in the upper-right corner of the program window.
   Or
1. Click the **Office Button**.
2. Click **Exit PowerPoint**.

TRYOUT

TASK 2

* Create and save a presentation
* Apply slide layouts
* Add slides to a presentation
* Change views
* Run a slide show

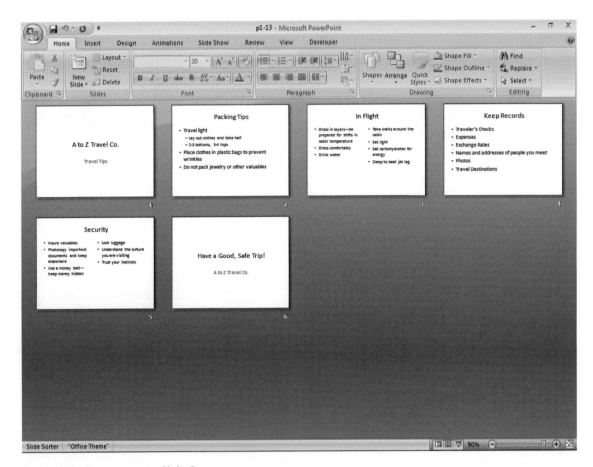

Figure 1.8: Presentation in Slide Sorter view

WHAT YOU NEED TO KNOW

Create and Save a Presentation

▶ The **Blank Presentation** option lets you build your own unique presentation from blank slides that contain standard default formats and layouts using the Office Theme.

▶ PowerPoint opens with a blank slide, as shown in Figure 1.9. Presentation1 appears in the title bar as the presentation name until you provide a filename during the save process.

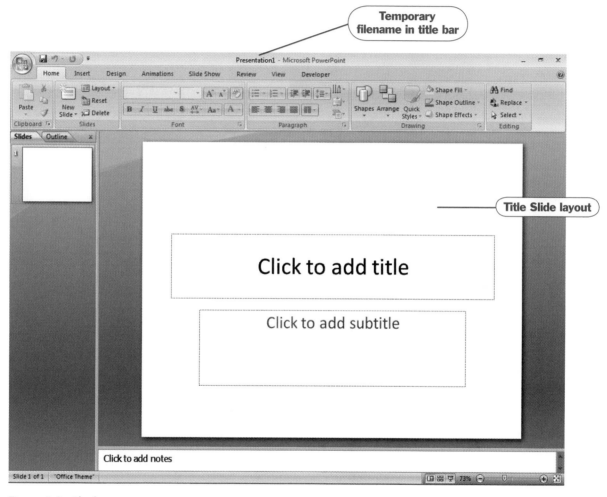

Figure 1.9: Blank presentation

▶ The first slide layout is formatted as a title slide (see Figure 1.9), which is generally the first slide in a presentation.

 To create a new presentation, **1.** click the **Office Button**. **2.** Click **New**. In the New Presentation dialog box that appears, as shown in Figure 1.10, **3.** select the **Blank Presentation icon**, if necessary, then **4.** click **Create**.

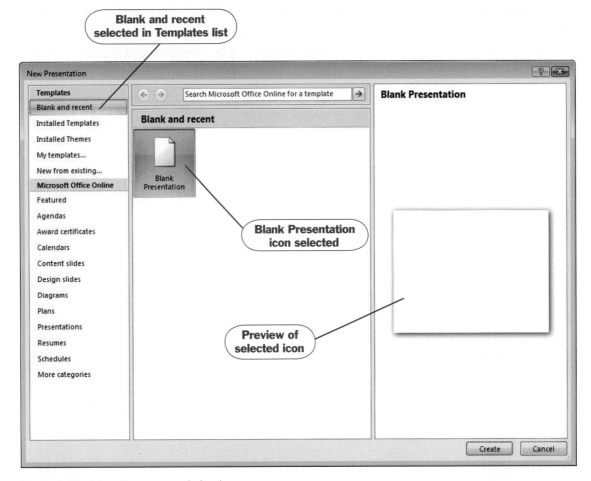

Figure 1.10: New Presentation dialog box

Save a Presentation

▶ You can save a presentation the same way that you save presentations in other Office programs, by using the Save or Save As command.

▶ When you use the Save command, the presentation is saved with the name it currently has. When you use the Save As command, the Save As dialog box opens and you can save the presentation with a new filename.

 To save the presentation with the same name, **1.** click the **Save** **button** on the Quick Access toolbar. Or, **1.** click the **Office Button**. **2.** Click **Save**.

 To save the presentation with a different name, **1.** click the **Office Button**. **2.** Click **Save As**. **3.** Type a filename. **4.** Click **Save**.

1. Start PowerPoint, if necessary. *A blank title slide appears, with Presentation1 indicated on the title bar.*

2. Click the **Save button** on the Quick Access toolbar, which opens the Save As dialog box.

3. Enter **p1-6.***yi* (*yi* = your initials) in the File name box, then click **Save**. *The dialog box closes and the filename you type appears in the title bar at the top of the window.*

4. Click the **Office Button**, then click **New** to open the New Presentation

dialog box. *The Blank Presentation thumbnail is selected by default.*

5. Click **Create**. *Another new presentation opens. Presentation2 is displayed on the title bar.*

6. Click the **Save button** on the Quick Access toolbar, enter **p1-6a.***yi* in the Filename box, then click **Save**.

7. Close all open files.

Apply Slide Layouts

▶ The Layout menu, shown in Figure 1.11, displays thumbnails of nine available slide layouts.

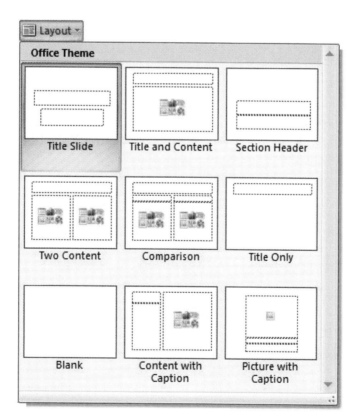

Figure 1.11: Layout menu

▶ A slide **layout** specifies how text or objects are positioned on the slide. The name of each layout appears under each thumbnail (see Figure 1.11).

▶ You can change the layout of the current slide or you can apply the same slide layout to multiple slides.

HOW To change the layout of the current slide, **1.** click the **Home tab**, and in the **Slides group**, click the **Layout button**. **2.** Click a **layout thumbnail**.

HOW To apply the same layout to multiple slides, **1.** select the slides on which to apply the layout (press and hold **[Ctrl]** as you click slides on the Slides tab). **2.** Click the **Home tab**, and in the **Slides group**, click the **Layout button**. **3.** Click a **layout thumbnail**.

TRY*it***OUT** *p1-7*

1. Open the file **p1-6.***yi*, which you created in the previous Try it Out. If this file is not available to you, open the data file **p1-7**. *A blank title slide should be displayed.*

2. On the **Home tab**, and in the **Slides group**, click the **Layout** button.

3. Click the **Title and Content layout**. *The Title and Content layout replaces the Title Slide layout.*

4. Click the **Layout button**, then click the **Title Slide layout**.

5. Do not close the presentation.

Add Slides to a Presentation

▶ You can easily add slides to a presentation. PowerPoint places the new slide immediately after the slide that is displayed or selected at the time you create the new slide.

▶ When you create a new presentation, it includes only one slide, the title slide. The title slide contains a title text placeholder and a subtitle text placeholder.

▶ When you add a new slide, it has the same layout as the current slide. However, if the layout of the current slide is the Title Slide layout, the layout of the new slide is the Title and Content layout, the typical layout for a slide following a title. The Title and Content layout contains a title text placeholder and a content placeholder.

▶ You can, however, change the layout of any slide in a presentation as explained previously. The number of slides is shown on the status bar (see Figure 1.12).

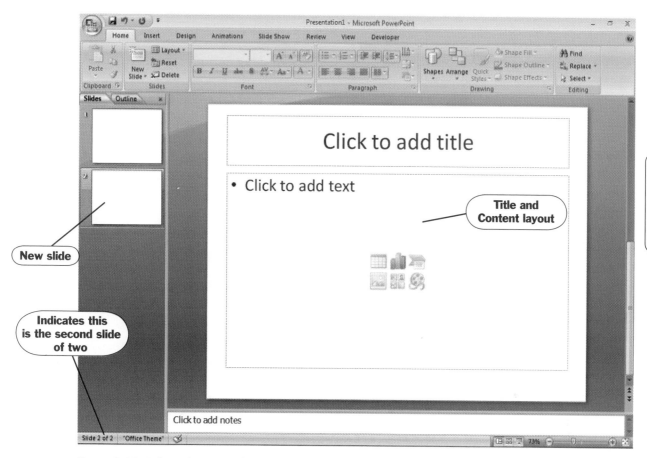

Figure 1.12: Title and Content slide added to presentation

HOW [Ctrl]+M   To add a slide with the default layout, click the **Home tab**, and in the **Slides group**, click the **New Slide button**.

HOW To add a slide and select a layout, **1.** click the **Home tab**, and in the **Slides group**, click the **New Slide list arrow**, which will display the layout thumbnails as shown in Figure 1.13. **2.** Click a **layout thumbnail**.

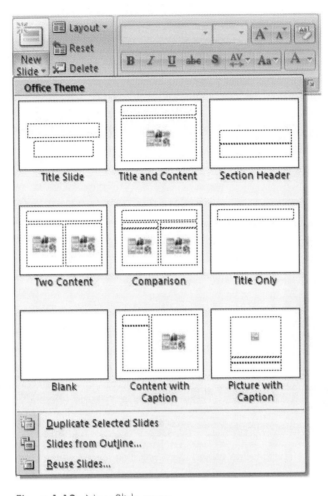

Figure 1.13: New Slide menu

TRY it OUT p1-8

Note: The presentation from the previous Try it Out should be displayed on your screen. If this file is unavailable, open the data file p1-8.

1. On the **Home tab**, and in the **Slides group**, click the **New Slide button** twice to add two new slides (Slides 2 and 3). *Note that these use the Title and Content layout.*

2. On the **Home tab**, and in the **Slides group**, click the **Layout button**, then click the **Two Content** layout thumbnail to change the slide layout of Slide 3.

3. On the **Home tab**, and in the **Slides group**, click the **New Slide button**.

4. Press and hold **[Ctrl]** as you select all the slides in the Slides tab.

5. On the **Home tab**, and in the **Slides group**, click the **Layout button**, then click the **Title Slide** layout thumbnail. *Scroll through the slides. Note that all the slides now have the Title slide layout.*

6. Close the file, but do not save it.

Work with Placeholders

▶ PowerPoint slides contain **placeholders**, which are empty boxes for text or objects on a slide, as shown in Figure 1.14. Each placeholder contains instructions to help you complete the slide. Placeholders are like text boxes, which you learned to use in Word.

Figure 1.14: Selected text placeholder

Add Text to Placeholders

▶ All title placeholders contain the formatting for title text, and all body text placeholders include formatting for subtitles or bulleted lists. You can add text, modify, and format placeholders to create a customized look for your slides.

▶ When you click inside a placeholder, **handles** appear to indicate that it is activated. An activated placeholder is ready for entering text. If you start typing without selecting a placeholder, PowerPoint automatically places the text in the first placeholder of the selected slide.

▶ As you add text to a placeholder, PowerPoint adjusts the size of the text to fit within the space of the placeholder. The first time PowerPoint automatically resizes text, the AutoFit Options button appears on the side of the placeholder. Clicking this button provides you with options to turn the AutoFit feature on or off, as shown in Figure 1.15. If you turn the AutoFit feature off, you will have to resize the placeholder manually to fit the text within it.

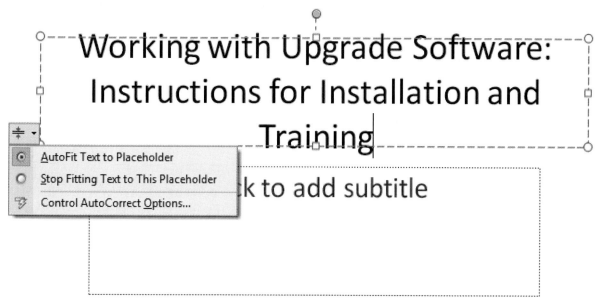

Figure 1.15: AutoFit options menu

HOW To replace a placeholder with text, **1.** click inside the placeholder to activate it. **2.** Enter the new text.

HOW To enter text for a bulleted list, **1.** press **[Enter]** to automatically generate another bullet on a new line. **2.** To create bulleted sublevels, press **[Tab]** or click the **Home tab**, and in the **Paragraph group**, click the **Increase Indent button**. *Different bullet shapes identify each sublevel, as shown in Figure 1.16.* **3.** To return to the previous level, press **[Shift]+[Tab]** or click the **Decrease Indent button**.

> • **Level 1**
>   – **Sublevel 2**
>   • **Sublevel 3**
>   – Sublevel 4
>   » Sublevel 5

Figure 1.16: Bullet levels

T R Y *it* O U T *p1-9*

1. Click the **Office Button**, click **New**, then click **Create**. *The title slide for a new blank presentation is displayed.*

2. Click in the **title placeholder** and enter: `Sales Overview: Developing Strategies for Successful Product Marketing`. *Notice that PowerPoint resizes the text to fit the placeholder and the AutoFit options button displays.*

3. Click in the **subtitle placeholder**, and enter your first and last name.

4. On the **Home tab**, and in the **Slides group**, click the **New Slide button** to create Slide 2. *Note that it is a Title and Content slide.*

5. Click in the **title placeholder** and enter: `Agenda`

6. Click in the **text placeholder**, and enter the following bullet points. Press **[Enter]** after each bullet point.
   - `Market by Market`
   - `New Products`
   - `Launch Dates`
   - `Next Steps`
   - `Conclusion`

7. Click the **New Slide button** to create Slide 3. *Note that it is a Title and Content slide.*

8. On the **Home tab**, and in the **Slides group**, click the **Layout button**, then click the **Two Content layout thumbnail** to change the slide layout.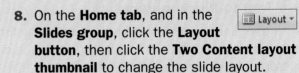

9. Click in the **title placeholder** and enter: `Market by Market`

10. Click in the **left content placeholder**, and enter the following bullet points. Press **[Enter]** after each bullet point.
    - `New York`
    - `Los Angeles`
    - `Chicago`
    - `Philadelphia`

11. Click in the **right content placeholder**, and enter the following bullet points. Press **[Enter]** after each bullet point.
    - `San Francisco`
    - `Dallas`
    - `Atlanta`
    - `Houston`

12. Click the **New Slide button** to create Slide 4. *Note that it is a Two Content slide.*

13. Save the file as **p1-9.*yi*** (*yi* = your initials). Close the file but do not exit PowerPoint.

Edit Placeholders

▶ You can easily move, copy, delete, size, rotate, and format placeholders to create a customized look for your slides. To edit a placeholder, you must first click to select it. A selected placeholder displays handles, which means that the placeholder or object is activated or in Edit mode (see Figure 1.17).

HOW To move a placeholder and its contents, **1.** select the placeholder. **2.** Place the mouse pointer on the border (not on a handle) until the pointer changes to a four-headed arrow. **3.** Press and hold the mouse button while you drag the placeholder to the location you want. *As you drag an object across a slide, a shaded box shows its new location, as shown in Figure 1.17.*

To copy a placeholder, **1.** select the placeholder. **2.** Press and hold **[Ctrl]**. **3.** Drag the placeholder to the new location.

Figure 1.17: Moving a placeholder

Shaded box shows movement

To delete a placeholder, **1.** select the text placeholder to display its handles. **2.** Click on a border (not on a handle). **3.** Press **[Delete]**. **4.** If the text placeholder contains text, repeat these steps to delete the placeholder itself.

To size a placeholder by dragging, drag a top- or bottom-middle handle to change the height, as shown in Figure 1.18 or drag a left- or right-middle handle to change the width or drag a corner handle to size the placeholder proportionally. *The text within the placeholder will adjust to its new borders.*

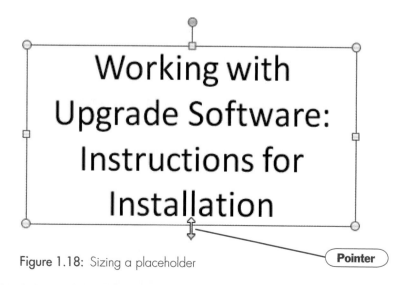

Figure 1.18: Sizing a placeholder

Pointer

To size the placeholder by a specific amount, **1.** select the placeholder. **2.** Drag a sizing handle. Or, **1.** select a placeholder. **2.** Click the **Drawing Tools, Format tab** as shown in Figure 1.19. **3.** In the **Size group**, select the measurement in the Shape Height or Shape Width box. **4.** Enter a new measurement. **5.** Press **[Enter]**.

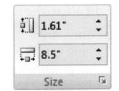

Rotate Placeholders

▶ You can **rotate** a placeholder in 90-degree increments by using the **Rotate button** in the Arrange group on the Drawing Tools, Format tab, as shown in Figure 1.20, or you can use the Free Rotate tool to rotate the box to any angle. If you choose the Free Rotate option, you can drag the green rotation handle on the placeholder, as indicated in Figure 1.20.

Figure 1.19: Size group on the Drawing Tools, Format tab

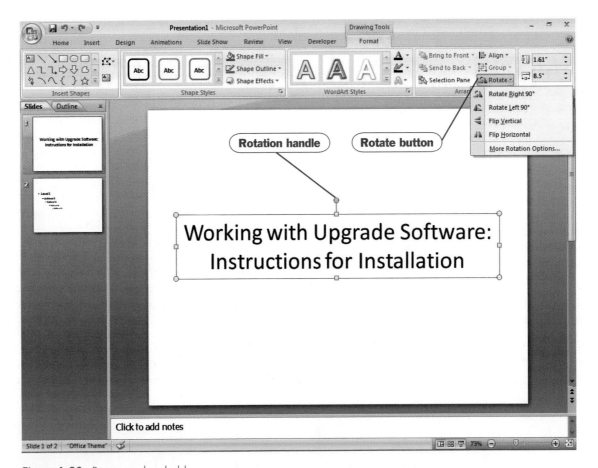

Figure 1.20: Rotate a placeholder

HOW **1.** Select the placeholder. **2.** Click the **Drawing Tools, Format tab**. **3.** In the **Arrange group**, click the **Rotate button**. **4.** Click a command on the menu. Or, **2.** click on the **green rotation handle**, but do not release the mouse button. **3.** Drag the **rotation handle** in the direction you want to rotate. **4.** Release the mouse button when the placeholder is rotated to the position you want.

1. Click the **Office Button**, click **New**, then click **Create**. *The title slide for a new blank presentation is displayed.*

2. Click in the **title placeholder** and enter: Palmetto Realty

3. Click in the **subtitle placeholder** and enter:

   450 Flora Boulevard
   Hollywood, FL
   30025

4. To modify the placeholders as shown below, do the following:

   a. Select the subtitle placeholder, then click the **Drawing Tools**, **Format tab**.

   b. In the **Size group**, click in the **Shape Height box** and enter **2**, click in the **Shape Width box** and enter **2**, then press **[Enter]**.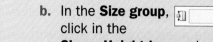

   c. Drag the resized placeholder to the top-right corner as shown.

   d. Select the title placeholder.

   e. On the **Drawing Tools**, **Format tab**, and in the **Arrange group**, click the **Rotate button**, then click **Rotate Left 90°**.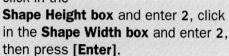

   f. Drag the handles to size the placeholder to fit the height of the slide, then drag it to the left of the slide as shown.

5. Do not close the file.

450 Flora Boulevard
Hollywood, FL
30025

Palmetto Realtors

POWERPOINT

Create Placeholders

▶ To add text to a slide in a location other than in a given placeholder, you can create a text box. A **text box** serves as a text placeholder, allowing you to insert text anywhere on a slide.

▶ After you create a text box, it appears with sizing handles and a green rotation handle (see Figure 1.20).

▶ If the text box is not located were you want or is not at the size or angle you want, you can move, resize, or rotate it.

▶ You can create text boxes only in Normal view.

HOW **1.** Click the **Insert tab**, and in the **Text group**, click the **Text Box button**. **2.** Click and drag the mouse diagonally on the slide to create the required box size. **3.** Release the mouse button. **4.** Enter new text.

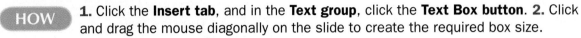

TRY *it* **OUT** *p1-11*

Note: The presentation from the previous Try it Out should be displayed on your screen. If this file is unavailable, open the data file **p1-11**

1. Click the **Insert tab**, and in the **Text group**, click the **Text Box button**.

2. Click and drag the mouse to draw a text box approximately 4½" wide in a blank area of the slide.

3. Enter **Finest Properties for Over 50 Years!**

4. Rotate and resize the box, and place it as shown.

5. Do not close the file.

450 Flora Boulevard Hollywood, FL

30025

Palmetto Realtors

Finest Properties for Over 50 Years!

Format a Placeholder

▶ You can format placeholders to create interesting effects, as shown in Figure 1.21.

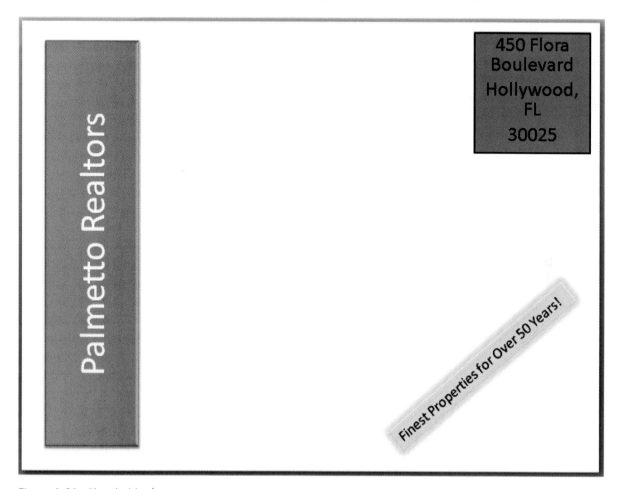

Figure 1.21: Placeholder format options

▶ You can add colorful border lines around the placeholder and fill the box with a color or pattern using buttons in the Shape Styles group on the Drawing Tools, Format tab, as shown in Figure 1.22. You can also add special effects, such as shadows, a glow, and a 3-D effect (with or without the border line). You can also use the Format Shape dialog box, as shown in Figure 1.23.

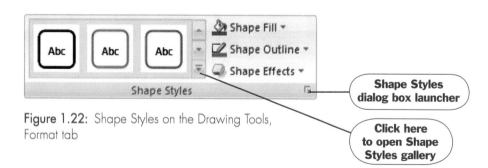

Figure 1.22: Shape Styles on the Drawing Tools, Format tab

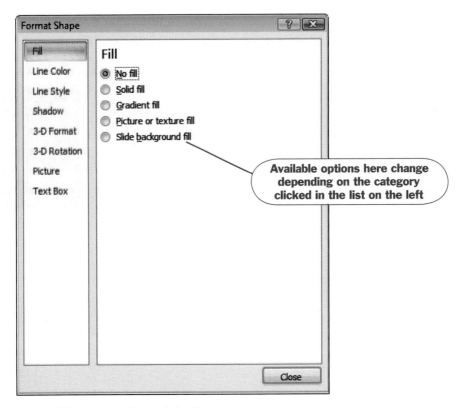

Figure 1.23: Format Shape dialog box

HOW To quickly format a placeholder, **1.** select the placeholder. **2.** Click the **Drawing Tools**, **Format tab**, and in the Shape Styles gallery shown in Figure 1.24, **3.** select a style. Or, **3.** in the Shape Styles group, click the **Shape Fill**, **Shape Outline**, or **Shape Effects button list arrow**. **4.** Make selections on the galleries that appear.

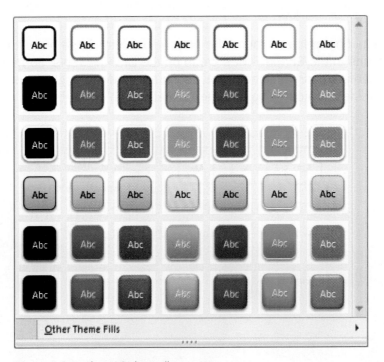

Figure 1.24: Shape Styles gallery

To format a placeholder using the Format Shape dialog box, **1.** select the placeholder. **2.** Click the **Shapes Styles dialog box launcher** to display the Format Shape dialog box shown in Figure 1.23. *As you click each category in the list on the left, different options appear in the pane on the right side of the dialog box. The bottom of the right side of the dialog box also changes as you select options at the top to allow you to customize the text box.* **3.** Make selections in the dialog box. **4.** Click **Close**.

▶ You can also format placeholder text using the buttons in the Font group on the Home tab.

T R Y *i t* O U T *p1-12*

Note: The presentation from the previous Try it Out should be displayed on your screen. If this file is unavailable, open the data file p1-12.

Refer to Figure 1.21 for this Try it Out.

1. Click in the text box that contains the words *Palmetto Realtors*, then click the **Drawing Tools**, **Format tab**.

2. In the **Shape Styles group**, click the **Shape Styles More button** (refer to Figure 1.22). The Shape Styles gallery opens (see Figure 1.24).

3. Click the last style in the last column (the ScreenTip identifies this as the Intense Effect - Accent 6). *The text box is formatted with an orange fill that gets darker from left to right, a shadow, and a bevel effect. In addition, the text is now white.*

4. Click in the box that contains the address. Format it as follows:
   a. In the **Shape Styles group**, click the **Shape Fill button list arrow**, then click the green square located second to the bottom in the green column in the Theme Colors section (the ScreenTip

identifies this as Olive Green, Accent 3, Darker 25%).
   b. In the **Shape Styles group**, click the **Shape Outline button list arrow**, then click the black square in the top row (the ScreenTip identifies this as Black, Text 1).
   c. In the **Shape Styles group**, click the **Shape Outline button list arrow** again, point to **Weight**, then click **2¼ pt**.

5. Click in the box that contains the text *Finest Properties for Over 50 Years!*
   a. In the Shape Styles group, click the **Shape Fill button list arrow**, then click the yellow square under Standard Colors.
   b. In the **Shape Styles group**, click the **Shape Effects button**, point to **Glow**, then click third glow style in the green column (the ScreenTip identifies this as Accent color 3, 11 pt glow).

6. Save the file as **p1-12.***yi* (*yi* = your initials), then close the file.

Change Presentation Views

▶ PowerPoint lets you view your presentation in several different ways. The three most frequently used views are the Normal, Slide Sorter, and Slide Show views.

- **Normal view**, the default, displays three panes: the Slide pane, the Outline and Slides tab pane, and the Notes pane, as shown in Figure 1.25. Use this view to enter and edit text on a slide.

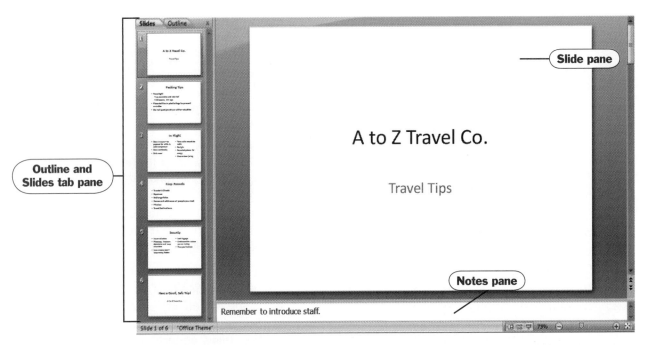

Figure 1.25: Normal view

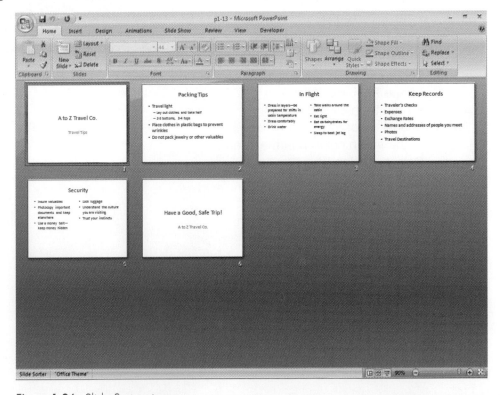

Figure 1.26: Slide Sorter view

- **Slide Sorter view** displays slides as thumbnails so that you can see the flow of the presentation, as shown in Figure 1.26. Use this view to move, copy, and delete slides. (Moving, copying, and deleting slides are explored in Lesson 2.) Double-clicking a slide displays that slide in Normal view.
- **Slide Show view** lets you see your slides as an on-screen presentation.
- In addition, **Notes Page view** lets you see your notes underneath each slide, as shown in Figure 1.27.

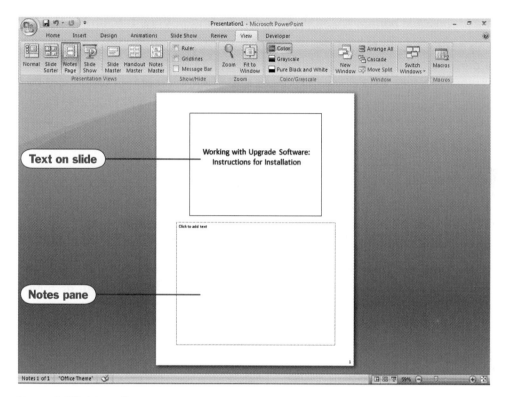

Figure 1.27: Notes Page view

▶ You can change from one view to another by clicking a view button in the status bar to the left of the Zoom slider, as shown in Figure 1.28, or by clicking a button in the Presentation Views group on the View tab.

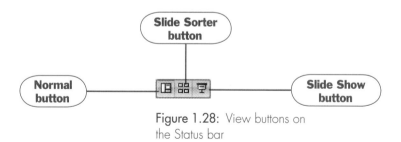

Figure 1.28: View buttons on the Status bar

HOW To change views, click the appropriate view button at the bottom left of the screen. Or, **1.** click the **View tab**. **2.** Click a button in the **Presentation Views group**.

1. Open the data file **p1-13**.

2. Click the **Slide Sorter button** in the status bar.

3. Double-click **Slide 2** to return to Normal view. *Slide 2, the slide you double-clicked, appears in the Slide pane.*

4. Click the **Slide Show button** in the status bar. *The slide show starts from the current slide, and Slide 2 fills the screen.*

5. Press **[Escape]** to end the slide show and return to Normal view.

6. Click the **View tab**, and in the **Presentation Views group**, click the **Notes Page button**.

7. On the **View tab**, and in the **Presentation Views group**, click the **Normal button**.

8. Close the presentation, but do not save it.

Run a Slide Show

▶ When you run a slide show, each slide fills the entire screen without showing the Ribbon or the status bar.

▶ You can start a slide show in several ways.

HOW [F5] Click the **Slide Show button** on the status bar. Or, click the **View tab**, and in the **Presentation Views group**, click the **Slide Show button**, as shown in Figure 1.29. Or, click the **Slide Show tab**, and in the **Start Slide Show group**, click the **From Beginning button** or the **From Current Slide button**. See *Figure 1.30*.

Figure 1.29: Presentation Views group on the View tab

Figure 1.30: Start Slide Show group on the Slide Show tab

▶ You can navigate through a slide show using any of several techniques.

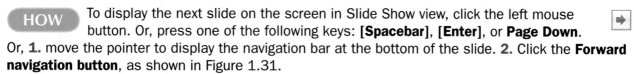 To display the next slide on the screen in Slide Show view, click the left mouse button. Or, press one of the following keys: **[Spacebar]**, **[Enter]**, or **Page Down**. Or, **1.** move the pointer to display the navigation bar at the bottom of the slide. **2.** Click the **Forward navigation button**, as shown in Figure 1.31.

To display the previous slide on the screen, press **Page Up**. Or, **1.** move the pointer to display the navigation bar at the bottom of the slide. **2.** Click the **Back navigation button**, as shown in Figure 1.31.

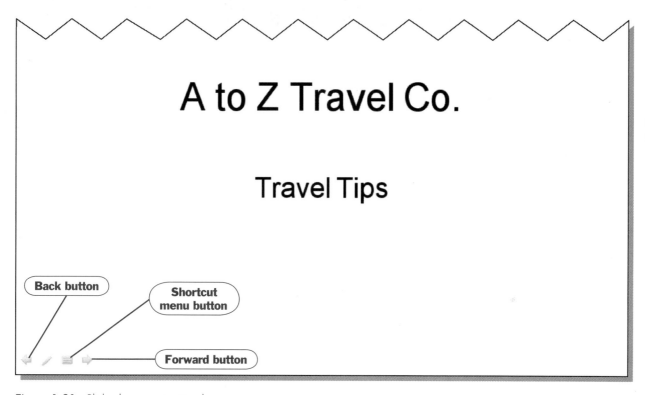

Figure 1.31: Slide show navigation bar

▶ The navigation bar appears only when the mouse is moved.

▶ You can also go to a specific slide during a slide show.

HOW **1.** Move the pointer to display the navigation bar at the bottom of the slide. **2.** Click the **Shortcut menu button**, as shown in Figure 1.31. **3.** Point to **Go to Slide** on the menu. **4.** Click the slide you want to display. Or, **1.** right-click anywhere on the slide. **2.** Point to **Go to Slide** on the menu. **3.** Click the slide you want to display, as shown in Figure 1.32.

Figure 1.32: Slide show shortcut menu

▶ You can end a slide show at any time.

HOW To end a slide show, press **[Escape]**.

TRY _it_ OUT _p1-14_

1. Open the data file **p1-14**.

2. Click the **Slide Show button** on the status bar.

3. Click the **left mouse button** to advance one slide.

4. Move the mouse to the lower left of the slide, then click the **Shortcut menu button** on the slide. Click **Go to Slide**, then click **3 Academic Program**.

5. Press **[Escape]** to end the slide show before it is finished and display the current slide, Slide 3.

6. Click the **View tab**, and in the **Presentation Views group**, click the **Slide Show button**.

7. Press **[Spacebar]** to advance one slide to Slide 2.

8. Press **[Enter]** to advance one slide to Slide 3.

9. Right-click anywhere on the slide. Click **Go to Slide** on the shortcut menu, then click **2 The School**.

10. Press **[Escape]** to end the slide show before it is finished and display the current slide, Slide 2.

Continued on next page

11. Click the **Slide Show tab**, and in the **Start Slide Show group**, click the **From Current Slide button**. *The slide show starts and displays Slide 2.*

displays on the screen identifying the end of the slide show. Press **Page Down** once more. *Slide Show view closes and Slide 2 appears again in Normal view.*

12. Press Page Down three times to advance to the end of the slide show. *A black slide*

13. Close the presentation but do not save it.

POWERPOINT

REHEARSAL

TASK 2

 GOAL
To create and save a presentation, apply slide layouts, add slides to a presentation, and work with placeholders to create a presentation as shown in Figure 1.33, then run the slide show

WHAT YOU NEED TO KNOW

▶ Marketing strategies are well-thought-out plans to sell or promote a product, company, or service.

▶ In this rehearsal activity, you will create an informative presentation about the programs available for students at the Fieldstone Zoo.

▼ DIRECTIONS

1. Start PowerPoint.

2. Add content to Slide 1 as follows:
   a. Enter the title and subtitle as shown in Figure 1.33.
   b. Draw a text box in a blank area of the slide, then enter the text **Open weekends until 8:00 all summer!**
   c. Rotate and reposition the text box in the upper-left corner of the slide, as shown in Figure 1.33.

3. Format the placeholders on Slide 1 as follows:
   a. Format the placeholder text box you created by using a Shape Style to match Figure 1.33.
   b. Fill both the title and subtitle placeholders with the lightest green color in the Theme Colors section.
   c. Add a 6-point green outline to the title placeholder using the darkest green color in the Theme Colors section.
   d. Add a shadow effect to the subtitle placeholder, as shown in Figure 1.33, then add the 50-point soft edge effect.

4. Add Slides 2 through 6.
   a. Slides 2, 3, and 5 use the Title and Content layout.
   b. Slide 4 uses the Two Content layout.
   c. Slide 6 uses the Title Slide layout.

5. Enter the slide content for Slides 2 through 6, as shown in Figure 1.33.

6. In Slide 6:
   a. Size the subtitle placeholder so that it is two inches high and four inches wide.
   b. Copy the title text placeholder, then rotate both title text placeholders as shown.
   c. Reposition both copies of the title text placeholder so the text appears as shown.

Continued on next page

7. Switch to Slide Sorter view.

8. Save the presentation as **p1r2-zoo**.

9. Run the slide show starting from Slide 1.

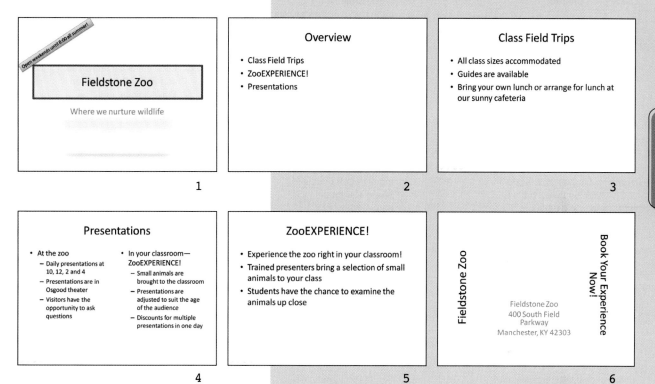

Figure 1.33: Zoo presentation

Create a Presentation

1. Click the **Office Button**.
2. Click **New**.
3. Click **Create**.

Save a Presentation

1. Click the **Save button** on the Quick Access toolbar.
   Or
1. Click the **Office Button**.
2. Click **Save**.
   Or
1. Click the **Office Button**.
2. Click **Save As**.
3. Type a filename.
4. Click **Save**.

Apply a Layout to a Slide

1. Click the **Home tab**, and in the **Slides group**, click the **Layout button**.
2. Click a layout thumbnail.

Apply a Layout to Multiple Slides

1. Press and hold **[Ctrl]**.
2. Click the slides on the Slides tab in the Outline and Slides tab pane to which you want to apply the layout.
3. Click the **Home tab**, and in the **Slides group**, click the **Layout button**.
4. Click a layout thumbnail.

Add Slides to a Presentation

1. Click the **Home tab**, and in the **Slides group**, click the **New Slide button**.
   Or
1. Click the **Home tab**, and in the **Slides group**, click the **New Slide button list arrow**.
2. Click a layout thumbnail.

Edit Placeholders

Move a Placeholder

1. Select the placeholder.
2. Place the mouse pointer on the border until the pointer changes to a four-headed arrow.
3. Click and hold the mouse button while you drag the placeholder to the location you want.

Copy a Placeholder

1. Select the placeholder.
2. Press and hold **[Ctrl]**.
3. Drag the placeholder to the new location.

Delete a Placeholder

1. Select the placeholder.
2. Click on a border.
3. Press **[Delete]**.
4. If the text placeholder contained text, repeat these steps to delete the placeholder itself.

Change the Size of a Placeholder

1. Select the placeholder.
2. Drag a sizing handle.
   Or
1. Select the placeholder.
2. Click the Drawing Tools, Format tab.
3. In the **Size group**, select the measurement in the **Shape Height** or **Shape Width box**.

4. Enter a new measurement.
5. Press **[Enter]**.

Rotate a Placeholder

1. Select the placeholder.
2. Click the Drawing Tools, Format tab.
3. In the **Arrange group**, click the **Rotate button**.

4. Click a command on the menu.
   Or
1. Select the placeholder.
2. Click on the green **rotation handle**, but do not release the mouse button.
3. Drag the **rotation handle** in the direction you want to rotate.
4. Release the mouse button when the placeholder is rotated to the position you want.

Change Views

1. Click the desired view button in the status bar:
   - Normal
   - Slide Sorter
   - Slide Show
   Or
1. Click the **View tab**, and in the **Presentation Views group**, click a view button.

Run a Slide Show from the Current Slide

Run a Slide Show from Slide 1

1. Click the **View tab**, and in the **Presentation Views group**, click the **Slide Show button**.
   Or
1. Click the **Slide Show tab**, and in the **Presentation Views group**, click the **From Beginning button**.

Run a Slide Show from the Current Slide

1. Click the **Slide Show button** on the status bar.
   Or
1. Click the **Slide Show tab**, and in the **Presentation Views group**, click the **From Current Slide button**.

Advance through a Slide Show

1. Click the left mouse button.
   Or
1. Press the **[Spacebar]**.
   Or
1. Press **[Enter]**.
   Or
1. Press Page Up or Page Down.
   Or
1. Move the pointer to display the navigation bar.
2. Click the **Forward** or **Back navigation button**.
   Or
1. Move the pointer to display the navigation bar.
2. Click the **Shortcut menu button**.
3. Point to **Go to Slide**.
4. Click the slide you want to display.
   Or
1. Right-click anywhere on the slide.
2. Point to **Go to Slide**.
3. Click the slide you want to display.

PERFORMANCE

TASK 2

BodyWorksFitnessCenters asked you to create a presentation as shown in Figure 1.34 that explains to the sales staff the marketing strategies that they will use to launch the opening of a new fitness center.

Follow these guidelines:

1. Start PowerPoint.

2. Add content to Slide 1 as follows:
   a. Enter the title **BodyWorksFitnessCenters**, and subtitle **Marketing Strategies**, as shown in Figure 1.34.
   b. Draw a text box in a blank area of the slide, then enter the text **Let us help you find the healthy you!**
   c. Rotate and reposition the text box in the lower-left corner of the slide as shown in Figure 1.34.

3. Format the placeholders on Slide 1 as follows:
   a. Format the placeholder text box you created using a Shape Style to match Figure 1.34.
   b. Fill the title placeholder with the lightest purple color in the Theme Colors section.
   c. Add the Cool Slant bevel effect to the title placeholder.
   d. Add a reflection effect to the title placeholder as shown in Figure 1.34.
   e. Reposition the subtitle placeholder as shown in Figure 1.34.

4. Add Slides 2 through 6.
   a. Slides 2, 3, 5, and 6 use the Title and Content layout.
   b. Slide 4 uses the Two Content layout.

5. Enter the slide content for Slides 2 through 6, as shown in Figure 1.34.

6. In Slide 6:
   a. Add a text box at the bottom of the slide with the text shown in Figure 1.34.
   b. Add a 4½-point dark purple outline to the text box.
   c. Add a shadow effect, using the Offset Bottom style from the Outer section in the Shadow submenu.

7. View the presentation in Slide Sorter view.

8. Save the presentation as **p1p2-bwstrategy**.

9. Run the slide show.

10. Close all files.

Slide 1

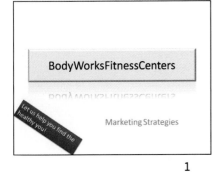

BodyWorksFitnessCenters

Let us help you find the healthy you!

Marketing Strategies

1

Slide 2

Overview

- Marketing Goals
- Current Promotions/Publicity
- Other Marketing Ideas
- Next Steps

2

Slide 3

Marketing Goals

- Image
  - Hip
  - Cutting-edge classes and equipment
  - Not just a place to work out
- Acquire new members
  - Those without existing gym memberships
  - Those who are members at other gyms
- Garner as much publicity as possible
- Attain strong promotional partners

3

Slide 4

Current Promotions/Publicity

- Running ads in several local newspapers and magazines
- Feature in
  - "US Health" magazine
  - "Get Fit" magazine
- Promotion with JUMP workout wear
- Limited time 2-for-1 membership incentive
- WNEW feature News segment on "What's New in New York"

4

Slide 5

Other Marketing Ideas

- Food product cross-promotion
  - Protein bars
  - Bottled water
  - Other health foods
- More health/news magazine features
- New membership incentives
  - Free dumbbells with membership
  - Seasonal promotions
- Local online advertising

5

Slide 6

Next Steps...

- Prep sales staff for opening day
- Meet with potential promotional partners
- Create premium items for giveaways
- Preliminary plans for launch party

HAVE A GREAT DAY!

6

Figure 1.34: Marketing presentation

TRYOUT

TASK 3

GOAL
To edit slide content and slides to create a presentation, as shown in Figure 1.35

* Change the orientation and select Page Setup options
* Move, copy, duplicate, and delete slides
* Check spelling
* Change text alignment and orientation

POWERPOINT

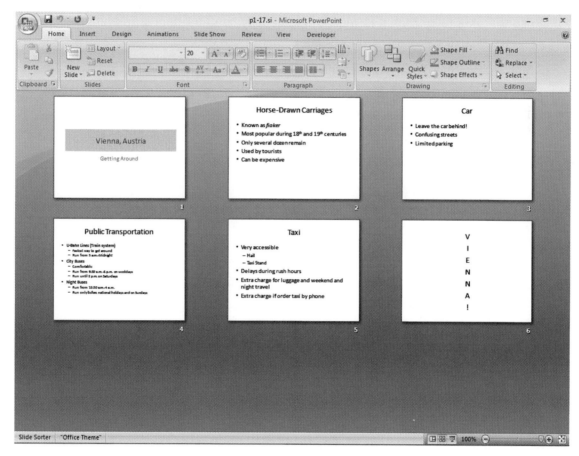

Figure 1.35: Six-slide presentation

WHAT YOU NEED TO KNOW

Change the Orientation and Select Page Setup Options

▶ Before creating a presentation, you must think about how you will deliver it. You can deliver a presentation as an on-screen slide show, over the Internet, or using overhead transparencies.

▶ The delivery method you choose will determine the output format. It may also require that you get additional viewing equipment.

▶ You can set the orientation of your slides, handouts, notes pages, and/or outline (handouts, notes pages and outlines will be covered in a later lesson). **Landscape orientation** positions the page so that it is wider than it is tall and is usually used for slides. **Portrait orientation** positions the page so that it is taller than it is wide and is usually used for handouts and notes pages.

▶ The default orientation for slides is landscape.

▶ You can also change the dimensions of the page.

HOW To change the orientation, **1.** click the **Design tab**. **2.** In the **Page Setup group**, click the **Slide Orientation button**, as shown in Figure 1.36. **3.** Click **Portrait** or **Landscape** from the menu. Or, **2.** in the **Page Setup group**, click the **Page Setup button**. In the Page Setup dialog box that opens as shown in Figure 1.37, **3.** click **Portrait** or **Landscape**. **4.** Click **OK**.

Figure 1.36: Slide Orientation menu

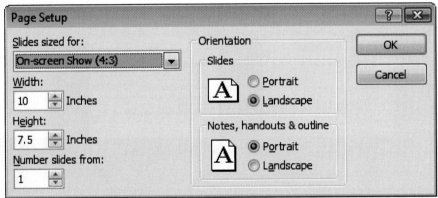

Figure 1.37: Page setup dialog box

HOW To change the dimensions of a page, **1.** click the **Design tab**, and in the **Page Setup group**, click the **Page Setup button**. In the Page Setup dialog box that opens (see Figure 1.37), **2.** click the **Slides sized for list arrow**. **3.** Click the desired size. **4.** Click **OK**.

T R Y *i t* **O U T** *p1-15*

1. Open the data file **p1-15**.

2. Click the **Design tab**.

3. In the **Page Setup group**, click the **Slide Orientation button**, then click **Portrait**. *The slide in the Slide pane changes to portrait orientation.*

4. On the **Design tab**, in the **Page Setup group**, click the **Page Setup button**.

5. Click the **Slides sized for list arrow**, then click **On-screen Show (16:9)**. *(This is the setting for wide-screen monitors.)*

Continued on next page

Note that the width and height measurements change in the dialog box.

6. Click the **Landscape option button** in the Slides section of the dialog box. *Note that the width and height measurements in the dialog box switch.*

7. Click **OK**. *The slide in the Slide pane resizes to the new dimensions and changes back to landscape orientation.*

8. Click the **Page Setup button**. Click the **Slides sized for list arrow**, scroll up, then click **On-screen Show (4:3)**. Click **OK**. *The slide in the Slide pane is resized to its original dimensions.*

9. Do not close the file.

Move, Copy, Duplicate, and Delete Slides

▶ You can move, copy, or delete slides in Slide Sorter view, or on the Outline tab or the Slides tab in the Outline and Slides tab pane. It is easiest and most efficient, however, to perform these tasks in Slide Sorter view because PowerPoint displays all slides as thumbnails and you can easily see the flow of the presentation as you move, copy, or delete slides.

▶ In Slide Sorter view, first you need to select the slide you want to move, copy, or delete. An orange border outlines the selected slide, as shown in Figure 1.38. To select multiple slides to move, copy, or delete as a group, press and hold [Ctrl] and click each slide you want to include.

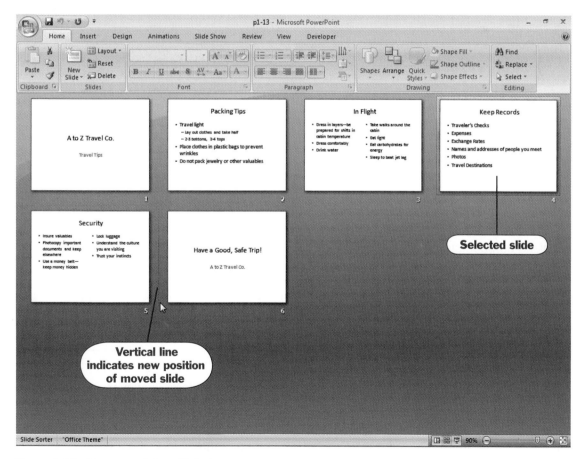

Figure 1.38: Moving a slide in Slide Sorter view

HOW To select slides, **1.** switch to Slide Sorter view. **2.** Click a slide. Or, **2.** press and hold **[Ctrl]**. **3.** Click multiple slides.

To move a selected slide, **1.** drag it to a new location. *When you move the slide, the mouse pointer arrow adds a slide icon and a vertical bar identifies the new position of the slide, as shown in Figure 1.38.* **2.** When the bar appears in the position where you want to place the slide, release the mouse button.

To copy a selected slide, press and hold **[Ctrl]**, as you drag the slide to its new location. *When you copy the slide, the mouse pointer arrow adds a slide icon with a plus sign [+].* Or, **1.** click the **Home tab**, and in the **Slides group**, click the **New Slide list arrow**. **2.** Click **Duplicate Selected Slides**. *PowerPoint inserts the duplicate slide or slides immediately after the selected slides.*

To delete a slide, **1.** click the **Home tab**, and in the **Slides group**, **2.** click the **Delete button**. Or, **1.** right-click the selected slide. **2.** Click **Delete Slide** on the shortcut menu.

▶ If you move, copy, or delete a slide then change your mind, use the Undo command to reverse the action.

T R Y *it* O U T *p1-16*

*Note: The presentation from the previous Try it Out should be displayed on your screen. If this file is unavailable, open the data file **p1-16**.*

1. Click the **Slide Sorter button** on the status bar.

2. Click **Slide 5** ("Bicycle/On Foot..."), then press **[Delete]**.

3. Click **Slide 4** ("Taxi") and drag it to become Slide 2. *Notice that the slide is moved and renumbered.*

4. Click **Slide 2** ("Taxi"), press and hold **[Ctrl]**, then drag Slide 2 so

that it becomes the last slide in the presentation. *The slide is copied.*

5. Double-click **Slide 6** (the copied "Taxi" slide) to display it in Normal view.

6. On the Slides tab, click **Slide 2**, then press **[Delete]**.

7. On the Slides tab, drag **Slide 4** ("Car") so it becomes Slide 3.

8. Save the file as **p1-16.*yi*** (*yi* = your initials). Do not close the file.

Check Spelling

▶ If automatic spell checking is activated, wavy red lines appear under words that PowerPoint recognizes as possible errors.

▶ The spelling and grammar feature in PowerPoint is used as in other Office applications.

HOW **1.** Click the **Review tab**, and in the **Proofing group**, click the **Spelling button**.

Change Text Alignment and Direction

▶ Each slide layout contains a default alignment for text placeholders. However, you can change both the horizontal and vertical alignment of text as well as its orientation.

▶ You can use the Align Text Left, Center, Align Text Right, and Justify buttons in the Paragraph group on the Home tab to position text horizontally in text placeholders left, right, centered, or justified.

▶ You can also use the **Align Text button** in the Paragraph group on the Home tab to position text vertically in text placeholders at the top, middle, or the bottom.

▶ PowerPoint also allows you to change the direction of text in a placeholder by clicking the **Text Direction button** in the Paragraph group on the Home tab by varying degrees. You can rotate text 90° or 270°, or you can arrange the text so that it is stacked one on top of another, as shown in Figure 1.39. After you choose the Stacked command, you usually need to enlarge the height of the placeholder so that the text will stack vertically from the top of the placeholder to the bottom rather than horizontally from left to right.

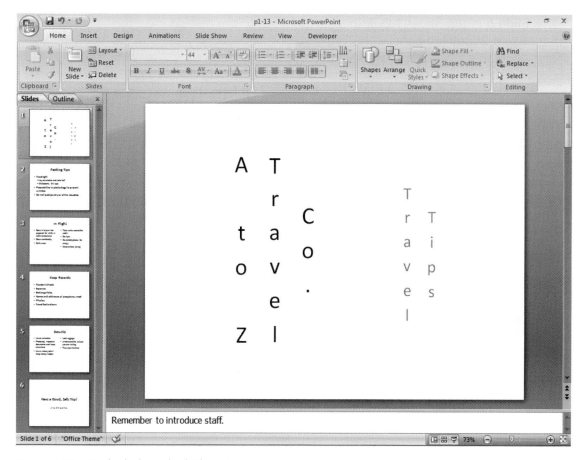

Figure 1.39: Stacked title and subtitle text

HOW To align text horizontally in a placeholder, **1.** select the placeholder. **2.** Click the **Home tab**, and in the **Paragraph group**, **3.** click the **Align Text Left**, **Center**, **Align Text Right**, or **Justify button**.

To align text vertically in a placeholder, **1.** select the placeholder. **2.** Click the **Home tab**, and in the **Paragraph group**, click the **Align Text button**. **3.** Click the **Top**, **Middle**, or **Bottom** command on the menu.

To change the direction of text in a placeholder, **1.** select the placeholder. **2.** Click the **Home tab**, in the **Paragraph group**, click the **Text Direction button**. **3.** Click a text direction on the menu.

T R Y *i t* **O U T** *p1-17*

*Note: The presentation from the previous Try it Out should be displayed on your screen. If this file is unavailable, open the data file **p1-17**.*

1. Click **Slide 5** in the Slides tab in the Outline and Slides tab pane.

2. Insert a new slide with the Title Only layout.

3. Click in the title placeholder, then enter `VIENNA!`

4. On the **Home tab**, and in the **Paragraph group**, click the **Text Direction button**, then click **Stacked**.

5. Drag the bottom-middle handle on the title placeholder down near the bottom of the slide, so that the bottom of the placeholder is the same distance from the bottom of the slide as the top of the placeholder is from the top of the slide.

6. Save the file as **p1.17.***yi* (*yi* = your initials), then close the file.

REHEARSAL

GOAL
To create and edit the presentation
shown in Figure 1.40

TASK 3

▼ **DIRECTIONS**

1. Open the data file, **p1r3-beads**.

2. Move Slide 2 so that it becomes Slide 5.

3. Move Slide 3 so that it becomes Slide 2.

4. Edit Slide 4 to match Slide 4 in Figure 1.40.

5. In Slide 5:
   a. Change the horizontal alignment of the bulleted
      list text so that it is center aligned.
   b. Change the vertical alignment of the bulleted list
      text so that it is centered.

6. Change the orientation to portrait.

7. Change the page setup so that the slides are sized
   for Letter Paper (8.5x11 in).

8. In Slide 1:
   a. Change the vertical alignment of the subtitle text
      to Bottom, change the horizontal alignment of
      the subtitle text to right, and drag the subtitle
      placeholder to the bottom right of the slide.
   b. Select the text placeholder containing the word
      "Beads," then change the text direction to
      Stacked.
   c. Change the text direction of the two text
      placeholders containing the words "Baubles"
      and "and More" to Stacked.

9. Save the presentation as **p1r3-bead store**.

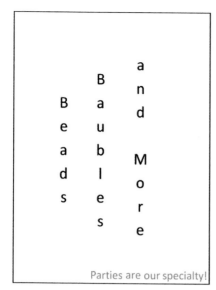

Slide 1

B e a d s

B a u b l e s

a n d

M o r e

Parties are our specialty!

Slide 2

Plan Your Next Party with Us!

- Several packages to choose from
  - Prices per guest
  - Prices per piece of jewelry made
    - Using beads from specified bins
    - Using limited selection of clasps
  - Prices per bead and accessory
- Come to our store or we'll come to you!

Slide 3

All Types of Beads

- Bugle
- Drop
- Swarovski crystal
- Seed
- Glass

- Pony
- Alphabet
- Faceted
- Sequins
- Wood

Slide 4

All the Supplies Needed for Finished Jewelry

- Clasps
- Chains
- Findings
- Wire
- Cord

Slide 5

Book Your Party Today!

- Beads, Baubles, and More
  - 534-3987

Figure 1.40: Bead store presentation

Change the Orientation
1. Click the **Design tab**, and in the **Page Setup group**, click the **Slide Orientation button**.
2. Click the desired orientation.

Select Page Setup Options
1. Click the **Design tab**, and in the **Page Setup group**, click the **Page Setup button**.
2. Select the desired options.
3. Click **OK**.

Move, Copy, Duplicate, or Delete Slides

Select Slides
1. Switch to Slide Sorter view.
2. Click a slide.
   Or
2. Press and hold **[Ctrl]**.
3. Click multiple slides.

Move Slides
1. Switch to Slide Sorter view.
2. Select a slide or slides.
3. Drag the selected slides to a new location.

Copy Slides
1. Switch to Slide Sorter view.
2. Select a slide or slides.
3. Press and hold **[Ctrl]**.
4. Drag the selected slides to a new location.

Or
4. Click the **Home tab**, and in the **Slides group**, click the **New Slide list arrow**.
5. Click Duplicate Selected Slides.

Delete Slides
1. Switch to Slide Sorter view.
2. Select a slide or slides.
3. Press **[Delete]**.
   Or
3. Click the **Home tab**, and in the **Slides group**, click the **Delete button**.
   Or
3. Right-click the selected slide.
4. Click **Delete Slide** on the shortcut menu.

Check Spelling
1. Click the **Review tab**, and in the **Proofing group**, click the **Spelling button**.

Change Text Alignment and Orientation

Align Text Horizontally
1. Select the placeholder.
2. Click the **Home tab**, and in the **Paragraph group**, click the **Align Text Left**, **Center**, **Align Text Right**, or **Justify button**.

Align Text Vertically
1. Select the placeholder.
2. Click the **Home tab**, and in the **Paragraph group**, click the **Align Text button**.
3. Click the **Top**, **Middle**, or **Bottom** command on the menu.

Change Text Orientation
1. Select the placeholder.
2. Click the **Home tab**, and in the **Paragraph group**, click the **Text Direction button**.
3. Click a text direction command on the menu.

TASK 3

EarthCare Services, a landscaping company, asked you to help create a presentation shown in Figure 1.41. They will show this presentation to apartment landlords and condominium boards as part of a marketing strategy.

Follow these guidelines:

1. Open the data file **p1p3-landscaping**.

2. Change the orientation to landscape.

3. Move Slide 6 ("All Your Landscaping Needs") so that it becomes Slide 2, then move the new Slide 6 ("As Green As Possible") so that it becomes Slide 3.

4. Copy Slide 1 to create a new Slide 7.

5. In Slide 7, edit the subtitle text as shown in Figure 1.41.

6. Change the page setup so that the slides are sized for an On-screen Show (16:10).

7. In Slide 7:
   a. Change the text direction of the title text as shown in Figure 1.41.
   b. Resize the title text placeholder so that it stretches from the top to the bottom of the slide, then reposition it as shown in Figure 1.41.
   c. Change the horizontal and vertical alignment of the subtitle text so it is centered in its placeholder.

8. Save the presentation as **p1p3-landscaping for landlords**.

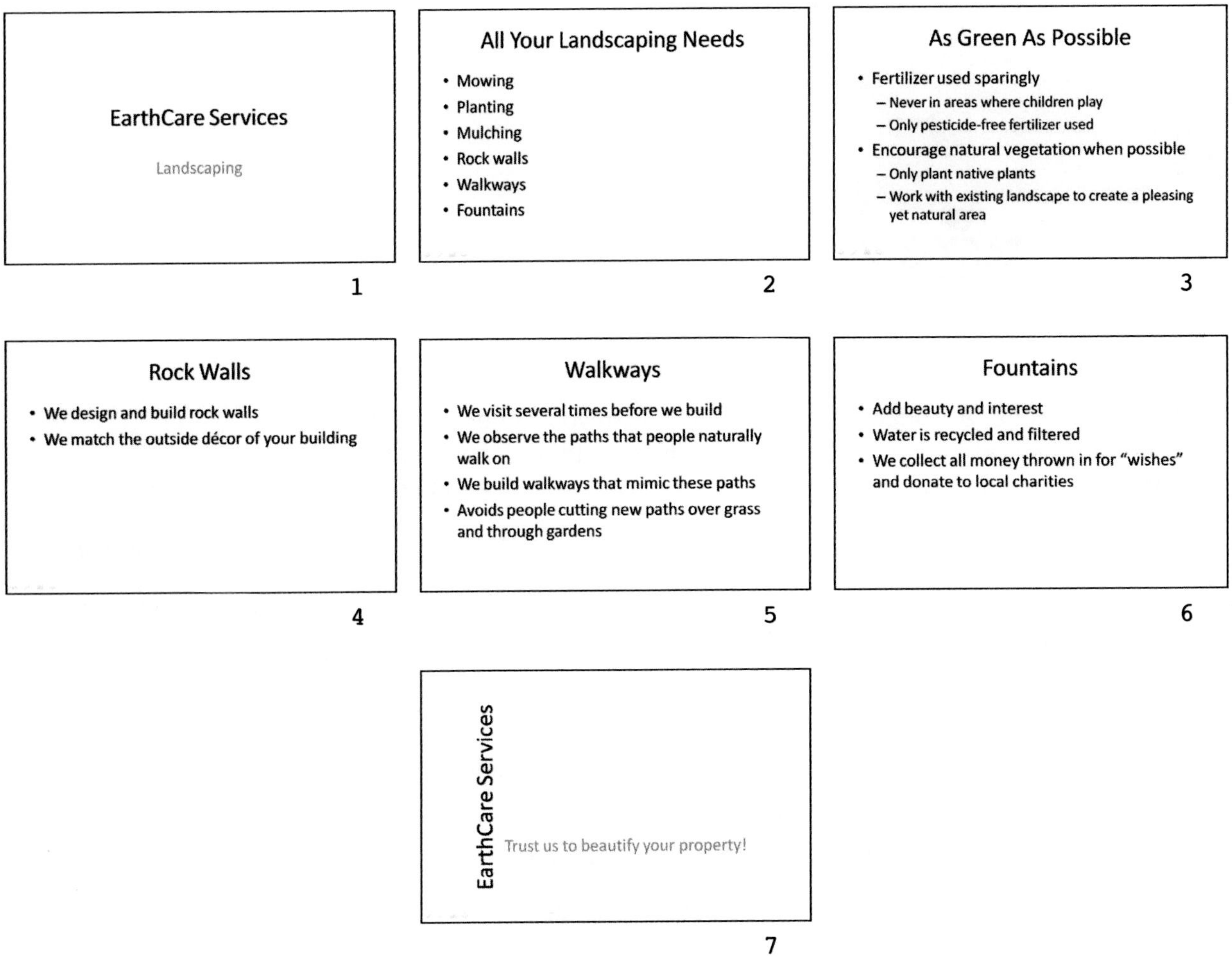

EarthCare Services

Landscaping

1

All Your Landscaping Needs

- Mowing
- Planting
- Mulching
- Rock walls
- Walkways
- Fountains

2

As Green As Possible

- Fertilizer used sparingly
  - Never in areas where children play
  - Only pesticide-free fertilizer used
- Encourage natural vegetation when possible
  - Only plant native plants
  - Work with existing landscape to create a pleasing yet natural area

3

Rock Walls

- We design and build rock walls
- We match the outside décor of your building

4

Walkways

- We visit several times before we build
- We observe the paths that people naturally walk on
- We build walkways that mimic these paths
- Avoids people cutting new paths over grass and through gardens

5

Fountains

- Add beauty and interest
- Water is recycled and filtered
- We collect all money thrown in for "wishes" and donate to local charities

6

EarthCare Services

Trust us to beautify your property!

7

Figure 1.41: Landscaping presentation

Act I

Upton Investment Group wants you to create a presentation explaining to new investors about the basic principles of compound investing and emphasizing that getting started at a young age is important. You will use Figure 1.42 as a guide.

Follow these guidelines:

1. Start PowerPoint.

2. Change the orientation to portrait.

3. Create the presentation shown in Figure 1.42.

4. In Slide 1:
   a. Copy the title text placeholder and enter the text as shown in Figure 1.42.
   b. Rotate both copies of the title text placeholder to match Figure 1.42. You'll need to resize the placeholders so that they fit on the slide.
   c. Center-align the subtitle text both horizontally and vertically.

5. In Slide 2:
   a. Use the Two Content layout.
   b. Center the text in both text placeholders both horizontally and vertically.
   c. Resize the text placeholders so that they are 1.5" in height.
   d. Use the rotation handle to rotate the text as shown in Figure 1.42.
   e. Fill both placeholders with a Shape Style as shown in Figure 1.42.

6. In Slide 5:
   a. Use the Title Slide layout or copy Slide 1.
   b. In the title placeholder, enter the text as shown, then resize the placeholder so that it stretches the width of the slide.
   c. Fill the title placeholder with third square in the first column (its ScreenTip labels it White, Background 1, Darker 15%).
   d. Change the color of the text in the title placeholder to the darkest gray color in the Theme Colors section.
   e. Enter the text as shown in Figure 1.42 in the subtitle placeholder.
   f. Drag the subtitle placeholder down so the bottom of the placeholder touches the bottom of the slide.

7. Save the presentation as **p1e1-investing**.

Compound Interest

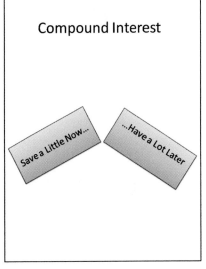

Save a Little Now...

- You invest a small amount and that amount earns interest to create a new, larger amount
- Then the new larger amount earns interest, creating a new, even larger amount
- Then the new, even larger amount earns interest... and so on
- If you start in your late teens, as little as $10 a week can ensure a wealthy retirement

1

2

3

...Have a Lot Later

- When you start saving at a young age, the money you invest has a chance to multiply
- Each year that you delay saving and investing reduces the final amount

Upton Investment Group

Give Your Money to Us and Watch It Grow!

4

5

Figure 1.42: Encore Act I

Act II

Palmetto Realtors run a course for new real estate agents. You need to refine their presentation so that it matches the one shown in Figure 1.43.

Follow these guidelines:

1. Open the presentation **p1e2-realestate**.
2. Change the page setup to On-screen Show (16:10).
3. Move Slide 3 so that it becomes Slide 4.
4. Create a new Slide 2, and enter the text shown in Figure 1.43.
5. Delete Slide 3.

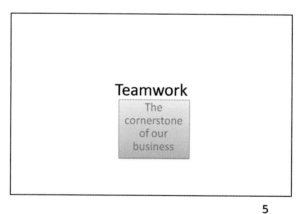

Figure 1.43: Encore Act II

6. Copy Slide 1 to create a new Slide 5.

7. In Slide 5:
   a. Edit the text to match Figure 1.43.
   b. Change the size of the subtitle text placeholder to 2" high by 2.5" wide.
   c. Reposition the subtitle text placeholder so that it is directly below the title.
   d. Format the subtitle placeholder with a Shape Style.

8. View the presentation in Slide Sorter view.

9. Save the presentation as **p1e2-realestate course**.

10. Run the slide show.

Creating Informative Presentations

In this lesson, you will learn to use features found in PowerPoint to create and enhance informative presentations. Informative presentations either report or explain. A presentation that reports brings the audience up to date about an issue or a product. An explanatory presentation provides information on a specific topic.

You will complete presentation projects that inform on the following topics:

- ✴ How to care for plants
- ✴ How to buy a diamond
- ✴ Overview of a company's services
- ✴ Product information

Upon completion of this lesson, you will have mastered the following skill sets

- ✴ Apply a slide theme
- ✴ Change theme colors and fonts
- ✴ Change the slide background
- ✴ Print preview
- ✴ Print a presentation
- ✴ Work with clip art
- ✴ Apply slide transitions
- ✴ Apply and edit animations
- ✴ Work with outlines
- ✴ Hide a slide
- ✴ Link slides

Terms
Software-related
- Animation
- Blank presentation
- Hyperlink
- Slide transitions
- Themes

TRYOUT

GOAL
To create, edit and print a five-slide informative presentation using a design theme, as shown in Figure 2.1

- Apply a slide theme
- Change theme colors and fonts
- Change the slide background
- Print preview
- Print a presentation

TASK 1

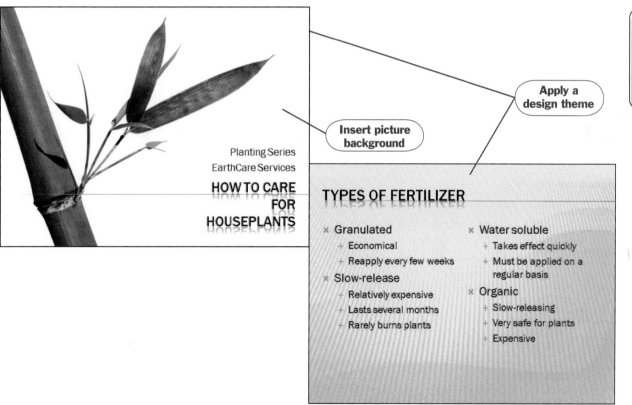

Figure 2.1: Two slides of a "how-to" presentation

WHAT YOU NEED TO KNOW

Apply a Slide Theme

▶ **Themes** in PowerPoint provide you with predesigned colorful backgrounds, fonts, (including font size settings), and a layout for your slides. You can choose from numerous predesigned built-in themes or find additional themes online. You can view a live preview of the theme to see its effect before you actually apply it to a presentation.

▶ By default, the Office theme is applied to new presentations. You can select a different theme to become the default, if you wish. You can apply a theme to the entire presentation or to selected slides in the presentation.

HOW To apply a theme to the entire presentation, **1.** click the **Design tab**, and in the **Themes group**, **2.** click **More**, as shown in Figure 2.2, which will display the Themes gallery (see Figure 2.3). **3.** Point to each theme to see a live preview, then **4.** right-click a theme, and **5.** select **Apply To All Slides**.

To apply a theme to selected slides only, **1.** select the slides on which to apply the theme, **2.** follow Steps 1–4 above and then **3.** select **Apply to Selected Slides**.

To set a new default theme, **1.** right-click a theme, and **2.** choose **Set as Default Theme** from the menu, as shown in Figure 2.3.

Figure 2.2: Design tab, Themes group

More

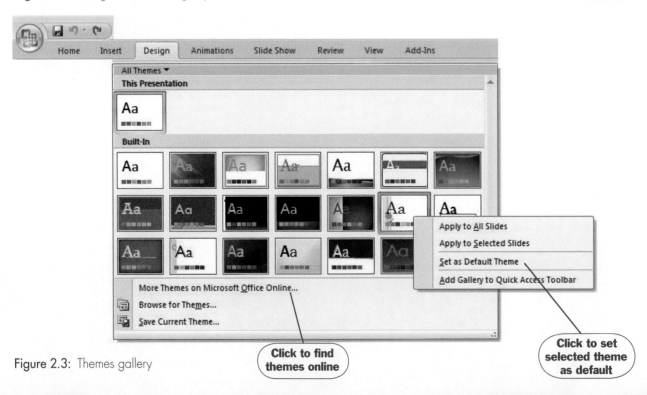

Figure 2.3: Themes gallery

Click to find themes online

Click to set selected theme as default

To find additional themes online, click the **More Themes on Microsoft Office Online** link on the Themes Gallery, as shown in Figure 2.3.

T R Y *i t* **O U T** *p2-1*

1. Open the data file **p2-1**.

2. Click the **Design tab**, and in the **Themes group**, click **More**.

3. Position your insertion point on each theme to see a live preview.

4. Click to select the **Median theme**. Notice that the new color scheme, font style, and formatting was applied to all six slides.

5. On the Slides pane, click to select the last slide ("Next Steps...").

6. Locate the **Civic theme** in the Themes Gallery. Right-click the thumbnail, then select **Apply to Selected Slides**. Note that only the last slide has the new theme.

7. Close the file without saving the changes.

Change Theme Colors and Fonts

▶ Each theme design has a predefined color scheme that affects the slide background, title text, fills, lines, shadows, accents, and hyperlinks. PowerPoint provides a set of colors that complement each other so your slides look professional.

▶ Each theme also applies specific fonts, font styles, and font sizes for various components on the slide (slide titles, bulleted lists, etc.).

▶ PowerPoint lets you change the color scheme and/or fonts of your applied theme. Color schemes can be changed on selected slides or all slides of a presentation, while font changes must be applied to all slides in a presentation.

HOW To apply new theme color to the entire presentation, **1.** click the **Design tab**, 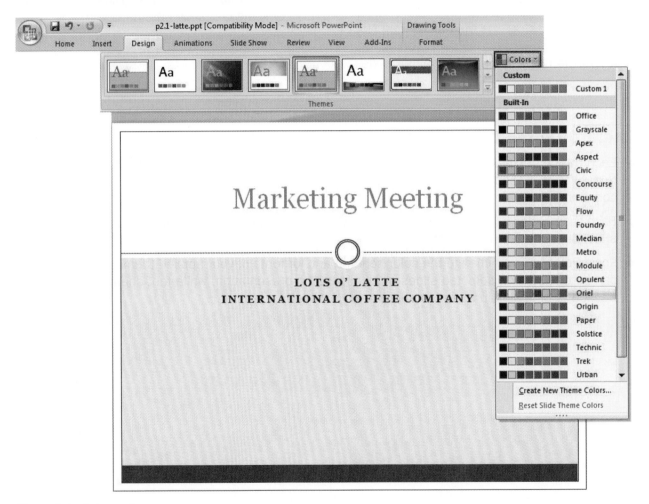 and in the **Themes group**, **2.** click the **Colors button**. **3.** Move your mouse pointer over each color theme in the gallery that appears, as shown in Figure 2.4, to see a live preview on your slide. **4.** Right-click a color scheme, and **5.** select **Apply to All Slides**.

To change a theme color on selected slides only, **1.** select the slides on which to apply the new theme color, **2.** follow Steps 1–4 above, and then **3.** select **Apply to Selected Slides**.

To change a theme font, **1.** click the **Design tab**, and in the **Themes group**, **2.** click the **Fonts button**. **3.** Move your mouse pointer over each font theme in the gallery that appears, as shown in Figure 2.5, to see a live preview. **4.** Click a font style to apply it to all slides.

Figure 2.4: Colors gallery

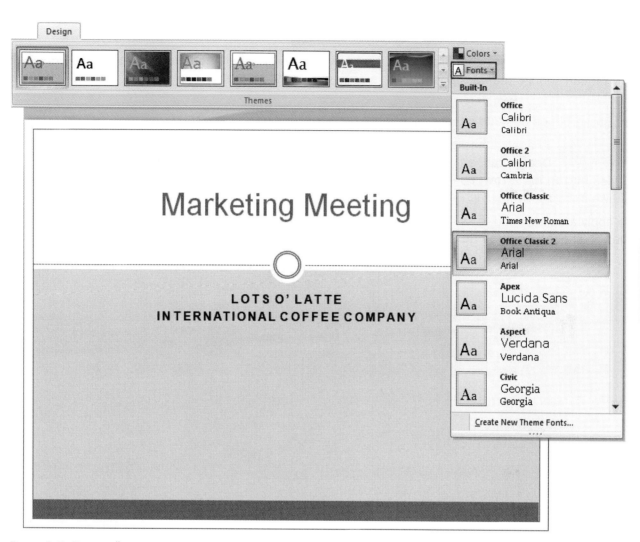

Figure 2.5: Fonts gallery

T R Y *it* O U T *p2-2*

1. Open the data file **p2-2**.

2. Click the **Design tab**, and in the **Themes group**, click the **Colors button**.

3. Position your insertion point on each color scheme to see its effect on your slides.

4. Click the **Urban** color scheme.

5. Click the **Fonts button**.

6. Position your insertion point on each font scheme to see its effect on your slides.

7. Click the **Apex** font scheme.

8. Cycle through your slides to see the effects of your newly applied theme color and font scheme.

9. Close the file without saving the changes.

Change the Slide Background

▶ Each theme design has a predefined background color, which is automatically applied. However, you can change the background to be a solid color or to have a gradient effect, picture, or texture.

▶ Backgrounds can add interesting effects to your slides.

HOW To apply a background style to an entire presentation, **1** click the **Design tab**, and in the **Background group**, **2.** click the **Background Styles button list arrow**, as shown in Figure 2.6. In the Background Styles gallery that appears, as shown in Figure 2.7, **3.** right-click a background style, and **4.** choose **Apply to All Slides**.

To apply a background to selected slides only, **1.** select the slides, **2.** follow Steps 1–3 above, and then **3.** choose **Apply to Selected Slides**.

Figure 2.6: Design tab, Background group

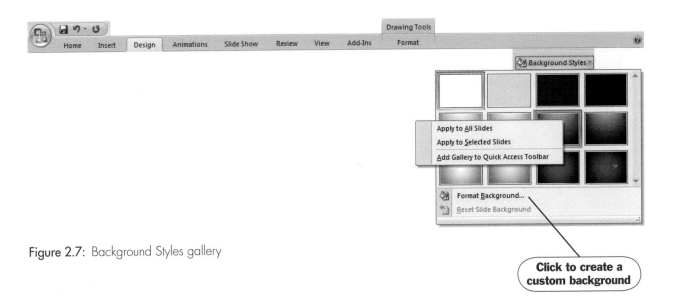

Figure 2.7: Background Styles gallery

Click to create a custom background

To create a custom background, **1.** click the **Format Background** link at the bottom of the Background Styles gallery (see Figure 2.7). In the Format Background dialog box that appears, as shown in Figure 2.8, **2.** select the type of fill you want to apply (Solid fill, Gradient fill, or Picture or Texture fill), then **3.** select the appropriate settings for that type of background.

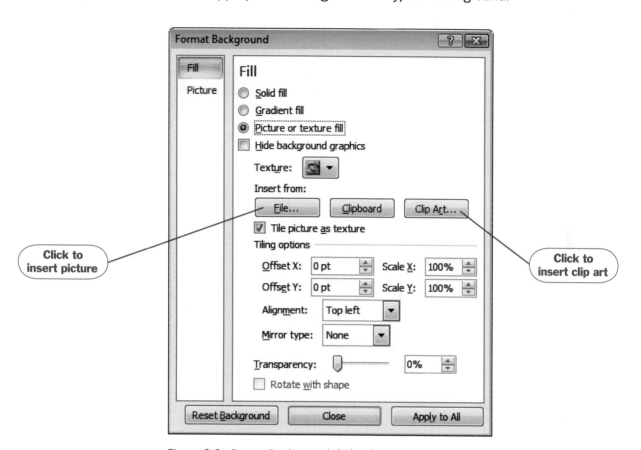

Figure 2.8: Format Background dialog box

TRY *it* **OUT** *p2-3*

1. Open the data file **p2-3a**.

2. Click the **Design tab**, and in the **Background group,** click the **Background Styles button** to display the Background gallery.

3. Position your insertion point on each background style to see its effect.

4. Right-click **Style 10**, and select **Apply to All Slides**.

5. Display Slide 1, and click the **Background Styles button** again.

6. Click the **Format Background** link.

7. In the Format Background dialog box, do the following:

   a. Click **Picture or texture fill**.

   b. Click **File**.

   c. Select the data file **p2-3b.png**, and click Insert.

   d. Click **Close**. *Notice that the picture became the slide background for the selected slide, as shown in Figure 2.9.*

8. Display Slide 2, and click the **Background Styles button** again.

9. Click the **Format Background** link.

10. In the Format Background dialog box, do the following:

   a. Click **Picture or texture fill**.

   b. Click the **Texture list arrow**.

Continued on next page

c. Select the **Water droplets** design from the gallery that appears.

d. Click **Close**. *Notice that the design was applied to Slide 2 only.*

11. Close the presentation without saving the changes.

Figure 2.9: Slide with picture background

Print Preview

▶ The Print Preview feature, new to PowerPoint 2007, allows you to preview your slides before you print them. You can also set the page orientation and other printing options from the Print Preview tab, which is shown in Figure 2.10.

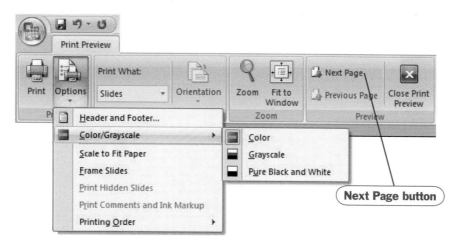

Figure 2.10: Print preview tab

▶ You can print your entire presentation in color, grayscale, or pure black and white. Typically, however, you will choose to print in either grayscale or black and white. **Grayscale** uses tones of gray to show the effects of color. It is useful to see how your slides will look if you plan to print your slides without color.

▶ You can also print from the preview window. The default is to print each slide as a page. However, you can choose to print 2-9 miniature slides per page, which is useful if you want to provide your audience with handouts. *Preparing handouts and other print options will be detailed in Lesson 5.*

HOW 1. Click the **Office button**, 2. highlight **Print**, then 3. click **Print Preview**. 4. Click the **Options button** in the **Print group**. 5. Highlight **Color/Grayscale**, then 6. choose a print color option (Color, Grayscale, Pure Black and White). 7. Click the **Next Page button** to cycle through the slides (see Figure 2.10).

To print from Print Preview, 1. click the **Print What list arrow** in the **Page Setup group**, and 2. choose how you want your slides printed (the default is Slides), as shown in Figure 2.11. 3. Click **Print**, and then click **OK**. 4. Click the **Close Print Preview button**.

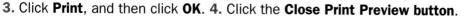

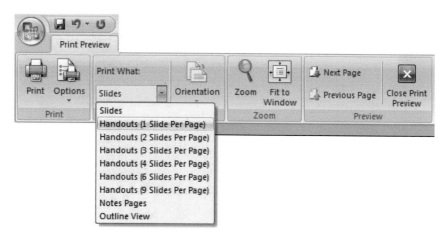

Figure 2.11: Print What option

1. Open the data file **p2-4**.

2. Click the **Office button**, highlight **Print**, then select **Print Preview**.

3. Click the **Options button**, highlight **Color/Grayscale**, then click **Grayscale**.

4. Repeat Step 3, and click **Pure Black and White**.

5. Click the **Next Page button** to view each slide in the presentation.

6. Click the **Print What list arrow**, and select **Handouts (2 Slides Per Page)**.

7. Click the **Close Print Preview button** to leave the Print Preview window without printing.

8. Close the presentation without saving the changes.

Print a Presentation

▶ Printing in PowerPoint is similar to other applications, but contains specific settings for choosing which slides to print and a print format (handouts, notes pages, or a presentation as an outline).

HOW 1. Click the **Office button**, 2. highlight **Print**, then 3. click **Print**. In the Print dialog box that appears, as shown in Figure 2.12, 4. choose which slides to print in the Print range section. 5. Click the **Print what list arrow**, and choose the type of output you want (see Figure 2.11). The default is set to print slides. 6. Click the **Color/grayscale list arrow**, and choose whether you wish to print in color, grayscale, or pure black and white, then 7. click **OK**.

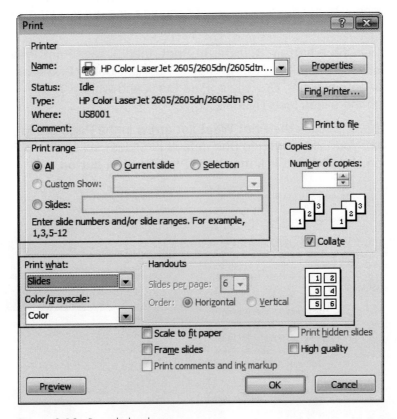

Figure 2.12: Print dialog box

▶ You can also print slides by clicking the Office button, and then clicking Quick Print. Doing this bypasses the Print dialog box and automatically prints your presentation as full pages of each slide using the default or most recent settings made in the Print dialog box.

T R Y *it* O U T *p2-5*

1. Open the data file **p2-5**.

2. Click the **Office Button**, highlight **Print**, then click **Print**.

3. In the Print dialog box, click the **Print what list arrow**, then click **Handouts.**

4. Click the **Slides per page list arrow**, then click **4**.

5. Click **Preview**. Click the **Next Page button** to view the last two slides.

6. On the **Print Preview tab**, click the **Print button** in the **Print group**. The Print dialog box reappears.

7. Click the **Slides per page list arrow**, click **6**.

8. Click the **Color/grayscale list arrow**, then click **Pure Black and White.**

9. Click **Preview** to view the six slides.

10. Click the **Close Print Preview button**, since you will not actually print this exercise. The presentation now appears in Normal view. (To print, you would click the **Print button**.)

11. Close the file, and do not save the changes.

REHEARSAL

 GOAL
To create and edit an informative
presentation, as shown in Figure 2.13

TASK 1

WHAT YOU NEED TO KNOW

▶ "How-to" presentations provide a
wealth of practical information on
a variety of topics.

▶ By default, the Office theme is
applied to new presentations. You
can apply a theme to the entire
presentation or to selected slides
in the presentation.

▶ Backgrounds can add interesting
effects to your slides.

▼ DIRECTIONS

1. Open a new presentation.

2. Click the **Design tab**, if necessary, and in the
Themes group, apply the **Trek** design theme.

3. Accept the default title slide layout for the first slide.

4. Enter the title and subtitle, as shown in Figure 2.13,
Slide 1.

5. Add new slides as shown in the figure, and apply
appropriate layouts.

6. Change the title slide background color, and add
a picture as a background. You may choose any
background color that complements the theme and
any relevant clip art. The illustration is only a guide.

7. Change the fonts in the presentation to any style
you want.

8. Move **Slide 4** ("Growing Basics") so that it becomes
Slide 2.

9. Preview your slides. View them in **Pure Black and
White**.

10. Print **Slide 5** ("Featured Plant-The Orchid") in **Pure
Black and White**.

11. Run the presentation.

12. Save the presentation as **2r1-houseplants**.

13. Close the presentation.

Planting Series
EarthCare Services
**HOW TO CARE
FOR
HOUSEPLANTS**

1

TYPES OF FERTILIZER

- Granulated
  - Economical
  - Reapply every few weeks
- Slow-release
  - Relatively expensive
  - Lasts several months
  - Rarely burns plants
- Water soluble
  - Takes effect quickly
  - Must be applied on a regular basis
- Organic
  - Slow-releasing
  - Very safe for plants
  - Expensive

2

WATERING TIPS

- Use warm water
- Water before plant wilts
- Know your plant, and water from above or below as necessary
- Soil should be thoroughly soaked, without overwatering

3

GROWING BASICS

- Bright light, but NOT direct sunlight
- 65 to 75 degrees Fahrenheit with relative humidity
  - Spray with water several times a day
  - Keep pot in a tray of damp pebbles
- Do not overwater
- Soil should be a mixture of dirt, peat, sand, and vermiculite
  - Good drainage
  - Air can circulate to roots
- Feed plants with fertilizer

4

FEATURED PLANT—THE ORCHID

- Thousands of orchid species
- Phalaenopsis is the best indoor orchid
- The Pot
  - Should be free-draining
  - Water cannot accumulate around roots
- Light
  - Moderate light
  - Not direct sunlight, but not dark
- Temperature
  - 75 degrees Fahrenheit during the day
  - 55-60 degrees Fahrenheit at night
  - Humidity at 50%
- Water
  - Depends on plant species
  - Depends on light

5

Figure 2.13: How to Care for Houseplants presentation

Apply a Slide Theme

1. Select the slide(s) on which to apply a theme (if applying to all slides, skip this step).
2. Click the **Design tab**, and in the **Themes group**, click **More** to display the gallery of themes.
3. Right-click the theme.
4. Select **Apply to All slides** or **Apply to Selected Slides**.

Change Slide Theme Color

1. Select the slide(s) on which to change the color scheme (if applying to all slides, skip this step).
2. Click the **Design tab**, and in the **Themes group**, click the **Colors button**.
3. Right-click a color scheme.
4. Select **Apply to All Slides** or **Apply to Selected Slides**.

Change Theme Fonts

1. Click the **Design tab**, and in the **Themes group**, click the **Fonts button**.
2. Click a Font scheme.

Change a Slide's Background

1. Click the **Design tab**, and in the **Background group**, click the **Background Styles button**.
2. Right-click a background style.
3. **Select Apply to All Slides** or **Apply to Selected Slides**.

Print Preview

1. Click the **Office button**.
2. Highlight **Print**.
3. Click **Print Preview**.
4. Click the **Print Preview tab** (if not already displayed).
5. Click the **Options button**.

6. Highlight **Color/Grayscale**.
7. Choose a preview option (Color, Grayscale, Pure Black and White).
8. Click **Next Page button** to cycle through slides.
9. Click **Print What list arrow**, and choose how you want your slides printed (default is Slides).
10. Click **Print**, and click **OK**.
11. Click the **Close Print Preview button**.

Print a Presentation

1. Click the **Office button**.
2. Highlight **Print**.
3. Click **Print**.
4. Select the Print range and Print what options.
5. Click **OK**.

TASK 1

Perfect Planning Group (PPG) is working with the sales training director of Prestige Jewelers, a national chain of fine jewelry stores, to organize their upcoming sales conference. PPG has agreed to create all sales presentations for the meeting. Because of your newly acquired expertise with PowerPoint 2007, you have been asked to help in this effort by creating a presentation titled "How to Buy a Diamond." Your contact at Prestige Jewelers tells you the following about the sales meeting:

- "As part of the Prestige Jewelers employee training program, new salespeople attending the sales meeting are given courses on gemstones and precious metals so that they are well-educated about the products they are selling. Most of our customers want to buy diamonds or diamond jewelry, but they do not know what to look for when buying a diamond. A common question customers ask is, 'Why are two diamonds that are the same size and same carat weight priced so differently?' To help our salespeople answer this and other questions, we need a presentation that focuses on the key issues facing customers who wish to purchase a diamond."

- In addition, Prestige Jewelers has provided you with the information you will need to create a presentation consisting of five slides.

Follow these guidelines:

1. Title the presentation: **How to Buy a Diamond**.

2. Include the following as the subtitle:

   Prestige Jewelers Sales Meeting
   Sales Presentation

3. Read through the information provided on the next page to get a basic understanding of the content the presentation will cover. Use the bold headings shown below as slide titles.

4. Use the information below the bold headings to create bullet points for that slide. For the last slide, use the information provided to create concise bullet points. Avoid using narrative text or long sentences.

5. Apply any design theme to the presentation.

6. Change theme colors and fonts.

7. Change the Slide 1 background. Use a picture as a background, if you want.

8. Make any adjustments necessary to better present the text.

9. Print your slides as handouts with six slides per page.

10. Save the presentation as **2p1-diamond**.

The 4 C's Determine Diamond Grade and Value

- Cut
  - Refers to a diamond's reflective qualities, not its shape
  - Angles and number of facets determine how diamond reflects light
    - In well-cut diamonds, light enters from the top, reflects from one side to the other, and exits out the top.
    - In poorly cut diamonds, light enters from the top and "leaks" out the bottom.
- Clarity
  - Refers to a diamond's flaws (or inclusions)
    - Internal air bubbles
    - Surface cracks
  - Diamonds range from Flawless (no inclusions) to Included 3 (flaws visible to the naked eye)
- Color
  - Refers to a diamond's color
    - Colorless is most valuable, reflecting the most light
  - Graded on alphabetical scale from "D" (colorless) to "Z" (traces of yellow or brown)
    - Fancy color diamonds do not follow this rule (i.e., blue, yellow, pink diamonds)
- Carat
  - Refers to the unit of weight by which a diamond is measured
  - The greater the carat weight, the more expensive the diamond (all other characteristics being equal)

Determining a Diamond's Quality

- Microscope/Loop
  - A microscope or jeweler's loop (10x magnifying glass) will show any inclusions in a diamond.
- Diamond Tester
  - Uses light to verify that the diamond is real
  - Does not guarantee quality of stone, just authenticity
- Certification
  - Certifies the quality of a diamond
  - Certificates should come from a reputable source
  - Certificates could cost up to $200

Buyer Beware of "Treated" Diamonds

- Filled with glass to enhance clarity
- Treated with heat to enhance color
  - Used to turn yellow or brown diamonds into a fancy-colored
  - Color may change over time
- Painted for color to offset yellow color
  - Wears off quickly
  - Easily detectable

Caring for Diamonds

After you purchase a diamond, be sure to care for it so that it does not get scratched or damaged. Remember, diamonds are brittle and can crack if banged. Diamonds should be stored separately so that they do not scratch other pieces of jewelry and do not get scratched. Finally, when a diamond needs to be cleaned, use a jeweler's polishing cloth or bring it to your jeweler.

TRYOUT

TASK 2

▶ GOAL

To create and enhance a six-slide informative presentation that includes clip art, transitions, and animations, as shown in Figure 2.14

❉ Work with clip art
❉ Insert clip art or a picture
❉ Edit clip art or pictures
❉ Add effects
❉ Apply slide transitions
❉ Apply animation scheme

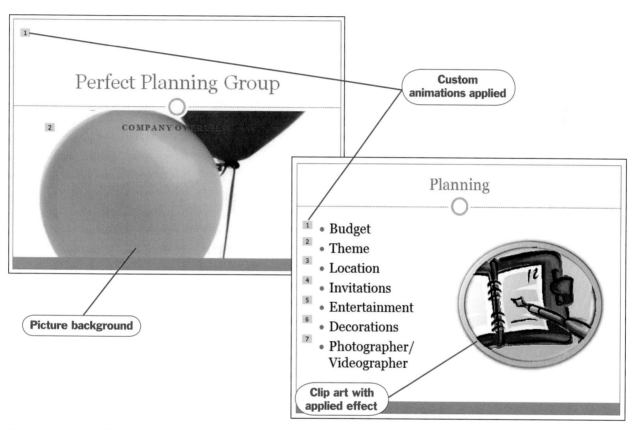

Figure 2.14: Two slides of an informative presentation enhanced with clip art

WHAT YOU NEED TO KNOW

Work with Clip Art

▶ To enhance a slide visually, you can insert graphic elements that include clip art, pictures, charts, diagrams, shapes, and drawn lines. *(Only clip art and pictures will be covered in this task; other graphic elements will be covered in Lesson 3).*

▶ The most frequently used graphic element is **clip art**, which is a collection of ready-made drawings, illustrations, photos, movies and sounds.

▶ PowerPoint installs a collection of clip art; however, you can access other clip art images and pictures from the Internet or download pictures from a digital camera. You can also use scanned images. If you scan an image, or download one from a digital camera or from the Web, PowerPoint automatically saves the image in the My Pictures folder.

► As you learned in Lesson 1, there are numerous slide layouts that contain placeholders. In addition to holding text for titles and bulleted lists, placeholders also hold slide content such as SmartArt graphics, tables, charts, pictures, shapes, and clip art.

► Layouts with content placeholders are shown in Figure 2.15. Figure 2.16 illustrates a Title and Content slide layout showing icons for various content elements (picture, clip art, SmartArt, table, etc.) that might be inserted.

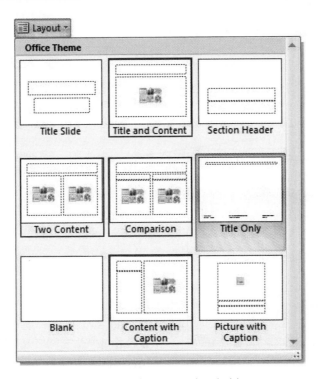

Figure 2.15: Layouts with content placeholders

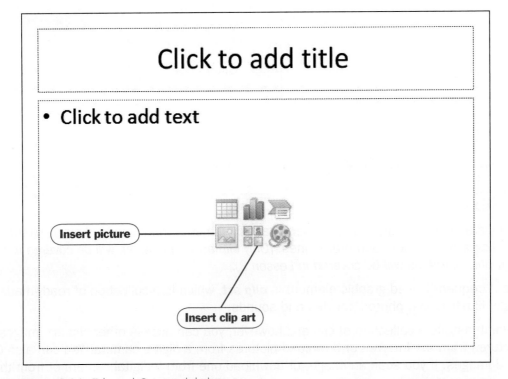

Figure 2.16: Title and Content slide layout

▶ Clip art and pictures are inserted on a slide in a content placeholder. However, you can also place clip art or a picture on a slide without inserting it into a placeholder.

HOW 1. Select a slide layout that contains a content placeholder, 2. click the **Clip Art icon**, which will open the Clip Art task pane, as shown in Figure 2.17. 3. Enter a topic or theme in the **Search for text box**. 4. Click the **Results Should be list arrow**, and choose the type of media you want to search, then 5. click **Go**. *PowerPoint displays those images that match your search word.* 6. Click the clip art image to insert it on the slide. The image appears with sizing and rotation handles (see Figure 2.18). Click off the image to hide the handles.

To insert clip art or a picture on a slide without inserting it into a content placeholder, 1. click the **Insert tab**, and in the **Illustrations group**, 2. click the **Picture button** to insert a picture from a file (a picture that has been saved to your computer), and 3. select the picture file to insert. Or, click the **Clip Art button**, then search for and select an image in the Clip Art task pane.

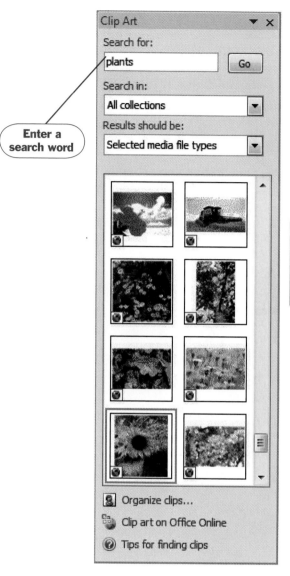

Enter a search word

Figure 2.17: Clip Art task pane

T R Y *i t* O U T *p2-6*

1. Open a new blank presentation.

2. Click the **Home tab**, and in the **Slides group**, click the **Layout button**, and select the **Title and Content** slide layout from the gallery that displays.

3. Click the **Clip Art icon** on the slide, which will open the Clip Art task pane. *(If the Clip Art task pane is already displayed, skip this step.)*

4. Enter **Tree** in the **Search for** text box, and click **Go**.

5. Click the tree of your choice.

6. Click off the image to hide the sizing handles. *The content options remain on the slide after the clip art has been inserted.*

7. Click the **New Slide button**.

8. Click the **Home tab**, and in the **Slides group**, click the **Layout button**, and select the **Blank slide layout** from the gallery.

9. Click the **Insert tab**, and in the **Illustrations group**, click the **Clip Art button**. *(If the Clip Art task pane is already displayed, skip this step.)*

Continued on next page

10. Enter **Plants** in the **Search for** text box. Click the **Results should be** list box, and check **Photographs**, if necessary. Deselect all other options, then click **Go**.

11. Click any image to insert it.

12. Display **Slide 1**.

13. Close the file without saving the changes.

▶ You can edit clip art and pictures (move, copy, delete, size, crop, rotate, adjust brightness or contrast and add special effects) using the same techniques that you used when working with clip art and pictures in Word. Using the Picture tools on the Ribbon, shown in Figure 2.18, you can make pictures that are too dark appear brighter, you can apply special effects, size an image, or crop it.

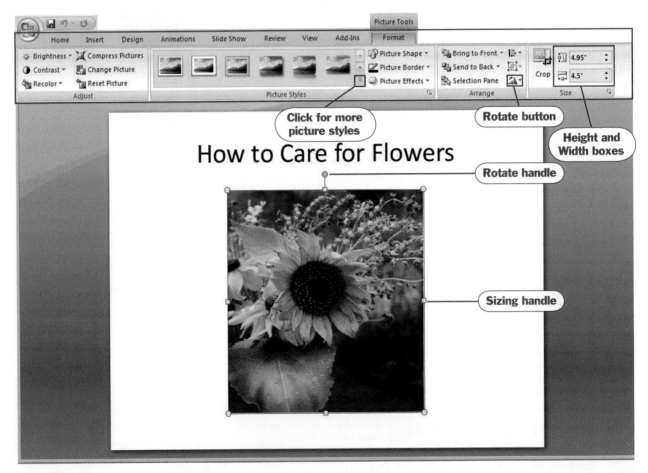

Figure 2.18: Picture Tools, Format tab on the Ribbon

▶ To edit clip art or a picture, you must first select it, which will display either Drawing Tools (for clip art images) or Picture Tools (for picture files). You can see a live preview of many of the effects before you actually apply them.

HOW Table 2.1 describes each button on the Picture Tools, Format tab that you can use to make adjustments to the images and how to apply the effect. Figure 2.19 illustrates the result of applying each effect.

Table 2.1: Effects available on the Picture Tools, Format tab

EFFECT	DESCRIPTION	BUTTON(S)	HOW
Brightness	Provides more or less brightness to an image.	☼ Brightness ▾	1. Click the **Brightness button**, and 2. select a brightness percentage.
Contrast	Provides more or less contrast to an image.	◑ Contrast ▾	1. Click the **Contrast button**, and select a contrast percentage.
Recolor	Allows you to add a color tone, such as grayscale or sepia, to an image.	Recolor ▾	1. Click the **Recolor button**, and 2. select a color mode or variation.
Picture Styles	This group of buttons provides a combination of different picture borders, orientations, and effects.		1. Click a Picture style or click **More**, and 2. select a style from the gallery.
Picture Shape	Changes the shape of the image.	Picture Shape ▾	1. Click the **Picture Shape button**, and 2. select a shape from the gallery.
Picture Border	Applies a border around the picture.	Picture Border ▾	1. Click the **Picture border button list arrow**, and 2. select a shape.
Picture Effects	Applies a visual effect to the picture, such as a shadow, glow, reflection, or 3-D rotation.	Picture Effects ▾	1. Click the **Picture Effects button**, 2. highlight an effect, then 3. click to select it.
Rotate	Rotates or flips selected picture in 90-degree increments. Click and select a rotation amount.	Rotate ▾	1. Click the **Rotate button**, then 2. select a rotation amount. You can also select the image, then drag the green rotation handle left or right to the appropriate angle.
Crop	Allows you to cut out any unwanted parts of a picture. While cropping makes the image look as if you resized it, its edges have actually been cut off. However, the edges of the image are not cut off permanently.	Crop	1. Click the **Crop button** (Pointer changes to a cropping tool). 2. Place the cropping mouse pointer over a cropping handle, and drag the sides, top, or bottom of the picture to crop off the parts you do not want. 3. Click the **Crop button** again to turn off cropping.
Height/Width	Allows you to size the height and width of the image.	▯ ⬍ ▭ ⬍	Enter an amount in the height and width box. You can also select the image and drag a corner or middle handle.
Reset Picture	Returns the picture to its original setting.	Reset Picture	Click **Reset Picture button** to reset.

Figure 2.19: Effects of using Picture Tools

TRY it OUT p2-7

1. Open the data file **p2-7**.

2. Select the image.

3. Click the **Format tab**, if necessary.

4. Click the **Brightness button**, and select **+30%**. [Brightness ▼]

5. Click the **Contrast button**, and select **+30%**. [Contrast ▼]

6. Click the **Reset Picture button** to remove all of the changes you made to the picture. [Reset Picture]

7. Click the **Recolor button**, and select **Sepia** from the **Color Modes** section. [Recolor ▼]

8. In the **Picture Styles group**, click **More**, then select **Soft Edge Oval** from the gallery.

9. Select the image, if necessary. Click the **Reset Picture button**.

10. Select the image, if necessary. Click the **Picture Shape button**, and click the **Heart shape** in the **Basic Shapes section**. [Picture Shape ▼]

11. Select the image, if necessary. Click the **Picture Border button list arrow**, and choose **Red** in the **Standard Colors** section. [Picture Border ▼]

Continued on next page

12. Click the **Picture Effects button**, highlight **Reflection**, and select **Tight Reflection, touching**.

Picture Effects ▾

13. Click the **Rotate button**. Position your mouse pointer on each option to see its effect, then select **Flip Vertical**.

Rotate ▾

14. Click the **Reset Picture button**.

15. Click the **Crop button**. Place the insertion point (now a cropping tool) on a cropping handle. Crop the photo to show only one flower.

Crop

16. Click in the **Height box**, and enter **5"**.

17. Click the image, then drag it to the right side of the slide.

18. Close the file without saving the changes.

Apply Slide Transitions

▶ **Slide transitions** control the way slides move on and off the screen during a slide show.

▶ You can apply transitions to all slides or to a single slide in all views. You can vary slide transitions for each slide or apply the same transition to all slides.

▶ You can also control the speed of a transition and/or add a sound to the transition effect by using the tools found on the Animations tab, shown in Figure 2.20.

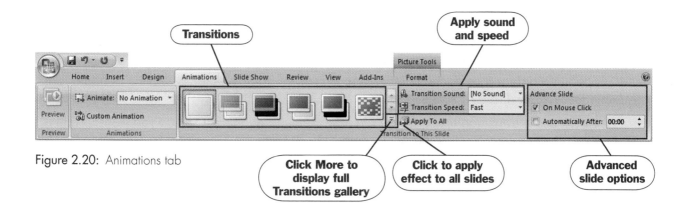

Figure 2.20: Animations tab

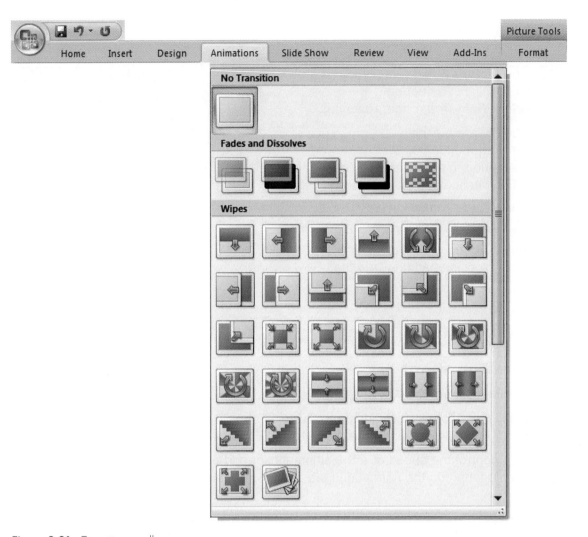

Figure 2.21: Transitions gallery

▶ PowerPoint provides you with a gallery of preset animations, as shown in Figure 2.21, which are divided into different categories (Fades and Dissolves, for example). Choosing Random, will automatically apply different styles.

HOW To add a transition to a slide, **1.** display or select the slide to which you want to add a transition, and **2.** click the **Animations tab**. **3.** Click the **Transition to This Slide More arrow** to display the entire gallery (see Figure 2.21). **4.** Move your insertion point over each transition to see its effect. **5.** Click a transition to apply it.

To add a transition to all slides in a presentation, **1.** click the **Animations tab**. **2.** Follow Steps 3–5 above, then **3.** click the **Apply To All button** (see Figure 2.20).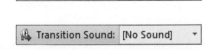

To modify the transition speed, **1.** click the **Transition Speed button list arrow**, and **2.** select a speed.

To add a sound to a transition, **1.** click the **Transition Sound button list arrow**, **2.** Move your insertion point over each sound to hear its effect, then **3.** click a sound to apply it.

▶ The Advance Slide options, as shown in Figure 2.20, allow you to specify how you want to move on to the next slide—manually or automatically.

If you choose to advance slides manually, select the **On Mouse Click** check box. To advance slides automatically, select the **Automatically after** check box, and specify the amount of time to elapse between slides.

TRY *it* **OUT** *p2-8*

1. Open the data file **p2-8**.

2. Display **Slide 1**, if it is not already displayed.

3. Click the **Animations tab**.

4. Click the **Transition to This Slide More button** to display the full gallery.

5. Move your insertion point over the different effects to see a live preview.

6. Click the **Dissolve** transition in the Fades and Dissolves section.

7. Press **[Page Down]** to advance to **Slide 2**.
   a. Click the **Transition to This Slide More button**, if necessary.
   b. Click the **Cover Up transition** in the Push and Cover section.

8. Press **[Page Down]** to advance to **Slide 3**.
   a. Click the **Transition to This Slide More button**, if necessary.
   b. Click the **Newsflash transition** in the Wipes section.

9. Press **[Page Down]** to advance to **Slide 4**. Apply any transition.

10. Press **[Page Down]** to advance to **Slide 5**. Apply any transition.

   a. Click the **Transition Sound button list arrow**, and click **Applause**.

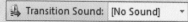

   b. Click the **Transition Speed button list arrow**, and click **Slow**.

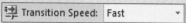

11. Display **Slide 2**.
   a. Select the **Automatically After** check box, and click the **up increment arrow** to display **02** seconds.
   b. Deselect **On Mouse Click**.

12. Drag the scroll bar up to return to **Slide 1**.

13. Click the **Slide Show view button** on the status bar.

14. Click the left mouse button to advance to the next slide. *Note: Wait two seconds; the slide will automatically advance without your clicking the mouse button.*

15. Click the left mouse button to advance to the next slide.

16. Repeat Step 15.

17. Press **[Escape]**.

18. Close the file without saving the changes.

Apply and Edit Animations

▶ **Animations** are visual or sound effects that affect the way text and objects appear on a slide during a slide show. You can use one of PowerPoint's built-in animation effects or you can create a custom effect, which allows you to combine animation schemes.

▶ If you want the same animation applied to all objects of a certain type, such as slide titles, you must apply the animation on the *slide master*. *You will learn to work with slide masters in Lesson 3.*

HOW To apply a built-in animation, **1.** select the text or object to animate. **2.** Click the **Animations tab**, and in the **Animations group**, select the animation effect that you want from the Animation list shown in Figure 2.22. **3.** Choose **All at Once** if you want the selected text or object to appear at once or **By 1st Level Paragraphs** if you want each bullet text item or object to appear one at a time.

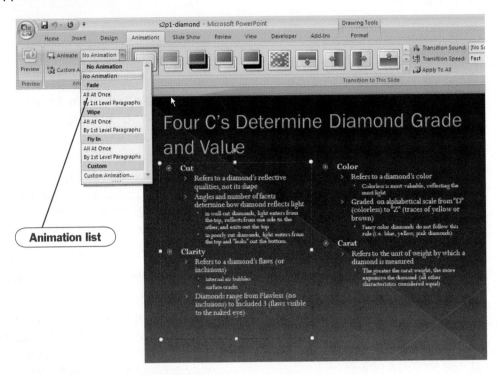

Figure 2.22: Built-in animation effects

To create a custom animation, **1.** select the text or object to animate. **2.** Click the **Animations tab**, and in the **Animations group**, click **Custom Animation**. On the Custom Animation task pane that appears, **3.** click **Add Effect**, and **4.** point to one of the following:

- **Entrance:** (to animate an item as it enters the slide), and click an entrance effect
- **Emphasis:** (to animate an item displayed on the slide), and click an emphasis effect
- **Exit:** (to animate an item as it exits the slide), and click an exit effect
- **Motion Paths:** (to animate text or an object to follow a specific path during the slide show), and click a motion path

Figure 2.23. shows the Custom Animation task pane and the animation effects that appear after you click **Add Effect**. If you point to Entrance, for example, you can choose animation effects such as Ascend, Blinds, Box, Checkerboard, Diamond, and Fly In. Click More Effects for options such as Boomerang, Bounce, Pinwheel, and Swivel.

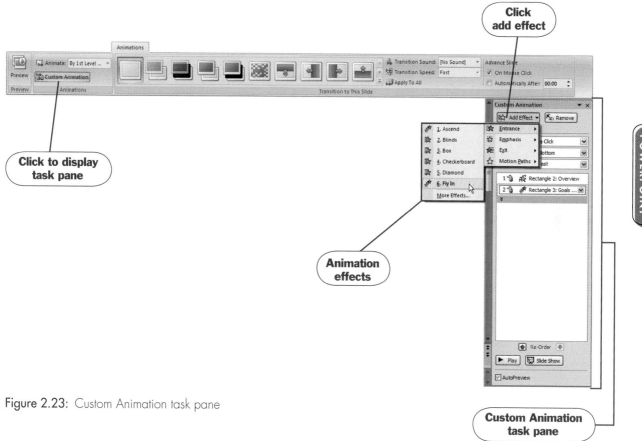

Figure 2.23: Custom Animation task pane

To specify settings for an entrance or exit effect, enter settings in the **Modify** section, as shown in Figure 2.24. **1.** Click the **Start list arrow**, and select how and when the effect will start. **2.** Click the **Amount** or **Direction list arrow** (the text box's name will vary depending on the selected animation), and select an amount or direction from which the text or object will start to animate. **3.** Click the **Speed list arrow**, and select an animation speed for the text or object. The effects appear in the Animation list in the order in which you add them, as shown in Figure 2.24.

To add a sound effect, **1.** right-click the animation effect in the **Custom Animation list**, and select **Effect Options** on the shortcut menu, as shown in Figure 2.25. In the dialog box that appears (the dialog box's name will vary depending on the effect you chose), **2.** click the **Effect tab**, **3.** click the **Sound list arrow**, and **4.** select a sound effect, as shown in Figure 2.26, then **5.** click **OK**.

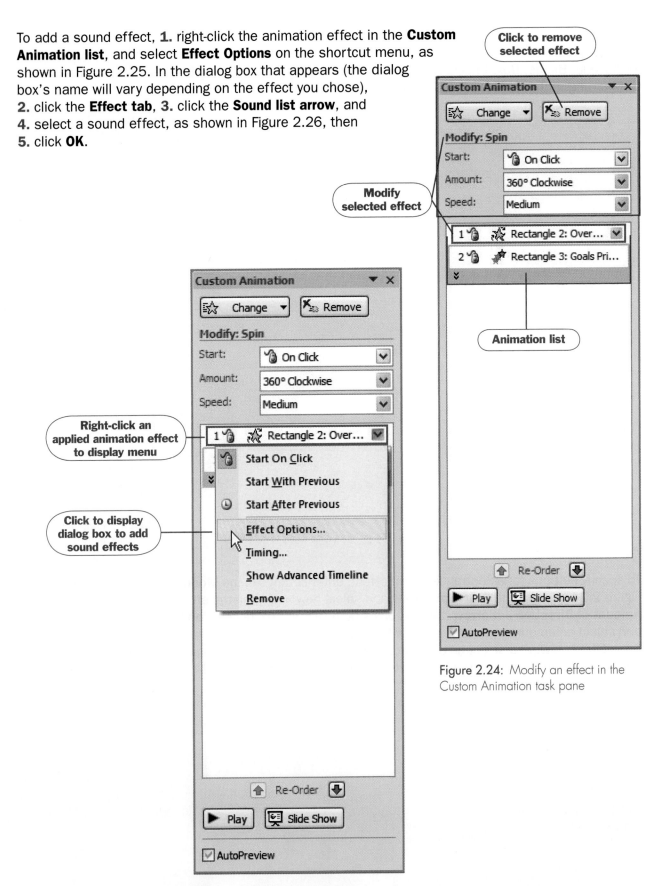

Figure 2.24: Modify an effect in the Custom Animation task pane

Figure 2.25: Add a sound effect through Effect Options

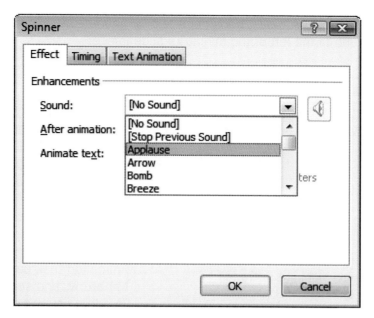

Figure 2.26: Dialog box used to set sound effects

▶ Effects appear in the Custom Animation list in the task pane with a number, timing icon, and animation effect icon, as shown in Figure 2.27.

- **Number:** Indicates the order in which the animation will play. The numbers also appear on the slide to help you visualize the order in which the animations will play.

- **Timing icon:** Indicates how the animation will be activated (a mouse icon indicates a mouse click).

- **Animation effect icon:** Indicates the animation type that you applied (Entrance, Emphasis, Exit, or Motion Paths).

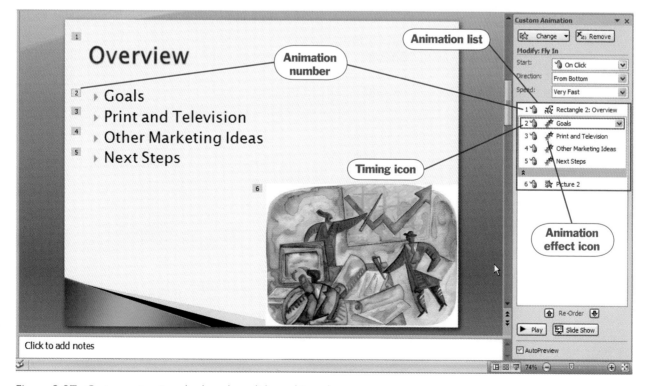

Figure 2.27: Custom animation displayed on slide and in task pane

▶ In Slide Sorter view, slides containing transitions and/or animations are marked by a star icon that appears below and to the left of the miniature slide image.

TRY*it*OUT *p2-9*

1. Open the data file **p2-9**.

2. Display **Slide 1**.
   a. Select the title.
   b. Click the **Animations tab**, and in the **Animations group**, click the **Custom Animation button**. [Custom Animation]
   c. On the Custom Animation task pane, click **Add Effect**, highlight **Entrance**, and click **Fly In**.

3. Display **Slide 2**.
   a. Select the title.
   b. Click **Add Effect**, highlight **Entrance**, click **More Effects**, and click **Checkerboard**.
   c. Select the bulleted text.
   d. Click **Add Effect**, highlight **Entrance**. Click **More Effects**. Click **Zoom** in the **Moderate group**, and click **OK**.

4. Display **Slide 3**.
   a. Select the title. Click **Add Effect**, highlight **Entrance**, and click **Checkerboard**.
   b. Select the title again. Click **Add Effect**, highlight **Emphasis**, select **Change Font Size**.
   c. Select the bulleted text. Click **Add Effect**, highlight **Entrance**. Click **More Effects**. Click **Zoom** in the **Moderate group**, and click **OK**.
   d. Select the graphic.
   e. Click **Add Effect**, highlight **Entrance**, select **More Effects**, select **Bounce** in the **Exciting** group, then click **OK**.
   f. In the **Modify** section of the Custom Animation task pane, click the **Speed list arrow**, and select **Very Slow**.
   g. To add a sound to the graphic animation, right-click the last animation effect (Picture) in the Animation list, select **Effect Options** on the shortcut menu. Click the **Effect tab**, if necessary, click the **Sound list arrow**, select **Wind**, then click **OK**.

5. Display **Slide 1**, then **Slide 2**, then **Slide 3**. For each slide, click **Play** at the bottom of the Custom Animation task pane to view your applied effects.

6. Switch to **Slide Sorter view**. Note that the slides containing an animation scheme are marked with a star icon.

7. Close the file without saving the changes.

Edit a Custom Animation

▶ Animation effects can be edited after you have applied them. You can change the animation effect, change the play order, or remove the animation.

▶ To edit a custom animation, you must display the Custom Animation task pane.

HOW To change the play order, **1.** click the effect in the Animation list in the Custom Animation task pane, then **2.** click the **Re-Order Up arrow** or **Re-Order Down arrow**, as shown in Figure 2.28.

To remove an effect, **1.** click the effect, then **2.** click **Remove** (see Figure 2.28).

To change an animation, **1.** click the effect, **2.** click **Change** (see Figure 2.28), then **3.** apply a new effect.

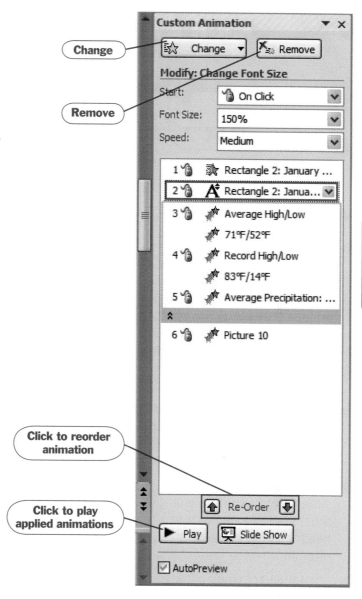

Figure 2.28: Change an animation effect on Custom Animation task pane

POWERPOINT

T R Y *it* O U T *p2-10*

1. Open the data file **p2-10**.
2. Display **Slide 3**.
   a. Click the **Animations tab**, and in the **Animations group**, click the **Custom Animation button** to display the Custom Animation task pane. [Custom Animation]
   b. Select animation number 2, and click **Remove**.

   c. Select animation number 5 (Picture). Click the **Reorder Up arrow** as many times as needed to move the animation to become number 2.
3. Click **Play**.
4. Close the file without saving the changes.

REHEARSAL

 GOAL
To create and enhance a six-slide informative presentation, as shown in Figure 2.29

TASK 2

WHAT YOU NEED TO KNOW

▶ Use clip art to enhance a presentation and make it more appealing. Pictures, if you use them correctly, can communicate an idea that words are unable to express. Visuals can also help make the presentation, or idea within the presentation, more memorable.

▶ It is important to use visuals that are relevant to the slide's topic. Do not add graphics just to fill space.

▶ Transitions and animation schemes transform a dull presentation into one that heightens the audience's attention.

▶ Animation schemes allow you to introduce text bullet by bullet so that the audience does not jump ahead of you as you deliver your presentation.

▼ DIRECTIONS

1. Open a new blank presentation, and apply the **Civic theme**.

2. For **Slide 1**, accept the default title slide layout. Enter the title and subtitle as shown in Figure 2.29.

3. Add new slides.
   a. Use relevant slide layouts, and enter the corresponding text for the slides shown in Figure 2.29.
   b. For **Slide 3** and **Slide 5**, use a slide layout that contains content placeholders.
   c. For **Slide 4**, insert clip art directly on the slide. *Hint: Click the **Insert tab**, and in the **Illustrations group**, click the **Clip Art button**, search for and select an image in the Clip Art task pane.*
   d. For **Slide 1**, insert a picture background. Insert relevant clip art where shown.

4. Display **Slide 2**.
   a. Draw a text box, and enter the text `We work with you from concept to completion!`, as shown in the figure.
   b. Use a **24-point** font size and any desired font color.
   c. Position the text box as shown.

5. Apply a different transition effect to each slide in the presentation.

6. Display **Slide 1**.
   a. Apply the **Spinner** entrance effect for the title, and add a **Drum Roll** sound effect.
   b. Apply the **Fly In** entrance effect for the subtitle, and apply a medium entrance speed.

7. For **Slides 2-6**, apply the **Ascend** entrance effect in the Moderate group to the bulleted text. Apply a Fast speed to the effect. Do not animate the text box on Slide 2.

Continued on next page

8. Display **Slide 5**.
   a. Apply the **Curvy Right** motion path effect for the graphic.
   b. Set the speed to **Medium**. *Hint: Select the graphic, click the **Animations tab**, click the **Custom Animation button**, click **Add Effect**, highlight **Motion Paths**, click **More Motion Paths**, click **Curvy Right**, then click **OK**.*

9. Click the **Animations tab**, if necessary, and in the **Transition to This Slide group**, select **On Mouse Click** below Advance Slide, if necessary.

10. Display **Slide 1**. Run the slide show.

11. Save the presentation as **2r2-ppg overview**.

12. Close the presentation.

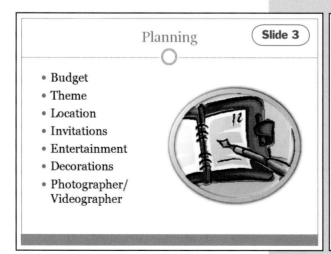

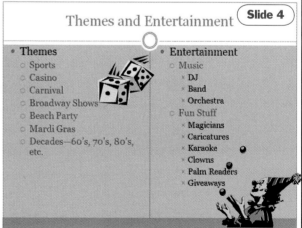

Figure 2.29a: Slides 1–4 of Perfect Planning Group presentation

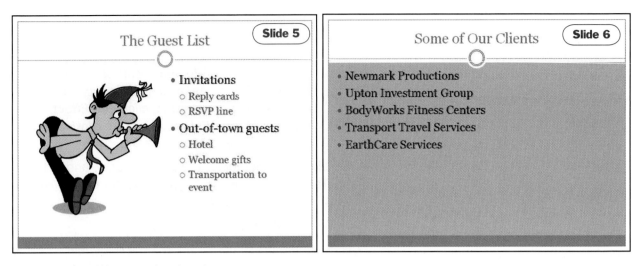

Figure 2.29b: Slides 5–6 of Perfect Planning Group presentation

Cues for Reference

Insert Clip Art or a Picture
Into a Content Placeholder
1. Select a slide layout that contains a content placeholder.
2. Click the clip art icon on the slide.
3. Enter a topic or theme in the Search for text box, and click **Go**.
4. Click desired clip art image.
   Or
1. Click the Picture icon on the slide.
2. Select the file to insert.
3. Click **Insert**.

Directly onto a Slide (Not into a Placeholder)
1. Click the **Insert tab**, and in the **Illustrations group**, click the **Clip Art button**.
2. Enter a topic or theme in the Search for text box, and click **Go**.
3. Click desired clip art image.
   Or
1. Click the **Picture button**.
2. Select the picture file to insert.
3. Click Insert.

Add Slide Transitions
1. Display the slide on which to add a transition.
2. Click the **Animations tab**, and then click the **Transition to This Slide More button**.
3. Click a transition to apply it.
4. Click the **Sound list arrow** to add a transition sound.
5. Click the **Speed list arrow** to modify the transition speed.
6. Click **Apply to All** to apply the transition effect to all slides.
   Or
6. Display another slide and repeat the steps above to apply a different slide transition to it.

Advance Slides Automatically
1. Click the **Automatically After check box**.
2. Click the **up** or **down** increment arrows to specify a time after which the slide will advance to the next one.

3. Click **Apply to All** to apply the transition effect to all slides.
   Or
3. Display another slide and repeat the steps above to apply a different transition to it.

Apply Custom Animations
1. Select the text or object to which to apply an animation.
2. Click the **Animations tab**, click the **Custom Animation button**.
3. Click **Add Effect** on the Custom Animation task pane.
4. Click one of the following animation options:
   • Entrance
   • Emphasis
   • Exit
   • Motion Paths
5. Click an animation, or click **More Effects** to view other animation options, then click an effect to apply it.

PERFORMANCE

TASK 2

You are the director of marketing at Palmetto Realtors. In an effort to solicit new business, you have been asked to create an informative presentation about the company and its services. Sales representatives will then use laptops to show the presentation to prospective buyers and sellers at open houses. You have compiled the information you will need to create a presentation consisting of six slides.

Follow these guidelines:

1. Title the presentation: **Palmetto Realtors**. Include the following subtitle: **Find the Perfect Home**

2. Read through the summary provided on the next page to get a basic understanding of the content the presentation will cover. Use the bold headings shown in the notes below as slide titles.

3. Use the information below the bold headings to create bullet points for that slide. For **Slide 4** ("Why Choose Palmetto?"), use the information provided to create concise bullet points. Use your own judgment with regard to wording.

4. Apply any design theme to the presentation.

5. Change the theme colors.

6. For **Slides 2–5**, insert relevant clip art where appropriate.
   - Apply a picture style and picture shape to at least one of the clip art images.

7. Apply a different slide transition to each slide.

8. Display **Slide 6** ("Contact Us").
   a. Add a text box that reads, **Call (305) 555-1234 and find an agent today!**, as shown in Figure 2.30. Apply any font color, font style, and font size to it as shown in the figure. (Figure 2.30 is provided only as an example; your design theme may differ.)
   b. Add three relevant clip art images directly on the slide. Use Figure 2.30 as a guide for placing your images.
   c. Add the **Drum Roll** transition sound.

9. Animate the bulleted text and clip art images throughout the presentation using entrance, emphasis, exit, and motion path effects. Do not animate the slide titles.

10. Save the presentation as **2p2-perfect home**.

Who We Are

- Leading residential real estate firm in Florida, serving Miami-Dade and Broward counties
- 1000 staff and employees
- 30 offices
  - South Miami
  - Miami Beach
  - Ft. Lauderdale
  - Aventura
  - Coconut Grove
  - Coral Gables

Our Services

- Residential real estate
- Relocation services
- International services
- Home mortgage
- Title closing services
- Property insurance

Why Choose Palmetto?

We have the best-trained brokers in Florida. Our company does exceptional marketing and advertising of properties to target the right buyers. With our centrally located offices, trained brokers are easy to reach. We do a quarterly analysis of the South Florida market to provide you with the most up-to-date information on condo and home sales. Our user-friendly Web site is another reason you will want to choose Palmetto for your home-buying and -selling needs.

Finding a Home with Palmetto

- Identify your budget, location, size, type of ownership, and amenities (if applicable).
- Choose *one* agent to work with to minimize overlap and create a good working relationship.
- Communicate with your broker. Be open about your budget, needs, interests, and anything else you might require in your new home or building.
- Schedule appointments during the week to avoid crowds and competition on weekends and during open houses.

Contact Us

- Search for a home 24 hours a day at **www.palmettorealtors.net**.

Figure 2.30: Palmetto Realtors final slide

T R Y O U T

GOAL

To create and modify an informative presentation as an outline, hide a slide, then link slides, as shown in Figure 2.31

* Work with outlines
* Hide a slide
* Link slides

TASK 3

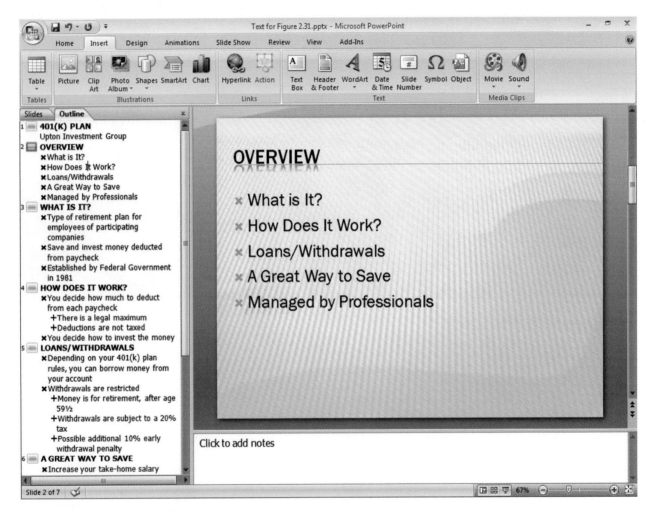

Figure 2.31: Outline of an informative presentation

WHAT YOU NEED TO KNOW

Work with Outlines

▶ You can view slide content as an *outline* to see the flow of your presentation by displaying the Outline tab, as shown in Figure 2.32.

▶ You can also enter text in the Outline tab. Slides are shown numbered down the left side of the screen, and slide icons identify the start of each new slide (see Figure 2.32). Slide content appears as plain text on the Outline tab, without formatting, graphics, text boxes, or enhancements. You can drag the outline window to show more of the outline and a smaller slide by positioning your insertion point on the vertical window divider. When you see a double-headed arrow, drag to the right.

▶ It is also possible to import an outline from Word to become a presentation. *Importing an outline from Word will be covered in Lesson 6.*

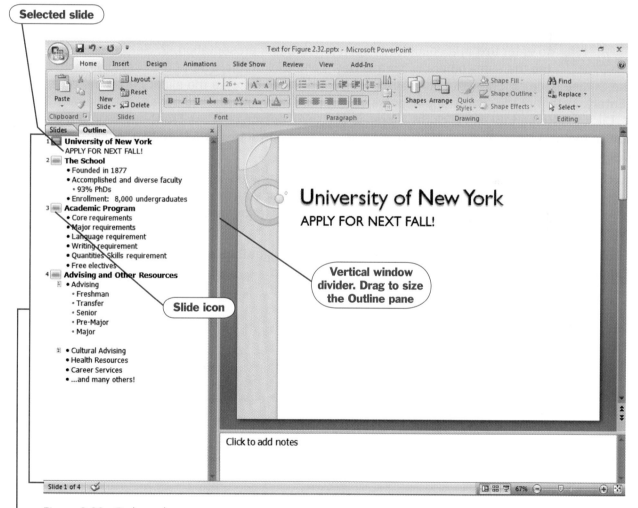

Figure 2.32: Outline tab pane

▶ Outlines can serve as a table of contents or agenda to be printed and distributed to an audience. To create a table of contents, you can collapse or hide subtext on all slides so that only slide titles appear, as shown in Figure 2.33. Working in outline view makes it easy to move headings to reorganize content.

▶ You may also want to create your presentation in the Outline tab pane. Text automatically is entered into the slide in the proper placeholders, and you can see the content of your entire presentation in this view.

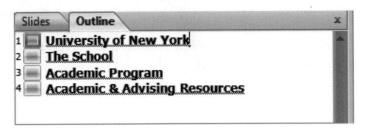

Figure 2.33: Text collapsed on all slides

HOW To enter text in an outline, **1.** open a new blank presentation. **2.** Select the **Outline tab** (be sure you are in Normal view), and click to the right of the first slide icon in the Outline pane. **3.** Enter `first-level text`, which will become the slide's title, and press **[Enter]**. Note that the slide's title appears on both the Outline and Slide panes (see Figure 2.32). **4.** Click the **Home tab**, and click the **Increase List level button** or press **[Tab]** to promote the text to the next level. **5.** Press **[Enter]**. **6.** Type the same level text (a new bullet), or click the **Decrease List Level button** to begin a new slide title.

To collapse an outline, **1.** click the **Outline tab** to display the outline. **2.** Right-click the text in the outline, **3.** highlight **Collapse**, then **4.** select **Collapse** to hide all the subheads for this slide, or select **Collapse All** to hide all the subheads for the presentation from the shortcut menu that displays, as shown in Figure 2.34.

To expand the outline, **1.** follow steps 1–2 above. **2.** Highlight **Expand**, and **3.** select **Expand** or **Expand All**.

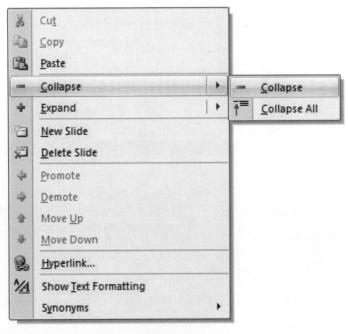

Figure 2.34: Outline shortcut menu

To move a slide title and subtext up or down, **1.** select the slide icon to highlight the slide title and subtext, then **2.** right-click. **3.** Select **Move Up** or **Move Down** from the shortcut menu (see Figure 2.34). You can also position your insertion point on a slide icon and drag it up or down.

To move subtext up or down, **1.** right-click the subtext to move, and **2.** select **Move Up** or **Move Down** from the shortcut menu.

To print an outline, use the same procedures that you use to print slides, but in the Print dialog box, select **Outline View** from the **Print what** list, as shown in Figure 2.35.

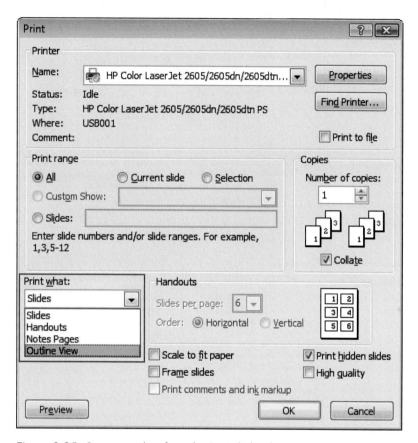

Figure 2.35: Print an outline from the Print dialog box

TRY *it* **OUT** *p2-11*

1. Open the data file **p2-11**.

2. Click the **Outline tab**, if necessary.

3. Click the **Slide 4 icon**.

4. Click the **Home tab**, and in the **Slides group**, click the **New Slide button** to create a new Slide 5. Apply a **Title and Content** layout.

5. On the **Outline pane**, enter Additional Programs as the title for **Slide 5.**

6. Press **[Enter]**, then click the **Increase list level button**.

7. Enter the text shown below, pressing **[Enter]** after each entry.
   - Study abroad
   - Undergraduate research opportunities
   - Individualized majors
   - Honors programs

8. Click the **Slide 5 icon** to highlight the slide title and subtext, then drag it up to become **Slide 4**.

Continued on next page

9. Right-click the last bullet in **Slide 2** ("Enrollment: 8,000 undergraduates"), and click **Move Up** once.

10. Right-click "Enrollment: 8,000 undergraduates" again, and click **Move Up** again. "Enrollment: 8,000 undergraduates" should be below "Founded in 1877."

11. Right-click the **Slide 4 title**, highlight **Collapse**, then select **Collapse All** from the shortcut menu.

12. Right-click the **Slide 4 title**, highlight **Expand**, then select **Expand All**.

13. Click the **Slide 1 icon**. Cycle through the slides using the **Page Down button**.

14. Click the **Office button**, then click **Print**.

15. In the **Print what box**, select **Outline View**. Click **Cancel**.

16. Close the file without saving the changes.

Hide a Slide

▶ A slide presentation created for one audience may not be suitable for another. You can use the same presentation for different audiences by hiding slides that are not relevant. Hiding slides does not delete them; it hides them during the presentation.

HOW 1. Select the slide you want to hide in Slide Sorter view. 2. Click the **Slide Show tab**, and in the **Set Up group**, 3. click the **Hide Slide button**, as shown in Figure 2.36. A diagonal bar across the slide number indicates that the slide is hidden (see Figure 2.36).

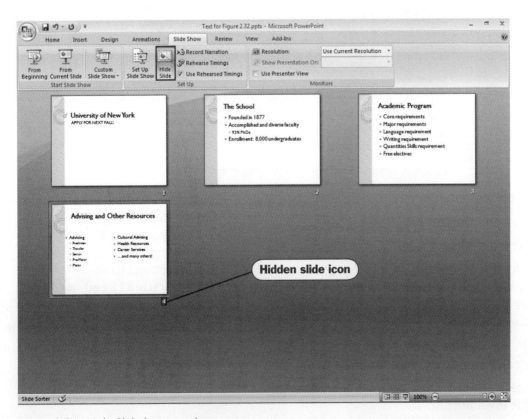

Figure 2.36: Hide Slide button and icon

▶ To unhide a slide, repeat the process you used to hide it. The diagonal bar will be removed from across the slide number.

 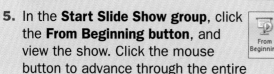
Link Slides

▶ A **hyperlink** is a shortcut that allows you to jump to another location. You can create a hyperlink on a slide to link to another slide within a presentation, a slide in another presentation, or a document in another software program. A hyperlink can also be created to link to a Web site. *(PowerPoint and the Web will be covered in Lesson 6.)*

▶ You can apply a hyperlink to text or objects. When you apply a hyperlink to text, the text appears underlined and in color. When you apply a hyperlink to an object, there is no visible change to the object.

▶ You can activate hyperlinks only in Slide Show view. When you position the mouse pointer over text or an object that contains a hyperlink while in Slide show view, the mouse pointer changes to a hand, as shown in Figure 2.37. Clicking on a hyperlink activates the link and brings you to the linked slide or program.

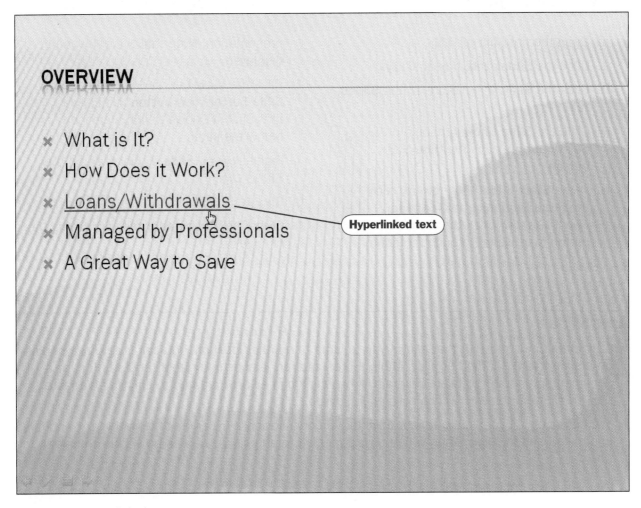

Figure 2.37: Hyperlinked text

HOW [Ctrl]+K   **1.** Select the text or object on which to create the link. **2.** Click the **Insert tab**, and in the **Links group**, **3.** click the **Hyperlink button**, as shown in Figure 2.38, or right-click and select **Hyperlink**. In the Insert Hyperlink dialog box that appears, as shown in Figure 2.38, **4.** click **Place in This Document** in the **Link to** section. This displays all of the slide titles within the presentation. In the **Select a place in this document** box, **5.** click the title of the slide to which you want to link, and then **6.** click **OK**.

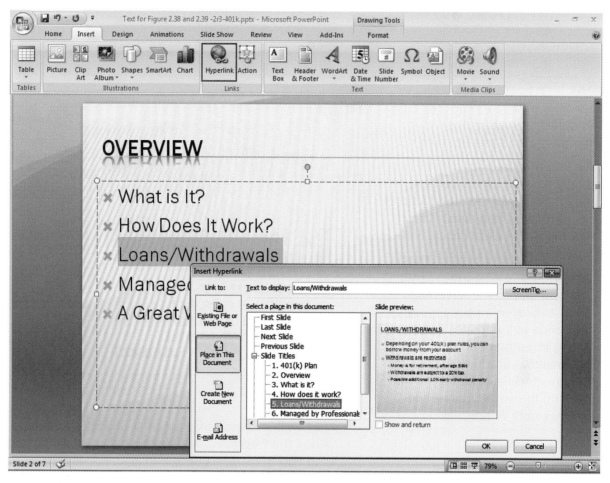

Figure 2.38: Insert Hyperlink dialog box

T R Y *i t* **O U T** *p2-13*

1. Open the data file **p2-13**.
2. Display **Slide 2** ("Overview").
3. Select "Loans/Withdrawals."
4. Click the **Insert tab**, and in the **Links group**, click the **Hyperlink button**.
5. In the **Link to** section, click **Place in This Document**.
6. In the **Select a place in this document** box, click **Loans/Withdrawals**.
7. Click **OK**.
8. Click the **Slide Show button** on the status bar.
9. On **Slide 2**, click the **Loans/Withdrawals** hyperlink.
10. Press **[Escape]**.
11. Close the file without saving the changes.

REHEARSAL

TASK 3

WHAT YOU NEED TO KNOW

▶ An outline serves as the framework for a presentation.

▶ The information in an outline should follow a logical pattern. It should begin with an introduction, include details and discussion, and end with a clear conclusion.

▶ A 401(K) is a type of retirement plan offered to employees. The employer deducts a percentage of the employee's salary every pay period and deposits it into a 401(K) investment account. Such a plan allows a worker to save for retirement while deferring income taxes on the saved money and earnings until withdrawal.

▽ DIRECTIONS

1. Open a new blank presentation.

2. Click the **Outline tab**.

3. Enter the titles for each slide, as shown in Figure 2.39.

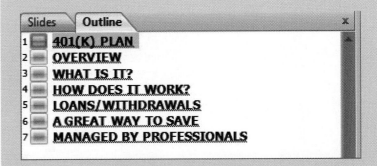

Figure 2.39: Slide titles

4. Click the **Home tab**, and in the **Paragraph group**, use the **Decrease** and **Increase List Level buttons** to add the subtext shown in Figure 2.40.

5. Right-click on **Slide 1** text on the Outline tab. Highlight **Collapse**, then click **Collapse All** to collapse all of the subtext.

6. Move **Slide 7** ("Managed by Professionals") so that it becomes **Slide 6.**

7. Apply a design theme to the presentation. Insert a background picture in the first slide in the presentation.

8. Expand all of the text.

9. Display **Slide 2** ("Overview"). Link each topic to the appropriate slide in the presentation.

10. Display **Slide Sorter view**.

11. Select **Slide 6**. Click the **Slide Show tab**, and click the **Hide Slide button**.

Continued on next page

BodyWorksFitnessCenters has developed a new corporate membership program that provides better rates and benefits for employees of companies that maintain 50 or more fitness center memberships. To inform businesses about this exciting program, you have been asked to create a presentation that describes the club and the benefits of corporate membership. In the next few weeks, your staff will be meeting with the human resources departments of companies in the area to share this information, which they can disseminate to their employees. You have been given the information you need to create a presentation consisting of five slides.

Follow these guidelines:

1. Read through the summary provided on the next page to get a basic understanding of the content the presentation will cover. Use an outline to create and organize the presentation content.

2. Each bold heading represents a slide title. Use the information below the heading to create the bulleted text for each slide.

3. Title the presentation: **BodyworksFitnessCenters**. Add the following subtitle: **The Corporate Membership**.

4. Apply a design theme to the presentation.

5. Display the **Outline tab**. Move **Slide 4** ("Corporate Membership") to become **Slide 5**.

6. Display **Slide 1**.
   a. Insert a hyperlink on the subtitle, "Corporate Membership" to link to **Slide 5** ("The Corporate Membership").

7. Display **Slide 2**.
   a. Insert a relevant clip art image, and apply a picture shape and border to it.
   b. Insert a hyperlink on the clip art image, and link it to **Slide 3** ("The Workout").

8. Insert additional clip art where appropriate.

9. Apply any slide transitions and custom animations to your presentation.

10. Display **Slide 1**, then run the slide show. Activate the hyperlinks during the presentation.

11. Save the presentation as **2p3-corporate join**.

The Club

We offer comfortable and clean clubs with multiple locations throughout Phoenix. We have a top-notch staff, state-of-the-art equipment, award-wining classes, and a newsworthy spa.

The Workout

We offer numerous classes per week:
- Boxing   14
- Step   9
- Yoga   12
- Pilates   8
- Spinning   10
- Dance   5

Our workout equipment includes:
- Treadmills
- Stairmasters
- Cross trainers
- Bikes
- Weight machines
- Free weights

Corporate Membership

There are two types of membership:

- Company Financed. The employer purchases memberships; memberships can be transferred to other employees; new employees can be added anytime.
- Paycheck Deductions. Employer pays total membership upfront for only those who join, and the employee gets a payroll deduction to cover the cost of the membership.

The Membership

We offer a month-to-month membership for our members. There is no additional charge for classes. All new members get a complimentary training session. Members can join one, two, or all of our gym locations. Members can also freeze their membership for up to 2 months per year.

ENCORE

Act I

You are the internship coordinator at Newmark Productions. Your company has just hired 20 interns for the summer. To orient the new interns to Newmark Productions, you have been asked to create a presentation that provides a company overview and lists each department's responsibilities. You have been given the information to create a presentation consisting of approximately nine slides.

Follow these guidelines:

1. Read through the information provided on the next page to get a basic understanding of the content the presentation will cover.

2. Use the information provided to create the slides. Use an outline to create and organize the presentation content.
   a. Create a relevant title slide for the presentation.
   b. Create the remaining slides. Use the bold headings as slide titles and the italicized words as bullet points. Amend the wording of the italicized words as needed.

3. Apply a design theme and a variety of slide layouts.

4. Insert appropriate clip art and a text box.

5. Change the theme colors, fonts, and slide background, if you want.

6. Apply animations to the bulleted text on all slides.

7. Save the presentation as **2e1-newmark**.

Newmark Productions

Summary

Fast Facts

CEO Alan Newman and CFO Mark Cohen founded Newmark Productions in 1990. Newmark maintains offices in New York and Los Angeles and currently employs more than 500 people. Since its founding, Newmark has released 50 feature films and 7 Emmy-winning television programs.

Departments

Six departments provide the foundation for Newmark's award-winning work: Production, Distribution, Marketing/Publicity/Promotions, Television, Merchandising, and Interactive.

Production

The Production Department is responsible for making the movies—from start to finish. The movie production process begins with *story and script development.* After a script is selected and purchased, *a budget is assigned and a production schedule is developed. A director and cast are then selected* and *pre-production begins.* After the movie is filmed, it goes into the final stage of *post-production,* where the director and Newmark agree on a final cut.

Distribution

The film is then ready to be distributed. The Distribution Department *books the theaters that will show the film.* As theaters are located all over the world, Newmark has *domestic distribution offices in New York, Los Angeles, Chicago, and Atlanta* and *international offices in London and Buenos Aires* to facilitate the distribution of the films. The Distribution Department also *calculates Newmark's film grosses* (money earned on the films).

Marketing/Publicity/Promotions

The Marketing, Publicity, and Promotions Departments work to promote the films. They are responsible for *creating the movie trailers* (commercials/previews) that play on television and in theaters and the *movie posters* that appear on billboards or newspapers. The departments also *plan and coordinate movie premieres, create giveaway items, write press releases, coordinate talent appearances on* TV talk shows and entertainment news programs, and *develop sweepstakes opportunities.*

Television

Newmark also has a strong Television Department that develops programming for network, cable, and syndication. The department also licenses movies to these TV outlets and does its own marketing and promotions for its current series.

Merchandising

The Merchandising Department works with various licensees to create products based on Newmark's film and television properties. It distributes these products (which can be T-shirts, Halloween costumes, posters, toys, etc.) to retail stores.

Interactive

Newmark's Interactive Department creates and maintains Web sites for current television series and movies. It also sends e-mails and e-newsletters to fans to promote the films and TV shows. Finally, it maintains an e-commerce site, which sells many of the products developed by the Merchandising Department.

Act II

You are the tour coordinator for Transport Travel Services. Your company wants to promote its new tour to Madrid, Spain. For travel agents to sell this trip to potential travelers, they must be well-informed about the city of Madrid. An assistant has researched the highlights of Madrid and has provided you with a summary of his research. You will use this summary, along with information you find on the Internet, to create a presentation consisting of approximately eight slides.

Follow these guidelines:

1. Read through the summary provided on the next page to get a basic understanding of the content the presentation will cover. Then use the summary information to create the slides that contain appropriate bulleted information.
   a. Create a relevant title for the presentation. Then create a title for each slide that summarizes slide information. Remember, the objective of this presentation is to inform travel agents about facts, highlights, and tourist attractions of Madrid.
   b. Conduct research on the Internet to create the first slide, which provides a snapshot of things to do and remember while in Madrid. To get this information, go to www.travelocity.com. Click the **Destination Guides** link, enter **Madrid** in the "Enter a destination here" box, and click **Search**. Print the page. Use the Madrid, Spain Snapshot information to create a slide titled "Snapshot." *If the Internet is not available to you, skip this step (and omit this slide).*
   c. Apply a design theme. Change the theme color.

2. Apply a background picture to the title slide. You may have to change the font color so the title is clearly visible.

3. Apply animations to bulleted text on all slides.

4. Apply transitions to all slides.

5. Insert relevant clip art where appropriate. Apply a picture effect and border effect to at least one clip art graphic.

6. Save your presentation as **2e2-madrid**.

Madrid, Spain

Summary

Madrid is the capital city of Spain, home to nearly five million people. The national government is a constitutional monarchy, the national language is Spanish, and the national currency is the peseta.

The city provides adequate public transportation. The bus system and the metro are the easiest and most efficient ways to get around. The fare for the bus or metro is 130 pesetas. The bus, however, offers a 10-trip booklet for 645 pesetas. Taxis are available at reasonable rates, but be sure to watch the meter, as taxi drivers might take advantage of tourists. *Do not* rent a car unless you plan to travel outside of the city. Traffic within Madrid is terrible. Overall, the best way to see the city is to walk.

While in Spain you should experience the things for which Spain is known. You might see a bullfight, eat tapas, shop the Rastro flea market, try or watch flamenco dancing, and spend some time at an outdoor café.

There are so many sights in Madrid worth visiting. If you are limited for time, however, you should be sure to see the following places: The Puerta del Sol, or "Gate of the Sun," marks the center of Spain. The Palacio de las Cortes is the home of the Spanish Parliament. The Prado museum, which was opened to the public in 1819, is a spectacular neoclassical structure that houses works by the famous Spanish painters Goya and Velázquez, among many, many others. Near the Prado is Retiro Park, which was a royal preserve built in 1636 for Philip IV. Plaza Mayor is a square in the city that hosts concerts, festivals, political rallies, and a Sunday market. Many shops and cafés also surround it. The Palacio Real, or Royal Palace, was built in 1738, has 2,800 rooms, and was home to Philip V. Casa del Campo, once a hunting preserve for Philip II, is now a fairground and amusement park that houses the Madrid Zoo.

The biggest meal of the day in Spain is consumed between 2 and 4 p.m., after which people take a siesta. Before dinner most Spaniards enjoy tapas, small dishes of food similar to appetizers. Dinner is eaten between 9:30 p.m. and midnight. When dining out, a gratuity is not usually included on the check; however, it is customary to tip about 10%.

There are many annual events in Madrid, and, depending on when you visit, you might be able to experience one! Do research on the Internet for the annual events in Madrid and place them on this slide.

Creating Sales and Marketing Presentations

In this lesson, you will learn to use PowerPoint features to create effective sales and marketing presentations. Businesses use sales and marketing presentations to promote products, services, or ideas.

Upon completion of this lesson, you will have mastered the following skill sets

- ✳ Format bullets
- ✳ Insert footers
- ✳ Work with Slide Masters
- ✳ Create and apply multiple Slide Masters
- ✳ Save a design or Slide Master as a template
- ✳ Create a custom show
- ✳ Link to a custom show
- ✳ Use multiple masters within a custom show
- ✳ Work with graphic objects
- ✳ Create shapes
- ✳ Create WordArt
- ✳ Format objects
- ✳ Rotate and flip objects
- ✳ Layer and group objects
- ✳ Use the grid and guides
- ✳ Align or distribute objects
- ✳ Work with tables, charts, and SmartArt
- ✳ Use action buttons

Terms
Software-related
Action button
Cell
Custom show
Data labels
Flip
Footer
Grid
Group
Guides
Layer
Master Layout slide
Rotate
Slide Master
Style
Table
Template
Title Master
Title slide layout
Ungroup
WordArt

TRYOUT

GOAL

To create and enhance a sales and marketing presentation, as shown in Figure 3.1

✱ Format bullets
✱ Insert headers and footers
✱ Work with Slide and Title Masters
✱ Save a design or slide Master as a template

TASK 1

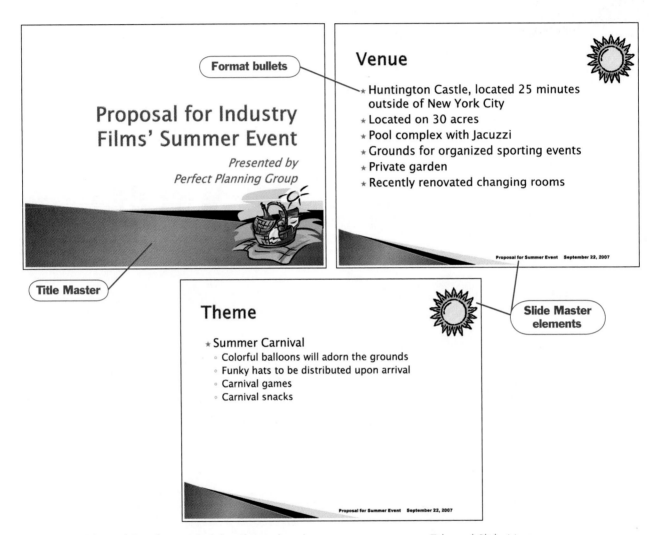

Figure 3.1: Three slides of an eight-slide sales and marketing presentation using Title and Slide Masters

WHAT YOU NEED TO KNOW

Format Bullets

▶ Many slide layouts contain bulleted text. You can change the style, size, and color of bullets to add visual excitement to your presentation on individual slides, or keep them consistent on all slides by working with a Slide Master. (Slide Masters will be covered later in this task.)

▶ You can use a symbol as a bullet or choose from numerous decorative bullets that PowerPoint provides. The same techniques for formatting bullets in Word are used in PowerPoint.

HOW To add or modify bullets, **1.** position the insertion point in the bulleted item or list level you want to change. **2.** Click the **Home tab**, and in the **Paragraph group**, **3.** click the **Bullets button list arrow**, or right-click and point to **Bullets**. **4.** In the gallery that appears, as shown in Figure 3.2, choose a different bullet style.

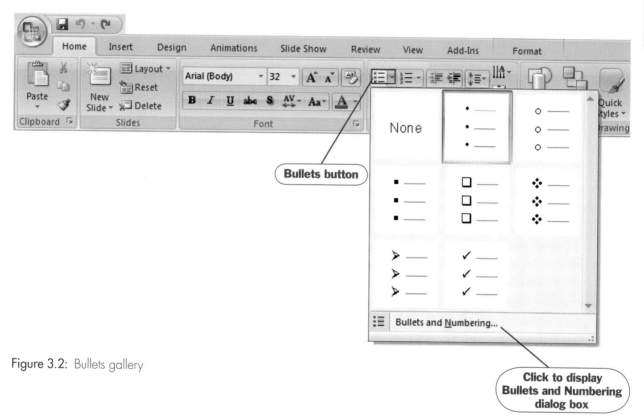

Figure 3.2: Bullets gallery

POWERPOINT

To customize a bullet, **1.** click the **Bullets and Numbering** link at the bottom of the gallery (see Figure 3.2). In the Bullets and Numbering dialog box that appears as shown in Figure 3.3, **2.** click the **Customize button** to select a symbol or graphical font, or click the **Picture button** to select a decorative bullet (see Figure 3.5). **3.** Select a symbol or a decorative bullet from the related dialog box that appears as shown in Figures 3.4 and 3.5. **4.** Click **OK**. **5.** Click **OK** again, if necessary.

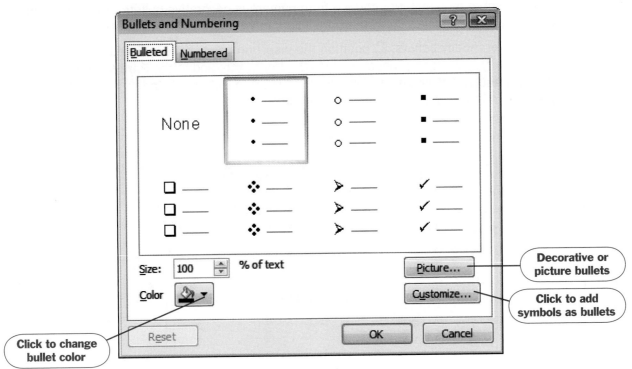

Figure 3.3: Bullets and Numbering dialog box

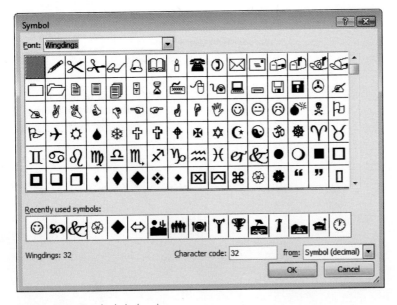

Figure 3.4: Symbol dialog box

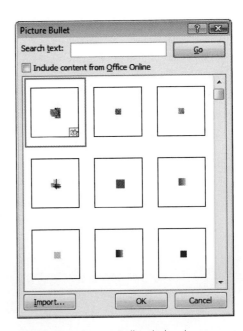

Figure 3.5: Picture Bullet dialog box

To change the color or size of bullets, **1.** select the bulleted text to affect, **2.** right-click, point to **Bullets**, and click the **Bullets and Numbering link** at the bottom of the gallery. **3.** On the **Bulleted tab**, click the **Color button**, and choose a color, **4.** use the Size increment arrows to change the bullet size, then **5.** click **OK**.

To remove a bullet, **1.** position the insertion point in the bulleted item or list level, or select the bulleted text to affect, **2.** click the **Home tab**, and in the **Paragraph group**, click the **Bullets button**.

T R Y *i t* **O U T** *p3-1*

1. Open the data file **p3-1**.

2. Display **Slide 2**.

3. Enter `January 15-18` as the first bullet point.

4. Click the **Home tab**, if necessary, and in the **Paragraph group**, click the **Bullets button list arrow**.

5. Click a bullet list style from the gallery that appears.

6. Press **[Enter]**.

7. Enter `Los Angeles Convention Center` as the second bullet.

8. Display **Slide 4**. Select all the bulleted text.

9. Click the **Bullets button list arrow**, click the **Bullets and Numbering** link, then click the **Customize button**.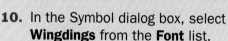

10. In the Symbol dialog box, select **Wingdings** from the **Font** list.

11. Click a smiley face symbol, then click **OK**.

12. Click the **Color button**, select **Green**, then click **OK**.

13. Close the presentation without saving the changes.

Insert Footers

▶ A **footer** is the same text that appears at the bottom of every slide.

▶ You can include slide numbers, the date or time, and other text that you want in the footer area on individual slides or all slides.

▶ PowerPoint provides footer placeholders for this information as shown in the preview window of the Header and Footer dialog box shown in Figure 3.6. Depending on the theme selected, the date and time generally appear on the bottom left of the slide, footer text appears in the middle of the slide, and the slide number appears on the bottom right. You can move footer placeholders the same way that you move any other placeholder.

▶ You can format the slide number, date and time, and footer text just like all other text within a placeholder.

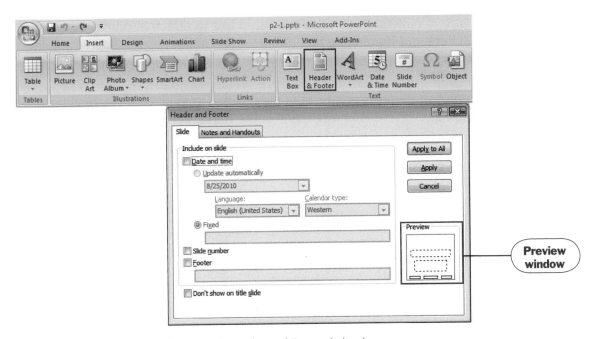

Figure 3.6: Header & Footer button and Header and Footer dialog box

HOW **1.** Click the **Insert tab**, and in the **Text group**, **2.** click the **Header & Footer button**, as shown in Figure 3.6. In the Header and Footer dialog box that appears (see Figure 3.6), **3.** click the appropriate check box to indicate whether you want to include the date and time, slide number, or footer. **4.** Enter the footer text in the appropriate box. **5.** Click the **Apply button** to apply the settings to the current slide, or click the **Apply to All button** to apply the settings to all the slides in the presentation. *Note: You cannot insert a header in PowerPoint even though the button says "Header & Footer" and you enter settings in a "Header and Footer" dialog box.*

▶ To have the date or time update automatically each time you open the presentation, click the Update automatically option button. To insert a date or time that is not updated automatically, click the Fixed option button and enter the date or time you want displayed.

▶ If you do not want your footer selections to appear on the title slide, click the Don't show on title slide check box.

TRY it OUT p3-2

1. Open the data file **p3-2**.

2. Click the **Insert tab**, and in the **Text group**, click the **Header & Footer button** to display the Header and Footer dialog box.

3. Click the **Date and time check box** to select it, if it is not already checked.

4. Click the **Fixed** option, if necessary, and enter today's date in the **Fixed** text box.

5. Click the **Slide number check box** to select it.

6. Click the **Footer check box** to select it, if it is not already checked.

7. Enter your name in the **Footer text box**.

8. Click the **Don't show on title slide check box**.

9. Click **Apply to All**.

10. Run the slide show. Notice that the footer appears on all slides except for the title slide.

11. Close the file without saving the changes.

Work with the Slide Masters

▶ The **Slide Master** feature enables you to achieve consistency on all slides in a presentation. Using this feature, you can change the content or formatting (font style, font size, color, position, tabs, indents, background, and color theme) of text or object placeholders on the Slide Master, and PowerPoint automatically reformats all slides throughout the active presentation with your changes.

▶ You can include elements such as clip art, your company's logo, a saying or quote, the date and time, footer text, and slide numbers on all slides or on specific slides in a presentation by adding them to the Slide Master.

▶ You can also apply an animation or transition to a Master Slide. Figure 3.7 shows a Slide Master and Slide Master thumbnails.

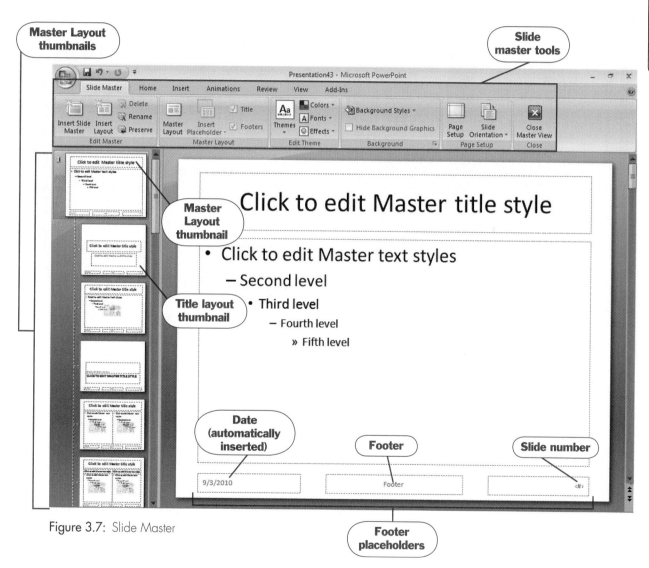

Figure 3.7: Slide Master

▶ Slide Masters are defined by the applied theme. The theme determines the font, font size, text formatting, bullet style, background and color scheme as well as the placement of the footer, page number, and date and time. Figure 3.8 shows how Slide Master elements appear on a slide in which a theme has been applied.

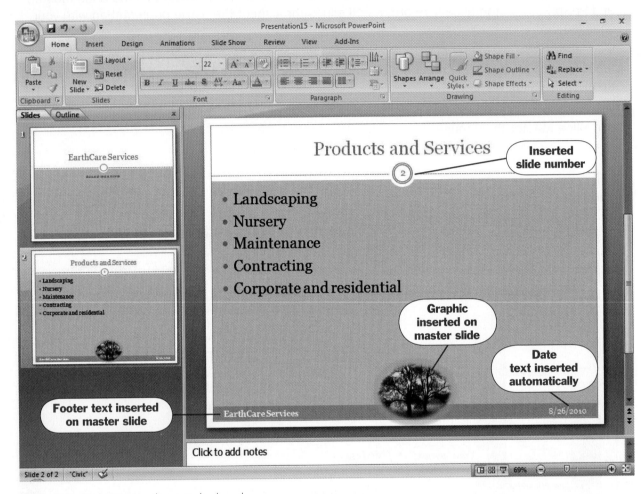

Figure 3.8: Slide Master elements displayed

▶ If you make changes to the Slide Master in a particular theme and want to apply the design to another presentation, you must save the presentation as a template (saving a presentation as a template will be covered later in this lesson).

▶ When you access Slide Masters, each layout's master is displayed as a thumbnail to the left of the slide pane, and Slide Master tools are displayed on a Slide Master tab on the Ribbon (see Figure 3.7).

▶ You can make changes to any of the Slide Master layouts so that any time you apply one of those layouts to a slide, whatever is on that layout's master will appear automatically on the slide. If you want to apply changes to all slides regardless of the layout, you must make those changes to the **Master Layout slide**, which appears at the top of the layout thumbnails.

▶ Formatting changes you make to individual slides after you create the Slide Master override changes you made on the Slide Master. The main Slide Master and Title Master cannot be deleted. Every other layout's master can be deleted by selecting it and clicking the Delete button in the Edit Master group.

▶ PowerPoint might automatically delete a Slide Master if it is not being used to format any slides in your presentation. The Preserve Master option allows you to save your Slide Master so that you do not lose it and all of the settings you applied to it. When you preserve a Slide Master, a pushpin icon appears next to the slide in the slide tab, as shown in Figure 3.9.

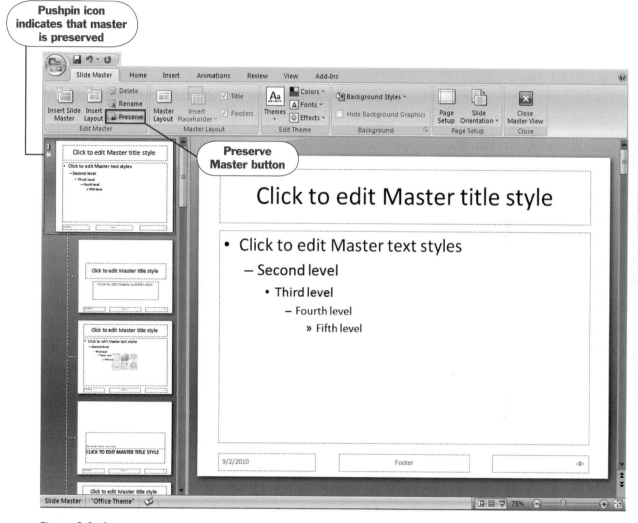

Figure 3.9: Preserve master

HOW To make changes to the Slide Master, **1.** click the **View tab**, and in the **Presentation Views group**, click the **Slide Master button** to display Slide Master thumbnails. **2.** Click a Slide Master layout to make changes to a particular layout, or on the **Slide Master tab** and in the **Master Layout group**, click the **Master Layout button** to make changes to all slides in the presentation. **3.** Use the tools in the **Edit Theme group** to change theme formatting, and deselect the **Title** and **Footers check boxes** in the **Master Layout group** if you do not want to include those items on your slides. The newly designed master appears as a thumbnail in the Slides pane. **4.** Click the **Close Master View button** to return to Normal view.

To insert footer information on the Slide Master, **1.** display the Slide Master, **2.** click the **Insert tab**, then in the **Text group**, **3.** click the **Header & Footer button**. In the Header and Footer dialog box, **4.** make selections for adding the date and time, slide number, and/or footer text. **5.** Click **Apply to All** to apply the settings to all layouts, or click **Apply** to apply them only to the selected layout.

To format footer text, slide numbers, and the date and time, **1.** select the placeholder or text to be affected on the Slide Master. **2.** Click the **Home tab**, and **3.** apply formatting changes using the tools in the Font and Paragraph groups.

To move footers, slide numbers, and/or the date and time placeholder, **1.** click and drag the placeholder to a new location. **2.** Be sure that the new placeholder location does not interfere with the design theme layout.

T R Y *i t* **O U T** *p3-3*

1. Start a new blank presentation.

2. Click the **View tab**, and in the **Presentation Views group**, click the **Slide Master button**.

3. Click the Master Layout slide (first slide in the Slide pane).
   a. On the **Slide Master Tab**, and in the **Edit Theme group**, click the **Themes button**, and apply the **Aspect** theme. *Note: Use ScreenTips to see the theme names.*
   b. Position the insertion point in the first bulleted item, if necessary.
   c. Click the **Home tab**, and in the **Paragraph group**, click the **Bullets button list arrow**, and choose a different bullet symbol.
   d. Click the **Insert tab**, and in the **Illustrations group**, click the **Picture button** and select the data file **p3-3**, then click **Insert**.
   e. Select the picture, if necessary, click the **Format Tab**, and in the **Size group**, enter the appropriate settings to resize the graphic to approximately **1"** high by **1.34"** wide.
   f. Move the graphic to the upper-right corner of the slide.

4. Click the **Insert tab**, and in the **Text group**, click the **Header & Footer button**. Click to select the

Date and time, Slide number, and **Footer** check boxes. Enter `Marketing Meeting` in the **Footer box**, and click **Apply to All**.

5. On the **Slide Master**, select **Marketing Meeting** in the footer. Click the **Home tab**, and in the **Font group**, change the font to **green**, and **12 point**.

6. Click the **Title Slide Master Layout**. On the **Home tab**, and in the **Font group**, change the title to a script font and change the title color to **green**.

7. Click the **Slide Master tab**, select the **Slide Master layout** in the Slide pane, and in the **Edit Master group**, click the **Preserve button** to save the Slide Master.

8. Click the **Close Master View button**.

9. Click the **Home tab**, and in the **Slides group**, click the **New Slide button list arrow**, and insert a Title and Content slide. Notice that the graphic you added and the changes you made to the footer and bullet appear on the Title and Title and Content slide of this presentation.

10. Close the file without saving the changes.

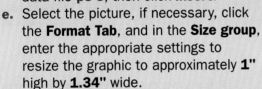

Create and Apply Multiple Slide Masters

▶ You can apply multiple slide designs within the same presentation. This is particularly useful if you want to differentiate or color-code certain sections or create custom shows within the presentation. *(Using multiple Slide Masters within a custom show will be covered in Task 3.)*

▶ By creating multiple Slide Masters as shown in Figure 3.10, you can create different design themes and apply them to one or more slides in your presentation.

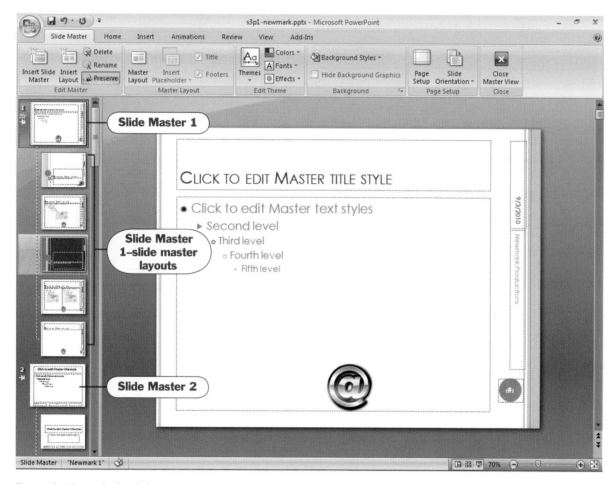

Figure 3.10: *Multiple Slide Masters*

▶ To easily identify each Slide Master you create, rename the master after you customize it.

HOW   1. Click the **View tab**, and in the **Presentation Views group**, 2. click the **Slide Master button**. 3. On the **Slide Master tab**, and in the **Edit Master group**, 4. click the **Insert Slide Master button** to insert a blank Slide Master, or in the **Edit Theme group**, 5. click the **Themes button** to insert a Slide Master with a predefined theme. 6. Make any edits to the master. 7. Click the **Close Master View button**.

To rename a Slide Master, **1.** click the **View tab**, and in the **Presentation Views group**, **2.** click the **Slide Master button**. **3.** Click the **thumbnail of the Slide Master** you want to rename, and in the **Edit Master group**, **4.** click the **Rename button**. In the Rename Master dialog box that appears as shown in Figure 3.11, **5.** enter a name for the master in the Master name box, and **6.** click the **Rename button**.

Figure 3.11: Rename Master dialog box

To apply a Slide Master layout, **1.** click the **Home tab**, and in the **Slides group**, click the **New Slide button list arrow**. **2.** Scroll down to see the new slide layouts as shown in Figure 3.12. **3.** Click a layout to apply it.

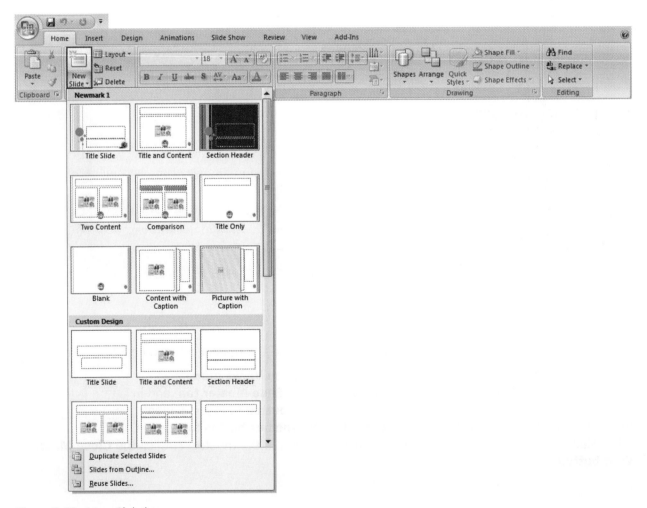

Figure 3.12: New Slide layouts

1. Open the data file **p3-4**.

2. Click the **View tab**, and in the **Presentation Views group**, click the **Slide Master button**.

3. In the **Edit Master group**, click the **Insert Slide Master button**.

4. Right-click the new Slide Master on the Slide pane, and select **Format Background** from the shortcut menu.

5. Click the **Picture or texture fill** option, click the **Texture list arrow**, select the **Papyrus texture**, then click **Close**.

6. Click the **Slide Master tab**, if necessary, and click the **Rename button**.

7. In the Rename Master dialog box that appears, type `Papyrus` in the **Master name** box, and click the **Rename button**.

8. Click the **Close Master View button**.

9. Click the **Home tab**, and in the **Slides group**, click the **New Slide button list arrow**, and under the **Papyrus section** of the gallery, select the **Title and Content** slide layout.

10. Close the file without saving the presentation.

Save a Design or Slide Master as a Template

▶ You can save your new presentation design or a Slide Master as a template that you can use to create new presentations or apply to existing presentations.

▶ If you create multiple Slide Masters within a presentation and save the presentation as a template, PowerPoint saves all of the masters along with it. This allows you to apply multiple templates to a presentation so that slides appear with different slide designs.

HOW To save a presentation as a template, **1.** click the **Office Button**, **2.** point to **Save As**, and click **Other Formats**. **3.** Enter a filename in the **File name** box. Click the **Save as type list arrow**, **4.** click **PowerPoint Template**, then **5.** click **Save**. *Note: It is recommended that you save your templates in the Templates folder to make them easier to locate in the future.*

To open a new template presentation, **1.** click the **Office Button**, then **2.** click **New**. In the New Presentation dialog box, under **Templates**, **3.** click **My templates**, as shown in Figure 3.13. In the New Presentation dialog box that appears, **4.** select a custom template that you created, as shown in Figure 3.14, then **5.** Click **OK**. *Note: If multiple Slide Masters were saved with the template, all of those Slide Masters will be available to you in the new presentation.*

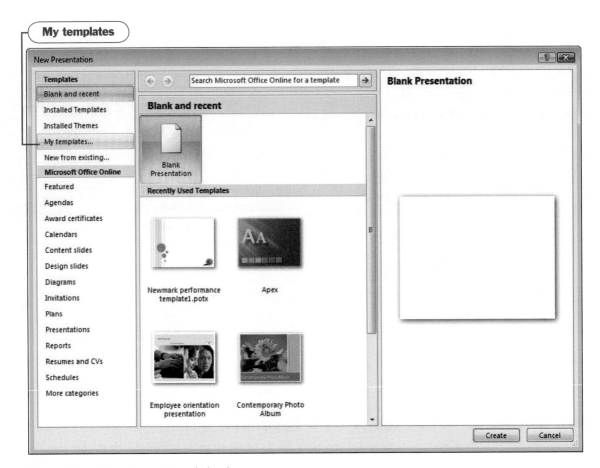

Figure 3.13: New Presentation dialog box

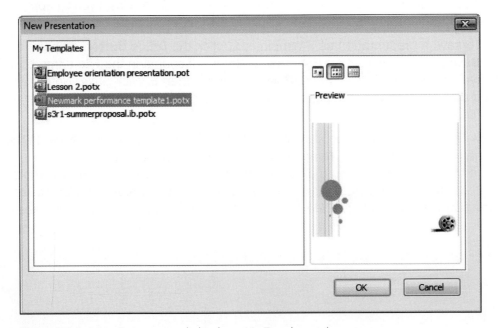

Figure 3.14: New Presentation dialog box, My Templates tab

1. Open the data file **p3-5**.

2. Click the **Office Button**, point to **Save As**, and select **Other Formats**.

3. Enter `Sample Template` in the **File name** box.

4. Click the **Save as type list arrow**, and choose **PowerPoint Template**.

5. Click **Save**.

6. Close the file without saving the changes.

7. Start a new blank presentation.

8. In the New Presentation dialog box, click **My templates**.

9. Click **Sample Template**, and click **OK**.

10. On the **Home tab**, and in the **Slides group**, click the **New Slide button list arrow**.

11. Click the **Title and Content** slide layout from the **Papyrus group**.

12. Close the file without saving the changes.

POWERPOINT

REHEARSAL

GOAL
To use the Slide Master to enhance an existing sales and marketing presentation, as shown in Figure 3.15, then save as a custom template

TASK 1

WHAT YOU NEED TO KNOW

▶ Each Slide Master has 11 slide layouts that accompany it, which can each be customized. The **title slide layout** defines the styles and layout for the title slide only.

▶ In this rehearsal, you will customize a Slide Master and save it as a template. You will then use the newly created template as the basis for a new presentation.

DIRECTIONS

1. Open a new blank presentation.
2. Click the **View tab**, and in the **Presentation Views group**, click the **Slide Master button**.
   a. On the **Slide Master tab**, and in the **Edit Theme group**, click the **Themes button**, and apply the **Concourse** design theme.
   b. In the **Edit Theme group**, click the **Colors button**, and change the color theme to **Oriel**.
   c. Click the **Concourse Slide Master**, and insert a summer-related clip art graphic in the top-right corner of the slide. Resize the title text placeholder so that it ends before the graphic.
   d. Select the master title text. On the **Home tab**, and in the **Font group**, apply a new font and a **dark blue** font color.
   e. On the **Home tab**, and in the **Font group**, change the bullet for the first level to a **star**, and color it **yellow**.
   f. Click the **Animations tab**, and in the **Transition to This Slide group**, apply the **Checkerboard Across** transition. *Note: Click the More button if necessary. The Checkerboard Across transition is in the Stripes and Bars section.*
   g. Click the **Insert tab**, and in the **Text group**, click the **Header & Footer button**.
      • Include the date in the footer to update automatically using a month, day, and year format and the slide number.
      • Enter `Proposal for Summer Event` as the footer text.
      • Click the **Don't show on title slide check box**, then click **Apply**.
   h. Click the title slide layout.
      • Insert and resize a relevant graphic in the lower-right corner of the slide.
      • Italicize the subtitle text.

Continued on next page

    i. Click the **Slide Master tab**, click the **Concourse** Slide Master, and in the **Edit Master group**, click the **Preserve button**.

    j. Close **Slide Master view**.

3. Save the presentation as a template, name it **3r1-summer proposal template**.*yi* (*yi* = your initials), and close the file.

4. Start a new blank presentation.

5. Open the New Presentation dialog box, and click **My templates**.

6. Click **3r1-summer proposal template.yi**, and click **OK**.

7. Enter the slide text as shown in Figure 3.15.

8. Display **Slide 8**. Remove the graphic from the background for this slide only.

9. Run the slide show, then print one copy of the presentation as handouts with four slides per page.

10. Save the presentation as **3r1-summer proposal**.

11. Close the file.

Slide 1

Proposal for Industry Films' Summer Event

Presented by
Perfect Planning Group

1

Slide 2

Venue

* Huntington Castle, located 25 minutes outside of New York City
* Located on 30 acres
* Pool complex with Jacuzzi
* Grounds for organized sporting events
* Private garden
* Recently renovated changing rooms

Proposal for Summer Event   September 22, 2007

2

Slide 3

Theme

* Summer Carnival
  ○ Colorful balloons will adorn the grounds
  ○ Funky hats to be distributed upon arrival
  ○ Carnival games
  ○ Carnival snacks

Proposal for Summer Event   September 22, 2007

3

Slide 4

Entertainment

* Palm Readers
* Magicians
* Caricaturists
* Circus clowns and mimes
* Karaoke
* DJ

Proposal for Summer Event   September 22, 2007

4

Slide 5

Catering

* Picnic Menu
  ○ Breakfast: 9 a.m. –11 a.m.
    ‣ coffee, tea, fruit, muffins, bagels, and pastries
  ○ Barbeque lunch: 12 noon – 3 p.m.
    ‣ burgers, frankfurters, grilled chicken, fries, cole slaw, mixed green salad, and corn on the cob
  ○ Dessert: 5 p.m. – 7 p.m.
    ‣ ice cream sundaes, cake, cookies, frozen yogurt, watermelon, coffee, and tea

Proposal for Summer Event   September 22, 2007

5

Slide 6

Team Building

* Work with the Individual
  ○ Games played with individual goals
  ○ Responsibility is not shared
* Work with Groups
  ○ Games where people work together
  ○ Leader provides direction
* Work with Teams
  ○ Highest level of performance
  ○ Team members share responsibilities and rewards

Proposal for Summer Event   September 22, 2007

6

Slide 7

Next Steps

* Set date
* Exact number of attendees
* Calculate total costs and budgets
* Hire caterer
* Hire all aspects of entertainment
* Coordinate itinerary for the day

Proposal for Summer Event   September 22, 2007

7

Slide 8

Perfect Planning Group For Your Corporate Needs

* Top-notch service
* Proven record of success with Fortune 500 clients
* Flawless execution of events

"You say yes, we do the rest!"

8

Figure 3.15: Eight slides of a sales and marketing presentation

Format Bullets

1. Position the insertion point in the desired bulleted item or select several bulleted items.
2. Right-click, and select **Bullets** from the shortcut menu. Click a bulleted list style from the gallery that displays.

   Or

1. Click the **Home tab**, and in the **Paragraph group**, click the **Bullets button list arrow**.
2. Click a bulleted list style from the gallery that appears.

Customize Bullets

1. Click the **Home tab**, and in the **Paragraph group**, click the **Bullets button list arrow**.
2. Click the **Bullets and Numbering link**.
3. Click the **Customize button**.
4. Click the **Font list arrow**.
5. Select a font.
6. Click a bullet style.
7. Click **OK** twice.

Insert Footers (Date and Time, Slide Numbers)

1. Click the **Insert tab**, and in the **Text group**, click the **Header & Footer button**.

2. In the Header and Footer dialog box, click to select items to be included in the footer.
   a. Click **Date and time** to insert the date or time:
      - Click **Update automatically**, or
      - Click **Fixed**, and enter the date and/or time.
   b. Click **Slide number** to insert slide numbers.
   c. Click **Footer**.
      - Enter the footer text in the **Footer** box.
   d. Click **Don't show on title slide** to omit the footer from the title slide.
3. Click **Apply to All** or **Apply**.

Use a Slide Master

1. Click the **View tab** and in the **Presentation Views group**, click the **Slide Master button**.
2. In the thumbnails that appear, click a Slide Master layout to make changes to a particular layout, or click the **Master Layout** (top of layout thumbnails) to make changes that will affect all slides in the presentation.

3. Using the tools in the Edit Theme and Background groups on the Slide Master tab as well as the tools found in the Text group on the Home tab, make desired format changes to font, size, alignment, slide background, and themes.
4. Click the **Close Master View button**.

Save as Template

1. Click the **Office Button**.
2. Point to **Save As**, then click **Other Formats**.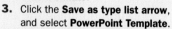
3. Click the **Save as type list arrow**, and select **PowerPoint Template**.
4. Enter the template filename in the **File name** text box.
5. Click **Save**.

Apply Saved Template

1. Click the **Office Button**, then click **New**.
2. In the New Presentation dialog box, under Templates, click **My templates**.
3. Select a template that you created.
4. Click **OK**.

POWERPOINT

P E R F O R M A N C E

TASK 1

You are the sales and marketing director at Newmark Productions. Your company has just relaunched its new website and is looking for advertisers to promote their products on it. Your boss has asked you to create a presentation outlining the advertising opportunities available on Newmark Production's website, which will be delivered to potential advertisers. Your boss has also asked you to create a corporate template, which will be used for all Newmark presentations.

Follow these guidelines:

1. Read through the information provided on the next page to get a basic understanding of the content the presentation will cover.

2. Start a new, blank presentation, and format a Slide Master using a design theme. Apply a new font theme. Change the title text color and bulleted text color.

3. Change the level 1 and level 2 bullets on the Slide Master; apply a new bullet color.

4. Insert a footer that reads **Newmark Productions**.
   - Include the slide number.
   - Do not include the footer or slide number on the title slide.
   - Italicize the footer text, and apply a new color to it.
   - Move the footer to the right edge and rotate it.

5. Apply a slide transition to all slides.

6. Insert a Web-related graphic on the Slide Master.

7. On the title slide layout master, insert a film-related graphic.

8. Preserve the Slide Master. Rename the Slide Master **Newmark 1**.

9. Insert a new Slide Master, and apply a different design theme. Apply the same font theme, footers, and transition as used on the first Slide Master. Preserve the Slide Master. Rename the Slide Master **Newmark 2**.

10. Save the file as a template. Name it **3p1-newmark performance template**.

11. Start a new presentation and apply the **3p1-newmark performance template**.

12. Use the paragraphs below to create and organize the presentation content.
    - Each bold heading represents a new slide.
    - Insert clip art where appropriate.

13. Apply the **Newmark 2** template to **Slides 4–6**.

14. Save the presentation as **3p1-newmark**.

Online Advertising Opportunities

Newmark Productions

Sponsorship of the New Releases Channel

New Releases section of the Web site has the highest reach. Advertisers can align their brand with this high-visibility content.

Targeted Impressions

Newmark Productions can target advertiser's message by: Section (New Releases, Now on DVD, etc.), Keyword, User profile.

E-Newsletter Opportunities

Weekly e-newsletter provides latest information on new releases and online content. Sent out every Thursday. 500,000 subscribers.

Video Opportunities

15 second pre-roll video: Before movie trailers. Before behind-the-scenes interviews with cast and crew. 300,000 video downloads per month. Ad banners to surround video content.

Additional Opportunities

Exclusive editorial opportunities. Custom microsite. Sweepstakes and contests.

T R Y O U T

GOAL
To create a custom show from a presentation, as shown in Figure 3.16

★ Create a custom show
★ Link to a custom show
★ Use multiple masters in a custom show

TASK 2

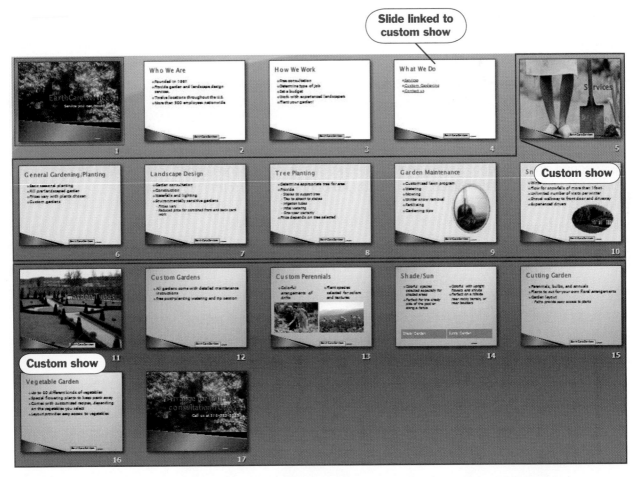

Figure 3.16: Custom slide show with multiple masters (Slides 5–10 is one custom show; Slides 11–17 is another custom show.)

WHAT YOU NEED TO KNOW

Create a Custom Show

▶ A **custom show** is a group of related slides within a presentation that you can deliver independently of the entire presentation. Think of a custom show as a presentation within a presentation. Custom shows are useful if you want to show different audiences slides that pertain only to them.

HOW **1.** Open the presentation from which you wish to create the custom show. **2.** Click the **Slide Show tab**, and **3.** click the **Custom Slide Show button**.
4. Click **Custom Shows**, as shown in Figure 3.17. In the Custom Shows dialog box that appears, as shown in Figure 3.18, **5.** click the **New button** to specify a new custom show. **6.** In the Define Custom Show dialog box that opens, as shown in Figure 3.19, all the slides in the presentation appear in the **Slides in presentation box**. **6.** Click each slide you want to include in the custom show, and **7.** click the **Add button**. (To select multiple slides, press and hold **[Ctrl]** as you click each slide; to select consecutive slides press and hold **[Shift]** as you click each slide.) **8.** Click a slide in the **Slides in custom show** list, and use the up and down arrows to change the order of slides. **9.** Enter a name in the **Slide show name box** to name the custom show, then click **OK**.

Figure 3.17: Custom Slide Show button

Figure 3.18: Custom Shows dialog box

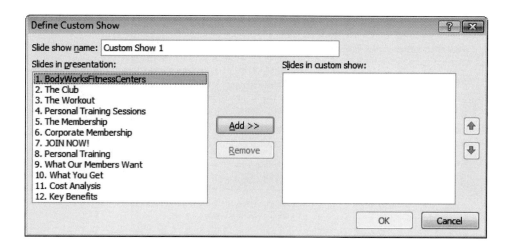

Figure 3.19: Define Custom Show dialog box

To remove a slide from the custom show, **1.** click the slide, and **2.** click the **Remove button**.

▶ Once you create a custom show, it appears in the Custom Shows dialog box, as shown in Figure 3.20. You can create multiple custom shows by repeating the procedures given on page 133 in the HOW section titled "Create a Custom Show."

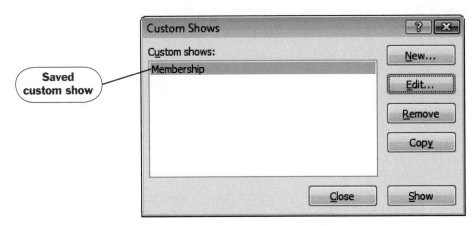

Figure 3.20: Custom Shows dialog box

Set Up and Run a Custom Show

▶ You can set up a slide show to run only the slides in a custom show rather than all the slides in the presentation. You can also run a custom show any time during a slide show.

HOW To set up a slide show, **1.** click the **Slide Show tab**, and in the **Set Up group**, **2.** click the **Set Up Slide Show button**. **3.** In the **Set Up Show dialog box** that opens, as shown in Figure 3.21, **4.** click the **Custom show** option, then **5.** click the **Custom show list arrow** to select the custom show, and **6.** click **OK**. *The Custom show option is only available if a custom show has been set up.*

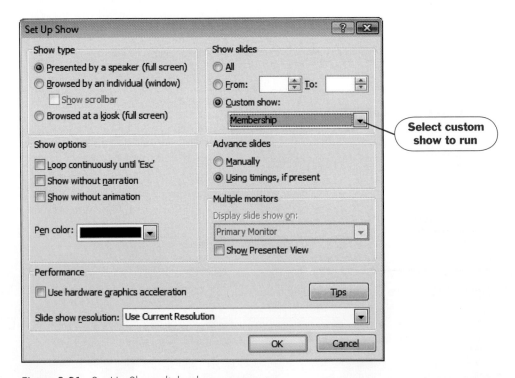

Figure 3.21: Set Up Show dialog box

To run a custom show, **1.** click the **Slide Show button** on the **status bar**, or **1.** click the **Slide Show tab**, and in the **Start Slide Show group**, **2.** click the **Custom Slide Show button list arrow**, and **3.** choose a show from the list that displays, as shown in Figure 3.22. This begins a slide show of only the slides in the specified custom show.

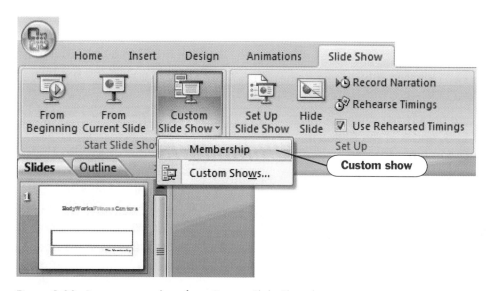

Figure 3.22: Run a custom show from Custom Slide Show button

To run a custom show during a slide show, **1.** right-click, and **2.** select **Custom Show**, then **3.** click the custom show you want to run, as shown in Figure 3.23. The slide show advances to the selected custom show and runs the slide show from that point forward.

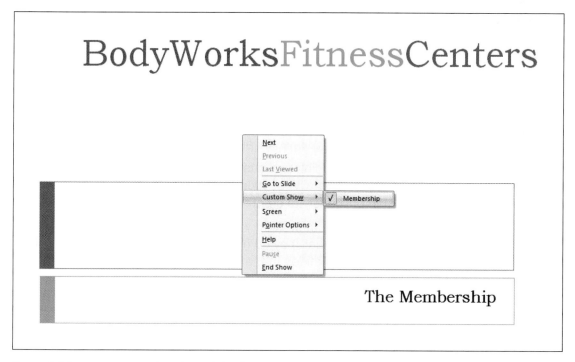

Figure 3.23: Run a custom show from Slide Show view

1. Open the data file **p3-6**.

2. Click the **Slide Show tab**, then click the **Custom Slide Show button**, then click **Custom Shows**.

3. Click the **New button**, and enter **Membership** in the **Slide show** name box.

4. Press and hold **[Ctrl]** while you click **Slides 1**, **5**, and **6** in the **Slides in presentation box**.

5. Click the **Add button**, and click **OK**.

6. Click the **Edit button**, click **Slide 2** in the **Slides in custom show** box, click the down arrow once, and click **OK**.

7. Click the **New button**, and enter **Personal Training** in the **Slide show name** box.

8. Click **Slide 8** in the **Slides in presentation box**, press and hold **[Shift]**, then click **Slide 12**.

9. Click the **Add button**, and click **OK**.

10. Click the **Membership** custom show, and click the **Show button**. View all slides in the Membership custom show.

11. On the **Slide Show tab**, and in the **Start Slide Show group**, click the **Custom Slide Show button**, then click **Custom Shows**.

12. Click the **Membership** custom show, if necessary, click the **Remove button**, and click **Close**.

13. Click the **Slide Show button** on the status bar, right-click, select **Custom Show**, and click **Personal Training**. View all slides in the **Personal Training** custom show.

14. Click the **Slide Show tab**, then in the **Set Up group**, click the **Set Up Show button**.

15. Click the **Custom show** option, select the **Personal Training** custom show from the drop-down list, and click **OK**.

16. Click the **Slide Show button** on the status bar, and view all slides in the **Personal Training** custom show.

17. Close the presentation without saving the changes.

Link to a Custom Show

▶ A presentation might begin with generic slides containing information for all audiences and link to different custom shows with information for specific audiences.

▶ To create a hyperlink on text or objects to link to a custom show, you must first create the custom show using the procedures in the HOW section titled "Set Up and Run a Custom Show." Then, use the procedures learned previously to create the hyperlink.

▶ Depending on the order in which you plan to present your slides and custom shows, you might have to hide the custom show slides so that they do not appear twice during the slide show (once with the custom show and once as slides in the presentation). Run the slide show and test the hyperlinks to determine whether or not you need to hide slides.

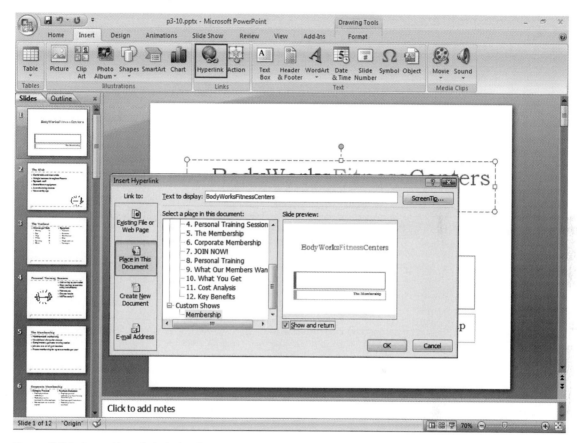

Figure 3.24: Insert Hyperlink dialog box

TRY *it* OUT *p3-7*

1. Open the data file **p3-7**.

2. Display **Slide 4**.

3. Select the words "Personal Training," click the **Insert tab**, and in the **Links group**, click the **Hyperlink button**.

4. Click the **Place in This Document button**, and select the **Personal Training Details** custom show from the **Select a place in this document** box.

5. Click the **Show and return** check box, and click **OK**.

6. On the **Slides tab**, select **Slides 8–12**.

7. Click the **Slide Show tab**, and in the **Set Up group**, click the **Hide Slide button**.

8. Display **Slide 1**.

9. Click the **Slide Show button** on the status bar.

10. View all the slides in the slide show, and activate the **Personal Training** link on **Slide 4**. *Notice that you automatically return to Slide 4 after viewing the custom show.*

11. Finish viewing the slide show.

12. Close the presentation without saving the changes.

Use Multiple Masters within a Custom Show

▶ As you learned previously, PowerPoint allows you to create multiple Slide Masters that you can apply within the same presentation. This is especially useful if you are creating different sections, or custom shows, in a presentation, as shown in Figure 3.25. The new master will be displayed among the Themes thumbnails in the Design tab.

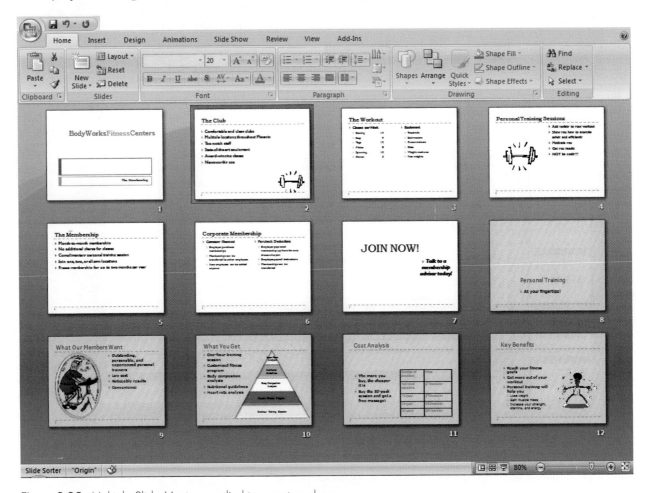

Figure 3.25: Multiple Slide Masters applied to a custom show

HOW 1. Open a presentation that contains a custom show and multiple Slide Masters. 2. On the **Slides pane**, select the slides to which you wish to apply a Slide Master design. 3. Click the **Design tab**, and in the **Themes group**, 4. right-click a thumbnail of one of the masters you created, and 5. click **Apply to Selected Slides**.

1. Open the data file **p3-8**.

2. Click the **View tab**, and in the **Presentation Views group**, click the **Slide Master button**.

3. Right-click the **Master Slide thumbnail**, and select **Duplicate Slide Master**.

4. Right-click the thumbnail of the new Slide Master (identified as number 2), click **Format Background** from the shortcut menu that displays.

5. Click the **Color list arrow** on the Format Background dialog box, and click **light yellow, Accent 4, lighter 40%**, then click **Close**.

6. Select the title placeholder text on the new Slide Master, and apply a new font style and font color to complement the background color.

7. Click the **Slide Master tab**, and in the **Edit Master group**, click the **Rename button**, then name the master `Personal Training`.

8. Click the **Rename button**.

9. Click the **Close Master View button**.

10. Display the Slides pane, if necessary, and select **Slides 8, 9, 10, 11**, and **12**.

11. Click the **Design tab**, and in the **Themes group**, right-click the **Personal Training** thumbnail, and select **Apply to Selected Slides**.

12. Click the **Slide Show tab**, and in the **Start Slide Show group**, click the **Custom Slide Show button**, and select the **Personal Training Details** custom show.

13. Run the slide show, then close the presentation without saving the changes.

REHEARSAL

TASK 2

GOAL
To create a sales presentation using custom shows and multiple Slide Masters, as shown in Figure 3.26

WHAT YOU NEED TO KNOW

▶ It is useful to create and apply multiple Slide Masters when you want to differentiate sections within a presentation.

▼ DIRECTIONS

1. Start a new presentation, and apply the **Concourse** design theme.

2. Change the color theme to **Foundry**.

3. Click the **View tab**, and in the **Presentation Views group**, click the **Slide Master button**.

4. Select the **Title Master**, if necessary.
   a. Insert a picture background that relates to gardening on the title slide. *Hint: Click the **Slide Master tab**, and click the **Background Styles button**, then use the Format Background dialog box to select a clip art picture.*
   b. Change the title font color to **red** and the subtitle color to **yellow**.

5. Select the **Concourse** Slide Master layout.
   a. Change the Level 1 bullet to the **Star bullet**, and change its color to **red**.
   b. Insert today's date as fixed on all slides.
   c. Create a text box, and insert the words **EarthCare Services** in any desired font, and position it in the footer area. Apply a **yellow** fill and a **green** border line.

6. Right-click the **Master Slide**, and select **Duplicate Slide Master**.

7. On the newly created Section Header layout, insert a different garden picture background. Change the color of the title and subtitle font to complement the picture.

8. On the newly created Master Slide, apply a **yellow** background.

9. Rename the new master **Services**.

10. Right-click the **Services** Master Slide, and select **Duplicate Slide Master**.

Continued on next page

11. On the newly created **Section Header** layout, insert a different garden picture background. *Hint: Click the **Slide Master tab**, and click the **Background Styles button**. Change the color of the title and subtitle font to complement the picture.*

12. On the newly created Master Slide, apply a **light green** background.

13. Rename the new master `Garden Types`.

14. Close **Master View**.

15. Enter the text on the slides, as shown in Figure 3.26, using appropriate layouts.
    a. Insert relevant clip art graphics where shown.
    b. Apply any picture effects you want.

16. Click the **Slide Show tab**, and in the **Start Slide Show group**, click the **Custom Slide Show button**, then click **Custom Shows**.

17. Create a custom show for **Slides 5–10**; name it `Services`.

18. Create a custom show for **Slides 11–16**; name it `Garden Types`.

19. Apply the **Services Section Header** layout to the Services slide (**Slide 5**). Apply the **Services Slide Master** to the Services custom show (**Slides 6–10**).

20. Apply the **Garden Types Section Header** layout to the Garden Types slide (**Slide 11**). Apply the **Garden Types Slide Master** to the Garden Types custom show (**Slides 12–16**).

21. Display **Slide 4** ("What We Do").
    a. Create a hyperlink on the word "Services" to link to the **Services** custom show. Choose to show the custom show and return to the linked slide.
    b. Create a hyperlink on the words "Custom Gardening" to link to the **Garden Types** custom show. Choose to show the custom show and return to the linked slide.
    c. Create a hyperlink on the words **Contact us** to link to the last slide in the presentation.

22. Display **Slide 1**, and run the slide show. Activate the links on **Slide 4**.

23. Save the presentation as **3r2-landscaping**.

1

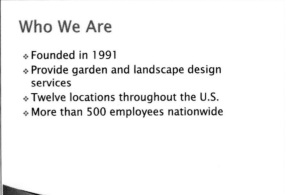

2

3

4

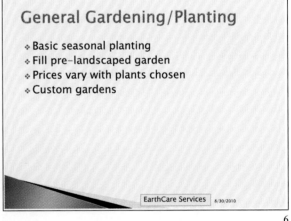

5

6

Figure 3.26a: Sales presentation for EarthCare Services (Slides 1–6)

Landscape Design

- ❖ Garden consultation
- ❖ Construction
- ❖ Waterfalls and lighting
- ❖ Environmentally sensitive gardens
  - ○ Prices vary
  - ○ Reduced price for combined front and back yard work

EarthCare Services 8/30/2010

7

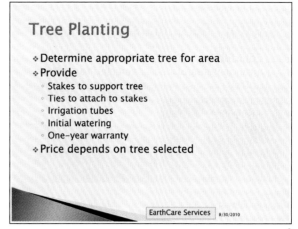

Tree Planting

- ❖ Determine appropriate tree for area
- ❖ Provide
  - ○ Stakes to support tree
  - ○ Ties to attach to stakes
  - ○ Irrigation tubes
  - ○ Initial watering
  - ○ One-year warranty
- ❖ Price depends on tree selected

EarthCare Services 8/30/2010

8

Garden Maintenance

- ❖ Customized lawn program
- ❖ Watering
- ❖ Mowing
- ❖ Winter snow removal
- ❖ Fertilizing
- ❖ Gardening tips

EarthCare Services 8/30/2010

9

Snow Removal

- ❖ Winter service
- ❖ Plow for snowfalls of more than one foot
- ❖ Unlimited number of visits per winter
- ❖ Shovel walkway to front door and driveway
- ❖ Experienced drivers

EarthCare Services 8/30/2010

10

EarthCare Services

11

Custom Gardens

- ❖ All gardens come with detailed maintenance instructions
- ❖ Free post-planting watering and tip session

EarthCare Services 8/30/2010

12

Figure 3.26b: Sales presentation for EarthCare Services (Slides 7–12)

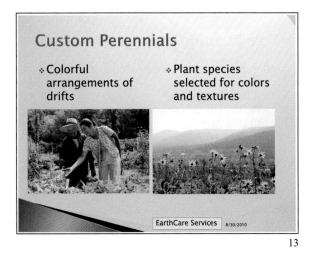

13

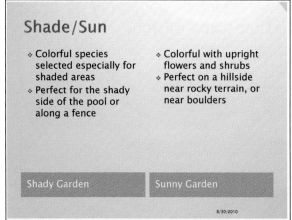

14

Cutting Garden

- ❖ Perennials, bulbs, and annuals
- ❖ Plants to cut for your own floral arrangements
- ❖ Garden layout
  - ▫ Paths provide easy access to plants

EarthCare Services 8/30/2010

15

16

17

Figure 3.26c: Sales presentation for EarthCare Services (Slides 13–17)

Create a Custom Show
1. Open the presentation from which you wish to create the custom show.
2. Click the **Slide Show tab**, and click the **Custom Slide Show button**.
3. Click Custom Shows.
4. In the Custom Shows dialog box, click the **New button**.
5. In the Define Custom Show dialog box, click each slide you want to include in the custom show.
6. Click the **Add button**.
7. Enter a name in the **Slide show name box**.
8. Click **OK**.

Set Up and Run a Custom Show
1. Click the **Slide Show tab** and in the **Set Up group**, click the **Set Up Slide Show button**.
2. In the Set Up Show dialog box, click the **Custom show option**.
3. Click the **Custom show list arrow** to select the custom show.
4. Click **OK**.

Run a Custom Show
1. Click the **Slide Show tab**.
2. In the **Start Slide Show group**, click the **Custom Slide Show button list arrow**.
3. Select a show from the list that displays.

Link to a Custom Show
1. Click the **Insert tab**, and in the **Links group**, click the **Hyperlink button**.
2. In the Insert Hyperlink dialog box, click the **Place in This Document button**.
3. Select the custom show from the **Select a place in this document box**.
4. Select the **show and return check box**.
5. Click **OK**.

Use Multiple Masters within a Custom Show
1. Open a presentation that contains a custom show and multiple slide masters.
2. On the **Slides tab**, select the slides to which you wish to apply a Slide Master design.
3. Click the **Design tab**, and in the **Themes group**, right-click a thumbnail of a master you created.
4. Click **Apply to Selected Slides**.

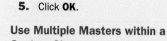

P E R F O R M A N C E

TASK 2

You are the sales director at Transport Travel Services. An increasing number of customers have been requesting information about bike tours. Your assistant has created an unformatted presentation about the bike tours that Transport Travel Services provides. You are responsible for enhancing and finalizing the presentation.

Follow these guidelines:

1. Open the data file **p3p2-bike**.

2. Display the Slide Master.
   a. On the Master Slide, apply a design theme.
   b. Change the color theme, and apply a new font style and color to the title text and bulleted text that complements the design theme.
   c. Change the level 1 bullet style and color.
   d. Insert a footer that reads: `Transport Travel Services`. Apply a new font style and color to the footer text.

3. Duplicate the Slide Master.
   a. Rename the master, `Destinations`.
   b. Apply a new theme color.
   c. Apply a new font color to the title text and bulleted text that complements the new design theme.
   d. Change the level 1 bullet style and color.
   e. Insert a relevant clip art image.
   f. Apply a slide transition.

4. Create a custom show for **Slides 5–9** called **Destinations**.

5. Display **Slide 2**. Create a hyperlink from the words **Variety of trips** to the **Destinations** custom show. Select the **Show and return** option.

6. Hide **Slides 5–9**.

7. Apply the Destinations Slide Master to the Destinations custom show (**Slides 5–9**).

8. Display **Slide 10**.
   a. Insert a relevant picture as the slide background.
   b. Change the title, and subtitle text color to make it more readable, if necessary.

9. Run the slide show, and activate the link on **Slide 2** to run the custom show.

10. Print one copy of the presentation as handouts with six slides per page.

11. Save the file as **3p2-bike trip**.

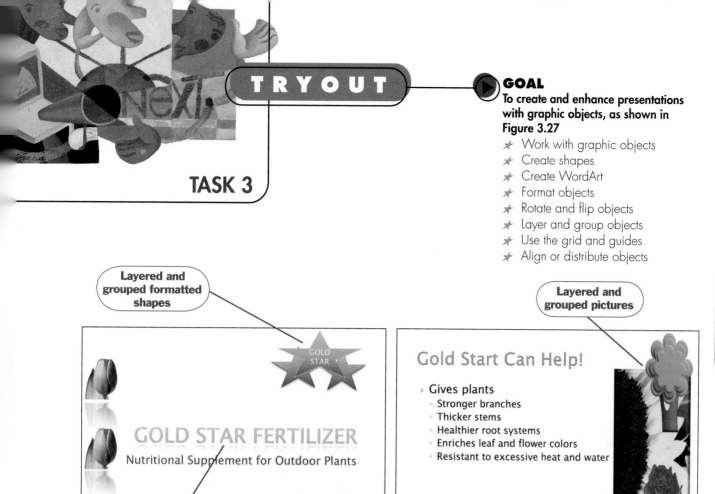

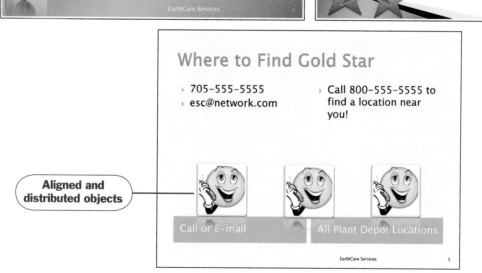
TRYOUT

GOAL

To create and enhance presentations with graphic objects, as shown in Figure 3.27

* Work with graphic objects
* Create shapes
* Create WordArt
* Format objects
* Rotate and flip objects
* Layer and group objects
* Use the grid and guides
* Align or distribute objects

Layered and grouped formatted shapes

Layered and grouped pictures

GOLD STAR

GOLD STAR FERTILIZER

Nutritional Supplement for Outdoor Plants

WordArt

EarthCare Services

Gold Start Can Help!

▸ Gives plants
  ◦ Stronger branches
  ◦ Thicker stems
  ◦ Healthier root systems
  ◦ Enriches leaf and flower colors
  ◦ Resistant to excessive heat and water

GOLD STAR

EarthCare Services 2

Rotated clip art

Where to Find Gold Star

▸ 705-555-5555
▸ esc@network.com

▸ Call 800-555-5555 to find a location near you!

Aligned and distributed objects

Call or E-mail

All Plant Depot Locations

EarthCare Services 5

Figure 3.27: Three slides of a six-slide presentation enhanced with graphic objects

WHAT YOU NEED TO KNOW

Work with Graphic Objects

▶ As you learned in Word, graphic objects include clip art, photographs, shapes, lines, charts, SmartArt diagrams, tables, and media such as video and sound clips. These same elements may be used on PowerPoint slides to visually and audibly enhance a presentation. You will learn to use tables, charts, and SmartArt later in this lesson. Media will be covered in Lesson 4.

▶ Objects generally behave the same way in every application. That is, you can edit objects (move, copy, delete, size, and rotate) and format them (change fill and border lines and apply 3-D effects) using the same techniques you learned in Word. Figure 3.28 shows graphic objects used on a slide with formatting applied.

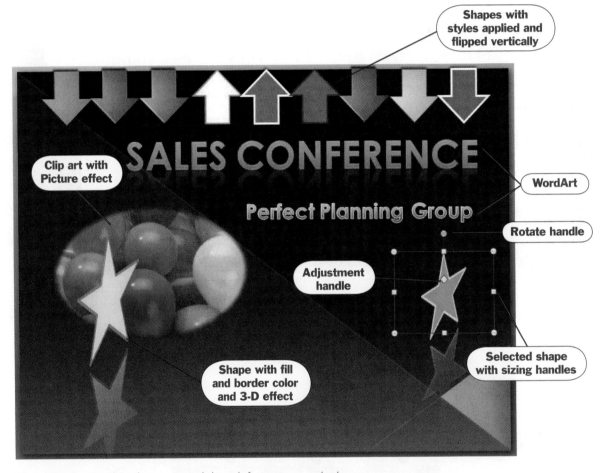

Figure 3.28: Graphic objects on a slide with formatting applied

Create Shapes

▶ You can draw simple shapes or create designs using shapes. These shapes can be drawn directly on individual slides or can be included on the Slide Master. As in Word, a drawn shape displays with sizing, adjustment, and rotation handles (see Figure 3.28). You will learn to format shapes later in this lesson.

▶ You can add text to a shape. When you do so, the text attaches to the shape and moves or rotates with the shape.

Use Multiple Masters within a Custom Show

▶ As you learned previously, PowerPoint allows you to create multiple Slide Masters that you can apply within the same presentation. This is especially useful if you are creating different sections, or custom shows, in a presentation, as shown in Figure 3.25. The new master will be displayed among the Themes thumbnails in the Design tab.

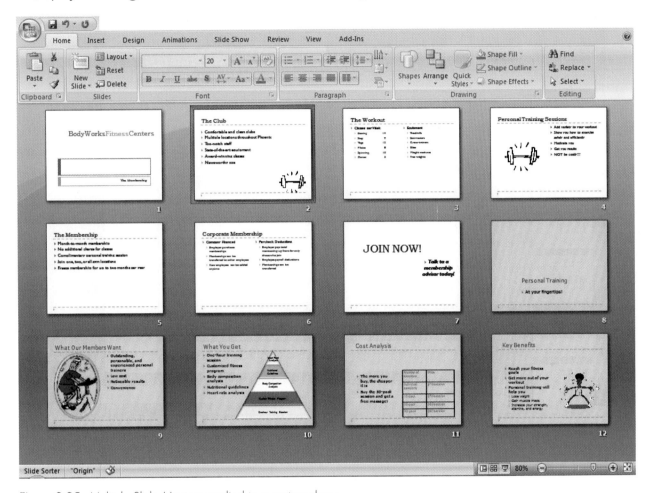

Figure 3.25: Multiple Slide Masters applied to a custom show

HOW 1. Open a presentation that contains a custom show and multiple Slide Masters. 2. On the **Slides pane**, select the slides to which you wish to apply a Slide Master design. 3. Click the **Design tab**, and in the **Themes group**, 4. right-click a thumbnail of one of the masters you created, and 5. click **Apply to Selected Slides**.

HOW 1. Click the **Insert tab**, and in the **Links group**, 2. click the **Hyperlink button**. In the **Insert Hyperlink dialog box**, 3. click the **Place in This Document button**, and 4. select the custom show from the **Select a place in this document box**, as shown in Figure 3.24. 5. Select the **Show and return check box** to return automatically to the slide that contained the link after viewing the custom show.

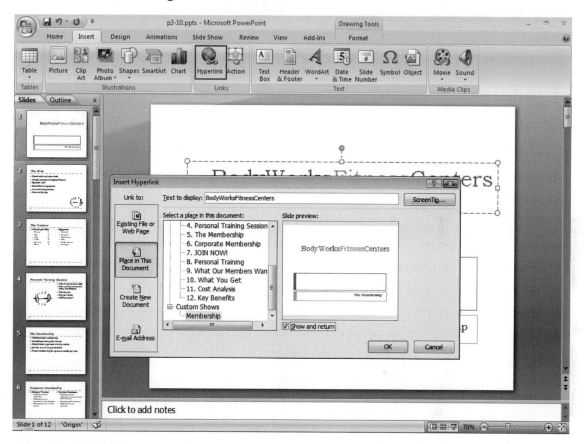

Figure 3.24: Insert Hyperlink dialog box

T R Y i t O U T *p3-7*

1. Open the data file **p3-7**.

2. Display **Slide 4**.

3. Select the words "Personal Training," click the **Insert tab**, and in the **Links group**, click the **Hyperlink button**.

4. Click the **Place in This Document button**, and select the **Personal Training Details** custom show from the **Select a place in this document** box.

5. Click the **Show and return** check box, and click **OK**.

6. On the **Slides tab**, select **Slides 8–12**.

7. Click the **Slide Show tab**, and in the **Set Up group**, click the **Hide Slide button**.

8. Display **Slide 1**.

9. Click the **Slide Show button** on the status bar.

10. View all the slides in the slide show, and activate the **Personal Training** link on **Slide 4**. *Notice that you automatically return to Slide 4 after viewing the custom show.*

11. Finish viewing the slide show.

12. Close the presentation without saving the changes.

HOW To draw a shape, **1.** click on the slide where you want to insert the shape. **2.** Click the **Insert tab**, and in the **Illustrations group**, click the **Shapes button**, as shown in Figure 3.29. **3.** Select a shape from the gallery that appears (see Figure 3.29). **4.** Press and hold the left mouse button, and drag diagonally to create the shape.

To add text to a shape, **1.** click the shape, and **2.** enter text.

To adjust the shape, **1.** click and drag a **sizing handle** to change the size of the shape, the **adjustment handle** to reshape the drawing, or the **rotation handle** to rotate the shape (see Figure 3.28).

To change the size of a shape by a specific amount, **1.** select the object. Then, **2.** click the **Drawing Tools Format tab**, and in the **Size group**, **3.** enter an amount in the **Height** and **Width boxes**, as shown in Figure 3.30.

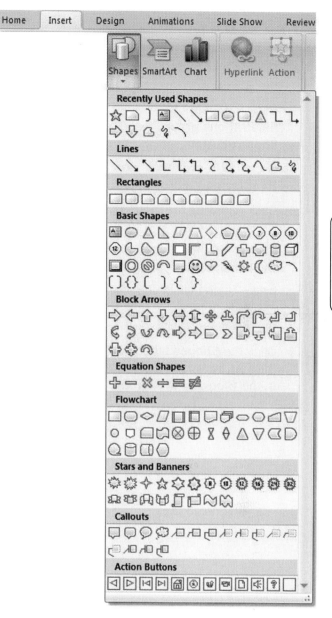

Figure 3.29: Shapes button and Shapes gallery

Figure 3.30: Format tab, Size group

1. Open a new blank presentation, and apply the **Blank** slide layout to the first slide.

2. Click the **Insert tab**, and in the **Illustrations group**, click the **Shapes button**.

3. Click the **Rectangle** shape in the **Rectangles group**.

4. Click and drag the mouse anywhere on the slide to draw a rectangle.

5. Click the **Shapes button**, and click the **Oval** shape in the **Basic Shapes group**.

6. Press **[Shift]** while you click and drag the mouse anywhere on the slide to draw a perfect circle.

7. Click the **Shapes button**, and click the third **Arrow** shape (upward pointing arrow) in the **Block Arrows group**.

8. Click and drag the mouse to draw the arrow.

9. Click the **Shapes button**, and click the **Down Ribbon** shape in the **Stars and Banners group**, if necessary, and resize it so that it is taller than it is wide.

10. Click and drag the top-middle adjustment handle down to make the ribbon thinner.

11. Click inside the ribbon shape, then enter: Congratulations.

12. Select the rectangle, click the **Drawing Tools, Format tab**, and in the **Size group**, enter 1" in the **Height** box and 1" in the **Width** box.

13. Close the file without saving the changes.

Create WordArt

▶ **WordArt** lets you create text with decorative effects. It is best used to call attention to words or phrases. After creating WordArt, you can apply various effects to it, which will be explained later in this lesson. You can also select text on your slide and create WordArt from it.

HOW **1.** Click the **Insert tab**, and in the **Text group**, **2.** click the **WordArt button**. In the WordArt gallery that appears, shown in Figure 3.31, **3.** click a WordArt style. **4.** Enter the text that you want to appear as WordArt in the placeholder that is displayed (replacing the words "Your Text Here"), as shown in Figure 3.32, then **5.** click outside the placeholder to view the WordArt. *The Drawing Tools, Format tab also appears, providing tools in the WordArt Styles group to help you customize or change the WordArt object (see Format Objects section below).*

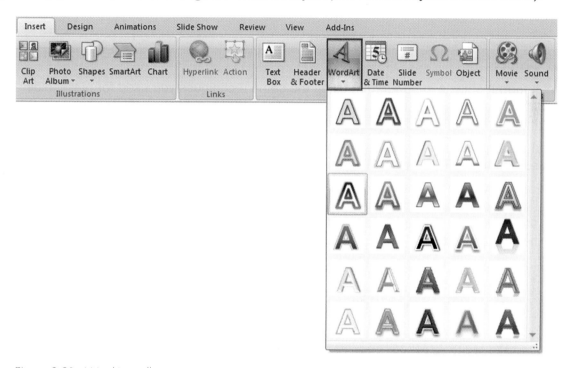

Figure 3.31: WordArt gallery

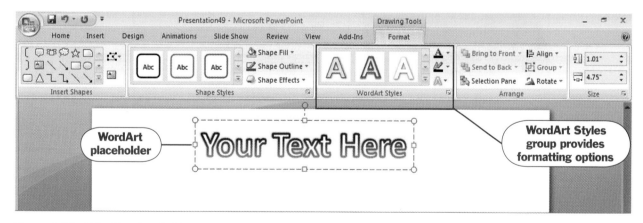

Figure 3.32: WordArt placeholder

To resize WordArt, **1.** select the WordArt text, **2.** click the **Home tab**, and in the **Font group**,   **3.** click the **Increase Font Size button** or **Decrease Font Size button**.

1. Open a new blank presentation, and apply the **Blank** slide layout as the first slide.

2. Click the **Insert tab**, and in the **Text group**, click the **WordArt button**.

3. Click a WordArt style.

4. Enter your first name in the placeholder.

5. Click the placeholder to select it, if necessary.

   a. Click the **Home tab**, and in the **Font group**, click the **Increase Font Size button**.

   b. Drag the placeholder to the top of the slide.

6. Close the file without saving the changes.

Format Objects

▶ You can format objects in PowerPoint using the same techniques you used for placeholders and clip art. You can change an object's fill to a color or pattern, apply an effect, or change the color, pattern, or thickness of an object's border.

▶ You can also apply one of PowerPoint's predesigned styles. A **style** is a combination of formats such as line weight, fill color, and line style.

▶ Table 3.1 reviews the formatting you can apply to objects in PowerPoint. Remember, there are several ways you can apply formatting. Regardless of the procedure you use, you must always select the object first before formatting it. Figure 3.33 shows examples of formatting options when they are applied.

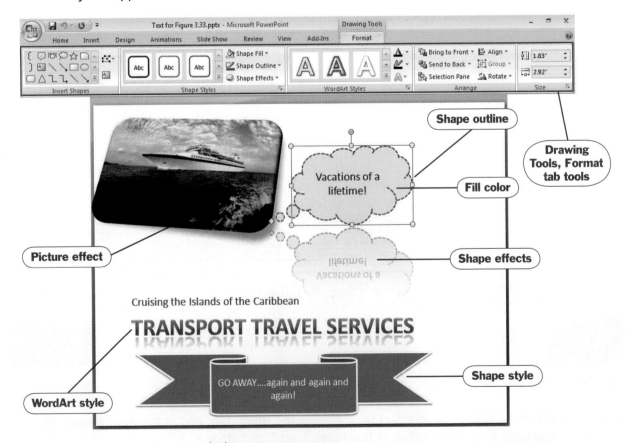

Figure 3.33: Formatting options applied

► After you draw the shape, the Drawing Tools, Format tab displays tools to help you customize the appearance of the shape. You can use buttons on the Ribbon to format shapes, right-click the object and select formatting options from the shortcut menu, or use the Format Shape dialog box shown in Figure 3.34.

► Many formatting options allow you to see a live preview before applying an effect.

HOW Table 3.1 summarizes the procedures for applying formatting options. For each procedure, do the following first: **1.** select a shape, text box, or WordArt object, and **2.** click the **Drawing Tools**, **Format tab**. Then, continue with the procedures shown in the table to carry out the application. *Note: Depending on the object you have chosen, the Picture Tools, Format tab or the Drawing Tools, Format tab, or both, will be available. They have similar tools that can be applied to selected objects.*

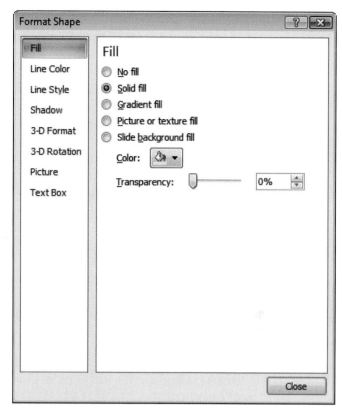

Figure 3.34: Format Shape dialog box

Table 3.1: Formatting options

FORMATTING OPTION	BUTTON	PROCEDURE
Fill Color	Shape Fill ▼	3. Click the **Shape Fill button list arrow**. 4. Make the appropriate selections from the gallery.
Outline	Picture Border ▼ Shape Outline ▼	3. Click the **Picture Border** or **Shape Outline button list arrow** (depending on whether you selected a picture or other object). 4. Make the appropriate selections from the gallery.
Effect	Picture Effects ▼ Shape Effects ▼	3. Click the **Picture Effects** or **Shape Effects button** (depending on whether you selected a picture or other object). 4. **Point to** an effect category, then 5. make the appropriate selections from the gallery.
Shape Styles	Abc	3. Click a shape style in the **Quick Styles group**, or click the **More button** to display the styles gallery. 4. Point to a style to see a live preview, then 5. select a style. You can also access Quick Styles from the Home tab, in the Drawing group.
WordArt Styles	A	3. Click a WordArt style in the **WordArt Styles group**, or click the **More button** to display the WordArt styles gallery. 4. Point to a style to see a live preview, then 5. select a style. Or 1. Select the **Text Effects button** in the **WordArt styles group**. 2. Point to an option on the menu, then 3. make the appropriate selections from the gallery.

1. Open the data file **p3-11**.

2. Select the WordArt shape.
   a. Click the **Drawing Tools Format tab**, if necessary, and in the **WordArt Styles group**, click the **Text Effects button**.
   b. Point to **Transform**, then select the **Stop** effect in the **Warp group**.

3. Click the **Insert tab**, and in the **Illustrations group**, click the **Shapes button**.

4. Click the **Rectangle** shape, then click and drag the mouse to draw a rectangle anywhere on the slide.
   • On the **Drawing Tools, Format tab**, and in the **Shape Styles group**, click the **More** arrow, point to several styles to see a live preview, then select **Subtle Effect, Accent 1**.

5. Draw another rectangle. Enter the word `Hello` in the shape.
   a. On the **Drawing Tools, Format tab**, and in the **Shape Styles group**, click the **Shape Fill button list arrow**, and select a color from the gallery that displays.
   b. Click the **Shape Outline button list arrow**, point to **Weight**, and select **6 pt**.
   c. Click the **Shape Outline button list arrow** again, and select any color.
   d. Click the **Shape Effects button**, point to **Soft Edges**, and select **25 Point**.

6. On the **Drawing Tools, Format tab**, and in the **Insert Shapes group**, click the **More** arrow, then select the **5-Point Star** shape in the **Stars and Banners group**.
   a. Click and drag the mouse to draw the shape anywhere on the slide.
   b. Click the **Shape Fill button list arrow**, and select a **red** color.
   c. Click the **Shape Effects button**, point to **3-D Rotation**, and select the **Off Axis 2 right** effect in the **Parallel group**.
   d. Click the **Shape Effects button** again, point to **Reflection**, and select the **Half Reflection, 8 pt Offset** effect.

7. On the **Drawing Tools, Format tab**, and in the **Insert Shapes group**, click **More**, then click the **Right Arrow** shape in the **Block Arrows group**:
   a. Click and drag the mouse to draw the shape anywhere on the slide.
   b. In the **Shape Styles group**, click the Format Shape dialog box launcher to display the **Format Shape dialog box**.
   • Click **Fill** in the left pane, if necessary, click the **Solid fill** option button, click the **Color list arrow**, and select **yellow**.
   • Click **Line Color** in the left pane, click the **Color list arrow**, and select **red**.
   • Select **Line Style** from the list of options, enter `3 pt` in the **Width** box, select the **Dash type list arrow**, and select **Dash**.
   • Click **Close**.

8. Close the file without saving the changes.

Rotate and Flip Objects

▶ The Rotate and Flip features allow you to reposition or angle an object to create interesting arrangements on your slide, as shown in Figure 3.35.

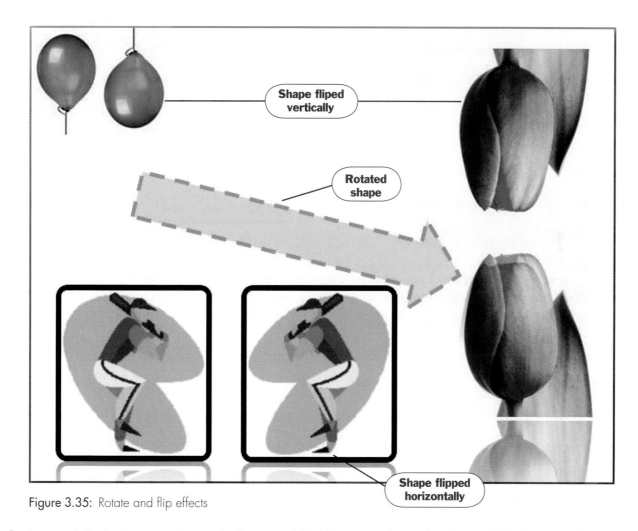

Figure 3.35: Rotate and flip effects

▶ The **Rotate** feature allows you to turn an object to a certain angle along a 360-degree axis.

▶ The **Flip** feature allows you to change the direction of an object horizontally (left to right) or vertically (top to bottom).

HOW To manually rotate an object, **1.** select the object to display the green rotation handle. **2.** Click the **rotation handle**, **3.** press and hold the mouse, and **4.** drag right or left to the desired angle, **5.** then release the mouse button.

To rotate an, and object by 90-degree increments, **1.** select the object, **2.** click the
appropriate **Format tab**, and in the **Arrange group**, **3.** click the **Rotate button**. **4.** Select
Rotate Right 90° or **Rotate Left 90°**, as shown in Figure 3.36.

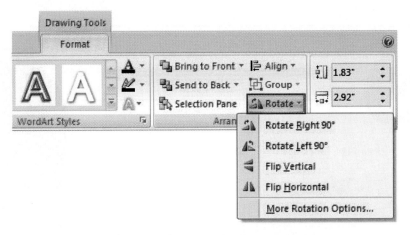

Figure 3.36: Rotate button and menu on the Format tab, Arrange group

To flip an object, follow Steps 1-3 above, then select **Flip Vertical** or **Flip Horizontal** (see
Figure 3.36). You can also use the Home tab to access the Flip and Rotate menus. To do
so, **1.** click the **Home tab**, and in the **Drawing group**, **2.** click the **Arrange button list arrow**,
and **3.** select from the menu, as shown in Figure 3.37.

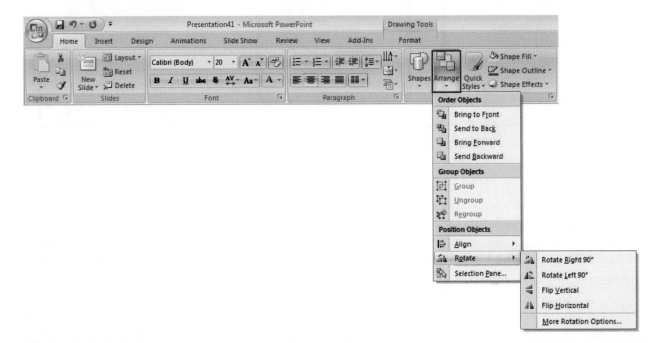

Figure 3.37: Rotate and flip options on the Home tab, Drawing group

1. Open the data file **p3-12**.

2. Select the **arrow** shape.

3. Position your mouse pointer on the rotation handle, and rotate left to point to the top tulip graphic.

4. Undo the action.

5. Click the **Drawing Tools, Format tab**, and in the **Arrange group**, click the **Rotate button**, and select **Rotate Right 90°**, then release the mouse button.

6. Undo the action.

7. Click the **Rotate button**, and select **Flip Horizontal**.

8. Undo the action.

9. Select the baseball player graphic. Click the **Picture Tools, Format tab**, then click the **Rotate button**, and select **Flip Horizontal**.

10. Select the top tulip graphic, click the **Rotate button**, and select **Flip Vertical**.

11. Select the **arrow**, then drag the rotation handle right so that the arrow points to the bottom tulip graphic.

12. Close the file without saving the changes.

Layer and Group Objects

▶ As in Word, you can **layer** or stack objects on top of one another to create interesting effects. When you layer objects, you can move one object behind another or bring one forward in the stack of objects. Table 3.2 lists layering options.

Table 3.2: Layering options

OPTION	BUTTON	EFFECT
Send to Back	Send to Back	Moves the graphic behind all other objects in the stack
Send Backward	Send Backward	Moves the graphic back one level
Bring to Front	Bring to Front	Moves the graphic on top of all other objects in the stack
Bring Forward	Bring Forward	Moves the graphic up one level

► When you **group** objects, you create one object out of individual objects, which you can then format, size, or move as a single item. You can **ungroup** grouped objects to edit the objects individually, then regroup them if you want. Figure 3.38 illustrates layered and grouped objects.

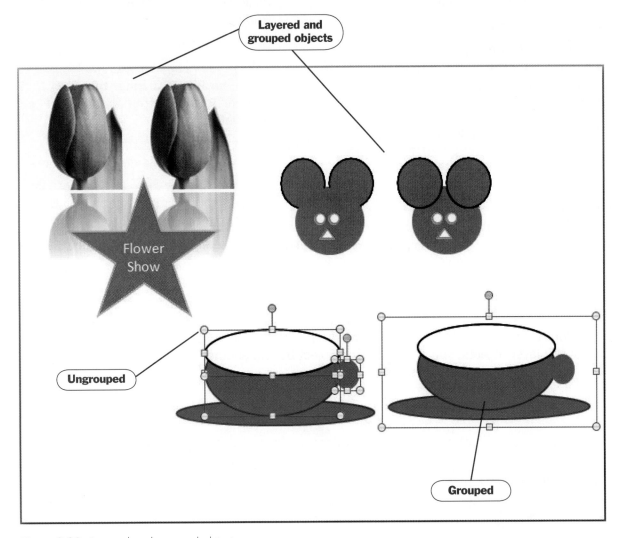

Figure 3.38: Layered and grouped objects

HOW To layer graphics, **1.** arrange the graphics where you want to position them on the slide. **2.** Select the graphic you want to move to another level in the stack. **3.** Click the appropriate **Format tab**, and in the **Arrange group**, **4.** click the **Send to Back list arrow** or the **Bring to Front list arrow**. **5.** Use Table 3.2 to choose a layering option.

To group objects, **1.** press and hold **[Ctrl]** as you select the individual objects. *You can select individual parts at once by dragging the pointer around all the objects.* **2.** Click the appropriate **Format tab**, and in the **Arrange group**, click the **Group button**, then **3.** click **Group**.

To ungroup objects, **1.** select the grouped object, **2.** click the **Format tab**, if necessary, and in the **Arrange group**, **3.** click the **Group button**, then **4.** click **Ungroup**.

1. Open the data file **p3-13**.

2. Click to select the saucer below the cup graphic. Click the **Drawing tools, Format tab**, and in the **Arrange group**, click the **Send to Back button**.

   Send to Back

3. For each ear shape on the mouse graphic, click to select it, then click the **Send to Back button**.

4. Click the **Home tab**, and in the **Editing group**, click the **Select button**, then click **Select Objects**.

   Select ▾

   a. Position the pointer at the bottom left of the cup and saucer. Drag to draw a box around the object to select all the parts.
   b. Click the **Drawing Tools, Format tab**, and in the **Arrange group**, click the **Group button**, and click **Group**.

   Group ▾

c. Move the cup and saucer to the lower-right corner of the slide.

5. Repeat Steps 4a and 4b to group the mouse.

6. Repeat Steps 4a and 4b to group the two flowers and the star graphic.
   a. Select the grouped object, then drag a corner handle to resize the graphic so that it is smaller. Then, move it to the top-right corner of the slide.
   b. Click the **Format tab**, and in the **Arrange group**, click the **Group button**, and click **Ungroup**.

7. Close the file without saving the changes.

Use the Grid and Guides

▶ The Grid and Guides feature allows you to position an object on a slide with more precision. A **grid** contains evenly spaced horizontal and vertical lines, which are hidden when you print a presentation but appear on screen to help align objects. **Guides** are invisible vertical and horizontal lines that you can also use to align objects.

▶ The grid and guides do not print or appear during a slide show. Figure 3.39 illustrates a slide with grids and guides displayed.

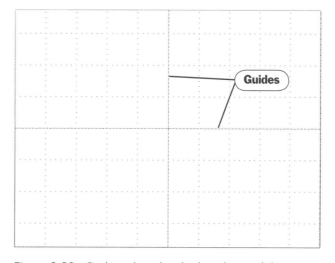

Figure 3.39: Grids and guides displayed on a slide

HOW **1.** Right-click the slide. **2.** Select **Grid and Guides** from the shortcut menu. **3.** In the Grid and Guides dialog box, as shown in Figure 3.40, **4.** click the appropriate check boxes to display the grid or drawing guides on screen. To set spacing between gridlines, click the **Spacing list arrow** and select a preset size. **5.** Click **OK**. *Note: The Snap objects to grid option allows you to position an object on the grid, regardless of whether or not you have chosen to display the grid. When you turn on the Snap objects to grid option and move an object, the object snaps to the nearest point on the grid. You can also choose to snap objects to other objects. This option aligns an object with another object as you move or draw it.*

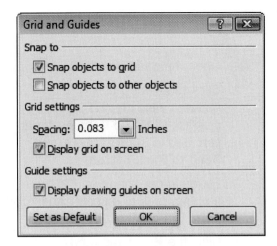

Figure 3.40: Grid and Guides dialog box

T R Y *it* O U T *p3-14*

1. Open a new blank presentation, and apply a blank slide layout as the first slide.

2. Right-click the slide, and select **Grid and Guides** from the shortcut menu.

3. Click to select all the check boxes, and click **OK**. Notice that the grid and guides display on the slide.

4. Close the file without saving the changes.

Align or Distribute Objects

▶ The Align or Distribute feature allows you to align or distribute objects in relation to each other, or to distribute them evenly on the slide. Figure 3.41 shows aligned and distributed objects.

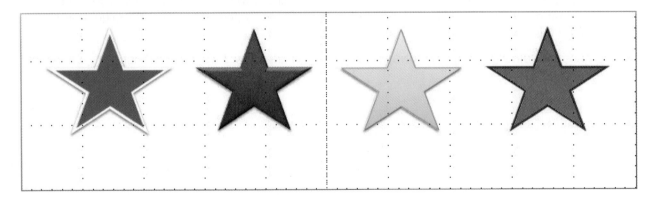

Figure 3.41: Aligned and distributed objects on a slide

HOW 1. Select each object you want to align or distribute. 2. Click the appropriate **Format tab**, and in the **Arrange group**, 3. click the **Align button**. In the menu that appears, as shown in Figure 3.42, 4. select **Align to Slide**. 5. Click the **Align button** again, and 6. select **Distribute Horizontally** or **Distribute Vertically**.

Figure 3.42: Align menu

T R Y *i t* **O U T** *p3-15*

1. Open the data file **p3-15**.

2. Move each star shape so that the bottom points are on the second horizontal gridline.

3. Press **[Ctrl]+A** to select all of the star shapes.

4. Click the **Drawing Tools, Format tab**, and in the **Arrange group**, click the **Align button**, then click **Align to Slide**. Click the **Align button** again and select **Distribute Horizontally**. Notice that the shapes align across the slide evenly.

5. Close the presentation without saving the changes.

REHEARSAL

GOAL
To use, edit, and work with shapes, WordArt, and alignment techniques to create and enhance a six-slide sales presentation as shown in Figure 3.43

TASK 3

WHAT YOU NEED TO KNOW

▶ It is important that your presentation have a professional and readable layout. When placing objects, be sure that they don't interfere with text.

▶ Objects generally behave the same way in every application. That is, you can edit objects (move, copy, delete, size, and rotate) and format them (change fill and border lines and apply 3-D effects) using the same techniques you learned in Word.

▼ DIRECTIONS

1. Start a new blank presentation, and apply the **Concourse** theme.

2. Change the theme color to **Metro**.

3. Create the slides shown in Figure 3.43.
   a. On **Slide 1** (the title slide), create a WordArt shape from the text in the title placeholder. (Select the text, click the **Insert tab**, and in the **Text group**, select the **WordArt button**, then select a WordArt style that uses a **green** font color.)
   b. On **Slide 2**, insert several relevant graphics and overlap them.
      • Select each graphic, click the **Drawing Tools, Format tab**, and in the **Arrange group**, click the **Group button**, then click **Group**.
      • Size the grouped image to fill the right side of the slide as shown.
   c. On **Slide 3**, insert a relevant clip art image.
   d. On **Slide 5**, insert a relevant clip art image, copy it twice, then align and distribute as shown.

4. Display the Slide Master, and select the Master Slide.
   a. Apply a **green** font color to the title.
   b. Insert a footer that reads **EarthCare Services**. Apply it to all slides, including the Title slide.
   c. Draw a star and place it at the bottom of the slide.
      • Size it wider than it is tall.
      • Apply any Quick Style with a **green** fill color.
   d. Copy the star twice. Apply any Quick Style with a **gold** color.
   e. Layer the stars as shown in the figure.
   f. Group the three stars.
   g. Insert the words **Gold Star** into the green star.
   h. Group the stars and position them as shown in the figure.

Continued on page 164

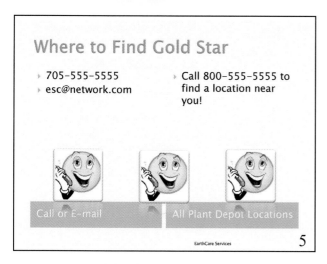

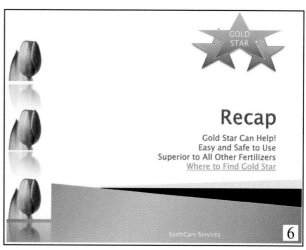

Figure 3.43: Six-slide sales presentation for EarthCare Services

i. Copy the grouped stars.
- Display the Title Master.
- Paste the grouped stars as shown.
- Insert a flower graphic, apply a reflection effect, size it appropriately, copy it twice and place the flowers one below the other as shown.

5. Apply animation effects for the bulleted text and transition effects to each slide.

6. On **Slide 6**, link the last line of text to the appropriate slide.

7. Run the slide show. Click the hyperlink on the last slide to display **Slide 5**.

8. Save the presentation as **3r3-goldstar**.

Cues for Reference

Create Shapes
1. Click the **Insert tab** and in the **Illustrations group**, click the **Shapes button**.
2. Select a shape from the gallery that appears.
3. Position the pointer where the shape will start.
4. Click and drag to create the shape.

Create WordArt
1. Click the **Insert tab**, and in the **Text group**, click the **WordArt button**.
2. Click a WordArt style from the gallery.
3. Enter the WordArt text into the placeholder.
4. Click outside the placeholder to view the WordArt.

Format Objects
1. Click the object to select it.
2. Click the **Format tab**, if necessary.
3. Make any changes using the tools on the Ribbon.
   Or
1. Right-click the object, and select **Format Shape**.

2. Make desired fill, line, and/or arrow formatting changes.
3. Click **Close**.

Layer Objects
1. Click the object you want to move to another level in the stack.
2. Click the **Format tab**, if necessary, and in the **Arrange group**, select a layering option.

Group Objects
1. Press and hold **[Ctrl]**, and click each object to group.
2. Click the **Format tab**, if necessary, and in the **Arrange group**, click the **Group button**, then click **Group**.

Ungroup Objects
1. Click the grouped object.
2. Click the **Format tab**, if necessary, and in the **Arrange group**, click the **Group button**, then click **Ungroup**.

Display Grid and Guides
1. Right-click a slide.
2. Select **Grid and Guides** from the shortcut menu.

3. Click the appropriate check boxes to display the grid or drawing guides.

Align/Distribute Objects
1. Press and hold **[Ctrl]**, and click each object to align or distribute.
2. Click the **Format tab**, and in the **Arrange group**, click the **Align button**.
3. Click **Align to Slide**, if objects should align in relation to slide. *Note: A check mark indicates that Align to Slide is selected.*
4. Click **Distribute Horizontally** or **Distribute Vertically**.

Rotate and Flip Objects
1. Select the object, and drag the rotation handle left or right.
   Or
1. Click the **Format tab**, if necessary, and in the **Arrange group**, click the **Rotate button**.
2. Select a Rotate or Flip option.

PERFORMANCE

TASK 3

Perfect Planning Group has asked you to enhance a seven-slide presentation with graphic objects. The presentation, which will provide account executives with marketing strategies for use when pitching new business, will be shown at the next new account executive orientation.

Perfect Planning Group

Follow these guidlines

1. Open the data file **p3r3-creative sales unformatted**.

2. Display the Slide Master.
   a. Select the Master Slide (first slide in the Slide pane), and apply the **Opulent** design theme.
   b. Change the background style to **Style 11**.
   c. Apply a decorative font to the title text (such as Frosty, Poornut, or Alba Matter).
   d. Create a WordArt object with the words **Perfect Planning Group** using any style you prefer that complements the theme.
   e. Size the WordArt font to **16 point**, then place it in the footer placeholder.
   f. Close Master view.

3. Display **Slide 1** ("Creative Sales").

4. Apply a relevant picture background on the title slide.

5. Use the following guidelines to create the balloons shown in Figure 3.44:
   a. Display the grid.
   b. Draw an oval to fit inside one of the grid squares.
   c. Draw a tiny triangle and send it behind the oval.
   d. Use the Scribble line to draw the balloon's string.
   e. Color the oval and triangle the same color; choose a color that complements the theme. Set the width of the line **2¼ point**, and color it **black**, if necessary.
   f. Group the oval, triangle, and scribble.
   g. Copy and paste the balloon twice.
   h. Align the tops of the first and third balloons as shown. Select all the balloons, click the **Format tab**, and in the **Arrange group**, click the **Align button**, and select **Align Selected Objects**. Click the **Align button** again, and select **Distribute Horizontally**.
   i. Position the second balloon slightly lower than the first one.

6. Display **Slide 2** ("Our Sales Strategy").

7. Draw a star, and apply a fill color that complements the theme, as shown in Figure 3.44.
   a. Size it **2" high by 2" wide**, then apply a shape effect.
   b. Copy and paste it twice.
   c. Position the stars as shown.
   d. Align the stars to the slide, if necessary, and distribute them vertically.

Continued on next page

8. Display **Slide 6** ("The Event Catalog").
   a. Insert a picture of a wedding cake.
   b. Apply a picture effect.
   c. Display **Slide 7** ("Making the Presentation").
   d. Insert a clip art image of a presenter.
   e. Apply two picture effects.

9. Insert relevant clip art or pictures on **Slide 3**.

10. Apply a different transition to each slide.

11. Run the slide show.

12. Save the file as **3p3-creative sales**.

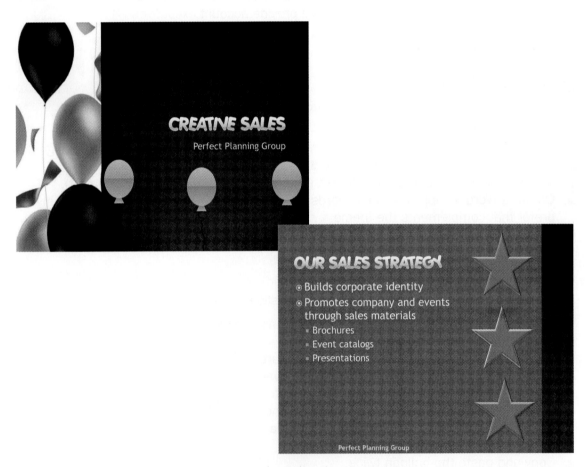

Figure 3.44: Two slides of the sales presentation for Perfect Planning Group

TASK 4

TRYOUT

GOAL

To create and enhance presentations with tables, charts, and SmartArt, as shown in Figure 3.45, and use action buttons to navigate during a slide show

✳ Work with tables, charts, and SmartArt

✳ Use action buttons

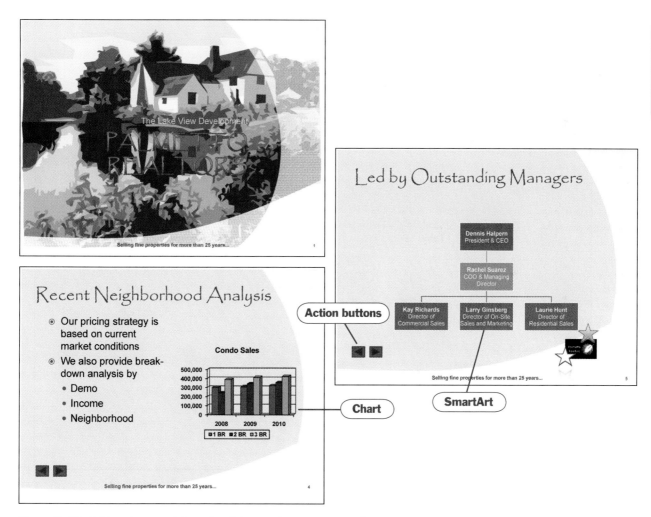

Figure 3.45: Table, chart, and SmartArt slides used to support a sales presentation

Work with Tables, Charts, and SmartArt

▶ Tables, charts, and SmartArt are visual elements that you can use to organize and analyze data in your presentation. As you learned in Word, SmartArt includes conceptual diagrams that help you visualize data. SmartArt is used to show a process, cycle, or hierarchy.

▶ Content slides, which you used when working with clip art, contain placeholders to work with one or more of these visual elements. The procedures you use to create and edit these elements are the same as those you used in Word. Figure 3.46 illustrates a Title and Content layout.

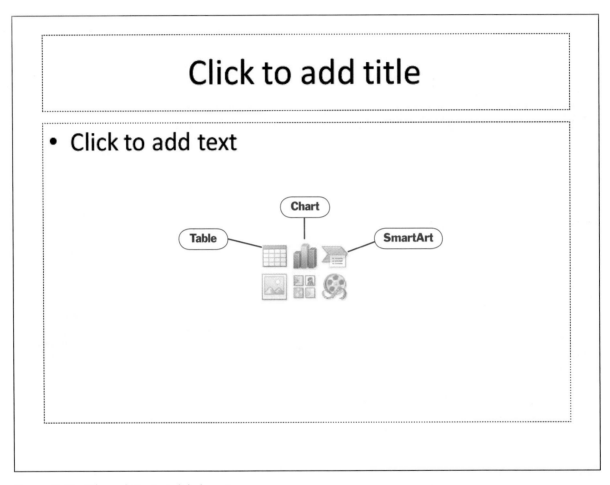

Figure 3.46: Title and Content slide layout

Tables

▶ A **table** organizes information in horizontal rows and vertical columns. The rows and columns intersect to form boxes, called **cells**. Tables offer a way to present information in columns and rows.

▶ Using PowerPoint's table styles, you can quickly apply attractive formatting to the table borders and text based on a color theme, or apply table borders and fills using other formatting tools found on the Ribbon or on the shortcut menus.

HOW 1. Apply a **Title and Content** slide layout, and 2. click the **Insert Table icon** on the slide. 3. In the Insert Table dialog box that opens, as shown in Figure 3.47, enter the number of columns and rows you want in the appropriate text boxes, then 4. click **OK**.

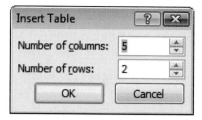

Figure 3.47: Insert Table dialog box

To create a table on a slide that does not contain a content or table placeholder, 1. click the **Insert tab**, and in the **Tables group**, 2. click the **Table button**. 3. On the **Insert Table menu**, click and drag across the squares to select the number of rows and columns you want. A live preview displays your selection, as shown in Figure 3.48. 4. Release your mouse and the table will appear on your slide, filling the slide area. The Table Tools, Design tab will also display, as shown in Figure 3.49.

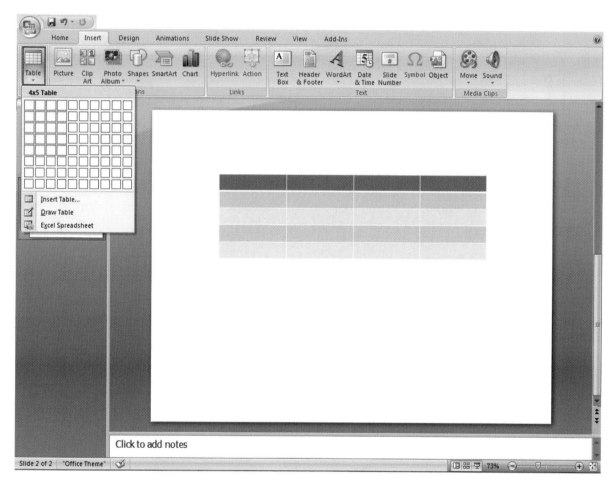

Figure 3.48: Table menu with live preview

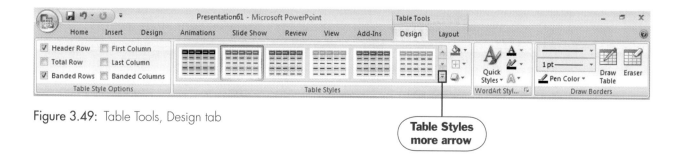

Figure 3.49: Table Tools, Design tab

Table Styles more arrow

POWERPOINT

Edit and Format a Table

▶ You can edit and format a table by inserting or deleting columns and rows, adding borders and shading, aligning text, and merging cells using the same techniques you learned in Word. Remember, pressing **[Tab]** in the last cell of the rightmost column creates a new row.

HOW To insert and delete columns and rows, **1.** click the table to select it, **2.** click the **Table Tools, Layout tab**, as shown in Figure 3.50. **3.** Position your mouse above a column or to the left of a row until the insertion point becomes an arrow, then **4.** click to select the column or row. **5.** In the **Rows & Columns group**, click the **Insert Left** or **Insert Right** button to insert a column to the left or right of the selected column, or click the **Insert Above** or **Insert Below button** to insert a row above or below the selected row.

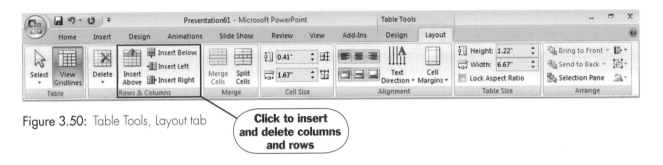

Figure 3.50: Table Tools, Layout tab

Click to insert and delete columns and rows

To format a table, **1.** select the table, then **2.** click the **Table Tools, Design tab** (see Figure 3.49) and use the appropriate buttons to change border style, add shading, apply a style, or make other changes.

TRYitOUT p3-16

1. Open a new blank presentation.

2. Insert a new slide using a **Title and Content** slide layout.

3. Click the **Insert Table icon** on the slide.

4. Enter 4 in the **Number of columns** box, enter 7 in the **Number of rows** box, then click **OK**.

5. Click in the top-left cell, if necessary, and enter: `Course Offering`.

6. Press **[Tab]**, then enter: `Professor`.

7. Press **[Tab]**, then enter: `Credits`.

8. Click to select the table, if necessary. Then click the **Table Tools, Design tab**.

9. In the **Table Styles group**, click the **More arrow**. Position your insertion point on each style to see a live preview, then select a style.

10. Select the first row.
   a. In the **WordArt Styles group**, click the **Quick Styles button list arrow**.
   b. Position your insertion point on each style to see a live preview, then select a style.

11. Click anywhere in Column 4.

12. Click the **Layout tab**.

13. In the **Rows & Columns group**, click the **Delete button list arrow**, and select **Delete Columns**.

14. Click anywhere in the first row.

15. Right-click, select Insert, then click **Insert Rows Below**.

16. Drag the table to the center of the slide.

17. Close the file without saving the changes.

Charts

▶ When you create a chart in PowerPoint, it is based on the chart feature in Excel. After you launch the chart feature and select a chart type, Excel opens with sample data to help guide you in entering your own information. You can select from numerous chart styles and formatting options to present your data visually.

HOW **1.** Apply a **Title and Content slide layout**, and **2.** click the **Insert Chart icon** on the slide, or **1.** click the **Insert tab**, then in the **Illustrations group**, **2.** click the **Chart button**. **3.** In the Insert Chart dialog box that displays as shown in Figure 3.51, **4.** click a chart type in the left pane, **5.** click a chart style in the right pane, then **6.** click **OK**. **7.** In the Excel datasheet window that appears, as shown in Figure 3.52, replace the sample data with your own. If your data does not fit within the blue data range border, resize the chart data range by dragging the lower-right corner of the range to include the number of columns and rows you need. **8.** Click the **Close button** in the Excel window to return to PowerPoint and view the chart on your slide, as shown in Figure 3.53. Notice that the Chart Tools, Design tab appears.

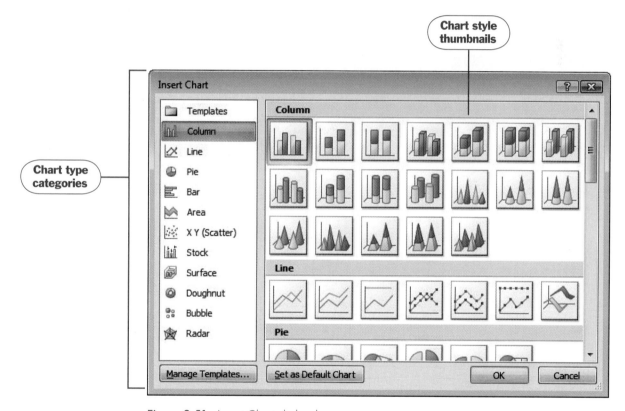

Figure 3.51: Insert Chart dialog box

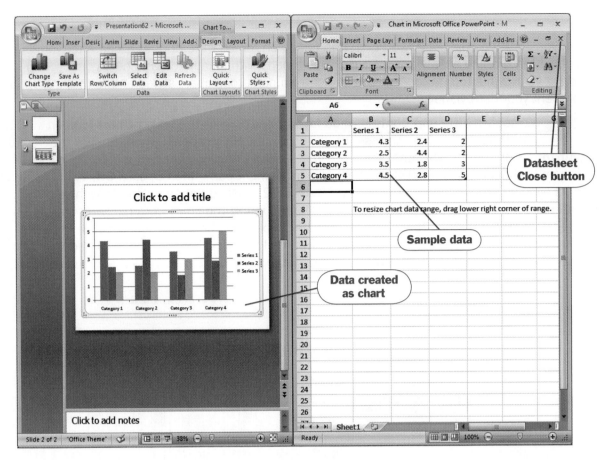

Figure 3.52: Datasheet window

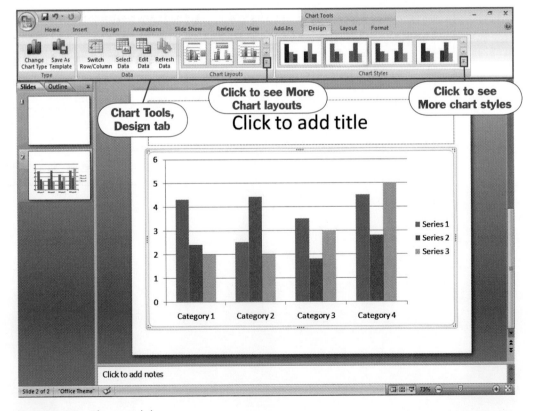

Figure 3.53: Chart on slide

Edit and Format a Chart

▶ You can change a chart's style and layout, as well as edit it to include a title, axes titles, a legend, and/or data labels using the tools found on the Chart Tools, Design, Layout and Format tabs. **Data labels** allow you to indicate the exact value of each data point.

HOW To apply a new chart style and layout, **1.** click a chart to select it. **2.** Click the **Chart Tools Design tab**. **3.** Click the **More arrow** on the **Chart Layouts group** to display the gallery, as shown in Figure 3.54. **4.** Click a new layout to apply it. **5.** Click the **More button** on the **Chart Styles gallery**, as shown in Figure 3.55. **6.** Click a new style to apply it.

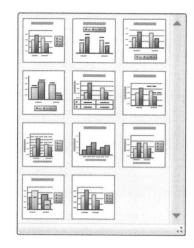

Figure 3.54: Chart Layout gallery

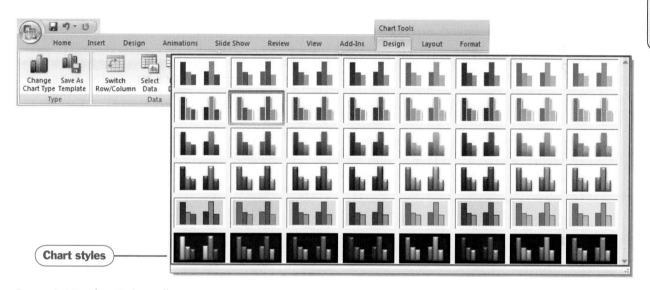

Figure 3.55: Chart Styles gallery

To apply chart labels, **1.** click the chart to select it. **2.** Click the **Chart tools, Layout tab**, and in the **Labels group** or **Axes group** shown in Figure 3.56, **3.** click an appropriate button, and add or modify the chart title, legend, data labels, and axes labels.

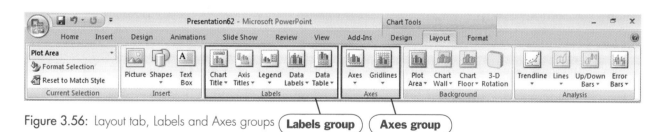

Figure 3.56: Layout tab, Labels and Axes groups **(Labels group) (Axes group)**

1. Open a new blank presentation.

2. Insert a new slide using a **Title and Content** slide layout.

3. Click the **Insert Chart icon** on the slide.

4. In the Insert Chart dialog box, select the default column type (Clustered Column), and click **OK**.

5. Drag the red box in the lower-right corner of the range to include the range **A1:E4**, then delete the data from the datasheet. Enter the new data shown below, and close the datasheet window.

	2007	2008	2009	2010
Internet	24	30	42	55
Catalog	50	40	30	20
Store	26	30	28	25

6. Select the chart, click the **Chart Tools, Layout tab**, and in the **Labels group**, click the **Chart Title button**, and select **Above Chart**.

7. Enter `Sales Analysis (by percentage)` in the chart title text box.

8. In the **Labels group**, click the **Legend list arrow**, and select **Show Legend at Bottom**.

9. In the **Labels group**, click the **Data Labels list arrow**, and select the **Center option**.

10. In the **Labels group**, click the **Data Table list arrow**, and select **Show Data Table**. *Note: You cannot modify the data table when it appears on the chart slide.*

11. Delete the slide title placeholder.

12. Select the chart, position your mouse on the chart frame, size it to fill the slide, then drag the chart to center it on the slide.

13. Close the presentation without saving the changes.

SmartArt

▶ As you learned in Word, SmartArt is a collection of diagrams that show process flows and relationships. An organization chart is a type of diagram you can use to illustrate a hierarchy or structure, flow of a project, or a family tree.

▶ After SmartArt is inserted on your slide or selected, a frame appears around the graphic, and the SmartArt Tools, Design and Format tabs also appear with the Design tab selected by default to help you customize the SmartArt graphic, as shown in the organization chart SmartArt graphic in Figure 3.58. Figure 3.57 shows the tools that appear on the SmartArt Tools, Format tab.

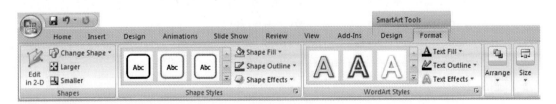

Figure 3.57: SmartArt Tools, Format tab

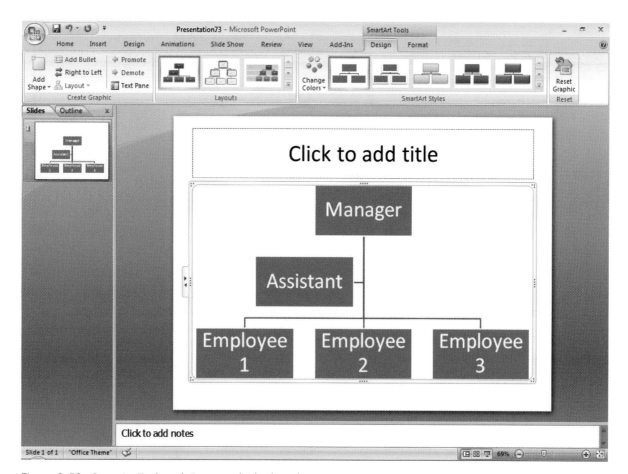

Figure 3.58: SmartArt Tools with Design tab displayed

▶ You can format a SmartArt graphic with preset styles, or format portions of it as you would format shapes by adding fill color and text, and change the line weight and style.

HOW To create a SmartArt graphic, **1.** click the **Insert tab** and in the **Illustrations group**, **2.** click the **SmartArt button**. **3.** In the **Choose a SmartArt Graphic dialog box** that appears, as shown in Figure 3.59, **4.** select a **SmartArt graphic type** (List, Process, Hierarchy, Cycle Relationship, Matrix, or Pyramid) in the left pane. **5.** Select a **SmartArt thumbnail** in the middle pane, then click **OK**. **6.** Click in a shape or text placeholder to enter text, or click the first item in the Text pane shown in Figure 3.60, and enter the text for that item. *Font is automatically resized based on the size of the boxes and the amount of text*. If the Text pane is not displayed on the **SmartArt Tools, Design tab**, and in the **Create Graphic group**, click the **Text Pane button**. **7.** Format the layout using the tools found on the SmartArt, Design and Format tabs.

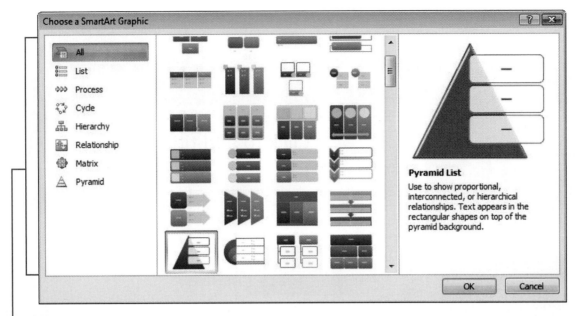

Figure 3.59: SmartArt graphic gallery

Graphic types

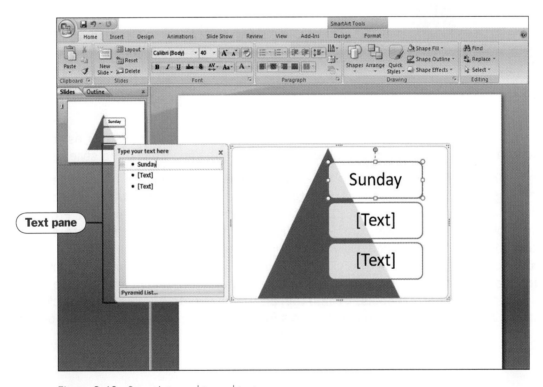

Figure 3.60: SmartArt graphic and text pane

Text pane

To create an organization chart, **1.** select **Hierarchy** in the left pane, and **2.** click the **Organization Chart thumbnail** in the middle pane, then **3.** click **OK** (see Figure 3.57).

To add a shape to the organization chart, **1.** select an existing shape to which you want to add a shape. **2.** Click the **Design tab**, and in the **Create Graphic group**, **3.** click the **Add Shape button list arrow**, then **4.** select a placement option. To add an assistant shape, click **Add Assistant**.

To delete a shape, **1.** click the shape border and **2.** press **[Delete]**.

1. Open a new blank presentation.

2. Right-click the first slide in the slide pane, point to Layout, and apply the **Title and Content** layout.

3. Click the **Insert SmartArt Graphic icon** on the slide.

4. Click the **Hierarchy** graphic type in the middle pane, and the **Organization Chart** thumbnail in the middle pane, then click **OK**.

5. Click in the top box, and enter the following on two lines:

   ```
   Jen Patton
   President
   ```

6. Click in the **Assistant** box, and press **[Delete]**.

7. Click in the left subordinate box, and enter the following on two lines:

   ```
   Darren Wong
   Vice President
   ```

8. Click the middle subordinate coworker box, and enter the following on two lines:

   ```
   Margaret Richards
   Vice President
   ```

9. Click the **SmartArt Tools, Design tab**, and in the **SmartArt Styles group**, click the **More** arrow, then select the **Inset 3-D effect**.

10. Click the **Change Colors button list arrow**, and select a color option from the **Colorful group**.

11. Click and drag a corner size handle to reduce the size of the SmartArt frame.

    • Position your insertion point on the frame until the pointer changes to a four-headed arrow. Then, click and drag the frame to better position the graphic on the slide.

12. Click the slide outside the graphic to hide the SmartArt frame.

13. Close the presentation without saving the changes.

POWERPOINT

Use Action Buttons

▶ You have already learned how to insert a hyperlink on text or objects to link to another slide in your presentation, another file, or a custom show. You can also place a hyperlink on an action button. **Action buttons** are ready-made buttons found in the Shapes gallery that contain common symbols that indicate specific actions such as advancing to the next slide, returning to the first slide, and so forth. Figure 3.61 shows action buttons on the Shapes gallery.

▶ Action buttons become active when you run your presentation in Slide Show view. When you place the mouse over an action button, the mouse pointer changes to a hand graphic. If you want the same action buttons to appear on all the slides of your presentation, insert the action buttons on the Slide Master.

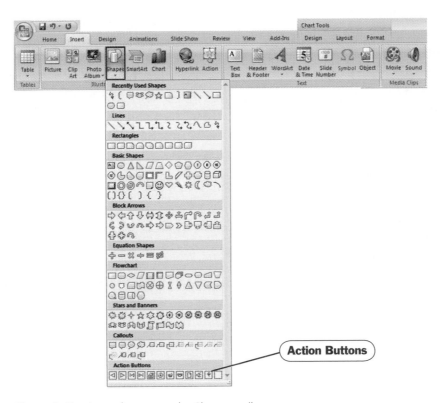

Action Buttons

Figure 3.61: Action buttons on the Shapes gallery

HOW To insert an action button, **1.** click the **Insert tab**, and in the **Illustrations group**, **2.** click the **Shapes button**. **3.** Click an action button from the **Action Buttons group**. **4.** Click the slide and drag the mouse diagonally to draw the button. **5.** When you release the mouse button, the Action Settings dialog box opens, as shown in Figure 3.62. **6.** To have the action button activate when you click it, select activation options on the **Mouse Click tab**. To have the action button activate when you place the mouse pointer over it, select activation options on the **Mouse Over tab**. **7.** Click **OK**.

Figure 3.62: Action Settings dialog box

To create a hyperlink on an action button, **1.** click the **Hyperlink to option button** in the Action Settings dialog box. **2.** Click the **Hyperlink to list arrow**, and select whether to link to another slide, a Web site, a custom show, or a file. If more information is needed, such as defining the URL of the Web site, or the location of a file, a dialog box will open, prompting you to enter the appropriate information. *If you insert one of the ready-made action buttons, the action settings reflect whatever the button indicates. For example, if you insert the Next Slide action button, the Action Settings dialog box is set so that clicking the action button advances you to the next slide.*

To play a sound when you activate an action button, **1.** click the **Play sound check box** in the Action Settings dialog box, **2.** click the **Play sound list arrow**, and **3.** select a sound effect.

T R Y *it* **O U T** *p3-19*

1. Open the data file **p3-19**.

2. Display **Slide 3**.

3. Click the Insert tab, and in the Illustrations group, click the **Shapes button**, then select the **Back** or **Previous button** in the **Action Buttons group**.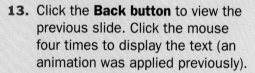

4. Drag the mouse to draw a button on the bottom-left corner of the slide. The Action Settings dialog box opens.

5. Click the **Mouse Click tab**, if necessary, and click **OK** to link to the previous slide.

6. Click the **Shapes button** again, and select the **Forward or Next button** in the **Action Buttons group**.

7. Drag the mouse to draw a button on the bottom-right corner of the slide.

8. Click the **Mouse Over tab**, click the **Hyperlink to** option button, and choose **Next Slide** from the **Hyperlink to** list.

9. Click the **Play sound** box, click the **Play sound list arrow**, select **Chime**, and click **OK**. *Note: The Sound Effects feature may need to be installed.*

10. Click the **Slide Show View button** on the status bar.

11. Place the mouse over the **Next button** to advance to the next slide. The slide will advance and play the chime sound.

12. Press **[Backspace]**.

13. Click the **Back button** to view the previous slide. Click the mouse four times to display the text (an animation was applied previously).

14. Press **[Escape]**.

15. Close the file without saving the presentation.

 GOAL
To create a presentation containing
a chart, table, action buttons, and
SmartArt, as shown in Figure 3.63

TASK 4

WHAT YOU NEED TO KNOW

▶ In this Rehearsal activity, you
will create a sales presentation
to be used to persuade a real
estate developer to hire Palmetto
Realtors as its exclusive sales
agent. You will use charts,
SmartArt, action buttons, and
hyperlinks to enhance the
presentation.

▼ DIRECTIONS

1. Open a new blank presentation, and apply the
Technic theme.
   a. Change the color theme to **Equity** and the
   background style to **Style 2**.
   b. Apply a picture background using a relevant
   graphic.

2. Enter the following title and subtitle in the
appropriate location on the title slide:
   Palmetto Realtors (title)
   The Lake View Development (subtitle)

3. Display the Slide Master, and select the Master
Slide.
   a. Enter the following footer on the Master Slide:
   **Selling fine properties for more
   than 25 years**. Set the text to a **12-point, red**
   font, and adjust the footer text box as necessary
   to fit the footer on one line.
   b. Include the slide number, but not the date, on all
   slides.
   c. Create an attractive design using the logo and a
   few shapes. The Palmetto Realtors logo can be
   found in the **Logos** folder in the data files.
   d. Include backward and forward action buttons
   on the bottom left of the slide as shown in the
   figure. Use the default action settings.
   e. Change the font for the title to **Papyrus**. If this
   font is not available to you, substitute another.
   Apply any theme font color that you want.
   f. Close Master view.

Continued on next page

4. Create the seven slides shown in Figure 3.63 using appropriate layouts.
   a. On **Slide 4** (Recent Neighborhood Analysis), replace the data on the datasheet, and enter the new data shown here:

	2008	2009	2010
1 BR	298,000	305,000	319,000
2 BR	238,000	339,000	354,000
3 BR	387,000	410,000	422,000

   • Include a chart title and legend.
   b. On **Slide 5**, create a SmartArt graphic using an **organization chart** layout, and enter the managers' names and their titles, as indicated in Figure 3.64.
      • Apply any SmartArt style and color.
   c. On **Slide 2**, insert hyperlinks from the slide text to its corresponding slide.
   d. On **Slide 7**, insert an appropriate graphic, and apply an effect.
   e. On the **Title slide**, apply a slow entrance animation for the title that includes a sound effect.

5. Apply a transition effect on all slides in the presentation.

6. Make any adjustments necessary to better present the data.

7. Run the slide show several times; activate the hyperlinks each time.

8. Print one copy of the presentation as handouts with six slides per page.

9. Save the file as **3r4-realty**.

10. Close the file.

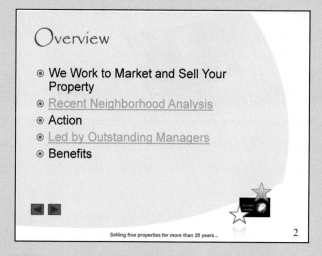

Figure 3.63a: Palmetto Realtors sales presentation (Slides 1 and 2)

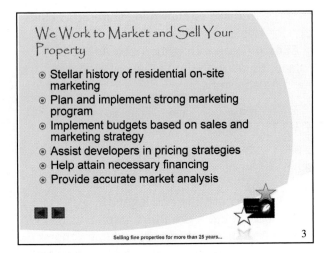

We Work to Market and Sell Your Property

- Stellar history of residential on-site marketing
- Plan and implement strong marketing program
- Implement budgets based on sales and marketing strategy
- Assist developers in pricing strategies
- Help attain necessary financing
- Provide accurate market analysis

Selling fine properties for more than 25 years...

3

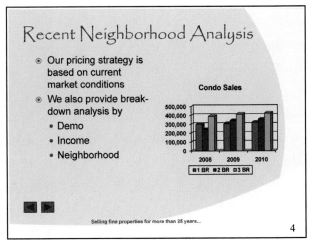

Recent Neighborhood Analysis

- Our pricing strategy is based on current market conditions
- We also provide breakdown analysis by
  - Demo
  - Income
  - Neighborhood

Condo Sales

1 BR 2 BR 3 BR
2008 2009 2010

Selling fine properties for more than 25 years...

4

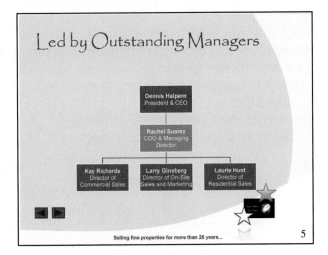

Led by Outstanding Managers

Dennis Halpern
President & CEO

Rachel Suarez
COO & Managing Director

Kay Richards
Director of Commercial Sales

Larry Ginsberg
Director of On-Site Sales and Marketing

Laurie Hunt
Director of Residential Sales

Selling fine properties for more than 25 years...

5

Benefits

- We are a full-service real estate company with a track record of new development sales success!
  - Early sales
    - Launch full-scale sales effort even before building begins
  - Competitive Pricing
    - Maximum dollars given market value
  - Flexibility
    - Adapt to your specific needs to market and sell your property

Selling fine properties for more than 25 years...

6

Choose the Right Broker!

- Experience
- Outstanding Staff
- Proven Success
- Detailed and respected marketing plans

Selling fine properties for more than 25 years...

7

Figure 3.63b: Palmetto Realtors sales presentation (Slides 3–7)

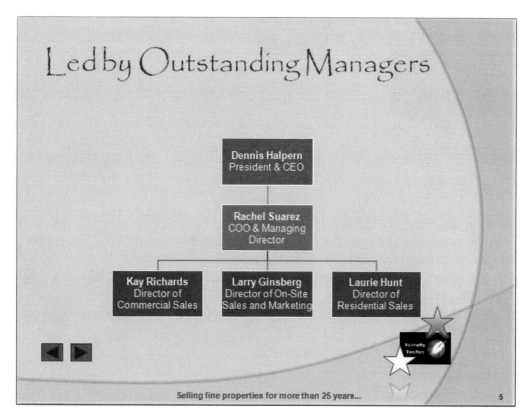

Figure 3.64: Slide with SmartArt

Cues for Reference

Insert a Table

1. Click the **Home tab**, and in the **Slides group**, click the **New Slide button list arrow**.
2. Click the thumbnail of a slide layout containing a content layout.
3. Click the **Insert Table icon**.
4. Enter the number of columns.
5. Press **[Tab]**.
6. Enter the number of rows.
7. Click **OK**.

Insert a Table without Using a Placeholder

1. Display the slide on which you want the table.
2. Click the **Insert tab**, and in the **Tables group**, click the **Table button**, and drag to select columns or rows.

Insert a Chart on a Slide

1. Click the **Home tab**, and in the **Slide group**, click the **New Slide button list arrow**.
2. Click the thumbnail of a slide layout containing a content layout, and click the **Insert Chart icon**.
   Or
2. On the **Insert tab**, and in the **Illustrations group**, click the **Insert Chart icon**.
3. Delete the sample data and enter the data you want to chart in the datasheet.

Edit a Chart

1. Select the chart, and click the **Chart Tools Design, Layout** or **Format tabs**.
2. Make your selections.

Insert SmartArt

1. Click the Home tab, and in the **Slides group**, click the **New Slide button list arrow**.
2. Click the thumbnail of a slide layout containing a content layout.
3. Click the **Insert SmartArt Graphic icon**.
4. Click a SmartArt category in the left pane; click a layout in the middle pane.
5. Click **OK**.

PERFORMANCE

TASK 4

You are the marketing assistant at Expedition Travel Gear. Your boss is preparing for a meeting with the president of Expedition Travel Gear to update him on the new camping equipment product launches. Your boss has already created the presentation, but she would like you to enhance it with a design theme, clip art images, action buttons, a chart, a table, and SmartArt objects.

Expedition

Travel Gear

Follow these guidelines:

1. Open the data file **p3p4-etg update unformatted**.

2. Display the Slide Master.
   a. On the Master Slide, apply a design theme.
   b. Change the color theme.
   c. Apply a new font style and color to the title and bulleted text that complements the design theme.
   d. Change the level 1 bullet style and color.
   e. Insert the following action buttons in this order: **Beginning, Previous, Next, End**. Align them on the bottom right of the slide, and apply a new shape style to them.
   f. Insert a footer that reads **ETG-Camping Equipment**. Do not include the footer on the title slide. Italicize the footer text, and change its font size to **10 pt**.

3. Display **Slide 4**.
   a. Insert the table, as shown in Figure 3.65a.
   b. Apply a new table style.

4. Display **Slide 5**.
   a. Insert a SmartArt object, as shown in Figure 3.65b.
   b. Apply a new color and SmartArt Style to it.

5. Display **Slide 7**.
   a. Use the information at the right to create a pie chart.
   b. Insert the following title: **2009 Sales Recap**.
   c. Apply a new Chart Style to it.

	SALES
Internet	$1,295,000
Store	$895,000
Catalog	$435,000

6. Display **Slide 11**.
   a. Insert the **Organization Chart**, as shown in Figure 3.65c.
   b. Apply a new SmartArt style to it.

7. Insert relevant clip art images throughout the presentation. Apply different picture styles to the images.

8. Run the slide show, and use the action buttons to advance to the next slide and to go back to a previous slide.

9. Print one copy of the presentation as handouts with six slides per page.

10. Save the file as **3p4-etg final**.

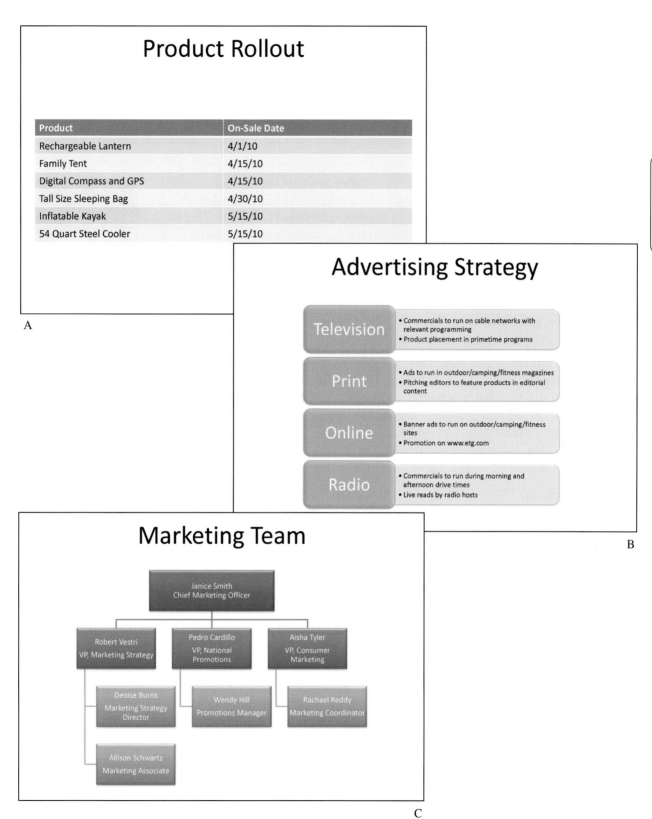

Figure 3.65: Table, SmartArt, and chart

ENCORE

Act I

You are the assistant to the director of television sales at Newmark Productions. Your boss must sell a new action/adventure television series called *Undercover* to television stations. The show is set in New York City, the perfect setting for mystery, adventure, and lots of action. She has asked you to create a sales presentation for potential station buyers. The production department has provided the information you need to create a presentation of approximately 12 slides.

Follow these guidelines:

1. Read through the information provided on the following page to get a basic understanding of the content the presentation will cover. Then create a presentation based on that content.
   - Each bold heading represents a new section, and should appear on a section header layout slide. The section header slide will precede each informational slide; there will be four section header layout slides in total.
   - The paragraph below each heading contains the information for each slide. Summarize the information into bullet points.

2. Apply a design theme. Use your creativity to design the slides using Slide Masters, footers, clip art, shapes, WordArt, text alignments, and any other embellishments.

3. Create a logo for the new show, *Undercover*, which you will place on all the section header slides.

4. Include a table as shown in Figure 3.66.

5. Create a relevant title (and title slide) for the presentation.

6. Add appropriate slide transitions and animations.

7. Save the presentation as **3e1-undercover**.

Action/Adventure Scores with Key Demos

- Most successful with women and men 25-54
- Of the top 10 programs of the year, more than half were action/adventure
- Staple genre that appeals to the masses

Rank	Show	Genre
1	The Hour	Action/Adventure
2	Married Life	Comedy
3	Crime Scene	Action/Adventure
4	Doctors & Nurses	Drama
5	Precinct 91	Action/Adventure
6	Miami Sunsets	Action/Adventure
7	Roommates	Comedy
8	The Robinson's	Drama
9	Cellular	Action/Adventure
10	The Search	Action/Adventure

Undercover – Premieres this Fall

Figure 3.66: Table on Slide 8

The Show

Undercover is a new action/adventure series about detectives from a New York City police department who go undercover to fight crime and injustice in the city streets. Each episode will bring exciting storylines, great action sequences, wit, irony, and romance. The show is set in New York City, the perfect backdrop for mystery, adventure, and lots of action. The series will be a feature film-quality production with a budget of $1 million per episode.

The show features talented, young stars including John Wagner, whose recent film credits include *The Diaries* and *The Breakfast Bunch*. The show also stars Alison Tepper, Janet Fine, and Maurice Banks.

The Credits

Undercover has hired an outstanding production team to bring this exciting program to TV. Jeff Grant is the executive producer. His credits include *Home Sweet Home* (TV), *The Long Ride Away* (film), and *Stalkers* (film). Susan Holmes is the director; her credits include *Wired* (film), *Crime Scenes* (TV), and *The Range* (TV). The head writer is Sloane Peterson, who has also written *Winter in Miami* (film), *The Wedding Fiasco* (film), and *Detective, Detective* (TV).

The Genre

Action/adventure programs do well with key demographics and are most successful with women and men age 25 to 54. Of the top 10 programs on TV this year, more than half were action/adventure. Action/adventure programming is a staple genre that appeals to the masses.

Newmark Productions has been successful with this genre. Our other two shows currently on the air are action/adventure programs, and they consistently rank among the top five in the genre. Our marketing campaigns and publicity stunts garner tremendous attention. Furthermore, every single one of our action/adventure films has been a blockbuster!

Perfect for Your Station

This show will play well in key time slots: early afternoons, evenings, and late at night. The show is advertiser-friendly and has flexible demographic appeal.

Act II

Expedition Travel Gear believes that a good way to sell its products is to partner with various travel agencies. With that goal in mind, the sales department wants to use a PowerPoint presentation to present its partnership proposal to travel agents who will attend a travel convention next month. The sales manager has provided you with the necessary information to create a sales presentation of approximately nine slides.

Expedition

Travel Gear

Follow these guidelines:

1. Read through the information provided on the next page to get a basic understanding of the content the presentation will cover. Then create a presentation based on that content.
   - Each bold heading represents a new slide. "The Partnership" should appear on a section header layout slide.
   - The paragraph below each heading contains the information for each slide. Summarize the information into bullet points.

2. Apply a design theme. Use your creativity to design the slides using Slide Masters, footers, clip art, shapes, text alignments, and any other embellishments.

3. Use WordArt to create Expedition Travel Gear's motto: `Whether you travel far or near, don't leave without Expedition Travel Gear!` Position the WordArt on **Slide 1**.

4. Insert action buttons on all slides that link to the previous slide and the next slide.

5. Insert an overview slide as the second slide in the presentation. The overview slide should contain all of the slide titles in the presentation as bulleted text. Title the slide **Overview**.

6. Insert a slide after the Partnership slide that contains a SmartArt graphic.
   a. Use the **Equation** graphic, which can be found in the **Process group**.
   b. Enter the text, `Expedition Travel Gear + Your Agency = Endless Opportunities`, as shown in Figure 3.67.

7. Use two Slide Masters for this presentation.
   a. Use the same design theme for these masters but apply different color themes to differentiate them.
   b. Apply one of the Slide Masters to **Slides 1–4**; apply the other Slide Master to **Slides 5–10**.

8. Save the presentation as **3e2-partnership**.

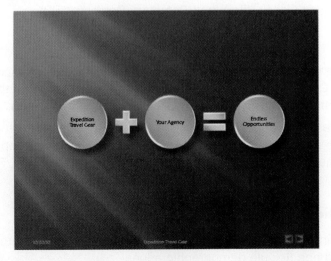

Figure 3.67: Slide containing SmartArt

Expedition Travel Gear

The presentation to launch this partnership proposal will be given on October 30, 2010.

What We Do

We offer high-quality travel products that make travel easier and more comfortable. We supply a wide range of travel products to meet the needs of all travelers. We pride ourselves on providing outstanding customer service and offer our products at extremely low prices. We will match any competitor's price.

Our Success Speaks for Itself

Within the past year, our catalog and Internet sales have doubled, and we have opened five more retail stores. We are consistently featured in top travel magazines including *Travel and Tourism*, *Voyages*, and *Around the World*. Furthermore, our products and exceptional service have received rave reviews from top travel critics.

The Partnership

We are seeking a mutually beneficial partnership that will offer your clients discounted products from Expedition Travel Gear.

Partner Benefits

This partnership will result in benefits for both Expedition Travel Gear and your travel agency. Both parties will profit from new advertising, cross-promotion, global reach, and revenue opportunities.

Your Role

The travel agency's contribution to the partnership will be as follows: Advertise Expedition Travel Gear to your clients as your exclusive travel gear supplier, distribute Expedition catalogs in all of your travel agencies, include an Expedition logo on all marketing materials generated by your agency, and include a link to Expedition's Web site from your agency's Web site.

What We'll Offer

Expedition's contribution to the partnership will be as follows: product discounts of up to 25% to your travel clients only, links from our Web site to your agency's Web site, a *Travel Specials* insert in our catalog that includes travel deals from your agency, and client referrals.

Make It Happen

It's now up to you to make this partnership a reality. If you are interested in moving forward or have any questions, call president and CEO Pamela Walters or marketing director Thomas Romano at 630-555-8888. You can also fax your name and agency information to 630-555-8787, and we'll contact you!

WHAT YOU NEED TO KNOW

Use Template Presentations

▶ A **template presentation** is a predesigned set of slides. Some template presentations use themes, and others include sample layout, text, and graphics about a particular topic.

▶ Some template presentations are installed with PowerPoint; most, however, must be downloaded from Microsoft Office Online to your computer. In order to download templates, Microsoft may verify that your software copy is properly registered.

HOW To access template presentations installed on your computer, **1.** click the **Office Button**, **2.** click **New**, **3.** click the **Installed Templates link** in the New Presentation dialog box, as shown in Figure 4.2, **4.** click one of the template thumbnails, then **5.** click **Create**.

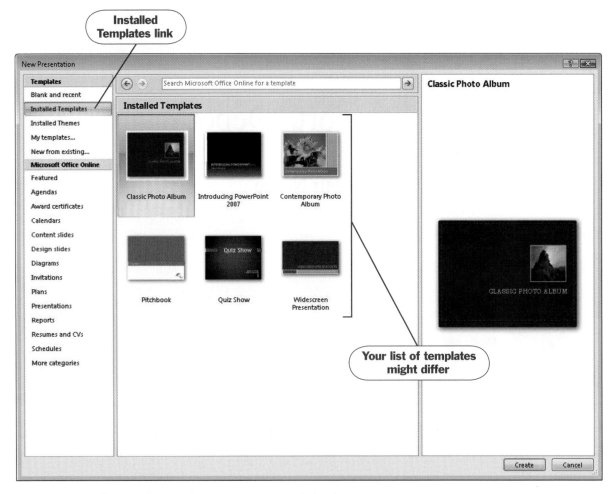

Figure 4.2: Installed templates in the New Presentation dialog box

To download template presentations from Microsoft Office Online to your computer, **1.** make sure that you are connected to the Internet, **2.** click any category in the left pane of the New Presentation dialog box to display additional categories of available templates in the middle pane, as shown in Figure 4.3, **3.** click a category, which will display thumbnails, **4.** click one of the template thumbnails, then **5.** click **Download**. **6.** If an alert box appears, click **Continue**.

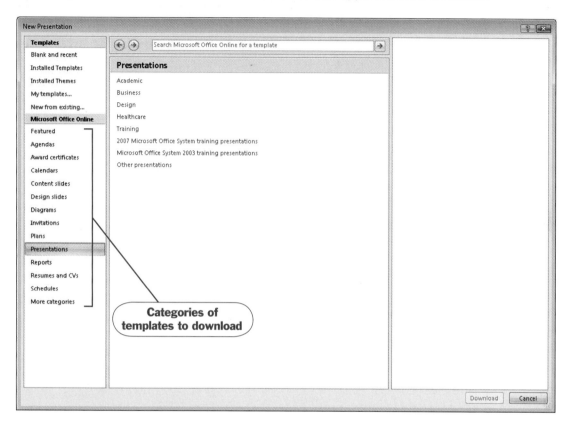

Figure 4.3: Accessing presentations from Microsoft Office Online

▶ After you choose a template, the presentation opens and the number of slides in the presentation appears on the status bar. Select the sample text on each slide and replace it with your own. You can make additional formatting changes to the presentation, if necessary.

TRY it OUT p4-1

Note: This activity will use an installed template.

1. Click the **Office Button**, then click **New** to display the New Presentation dialog box.

2. Click the **Installed Templates** link.

3. Click the **Introducing PowerPoint 2007** template.

4. Click **Create**.

5. Select the title text on the first slide, then enter: **Product Development Meeting**.

6. Select the subtitle text on the first slide, then enter your name.

7. Scroll through the slides, and note the sample text and any graphics on each slide.

8. Close the presentation without saving the changes.

POWERPOINT

Work with Media

▶ Media include sound effects, music, video, or **animated .gifs** (pictures that have animation effects) that you can add to slides. The media are activated during a slide show.

▶ You can add media clips to slides in the same way that you add clip art images. Like clip art, media clips come preloaded with Office and are located in the Microsoft Clip Organizer. Video clips and animated .gifs are indicated by a star icon in the bottom-right corner of the thumbnail (see Figure 4.4).

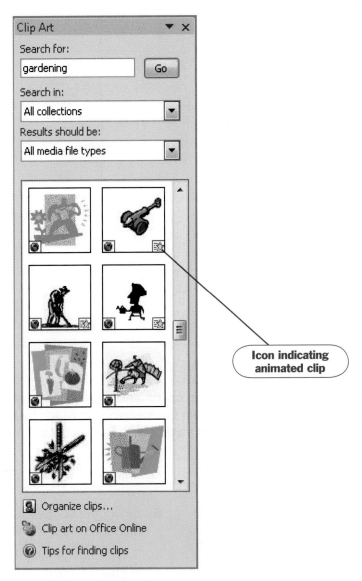

Figure 4.4: Clip Art task pane

▶ After you select a media clip, PowerPoint prompts you to choose whether to play the media clip in the slide show automatically when the slide appears or only when you click it.

HOW To add a media clip from clip art using a slide layout that contains a media clip icon, **1.** click the icon on the slide to open the Clip Art task pane shown in Figure 4.4, **2.** enter search criteria, **3.** click the **Results should be list arrow**, **4.** select the **Movies** and **Sounds check boxes**, and **5.** click **Go. 6.** Click to select the clip, and then **7.** click **Automated** or **When Clicked**.

To add a media clip from your files, **1.** click the **Insert tab**, and in the **Media Clips group**, click the **Movie** or **Sound button**. In the Insert Movie or Insert Sound dialog box that opens, (see Figure 4.5), **2.** navigate to locate an existing video, sound, or animated. gif, **3.** click the media clip, then **4.** click **OK**.

Figure 4.5: Insert Movie dialog box

► Media clips appear on slides, as shown in Figure 4.6. To play a media clip, you must be in Slide Show view. You can, however, preview a media clip in Normal view by double-clicking it, or by right-clicking the media clip and clicking Preview.

► An animated .gif plays automatically in Slide Show view.

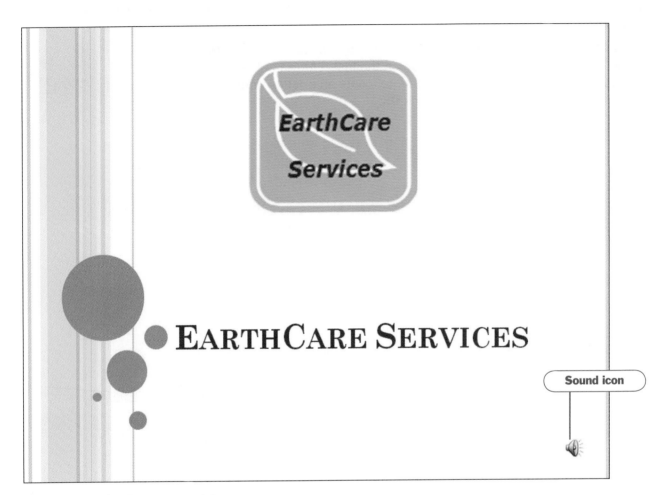

Figure 4.6: Media clip icon on a slide

Looping Media

▶ **Looping** allows you to play a sound or movie continuously until you advance to the next slide.

HOW To loop a sound or movie, **1.** click the media clip, **2.** click the **Sound Tools, Options tab** or the **Movie Tools, Options tab**, then **3.** click the **Loop Until Stopped check box**, as shown in Figures 4.7 and 4.8.

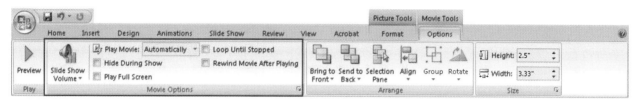

Figure 4.7: Movie Tools, Options tab

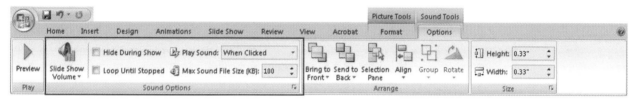

Figure 4.8: Sound Tools, Options tab

T R Y *i t* O U T *p4-2*

1. Open a new blank presentation.

2. On the **Home tab**, and in the **Slides group**, click the **Layout button**.

3. Click **Title and Content** on the **Layout menu**.

4. Click the **Insert Clip Art icon**.

5. In the Clip Art task pane, type **Animated** in the Search for text box, then click **Go**.

6. Scroll and select any animated.gif.

7. Click the **Slide Show View button** on the status bar.

8. Press **[Esc]** to end the slide show.

9. Click the **Insert tab**, and in the **Media Clips group**, click the **Sound button list arrow**, then click **Sound from Clip Organizer**.

10. Click a music clip.

11. Click **When Clicked** in the alert box.

12. Click and drag the sound object to the bottom-right corner of the slide.

13. Click the **Slide Show View button** on the status bar.

14. Click the sound object to play it.

15. Press **[Esc]** to end the slide show.

16. Close the file without saving the changes.

Insert Music from a CD

▶ To enhance your presentation with music from a CD, first insert a CD in the computer's CD-ROM drive, then display the slide on which you want the music to play. Figure 4.9 shows a setting to start a CD audio clip at the beginning of Track 1 and end it during Track 2, with a total playing time of 10:58.25 seconds.

Figure 4.9: Insert CD Audio dialog box

HOW To add a sound clip from a CD, **1.** click the **Insert tab**, and in the **Media Clips group**, **2.** click the **Sound button** list arrow, then **3.** click **Play CD Audio Track**. In the Insert CD Audio dialog box, shown in Figure 4.9, **4.** enter the track number of the song you want to play in the **Start at track box** and the starting point in the **time box**. **5.** Enter the track number where the music will end in the **End at track box** and the ending point in the **time box**. **6.** Click the **Loop until stopped check box** if desired, then **7.** click **OK**.

TRY*it* OUT *p4-3*

Note: You must have a CD-ROM drive and a music CD available to complete this activity.

1. Open the data file **p4-3**. Display **Slide 1**, if necessary.

2. Insert a music CD into the CD-ROM drive.

3. Click the **Insert tab**, and in the **Media Clips group**, click the **Sound button list arrow**, then click **Play CD Audio Track**.

4. Click the **Start at track** up arrow to display **2**, click the **End at track** up arrow twice to display **3**, then click **OK**.

5. Click **Automatically** in the alert box. A CD icon appears on the slide.

6. Click and drag the **CD** icon to the bottom-right corner of the first slide.

7. Click the **Slide Show View button** on the status bar. *The music will begin automatically.* Click the mouse to advance to the next slide.

8. Press **[Esc]**.

9. Close the presentation without saving changes.

REHEARSAL

TASK 1

GOAL
To create a presentation containing media, as shown in Figures 4.10 and 4.11

WHAT YOU NEED TO KNOW

▶ A persuasive presentation is used to convince the audience of something in some way. It should clearly state your goals and expectations, and the benefits of your proposal.

▶ Media clips can be used to get the audience's attention and emphasize points within your presentation. Be sure that the media clips complement the subject of your presentation, but do not overshadow the presentation.

▶ If you are using music from a CD in your presentation, you must give credit to the source of the material (in this case, the musician). Also, some music may be copyrighted, which means that, depending on how you plan to use the presentation, you may need to obtain permission to use it.

▶ In this Rehearsal activity, you will use a template to create a presentation that outlines the goals for All Sports Depot. You will use media clips to enhance the presentation.

▼ DIRECTIONS

*Note: You must be connected to the Internet to download the template for this activity. If not, open the **p4r1-company meeting template**, which can be found in the data files, and skip to Step 1b.*

1. Open the New Presentation dialog box, click the **Presentations** link, then click the **Business** category.
   a. Select the **Company meeting presentation** template, then click **Download**. Click **Continue** in the alert box, if necessary.
   b. Enter the following presentation title: **All Sports Depot**.
   c. Enter the following presentation subtitle: **Your Name, Presenter**.
   d. Include the following footer on all slides: **Company Meeting, January 2010**. Include the slide number, but not the date, in the footer on all slides.

2. Replace the slide text on Slides 2–5 as indicated in Figure 4.10. Notice the new text corresponds to the template slide text. Delete slides as appropriate so that your presentation looks like Figure 4.10.

3. On **Slide 6** insert a new table, as shown in Figure 4.11, and enter the new data shown here.

	2008	2009	GOAL: 2010
Equipment	$1.5 million	$1.8 million	$2.3 million
Apparel	$643,000	$720,000	$1 million
Footwear	$790,000	$994,000	$1.2 million

4. On **Slide 2**, enter the titles of Slides 3 through 6.

5. Include hyperlinks on **Slide 2** from the slide title to its corresponding slide.

6. On **Slide 1**, insert a sound clip to play upbeat music using a music CD you own. *(If a music CD is not available, skip this step.)*

Continued on next page

a. Loop the sound to play automatically throughout the slide show when the slide show begins.

b. Place the sound object in the bottom-left corner of the slide.

7. Run the slide show, and activate the hyperlinks. Notice that object animations are built into the template.

8. Print one copy of the presentation as handouts with six slides per page.

9. Save the file as **4r1-sports**, then close the file.

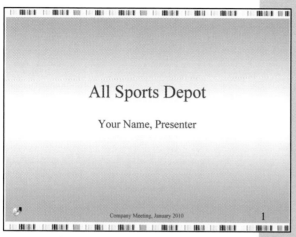

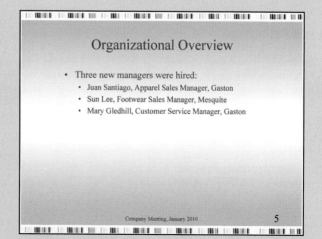

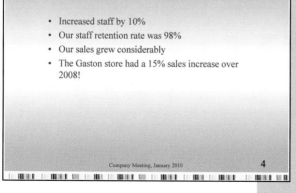

Figure 4.10: Slides 1–5

Figure 4.11: Slide with a table

PERFORMANCE

TASK 1

Perfect Planning Group (PPG) has accepted an invitation to make a presentation at an upcoming Event Planning conference. You have been asked to create a presentation to showcase PPG's offerings for children's parties. You will use a template and add sound to run during the looped presentation.

Follow these guidelines:

1. Apply a template to a new presentation as follows:
    a. Open the **New Presentation** dialog box.
    b. If connected to the Internet, click the **Design slides link**, then in the **Whimsy** category, click the **Balloons** thumbnail, then click **Download**. Click **Continue** in the alert box, if necessary. (If not connected to the Internet, use the file **p4p1-balloons template** in the data files.)
    c. Save the presentation as **4p1-childrens presentation**.

2. Add text and slides to the presentation as follows:
    a. Enter `Perfect Planning Group` as the title. Enter `Children's Entertainment` as the subtitle.
    b. Insert three Title and Content slides, and enter text as shown in Figure 4.12.

3. Insert a sound clip and set it to start automatically and loop.

4. Run the slide show.

5. Print one copy of the presentation as handouts with six slides per page.

6. Save the presentation, and then close the file.

Perfect Planning Group

Children's Entertainment

1

Activities

- All of our entertainers are top-notch, love children, and will take special requests
- Choose from:
  - Clown
  - Magic
  - Music
  - Gymnastics

2

Food

- A varied menu with options for allergies or special diets
- Some menu choices:
  - Grilled cheese
  - Pizza
  - Wraps

3

Favors

- Each child gets a custom favor bag depending on the ages and theme
- Request from:
  - No candy options
  - Age-appropriate toys
  - Personalized items

4

Figure 4.12: Children's presentation

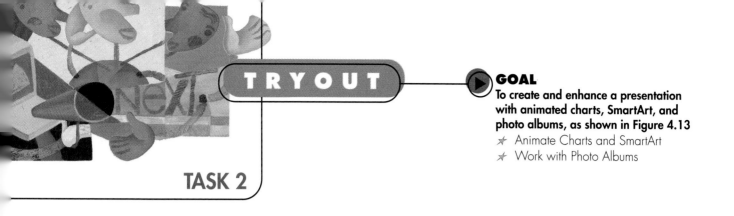

TRYOUT

GOAL
To create and enhance a presentation with animated charts, SmartArt, and photo albums, as shown in Figure 4.13
✶ Animate Charts and SmartArt
✶ Work with Photo Albums

TASK 2

POWERPOINT

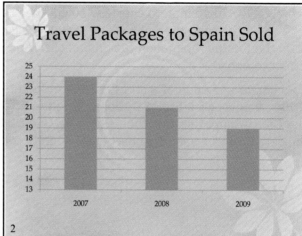

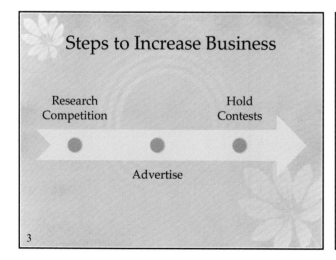

Figure 4.13: Selected slides with photos, animated charts, and SmartArt

WHAT YOU NEED TO KNOW

Animate Charts and SmartArt

▶ As you learned in Lesson 2, animations are visual or sound effects that you can add to text or objects during a slide show. You also learned to apply preset animations with transition effects.

▶ You can animate charts and SmartArt (diagrams) with the same techniques used to animate text and objects. You can also animate individual sections of a chart or diagram and/or add sound effects, which can add interest when emphasizing data during your slide show. When an animation is added to a slide or object, it appears in the Custom Animation task pane with a descriptive name for the animation.

HOW To animate a chart, **1.** select the chart, **2.** click the **Animations tab**,  and in the **Animations group**, **3.** click the **Custom Animation button**.
4. In the Custom Animation task pane, click **Add Effect**, and then **5.** select the animation effect to apply.

To animate a section of a chart, **1.** in the Custom Animation task pane, click the **animation list arrow**, then **2.** click **Effect Options**. **3.** In the Effect Options dialog box, shown in Figure 4.14, click the **Chart Animation tab**, then select **As One Object** or **By Category** from the Group chart list to indicate how you want the chart animated.

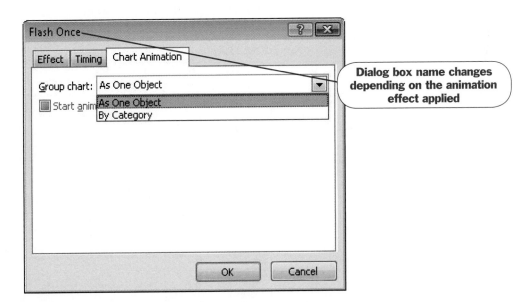

Figure 4.14: Chart Animation tab

To add a sound effect to a chart, **1.** in the Custom Animation task pane, click the **animation list arrow**, then **2.** click **Effect Options**. **3.** In the Effect Options dialog box, click the **Effect tab**, then select a sound from the **Sound list arrow** in the **Enhancements group**.

1. Open the data file **p4-4**.

2. On **Slide 6**, click the pie chart. Click the ⎡**Custom Animation**⎤ **Animations tab**, and in the **Animations group**, click the **Custom Animation button**.

3. In the Custom Animation task pane, click **Add Effect**, point to **Entrance**, click **More Effects**, click **Dissolve In**, then click **OK**.

4. Click the **Chart 3 animation list arrow** in the **Custom Animation** list, then click **Effect Options**. On the **Effect tab**, click the **Sound list arrow**, then select a sound.

5. Click the **Chart Animation tab**, click the **Group chart list arrow**, click **By Category**, then click **OK**.

6. Click the **Slide Show View button** on the status bar to run the slide show.

7. Close the presentation without saving the changes.

Animate SmartArt

▶ As you learned in Lesson 3, **SmartArt** objects are different types of diagrams, such as hierarchies, organizational charts, and cycles.

▶ You can animate sections of SmartArt, just as you can animate sections of a chart.

HOW To add SmartArt to your presentation, **1.** click the **Insert tab** and in the **Illustrations group**, **2.** click the **SmartArt button**. **3.** In the Choose a SmartArt Graphic dialog box, select a diagram type in the left pane, **4.** click a SmartArt thumbnail, apply a theme if necessary, then **5.** click **OK**. **6.** Enter the information for your SmartArt diagram, as shown in Figure 4.15.

SmartArt

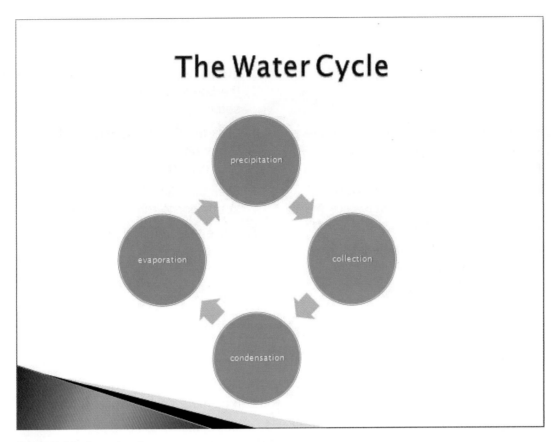

Figure 4.15: SmartArt object

To animate SmartArt, **1.** select the SmartArt object or SmartArt section you want to animate, **2.** click the **Animations tab**, and in the **Animations group**, **3.** click the **Custom Animation button**. **4.** In the Custom Animation task pane, click **Add Effects**, then **5.** select the effect to apply. **6.** Click the *animation* **list arrow**, then **7.** click **Effect Options**. **8.** In the Effect Options dialog box, click the **SmartArt Animation tab**, then **9.** select an element from the Group graphic list, as shown in Figure 4.16.

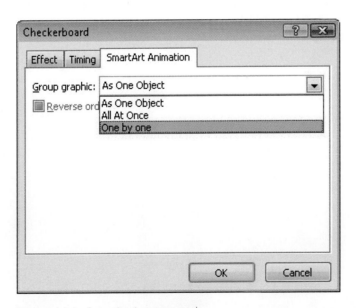

Figure 4.16: SmartArt Animation tab

To add a sound effect to SmartArt animations, follow the same procedures provided for adding sound to charts.

T R Y *i t* **O U T** *p4-5*

1. Open the data file **p4-5**.

2. Display **Slide 4**.

3. Click the SmartArt object or SmartArt section to select it.

4. If the Custom Animation task pane is not displayed, click the **Animations tab**, and in the **Animations group**, click the **Custom Animation button** to display the Custom Animation task pane, if necessary.

5. Click **Add Effect**, point to **Entrance,** then click **Fly In**.

6. Click the **1 animation list arrow** in the Custom Animation task pane, then click **Effect Options**.

7. Use the **Sound list arrow** on the **Effect tab** to add a sound to accompany the animation.

8. Click the **SmartArt Animation tab**, click the **Group graphic list arrow**, click **By branch one by one**, then click **OK**.

9. Click the **Slide Show View button**, then click the mouse to run the animation for the entire organization chart.

10. Close the presentation without saving the changes.

Work with Photo Albums

▶ A **photo album** is a collection of pictures that you can create from a file or from a device such as a scanner or digital camera. You can customize the photo album with special layout options, including oval frames and captions.

▶ A photo album is an independent presentation that you can add to an existing presentation, publish to the Web, e-mail, or print.

▶ The pages of your photo album are slides. You can customize the layout of the photo album pages to include frame options, captions, and/or text boxes. The layout you create applies to the entire photo album. You cannot customize individual pages. Figure 4.17 illustrates a photo album slide.

▶ You can rotate a picture and adjust the contrast and/or brightness of a picture.

▶ You can modify a photo album by changing the layout, slide numbers, slide order, and adding and deleting pictures, captions, and text boxes.

POWERPOINT

Figure 4.17: Photo album slide

HOW To create a photo album, **1.** click the **Insert tab**, and in the **Illustrations group**, **2.** click the **Photo Album button list arrow**, then **3.** click **New Photo Album**. In the Photo Album dialog box shown in Figure 4.18, **4.** click the **File/Disk button** to indicate the source of your photos. **5.** Navigate to the folder, disk, or device drive, and **6.** click the desired picture. To select additional pictures, **7.** press and hold **[Ctrl]** while you click them, **8.** click **Insert**, **9.** select options (see procedures below for applying various options in the Photo Album dialog box), then **10.** click **Create**, which will open a new presentation with a custom title slide, as shown in Figure 4.19. Change the title and subtitle on the slide, as desired.

To apply a design theme to your photo album, **1.** click the **Browse button**, then **2.** select a theme design (see Figure 4.18).

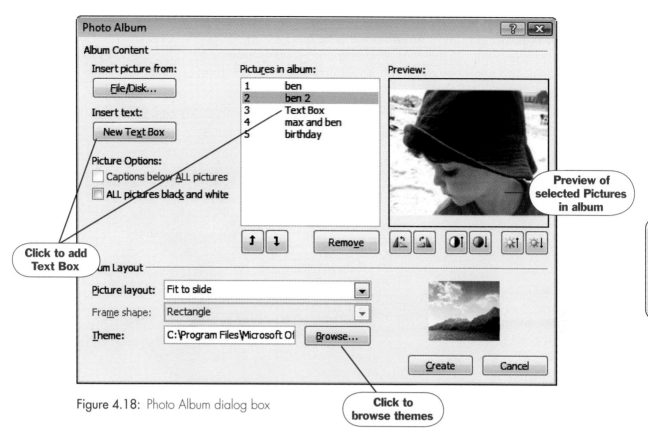

Figure 4.18: Photo Album dialog box

Figure 4.19: Title slide of photo album with theme applied

HOW To include a text box placeholder as part of a photo album layout, **1.** click the **New Text Box button** in the **Photo Album dialog box**, and then **2.** click **Create**. The text box and picture filenames that you are including in your photo album appear in the Pictures in album list box (see Figure 4.18). After you create the photo album, you can click the text box on a slide and insert your own text.

To rotate a picture, click the **Rotate buttons**, as shown in Figure 4.20. To adjust the contrast and/or brightness of a picture, click the appropriate buttons as many times as necessary.

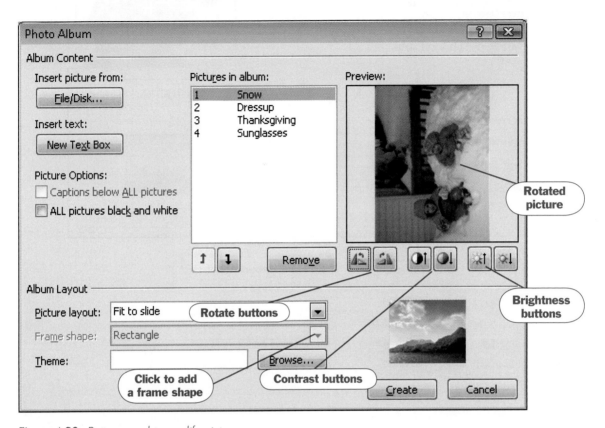

Figure 4.20: Buttons used to modify pictures

To specify the number of pictures on a slide, **1.** click the **Picture layout list arrow** in the Edit Photo Album dialog box, as shown in Figure 4.21, and **2.** select the number of pictures you want. The number on the left side of the Pictures in album list box indicates the slide on which the pictures will appear. The default is for one picture to fill an entire slide.

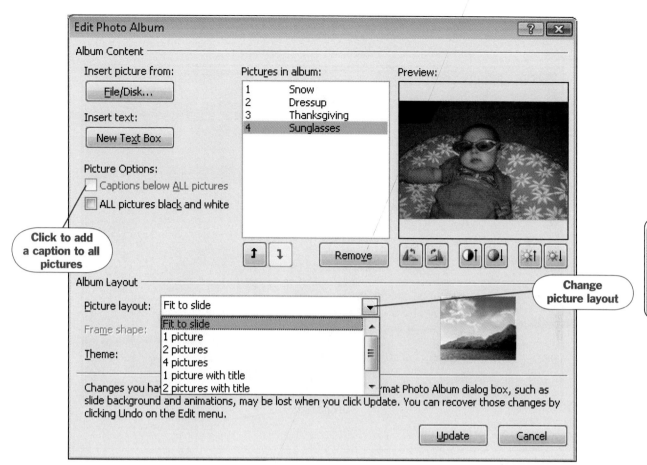

Figure 4.21: Picture layout list

To add a caption to each picture in the album, **1.** click the **Captions below ALL pictures check box** (see Figure 4.21). Your pictures will appear with a caption placeholder that contains the filename of the picture, as shown in Figure 4.22. **2.** Click the placeholder, and **3.** enter your caption to replace the filename.

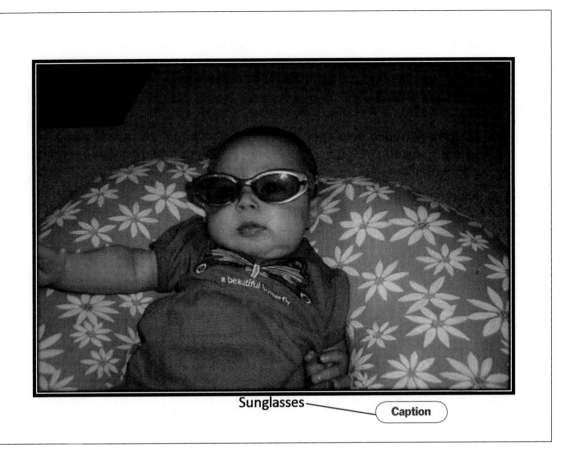

Figure 4.22: Album photo with a picture caption

To reorder a picture, **1.** click the picture, then **2.** use the arrow buttons to move it up or down in the list.

To display pictures in black and white, click in the **ALL pictures black and white** check box.

To change the frame that surrounds each picture, **1.** click the **Frame shape list arrow**, and **2.** select an option (see Figure 4.20).

To modify a photo album, **1.** click the **Insert tab**, and in the **Illustrations group**, **2.** click the **Photo Album button list arrow**, and **3.** click **Edit Photo Album**. **4.** Make changes in the Edit Photo Album dialog box, then **5.** click **Update**.

To insert a photo album into another presentation, **1.** click the **Home tab**, and in the **Slides group**, **2.** click the **New Slide list arrow**, then **3.** click **Reuse Slides** from the menu. **4.** In the Reuse Slides task pane, click **Open a PowerPoint File**, **5.** double-click the photo album file, then in the Reuse Slides task pane, **6.** click a thumbnail.

1. Open a new blank presentation.

2. Click the **Insert tab**, and in the **Illustrations group**, click the **Photo Album button list arrow**.

3. Click **New Photo Album**.

4. In the Photo Album dialog box, click the **File/Disk button**.

5. Navigate to your data files, press and hold **[Ctrl]** as you select the following files: **p4-6-puddle.bmp**, **p4-6-pumpkin.bmp**, and **p4-6-stroller.bmp**, then click the **Insert button**.

6. Click the **New Text Box button**.

7. Click the **Picture layout list arrow**, then click **2 pictures**.

8. Click the **Frame shape list arrow**, then click **Soft Edge Rectangle**.

9. Use the arrow buttons to reorder the items in the **Pictures in album** list box as follows: **p4-6-stroller**, **p4-6-pumpkin**, **Text Box**, and **p4-6-puddle**.

10. Click the **Captions below ALL pictures check box** to select it.

11. Click the **Browse button**, click a template design theme to apply to the photo album, then click **Select**.

12. Click **Create** in the Photo Album dialog box, then scroll through the slides to view the photo album.

13. Add your name to the first slide.

14. Print one copy of the photo album as handouts.

15. Close the presentation without saving the changes.

REHEARSAL

GOAL
To create a presentation that contains animated charts and SmartArt, and a photo album, as shown in Figure 4.23

TASK 2

WHAT YOU NEED TO KNOW

▶ The special layout options you choose to add to your photo album such as frames and captions should enhance your overall presentation message.

▶ In this Rehearsal activity, you will finalize a presentation about group travel packages to Spain. You will add a chart, SmartArt, and animation to selected slides. You will also create a photo album with pictures from Spain.

▼ DIRECTIONS

1. Open the data file **p4r2-spain**.

2. Apply a new template design of your choice.

3. Click **Slide 2**, then apply the **Fly In** Entrance animation to the chart.

4. Click **Slide 3**.
   a. Insert the **Basic Timeline** SmartArt graphic from the **Process** category, then add the following information to complete the diagram:
      Research Competition
      Advertise
      Hold Contests
   b. Apply the **Spin Emphasis** animation to the SmartArt object.

5. Insert a sound clip on **Slide 1** that plays automatically when the slide show begins.

6. Insert the photo album **p4r2-album** from your data files.

7. Apply a picture effect to each photo in the album.

8. Add your name to the title slide of the album.

9. Save the presentation as **4r2-travel**.

10. Run the slide show and navigate through to display the animations.

11. Close the presentation.

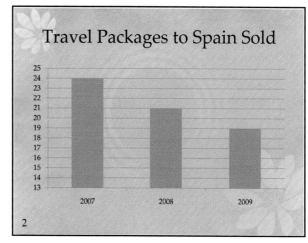
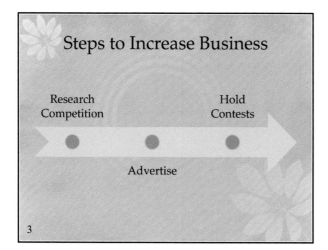

Figure 4.23a: Slides with a photo album, animated chart, and SmartArt

Figure 4.23b: Slides with a photo album, animated chart, and SmartArt

Create a Photo Album
1. Click the **Insert tab**, and in the **Illustrations group**, click the **Photo Album button list arrow**, then click **New Photo Album**.
2. Click the **File/Disk button**.
3. Select photograph(s) to insert, then click **Insert**.
4. Select appropriate rotate, contrast, and brightness options.
5. Click the **Picture layout list arrow**, and select a layout.
6. Click the **Frame shape list arrow**, and select a frame.
7. Click the **Browse button** to select a design template. Double-click a template.
8. Click **Create**.

Insert a Photo Album into a Presentation
1. On the **Home tab**, in the **Slides group**, click the **New Slide button list arrow**, then click **Reuse Slides**.
2. Select a photo album, then click **Open**.
3. Right-click a slide, then click **Insert Slide** or **Insert All Slides**.

Animate Charts and SmartArt
1. Click the **Animations tab**, and in the Animations group, click the **Custom Animation button**.

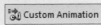

2. Click the **Add Effect button**, then select an effect.
3. Click the **Animation list arrow**, then click **Effect Options**.
4. Make any selection in the Effect Options dialog box, then click **OK**.

Insert SmartArt
1. Click the **Insert tab**, and in the Illustrations group, click the **SmartArt button**.
2. Select a SmartArt category and thumbnail, then click **OK**.
3. Enter the text for the SmartArt object.

PERFORMANCE

TASK 2

Palmetto Realtors is having an open house at 1984 Red Robin Lane in Ithaca, New York. You have been asked to prepare a presentation for the local salesperson to use to showcase the property during the open house. You will design the presentation, add and animate charts and SmartArt that show the sales trends for the area for similar properties, and add a photo album that shows different rooms of the house. Figure 4.24 is provided as a guide.

Follow these guidelines:

1. Create a new photo album with the **Median** theme.
   a. Insert the following pictures from your data files: **p4p2-living room.bmp**, **p4p2-dining room.bmp**, and **p4p2-bedroom.bmp**, then create the photo album.
   b. Select 1 picture per slide with captions below all pictures.
   c. Insert appropriate captions.
   d. Save the album as **4p2-house album**, then close it.

2. Start a new blank presentation:
   a. Apply the **Median** design theme.
   b. Enter `Palmetto Realtors Presents` as the title, and center the text.
   c. Enter `1984 Red Robin Lane, Ithaca, NY` as the subtitle.

3. Insert a new slide, **Slide 2**:
   a. Insert a bar chart, as shown in Figure 4.24, using the following data:
      ```
      Year          2006    2007    2008
      Houses Sold  100     134     117
      ```
   b. Add an animation to the chart.

4. Insert a new slide, **Slide 3**:
   a. Add a **Vertical Chevron List** SmartArt graphic, and enter the text shown in Figure 4.24.
   b. Choose the **Box Entrance** animation effect, then make the objects on the list enter one by one.

5. Display Slide Sorter view.
   a. Place the insertion point in the slide sorter after **Slide 3**.
   b. Insert the album you created and named **4p2-house album**.

6. Run the slide show, and navigate through it to display the animations.

7. Save the presentation as **4p2-open house**, then close it.

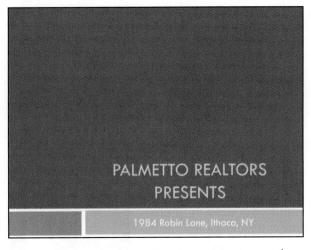

1

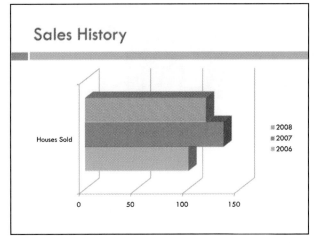

2

3

4

5

6

Figure 4.24: Slides with a photo album, animated charts, and SmartArt

Act I

Expedition

Travel Gear

You are the human resources manager at Newmark Productions, corporate headquarters. In the next few weeks, you plan to visit several colleges to recruit future employees. You have decided to create a presentation to persuade college seniors to work at Newmark. Ms. Wallace has provided you with basic information about Newmark and its operations. You will use this summary, along with information you find on the Internet, to create a presentation consisting of approximately nine slides.

Follow these guidelines:

1. Read through the summary provided below to get a basic understanding of the content the presentation will cover.

2. Use any design template. The first three slides (shown in Figure 4.25) are provided as a sample.

3. Include an appropriate presentation title, the company name, and the company logo (found in the **Logos** folder in the data files).

4. Use clip art and media clips, color schemes, and animation to enhance the presentation.

5. Include a slide entitled "Our Training Program."
   a. Add your own information, or go to www.bls.gov/oco/cg/cgs038.htm to access information from the Career Guide on the U.S. Department of Labor Statistics Web site. Read about careers in motion picture production and distribution and include any relevant information on the slide.
   b. Use statistics you find from the Web site or make up your own to create a pie chart and animate the chart.

6. Save the presentation as **4e1-recruit**.

7. Run the slide show and navigate through it to display the animations.

8. Print one copy as handouts with six slides per page.

Newmark Productions

Corporate Recruiting

1

About Newmark Productions

* Motion picture and television production company
* We deal with a number of Hollywood's top talent, including writers, directors, and filmmakers
* Released roughly 50 feature films and numerous Emmy-winning television programs.
* Offices in New York and Los Angeles
* We have more than 500 employees

2

Our Corporate Staff

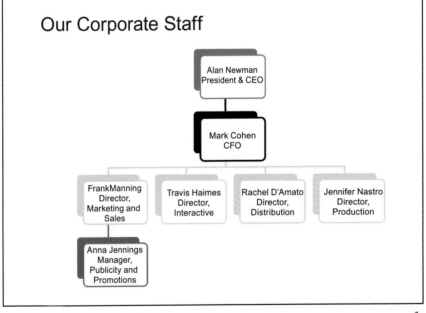

3

Figure 4.25: Slides 1–3

A Career at Newmark Productions

Newmark is a motion picture and television production company. We release approximately 50 feature films per year and have produced numerous Emmy-winning television programs. Our offices are located in New York and Los Angeles, and we currently employ more than 500 people.

Our corporate staff is as follows: Alan Newman is the President and CEO. Mark Cohen, CFO, reports to Alan. Reporting to Mark are Frank Manning, Director of Marketing and Sales; Travis Haimes, Director of Interactive; Rachel D'Amato, Director of Distribution; and Jennifer Nastro, Director of Production. Anna Jennings is Manager of Publicity and Promotions, and she reports to Frank.

Our growth over the past few years is a result of our philosophy. We produce movies and television programs to please our audiences. We foster a fun and challenging work environment. As a result, our films continue to break box-office records, and our television programs earn critical acclaim.

Newmark offers a training program to a select group of individuals. This is a very rare opportunity—especially in the entertainment field. The program is well known throughout the industry and very well respected. The training is a 12-month program in which there is formal classroom training once a week. Trainees are rotated to gain experience, giving them broad exposure before we place them permanently.

Just to give you an idea of how competitive the training program is, here are some statistics on last year's recruits. We received 2,578 résumés. Of those, we granted interviews to 100 candidates (3.5%). Of those interviewed, we offered jobs to 10 individuals (0.5%). All 10 candidates accepted our offer.

We are looking for individuals who are energetic, articulate, creative, motivated, outgoing, and able to manage multiple projects.

Working at Newmark is truly a unique opportunity. We are a top entertainment company, we offer the best possible training, and we provide outstanding medical, dental, and 401(K) benefits.

To apply for the training program, fax your resume to 212-555-8100. We look forward to meeting you!

Act II

Background: A **business plan** is a summary of the goals and objectives of a business and outlines how the business will operate and how resources will be organized. Visit the following Web sites to view sample business plans and get an idea of how business plans are structured: www.sba.gov and www.bplans.com.

Expedition Travel Gear has decided to create a travel magazine for rugged sports enthusiasts. The magazine, to be named *Expeditions Unlimited,* will profile fun and exotic places to travel to engage in outdoor sporting activities. To attract potential investors, Expedition Travel Gear must develop a business plan for the new magazine. Pamela Walters, President and CEO of Expedition Travel Gear, has asked you to create a business plan for *Expeditions Unlimited* with information that she has provided. Your presentation should have approximately 11 slides.

Follow these guidelines:

1. Read through the summary provided below to get a basic understanding of the content the presentation will cover.

2. Use the **Business Plan** template (download it from Microsoft Office Online, or use the **p4e2-business plan template** in the data files) to create the presentation. Replace the sample template text with the information Ms. Walters has provided.

3. Include an appropriate presentation title and the company logo (found in the **Logos** folder in the data files).

4. Include a slide titled "Sales Projections." Use the following information to create an animated chart:

	YEAR 1	YEAR 2	YEAR 3
Subscriptions	$1,525,500	$1,876,000	$2,455,500
Newsstand	$55,935	$60,290	$65,325
Ad Revenue	$265,770	$275,000	$300,000
TOTAL	**$1,847,205**	**$2,211,290**	**$2,820,825**

5. Include a slide titled "Our Team." Add an organization chart, and animate it.

6. Use any clip art and media clips to enhance the presentation.

7. Save the presentation. Name it **4e2-expeditions plan**.

8. Run the slide show, and navigate through to display the animations.

9. Print one copy as handouts with six slides per page.

Expeditions Unlimited

Our Mission: *Expeditions Unlimited* is a travel magazine for the rugged sports enthusiast. This magazine will profile enjoyable and exotic places to travel to engage in outdoor sporting activities. Our mission is to promote the concept of sports vacations for all types of travelers.

Our Team: Pamela Walters, President and CEO of Expedition Travel Gear, will function as President and CEO of the magazine. She has successfully led Expedition Travel Gear for 10 years, during which time the company has grown steadily. Reporting to her as the Editor-in-Chief of *Expeditions Unlimited* will be Daryl Shinen. He is the former Editor-in-Chief of *Sports Extra magazine*. Both Melissa Tusk (Managing Editor) and Jane Williams (Projects Editor) will report to Daryl.

Our Market: Our target market is primarily Expedition Travel Gear customers and outdoor sports enthusiasts. Sports interests define market segments, so our media strategy and execution will vary by segment.

Now is the time to launch this magazine, as opportunities in the market have presented themselves—people are increasingly health conscious, people are economically able to take trips, and there are hundreds of fun and exotic destinations, both warm and cold, to visit for active vacations.

Our business concept: We want to create a spin-off of the already existing and successful Expedition Travel Gear. We are looking to serve a clearly defined niche market. We already have distribution channels and we already reach those who buy from Expedition Travel Gear and those who receive the Expedition Travel Gear catalog.

Competition: *Expeditions Unlimited* has a competitive advantage, as Expedition Travel Gear already has a successful franchise and existing distribution channels. Furthermore, though there are sports magazines and travel magazines, there are no magazines that are a combination of the two.

Once established, our goals and objectives are to reach and inform our target market, cross-promote with Expedition Travel Gear, and consistently increase the distribution and sales of *Expeditions Unlimited.*

Because we already print catalogs for Expedition Travel Gear, our printing requirements are already fulfilled. We plan to hire 30 new employees to help run *Expeditions Unlimited*. These employees will work out of Expedition Travel Gear's offices. We will, however, need to order additional technology resources as we see fit.

Finally, the key issues that are facing us as we start *Expeditions Unlimited* are twofold. We have near-term issues of initial funding and the hiring of new employees. Long term, we might face changes in the economy that could affect people's ability to go on vacation, the ability of people to get information on active vacations from the Internet, and the ever-present threat of new competition.

Collaborating On and Delivering Presentations

In this lesson, you will learn to use PowerPoint features to review a presentation, prepare a presentation with printed materials, and finalize a presentation for delivery.

Upon completion of this lesson, you will have mastered the following skill sets

✳ Add, edit, delete, cycle through, and print comments
✳ Use handouts
✳ Use notes pages
✳ Work with handout master and notes master
✳ Work with the pen and annotations
✳ Rehearse timings
✳ Use slide show set-up options
✳ Save a presentation to CD
✳ Prepare a presentation as read-only

Terms
Annotations
Comments
Handout master
Handouts
Kiosk
Loop
Notes master
Notes pages
Read-only
Speaker notes

TRYOUT

GOAL
To review and edit a presentation,
as shown in Figure 5.1

✦ Add, edit, delete, cycle through,
and print comments

TASK 1

POWERPOINT

Figure 5.1: Slide 1 of presentation showing comment

WHAT YOU NEED TO KNOW

Add, Edit, Delete, Cycle through, and Print Comments

▶ **Comments** are notes that you or a reviewer can add to a presentation. You can read these comments on the screen, hide them when you print the presentation, print them with the presentation, or incorporate them into the presentation. Comments do not show in Slide Show or Slide Sorter view. To add a comment, you must be in Normal view.

▶ The comment feature is particularly useful when you are collaborating with others on the development of a presentation.

HOW 1. Click on the slide where you want to attach the comment (to attach a comment to an object or placeholder, click to select it). If you do not select an object or placeholder, PowerPoint will insert the comment at the top-left corner of the slide. 2. Click the **Review tab**, then 3. click the **New Comment button** (see Figure 5.2). 4. Enter your comment as shown in Figure 5.2, then 5. click anywhere outside the comment box to resume working on the slide. The comment box changes to a small icon showing the initials of the author and the comment number as shown in Figure 5.3. To view the full comment, place your mouse pointer over the icon. PowerPoint uses information in the User Information Profile to identify the author of the comments.

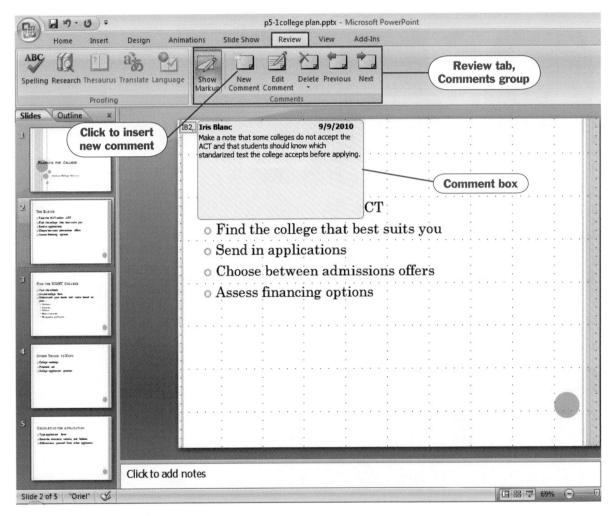

Figure 5.2: Insert a comment

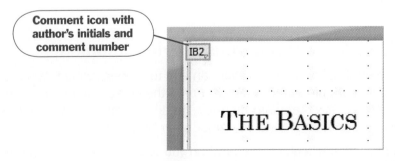

Figure 5.3: Comment icon

Edit, Delete, and Cycle through Comments

▶ Once a comment has been entered on a slide, a reviewer can edit, delete, or cycle through the comments.

HOW To edit a comment, insert a new comment, or delete a comment, **1.** right-click the **comment icon**, and **2.** select an option from the shortcut menu, as shown in Figure 5.4. You can also click the appropriate button on the **Review tab**, and in the **Comments group**, as shown in Figure 5.4.

To move the comment, click and drag the icon or comment box.

To cycle through comments, click the **Next Comment button** or **Previous Comment button** in the **Comments group** (see Figure 5.4).

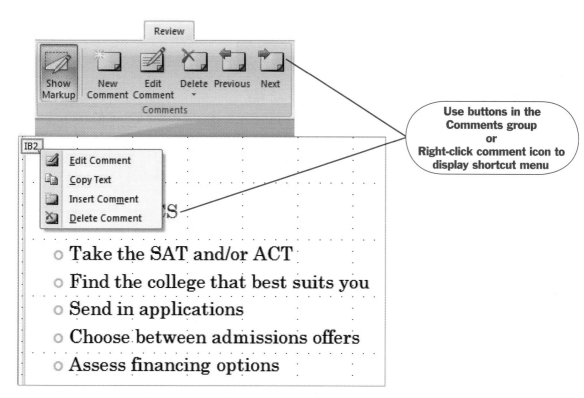

Figure 5.4: Comments shortcut menu and Review tab, Comments group

Print Comments

▶ Comments print with slides unless you choose to hide them.

▶ If you choose to print a comment, the slide prints showing the comment box and a separate page is also printed showing the actual comment, the author's name and the date the comment was made as shown in Figure 5.5.

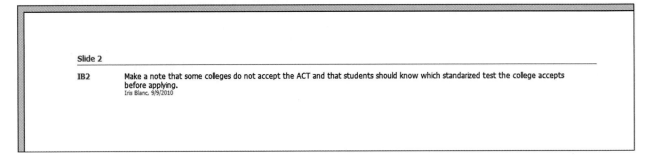

Slide 2

IB2   Make a note that some colleges do not accept the ACT and that students should know which standarized test the college accepts before applying.
Iris Blanc, 9/9/2010

Figure 5.5: Printed comment

HOW To hide a comment, **1.** click the **Review tab**, and in the **Comments group**, **2.** click the **Show Markup button** to activate it. **3.** Click the **Show Markup button** again to deactivate it.

Show Markup

To print comment pages, **1.** click the **Office Button**, then **2.** click **Print**. In the Print dialog box, shown in Figure 5.6, select the **Print comments and ink markup check box**. The slide will print along with the printed comments page (see Figure 5.5).

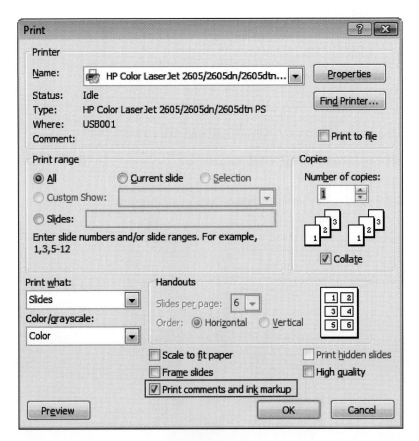

Figure 5.6: Print dialog box with Print comments and ink markup check box selected

1. Open the data file **p5-1**.

2. Display **Slide 2** (The Basics).

3. Click the **Review tab**, and in the **Comments group**, click the **New Comment button**.

4. Enter the following in the comment box: `Make note that some colleges do not accept the ACT and that students should know which standardized test the college accepts before applying.`

5. Click on the slide to close the comment box.

6. Click and drag the comment box, and place it next to the _Take the SAT and/or ACT_ bullet.

7. Place the mouse pointer over the comment to view it.

8. Display **Slide 3** (Find the RIGHT College).

9. Repeat Step 3 to insert another comment.

10. Enter the following in the comment box: `Insert a table showing the date, time, and location of upcoming college fairs. Also include a picture of a past college fair.`

11. Click on the slide to close the comment box.

12. Display **Slide 2**.

13. Right-click the comment, and click **Edit Comment**.

14. Add the following to the comment: `Include a chart or table that compares and contrasts the ACT and SAT.`

15. Click on the slide to close the comment box.

16. Display **Slide 1**.
    a. Click the **Review tab**, if necessary, and in the **Comments group**, click the **Next Comment button** to see the first comment on the slide.
    b. Click the **Next Comment button** again until you cycle through and view each comment.

17. Display **Slide 2**. Right-click on the comment, and click **Delete Comment**.

18. Close the file without saving the changes.

REHEARSAL

TASK 1

GOAL
To review a presentation and add comments

WHAT YOU NEED TO KNOW

▶ The ability to have multiple people, located anywhere in the world, make changes to a presentation independently using comments, results in a true project collaboration.

▶ In this Rehearsal activity, you will add comments and edit comments in an existing presentation.

DIRECTIONS

1. Open the data file **p5r1-creative sales with comments**.
2. Save the presentation as **5r1-cs comments updated**.
3. Add the following comments:
   a. **Slide 1:** `Include the name and title of the presenter and the date of the presentation.` Move the comment so that it appears next to the subtitle.
   b. **Slide 4:** `Insert a picture of some examples of the sales materials.` Move the comment below the last line of text.
   c. **Slide 5:** `Insert a picture of a sales brochure.` Move the comment below the last line of text.
   d. **Slide 7:** `Insert a new slide as the last slide with Perfect Planning Group's contact information.`
4. Display **Slide 1**.
   a. Edit the comment to read: `Include "John Stone, VP Marketing" as part of the subtitle, as well as the date of the presentation.`
5. Display **Slide 4**. Read the comment from reviewer, Iris Blanc. Delete it. Then, insert a comment that says, `Per John, insert a picture of a brochure and a business card.`
6. Display **Slide 5**. Delete the comment on this slide.
7. Print the presentation with comments.
8. Close the presentation, and save the changes.

You are the assistant to Lara Morales, the director of marketing and sales at EarthCare Services. Ms. Morales and Iris Blanc, a consultant who was hired to help develop the EarthCare Services marketing presentation, have reviewed the presentation and made numerous comments. Ms. Morales would like you to review the comments and make the changes to the presentation as instructed in each comment. Ms. Morales has also asked that you insert any additional comments you have into the presentation.

Follow these guidelines:

1. Open the data file **p5p1-earthcare with comments**.

2. After you have read and followed the instructions indicated in each comment, delete the comment.

3. Display **Slide 2**. The information you need to respond to the comment is noted in Steps 3a and 3b.
   a. Insert a map graphic of the U.S., as indicated in the comment, which can be found on the data files as **usmap.gif**.
   b. EarthCare Services has locations in each of the following states: New York, California, Texas, South Florida, Georgia, Tennessee, Utah, Washington, Pennsylvania, North Carolina, Illinois, and Colorado.

4. To apply the gradient background fill to **Slide 14**, as shown in Figure 5.7, right-click the slide, and select **Format Background** from the menu. In the Format Background dialog box that appears, do the following:
   a. Apply the **Moss** preset color.
   b. Apply the **Linear** gradient type.
   c. Set the Angle to **180°**.
   d. Set the Stop position to **32%**.
   e. Select a bright **green** color from the **Color drop-down list**.

5. Insert three of your own comments for Lara Morales to review. The comments should make suggestions about how the bullets might be revised for better clarity or how a slide or slides might be enhanced with a graphic or charts or SmartArt.

6. Print one copy of the presentation as handouts with six slides per page. Print the comments.

7. Save the presentation as **5p1-earthcare with comments updated**, then close it.

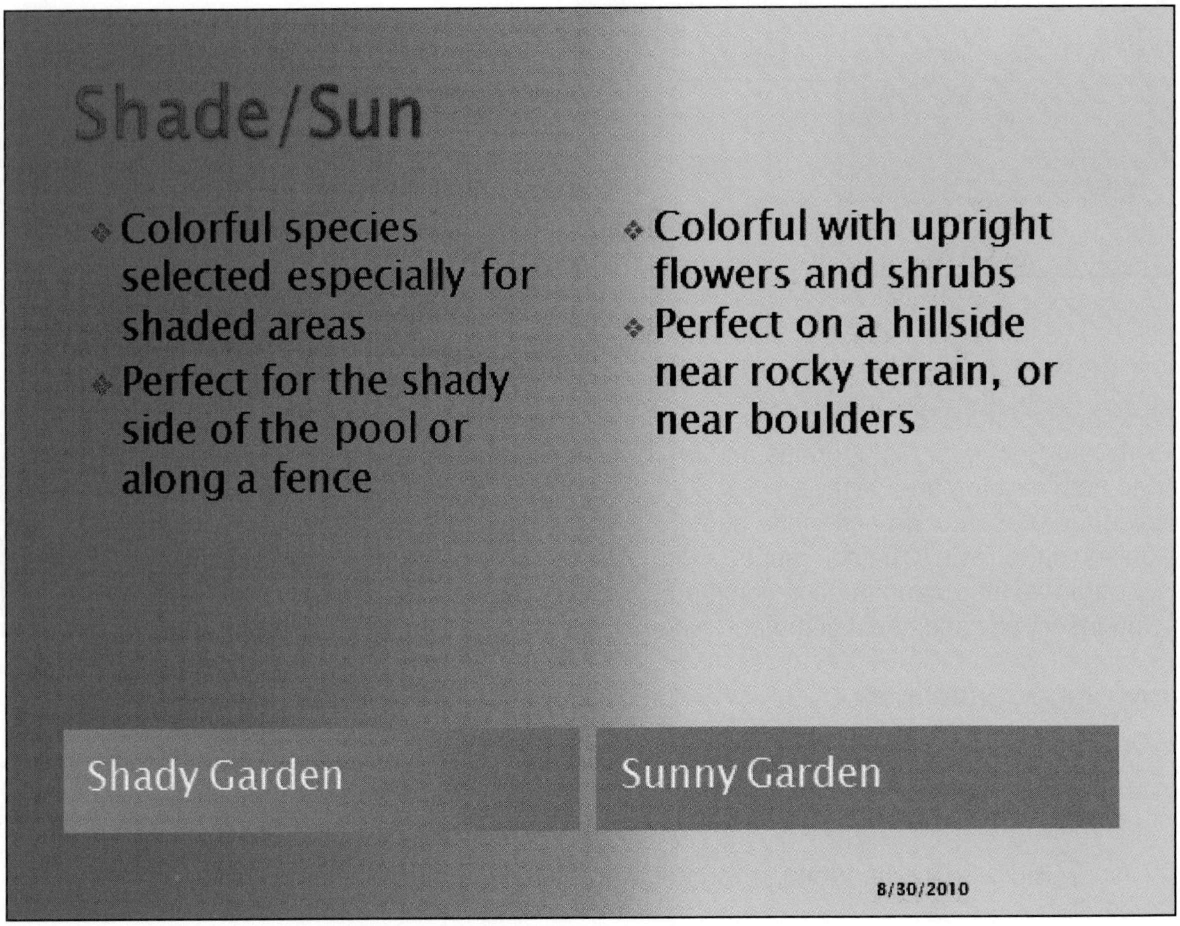

Figure 5.7: Slide with gradient background fill effect

TRYOUT

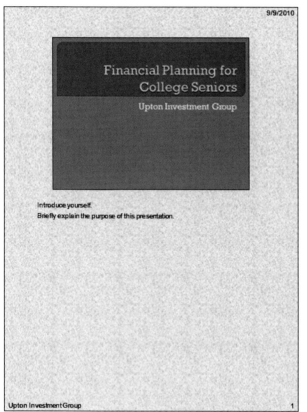

GOAL

To prepare a presentation with notes pages, as shown in Figure 5.8, then print the presentation as handouts

✴ Use handouts
✴ Use notes pages
✴ Work with handout master and notes master

TASK 2

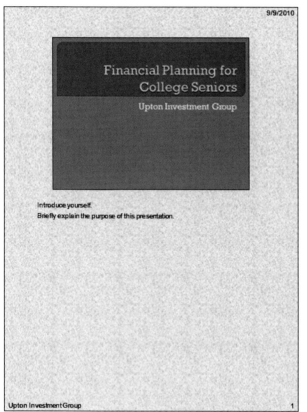
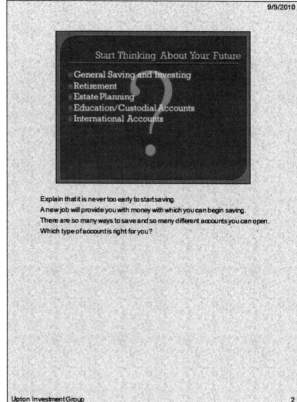

Figure 5.8: Two slides of a seven-slide presentation with notes pages

WHAT YOU NEED TO KNOW

Use Handouts

▶ PowerPoint allows you to print your presentation as **handouts** with 1, 2, 3, 4, 6, or 9 slides on a page. This printing option allows you to distribute the printouts to the audience so that they can follow along with your on-screen presentation and have material to which they can refer at a later time.

▶ In previous lessons, you printed your presentation as handouts with six slides per page. You can use the same procedure to print handouts with other options. Figure 5.9 shows slides printed as handouts with six slides per page.

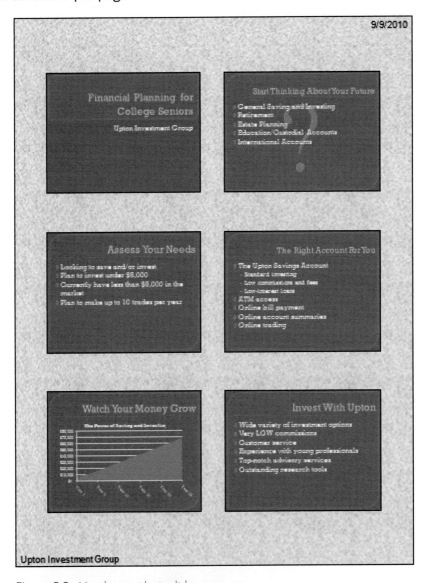

Figure 5.9: Handouts with six slides per page

HOW 1. Click the **Office Button**, then 2. click **Print**. In the Print dialog box that appears, as shown in Figure 5.10, 3. click the **Print what list arrow**, then 4. select **Handouts**. 5. Click the **Slides per page list arrow**, 6. select the number of slides per page, then 7. click **OK**.

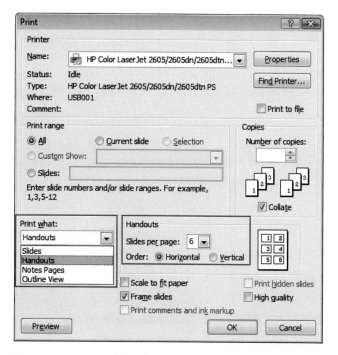

Figure 5.10: Print dialog box

Use Notes Pages

▶ **Notes pages**, often referred to as **speaker notes**, are printouts that contain the slide image in the top half of the page and notes that you have created (in the Notes pane), in the lower half of the page. They are often used to assist the speaker in delivering a presentation. You can also distribute speaker notes to the audience, providing them with detailed information about each slide.

▶ The notes can be entered in the Notes pane in Normal view, as shown in Figure 5.11, or directly in the notes page placeholder of the notes page (see Figure 5.12).

▶ Use the same procedures to print the notes pages that you use to print slides and handouts.

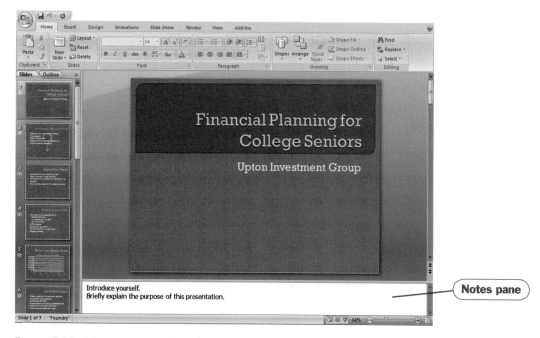

Figure 5.11: Notes pane in Normal view

HOW To enter text in the notes pane, **1.** click in the Notes pane and **2.** enter notes. To display more or less of the notes pane, drag the top border of the pane up or down.

To enter text directly in the notes placeholder, **1.** click the **View tab**, and in the **Presentation Views group**, **2.** click the **Notes Page button**. A notes page, which contains a slide and a text placeholder, appears, as shown in Figure 5.12. **3.** Click in the text placeholder to enter and/or format your notes.

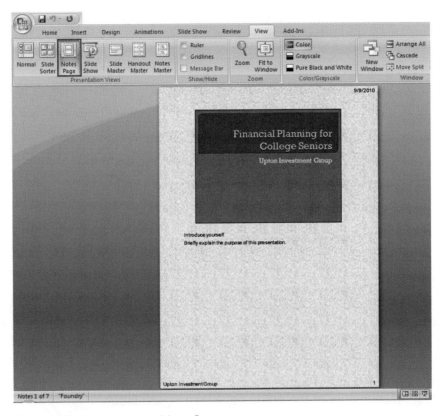

Figure 5.12: Notes page in Notes Page view

TRY *it* OUT *p5-2*

1. Open the data file **p5-2**.

2. Click in the Notes pane on **Slide 1**.

3. Enter the following: `Introduce yourself. Briefly explain the purpose of the presentation.`

4. Drag the top border of the Notes pane to expand it.

5. Display **Slide 2**.

6. Click the **View tab**, and in the **Presentation Views group**, click the **Notes Page button**.

7. Click in the text placeholder. Click the **Zoom In button** on the status bar, if necessary to enlarge the notes page.

8. Enter the following:

`Give examples of other funds that have not been performing as well in our unstable economy:`

`The Parker Fund`

`Westinghouse Fund`

`Emphasize that despite downturns in the market, Devon has been profitable.`

9. In the **Presentation Views group**, click the **Normal button** to return to Normal view.

Continued on next page

10. Click the **Office Button**, then click **Print**.

11. In the Print dialog box, click the **Print what list arrow**, and select **Handouts**.

12. Click the **Slides per page list arrow**, and click **9**.

13. Click **Cancel**.

14. Close the file without saving the changes.

Work with Handout Master and Notes Master

▶ In Lesson 3, you learned to use the slide master to customize all slides of a presentation by adding text, objects, and/or color themes to a master slide. Similarly, the **handout master** and the **notes master** allow you to customize your handouts and notes pages.

Handout Master

▶ Using the tools on the Handout Master tab, shown in Figure 5.13, you can choose to include a header, date, footer, and/or page number. You can also change the handout orientation, select the number of slides per page, edit the theme, and/or include a background style.

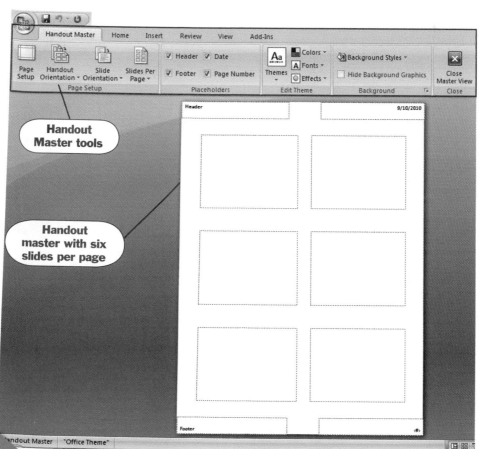

Handout Master tools

Handout master with six slides per page

Figure 5.13: Handout Master tab

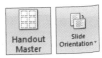

HOW **1.** Click the **View tab**, and in the **Presentation Views group**, **2.** click the **Handout Master button**. **3.** On the **Handout Master tab**, and in the **Placeholders group**, **4.** click to deselect all of the four placeholders from the handout. In the **Page Setup group**, **5.** click the **Slide Orientation button** or **Handout Orientation button**, and choose **Portrait** or **Landscape**. **6.** Click the **Slides Per Page button**, and choose an option. Optional: Use the buttons in the **Edit Theme or Background groups** to choose formatting options, then **7.** click the **Close Master View button**.

Notes Master

▶ The notes master is used to make global changes to all notes pages in the presentation. Using the tools on the Notes Master tab, shown in Figure 5.14, you can choose to include a header, slide image, footer, date, body, and/or page number on your notes pages. You can also change the notes page and slide orientation, edit the theme, and/or include a background style. To actually insert the header and/or footer on your handout, you must access the Header and Footer dialog box (see Figure 5.15).

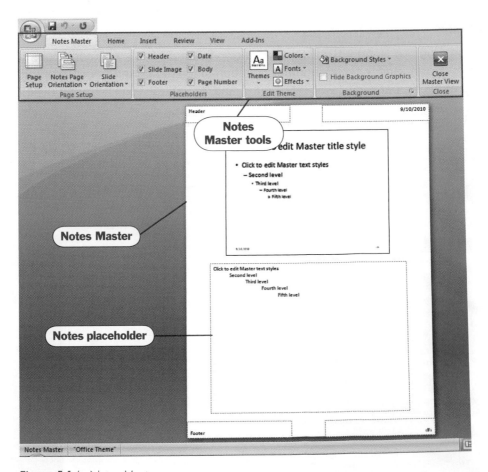

Figure 5.14: Notes Master

HOW **1.** Click the **View tab**, and in the **Presentation Views group**, **2.** click the **Notes Master button**. **3.** On the **Notes Master tab**, and in the **Placeholders group**, **4.** click to deselect those items that you do not want to include on the page (which will remove the placeholder). In the **Page Setup group**, **5.** click the **Slide Orientation button** or **Notes Page Orientation button**, and choose **Portrait** or **Landscape**. Optional: Use the buttons in the **Edit Theme group** to choose formatting options, click the **Background Styles button**, and choose an option. **6.** Enter text in the notes placeholder. To enter a header and/or footer, follow the steps below. **7.** Click the **Close Master View button**.

Add Headers and Footers

▶ You can add headers and footers to the handout master and the notes master by using the Header and Footer dialog box. You should do so while you are in notes master or handout master view so that you can apply formatting to the text in the view.

HOW **1.** In Notes Master or Handout Master view, click the **Insert tab**, and in the **Text group**, **2.** click the **Header & Footer button**. **3.** In the Header and Footer dialog box that appears, as shown in Figure 5.15, **4.** use the **Notes and Handouts tab** to create your header and footer. **5.** Select the **Header** check box, and enter the header in the text box. **6.** Click **Apply to All**. **7.** Click the **Notes Master tab**, then **8.** click **Close Master view**.

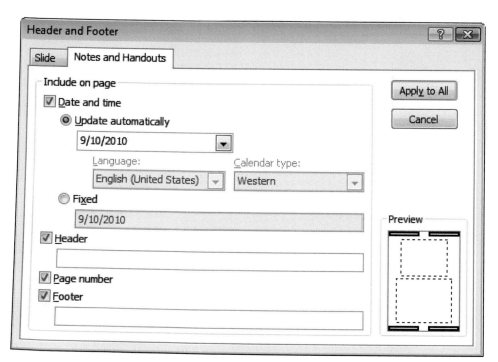

Figure 5.15: Header and Footer dialog box, Notes and Handouts tab

1. Open the data file **p5-3**.

2. Click the **View tab**, and in the **Presentation Views group**, click the **Notes Master button**.

Notes Master

3. Click the **Insert tab**, and in the **Text group**, click the **Header & Footer button**.

Header & Footer

   a. Select the **Date and time check box**, if necessary.
   b. Click **Fixed option button**, if it is not already selected.
   c. Click in the **Fixed text box**, and enter today's date.
   d. Click the **Header check box**, if not already selected.
   e. Click in the **Header text box** and enter: Devon Mutual Funds.
   f. Click **Apply to All**.

4. Click the **Notes Master tab**.

5. Click the **Background Styles button**, and select the **Style 5** background effect from the gallery that appears.

6. Select the header text, and change the font size to **16 point**. Apply a **red** color.

7. Close Master view.

8. Display **Slide 1.**

9. Click the **Office Button**, point to **Print**, then click **Print Preview**.

   a. Click the **Print What list arrow**.
   b. Click **Notes Pages**.

10. Scroll down to view all pages.

11. Click the **Close Print Preview button**.

12. Close the file without saving the changes.

REHEARSAL

TASK 2

GOAL
To create a presentation with speaker notes, as shown in Figure 5.16, then print the notes pages and handouts

WHAT YOU NEED TO KNOW

► Speaker notes can include quotes, statistics, or lists, which help to further explain an item on the slide.

► Handouts are distributed to the audience so that they can follow along with your presentation. You can also distribute handouts with space for the audience to take notes.

► In this Rehearsal activity, you will create a seven-slide presentation for college seniors to persuade them to invest their money in an Upton Investment Group account. You will add notes as you create the presentation and customize the handouts pages, which you will distribute to the audience.

▼ DIRECTIONS

1. Start a new blank presentation, and apply a design theme to it.

2. Create the presentation shown in Figure 5.16. Insert the notes for each slide, as shown in Figure 5.17.

3. Display **Slide 2**.
   a. Create a text box and enter a question mark.
   b. Size it to **400 pt**, and color it a **light purple**. Center it on the page, and send it to the back.

4. Display **Slide 5**.
   a. Create an Area chart using the following data:

YEAR 1	YEAR 5	YEAR 10
$5,500	$16,000	$29,260
YEAR 15	**YEAR 20**	**YEAR 25**
$42,460	$55,600	$68,860

   Insert the following title: `The Power of Saving and Investing`
   b. Format the **y-axis** to currency with no decimal points.
   c. Hide the legend.
   d. Format the **x-axis** titles to align at a **45-degree** angle.

5. Click the **View tab**, and in the **Presentation Views group**, click the **Handout Master button**.
   a. Set the page to display six slides per page.
   b. Include a header/footer on all slides with the date (to update automatically), the page number, and a footer that reads: `Upton Investment Group`
   c. Format the handout background, and apply the **Newsprint** texture to all pages, then close Handout Master view.

Continued on next page

6. Click the **View tab** if necessary, and in the **Presentation Views group**, click the **Notes Master button**.

   a. Apply the same background that you used for the handouts pages to the notes page.

7. Apply any animation scheme to all slides.

8. Print one copy of the notes pages.

9. Run the slide show.

10 Print one copy of the presentation with four slides per page.

11. Save the presentation as **5r2-seniors**, then close the file.

Cues for Reference

Print Handouts

1. Click **the Office Button**, then click **Print**.
2. Click the **Print what list arrow**.
3. Click **Handouts**.
4. Click the **Slides per page list arrow**, and click the number of slides per page.
5. Click **OK**.

Create Notes Pages

1. Click in the notes pane and enter your notes.
   or
1. Click the **View tab**, and in the **Presentation Views group**, click the **Notes Page button**.
2. Click in the text placeholder and enter your notes.

Print Notes Pages

1. Click the **Office Button**, then click **Print**.

2. Click the **Print what list arrow**.
3. Click **Notes Pages**.
4. Click **OK**.

Create a Handout Master

1. Click the **View tab**, and in the **Presentation Views group**, click the **Handout Master button**.
2. Make the desired changes using the tools on the Handout Master tab.

To add headers/footers:
   a. Click the **Insert tab**, and in the **Text group**, click the **Header & Footer button**.
   b. Click the **Notes and Handouts tab**.
   c. Make the necessary changes.
   d. Click **Apply to All**.
3. Click **Close Master View** on Handout Master tab.

Customize Notes Master

1. Click the **View tab**, and in the **Presentation Views group**, click the **Notes Master button**.
2. Make the necessary changes.

To add headers/footers, follow Steps a–d in To add headers/footers.
3. Click **Close Master View**.

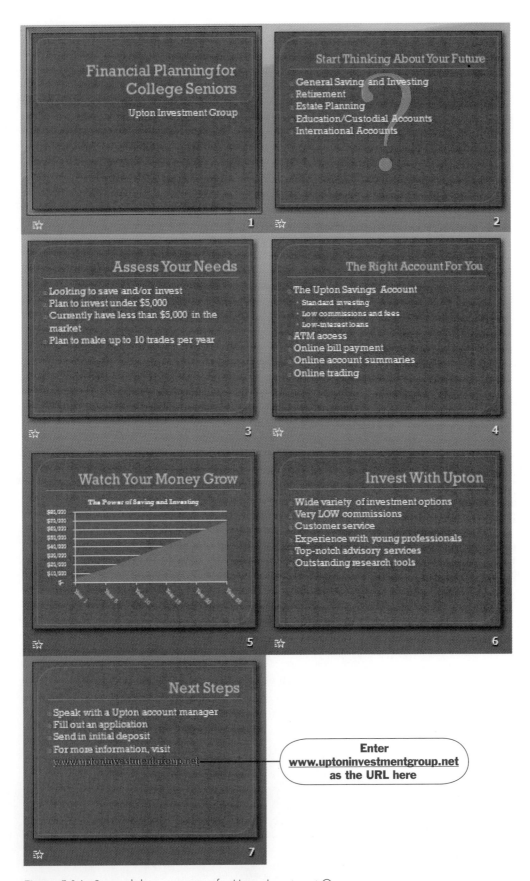

Figure 5.16: Seven-slide presentation for Upton Investment Group

Slide 1
Introduce yourself.
Briefly explain the purpose of this presentation.

Slide 2
Explain that it is never too early to start saving.
A new job will provide you with money with which you can begin saving.
There are so many ways to save and so many different accounts you can open.
Which type of account is right for you?

Slide 3
As a college senior, your needs are different than your parent's or grandparent's needs.
Think about these things...
Bullet 1: What is the purpose for this account?
Bullet 2: How much can you invest initially?
Bullet 3: How much money do you currently have invested?
Bullet 4: How many trades do you expect to make each year?

Slide 4
Explain why we recommend the Upton Savings Account.
• Allows you to invest in stocks, bonds, mutual funds, etc.
• Access to account information and trading can be done online.

Slide 5
Explain that long term investing is easy.
Start out with $5,000.
Add $200/month for 25 years, assuming an average of 10% annual interest.
After 25 years, $5,000 will become nearly $70,000!

Slide 6
Review Upton's outstanding reputation as a leader in the industry.

Slide 7
Explain that setting up an account is easy.
You can set up an account today, or when you get your first paycheck from your new job!
Good luck to you!

Figure 5.17: Text for notes

PERFORMANCE

TASK 2

You are the marketing director at Perfect Planning Group. On September 14, 2010, John Smith, head of sales, will be delivering a presentation to new salespeople at the company explaining Perfect Planning Group's capabilities and how to pitch new business. Your boss, Jaime Blanc, reviewed John's presentation and made several comments to it. She would like you to review her comments, make the requested changes, add speaker notes for John, and create notes pages and handouts.

Perfect Planning Group

Follow these guidelines:

1. Open the data file **p5p2-pitch**.

2. Review the comments on **Slides 1** and **4**, and make the requested changes. Delete each comment after you read it.

3. Review the comments on **Slide 7**. Delete them, and make the changes as follows:
   a. Insert a new **Slide 8**.
   b. Use a **Title and Content layout**, and enter the title, **Sales Compensation**.
   c. To show year-to-year compensation growth, create a column chart, using the **Clustered Column layout**. Enter the information below to create the chart.

	COMMISSION PAID	AVG. COMMISSION PER SALES REP
2006	$ 534,779.63	$ 106,955.93
2007	$ 582,890.00	$ 116,578.00
2008	$ 757,876.00	$ 126,312.67
2009	$ 872,395.44	$ 345,399.24

4. Insert a new **Slide 9**.
   a. Use a **Section Header** layout. Enter **Any Questions?** on the slide, and include John Smith's e-mail address (jsmith@ppg.world.com) and his phone number (212-555-1234). Enter the information in a way that best presents the data.

5. Apply custom animations to slide text and objects.

6. Apply slide transitions to all slides.

7. Add speaker notes for John, as follows:
   a. **Slide 2:** Explain Perfect Planning Group's mission and the way PPG builds corporate identities for clients. Give examples.

b. **Slide 3:** Show examples of sales kits you have created. Explain that sales kits can range from simple to extravagant depending on client and budget. Salespeople should always bring samples of materials on sales calls.

c. **Slide 4:** Show examples of those items that are pictured.

d. **Slide 5:** Explain that the sales brochure is the most requested item from clients. Show examples of brochures you have made, from the simple four-page color brochure, to die-cut and Velcro-sealed brochures.

e. **Slide 6:** This is a very impressive catalog that shows the breadth of PPG's capabilities. Not only do we create all kinds of sales materials, but we also can produce events for clients.

f. **Slide 7:** Salespeople should use visuals in their pitch. Premium items act as a gift for clients while also providing ideas.

g. **Slide 8:** Explain that a 7% commission is paid to all salespeople.

8. Display the handout master:
   a. Apply a gradient fill to the background.
   b. Show six slides per page.
   c. Insert the page number, date and time (fixed to today's date), and a footer that reads, **Creative Sales**.

9. Display the notes master:
   a. Apply the same background and header and footer as the handout master.

10. Print one copy of the notes pages.

11. Run the slide show.

12. Save the presentation as **5p2-pitch updated**.

TRYOUT

TASK 3

GOAL

To prepare a presentation for delivery to a live audience and on a kiosk, as shown in Figure 5.18

* Work with the pen and annotations
* Rehearse timings
* Use slide show set-up options

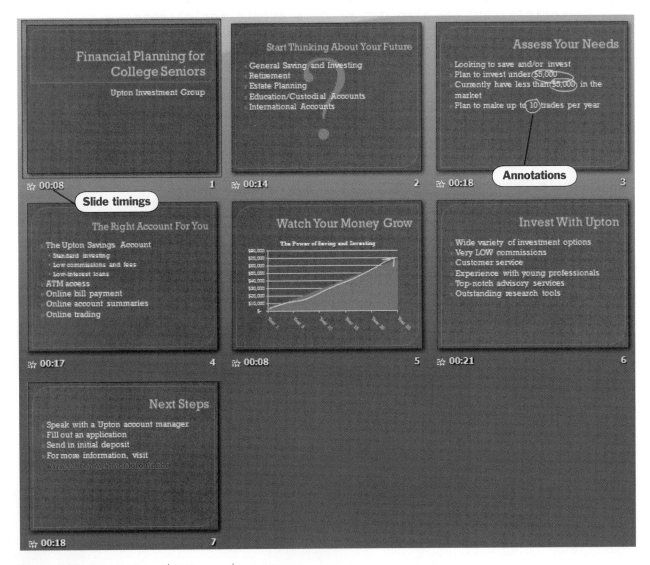

Figure 5.18: Presentation with timings and annotations

WHAT YOU NEED TO KNOW

Work with the Pen and Annotations

▶ **Annotations** are written comments that you can write on slides during a slide show, and later choose to erase or save.

▶ PowerPoint provides a pen tool that allows you to use your pointer as a writing instrument. You can select from three different pen types: ballpoint, felt tip, and highlighter. You can also change the ink color. Figure 5.19 shows a slide with an annotation that was made using the felt tip pen option.

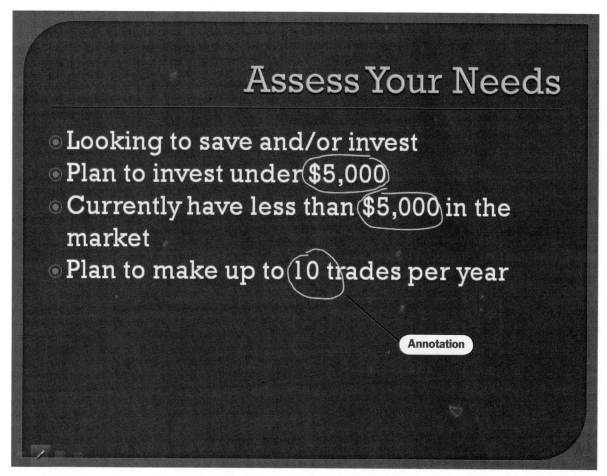

Figure 5.19: Slide with annotation made using the felt tip pen option

▶ To apply annotations, you must be in Slide Show view. On the lower-left corner of the slide, there is a hidden toolbar. Place the insertion point in the lower-left corner to display and activate the toolbar.

▶ Annotations made on the screen during a slide show do not alter the slide in any way, and they disappear when you move on to another slide. PowerPoint suspends slide transition and animation timings when you are annotating; they begin again when you turn off the annotation pen.

► When you end the slide show, you will be prompted to keep your annotations or discard them. If you keep them, they will display first on the slide before any transitions take place. Keep this in mind, and always practice a presentation with saved annotations before giving a live presentation to make sure that the effect is what you want.

HOW To choose a pen style and color, **1.** click the **Slide Show view button** on the status bar to begin your presentation. **2.** Position the pointer in the lower-left corner of the slide, then **3.** click the **Pen button** on the toolbar that appears, as shown in Figure 5.20. **4.** Select a pen style from the shortcut menu that appears (see Figure 5.20). **5.** Click the **Pen button** again, then **6.** point to **Ink Color**, and choose a color from the palette that appears, as shown in Figure 5.21.

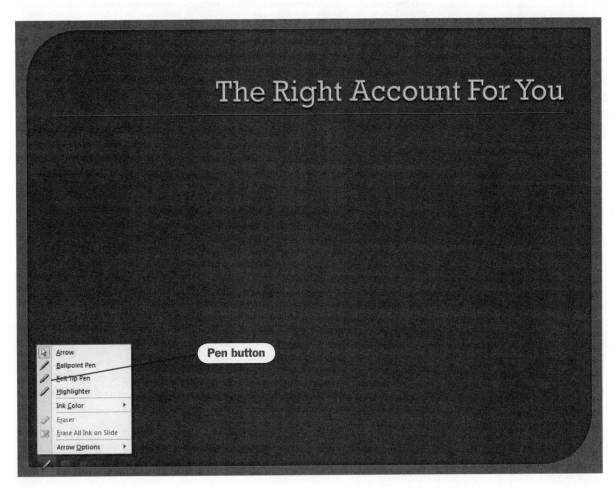

Figure 5.20: Pen button and shortcut menu

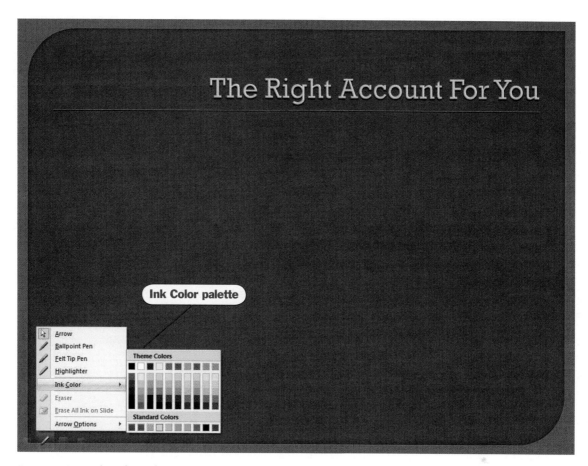

Figure 5.21: Ink Color palette

To make an annotation on a slide, **1.** click the **Slide Show view button** on the status bar. **2.** Click the **Pen button**, and then **3.** click on the slide and draw, write, or highlight what you want to add or emphasize. **4.** Click the **Pen button** again, and select **Arrow** to turn off the pen. **5.** Continue showing the presentation until the last slide appears. When prompted at the last slide in the dialog box, **6.** click **Keep** to save your annotations or **Discard** to not save them. You can also press **[E]** to erase your annotation on a slide. A saved annotation displays on each slide in Normal view.

T R Y *i t* **O U T** *p5-4*

1. Open the data file **p5-4**.

2. Display **Slide 4**.

3. Click the **Slide Show view button** on the status bar.

4. Position the pointer in the lower-left corner of the slide, then click the **Pen button**.

5. Select **Felt Tip Pen**.

6. Click the mouse and draw or write on the slide **Note: You might want**

to draw a line following the Fund's increase over the years.

7. Press **[E]** to erase your annotation on this slide.

8. Click the **Pen button** again, then select **BallPoint Pen**.

9. Click the **Pen button** again, point to **Ink Color**, select another pen color, then write something on the slide.

10. Close the file without saving the changes.

Rehearse Timings

▶ If you have to deliver a presentation with time constraints, you can rehearse how long it takes for you to deliver it. When you use the Rehearse Timings feature, PowerPoint records how long you stay on each slide and saves the timings. Once the timings are saved, you can have your slides advance automatically. This is particularly useful if you want to show a presentation as a self-running show which can be viewed at a trade show or on a sales counter.

▶ When timings are saved, they display below each slide in Slide Sorter view.

HOW **1.** Click the **Slide Show tab**, and in the **Set Up group**, **2.** click the **Rehearse Timings button** to start your slide show and display the

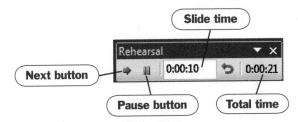

Rehearsal dialog box as shown in Figure 5.22. **3.** Leave each slide displayed for as long as necessary to present the slide content. *Notice that the second counter is timing how long the slide is displayed.* **4.** Click the **Next button** on the Rehearsal dialog box to advance to the next slide. *Notice that the clock in the Slide Time box resets (goes back to 00:00), while the clock measuring the presentation's total running time continues.* At the end of the show, a dialog box displays showing the total time of the show as shown in Figure 5.23. **5.** Click **Yes** to save the timings, or click **No** to discard them.

Figure 5.22: Rehearsal dialog box

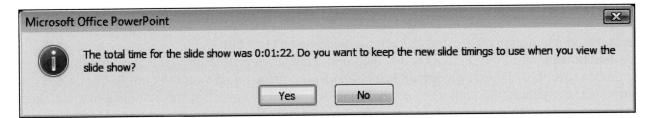

Figure 5.23: Microsoft Office PowerPoint dialog box

1. Open the data file **p5-5**.

2. Print one copy of the presentation as Notes Pages.

3. Click the **Slide Show tab**, and in the **Set Up group**, click the **Rehearse Timings button**.

4. Read the text on **Slide 1** as if you were presenting it.

5. Click the **Next button** in the Rehearsal dialog box.

6. Continue to deliver the presentation using your notes pages as a guide. Click each slide to advance to the next one.

7. Click **Yes** when prompted to save the new slide timings, then click **Slide 1** in Slide Sorter view.

8. Run the slide show again. Notice that the slides advance automatically. Each slide stays on screen based on each saved slide timing.

9. Close the file without saving the changes.

Use Slide Show Set-Up Options

▶ Before showing your presentation, you must set options for how the show will be presented. You can have the show loop continuously (creating a self-running presentation) or specify that the show will be presented by a speaker or browsed by an individual.

▶ You can specify how many slides you want included in the show. Finally, you can set up the show to advance slides manually (based on the clicking of the presenter) or automatically (based on saved timings).

HOW 1. Click the **Slide Show tab**, then 2. click the **Set Up Slide Show button**. In the Set Up Show dialog box that appears, as shown in Figure 5.24, 3. select a **Show type option button**, 4. select a **Show option check box**, 5. select how many slides to show in the **Show slides** section, 6. select how to **Advance slides**, then 7. click **OK**.

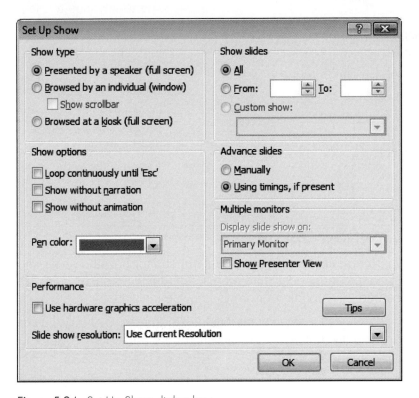

Figure 5.24: Set Up Show dialog box

TRY*it*OUT *p5-6*

1. Open the data file **p5-6**, which contains saved slide timings.

2. Click the **Slide Show tab**, and in the **Set Up group**, click the **Set Up Slide Show button**.

3. Click the **Loop continuously until 'Esc' check box**, then click **OK**.

4. Click the **Slide Show view button** on the status bar to run the slide show. *Note that the slide show will run continuously until you press [Esc].*

5. After viewing the show twice, press **[Esc]**.

6. Close the file without saving the changes.

REHEARSAL

 GOAL
To prepare a presentation for delivery
for a live audience and for a kiosk

TASK 3

WHAT YOU NEED TO KNOW

▶ The best way to ensure that you do not exceed your time limit is to rehearse the presentation.

▶ When practicing your presentation, be sure to speak slowly and clearly. Leave time to make eye contact with your audience and to incorporate the speaker notes into the presentation. A good presenter will not just read the slides on the screen, speak too quickly, or speak without pausing.

▶ A **kiosk** is a publicly accessed, freestanding computer terminal seen at trade shows or on a sales counter. Presentations shown on a kiosk are set up to **loop**, or run continuously.

▼ DIRECTIONS

1. Open the data file **p5r3-seniors**.

2. Print one copy of the presentation as notes pages.

3. Rehearse and time the presentation using your notes, then save the timings.

4. Run the slide show.
   a. On **Slide 3**, click to display four bullets of text, then click the **Pause button** on the Rehearsal toolbar.

5. Click the **Pen button** on the lower-left corner of the slide.
   a. Select **Felt Tip Pen** as the pen style.
   b. Click the **Pen button** again.
   c. Point to **Ink Color**, and select **Yellow**.

6. Draw a circle around each occurrence of $5,000 and around the number 10.

7. Click the **Next button** on the Rehearsal toolbar. Then, click to continue with the show.
   a. On **Slide 5**, use the pen to emphasize the growth displayed on the chart.

8. Continue with the show until the end. When prompted, save the annotations.

9. Click the **Slide Show tab**, then click the **Set Up Slide Show button**. In the Set Up Show dialog box that appears, select the following options:
   a. Loop continuously until 'Esc.'
   b. Advance slides using timings, if present.

10. Run the slide show again, and let the slides display automatically.

11. Save the file as **5r3-seniors with timing**.

12. Close the file.

Work with the Pen and Annotations

1. Click the **Slide Show view button** on the status bar to begin your presentation.
2. Click the **Pen button** on the lower-left of the slide.
3. Select a pen style from the shortcut menu.
4. Click the **Pen button** again.
5. Point to **Ink Color**.
6. Choose a color from the palette.

Make an Annotation on a Slide

1. Click the **Slide Show view button** on the status bar.
2. Click the **Pen button**, and select a pen style.
3. Click on the slide and draw, write, or highlight what you want.

4. Click the **Pen button** again.
5. Select **Arrow** to turn off the pen.
6. Continue showing the presentation until the end.
7. When prompted after the last slide, click **Keep** to save annotations or **Discard** not to save them.

Rehearse Timings

1. Click the **Slide Show tab**, and in the **Set Up group**, click the **Rehearse Timings button**.
2. Leave each slide displayed as long as necessary to present the slide content and all animations.

3. Click the **Next button** on the Rehearsal dialog box to advance to the next slide.
4. At the end of the show, when prompted, click **Yes** to save the timings, or **No** to discard them.

Use Slide Show Set Up Options

1. Click the **Slide Show tab**.
2. Click the **Set Up Slide Show button**.
3. Select a Show type, Show option, how many slides to show in the Show slides section, and how to Advance slides.
4. Click **OK**.

PERFORMANCE

TASK 3

You work for Ethan Jasta, vice president of Domestic Investments at Upton Investment Group. Mr. Jasta has created a presentation to persuade clients to consider investment opportunities in a new company called Copyit, Inc. You have been asked to put the finishing touches on the presentation, create notes pages, rehearse timings, and practice presenting the show using the annotation pen to emphasize certain slide data.

Follow these guidelines:

1. Open the data file **p5p3-copyit**.

2. Display the slide master and format it as follows:
   a. Create a design using shapes, and position it on the bottom right of the slide.
   b. Insert the slide number.
   c. Create a footer that reads, `Copyit, Inc`. Set the footer to a **14-point**, script font.
   d. Apply an animation effect to the slide title and bulleted text.

3. Apply the same transition effect to all slides in the presentation.

4. Display the notes master.

5. Format the notes master page as follows:
   a. Insert the company name (`Copyit, Inc.`) in the footer area. Set the text to **14-point**, script, and bold.
   b. Insert a page number.

6. Display notes page view. Add the following notes to the slides indicated:
   a. **Slide 1:** Introduce yourself and your position in the company. Explain the purpose of today's presentation.
   b. **Slide 2:** Emphasize the unique feature of the company—all branches are open 24 hours.
   c. **Slide 3:** Introduce the corporate staff.
   d. **Slide 5:** Explain that a new initiative—classes in design and production services—will start next year.
   e. **Slide 9:** Emphasize the positive feedback from customers who comment on the environmental commitment.

7. Print one copy of each notes page in black and white.

8. Display **Slide 1**.

9. Go to Slide Show view, and rehearse timings.
   a. Read the text on the slides (using the notes pages) as if you were presenting it. *Note: Leave time to make annotations on Slides 3 and 6.*
   b. Click the **Next button** on the Rehearsal toolbar to advance to the next slide.
   c. Continue to deliver the presentation.
   d. Click **Yes** when prompted to save the new slide timings.

10. Run the slide show.
    a. On **Slide 3** (our Corporate staff), use the felt tip pen style with red ink to circle the names of each person as you introduce them.
    b. On **Slide 6**, use the highlighter pen style (in green) to highlight the bulleted text: 2008, 100 square feet, 2,500 square feet.
    c. When prompted, save the annotations.

11. Print the presentation as handouts with six slides per page.

12. Save the file as **5p3-copyit updated**.

POWERPOINT

TRYOUT

TASK 4

GOAL

To finalize a previously created presentation, copy it to a CD, then mark it as final (read only)

⁎ Save a presentation to CD

⁎ Prepare a presentation as read-only

WHAT YOU NEED TO KNOW

Save a Presentation to CD

▶ Often you must give your presentation using a computer other than the one you used to create it, which requires you to take the presentation file with you. PowerPoint allows you to save your presentation to a blank recordable CD (CD-R), a blank rewritable CD (CD-RW), or a CD-RW with existing content that can be overwritten. *Note: If you use a CD-R, make sure you copy all the files you need onto the CD the first time. After the files are copied, you cannot add more files to the CD.*

▶ When you copy a presentation to a CD, Microsoft Office PowerPoint Viewer and any linked files (such as movies or sounds) are copied also. You can also choose to embed fonts, which ensures that the fonts you use in a presentation are available no matter what computer you use to deliver it.

▶ PowerPoint Viewer is the program that allows you to view a presentation on a computer that does not have PowerPoint installed, or which has a different version of PowerPoint than the one you used.

HOW **1.** Click the **Office Button**, **2.** point to **Publish**, and **3.** select **Package for CD**, as shown in Figure 5.25. In the Package for CD dialog box, shown in Figure 5.26, **4.** enter a CD name in the **Name the CD** box. **5.** To add more presentations or other files, **6.** click **Add Files**. Then, **7.** select the files you want to add, and **8.** click **Add**. The presentations to be copied will display in the Files to be copied list, as shown in Figure 5.27. *Note: By default, the presentation that is currently open is already in the Files to be copied list and presentations are set up to run automatically in the order in which they are listed. You can change that order by clicking the up or down arrow to move it to a new position in the list. Files linked to the presentation are included automatically and will not appear in the Files to be Copied list.* Click the Options button to change default settings. **9.** Click **Copy to CD**. **10.** Click **Yes** when prompted to include linked files. Optional: To embed fonts, click the **Options button** (see Figure 5.27). In the Options dialog box that appears, shown in Figure 5.28, select the **Embedded TrueType fonts check box**, then click **OK**. **11.** Click **Close**.

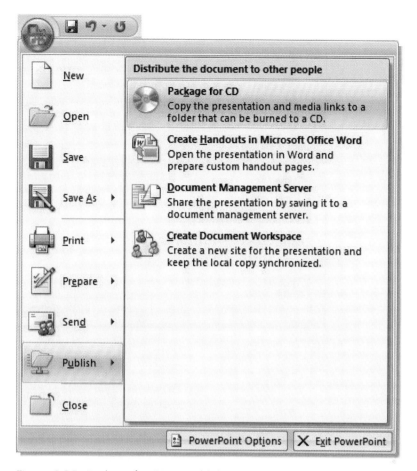

Figure 5.25: Package for CD on Publish menu

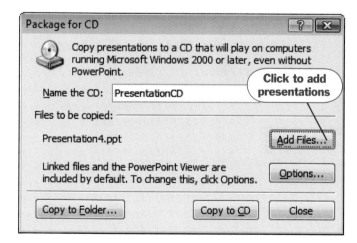

Figure 5.26: Package for CD dialog box

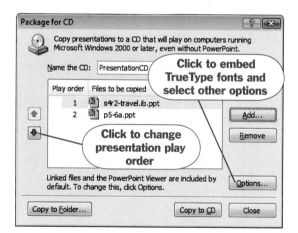

Figure 5.27: Presentations to be copied listed in Package for CD dialog box

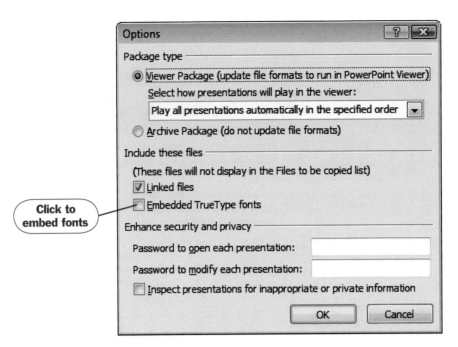

Figure 5.28: Options dialog box

TRY i t OUT p5-7

Note: You must insert a blank CD in the CD drive to complete this Try it Out. If you do not have a CD, read, (but do not complete) Steps 1–8.

1. Open the data file **p5-7**.

2. Click the **Office Button**, point to **Publish**, then select **Package for CD**.

3. Enter `Sales Related` in the **Name the CD box**.

4. Click **Add Files**.

5. Select the data file **p5-7a**, then click **Add**.

6. Click the **Options button**.

7. Select the **Embedded TrueType fonts check box**, and click **OK**.

8. Click **Copy to CD** if you have a blank CD in the CD drive. Otherwise, click **Close**.

9. Close all files.

Prepare a Presentation as Read-Only

▶ A **read-only** file can be viewed, but cannot be modified unless you save it with a new name or turn off read-only status. PowerPoint enables you to protect your file from further editing by using the Mark as Final command to make the document read-only and prevent inadvertent changes. When a document is marked as final, editing commands are disabled. The Mark as Final command can be removed from the document so that a reviewer who wants to make a change can do so.

HOW To mark a file as read-only,
1. display the presentation you want to mark. **2.** Click the **Office Button**, point to **Prepare**, then **3.** click **Mark as Final**, as shown in Figure 5.29. Click **OK** in any dialog boxes that open. *Note: A read-only document will display a Marked as Final icon in the status bar, as shown in Figure 5.30.*

To edit a read-only file, save it with a new filename, or
1. open the document that is marked as final,
2. click the **Office Button**, point to **Prepare**, then
3. click **Mark as Final**.

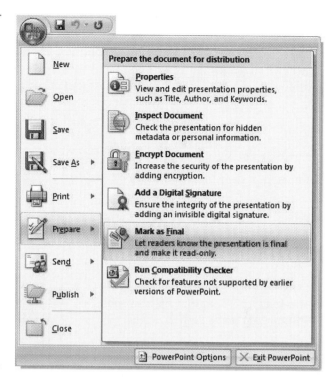

Figure 5.29: Mark as Final on Prepare menu

Figure 5.30: Marked as Final icon on status bar

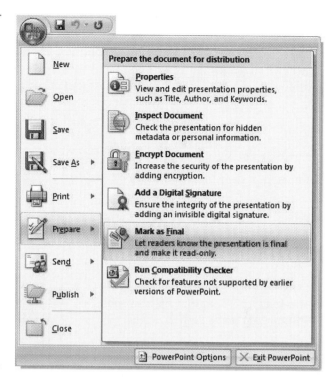

POWERPOINT

TRY it OUT *p5-8*

1. Open the data file **p5-8**.

2. Click the **Office Button**, point to **Prepare**, then click **Mark as Final**.

3. Display **Slide 1**. Attempt to change the title.

4. Repeat **Step 2** to remove the Read-only status.

5. Close the file.

Tryout Task 4   **Collaborating On and Delivering Presentations Lesson 5   PowerPoint–265**

REHEARSAL

TASK 4

WHAT YOU NEED TO KNOW

▶ If you receive a read-only file and want to make changes to it, save it under a new filename. In that way, the original file remains intact.

▶ In this Rehearsal activity, you will finalize a presentation, copy the presentation to CD, then mark it as final.

▼ DIRECTIONS

1. Open the data file **p5r4-realty**.

2. Save the file as **5r4-realty final**.

3. Respond to the comment on **Slide 1**, which is shown in Figure 5.31.

4. Add speaker notes to the slides as follows:
   a. **Slide 1:** Selling your ideas is challenging. First, you must get your listeners to agree with you in principle. Then, you must move them to action.
   b. **Slide 3:** Provide the audience with a motivational incident. Then go through the bullets.
   c. **Slide 6:** Support the benefits with evidence such as statistics, demonstrations, testimonials, incidents, analogies, and exhibits.

5. Add relevant clip art to **Slide 3** and **Slide 6**.

6. Format the Notes Master to include the same footer used on the slides, and apply any color background you want.

7. Print one copy of the presentation as notes pages.

8. Using the notes pages, rehearse timings, then save them.

9. Run the slide show. Use the pen tool in any style and color to annotate the chart and bullets. Do not save the annotations.

10. Click the **Office Button**, point to **Publish**, then click **Package for CD**. Copy the presentation to a CD if a CD is available to you. Otherwise, skip this step.
    a. Include linked files and embed TrueType fonts. *Some fonts have licensing restrictions and cannot be saved with a presentation. If you try to embed a font that has such a restriction, PowerPoint will prevent you from doing so. If this happens, click OK and embed just those fonts that are available.*

Continued on next page

11. Click the **Office Button**, point to **Prepare**, then click **Mark as Final**.

12. Save the file, then close it.

Figure 5.31: Slide with comment

Cues for Reference

Save a Presentation to CD
1. Click the **Office Button**.
2. Point to **Publish**.
3. Select **Package for CD**.
4. Enter a CD name in the **Name the CD** box.
5. Click **Add Files** to add other presentations.
   a. Select the file(s) you want to add.
   b. Click **Add**.

6. Click the **Options button**, and make desired selections.
7. Click **OK**.
8. Click **Copy to CD**.
9. Click **Close**.

Prepare a presentation as Read-Only
1. Display presentation to mark.
2. Click the **Office Button**.
3. Point to **Prepare**.

4. Click **Mark as Final**.
5. Repeat Steps 2-4 to remove Mark as Final status.

PERFORMANCE

TASK 4

You are the tour coordinator for Transport Travel Services. Before each tour begins, you conduct an orientation to familiarize tour participants with their destination city. Next Monday, a tour group leaves for a one week trip to New York City. Your presentation must tell these travelers something about New York City—including fun facts, places to visit, how to get around, and where to eat and shop. Use the information provided to develop the content for the presentation.

Follow these guidelines:

1. Read through the information provided on page 270 to get a basic understanding of the content the presentation will cover. Then create a presentation based on that content.

2. Open a new blank presentation.

3. Create a slide master for the presentation.
   a. Apply a background picture of New York City to all slides in the presentation, as shown in the sample title slide in Figure 5.32.
   b. Create a WordArt object to be used as the footer that reads, **New York City**.
   c. Include a slide number on all but the title slide.
   d. Include Action Buttons that link to the next slide and previous slide.
   e. Apply any desired theme.

4. Create a seven-slide presentation using the information below to create the slide content.
   a. Enter the presentation title: **The New York City Tour**.
   b. Create a relevant slide title for each slide after you read the slide content.

5. Insert relevant clip art on some slides. Be sure the clip art does not interfere with your slide background.

6. Use tables and SmartArt where appropriate to organize slide content.

7. Apply slide transitions and custom animations to text and objects.

8. Format the handout master with six slides per page. Apply a gradient background. Include the page number, a fixed date, and a footer that reads: **Transport Travel Services**.

9. Create notes pages that you can use when you rehearse and deliver the presentation. Search the Web for information about New York City to include in your notes.

10. Make any adjustments necessary to better present the information.

11. Rehearse the presentation, and use the pen tool as a highlighter (in any ink color) to emphasize specific places of interest on the tour information slides. Save the slide timings, but not the annotations.

12. Run the slide show.

13. Print one copy of the presentation as handouts.

14. Mark the presentation as Final (read-only).

15. Save the presentation to a CD, and embed fonts in the presentation. *If a CD is not available to you, skip this step.*

16. Save the presentation as **5p4-nyc**.

17. Close the file.

Figure 5.32: Sample title slide

Slide 1: Title Slide

Slide 2: New York City is made up of five boroughs: Bronx, Brooklyn, Manhattan, Queens, and Staten Island. New York City has more than 8 million inhabitants.

Slide 3: There is so much to see in NYC. The best way to see the city is on foot, but you can also take a taxi, the subway, a bus, or the ferry.

Slide 4: New York City is the shopping capital of the world! The best places to shop are at department stores, such as Macy's, Bloomingdale's and Saks Fifth Avenue. The best stores for kids are FAO Schwartz, Toys 'R' Us and The Disney Store. The best shopping areas are Nolita, Greenwich Village, Fifth Avenue, Madison Avenue, and Soho.

Slide 5: Here are some of our most popular NYC tours: (*Create a table on the slide to show these tours.*)

TOUR	DESCRIPTION	START TIME
NYC Buildings	Tour the city's most famous structures-including the Empire State Building and the Chrysler Building.	12 p.m.
The Financial Capital	Tour Wall Street and visit the NY Stock Exchange.	8:30 a.m.
The Lower East Side	Visit the neighborhood that bustled during the massive wave of immigration in the early 1900s.	9 a.m.
Lincoln Center Spectacular	Tour all the buildings that comprise this performing arts complex. After the tour, see the world famous NYC ballet.	4 p.m.

Slide 6: Here are two examples of our popular day trips: (Create a table on the slide to show these day trips.)

THE UPPER EAST SIDE	TIMES SQUARE
Meet at the Metropolitan Museum of Art	Meet in Times Square
Lunch in Central Park	See Carnegie Hall
Shopping on Madison Avenue	Lunch at Carnegie Deli
Tea at the Pierre Hotel	See a Broadway show (matinee)
Bloomingdale's Shopping Break	Horse and buggy ride through Central Park

Slide 7: Have a wonderful stay in New York City!

Act I

You work for the director of new business development at Transport Travel Services. Due to Transport's relationships within the travel industry and the recent increase in recreational flying, your boss has decided to start an aviation company. In order to obtain the financing to create this new company, your boss has asked you to help him create a business plan that he will present to potential investors. He has provided you with information to include in the business plan. Slides 1, 6, 10, 13, and 15 are shown in Figure 5.33 as a guide.

Follow these guidelines:

1. Read through the information provided on page 273 to get a basic understanding of the content the presentation will cover. Then create a presentation based on that content. Each slide heading represents a new slide. A "Section Header" designation indicates a new section in the presentation.

2. After creating the presentation, create a title slide, and enter an appropriate title for the presentation.

3. Create and apply a different slide master for each section within the presentation. You may use a background design to differentiate the sections, if you want.

4. Insert relevant clip art on some slides, and use a money-related clip art object on the Financial Overview slide.

5. Use bullets, font or color themes, headers, footers, WordArt, SmartArt to enhance the presentation where relevant. Apply any effect to objects you use.

6. Apply slide transitions and custom animations to text and objects.
   a. Animate the pie chart to introduce one pie slice at a time.
   b. Animate the organization chart to introduce one level at a time.
   c. Animate the stacked bar graph to introduce one category at a time.

7. Apply the cash register sound clip to the money-related clip art object on the Financial Overview slide.

8. Apply slide timings so that clip art objects animate automatically (without a mouse click).

9. Insert a music sound clip on **Slide 1** to play automatically in the slide show. Customize the animation to play across slides. Do not loop the sound.

10. After you create the presentation, enter notes that you think would help you deliver the presentation.

11. Print one copy of your presentation as notes pages.

12. Using the notes pages, rehearse the presentation, and save the slide timings.

13. Run the slide show; use the pen tool using any style and color, to emphasize slide chart data. Do not save the annotations.

14. Copy the presentation to a CD (if you have one available; otherwise, skip this step). Include linked files and embed TrueType fonts.

15. Prepare the presentation as Read-only (Mark as Final).

16. Save the file as **5e1-aviation**.

Executive Summary (Section Header)

TTS Aviation is a division of Transport Travel Services. We provide aircraft for rental and training. We have a state-of-the-art training center and outstanding, experienced instructors.

Mission

Our mission is to provide affordable aircraft rental, to offer flight training and instruction, and to adhere to state and federal aviation requirements.

Keys to Success

Our airplanes will be serviced by commercial aircraft maintenance crews, our instructors will be experienced, certified pilots, and we will conduct thorough screenings of our rental customers. We also plan to do extensive cross-promotions with Transport Travel Services to boost our business.

The Company (Section Header)
Location

The aircraft rental and training will take place at Hanger 117, adjacent to the Dallas-Ft. Forth Airport. Our main office will be located at 1890 Airport Highway in Dallas, TX.

Services

TTS Aviation will provide aircraft rental for licensed flyers and students. We will also provide flight instruction for those seeking pilot certification, as well as for leisure flyers.

Our Competitive Edge

All of our aircraft are well maintained. We will never fly damaged planes, as safety is our #1 concern. We will provide insurance for renters, students, and instructors. We will also operate 24-hour flight schedules, which will allow our customers to fly any time of day or night.

Market Analysis (Section Header)
Market Segmentation

Our clients will include Transport Travel Services referrals (their customers, pilots, and/or flight attendants), competitors' students, leisure flyers, aspiring pilots, and others. We feel that the breakdown of our client base will be 40% Transport Travel Services referrals, 15% competitors' students, 18% leisure flyers, 22% aspiring pilots, and 5% others.

(Use a pie chart to show this breakdown.)

Continued on next page

Market Trends

Currently, there is a shortage of pilots in the aviation industry, which has created a need for accessible training facilities. There is also an increase of flight students in the Dallas-Ft. Worth area. Furthermore, there has been an increase in disposable income, personal aircraft, and leisure flying.

Management Summary (Section Header)
Organizational Structure

Dennis Watkins is the president of TTS Aviation. Roger Davidson is the SVP (Senior Vice President) of Facilities and Administration, Alexander Parker is the SVP of Aviation Training, and Regina Anderson is the SVP of Aviation Rental. Patrick Fitzsimmons is the Manager of Instructor Recruitment, and works for Mr. Parker. Lauren Thames is the Manager for Marketing and works for Ms. Anderson.

Financial Overview (Section Header)
Sales Forecast

Use a stacked bar graph to show the projected 2011 monthly sales:

	RENTAL	TRAINING
January	$ 500.00	$ 1,500.00
February	$ 1,200.00	$ 1,500.00
March	$ 1,400.00	$ 2,750.00
April	$ 5,400.00	$ 4,500.00
May	$ 5,700.00	$ 5,000.00
June	$ 6,000.00	$ 5,000.00
July	$ 7,000.00	$ 4,500.00
August	$ 7,200.00	$ 4,500.00
September	$ 5,800.00	$ 5,000.00
October	$ 4,000.00	$ 4,000.00
November	$ 3,800.00	$ 3,000.00
December	$ 1,000.00	$ 2,500.00

1

6

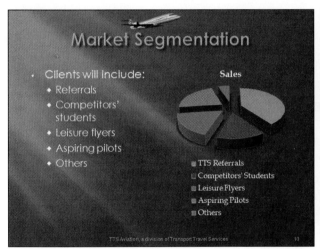

10

13

15

Figure 5.33: Selected sample slides

Act II

You work in the Marketing Department at Expedition Travel Gear and have just learned that Expedition will be the exclusive retailer of Solar Eyes sunglasses, the latest sports-inspired sunglasses to hit the market. Because of your PowerPoint skills, you have been asked to create a presentation that salespeople can deliver to customers to persuade them to purchase this new product.

Expedition

Travel Gear

You have been given product information shown below to create the presentation. Each bold heading represents a slide title; each paragraph represents information for that slide. Slides 1, 2, and 6 are shown in Figure 5.34 as a guide.

Follow these guidelines:

1. Read through the information provided on page 278 to get a basic understanding of the content the presentation will cover. Then create a presentation based on that content. Each slide heading represents a new slide.

2. After creating the presentation, create a title slide and enter an appropriate title for the presentation.

3. Prepare a final slide that reads:
   a. `Expedition Travel Gear`
   b. `ASK A SALESPERSON ABOUT SOLAR EYES TODAY!`

4. Apply any design theme.

5. Use a variety of slide layouts, as appropriate.

6. Use any clip art, bullets, media clips, font or color themes, headers, footers, WordArt, and/or SmartArt to enhance the presentation where appropriate.

7. Create a custom show using **Slides 6-11**.
   a. Name the custom show `Solar Lenses`.
   b. Apply a different design theme to the slides in the custom show. You may apply a background to differentiate the shows.

8. Create and format five WordArt objects on **Slide 6** for each lens type—polarized, gray, brown, amber, and yellow (see Figure 5.34 as a sample). Create a hyperlink on each object to link to the appropriate slide.

9. Apply any transitions and/or custom animations.

10. Insert a music clip or song on the first slide, and have it play for the duration of the presentation.

11. After you create the presentation, enter notes that you think would help you deliver the presentation.

12. Format the handout master to print six slides per page.
    a. Apply any background.
    b. Include the date and a footer that reads, `Solar Eyes`.

13. Print one copy of the notes pages.

14. Rehearse and time your delivery of the presentation using your notes.

15. Deliver the presentation.
    a. Use the pen tool to emphasize chart data. Do not save the annotations when prompted.
    b. Activate one of the hyperlinks during the slide show.

16. Print a copy of the presentation as handouts with six slides per page.

17. Save the presentation as **5e2-eyewear**.

18. Close the file.

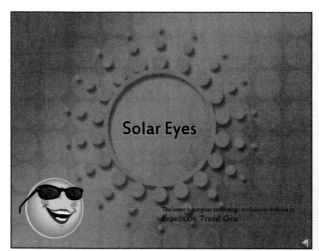
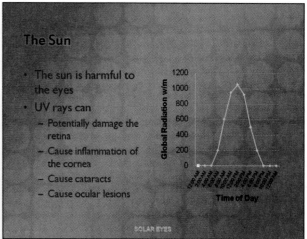

Figure 5.34: Selected sample slides

Solar Eyes

Solar Eyes sunglasses provide the latest in sunglass technology, and Expedition Travel Gear will be the exclusive retailer of these glasses.

The Sun

The sun is harmful to the eyes. UV rays can potentially damage the retina and cause inflammation of the cornea, cataracts, and ocular lesions. *Create a line graph that shows the times of day when we are most exposed to radiation. Use the following information to create the chart and then animate it by category.*

TIME OF DAY	GLOBAL RADIATION W/M
12:00 AM	0
2:00 AM	0
4:00 AM	0
6:00 AM	200
8:00 AM	600
10:00 AM	950
12:00 PM	1050
2:00 PM	925
4:00 PM	500
6:00 PM	200
8:00 PM	0
10:00 PM	0
12:00 AM	0

Solar Eyes

With Solar Eyes, you can protect your eyes from the sun's harmful rays. Solar Eyes are high-performance sunglasses that provide visual comfort and extreme protection against the sun. They filter out all harmful UVA, UVB, and UVC radiation. *Your boss suggested you go to* http://www.epa.gov/sunwise/uvradiation.html *to find definitions of UV radiation, UVA, and UVB. Explain the differences when delivering your presentation. Provide a reminder to yourself on the note page.*

Perfect for the Sports Enthusiast

Solar Eyes are perfect for the sports enthusiast. Our lenses filter differently depending on the activity (skiing, hiking, tennis).

Features

The frames are adjustable, have nose pads, accommodate all lenses, and are durable. Our lenses have an anti-reflective coating, which eliminates reflection and allows light to pass through them.

All Lenses
- Our lenses provide 100% UV protection. They all offer visual clarity so that there are no distortions, no eyestrain, and no headaches. You will also experience color stability, as these lenses do not fade after years of use. The lenses are also scratch- and impact-resistant.

Polarized Lenses

- Polarized lenses are made of optical-quality glass. They filter out reflected light or glare and are especially useful for boating, fishing, and night driving. These lenses reduce eyestrain and improve contrast and clarity.

Gray Lenses

- Gray lenses are versatile and good for everyday use. They provide true color transmission, as well as glare and UV protection.

Brown Lenses

- Brown lenses block glare and blue light, as well as sharpen details and enhance colors. They are perfect for low-light conditions and good for fast-reaction activities.

Amber Lenses

- Amber lenses eliminate glare and reflection, improve contrast, and enhance depth. They are perfect for boating.

Yellow Lenses

- Yellow lenses are all-weather lenses. They protect against reflection from water and snow, and protect against glare from fog. They are the perfect lenses for water sports.

Outlook Basics

In this lesson, you will be introduced to Microsoft Outlook 2007 and its basic features.

Upon completion of this lesson, you should have mastered the following skill sets

* Start and exit Outlook
* Explore the Outlook window
* Hide and show Outlook toolbars
* Minimize and expand the Navigation Pane and the To-Do Bar
* Work with Outlook folders
* Add and delete notes and shortcuts
* View the Calendar
* Work with Tasks
* Use Outlook Help

Terms
Software-related

Address book
Advanced toolbar
Calendar
Contacts
Folder List
Inbox
Information manager
Internet
Navigation Pane
Notes
Reading Pane
Shortcut
Standard toolbar
Tasks
View buttons
Web toolbar

T R Y O U T

▶ **GOAL**
To explore the Outlook screen and work with toolbars, folders, notes, and shortcuts

TASK 1

WHAT YOU NEED TO KNOW

About Outlook

▶ Outlook is the **information manager** program in the Office suite. You can use Outlook to send and receive e-mail, maintain an **address book**, organize and schedule meetings, keep track of appointments, list tasks, and create reminders.

▶ Outlook also lets you integrate data with other Office applications and with an instant message application, and manage links to the **Internet**.

Start and Exit Outlook

▶ There are four ways to start Outlook:

HOW **1.** Click the **Start button** on the taskbar. **2.** Point to **All Programs**. **3.** Click **Microsoft Office**. **4.** Click **Microsoft Office Outlook 2007**, as shown in Figure 1.1. Or **2.** Click **E-mail**, as shown in Figure 1.2. *Microsoft Office Outlook appears under E-mail.* Or **1.** Double-click the **Microsoft Office Outlook 2007 program icon** on the desktop, as shown in Figure 1.3. Or **1.** Click the **Microsoft Office Outlook program icon** on the Quick Access toolbar, as shown in Figure 1.3.

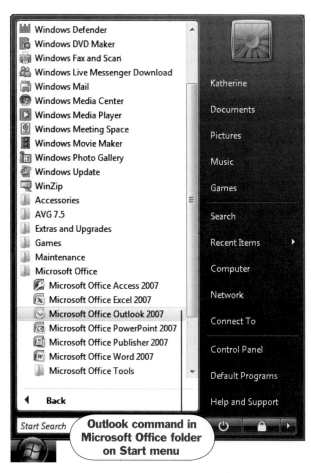

Figure 1.1: Start Outlook from Microsoft Office folder on Start menu

Figure 1.2: Start Outlook from Start menu

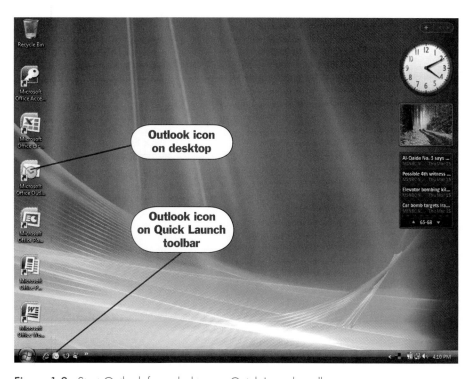

Figure 1.3: Start Outlook from desktop or Quick Launch toolbar

▶ There are two ways to exit Outlook.

HOW [Alt]+[F4] **1.** Click the **Close button** in the upper-right corner of the program window. Or **1.** Click **File** on the menu bar. **2.** Click **Exit**.

TRY *it* OUT *o1-1*

1. Click the **Start button**.
2. Point to **All Programs**.
3. Click **Microsoft Office**.
4. Click **Microsoft Office Outlook 2007**.

5. Click the **Close button** in the upper-right corner of the program window to exit Outlook.

Explore the Outlook Window

▶ When you start Outlook, the Outlook Today window appears, similar to the one shown in Figure 1.4, providing you with a preview of your day. This preview includes a calendar listing of events such as appointments, a list of tasks to be performed, and the number of new e-mail messages you have received.

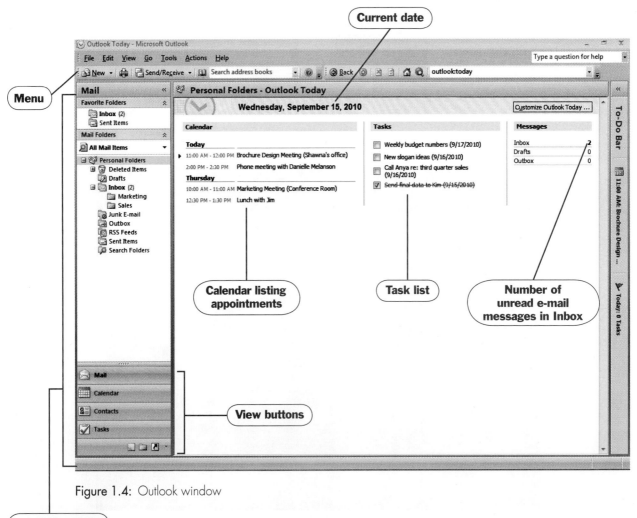

Figure 1.4: Outlook window

▶ Unlike other Office programs, the main Outlook window has a menu bar at the top instead of the Ribbon. As you work with Outlook, you'll see that some windows in Outlook do have a Ribbon at the top.

▶ Outlook displays the **Navigation Pane** in a column on the left side of the screen. The Navigation Pane allows quick access to the various Outlook features. The lower portion of the Navigation Pane contains **View buttons** to access Mail, Calendars, Contacts, Tasks, Notes, the Folder List, and Shortcuts. When Outlook Today is displayed, the Mail button is selected (see Figure 1.5).

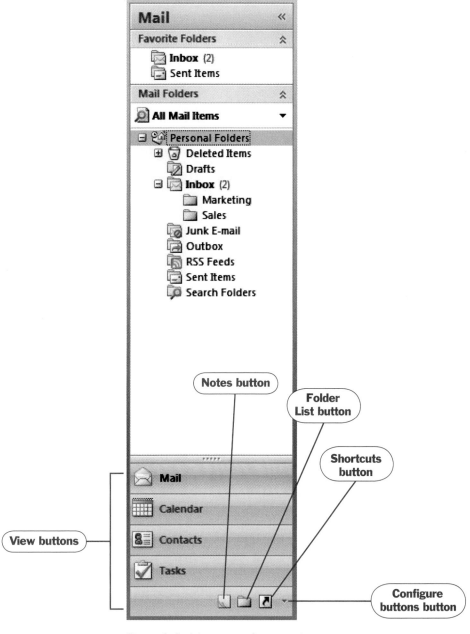

Figure 1.5: Navigation Pane with Mail button selected

▶ Table 1.1 lists the View buttons on the Navigation Pane:

Table 1.1: View Buttons in the Navigation Pane

CLICK THIS BUTTON...	TO DISPLAY...	
Mail	The Mail folders in the upper portion of the Navigation Pane, as shown in Figure 1.5. The main Mail folder is called Inbox. If you click one of the folders in the upper portion of the Navigation Pane, the screen opens into three panes; the Navigation Pane on the left, the Mail folder pane in the middle, and a Reading Pane on the right.	
Calendar	Thumbnail calendars in the upper portion of the Navigation Pane for the current and the following month. You can switch to view the appointments by day or week. The right side of the screen displays the working calendar.	
Contacts	Options for displaying your contacts in the upper portion of the Navigation Pane. All the contacts in your address book are displayed in the Contacts pane on the right. A list of buttons on the right allows you to jump to contacts in that section of the alphabet.	
Tasks	The screen in three panes. The upper portion of the Navigation Pane contains options for displaying your tasks. The middle pane is the To-Do List pane and lists your tasks. Selected tasks are displayed in the Reading Pane on the right.	
Notes	A new note. The Notes feature is the electronic equivalent of yellow paper sticky notes and is used to jot down thoughts or questions that you don't want to forget. A new note can be created while working in any other Outlook section and can be attached to an e-mail, inserted into a document, or displayed on your desktop.	
Folder List	All of the Outlook folders in the Navigation Pane. Click a folder to view its contents.	
Shortcuts	Shortcuts that you have created to quickly access certain Outlook folders in the Navigation Pane. The Navigation Pane also displays options to create additional shortcuts.	
Configure buttons	Commands for viewing more or fewer buttons on the Navigation Pane, configuring the Navigation Pane, and adding or removing buttons from the Navigation Pane.	

TRY _it_ OUT _o1-2_

1. Start Outlook. Note that the Mail button is selected by default and the Mail folders are displayed.

2. Click the **Inbox folder** (one of the Mail folders) in the Navigation Pane. _Note the three-pane configuration that may or may not contain e-mails._

3. Click the **Calendar button**.

4. Click the **Contacts button**.

5. Click the **Tasks button**.

6. Click the **Notes button**.

7. Click the **Folder List button**. Note the folders for Calendar, Contacts, Notes, and Tasks.

8. Click the **Shortcuts button**.

9. Click the **Configure buttons button**.

10. Press **[Escape]**. _The Configure buttons menu closes._

11. Click the **Mail button**, then click **Personal Folders** near the top of the Navigation Pane. _Outlook Today is displayed again._

Hide and Show Outlook Toolbars

▶ Outlook has the following toolbars: Standard, Advanced, and Web. You can choose to show or hide any or all of these toolbars on the Outlook screen.

HOW **1.** Click **View** on the menu bar, then point to **Toolbars**. *The toolbar names display, as shown in Figure 1.6.* **2.** Click any of the displayed toolbar names. *A checkmark next to the toolbar name indicates that the toolbar is displayed.*

▶ The **Standard toolbar** contains buttons for creating new items, printing, deleting, and finding contacts regardless of which View button is selected in the Navigation Pane. Figure 1.7 shows the Standard toolbar when the Inbox folder is selected in Mail view.

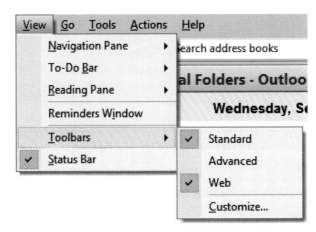

Figure 1.6: Toolbars submenu on View menu

Figure 1.7: Standard toolbar in Mail view

▶ The **Advanced toolbar** always contains buttons to access the Outlook Today window, move backward and forward, move up the folder lists, control the Reading Pane, and undo certain actions. Other buttons are displayed depending on the View button selected. Figure 1.8 shows the Advanced toolbar in Mail view. The Outlook Today button returns you to the Outlook Today screen from any view option.

Figure 1.8: Advanced toolbar in Mail view

▶ The **Web toolbar**, shown in Figure 1.9, provides navigation buttons for working online and does not change when different View buttons are selected.

Figure 1.9: Web toolbar

T R Y *it* O U T *o1-3*

1. Click **View** on the menu bar, then point to **Toolbars**.

2. Click to display **Standard**, **Advanced**, and **Web** toolbars, if necessary.

3. Click the **Calendar button**. Note the change in the Standard toolbar.

4. Click **View** on the menu bar, then point to **Toolbars**. *Note which toolbars are checked in Calendar view.*

5. Click the **Contacts button**. *Note the change in the Standard toolbar.*

Continued on next page

6. Click the **Outlook Today button** on the Advanced toolbar to return to Outlook Today.

7. Click the **Mail button**.

8. Click **View** on the menu bar, point to **Toolbars,** then click **Advanced**. *The Advanced toolbar disappears.*

Work with Outlook Folders

▶ You can create, rename, and delete Outlook folders to organize your information.

▶ Deleted folders and files are stored in the Deleted Items folder until you empty the folder.

HOW To create a new folder, **1.** click **File** on the menu bar, point to **New**, then click **Folder**. Or **1.** Click **File** on the menu bar, point to **Folder**, then click **New Folder**. Or **1.** Right-click a folder, then click **New Folder**. *The Create New Folder dialog box opens, as shown in Figure 1.10.* **2.** Type a name for the new folder in the Name box. **3.** Click the **Folder contains list arrow**, then click the type of folder you want to create. *This option is automatically set depending on the folder you have selected.* **4.** Click a folder in the list to place the new folder. **5.** Click **OK**.

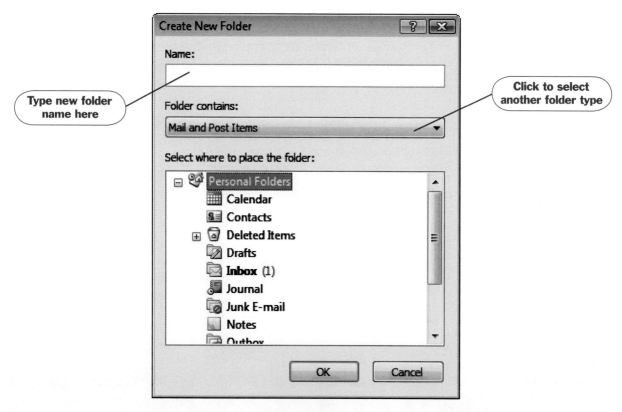

Figure 1.10: Create New Folder dialog box

To rename a folder that you create, **1.** select the folder, **2.** click **File** on the menu bar, point to **Folder**, then **3.** click **Rename "*folder name*"**. *The Rename dialog box opens.* **4.** Type a new folder name. **5.** Click **OK**. Or **1.** Right-click a folder, then **2.** click **Rename "*folder name*"**. *The folder name is selected, as shown in Figure 1.11.* **3.** Type a new folder name. **4.** Press **[Enter]**.

To delete a folder that you create, **1.** select the folder, **2.** click **File** on the menu bar, point to **Folder**, then **3.** click **Delete "*folder name*"**. *A confirmation dialog box opens.* **4.** Click **Yes**. Or **1.** Right-click a folder, then **2.** click **Delete "*folder name*"**. *A confirmation dialog box opens.* **3.** Click **Yes**.

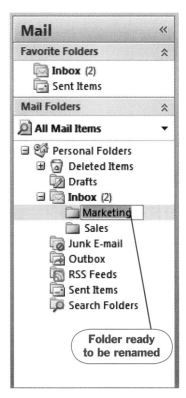

Figure 1.11: Selected folder ready to be renamed

T R Y *i t* O U T *o1-4*

1. Click the **Inbox folder** in the Navigation Pane.

2. Click **File** on the menu bar, point to **New**, then click **Folder**. *The Create New Folder dialog box appears.*

3. Type **Test** in the Name box, leave the folder type as **Mail and Post Items**, then verify that **Inbox** is selected in the list at the bottom of the dialog box.

4. Click **OK**. *The new Test folder appears as a subfolder of the Inbox folder.*

5. Right-click the **Test folder** in the Navigation Pane, then click **Rename "Test"**.

6. Type **Test2**, then press **[Enter]**. *The Test folder is renamed Test2.*

7. Right-click the **Test2 folder** in the Navigation Pane, then click **New Folder**.

8. Type **Subtest2**, then click **OK**.

9. Right-click the **Subtest2 folder** in the Navigation Pane, then click **Delete "Subtest2"**.

10. Confirm the deletion by clicking **Yes**. *The Subtest2 folder is deleted.*

11. Click the **Test2 folder**, click **File** on the menu bar, point to **Folder**, click **Delete "Test2"**, then click **Yes** to confirm the deletion. *The Test2 folder is deleted.*

12. Click the plus sign next to the **Deleted Items folder** in the Navigation Pane. *The two folders you deleted appear below the Deleted Items folder.*

13. Right-click the **Deleted Items folder**, click **Empty "Deleted Items" Folder**, then click **Yes** to confirm the deletion. **The folders disappear from the list**.

14. Click **Personal Folders** in the Navigation Pane to return to the opening screen.

Adding and Deleting Notes and Shortcuts

▶ You can add **notes** as you work to record information that you do not want to forget. Notes may be attached to e-mails and updated while working in Outlook or any other application.

▶ You can delete notes when you are finished with them.

HOW [Ctrl]+[N] or [Ctrl]+[D] To create a note, **1.** click the **Notes button** in the Navigation Pane. **2.** Click the **New button** on the Standard toolbar. **3.** Type text in the note. *A yellow note with text displays, as shown in Figure 1.12.*

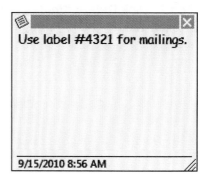

To delete a note, **1.** click the **Notes button** in the Navigation Pane. **2.** Click the note. **3.** Click the **Delete button** on the Standard toolbar. Or **2.** Right-click the note, then **3.** click **Delete**.

▶ You can add a **shortcut** to a folder to quickly access it.

▶ You can delete notes when you are finished with them.

Use label #4321 for mailings.

9/15/2010 8:56 AM

Figure 1.12: Note with text

HOW To create a shortcut, **1.** click the **Shortcuts button** in the Navigation Pane. **2.** Click **Add New Shortcut** in the Navigation Pane. *The Add to Navigation Pane dialog box opens.* **3.** Click the folder to which you create a shortcut in the Add to Navigation Pane dialog box, as shown in Figure 1.13. **4.** Click **OK**.

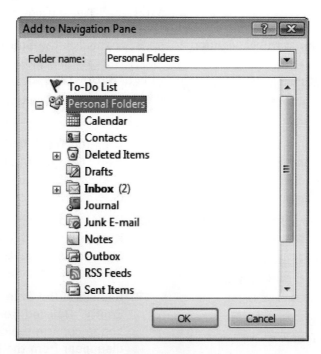

Figure 1.13: Add to Navigation Pane dialog box

To delete a shortcut, **1.** right-click the shortcut in the Shortcuts folder, then **2.** click **Delete Shortcut**. **3.** Click **Yes** to confirm the deletion.

1. Click the **Notes button**.

2. Click the **New button** on the Standard toolbar.

3. On the note, type `Use label #4321 for mailings`.

4. Click the **Close button** on the note.

5. Click the **Shortcuts button** in the Navigation Pane.

6. Click **Add New Shortcut** in the Navigation Pane.

7. Click **Notes** in the Add to Navigation Pane dialog box, if necessary, then click **OK**.

8. Click the **Outlook Today shortcut** in the Navigation Pane.

9. Click the **Notes shortcut** in the Navigation Pane. *The Notes pane appears to the right of the Navigation Pane.*

10. Click the note, then click the **Delete button** on the Standard toolbar.

11. Right-click the **Notes shortcut**, then click **Delete Shortcut**. Click **Yes** to confirm the deletion.

12. Click the **Folder List button**, then click **Deleted Items**. *The note you deleted appears in the Deleted Items pane.*

13. Right-click **Deleted Items**, click **Empty "Deleted Items" Folder**, then click **Yes**. *The note is permanently deleted.*

View the Calendar

▶ You can view the **Calendar** a day at a time, a week at a time, or a month at a time.

HOW **1.** Click the **Calendar button** in the Navigation Pane. **2.** Click the **Day button** below the Standard toolbar. *The Calendar pane changes to display the current day, similar to Figure 1.14.* **3.** Click the **Week button** below the Standard toolbar. *The Calendar pane changes to display the current week, similar to Figure 1.15.* **4.** Click the **Month button** below the Standard toolbar. *The Calendar pane changes to display the current month, similar to Figure 1.16.*

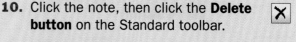
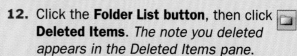

OUTLOOK

Day button

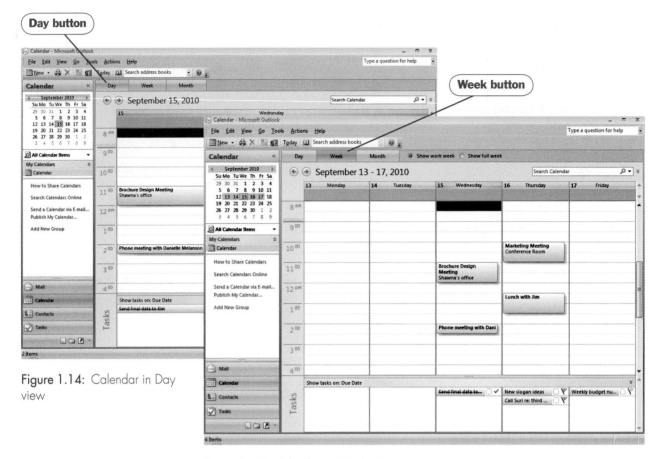

Week button

Figure 1.14: Calendar in Day view

Figure 1.15: Calendar in Week view

Month button

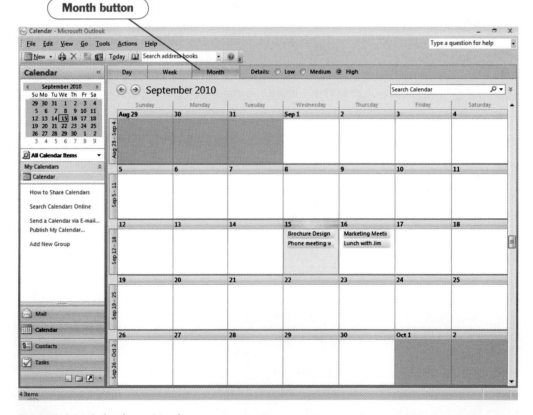

Figure 1.16: Calendar in Month view

1. Click the **Calendar button** in the Navigation Pane.

2. Click the **Day button** at the top of the Calendar pane. *The current day is shown in the Calendar pane.*

3. Click the **Week button** at the top of the Calendar pane. *The*

current week is shown in the Calendar pane.

4. Click the **Month button** at the top of the Calendar pane. *The current month is shown in the Calendar pane.*

Working with Tasks

▶ You can add **tasks** to remind yourself of things you need to accomplish. You use the Tasks pane to do this. See Figure 1.17.

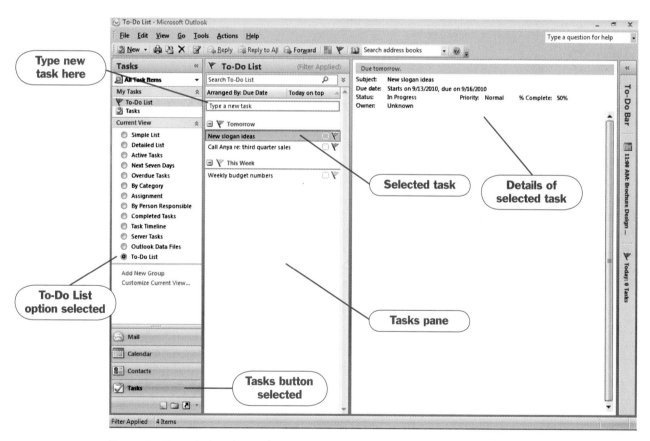

Figure 1.17: Tasks listed in Tasks pane

▶ You can mark tasks as completed after you have completed them. You can also delete them.

HOW [Ctrl]+[N] or [Ctrl]+[D]

To create a new task, **1.** click the **Tasks button** in the Navigation Pane. **2.** Click the **To-Do List option button** in the Navigation Pane, if necessary. **3.** Type the task in the Type a new task box at the top of the To-Do List pane. **4.** Press **[Enter]**. Or **2.** Click the **New button** on the Standard toolbar. *A new Task window opens, as shown in Figure 1.18.* **3.** Type the task in the Subject box at the top of the window. **4.** Click the **Save & Close button** on the Task tab on the Ribbon.

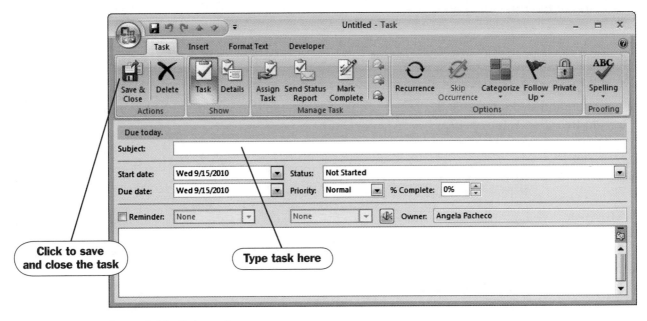

Figure 1.18: Task window

To mark a task as complete, **1.** click the **Tasks button** in the Navigation Pane. **2.** Click the **To-Do List option button** in the Navigation Pane, if necessary. **3.** Click the task in the To-Do List pane. **4.** Click the **Mark Complete button** on the Standard toolbar. Or **3.** Right-click the task in the To-Do List pane. **4.** Click **Mark Complete**. *The tasks disappear from the To-Do List pane and are moved to the Completed Tasks To-Do List.*

To view completed tasks, **1.** click the **Tasks button** in the Navigation Pane. **2.** Click the **Completed Tasks option button** in the Navigation Pane. *The completed tasks appear in the To-Do List pane, as shown in Figure 1.19.*

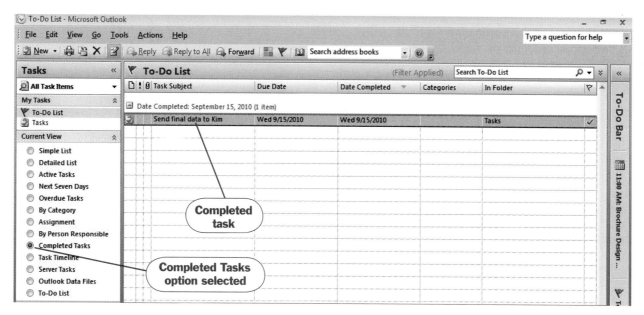

Figure 1.19: Completed task

To delete a task, **1.** click the **Tasks button** in the Navigation Pane. **2.** Click the task in the To-Do List pane. **3.** Click the **Delete button** on the Standard toolbar. Or **2.** Right-click the task in the To-Do List pane. **3.** Click **Delete**.

T R Y *i t* O U T *o1-7*

1. Click the **Tasks button** in the Navigation Pane.

2. Click the **To-Do List option button** in the Navigation Pane, if necessary.

3. Type **Task1**, then press **[Enter]**. *The task appears in the To-Do List pane under Today.*

4. Click **Task1** in the To-Do List pane. *The details of the task appear in the Reading Pane on the right.*

5. Click the **Mark Complete button** on the Standard toolbar. *The task disappears from the To-Do List.*

6. Click the **Mail button** in the Navigation Pane, then click

Personal Folders. *Task1 is listed in the Tasks list in the middle of the Outlook Today window. It has a line through it and a check mark next to it to indicate that it is completed.*

7. Click the **Tasks button** in the Navigation Pane, then click the **Completed Tasks option button** in the Navigation Pane. *The task is listed in the To-Do List pane.*

8. Click **Task1** in the To-Do List pane, if necessary, then click the **Delete button** on the Standard toolbar.

9. Click the **Mail button** in the Navigation Pane, then empty the Deleted Items folder.

Use Outlook Help

▶ As with all the other Office applications, you can find help for working with Outlook by clicking the Microsoft Office Help button. In Outlook, the button appears on the Standard toolbar. When you click the Microsoft Office Help button, the Help window appears. You can type text in the Search box to search for specific information. You can click the Search button to search Microsoft Office Online to get current solutions, click Outlook Training for a mini course, or search only on the computer.

FINAL PROJECT

FINAL PERFORMANCE

You are the assistant to Sara Vickers, the conference coordinator at Perfect Planning Group in New York, NY. Your New Jersey office has been hired by the New Jersey Small Business Development Association to assist in planning the 10th Annual Small Business Ownership Conference, which will be held on May 22, 2010, from 7:30 a.m. to 5:00 p.m. at the Teaneck Marriott at Glenpointe, a hotel and conference center in New Jersey.

The purpose of this conference is to give small business owners from the state the opportunity to attend workshops and exhibits that will provide the tools needed to grow their businesses and to provide networking opportunities with fellow entrepreneurs.

In preparation for this event, you will complete numerous projects that will require you to use various Office tools, as follows:

Internet

* Research and gather contact information for the New Jersey Chambers of Commerce
* Research the conference facility to locate the meeting floor layout

Word

* Develop a Web site
* Create a logo
* Create a press release
* Design a flyer
* Send a merged letter to recipients
* Develop the conference program

Excel

* Create an RSVP list, including fees collected
* Develop a budget
* Prepare a comparative income statement

PowerPoint

* Create a 10-12 slide multimedia presentation

Access

* Create and query a table

Outlook

* Schedule meetings

The next few pages will provide detailed information to assist you with finalizing these projects. The projects are divided into three parts and follow the sequence of events as they would occur if you were truly planning a conference.

Follow these Guidelines

1. Before starting any of the projects, you will need to read the "Conference Details" section on pages 2–5. This section provides facts that you will need to include in some of the projects.

2. Complete the projects in the order they are presented on pages 5–16.

3. For each project, do the following:

   a. Include your first and last name as a header.

   b. Keep all first drafts. Place all first drafts and final projects in a folder. These may be used as portfolio work samples.

   c. Print one copy.

Note: You can copy information contained in the **Conference Details** *Word data file and paste it into the project(s) where appropriate.*

Conference Details

✦ The conference will open with a keynote address by Thomas McLeod, president of the New Jersey Commerce Commission and a member of the governor's cabinet. Anthony Ericson, the president of the New Jersey Small Business Development Association, will make the closing remarks.

✦ The luncheon will include remarks by BBN-TV business reporter Marcie Thomas, who will recount local success stories.

✦ Throughout the day, there will be numerous one-hour breakout sessions. Attendees may choose to attend any one of the 10 sessions listed on the next page. Each session will be repeated three times throughout the day.

✦ Below is the list of all sessions, the room in which each session will be held, the speaker's name, and a brief description of each session.

   1. **Business Plans for Small Businesses** (Montclair Room) *Speaker: Pamela Areana* Looking for investment capital, loans, or a direction for your business? Create a simple business plan to formulate your ideas and detail your financial plans.

   2. **Buying and Selling a Business** (Alpine Room) *Speaker: Joseph Kubiak* What are the considerations when buying an ongoing business or franchise? What steps should you take when you want to sell a business?

   3. **E-Business for Small Businesses** (Morris Room) *Speaker: Gregory Martinez* How can your business profit by having a Web site? How can you use e-mail for advertising and marketing your product?

   4. **Finance for Small Businesses** (East Ballroom, Section III) *Speaker: Ann McConnell* What software will help you maintain business records? What records are necessary? How can you minimize accounting service fees?

   5. **How to Start Your Own Business** (East Ballroom, Section I) *Speaker: Norman Posner* What do you need to get started? What steps should you take?

   6. **Interviewing and Hiring for Employee Retention** (Essex Room) *Speaker: Fran Suraci* Learn how to tailor your interviewing questions and how to interpret answers to select the ideal candidate.

7. **Managing Work, Life, and Family** (Palisades Room) *Speaker: Jonathan Lismore* Is balancing all your commitments creating stress in your life? Learn how to manage your business so that you have more time for life and family.

8. **Networking** (Hospitality Suite) *Hosts: Mary Ann Kingsley and Lawrence Treacy* Make business contacts by attending this brief get-acquainted session, which includes tips for networking. Most of the session will be free-form for meeting and greeting the participants.

9. **Your Professional Image: Entrepreneur** (Princeton Room) *Speaker: Robert Martinson* How do you create and promote your professional business image? Learn image-enhancing tips for company policies, promotions, publications, etc.

10. **Web Page Design for the Small Business** (East Ballroom, Section II) *Speaker: Gregory Lee* Keep up with the competition by getting on the Web! Learn the basics for creating your company's very own Web page and the advantages of doing so.

Twenty-five local businesses will be exhibiting their products and services. These businesses include local banks, software vendors, accounting firms, human resources companies, business-to-business services, Web site designers, telecommunications companies, and financial planning companies. Conference exhibitors are listed below.

- Areana Business Plan Consultants
- Bergenfield Community College
- Brandt and Brandt
- Business Software, Ltd
- Business Management Consultants, Inc
- Commerce Bank
- Computer Gurus
- First State Bank
- Financial Umbrella, Inc
- Greg, Parsons, and Holtz
- Human Resources Consulting, Inc
- Ippolino Insurance Agency
- Kerrigan Internet Consultants
- Lee Web Site Design
- Nunez Central Supply Company
- Office Supplies Depot
- PeopleSoft
- Personnel Associates, Inc
- PriceWaterhouseCoopers
- Security Insurance Group
- Software Solutions, Inc
- State of New Jersey Economic Development Board
- Tenafly Chamber of Commerce
- Wassau Bank and Trust Company
- Web Design Services, Inc

✴ Participants can register for the conference by completing and mailing the registration form on the flyer or from the Web site. The registration form is shown below.

- -

Send or fax this form to:

SARA VICKERS, Conference Coordinator   Telephone: (201) 555-4322
Perfect Planning Group, NJ Office   Fax: (201) 555-4323
1045 Palisades Avenue
Fort Lee, NJ 07024

CONFERENCE REGISTRATION INCLUDES LUNCHEON AND ALL SESSIONS

Name _____ Company _____

Address _____

City _____ State _____ Zip _____

❏ New Jersey Small Business Development Association Member: $60   ❏ Other: $85

❏ Check enclosed (made out to Small Business Ownership Conference)
❏ Charge my credit card: Amex, Discover, Visa, or MasterCard (circle one)

Acct # _____ Exp. date _____

Signature _____

- -

✴ The corporate sponsors, to be credited in the conference program, are listed below.

Commerce Bank

PeopleSoft

Sam Malone Mercury

Software Solutions, Inc

State of New Jersey Economic Development Board

Tenafly Chamber of Commerce

✴ The conference schedule and room assignments are as follows:

7:30–8:30	Conference registration/ Continental breakfast	Conference center lobby
8:30–9:15	Keynote address— *Speaker: Thomas McLeod*	Grand Ballroom, Section A
9:30	Exhibits open	Grand Ballroom, Section C
9:30–10:30	Breakout session #1	Various
10:45–11:45	Breakout session #2	Various
12:00–1:30	Luncheon— *Speaker: Marcie Thomas*	Grand Ballroom, Section B
1:45–2:45	Breakout session #3	Various
3:00	Exhibits close	Grand Ballroom, Section C
3:00–3:45	Closing session— *Speaker: Anthony Ericson*	Grand Ballroom, Section A
4:00–5:00	Networking and cocktail party	Grand Ballroom, Section B

- The *room* layout of the conference facility is on the hotel's Web site. To locate the hotel's conference facility layout, do the following:
  a. Go to www.marriotthotels.com.
  b. Click on Events & Meetings.
  c. Choose New Jersey from the State drop-down list.
  d. Enter 10,000 in the Largest Meeting Room Needed text box, make sure the square feet option button is selected, then click Find.
  e. Click the Meeting Space link for the Teaneck Marriott at Glenpointe.

PROJECTS

Part I

The Logo

Create or locate a colorful logo for the 10th Annual Small Business Ownership Conference to use on the flyer, letter, conference program, Web site, and title slide of the presentation.

The Press Release

1. Create a press release.

2. It should be dated May 22, 2010, and should announce the 10th Annual Small Business Ownership Conference.

3. Indicate the highlights of this year's program (found in Conference Details).
   - Include a quote from the Conference Chairperson for the event, Wendy Pilgrim: "This year's 10th anniversary conference is sure to be our most successful one yet. We are excited to have such an extensive program with impressive and inspiring speakers."
   - Indicate that the announcement was made today by Anthony Ericson, President of the New Jersey Small Business Development Association in Newark, the sponsoring organization for the conference.

4. The press contact is Christine Powell from the New Jersey Small Business Development Association, (973) 555-1232.

The Flyer

1. Design a one-page flyer, which will be mailed to New Jersey and New York Chambers of Commerce members, encouraging them to attend the conference. It will also be included in the letter sent to members of the New Jersey Small Business Development Association.

2. Include the conference logo, conference date, conference location, and the breakout session titles, as well as the keynote and closing speakers.

3. Include a tear-off with the registration form, so people can register by fax or mail. (You can find needed conference information in the Conference Details section.)

Note: The flyer shown on the next page is a guide.

10th Annual
Small Business Ownership Conference

May 22, 2010, 7:30 a.m. – 5:00 p.m.
Marriott Glenpointe Hotel, Teaneck, NJ

KEYNOTE SPEAKER: Thomas McLeod, President of the NJ Commerce Commission

LUNCHEON SPEAKER: Marcie Thomas of BBN-TV

Business Plans for Small Businesses

Buying and Selling a Business

E-Business for Small Businesses

Finance for Small Businesses

How to Start Your Own Business

Interviewing and Hiring for Employee Retention

Managing Work, Life, and Family

Networking

Your Professional Image: Entrepreneur

Web Page Design for the Small Business

Send or fax this form to:

SARA VICKERS, Conference Coordinator   Telephone: (201) 555-4322

Perfect Planning Group, NJ Office   Fax: (201) 555-4323

1045 Palisades Avenue

Fort Lee, NJ 07024

CONFERENCE REGISTRATION INCLUDES LUNCHEON AND ALL SESSIONS

Name _____ Company _____

Address _____

City _____ State _____ Zip _____

❑ New Jersey Small Business Development Association Member: $60   ❑ Other: $85

❑ Check enclosed (made out to Small Business Ownership Conference)

❑ Charge my credit card: Amex, Discover, Visa, or MasterCard (circle one)

Acct # _____ Exp. date _____

Signature _____

Planning Meetings

Use Outlook to schedule the following meetings:

January 4 – Meeting with Hotel Event Planner and NJ Small Business Association representative at the Glenpointe Marriott – 11:00 a.m.

January 11 – Meet with corporate sponsor representatives at Perfect Planning Group NY office. 10:00 a.m.

Participants:

Commerce Bank

PeopleSoft

Sam Malone Mercury

Software Solutions, Inc

State of New Jersey Economic Development Board

Tenafly Chamber of Commerce

The Letter and Data File

You will send letters to members of the New Jersey Chambers of Commerce, who are also members of the New Jersey Small Business Development Association, inviting them to the conference. To complete the project, do the following:

1. Open the Access data file, **chofcom**. This data file contains a list of the members of the New Jersey and New York Chambers of Commerce Association. The illustration below shows the **NYNJTable** within the chofcom database file.

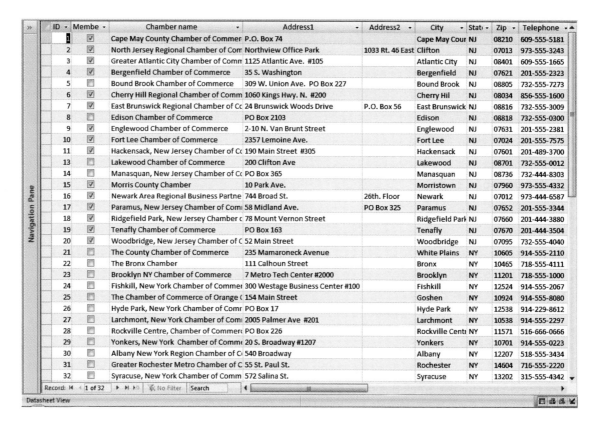

2. Edit the table to include information for additional chambers of commerce who have joined the association.
   a. Create a form (using the **NYNJTable**) and add each chamber of commerce and the name of its president into the database as follows:
      • New Brunswick, Nat Zanardi
      • Toms River, Judy Gordon
      • Westfield, John Carling

b. Search the New Jersey page of the U.S. Chambers of Commerce Directory on the Internet at www.2chambers.com to find the address, zip, telephone, and fax numbers of New Brunswick, Toms River, and Westfield chambers of commerce; add this information to the database using the form.

3. Create a query of only New Jersey members. (Query the database on the MEMBER and STATE fields and save the query.)

4. Complete the invitation letter. The incomplete letter is available as a Word data file, **chcomlet**. You must insert the merge codes and the conference logo that you designed, similar to the figure shown here. You should redesign the letterhead to accommodate the logo you desgined, if you want. You will note that the letter invites members of the New Jersey Chambers of Commerce, who are also members of the New Jersey Small Business Development Association, to the conference.

5. Merge the completed letter with the New Jersey members query table to produce your mailing.

6. Save the merged file, if you wish.

10TH ANNUAL SMALL BUSINESS OWNERSHIP CONFERENCE

May 22, 2010, 7:30 a.m. to 5:30 p.m.
Teaneck Marriott at Glenpointe

February 1, 2010

<<TITLE>> <<FIRST>> <<LAST>> <<SUFFIX>>
<<COMPANY>>
<<STREET1>>
<<STREET2>>
<<CITY>>, <<STATE>> <<POSTAL>>
<<COUNTRY>>

Dear <<TITLE>> <<LAST>> <<AFTER>>:

We are happy to invite you and all the members of your Chamber to the 10th Annual Small Business Ownership Conference. This is an anniversary year and the events planned for this conference reflect our goal to make this the biggest and best conference ever. This year, the conference will be held on May 21 at the Teaneck Marriott at Glenpointe, the hotel and conference center.

Please read the enclosed flyer, which highlights the day's keynote speaker and other impressive guests. We are confident that this year's convention is going to be a tremendous success, due to the informative sessions and the outstanding conference exhibitors that will be present. If there are any { MERGEFIELD Chamber_Name } members who are interested in reserving a booth for the conference, contact Wendy Pilgrim at the N.J. Small Business Development Association to receive all of the necessary exhibit information.

We are offering members of the N.J. Small Business Development Association a reduced registration fee of $45. All the members of your Chamber of Commerce are included at this rate. Please reproduce the flyer for your members and have them fax or mail the registrations as per the instructions on the flyer.

The Small Business Ownership Conference is, as always, a great opportunity to network, but this year the sessions, speakers and exhibitors make it a "must". We look forward to seeing you and the members of your group at our 10th Annual conference in May.

Cordially,

Anthony Ericson
President

ae/

Enclosure

New Jersey Small Business Development Association ✻ 134 Market Street ✻ Newark, NJ 07012
PHONE: 973-555-1232 ✻ FAX: 973-555-1233

The Web Site

1. Create a home page for the Small Business Ownership Conference. You may use a Web template if you want. Include the following on the home page:

   a. The name, date, and time of the conference.

   b. The conference logo.

   c. A navigation bar that links to all pages (see step 2).

   d. A "welcome to the home page" statement.

   e. Location of the event, the Teaneck Marriott at Glenpointe. Create a hyperlink to the Teaneck Marriott's home page at www.marriott.com/hotels/travel/ewrgp.

f. Contact Information
  • The Small Business Development Association
  • Wendy Pilgrim, Vice President and Event Coordinator
  • 134 Market Street, Newark, NJ 07012
  • Telephone: (973) 555-1232
  • Fax: (973) 555-1233
  • E-mail: pilgrim@sbda.biz

2. Create additional Web pages for each of the following aspects of the conference that can be accessed by the navigation bars on all pages. Use the names below for the navigation bar and use each name as the respective page title. (The information for each of these pages can be found in the Conference Details section.)
  • Exhibitors
  • Schedule of Events
  • Breakout Sessions
  • Registration Information (Include the registration form here.)

Part II

The conference preparation is well under way, and responses are beginning to come in. As more people register for the conference, you will need to update various documents. Therefore, you need to complete the following projects at this time.

The RSVP List

1. A spreadsheet has been created to keep track of those who have responded so far and the amount of their checks. To complete the spreadsheet, open the Excel data file **chcomdata**, and select the **RSVP** worksheet, shown here.

2. Enter the fee for each respondent. (Remember, New Jersey Small Business Development Association members pay $60, while non-members pay $85.) To enter the fees, create an IF statement to test if the Member column contains a "Y." If it contains a "Y," enter 60.00; otherwise, enter 85.00.

3. After all fees are entered, total them in Cell E51, leaving room for additional respondents.

4. Alphabetize the RSVP list by last name.

	A	B	C	D	E
1			RSVP List		
2					
3	NJ-SBDA Members			$60	
4	Non- Members			$85	
5				NJ-SBDA	
6	Last	First	Firm Name	Member	Fee
7	Berlin	Susan	Susan's Beauty Parlor		
8	Axelrod	Martin	Boat Supply Depot	Y	
9	Savarino	Vincent	Triumph Auto Glass	Y	
10	Tryon	Bradley	Litespeed Technologies	Y	
11	Roland	Robert	Robert Interiors	Y	
12	Fox	Marilyn	Antiques and Stuff		
13	Gibson	Gilbert	Gil's Kitchens		
14	Cassata	Patricia	Medical Supply Center	Y	
15	Dominquez	Nunzio	Nunzio's Landscapers	Y	
16	Rojas	Saul	R and T Movers		
17	Roisland	Janice	Shore Music Studios	Y	
18	Trainor	Diane	Pack and Ship Center	Y	
19	Johnson	Brenda	Flowers by Brenda	Y	
20	Shahid	Ahmed	Health Care Supplies	Y	
21	Ling	David	Bicycles Unlimited		
22	Sergio	Anthony	none		
23	Shalda	Doris	Ace Photography		
24	Castillo	Ann	Get Away Travel	Y	
25	Fredrico	Carl	Carl's Antiques	Y	
26	DeBernardis	Bill	PrintShop Plus		
27	Crowell	Ronald	Crowell Marina		
28	Dussault	Barbara	Westfield Interior Design	Y	
29	Duran	Brad	Caretenders		
30	Kaftan	George	Hillside Dental Labs		
31	Horton	Roger	Chemical Sales Co.		
32	Zanardi	Nat	Seasons Lighting	Y	
33	Gordon	Judy	Gordon Preschool	Y	
34	Miller	Richard	Software Solvers	Y	
35	Eguchi	Robert	Computer Repair Depot	Y	
36	Garson	Ronald	Mail Services Unlimited	Y	
37					

|◀ ◀ ▶ ▶| Budget **RSVP**

Budget Analysis

1. The actual budget and the estimated budget are compared in the Excel file, **chcomdata** on the worksheet titled **Budget**, which is shown below.

2. Switch to the **RSVP** worksheet. Copy the total in Cell E51 and paste link it to the Actual Registration Fee cell on the **Budget** worksheet.

Note: The budget estimate was based on 100 attendees; the actual numbers are not known at this time. By creating a link, each time you update the RSVP list, the budget analysis page also changes.

	A	B	C	D	E
1		Small Business Ownership Conference			
2		Budget Analysis 2010			
3					
4	INCOME		Estimated Budget *	Current Year Actual to Date	Variation
5		Registration Fees	$ 7,000		
6		Donations for Event	$ 6,000	$ 5,070	
7		Convention Funds	$ 4,000	$ 2,500	
8					
9		Total Income			
10					
11	EXPENSES				
12	Variable Expenses				
13		Luncheon @ $25 per person	$ 2,500		
14					
15	Fixed Expenses				
16		Event Planning Fees	$ 2,500		
17		Hotel Charges	$ 3,500		
18		Insurance	$ 650	$ 650	
19		Postage	$ 80	$ 65	
20		Advertising	$ 400	$ 300	
21		Marketing/Promotion	$ 500	$ 425	
22		Professional Fees	$ 1,800		
23		Entertainment/Food	$ 1,000		
24		Miscellaneous	$ 1,400	$ 500	
25					
26		Total Expenses			
27					
28	NET PROFIT				
29					
30					

Paste link total D51 on RSVP sheet here

Budget / RSVP

Update the RSVP List

The following people have just responded. Add their names and the fees collected to the RSVP list. Those who have a Y next to their names are NJ-SBDA members. *Note: The total is automatically updated when the fees are entered, and the increased total is reflected in the budget spreadsheet because of the link.* After entering the fees, re-alphabetize the list by last name.

Mr. Tyrone Thompson, Newark Glass Associates, Y

Mr. John Vincenza, Gazebo Gardening Supply, Y

Mr. James Josephs, Josephs Medical Supplies

Ms. Connie Williams, Isolde Spa and Beauty Salon, Y

Mr. Larry Vasalotos, Vasalotos Insurance Agency, Y

Ms. Sally Ciratoz, no affiliation (enter "none" in the field)

Part III

It is now 10 days before the conference and you will be finalizing all necessary documents.

The Conference Program

Now that the conference details are established, you can complete the conference program that will be distributed to all conference attendees.

You have been asked to work with a few members of your department on this project. Ask each member to plan a page by sketching the content on a plain sheet of paper. After discussing the layout and all the design elements you plan to use, you can start creating the document on the computer.

1. Design a conference program using the information found in the Conference Details section on pages 2–5. Enhance the program with clip art and any relevant design elements.

    a. The program should be in the form of an eight-page brochure.

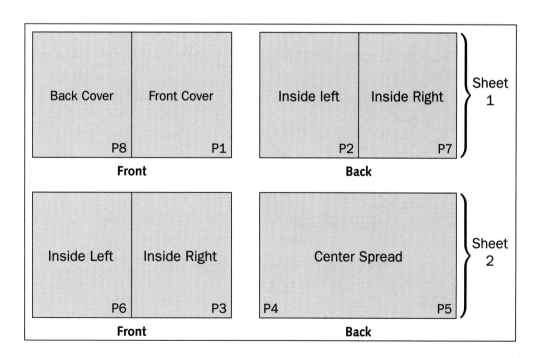

b. Each page should contain the following information:

- Sheet 1, Page 8, Back Cover
  - Insert a map showing the location of the Teaneck Marriott at Glenpointe. Both the map and the directions are on the hotel's Web site at: www.marriott.com/hotels/travel/ewrgp. If you cannot obtain the map, use the Word data file **map**.
  - Insert the hotel name, address, telephone number, name of the sponsoring organization (New Jersey Small Business Development Association), and the conference title (Small Business Ownership Conference) at the bottom of the page.
- Sheet 1, Page 1, Front Cover
  - Insert the conference name, logo, date, and location.
- Sheet 1, Page 2, Inside Left
  - Insert the following text:

Welcome to the 10th Annual Small Business Ownership Conference!

The Association greets all the small business owners and their employees here today. We are happy to announce another increase in registration over last year's conference. Based upon last year's evaluations, we have added workshops in Web page design and business plan development.

This year's keynote speaker, Thomas McLeod, brings greetings from the governor of our state and will discuss the economic climate for small business in New Jersey. Twenty-five local businesses are displaying and selling their products and services, including banks, accounting firms, office suppliers, software solution providers, Web designers, and financial planners.

Relax and visit with friends at the luncheon and networking session. Along with a wonderful luncheon, we will enjoy hearing from local BBN-TV reporter, Marcie Thomas, who will speak about local success stories.

Finally, Anthony Ericson, our president, will make brief closing remarks and award attendee prizes.

Don't forget!! Enter your name in the drawing for a free weekend at the Marriott in New York City.

And enjoy your day!

- Sheet 1, Page 7, Inside Right
  - Insert the conference sponsors and exhibitors.
- Sheet 2, Page 6, Inside Left
  - Insert the room layout, found on the hotel Web site.
- Sheet 2, Page 3, Inside Right
  - Insert the conference schedule.
- Sheet 2, Page 4, Left Center Spread
  - Insert five breakout sessions and room assignments.

- Sheet 2, Page 5, Right Center Spread
  - Insert remaining breakout sessions and room assignments.

2. After creating the front and back of each sheet, print them back-to-back and fold them in half to create the brochure.

Budget Analysis

The final income and expense data is shown on the **Budget** worksheet in the Excel data file, **finalbud**, shown below. To date, 120 participants have registered. The shaded areas require formulas as follows:

- Complete the actual variable expense data in D12. Enter a formula to calculate the luncheon expense based on 120 participants.

- Calculate the total income, total expenses, and net profit.

- Enter a formula to calculate the variations between the budgeted and actual values.

- Remove all shading from cells.

	A	B	C	D	E
1	**Small Business Ownership Conference**				
2	**Budget Analysis 2010**				
3	INCOME		Estimated Budget	Actual	Variation
4		Registration Fees	$ 7,000	$ 8,200	
5		Donations for Event	$ 6,000	$ 8,870	
6		Convention Funds	$ 4,000	$ 2,500	
7					
8		**Total Income**			
9					
10	EXPENSES				
11	Variable Expenses				
12		Luncheon @ $25 per person	$ 2,500		
13					
14	Fixed Expenses				
15		Event Planning Fees	$ 2,500	$ 3,000	
16		Hotel Charges	$ 3,500	$ 3,500	
17		Insurance	$ 650	$ 650	
18		Postage	$ 80	$ 70	
19		Advertising	$ 400	$ 300	
20		Marketing/Promotion	$ 500	$ 425	
21		Professional Fees	$ 1,800	$ 2,000	
22		Entertainment/Food	$ 1,000	$ 2,000	
23		Miscellaneous	$ 1,400	$ 1,500	
24					
25		**Total Expenses**			
26					
27	NET PROFIT				
28					
29					
30					

Use 120 for the number of actual lunches

Budget / Comparative IS

Comparative Income Statement

1. Complete the comparative income statement on the **Comparative IS** worksheet in the Excel file, **finalbud**, shown below, to compare this year's income and expenses with last year's.

	A	B	C	D	E
1		**Small Business Ownership Conference**			
2		**Comparative Income Statement**			
3		*Copy Actual column data from Budget worksheet to this column*			
4			This Year	Last Year	
5	INCOME				
6		Registration Fees		$ 6,580	
7		Donations for Event		$ 5,225	
8		Convention Funds		$ 2,000	
9					
10		Total Income		$ 13,805	
11					
12	EXPENSES				
13	Variable Expenses				
14		Luncheon @ $25 per person		$ 1,800	
15					
16	Fixed Expenses				
17		Event Planning Fees		$ 2,000	
18		Hotel Charges		$ 2,100	
19		Insurance		$ 500	
20		Postage		$ 50	
21		Advertising		$ 200	
22		Marketing/Promotion		$ 225	
23		Professional Fees		$ 1,600	
24		Entertainment/Food		$ 1,500	
25		Miscellaneous		$ 1,250	
26					
27		Total Expenses		$ 11,225	
28					
29	NET PROFIT			$ 2,580	
30					
31					
32					

Budget   Comparative IS

2. Copy the Actual column data from the **Budget** worksheet and paste link it to the This Year column on the **Comparative IS** worksheet. This will allow for updating if values are changed on the **Budget** worksheet.

3. Create a chart (as a separate chart sheet) comparing the income sections for this year and last year.

GLOSSARY

3-D reference A formula that calculates values in a workbook to a summary worksheet.

Absolute cell reference In an Excel formula, a link to a particular cell or group of cells that remains constant even if the contents or formula are copied from one cell to another cell.

Access keys Microsoft Office feature that allows tabs and commands on the Ribbon, Office Button, and the Quick Access toolbar to be accessed using the keyboard.

Access opening screen The first screen that appears when Access is opened; contains links to help and training, templates, a blank database, and a list of recently saved databases.

Accounting format In Excel, a number format that displays a $ in front of a monetary value; each dollar sign is aligned in the column.

Accounting software Application program used to organize and manage money and finances.

Active cell Location of the current worksheet insertion point.

Active cell reference Row and column location of the current cell; the cell address appears in the name box.

Active document Window containing the insertion point and a darkened title bar.

Address Block A combination of several fields that includes Title, First Name, Last Name, Company, Address, City, State, and ZIP code.

Address Book A collection of names, contact information, and e-mail addresses in Outlook.

Advanced toolbar In Outlook, buttons that provide access to the Outlook Today window, move backward and forward, move up folder lists, and control the Reading pane.

Aggregate function A built-in formula that calculates a summary value for a group of data.

Align center Text alignment in which text is centered between the margins.

Align left Text alignment in which text is even at the left margin and uneven at the right margin.

Align right Text alignment in which text is uneven at the left margin and even at the right margin.

Alignment The placement of text relative to the margins of a page, tab, cell, or column.

Animated.gif The addition of sound or special effects to a graphic. *See also* Graphic Interface Format.

Annotations Notes that are written on slides during a presentation using the pen tool, and that can be saved or erased.

Append Access feature that allows Excel data to be added to an existing table in a database.

Application software A program, such as word processing, spreadsheet, or database, that is used to perform a specific task.

Ascending order A sort order that arranges text alphabetically from A to Z, or numbers/figures from smallest to largest.

Attachment A file sent with an outgoing e-mail message, or, in Access, a data-type setting that allows files, such as images, spreadsheets, and charts, to be embedded.

AutoArchive An Outlook feature that moves old Outlook items at scheduled intervals to the archive location, and discards items that have expired and are no longer valid.

AutoComplete Excel feature that enters text automatically in a column using previously entered data.

AutoCorrect A feature that automatically replaces common capitalization, spelling, and grammatical errors with the correct text.

AutoFill Excel feature that automatically continues a series of text or data based on an established pattern in a row or column.

AutoFilter Sorting system provided in Excel tables that hides all items not in the set criteria.

AutoFit Feature used to widen columns to fit the data in a column or text box.

AutoFormat A feature that provides a predefined format to a letter, report, form, worksheet, or table.

AutoNumber Access data type in which a sequential identification number is entered automatically when a new record is added.

AutoShapes Predesigned shapes and symbols on the Drawing toolbar.

AutoSum Excel feature that allows users to enter a function such as sum and average to calculate the value of a group of cells.

AutoText Frequently used text, graphics, fields, tables, or bookmarks that are saved using a unique name, which you can insert into a file when needed.

Background A pattern, texture, or graphic that appears behind text in a file.

Back up The process of copying data from one storage location to another to prevent loss of data.

Banded Rows or columns in a table that are displayed with alternating colors.

Bar chart A type of graph in which values are represented by horizontal rectangular bars.

Bibliography Summary list of sources used, quoted, or paraphrased within a document.

Bitmap (.BMP) The graphics file format recognized by almost all Windows applications and commonly used for photographs and images. Bitmapped images and photographs are made up of a series of dots that create an image.

Blank presentation A PowerPoint option that allows the user to build a unique slide show using slides that contain standard default formats and layouts.

Bold Text enhancement in which text is darkened.

Bookmark A placeholder that marks specific text on a page, a page in a document or workbook, or a Web site so that the user can easily return to that place at a later time.

Boolean operator A word or symbol that modifies the search for information on the Web or in a database.

Border A variety of line styles that surround the edge of a cell, range of cells, paragraph, or page.

Bound control In Access, an object that is connected to a field in a table and is generally a text box. *See also* Controls.

Browser *See* Web browser.

Bulleted list A list of items marked by a round dot or other symbol.

Cache Region of the hard drive that temporarily stores frequently accessed data so that it can be retrieved quickly and efficiently.

Calculated control In Access, an object in a database that derives its value from an expression rather than a field. *See* Expression.

Calculated field A field defined in an Access query that displays the result of an expression. If values in the expression change, the value in the field is recalculated automatically.

Calendar In Outlook, the view that allows users to make entries of appointments or other date-specific information.

Caption In Access, this feature allows the user to assign a name to a field other than its field name, for use in reports.

Category A tool for organizing objects into sets that make managing a database easier.

Category label Identifies individual values in a chart data series as shown on the horizontal axis.

CD *See* Compact disc.

Cell The intersection of a row and column.

Cell address The location of a cell as identified by the column letter and row number.

Cell comment A notation added to a cell in a worksheet.

Cell style In Excel, a feature that defines a set of formats, such as font, font size, or font color, that can be applied to cells.

Center alignment *See* Align center.

Central processing unit (CPU) Referred to as the brain of the computer, this hardware device contains computer chips and circuits that control and manipulate data to produce information.

Chart A visual representation of data in a graphic format.

Chart sheet A separate worksheet created to display a chart on a full page.

Citation A reference to the source of quoted material in a report.

Click and type Easy method for changing the insertion point placement in a document. Move the mouse to the desired position, click once, and type.

Clip Art Pictures and drawings that can be inserted into a document.

Clipboard An area of the computer's memory where data that has been cut or copied is stored temporarily.

Clock speed Rate at which a computer processes instructions or stores data. Speeds are measured in megahertz and gigahertz.

Close button A button (represented by an "X") that closes the document or program window.

Collaborative Groupware Application program that helps groups communicate and organize activities, meetings, and events.

Column Vertical area for data and text organization. In Excel, these are identified by letter(s) across the top of the worksheet. In Word, the Columns feature allows text to flow down one column and into the next.

Column chart A graph in which values are represented by vertical rectangular bars.

Comma format In Excel, a number format that displays a value with commas and two decimal places; for example, 1,234.50.

Command A button on the Ribbon used to complete a task, such as choosing Font, Alignment, Number, and Style. Buttons are arranged on command tabs in groups of similar tasks.

Comment Notes or annotations that a user or a reviewer can add to a file.

Communication software Application program used to transmit and receive information between computers in real time.

Compact disc (CD) A storage device that can hold approximately 650 MB of data; often used by software and music industries; CDs can be used to store data and backup system files.

Compacting In Access, the process of defragmenting a database to eliminate unnecessary space.

Computer An electronic device that can perform tasks and calculations to provide logical information based on the instructions it has been given.

Contacts In Outlook, the view that displays entries in a user's address book.

Control Object in an Access form that displays data, performs actions, and enhances the view of form data.

Copy and paste A method of creating a duplicate of text or a graphic and placing it in another location in a document.

CPU *See* Central processing unit.

Criteria Restrictions placed on an Access query that specify which records are sought.

Crop A drawing tool used to trim parts of a graphic image.

Crosstab query In Access, a method of sorting and returning fields in a spreadsheet format with summary options.

Currency format Number format in Excel that displays a $ to the immediate left of the number.

Custom tab A setting that affects the way text aligns when the tab key is pressed; for example: center, right, left, bar, and decimal.

Cut and paste A method of moving text or a graphic. The "cut" procedure deletes the object from a document and places it on the computer's clipboard. The "paste" procedure places it in another location.

DAT *See* Digital audio tape.

Data series A group of values in a chart identified by a label.

Data source Document used in the merge process that contains variable information that is inserted into a main document.

Data type In Access, attributes that determine the type of information a field contains; for example, text, currency, or date.

Database Organized collection of facts about a particular subject.

Database management system A program that provides functions to store, search, filter, query, and report on data.

Database object A tool used to store, maintain, search, analyze, and report on databases.

Database software Application program used to collect, store, organize, modify, extract, and manage information.

Database view A layout used to change the data or structure of a table, form, query, or report.

Datasheet Another name for a table.

Date/Time In Access, a data type containing values for dates and times.

Decimal tab A tab type in which data is aligned at a decimal point.

Decrease Decimal format Excel number format that decreases a numeric value one decimal place. Values are rounded when decimal places are decreased.

Default printer setting Setting that will be applied by default when creating a paper printout of your file.

Default settings Settings that are established within software; for example, specific fonts, font size, and alignment. Default settings can be modified by the user.

Descending order A sort order used to organize text alphabetically from Z to A or numbers/figures from largest to smallest.

Design view Used to create or modify the design of a new or existing database object or report.

Desktop The first window that appears on the computer screen after a user has logged on. The Desktop can be personalized to help the user easily move between applications and files.

Destination file The file that receives data from another file when data is integrated. *See* integration.

Detail Section The main body of an Access report.

Dialog box A window that contains options to change current settings.

Dialog box launcher Button in the lower-right corner of a group that allows the user to change settings.

Dictionary A feature that provides the user with definitions for selected words. It can be accessed by right-clicking on a word or pressing [Alt] and the word.

Digital audio tape (DAT) A standard magnetic medium that has the ability to hold large amounts of information. These devices are often used by businesses to perform hard drive backups.

Digital camera A device that captures images in a format that can be read by a computer.

Digital video camera A device that can record live audio and video, which can be downloaded to a computer.

Digital video disc (DVD) A storage device that holds approximately 4.7 gigabytes, often used by the movie industry because of their ability to store and play high-quality video.

Directory Displays information by major topic headings or categories, which are broken down into increasingly smaller topics.

Document map Feature that allows a user to see a structural view of a document.

Domain name Part of a URL (Uniform Resource Locator) that identifies the business or organization. Each domain name has a unique identifier plus a suffix which identifies the type of Web site; for example commercial (.com), government (.gov), educational (.edu), U.S. military (.mil), or network (.net).

Downloading The process of copying files from the Internet to a computer.

Draft document A document that is not yet finalized.

Draft view In Word, a document view that allows the user to view a document as a draft without graphics, headers, and footers.

Drag-and-drop A method of moving selected text, graphics, or cells in a spreadsheet, using the mouse. Selected material is "dragged" from its original location and "dropped" into a new location by releasing the mouse.

Drop cap A formatting effect that changes the first letter of a paragraph so that it is larger than the rest of the text.

Duplicates query In Access, a sort that can detect duplicate entries in a field when duplication presents an error.

DVD *See* Digital video disc.

Edit mode In Excel, technique used to change cell contents by placing the insertion point at the end of an incorrect entry and making corrections.

Electronic mail (e-mail) software Application program used to send and retrieve e-mail from a mail server.

Ellipsis points Three periods following a menu item that indicate a dialog box will open.

E-mail address An address used to send and receive electronic mail.

Embedded file A file, chart, or other object placed into a destination file that becomes part of that file but can be edited in its source application.

Endnote A citation located in a list at the end of a document.

Export To copy data and database objects from Access to another database, spreadsheet, or file.

Expression Tool used to calculate a value. Expressions contain operators (such as = and *), control names, field names, functions, and constant values.

External reference Similar to a link, this refers to a cell in another workbook that can be used in formulas.

Favorite A link to a Web site that is stored on a computer for easy access.

Fax Device that can scan a document and translate the visual image into electronic impulses, which are sent to another machine at a different location by means of a phone line.

Field In Access, a category of information that makes up a record.

Field content The specific data in a field.

Field name The identifier for a specific field in a database.

Field properties Settings that can be modified to define how data is stored, manipulated, or displayed.

Field template Field definitions for commonly used categories found in the table templates.

File A collection of data, text, or information that has a name and is saved.

File extension A suffix following a filename that identifies the file type.

File management System of organizing and keeping track of files and folders.

Filename A unique name given to saved data.

File server A shared network computer that provides access to storage for users in a common environment.

File Transfer Protocol A format for transferring files across the Internet.

Fill handle The small black square in the bottom-right corner of a cell that is used with AutoFill.

Filter A feature that sets criteria to select or sort data and isolates records that meet a certain set of conditions.

Filter by form Access feature that allows users to use a sample of a form or datasheet to indicate selection criteria; used to filter more than one field.

Filter by selection Access feature that allows users to filter all or part of a set of values to obtain only those that meet specific criteria.

Find and replace A feature that scans a document and searches for occurrences of specified text, symbols, or formatting and replaces it with other specified text, symbols, or formatting.

First-line indent A feature used to set a specific indent for the first line of text in a paragraph.

Flash drive A durable, rewritable storage device that can easily fit in a pocket or on a keychain; also known as a jump or thumb drive.

Floating point operations per second (FLOPS) Measure of speed at which a supercomputer can perform specific operations.

Folder An object that is created to hold and organize related files.

Font A set of characters in a specific style.

Font color The color of text in a document.

Font size The height of the characters in a font, usually measured in points.

Font style A formatting effect that emphasizes characters, such as bold, italic, and underline.

Footer Text or graphics that appear at the bottom of a page or slide.

Footnote A reference that appears at the bottom of a page and gives credit to the source of information.

Foreign key In Access, a field in one or more tables that refers to the primary key field in another table. The data in the foreign key and primary key fields must match.

Form A format that displays one record at a time; used to enter or update data.

Form footer In Access, a section that appears at the bottom of each form and includes identification data that is repeated on each form.

Form header In Access, a section that appears at the top of each form and includes identification data that is repeated on each form.

Form Selector The tool used in Access to define the characteristics of a form.

Form Tool In Access, a feature that allows users to automatically create a form to display all fields in a table.

Form Wizard Access tool that allows users to create a customized form. It is useful when not all fields in a table are required, choices are needed in layout and style, or fields from more than one table will be used.

Format Changing the display of text or objects in order to create emphasis.

Format Painter A feature that allows the user to copy formatting such as font, style, and size from one block of text, or cell, to another.

Formula An equation or instruction in a worksheet that performs numeric calculations, such as adding, subtracting, and averaging.

Formula bar Area below the Excel Ribbon that displays the contents of the active cell.

Fraction format Number format in Excel that changes a decimal to its fractional equivalent. Found on the Format Cells dialog box or the Number format gallery.

Fragmentation In Access, the possible degradation of data that can result from regular use that involves adding and deleting objects or moving the data to different areas on a disk drive.

Freeze panes A command that locks a group of rows or columns to the left or above a selected cell, so that the area does not move during scrolling.

FTP *See* File Transfer Protocol.

Full screen Hides all commands and provides a full view of a document.

Function In Excel or Access, a built-in formula that performs special calculations automatically.

Function argument In Excel, the cell range that supplies the data for a formula.

Graphic An illustration such as a picture, piece of clip art, or shape that can be inserted into a document.

Graphics Interchange Format (GIF) An image file format that can be viewed in a Web browser. GIFs are usually used for drawings or illustrations.

Graphics software Application program used to create charts, pictures, illustrations, drawings, and 3-D images.

Gridline Horizontal and vertical outlines that outline boxes in Word or cells in Excel.

Group A cluster of command buttons that are displayed once a tab is selected. Commands tabs are organized by related tasks. Also, a command that allows graphics to become one object and behave as a single object.

Group footer Presents information at the end of a group of records.

Group header Presents information at the beginning of a group of records.

Group sheets A process used to select multiple worksheets in order to make changes such as using the same headings, data, formats, or formulas.

Hacker A user who breaks into classified and secret computer systems for malicious purposes.

Handle A box on the outside of an object indicating that it has been selected and is ready for text entry or resizing.

Handout A printout of a presentation in which slides are printed with one, two, three, four, six, or nine slides on a page, and given to an audience for future reference.

Handout master Tool in PowerPoint that allows presenter to include a header, date, footer, and/or page number on materials for an audience.

Hanging indent An indentation style in which all lines in a paragraph are indented except the first line.

Hard drive A storage device that usually resides inside a computer and is capable of storing large amounts of information.

Hard page break A term used to indicate a manually inserted page break.

Hardware The physical parts of a computer, including devices for input, output, and storage as well as the processing unit.

Header Identical text or a graphic that appears at the top of every page or every other page in a document.

Hidden An option to hide text in a document.

Home page The first page of a Web site that contains general information as well as links to other related pages.

Horizontal (category) axis Often referred to as the x-axis, this area of a chart represents the data series categories.

HTML *See* Hypertext Markup Language.

Hyperlink A shortcut used to easily change location; for example, to another Excel worksheet, a file on your hard drive or network, or an internet address.

Hypertext Text formatted as a hyperlink.

Hypertext Markup Language (HTML) The programming language used to write content for the World Wide Web.

Impact printer A printer that uses a device that strikes a ribbon on paper to transfer text or illustrations.

Importing To copy data from a text file, spreadsheet, or database table into another file.

Inbox An Outlook folder that receives and stores e-mail messages.

Increase Decimal format Number format in Excel that adds one decimal place to numerical values.

Index In Access, the feature that places primary key fields in order for easy access so that there are no duplicates and values are unique for each record.

Information manager An application, such as Outlook, that allows users to organize information, manage time, and communicate with others.

Inner join In Access, a way of editing relationships between tables to include only records in one table that match records in another.

Input device Hardware that transports data into the computer.

Input mask In Access, a pattern or template to which data must conform.

Input Mask Wizard In Access, a tool that allows the user to work with different data types.

Insert Function button Button used to search for uncommon functions and to view an explanation of the function selected.

Insertion point Blinking vertical line that appears in a document window and indicates where text will be placed.

Integration Sharing or combining data between Office applications.

Internet A global network of computers developed to share information.

Internet Explorer A Web browser that is included with the Microsoft Office suite.

Internet Protocol (IP) A format that enables information on the Internet to be routed from one network to another.

Internet service provider (ISP) A business that provides access to the Internet for electronic mail and use of the World Wide Web.

Intranet An internal network system confined within a specific location, usually one particular office or business.

Italic A text enhancement in which text is slanted.

Joint Photographic Experts Group (JPG or JPEG) An image file format used to compress and store images that include thousands of colors. Most Web browsers support this format.

Journal An accounting record that tracks financial events or transactions.

Justify An alignment option in which text is even at the left and right margins.

Keyboard Input device with typewriter-like keys as well as special function keys for entering data.

Keyboard shortcut A combination of keystrokes to perform a specific command; for example, Ctrl+C to copy selected text.

KeyTips Labels that show the access key for each tab or command.

Keyword Term that identifies the information used in a search.

Label In Excel, a text entry such as an alphabetic character or non-mathematical symbol.

Label control In Access, an object in a form that displays a title or caption and is not connected to a data source.

Label prefix Excel tool needed to create a label by inserting an apostrophe at the beginning of a numerical cell entry; for example, entering '2010 in the formula bar will make the entry appear as 2010 in the cell.

Label Wizard A tool used to create mailing and other labels, in standard or custom sizes, based on the data in the database.

Landscape orientation Position of a page or slide in which the display is wider than it is tall.

LAN *See* Local area network.

Laptop computer A portable computer, also known as a notebook.

Layer This feature allows graphics to be stacked on top of each other to create shadows and other effects.

Layout In PowerPoint, the menu that specifies how text or objects are positioned on a slide.

Layout view In Access, a Report view that allows the user to change the way a report is displayed.

Leader A series of dotted, dashed, or solid lines that connect one column to another to keep the reader's eye focused.

Left alignment *See* Align left.

Left outer join In Access, a way of editing relationships between tables to include all records from a table on the left with only those where the joined fields are equal in the other table.

Legend In Excel charting, the key that identifies the color or pattern assigned to a data series.

Line break A format applied to the end of a line. It ends a line of text without inserting a new paragraph at the end of the line.

Line A horizontal, vertical, curved, and freeform element added to documents using the line tool available on the Shapes gallery.

Line spacing The amount of vertical spacing between lines of text or data, measured in lines or points.

Link Connecting data and objects between files so that a change made in one file automatically updates the other.

Logical function Excel action that tests data and returns results based on the outcome of the test; for example, "if" an argument is "true," then a certain action will be taken.

Local area network (LAN) A computer system that covers a small area such as a company, school, or small business.

Lookup field An option that allows the user to enter the value for a field from a list of values or from another table.

Lookup Wizard A tool that automates the process of creating lookup fields.

Looping PowerPoint feature that allows a presentation, sound, or movie to be played repeatedly until the mouse is clicked.

Machine language *See* programming language.

Main document In the merge process, the file that contains elements that do not change as well as merge codes where the variable information will be inserted.

Mainframe A computer capable of storing and processing large amounts of data; it can have several hundred simultaneous users.

Many-to-many relationship In Access, a relationship in which a record in one table has many matching records in another, and a record in the second table has many matching records in the first.

Margin The parameters that are set to position data on a page and allow for blank space around the edges of a page.

Match Box In Access, the feature that allows users to find, and replace, information in a record.

Match Case Search feature that ensures that all items found in a scan of a document will have the same uppercase and lowercase entries.

Mathematical priority Order of operations that must be followed in entering formulas. *See* Order of mathematical operations.

Maximize button A button that enlarges a document or application to fill the screen. Replaces the Restore button after the Restore Down button is clicked.

Memo In Access, a data type used for long strings of text such as notes or descriptions.

Merge A feature that combines a source document with a main document to produce personalized letters, envelopes, or labels.

Merge and Center button This command, found in the Alignment group in Excel, centers text over a selected range by merging the cells into one large cell.

Merge field code Text that acts as a placeholder for variable information that will be inserted into a document.

MHTML An encapsulated aggregate document that includes all the elements of a Web site in a single file.

Microcomputer *See* Personal computer.

Microphone A device that accepts audio input for use in a computer program.

Mini toolbar A context-sensitive toolbar that appears when text or data is selected.

Minicomputer Smaller than a mainframe, but more powerful than a PC, these computers, also referred to as servers, support multiple users at their own terminals and can provide access to network resources such as file and application sharing as well as shared printing.

Minimize button A button that reduces the window to a button on the taskbar.

Millions of instructions per second (MIPS) Refers to the speed with which computers can perform specific tasks.

Mobile e-mail device A tool that provides access to e-mail accounts, allowing users to read and send e-mails, view calendars, and access contact information.

Modem A communication device that connects computers by means of a standard telephone line or cable.

Monitor Output device that allows the user to view computer information; also known as a display, video display terminal (VDT), or computer screen.

Mouse An input device that controls the movement of the pointer and allows the user to make selections from a menu.

Multiple items form Access view option that is similar to a datasheet and shows all items in the table. It has more customization and format options than a datasheet provides.

Multi-table select query An Access feature that give options for creating a query based on more than one table.

Name box In Excel, the area to the left of the formula bar that identifies the cell reference of the active cell.

Navigation pane Usually displayed on the left side of an application, this area displays various features or objects used by the application. In Access, the view lists the database objects present in the file. In Outlook, users see the different tasks that Outlook performs.

Negative numbers Value less than zero; in Excel, these values are displayed, by default, with parentheses.

Network A group of linked computers.

New Window A copy of a document.

Nonadjacent selection A selection of data which is not contiguous; to select nonadjacent text, objects, or cells, press and hold [Ctrl] while selecting.

Non-impact printer A printer that uses laser or ink-jet technology.

Normal view The default view in Word and PowerPoint.

Notebook *See* Laptop.

Notes Electronic tool that allows users to jot down questions, ideas, reminders, and other bits of information.

Notes master Tool in PowerPoint that allows presenters to include a header, date, footer, slide image, and/or page number on materials for the speaker. Page orientation, themes, and backgrounds can also be selected.

Notes Page *See* Speaker notes.

Notes Page view The PowerPoint view that displays notes attached to a slide.

Notes pane In PowerPoint, the area below the Slide pane; this window can be used to add additional notes for a speaker.

Number In Access, a data type that contains general numeric data used for nonfinancial calculations.

Number format In Excel, a number format that displays a value with two decimal places.

Numbered list A list of items marked by a number or letter.

Numeric label In Excel, a value or number, that is not used for calculations and is treated as text.

Over All Access feature that calculates a running sum of values that accumulate until the end of a report.

Over Group Access feature that calculates record-by-record or group-by-group totals.

Object dependencies Relationships between data in tables in Access that make it important for the user to determine which objects are related.

Office Button A button in the upper-left corner of an application window or dialog box that contains commands that relate to whole documents such as open, save, and print commands.

Office Clipboard *See* Clipboard.

OLE object In Access, a data type where data is linked to an object in another file, such as an Excel worksheet, using the object linking and embedding procedure.

One-to-many relationship In Access, a relationship in which a record in one table matches many records in a second table, with the second table having only one match to the first.

One-to-one relationship In Access, a relationship in which each record in one table has only one matching record in a second table, with each record in the second table having only one matching record in the first table.

Online service software Application program that provides subscribers with the ability to communicate with one another through e-mail, as well as receive news, weather, and sports information.

Operating system software The program that controls the basic operation of the computer, including file management and use of application software.

Optical character recognition (OCR) A system that allows printed pages to be scanned and translated into text or image files.

Order of mathematical operations Order in which Excel calculations are made based on the way a formula is written. Order is determined first by parentheses, exponents, multiplication and division, then addition and subtraction, then from left to right.

Organization chart SmartArt graphic that illustrates hierarchical structures.

Orientation The direction that text is printed on a page.

Orphan The last line of a paragraph appearing by itself at the top of a column or page.

Outline and Slides tab pane Window in PowerPoint to the left of the Slide pane, used to navigate through slides or topics.

Output device A device that allows the user to see or hear the information the computer compiles.

Page break The location in a document where one page ends and another begins. Breaks can be inserted manually.

Page footer A text box that displays information, such as the current date and page number, at the bottom of every printed page.

Page header A text box that displays information, such as the title or page number, at the top of every printed page.

Pane A section of a window that can be resized.

Paragraph spacing The amount of space, measured in points, that will appear above or below a paragraph.

Paste link Reference to a cell in another workbook or worksheet; if the original data is changed in the source cell, the linked cell will be updated automatically.

Paste Special Dialog box that displays custom pasting options such as formulas or values.

Paste values Numeric values that are posted without formulas.

PDF *See* Portable Document Format.

Percent Style Format Number format in Excel that changes numerical values to percentages.

Personal computer (PC) A computer small enough to fit on a desk that is relatively inexpensive and is designed for an individual user.

Personal digital assistant (PDA) Handheld device that combines functions such as computing, telephone, e-mail, and networking features.

Photo Album A collection of graphics that can be inserted into documents or used as a slide show in PowerPoint.

Picture Illustration such as a drawing, piece of clip art, or photograph that can be saved in a file format reserved for graphics such as a .tif, .jpeg, or .gif.

Pie chart Circular graphs that display the percentage of each data item in relation to the total of all items.

PivotChart view In Access, the feature that graphically represents information in chart form.

PivotTable view In Access, the feature that allows users to interactively summarize and analyze data from tables.

Placeholder In templates or presentations, boxes that define the placement and formatting of text or objects, and that sometimes provide sample text or graphics.

Plot area In an Excel chart, the space where values are charted.

Point size The measurement of the height of characters. A point is approximately $\frac{1}{72}$ of an inch.

Portable Document Format (PDF) A file format that preserves document formatting and content.

Portrait orientation Position of a page or slide in which it is taller than it is wide.

Presentation software Program, such as PowerPoint, used to create and save on-screen slides and handouts to accompany a speech or lecture.

Primary key In Access, a field that provides a unique code or number to identify each record.

Print Preview Screen display that shows how a document will appear on the page before it is printed.

Print titles A page setup feature used to print row or column titles on subsequent pages of a multiple page worksheet.

Printer An output device that transfers text or illustrations to paper.

Programming language Code written with a specific vocabulary and set of grammatical rules that instructs computers to perform tasks.

Query A structured search method that uses keywords or phrases to find information that meets certain criteria.

Query Design grid The area in Design view where users set criteria, indicate if a field is to be shown or not, and add totals.

Query Design view Access feature that allows users to structure a query.

Query Wizard Access feature that provides step-by-step dialog boxes to request information that will retrieve and analyze data.

Quick Access toolbar A customizable toolbar that provides a set of frequently used commands independent of the tab that is open.

Quick Parts Feature that allows a user to save and quickly insert frequently used text and graphs.

Quick Styles Predefined table formats that can be applied to data.

Quick Tables Predesigned tables with sample data that can be replaced and formatting that can be customized.

Random access memory (RAM) Computer memory that is used only when a computer is turned on. The amount of information and number of operations that can be used at any one time is limited by the amount of RAM a computer has.

Range In Excel, one or more contiguous cells; ranges can be saved with a name and used in a formula.

Read-only Designation given to a file that can be viewed, but not modified, unless it is saved with a different name.

Read-only memory (ROM) Computer memory on which data has been prerecorded. Once data has been written on a ROM chip, it cannot be deleted or edited.

Record A complete set of related information about one person or item. In Access, each row in a table represents one record.

Record selector In Access, the small box to the left of the first field in a record used to choose a record for editing or to delete it.

Redo A feature that allows the user to reverse the previously undone action.

Relational database management system An Access tool for dividing data into separate, subject-based tables that can be brought together in reports, as needed.

Relationship In Access, a correlation established between shared fields or columns in two or more tables.

Relative cell reference In formulas, the specific cell (or group of cells) location that changes in relation to their new locations when a formula is copied. By default, all cell references are relative unless a $ precedes the column and row reference for a cell. *See* Absolute reference.

Repeat A feature that allows the user to duplicate the last action made.

Report footer In Access, the bottom of the last printed page, above the page footer; this contains the summary values for a report.

Report header In Access, the top of the first printed page; displays the report title, logo, and current date.

Report section In Access, the section that includes the report header and footer, Group header and footer, page header and footer, and detail sections.

Report selector In Access, the box where the rulers meet in the upper-left corner of a report in Design view. The report selector allows the user to see the properties of a report.

Report view The display option for an Access report in which no modifications can be made.

Report Wizard In Access, a tool that builds a report by asking questions about information that should be included as well as the method of formatting and presentation.

Report In Access, a display of information retrieved from a database.

Restore Down button A button that reduces the size of a document or application.

Ribbon An area located below the Title bar, which contains a band of tabs and commands used to complete tasks.

Rich Text Format (RTF) A file format used for document interchange between applications and/or types of word processing programs.

Right alignment *See* Align right.

Right outer join In Access, a way of editing relationships between tables to include all records from a table on the right with only those where the joined fields are equal in the other table.

ROM *See* Read-only memory.

Rotate Drawing tool used to turn a placeholder in 90-degree increments.

Rotation handle Tool that allows the user to change the angle at which a graphic is positioned. The pointer becomes a four-headed arrow for moving a graphic.

Row Horizontal area for data organization. In Excel, these are identified by a number along the left side of the worksheet.

Row Source Type property In Access, the property that specifies the entries in a list to be used for field lookup.

Ruler Horizontal and vertical tools used to gauge the position of text on a page.

Running Sum In Access, the feature used to calculate totals of an entire list or group of items in a database.

Sans serif A type of font without lines, curves, or edges extending from the ends of the letters.

Save As Feature that allows a document to be saved with a different filename, file format, or location while keeping the original file intact.

Scanner An input device that can convert text or illustrations into digital formats that can be read by a computer.

ScreenTips Small windows that display descriptive information when the mouse pointer is positioned on a command or control.

Script A type of font that resembles handwriting.

Scroll To move a document in order to view different parts, scroll bars move the page horizontally and vertically. Scroll arrows move the document in incremental amounts.

Search engine A software program that uses keywords and queries to find relevant Web sites.

Section break A feature that creates multiple sections in a document so that they can be formatted differently.

Section selector In Access, the box to the left of a section bar. This box can be used to view the properties of a section.

Select query In Access, a search used to find data or make calculations.

Select A tool used to highlight a character, cell, word, or block of text/data in order to edit or modify it.

Series labels Text boxes that identify each data series in a chart.

Serif A type of font with lines, curves, or edges extending from the ends of the letters.

Server *See* Minicomputer.

Shading Tint or color added to text or data.

Shapes Predefined graphical images that can be formatted, placed, and sized.

Sheet tabs Labels at the bottom of a workbook that show the names of the worksheets in a workbook.

Shortcut A quick link to a document, folder, or application.

Shortcut menu Displays commands needed while performing tasks. Shortcut options vary, depending on where the mouse is pointing and what task is being performed.

Shutter Bar Open/Close button Feature that expands or collapses the Navigation Pane.

Simple Query Wizard Access feature that allows users to ask a question about data stored in one or more tables.

Sizing handles Small squares in the corners and outside borders of graphics; these allow users to change the height, width, or proportional size of the graphic.

Slide pane Window in PowerPoint that contains the current slide.

Slide show view A layout that displays PowerPoint slides as an on-screen presentation.

Slide sorter view A layout that displays PowerPoint slides as thumbnails so they can be moved, copied, or deleted.

Slide transition A feature that can be applied in presentations to control the way slides move on and off the screen.

SmartArt Editable graphic designs found under the Insert Menu in Microsoft Office Applications.

Soft page break A term used to indicate an automatic new page.

Software A set of instructions written by computer programmers in machine or programming language.

Software program A detailed set of computer instructions that resides in the computer and determines the way a computer performs.

Sorting (Sort) Feature that allows users to rearrange the order of words or numbers in a list, table, or records in a database.

Source file A file that provides the data for integration into another file. *See* integration.

Speaker notes Written notes that correspond to slides in a presentation.

Split A feature used to unmerge cells that you have joined.

Split screen A divided window with multiple resizable panes to view all parts of a document.

Split Form In Access, an option that displays both the form view and datasheet view at the same time.

Spreadsheet software Application program, such as Excel, used to organize, analyze, and report statistical and numerical data.

Standard toolbar In Outlook, the set of selectable buttons used to create, print, delete, and find items.

Start button A button that displays menu options to start programs on the computer and work with computer settings.

Status bar An area that displays information about the current document at the bottom of a program window.

Storage devices Tool that allows instructions and data to be saved and retrieved for future use.

Structured data Formatted data that can be imported to Access from other programs and file formats.

Style A set of formats that can be applied to selected text. Styles can be preselected from the Quick Styles gallery or created and saved by the user.

Subscript Characters that print slightly below a line of type.

Summary query Access feature that totals (sums), counts, averages, or finds minimum or maximum values in a sort.

Supercomputer The fastest type of computer. These machines are capable of storing data and performing numerous tasks simultaneously and are used for specialized tasks such as weather forecasting and medical research.

Superscript Characters that print slightly above a line of type.

Symbol Special characters used to separate items on a page, emphasize items on a list, or enhance a document.

System software A program that controls the way computer parts work together.

Tab A mark on the ruler that positions the insertion point relative to the margin. *See* Custom tabs.

Table Data organized in columns and rows.

Table properties Tool that provides descriptive information about a table, such as date created or modified.

Table template In Access, a tool for quickly organizing information. These templates can be customized and are found under the Create tab.

Tagged Image File Format (TIF or TIFF) An image file format used to compress and store color

images; recognized by most Windows applications but not usable by Web browsers.

Task A reminder in Outlook.

Taskbar The desktop toolbar that appears at the bottom of the Windows screen and is used to change between open applications and documents.

Template presentation Predesigned sets of PowerPoint slides.

Template A predesigned and formatted document that serves as the structure for a new document.

Text A data type or entry that is a mix of text and numbers and that cannot be used in calculations.

Text box A placeholder containing text that can be positioned, sized, and edited.

Text data type Used for alphabetic characters or a mix of alphabetic and numeric characters (street addresses), or for numbers that will not be calculated (ZIP codes).

Text highlight Word feature that marks text or graphics for emphasis as though they were marked with a highlighter pen.

Text string Multiple-word entry that is used to search for documents, data, or other information.

Text wrap An option for controlling whether and how text wraps around a graphic or other object.

Theme A combination of font, color, and style formatting choices for an entire document.

Thesaurus A feature that provides the user with synonyms for selected words. The thesaurus can be accessed by right-clicking on a word or pressing [Alt] and the word.

Thumbnails A feature that will display a document page in miniature.

TIFF or TIF *See* Tagged Image File Format.

Title bar The shaded area at the top of a dialog box or application window that displays the title of the box, or the name of the file, and the application.

Total row In Access, used to perform calculations on the values in a field.

Transpose An option that displays vertical data as horizontal data or vice versa.

Unbound control In Access, a field object not connected to a data source and used to display information such as text, lines, rectangles, and pictures.

Undo A feature that lets the user reverse an action.

Uniform Resource Locator The global address of resources or pages on the Web.

Unmatched query In Access, a sort that finds records in one table that do not match records in another.

URL *See* Uniform Resource Locator.

Value In Excel, a numeric entry that is able to be calculated.

Vertical (value) axis Often referred to as the y-axis, this area of a chart represents the data scale.

View buttons Buttons that allow a user to change the file display or program tool.

Virtual reality (VR) software A program that uses three-dimensional real-world graphics and special devices to interact in a computer simulation.

Voice recognition software Application program used to create, edit, and format documents using voice input that is transmitted through a microphone.

WAN *See* Wide area network.

Watermark Text or graphics used as a background image on printed documents.

Web address An Internet address that is unique for a particular Web site.

Web browser Application program that is used to locate and display Web pages.

Web crawler *See* Search engine.

Web Layout view A document view in Word that shows how a document will look as a Web page.

Web page A location on an Internet server that can be reached and identified by a Web address.

Web page software Application program used to design and manage Web sites.

Web server A dedicated computer that stores and delivers Web pages.

Web site A collection of Web pages connected by hyperlinks.

Web toolbar In Outlook, navigation buttons used to work online.

Wide area network (WAN) A computer system that links computers outside a local area.

Widow The first line of a paragraph appearing by itself at the bottom of a column or page.

Wildcard A character or symbol used in a search string to substitute for unknown characters.

Window control buttons Located in the title bar, these buttons control the way a program behaves. *See* Maximize button, Minimize button, and Restore down button.

Wireless computing Technology that allows users to access network resources without hardwired connections.

WordArt Feature that allows text to be created as a graphic image using predesigned styles.

Word count A feature that allows the user to calculate pages, characters, paragraphs, and lines in a document or selected text.

Word processing software Application program, such as Word, used to create, edit, and print text-based documents, including letters, reports, and memos.

Word-wrap A feature that automatically advances text that is entered beyond the right margin to the next line without pressing [Enter].

Workbook In Excel, a file that can contain one or more worksheets.

Work pane In Access, the pane on the right side of the screen of an open database; this area is the display area for the active object.

Worksheet Separate documents within an Excel workbook.

World Wide Web A system of linked documents and files located on computers connected through the Internet. *See also* Internet.

Wrap Text In Excel, a button that displays text on more than one line in a cell.

Yes/No In Access, a data type in which each entry is one of two values; for example, Yes/No, or True/False.

Zoom Feature used to magnify (zoom in) or reduce (zoom out) the size of the document on screen.

INDEX

★Downloadable from the Student Online Companion.

★Downloadable from the Student Online Companion.

★Downloadable from the Student Online Companion.

★Downloadable from the Student Online Companion.

★Downloadable from the Student Online Companion.